1866 - 1991

125th

ANNIVERSARY

5OO1 NIGHTS
AT THE MOVIES

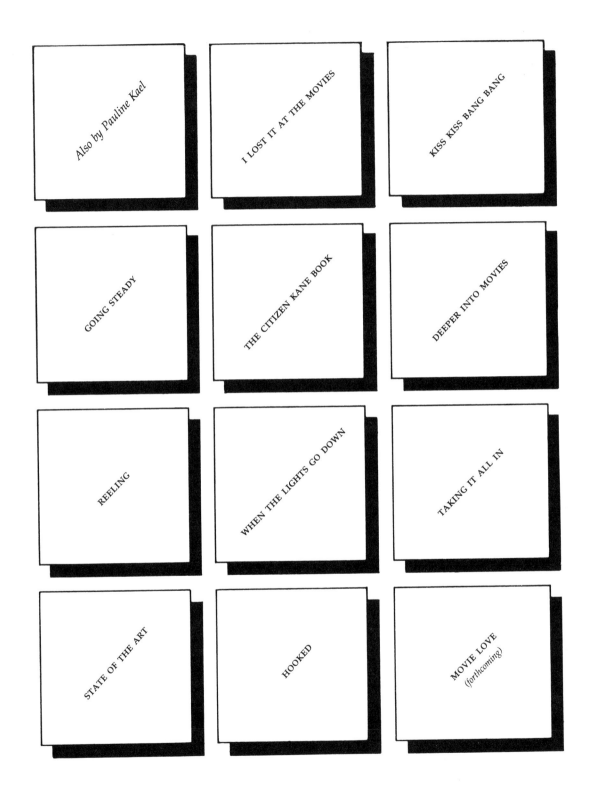

Also by Pauline Kael

I LOST IT AT THE MOVIES

KISS KISS BANG BANG

GOING STEADY

THE CITIZEN KANE BOOK

DEEPER INTO MOVIES

REELING

WHEN THE LIGHTS GO DOWN

TAKING IT ALL IN

STATE OF THE ART

HOOKED

MOVIE LOVE
(forthcoming)

PAULINE KAEL

5001 NIGHTS
AT THE MOVIES

An Owl Book
A William Abrahams Book

HENRY HOLT and COMPANY · NEW YORK

Published by Henry Holt and Company, Inc.,
115 West 18th Street, New York, New York 10011.
Published in Canada by Fitzhenry & Whiteside Limited,
195 Allstate Parkway, Markham, Ontario L3R 4T8.

Library of Congress Cataloging-in-Publication Data
Kael, Pauline.
5001 nights at the movies.
"A William Abrahams/Owl Book."
1. Moving-pictures—Reviews.   I. Title.   II. Title:
Five thousand one nights at the movies.   III. Title: Five
thousand and one nights at the movies.
PN1995.K19   1985   791.43'75   84-10179
ISBN 0-8050-1366-0
ISBN 0-8050-1367-9 (An Owl Book: pbk.)

Henry Holt books are available at special discounts
for bulk purchases for sales promotions, premiums,
fund-raising, or educational use. Special editions
or book excerpts can also be created to specifications.
For details contact:
Special Sales Director, Henry Holt and Company, Inc.,
115 West 18th Street, New York, New York 10011.

First published in hardcover by Holt, Rinehart and Winston
in 1982. First Owl Book Edition—1985.

Designed by Joy Chu

Printed in the United States of America
Recognizing the importance of preserving the written word,
Henry Holt and Company, Inc., by policy, prints all of its
first editions on acid-free paper.∞

1   3   5   7   9   10   8   6   4   2

FOREWORD

It is unlikely that anyone in the world has reviewed more movies than Pauline Kael. It is also unlikely that anyone in the world carries around in his or her head more information about movies. When Pauline Kael sits down to review a new film, she is able to sum up pertinent details from the thousnds of American and foreign films that preceded it. She remembers, and can describe, scenes, sequences, performances, shots, images, touches, gestures, effects. In herself, she is the international history, library, archive, encyclopedia of film—the cinemathèque. If numbers, or even knowledgeability, were all that mattered, she would be the champion. But these are merely a point of departure. She brings to her criticism more than stamina and a phenomenal memory, more than scholarship. What is most important, perhaps, is that she loves movies. Good and bad, they are her passion. Movies sustain her, and she, in turn, sustains many of the people who make them. Moviemakers may be satisfied or dissatisfied with her reaction to any given picture, but they are not inclined to dismiss it, and they never question her rapt involvement with movies. They know that she takes their work seriously, that she judges it by the most rigorous standards, that she gives it the attention it deserves. When she thinks that a picture has failed, she can become so intent on getting to the bottom of what went wrong that now and then, to her own astonishment, she wounds somebody's feelings, but even on those occasions the charms of her criticism are such that she is apt to be forgiven. And when she thinks that a picture succeeds she rejoices.

The originality of Pauline Kael's mind and temperament, her formidable intelligence, her eloquent use of the vernacular, her extraordinary analytical powers, her insight into character, her ability to shed light wherever the real world intersects with the world on film, her enormous gift for social observation, the wit and energy and clarity of her prose all go into making her the singular critic she is. What she is primarily is a writer; one reads her for the sheer pleasure her writing affords. Her opinions are forceful, convincing, often unexpected, but whether or not one agrees with them one comes away from her writings in a state of exhilaration.

Pauline Kael's reviews are normally longer than most—long enough to daunt the uninitiated but not too long for her admirers.

Yet in this volume she has assembled several thousand reviews—written for the Going On About Town department of *The New Yorker*—that are not only dazzling but brief, are models of compression. Nothing like this collection of short reviews has ever been seen before. They can be read by moviegoers or television viewers as a guide or they can be read for their own sake: either way they are a marvel. A master of synopsis, Pauline Kael has contrived to tell us between the covers of one book what eight decades of film are about and who is in them and behind them, and to reflect, swiftly but astutely, on what they signify. No one else has done that; no one else could have done that.

—WILLIAM SHAWN

AUTHOR'S NOTE

To the 1991 edition

I'm grateful to the people who took me up on the suggestion that they let me know about errors. I'm grateful also to those who wrote in suggesting titles to be included in this expanded edition. Whenever time and memory made it possible, I've complied. Roughly eight hundred titles have been added; they include most of the important films of the '80s. I know that there are still major omissions from every period, but I've done my damnedest. (If I go on, I'll never stop.)

To the original edition

For a long time, despite persistent requests by the readers of *The New Yorker*, I resisted the idea of a collection of these notes, which were printed (anonymously) in the Goings On About Town section of the magazine, because they are often written hurriedly and are frequently dependent on my old, spotty memories. Also, there are so many different versions of them that I knew it would be a nightmare to sort out what should be reprinted. (Before I began writing for the magazine I had been doing short descriptions for theatres and colleges. Then, in my first years at the magazine I wrote three notes for each new film, so that they could be rotated, and if I wrote a longish note, this would gradually be cut down if the film continued to play.) And there was another reason: many of the notes are vandalized from my own reviews, and, in my first years at *The New Yorker*, when the Goings On was expanded to include revivals—partly because of my feeling that readers might be missing out on older films that they hadn't heard of—I sometimes tried to blend my view of a movie with some of the language from the magazine's initial review of it. So I've had to check those reviews to give the proper credits.

Phrases from other reviewers still appear in eighty-odd cases—from Russell Maloney in *Alexander's Ragtime Band, Here Comes Mr. Jordan,* and *They Drive By Night;* from Theodore Shane in *Ben-Hur* (1925); from Philip Hamburger in *Ivanhoe;* from Brendan Gill in *The Agony and the Ecstasy, The Appaloosa, Hush . . . Hush, Sweet Charlotte, Sweet Bird of Youth,* and *To Kill a Mockingbird;* from David Lardner in *Air Force, Lady of Burlesque,* and *This Is the Army,* from John Lardner in *Kismet* (1944) and *Step Lively;* from Edith Oliver in *The Blue Max;* from Wolcott Gibbs in *Over 21, Practically Yours,* and *The Thin Man Goes Home;*

from John McCarten in *Anna and the King of Siam*, *Autumn Leaves*, *Blithe Spirit*, *A Connecticut Yankee in King Arthur's Court* (1949), *Down to the Sea in Ships*, *Forever Amber*, *Friendly Persuasion*, *Green Dolphin Street*, *Humoresque* (1946), *It Should Happen to You*, *Lady in the Lake*, *Lady on a Train*, *Leave Her to Heaven*, *Mighty Joe Young*, *Miss Sadie Thompson*, *Night and Day*, *The Outlaw*, *Possessed*, *The Razor's Edge*, *The Revolt of Mamie Stover*, *Ride the Pink Horse*, *Samson and Delilah*, *The Sea of Grass*, *Smash-Up*, *The Spiral Staircase*, *The Strange Love of Martha Ivers*, *The Teahouse of the August Moon*, *The Ten Commandments*, *The Three Musketeers* (1948), and *Titanic*; from John Mosher in *Blockade*, *Cleopatra* (1934), *Dr. Cyclops*, *Drums Along the Mohawk*, *The Garden of Allah*, *The Gracie Allen Murder Case*, *Hold Your Man*, *Hollywood Party*, *The Informer*, *Intermezzo* (1939), *Invitation to Happiness*, *Jamaica Inn*, *Lillian Russell*, *The Mad Miss Manton*, *Made for Each Other* (1939), *Maid of Salem*, *Mannequin*, *The Mark of Zorro* (1940), *Meet Nero Wolfe*, *Mrs. Miniver*, *Mr. Smith Goes to Washington*, *Our Modern Maidens*, *Road to Singapore*, *The Shining Hour*, *The Sign of the Cross*, *Strange Cargo*, *A Tale of Two Cities* (1935), *Tarzan and His Mate*, *This Gun for Hire*, *Up the River*, *Weekend in Havana*, *Zaza*, and *Zoo in Budapest*. Most of the time, these borrowings are no more than a few words, but in some I lifted descriptive passages that I liked. To these predecessors and colleagues I offer my thanks.

There were no strict rules in selecting the batch of brief notices from among the thousands more that I've got piled up. I wanted to suggest the range of what movies have done, and so I've brought together silent films and talkies, foreign films and American ones, and even some shorts. You won't find *Gone With the Wind* or *The Wizard of Oz.* Omitting them is a gesture: I wouldn't want anyone to take this book for a complete guide to movies. But I hope that it is a guide to the varieties of pleasures that are available at the movies—from the fun to be had at the juicier forms of trash to the overwhelming emotions that are called up by great work.

For those who may want a fuller analysis of a film: if I have written a review and it's included in one of my collections, this is indicated at the end of the notice.

No doubt errors have crept in—faulty recollections as well as typos. If you'll write to me (at *The New Yorker*, 25 West 43 St., New York, NY 10036), I'll do my best to see that such mishaps are corrected in any subsequent editions. And if there are films you'd particularly like to see added, please let me know and if (as I hope) I get the chance to expand this book I'll try to fit them in.

This book is for my daughter Gina and for the one to whom I hope it will prove most useful, her son William.

5001 NIGHTS
AT THE MOVIES

À bout de souffle, see *Breathless*

A Ciascuno il Suo, see *We Still Kill the Old Way*

À double tour, see *Léda*

À nous la liberté (1931)—René Clair's imaginative social satire on the mechanization of modern life begins with a man (Raymond Cordy) who escapes from prison and builds a phonograph-record business with an assembly line that's as regimented as the prison. This factory owner is modelled on Charles Pathé, who said of his phonograph-cinema empire, "Only the armaments industry made profits like ours." The tycoon's pal from his prison days is a softhearted "little man" (Henri Marchand)—the underdog embodiment of a free, humanistic spirit. Beautifully made, the picture has elegantly futuristic sets by Lazare Meerson, and Georges Périnal's cinematography has a simplified, formal perfection; the whole film is paced to Georges Auric's memorable score—one of the earliest (yet best) film scores ever written. Clair's directing demonstrates that sound pictures can be as fluid as silents were, and this picture is rightly considered a classic.

Yet it isn't as entertaining as his earlier (silent) *The Italian Straw Hat* or his later *Le Million;* the scenario (which he wrote) turns a little too carefree and ironic—the film grows dull. *À nous la liberté* was obviously the source of some of the ideas in Chaplin's 1936 *Modern Times;* the producing company filed suit against Chaplin for copyright infringement, but Clair had the suit dropped, saying that "All of us flow" from Chaplin, and "I am honored if he was inspired by my film." In French. b & w

The Abdication (1974)—This Warners picture about Queen Christina's stepping down from the Swedish throne, in 1654, is embalmed in such reverence for its own cultural elevation that it loses all contact with the audience. Liv Ullmann is the virgin queen who becomes a Catholic hoping to find ecstasy in God, and Peter Finch is the cardinal who examines her motives. Anthony Harvey directed, on his knees. We're never allowed to forget the exalted rank of the characters, and nothing like human speech intrudes upon the relentless dignity of Ruth Wolff's script (adapted from her own play). Ullmann doesn't have the high style or the mystery that her grand-gesture role requires; her performance is dutifully wrought and properly weighted—she's like a hausfrau who's too conscientious to give good parties. With Cyril Cusack, Paul Rogers, Michael Dunn, and Edward Underdown. The turbulent, pseudo-liturgical score is by Nino Rota; the pictorial cinematography is by Geoffrey Unsworth. color (See *Reeling*.)

About Last Night . . . (1986)—In *Sexual Perversity in Chicago*, David Mamet's one-act play about singles bars and the hostility between the sexes, Bernie, the major character, is a macho braggart; his stooge, the passive Danny, soaks up Bernie's poison—his obsession that women are out to trap them. In this adaptation, written by Tim Kazurinsky and Denise DeClue, and directed by Edward Zwick (it's his first picture), Danny, played by Rob Lowe, is the major character—and a hero. He's intimidated by his pal Bernie (Jim Belushi), but he learns to trust his love for Debbie (Demi Moore) and get off the singles treadmill. And Debbie casts out the doubts that are engendered by her roommate, the caustic Joan (Elizabeth Perkins). The movie is close to being a conventional romance about the adjustments that lovers have to make in their first year together—except that Bernie is around yelling, and Joan keeps putting everybody down. The screenwriters retain much of Mamet's dialogue, but they piece it out, and the director punches up the breaks between scenes with rock music. It's like being pounded on the back every two minutes when your back is already sore (because the dialogue has been whacking you so hard). If anyone comes out of this enterprise with honor it's Perkins, who, in her first screen appearance, brings appealing, plaintive undercurrents to a ghastly role. Tri-Star. color (See *Hooked*.)

Absence of Malice (1981)—A trim, well-paced newspaper melodrama that queries journalistic practices. Sally Field is the basically insensitive, eager-beaver Miami reporter who snaps up a story that the head of a federal strike force investigating the disappearance of a union leader leaks to her. The story is false—the federal man's purpose is simply to stir things up by putting pressure on an honest businessman who has Mafia relatives. Paul Newman is the victim, and the movie is about how he turns the methods of the authorities and the newspaperwoman against them. It's doubtful that people who are out to get even are as calm and well-balanced as this character; Newman gives revenge class, so we can all enjoy it. The script, by Kurt Luedtke, a former newspaperman, is crisply plotted, but he doesn't write scenes to reveal anything more in the characters than the plot requires. Sydney Pollack's directing is efficient and the film is moderately entertaining, but it leaves no residue. Except for the intensity of Newman's sly, compact performance (especially in the one scene when he blows up at the reporter and hisses his rage right into her ear), and the marvellously inventive acting of Melinda Dillon in the role of an achingly helpless, frightened woman, and the character bits by Barry Primus, Luther Adler, Josef Sommer, Wilford Brimley, Don Hood, and John Harkins you could get it all by reading an article. As the head of the strike force, Bob Balaban must think that he's doing Captain Queeg. He has devised an attention-getting nervous shtick—he spins his hands around while playing with rubber bands—and he never gives it a rest. Columbia. color (See *Taking It All In*.)

Absolute Beginners (1986)—Colin MacInnes's 1959 novel—an inventive, slangy, poetic celebration of youth and jazz and London, and a cry of disgust at the way teenagers, who didn't emerge as a group with money to spend until the 50s, are already being commercialized and corrupted—has been turned into a stylized, widescreen musical by Julien Temple. Whether because of the fast-cutting style that Temple developed from his work in rock videos or because of the generally undistinguished choreography, it's peculiarly unlyrical and ephemeral. The film has a glossy immediacy, and you can feel the flash and determination that went into it. What you don't feel is the tormented romanticism that made English adolescents in the 70s swear by the novel the way American kids had earlier sworn by *The Catcher in the Rye.* David Bowie, James Fox, Ray Davies, Anita Morris, and Sade provide entertaining moments; Lionel Blair, Bruce Payne, and Graham Fletcher-Cook come through with glints of humor. But the two central teen-age characters—Colin (Eddie O'Connell) and the girl he loves, Suzette (Patsy Kensit)—seem generic. Musical arrangements by Gil Evans; cinematography by Oliver Stapleton; screenplay by Richard Burridge, Christopher Wicking, and Don MacPherson. Also with Slim Gaillard, Steven Berkoff, and Mandy Rice-Davies. Released in the U.S. by Orion. color (See *Hooked.*)

Accident (1967)—Joseph Losey and his scenarist, Harold Pinter, use sexual desperation amid the beauty of Oxford in summertime to make our flesh crawl. A cleverly barbed comedy of depravity—uneven, unsatisfying, but with virtuoso passages of calculated meanness and, as the centerpiece, a long, drunken Sunday party, with people sitting down to supper when they're too soused to eat. As a weakling philosophy don, Dirk Bogarde goes through his middle-aged-frustration specialty brilliantly, gripping his jaw to stop a stutter or folding his arms to keep his hands out of trouble. With Stanley Baker, who is properly swinish as another academic, and Vivien Merchant, Jacqueline Sassard, Michael York, Alexander Knox, and Delphine

Seyrig as a dumb blonde. From the novel by Nicholas Mosley; cinematography by Gerry Fisher; music by Johnny Dankworth. color (See *Kiss Kiss Bang Bang.*)

The Accidental Tourist (1988)—It begins with the numb grief of a punctilious Baltimore travel writer, Macon Leary (William Hurt), whose 12-year-old son was senselessly shot by a gunman in a Burger Bonanza. Macon has become such a depressed loner that his wife (Kathleen Turner) leaves him. The movie, directed by Lawrence Kasdan, who wrote the screenplay with Frank Galati, closely follows the 1985 Anne Tyler novel, and it's about Macon's coming to life. A fiercely eager oddball (Geena Davis) who pulls him into her bed turns out to be his salvation. The plot construction is that of a screwball comedy of the 30s: poor working girl has the life force that upper-class prig needs. But people talk a formal, affected English that sounds counterfeit and everyone seems catatonic—even the skinny oddball, whose tense talkativeness is as panicked as Macon's recessiveness and silence. This picture's ponderousness doesn't keep it from affecting some people deeply. It provides a new romantic myth of the 80s—a time of widespread remarriage and hoped-for rebirth. Essentially, this is a dating movie, like Claude Lelouch's *A Man and a Woman,* but for darker times, for times of lower expectations. The film's minimal fun has to do with the wry, pixillated family humor of Macon and his siblings (Amy Wright, Ed Begley, Jr., and David Ogden Stiers). The cast includes Bill Pullman and Robert Gorman. Cinematography by John Bailey; the offensive rippling score is by John Williams. Warners. color (See *Movie Love.*)

The Ace, see *The Great Santini*

Ace in the Hole Also known as *The Big Carnival.* (1951)—Billy Wilder produced and directed this box-office failure right after *Sunset Boulevard* and just before *Stalag 17.* Some people have tried to claim some sort of satirical brilliance for it, but it's really just nasty, in a sociologically pushy way. Kirk Douglas is the big-time New York reporter who is so opportunistic that when he gets to where a collapsed roof has buried a man in New Mexico, he arranges to have the rescue delayed so that he can pump the story up. The trapped man dies, while Douglas keeps shouting in order that we can all see what a symptomatic, cynical exploiter he is. With Jan Sterling as the trapped man's wife, Porter Hall, Richard Benedict, Ray Teal, and Frank Cady. Script by Wilder, Lesser Samuels, and Walter Newman. Filmed on location near Gallup, New Mexico. Paramount. b & w

Across the Bridge (1957)—Graham Greene's protagonist is a crooked international financier (Rod Steiger) who runs to Mexico, and the film is one long chase after this disintegrating quarry. Ken Annakin directed this English production, photographed in Spain, which some English critics regarded as their best thriller since *The Third Man.* (There may not have been much competition.) If the film had sustained the tension of its opening scenes the comparison with *The Third Man* might be apt, but the middle of the picture (and it's an extended middle) falls apart. It was invented by the screenwriters, Guy Elmes and Denis Freeman, who filled out Greene's 1938 short story. Steiger gives a dominating performance; Bill Nagy plays Scarff, whose identity the financier takes, not knowing that Scarff is a revolutionary, who is wanted in Mexico. Noel Willman is the vicious police chief; David Knight and Marla Landi are young lovers (she is beautiful, he is dreary). b & w

Across the Pacific (1942)—After his exhilarating début film, *The Maltese Falcon* (1941), John Huston had a commercial failure with *In This Our Life*; then he tried to repeat the success of the *Falcon* with an action-adventure story, using some of the *Falcon* cast—Humphrey Bogart, Mary Astor, Sydney Greenstreet. The film was supposed to be about a group sailing to Honolulu to thwart a Japanese plan to blow up Pearl Harbor; during the second week of shooting, the Japanese *did* blow up Pearl Harbor. The production was shut down and there was a hasty rewrite. The result is a complicated plot about spies who plan to blow up the Panama Canal, and there are assorted captures and hairbreadth escapes. Huston manages to give the sequences some tension, and though the shipboard scenes were—in the custom of the time—filmed on the studio back lot, the images are airy and spacious. But Huston couldn't do anything about the essential mediocrity of the material, and when he was drafted into the Army Special Services before the picture was finished, he showed what he thought of the mess: he hurriedly shot a scene with Bogart trussed up and about to be killed, and then left his replacement director, Vincent Sherman, to figure out how to save Bogart in time to prevent the bombing of the Canal. The movie isn't really bad—just bewildering. Mary Astor comes off the worst; cast as a conventional heroine, she looks heavy and uncomfortable, and too big for Bogart, who, incidentally, was called Rick here—the name that was carried over the next year in *Casablanca.* With Victor Sen Yung, Charles Halton, Richard Loo, Keye Luke, and Monte Blue. Script by Richard Macaulay, from Robert Carson's *SatEvePost* serial *Aloha Means Goodbye*; montages by Don Siegel; cinematography by Arthur Edeson; music by Adolph Deutsch. Produced by Jerry Wald and Jack Saper, for Warners. b & w

Act of the Heart (1970)—Geneviève Bujold, in one of those passionate, spiritual jobs about a girl who is "different." The heroine sings the solo with the church choir; she suffers while singing in a nightclub; she even—God help us—makes love with an Augustinian monk (in the unlikely, affable person of Donald Sutherland) at the front of the altar. After hours of fire symbolism, she finally pours kerosene on herself to create a new sacrifice for a world that has forgotten Jesus; by then you're ready to toss her a match. This Canadian film was written and directed by Paul Almond (Bujold's husband at the time) who goes for obsessions and fatalities and an elliptical style, and is very high on portents. Bujold has some lovely bits, but the masochistic feminine-fantasy material forces her to fall back on the old fragile, incandescent child-woman shtick. color (See *Deeper into Movies*.)

The Actress (1953)—Ruth Gordon adapted her autobiographical play *Years Ago*, which dealt with a young girl in New England determined to make her way in the theatre, and it was turned into a pleasantly modest though disappointing picture by the director, George Cukor. Jean Simmons plays the title role with grace, but the author has neglected to provide indications of talent and drive in the character; this girl seems too nice, too ordinary—she could never grow up to be that tough, indefatigable trouper Ruth Gordon. (The heroine sets out on her own in 1911.) Despite the title, the central character is the girl's gruff, lovable father (Spencer Tracy); Tracy overdoes it, but he shows some energy, and the film is sadly short of it. With Teresa Wright giving a wan performance as the mother, Anthony Perkins making his first screen appearance, Ian Wolfe, Mary Wickes, Jackie Coogan as the joker in the gymnasium,

and, in the best sequence, Kay Williams as a musical-comedy star. M-G-M. b & w

Adalen 31 (1969)—An extraordinarily sensitive re-creation of a strike and riot that altered the course of Swedish political life, seen through the eyes of an adolescent boy whose father dies in the events. Bo Widerberg, whose previous film was *Elvira Madigan*, wrote and directed this beautiful yet uninspired piece of work; lush and lyrical as it is, it's fundamentally didactic, with stereotyped social-realist characters. And because Widerberg seems to work best in vignettes and to have architectural problems when he's working on such a large scale, his argument isn't clear; he makes the little points but not the big ones. So when the violence erupts, we don't really understand its political significance—we're left "appreciating" it, in a rather embarrassed way, for its pictorial values. In Swedish. color (See *Deeper into Movies*.)

Adam's Rib (1949)—George Cukor directed this "uncinematic" but well-played and often witty M-G-M comedy about the battle of the sexes. Katharine Hepburn, thin, nervous, and high-strung, keeps pecking away at Spencer Tracy, who is solid, imperturbable, and maddeningly sane. She attacks, he blocks; their skirmishes are desperately, ludicrously civilized. They are married lawyers on opposing sides in a court battle; the case involves equal rights for women, i.e., does Judy Holliday have the right to shoot her two-timing husband, Tom Ewell, in order to protect her home against Jean Hagen? The script by Ruth Gordon and Garson Kanin is lively and ingenious (though it stoops to easy laughs now and then). Cukor's work is too arch, too consciously, commercially clever, but it's also spirited, confident. Holliday and Ewell have roles that seem just the right size for them; intermittently, Holliday lifts the picture to a higher, free-style wit. And as a composer-neighbor of the married lawyers David Wayne airily upstages the two stars; Hepburn is overly intense and Tracy does some coy mugging, but Wayne stays right on target. With Polly Moran, Clarence Kolb, and Hope Emerson (as a circus strong woman). b & w

The Admirable Crichton, see *Paradise Lagoon*

The Adventure of Sherlock Holmes' Smarter Brother (1975)—Gene Wilder's talent is evident in the many nice leafy touches, but in his first attempt at a triple-header (writer-director-star) he shows poor judgment and he gets bogged down in an overelaborate production. The idea—Holmes' bringing in his insanely jealous younger brother, Sigerson, to help on a case involving Queen Victoria's state secrets—has mouth-watering possibilities, but they aren't developed. There's no mystery, and since you can't have a parody of a mystery without a mystery, there's no comic suspense. And Wilder, keeping his eye on his responsibilities as a director, loses his performing rhythm. A vaudeville number is disconcertingly like the specialty number in Mel Brooks' *Young Frankenstein* (which Wilder co-wrote and starred in) and calls attention to the general similarity between the two films. With Madeline Kahn, Marty Feldman, Dom DeLuise, Leo McKern, and Roy Kinnear. 20th Century-Fox. color (See *When the Lights Go Down*.)

The Adventurers (1970)—This Paramount–Joseph E. Levine release seems to have been put together by scavengers with computers. It cuts back and forth between the massacres and upheavals of a mythical poor country in South America and the tortured sex lives of the international celebrity set in Europe and America, and every 15 minutes or so there's carnage or a cloddish sex scene to keep you from losing interest in the slack story. Sleazy (the Harold Robbins novel) and square (the approach of the director, Lewis Gilbert) don't blend entertainingly here; the film lacks crude dynamism—it's dispiriting. There are only a couple of amusing scenes: a nice moment when Thommy Berggren, as a gigolo, tips his doorman father (Ferdy Mayne), and a villainous moment or two by Alan Badel, as a Trujillo-style dictator. The international cast of this $10 million clinker includes Bekim Fehmiu as the Porfirio Rubirosa–like hero, Candice Bergen, Charles Aznavour, Rossano Brazzi, Olivia de Havilland, Leigh Taylor-Young, Fernando Rey, Sydney Tafler, Ernest Borgnine, Anna Moffo, and John Ireland. The script is by Michael Hastings and Gilbert, the music is by Jobim, and the cinematographer, Claude Renoir, gives it all a better look than it deserves. color (See *Deeper Into Movies*.)

The Adventures of Baron Munchausen (1989)—The Baron, who lived from 1720 to 1797, was a fibber of genius—a fabulist. Terry Gilliam, who directed this special-effects extravaganza, sees his theme as the liar as artist; his Munchausen (John Neville) is a poet, a man of imagination. He's pitted against the practical men who believe in facts and compromise and conformity (i.e., the men who finance movies). The elements are here for a fantasy on the order of *The Wizard of Oz* and *Pinocchio* and the 1940 *Thief of Bagdad*; the Baron and a 10-year-old girl (Sarah Polley) voyage to a city on the moon, fall into the fire god Vulcan's foundry inside the belching Mt. Etna, and are swallowed by a monster fish. Yet the picture is dry and choppy and remote. The design (by Dante Ferretti) and the cinematography (by Giuseppe Rotunno) are sometimes magnificent, and there are scenes that are near-inspired. Something is missing, though: a bit of conviction—of ardor and awe. Gilliam's hip silliness is deflating; his gifts—his gagster's prankishness and his sense of beauty—don't harmonize. The picture is almost devoid of emotional shadings. With Oliver Reed, who's a great rampaging Vulcan, Robin Williams (uncredited) as the King of the Moon, Uma Thurman as Venus, and Eric Idle, Jonathan Pryce, Sting, Valentina Cortese, Bill Paterson, Winston Dennis, Jack Purvis, Alison Steadman, and Charles McKeown, who co-wrote the script with Gilliam. Released by Columbia. color (See *Movie Love*.)

The Adventures of Buckaroo Banzai Also known as *Buckaroo Banzai*. (1984)—Making his début as a director, W. D. (Rick) Richter doesn't bring out the baroque lunacy of the material—a kind of fermented parody of *M*A*S*H*, *Star Wars*, *Raiders of the Lost Ark*, and the TV series "The A-Team"—but though the characters don't develop and the laughs don't build or come together, the film's uninflected deadpan tone is somehow likable. Dr. Buckaroo Banzai (Peter Weller), the half-Japanese, half-American hero, is a neurosurgeon, a physicist, a jet-car racer (who goes right through a mountain), and the leader of the Team Banzai—seven dapper whizbang Renaissance men. For relaxation, Buckaroo and a few of the others have formed their own rock group, the Hong Kong Cavaliers, and it's at a Cavaliers' performance in a New Jersey night spot that the hypersensitive Buckaroo picks up the disturbed vibes of someone in the audience; that's how he meets the heroine, Penny Priddy (Ellen Barkin). Richter and the scriptwriter Earl Mac Rauch don't seem to have an angle of vision on the interplanetary fantasy world they present; what they've got are an unmoored hipsterism and a lot of inventiveness. As Dr. Lizardo, the mad-genius villain (a comic-strip mixture of Eisenstein, Klaus Kinski, and a Wagnerian tenor), John Lithgow gives the movie the anchor it needs. White-faced, with bloodshot eyes, dark greenish teeth, and a

wild foreign accent, Lithgow's Dr. Lizardo can make you crazy with happiness. With Jeff Goldblum, Matt Clark as the Secretary of Defense, Carl Lumbly as the friendly alien who disguises himself as a Rastafarian, Christopher Lloyd, Vincent Schiavelli, Rosalind Cash, Ronald Lacey, and the platinum-blond Lewis Smith. The picture went through a change of cinematographers (it was completed by Fred J. Koenekamp), but the young production designer J. Michael Riva has given it a consistent—and radiant—whimsicality. 20th Century-Fox. color (See *State of the Art*.)

Adventures of Don Juan (1948)—By this time, Errol Flynn's offscreen life had colored the public's view of him, and this wry, semi-satirical swashbuckler was designed to exploit his reputation for debauchery. William Faulkner and Frederick Faust (Max Brand) were among the writers whom the Warners producer, Jerry Wald, brought in to work on various drafts of the screenplay, which was finally credited to George Oppenheimer and Harry Kurnitz. Flynn looks far from his best, and the whole lavish production has a somewhat depressed tone. The story has Juan saving Queen Margaret of Spain (Viveca Lindfors) from a traitor's skulduggery. With Romney Brent, Ann Rutherford, Alan Hale, Robert Warwick, Robert Douglas, Helen Westcott, Raymond Burr, Una O'Connor, Fortunio Bonanova, and Monte Blue. Those with keen eyes may spot bits of footage lifted from *The Private Lives of Elizabeth and Essex* and *The Adventures of Robin Hood*. The director Vincent Sherman's work is no more than adequate. color

The Adventures of Robin Hood (1938)—One of the most popular of all adventure films—stirring for children and intensely nostalgic for adults. As Robin, Errol Flynn slings a deer across his shoulders with exuberant aplomb; he achieves a mixture of dar-

A

ing and self-mockery, like that of Douglas Fairbanks, Sr., in the 20s. The film gives the legend a light, satirical edge: everyone is a bit too much of what he is. (The archetypal roles that the actors played here clung to their later performances.) With improbably pretty Olivia de Havilland as Maid Marian, Alan Hale as Little John, Ian Hunter as Richard the Lion-Hearted, Basil Rathbone and Claude Rains as the villains, and Herbert Mundin, Patric Knowles, Melville Cooper, Una O'Connor, Montagu Love, and Robert Warwick. The story is clear, the color ravishing, the acting simple and crude. Erich Wolfgang Korngold did the marvellous score; the script is by Norman Reilly Raine and Seton I. Miller; the rousing, buoyant direction is credited to Michael Curtiz and William Keighley, the former having replaced the latter. Hal B. Wallis produced, for Warners.

The Adventures of Robinson Crusoe (1952)—Luis Buñuel's version of the Defoe novel (made in English) is free of that deadly solicitude that usually kills off classics. The film is a simple, unsentimental account of Defoe's basic themes: a man alone face to face with nature; then a man terribly alone, unable to face lack of love and friendship; and finally, after the lacerations of desire, a man ludicrously alone. Buñuel used Dan O'Herlihy, a fine actor with a beautiful voice, and photographed him in the jungle of Manzanillo, near Acapulco. In the delirium sequence, Buñuel is the same startling director who made film history. When Crusoe shouts to the hills in order to hear the companionable echo, and when he rushes to the sea in desperate longing for a ship, loneliness is brought in sudden shocks, to the pitch of awe and terror. Crusoe's eventual meeting with Friday (James Fernandez) changes the tone to irony. color

The Adventures of Tom Sawyer (1938)— Norman Taurog, who had scored at the box office with *Skippy* and other films starring children, directed this fairly straightforward version, for David O. Selznick. It's a reasonably good family-style comedy-melodrama of its period, and the humor in many of Mark Twain's episodes survives the studio-made scenery, the Technicolor sunsets, and the obviousness of the tone. May Robson is Aunt Polly, tapping her thimble briskly; Tommy Kelly plays Tom, and Ann Gillis is Becky Thatcher. The adaptation is by John Weaver.

The Adventuress, see *I See a Dark Stranger*

Advise and Consent (1962)—Mindless "inside" story of Washington political shenanigans, directed by Otto Preminger. Accused of having been a Communist, Leffingwell (Henry Fonda), the nominee for Secretary of State, perjures himself. A senator (Don Murray) is victimized because of a homosexual episode in his past. (When he goes to a gay bar, it's such a lurid, evil place that the director seems grotesquely straight.) There are noteworthy performances by Burgess Meredith, as Leffingwell's accuser, and by Franchot Tone, as the President; Charles Laughton is entertainingly flamboyant as a Southern senator. With Lew Ayres as the Vice-President, and Walter Pidgeon, Gene Tierney, Peter Lawford, Paul Ford, George Grizzard, Inga Swenson, Will Geer, Betty White, and some actual Washington personages. The procession of people helps to take one's mind off the overwrought melodrama. Wendell Mayes adapted Allen Drury's bestseller. Columbia. b & w

The African Queen (1951)—An inspired piece of casting brought Humphrey Bogart and Katharine Hepburn together. This is a comedy, a love story, and a tale of adventure, and it is one of the most charming and entertaining movies ever made. The director, John Huston, has written that the comedy was not present either in the novel by C. S. Forester or in the original screenplay by James Agee, John Collier, and himself, but that it grew out of the relationship of Hepburn and Bogart, who were just naturally funny when they worked together. Hepburn has revealed that the picture wasn't going well until Huston came up with the inspiration that she should think of Rosie as Mrs. Roosevelt. After that, Bogart and Hepburn played together with an ease and humor that makes their love affair—the mating of a forbidding, ironclad spinster and a tough, gin-soaked riverboat captain—seem not only inevitable, but perfect. The story, set in central Africa in 1914, is so convincingly acted that you may feel a bit jarred at the end; after the lovers have brought the boat, the African Queen, over dangerous rapids to torpedo a German battleship, Huston seems to stop taking the movie seriously. With Robert Morley as Hepburn's missionary brother, and Peter Bull. Cinematography by Jack Cardiff. Bogart's performance took the Academy Award for Best Actor. (Peter Viertel, who worked on the dialogue while the company was on location in Africa, wrote *White Hunter, Black Heart*—one of the best of all moviemaking novels—about his experiences with Huston.) Produced by Sam Spiegel, for United Artists. color

After Hours (1985)—Martin Scorsese directed, and his work here is lively and companionable; the camera scoots around, making jokes—or, at least, near-jokes. But this skittish paranoid fantasy is just a classroom exercise of a movie: elegant, crisp, and flashy, with perky zooms and cute little dissolves. Scorsese uses his skills (and even his personality) like a hired hand, making a vacuous, polished piece of consumer goods—all surface. Griffin Dunne plays a young word-processor operator in midtown New York, who goes down to SoHo for a date and finds himself trapped in a nightmare world, where he has to contend with one flaky, threatening woman after another: Rosanna Arquette, Linda Fiorentino, Teri Garr, Catherine O'Hara, and Verna Bloom. The cast includes John Heard, who gives the movie its only rooted moments, and Cheech and Chong, Dick Miller, and Bronson Pinchot. Script by Joseph Minion; cinematography by Michael Ballhaus. Released by Warners. color (See *Hooked.*)

After the Fox (1966)—An international collaboration that turned into a box-office calamity, yet, for a messy satirical farce, this picture has a surprising number of funny moments. Neil Simon and Cesare Zavattini wrote the screenplay about a crook who pretends to be a moviemaker. Vittorio De Sica directed, and the cast includes Peter Sellers as the crook, his then-wife, Britt Ekland, playing his sister, Martin Balsam, Victor Mature (who parodies himself and earns the biggest laughs), Paolo Stoppa, Akim Tamiroff, and De Sica himself. The score is by Burt Bacharach. color

After the Thin Man (1936)—This second of the six films that make up the *Thin Man* series, starring William Powell and Myrna Loy as Nick and Nora Charles, doesn't live up to the first. It isn't particularly entertaining; it's just busy. Elissa Landi (who has peculiarly mushy, ladylike diction) is in distress because she has lost her husband (Alan Marshal) to Penny Singleton. There are a couple of murders, and Asta's mate has puppies. The cast includes James Stewart, Joseph Calleia, Sam Levene, and Jessie Ralph. Like the first film, this one was directed by W. S. Van Dyke, from a screenplay by Albert Hackett and Frances Goodrich. M-G-M. b & w

Against All Odds (1984)—Suggested by the 1947 Jacques Tourneur suspense film *Out of the Past*, this revved-up picture is of the "everybody uses everybody" genre, set in swank surroundings and outfitted with electronic music to make you twitch. With a plot that borrows from *Chinatown* and *North Dallas Forty*, it has so many convoluted double crosses that each time you're told what was "really" going on behind the scene you just witnessed you care less. Rachel Ward is the woman who steals and kills, lies all the time, and makes love alternately to Jeff Bridges, a pro football player, and to James (The Snake) Woods, a gamblin' man. It turns out that she's just confused, from having grown up in a nest of vipers, with a real-estate-tycoon mother (played with considerable cool by Jane Greer) and a smoothly villainous stepfather (a hambone special by Richard Widmark). The scenes aren't shaped to get anywhere, so even though the movie hops about L.A. and Mexico, the effect is static, and some sequences—such as the lovemaking set in the ancient Mayan steam house at Chichén Itzá—should earn their place in the annals of camp. With Dorian Harewood, Saul Rubinek, Alex Karras, and Swoosie Kurtz, who has only two or three minutes onscreen (as a lawyer's secretary) but gets a relationship going with the audience; she's the only member of the cast who doesn't seem to have been pulped. Directed by Taylor Hackford, from a script by Eric Hughes. Columbia. color (See *State of the Art*.)

Agatha (1979)—Vanessa Redgrave has a luminously loony quality as the distraught heroine of this fictional romantic mystery, which purports to be about the 11 days in 1926 when Agatha Christie, whose husband wanted a divorce so he could marry his mistress, took off for a Yorkshire spa, where she used the mistress's name. Dustin Hoffman is furiously theatrical in the role of a preening star journalist from America who trails Agatha to the spa and falls in love with her. There is a blissful romantic moment when the goddess-tall, swan-necked Agatha responds to the journalist's (previously denied) request for a kiss by coiling over and down to reach him. The movie has a general air of knowingness, and some of the incidental dialogue is clever, though it doesn't seem to have a story—with its lulling tempo and languid elegance, it seems to be from a musing. The talent of the director, Michael Apted, is for the tactile, the plangent, the indefinite; when the action dawdles, he lets the cinematographer, Vittorio Storaro, take over. The rooms look smoked, and everything is in soft movement; this is the rare movie that is too fluid. Yet there's a gentle pull to it, and Redgrave endows Agatha Christie with the oddness of genius. With Timothy Dalton, who gives a strong, funny performance as the husband exhausted by his wife's high-powered sensitivity, and the curly-mouthed Helen Morse as the friendly woman Agatha meets at the spa, and Celia Gregory, Carolyn Pickles, Tony Britton, Timothy West, and Alan Badel. The script is credited to Kathleen Tynan, who initiated the project, and Arthur Hopcraft; additional writers were also involved. The production designer was Shirley Russell. A First Artists Production, for Warners. color (See *When the Lights Go Down*.)

L'Age d'or (1930)—The most anti-religious, most anti-bourgeois of all Luis Buñuel's films and, naturally, the most scandalous. This episodic 60-minute film—surreal, dreamlike, and deliberately, pornographically blasphemous—was written by both Buñuel and Salvador Dali, who had collaborated two years before on *Un Chien andalou*. With Gaston

Modot, Lya Lys, Max Ernst, Pierre Prévert, and Jacques Brunius. In French. b & w

Age of Infidelity, see *Death of a Cyclist*

The Agony and the Ecstasy (1965)—There is a dreadful discrepancy between Michelangelo's works and the words put in the mouth of Charlton Heston, who represents him here, and this picture—which is mostly about a prolonged wrangle between the sculptor and Pope Julius II (Rex Harrison), who keeps sweeping into the Sistine Chapel and barking, "When will you make an end of it?"—isn't believable for an instant. It was a terrible fiasco for all concerned—the financiers as well as the artists. Carol Reed directed, from Philip Dunne's lugubrious adaptation of the massive Irving Stone best-seller. With Diane Cilento and Harry Andrews. Released by 20th Century-Fox. color

Ah Wilderness! (1935)—This piece of ordinary-family-life Americana, centering on the sweet love pangs of adolescence, is so remote from Eugene O'Neill's life and his other work that it's something of a freak. O'Neill said that the play came to him at night, as a dream, but it seems to be a dream based on Booth Tarkington's world. Eric Linden (who always looks as if he's just about to cry) plays the mooning high-school-valedictorian hero in the era of choking starched collars; that cloying old fraud Lionel Barrymore is his father; Wallace Beery is his tippling uncle; Mickey Rooney is his little brother; and Aline MacMahon and Spring Byington wear neat shirtwaists and make themselves useful about the house. If it sounds Andy Hardyish, it is, and more than a little; in 1948, M-G-M tried to capitalize on the resemblance by starring Rooney in a musical version of the play, called *Summer Holiday*. The musical turned out to be an abomination, but this early version, directed by Clarence Brown, while not

a world-shaker, and rather dim as entertainment, has at last a nice, quiet, comic sense of period. With Cecilia Parker, Charley Grapewin, Frank Albertson, Bonita Granville, and Eddie Nugent. The adaptation is by Albert Hackett and Frances Goodrich. M-G.M. b & w

L'Aigle à deux têtes, see *The Eagle with Two Heads*

Air Force (1943)—One of the "contribution-to-the-war-effort" specials—the biography of a Flying Fortress, a Boeing B-17 nicknamed Mary Ann, that heads out into the Pacific on the eve of Pearl Harbor and goes on to Wake Island and then takes part in the Coral Sea battle and, at the last, is about to participate in the raid on Tokyo. The film is one crisis after another, and the director, Howard Hawks, stages the air battles handsomely, but for the rest it helps if you're interested in the factors involved in getting a bomber somewhere and back. This is one of the most impersonal of the Hawks films; it feels manufactured rather than made. The script by Dudley Nichols, with dialogue by William Faulkner, provided what is meant to be a microcosm of democracy in motion—a melting-pot crew; on board are John Garfield as aerial gunner Winocki, George Tobias as assistant crew chief Weinberg, Gig Young as co-pilot Williams, John Ridgely as Captain Quincannon, Arthur Kennedy as bombardier McMartins, Harry Carey as crew chief White, Charles Drake as the navigator, and James Brown as Rader, who replaces the pilot. Stereotypes all, though acted with professional conviction. The cast includes Edward S. Brophy, Faye Emerson, Dorothy Peterson, Addison Richards, Ann Doran, Stanley Ridges, Willard Robertson, and Moroni Olsen. Cinematography by James Wong Howe. Warners. b & w

Airplane! (1980)—If you were a teen-ager in the late 50s and read the movie lampoons in *Mad* and watched a lot of TV series shows and a lot of cheapie old movies on television and remembered parts of all of them, jumbled together into one dumb movie—that's *Airplane!* It's compiled like a jokebook. Except for a genuinely funny sequence that parodies *Saturday Night Fever*, it has the kind of pacing that goes with a laughtrack. But the three writer-directors (Jim Abrahams and David and Jerry Zucker) keep the gags coming pop pop pop, and the picture is over blessedly fast. With Julie Hagerty and Robert Hays as the young lovers, and Leslie Nielsen, Peter Graves, Robert Stack, Lloyd Bridges, and Kareem Abdul-Jabbar; celebrities such as Howard Jarvis, Maureen McGovern, Jimmie Walker, and Ethel Merman turn up in bits. Based on the 1957 movie *Zero Hour*. Paramount. color (See *Taking It All In*.)

Airport (1970)—Arthur Hailey, the author of the novel on which it's based, publicly explained his methods of work—the number of hours of research per character, the amount of time spent on plotting, etc. The result was the No. 1 best-seller—it sold over 4 million copies—and was bought by the producer Ross Hunter, who assembled a cast and crew with 23 Oscars among them. The baldness of all this might lull you into imagining that the result would be slick fun, but there's no electricity in it, no smart talk, no flair. Written and directed by George Seaton, it's bland entertainment of the old school: every stereotyped action is followed by a stereotyped reaction—clichés commenting on clichés. The actors play such roles as responsible, harried executive (Burt Lancaster), understanding mistress (Jean Seberg), spoiled, selfish wife (Dana Wynter), man who needs to care for someone (Dean Martin), and the someone (Jacqueline Bisset), with Helen Hayes doing her lovable-old-pixie act. The only performer

who suggests a human being is Maureen Stapleton; she manages to bring some intensity out of herself—it certainly isn't in the lines. The picture was a huge success. The cast includes Barry Nelson, George Kennedy, Lloyd Nolan, Barbara Hale, and Jessie Royce Landis. Universal. color

Airport 1975 (1974)—Processed schlock. This could only have been designed as a TV movie and then blown up to cheapie-epic proportions. One can have a fairly good time laughing at it, but it doesn't sit too well as a joke, because the people on the screen are being humiliated. Jack Smight directed, fumblingly; Karen Black and Charlton Heston do the most emoting. The cast includes George Kennedy, Myrna Loy, Linda Blair, Helen Reddy, Gloria Swanson, Dana Andrews, and Sid Caesar. Universal. color (See *Reeling*.)

Alex & the Gypsy (1976)—Off the beaten track, but that's just about the only thing you can give it points for. Jack Lemmon is Alex, a cynical, loquacious bailbondsman, whose character is taken from the Stanley Elkin short novel *The Bailbondsman*, but the movie involves him with a gypsy (Geneviève Bujold) invented by the screenwriter, Lawrence B. Marcus. Lemmon is always up, and works desperately hard. And so Bujold, who's meant to be the vibrant, tempestuous one, has to fight him for every bit of audience attention, and what should be a love story is a shouting match—ersatz D. H. Lawrence and ersatz Billy Wilder. Directed by John Korty; cinematography by Bill Butler. With James Woods, Robert Emhardt, and Gino Ardito. Produced by Richard Shepherd; released by 20th Century-Fox. color (See *When the Lights Go Down*.)

Alex in Wonderland (1970)—Paul Mazursky's account of a movie director (Donald Sutherland), who has just made his first picture (Mazursky had just made his first, *Bob & Carol & Ted & Alice*), fretting and fantasizing over his next project. Alex's fantasy life has no intensity—it's a series of emotionally antiseptic reveries, staged like the big production numbers in a musical. And the film is so loose that one's attention wanders. (It was a total commercial failure.) But Mazursky and his co-writer, Larry Tucker, have an affectionate, ambivalent way of observing the contradictions in how people live—especially in the domestic scenes of Alex and his wife (Ellen Burstyn) and their two daughters, and in the chaotic ambiance of the late-60s Hollywood, where bearded executives wear Indian headbands and consider themselves anti-Establishment. The film has very funny moments, and at least one satiric triumph: a long revue skit in which Alex goes to lunch with a manic producer (played by Mazursky). Sutherland isn't bad—he has a soft-spoken way with dialogue and he's wonderful when he leans back in fatuous satisfaction as Jeanne Moreau (who appears briefly as herself) sings to him, though he's so cool he drifts away while you're watching him. With Federico Fellini (as himself), Meg Mazursky, Glenna Sergent, and Viola Spolin. Cinematography by Laszlo Kovacs. Produced by Tucker, for M-G-M. color (See *Deeper into Movies*.)

Alexander Nevsky (1938)—Sergei Eisenstein's ponderously surging epic has a famous score by Prokofiev and a stunning battle on ice. When it's great it's very great, but there are long deadly stretches (which isn't the case with Eisenstein's other films). The plot has something to do with the 13th-century invasion of Russia by German knights; needless to say, the Russians drive the invaders out. The propaganda isn't Communist but nationalist: the medieval story was used to warn Hitler to stay out. Photographed (as were all Eisenstein's feature films) by Eduard Tisse; with Nikolai Cherkassov as Prince Nevsky. In Russian. b & w

Alexander's Ragtime Band (1938)—The twenty Irving Berlin songs are reason enough for seeing the film, but you have to be prepared for the persistent, mosquito-like irritation of the plot—from 1911 to 1939 two songwriters (Tyrone Power and Don Ameche) are rivals for the affections of Alice Faye, who smiles her overripe, slow smile. Her mellow voice is wonderful on the title song and you want to cheer her rendition of "When That Midnight Choo-Choo Leaves for Alabam'," but you may get to shuddering when she ponders the First World War (exhibited to us in three seconds of newsreel shots) and murmurs, "It was all so futile, wasn't it?" This big, lavish 20th Century-Fox musical, directed by Henry King, has Ethel Merman, Jack Haley, Dixie Dunbar, Chick Chandler, Douglas Fowley, John Carradine, Helen Westley, Ruth Terry, Wally Vernon, and Jean Hersholt. Sets by Boris Leven; dances staged by Seymour Felix; the writers include Kathryn Scola, Lamar Trotti, Richard Sherman, and Irving Berlin. b & w

Alfie (1966)—Michael Caine gives us Alfie, the swaggering Cockney Don Juan, as he sees himself. Alfie doesn't know his own limitations; that's what makes it possible for him to charm so many "birds." Bill Naughton adapted his own material (it had already been a radio play, a stage play, and a novel—in that order) for this British picture, directed by Lewis Gilbert. It's still basically oral—Alfie addresses us, narrating his own story, and his sexual encounters are used as illustrations of his character. But Caine brings out the gusto in Naughton's dialogue and despite the obvious weaknesses in the film (the gratuitous "cinematic" barroom brawl, the clumsy witnessing of the christening, the symbolism of the dog), he keeps the viewer absorbed in

Alfie, the cold-hearted sexual hotshot, and his self-exculpatory line of reasoning. The supporting performers, who appear in a series of sketches and have highly individualized roles, include Julia Foster, Jane Asher, Vivien Merchant, Millicent Martin, Eleanor Bron, Shirley Anne Field, Shelley Winters, Denholm Elliott, Alfie Bass, Graham Stark, Murray Melvin, and Sydney Tafler. The score is by Sonny Rollins. color

Alfredo Alfredo (1973)—Dubbed with a mellifluous Italian voice, Dustin Hoffman gives a warm and friendly performance as a shy young Italian bank clerk, and the novelty of seeing him without his own frightened, choked-up voice adds an extra dimension to this Pietro Germi comedy. Germi's method pits individuals—heaping collections of foibles—against the rigid Italian legal system, with its irrational laws governing marriage, divorce, and cohabitation. But the comic tone is a bit used; everything Germi does here he has done before, and better (especially in *Divorce—Italian Style*). Stefania Sandrelli plays the flighty, extravagantly romantic girl Alfredo marries; his bride's exquisite features give her a look of mystery, but she's an imbecile sphinx, mysterious yet dumb as a cow. The early scenes of her imperiousness and her enslavement of the deliriously impressed Alfredo are high slapstick. But since this character's comedy is all based on the one gag of her insatiability, she becomes as wearying to us as to the exhausted Alfredo. After the first third, the picture sags under a load of uninspired, forced gaiety. It has some beautiful gags, though. Carla Gravina plays the modern independent working woman who liberates Alfredo. Written by Leo Benvenuti, Piero De Bernardi, Tullio Pinelli, and the director. In Italian. color (See *Reeling*.)

Algiers (1938)—An entertaining piece of kitsch, featuring a torrid romance between Charles Boyer and Hedy Lamarr, making her American film début. Directed by John Cromwell, it's a remake of the infinitely superior French film, *Pépé le Moko*, directed by Julien Duvivier—and so close a remake that many of the original sequences are followed shot by shot. Yet this version is pure Hollywood, sacrificing everything to glamour, and the heavy makeup and studio lighting make it all seem so artificial one can get giggly. In the role that Jean Gabin made famous, Boyer (who may be an even greater actor than Gabin) is reduced to giving so many passionate, hot glances at the inhumanly beautiful Lamarr that he almost becomes a self-caricature. He plays Pépé, the French crook who is safe in the Casbah, where he lives like a lord, but who longs for Paris. And Lamarr, with her slurry German-English, plays a Parisienne visiting Algiers. Sigrid Gurie is the native girl in love with Pépé, Joseph Calleia slinks about corners as the suave detective, and Gene Lockhart is the rotten squealer. With Johnny Downs, Alan Hale. Cinematography by James Wong Howe; adaptation by John Howard Lawson, with additional dialogue by James M. Cain. (A 1948 remake, *Casbah*, with Tony Martin as a singing Pépé, tried for—but missed—the heat and glamour.) A Walter Wanger Production; released by United Artists. b & w

Ali Baba and the Forty Thieves (1944)—Maria Montez and Jon Hall in a follow-up to *Arabian Nights*, a picture of such dreamy fatuousness that Universal made a bundle out of it. This time, plump-cheeked, slit-eyed Turhan Bey is the camp treat. With Andy Devine and Fortunio Bonanova. Directed by Arthur Lubin. color

Alice Adams (1935)—Katharine Hepburn, with her young, beautiful angularity and her faintly absurd Bryn Mawr accent, is superbly cast as Booth Tarkington's eager, desperate, small-town social climber. Her Alice is one of the few authentic American movie heroines. George Stevens directed with such a fine sense of detail and milieu that the small-town nagging-family atmosphere is nerve-rackingly accurate and funny. Alice is cursed with a pushing mother (Ann Shoemaker), an infantile father (Fred Stone), and a vulgar brother (Frank Albertson). The picture is cursed only by a fake happy ending: Alice gets what the movie companies considered a proper Prince Charming for her—Fred MacMurray, as a wealthy young man. Even with this flaw, it's a classic, and Hepburn gives one of her two or three finest performances—rivalled, perhaps, only by her work in *Little Women* and *Long Day's Journey Into Night*. With Hattie McDaniel, Evelyn Venable, and Hedda Hopper as a rich bitch. (A 1923 silent version, with Florence Vidor, had a more realistic ending.) R K O. b & w

Alice Doesn't Live Here Anymore (1975)— Ellen Burstyn stars in this Martin Scorsese comedy, from an original script by Robert Getchell, about a 35-year-old widow who sets out with her young son to make a new life. Full of funny malice and breakneck vitality, it's absorbing and intelligent even when the issues it raises get all fouled up. With Harvey Keitel, Kris Kristofferson, Valerie Curtin, Lelia Goldoni, Lane Bradbury, Diane Ladd, Jodie Foster, and, as the son, wire-drawn little Alfred Lutter, who has crack comedy timing. Warners. color (See *Reeling*.)

Alice in Wonderland (1933)—Charmless, wooden version, with Paramount's most famous stars barely recognizable—and then only by their voices, since they appear in huge false heads. And though it's fun to recognize them that way, those voices don't do much for the Lewis Carroll lines. The film was lavishly produced, with great care given to the sets and costumes and makeup, but the spirit is missing. Charlotte Henry plays Alice (with plucked eyebrows), Cary Grant is the Mock Turtle, Gary Cooper is the White Knight, Louise Fazenda is the White Queen, Richard Arlen is the Cheshire Cat, Ned Sparks is the Caterpillar, Jack Oakie is Tweedledum, and Alison Skipworth is the Duchess. Perhaps the best remembered, however, are W. C. Fields as Humpty Dumpty, Edna May Oliver as the Red Queen, Sterling Holloway as the Frog, and Baby Le Roy as the Joker. Norman McLeod directed; the text, by Joseph L. Mankiewicz and William Cameron Menzies, includes material from *Through the Looking Glass*. b & w

Aliens (1986)—An inflated sci-fi action-horror film, this sequel to Ridley Scott's 1979 *Alien* is more mechanical than the first film—more addicted to "advanced" weaponry and military hardware. The movie is really a combat picture set in the future, in space. The writer-director James Cameron pits a platoon of United States Marines (ethnically assorted, of course) against a family of extraterrestrial monsters—a queen and her slimy brood. He does it in an energetic, systematic, relentless way, with an action director's gusto, and a shortage of imagination. The imagery has a fair amount of graphic power, but there's too much claustrophobic blue-green dankness. As Warrant Officer Ripley, the only human survivor of the spaceship that voyaged forth in the earlier picture, Sigourney Weaver seems to take over by natural authority and her strength as an actress. She gives the movie a presence, and Cameron toys with the sex-role reversal by turning the final confrontation with the queen into the Battle of the Big Mamas. But at 2 hours and 17 minutes this is just a very big "Boo!" movie, with bum dialogue. With Michael Biehn, Paul Reiser, Lance Henriksen, Jenette Goldstein as Vasquez the bodybuilder, and Carrie Henn as the wraithlike little girl, Newt, who is out there in space to arouse Ripley's maternal instinct. Produced by Gale Anne Hurd, for 20th Century-Fox. color (See *Hooked*.)

All About Eve (1950)—Ersatz art of a very high grade, and one of the most enjoyable movies ever made. A young aspiring actress, Eve Harrington (Anne Baxter), intrigues to take the place of an aging star, Margo Channing (Bette Davis), on stage and in bed, and the battle is fought with tooth, claw, and a battery of epigrams. The synthetic has qualities of its own—glib, overexplicit, self-important, the "You're sneaky and corrupt but so am I—We belong to each other darling" style of writing. The scriptwriter-director Joseph L. Mankiewicz's bad taste, exhibited with verve, is more fun than careful, mousy, dehydrated good taste. His nonsense about "theatre" is saved by one performance that is the real thing: Bette Davis is at her most instinctive and assured. Her actress—vain, scared, a woman who goes too far in her reactions and emotions—makes the whole thing come alive (though it's hard to believe Anne Baxter could ever be a threat to Bette Davis). With George Sanders (as the critic Addison De Witt), Celeste Holm, Gary Merrill, Thelma Ritter, Gregory Ratoff, Hugh Marlowe, Barbara Bates, Walter Hampden, and Marilyn Monroe, who has one of her best early roles. Based on a short story and radio play by Mary Orr. Academy Awards: Best Picture, Director, Screenplay, Supporting Actor (Sanders), Costume Design (Edith Head, Charles Le Maire), Sound Recording. 20th Century-Fox. b & w

The All-American Boy (1973)—Jon Voight is a prizefighter suffering from a type of working-class alienation that is indistinguishable from bellyache. He mopes through the picture looking puffy, like a rain cloud about to spritz. Charles Eastman wrote and directed this disgracefully condescending view of America as a wasteland populated by grotesques, stupes, and sons of bitches; they are incapable of love and have false values—and to prove it Eastman sets Voight to walking the Antonioni walk. This is probably the only movie on record in which you can watch boxers working out in a gym while you hear a Gregorian chant. With Carol Androsky, Art Metrano, E. J. Peaker, Anne Archer, Ned Glass, Harry Northup, Rosalind Cash, Jeanne Cooper, and Jaye P. Morgan. Warners. color

All Fall Down (1962)—Adapted by William Inge from a James Leo Herlihy novel, this ambitious and elaborately staged John Frankenheimer film is set deep in the Inge territory of homespun and gothic—that strange area of nostalgic Americana where the familiar is the Freudian grotesque. It's also a peculiar kind of fantasy, in which hideous, lecherous women (schoolteachers seem to be the worst offenders) paw handsome young men, and the one girl who might seem attractive (played by Eva Marie Saint) disqualifies herself by becoming pathetically pregnant. As the mother, Angela Lansbury at times steps free of the howling caricature she's playing and becomes extraordinarily moving. But the film turns out to be a portrait of the writer as an adolescent (Brandon deWilde plays the part) who grows up— "matures"—when he learns that the older brother he idolizes (Warren Beatty) is an empty wreck. Does *anybody* really grow up the way this boy grows up? He learns the truth, squares his shoulders, and walks out into the bright sunlight, as Alex North's music rises and swells in victory. How many movies have pulled this damned visual homily on us, this synthetic growing-into-a-man, as if it happened all at once and forever? Suggested party game: ask your friends to tell about the summer they grew up. The one who tells the best lie has a promising career ahead as a Hollywood screenwriter. With Karl Malden, Barbara Baxley, and Madame Spivy; cinematography by Lionel Lindon. Produced by John Houseman, for M-G-M. b & w

All My Sons (1948)—Edward G. Robinson is the money-hungry industrialist who ships a batch of defective airplane-engine cylinders to the Air Force, blames his partner for the crime, and causes one of his sons, an aviator, to commit suicide out of shame. Another son, Burt Lancaster, newly returned from the war, refuses to believe in his father's guilt until overwhelmed by incriminating facts, whereupon he tries to kill the old man. Meanwhile Lancaster has fallen in love with the partner's daughter (Louisa Horton), and has also had a soggy time of it at home, owing to the iron refusal of his mother (Mady Christians) to believe in the death of his aviator brother. Arthur Miller conceived this idea-ridden melodrama, and Irving Reis directed it. Surprisingly, it does work up some energy, but by then you have to be a little saintly to care. With Howard Duff and Frank Conroy. Adapted by Chester Erskine. Universal. b & w

All Night Long (1981)—This sophisticated slapstick romance starring Gene Hackman and Barbra Streisand is a happy surprise. Hackman, doing the kind of comic acting that rings true on every note, plays a Los Angeles business executive who gives up the phony obligations he has accumulated, drops out, and tries to find a way to do what he enjoys. Streisand plays a soft-spoken bleached blonde—intuitive and cuddly—who joins him. Directed by Jean-Claude Tramont and written by W. D. (Rick) Richter, it has a distinctive comic sensibility; at times it suggests Tati, at other times W. C. Fields, and then, maybe, Lubitsch or Max Ophuls. With Dennis Quaid as Hackman's muscular, inarticu-

late son; Diane Ladd as Hackman's wife; Kevin Dobson as Streisand's husband; and William Daniels as a lawyer. The poignant music that is heard is José Padilla's "La Violetera," which was also heard in Chaplin's *City Lights*. Universal. color (See *Taking It All In*.)

All of Me (1984)—Steve Martin is Roger, a lawyer who has been sent to revise the will of Edwina (Lily Tomlin), a rich, bedridden spinster. Edwina has imported a Tibetan swami (Richard Libertini), who at the moment of her death is supposed to capture her spiritual substance in a bronze pot and transfer it into the curvy body of the lovely Terry (Victoria Tennant), who has agreed to vacate it. Edwina instructs Roger to arrange for Terry to inherit everything she has, but he thinks she's crazy and refuses. The argument precipitates her demise, and in the confusion her spirit pops into Roger's body, and enters into joint occupancy with him. This is the nifty premise of a romantic comedy about how two antagonists in the same body fall in love. Martin and Tomlin are both uninhibited physical comics. They tune in to each other's timing the way lovers do in life, only more so, and in her early scenes Tomlin presents a distinctive enough caricature for us to sense Edwina's presence when Martin simulates her being inside him. He's a wizard at keeping her vivid for us. And the director, Carl Reiner, seems to have an intuitive rapport with the two leads, with Libertini as the disoriented Tibetan, with Jason Bernard, who plays a black musician pal of Roger's, and with the talented Madolyn Smith, who plays Roger's nasty fiancée. Reiner's weakness is that the gags aren't thought out visually in terms of the L.A. locations; the camera setups are often klunky, especially in Edwina's mansion (it's Greystone, where *The Loved One* was also shot, and which was for some years the base of the American Film Institute). The film has a halfhearted subplot about Dana Elcar as Roger's philandering boss; it also suffers a dip in energy when Edwina's spirit finally enters Terry's body, because the beautiful, mild Victoria Tennant doesn't indicate that Terry is at all changed. Edwina seems to disappear (but she comes back). Parts of this picture give viewers the kind of giddy pleasure that is often what we most want from the movies. The ingenious script, by Phil Alden Robinson, was adapted from an unpublished novel, *Me Two*, by Ed Davis. Universal. color (See *State of the Art*.)

All Quiet on the Western Front (1930)— Over a hundred million people have gone to theatres to see it and have—perhaps— responded to its pacifist message. One could be cynical about the results, but the film itself does not invite cynical reactions, and the fact that it has frequently been banned in countries preparing for war suggests that it makes militarists uncomfortable. Erich Maria Remarque's 1929 novel, on which it is based, was already famous when Lewis Milestone directed this attack on the senseless human waste of war, made in Hollywood. It follows a handful of young German volunteers in the First World War from school to battlefield, and shows the disintegration of their romantic ideas of war, gallantry, and fatherland in the squalor of the trenches. Except for Louis Wolheim, who is capable of creating a character with a minimum of material, the actors—Lew Ayres, Slim Summerville, Russell Gleason, Billy Bakewell, John Wray, Raymond Griffith, Ben Alexander—are often awkward, uncertain, and overemphatic, but this doesn't seem to matter very much. The point of the film gets to you, and though you may wince at the lines Maxwell Anderson wrote (every time he opens his heart, he sticks his poetic foot in it), you know what he means. (The year 1930 was, of course, a good year for pacifism, which always flour-

ishes between wars; Milestone didn't make pacifist films during the Second World War— nor did anybody else working in Hollywood. And wasn't it perhaps easier to make *All Quiet* just because its heroes were German? War always seems like a tragic waste when told from the point of view of the losers. It would be an altogether different matter to present the death of, say, R.A.F. pilots in the Second World War as tragic waste.) George Cukor was dialogue director, coaching Lew Ayres, in particular; Arthur Edeson did the cinematography; George Abbott, Del Andrews, and Milestone also had a hand in the script. The cast includes Beryl Mercer, Vince Barnett, Heinie Conklin, Edwin Maxwell, Marion Clayton, Yola D'Avril, and Fred Zinnemann, who had just arrived in Hollywood after studying film in Paris and Berlin—he does double duty as a German soldier and a French ambulance driver. Academy Awards: Best Picture, Best Director. Originally 145 minutes; cut when it was reissued in 1939. (Remade in 1979 as a film for TV, with Delbert Mann as director.) Universal. b & w

All Screwed Up *Tutto a Posto e Niente in Ordine* (1974)—Lina Wertmüller finished this film early in 1974, just before starting *Swept Away*. It's a noisy, sprawling, incident-filled, slice-of-life comedy-melodrama about the corruption of the Sicilians who go to Milan. Several aspects of the film, such as its poignant hero, Carletto (Nino Bignamini), and the scene showing the monotonous dehumanization of labor, are reminiscent of René Clair's *À nous la liberté* (which also influenced Chaplin's *Modern Times*). But Wertmüller's point of view is chaotic. The women workers are shown as tightfisted petit-bourgeois schemers who manipulate and exploit their likable proletarian men, and there's a ballet in a slaughterhouse, which has comic bravura but is so ambiguous that we seem to be asked to laugh at the dead animals. Lina

Polito, who was the dark Tripolina in *Love and Anarchy*, is here thin and blond as the lovely Mariuccia, who has quintuplets; Isa Danieli is the dark, soft-faced Elizabeth Taylor–type who turns prostitute. Cinematography by Giuseppe Rotunno. In Italian. color

All That Heaven Allows (1955)—A trashy love story about the attraction between a natural man (Rock Hudson, as a New England tree surgeon) and a frustrated-by-respectability rich widow (Jane Wyman) who is some fifteen years older than he and has two grown children. Hudson and Wyman are hardly an electric combination, but this Ross Hunter production is made with so much symbolism that some people actually see it as allegorical. Its reputation derives from the slurpy, peculiarly glossy intensity of Douglas Sirk's direction—the same sort of pop spirituality that he had brought to Ross Hunter's *Magnificent Obsession*, with the same two stars, the year before. Sirk's blend of Germanic kitsch and Hollywood kitsch was a major influence on the young German director Fassbinder, whose work is a further formalization of Sirk's schematic sentimentality. With Agnes Moorehead, Conrad Nagel, Virginia Grey, Gloria Talbott, and Charles Drake. Written by Peg Fenwick. Universal. color

All the King's Men (1949)—Broderick Crawford's Willie Stark might just make you feel better about the President you've got. Robert Penn Warren's novel about the rise of a bullheaded demagogue (modelled on Huey Long) was turned into a rousing melodrama, full of graft, double-dealing, and strong-arm excitement. Robert Rossen adapted the novel and directed; the film took the Academy Award for Best Picture, with Broderick Crawford also winning Best Actor, and Mercedes McCambridge, as tough Sadie, winning Best Supporting Actress. It's by no means a great film, but it moves along. With John Ireland, Joanne Dru, John Derek, and Shepperd Strudwick; cinematography by Burnett Guffey. Columbia. b & w

All the Way Home (1963)—This adaptation of the Tad Mosel play, set in Knoxville in 1915 and based on James Agee's semi-autobiographical novel *A Death in the Family*, is terribly earnest, pictorial, and well-intentioned. And a terrible mistake. Robert Preston had been a favorite actor of Agee's, but he's clearly in the wrong age bracket to play a young married man, and even the lovely Jean Simmons can't do anything to save her role as his wife, who soon becomes his widow. Michael Kearney is extremely unengaging as the bereaved child. With Aline MacMahon and Pat Hingle. Directed by Alex Segal; adapted by Philip Reisman, Jr.; cinematography by Boris Kaufman. Paramount. b & w

All Through the Night (1942)—The title of this Humphrey Bogart picture is taken from the Johnny Mercer and Arthur Schwartz song (which is sung in a nightclub sequence) and doesn't provide a clue to what the story is about. Some people might think this is one of the good Bogarts that they've missed; on the contrary it's a sugar-coated anti-Nazi message comedy, and so negligible that you've forgotten it ten minutes after you've staggered out. (It feels *long*.) Concocted by Leonard Spigelgass and Edwin Gilbert from a rattlebrained screen story by Spigelgass and Leonard Ross, and directed (ineptly) by Vincent Sherman, it's set in New York (a studio version) during the Second World War. Bogart is "Gloves" Donohue, a Broadway gambler-promoter, and he and his bunch of meant-to-be-lovable Damon Runyonesque demi-racketeers (among them, Frank McHugh, William Demarest, Jackie Gleason) rout an entire Nazi fifth column organization, headed by the supersuave Conrad Veidt, dachshund-loving Judith Anderson, and baby-face hit-man Peter Lorre, who operate under cover of an antiques-auction business. This movie oozes sentimentality, and the coy, frolicsome music is like a TV laugh track. With Jane Darwell at her folksy phoniest as Bogart's Irish ma, Phil Silvers as a near-sighted waiter, Kaaren Verne as the heroine, and Martin Kosleck, Sam McDaniel, Barton MacLane, Wallace Ford, and Ludwig Stossel. Produced by Hal B. Wallis and Jerry Wald, for Warners. b & w

The Alphabet Murders (1965)—Tony Randall as Agatha Christie's Hercule Poirot, with Robert Morley as Major Hastings. Frank Tashlin directed this attempt at a stylish comedy-thriller; it goes very wrong—there's no suspense, because we have no idea what's going on, and the spoofy, slapstick embellishments are almost painfully self-conscious. Randall—perhaps just because he's so talented and inventive—mugs too much: he's always doing something, and then when he does something really good, we're too tired of him to react. Adapted from *The ABC Murders*, by David Pursall and Jack Seddon. With Anita Ekberg, Maurice Denham, James Villiers, and Guy Rolfe. Made in England. b & w

Alphaville (1965)—Jean-Luc Godard ventures into science fiction, with mixed results. The picture is brilliant, yet it's no good. Godard found enough of the future in present-day Paris to create a vision of a new world without constructing sets; it's a sleek, dark, glittering society—at first, the dehumanization is funny and alluring and a little eerie. The modern corridors and ramps and the flickering lights suggest something almost supernaturally impersonal. But the people of Alphaville are ruled by a giant computer, and soullessness can be very monotonous. The movie was shot at night, and it seems to give off powerfully soporific vapors, especially since the comic-strip story is an uninspired mixture of sci-fi and private eye that never takes hold. With Eddie Constantine as cool, tough Lemmy Caution (his face is so tired and leathery he's like an old shoe); Anna Karina—she's the most radiant of robots; Akim Tamiroff; Laszlo Szabo; Michel Delahaye; and Howard Vernon. Written and directed by Godard; cinematography by Raoul Coutard; the score, which has elements of parody, is by Paul Misraki. (In the 1968 *Weekend*, Godard has a very different vision of the dehumanized future: the consumer society regresses to barbarism and cannibalism.) In French. b & w

Altered States (1980)—An aggressively silly head-horror movie, the result of the misalliance of two wildly different hyperbolic talents—the director Ken Russell and the writer Paddy Chayefsky. The picture deals with the efforts of a psychophysiologist (William Hurt), who has lost his belief in God, to find the source and meaning of life by immersing himself in an isolation tank, and ingesting a brew of blood and sacred mushrooms. Chayefsky's dialogue is like a series of position papers. Russell uses a lot of tricks to spare you the misery of hearing the words declaimed straight, but no matter how hopped up the delivery is, you can't help feeling that you're in a lecture hall and that the characters should all have pointers. There are some effectively scary Jekyll-and-Hyde tricks, and Hurt, making his movie début, brings a cool, quivering untrustworthiness to his revved-up mad-scientist role; this young scientist is neurasthenic, charismatic, and ready to try anything. But Russell clomps from one scene to the next, the psychedelic visions come at you like choppy slide shows, and the picture has a dismal, tired humanistic ending. With Bob Balaban and Charles Haid, and with Blair Brown in an updated version of the thankless role of the worrying, hand-wringing wife. She's an anthropologist with a job at Harvard, but all she does is fret. Cinematography by Jordan Cronenweth. Released in the U.S. by Warners. color (See *Taking It All In*.)

Altri Tempi, see *Times Gone By*

Alvin Purple (1974)—Soft-core porno from Australia, said to be the most financially successful film made there up to that time. It's reminiscent of Russ Meyer's *The Immoral Mr. Teas*, but the director, Tim Burstall, isn't innocently clunky like Meyer; his film gives one the impression of a director who is trying to regress to a pubescent state. The premise is that every girl and woman, and even a fella, wants Alvin (Graeme Blundell); as a high-school boy, he is besieged, and when he goes out into the world it's even worse. He functions without a visible erection, which probably accounts for the R rating. A half hour of this picture, and you feel sentenced to eternal giggly imbecility. color

Always (1989)—*A Guy Named Joe* made Steven Spielberg cry when he was 12; his remake can make you want to cry at the waste of his talent and your time. All he seems to want to do in each scene is get an audience reaction; almost everything is grandiloquent, rushed, confusing. And the whole idea has a voyeuristic queasiness. A miscast Richard Dreyfuss is the daredevil hero. The ace pilot of the wilderness-fire-fighting service, he is in love with Holly Hunter. He dies, but returns to serve as the spiritual guide of a shy young pilot (amateurish Brad Johnson), who replaces him in her (grief-stricken) affections. As Dreyfuss's supervisory angel, Audrey Hepburn delivers transcendental inanities in the cadences that have stoned audiences at the Academy Awards; she's become a ceremonial icon. As Dreyfuss's best friend, John Goodman is turned into a fat-jolly-buddy icon; he saves himself from darlingness, but just barely. With Marg Helgenberger as Rachel. The new screenplay is credited to Jerry Belson, though it plays like an amalgam. Amblin Entertainment, for Universal. color (See *Movie Love*.)

Always a Bride (1953)—Peggy Cummins is the girl who goes from hotel to hotel playing a deserted bride in a suave little confidence game. The English had a phenomenal streak during the 50s; they made so many pleasant, deft comedies that this one didn't get much attention here. Peggy Cummins is a fresh comedienne; it's a pity she couldn't have been paired with someone livelier than Terence Morgan, but she does have Ronald Squire as her father, and the cast includes James Hayter, Marie Lohr, Jacques Brunius, Charles Goldner, and Sebastian Cabot. The director, Ralph Smart, wrote the script with Peter Jones. b & w

Amadeus (1984)—The lofty playwright Peter Shaffer has the minor composer Salieri (F. Murray Abraham) declaring war on Heaven for gypping him, and determined to ruin the incomparable Wolfgang Amadeus Mozart (Tom Hulce) because God's voice is speaking through him. The story is told to a priest (and to us) many years later, by the mad, suicidal old Salieri, and there is the suggestion that what we're seeing is his delusion, but the weight of the production, which is reminiscent of big biographical movies such as *The Life of Emile Zola* and *A Song to Remember*, asserts its own kind of authority. The director, Miloš Forman, trudges through the movie as if every step were a major contribution to art, and he keeps the audience hooked. Some redeeming qualities: Mozart's music, Twyla Tharp's staging of the dances and opera excerpts, Abraham's eager, slimy Salieri, Jeffrey Jones' amusingly vapid Emperor Joseph II, and downtown Prague as 18th-century Vienna. Academy Awards: Best Picture, Director, Actor (Abraham), Adapted Screenplay, Art Direction, Costume Design, Makeup, Sound. Produced by Saul Zaentz; an Orion release. color (See *State of the Art.*)

L'Amant de cinq jours, see *The Five-Day Lover*

Les Amants de Teruel, see *The Lovers of Teruel*

Les Amants de Vérone, see *Lovers of Verona*

America America (1963)—Elia Kazan's account, drawn from his own family background, of the fierce struggle of a Greek boy at the turn of the century to escape the persecutions that the Greeks suffered in Turkey and to make his way to the fabled land of opportunity. Though the picture is flawed by the miscasting of the central role (Stathis Giallelis doesn't convince you that he has the will or the passion—or the brains—to realize his dream), and the main narrative line is unconvincing melodrama, there are some fine images, such as the sealed, stifling, yet warm and inviting interiors of a rich merchant's home in Constantinople, and some memorable performances, such as Paul Mann's as the merchant and Linda Marsh's as his daughter. You can feel the desperate ambitiousness to create an epic (this film was intended as the first of a trilogy), and some of the crowd scenes that the cinematographer, Haskell Wexler, has shot have scale and turmoil and a feeling of authenticity. Yet the hero is so blandly uninteresting that there's nothing to hold the movie together, and the tired ideas in the script (by Kazan)—such as a Judas figure who robs the hero and a Christ figure who gives his life for the hero—become embarrassing. With Lou Antonio, Salem Ludwig, Frank Wolff, and John Marley. Music by Manos Hadjidakis; editing by Dede Allen; production design by Gene Callahan. (168 minutes.) Warners. b & w

America at the Movies (1976)—An anxiously inspirational compilation film put together by the American Film Institute for the American Revolution Bicentennial Administration; you can't just enjoy the clips as reminders of the 83 movies they're from, because the whole enterprise has such an official, high moral tone. You feel as if you're supposed to go out determined to do better on your next report card. color and b & w (See *When the Lights Go Down.*)

The American Friend (1977)—The young German director Wim Wenders is attracted to the idea of telling a story, but he can't quite keep his mind on it; he overdoses on mood—poetic urban masochism—in this adaptation of Patricia Highsmith's crime novel *Ripley's Game.* Wenders' unsettling compositions are neurotically beautiful visions of a disordered world, but the film doesn't have the nasty, pleasurable cleverness of a good thriller; dramatically, it's stagnant—inverted Wagnerianism. Bruno Ganz is impressive as the watchful, anxious-eyed hero; with more than a half-dozen directors (including Dennis Hopper, Nicholas Ray, Gérard Blain, and Samuel Fuller) playing crooks. Script by Wenders; cinematography by Robby Müller. In English, German, and French. color (See *When the Lights Go Down.*)

American Hot Wax (1978)—Cheerfully, trashily enjoyable, even though the hero, the disc jockey Alan Freed (well played by Tim McIntire), is made so righteous that he's like Buford Pusser fighting the enemies of rock 'n' roll. The moviemakers (the director Floyd Mutrux, the producer Art Linson, the screenwriter John Kaye) should have had more trust in the 50s rock milieu and in their own talents. Freed's secretary, Sheryl (Fran Drescher), is so entertainingly shrill that she might have had Jean Harlow for a voice teacher; his shovel-faced chauffeur, Mookie (Jay Leno), teases her and keeps her shrieking in outrage. This is a super B-movie. With Laraine Newman, Chuck Berry, Jerry Lee Lewis, and Moosie Drier as the 12-year-old president of the Buddy Holly Fan Club (5,000 members). The lively cinematography is by William A. Fraker. Paramount. color (See *When the Lights Go Down*.)

An American in Paris (1951)—The Academy Award–winning musical, directed by Vincente Minnelli, about a romance between an American painter (Gene Kelly) and a French girl (Leslie Caron). Too fancy and overblown (there's a ballet with scenes in the styles of Dufy, Renoir, Utrillo, Rousseau, van Gogh, and Toulouse-Lautrec), but the two dancing lovers have infectious grins and the Gershwin music keeps everything good-spirited. The songs include "I Got Rhythm," "Embraceable You," and " 'S Wonderful," and Georges Guétary sings a spiffy arrangement of "I'll Build a Stairway to Paradise." With Nina Foch as a rich, decadent American, and Oscar Levant thumping away happily on the piano. Written by Alan Jay Lerner; choreographed by Kelly; art direction by Cedric Gibbons and Preston Ames; produced by Arthur Freed. M-G-M. color

American Madness (1932)—A topical melodrama of the Depression. It's about a run on a bank—and with a twist that is purest Hollywood. The big banker (Walter Huston) is the hero, and it's his lower-echelon employees who are the villains. Frank Capra directed, and Robert Riskin wrote the script. Capra's dramatic use of the bank, where almost all the action is set, is ingenious, and the sequences of the mounting panic and the storming of the bank are effectively staged, but the resolution is the usual Capra-Riskin populist hokum: the small depositors, grateful to Huston for his help in the past, bring in their savings to preserve his bank from ruin. (Even this early in his career, Capra often underestimated the audience.) In some cities, the picture was *too* topical: in Baltimore, it opened the day after a bank panic and closed in 48 hours. With Pat O'Brien, Constance Cummings, Kay Johnson, and Gavin Gordon. Columbia. b & w

An American Tragedy (1931)—This version of the Dreiser novel, scripted by Samuel Hoffenstein and directed by Josef von Sternberg, is best in the scenes relating to the poor, pregnant factory girl, Roberta (Sylvia Sidney), and her drowning; Sylvia Sidney is so appealing that the pathos of Roberta's situation is intensified. However, the film vulgarizes Dreiser's conception of Clyde Griffiths (the handsome, long-jawed, blond Phillips Holmes, who died young), and turns his drives and actions into tabloid commonplaces. Von Sternberg shows surprisingly little of the feeling for psychological complexity that he had brought to *The Blue Angel* the year before, and Dreiser furiously protested this picture (he sued Paramount). Although the film respects his framework, it seems indifferent to what it meant in the novel. What's left—a tragic romance—is still very affecting. Frances Dee is the rich Sondra (the role Elizabeth Taylor played in a later version, *A Place in the Sun*), and the cast includes Irving Pichel. Lee Garmes is the cinematographer. b & w

Amici per la Pelle Also known as *Friends for Life* and *The Woman in the Painting*. (1955)—Franco Rossi's film is an intuitive study of the emotional involvement of two boys—glittering little fawns who suggest an earlier stage in the lives of the schoolboys of *Les Enfants terribles*. Films that deal with the pains of love in the undifferentiated period of early adolescence are usually crude and coy; this one is almost too tender, too "sensitive" to the beauty of youthful agony. But it respects the dreams and the humor of its subjects. Dark, incredibly beautiful Geronimo Meynier is the assured Mario; blond Andrea Scire (the more gifted actor of the two) is Franco. This movie is conceived on a small scale and it never attracted much of an audience here except among homosexuals—although it doesn't have any overt homosexual content. In Italian. b & w

Among the Living (1941)—Forgettable horror item about two brothers, one of them a homicidal maniac, the other a prosperous, married citizen; Albert Dekker, unshaved when mad, shaved when sane, plays the pair. With Frances Farmer and Harry Carey. Directed by Stuart Heisler. Paramount. b & w

D'Amore e d'Anarchia, see *Love and Anarchy*

The Amorous Bus Driver (1953)—(From *Tempi Nostri*, the omnibus of five short stories directed by Alessandro Blasetti, released in the U.S. in 1959 as *Anatomy of Love*.) In middle age, Vittorio De Sica exhibited a facility for romantic self-satire (Gina Lollobrigida and Sophia Loren bloomed when he leered). His performance here is a demonstration of the traditional (and highly enjoyable) Italian overacting in which character is subordinate to the florid gestures of gallantry. He's a happy Neapolitan bus-driver who swerves from his prescribed route whenever he sees a woman he deems worth following. With Maria Fiore (who did some chasing of her own in *Two Cents Worth of Hope*) and Eduardo de Filippo. In Italian. b & w

Un Amour de Swann, see *Swann in Love*

L'Amour fou (1968)—During the first half hour, there's a strong temptation to flee from this legendary Jacques Rivette film, which moves back and forth between the rehearsals for an experimental production of Racine's *Andromaque* and the disintegrating marriage of the actor-director (Jean-Pierre Kalfon) and his actress-wife (Bulle Ogier). But those who stick with the film may find that Rivette's measured, unemphatic style begins to take hold. Tight little Bulle Ogier is ominously compelling; she gives a superlative performance. And there has never been anything like the *folie-à-deux* sex-and-destruction orgy that climaxes the marriage. The purpose of the juxtapositions remains damned elusive, but a highly intellectualized horror story develops inside the smooth, elegantly patterned, abstract camera movement. Rivette has a hypnotic style, partly because of his unusual spatial sense and his "normal" use of time. (4 hours and 12 minutes.) In French. b & w

L'Amour, l'après-midi, see *Chloe in the Afternoon*

Anatahan (1953)—Josef von Sternberg's last film; he did not, regrettably, go out in glory. He wrote the screenplay, directed, photographed, and narrated this story, which was shot in a Japanese studio and is based on an actual incident involving a group of Japanese soldiers who were castaways for seven years on a tiny Pacific island during and after the Second World War. However, as he tells it, the men's battles over a sulky, lusting femme fatale called Keiko (Akemi Negishi, who is photographed as if she were Marlene Dietrich in a 30s Paramount swampy jungle) are so pointless and unbelievable that you barely react as they kill one another off. The island has so many dead trees, shining leaves, and writhing shadows that you just want to get out of there. b & w

Anchors Aweigh (1945)—This Gene Kelly–Frank Sinatra musical has an abundance of energy and spirit, and you may feel it could be wonderful if it weren't so stupidly wholesome, and if you could just *do* something about Kathryn Grayson and José Iturbi—like maybe turn Terry Southern loose on them. The sugary wholesomeness was the stock in trade of the producer, Joe Pasternak; characters in his movies always look scrubbed and sexless, and act embarrassingly young. Pasternak doesn't destroy Kelly's bounding vitality, however; this was the hit movie that made him a hugely popular star. He and Sinatra play sailors on shore leave in Hollywood who get involved with Grayson, a singer working as an extra and living with her chubby-faced angelic little nephew (Dean Stockwell). In the worst sequence, Sinatra sings Brahms' "Lullaby" to Stockwell. Kelly has three big dance numbers, including the famous Jerry the Mouse cartoon dance, and he and Sinatra perform together amiably. With Pamela Britton, Edgar Kennedy, Grady Sutton, Rags Ragland, Billy Gilbert, and Sharon McManus—the little girl who dances with Kelly. George Sidney directed; Kelly choreographed, with Stanley Donen assisting. The songs are mostly by Sammy Cahn and Jule Styne. M-G-M. color

And Then There Were None (1945)—The Agatha Christie murder mystery and play *Ten Little Indians* (known in England as *Ten Little Niggers*) gathers together a group of characters and then ticks them off to the nursery rhyme. Ten people are invited to spend a weekend on an island by a host none of them knows; on arrival, they are notified by phonograph that their host, in absentia, is going to punish them for various crimes they have committed, and they start keeling over like plague victims. This René Clair version isn't exactly full of life to start with, despite the cast—Judith Anderson, June Duprez, Roland Young, Walter Huston, Mischa Auer, Barry Fitzgerald, Richard Haydn, Louis Hayward, C. Aubrey Smith, Queenie Leonard, and Harry Thurston. The efforts at sprightly, stylish comedy don't gain much momentum. Adapted by Dudley Nichols. (There were English versions made in 1965 and 1974. The Christie material was also parodied in the boisterous, unfunny 1976 *Murder By Death*, written by Neil Simon.) 20th Century-Fox. b & w

The Anderson Tapes (1971)—An energetic but coarsely made comic melodrama about an attempt to rob all the tenants of a New York apartment house. As the gang leader, Sean Connery manages to rise above the material; most of the rest of the cast plays in a broad style, and there have rarely been so many small, sleazy performances in one movie. (They're so bad they stand out.) A lot of time is spent on a gimmick—everybody's conversations are being recorded—which turns out to be totally irrelevant to the plot. Some may be willing to call this irony. Directed by Sidney Lumet; screenplay by Frank R. Pierson, from a novel by Lawrence Sanders. With Martin Balsam, Dyan Cannon, Alan King, Ralph Meeker, Christopher Walken, Garrett Morris, Val Avery, Dick Williams, Richard B. Schull, Margaret Hamilton, Anthony Holland, Max Showalter, Stan Gottlieb, and Conrad Bain. Columbia. color

Androcles and the Lion (1952)—After Shaw's death, Gabriel Pascal, who had produced Shaw adaptations in England with considerable success but had come a cropper with the lavish *Caesar and Cleopatra*, produced his last Shaw work in Hollywood, at R K O. He hired Jean Simmons, who had had a small part in *Caesar and Cleopatra*, and Robert Newton, who had attracted attention in *Major Barbara*, and Maurice Evans, Elsa Lanchester, Alan Mowbray, Reginald Gardiner, and John

Hoyt. The part of Androcles was assigned to the American comedian Alan Young, but since Victor Mature was put in as a Roman captain, opposite Jean Simmons, and his role beefed up to match his physique, Androcles dwindled in importance. Shaw's comedy of ancient Rome came to resemble the Hollywood Roman spectacles of the early-50s period. But if the film isn't one thing or the other, it isn't a total travesty, either—it's rather pleasant. Simmons is lovely to watch and to listen to, and some parts have the Shaw waggishness and charm. Chester Erskine directed, and did the adaptation with Ken Englund; cinematography by Harry Stradling. The cast includes Jim Backus and Gene Lockhart. b & w

The Andromeda Strain (1971)—Biological invasion from outer space. The rapidly expanding green muck is like the various slimy menaces in the unpretentious sci-fi thrillers of the 50s, but Robert Wise, who made this expensive version of the Michael Crichton novel, having chosen a fanatically realistic documentary style, has failed to solve the dramatic problems in the original story. The suspense is strong, but not pleasurable. With Arthur Hill, David Wayne, James Olson, Kate Reid, and Paula Kelly. Universal. color (See *Deeper into Movies*.)

Angel (1937)—The only Marlene Dietrich movie directed by Ernst Lubitsch (though the year before he was the producer of *Desire*). One might expect them to bring out the scintillating best in each other, but the picture is too prettily contrived, and the craftsmanship is right on the surface. Dietrich plays the lonely foreign wife of an eminent English diplomat (Herbert Marshall); she skips off for a day to Paris and visits a house of assignation (euphemistically called a salon) presided over by Laura Hope Crews. There she meets Melvyn Douglas (another government official),

and he falls passionately in love with her. Naturally, he turns up at her London home. This is one of Dietrich's stiffest, most impassive performances; the role doesn't give her anything to do but look blankly frightened that her husband will discover her guilty secret. Boredom must have set in for her, because when she has to express emotional turmoil she rattles off her lines without conviction. For want of action, the movie keeps cutting to what's going on among the fleet of servants, which includes Ernest Cossart and also Edward Everett Horton, who playacts as if to an audience of fey 3-year-olds. This movie isn't essentially different from the best of Lubitsch, but it's attenuated. It's the sort of cultivated triangular love affair in which each of the three has a turn at the piano, and Marshall and Douglas, whose acting is a matter of lifted eyebrows and the smallest shifts of inflection, have the affable man-of-the-world conversations that were a feature of "polished" 30s comedies. With Herbert Mundin, Ivan Lebedeff, Dennie Moore, and Herbert Evans. The screenplay is by Samson Raphaelson, from a play by Melchior Lengyel. Paramount. b & w

Angel and the Badman (1947)—Pleasantly unslick minor Western, with John Wayne as Quirt, the gunfighter who reforms, matched against Bruce Cabot as the villainous Laredo. It's easily distinguishable from other Wayne Westerns: Gail Russell, of the sexy-sad eyes, is the Quaker heroine—one of the few Western heroines who suggests softness and body warmth. James Edward Grant, who worked on many Wayne films as a writer, was both writer and director this time; he did not excel in the latter capacity, though he did stage a classic Wayne walk to meet the villains for the final shootout. Wayne is in a dark shirt and dark wide hat, and he moves fast, swivel-hipped, like a broken-field runner. With Irene Rich, Harry Carey, Lee Dixon, Tom

Powers, and Paul Hurst. The second unit director, Yakima Canutt, was responsible for the big action sequences. A John Wayne Production, for Republic. b & w

Angel Heart (1987)—There's no way to separate the occult from the incomprehensible in this Alan Parker film set in 1955. Mickey Rourke plays a private eye who is hired by a mysterious client (Robert De Niro) to search for information about a crooner of the prewar era who has disappeared. Rourke searches in the murkiest holes in America—New Orleans is almost as dim as the New York slums. Every place Rourke goes is artfully arranged to be scuzzy, and *he's* scuzzy, although women don't seem to mind. He has a cajoling, intimate manner with Elizabeth Whitcraft as a ready-for-action blonde, with Charlotte Rampling as a sullen psychic, and especially with the sexpot Lisa Bonet as a teen-age Mambo priestess who has a penchant for smearing herself with chicken blood. This is a lavishly sombre piece of hokum—funereal and loony. Parker broods while serving up slit throats, bodies with hearts cut out (and placed nearby for your delectation), a man plunged face down in a vat of scalding gumbo, chickens being drained in voodoo rites, and assorted solemn mutilations. And it all looks fussed over. Parker simply doesn't have the gift of making evil seductive, and he edits like a flasher. With Brownie McGhee, Michael Higgins, and Stocker Fontelieu in the vat. Parker wrote the screenplay, based on William Hjortsberg's *Falling Angel*. Cinematography by Michael Seresin; music by Trevor Jones. Tri-Star. color (See *Hooked*.)

Angel on My Shoulder (1946)—Gangster whimsey—which is to say the very worst kind. Paul Muni is depressingly arch as a tough-talking gangster who is shot, sent to Hell, and there discovered by the Devil (Claude Rains) to be a dead ringer for an upstanding judge who has been saving people and sending them to Heaven. In order to spread evil on earth, the Devil arranges to get the bad guy into the body of the judge; pretty soon the gangster is involved in a political campaign, and with the judge's fiancée (Anne Baxter), too. The picture was a deserved flop. Archie Mayo directed. United Artists. b & w

Angels Over Broadway (1940)—Ben Hecht wrote, produced, and, with the famous cinematographer Lee Garmes, directed this night-life story about a poor clerk (John Qualen) who is going to kill himself if he can't get $3,000, and a drunken playwright (Thomas Mitchell) who takes him in charge. The playwright thinks that since sharp gamblers always let you win at poker before they trim you, the trick is to leave the game early. Rita Hayworth and Douglas Fairbanks, Jr., are the young lovers who complicate the playwright's plan. Hecht's characters talk too much, but he was a compulsive gambler himself, and there's a genial, original spirit to this movie. Columbia. b & w

Angels with Dirty Faces (1938)—An entertaining picture lurks behind that uninviting title. Warners threw its assets together in this one: James Cagney at his cockiest as a gangster, Pat O'Brien as a priest, and Humphrey Bogart, Ann Sheridan, George Bancroft, and the Dead End Kids, too. It has jokes and romance and a smashing big last sequence on Death Row—the priest asks the gangster to act cowardly when he's executed, so that he won't be a hero to the Dead End Kids, and Cagney comes through with a rousing finale. Michael Curtiz directed; John Wexley and Warren Duff wrote the screenplay, based on Rowland Brown's story. (It was followed the next year by *The Angels Wash Their Faces*.) b & w

Animal Crackers (1930)—The Marx Brothers in their pre-Hollywood period; like *The Cocoanuts* of the year before, it was a Broadway musical comedy, slightly adapted, and filmed in Astoria—and it looks stagey. But the film is too joyous for cavilling. Groucho is the fearless African explorer Captain Spaulding, who deigns to attend a party at Rittenhouse Manor on Long Island; Margaret Dumont is Mrs. Rittenhouse and Lillian Roth is her daughter Arabella. Arguably the best line: "Signor Ravelli's first selection will be 'Somewhere My Love Lies Sleeping' with a male chorus." Once again, the writers were George S. Kaufman and Morrie Ryskind; this time the songs (the justly celebrated "Hooray for Captain Spaulding" and "Why Am I So Romantic") were by Bert Kalmar and Harry Ruby. Directed by Victor Heerman. Paramount. b & w

Anna and the King of Siam (1946)—In this first movie version of Margaret Landon's account of the Englishwoman who went to Siam in 1862 to teach the multitudinous children of the barbaric king, Irene Dunne is Anna to Rex Harrison's king. Harrison wears a dusky makeup and a pair of short pants that wrap around his haunches, and he speaks in a quaint dialect—a sort of pidgin Piccadilly—but he's never less than magnetically ridiculous. You don't want to take your eyes off him—certainly not to watch Irene Dunne curtsying in her starched petticoats. It's pitifully unauthentic, and not a very good movie, either, but the story itself holds considerable interest. Linda Darnell is brashly American but luscious as the king's favorite wife; with Lee J. Cobb, well-tanned, as the bare-chested Siamese prime minister, and Gale Sondergaard, Mikhail Rasumny, and John Abbott. Directed by John Cromwell, from the script by Talbot Jennings and Sally Benson; score by Bernard Herrmann. (In the 1956 musical version, *The King and I*, the leads

were Deborah Kerr and Yul Brynner.) 20th Century-Fox. b & w

Anna Christie (1930)—One waits for an eternity for Garbo to show up and utter her first talking-picture line—"Give me a whiskey, ginger ale on the side. And don't be stingy, baby." This is not one of Eugene O'Neill's best plays, and dat-ole-davil-sea stuff is pretty hard to take in this version, directed by Clarence Brown. The cast includes Charles Bickford, Marie Dressler, and George F. Marion. M-G-M. b & w

Anna Karenina (1935)—Greta Garbo is Anna in this version, directed by Clarence Brown from a screenplay that S. N. Behrman, Clemence Dane, and Salka Viertel all worked on. The picture is more M-G-M than Tolstoy; the cast includes Fredric March as Vronsky and Basil Rathbone as Karenin, and also Maureen O'Sullivan, Constance Collier, May Robson, Mischa Auer, and Freddie Bartholomew. God knows it isn't all it might be, and Garbo isn't even at her best, but she's there to be gazed upon. b & w

Anne of the Thousand Days (1970)—This version of the events that led Henry VIII to make himself head of the Church of England is intelligent from line to line, but the emotions that are supplied seem hypothetical, and the conception lacks authority. Richard Burton's Henry is conceived as a weak, tentative, somewhat apologetic monarch, and though Burton delivers his speeches with considerable sureness and style, his performance is colorless; it's almost as if he *remembered* how to act but couldn't work up much enthusiasm or involvement. Geneviève Bujold's Anne Boleyn is a clever, wily, sexually experienced young girl who keeps the King waiting for her sexual favors for six years—until he can marry her and make their children heirs to the throne. Bujold works at the role with all her will and intelligence, and her readings are often extraordinary, but she's too tight and too self-contained; one admires her as an actress but does not really warm to her performance. The adapters sharpened Maxwell Anderson's play, and the dialogue is often much crisper than one anticipates, but the script has a structural weakness: it does not convince us that after all those years of waiting for Anne the King would turn against her when she gives birth to a daughter. And at the end we're left with Maxwell Anderson's glowing, fatuous hindsight: a final shot of Anne's posthumous triumph—the baby Elizabeth wandering about, deserted, as her foolish father, who doesn't know what *we* know, goes off to beget a male heir. The director is Charles (Static Camera) Jarrott; with Irene Papas, Michael Hordern, John Colicos, and Anthony Quayle. Script by John Hale and Bridget Boland. Produced by Hal B. Wallis, for Universal. color (See *Deeper into Movies*.)

L'Année dernière à Marienbad, see *Last Year at Marienbad*

Annie (1982)—As the soused, man-hungry Miss Hannigan, the head of the New York City orphanage where Annie lives till the age of 10, Carol Burnett is both hag and trollop, and her inflections spin around and make her the butt of her own sarcasm; she's gloriously macabre. But the rest of this big movie (which is set in 1933) has the feel of a manufactured romp. Annie (Aileen Quinn) and the other little orphans seem to have been trained by Ethel Merman; they belt in unison. And when they dance it's showy leaping about, and the editing breaks it up, making it more hectic. When Annie, who is invited to the mansion of the billionaire Daddy Warbucks, arrives, his household staff dances, and the cutting is so choppy that the pump-and-tumble dancing—arms like pistons, and

stamping feet—turns into commotion. Children from about 4 to about 11 will probably enjoy the picture—how often do they get to see a musical that features a little girl conquering all? Produced by Ray Stark and directed by John Huston. As Daddy Warbucks, Albert Finney (with a shaved head) gives a smooth, amused performance and models his manner of speech on Huston's awesome velvet growl. With Ann Reinking as Warbucks' secretary, Tim Curry as Rooster, Geoffrey Holder as Punjab, Bernadette Peters as Lily, Edward Herrmann as F. D. R., and the little scene-stealer Toni Ann Gisondi as Molly. The script is by Carol Sobieski; music by Charles Strouse and lyrics by Martin Charnin; choreography by Arlene Phillips and musical sequences by Joe Layton. Columbia. color (See *Taking It All In*.)

Annie Get Your Gun (1950)—The historical Frank Butler behaved very sensibly: when he realized that his wife, Annie Oakley, was a better shot than he, he retired from competition and managed her career. (He was an excellent manager: when the remarkable old lady died in 1926, she left a half million dollars.) In this M-G-M version of the Broadway musical, Annie, discovering that "you can't get a man with a gun," convinces Frank that he's a better shot; this plot allows for 10 Irving Berlin songs, which are surprisingly exhilarating in their simple crudity. The whole movie has a kind of primer mentality ("Folks are dumb where I come from/They ain't had any learnin'./Still they're happy as can be/ Doin' what comes natur'lly."), but it comes across as a rousing, good show. Betty Hutton's all-out comic desperation is very appealing; she seems emotionally naked and even strident, but in a way that works for her (as it did also in *The Miracle of Morgan's Creek*). Her performance didn't get the praise it deserved, though—probably because she had replaced Judy Garland (who had suffered a breakdown). There were other calamities on this production, which started with Busby Berkeley as director; then Charles Walters took over, and then George Sidney—who is probably the one to thank for the film's happy spirit. Howard Keel was a fine choice for Frank Butler; cast against type, Louis Calhern is an effective Buffalo Bill. (Frank Morgan, who started in the role, died, and his scenes had to be reshot.) The cast includes Edward Arnold, Keenan Wynn, Clinton Sundberg, Benay Venuta, and J. Carrol Naish. Produced by Arthur Freed; adapted by Sidney Sheldon, from the Herbert and Dorothy Fields text for the Broadway show; choreography by Robert Alton; the Irving Berlin songs were scored by Adolph Deutsch and Roger Edens. color

Annie Oakley (1935)—Barbara Stanwyck was an amazing vernacular actress. As the backwoods girl who joins Buffalo Bill's Wild West Show and becomes internationally famous for her marksmanship (and showmanship), she's consistently fresh and believable, and she brings a physical charge to the role. The film, directed by George Stevens, makes some of the points about race he made later in *Giant* (and that Arthur Penn made in *Little Big Man*), but here they're lighter and better. They seem to grow casually out of the American material; the movie feels almost improvised. (It covers much of the material that seems strained in the improvisational style of Robert Altman's 1976 *Buffalo Bill and the Indians*.) The screenplay, by Joel Sayre and John Twist, from a story by Joseph A. Fields and Ewart Adamson, emphasizes Annie's instinctive unwillingness to humiliate the handsome World's Champion Sharpshooter (Preston Foster) by outshooting him. She settles for the title of the World's Greatest Woman Rifle Shot. (The movie makes the case that she's a realist even when she's in love—that she's a realist because she's so completely in love.) Maybe the cast intu-itively responded to Stanwyck's talent: everyone in the Wild West troupe seems to know that Annie Oakley is no ordinary person. As for Preston Foster, he's blandly unexciting yet he brings a masculine charm to his role. With Moroni Olsen as Buffalo Bill, Chief Thunder Bird as Sitting Bull, and Melvyn Douglas, Pert Kelton, and Andy Clyde. R K O. b & w

Another Part of the Forest (1948)—Apparently, Lillian Hellman couldn't shake off the predatory Hubbards after *The Little Foxes*; she wrote this play about the same family, setting it back 30 years earlier in their dark history. The Hubbards, who are supposed to be rising Southern capitalists, are the greatest collection of ghouls since *The Old Dark House* of 1932. Hellman must combine witchcraft with stagecraft—who else could keep a plot in motion with lost documents, wills, poisonings, and pistols, and still be considered a social thinker? Fredric March is the profiteer paterfamilias (he betrayed 27 local soldiers during the Civil War); son Ben (Edmond O'Brien) robs and blackmails Papa; son Oscar (Dan Duryea) organizes Ku Klux Klan raids—need we go on with this? The others are Ann Blyth, Florence Eldridge, John Dall, Betsy Blair, Dona Drake, etc. Mostly, they act as if they were warming up for an American version of *Ivan the Terrible*. Michael Gordon directed. Universal. b & w

Another Thin Man (1939)—The third in the series, and without any new ideas except a bad one: still airily casual, Nick and Nora Charles (William Powell and Myrna Loy) are now the parents of a baby boy. The screenplay (once again by Frances Goodrich and Albert Hackett) tosses shootings and skulduggery and repartee at us before we're ready, and then Nick Charles takes an unconscionable amount of time sorting things out. The plot involves a weekend at the estate of an explosives manufacturer (C. Aubrey Smith) who expects Sheldon Leonard (looking very young and sleek) to kill him. The film is dispiriting, but a lot of amusingly familiar faces turn up, among them Otto Kruger, Ruth Hussey, Virginia Grey, Nat Pendleton, Tom Neal, Marjorie Main, Abner Biberman, and, of course, Asta. Directed by W. S. Van Dyke. M-G-M. b & w

Another Woman (1988)—Woody Allen's (unofficial) version of Ingmar Bergman's *Wild Strawberries* features Gena Rowlands as a firm-minded, judgmental philosophy professor who has just turned 50. Having taken a year off to write a book, she has rented a workplace, but "reality" leaks through: the voices of an analyst's patients come through an air vent, and she becomes obsessed with the voice of a distraught pregnant woman (Mia Farrow), whose confused feelings awaken the professor to the risk-taking she has put out of her own fearful, prudent life. As if by magic, she begins to encounter people she used to know and to flash back to scenes from her past. And she realizes she has missed out on passion, on motherhood, on everything that matters. The picture is meant to be about emotion, but it has no emotion. It's smooth and high-toned; it's polished in its nothingness. The only resonance comes from a few of the performers—especially from Gene Hackman, who comes through with some sexual magnetism, and Sandy Dennis, who lets loose with bursts of smudgy, chaotic anger. The huge cast includes Martha Plimpton, Blythe Danner, Bruce Jay Friedman, Ian Holm, Harris Yulin, Philip Bosco, Kenneth Welsh, Betty Buckley, John Houseman, and David Ogden Stiers. Cinematography by Sven Nykvist. Orion. color (See *Movie Love*.)

Ansiktet, see *The Magician*

Anthony Adverse (1936)—Not Fredric March's finest 2 hours and 20 minutes: he wasn't a physical enough presence to play a dashing, swashbuckling hero. This turgid story involves a lot of crowds and plenty of travel. March takes part in the Napoleonic Wars, as well as in the slave trade, and along the way he misplaces his wife, Olivia de Havilland. When he finds her, it turns out that she has been even busier than he; she has managed to become a great opera star and a famous shady lady. Which might have been an entertaining plot development if the director hadn't been humorless Mervyn LeRoy, drudging away. Claude Rains plays a haughty, gout-ridden marquis, and Gale Sondergaard, whose leer was her fortune, is the superwicked villainess; with Anita Louise, Louis Hayward, and Akim Tamiroff. The novel by Hervey Allen was adapted by Sheridan Gibney. Warners. b & w

Antigone (1961)—An unjustly neglected version of the Sophocles drama, adapted and directed by George Tzavellas so that the action is lucid and uncluttered, the characters are driven by instinct and passion, and the voices (speaking modern Greek) are eloquent. The commenting chorus (the bane of movie adaptations of classic Greek plays and of many stage versions, too) has been reduced to a minimum. The action moves from the formalized setting of the palace at Thebes to the natural landscape of hills and plains without sacrificing the formal power of the performances, though it may take viewers a little while to adjust to this mixture of stylization and naturalism. The young Irene Papas is the strong yet defenseless Antigone, daughter of Oedipus, who rebels against the kingly authority of her uncle Creon (the great Manos Katrakis); she breaks an unjust law— a law that violates her deepest feelings and her sense of justice and obligation—and is condemned to be buried alive. Papas and Katrakis give splendidly matched antagonistic performances, and there are memorable sequences, such as that of Antigone stealing into the countryside to bury her dead brother, who has been left exposed in the sun, and powerful images, such as that of the blind, decrepit Teiresias in the shocking daylight. The English subtitles, by Noelle Gillmor, are a demonstration that subtitling can be a branch of the fine craft of translation. b & w

Any Wednesday (1966)—Jane Fonda is millionaire businessman Jason Robards' tax deductible mistress, in the film version of Muriel Resnik's long-running boudoir farce. Most of the movie takes place in the mistress's apartment (which is charged to Robards' company); maybe the various characters' entrances and confusions had some fizziness on the stage, but here there's an element of embarrassment in watching Fonda and Robards trying to activate the static, thudding material. The film would be easier to take if it weren't for the unpleasant moralizing tone: the businessman is sulky and selfish, and our sentiments are meant to be with his supposedly adorable, foolish mistress who wants babies and with his wife (Rosemary Murphy, who does more for her role than the others do with theirs). Dean Jones is the juvenile provided to replace Robards in Fonda's love life; also with King Moody. Directed by Robert Ellis Miller; the adaptation is by Julius J. Epstein. Warners. color

Anything Goes (1936)—Bing Crosby, in a mildly entertaining version of the Cole Porter Broadway musical comedy, with a book by Howard Lindsay and Russel Crouse, about multiple cases of mistaken identity on board a liner crossing from New York to Southampton. Paramount 30s musical comedies like this one are so openhearted in their disor-

ganized frivolous silliness that they're not offensive, and sometimes the performers lift them to a surreal, happy state. However, the craziness here isn't crazy enough; the gags often suggest a dog-eared jokebook. Crosby's relaxed, lackadaisical manner sets the tone for the whole revue-like production; he's likable though he doesn't supply any tension. Ethel Merman (in weird puffy little short sleeves that stick up and out from her shoulders) has more energy than the others in the cast, but it's a gruesome sort of belting energy (her version of ''I Get a Kick out of You'' has no romance), and even when she lowers her high, strident speaking voice she sounds bossy. With Ida Lupino, very shiny-blond and pretty as the ingenue, Charles Ruggles as Public Enemy No. 13 disguised as a clergyman, Arthur Treacher (looking like a moose), Grace Bradley, the Avalon Boys, Chill Wills, and, in a bit, Jack Mulhall. Lewis Milestone directed, from the adaptation (i.e. bowdlerization) that Guy Bolton, Lindsay, and Crouse did. There are a few classic Porter songs; also, Richard Whiting and Leo Robin's ''Sailor Beware'' and Edward Heyman and Hoagy Carmichael's ''Moonburn.'' Shown on TV as *Tops Is the Limit*; without the visual vitality—the Art Deco black and silvery contrasts—of the original 35 mm prints, things really sag between the musical numbers. (Remade in 1956, also with Crosby.) b & w

Aparajito (1957)—The central film of Satyajit Ray's great Apu Trilogy is transitional in structure, rather than dramatic, but it's full of insights and revelations. Ray takes the broken family of *Pather Panchali* from its medieval village life to the modern streets of Benares and follows the boy Apu in his encounter with the school system, and, later, when he has left his mother, with the intellectual life at the University of Calcutta. (There is a luminous moment when Apu recites a poem in a classroom—you understand how it is that art survives in the midst of poverty.) The film chronicles the emergence of modern industrial India, showing it to be not a primitive society but a corrupted society. However, Apu himself embodies Ray's belief that individuals need not become corrupt. Adapted from a novel by B. B. Bandapaddhay, by Ray; music by Ravi Shankar. In Bengali. b & w

Der Apfel Ist Ab *The Original Sin* (1949)—There are many who think that Germans are incapable of comedy, and this film may not dissuade them, but it's so unusual a piece of kitsch that it's worth a look. Helmut Käutner (*The Devil's General, The Captain From Koepenick*) made this satirical musical comedy in American-occupied Bavaria. Adam (Bobby Todd), a cider manufacturer, has a wife, and also a secretary named Eve (Bettina Moissi); most of the film is his dream of Paradise and Hell—the latter is a nightclub that he attends with Eve, who is dressed in cellophane. The Devil is the headwaiter, and if you've seen *Damn Yankees* you may be startled at the diabolic coincidences. *Life* described this movie as a "bebop translation of Genesis" and reported that it was denounced from pulpits all over Bavaria. Here, the few who saw it were probably more amused than shocked. Käutner himself has a role in it. In German. b & w

The Appaloosa (1966)—A dog of a movie about a horse. Marlon Brando is a sullen misfit cowboy who, along about 1870, enters a border-town church to do penance for his sins and has his horse stolen by a girl (Anjanette Comer) who is trying to get away from a sadistic bandit (John Saxon). Brando broods and suffers a multiplicity of physical humiliations. Presumably out of despair, the director, Sidney J. Furie, abandoned himself to closeups of tequila bottles, decayed teeth, and bloodshot eyes. The screenplay by James Bridges and Roland Kibbee was based on a novel by Robert MacLeod. Cinematography by Russell Metty. Universal. color

Appointment for Love (1941)—This is one of those heavily contrived romantic comedies in which everything rests upon postponing sexual consummation. There's nothing memorable about the picture, but under the circumstances the teamwork of Margaret Sullavan (she's a doctor) and Charles Boyer (he's a playwright) is amazing. They had worked together earlier in 1941 in *Back Street*, and they seem to have kept their rapport going here; they act as if they were in a wonderful movie. Directed by William Seiter, from a script by Bruce Manning and Felix Jackson, based on a short story by Ladislaus Bus-Fekete. With Rita Johnson and Reginald Denny. Universal. b & w

The Apprenticeship of Duddy Kravitz (1974)—No matter how phenomenal Richard Dreyfuss is in other roles, it's not likley that he'll ever top his performance in this teeming, energetic Canadian film. His baby-faced Duddy is a force of nature, a pushy 18-year-old con artist on his way to becoming an entrepreneur. Mordecai Richler's screenplay, based on his exultant, Dickensian 1959 novel, really enables us to understand "what makes Sammy run." Duddy waits on tables, he drives a taxi, he deals in pinball machines, he sets up a company to film weddings and bar mitzvahs. He jiggles impatiently and sweats and scratches himself. His drive for success is a comic passion. We feel with him every step of the way; he's a little monster, yet we share his devastation when his suave uncle (Joseph Wiseman) tells him, "You're a *pusherke*, a little Jew-boy on the make. Guys like you make me sick and ashamed." The work of the director, Ted Kotcheff, is often crude but it has electricity. And the film has real wit; it even has visual wit when we see a bar mitzvah film made by a drunken, half-mad blacklistee (Denholm Elliott). With Randy Quaid, Jack Warden, Micheline Lanctôt, Joe Silver, Henry Ramer, and, as the grandfather, Zvee Scooler. (The adaptation is credited to Lionel Chetwynd.) Shot mostly in and around Montreal, on a budget of less than $1 million. color

The April Fools (1969)—An attempt to revive the madcap-romantic comedy, with Catherine Deneuve (a bit glazed) and Jack Lemmon (rather mournful and too sappy) as the lovers. The director, Stuart Rosenberg, didn't have the right light touch, but one can still perceive what was intended in Hal Dresner's script, despite the movie's lumpiness. With Charles Boyer, Myrna Loy, Sally Kellerman, Peter Lawford, Jack Weston, and Harvey Korman, who almost makes the picture worth seeing. Produced by Gordon Carroll; released by National General. color

The Apu Trilogy, see *Pather Panchali, Aparajito,* and *The World of Apu (Apur Sansar)*

Apur Sansar, see *The World of Apu*

Arabian Nights (1942)—Part of what makes the Universal–Maria Montez movies camp classics is that they're elaborately produced, yet every word and every plot device is stamped Grade-B. In this sumptuous comedy-extravaganza, Sabu scampers about as Ali the acrobat, muscle-bound Jon Hall is Caliph Harun al-Rashid, and the blankly sensuous Maria Montez is Scheherazade (not a storyteller in this version, but only a dancing girl). The picture is filled with harem cuties, horses, Technicolor Arizona scenery, and blissfully dumb lines. But then, perfection belongeth only to Allah the Most High. Produced by Walter Wanger and directed with complete lack of conviction by John Rawlins, from Michael Hogan's script. With the matchless Turhan Bey, and Leif Erickson, Edgar Barrier, Thomas Gomez, John Qualen, and for slapstick, Billy Gilbert (who has a drag sequence), and Shemp Howard (one of the Three Stooges) as Sinbad.

Arachnophobia (1990)—It's O.K. You don't feel suckered, though you don't feel elated, either. A deadly arachnid that is discovered in Venezuela kills a young photographer, crawls into his coffin, and travels from the Amazon to the fictional little town of Canaima, California. There, the hairy-legged intruder—a tarantula as big as a big-guy's fist—breeds with a harmless domestic spider, and troops of poisonous bugs begin marching out of the bathroom drains. But when it comes down to the basics of scare comedy, the arachnids are short on personality, and so is the movie. The script, credited to Don Jakoby and Wesley Strick, has too many B-picture precursors, and the first-time director, Frank Marshall, is like a Boy Scout remaking *Jaws*. The tricks and teases aren't hip enough to spook your imagination. Jeff Daniels is smooth as the doctor with the phobia, but his dread seems shallow. The doctor's wife (Harley Jane Kozak) is presented as the fearless, competent one; then she's dropped from view. John Goodman, in the role of the local exterminator, brings up the energy level; he gives the picture a shot of authentic American grunge. Also with Julian Sands as the uppity entomologist, Brian McNamara as his assistant, and Henry Jones and Mary Carver. The witless musical score, by Trevor Jones, is a flat-out insult. Amblin Entertainment, for Hollywood (Disney). color

Aranyer din Ratri, see *Days and Nights in the Forest*

L'Argent de poche, see *Small Change*

Armored Attack, see *The North Star*

The Arrangement (1969)—Kirk Douglas is a successful Los Angeles advertising man in his early 40s who tries to kill himself, and as he recovers we begin to see the tensions that have made him self-destructive—on one side a girl (Faye Dunaway) who is contemptuous of his lucrative job and conventional life, and on the other a wife (Deborah Kerr) who wants security, and in the background his Greek immigrant father (Richard Boone), who measures worth in dollars. Even more blatantly than the novel, by Elia Kazan, this movie, which he directed, is a noisy glorification of anguish over selling out. Kazan probably believes that people can't hear unless they're shouted at, and since he wants to be heard he shouts. He mistakes the noise for having something to say. This is a monstrously unconvincing movie. With Hume Cronyn, Michael Higgins, Carol Rossen, Harold Gould, Philip Bourneuf, Charles Drake, Ann Doran, Barry Sullivan, and Michael Murphy. Warners. color (See *Deeper into Movies*.)

Arsenal (1929)—The writer-director Alexander Dovzhenko was the poet of the Russian revolutionary film movement—a poet whose startling imagery had a heat and pitch and lyricism that Eisenstein and Pudovkin never approached. This classic film, set during the war of 1914, is an original and experimental celebration of social revolution. (It ranks just below his great *Earth* of 1930.) Silent. b & w

Arsène Lupin (1932)—John Barrymore as a suave gentleman thief who poses as a duke in Paris in order to fleece the rich; his techniques are suspiciously easy—at one point he saunters out of the Louvre with the Mona Lisa tucked under his arm, wrapped around an umbrella. Lionel Barrymore plays an agonized, limping detective on the lighthearted thief's trail. The contrast should be more entertaining than it is. This was the Barrymore brothers' first film together and John gets to show a little of his humor but Lionel was already making a profession out of crankiness. The movie is mildly amusing in spots but it isn't much fun. Directed by Jack Conway, for M-G-M. From the play by Maurice Le Blanc and Francis de Croisset (which had already done service in the silent period), adapted by Carey Wilson, with dialogue by Bayard Veiller and Lenore Coffee. With Karen Morley, John Miljan, and Tully Marshall. b & w

Arsenic and Old Lace (1944)—Adapted from Joseph Kesselring's black comedy, this laborious farce was actually made in 1941, but by contract it couldn't be released until the Broadway production—which ran and ran—finally closed. Maybe the success of the play magically rubbed off on the movie, because it has always been inexplicably popular. The sane theatre-critic hero, Cary Grant, tries to convince his sweetly lethal little aunts (Josephine Hull and Jean Adair) that it isn't nice to put arsenic in the elderberry wine that they serve their guests, but they just don't understand why he gets so upset. You may not, either; the director, Frank Capra, has Grant performing in such a frenzied, dithering manner that during much of the action he seems crazier than anybody else. His role was shaped as if for Fred MacMurray, and Grant was pushed into overreacting—prolonging his stupefied double-takes, stretching out his whinny. Capra's hick jollity turns Grant into a manic eunuch. The hero's aggressive fiancée, here rewritten into a cuddly, innocuous little dear, is played by Priscilla Lane. The villains—murderers who are less couth in their methods than the innocently mad aunts—are Peter Lorre, as himself, and Raymond Massey, impersonating Boris Karloff; some people roar at their antics. With James Gleason, Edward Everett Horton, Jack Carson, John Alexander, Grant Mitchell, and the famous thirteen corpses. Adapted by Julius J. and Philip G. Epstein; score by Max Steiner. Warners. b & w

Arthur (1981)—John Gielgud can steal a scene by simply wearing a hat; it's so crisply angled that you can't take your eyes off him—you want to applaud that perfect hat. As Hobson, the valet to a drunken millionaire playboy, he may be the most poised and confident funnyman you'll ever see. And as the top-hatted lush, Arthur, Dudley Moore has a mad sparkle in his eyes. There's always something bubbling inside Arthur—the booze just adds to his natural fizz. This was the only film directed by Steve Gordon (who also wrote the script); he was a long way from being able to do with images what he could do with words, but there are some inspired bits and his work has a friendly spirit, and with Moore and Gielgud bouncing off each other like Bertie Wooster and Jeeves, the first part is fairly lively. But Gordon's attempt to reactivate the romantic mechanisms of the screwball comedies of the 30s doesn't work with the women characters—particularly with Liza Minnelli and Geraldine Fitzgerald. As the poor-girl heroine, Minnelli doesn't have her share of the good lines and she's electrifying when she only needs to be charming; as the playboy's grandmother, Fitzgerald has the worst scenes and the zest she gives them goes peculiarly wrong. With Barney Martin, Anne DeSalvo as Gloria, Jill Eikenberry, Thomas Barbour, Ted Ross, Stephen Elliott, Peter Evans, Lou Jacobi, and, in a bit, Lawrence Tierney. Cinematography by Fred Schuler; he makes the New York locations look elegant even when the staging suggests a waxworks museum. An Orion Picture; released by Warners. color (See *Taking It All In*.)

Artists and Models (1937)—A lavish mess of loosely strung together vaudeville acts and a story centering on the selection of a queen for a charity ball and on Jack Benny as the head of an advertising agency trying to land an account with a silverware company, run by Richard Arlen. The cast includes Louis Armstrong, Martha Raye, Ben Blue, Ida Lupino, Gail Patrick, Judy Canova, Connee Boswell, Peter Arno, and Rube Goldberg, but the plot makes you feel as if you're back in grammar school. Raoul Walsh directed. (There was actually a sequel the following year.) Paramount. b & w

As You Like It (1936)—Shakespeare cleaned up and made rather too respectably light-hearted. Still, this British production is by no means contemptible; it's enjoyable even in its disappointing moments. As Rosalind, Elisabeth Bergner, a great theatrical technician who specialized in heartbreaking gamine charm, can't resist being more adorably mischievous than is necessary and she's handicapped by her age (she was close to 40) and by her German accent, which dims the sparkle of some of her lines. One doesn't think of her as Fräulein Rosalind—one just doesn't make contact with her Rosalind. The young Laurence Olivier is triumphantly angelic as that amorous, brooding goof Orlando; there's a real interpretation at work here—his reactions make one grin. With Henry Ainley, Richard Ainley, Sophie Stewart, Mackenzie Ward, Leon Quartermaine, Felix Aylmer, Aubrey Mather, John Laurie, and Peter Bull. Directed by Bergner's husband, Paul Czinner, who—as in his movie versions of operas—never really seems to get the hang of the medium. Adapted by J. M. Barrie and Robert Cullen. b & w

Ascenseur pour l'échafaud, see *Elevator to the Gallows*

Ash Wednesday (1973)—In a few scenes, Elizabeth Taylor is done up like Arletty playing Garance in *Children of Paradise*, and she's absolutely ravishing, in an unearthly, ageless way. But the film is a long-drawn-out ghoulish commercial for cosmetic surgery—made, apparently, for people who can't think of anything to do with their lives but go backward. Jean-Claude Tramont is credited with the script and Larry Peerce is credited with the direction, but there is no script and there is no direction. With Keith Baxter, Helmut Berger, and Henry Fonda giving a sour, dumb performance. Produced by Dominick Dunne; released by Paramount. color

Ashani Sanket, see *Distant Thunder*

The Asphalt Jungle (1950)—A competent (often overrated) thriller by John Huston about a group of crooks who plan a jewel robbery and how their characters determine the results. Sterling Hayden is the central figure; the cast includes Sam Jaffe, Louis Calhern, Jean Hagen, Marilyn Monroe, James Whitmore, John McIntire, and Marc Lawrence. The screenplay, by Ben Maddow and Huston, was adapted from the W. R. Burnett novel. (Remade as *The Badlanders* in 1958, *Cairo* in 1962, and, with a black cast, as *A Cool Breeze*, in 1972.) M-G-M. b & w

The Assassination of Trotsky (1972)—Not for anyone who knows, or cares, anything about Leon Trotsky. With Richard Burton as a stuffed-shirt Trotsky; Alain Delon as an angel-of-death assassin; Romy Schneider, and Valentina Cortese. Directed by Joseph Losey; cinematography by Pasqualino De Santis; screenplay by Nicholas Mosley and Masolino D'Amico. A French, Italian, and British co-production. color

Assassins et voleurs, see *Lovers and Thieves*

At Long Last Love (1975)—Peter Bogdanovich's stillborn musical comedy—a relentlessly vapid pastiche of 30s Art Deco romantic-mixup movies. With Burt Reynolds as a bored millionaire playboy, Cybill Shepherd as a spoiled heiress, Eileen Brennan as a comic Irish maid, John Hillerman as an unflappable valet, Duilio Del Prete as a debonair gambler, and 16 Cole Porter songs. Performed as they are here, they sound smug, though Madeline Kahn, as a Broadway songstress nudging her thighs together while she sings "Find Me a Primitive Man," is fairly funny. Also with Mildred Natwick and M. Emmet Walsh. Script by Bogdanovich; cinematography by Laszlo Kovacs. 20th Century-Fox. color (See *Reeling*.)

At the Circus (1939)—The Marx Brothers. They do get to shoot Margaret Dumont out of a cannon, but it's all fairly ponderous. Edward Buzzell directed, from Irving Brecher's weary script. With Kenny Baker, Eve Arden, Florence Rice, Nat Pendleton, and Fritz Feld. The music is by Harold Arlen; Groucho sings the famous ditty about "Lydia, the Tattooed Lady." Mervyn LeRoy was the producer. M-G-M. b & w

L'Atalante (1934)—Jean Vigo, who died in his twenties, made only this one feature-length film—a sensuous, poetic love story about a young barge captain on the Seine, who marries and takes his bride with him; after a quarrel she runs off and they lose each other. Jean Dasté and Dita Parlo are the lovers, Michel Simon is the tattooed barge hand who finds her and brings her back. It's a wonderfully spontaneous, unarranged-looking film, photographed by Boris Kaufman, and with a lovely score by Maurice Jaubert. It's also a strange film—much slower and more consciously dreamlike than Vigo's short works. In some ways it's more pleasurable in the memory than while you're seeing it. Its surreal lyricism was described by Elie Faure: "The spirit of Jean Vigo's work is classical, almost violent and always tormented, fevered, overflowing with ideas and with fantasy; truculent; a virulent and even demonical romanticism that still remains humanistic." With Louis Lefèvre. (Not released in the U.S. until 1947.) In French. b & w

Atlantic City (1981)—This spa that became a racketeers' paradise during Prohibition and in 1981 was on its chaotic way to becoming Vegas with a beach is an improbable place, and in this lyric farce, directed by Louis Malle, from John Guare's script, it gives a hallucinatory texture to the lives of the characters. The story is a prankish wish-fulfillment fantasy about prosperity—what it does to cities, what it can do for people. It takes Malle a little while to set up the crisscrossing of the 10 or 12 major characters, but once he does, the film operates by its own laws in its own world, and it has a lovely fizziness. Everything goes wrong and comes out right. The casting is superb. As an old numbers runner who dreams of the days when he was a flunky and bodyguard for big-time racketeers, Burt Lancaster gives what is probably his funniest (and finest) performance. Susan Sarandon plays an uneducated girl studying to become a croupier, and for once her googly-eyed, slightly stupefied look seems perfect. With Kate Reid as the widow of a mobster, Hollis McLaren as a dippy flower child born into the wrong era, Robert Joy, Michel Piccoli, and many fine character actors, and an appearance by Robert Goulet as himself. Cinematography by Richard Ciupka. Produced by Denis Heroux; a French and Canadian co-production, released by Paramount. color (See *Taking It All In*.)

Atlas (1961)—A yawner. It's hard to believe that *Hercules* with Steve Reeves could have

inspired imitations, but here's Roger Corman's quickie version, with earnest, scrawny Michael Forest trying to save the Grecian city of Thenis from the power-mad Praximedes (Frank Wolff, who is occasionally amusing). color

L'Attentat, see *The French Conspiracy*

Au hasard, Balthazar (1966)—Robert Bresson's grave, oblique account of the life and suffering of a donkey, and the life and suffering of the people who mistreat him. It's a meditation on sin and saintliness. Considered a masterpiece by some, but others may find it painstakingly tedious and offensively holy. With Anne Wiazemsky as the passive, puffy-mouthed girl who falls in love with the cruel, thieving boy who is bound to make her miserable. In French. b & w

Au revoir les enfants *Goodbye, Children* (1987)—It's set in Occupied France in 1944, when the writer-director Louis Malle was an 11-year-old at a Catholic boys' boarding school near Fontainebleau that sheltered several Jewish boys. The Gestapo learned they were there, and sent the ones they found to Auschwitz, and the headmaster to a work camp. One of the Jewish boys was in Malle's class, but Malle didn't get to know him well and didn't realize that he was Jewish. For the dramatic purposes of the movie, he has conceived a close friendship between his alter ego, the fair-haired Julien Quentin (Gaspard Manesse), and the dark boy who is using the false name Jean Bonnet (Raphaël Fejtö). But nothing comes into clear focus—not the boys' attitudes, not even the images. The film (especially the first half) seems padded, formal, discreet. It's like watching a faded French classic. And there's something unseemly about the way Jean is used as an aesthetic object—spiritual, sensitive, exotic. With Francine Racette as Julien's mother and François Négret as the informer. In French. color (See *Hooked*.)

L'Auberge rouge, see *The Red Inn*

Au-delà des grilles, see *The Walls of Mala-paga*

Author! Author! (1982)—As the hero, a playwright who's a genial, children-loving jokester, Al Pacino reads his lines very skillfully, but he can't seem to get the message to his face or his body. He's like a man who's looking for something and has forgotten what; he prowls, distractedly. And when he tries for warmth, his smile is so self-conscious that at times his teeth seem to be stranded on the screen, left behind. Most of the scenes in which he is shown in his theatrical dealings have a quick, satirical snap, and in the first half, the dialogue has a sense of give-and-take, but then the film follows up on all the stuff we're not interested in. The playwright chases after his wife (Tuesday Weld), who has casually gone off with another man, leaving behind her four children by three earlier husbands. The playwright also has one child of his own, and by the time he is hauling kids onto the roof of his Greenwich Village house to protect them from being dispersed to homes they don't want to go to, the picture has turned into a *New York Times Magazine* article on male parenting. The script, by Israel Horovitz, has trim, funny lines but also terrible, overingratiating ones, and some of the most doddering, bonehead situations to be seen on the big screen in years. Directed by Arthur Hiller, the film is blotchy in just about every conceivable way; you'd have to conduct an exhaustive search to find a movie with scuzzier lighting (the cinematography is by Victor J. Kemper). With Dyan Cannon, who gives her scenes an infusion of spirit, and also Alan King, André Gregory, Bob Dishy, Eric Gurry, and Bob and Ray. Produced by Irwin Winkler; 20th Century-Fox. color (See *Taking It All In*.)

The Autobiography of Miss Jane Pittman (1974)—Cicely Tyson plays a woman who was born in slavery and lived to take part in a civil-rights demonstration in 1962; the role spans Jane Pittman's life from the age of 20 to the age of 110, and Cicely Tyson knows what she's doing every inch of the way. Jane isn't a deep woman; childless, uneducated, she's an enjoyer of life. It isn't until extreme old age gives her a privileged status that she loses her fear and becomes—briefly, just before her death—free enough to speak her mind and to crack a joke and to find herself. When she walks up to a whites-only drinking fountain in front of a Southern courthouse, and drinks from it, all of us in the audience can taste the good water. And the way the tough-minded Tyson plays the part, you feel you're inside skinny old Jane's head. Based on a novel by Ernest J. Gaines and made for television, the film was directed by the self-effacing John Korty; his plain, uncoercive approach suggests a principled reticence. Tyson's performance and Korty's tact are more than enough to compensate for the flaws: the anachronisms and naïveté in parts of Tracy Keenan Wynn's adaptation; some nondescript casting and acting; the device of using a journalist (Michael Murphy) to link the episodes. The character of Jane Pittman is synthesized from stories that Gaines heard while growing up on a plantation in Louisiana, but watching the film (which was all shot in Louisiana), you forget (as readers of the novel did) that it's fiction. It seems to be a slightly awkward re-enactment of the life of an actual person. color (See *Reeling*.)

Autumn Leaves (1956)—Robert Aldrich piling on the garish melodrama and working up a storm of emotional anguish. He holds your attention even though some part of you is giggling while you watch Joan Crawford take as her husband Cliff Robertson, who is not well in the head. He tosses objects at her (including a standard typewriter), and she heaves, gasps, and rolls her large eyes, but persists in being understanding. What's eating him is that in his first marriage (to Vera Miles) he was cuckolded by his own rotten dad (Lorne Greene). It eventually becomes evident to the hand-wringing, knuckle-gnawing Crawford that *something* has to be done, but not until after she does a lot of striding up and down. Columbia. b & w

Autumn Sonata *Höstsonaten* (1978)—Just when Americans seemed to be getting over that 50s craziness of children's blaming everything on their parents, we got it back from Ingmar Bergman. Eva (Liv Ullmann), a spiritually distraught, dowdy woman of perhaps 35 or 40, the wife of a pastor in rural Norway, invites Charlotte (Ingrid Bergman), her majestically worldly concert-pianist mother, to come for a visit. Then Eva goes at her mother with the impacted rage of a lifetime, accusing Charlotte of having deserted her when she was a child by going off to give concerts, and of never loving her. The whole film is like the grievances of someone who has just gone into therapy—Mother did this to me, she did that to me, and that and that and that. Ullmann enters into Ingmar Bergman's disturbed emotions and puts them on the screen just as he desires; neither of them does the shaping job of an artist here. It's a grueling, unconvincing movie. Ingrid Bergman is the one likable performer. With Lena Nyman and Halvar Björk. Cinematography by Sven Nykvist. In Swedish. color (See *When the Lights Go Down.*)

Avalon (1990)—In legend, Avalon is an earthly paradise. The writer-director Barry Levinson uses the name as his Rosebud: it's carved into the facade of the castle-like Bal-timore apartment house where the five Krichinsky brothers, Jews who emigrated from Eastern Europe before the First World War, make their first American home. In Levinson's view, those early years were a golden age. The film is set mostly during his own childhood, in the late 40s, when his parents move to the suburbs, and TV breaks up the clan's social patterns, and the surviving brothers have divided into feuding factions. The scattered fine comic moments don't make up for the wide streak of fuddy-duddyism in the notion that the family used to be the bulwark of the nation's value system. The movie is an elegy to a mythical past, and people emerge from the theatre sniffling. They've been told they're suffering from soul-sickness—the loss of unity, harmony, family music. With the quietly witty Elizabeth Perkins as the American-born young wife who doesn't buy into Levinson's vision of how great the past was. Trapped living with her bickering Old World in-laws, she's practically stiff from repressed annoyance, but she's too decent and too timid to explode. Aidan Quinn is persuasive as her affable, salesman husband who's not going to get caught between his wife and his mother (Joan Plowright); his specialty is keeping the peace. The peppy Kevin Pollak is Quinn's cousin and business partner. Armin Mueller-Stahl is the paperhanger grandfather Sam Krichinsky, the life-spirit central character who makes the points that Levinson wants to put across. Also with Lou Jacobi, and Elijah Wood as the child Michael. Cinematography by Allen Daviau. Tri-Star. color (See *Movie Love.*)

The Avenging Conscience (1914)—D. W. Griffith was so extraordinarily fertile and imaginative that when he saw *The Cabinet of Dr. Caligari*, in 1919, he could complain, with justice, that he had already tried and discarded that approach. And here's the evidence—a dream film, derived from Poe's "The Tell-tale Heart" and *Annabel Lee*, in which inanimate objects are used in a hallucinatory way. With Henry B. Walthall, Mae Marsh, and Blanche Sweet. (Vachel Lindsay analyzed this film in his 1915 book *The Art of the Motion Picture*.) Silent. b & w

L'Aveu, see *The Confession*

L'Avventura (1959)—Antonioni's study of the human condition at the higher social and economic levels—a study of adjusted, compromising modern man, afflicted by short memory, thin remorse, the capacity for easy betrayal. The characters are active only in trying to discharge their anxiety: sex is their sole means of contact. Too shallow to be truly lonely, they are people trying to escape their boredom by reaching out to one another and finding only boredom once again. Because the film is subtle and ascetic, yet laborious about revealing its meanings, it suggests Henry James when he "chewed more than he bit off." Visually, it's extraordinary: a calm hangs over everything—Antonioni's space is a vacuum in which people are aimlessly moving. Searchers and lost are all the same: disparate, without goals or joy. This is upper-class neo-realism—the poetry of moral and spiritual poverty. There had been nothing like it before, and it isn't fair to blame this movie for all the elegant sleepwalking and desolation that followed. There's something great here—a new mood, a new emotional rhythm—even with all the affectation. Léa Massari is the woman who quarrels with her architect lover (Gabriele Ferzetti) and then disappears from the uninhabited island they're visiting; Monica Vitti is her friend who takes up the search and then takes her place with the architect. Also with Dominique Blanchar. Cinematography by Aldo Scavarda; script by Elio Bartolini, Tonino Guerra, and Antonioni. In Italian. b & w (See *I Lost it at the Movies*.)

The Awful Truth (1937)—A classic screwball comedy, about one of old Hollywood's favorite subjects: the divorced couple who almost bed down with new mates but get back together. Irene Dunne and Cary Grant are the sparring partners, and Ralph Bellamy plays just about the same role he later played in *His Girl Friday*. Irene Dunne's way with a quip is to smile brightly and wring it dry, but she's at her best here. Joyce Compton plays the nightclub performer whom Dunne parodies, and the cast includes Esther Dale, Cecil Cunningham, and Alex D'Arcy. Leo McCarey's direction is first-rate; in a memorable sequence toward the end, Grant tries to persuade a door to open without visible assistance. Viña Delmar did the screenplay, from Arthur Richman's 1922 play. (There was a forgettable remake in 1953 with the shame-faced title *Let's Do It Again*.) Columbia. b & w

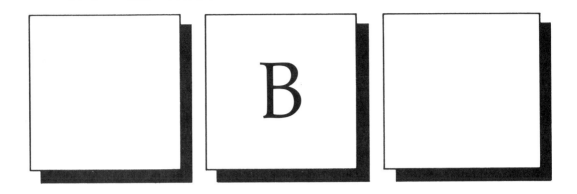

B

Babes in Arms (1939)—This version of the Rodgers and Hart Broadway musical didn't retain much of their material, but it starred Judy Garland (it was her big year, the year of *The Wizard of Oz*) and Mickey Rooney as the children of vaudevillians, and it has great charm. Busby Berkeley directed and choreographed; the direction is likably naïve, the choreography is primitive-surreal. The songs (from an assortment of sources) include "Where or When," "The Lady Is a Tramp," "I Cried for You," "Good Morning," and "You Are My Lucky Star." With June Preisser, Charles Winninger, Guy Kibbee, and Margaret Hamilton. This was Arthur Freed's début as a producer; the script is by Jack McGowan and Kay Van Riper. M-G-M. b & w

Babes on Broadway (1941)—The third of the three Judy Garland and Mickey Rooney M-G-M musicals produced by Arthur Freed and directed by Busby Berkeley. The plot is something forgettable about Judy and Mickey and other youngsters putting on a musical as a benefit for a settlement house for poor children, and there's also a patriotic number about British refugee kids. But Garland and Rooney dancing together are a happy sight.

He, Richard Quine, and Ray McDonald are three young hoofers billed as "The Three Balls of Fire," and he gets to do some terrific rowdy dancing, especially in the jive number "Hoe Down." He also has a wild impersonation of Carmen Miranda, the "Bombshell from Brazil," as well as somewhat more subdued takeoffs on George M. Cohan, Walter Hampden's Cyrano de Bergerac, and Harry Lauder. Garland's impressions (of Sarah Bernhardt, Fay Templeton, and Blanche Ring) are less vivid but pleasant enough; her solo songs were directed by Vincente Minnelli, then new to films. With James Gleason, Virginia Weidler, Fay Bainter, and Donald Meek. The script is by Fred Finklehoffe and Elaine Ryan; the songs, from a variety of sources, include Harold Rome's "Franklin D. Roosevelt Jones" and Ralph Freed and Burton Lane's "How About You?" b & w

Baby Boom (1987)—Diane Keaton gives a glorious comedy performance that rides over many of the inanities in this picture conceived by the monarchs of Yup: the writer-producer Nancy Meyers and the writer-director Charles Shyer. Their subject is the feminist as darling. Keaton is a Manhattan management-consulting firm's Tiger

Lady until she's entrusted with the care of a baby girl. Then, her single-minded concentration gone and her status diminished, she quits, moves to a farmhouse in Vermont, meets a calm, steadying Gary Cooperish veterinarian helpfully named Cooper (Sam Shepard), and starts a venture that turns her into the biggest employer in town. Soon she's a tycoon, rejecting astronomic offers to sell out. She, her child, her lover, and her business are all booming, and the picture rattles along cheerily, cutting to the child for clever reactions, the way movies used to cut to the family dog. But Keaton is smashing: the Tiger Lady's having all this drive is played for farce and Keaton keeps you alert to every shade of pride and panic the character feels. She's an ultra-feminine executive, a wide-eyed charmer, with a breathless ditziness that may remind you of Jean Arthur in *The More the Merrier*. With Sam Wanamaker as Fritz, Harold Ramis as the heroine's apartment mate, James Spader as her baby-faced assistant, Britt Leach as her Vermont plumber, and the twins Kristina and Michelle Kennedy as the baby. Also with Pat Hingle, Mary Gross, and, in quick flashes, Victoria Jackson, Dori Brenner, Robin Bartlett, Constance Forslund, Margaret Whitton, and many other underused talents. Cinematography by William A. Fraker. United Artists. color (see *Hooked*.)

Baby Doll (1956)—Tennessee Williams' droll and engrossing carnal comedy, set low-down in Mississippi. The infantile, flirtatious heroine (Carroll Baker) sucks her thumb and sleeps in a crib. Her balding, middle-aged husband (Karl Malden) has agreed not to consummate the marriage until she is 20; meanwhile her husband's enemy, a sharp Sicilian (Eli Wallach), lays expert hands on her. (His performance is also expert.) Carroll Baker as the lazy girl who couldn't get through long division and Malden as a grotesque simp (lust makes him helpless) are all-out funny—it's

unlikely that either of them ever gave another performance this good or had such wonderful material again, either. And when the mustachioed Wallach—his beady eyes shining with lechery—makes his move on Baby Doll, pushing her in a swing until she's sweetly dizzy, he seems a master of barnyard seduction. (This must be the only movie ever made in which the heroine invites a man into her crib.) With Mildred Dunnock as Baby Doll's half-crazed old aunt, the young Rip Torn as the dentist, and Madeleine Sherwood, Lonny Chapman, and a number of residents of Benoit, Mississippi, whom the director, Elia Kazan, employed as extras. There are some wobbly moments toward the end, and although the film doesn't make too much of the score by Kenyon Hopkins (the music of Williams' dialogue is all you have needed), there's a scene inside the house that plays too slow and the music is brought up to cover the dead spot, and then brought up again when Malden is running around with a gun. Williams doesn't seem sure how to resolve the movie, but it's wonderfully entertaining. When it came out, it was condemned by the Catholic Legion of Decency, and *Time* said that it was "just possibly the dirtiest American-made motion picture that has ever been legally exhibited," with "Priapean detail that might well have embarrassed Boccaccio." It's not quite all that, but it is a delight. The look of the film is amazing—the black-and-white cinematography by Boris Kaufman is unusually sunny and bright; the images seem free and natural yet stylized, like a cartoon. Kazan does some of his finest work here—not just with the principal actors, but also with the hired hands, and the townspeople who laugh at Malden, and the happy gawkers at a fire. At one point—almost out of nowhere—we hear a black woman singing "I shall not be moved" in a harsh, plain, strong voice. Kazan's choices seem miraculously right. Art direction by Richard Sylbert, working with

Paul Sylbert. Williams' script is based on two of his one-act plays—27 *Wagons Full of Cotton* and *The Unsatisfactory Supper*. Warners.

The Baby Maker (1970)—Pseudo-serious-ness about a life-loving young hippie (Barbara Hershey) who agrees to make a baby for a childless couple (Collin Wilcox-Horne and Sam Groom). Cellophane-wrapped little insights into everybody's feelings, and enough poignant touches and discreetly meaningful facial expressions to cover the writer-director, James Bridges, with medals for sincerity. With Brenda Sykes, Jeannie Berlin, and Scott Glenn. A Robert Wise Production, for National General. color (See *Deeper into Movies*.)

The Bachelor and the Bobby-Soxer (1947)—Right after doing himself proud in *Notorious*, Cary Grant made the mistake of appearing in this meant-to-be-bubbling farce by Sidney Sheldon. He's cast as a roué painter, and there's no core of plausibility in the role; Grant doesn't have the eyes of a masher, or the temperament. When he's accused of chasing skirts it seems like some kind of mistake. Shirley Temple is the bobby-soxer who develops a crush on him, and Myrna Loy (prissy and dull here) is her older sister, a judge. The painter is coerced into dating the bobby-soxer until she gets over her infatuation; wearing his shirt open and acting like an adolescent, he escorts her to various teen functions and competes with high-school athletes in an obstacle race at a school picnic. It's degradingly unfunny, and Grant doesn't even get a chance to show his romantic style when he finally pairs off with the older sister. With Rudy Vallee, Ray Collins, Harry Davenport, Veda Ann Borg, William Bakewell, Johnny Sands, and Don Beddoe. Produced by Dore Schary, for R K O; directed by Irving Reis. (It's hard to believe that Sheldon's script won the Academy Award for Best Original Screenplay.) b & w

Bachelor Mother (1939)—Ginger Rogers was an astonishingly straightforward, good-natured comedienne. She played dozens of variations on Cinderella, and looked surprised each time she caught the prince. This time he's David Niven, the heir to the department store founded by his old-codger father (Charles Coburn). Ginger, who works at the toy counter, happens to find an infant who has been deserted; her employers, taking her for an unmarried mother, are indignant at her assertions that the baby isn't hers, and to keep her job she has to keep the baby. Contrived by Norman Krasna (from Felix Jackson's story) and directed by Garson Kanin, this is a rollicking, warm, obvious comedy; it's heavy-handed yet ingenious and enjoyable, partly because of good punch lines and realistic gags, such as Ginger and her boyfriend, Frank Albertson, being disgusted when they win the first-prize loving cup in a dance contest, because the second prize is cash. With June Wilkins as Niven's pill of a girlfriend, Ernest Truex as a social worker, and E. E. Clive. (Remade in 1956, under the title *Bundle of Joy*.) R K O. b & w

Back Street (1932)—Irene Dunne does the suffering in this version of the Fannie Hurst classic weeper about a woman who loves a selfish married man (John Boles) and spends her whole life in the shadow of his. Fannie Hurst had a shameful genius for this sort of muck. John M. Stahl directed, and the great Karl Freund did the cinematography. With ZaSu Pitts, William Bakewell, Jane Darwell, Walter Catlett, Robert McWade. (It was remade in 1941 and 1961; the 1941 version, with Margaret Sullavan and Charles Boyer, is delicately acted and considerably easier on the stomach than this one.) Universal. b & w

Back to School (1986)—Rodney Dangerfield, the archetypal complaining loser, who has always been a little sweaty and berserk, plays a winner here—a jovial, avuncular multimillionaire merchant, with a short fluffy coiffure; he discovers that his son (Keith Gordon) is miserable at college, and enrolls as a freshman so he can change things for the kid. It's Dangerfield's movie, and when he can't say a line directly to the camera he seems worried that he's not doing enough, and so he does some eyeball mugging. The picture's inertia is overpowering, but Dangerfield enthusiasts don't seem to mind the cornpone script or the deadening moviemaking. It's like a beer bust to them. As the son's blue-haired punker roommate, Robert Downey, Jr., has zapped big eyes and a serene, dreamy smile; he gives the movie its only airy touches. Sally Kellerman helps out as a throaty-voiced literature professor, and Paxton Whitehead and Sam Kinison provide marginal distractions. Also with Ned Beatty, Burt Young, M. Emmet Walsh, Adrienne Barbeau, Severn Darden, and, as himself, Kurt Vonnegut, Jr. Directed by Alan Metter; screenplay credited to Steven Kampmann, Harold Ramis, and others, from a story credited to Dangerfield and others. Orion. color (See *Hooked*.)

Back to the Future (1985)—Directed by Robert Zemeckis, from a script he wrote with his regular teammate Bob Gale, this piece of Pop Art Americana is a clever, generally engaging screwball comedy. Christopher Lloyd is the small-town crackpot inventor who builds a time machine on the chassis of a gull-winged DeLorean, and Michael J. Fox is Marty, the 17-year-old Hill Valley, California, high-school boy who is hurtled back 30 years to Hill Valley, 1955, where his parents are 17-year-olds at the same school. The movie has the structure of a comedy classic, but it doesn't have the rambunctiousness or the maniacal edge of Zemeckis and Gale's 1980 *Used Cars*; despite their wit in devising intricate structures that keep blowing fuses, the thinking is cramped and conventional. Christopher Lloyd is a blissful silly, though, and Lea Thompson's woozy-faced young Lorraine (Marty's mother-to-be) has a sly lustiness that's entrancing; as the tall, skinny, sad-sack George McFly (Marty's father-to-be), Crispin Glover is almost too painful a caricature, but he has more force than anyone else in the movie. With Claudia Wells, Wendie Jo Sperber, Marc McClure, Thomas F. Wilson, and Frances Lee McCain. There couldn't have been many people on the movie set who were old enough to remember the 50s: Patti Page's first name is spelled Patty in the record store window on the town square. Cinematography by Dean Cundey; production design by Lawrence G. Paull. Amblin Entertainment, for Universal. color (See *Hooked*.)

Back to the Future Part II (1989)—It's all manic and wacky; it's all twists. The amiably mad inventor Doc Brown (Christopher Lloyd) rushes into the frame to tell teen-age Marty McFly (Michael J. Fox) about new emergencies in the year 2015 or 1955 or an alternate 1985 (brought about by their disrupting the space-time continuum), and they go hurtling off to set things right. The picture is fast and furious, but low in spirit; the inventiveness of the director, Robert Zemeckis, and his writing partner, Bob Gale, seems to be on a treadmill in a void. And yet the construction keeps you going—it's like a frenzied daydream that you don't want to break off. With Elizabeth Shue, Lea Thompson, and Thomas F. Wilson as the bullies Biff and Griff. Amblin Entertainment, for Universal. color (See *Movie Love*.)

The Bad and the Beautiful (1952)—Early in the year the great Hollywood Dunciad, *Singin' in the Rain*, came out, and then came this spangled, overwrought piece of Hollywoodian self-analysis. The first was a satire, the second a satire in spite of itself—which recalls the fabled little old lady who said in the middle of *Quo Vadis?*, "Look, there's a sweet little lion who hasn't got a Christian." *The Bad and the Beautiful*, a glossy melodrama about a "bad" megalomaniac Hollywood producer (Kirk Douglas) and a "beautiful" alcoholic star (Lana Turner), is one of those movies that set out to explain what Hollywood is *really* like. It's a piquant example of what it purports to expose—luxurious exhibitionism—and the course of what is described as a "rat race" to success is the softest turf ever. The structure is all too reminiscent of *Citizen Kane*, and there is the "Rosebud" of Douglas's ill-defined Oedipal confusion, but there are also flashy, entertaining scenes and incidents derived from a number of famous careers. And the director, Vincente Minnelli, has given the material an hysterical stylishness; the black-and-white cinematography (by Robert Surtees) is more than dramatic—it has temperament. With Dick Powell as an author; Gloria Grahame as his Southern wife; Walter Pidgeon as a studio head; Barry Sullivan as a director; Gilbert Roland as Gaucho, the actor; Elaine Stewart as a starlet; and Leo G. Carroll, Paul Stewart, and Vanessa Brown. Music by David Raksin; produced by John Houseman, for M-G-M. Academy Awards: Best Supporting Actress (Grahame), Screenplay (Charles Schnee), Cinematography, Art Direction (Cedric Gibbons and others), Costume Design (Helen Rose). (In 1962, Houseman, Minnelli, and Schnee collaborated on another melodramatic inside view of moviemaking, *Two Weeks in Another Town*.)

Bad Boys (1983)—At 22, Sean Penn is probably the best actor in American movies who is still young enough to play adolescents. He gets so far inside a role that he can make even a sociological confection such as the 16-year-old hero, Mick—a proud, tough juvenile delinquent who commits crude, reckless crimes—someone an audience can care about. Penn is given so little to work with here that it's practically a pantomime performance: he holds us by the depth of Mick's grief over the way things have worked out in his life. He sits in his cell at the reformatory—hypersensitive, intelligent, and bitter. He's worth watching, even though the picture is singularly unimaginative. Directed by Rick Rosenthal, from a script by Richard DiLello, it has been made in a brutal, realistic, neo-Warners style, with shock cuts, a pungent visual surface (using Chicago locations and Illinois correctional institutions), and Bill Conti's snazzy, aren't-you-lucky-I'm-here music, which gets anxious and excited for us, whipping itself into snits and furies. Even when episodes are powerful, they're banal. With Eric Gurry, Esai Morales, Ally Sheedy, Reni Santoni, and Jim Moody. Produced by Robert Solo; Universal. color (See *Taking It All In*.)

Bad Company (1972)—A hip-picaresque comedy set in the Civil War period, with the lively, talented Jeff Bridges as the bumpkin Fagin of a gang of thieving orphans and runaways. There's dazzle in the script by Robert Benton and David Newman, but Benton's direction is tepid, and the yellow-brown autumnal West is getting very tired. The movie is sparked by a caricature of a big-time movie director (Joseph L. Mankiewicz, to be specific) in the character of the cynical robber chief, Big Joe (David Huddleston). With Barry Brown, Jim Davis, and John Savage; cinematography by Gordon Willis. Paramount. color (See *Reeling*.)

Bad Day at Black Rock (1954)—The title may suggest a banal Western, but this was the first film to bring up the wartime outrages against Japanese-Americans (treated also in 1960 in Phil Karlson's *Hell to Eternity*). The story is set in the mythical Southwestern town of Black Rock where the inhabitants are bound together by the guilty secret of their mistreatment of a Japanese farmer; on this bad day a one-armed stranger (Spencer Tracy) arrives and begins to ask questions. Though *Bad Day at Black Rock* is crudely melodramatic, it is a very superior example of motion picture craftsmanship. The director, John Sturges, is at his best—each movement and line is exact and economical; the cinematographer, William C. Mellor, uses CinemaScope and color with intelligent care—the compositions seem realistic, yet they have a stylized simplicity. In part because of this, when the violence erupts, it's truly shocking. With Robert Ryan, Dean Jagger, Walter Brennan, Anne Francis, John Ericson, Lee Marvin, and Ernest Borgnine. Written by Millard Kaufman; produced by Dore Schary, for M-G-M.

Bad Night, see *Mala Noche*

The Bad Sleep Well *Warui Yatsu Hodo Yoku Nemuru* (1960)—Kurosawa takes on the theme of corruption in business and government in this melodrama about how Toshiro Mifune tries to track down the men responsible for murdering his father. He finds them, all right, but here's the Japanese twist on a basically American-type story: Mifune is eliminated and business goes on as usual. It's a strangely mixed movie—an attempt at social significance but with several borrowings from *Hamlet* that take bizarre forms: a giant wedding cake in the shape of an office building serves the plot function of the play within the play in *Hamlet*. (The groom's father had committed suicide by jumping from a window of an office building.) The cast includes Masayuki Mori and Takashi Shimura. In Japanese. b & w

Badlands (1973)—Probably we've all seen those convicted killers in prison documentaries on TV who sound uninvolved and mechanical when they talk about their crimes; Terrence Malick's début picture extends that uninvolvement to the whole culture. Set at the end of the 50s, it's about an emotionless young killer (Martin Sheen) and his 15-year-old girlfriend (Sissy Spacek), whose killing spree starts in South Dakota. The young lovers are psychologically aberrant and yet just like everybody else; their moral vacuum spreads over the flat, dead landscape. Malick appears to be saying that mass-culture banality is killing our souls and making everybody affectless, but his detached tone puts the viewer in the ugly position of feeling culturally superior to the people on the screen. An intellectualized movie—shrewd and artful, carefully styled to sustain its low-key view of dissociation—but so preconceived that there's nothing left to respond to. With Warren Oates; art direction by Jack Fisk. The music is by Carl Orff and Erik Satie. A Pressman-Williams Production; released by Warners. color (See *Reeling*.)

La Baie des anges, see *Bay of the Angels*

Baisers volés, see *Stolen Kisses*

The Baker's Wife *La Femme du boulanger* (1938)—The village baker (Raimu) cannot work because he laments his wife's departure with a stupid, sexy shepherd; the villagers, who want their bread, organize to bring her back. Raimu's baker is an acting classic—a true tragicomic hero—and it's easy to agree with Orson Welles, who cited this comedy as proof that "a story and an actor, both superb," can result in "a perfect movie" even if the direction and the editing are not "cinematic." Marcel Pagnol, a playwright who turned scenarist and then writer-director, adapted this classic of cuckoldry from Jean Giono's *Jean le Bleu* and directed it very simply. With Ginette Leclerc (who can pout with her mouth open) as the wife; Charpin; and Charles Moulin. In French. b & w

Balalaika (1939)—Perfect for a mixed-media show at the Russian Tea Room—but at a theatre, without distraction? Nelson Eddy, in another uniform, smiling vacuously, and that beautiful, blank songbird, Ilona Massey, in an overdressed adaptation of Eric Maschwitz's play about Russian exiles in Paris. M-G-M loaded this flop operetta with such sure-disaster songs as "Ride, Cossack, Ride," "In a Heart as Brave as Your Own," "Shadows on the Sand," "The Magic of Your Love," and, to cap it all, "My Heart Is a Gypsy." The cast includes Charles Ruggles and the inevitable Frank Morgan, as well as Walter Woolf King, C. Aubrey Smith, Joyce Compton, Lionel Atwill, George Tobias, Alma Kruger, and Phillip Terry. Produced by Lawrence Weingarten; directed by Reinhold Schunzel; script by Jacques Deval and Leon Gordon. b & w

Ball of Fire (1942)—The romantic collision of Sugarpuss O'Shea, a burlesque dancer (Barbara Stanwyck), and Bertram Potts, a fuddy-duddy professor (Gary Cooper), is played as if it were terribly bright, but it's rather shrill and tiresome. Howard Hawks directed, but Brackett and Wilder did the script, and Wilder's influence seems strong. The professor's colleagues have corny cute names and carry on like people left over from a stock-company Viennese operetta. The cast includes Dana Andrews, Dan Duryea, and Allen Jenkins, and, as the professors, Oscar Homolka, Henry Travers, S. Z. Sakall, Tully Marshall, Leonid Kinskey, Richard Haydn, and Aubrey Mather. Gene Krupa and his band are also on the screen. Gregg Toland was the cinematographer for this expensive Samuel Goldwyn production. (Remade in 1948, as *A Song Is Born*.) Released by R K O. b & w

The Ballad of Cable Hogue (1970)—Sam Peckinpah is in a relaxed and playful mood in this rambling comedy-Western with Jason Robards (in fine form) as a desert rat who discovers a mudhole and turns water merchant, Stella Stevens as an ambitious whore, and David Warner as a lecherous self-ordained preacher. The picture needs more invention, more variety; it's a little too pleased with itself, and shots are held too long. Also with Strother Martin, L. Q. Jones, Slim Pickens, Kathleen Freeman, Gene Evans, Peter Whitney, R. G. Armstrong, and Max Evans. Cinematography by Lucien Ballard; script by John Crawford and Edward Penney; music by Jerry Goldsmith, with songs by Goldsmith and Richard Gillis. Warners. color

Le Ballon rouge, see *The Red Balloon*

La Bamba (1987)—Written and directed by Luis Valdez, this is the life story of the Chicano rock 'n' roller Ritchie Valens (Lou Diamond Phillips), who had three hit records before he died at 17 in a plane crash, in 1959. Valdez isn't primarily concerned with Ritchie Valens as the bullet of talent he must have been. The film's Ritchie is simply a warm, friendly Latino version of the boy next door. Ritchie Valens' music, as it's performed by the group Los Lobos, with David Hidalgo singing for Phillips, is what carries the movie along, but even with the music and brief appearances by Stephen Lee, Brian Setzer, and Howard Huntsberry, this is a leaden, lachrymose piece of filmmaking. (No doubt many people are susceptible to the film's mythmaking; you can hear their enthusiastic weeping in the theatre.) With the fiery, hammy Esai Morales as Ritchie's tormented, bad-boy half brother, Bob; Elizabeth Peña (she has a comic side) as Bob's wife, who keeps looking at him with disgust; Rosana De Soto as the boys' mother; Joe Pantoliano as Bob Keene; and Marshall Crenshaw as Buddy Holly. color (See *Hooked*.)

Bambi (1942)—The animals in this animated Disney feature have Walter Keane eyes and fluttering long eyelashes. None has a gooier gaze than the little fawn, Bambi. His relationship with his mother is tender and close, and when she is killed by hunters, small children in the audience frequently scream and cry. It all ends happily when Bambi, grown to staghood, marries the virginally sweet doe Faline. The picture is a classic of sorts, if only for the uncannily awful sound of the young woodland creatures in conversation; when puberty sets in and these voices suddenly change, Walt Disney begins to seem as berserk as Busby Berkeley. Still there's no denying that for many people sequences such as Bambi's birth have an enduring primal power. From the Felix Salten novel. color

I Bambini ci Guardano, see *The Children Are Watching Us*

Band of Outsiders *Bande à part* (1964)—The two heroes (Claude Brasseur and Sami Frey) begin by playacting crime and violence movies, then really act them out in their lives. Their girl (Anna Karina), wanting to be accepted, tells them there is money in the villa where she lives. And we watch, apprehensive and puzzled, as the three of them go through the robbery they're committing as if it were something in a movie—or a fairy tale. The crime doesn't fit the daydreamers or their milieu: we half expect to be told it's all a joke—that they can't really be committing an armed robbery. This Jean-Luc Godard film is like a reverie of a gangster movie—a gangster movie as students in an espresso bar might remember it or plan it. It has the gangster-film virtues (loyalty, daring) but they are mixed with innocence, amorality, lack of equilibrium. It's as if a French poet took a banal American crime novel and told it to us in terms of the romance and beauty he read between the lines; Godard re-creates the gangsters and the moll with *his* world of associations—seeing them as people in a Paris café, mixing them with Rimbaud, Kafka, Alice in Wonderland. This lyrical tragicomedy is perhaps Godard's most delicately charming film. Script by Godard (he's also the narrator), based on the novel *Fool's Gold* by Dolores Hitchens. Cinematography by Raoul Coutard; music by Michel Legrand. In French. b & w (See *Kiss Kiss Bang Bang*.)

The Band Wagon (1953)—The Comden-Green script isn't as consistently fresh as the one they did for *Singin' in the Rain*, but there have been few screen musicals as good as this one, starring those two great song-and-dance men Fred Astaire and Jack Buchanan. Actually, Buchanan's dancing and his rosy-ripe way with his lines (satirical cant about the theatuh) have such style and flourish that he steals the picture. (His role is a spoof of Orson Welles.) The plot, about a movie star (Astaire) trying for a comeback on Broadway and falling in love with a ballerina (Cyd Charisse), is a relaxed excuse for a series of urbane revue numbers, which includes "I Guess I'll Have to Change My Plan," "That's Entertainment," "Triplets" (featuring Astaire, Buchanan, and Nanette Fabray), and culminates in the "Girl Hunt" dance sequence—a parody of Mickey Spillane's bloody boudoir fiction, with Astaire as the detective and Charisse as the good-bad women in his life. When the bespangled Charisse wraps her phenomenal legs around Astaire, she can be forgiven everything, even her three minutes of "classical" ballet and the fact that she reads her lines as if she learned them phonetically. With Oscar Levant, in one of his best movie roles (he and Fabray play at being Comden and Green), and James Mitchell. The black shoeshine dancer is LeRoy Daniels. Directed by Vincente Minnelli; the choreography is by Michael Kidd; the songs are by Howard Dietz and Arthur Schwartz. The title and three of these songs are from a 1931 Broadway revue that starred Astaire and his sister Adele; Cyd Charisse's singing was dubbed by India Adams. M-G-M. color

Bande à part, see *Band of Outsiders*

The Bandit, see *O Cangaceiro*

Banditi a Orgosolo, see *Bandits of Orgosolo*

Bandits of Orgosolo *Banditi a Orgosolo* (1961)—The story is about a young shepherd wrongly suspected of being a bandit and of having killed a policeman; terrified of the police, he attempts to escape and is forced to become a bandit. It's a good, basic neo-realist subject, and the young director-cinematographer, Vittorio De Seta, who shot the film in the mountains of Sardinia, has an eye for harsh beauty. The film has a distinctive look and mood that stay with one. De Seta spent nearly two years among the Sardinian peasants who play the roles, and he communicates their impassive suspiciousness toward authority; this is one of the rare films in which hard, taciturn people reveal themselves to us, and they do it without sentimentality. In Italian. b & w

Bang the Drum Slowly (1973)—Pathos poured on by the bucketful. This picture has a moral—Be kind. The baseball-player hero (blue-eyed Michael Moriarty, in the role Paul Newman played on TV in 1956) behaves like a saint to his doltish buddy (Robert De Niro), who is dying of Hodgkin's disease, and then is made to suffer remorse anyway. It seems he had neglected to send the buddy the score-card of his last game on earth. And the ball

team who had done their slobby best to behave like comrades to the dying man fail, unaccountably, to send a delegation to the funeral. This baseball weeper was very clumsily directed by John Hancock; everything stops dead for the dialogue scenes. De Niro gives what may be his only bad screen performance; he overworks the tobacco chewing and the idiotic smile. With Vincent Gardenia, Phil Foster, Ann Wedgeworth, Heather MacRae, Tom Ligon, Selma Diamond, Patrick McVey, and Marshall Efron. Adapted by Mark Harris, from his own novel. Produced by Maurice and Lois Rosenfield; released by Paramount. color

Barbarella (1968)—The decor and effects in Roger Vadim's erotic comic strip are disappointing, but Jane Fonda has the skittish naughtiness of a teen-age voluptuary. She's the fresh, bouncy American girl triumphing by her innocence over a lewd, sadistic world of the future. David Hemmings shows unexpected comic talent as an absent-minded revolutionary. With John Phillip Law, Anita Pallenberg, Milo O'Shea, Marcel Marceau, Ugo Tognazzi, and Claude Dauphin. Produced by Dino De Laurentiis. color (See *Going Steady*.)

Barbarosa (1982)—The most spirited and satisfying Western epic in several years—it may seem a little loose at first, but it gets better and better as it goes along and you get the fresh, crazy hang of it. Directed by the Australian Fred Schepisi, from a script by the Texas-born William D. Wittliff, it has some of the psychedelic ambiance of Sergio Leone's spaghetti Westerns—the West seen in a fever. Willie Nelson has a great screen presence; he has an aura—his scruffiness is part of his grace. As the legendary outlaw Barbarosa, a desert rat mythologized by those who grow up fearing him, he's like the dragon in the fairy tale who threatens the community (and keeps it strong). The period is the 1880s and the film was shot along the Rio Grande, in an area of extremes that's either steep Texas mountains or mustard-colored mesa and desert. Gary Busey plays a lumpy, raw farm boy who gets in trouble with his in-laws and has to run off to hide; he joins up with Barbarosa, and without intending to becomes an apprentice desperado. Busey makes a certain kind of American huskiness and uncouthness seem the best part of the national character; as the farm boy he's an outlaw-galoot—Mark Twain might have dreamt him up. Working with the cinematographer Ian Baker and the composer Bruce Smeaton, Schepisi shows the fullness of his approach to moviemaking; Willie Nelson doesn't need to sing here—the whole picture is a ballad. With Gilbert Roland, Howland Chamberlin, Isela Vega, Danny De La Paz, and George Voskovec. Produced by Paul N. Lazurus III, for Universal. color (See *Taking It All In*.)

Barbary Coast (1935)—Lavish, unconvincing re-creation of San Francisco's vice dens in the 1850s. The picture was designed as a showcase for Edward G. Robinson's talents, and he gives a juicy performance as a lovable gangland boss. But the material is too false and studied—and too polite. Miriam Hopkins is Swan, the disillusioned queen of the Coast, who presides over a crooked roulette wheel; Joel McCrea courts her with a volume of Shelley. Howard Hawks directed, from a script by Hecht and MacArthur, and there's plenty of action, but you feel as if you've seen it all before. With Walter Brennan, Frank Craven, Brian Donlevy, Donald Meek, and, in a bit part, David Niven. A Samuel Goldwyn Production. b & w

Barfly (1987)—The 67-year-old L.A. poet Charles Bukowski wrote this semi-autobiographical script about his heavy-drinking skid-row days just after the Second World War, when he was a scrappy young man, in his mid to late 20s—a budding writer who was beginning to be published. But Mickey Rourke, who plays the role, imitates the tortoise movements of the battle-scarred survivor Bukowski, the writer-philosopher, the sage. This howler gives the movie a comic boost. Rourke twinkles with amusement at doing Bukowski, and the two principal women (Faye Dunaway as a burnt-out drinker, Alice Krige as the wealthy publisher of a literary magazine) twinkle back. The movie, though, is big on life affirmation. The hero isn't afraid to lose a fight or to hit bottom. And he isn't tempted by security. Offered the guesthouse on the publisher's estate, he snubs her; he calls her world "a cage with golden bars." (Of course, she's infatuated with his integrity.) Waking in her bed, he gets up saying, "I belong on the streets. I don't feel right here. It's like I can't *breathe!*" He goes back to his grimy haunts, where—we're supposed to believe—the real people are. This might be a film about the leader of a religious cult which was made by an altar boy. The director, Barbet Schroeder, wanting to please the Master, inadvertently exposes Bukowski's messianic windbag sensibility at its most self-satisfied. You wouldn't guess at Bukowski's talent from this movie. With Frank Stallone, J. C. Quinn, Jack Nance, and Fritz Feld. Cinematography by Robby Müller. Cannon Films, in association with Zoetrope. color (See *Hooked*.)

The Barefoot Contessa (1954)—Writer-director Joseph L. Mankiewicz tries to tell all about Hollywood—where the men aren't men and the women are magnificent, frustrated animals. Flamenco dancer Ava Gardner is discovered in the slums of Madrid by a vicious millionaire producer (Warren Stevens), a gutless, sycophantic press agent (Edmond O'Brien), and an alcoholic, broken-down director (Humphrey Bogart). She becomes a glamorous star but only feels at home with her feet in the dirt (symbolized by a guitar player, a chauffeur, and a gypsy dancer). The movie is so ornate and so garrulous about telling the dirty truth that it's a camp classic: a Cinderella story in which the prince turns out to be impotent. It's hard to believe Mankiewicz ever spent an hour in Hollywood; the alternative supposition is that he spent too many hours there. With Rossano Brazzi as the castrated Italian count, Marius Goring as a rich South American playboy, Valentina Cortese, Elizabeth Sellars, Franco Interlenghi, Bessie Love, Tonio Selwart, Enzo Staiola, and Riccardo Rioli. United Artists. color

Barefoot in the Park (1967)—Jane Fonda and Robert Redford are the spatting newlyweds—he's a hardworking lawyer and she, living in a romantic fantasy, has rented them a miserable fifth-floor walk-up in Greenwich Village. This movie version of a Neil Simon comedy hit is a trifle and almost amusing in a harmlessly, pleasantly stupid way. What Neil Simon can't seem to get rid of are those terrible moments of dramatic untruth—"I love you very much" and "I want a divorce"; they crunch like nutshells in a candy bar. If he could manage without them, he'd have candy so perfectly digestible people wouldn't know if they'd eaten it or just seen an ad for it. You can still feel the stage origins of this material and the director, Gene Saks, leaves pauses for laughs that don't come. But, at least, it's livelier than Fonda's 1966 picture *Any Wednesday*, and Mildred Natwick, as Fonda's mother, and Charles Boyer, as a Village neighbor, do their damnedest to make the lines seem witty. Also with Herbert Edelman, Mabel Albertson, Fritz Feld, and James Stone. Adapted by Simon; the play, directed by Mike Nichols, ran on Broadway from 1963 to 1967—Redford, Natwick, and Edelman were in the original cast. Produced by Hal B. Wallis, for Paramount. color

Le Baron fantôme, see *The Phantom Baron*

Barrage contre le Pacifique, see *The Sea Wall*

The Barretts of Wimpole Street (1934)—The war-horse of the stage-matinée trade tells the story of how the invalid Elizabeth Barrett escaped from her domineering father by miraculously getting up and eloping with the dashing Robert Browning. In this overproduced, unleavened version from M-G-M, Norma Shearer is the tremulous, bedridden poet, and Fredric March comes to the rescue. The glowering Papa is Charles Laughton. The cast includes Maureen O'Sullivan, Ralph Forbes, Una O'Connor, Katharine Alexander, Ian Wolfe, and Leo G. Carroll. Irving Thalberg produced, with his favorite dull company man, Sidney Franklin, directing. From the Rudolf Besier play (which Katharine Cornell made famous), worked over by Ernest Vajda, Claudine West, and Donald Ogden Stewart. (A 1956 version, also directed by Franklin, and starring Jennifer Jones, with John Gielgud as her father, was the box-office failure it deserved to be.) b & w

Barry Lyndon (1975)—Thackeray wrote a skittish, fast-moving parody of romantic, sentimental writing. It was about the adventures of an Irish knave who used British hypocrisy for leverage. However, it must have been Barry's ruthless pursuit of wealth and social position rather than his spirit that attracted Stanley Kubrick. His images are fastidiously delicate in the inexpressive, peculiarly chilly manner of the English painters of the period—the mid-18th century—and it's an ice-pack of a movie, a masterpiece in every insignificant detail. Kubrick suppresses most of the active elements that make movies pleasurable. The film says that people are disgusting but things are lovely. And a narrator (Michael Hordern) tells you what's going to happen before you see it. It's a coffee-table movie; the stately tour of European high life is like a three-hour slide show for art-history majors. With Ryan O'Neal, Marisa Berenson, Patrick Magee, Hardy Krüger, Diana Koerner, André Morell, Murray Melvin, Godfrey Quigley, Leonard Rossiter, Gay Hamilton, and Marie Kean. Production design by Ken Adam; cinematography by John Alcott; adaptation by Kubrick. (185 minutes.) Warners. color (See *When the Lights Go Down.*)

Bartleby (1970)—The shock when you first read the story—Melville's "Bartleby, the Scrivener"—may be in the recognition that Melville had this pre-vision of modern alienation back in 1853. The character is a precursor of Kafka's central figures, of Oblomov, of Dostoevski's underground man, of Camus's Meursault, and you can't grasp how this specifically modern man was formed in that mid-19th-century setting. What is he doing in that world, passively resisting, and withdrawing into courteous, stubborn catatonia? The English movie, directed by Anthony Friedman, from a script he wrote with Rodney Carr-Smith, is set in modern London, and that kills the visionary quality right off the bat. This disappointment doesn't diminish as the picture goes on, because the story is never made to belong to its new setting. John McEnery, in the title role, is successful in bringing the clerk up to date: he suggests both the mournful, bleached-out intransigence of the character and all the wan, misfit loners in their seat-sprung pants who wander through the big cities. And Paul Scofield is very fine as Bartleby's amiable, confused employer. But Melville's story moves logically and inexorably: it records the movement of a wage slave toward the freedom of total negation. When it's padded to feature-film length it gets thin. The movie was obviously made on

a shoestring and with honorable intentions, yet it's tentative and lame; it has little to recommend it but the two actors, Melville's dialogue, and the remnants of his great spooky conception. color (See *Deeper into Movies.*)

Les Bas-Fonds, see *The Lower Depths*

Basileus Quartet *Il Quartetto Basileus* (1982)—We may never get to see another movie about a string quartet, and so it's disappointing that this one turns out to be less interested in music and musicians than in demonstrating the perils of asceticism, but it's fairly pleasing anyway. The quartet has toured together for 30 years—the four men have given up everything for their musical careers—when the first violinist (François Simon) has a fatal heart attack. He is replaced by a 20-year-old virtuoso (Pierre Malet) with long ringlets, flaring nostrils, and the animal sensuality of a young Nureyev. This young man denies himself nothing; he has his pick of the beautiful women of Europe, he drinks, he gambles, he smokes pot—and his music does not suffer. The life in him is, of course, too much of a shock to the three older men, and, with no ill will on his part, he brings them to grief. The writer-director Fabio Carpi is somewhat too measured and solemn in his approach (the movie really should be a comedy—it's a bit like *Death in Venice* with three Gustav von Aschenbachs), and the material sags when one of the three (Michel Vitold) deludes himself that the young fiddler is his lover. But the other two—Omero Antonutti and Hector Alterio, both with trim, lordly beards—bring the film force and dignity; the rounded domes of their high foreheads and partly bald heads loom in the richly varnished, wood-panelled rooms. If you're going to give a movie Old Master lighting, these are certainly the actors to soak up the light. The cast also includes Gabriele Ferzetti as a weary, bitter old fellow, and that absurdly magnetic bad actor Alain Cuny, as the host at a couple of private musicales. In Italian. color (See *State of the Art*.)

I Basilischi, see *The Lizards*

La Batalla de Chile, see *The Battle of Chile*

Bathing Beauty (1944)—More simperingly girlish than even Doris Day, Esther Williams had one contribution to make to movies—her magnificent athletic body—and for over 10 years M-G-M made the most of it, keeping her in clinging, wet bathing suits and hoping the audience would shiver. This first starring extravaganza is simple compared to her later big splashes; it features Red Skelton and a nitwit plot about a man enrolling in a girls' college. The Johnny Green songs are sadly undistinguished. George Sidney directed; with Basil Rathbone, Helen Forrest, Ethel Smith, and Xavier Cugat and his orchestra. color

Batman (1989)—Tim Burton's powerfully glamorous comic-book epic, with sets angled and lighted like *film noir*, goes beyond pulp. It has a funky, nihilistic charge, and an eerie, poetic intensity. Michael Keaton is the fabulously wealthy Bruce Wayne, who patrols the sinister, nighttime canyons of Gotham City in the guise of Batman, and Jack Nicholson is the sniggering mobster Jack Napier, who turns into the leering madman the Joker. The two are fighting for the soul of the city that spawned them. The movie is underwritten, but it has so many unpredictable spins that what's missing doesn't seem to matter much. It's mean and anarchic and blissful. Written by Sam Hamm, Warren Skaaren (and uncredited others), based on characters created by Bob Kane. With cinematography by Roger Pratt; design by Anton Furst; costumes by Bob Ringwood; a plangent score by Danny Elfman, and songs by Prince.

The cast includes Jack Palance, Kim Basinger, Jerry Hall, and Robert Wuhl. Warners. color (See *Movie Love*.)

The Battle of Algiers (1966)—Like *Potemkin*, it's an epic in the form of a "created documentary"; it's a reconstruction of the events of 1954 to 1957 in the guerrilla war waged by the National Liberation Front against the French authorities, with the oppressed, angry masses as the hero. The enemy of the Algerian N.L.F.—the hyper-intelligent French colonel played by Jean Martin—isn't really a character; he represents the cool, inhuman manipulative power of imperialism versus the animal heat of the multitudes rushing toward us as they rise against their oppressors. The director, Gillo Pontecorvo, and his co-writer, Franco Solinas, are almost too clever in their use of this device of the colonel—yet it works, and brilliantly. The revolutionaries forming their pyramid of cells don't need to express revolutionary consciousness, because the French colonel is given such a full counter-revolutionary consciousness that he says it all for them. He even expresses the knowledge that history is on the side of the oppressed colonial peoples, who will win; he himself is merely part of a holding action, preserving imperialism a little longer but bound to fail. To put it satirically but, in terms of the movie, accurately, the Algerian people are spontaneously turned into revolutionaries by historical events, and if they haven't studied Marx, the counter-revolutionaries have, and know they are on the wrong side and are doomed by history. The movie hardly seems to be "saying" anything, yet the historical-determinist message seeps right into your bones. As a propaganda film, it ranks with Leni Riefenstahl's big-game rally, the 1935 *Triumph of the Will*, and it's the one great revolutionary "sell" of modern times. If has a firebrand's fervor; it carries you with it, and doesn't give you time to think. You may even accept the movie's implicit message that the N.L.F.'s violent methods are the only way to freedom. Pontecorvo's inflammatory passion works directly on your feelings. He's the most dangerous kind of Marxist, a Marxist poet. Cinematography by Marcello Gatti; music by Ennio Morricone and Pontecorvo. In French and Arabic. b & w (See *Reeling*.)

The Battle of Chile *La Batalla de Chile* (1976)—A great two-part 3-hour-and-10-minute documentary about the events leading to the fall of Allende; this cross-section view of a collapsing government must be unprecedented—we actually see the country cracking open. The young director, Patricio Guzmán, and his team have put a strict Marxist vise on the material; the film is structured to demonstrate that workers have to be prepared to use force of arms to defend their legally won gains, and much of what is presented as fact is highly questionable. But as a piece of epic filmmaking it is superb, and the editing is so subtle and fluid that the second half has the effect of one long, continuous shot. b & w (See *When the Lights Go Down*.)

The Battle of San Pietro Also known as *San Pietro*. (1943)—This record of one of the fights engaged in by a regiment of infantrymen for the capture of a 700-year-old Italian village is generally regarded as perhaps the greatest wartime documentary ever made. It was shot by six Signal Corps cameramen, under Major John Huston's direction. He wrote and spoke the factual narration, which shades into austere irony. The film got into trouble with the Army and was cut from five reels to the 33 minutes that remain, but you wouldn't guess it. This doesn't seem like a cut film; it has its own perfection. James Agee referred to part of it as "the first great passage of war poetry that has got on the screen,"

and it's as war poetry that the whole brief film is experienced. b & w

The Battle of the Sexes (1960)—The old order, represented by Peter Sellers as the head accountant of a Scottish firm rich in tradition, triumphing over the new, represented by Constance Cummings as an interloping American efficiency expert. This British film was adapted from the James Thurber story "The Catbird Seat," but as directed by Charles Crichton it's not as funny as it's meant to be. With Robert Morley as the laird in charge of the firm. b & w

The Battleship Potemkin, see *Potemkin*

Battling Butler (1926)—Rarely seen Buster Keaton film that he sometimes said was his favorite but that is probably no one else's favorite; the story is slight enough to hang gags on (including a famous duck shoot), but there's some discomfort—almost masochism—built into it. Keaton plays puny, defenseless Alfy Butler, a rich, soft simpleton whose father sends him into the woods to make a man of him; through love (for broad-faced Sally O'Neil) and mistaken identity, he becomes embroiled in prizefighting and is pitted against the sadistic world champion. He wins, of course, but not until after he's taken a cruel beating. Keaton directed, and there are cleverly worked out compositional techniques, including the sort of deep focus that was later to be associated with Orson Welles and Gregg Toland. With Snitz Edwards as the valet. Silent. b & w

Bay of the Angels *La Baie des anges* (1962)— What would this film be like without Jeanne Moreau? Even if the dialogue and direction were the same, the meanings wouldn't be. The picture is almost an emanation of Moreau, is inconceivable without her. Written and directed by Jacques Demy, it's rather like a French attempt to purify, to get to the essence of, a Warners movie of the 30s. Demy not only gets to it, he goes beyond it. His virtuoso sense of film rhythm turns this flimsy, capricious story about a gambling lady into a lyrical study in compulsion and luck. The concept of gambling as almost total spontaneity and irresponsibility—as giving in to chance (as if that were the most complete acceptance of life)—is oddly suggestive, and we begin, in this film, to feel its appeal, to feel that gambling is a bum's existentialism. And Jeanne Moreau, in a very Bette Davis sort of way, dramatizes herself superbly. (There are times when she's as white and unreal as Constance Bennett in her satins and you think how marvellous she'd be singing "The Boulevard of Broken Dreams.") This is a magical, whirling little film, a triumph of style, even though it runs down to nothing in the last, too quick, too ambiguous shot. With Claude Mann. Photographed, in dazzling sunlight, by Jean Rabier, and with one of Michel Legrand's best scores. In French. b & w

Beach Red (1967)—Sincere to a fault; the worst speeches always seem to be underlined. Cornel Wilde directed, and stars in, this anti-war Second World War movie about a battalion of Marines on a Japanese-held island off the Philippines. Rip Torn plays a sadistic sergeant who gratuitously murders a wounded Japanese soldier. United Artists. color

The Beachcomber (1938)—A charming, neglected romantic comedy. The happiest screen collaboration of Elsa Lanchester and Charles Laughton—they're both wonderful—is in this adaptation of a Somerset Maugham story, "The Vessel of Wrath." It's set on an island in the Pacific, which Maugham calls Baru, and it's concerned with the efforts of the prim missionary (Lanches-

ter) to reform the carnal, ribald beachcomber (Laughton). The situation is the reverse of that in Maugham's Sadie Thompson story, but with a light, comic tone. The Hepburn-Bogart *African Queen* probably took a few notions from it. Erich Pommer directed; with Robert Newton. (A 1954 version, starring Glynis Johns, with Newton in the Laughton role, isn't in the same class.) Paramount. b & w

Beaches (1988)—This movie about the lifelong friendship between two women of contrasting backgrounds—Bette Midler as CC Bloom, a show-biz-crazy Jewish redhead from New York, and Barbara Hershey as Hillary Whitney, a repressed wealthy Wasp from San Francisco—suggests the kind of material that Midler might be using for a takeoff. Instead, it's being played for maudlin soulfulness. After a while, it turns into an all-girl *Love Story*, with Hillary becoming ghoulishly pale from heart disease and CC (now a singing star) staying at her side. Through this (slow, slow) deathwatch, CC learns to transcend her self-involvement; she becomes a better person, and—implicitly—a bigger star. If you admired Midler in *The Rose* and *Down and Out in Beverly Hills*, you may want to bash your head against the wall. With Mayim Bialik, who must have been specially created to be CC at 11, and John Heard. The director, Garry Marshall, shows no feeling for the material—not even false feeling; the script, by Mary Agnes Donoghue, is from Iris Rainer Dart's novel. Touchstone (Disney). color (See *Movie Love*.)

The Bear (1989)—This French-made version of the romantic-wilderness pictures that Hollywood turned out in the silent era is a combination of raw pulp and gooey kitsch. A whimpering orphaned bear cub tries to attach himself to a huge male bear (9 feet 2 and weighing 2,000 pounds), who has been shot in the shoulder and growls, rebuffing the infant. The plucky cub's feelings are hurt, but he ignores the threats, and follows the big bear, pleading for acceptance; he comes close enough to clean the wound with his tongue, and soon the two are kissing and licking. They have "bonded"; the music swells, and our hearts are supposed to be swelling, too. The director, Jean-Jacques Annaud, and the screenwriter, Gérard Brach, devised the plan for a gory, sentimental myth and then tried to get animals to act out the parts of the story that couldn't be faked; they fell back on sleight-of-hand cutting that never quite covers up the gaps. The human grunts and groans of the cornered big bear and the cub's constant crying out in terror are usually as close to telling the story as the film gets. The movie doesn't exist except for its dubbed sound effects. Set in British Columbia in 1885; shot in the Austrian Tyrol and Northern Italy. Based on James Oliver Curwood's 1916 novel *The Grizzly King*. Tri-Star. color (See *Movie Love*.)

Beat the Devil (1954)—"The formula of *Beat the Devil*," its director, John Huston, once remarked, "is that everyone is slightly absurd." The plot of the picture was unknown to the cast, but presumably known to Huston and his co-writer, Truman Capote; however, Capote later remarked that he had "a suspicion that John wasn't too clear about it." Commercially speaking, the movie courted—and achieved—disaster. According to most accounts, Capote wrote the script as they went along (reading it aloud to the cast each morning, Robert Morley says), and Huston didn't show any signs of anxiety. This improvisation was not necessarily an actor's delight, and Humphrey Bogart, who looks rather bewildered through much of it, as if he hadn't been let in on the joke, said, "Only the phonies think it's funny. It's a mess." Yes, but it may be the funniest mess of all time. It

kidded itself, yet it succeeded in some original (and perhaps dangerously marginal) way by finding a style of its own. Bogart and his wife, Gina Lollobrigida, are on a ship bound for British East Africa; their travelling companions are a gang of uranium swindlers— Morley, Peter Lorre, Marco Tulli, and Ivor Barnard. The funniest performer is Jennifer Jones (in a blond wig) as a creative liar; she's married to a bogus British lord (Edward Underdown). Then there's a shipwreck. This straight-faced parody of the international thriller killed off the whole genre. (It also ended the Huston-Bogart working relationship. Bogart had had his own money in the picture.) With Bernard Lee. Cinematography by Oswald Morris and Freddie Francis; from a novel by James Helvick (a pseudonym for Claud Cockburn). A Santana-Romulus Production, for United Artists. b & w

Beau Geste (1939)—Gary Cooper had had three flops in a row when he decided to play it safe with this remake of the 1926 Ronald Colman hit about a valiant Foreign Legionnaire's life in the midst of Arab attacks, garrison floggings, desert deaths, and assorted fortress crises. The picture, rousingly directed by William Wellman, was indeed a success, but Cooper, horribly miscast as a dashing young British gallant—saying things like "You young pup!" to Ray Milland—was embarrassingly callow, almost simpering, and he looked too old for the part. Besides, times had changed, and his somewhat delirious courage didn't entertain audiences nearly as much as Brian Donlevy's ruthless villainy. Donlevy's sadistic Russian officer shocked audiences, and at the same time persuaded them that he was a superb soldier; the role had some of the fascination of George C. Scott's later Patton. Donlevy got the notices and an Academy Award nomination. With Robert Preston as Cooper's brother, Susan Hayward, Albert Dekker, Broderick

Crawford, J. Carrol Naish, and Donald O'Connor playing Beau as a child. The Percival C. Wren novel was adapted by Robert Carson. (A 1966 version starred Guy Stockwell, and Telly Savalas in the Donlevy role.) Paramount. b & w

Le Beau Mariage (1982)—Béatrice Romand plays Eric Rohmer's heroine, Sabine, a bright working girl who is studying for her Master's in art history. At 25, Sabine is weary of freedom and insecurity and married men; she wants to be taken care of and to make a home for a man and have children. When she meets a lawyer who she decides is her type, she goes after him so briskly and transparently that she might seem a madwoman, except that she has such a dumb little obsession. There's no passion in it, and she's an orderly little campaigner—watching her lay siege to this man is like watching someone arrange his desk. The film is full of glib, precise chatter and the clickety-click of Sabine's high heels. Rohmer, who wrote the script, never gives us a clue to why she doesn't draw upon her knowledge of men to be more elusive. Since we see her humiliating herself, she becomes poignant, and at the end, when she comes to her senses, we want to see her play the game right. But what we get seems only the first act—the movie ends just when it begins to be interesting. Serio-comic triviality has become Rohmer's specialty. His sensibility would be easier to take if he'd stop directing to a metronome. In French. color (See *Taking It All In*.)

La Beauté du diable, see *Beauty and the Devil*

The Beautiful Blonde from Bashful Bend (1949)—It's hard to believe that Preston Sturges wrote, produced, and directed this botched parody Western, but he was trying to recoup after the shattering critical and box-office failure of his most high-style slapstick comedy—the 1948 *Unfaithfully Yours*—and he seems to have lost his bearings totally. A hot-tempered barroom singer (Betty Grable) takes a shot at her rival for the affections of a card shark (Cesar Romero) and accidentally hits a judge (Porter Hall) in the rear end. She escapes from prison and goes to Snake City (populated with many of the Sturges regulars), where she pretends to be a schoolteacher named Hilda Swandumper. Sturges tries for the frantic comic atmosphere he got in *The Miracle of Morgan's Creek*, but everything is mistimed. The film was such a disaster that 20th Century-Fox cancelled his contract and he was finished in Hollywood. His career as an American writer-director began and ended in the 40s. Among the performers struggling desperately to be funny are Rudy Vallee, Olga San Juan, Sterling Holloway, El Brendel, Hugh Herbert, Margaret Hamilton, Esther Howard, J. Farrell MacDonald, Marie Windsor, Chester Conklin, Chris-Pin Martin, and Dewey Robinson. Sturges's only film in color.

Beauty and the Beast *La Belle et la bête* (1946)—Jean Cocteau's first full-length movie (he wrote and directed it) is perhaps the most sensuously elegant of all filmed fairy tales. As a child escapes from everyday family life to the magic of a storybook, so, in the film, Beauty's farm, with its Vermeer simplicity, fades in intensity as we are caught up in the Gustave Doré extravagance of the Beast's enchanted landscape. In Christian Bérard's makeup, Jean Marais is a magnificent Beast; Beauty's self-sacrifice to him holds no more horror than a satisfying romantic fantasy should have. The transformation of the Beast into Prince Charming is ambiguous—what we have gained cannot quite take the place of what we have lost. (When shown the film, Greta Garbo is reported to have said at the end, "Give me back my Beast.") The delicate Josette Day is, quite properly, Beauty. With

Marcel André as the father, Michel Auclair as the brother, and Mila Parély as a sister. Alekan was the cinematographer; Georges Auric wrote the score; Bérard did the decor and costumes. (A running account of the making of the picture—anxieties, physical ailments, mistakes and all—is given in Cocteau's entertaining 1950 book, *Diary of a Film.*) In French. b & w

Beauty and the Devil *La Beauté du diable* (1949)—The American title is deceptive; the film was probably given the confusing title here so that it would seem like a sex film. Michel Simon, as Mephistopheles, offers old Faust youth, then shows him how little he can do with youth without wealth; he hooks him. Mephistopheles then assumes the shape of the aging Faust, while Faust becomes the dashing young Gérard Philipe. There are no spiritual conflicts in this René Clair film; the dangers of science and of absolute power are the targets, and the fantasy is urbane. The twistings of the plot become tedious and the whole elaborate joke gets awfully smug. With Gaston Modot, Simone Valère, Paolo Stoppa, Nicole Besnard, Raymond Cordy, Carlo Ninchi, and Tullio Carminati. Written by Clair and Armand Salacrou. In French. b & w

Becky Sharp (1935)—More famous for its color design and its experimental use of Technicolor than for its dramatic qualities. Rouben Mamoulian directed this only intermittently compelling version of *Vanity Fair.* Miriam Hopkins is the naughty witch herself, and the cast includes Frances Dee, Cedric Hardwicke, Alison Skipworth, Nigel Bruce, and Billie Burke. R K O.

Bed and Board *Domicile conjugal* (1970)—About the married life of Truffaut's hero, Antoine Doinel (Jean-Pierre Léaud). Léaud appears to have developed a dogged resistance to acting, but, as Antoine's bride, Claude

Jade, who looks like a less ethereal, more practical Catherine Deneuve, is lovely. The movie is cheerful, if conventionally "beguiling." With Hiroko Berghauer, Barbara Laage, and Daniel Boulanger; cinematography by Nestor Almendros. In French. color (See *Deeper into Movies.*)

The Bed Sitting Room (1969)—The ghastly kind of far-out humor that makes you feel as if you've got a pain in your side when you haven't even laughed. Richard Lester directed this apocalyptic after-the-bomb farce. Some twenty-odd straggling survivors in London wander in and out of blackout sketches. With Michael Hordern, Rita Tushingham giving birth to something unspecified, and Ralph Richardson—until he mutates into a bed-sitting room. The absurdist chaos becomes numbing; this perpetual giggle almost seems to require a bomb. Also with Mona Washbourne, Peter Cook, Dudley Moore, Arthur Lowe, Harry Secombe, Marty Feldman, and Spike Milligan. From the Milligan–John Antrobus play, adapted by Antrobus. Cinematography by David Watkin. Released by United Artists. color (See *Deeper into Movies.*)

Bedazzled (1967)—Dudley Moore and Peter Cook, who had performed in the Beyond the Fringe cabaret-comedy troupe, probably did their best screen teamwork in this movie, written by Cook, from a story they devised together, and directed by Stanley Donen. It's a very deft and silly and likable Faustian vaudeville—a series of skits in which the tall, skinny Cook, as the Devil, makes a sucker of the shy, little-boyish Faust (Moore). The scenes are quick, and even though the rhythm is frequently stagey little bits of verbal wit seem to be flying about. Moore starts out as a timid, working-class fellow who's helplessly in love with a girl (Eleanor Bron) who likes intellectuals; he sells his soul for her, and of course he never gets her. (He and Bron—whose hair seems to be twisted into different shapes in every scene—are like a British Nichols and May.) The Devil grants him the fulfillment of seven wishes, and the fun of the plot is in Moore's seven different incarnations and in the Devil's cool deviousness and the pleasure he takes in frustrating him. The movie is no more than a novelty, but it may surprise you by making you laugh out loud a few times. With Raquel Welch, who appears briefly as Lust, Barry Humphries as Envy, and Lockwood West as St. Peter. color

Bedknobs and Broomsticks (1971)—Angela Lansbury as an apprentice witch in a fantasy from the Disney studios set in Second World War England. It's a big, mongrel production, combining live action and animation and with an elaborate ballet in a mockup of Portobello Road, and a sequence, perhaps influenced by Russian and Central European movie fantasies, that is magical animation in a tradition different from the usual Disney work. Lansbury, on a broomstick, commands a ghostly army of knights on steeds against the Nazis. There's no logic in the style of the movie, and the story dribbles on for so long that it exhausts the viewer before that final magical battle begins. The story is suffused with patriotic sentimentality circa *Mrs. Miniver*. Lansbury gives up witchcraft when she gets a man, David Tomlinson, who twinkles like a sexless pixie and, of course, the movie includes the Disney inevitable—this time in the shape of three lovable Cockney orphans. The director, Robert Stevenson, found an appallingly simple solution to the problem of enabling Americans to understand the children's Cockney intonations: every time one of them speaks we get a closeup, so that our full attention is focussed on the piping little speaker and we can practically read the lips. It's as if a TV show had been cut into the movie every few seconds. This whole production is a mixture of wizardry and ineptitude; the picture has enjoyable moments but it's as uncertain of itself as the title indicates. With Sam Jaffe, Roddy McDowall, Reginald Owen, and Tessie O'Shea. Choreography by Donald McKayle. color (See *Deeper into Movies*.)

The Bedroom Window (1987)—This suspense film by the writer-director Curtis Hanson has a good premise. A married woman (Isabelle Huppert) who has seen an assault from her lover's window can't give her testimony to the police without endangering her marriage, so her lover (Steve Guttenberg) reports all the details she has given him but pretends that he was the observer. His apparently innocent lie gets them both into a mess. It's an erratic and, finally, disappointing picture (it loses its snap). Yet you keep rooting for it, because Elizabeth McGovern, as the assault victim, a cocktail waitress, has the style and resources that the other two leads lack, and the cinematography, by Gil Taylor, his a snazzy verve, and Hanson has some clever ideas, such as the way he sets up a courtroom sequence (with Wallace Shawn demonstrating a new witty suavity as the attorney for the assailant) and the way he directs the almost mute psycho (the chilling, well-cast Brad Greenquist). Also with Paul Shenar, Carl Lumbly, Frederick Coffin, Sara Carlson, and Maury Chaykin; adapted from the English novel *The Witnesses*, by Anne Holden. The Baltimore locations, and the scenes in Wilmington and Winston-Salem, North Carolina, doubling for Baltimore, provide a colorful architectural mix. De Laurentiis. color (See *Hooked*.)

Beetlejuice (1988)—Set in an idyllic New England town, this farce about the afterlife is a variant on *Topper* (1937) and *The Old Dark House* (1932). A devoted, home-loving young couple (Alec Baldwin and Geena Davis) are drowned in a car accident, and when they return to their house as ghosts they are miffed by the redecorating of the New Yorkers who have bought it. Too mild to scare these intruders away, they call upon the services of the rutty little demon Betelgeuse. Michael Keaton plays the part, and his uninhibited comic performance is like an exploding head. He isn't onscreen nearly enough—when he is, he shoots the film sky-high. The story is bland and the movie is slow to get going, but with crazy comedy you settle for the moments of inspiration, and this picture has them. The young director, Tim Burton, takes stabs into the irrational and the incongruous; the film's blandness is edged with near-genius (and some great special effects). The smudge-faced blond Catherine O'Hara, who's the possessor of the freakiest blue-eyed stare since early Gene Wilder, is brilliant as the madwoman who is the new lady of the house. Also with Sylvia Sidney as a caseworker in the social-services bureaucracy of the dead, and Winona Ryder, Jeffrey Jones, Glenn Shadix, Adelle Lutz, and Robert Goulet and Dick Cavett. The story is by Michael McDowell and Larry Wilson; the screenplay is by McDowell and Warren Skaaren. The cinematography is by Thomas Ackerman; the production design is by Bo Welch. Warners. color (See *Hooked*.)

Before the Revolution *Prima della Rivoluzione* (1964)—A sweepingly romantic movie about a young man's rebellion against bourgeois life and his disillusion with Communism, set in Parma and written and directed by Bernardo Bertolucci at the astonishing age of 22. He captures what has rarely been seen on the screen—the extravagance and poetry of youthful ardor. The hero, Fabrizio, discovers that he is not single-minded enough to be a revolutionary, that he is too deeply involved in the beauty of life as it is *before* the revo-

lution. He has "a nostalgia for the present." (The characters of Fabrizio and his young aunt Gina are loosely derived from Stendhal's *The Charterhouse of Parma*.) With Francesco Barilli, Adriana Asti, Allen Midgette, and Morando Morandini; cinematography by Aldo Scavarda; music by Gino Paoli and Ennio Morricone. This was Bertolucci's second feature; his first was *La Commare Secca (The Grim Reaper)*. In Italian. b & w (See *Kiss Kiss Bang Bang*.)

The Beggar's Opera (1953)—Pure pleasure— the ballad-opera about the highwayman Captain Macheath and his escapes from the law and the ladies, with Laurence Olivier doing his own singing (he has a pleasant light baritone) as the dashing Macheath. This is one of his most playful, sophisticated, and least-known roles. It was Swift who suggested that a "Newgate pastoral might make an odd pretty sort of thing," and John Gay worked out the idea in a new form—a musical play with the lyrics fitted to existing music. To Londoners weary of the bombast of Italian opera, Gay's corrupt gang of thieves, highwaymen, whores, and informers was the fresh, sweet breath of England. Gay satirized the politics of the day as well as the heroics of Italian opera; many of his targets are now a matter for historians, but the large butt of the joke—the corruption and hypocrisy of mankind—still sits around. And by the time Peter Brook directed this film (his first, and the only comedy he has ever made), a new set of conventions, as tired and inflated as Italian opera, was ready for potshots—the conventions of the movies: the chaste heroines, the intrepid Robin Hood heroes, the phony realism. Dennis Cannan and Christopher Fry adapted the text freely, retaining the mocking, raffish spirit, and Arthur Bliss arranged the score so that we come out humming the pretty airs. And the actors are having such a good time playing scoundrels that their zest for villainy is infectiously satiric. Stanley Holloway is a magnificent Lockit, and shows off his fine, deep voice. Most of the others are dubbed, but they perform in such an offhand manner that the dubbing is inoffensive. It even comes in for a bit of parody when Dorothy Tutin, as dear Polly Peachum, sings while rowing a boat. She obviously isn't singing the way someone rowing would sing; she smiles like a cat who has swallowed a canary, as indeed she has. Athene Seyler is a great Mrs. Trapes; George Devine is Peachum; Yvonne Furneaux is Jenny Diver; Daphne Anderson is Lucy Lockit; Hugh Griffith is the Beggar; Mary Clare is Mrs. Peachum; Margot Grahame is the Actress. The cinematography is by Guy Green, with art direction by Georges Wakhévitch and William C. Andrews. Commercially, the film was a disaster, and it has rarely been revived. color (See *I Lost it at the Movies*.)

Bell' Antonio (1960)—Antonio (Marcello Mastroianni, in perhaps his most delicate, muted performance) is a Sicilian Don Juan whose life is destroyed by the conflict between sacred and profane love. He is expected to profess the Church's belief in purity while acting out his father's belief that sexual prowess is the measure of a man, but Antonio really believes in purity and love. And so, although he is a great ladies' man with "loose" women or women of a lower social class, he is impotent with the pure, highborn girl whom he loves and marries. In Pier Paolo Pasolini's adaptation of Vitaliano Brancati's novel, Antonio represents the whole pattern of social and religious decadence; he is the victim of the system. This proud, handsome hero is never for an instant comic; what is so often treated from the outside as a subject for comedy is here treated from the inside—from the point of view of the humiliated, desolate man. All his life, Antonio will long to possess the ideal, and the very intensity of his longing

for idealized love will defeat him. Mauro Bolognini directed this gentle satirical study of virility and social position in a Catholic culture. With Pierre Brasseur as the strutting rooster of a father, Rina Morelli as the mother, Claudia Cardinale as the pure bride, and Tomas Milian as the cousin. In Italian. b & w

La Belle et la bête, see *Beauty and the Beast*

Belle of the Nineties (1934)—The Mae West pictures without Cary Grant didn't have much class, and in this tawdry melodrama, with Roger Pryor and Johnny Mack Brown opposite her, she isn't funny enough, either. But the tawdriness is so explicit in her low-down script (about a 19th-century entertainer's romance with a prizefighter) that the movie is rather fascinating, and once again Miss West sings marvellous honky-tonk blues—perhaps even better than usual. This time, the songs include "When a St. Louis Woman Goes Down to New Orleans," "Troubled Waters," "My Old Flame," and "Memphis Blues," and Duke Ellington and his orchestra (sometimes on screen, sometimes off) provide the backing, so one can see Johnny Hodges, Barney Bigard, Cootie Williams, and the whole troupe. Scott Joplin's "Maple Leaf Rag" can be heard on the soundtrack. Directed by Leo McCarey, for Paramount. With John Miljan and Katherine De Mille. b & w

Bellissima (1951)—It is said that this Luchino Visconti film (it was his third) was conceived when the director was looking for a child actress for a different production and found himself surrounded by 4,000 mothers, each shouting "Mine is *bellissima*!" The film is a satirical view of the movie-studio world of Cinecittà, and is also perhaps Visconti's warmest comedy. It's full of contradictory impulses, and is marred by a too pat ending glorifying the wisdom of the common people, but at its center is the great Anna Magnani as a screen-struck mother, determined to make a star of her plain little 5-year-old (Tina Apicella). Magnani enters the child in a contest to find "the prettiest child in Rome"; there is a devastating sequence when the mother, who has finagled her way into the screening room where her daughter's screen test is being run, is listening to the laughter—Magnani is at her most extraordinary. With Alessandro Blasetti, a highly respected director and precursor of neo-realism, playing himself, but with overtones of Visconti. And with Walter Chiari and Gastone Renzelli. From a script by Suso Cecchi d'Amico, Francesco Rosi, and Visconti, based on a story by Cesare Zavattini. The assistant directors were Rosi and Franco Zeffirelli. In Italian. b & w

Ben-Hur (1925)—The Ramon Novarro–Francis X. Bushman version; it was a remake even then, but M-G-M put $5 million into it, and so much Amazing, Gargantuan, Stupendous, and Mighty Biblical Pageantry that vast numbers of viewers were swept off their feet. There's the galley manned by a thousand slaves, the sea battle between Romans and ancient pirates, the Valley of the Lepers, and the chariot race staged in a mammoth stadium, with every L.A. man, woman, and child lying about as a super. Novarro has his adolescent charm and beauty, and Bushman's nose is majestically Roman. With Betty Bronson, May McAvoy, Carmel Myers, and Claire McDowell. Directed by Fred Niblo. Silent. b & w and color

Ben-Hur (1959)—Movie moguls have always had a real affinity for the grandiosity of the old Roman Empire. Charlton Heston plays the Jewish prince Ben-Hur; when he refuses to rat on the Jews opposed to Roman domination, his childhood friend Messala (Stephen Boyd) packs him off to the galleys

and sends his mother (Martha Scott) and his sister (Cathy O'Donnell) to a dungeon. After prolonged slaving at the oars, Ben-Hur escapes and saves the life of a bigwig in the Roman navy (Jack Hawkins), who adopts him. Eventually we get to the chariot race, with Ben-Hur pitted against the treacherous Messala. Lew Wallace's hectic potboiler-classic has everything—even leprosy. M-G-M laid on the cash and William Wyler directed, with several busy assistants; the cast includes Sam Jaffe, Haya Harareet, Hugh Griffith, Finlay Currie, and a corps of stunt men. Has anyone ever been able to detect the contributions to the script of Gore Vidal, Christopher Fry, and S. N. Behrman? Could *they*? color

Benjamin (1967)—Pierre Clémenti and Catherine Deneuve are the virgins who eventually get deflowered, while Michel Piccoli and Michèle Morgan have their mature love problems. For people who like Gallic romps and aphorisms about the relations of the sexes. Directed by Michel Deville; cinematography by Ghislain Cloquet. In French. color (See *Going Steady*.)

The Bespoke Overcoat (1955)—This 37-minute film directed by Jack Clayton (his next was his first feature, *Room at the Top*) is one of the best short-story films ever made. Wolf Mankowitz adapted Gogol's "The Overcoat" to Jewish characters in the East End of London; David Kossoff is the tailor and Alfie Bass (of *The Lavender Hill Mob*) is the clerk. The music is by Georges Auric. b & w

Best Foot Forward (1943)—No one who saw it is likely to have forgotten "Buckle Down Winsocki"—the best of all the school songs in all the cheery-silly, hip-hip-hoorah musicals. The women excel in this one, an M-G-M picture with a cast that includes Lucille Ball, June Allyson, Gloria De Haven,

Nancy Walker, William Gaxton, and Harry James and his orchestra. Eddie Buzzell directed. color

Best Friends (1982)—The script raises the question: Why does formalizing a living-together relationship by marriage often wreck it, leaving both partners feeling trapped? But the scriptwriters (Barry Levinson and Valerie Curtin) have nothing but sit-com answers. It's a Velveeta comedy, processed like a Neil Simon picture, with banter and gags and an unctuous score. All its smart talk is low-key and listless. It stays on the surface, yet it's dissatisfied with the surface; it's a deeply indecisive movie that starts escaping its subject as soon as the newlywed screenwriting partners—Burt Reynolds and Goldie Hawn—go off on their wedding trip and into a series of comic nightmares. The two have been made so lightweight that there's nothing at stake when they recoil from each other, and Reynolds gives a flabby, mildewed performance. Directed by Norman Jewison; with Jessica Tandy, Barnard Hughes, Audra Lindley, and Keenan Wynn. Two performers give the film a little bounce—Ron Silver as a hotshot movie producer and Richard Libertini as the Hispanic who conducts the marriage ceremony. Warners. color (See *Taking It All In*.)

The Best Little Whorehouse in Texas (1982)—The moviemakers pile on the coy Americana; they appear to have distrusted anything original in the material—the movie is adapted from the long-running Broadway musical based on Larry L. King's 1974 *Playboy* article about a crackbrained crusading TV newsman who attacked a time-honored brothel with such fervor that the authorities had to force the madam to close it. The film's rambunctiousness is off-color yet wholesome, in the worst sense: this is the sort of movie romp in which the frolicking prosties can hardly wait to jump into bed with the fellas. But dimples, wigs, bazooms, and all, Dolly Parton is phenomenally likable as the madam; her whole personality is melodious, and her acting isn't bad at all, even though the director, Colin Higgins, has made her chest the focal point of her scenes. She has the charm to transcend her own cartoonishness and the additional portion inflicted on her. As the local sheriff, Burt Reynolds doesn't give an ostentatiously bad performance—just his usual low-key, embarrassed-to-be-up-here-doing-this-dumb-stuff performance. While Reynolds underplays and looks mortified, Charles Durning, as governor of Texas, steals the honors with his "Sidestep" song-and-dance routine—a demonstration of how a corrupt-to-the-bone politico evades answering probing questions and takes joy in his own slippery skill. This sequence is the only part of the movie that's satisfyingly shaped and has a musical-comedy rhythm. With Dom DeLuise, Jim Nabors, Theresa Merritt, and Lois Nettleton. The script is by King and Peter Masterson (who wrote the Broadway show) and Higgins; 7 of the 14 songs that Carol Hall wrote for the stage version have been retained, and 2 new ones by Dolly Parton have been added. Universal-R K O. color (See *Taking It All In*.)

The Best Man (1964)—Gore Vidal's political melodrama is about a convention at which the two chief contestants for the party's nomination for the Presidency are an Adlai Stevenson type (Henry Fonda) and a Joe McCarthy type (Cliff Robertson). The film has a lot of verve. It has the look of crackling intelligence thanks to Haskell Wexler's black-and-white cinematography and Franklin Schaffner's sure, fast-paced direction. It seems like a hot, inside view even though Vidal sets the issues in terms of a slick, simplistic ends-and-means morality play, and throws in the kind of clever, self-congratu-latory topical jokes that sound dated the first time you hear them. With Lee Tracy as the hard-bitten old-pro ex-President, Margaret Leighton, Ann Sothern, Edie Adams, Kevin McCarthy, Gene Raymond, George Kirgo (who is said to have had a hand in the script) as the speechwriter, and Shelley Berman, as an obsequious weakling. There's also an ap-pearance by the magnificent Mahalia Jack-son. United Artists.

The Best of Times (1986)—An enjoyable soft-shoe farce, directed by Roger Spottis-woode and written by Ron Shelton—the team who made the 1983 *Under Fire*. Every smart aleck in the town of Taft, California, has been ribbing the smarmy bank vice-pres-ident Jack Dundee (Robin Williams) for 13 years—ever since he fumbled the beautiful touchdown pass that the high school's star quarterback, Reno (Kurt Russell), threw to him at the end of the Big Game with Bakers-field, in 1971. Jack fastens on the addlepated notion of replaying the game, and won't let go of it. His loony psyche operates at full tilt, and he's so nervous he's unstoppable. The mellow Russell is a great straight man to him: the way Russell plays Reno, you see his trans-parent normality in every curve of his face. What makes this movie more than a football fantasy and puts you in mind of Preston Sturges and of Jonathan Demme's *Citizens Band* is how the rematch affects the two men's marriages. As the two pairs of high-school sweethearts who are now married lovers, Robin Williams and Holly Palance and Kurt Russell and Pamela Reed are as close to comic perfection as movie couples are likely to get. With Donald Moffat as Jack's father-in-law, M. Emmet Walsh as the head Caribou of the Caribou Lodge, and Margaret Whitton, Dub Taylor, R. G. Armstrong, and Kathleen Free-

man. Cinematography by Charles F. Wheeler. Universal. color (See *Hooked*.)

The Best Years of Our Lives (1946)—A hefty (172 minutes) piece of moviemaking that seemed to satisfy the public desire to see what changes the Second World War had made in people's lives. Despite its seven Academy Awards, it's not a great picture; it's too schematic and it drags on after you get the points. However, episodes and details stand out and help to compensate for the soggy plot strands, and there's something ab-sorbing about the banality of its large-scale good intentions; it's compulsively watchable. And it's by no means a rah-rah film—there's an undercurrent of discontent. Fredric March is the infantry sergeant who comes home to his small (apocryphal) Midwestern city and the love of his wife (Myrna Loy) but finds no pleasure in his job as vice-president of a bank. Dana Andrews, an Air Force captain who had been a soda jerk before the war, discovers that his hard-as-nails wife (Virginia Mayo) doesn't want him any more than he wants her; he turns to the sergeant's daughter (Ter-esa Wright). Harold Russell is the machinist's mate second class who has lost his hands but has retained the love of his childhood sweet-heart. Directed by William Wyler, it's clean and unmannered. In 1944, Sam Goldwyn had seen a photograph in *Time* showing a group of Marines coming home, and the accompa-nying news story had suggested that they might be returning to their families and jobs with mixed emotions. Goldwyn commis-sioned MacKinlay Kantor to write a screen treatment based on this idea; Kantor, instead, wrote *Glory for Me*, a novel in verse, which Goldwyn then hired Robert E. Sherwood to adapt. With Cathy O'Donnell, Gladys George, Hoagy Carmichael, Roman Bohnen, Ray Collins, Steve Cochran, Minna Gombell, Don Beddoe, and Erskine Sanford. Cinematography by Gregg Toland. A Samuel Goldwyn Production; released by R K O. b & w

La Bête humaine *The Human Beast* (1938)—Jean Renoir's version of the Zola novel, transferred from the Second Empire to the 30s, has a memorable beginning, with Jean Gabin driving the express on the run from Le Havre to Paris. The train sequences, which are superb—realistic yet poetic—were shot on location and include views of the Gare St. Lazare in Paris in 1938. The film has marvellous atmosphere and a fine cast (Simone Simon, Carette, Fernand Ledoux, Blanchette Brunoy, Renoir himself), but the material, which involves brutal, uncontrollable passion seen in a social framework, turns oppressive, and at times Gabin is a lump. (Remade in Hollywood in 1954 as *Human Desire*, directed by Fritz Lang with Glenn Ford and Gloria Grahame.) In French. b & w

The Betsy (1978)—The director, Daniel Petrie, aims low and misses his target—maybe through taste and halfheartedness as much as ineptitude. This adaptation of Harold Robbins' novel about three generations of a Detroit automobile dynasty lacks the juicy vulgarity of soul which Robbins requires—it's so tranquil it's like a reverie on the clichés of the genre. As the superabundantly sexed patriarch of the family, Laurence Olivier keeps on acting after everyone else has given up. He must be doing it for himself—for the sheer love of testing himself as an actor. His energy blasts through the film's largo style; it's a personal triumph. With Tommy Lee Jones, Robert Duvall, Katharine Ross, Jane Alexander, Lesley-Anne Down, Kathleen Beller, Paul Rudd, Edward Herrmann, and Joseph Wiseman. Cinematography by Mario Tosi; screenplay by William Bast and Walter Bernstein; produced by Robert R. Weston. Allied Artists. color (See *When the Lights Go Down*.)

Beverly Hills Cop (1984)—The plot—Eddie Murphy is a Detroit cop who takes a vacation to go to Beverly Hills and hunt down the men who killed his best friend—is just a peg for little set pieces in which the street-smart Murphy, in his worn-out sweatshirts, saunters through swank Beverly Hills locations, tells whopping lies, and outsmarts the white dumbos. Yelling and fast-talking, and hotfooting the picture to keep it going, he rattles off pitifully undistinguished profanity, but we're cued to react to every stupid four-letter word as riotous. And, with Murphy busting his sides laughing in self-congratulation, and the camera jammed into his tonsils, damned if the audience doesn't whoop and carry on as if, yes, this is a wow of a comedy. There are a few likable, unforced funny scenes with Judge Reinhold as a credulous, velvet-voiced cop, Stephen Elliott as the police chief, and Bronson Pinchot as Serge. Also with Ronny Cox, Steven Berkoff, Paul Reiser, Lisa Eilbacher, James Russo, Jonathan Banks, and John Ashton. Directed by Martin Brest, from a lame script by Daniel Petrie, Jr. Produced by Don Simpson and Jerry Bruckheimer, for Paramount. color (See *State of the Art*.)

Beyond the Forest (1949)—Consistently (though inadvertently) hilarious; there's not a sane dull scene in this peerless piece of camp. This is the melodrama in which Bette Davis tosses her black wig and snarls the line "What a dump!"—which Edward Albee took for the opening of *Who's Afraid of Virginia Woolf?* An evil Emma Bovary, she's a sloven married to a Midwestern doctor (Joseph Cotten); she treats him abominably, and every time she has a chance, she surrenders herself with hysterical enthusiasm to the hot-eyed embraces of a Chicago magnate (David Brian). Her obsession is to blow town, join her lover, and be a fancy kept woman; she nearly obsesses the soundtrack with variations of "Chicago, Chicago." The director,

King Vidor, seems to be inventing his own brand of hog-wild Expressionism; covered with droplets of erotic sweat, Davis shakes her ample hips, kills an old man (Minor Watson), plunges down a mountainside to end an unwanted pregnancy, and dies within sight of a choo-choo pulling out for Chicago, Chicago. Max Steiner's music cues her every stormy mood. With Dona Drake, Ruth Roman, and Regis Toomey. The screenplay is by Lenore Coffee, from a novel by Stuart Engstrand. Warners. b & w

The Bible (1966)—John Huston's agnostic version of the stories of Genesis. There are times when God seems to be smiling, such as during the dispersal of the animals after the landing of the Ark, and other times when God demands cruel proofs of obedience, such as in the story of Abraham (George C. Scott). A sprawling, flawed epic, but with some breathtaking conceptions and moments of beauty. With Michael Parks, Ulla Bergryd, Richard Harris, Ava Gardner, Stephen Boyd, and Peter O'Toole; cinematography by Giuseppe Rotunno. A Dino De Laurentiis Production; released by 20th Century-Fox. color (See *Kiss Kiss Bang Bang*.)

Les Biches (1968)—Saint-Tropez in December, and a sexually ambiguous threesome: a mope (Jacqueline Sassard), a dope (Jean-Louis Trintignant), and a chic, slinky lesbian (Stéphane Audran). Claude Chabrol directed this languorous exercise in classy eroticism; very little of anything goes on. Cinematography by Jean Rabier. In French. color (See *Going Steady*.)

The Bicycle Thief *Ladri di Biciclette* (1949)— This story of a poor man's search for his stolen bicycle is deceptively simple. At first, there is ironic tenderness: humanity observed with compassion but without illusion. Then the search becomes an odyssey of pov-

erty, encompassing much more than the realistic method leads you to expect. And the richness and the enigmas sneak up on you. What is the meaning of the seeress's words? How is it that the hero who is searching for the bicycle thief becomes the bicycle thief? This neo-realist classic, directed by Vittorio De Sica and written by Cesare Zavattini, is on just about everybody's list of the greatest films. It isn't a movie that warms you, though; it doesn't have the flawed poetry that De Sica's *Shoeshine* and *Miracle in Milan* have. It's a more impersonal great film. In Italian. b & w

Il Bidone *The Swindlers* (1955, though not released in the U.S. until 1964)—This Fellini film, made directly after *La Strada*, wasn't a success in Italy, or in this country, either. The tone is uncertain; one keeps expecting the movie to be something different from the harsh story it turns out to be. Broderick Crawford (in a role conceived for Bogart), Richard Basehart, and Franco Fabrizi are con artists who cheat gullible peasants. The film doesn't quite work, but it isn't negligible; it has some of Fellini's most realistic passages, and Broderick Crawford's remorse for his crimes, and his end, alone on a mountain road, are painful in a simple, direct way. Giulietta Masina plays Basehart's wife. Written by Fellini, Tullio Pinelli, and Ennio Flaiano. In Italian. b & w

Big (1988)—A formula fantasy film that has been directed very gently and tactfully by Penny Marshall; she sleepwalks you through the script (by Gary Ross and Anne Spielberg) about a 12-year-old boy who wishes he were big and is magically given the body of a man in his 30s—Tom Hanks. There are neat, flaky moments, but everything has a tepid inevitability, and even as you smile you may be groaning inwardly, because *Big* is dedicated to awakening the child in all of us. Of course, the Hanks character isn't ready to function as an adult; he wants to go back. The movie wants to go back, too. It's nostalgic for childhood, for suburbia, for innocent fun. (It isn't about kids wanting to be big; it's about grown-ups feeling little.) In its wholesome way, *Big* is selling the slick wonders of immaturity. It turns prepubescence into a dream state. With the slyly sexy Elizabeth Perkins, and good comic work by Robert Loggia and Jared Rushton. Also with John Heard, David Moscow, Jon Lovitz, and Mercedes Ruehl. 20th Century-Fox. color (See *Hooked*.)

The Big Broadcast of 1938—One of the best of the pleasantly anarchic Paramount vaudeville shows. This one features W. C. Fields, Kirsten Flagstad, Martha Raye, Dorothy Lamour, and Bob Hope and Shirley Ross singing "Thanks for the Memory," and most of it takes place on an ocean liner. Mitchell Leisen directed. b & w

The Big Bus (1976)—This slapstick satire of disaster movies is full of gags that seem potentially hilarious, and the script, by Fred Freeman and Lawrence J. Cohen, may have looked really promising, in an all-out sophomoric-surreal way. But only a very few of the gags get their laughs—and when slapstick goes flat, the effect is grim. Right from the start, you get the feeling of indecisiveness; the director, James Frawley, doesn't stylize the clichés he's parodying, and so they remain clichés. Intermittently, some of the actors come through. Joseph Bologna and John Beck are the drivers of a nuclear-powered bus on its maiden run from New York to Denver. Bologna is a remarkably easy, unactorish actor; at times, he's like a smaller Sid Caesar or a deadpan Alan Alda. And the long-chinned Beck knows how to use his dumb-lug face for amiable stupor. But the heroine, Stockard Channing, has an abrasive

voice, and it's hard to know how one is meant to respond to her smug whimsicality, or to her eyebrows, or to the way she crumples her lower face. With Bob Dishy, who wins at least a smile from the audience, and Lynn Redgrave, José Ferrer, Sally Kellerman, Ruth Gordon, René Auberjonois, Harold Gould, Larry Hagman, Ned Beatty, and Richard Mulligan. Paramount. color

Big Business (1988)—Bette Midler and Lily Tomlin in a farce about two sets of identical twins accidentally mismatched at birth. They're the Ratliffs, who live in a backwoods Southern town, and they're the Sheltons, who run the New York conglomerate Moramax. The four women and their various courtiers, flunkies, and love objects wind up spending the weekend at the Plaza Hotel. (Actually, it's a more spacious, vacuously glamourized Plaza—most of the interiors were constructed at the Disney Studios in Burbank.) The film often looks third class, and the director, Jim Abrahams, doesn't have the knack of making the details click into place. You're aware of an awful lot of mistaken-identity plot and aware of how imprecise most of it is. Yet the picture moves along, spattering the air with throwaway gags, and a minute after something misfires you're laughing out loud. Fred Ward, who plays Tomlin's down-home suitor, is serenely unself-conscious, and takes over as the film's hero. And Midler breezes through, kicking one gong after another. Free and inspired, she plays the poor girl as a supplicant abasing herself before the world's goodies. She's pure appetite. And as the mogul of Moramax she flips up her collar and her gesture bespeaks perfect self-satisfaction. (Chaplin did this sort of thing, and he didn't do it better.) With Michele Placido, Deborah Rush, Edward Herrmann, Daniel Gerroll, Michael Gross, Barry Primus, Mary Gross, and Leo Burmester as the bum. Script credited to Dori Pierson and Marc Rubel. Touchstone (Disney). color (See *Hooked*.)

The Big Carnival, see *Ace in the Hole*

The Big Chill (1983)—An amiable, slick comedy with some very well-directed repartee and skillful performances. It's ostensibly about how the late-60s campus activists have adjusted to becoming the kind of people they used to insult, but it isn't really political. Directed by Lawrence Kasdan, who wrote the script with Barbara Benedek, it's set in South Carolina, where a group of seven former friends from the University of Michigan gather for the funeral of Alex, the campus radical who brought them together, and who has now, after years of flailing about disconsolately, slit his wrists. The friends bury the 60s (which Alex symbolizes) and then dredge them up to talk about during the weekend. The movie may pretend to be about "life," but it's really about being clever (even the title tells you that), and about the fun of ensemble acting. Jeff Goldblum, William Hurt, and Kevin Kline do some of their best work here; Tom Berenger, Glenn Close, Mary Kay Place, and JoBeth Williams do remarkably well with what they've got to work with. And Meg Tilly, who plays Alex's young girlfriend, is an extraordinarily lovely presence; it's easy to see why Alex turned to this restful girl— she's a refuge from ideas. The picture offers the pleasures of the synthetic. It's overcontrolled, it's shallow, it's a series of contrivances. And whenever Kasdan tries for depth the result is phony. But a lot of the time he manages to turn phoniness into wisecracking fun. A Carson Production, released by Columbia. color (See *State of the Art*.)

Big City (1937)—Luise Rainer, wanly dying of leukemia, as the immigrant wife of a taxi-driver (Spencer Tracy) involved in a taxi war. William Demarest turns up, and in the final

scramble on the New York docks, so do Jack Dempsey, Man Mountain Dean, Maxie Rosenbloom, and sundry other sporting figures. The picture doesn't hold together, and although Tracy struggles with the material, he can't win. Directed by Frank Borzage. M-G-M. b & w

The Big City, see *Mahanagar*

The Big Day, see *Jour de fête*

The Big Deal on Madonna Street (1958)— The Italian title is *I Soliti Ignoti*, the police term for "the usual unidentified persons." Mario Monicelli's gentle, casually underplayed comedy is about a group of petty thieves eager to move up in status—to rob a safe in a loan office. The thieves are ambitious, good-natured, and hopeful, but they are easily distracted; when they should be concentrating on plans, they become hungry or fall in love or quarrel or fuss over a sleepless baby. This is a shaggy *Rififi*. With Marcello Mastroianni (as a simpleton), Vittorio Gassman, Renato Salvatori, Claudia Cardinale, Carla Gravina, and, as the leading safecracker in Italy (now near-senile), whom the small-time thieves hire to show them how to pull off their big job, the superb clown Totò—a stylized image of fatigue, sadness, decadence. From a screenplay by Age and Scarpelli, Cecchi D'Amico, and Monicelli. In Italian. b & w

The Big Easy (1986)—It has an amateurish, 50s-B-movie droopiness. Dennis Quaid plays a vain, irresistible New Orleans police lieutenant, half-Irish, half-Cajun, who is relaxed about accepting free meals and small favors; to him that's friendly, it has nothing to do with crime. Ellen Barkin plays a new assistant district attorney from up North who believes in the letter of the law—you can tell that from her drab tailored suits and her asexual prissiness. The lieutenant goes to work on her immediately in a few fairly explicit devilish-charmer-and-nervous-novice scenes, and her inhibitions melt away. The carnal humor of these moments gives the film a distinctive amiability, but there's too much TV-style drugs and killing, and the director, Jim McBride, has Quaid and Barkin playing too broadly; he also has the camera too close in—the performers stick out of the film frame. With Ned Beatty, John Goodman, Grace Zabriskie, Lisa Jane Persky, and the great Charles Ludlam, who thrives on broadness. As a gentleman lawyer of Old Dixie, he rolls his eyes and wraps the picture like a ribbon around his panama hat. The script is by Daniel Petrie, Jr., and Jack Baran. Released by Columbia. color (See *Hooked*.)

The Big Fix (1978)—A counterculture detective story, with a wisecracking detective—Moses Wine (Richard Dreyfuss)—who isn't the usual cynical down-at-the-heels private eye; he's warm and Jewish and disillusioned, with two sons to support from a failed marriage. The film's nostalgia for the great days of Berkeley in the late 60s—for the sit-ins, the strikes, the anti-war demonstrations—is like a form of intellectual mildew. The film uses "Berkeley" the way Stalinists used "Spain"—to set off waves of guilt and sadness. The plot involves someone's attempt to sabotage the campaign of the liberal candidate for Governor of California by dirty tricks, but the director, Jeremy Paul Kagan, doesn't draw our attention to the vital plot elements or provide enough visual emphasis and clarity for us to see who is chasing whom, or even who is in a sequence. The movie seems to have been photographed through sludge. Dreyfuss acts like a puppy surprising his master with little tricks he's thought of all by himself; you feel he wants petting after each scene. With a remarkable satirical performance by F. Murray Abraham as an Abbie Hoffman–

like sloganeering radical, who bounces up and down gleefully, out of sheer kinetic high spirits, and with Susan Anspach, Bonnie Bedelia, John Lithgow, Rita Karin, Fritz Weaver, Ofelia Medina, Nicolas Coster, and Michael Hershewe. Produced by Carl Borack and Dreyfuss; from Roger L. Simon's adaptation of his own 1973 novel. Universal. color (See *When the Lights Go Down*.)

The Big Heat (1953)—Sidney Boehm's solid, hard-nosed script might have been made into a routine cops-and-robbers thriller, but the director, Fritz Lang, gave it a formalized style. The movie is all of a piece; it's designed in light and shadows, and its underworld atmosphere glistens with the possibilities of sadism—this is a definitive *film noir*, with a few stunningly choreographed nasty scenes. Glenn Ford is Dave Bannion, a police lieutenant who ignores the orders of his superiors and investigates a big-time gangster (Alexander Scourby). A bomb is planted in Bannion's car, and his wife (Jocelyn Brando) is blown up. Full of hate, Bannion leaves the department to find revenge. When one of the gangster's henchmen (Lee Marvin) throws scalding coffee at his mistress, a high-living tough-girl lush (Gloria Grahame), and she wants vengeance, too, she joins up with Bannion. And the film accumulates corpses and arrests. With Carolyn Jones and Dan Seymour. From a novel by William P. McGivern; cinematography by Charles Lang, Jr. Columbia. b & w

The Big Knife (1955)—It's in the same garish genre as *The Bad and the Beautiful*. It's paced too fast and pitched too high, immorality is attacked with almost obscene relish, the knife turns into a buzz saw. Maybe because of all these faults of taste, you can't take your eyes off it. Rod Steiger gives a classic performance as a destructive, self-righteous Hollywood magnate; Jack Palance is surprisingly effective as the overwrought John Garfield–type star. With Wendell Corey, Shelley Winters, Everett Sloane, Jean Hagen, Ilka Chase, and Ida Lupino and Wesley Addy as sanctimonious characters who, regrettably, are the authors' mouthpieces. James Poe adapted Clifford Odets' play. Robert Aldrich directed, overdoing everything in sight; he just about turns hysteria into a style. United Artists. b & w

The Big Pond (1930)—The pond is the Atlantic, and in this musical starring Maurice Chevalier he's a Frenchman whose intentions are often misunderstood in the United States, particularly by George Barbier, the rich, chewing-gum-manufacturer father of the girl Chevalier loves (Claudette Colbert). Preston Sturges did part of the rewrite job on the 1928 Broadway play, but the spoofy film is remembered chiefly for the charming songs that Chevalier introduced, especially "You Brought a New Kind of Love to Me" and "Livin' in the Sunlight, Lovin' in the Moonlight." With Nat Pendleton. Directed by Hobart Henley. Paramount. b & w

The Big Sleep (1946)—Humphrey Bogart is Raymond Chandler's private eye in this witty, incredibly complicated thriller. You may not be able to figure out the plot even after the dénouement (Chandler reported that while the film was in production, William Faulkner and the other screenwriters had to appeal to him for guidance, and apparently Chandler couldn't exactly figure it out either), but it's the dialogue and the entertaining qualities of the individual sequences that make this movie. It takes place in the big city of displaced persons—the night city, where sensation is all. The action is tense and fast, and the film catches the lurid Chandler atmosphere. The characters are a collection of sophisticated monsters— blackmailers, pornographers, apathetic soci-

ety girls (Lauren Bacall and Martha Vickers are a baffling pair of spoiled sisters; the latter sucks her thumb), drug addicts, nymphomaniacs (a brunette Dorothy Malone seduces the hero in what must surely be record time), murderers. All of them talk in innuendoes, as if that were a new stylization of the American language, but how reassuring it is to know what the second layer of meaning refers to. Howard Hawks directed—and so well that you may even enjoy the fact that, as he says, "Neither the author, the writer, nor myself knew who had killed whom." (The 1978 Michael Winner remake, starring Robert Mitchum, is easily forgotten.) Warners. b & w

The Big Store (1941)—The Marx Brothers take over a department store. But they never quite take over the movie, which is far from inspired, though it does have Margaret Dumont and that great slimy villain Douglass Dumbrille. Directed by Charles Reisner; from a script by Sid Kuller, Hal Fimberg, and Ray Golden. M-G-M. b & w

A Bill of Divorcement (1932)—The dialogue has the creaky sound of classy, overcivilized theatre; the film is just barely adapted from Clemence Dane's play about a father and daughter doomed by hereditary insanity— the kind of play in which the daughter is named Sydney Fairchild, her father Hilary Fairchild, and the daughter's boyfriend Kit. But as Sydney, Katharine Hepburn, in her film début, was like nothing that had ever been seen on the screen. It wasn't that she was good, exactly (in fact, her acting was mostly awful), but she was so angular and mannered, with her mouth a scar of suffering, that she was rivetting. And John Barrymore, who plays the father, was a fairly rivetting performer himself—though his role here is drearily subservient. Young George Cukor directed, in the insulated style all too appropriate to the material. With David Manners (Kit, of course), Billie Burke, Elizabeth Patterson, Paul Cavanagh, and Henry Stephenson. R K O. b & w

Billion Dollar Brain (1967)—Ken Russell's second picture. (The first was *French Dressing*, which didn't open in the U.S.) It stars a wearily nonchalant Michael Caine, as the seedy spy Harry Palmer, and it was a sequel to *The Ipcress File* and *Funeral in Berlin*. Russell finished off the series; he hurled the audience from one crisis to the next, and things went by so fast that the story line got befuddled and nothing at all seemed to be happening. It was Françoise Dorléac's last role; though part of the film was shot in Helsinki in winter and she's all bundled up, she looks lovely. The cast includes Oscar Homolka as the Russian Colonel Stok, Karl Malden, Ed Begley, Vladek Sheybal, and some lively Honeywell electronic calculators. Screenplay by John McGrath, based on Len Deighton's novel; cinematography by Billy Williams. color

Billy Budd (1962)—Melville's short novel is stripped for action in this tense, straightforward shipboard narrative, directed by Peter Ustinov. Ustinov's efficiency and Robert Krasker's stylized black-and-white cinematography help to release the ambiguities without clogging the film with metaphysical speculation or too many homoerotic overtones. As Billy, the beautiful sailor, an American Prince Myshkin, Terence Stamp wears white pants and suggests angelic splendor without falling into the narcissistic poses that juveniles often mistake for grace. Robert Ryan is the depraved master-at-arms, Claggart, whose self-hatred makes it necessary for him to destroy Billy, the image of goodness; Ryan gives the role the requisite satanic ugliness. Unfortunately, Ustinov miscasts himself as Captain Vere; as he plays the part, the Captain is a humane man, a good liberal trag-

ically torn by the demands of authority. But what gives Melville's story its fascination and its greatness is the suggestion that Claggart is merely the underling doing the evil Captain's bidding. As actor, director, and co-scenarist, Ustinov may be too much the relaxed, worldly European to understand Melville's raging emotions; in Ustinov's view, Billy is just a victim of unfortunate circumstances. The film doesn't approach Melville's passion, but it's a good movie anyway. With Paul Rogers, Ronald Lewis, Melvyn Douglas, David McCallum, John Neville, and Niall MacGinnis. The adaptation by Ustinov, Robert Rossen, and DeWitt Bodeen comes via a play version by Louis O. Coxe and Robert H. Chapman. Allied Artists. (See *I Lost it at the Movies*.)

Billy Jack (1971)—A fascinating, primitive, mixed-up movie, made by the director, Tom Laughlin, and his co-writer, co-producer wife, Delores Taylor. (The screen credits are pseudonyms.) They also star in it, he as Billy Jack, a half-breed who is also half man of action, half mystic, and she as a pacifist Southwestern woman who runs an experimental "freedom school." Its racially mixed students are being persecuted by the vicious bigots of the neighboring town. In plot and structure, the picture is a crude, shapeless mess, but the freedom school teachers (comedians from The Committee) and some loose, good-humored children (actually Herbert Kohl's students from The Other Ways school) give it a disarming, hip innocence. There's a sweet, naïve feeling to the movie even when it's violent and melodramatic and atrocious, and when it's good it's good in an unorthodox, improvisatory style. This may be the first movie in which a rape victim talks about what happened to her in terms of a specific feminine anger at her violation: Delores Taylor speaks haltingly in a singsong monotone, as if she were working it out, and by normal dramatic standards the scene is a drag. Yet it stays with one. The picture has a special fairy-tale appeal to very young audiences, in part because Billy Jack uses his mystical powers on behalf of the young. Billy Jack, who wears his cowboy hat flat across his forehead, appeared for the first time in the Laughlins' first picture, the motorcycle-gang film *Born Losers* (1967), and then, after *Billy Jack*, in the grandiose sequel, *The Trial of Billy Jack* (1974), which had none of the charm of this film. Released by Warners. color (See *Deeper into Movies*.)

The Bingo Long Traveling All-Stars and Motor Kings (1976)—Rowdy, good-natured comedy-melodrama about a barnstorming black baseball team. Set in 1939, in the period just before major-league clubs admitted black players, it shows the players' attitudes toward the cakewalking and clowning expected of them by white crowds. It's like a modern, black variant of the 30s lunatic football comedies, such as *Pigskin Parade*. The cast is headed by Richard Pryor, Billy Dee Williams, Stan Shaw, and James Earl Jones, whose great, deep voice functions as a joke all by itself. The script, by Hal Barwood and Matthew Robbins, has some sophisticated, double-edged ideas but is short on characterization; it settles for a few too many cheap laughs, such as those involving a loud, fat black woman, and too many cartooned black capitalistic club owners as well as sadistic white villains (who, for unexplained reasons, have sinister Scandinavian accents). Directed by John Badham (it was his first picture, followed by *Saturday Night Fever*); cinematography by Bill Butler. Universal. color

Bird (1988)—Clint Eastwood, who directed, gives the life of the master of jazz improvisation—the bebop alto saxophonist Charlie Parker—the art-film treatment: flashbacks, rain, darkness, and a running time of 161 minutes. With the film flashing back and forth, you can't get the hang of Parker's life story, and you don't come out with much understanding of his achievement or what made him a legend—the potent archetype of the self-destructive jazz artist. As Parker, Forest Whitaker trudges off to his gigs like a jazz version of Willy Loman; he's always fouling up—boozing and doping and smashing things. Whitaker gives a richly felt performance, yet he comes across as just a genial big blob of a fellow who can't get his life together. Some of his scenes with Diane Venora (as Chan Parker) have tension and a pricklish originality, and a few of his scenes with Michael Zelniker (as Red Rodney) have something comic and unresolved in them—Parker shows a streak of ''just kidding'' sadism. But mostly it's an earnest, lifeless movie. Joel Oliansky wrote the script; the cast includes Samuel E. Wright as Dizzy Gillespie. Warners. color (See *Movie Love*.)

Bird Man of Alcatraz (1962)—Intelligent, affecting, clearly well-meaning—too well-meaning as it drones on and on, upliftingly. The director, John Frankenheimer, and the scenarist, Guy Trosper, are so sympathetic and discreet in their near-documentary approach to Robert Stroud (who was still in prison, at 75, when the film was made) that they never solve the problem of how to dramatize the life of a convicted killer who spent more than 40 years in solitary confinement, with birds as his only companions. We don't get enough understanding of Stroud (Burt Lancaster) to become involved in how he is transformed over the years. (Stroud wrote a book on bird diseases.) And though Lancaster has to get points for his willingness to tackle the diffcult role, he doesn't have much expressive range, and when he's cooped up like this and can't use his intense physicality he seems numb—half dead. With Karl Malden, Thelma Ritter, Betty Field, Edmond

O'Brien, Neville Brand, Whit Bissell, Hugh Marlowe, and Telly Savalas. Based on the book by Thomas E. Gaddis; cinematography by Burnett Guffey. Released by United Artists. b & w

Bird of Paradise (1932)—The director, King Vidor, and his associates performed near-miracles on this outdated story (an adaptation of a stage melodrama) about a Polynesian princess (Dolores Del Rio) whose love for a white man (Joel McCrea) results in her being punished by the Polynesian priests (she's thrown into a volcano). The talk is fearfully silly, but Clyde De Vinna's rich, tactile cinematography, the foliage of the locations, and Max Steiner's overblown score contribute to some high romantic effects. (Remade by Delmer Daves in 1951, with Louis Jourdan and Debra Paget.) R K O. b & w

The Birds (1963)—Some of the special effects are amusing, and a few are perverse and frightening, but the effects take over in this Hitchcock scare picture, and he fails to make the plot situations convincing. The script (by Evan Hunter) is weak, and the acting is so awkward that often one doesn't know how to take the characters. With Rod Taylor, Tippi Hedren, Suzanne Pleshette, and Jessica Tandy. Universal. color

Birds in Peru *Les Oiseaux vont mourir au Pérou* (1968)—An atrocity perpetrated by Romain Gary in which Jean Seberg plays a frigid nymphomaniac goddess who lures men to their doom. Sample dialogue: "Take me." With Maurice Ronet, Pierre Brasseur, Danielle Darrieux, and Jean-Pierre Kalfon; cinematography by Christian Matras. In French. Universal. color

Birdy (1984)—Part satire, part Christ myth, it's like *The Little Prince* rewritten by Kurt Vonnegut. It's about two boys from the drab working-class suburbs of Philadelphia; they have both been maimed in Vietnam. Al (Nicolas Cage), his mutilated face wrapped in bandages, comes to see the psychically injured Birdy (Matthew Modine), who squats naked on the floor of a military hospital, crumpled like a broken bird. The movie is about the purity of madness, about male bonding, sadism, violation, and so on. And, with Al sitting on the hospital floor holding the catatonic Birdy in his arms, it's one Pietà after another. In flashbacks, through the two boys' thoughts and fantasies, we see them in their high-school days, when Birdy used to escape the meanness of the corrupt society by creating an aviary world of his own. Directed by Alan Parker, the movie takes itself inordinately seriously as a moral fable expressing eternal truths. It feels morose and unrelieved, despite the efforts of the two actors. (In the flashback scenes, when Al and Birdy are just kids doing reckless teen-age things, the actors have matching smiles, the way best friends with shared secrets often do. And they move together, as if they were both hearing the same signals, the same music.) The movie is based on the late-70s novel by William Wharton (a pseudonym). It probably needed a director who found the story lulling, tantalizing, its meanings hidden; Parker's technological sophistication nails everything down. The score is by Peter Gabriel; the cinematography is by Michael Seresin. The screenwriters, Sandy Kroopf and Jack Behr, updated the material from the Second World War. With John Harkins and Sandy Baron. Tri-Star. color (See *State of the Art.*)

Birth of the Blues (1941)—Harmless enough, though the trip from Basin Street recorded here is a puny, disingenuous fairy tale about a struggling band and its vocalist, demure Mary Martin, who makes the Dixieland style a public success. This is too stupid to function

B

as an insult to history. Bing Crosby (with his clarinet playing dubbed by Danny Polo) comes off considerably better than smiling Mary, and among the cast are Jack Teagarden and Harry Barris, along with Eddie Anderson and Brian Donlevy (with his trumpet playing dubbed by Poky Carriere). The songs—a mixed bag—include "St. James Infirmary," "That's Why They Call Me Shine," "The Waiter and the Porter and the Upstairs Maid," and "Cuddle Up a Little Closer." Directed by Victor Schertzinger, who was probably responsible for the nauseating full-choir rendition of "St. Louis Blues." Paramount. b & w

The Birthday Party (1968)—The early Harold Pinter play, directed by William Friedkin, with an expert cast (Sydney Tafler, Robert Shaw, Patrick Magee, and Dandy Nichols). Lacking the excitement that Pinter's plays usually generate on the stage, the material became frozen and arbitrary. Cinematography by Denys Coop. color (See *Going Steady*.)

Bitter Sweet (1940)— It is said that when Noël Coward saw how his ironic, romantic costume operetta of 1929 (the book, the lyrics, and the music are all his) had been turned into a clumsy, sentimental vehicle for the overgrown kitten Jeanette MacDonald and dim, stalwart Nelson Eddy he wept. He also vowed to sell nothing more to Hollywood and—surprisingly—he kept that vow. MacDonald (born in 1903) is meant to be a proper, inexperienced English girl of 18, and Eddy, who could never manage dash or fire (he always looked pained from the effort; you could see the dull ache of someone who recognized his limitations), is supposed to be a Viennese rake. This is by no means the worst of the MacDonald-Eddy love-duet films—the songs are still mostly by Coward, and they include "I'll See You Again"—but this isn't one of the rare ones redeemed by high spirits,

either. It's bad enough: you pass the time watching the actors ladling on their characterizations. And this being a big M-G-M production, MacDonald, even when she is supposed to be starving, is dressed in Adrian's plushiest low-camp creations. All the women in the large cast are decked out in ruffles and puffs and bows. Victor Saville produced; W. S. Van Dyke directed from Lester Samuels' adaptation. The cast includes George Sanders, Ian Hunter, Felix Bressart, Curt Bois, Veda Ann Borg, Sig Rumann, Herman Bing, Fay Holden, Edward Ashley, Janet Beecher, Diana Lewis, Lynne Carver, Greta Meyer, Paul Oman as the Zigeuner, and, in bits, Hans Conried and Jeff Corey. (Also filmed in England in 1933, with Anna Neagle.) color

The Bitter Tea of General Yen (1933)—This story about a cool, straitlaced girl from New England (Barbara Stanwyck) who is sexually drawn to the Chinese warlord who kidnaps her was the opening attraction at Radio City Music Hall. Tall, Swedish Nils Asther was a very peculiar Oriental, but he was certainly dazzlingly elegant and a highly exotic love object—too exotic, maybe, for moviegoers of the time, because despite the tensions of the daring interracial romance, the picture was not a box-office success. One of the most sensuously atmospheric (and least cloying) of Frank Capra's films, it suggests the influence of von Sternberg's *Shanghai Express* (1932). With Gavin Gordon, Walter Connolly, Toshia Mori, Richard Loo, and Lucien Littlefield. The screenplay by Edward Paramore was adapted from a story by Grace Zaring Stone. Cinematography by Joseph Walker; produced by Walter Wanger for Columbia. b & w

Bizarre, Bizarre *Drôle de drame* (1937)— Dadaist frivolity, with sequences that one giggles over happily for years. Jacques Prévert wrote and Marcel Carné directed this romantic, satirical comedy about the English mania for detective fiction, set in Edwardian England. Jean-Louis Barrault is the detective-story reader who decides to commit his own perfect crime by murdering the author (Michel Simon). With Françoise Rosay as Barrault's inamorata (he gathers a bouquet for her by stealing the boutonnieres of men who have been clobbered in the Limehouse alleys); Louis Jouvet as a clergyman; and Jean-Pierre Aumont as a lovesick milkman. A memorable, deadpan dinner conversation about Duck à l'Orange is the source of the American title. In French. b & w

Bizet's Carmen (1984)—Directed by Francesco Rosi, this version has a clean, raw vivacity and is supremely romantic. Julia Migenes-Johnson's freckled street urchin Carmen revitalizes the story. Her strutting, her dark, messy frizzy hair—her sexual availability—attract the middle-class clod Don José (Plácido Domingo) and drive him crazy; Carmen, who's true to her instincts, represents everything he tries to repress. Rosi lets the music carry the passion; what he supplies is ideal conditions for the viewer to experience the opera as a totality. The natural settings have an extra, formal dimension: the luster of 19th-century paintings with the near-abstract clarity of 20th-century art. Rosi's handling suggests the most fluently stylized movie musicals. (Collaborating with the cinematographer Pasqualino De Santis, and with Enrico Job supervising the sets and costumes, he achieves lighting so beautiful (and so evocative) that the images seem serenely right—just what the arias call for. With Faith Esham as Micaëla and Ruggero Raimondi as Escamillo. The straightforward screen adaptation is by Rosi and Tonino Guerra. In French. color (See *State of the Art*.)

The Black Bird (1975)—George Segal is engagingly peppy as Sam Spade, Jr., in this attempted takeoff on *The Maltese Falcon*. Spade Junior's San Francisco is the zonked city of fantasists, and he's scrounging around for a living in an inherited trade that makes no sense to him. Something could have been done with the idea of a renewed search for the falcon in these changed circumstances if this new film, written and directed (more or less) by David Giler, had been able to roll along, moving among the street people and their throwaway conversations, and parodying modern filmmaking techniques as against the controlled studio style of the Huston film. There are bits of this attempted, and there's potential humor in seeing Effie (Lee Patrick), who was Bogart's proper, adoring secretary, arrive at Segal's office in a hostessy caftan and make no bones about her loathing of her boss. But the movie was shot in L.A., with only a few days of actual location work in San Francisco, and Giler, a writer making his début as a director, is too inexperienced to achieve anything like the slouchy, wacked-out style that might have released the humor in some of his gag ideas. Instead, it's a dumb comedy, with an insecure tone and some good ideas mixed with some terrible ones. With Stéphane Audran, Lionel Stander (dressed in a frogman's suit, he's grotesque to the point of adorability), the enigmatic John Abbott, Elisha Cook, Jr., as Wilmer the Gunsel again, and Signe Hasso, who speaks with a precision that recalls the gilt-edged intonations of the 40s. Produced by Ray Stark; Columbia. color (See *When the Lights Go Down*.)

The Black Cat (1934)—Boris Karloff and Bela Lugosi were fated to meet; the encounter took place in this nutty, nightmarish mélange of Black Masses and chess games, shadows and dungeons, Satanism and necrophilia.

(They actually stalk each other.) It's a crepe-hangers' ball. Edgar G. Ulmer directed. With David Manners, being as ineffectual as ever, and Jacqueline Wells (later Julie Bishop). Universal. b & w

Black Girl (1972)—Peggy Pettitt is the young girl, living in a matriarchal family, who tries to free herself from the patterns of ghetto apathy and become a dancer. The structure resembles the well-made second-rate serious play of thirty years ago, and the movie is faltering and clumsy, but it's an honest, straightforward attempt to express black experiences. The actors embody these experiences even when the theatrical mechanisms get in the way. Ossie Davis directed, from J. E. Franklin's adaptation of her own off-Broadway play. With the talented, queenly Louise Stubbs as the girl's mother; that powerhouse Claudia McNeil as the grandmother; Brock Peters; and, regrettably, the miscast Leslie Uggams. Produced by Lee Savin; released by Cinerama. color (See *Reeling*.)

Black Legion (1936)—In 1936, there were press accounts that a new Klan had sprung up, selecting Jews, Catholics, and Communists as its targets, and Warners, always eager for topical stories, leaped in. In the movie, the organization is against foreigners in general, and Humphrey Bogart is the young factory worker who joins up in anger because a Pole got the job he wanted. He is soon involved with black sheets, masks, copper-studded whips, and guns. Though the film flaunts its cautionary message and assumes a virtuous, civics-lesson stance, the story is tacky and primitive. Tolerable, but not in a class with the best of the Warners socially conscious melodramas. Archie Mayo directed; with Ann Sheridan, Erin O'Brien-Moore, and Dick Foran. b & w

Black Moon (1975)—Louis Malle is temperamentally unsuited to the meandering, enigmatic, post-apocalypse fantasy he attempts here; he's a sane man trying to make a crazy man's film. Fifteen-year-old Cathryn Harrison is Alice in a bombed-out Wonderland, where flowers squeal when they're stepped on and a unicorn talks. There's no obsessive quality in the disordered vision, and no wit. It's deadly. With Joe Dallesandro, Alexandra Stewart, and Thérèse Giehse; cinematography by Sven Nykvist. color (See *When the Lights Go Down*.)

The Black Pirate (1926)—Douglas Fairbanks, Sr., in an exhilarating, lighthearted swashbuckler, filmed in a soft, golden, early Technicolor process. This is the film with the memorable sequence of the hero sliding down a sail on a knife, and it's probably the Fairbanks film that children like best. Billie Dove is the beautiful leading lady; Sam de Grasse is the sour, sneering villain, and Donald Crisp plays an aged, goodhearted pirate who scratches himself a lot. Albert Parker directed. Silent.

The Black Stallion (1979)—One of the rare movies that achieves a magical atmosphere. Seeing it is like being carried on a magic carpet; you don't want to come down. (It may be the greatest children's movie ever made.) In this first feature by Carroll Ballard (as in his earlier short films and documentaries), the visual imagination that he brings to the natural landscape is so intense that his imagery makes you feel like a pagan—as if you were touching when you're only looking. His great scenes have a sensuous, trancelike quality: the movie is set in 1949, but it seems outside time. And this distilled atmosphere makes it possible for a simple boy-and-animal story to be transformed into something mythological. The boy's sense of wonder recalls

Pather Panchali, but there are also elements of Arabian Nights fantasy that suggest the 1940 *Thief of Bagdad*, without that film's theatricality. When the boy, alone on a desert island with the horse, woos him with a gift of seaweed and finally rides him, you may agree with the man who said that when he saw this movie he felt that he was rediscovering the emotional sources of mystery and enchantment. With Kelly Reno as the 11-year-old boy, and Mickey Rooney, Hoyt Axton, Teri Garr, and Clarence Muse. Based on the 1941 novel by Walter Farley; the screenplay is by Melissa Mathison (who later wrote *E.T.*), Jeanne Rosenberg, and William D. Wittliff. The cinematography is by Caleb Deschanel; the editing is by Robert Dalva. (A 1983 sequel, *The Black Stallion Returns*, was not directed by Ballard.) Produced under the aegis of Francis Ford Coppola (he had been at U.C.L.A. at the same time as Ballard), and released by United Artists. color

Black Sunday *La Maschera del Demonio* (1960)—A rich draught of vampire's blood. With its crypts and cobwebs and eerie old castles set in batty, steamy forests, it's sumptuous enough to have acquired a considerable reputation. The resurrected 200-year-old witch Princess Asa and the beautiful Princess Katia are both played by the English actress Barbara Steele in a deadpan manner that makes evil and good all but indistinguishable; in both roles, she looks like Jacqueline Kennedy in a trance. But you wouldn't want her to be any different in this studio-made Moldavia of 1830. The cinematographer-director, Mario Bava, who specialized in occult horror, and most of the actors are Italian; the story is derived from Gogol. Dubbed into English. Released by A.I.P. b & w

Black Widow (1954)—This gaudy whodunit features a group of murderous, lascivious upper-crusters in the kind of Manhattan apartments that are found only in Hollywood. Van Heflin and Gene Tierney live on one floor, Ginger Rogers and Reginald Gardiner above them, and the remarkable Peggy Ann Garner commutes from one to the other. Nothing in this hothouse movie is remotely believable, but nothing is meant to be, either. Ginger Rogers, who is somewhat more fleshy than one expects, dominates the film in a rather entertaining way. The cast includes George Raft, Virginia Leith, Otto Kruger, Cathleen Nesbitt, Hilda Simms, Skip Homeier. Nunnally Johnson directed and wrote the screenplay, based on Patrick Quentin's novel *Fatal Woman*. 20th Century-Fox. (Caution: Some of the Fox films of this period have faded to pale, pale blue.) CinemaScope, color

Black Widow (1987)—Theresa Russell plays a slinky, cat-eyed dame who is somehow driven to marry a series of the richest millionaries in the country and murder them; Debra Winger plays an investigator at the Justice Department who notices the pattern in the sudden deaths and gets on the widow's trail. This may sound irresistibly succulent and trashy, but the director, Bob Rafelson, can't seem to give trash its due; he intellectualizes it. You expect the women to share identities or the picture to go lesbian, or *something*. But you're wrong. This is postmodernist *film noir*. Rafelson and the writer, Ronald Bass, disdain motivation and they don't develop the characters. The picture doesn't bother with suspense, either, but it has a high-tech swank, and though you may want to giggle at the fanciness, there are a few moments when the near-pornographic texture is actually amusing. Dennis Hopper and Nicol Williamson liven up their brief scenes as two of the widow's husbands; also with James Hong as a drugged-out private investigator, Terry O'Quinn as Winger's boss, and Sami Frey, Diane Ladd, Lois Smith, Leo Rossi, Rutanya Alda, Mary Woronov, and

David Mamet as a poker player. Cinematography by Conrad Hall. 20th Century-Fox. color (See *Hooked*.)

Blackboard Jungle (1955)—It was a shocking movie at the time and was said to provoke violence, and when Clare Boothe Luce, then American ambassador to Italy, protested its showing at the Venice Film Festival, its international fame was assured. The subject—contempt for authority (in a metropolitan trade school)—is treated as a problem with a definite solution. Surrounded by hostile and delinquent boys, the hero, an idealistic teacher, played by Glenn Ford, tries to reach the salvageable one among them—Sidney Poitier, who gives an angry, exciting performance. (He makes you feel his tensions and heat.) The director, Richard Brooks, wrote the script, adapted from Evan Hunter's novel, and it's sane and well worked out, though it's hard for audiences to believe in the hero's courage, and not hard at all for them to believe in the apathetic cowardice of the other teachers. If you excavate Evan Hunter's short story on which the rather shoddy novel was based, it's no big surprise to find that in the original account, "To Break the Wall," the teacher did not break through. Once again, a "daring" Hollywood movie exposes social tensions—touches a nerve—and then pours on the sweet nothings. But along the melodramatic way, there are some startling episodes (and one first-rate bit of racial interchange), and recordings by Bix Beiderbecke, Stan Kenton, Bill Holman, and others set quite a pace. (The music behind the opening titles—Bill Haley and the Comets on "Rock Around the Clock"—really made people sit up.) Glenn Ford seethes all the time, but he's fairly competent. With Louis Calhern, who's always fun to watch; Margaret Hayes, as the teacher who's a candidate for rape; Anne Francis in the tiresome role of Ford's pregnant wife; Richard Kiley, as the embarrassingly weak-kneed teacher whose jazz records get smashed. Also with John Hoyt, Paul Mazursky, Emile Meyer, Horace McMahon, Warner Anderson, and Vic Morrow as the Brando-style hoodlum. Cinematography by Russell Harlan. Produced by Pandro S. Berman, for M-G-M. b & w

Blackmail (1929)—A London-set Hitchcock silent thriller that was in part reshot and in part dubbed to make it a sound film—and an unusually imaginative and innovative one. With its trick shots in the British Museum and a chase on the museum roof, the film seems almost German in its pictorial style, and the heroine is indeed played by the German actress Anny Ondra, who married Max Schmeling. (Her voice is dubbed.) Cyril Ritchard, who didn't look very different half a century later, plays the artist who tries to rape the heroine. Also with Sara Allgood, John Longden, and Donald Calthrop. Hitchcock turns up being pestered by a little boy while he tries to read a book. b & w

Blade Runner (1982)—Ridley Scott's futuristic thriller is set in a hellish, claustrophobic city, dark and polluted, and with a continual drenching rainfall—it's Los Angeles in the year 2019. The congested-megalopolis sets are extraordinary: this is the grimy, retrograde future—the future as a black market, made up of scrambled, sordid aspects of the present. A visionary sci-fi movie that has its own look can't be ignored: it has its place in film history. But you're always aware of the sets as sets—it's 2019 back lot. And the movie forces passivity on you. It puts you in this lopsided maze of a city, with its post-human feeling, and keeps you persuaded that something bad is about to happen. Harrison Ford is the blade runner—a police officer who kills "replicants," the powerful humanoids manufactured by genetic engineers, if they rebel against their drudgery in the space colonies and show up on Earth. He tracks down four of these replicants (Brion James; Joanna Cassidy; Daryl Hannah, who has killer thighs and does a punk variation on Olympia, the doll automaton of *The Tales of Hoffmann*; and the blue-eyed scenery-chewer Rutger Hauer), but Ford's mission seems of no particular consequence. The whole movie gives you the feeling of not getting anywhere—of being part of the atmosphere of decay. With Sean Young as Rachael and William Sanderson as the toymaker. From the 1968 novel *Do Androids Dream of Electric Sheep?*, by Philip K. Dick; adapted by Hampton Fancher and David Peoples. Produced by Michael Deeley; a Ladd Company Release (in association with Run Run Shaw), through Warners. color (See *Taking It All In.*)

Blame It on Rio (1984)—Travel-folder footage of Rio mixed with father-daughter incest (in a disguised form). The movie is about a 43-year-old father's guilt and confusion because of his affair with his best friend's 15-year-old daughter, who is also his own teenage daughter's best friend. Michael Caine and Joseph Bologna are the fathers who take their daughters (Demi Moore and Michelle Johnson, respectively) for a month's holiday in Rio. On the beach, ogling the bare-breasted women, the fathers see the backs of two beauties, who turn, and their bare-breasted daughters come bobbing over to them, laughing at their discomfort and hugging them. It's as if a Doris Day–Rock Hudson comedy of the early 60s had gone topless. Most of the movie is an attempt to squirm out from under its messy erotic-parental subject. Directed by Stanley Donen, from a final script by Larry Gelbart (a revision of Charlie Peters' version), the picture degenerates into a smarmy sit-com. It oozes self-consciousness. Caine's near-incest keeps him sweating and rushing about anxiously, while the ripe-to-bursting Michelle Johnson pouts and wig-

gles. With Valerie Harper. Cinematography by Reynaldo Villalobos. (Claude Berri's 1977 film *One Wild Moment*, which has the same plot, isn't credited on the screen.) A Sherwood Production, released by 20th Century-Fox. color (See *State of the Art.*)

Der Blaue Engel, see *The Blue Angel*

Blaze (1989)—The love story of that old raspy-voiced rooster Earl K. Long, three-time governor of Louisiana, and the young red-headed stripper Blaze Starr is bawdy and satirical—it's Rabelaisian. Life was a banquet for Earl, and when he met Blaze he'd found the centerpiece. Ron Shelton, who wrote and directed, cherishes Blaze (Lolita Davidovich, in her first major screen role), and he adores Ol' Earl (Paul Newman), who used his swamp smarts to fight the white supremacists. But Shelton doesn't quite engage with the material; the picture is lame and rhythmless. Still, it's never boring, and it offers a ribald view of Southern politics that contrasts with the stern, melodramatic portrait of Earl's older brother Huey as a fascistic demagogue in the 1949 film *All the King's Men*. Newman, using the low, hoarse voice of a lifelong stump speaker, seems an eccentric husk of a man. He begins too far into the character; we have to catch up. By the end, we're with him. With Robert Wuhl, Jerry Hardin, Gailard Sartain, Jeffrey DeMunn, Garland Bunting, and, in one scene, the real Blaze Starr. Touchstone (Disney). color (See *Movie Love.*)

Blazing Saddles (1974)—Mel Brooks' comedy of chaos, with a surfeit of chaos and a scarcity of comedy. The story is about a modern black hipster (Cleavon Little) who becomes sheriff in a Western town in the 1860s; Gene Wilder and Madeline Kahn manage to redeem some of the film, but most of the cast (including Brooks himself) mug and smirk and shout insults at each other. Brooks' celebrated spontaneous wit isn't in evidence: the old gags here never were very funny; rehashed, they just seem desperate. The picture was a hit, though. Also with Dom DeLuise, Harvey Korman, Slim Pickens, David Huddleston, Alex Karras, Liam Dunn, George Furth, and John Hillerman. From a story by Andrew Bergman, who worked on the script with Brooks, Richard Pryor, Norman Steinberg, and Alan Uger. Warners. color (See *Reeling*.)

Le Blé en herbe, see *The Game of Love*

Blessed Event (1932)—Probably nobody in Hollywood history was better at the art of timing and placing a wisecrack than Lee Tracy. (He used his hands as much as his voice.) In this newspaper comedy-satire based on the rise of the fast-talking gossip columnist Walter Winchell, Tracy shows his peerless style—he can get a sob in his voice for the benefit of his radio listeners while grinning at his intimates. The columnist has a pet peeve—a bright-eyed young crooner with an idiotic smile, played by Dick Powell. It's quick and breezy and very likable. With Mary Brian, Ruth Donnelly, Ned Sparks, Emma Dunn, and Isabel Jewell. Directed by Roy Del Ruth, from a play by Manuel Seff and Forrest Wilson, adapted by Howard Green. Warners. b & w

Blind Husbands (1918)—Erich von Stroheim's first film as writer, director, and star, and he was the designer besides. The setting is a resort in the Dolomites, and von Stroheim plays an immaculately groomed Army officer who makes advances to the naïve, dark young wife (Francilla Billington) of a vacationing American doctor (Sam de Grasse). Gibson Gowland plays the Alpine guide. The film is a catalogue of the themes von Stroheim later developed, as well as a predecessor of the German mountain films, such as the ones

starring Leni Riefenstahl. It isn't likable, exactly, but you certainly can't mistake it for a film by any other director. Silent. b & w

The Bliss of Mrs. Blossom (1968)—A stagebound whimsey about Harriet Blossom (Shirley MacLaine), the wife of a bra manufacturer (Richard Attenborough). Mrs. Blossom keeps a lover (James Booth) in the attic. Joe McGrath directed this frivolous comedy with an uncertain hand; some sequences are wayward and kinky in a way that works, but when the kinkiness doesn't work the picture is just harmlessly stupid. Based on a play by Alec Coppel. Paramount. color

Blithe Spirit (1945)—Noël Coward wrote this flippant, ectoplasmic comedy in 1941 to provide some relief for war-torn London; it seemed pleasantly airy in stage productions at the time, but it sags more than a little in this arch David Lean version. You're terribly aware that you're listening to repartee. Rex Harrison plays the English novelist who, in order to gather material for a story, jestingly arranges for a medium to conduct a séance. Inadvertently, he conjures up the ghost of his pouty, blond first wife (the husky-voiced Kay Hammond), and she ensconces herself in the home he now shares with his second wife (Constance Cummings), and flits about, making salacious comments. The novelist finds himself in an involuntary state of "astral bigamy." Margaret Rutherford provides some desperately needed gusto. She plays Madame Arcati, the brisk, exuberant medium, who wears long woollen scarves, moves with a skating motion, and whoops clichés like a football coach. "Let's make it a real rouser!" she cries at the start of a séance. color

Blockade (1938)—"Where is the conscience of the world?" Henry Fonda cries. In Hollywood, obviously. This film represents Hollywood's treatment of the war in Spain; it's a war in some other Spain, with hats by John-Frederics. Madeleine Carroll is the virtuous young woman who is compelled to spy for the nameless "wrong" side; she attempts to destroy the ship that is bringing food to the starving people of a besieged town. The wear and tear of espionage add a deeper throb to her voice, and as her love for the very man who is her enemy—Fonda, the upstanding fellow on the nameless "good" side—becomes more excitingly disturbing to her, she grows radiantly, glossily beautiful. The mixture here—of studio sets, hokum, romance, a stirring sequence or two featuring the faces of the hungry people as they watch the ship, and declamations against war—doesn't work in any terms. With John Halliday as the suave mastermind of the spy ring, and Vladimir Sokoloff and Leo Carrillo. A United Artists release, produced by Walter Wanger and directed by William Dieterle, from John Howard Lawson's script. Hazy and unspecific though the film is, it was protested by Catholic groups. b & w

Blonde Bombshell, see *Bombshell*

A Blonde in Love, see *Loves of a Blonde*

Blonde Venus (1932)—Marlene Dietrich in one of those forgettable stories about women who "sacrifice" their bodies for the noblest of reasons (sick husband Herbert Marshall, child Dickie Moore); the man she sells herself to is played by the young and not yet sufficiently stylized Cary Grant. Once degraded, she sinks down to flophouse level before she pulls herself together and becomes the toast of the nightclub world. The director, Josef von Sternberg, caps the silliness by putting Dietrich into a monkey suit to sing "Hot Voodoo"—a number that may define camp. (It's the only memorable sequence in the movie.) With Sidney Toler as a detective, Cecil Cun-

ningham as a nightclub hostess, and Hattie McDaniel, Sterling Holloway, and Dewey Robinson. The screenplay is by Jules Furthman and S. K. Lauren, based on von Sternberg's story. Paramount. b & w

Blondie of the Follies (1932)—An unjustly forgotten film—a backstage story with an F. Scott Fitzgerald feeling to it. (It was written by Frances Marion and Anita Loos.) Marion Davies and Billie Dove are a marvellously contrasting pair of Follies girls, and Robert Montgomery is the male lead. Also with Jimmy Durante, James Gleason, ZaSu Pitts, and Douglass Dumbrille. Edmund Goulding directed. M-G-M. b & w

Blood and Roses *Et mourir de plaisir*. Literally, "And Die of Pleasure." (1960)—There's a special reason to see this vampire pastiche: the exteriors were shot at Hadrian's Villa, in color, by the great cinematographer Claude Renoir. The gardens are so fabulously beautiful that this horror film has no horror. But the director, Roger Vadim, is more interested in sensuousness anyway—lush, naughty, hypnotic sensuousness. Possessed by an ancestral vampire, Carmilla (Vadim's wife, Annette Stroyberg, who seems to imitate his earlier wife, Bardot), is a very confused girl looking for love. She secretly longs for her cousin (Mel Ferrer) and is jealous of his fiancée (Elsa Martinelli). The girls kiss and bite, but Martinelli, who wanders around looking like a *Harper's Bazaar* model, is so gaunt that Stroyberg couldn't squeeze a drop of blood out of her. The film only wants to turn you on. It's creamy-artistic, with an innocent, playful perversity: there's an elaborate dream sequence with spectral bicycles and dummies of the girls—one pinches the other's nipple. The screenplay, by Vadim and Roger Vailland, is based on the novel *Carmilla* by Sheridan Le Fanu. The art direction is by Jean Andre; the Irish-harp score is by Joan Podromines; the costumes are by Marcel Escoffier. A French-Italian co-production, released by Paramount. Partially dubbed into English.

Blood and Sand (1941)—In 1922, Valentino had starred as Juan, the poor Spanish boy who rises to fame in the bullring; in this later version, Tyrone Power played the part but color was the real star of the film. Rouben Mamoulian, who had directed the spectacularly bright *Becky Sharp*, the first feature made in the three-color Technicolor process, planned this new film to resemble the works of the great Spanish painters, using dark, ominous tones and splashy, symbolic reds. As the bullfight critic, the huge Laird Cregar pirouettes, whirling Juan's red cape; as a rich, lusciously decadent vampire who represents "death in the evening," Rita Hayworth wears deliberately jarring crimsons. Unfortunately, the script doesn't have the energy of the color design; Tyrone Power looks weary and lacks romantic charge; the pace is draggy, and the presentiments of doom make one groan. In the role of Juan's saintly wife, Linda Darnell is beautiful and ludicrously American, and although, as Juan's mother, Nazimova (in her last screen appearance) manages to bring some emotion into her few scenes, it's embarrassing to see this legendary actress as a cliché peasant, on her knees scrubbing floors. Jo Swerling did the adaptation of the Ibañez novel; Hermes Pan choreographed the dances and Budd Boetticher choreographed the crowds. With John Carradine, Anthony Quinn, J. Carrol Naish, Vicente Gomez, Lynn Bari, Pedro de Cordoba, Victor Kilian, and Fortunio Bonanova. 20th Century-Fox.

The Blood of a Poet *Le Sang d'un poète* (1930)—Jean Cocteau's first film is an enigmatic account of a poet's dreams and ecstasies and obsession with the unknown, composed in four illogical, timeless sequences that happen in the instant that a chimney topples. Here is Cocteau's own interpretation: "The poet's solitude is so great, he so lives what he creates, that the mouth of one of his creations lives in his hand like a wound, and that he loves this mouth, that he loves himself in short, that he wakes up in the morning with this mouth against him like a pickup, that he tries to get rid of it on a dead statue—and that this statue begins to live—and that it takes its revenge, and that it sets him off upon awful adventures. I can tell you that the snowball fight is the poet's childhood, and that when he plays the game of cards with his Glory, with his Destiny, he cheats by taking from his childhood that which he should draw from within himself." The first time you see this film, you're likely to find it silly, autoerotic, static, absurd, and you may feel cheated after having heard so much about it. But though it may seem to have no depth, you're not likely to forget it—it has a suggestiveness unlike any other film. Almost 20 years later, in *Orpheus*, Cocteau orchestrated the themes of the dreams and ecstasies of the poet and his obsession with the unknown. Music by Georges Auric. Cinematography by Georges Périnal. In French. b & w

Blood Simple (1984)—A splatter-movie art movie. The director, Joel Coen, wrote the screenplay with his brother Ethan, who was the producer; they made the film independently, but it's a Hollywood by-product. A Texas roadhouse owner (Dan Hedaya) wants to have his young wife (Frances McDormand) and her lover (John Getz) murdered; he hires a killer, a good-ol'-boy private detective (M. Emmet Walsh) who takes his money and double-crosses him. The one real novelty in the conception is that the audience has a God's-eye view of who is doing what to whom, while the characters have a blinkered view and, misinterpreting what they see, sometimes take totally inexpedient actions. Joel Coen doesn't know what to do with the actors (they give their words too much deliberation and weight), but he knows how to place the characters and the props in the film frame in a way that makes the audience feel knowing and in on the joke. His style is deadpan and klutzy, and he uses the klutziness as his trump card. It's how he gets his laughs—the audience enjoys not having to take things seriously. The film provides a visually sophisticated form of gross-out humor; the material is thin, though, and there isn't enough suspense until about the last ten minutes, when the action is so grisly that it has a kick. M. Emmet Walsh is the only colorful performer; he lays on the loathsomeness, but he gives it a little twirl—a sportiness. The grimy, lurid cinematography is by Barry Sonnenfeld. With Samm-Art Williams. color (See *State of the Art*.)

Bloodbrothers (1978)—The director, Robert Mulligan, is trying for something crude, powerful, volatile—but it goes terribly wrong. The story is of a brawling Italian Catholic family living in Co-op City, in the Bronx, and the actors—Richard Gere as the sensitive, imaginative 19-year-old, and Tony LoBianco as his father, and Paul Sorvino as his uncle—pour on the Mediterranean sensuality and act at their highest pitch. The father and uncle, who are electricians on construction jobs, are frustrated, boozing, skirt-chasing, braggart hardhats; the boy is trying to save himself. This is an ethnic variant of all those the-summer-the-adolescent-became-a-man pictures, done in a messagey, exploitation manner. People laugh with hysterical heartiness, or they've learned their lessons and say things like "Life can hurt. It's made me feel close to all those doin' the hurtin' dance." Gere's performance is all mannerisms—defenseless, sunshiny grins and juvenile torment; LoBianco is reaching so frenziedly for large-scale emotions that he seems three feet

off the ground; and Sorvino appears to equate hardhat with wide-eyed simpleton. The only actor who gets inside his role is Kenneth McMillan in the minor part of Banion, the crippled barkeeper. With Lelia Goldoni, Marilu Henner, Michael Hershewe, Robert Englund, Yvonne Wilder, and Floyd Levine. From Richard Price's novel, adapted by Walter Newman. Warners. color (See *When the Lights Go Down*.)

Blossoms in the Dust (1941)—Greer Garson, gowned by Adrian, coiffured by Sydney Guilaroff, and at her most sickeningly prissy. She plays a widow who battles for the legal rights of the homeless waifs of Texas; with her nostrils flaring and her eyebrows poised near her hairline, she enunciates such virtuous sentiments as "There are no illegitimate children, only illegitimate parents." Anita Loos, to her shame, wrote this high-minded prattle, and Mervyn LeRoy directed, in a dreary, inspirational style, for M-G-M. Walter Pidgeon is the husband who dies early. With Marsha Hunt, Felix Bressart, and Cecil Cunningham. color

Blow Out (1981)—It's hallucinatory, and it has a dreamlike clarity and inevitability, but you'll never make the mistake of thinking it's only a dream. John Travolta is Jack, a sound-effects man who happens to record the noise of a car speeding across a bridge, a shot, a blowout, and the crash of the car to the water below. The driver—the governor who is the most popular candidate for the Presidency—is dead, but Jack is able to rescue the governor's passenger, a cuddly blonde (Nancy Allen). On paper this movie, written and directed by Brian De Palma, might seem to be just a political thriller, but it has a rapt intensity that makes it unlike any other political thriller. Playing an adult (his first), and an intelligent one, Travolta has a vibrating physical sensitivity like that of the very young

Brando, and Nancy Allen, who gives her role a flirty iridescence, is equally vivid. It's as if De Palma had finally understood what technique is for; this is the first film he has made about the things that really matter to him. It's a great movie (and probably the best of all American conspiracy movies). With John Lithgow, Dennis Franz, and Deborah Everton as the unlucky hooker. Set in Philadelphia; cinematography by Vilmos Zsigmond. A George Litto Production, for Filmways. color (See *Taking It All In*.)

Blow-Up (1966)—When the film came out, Michelangelo Antonioni's mixture of suspense with vagueness and confusion seemed to have a numbing fascination for some people which they associated with art and intellectuality. He conducts a leisurely tour of "swinging" London, lingering over the flashiest routes and dawdling over a pot party and a mini-orgy, while ponderously suggesting that the mod scene represents a condition of spiritual malaise in which people live only for the sensations of the moment. Yet despite Antonioni's negativism, the world he presents looks harmless, and sex without "connecting" doesn't really seem so bad. The best part of the movie is an ingeniously edited sequence in which the fashion-photographer hero (David Hemmings) blows up a series of photographs and discovers that he has inadvertently photographed a murder. With Vanessa Redgrave, Sarah Miles, Verushka, Jane Birkin, and Peter Bowles. Freely adapted by Antonioni and Tonino Guerra from a short story by Julio Cortázar, with English dialogue by Edward Bond. Cinematography by Carlo Di Palma. color (See *Kiss Kiss Bang Bang*.)

The Blue Angel *Der Blaue Engel* (1929)—The director, Josef von Sternberg, had been working in Hollywood for more than 15 years when he went to Germany, at Emil Jannings' request, to direct this film; he had directed

Jannings in *The Last Command*, one of the two American silent films that had won Jannings the Academy Award in 1927–28, and Jannings wanted him to guide his first sound film. They set in motion the Marlene Dietrich myth that was eventually to surpass their fame. Adapted from Heinrich Mann's novel *Professor Unrath*, this film deals with the breakdown of an authoritarian personality. Jannings plays the inhibited, tyrannical high-school instructor who is prudishly indignant about his students' visiting Lola Lola (Dietrich), the singer at the Blue Angel; he goes to the café to put a stop to it and instead succumbs to her callous, impassive sexuality. Dietrich's Lola Lola is a rather coarse, plump young beauty; as she sings "Falling in Love Again," her smoldering voice and sadistic indifference suggest sex without romance, love, or sentiment. The pedant becomes her husband, her slave, her stooge; he travels with the café troupe, hawking dirty pictures of his wife. Dietrich is extraordinary, and *The Blue Angel* is a movie you can admire sequence by sequence, because it's made in an imaginative, atmospheric style, yet you may feel that you don't really like it on an emotional level; the sexual humiliation gets very heavy in the scenes in which the teacher, now a clown, returns to his home town and to his old classroom. With Hans Albers. Songs by Friedrich Hollaender (later Frederick Hollander). (A 1959 American remake directed by Edward Dmytryk starred Curt Jurgens and Mai Britt.) In German. b & w

Blue Collar (1978)—The phenomenally successful young screenwriter Paul Schrader in his début as a director, with a script he wrote with his brother Leonard. It's about three Detroit auto workers (Richard Pryor, Yaphet Kotto, and Harvey Keitel) who rob their union headquarters; the destruction of their friendship as a result of the robbery is used to illustrate the you-can't-win thesis. Shot in an ominous, fatalistic style, the film says that the system grinds all workers down, that it destroys their humanity and their hopes. Schrader's jukebox Marxism carries the kind of cynical charge that encourages people in the audience to yell "Right on!" His hostile, melancholy tone unifies this amalgam of pilfered pieces of old pictures and ideologies, but he has imposed his personal depression on characters who, in dramatic terms, haven't earned it. The picture seems dogged and methodical, though it is graced with a beautiful performance by Kotto, as a man who's gentle and pleasure-loving, and an unusual one by Pryor, who plays a turncoat with mean, calculating little eyes. With Harry Bellaver, George Memmoli, Lucy Saroyan, Cliff DeYoung, Ed Begley, Jr., Lane Smith, Borah Silver, Leonard Gaines, and Harry Northup. Script suggested by Sydney A. Glass's source material. Universal. color (See *When the Lights Go Down*.)

The Blue Dahlia (1946)—This untidily complicated thriller threatens to turn into something, but it never does. The director, George Marshall, doesn't provide a tense atmosphere or a hard-boiled pace, and though the screenplay is by Raymond Chandler, the picture just drags along. The performers' responses are too slow; the acting throughout seems lifeless, narcotized. The plot involves Alan Ladd as a Navy flyer whose adulterous wife (Doris Dowling) is murdered; a nightclub proprietor (Howard Da Silva) whose own estranged wife (Veronica Lake) is attracted to the flyer; and the flyer's psychoneurotic buddy (William Bendix) who can never remember just what he's been up to. There are also voyeurs, blackmailers, baffled cops, and mugs in the pay of the nightclub proprietor. Ladd takes many a mauling before he gathers the heroine (Lake) in his arms. With Frank Faylen, Hugh Beaumont, Will Wright, Howard Freeman, and Tom Powers.

Three of the players—Dowling, Da Silva (who wears a mustache here), and Faylen—had appeared in *The Lost Weekend* the year before and each had done good, distinctive work, but, like the rest of the cast here, they sink without a trace. Produced by John Houseman, for Paramount. b & w

The Blue Lagoon (1980)—The central and virtually the only characters are two little cousins; shipwrecked, they grow up alone together on a South Seas island, and turn into Brooke Shields and Christopher Atkins. The film has an inevitable, built-in prurience. All we have to look forward to is: When are these two going to discover fornication? The director, Randal Kleiser, and his scenarist, Douglas Day Stewart, have made the two clean and innocent by emptying them of any dramatic interest. Watching them is about as exciting as looking into a fishbowl waiting for guppies to mate. It's Disney nature porn. The cinematography, by Nestor Almendros, is so inexpressive that we seem to be looking at the scenic wonders of a vacation spa in a travelogue. Taken from a popular novel of 1908, by Henry de Vere Stacpoole, which was adapted to the screen once before, in 1948, with Jean Simmons. Columbia. color (See *Taking It All In*.)

The Blue Max (1966)—The time is 1918, the Blue Max is the nickname for the highest medal a German Air Corps flyer can get, and the leading role is that of a lowborn oddball (George Peppard), whose only ambition is to get it. Addicts of flying movies swear by this one, but for others, the monoplanes and biplanes can't smash or burn fast enough. Directed by John Guillermin; cinematography by Douglas Slocombe. With Ursula Andress and James Mason. Music by Jerry Goldsmith. 20th Century-Fox. CinemaScope, color

Blue Thunder (1983)—There's electricity in the air, and L.A. at night has a psychedelic, futuristic quality, like Godard's Alphaville. But the plot is no more than hints and eaves-droppings about a sinister right-wing conspiracy within the government—it involves the use of a sumptuous test-model helicopter with the deceptively romantic name Blue Thunder. The director, John Badham, does a glamorous, showy job, and, what with all the stunt flying and the hair-trigger editing (by Frank Morriss and Edward Abroms), this is the sort of action film that can make you feel sick with excitement, yet it's all technique—suspense in a void. The battle between good and evil rages in the dirty looks that Roy Scheider, a police-officer pilot, exchanges with Malcolm McDowell as an Army colonel, a mad-twit racist. With Daniel Stern in an engaging performance as a rookie police pilot, Warren Oates as a scowling, good-guy police captain, and Candy Clark. The cinematography is by John A. Alonzo; the script is by Dan O'Bannon and Don Jakoby—they obviously don't do people. Columbia. color (See *Taking It All In*.)

Blue Velvet (1986)—Written and directed by David Lynch, this is possibly the only only com-ing-of-age movie in which sex has the danger and heightened excitement of a horror picture. The charged erotic atmosphere makes the film something of a trance-out, but Lynch's humor keeps breaking through, too. His fantasies may come from his uncon-scious, but he recognizes them for what they are, and he's tickled by them. The film is consciously purplish and consciously funny, and the two work together in an original, down-home way. The setting is an archetypal small, sleepy city in an indefinite mythic present that feels like the past, and Kyle MacLachlan is Jeffrey, the clean-cut young man who's scared of his dirty thoughts (but wants to have them anyway). He commutes

between the blue lady of the night (Isabella Rossellini, who's a dream of a freak) and the sunshine girl he loves (Laura Dern). The movie has so much aural-visual humor and poetry that it's sustained despite the wobbly plot and other weaknesses. Lynch skimps on commercial-movie basics and fouls up on them, too. But his use of irrational material works the way it's supposed to: at some not fully conscious level we read his images. With Dennis Hopper, who gives the movie a jolt of horrific energy, and Dean Stockwell, who is a smiling wonder as Ben the sandman. Also with Hope Lange, Priscilla Pointer, Brad Dourif, and Jack Nance. The cinematography is by Frederick Elmes; the production de-signer is Patricia Norris; the sound design is by Alan Splet; the score is by Angelo Bada-lamenti. De Laurentiis. color (See *Hooked*.)

Bluebeard's Eighth Wife (1938)—A miscast Gary Cooper in a flat comedy, adapted by Brackett and Wilder from the Alfred Savoir play, and directed by Lubitsch. The gimmick is that Cooper has been divorced seven times; his eighth wife, Claudette Colbert, tries to make their marriage last by the supposedly hilarious expedient of refusing to consum-mate it. Her ruses, which include munching on scallions, finally drive him to a nervous breakdown. The cast includes David Niven, Herman Bing, Elizabeth Patterson, Edward Everett Horton, Franklin Pangborn, and War-ren Hymer, so there are some alleviating comic moments. The film bears a heavy mark of the studio, but there are background shots of France. (Sacha Guitry may be glimpsed coming out of a hotel in Cannes.) Paramount. b & w

The Blues Brothers (1980)—A musical slap-stick farce, set in Chicago and starring Dan Aykroyd and John Belushi as deadpan hip-ster musicians—characters they first used in skits on the television show "Saturday Night

Live." But their taciturn style doesn't allow them to show enough personality for this full-length movie, and they don't really click together in the slightly hallucinated way one expects them to. It's a good-natured, sentimental folk-bop movie, in which the Blues Brothers antagonize so many people in the course of rounding up their old band that thousands of vehicles chase them and converge on unlucky streets and plazas. The director, John Landis, has a lot of comic invention and isn't afraid of silliness, but in terms of slapstick craft he's still an amateur. The film's big joke is how overscaled everything in it is; this has an unfortunate result—Landis is working with such a lavish hand that his miscalculations in timing are experienced by the audience as a form of waste. There are too many jokes that miss, too many musical numbers that fizzle. The film, however, brings Aretha Franklin to the screen, and she's so completely there and so funny as she sings "Think" that she transcends the film's incompetence. The picture's tragedy is that she has only one number. With Carrie Fisher, Henry Gibson, Ray Charles, Cab Calloway, James Brown, and many other celebrated musicians. Written by Aykroyd and Landis. Produced by Robert K. Weiss; released by Universal. color (See *Taking It All In*.)

Blues in the Night (1941)—Jazz and melodrama, in a fermented mixture. Directed by Anatole Litvak and written by Robert Rossen, this self-serious, overheated Warners picture about the life of travelling musicians was released just before Pearl Harbor. Richard Whorf is the tormented pianist who cracks up, and Betty Field is the bad, bad girl who not only leads him astray but kills Lloyd Nolan, and is herself killed in a car crash with Wallace Ford. Whorf's band includes Elia Kazan; the vocalist is Priscilla Lane. The songs are by Johnny Mercer and Harold Arlen. Also with Jack Carson, whose trumpet playing is by Snooky Young; and Jimmy Lunceford and his band. Whorf's piano playing is dubbed by Stan Wrightsman. b & w

Blume in Love (1973)—This romantic, marital-mixup comedy, written and directed by Paul Mazursky, is like a hip updating of *The Awful Truth*. Now the institution of marriage itself is in slapstick disarray. Blume (George Segal), an L.A. divorce lawyer, is berserkly in love with his ex-wife, the stiff-jawed Nina (Susan Anspach). An inscrutably frustrated, humorless woman, she has taken up with Elmo (Kris Kristofferson), a roly-poly drifter-musician. He's just the right lover for tense Nina: his stoned contentment is the best protection against her high-mindedness. And he's so likable that even Blume, who's obsessed with winning Nina back, has to like him. Mazursky gets L.A. just right; he sees the pratfall folly of his educated, liberal characters who are up to their ears in social consciousness. This is his most messily romantic movie: he's "too close" to the subject—he's gummed up in it, and the chaos feels good. The scattier his characters are, the more happily he embraces them. They include Marsha Mason (in her film début) as a giggly, compliant woman who has an affair with Blume, and Shelley Winters as a legal client. Also with Donald F. Muhich as the divorced couple's deadpan analyst, Mazursky himself as Blume's law partner, Anzanette Chase, and Erin O'Reilly. There are scenes that dawdle, but in Mazursky's best films craziness gives life its savor and a little looseness hardly matters. The cinematography is by Bruce Surtees; the production design is by Pato Guzman. Warners. color

The Boat, see *Das Boot*

Bob & Carol & Ted & Alice (1969)—A lively, unabashedly commercial American comedy on the subject of modern sexual mores—the first feature directed by Paul Mazursky. The period is 1969, when the concept of legal marriage is being undermined and Southern California middle-class people are culturally uneasy about clinging to something square, and personally tantalized by thoughts of the sex possibilities they're missing; swinging is in the air. The film contrasts the marriage of Robert Culp, as a documentary filmmaker, and his wife, Natalie Wood, with the mismatch of Dyan Cannon and her lawyer-husband, Elliott Gould—she's bored and he's bewildered. Mazursky and his co-writer, Larry Tucker, who served as producer, designed the picture as a series of sketches, letting the rhythm of the actors' interplay develop as it does in satiric improvisational-revue theatre. Natalie Wood is the wrong kind of actress for this material; she's still doing what she was doing as a child—still telegraphing us that she's being cute—and when she tries hard she just becomes an agitated iron butterfly. But the scenes involving Gould and Cannon are small miracles of timing; Cannon (who looks a bit like Lauren Bacall and a bit like Jeanne Moreau, but the wrong bits) is also remarkably funny in her scenes with an analyst (played by the analyst Donald F. Muhich). You can feel something new in the comic spirit of this film—in the way Mazursky gets laughs by the rhythm of clichés, defenses, and little verbal aggressions. With Horst Ebersberg, K. T. Stevens, Lee Bergere, Greg Mullavey, and Garry Goodrow. The executive producer was Mike Frankovich, for Columbia. color (See *Deeper into Movies*.)

Bobby Deerfield (1977)—A rich-meets-rich picture, and worse than one imagines. Al Pacino gives a torpid performance as a spiritually depleted Grand Prix racing-car driver who falls in love with a well-heeled free spirit (Marthe Keller), a metaphysical kook.

Though she's dying, she asks him such meaningful questions that he is restored to life. The director, Sydney Pollack, tries for a Lelouch atmosphere but settles for the glitter of cash outlay. From Remarque's *Heaven Has No Favorites*, adapted by Alvin Sargent; cinematography by Henri Decaë. With Anny Duperey and Romolo Valli. Produced by Pollack; presented by Columbia and Warners. color (See *When the Lights Go Down*.)

Boccaccio '70 (1962)—A celebrated three-part film, directed by the three reigning Italian directors of the time. The Fellini segment features Anita Ekberg as a big blonde on a gigantic poster advertising milk; the skit is as padded as Ekberg. The Visconti segment is an elegant though overextended sketch featuring Romy Schneider in an attractive performance as a wife who holds her husband (Tomas Milian) by making him pay for her favors. The De Sica segment—the liveliest, and the only one with a Boccaccio flavor—features Sophia Loren as a girl who works with a travelling carnival; in each town she is the prize of a Saturday-night raffle. The way she looks, the whole world would buy tickets. Produced by Carlo Ponti and Antonio Cervi. In Italian. color

Body Double (1984)—Brian De Palma, working with material that he has grown past: a murder mystery set in L.A., in the overlapping worlds of "serious" acting and performing in porno films. The big, showy scenes recall *Vertigo* and *Rear Window* so obviously that the movie is like an assault on the people who have put De Palma down for being derivative. This time, he's just about spiting himself and giving them reasons not to like him. The central role—that of an actor who suffers from claustrophobia—is played by Craig Wasson, whose conscientious acting is a drag on the movie. Things pick up close to the midway point, when Melanie Griffith arrives and gives a tickling performance as Holly Body, a porno star with a punk-vamp haircut and a sprig of holly tattooed on her rump. Holly is like a dirty-minded teen-age seductress, and what she says has an element of surprise even for her; her talk is so sexy it gives her ideas and drives her eyebrows up. But most of the movie lacks zest. In De Palma's *Carrie*, when the camera moves languorously around teen-age girls in a high-school locker room there's a buzz between the camera and what it's filming. Here, De Palma saves the languorous camera for the sleek, expensive settings, such as the Beverly Hills shopping mall called the Rodeo Collection, and there's not only no comic buzz—the camera seems wowed, impressed. The voyeuristic sequences, with Wasson peeping through a telescope, aren't particularly erotic; De Palma shows more sexual feeling for the swank buildings and real estate. With Deborah Shelton, Gregg Henry, Guy Boyd, David Haskell, B. J. Jones, and Dennis Franz. The script by Robert J. Avrech and De Palma is from De Palma's story (a contraption). Cinematography by Stephen H. Burum; the score, by Pino Donaggio, seems to be ladled on. Columbia. color (See *State of the Art*.)

Body Heat (1981)—Lawrence Kasdan wrote and directed this 40s pastiche that verges on camp but takes itself straight. He has devised a style that is a catalogue of *noir* clichés—Deco titles, flames and a heat wave, ceiling fans, tinkling wind chimes, old tunes, chicanery in muted voices, a weak man (William Hurt) and a femme fatale in white (Kathleen Turner), and insinuating, hotted-up dialogue that it would be fun to hoot at if only the hushed, sleepwalking manner of the film didn't make you cringe or yawn. Kasdan has modern characters talking jive talk as if they'd been boning up on Chandler novels, and he doesn't seem to know if he wants laughs or not. It's like listening to Mae West

deliver her bawdy innuendoes in a sincere tone. He poses Turner as a hot number, and she proceeds to lure Hurt, who's a chump, to murder her rich husband (Richard Crenna) as if she were following the marks on the floor made by the actresses who preceded her. As Teddy, a professional arsonist, Mickey Rourke almost makes you feel that you're at a real movie. With Ted Danson and J.A. Preston. Cinematography by Richard H. Kline. Warners. color (See *Taking It All In*.)

Bolero (1934)—George Raft, wearing pants that start at the armpits, and Carole Lombard (before she became a star comedienne), in clinging satin. The Astaire and Rogers pictures were making money for R K O, so somebody at Paramount got the idea of passing off Raft and Lombard as a dance team. The studio poured every sultry effect shameless people could dream up into this movie, and, almost incredibly, got by with it—though it was low camp even then. In the big number, set to Ravel's "Bolero," Raft and Lombard gyrate on a circular elevated platform while bare-chested black men sit around them, pounding on drums. Some of those who saw the picture in the 30s could never again keep a straight face when they heard that music. With Ray Milland, Sally Rand, and William Frawley; directed by Wesley Ruggles. b & w

Bombay Talkie (1970)—A James Ivory film about a bored English woman novelist (Jennifer Kendal) who destroys the life of a young Indian film star (Shashi Kapoor). Ivory's attempt to use the clichés of early Hollywood melodramas for an ironic effect doesn't work out, but the film is full of fine marginal details—a guru showing his followers color slides of his conquest of Los Angeles, the preparations for a musical film, with plump-bottomed Indian girls dancing on giant typewriter keys. Screenplay by R. Prawer Jhabvala and Ivory; cinematography by Subrata

Mitra. Produced by Ismail Merchant. color (See *Deeper into Movies*.)

Bombshell Also known as *Blonde Bombshell*. (1933)—A wisecracking comedy-satire, with Jean Harlow in the title role as a goodhearted, dumb-blond movie star. Great fun in the uninhibited early-30s style, made at M-G-M before fear of church pressure groups turned the studio respectable and pompous. Lee Tracy is the star's finger-wagging, fast-talking press agent, and Franchot Tone is slickly funny as the man who woos her with lines such as "Your hair is like a field of daisies—I should like to run barefoot through your hair." With Frank Morgan, Una Merkel, Ted Healy, Isabel Jewell, Pat O'Brien, Louise Beavers, Ivan Lebedeff, Mary Forbes, and C. Aubrey Smith. Victor Fleming directed rather stridently and unimaginatively, but from an enjoyably snappy, rude script by John Lee Mahin and Jules Furthman, adapted from a play by Caroline Francke and Mack Crane. b & w

Bone (1974)—The four principal characters taunt each other with what are meant to be hideous truths. Larry Cohen, who wrote, produced, and directed, mates the lurid exploitation film with a high-pitched attack on hypocrisy and American values. Excruciatingly shrill. With Yaphet Kotto, Jeannie Berlin, Joyce Van Patten, and Andrew Duggan. Cinematography and editing by George Folsey, Jr. color (See *Reeling*.)

Les Bonnes Femmes (1960)—This early episodic Claude Chabrol film, dealing with the yearnings and vulnerabilities of a group of shopgirls, is uneven and, in parts, somewhat tedious and tawdry, yet it has more tenderness and is more emotionally compelling than much of Chabrol's more refined work. The girls are Bernadette Lafont, Clotilde Joano, Stéphane Audran, and Lucile Saint-Simon; the cast includes Claude Berri and Pierre Bertin. Cinematography by Henri Decaë. In French. b & w

Bonnie and Clyde (1967)—A landmark movie, this account of the lives of the 30s outlaws Bonnie Parker (Faye Dunaway) and Clyde Barrow (Warren Beatty) keeps the audience in a state of eager, nervous imbalance; it holds our attention by throwing our disbelief back in our faces. In a sense it's the absence of sadism—it is the violence without sadism—that throws the audience off balance. The brutality that comes out of the innocent "just-folks" Barrow-family gang is far more shocking than the calculated brutalities of mean killers. And there is a kind of American poetry in a stickup gang seen chasing across the bedraggled backdrop of the Depression—as if crime were the only activity in a country stupefied by poverty. Arthur Penn directed, from a screenplay by David Newman and Robert Benton, with some rewriting by Robert Towne (who is credited as Special Consultant). With Gene Hackman, Estelle Parsons, Michael J. Pollard, Gene Wilder, Denver Pyle, Dub Taylor, and Evans Evans. Cinematography by Burnett Guffey; editing by Dede Allen; art direction by Dean Tavoularis; music by Charles Strouse. Produced by Warren Beatty, for Warners. color (See *Kiss Kiss Bang Bang*.)

Boomerang! (1947)—Elia Kazan was still a fledgling movie director when he did this modest, cleanly made, rather simplistic crime picture, produced by Louis de Rochemont (long associated with the "March of Time" series), who specialized in the use of documentary locations. It's based on an episode in the career of Homer Cummings (who was Franklin Roosevelt's first Attorney General); as a state's attorney in Connecticut, Cummings became convinced that a man he was about to prosecute was innocent, and set about gathering evidence to clear him. The film was shot in Stamford (the actual events took place in Bridgeport). With Dana Andrews, Jane Wyatt, Lee J. Cobb, Sam Levene, Arthur Kennedy, Cara Williams, Taylor Holmes, Ed Begley, Karl Malden, Robert Keith, Anthony Ross, Bert Freed, and non-professionals from the area, and with Joe Kazan (the man later celebrated in *America America*). The script, by Richard Murphy, was based on the *Reader's Digest* article "The Perfect Case," written by Fulton Oursler under the pseudonym Anthony Abbott; the cinematography is by Norbert Brodine. 20th Century-Fox. b & w

Das Boot *The Boat* (1980)—If you want to experience the tedium of life in a German submarine, this is the movie that will give it to you—you're trapped for 2½ hours in a Second World War U-boat that's 10 feet wide by 150 feet long. And with men who have the same kind of anti-war nobility that the men had in American submarine epics of the 50s. About ten minutes in, you may feel that you've already seen this picture. It even has the same kind of heroic man-of-few-words-but-strong-deep-feelings captain (Jürgen Prochnow). The camera keeps moving, yet the whole feeling is claustrophobic—the movement of the camera (deliberately) calls *more* attention to how cramped everything is. The director, Wolfgang Petersen, did the adaptation of the best-selling autobiographical novel by Lothar-Günther Buchheim, a former war correspondent. (Petersen had an international success with this film.) The set was constructed at the Bavaria Studios in Munich. In German. A dubbed-into-English version was released as *The Boat*. color

The Border (1982)—In this solid, impressive muckraking movie directed by Tony Richardson and filmed largely on location in El Paso, Texas, Jack Nicholson plays a U.S. border patrolman whose job it is to shove Mexicans back to their side of the Rio Grande. The patrolman hates his work; it fills him with disgust, because most of the patrolmen are in cahoots with the American businesses that hire wetbacks, and the patrolmen make their money—their big money—by closing their eyes to vans full of workers earmarked for their business partners. It's an ugly life—persecuting enough Mexicans to keep the government bureaus happy while functioning as slave dealers. Working from a script by Deric Washburn, Walon Green, and David Freeman, and with the cinematographers Ric Waite and Vilmos Zsigmond, Richardson is able to encompass so much in the widescreen frame that he shows how the whole corrupt mess works. Nicholson's role is rather like that of the hero of Kurosawa's *Ikiru*, who knew that he couldn't do anything big to fight the bureaucracy but was determined to do one small thing. Nicholson tries to help an unspoiled young Mexican girl (Elpidia Carrillo) who is the opposite of his giggly sexpot wife (Valerie Perrine), and he has to fight his pals and go through hell to do it. Nicholson is completely convincing as a man who has been living in dung up to his ears, and so when he feels he has to do something decent before it covers his head, there's nothing sentimental about his need. It's instinctive—like a booze-soaked man's need for a drink of water. With Harvey Keitel, Warren Oates, Shannon Wilcox, and Jeff Morris. Production design by Toby Rafelson; music by Ry Cooder; the theme song is sung by Freddie Fender. Universal. color (See *Taking It All In.*)

Born Losers (1967)—Featuring teen-age girls being raped and tormented by rampaging sadistic motorcyclists (with nicknames such as Gangrene and Crabs), this exploitation picture—a mixture of vigilantism, paranoia, liberalism, and feminist consciousness—must be the most *amateurish* bad movie that ever wound up on *Variety*'s list of the highest grossing films of all time. It's so pokey (112 minutes) and crudely obvious that it seems almost guileless—helplessly inept. Yet with an appealingly masochistic title, and the lure of the subject, it not only cleaned up financially, but spawned two more films featuring its hero, Billy Jack (Tom Laughlin), a deceptively quiet half-breed Indian. In this first appearance, Billy Jack, the protector of the innocent and abused, single-handedly takes on the whole outlaw motorcycle gang. With Elizabeth James, Jane Russell, Jeremy Slate, Robert Tessier, Jeff Cooper, and William Wellman, Jr. The credits on this A.I.P. production are beefed up with the names Donald Henderson as producer, T. C. Frank as director, and E. James Lloyd as screenwriter, but those are all pseudonyms for Laughlin; Mrs. Laughlin—Delores Taylor—served as executive producer. color

Born on the 4th of July (1989)—An anti-war epic, it's like one of those commemorative issues of *Life*. This one covers 1956 to 1976, and the counterculture is presented in a nostalgic, aesthetically reactionary way: it's made part of our certified public memories. The director, Oliver Stone, plays bumper cars with the camera and uses cutting to jam you into the action, and you can't even enjoy his uncouthness, because it's put at the service of sanctimony. The pure of heart, Catholic, and patriotic hero Ron Kovic (Tom Cruise) thinks war is how he'll prove himself a man. He joins the Marine Corps and is sent to Vietnam; in 1968, his spine is severed, and he's left in a wheelchair, impotent, paralyzed from the chest down. The movie is a scream of rage at how he was betrayed, mutilated, neglected; it's also an uplifting account of how he boozed, quarrelled with everyone, and despaired until he stopped being contemptuous of the war protesters and became active in Vietnam Veterans Against the War.

Overblown right from the start, this story is constructed as a series of blackout episodes that suggest the Stations of the Cross; rising strings alert you to the heavy stuff. Then the finale—Resurrection—takes Ron into white light, and John Williams lays on the trumpets. The script, by Stone and Kovic, is based on Kovic's autobiography. With Willem Dafoe, Tom Berenger, Raymond J. Barry as the gentle father, Caroline Kava as the castrating Mom, Kyra Sedgwick as Donna, Frank Whaley as Timmy, Cordelia Gonzalez as the whore, Tony Frank as Mr. Wilson, and Abbie Hoffman. Cinematography by Robert Richardson. Universal. color (See *Movie Love*.)

Born to Dance (1936)—The plot of this big, unimaginative M-G-M musical is a half-hearted reprise of *42nd Street* and *On With the Show*; this time Eleanor Powell is the understudy who replaces the star (Virginia Bruce). The scriptwriters, Jack McGowan, Sid Silvers, and B. G. DeSylva, didn't even try for plausibility: they had a dancer stepping in for a singer. Produced by Jack Cummings and directed by Roy Del Ruth, the movie was designed to show off Eleanor Powell, who had just scored a success in *Broadway Melody of 1936*; the chief woman tapper of the period, she had little natural grace and a rather horsy manner—all wholesome high spirits—but she was certainly proficient. Here she falls for a sailor on leave (James Stewart) and in the finale she taps on a battleship; the number is called "Swingin' the Jinx Away." By the time she finishes, you're overpowered and feel you should cheer. Fortunately, Buddy Ebsen is around. Also Frances Langford, Una Merkel, Reginald Gardiner, Raymond Walburn, and Sid Silvers himself. The Cole Porter score includes the great "I've Got You Under My Skin," as well as "Easy to Love"; the other songs were instantly forgettable. b & w

Born to Win (1971)—An unjustly neglected film. Maybe the mixture of moods (comedy and horror) frightened off the producers; they didn't open it, they just let it out. George Segal gives his most prodigious and imaginative performance as a hipster junkie who is so giddy that he really digs the hustling lower depths he inhabits. The film isn't totally satisfying, but even at its most ragged, it holds one's interest. With Karen Black, Jay Fletcher, Paula Prentiss, and Hector Elizondo. Directed by Ivan Passer, from David Scott Milton's screenplay. United Artists. color (See *Deeper into Movies*.)

Born Yesterday (1950)—Judy Holliday's classic portrait of the dumb blonde—brassy, vacuous Billie Dawn. Broderick Crawford plays the man who "keeps" her—a junkman lately become "a dealer in scrap metal" in the world of cartels. Afraid that Billie will disgrace him in Washington, he hires a newspaperman, William Holden, to make Billie more "couth." Unfortunately, both for the junkman and the picture, the journalist reforms Billie, and as she gains in virtue she diminishes in interest. The second half is pretty dreary: the movie, like the Garson Kanin hit play that it's based on, turns into a civics lesson. Broderick Crawford is too heavy and mean to be funny, and Holden's role is colorless. But you'll remember the early, acquisitive Billie with her truculent voice and glassy eyes, and her gin-rummy game. Directed by George Cukor, who's not in top form; the movie is visually dead. The play was adapted (insufficiently) by Albert Mannheimer. (Judy Holliday had played the role on Broadway; her inflections are so set that there's not much surprise left in her performance.) Columbia. b & w

The Bostonians (1984)—Another of the film adaptations of great novels that fail to communicate what's great about the book—in this case, Henry James's liveliest novel, which is set in the period after the Civil War, among the abolitionists who are now turning their energies to the emancipation of women. It must certainly be the best novel in the language about the cold anger that the issue of equal rights for women can stir in a man, but you wouldn't know that from the movie, which was produced by Ismail Merchant and directed by James Ivory, from a script by Ruth Prawer Jhabvala. Although it's not as limp as some of their other collaborations, they don't dramatize the material, and Ivory doesn't shape the performances. As the tall, distinguished-looking, and intelligent young Mississippian Basil Ransom, who thinks women essentially inferior to men, Christopher Reeve has such a likable, wholesomely romantic presence that he takes the sting out of his lines. And as Verena, the sparkling, flirtatious young girl who has been trained by her mesmerist father to surrender her mind, Madeleine Potter is odd and overcontrolled. The only good reason to see the insignificant, washed-out film is Vanessa Redgrave's performance as the repressed lesbian Olive Chancellor, who takes Verena into her fine house on Charles Street and grooms her to be a spokesperson for the suffragettes. Her voice shaking with emotion, Redgrave gives this woman who is "unmarried by every implication of her being" mythological size. James's story is, of course, a tug-of-war between Ransom and Olive, who are both drawn to Verena. With some fine performers: Jessica Tandy as Miss Birdseye, Linda Hunt as Dr. Prance, Nancy Marchand as Mrs. Burrage (she has one remarkable scene with Olive), and Wesley Addy (who brings just enough grotesquerie to his facial contortions) in the role of Verena's father. Also with Wallace Shawn (Mr. Pardon), Barbara Bryne (Verena's mother), Nancy New (Olive's sister), and John Van Ness Philip (young Burrage). The handsomely lighted cinematography is by Walter Lassally; the costumes are by Jenny Beavan and John Bright. color (See *State of the Art*.)

Le Boucher (1969)—Another tone poem on a thriller theme by Claude Chabrol; he provides all the elements for a thriller except the zinger. This fluid, beautifully controlled, but very minor film was shot in a serene village in the Périgord and features the exquisite Stéphane Audran, with Jean Yanne as the melancholy, frustrated butcher. Cinematography by Jean Rabier. In French. color (See *Deeper into Movies*.)

Boudu Saved from Drowning *Boudu sauvé des eaux* (1931)—Despite the problems of sound recording in 1931, Jean Renoir went out of the studio and shot this film on the streets and along the banks of the Seine, and so it is not only a lovely fable about a bourgeois attempt to reform an early hippie (Michel Simon is the shaggy-bearded tramp who spills wine on the table and wipes his shoes on the bedspread) but a photographic record of an earlier France. A beautifully rhythmed film that makes one nostalgic for the period when it was made. Cinematography by Marcel Lucien; with Charles Grandval, Marcelle Hainia, Jean Gehret, Max Dalban, Jean Dasté, and Jacques Becker. Not released in the U.S. until 1967. In French. b & w (See *Kiss Kiss Bang Bang*.)

Boulevard Nights (1979)—Earnest, uninspired movie about the Chicano gangs of the east Los Angeles barrio. There's a well-shot sequence—a psychedelic parade of the decorated, customized low-rider cars cruising on Whittier Boulevard on Saturday night. But the story, about the strivings of the poor and the tragic macho explosions that trap them, is grindingly familiar; it's reminiscent of the Warners working-class-family dramas of the 30s and the later black-family dramas, such

as *A Raisin in the Sun*. There's the hardworking young man (Richard Yñiguez) and his mixed-up, loser brother (Danny De La Paz), who feels like a real somebody only when he's with his gang. De La Paz has a poignant self-destructive quality, like John Garfield in *Four Daughters*; he's seen in closeup so much, though, that he becomes wearying. With Marta Du Bois. Directed by Michael Pressman, from a script by Desmond Nakano; cinematography by John Bailey; music by Lalo Schifrin. Warners. color

Bound for Glory (1976)—As the singer-composer-writer Woody Guthrie, David Carradine has an ornery intransigence that gives this Hal Ashby film a core, and the re-creation of the late 30s is superbly lighted and shot (by Haskell Wexler). The film has a feeling for detail—the matching profiles of two young Baez-like sisters in a squatters' camp, Carradine's lived-in, seat-sprung pants. There's real love in Ashby's staging of the incidents, and a unifying romanticism. Though the story doesn't build dramatically—it straggles just when you want it to soar and it bogs down in backward and forward movement and it's filled in with woozy generalities—this is an absorbing and impressive piece of work. With Melinda Dillon as Mary Guthrie and also as Memphis Sue, and Lee McLaughlin as the fat man who has newsreels going in his head. Ashby deploys huge numbers of extras—900 were used in the camp sequences, and nobody looks anachronistic—yet two of the principals stick out every time they turn up. As a singer-organizer who recruits Guthrie to work for the union, Ronnie Cox beams with a Scoutmaster's fervor, and as an all too symbolic member of the working masses, Randy Quaid is like a stock-company peasant. It's also regrettable that the tautness of Carradine's singing voice is betrayed by the Leonard Rosenman score, which uses conventional instrumentation on Woody Guthrie themes. The script, based on Guthrie's (highly readable) autobiography, is by Robert Getchell; however, Ashby and his editor, Robert C. Jones, wrote the explicit messagey material of the latter part. United Artists. color (See *When the Lights Go Down*.)

The Bounty (1984)—Based on a script condensed from Robert Bolt's scripts for two projected films about the 1789 mutiny, this misshapen movie doesn't work as an epic—it doesn't have the scope or the emotional surge of epic storytelling. It's certainly not boring, though. The director, Roger Donaldson, shoots very close in for dynamic power—you're thrust right in among the men on the crowded British naval vessel—and Anthony Hopkins, who plays Captain Bligh, gives his vocal cords a workout, ordering Fletcher Christian (Mel Gibson) to stop "mixing with the damned degenerate natives" and shouting that "the ship is filthy." In this version, Bligh is no worse than ambitious, repressed, and somewhat harsh, and Christian is an open-shirted man of impulse—a moody flower child who's drugged on love. Whether because of the condensing or cuts in the editing room or just plain miscalculation, Gibson's romanticism seems faintly absurd, and in his big scene—his emotional outburst during the mutiny—he seems to be having a nervous breakdown. With Wi Kuki Kaa as King Tynah, Tevaite Vernette as Princess Mauatua, skinny-faced Daniel Day-Lewis as Fryer, and, among the effete aristocrats who sit on the court-martial, Laurence Olivier and Edward Fox (who has this performance down pat by now—he lets his crooked front tooth do his acting for him). Adapted from Richard Hough's 1972 book, *Captain Bligh and Mr. Christian*. The music is by Vangelis, who goes in for effects such as ominous boom-booms when Christian first touches Mauatua's hair; the cinematography

is by Arthur Ibbetson. Orion–Dino De Laurentiis. color (See *State of the Art*.)

Le Bourgeois Gentilhomme *The Would-Be Gentleman* (1960)—An enjoyable photographed performance, in color and with the exquisite Lully music, by the Comédie-Française of the famous Molière comedy about the rich man (Louis Seigner) who wants to become a gentleman. Jean Meyer, who directed the play and the film, appears as the valet. The exaggerated balletic movement and the elegant diction are intact; the subtitles are witty and idiomatic. In French.

The Boy Friend (1971)—It might have been a lovely little musical, with the bittersweet jazz-age gaiety that is foolish and yet heartbreakingly winning. But Ken Russell turned the Sandy Wilson show (first produced in London in 1953) into an anti-musical and destroyed most of the pleasure the audience might have had. Russell's greatest deficiency is that he doesn't understand the charm of simplicity. The glittering, joyless numbers keep coming at you; you never get any relief from his supposed virtuosity. Twiggy sings adequately (though not well enough for the load of singing she's asked to carry), and she dances rather better, but Russell doesn't develop her possibilities, and she remains an appealing blank. With Christopher Gable, Max Adrian, Georgina Hale, Vladek Sheybal, Tommy Tune, Barbara Windsor, Antonia Ellis, and Glenda Jackson in a wonderful cameo as the injured star who is replaced by Twiggy. Cinematography by David Watkin; sets by Tony Walton; costumes by Shirley Russell. Made in England, for M-G-M. color (See *Deeper into Movies*.)

A Boy Named Charlie Brown (1969)—A very sad excuse for a children's picture—a pathetically limp animation feature that barely taps the verbal wit or the great charm of the comic strip it is derived from. Directed by William Melendez; written by Charles M. Schulz; songs by Rod McKuen; musical score by Vince Guaraldi. National General. color (See *Deeper into Movies*.)

The Boys from Brazil (1978)—Franklin J. Schaffner's large-scale version of Ira Levin's novel about Nazi experiments in cloning is too logy and literal-minded for suspense, and when an actor like Gregory Peck plays a sadistic Nazi geneticist and speaks in an archvillain's sibilant German accent, you can't keep from laughing. Peck, in his jungle hideaway, staring into the future as he walks unconcernedly among the mutants he has created, just doesn't have it in him to inspire primitive terror; his effects are all on the surface, and he looks particularly bad because he's playing opposite Laurence Olivier, who is the aged hero, a famous Nazi-hunter (a fictional counterpart of Simon Wiesenthal). Olivier does a flirtatious impersonation of such actors as the late Albert Basserman and Felix Bressart, with their querulous, whiny voices and their fussiness—their way of seeming almost helpless yet resourceful, sagacious, and totally *good*. He takes off on this cloying humanistic style just enough to be very funny, and then, in the key sequences, he rises above his Viennese singsongy charm and demonstrates that the harmless-old-bore act of the aged can be a way of saving oneself for the things that count. He's the only reason to see this movie. It starts from the dumb idea that Hitler's closest associates—whom he dragged down with him—would want him cloned. Nazism here is comic-book mythology, a consumer product. With James Mason, and an enormous international cast that includes Rosemary Harris, Bruno Ganz, Uta Hagen, Lilli Palmer, Jeremy Black, Steven Guttenberg, Denholm Elliott, John Dehner, John Rubinstein, David Hurst, Michael Gough, Anne Meara, and Prunella Scales.

Screenplay by Heywood Gould. A Lew Grade Production; released by 20th Century-Fox. color (See *When the Lights Go Down.*)

The Boys from Syracuse (1940)—Hollywood, or at least Universal, should be hanged for what it did to the celebrated Broadway show by George Abbott and Rodgers and Hart (based on *The Comedy of Errors*). The rewriting was so disastrous that the studio finally cut the picture down to 74 minutes, which doesn't leave much time for Martha Raye and Charles Butterworth or for the wonderful songs—"Falling in Love with Love," "Sing for Your Supper," and "This Can't Be Love." The cast includes Allan Jones, Joe Penner, Rosemary Lane, Irene Hervey, and Alan Mowbray. Directed by Eddie Sutherland; the dance director was Dave Gould. b & w

The Boys in Company C (1978)— While taking anti-Vietnam-war attitudes, this comedy-melodrama about a group of Marine recruits who go to Vietnam in 1967 attempts to show how comradeship builds character—as in Second World War movies. Rambunctious service-comedy situations are given a raucous, hip updating and encrusted with four letter words. The director, Sidney J. Furie, brings the film energy and he keeps the gags and the sentiment coming. It's an exploitation war movie, with a soccer game that turns into a blood bath, maniacal American officers, and vile South Vietnamese officers who gloat over their profits from dope deals. Mostly, it's like dirty TV, and the highly volatile, predominately male audiences it attracted really got with it. The relatively fresh cast includes Stan Shaw as a black soldier who's as strong a natural leader as John Wayne; James Whitmore, Jr., as the intelligent officer; Santos Morales as a Chicano drill sergeant; Andrew Stevens (who becomes a junkie); Craig Wasson; James Canning; Michael Lembeck; and an ex–Marine sergeant,

Lee Ermey, whose voice is wrecked from years of shouting at recruits—he gives his scenes an unusual emotional texture. The mixed-up, messagey script is by Rick Natkin and Furie. (With a John Wayne movie, you at least knew where you were.) Shot in the Philippines. A Golden Harvest Production, with Raymond Chow as executive producer; released by Columbia. color

The Boys in the Band (1970)—A gathering of homosexuals at a birthday party; it's like the gathering of bitchy ladies in *The Women*, but with a 40s-movie bomber-crew cast: a Catholic, a Jew, a Negro, a hustler, one who is butch, and one who is nellie, and so on. They crack jokes while their hearts are breaking. The message appears to be that the spirit of M-G-M in the 40s still lives in the hearts and jokes of homosexuals. William Friedkin directed Mart Crowley's adaptation of his own play; Crowley preserves the text as if the quips were ageless. With Leonard Frey, Cliff Gorman, and Laurence Luckinbill. Cinema Center. color (See *Deeper into Movies*.)

The Brave Bulls (1951)—Robert Rossen's overblown production of Tom Lea's novel stars Mel Ferrer as a Mexican matador—a performance that recaptures some of the glamour of early screen idols but is short on strength. There is some nonsense about a heartless blond aristocrat (Miroslava) who two-times the hero with his manager (Anthony Quinn), though it's easy to overlook all that when the bulls pound across the screen. They're the only believable characters. Cinematography by James Wong Howe and Floyd Crosby; script by John Bright. Columbia. b & w

Brazil (1985)—Terry Gilliam, of the Monty Python troupe, presents a retro-futurist fantasy—a melancholy, joke-ridden view of the horribleness of where we are now and the worse horribleness of where we're heading. It's like a stoned, slapstick *1984*; a nightmare comedy in which the comedy is just an aspect of the nightmarishness. The title refers to pop escapism of the past—what you can only dream about in the squalor and sporadic terrorist violence of an Anglo-American police state "somewhere in the 20th century." Visually, it's an original, bravura piece of moviemaking, with a weirdly ingenious vertical quality: the camera always seems to be moving up and down, rarely across. You get the feeling that people live and work squashed at the bottom of hollow towers. The clothes, like the furnishings and the ancient TV sets and assorted gadgetry, suggest that nothing has been made or manufactured since the 40s. It's a thrift-shop world of the future. The central character (Jonathan Pryce) is a lowly clerk, a drone; in pursuit of the girl (Kim Greist) he has glimpsed in his dreams, he runs afoul of the state apparatus, and there's a super-realistic inevitability about this. The episodes lack dramatic definition, just as the gags do; they all run together and blur. And the film is both torpid and frantic. Yet Gilliam's vision is an organic thing on the screen—and that's a considerable achievement. Pryce's dead-eyed performance is charmless, but Robert De Niro turns up in a cameo role as a prankster daredevil, a freedom fighter; chomping on a cigar and all revved up, he's the life of the party. And Katherine Helmond, as Pryce's mother, delivers an elegant, broad caricature of a woman obsessed with plastic surgery. Also with Michael Palin, Ian Holm, Ian Richardson, and Kathryn Pogson. The script is by Gilliam, Tom Stoppard, and Charles McKeown; the production designer is Norman Garwood. Released in the U.S. by Universal. color (See *Hooked*.)

Break of Hearts (1935)—Katharine Hepburn as a tender, guileless young composer, and

Charles Boyer as a worldly, philandering symphony conductor. They marry, she leaves him in disillusionment, he drinks and goes to the dogs, she returns to save him. It's dreadful, turgid stuff, yet these two make something of it anyway. She's so intuitive and girlish and wistful that you want to conk her one, but she's so flamingly intense that you find yourself surrendering. With John Beal; directed by Philip Moeller; music by Max Steiner. R K O. b & w

Breakfast at Tiffany's (1961)—Audrey Hepburn's Holly Golightly is a tad refined for a girl who lives so improvisationally (on the money men give her), but for about the first three-quarters of an hour, this picture, directed by Blake Edwards, has a fair amount of sophisticated slapstick comedy, especially at a cocktail party that ranks with the best screen parties of the era. If you've read the Truman Capote novella that the movie is based on (and even if you haven't) you may be dismayed to see things go soft and romantic. The film wanders, and Hepburn is forced to become too frail and too enchantingly raffish before it comes to its makeshift, fairy-tale end. The madcap Holly, with her attachment to a writer (George Peppard) whose apartment is just below hers, is, of course, very similar to Sally Bowles with her Isherwood, except that the setting here is New York not Berlin. Patricia Neal is amusing in the rather impenetrable role of an interior decorator who appears to be a lesbian but is also keeping Peppard. (It may be wise not to let the mind linger too long over that.) Mickey Rooney does a wild bit of racial caricature as the Japanese photographer who lives in the apartment above Holly's; it's the most low-down and daring thing in the movie. The cast includes Buddy Ebsen, John McGiver, Martin Balsam, José-Luis de Villalonga, and Gil Lamb. The script is by George Axelrod; the cinematography is by Franz Planer; the song

"Moon River" is by Johnny Mercer and Henry Mancini; Hepburn's clothes are by Givenchy and Neal's are by Pauline Trigere. Paramount. color

The Breakfast Club (1985)—Set mostly in the library of a suburban Chicago high school, this encounter-session movie by the writer-director John Hughes is about five students—a cross-section of the student body—who in the course of serving a 7 A.M.–4 P.M. Saturday detention peel off their layers of self-protection, confess their problems with their parents, and are stripped down to their "true selves." The five are: a champion wrestler (Emilio Estevez), a popular redhead "princess" (Molly Ringwald), a grind (Anthony Michael Hall), a glowering rebel-delinquent (Judd Nelson) who wears an earring, and a shy, skittish weirdo (Ally Sheedy). With the exception of Sheedy, who's a marvellous comic sprite and transcends her role until she is jerked back into the script mechanics, the movie is about a bunch of stereotypes who complain that other people see them as stereotypes. Hughes has talent, and when the kids are just killing time the dialogue has an easy, buggy rhythm, but this is a very wet enterprise. It appeals to young audiences by blaming adults for the kids' misery and enshrining the kids' most banal longings to be accepted and liked. Judd Nelson, who is supposed to represent what authorities want to crush, has the worst-conceived role, though Paul Gleason's part as the callous dean is a close runner-up. Also with John Kapelos as the school janitor. Universal. color (See *State of the Art.*)

Breaking In (1989)—The John Sayles script about how professional small-time criminals live and practice their trades is confident, offbeat, and shallow, all at the same time. The director, Bill Forsyth, does a beautiful, clean job; he brings out everything there is to be brought out, but it isn't enough. Burt Reynolds plays an old-pro safecracker who lives in a tract home in Portland, Oregon, and doesn't call attention to himself; he trains a fluky adolescent, played by Casey Siemaszko, who can't resist flashing his new wealth. The film's patterning seems consciously quaint: an experienced prostitute (Lorraine Toussaint) who is training a novice (Sheila Kelley); a pair of retired crooks (Albert Salmi and Harry Carey); a pair of adversarial lawyers (Maury Chaykin and Stephen Tobolowsky). Forsyth may have imagined that he could go around the margins of the quaintness and show us American life out of the mainstream—the stuff you don't usually see in movies, the life behind the billboards. But with a Sayles script you go behind the billboards and there's nobody there. Samuel Goldwyn Company. color (See *Movie Love*.)

Breaking the Sound Barrier Also known as *The Sound Barrier*. (1952)—The screen heroes who had been winning the war by killing Japanese or Germans gave way to quiet, worried-eyed heroes in this David Lean epic of the air. The most worried of them all is Ralph Richardson—the courageous, civilized modern man. Sober-faced and businesslike, he keeps his inner tensions under exquisite control (though we are always tipped off that he is suffering more than men who crudely vent their emotions). Terence Rattigan, who wrote the film, didn't exactly break any new ground in the air: he provides Ann Todd with that inevitable role of the prescient wife (the "please don't go up to break the sound barrier tonight, dear" type), and Nigel Patrick, John Justin, Denholm Elliott, and Dinah Sheridan and the others say and do just what you might expect were they carrying the White Man's Burden in remote Outposts of Empire. If you're tolerant, you'll just relax through all this low-keyed English valor and enjoy the soaring cinematography and the supersonic sound effects. Cinematography by Jack Hildyard. b & w

Breathless *À bout de souffle* (1959)—Jean-Luc Godard's first feature—a witty, romantic, innovative chase picture with the 26-year-old Jean-Paul Belmondo as a Parisian hood, and Jean Seberg as the American girl who casually lives with him and just as casually turns him in to the police when he becomes an inconvenience. Godard, who dedicated this film (made for $90,000) to Monogram Pictures, saw something in the cheap American gangster movies of his youth that French movies lacked; he poeticized it and made it so modern (via fast jump cutting) that he, in turn, became the key influence on American movies of the 60s. Here, he brought together disharmonious elements—irony and slapstick and defeat—and brought the psychological effects of moviegoing into the movie itself. (His hero was probably the first to imitate Bogart.) The film is light and playful and off-the-cuff, even a little silly. Yet the giddy, gauche characters who don't give a damn— the hood who steals a car, kills a highway patrolman, and chases after some money that is owed him for past thefts so he and his impervious, passively butch girl can get to Italy—are not only familiar in an exciting, revealing way, they are terribly *attractive*. The well-known director Jean-Pierre Melville appears as a celebrity being interviewed; Daniel Boulanger appears as the police inspector. Jean-Louis Richard and Philippe de Broca turn up, and there are also bit appearances by Godard, as an informer, by Truffaut (who supplied the news item on which Godard based the script), and by Chabrol (who lent his name as supervising producer). In French. b & w (See *I Lost it at the Movies*.)

Una Breve Vacanza, see *A Brief Vacation*

Brewster McCloud (1971)—Robert Altman's film was shot in Houston. Gentle Brewster (Bud Cort), who is building wings for himself, is a boy Phantom of the Astrodome who is also an imperilled virgin—a sort of mad, murderous Peter Pan, or Rima the Bird Boy. Sally Kellerman is his bird-mother, who deserts him when he loses his virginity. The idea seems to be left over from a Victorian fable, but the style of the picture is parodistic and manic—like a Road Runner cartoon. The whole thing is amorphous and rather silly, but it's clearly a trial run for some of the effects that Altman brings off in *Nashville*. M-G-M. color (See *Deeper into Movies*.)

The Bride Came C.O.D. (1941)—Bette Davis, taking time off from her big dramatic roles, as an eloping heiress in a screwball farce, with James Cagney opposite her. The heiress is about to marry an obnoxious bandleader (Jack Carson) when her father arranges with a pilot (Cagney) to kidnap her and bring her home. The plane makes an emergency landing in Death Valley, and Davis and Cagney battle each other with wisecracks, and her rump hits a bed of cactus. The material is very tired and the production is so unpretentious it suggests financial embarrassment, but Davis shrieks her lines happily, and Cagney sticks out his ample gut and holds his ground. Both of them mug good-naturedly, and it's pleasantly fast. Directed by William Keighley, from a screenplay by Julius J. and Philip G. Epstein, from a story by Kenneth Earl and M. M. Musselman. With Stuart Erwin, George Tobias, Eugene Pallette, Harry Davenport, William Frawley, Chick Chandler, and Edward Brophy. Warners. b & w

The Bride Comes to Yellow Sky (1952)—When the sheriff (Robert Preston) brings home a bride (the charmingly toothy Marjorie Steele), the town drunkard, Scratchy (Minor Watson), the last roaring, gun-toting bad man left in Yellow Sky, takes it as the final encroachment of civilization and goes on a rampage. The tang of James Agee's adaptation of the Stephen Crane story helps to make this one of the most entertaining American short-story films, despite rather laborious direction by Bretaigne Windust. With Olive Carey and Dan Seymour, and Agee in a small part. Produced by Huntington Hartford, as half of the feature *Face to Face*, along with Joseph Conrad's *The Secret Sharer*. (The script is available in *Agee on Film, Vol.II*.) Released by R K O. b & w

The Bride of Frankenstein (1935)—This caricature by some very knowing people is a macabre comedy classic. The monster (Boris Karloff) is the only sympathetic character. James Whale, who had a good gothic sense of humor, directed, with Elsa Lanchester as Mary Shelley in the prologue, and then as the Bride. A character in Elizabeth Macklin's story "Circle of Friends" describes the Bride's birth, how she is "zapped into life by the lightning coming down the kite wires into the laboratory." And then "she's standing there, the bandages are just off, the bells are ringing, and her hair is flying all around her face and she's actually scintillating, moving her head around in quick jerks, like some kind of electrified bird!" For many of us this scene—and the way she said "Eeeek" in revulsion when she saw her intended—was so satisfyingly silly that whenever we saw Elsa Lanchester in other roles we were likely to break out in a grin of childish pleasure. She won our hearts forever, as Margaret Hamilton did as the wicked witch in *The Wizard of Oz*. (Who cared about the icky sweet Glinda?) This Bride drives the poor monster to despair. With Colin Clive as Baron Frankenstein, Valerie Hobson as his wife, the deliciously desiccated Ernest Thesiger as Dr. Pretorius, Una O'Connor, Dwight Frye, O. P. Heggie, E. E. Clive, Gavin Gordon as

Byron, and Douglas Walton as Shelley. Written by John L. Balderston and William Hurlbut. Universal. b & w

The Bridge *Die Brücke* (1959)—Bernhard Wicki directed this brutally cool and lucid account of how German schoolboys were drafted in the last days of the Second World War and insanely and absurdly sacrificed. Oddly, the film has acquired a following among conservatives and militarists who think the massacred innocents died nobly. Adapted from a novel by Manfred Gregor. In German. b & w

The Bridge on the River Kwai (1957)— David Lean's big and engrossing Academy Award winner, adapted from Pierre Boulle's novel about prisoners of war held in Burma by the Japanese. The film is rather misshapen, particularly in the sections featuring William Holden, and the action that detonates the explosive finish isn't quite clear. However, Alec Guinness is compelling as the English Colonel Nicholson, a stickler for rules who courageously defies the Japanese by legalistic means, and then goes haywire and restores morale among the men in the prison camp by putting them to work building a bridge for their captors—a bridge that will enable the Japanese to bring up troop reinforcements. With Sessue Hayakawa, Jack Hawkins, James Donald, André Morell, and Geoffrey Horne. Produced by Sam Spiegel; cinematography by Jack Hildyard; the screenplay, credited to Boulle, was written by the blacklisted Carl Foreman and Michael Wilson, who received their Academy Awards, posthumously, in 1985. Filmed in Ceylon. Columbia. color.

Brief Encounter (1946)—David Lean directed this romantic expansion of Noël Coward's one-act play *Still Life* (from *Tonight at 8:30*)—an evocation of the emotions that lie dormant in respectable, middle-class existence. Celia Johnson and Trevor Howard play the pair who fall passionately in love but agree not to see each other again and return to their responsibilities. And they do this with such touching restraint that they broke many hearts. A celebrated, craftsmanlike tearjerker, and incredibly neat. There's not a breath of air in it. Coward's material is implicitly condescending even while he's making the two heroic. With Stanley Holloway, Joyce Carey, Cyril Raymond, Irene Handl, and Valentine Dyall. Cinematography by Robert Krasker; adaptation by Coward; the music is Rachmaninov's Piano Concerto No. 2. b & w

A Brief Vacation *Una Breve Vacanza* (1973)—Vittorio De Sica's final collaboration with the scriptwriter Cesare Zavattini was on this story of Clara (Florinda Bolkan), a Calabrian peasant who is a factory worker in Milan; resentful, beaten down to a morose stupor, she's also oppressed by her husband (Renato Salvatori), who uses her sexually as if she were a farm beast he owned. When she collapses and is sent to a sanatorium in northern Italy to be cured of tuberculosis, the schizoid picture leaves this working-class grimness behind; it's swoony romanticism from then on. Clara discovers art and spirituality, and she finds a frail, dewy-eyed lover (Daniel Quenaud) who drips nobility as only a narcissistic bad actor can. Sedately sentimental, with Adriana Asti playing a feverishly frisky, dying music-hall entertainer in the gallant-waif Piaf style. Cinematography by Ennio Guarnieri. In Italian. color (See *Reeling*.)

Brigadoon (1954)—M-G-M was having an economy drive, and this adaptation of Lerner and Loewe's Broadway hit musical fantasy, which was scheduled to be shot on location in Scotland, was instead done in the studio.

Also by executive decree, the director, Vincente Minnelli, had to do it in Cinema-Scope—which, for dance in studio settings, was disastrous. Gene Kelly and Van Johnson play the two Americans hunting in the Scottish Highlands who stumble into Brigadoon, a magical village that went to sleep in 1754 and wakes for a day each century. Kelly falls in love with a local girl (Cyd Charisse), while Johnson maintains a cynical attitude. Probably the material was too precious and fake-lyrical to have worked in natural surroundings, either, but the way it has been done it's hopelessly stagey. The movie has one sensational sequence, when the action gets away from that damned idyllic village and Kelly and Johnson go to a jangly, noisy Manhattan nightclub with Elaine Stewart; you can feel Minnelli's relief at being able to do something funny and bitchy after staging all those wholesome scenes with grinning men in tartans. Arthur Freed produced; Lerner wrote the script; Kelly choreographed. With Hugh Laing, Barry Jones, Eddie Quillan. color

Bright Lights, Big City (1988)—The Jay McInerney book came out in 1984, in paperback—and that was right for it, because the story has no heft, no substance. Smart and maudlin, it's a just about perfect pop novel—so pop it's almost nothing. The hero works as a fact checker at a magazine modelled on *The New Yorker* (McInerney worked at the magazine for a little under six months in 1980) and spends his nights in the coke-snorting high wild life of the disco-party scene. The movie version, directed by James Bridges, from a script he devised with McInerney, follows the novel very closely but drugs and AIDS have created a time warp between the early 80s and the late 80s, and the movie doesn't provide the seductiveness, the kick, the high. And, without that sexy glow, the movie has no vision. As the hero, Michael J. Fox does fine work; onscreen in every scene,

he keeps the character from being an obnoxious crybaby, and he suggests some interior life. The sly John Houseman has become a comedian at 85; he gives the standout performance in the brief role of the magazine's imposing editor-in-chief, his shoulders slumped in sorrow over the factual errors that the hero has allowed to creep into the magazine. And Jason Robards gives the movie a flourish: he's a talkative, lonely old swill-pot—a onetime writer, now a hanger-on in the fiction department, who guzzles vodka Martinis until his eyes glaze over. The picture isn't terrible, just terribly dull. It feels dated, especially in the scenes that "explain" the hero and show his redemption—the banality comes down on you like drizzle. With Kiefer Sutherland, Dianne Wiest, Frances Sternhagen, Charlie Schlatter, Swoosie Kurtz, Phoebe Cates, William Hickey, and Tracy Pollan. Cinematography by Gordon Willis; the score, which seems buried, is by Donald Fagen. United Artists. color (See *Hooked*.)

Brighton Beach Memoirs (1986)—The 1982 play—the first in Neil Simon's semi-autobiographical trilogy—was acclaimed as a deepening of Simon's talent, a move beyond wisecracking Broadway entertainment to something true. The film is a faithful version, adapted by Simon himself and directed by Gene Saks, who staged the play for L.A. and Broadway, and it features such celebrated performers as Blythe Danner, Bob Dishy, and Judith Ivey. They certainly help, but the whole experience of this lower-middle-class-family drama set in 1937 is so drab that even these performers finally fade into the dark wallpaper. The material doesn't have the noisy abrasiveness of many of Simon's earlier plays-into-films; you're not subjected to verbal exchanges that beat a tattoo on your skull. However, it's not exactly an improvement to get near-realistic misery: his life as a horny 15-year-old (Jonathan Silverman), with a closed-minded, suspicious mother (Danner). This woman who kills any possibility of domestic pleasures—it's like living with a hanging judge—would breed rage. But Simon doesn't seem to know what to do with her (or with the boy's responses to her). The film's tone is jokey nostalgia. The boy sees the lunacy in his mother's behavior, but he sees it humorously, as if it gave him no pain. Simon instinctively makes things easy and palatable, and there's a penalty: it's the retrograde, pepless snooziness of the picture. You come out feeling half dead. Universal. color (See *Hooked*.)

Brighton Rock Also known as *Young Scarface*. (1947)—Graham Greene's 1938 novel about a man who goes to hell was filmed with the young and chilling Richard Attenborough as the vicious teen-age leader of a gang of slashers. In this tense thriller, the suspense is indistinguishable from dread—everything is tinged with evil. With Hermione Baddeley as the blowsy singer, Harcourt Williams as the dilapidated lawyer, and William Hartnell and Carol Marsh. John and Roy Boulting produced and directed; adapted by Greene and Terence Rattigan. b & w

Bringing Up Baby (1938)—Lunatic comedies of the 30s generally started with an heiress. This one starts with an heiress (Katharine Hepburn) who has a dog, George, and a leopard, Baby. Cary Grant is a paleontologist who has just acquired the bone he needs to complete his dinosaur skeleton. George steals the bone, Grant and Baby chase each other around, the dinosaur collapses—but Grant winds up with Hepburn, and no paleontologist ever got hold of a more beautiful set of bones. The director, Howard Hawks, keeps all this trifling nonsense in such artful balance that it never impinges on the real world; it may be the American movies' closest equiv-

alent to Restoration comedy. With Charles Ruggles as an explorer, Barry Fitzgerald as a drunk, May Robson as a dowager, Walter Catlett as a sheriff, and Fritz Feld as a frenzied psychoanalyst. George is played by Asta, of the *Thin Man* series. The screenplay is by Dudley Nichols and Hagar Wilde, from Wilde's story. (This picture was the taking-off point for Peter Bogdanovich's comedy *What's Up, Doc?*) R K O. b & w

Brink of Life *Nära Livet* (1957)—Ingmar Bergman directed this study of women in a maternity hospital—and a gory, dreary film it is. With Eva Dahlbeck, Ingrid Thulin, Bibi Andersson, Erland Josephson, and Max von Sydow. Screenplay by Bergman and Ulla Isakssom (from her short story). In Swedish. b & w

Broadcast News (1987)—The writer-producer-director James L. Brooks puts us inside the world of a network's Washington bureau and sets up an adversarial relationship between the reddish-blond charmer Tom (William Hurt), who represents TV's corruption of the news into entertainment, and dark, broody Aaron (Albert Brooks), a near-genius newsman who, on the surface, at least, represents substance and integrity. The heroine, Jane (Holly Hunter), is a producer, and she and Aaron are supposed to be high-principled professionals, as well as close friends. The satirical, romantic-comedy dilemma is that Jane finds herself falling in love with Tom, who incarnates everything that she despises. It's fun to see a workaday world presented so that it moves and keeps you off balance and looks authentic, and the picture has some witty dialogue. But basically all it's saying is that beautiful, assured people have an edge over the rest of us, no matter how high our I.Q.s are. And it lacks any filmmaking excitement. With all the surface authenticity Jim Brooks gives us, he himself represents the corruption of movies into TV. The actors are vivid; they're like pop-up figures in a child's book, as they often are in sit-coms. (Albert Brooks is the only one who goes beyond that: he gives the picture its bit of soul.) With Joan Cusack, Lois Chiles, Robert Prosky, Peter Hackes, and, as the big cheese, the New York anchorman, Jack Nicholson, who's not listed in the opening credits. Released by 20th Century-Fox. color (See *Hooked.*)

Broadway Danny Rose (1984)—Danny Rose is a small-time booking agent, a little schmo in loud plaids who nurtures his more promising clients until they're on the brink of stardom, at which point they invariably leave him and sign up with big-time agents. The new Judas in his life is Lou Canova (Nick Apollo Forte), a barrel-chested singer in his forties with a dimply, piggy Vegas smile and a voice to make musicians shudder. Woody Allen, who plays Danny and who also wrote and directed this Damon Runyonesque movie, isn't working with post-Freudian comedy here; he has left out the hostility that made him famous, and the imagination and freak lyricism, too. Danny is Mr. Goodness-and-Poignancy; he's a Chaplinesque moral presence in a world of Catskills comics and Mafia hoods. The movie is about how Lou Canova's ruthless, tough girlfriend Tina (Mia Farrow, disguised with a nasal accent, fright wig, shades, and some padding) learns to appreciate Danny. Shot in grainy black and white, the material is rather unformed. It's dim and larval, like Danny. Allen leaves us in the uncomfortable position of waiting for laugh lines and character developments that aren't there. The picture has a curdled, Diane Arbus bleakness, but it also has some good fast talk and some push. Allen plugs up the holes with gags that still get laughs; he remembers to pull the old Frank Capra, cut-

rate Dickens strings, and he keeps things moving along. Orion (See *State of the Art.*)

Broadway Melody (1929)—When talkies were new, this was the musical that everyone went to see. It's the one with ''The Wedding of the Painted Doll'' and ''Broadway Melody,'' of course, and ''You Were Meant for Me,'' all by Arthur Freed and Nacio Herb Brown. It's the one with Anita Page and Bessie Love as the sisters from tank-town vaudeville whose hearts are broken in the big city. With Charles King, Kenneth Thomson, Jed Prouty, and Mary Doran. Directed by Harry Beaumont, with ensemble numbers staged by George Cunningham; produced by Harry Rapf. M-G-M. (Some sequences were in an early Technicolor process.)

Broadway Melody of 1936 (1935)—An M-G-M musical with Eleanor Powell (a dynamo, all right, but she manages to be wholesome even in glittering top hat and tails), Robert Taylor, Buddy Ebsen, Jack Benny, Frances Langford, Una Merkel, and June Knight. A good score by Arthur Freed and Nacio Herb Brown includes ''I Gotta Feelin' You're Foolin','' ''You Are My Lucky Star,'' and ''Broadway Rhythm.'' Roy Del Ruth directed. b & w

Broadway Melody of 1938 (1937)—The script is something dim about backstage troubles before the opening of a giant musical, and this follow-up to the hit *Broadway Melody of 1936*, which had also featured Eleanor Powell, Robert Taylor, and Buddy Ebsen, and been directed by Roy Del Ruth, seems routine. The score, once again by Arthur Freed and Nacio Herb Brown, doesn't have the same excitement. But something startling and joyful happens when the 15-year-old Judy Garland, in bobby socks, lets out her huge voice on the memorable love letter, ''Dear Mr. Gable'' (to the tune of ''You Made

Me Love You"). She had made her feature-film début the year before in *Pigskin Parade*, but this was her first feature at M-G-M. In the finale the little bobby-soxer is paired with the tall Ebsen (whose gangly loose dancing was always a high spot of these M-G-M musicals) and she looks like the most radiantly normal of children. With George Murphy, Sophie Tucker, Binnie Barnes, Billy Gilbert, Raymond Walburn, Charley Grapewin, Willie Howard, Sid Silvers, Igor Gorin, and Robert Benchley. Produced by Jack Cummings; written by Jack McGowan and Silvers. b & w

Broadway Melody of 1940—Fred Astaire, Eleanor Powell, and George Murphy. That's a lot of tapping. Astaire and Murphy are both hoping to get the Broadway role opposite the dancing star, Powell; by mistake, the producers hire Murphy, but Astaire gets to play it, after all. This is a big, lavish M-G-M musical, with a Cole Porter score and lots of spectacular dancing; what's missing is romance, sensuousness, magic. The indefatigable, intensely dull Eleanor Powell is better on her own than when she has a partner and is still on her own. With Astaire nearby, you're terribly aware of what long arms she has and what a jolly, good-natured, big, all-American girl she is. (Her costumes always suggest uniforms.) Their dancing together does have vitality and verve, and at times it's good, carefree hoofing, but it seems healthy and impersonal. Even in the finale, when they dance to "Begin the Beguine"—the only song that Porter didn't write specially for the film—it isn't memorable. The new songs include "I Concentrate on You," sung by Douglas McPhail, and "I've Got My Eyes on You," and a real bummer that Astaire and Murphy team up for—it's called "Please Don't Monkey with Broadway." With Frank Morgan, Ian Hunter, Florence Rice, Lynne Carver, Herman Bing, Jack Mulhall, Joe Yule, and Barbara Jo Allen (Vera Vague) as a reception-ist. Produced by Jack Cummings; directed by Norman Taurog; script by Leon Gordon and George Oppenheimer, from a story by Dore Schary and Jack McGowan. The choreography is by Astaire and Bobby Connolly. b & w

Broadway Rhythm (1944)—An M-G-M musical hodgepodge that enlisted the dubious talents of popular performers from radio, and other lesser luminaries. It starred Ginny Simms, who had a lot of teeth for the camera, and George Murphy, who was always short on charisma. The score is mostly mediocre, but with some big exceptions—"All the Things You Are," "Irresistible You," and "Pretty Baby." The picture has some genuine attractions: Ben Blue, Gloria De Haven, Kenny Bowers, the very young Nancy Walker, and Lena Horne, singing, of course, and hoofing (with John Thomas and Archie Savage). The seductive Miss Horne is more full-bodied here than in her later streamlined, agelessly beautiful incarnation, and she's bouncier, too. Also with Hazel Scott, Eddie "Rochester" Anderson, Charles Winninger, Tommy Dorsey and His Orchestra. Produced by Jack Cummings; directed by Roy Del Ruth; screenplay by Dorothy Kingsley and Harry Clork; remotely based on the Jerome Kern and Oscar Hammerstein II show *Very Warm for May*. color

Broadway to Hollywood (1933)—Three generations of a theatrical family, headed by Alice Brady and Frank Morgan; there are song-and-dance interludes, but mostly it's about the domestic loyalties of stupefyingly dull people. With Mickey Rooney, at 10 (it was his first M-G-M picture), and Jimmy Durante, Madge Evans, Jackie Cooper, Fay Templeton, Eddie Quillan, Russell Hardie, May Robson, Una Merkel, and—in his screen début—Nelson Eddy. Produced by Harry Rapf; directed by Willard Mack, from a script he wrote with Edgar Allan Woolf; lacklustre score. b & w

Broken Arrow (1950)—Everybody seems to enjoy this movie. It's full of legend and romance and action. The setting is Arizona in those confused days after the Civil War when renegades from both armies were causing trouble among the Indians. James Stewart plays the ex–Union officer who befriends the Apache Cochise (Jeff Chandler) and marries an Apache princess (Debra Paget). Delmer Daves directed this adaptation by Michael Blankfort of the novel *Blood Brother*, by Elliott Arnold, and though the picture never won any Academy Awards or brotherhood awards, it has probably done more to soften the hearts of racists than most movies designed to instruct, indict, and inspire. (That Indian princess was no squaw.) Part of the pleasure of the film is that its treatment of the Indians-vs.-settlers theme doesn't violate the conventions of the genre. 20th Century-Fox. color

Broken Blossoms (1919)—D. W. Griffith's stylized lyric tragedy—a small-scale film that is one of his most poetic, and one of his finest. With Lillian Gish as the childish waif (the source, possibly, of the Giulietta Masina role in *La Strada*), Donald Crisp as the brutal Zampanò-like prizefighter, and Richard Barthelmess as the lonely Chinese dreamer. (The original prints were tinted and it was first exhibited with additional color—a "Chinese blue" glow thrown from the projection booth onto the screen.) Silent.

Broken Lullaby Originally called *The Man I Killed*. (1932)—Ernst Lubitsch, the master of light and frivolous film art, seems to be doing penance for his own wit in this pacifist drama, adapted from a play by Maurice Rostand. Phillips Holmes, unspeakably handsome but an even more unspeakable actor, is the sickly, sensitive French musician who kills a German soldier (also a musician . . .) in the trenches. Remorseful, he goes to Germany and settles in with the dead man's family (Lionel Barrymore is the father) and fiancée (Nancy Carroll, miserably miscast, with a fat braid around her head). Lubitsch can't entirely escape his own talent, and the film is beautifully crafted, but he mistook drab, sentimental hokum for ironic, poetic tragedy. The picture was a box-office fiasco, despite the excessive praise of Robert E. Sherwood, who said, "It is the best talking picture that has yet been seen and heard." Not by a long shot. With ZaSu Pitts, Lucien Littlefield, and Emma Dunn. Adapted by Ernest Vajda and Samson Raphaelson; art direction by Hans Dreier. Paramount. b & w

Bronenosets Potyomkin, see *Potemkin*

The Browning Version (1951)—The cuckolded schoolmaster of Terence Rattigan's play requires a virtuoso actor, and in this British film version, directed by Anthony Asquith, it got one. If the sustained anguish of the role does not allow Michael Redgrave a great deal of room to move around in, it does give him a chance to show what he can do in tight quarters, and that, it turns out, is considerable. He is superb. With Jean Kent as his wife, Nigel Patrick as her lover. b & w

Brubaker (1980)—Suggested by the Arkansas prison scandals of the late 60s, this muckraking melodrama has considerable power and some strong performances. In the film, the prison, which is under the control of gun-carrying convict guards who supply slave labor to nearby farms and businesses, is in an unidentified Southern state. Robert Redford plays the warden who tries to clean up the place, but he's the wrong kind of actor for a prison movie—he isn't a tough man of action, and so the character has been mythologized, softened, and honeyed, and he seems to be the selfless white knight of the Westerns. Despite some perplexing scenes—probably occasioned by the fact that the director, Stuart Rosenberg, took over a project that had been shaped for a different director (Bob Rafelson) and tried to mold the material his way—there are individual sequences that may be the best work Rosenberg has ever done on the screen. The script, by W. D. Richter, has offhand dialogue with a warm, funny edge; the cinematography, by Bruno Nuytten, has a marvellous ease. And the remarkable cast includes Morgan Freeman, Richard Ward, Yaphet Kotto, David Keith, Tim McIntire, David Harris, M. Emmet Walsh, and Matt Clark. There are also performers who are used poorly (Murray Hamilton, John McMartin, and Jane Alexander) or use themselves poorly (Everett McGill). 20th Century-Fox. color (See *Taking It All In*.)

Die Brücke, see *The Bridge*

Brute Force (1947)—The title is accurate: this is a crudely powerful prison picture, produced by Mark Hellinger, written by Richard Brooks, and directed by Jules Dassin. The essentially old-fashioned material was modernized by the use of sadistic scenes and such devices as having the power-mad warden (Hume Cronyn) suggest a home-grown Hitler. This is the kind of movie that is often called a man's picture; that is, fast, action-packed, pseudo-realistic. With Burt Lancaster, Charles Bickford, Roman Bohnen, Ella Raines, Yvonne De Carlo, Ann Blyth, Anita Colby, Sam Levene, Howard Duff, John Hoyt, Jeff Corey, Whit Bissell, and Vince Barnett. Universal. b & w

Die Büchse der Pandora, see *Pandora's Box*

Buckaroo Banzai, see *The Adventures of Buckaroo Banzai*

Bugsy Malone (1976)—An aberration from England, set in New York in 1929 and made with a cast of children, average age 12. The children don't play children, though. Little boys with their hair slicked down impersonate the Hollywood-movie racketeers of the Prohibition era; in their fedoras and double-breasted suits, these hoods look like midgets, and the speakeasies, molls, automobiles are all slightly miniaturized. This picture is a kiddie-gangster musical, with slapstick gang wars; it operates on darlingness and the kitsch of innocence. The almost pornographic dislocation, which is the source of the film's possible appeal as a novelty, is never acknowledged, but the camera lingers on a gangster's pudgy, infantile fingers or a femme fatale's soft little belly pushing out of her tight satin dress, and it roves over the pubescent figures in the chorus line. Alan Parker wrote and directed (it's his first film); the score (sung by adults) is by Paul Williams. With Jodie Foster as the vamp Tallulah, Martin Lev as the villain Dandy Dan, Scott Baio as the good guy, and the appealing Florrie Dugger as the complacent ingenue Blousey. Released by Paramount. color (See *When the Lights Go Down*.)

Bull Durham (1988)—Written and directed by Ron Shelton, this sunny romantic comedy has the kind of dizzying off-center literacy that Preston Sturges's pictures had. It's a satirical celebration of our native jauntiness and wit; it takes us into a subculture that's like a bawdy adjunct of childhood—minor-league baseball. Kevin Costner plays the smart, hyper-articulate catcher Crash, and comes through with his first wide-awake, star performance; at his best, he's as berserkly ironic as Jack Nicholson is at some of his peaks. After playing for 12 years, Crash arrives in Durham, North Carolina, to join the Durham Bulls and learns that he's been brought in to train baby-faced Nuke (Tim Robbins), a wild young rookie pitcher who is destined to move up. Susan Sarandon plays the beautiful, passionate Annie Savoy, a baseball fanatic who has her own scorecard: "There's never been a ballplayer slept with me who didn't have the best year of his career." What you keep reacting to is the film's exuberant doodles. With Jenny Robertson, Trey Wilson, William O'Leary, Robert Wuhl, and Max Patkin. Cinematography by Bobby Byrne. Orion. color (See *Hooked*.)

Bullfight (1956)—You begin to understand—or rather to feel—the magnetism of this archaic sport as you watch the great Manolete, who died in 1947 at the age of 30. Thin, reserved, sad, he performs the rites of the game with subtle, pure movements. His classic style is contrasted with that of the glamorous, artful Dominguín, and Belmonte, Arruza, and others. This feature-length documentary, compiled in Europe, has some remarkable footage; it succeeds where fictional treatments have failed—in communicating the elation and the desperation of bullfighters testing themselves. b & w

The Bullfighter and the Lady (1951)—Produced and directed by Budd Boetticher, this film came out in the same year as Robert Rossen's much more expensive *The Brave Bulls*; though marred by a synthetic plot, it's a more enjoyable film than its heavily glamourized and publicized rival, and has moments of an authentic seaminess. Robert Stack plays an American who wants to be a bullfighter; Gilbert Roland, in possibly the best performance of his amazingly long career, is an aging matador. With Katy Jurado, Joy Page, Virginia Grey, and John Hubbard. Script by James Edward Grant. Republic. b & w

Bullitt (1968)—A competent director (Peter Yates), working with competent technicians, gives a fairly dense texture to a vacuous script

about cops and gangsters and politicians. The stars are Steve McQueen with his low-key charisma, as the police-officer hero, and the witty, steep streets of San Francisco. There's a big car-chase sequence, which helped to make the movie a hit. With Robert Vaughn as a slimy Mr. Big whose technique of bribery is so blatantly insulting he couldn't give away a lollipop, and Jacqueline Bisset, Robert Duvall, Georg Stanford Brown, Simon Oakland, Norman Fell, and Don Gordon. Script by Alan Trustman and Harry Kleiner, from Robert L. Pike's *Mute Witness*; cinematography by William Fraker; music by Lalo Schifrin; titles by Pablo Ferro. Warners. color (See *Going Steady*.)

Il Buono il Brutto il Cattivo, see *The Good, the Bad and the Ugly*

Burden of Dreams (1982)—Les Blank's feature-length documentary on the making of Werner Herzog's *Fitzcarraldo* isn't a major work on its own, but it has an unusual effect: it makes *Fitzcarraldo* crumble in the memory—it merges with it. Blank shows more sensitivity in his shots of the Peruvian Indians than Herzog does, and Blank's footage of Herzog himself, standing and addressing the camera (though with eyes averted), is stronger than anything in *Fitzcarraldo*. In these monologues, Herzog seems almost priggish in his dissociation from his own filmmaking methods; he speaks of the mammoth physical challenges he sets up as if they had been imposed on him—as if he had been cursed. He turns the production of a film into a mystical ordeal. color (See *Taking It All In*.)

Burn! *Queimada!* (1970)—Gillo Pontecorvo's luxuriant, ecstatic epic about a mid-19th-century slave uprising on a fictitious Spanish-speaking Caribbean island is told from a neo-Marxist, Frantz Fanonian point of view. It is an attempt to plant an insurrectionary fuse within a swashbuckler—to use a popular costume-adventure form to arouse black revolutionary passions. Marlon Brando plays a British *agent provocateur* who instigates the revolt and then cynically crushes it; he personifies colonial manipulative policies as well as, by implication, the American involvement in Vietnam. As Pontecorvo demonstrated in *The Battle of Algiers*, he has a true gift for epic filmmaking: he can keep masses of people in movement so we care about them. And here, in his feeling for crowds and battles, for color and images, and for visual rhythms, he's a sensuous, intoxicating director. When blacks ride white horses that prance to what sounds like a syncopated Gregorian chant, the sequence is so shimmering and showy that one knows Pontecorvo and his cinematographer, Marcello Gatti, and his composer, Ennio Morricone, couldn't resist it. *Burn!* is politically schematic, and almost every line of dialogue jogs us to fit it into a deterministic theory of history, yet the film is large-spirited, and it might have reached a much wider audience if the Spanish government, sensitive about Spaniards being cast as heavies, hadn't applied economic pressure against the producing company, United Artists. So parts of this picture were deleted and others reshot, and the Spaniards, who had traditionally dominated the Antilles, were replaced by the Portuguese, who hadn't but aren't a big movie market. After these delays the picture was given a nervous, halfhearted release. Produced by Alberto Grimaldi; written by Pontecorvo, Franco Solinas, and Georgio Arlorio; production design by Piero Gherardi. With Evaristo Marquez as the black leader, and Renato Salvatori as the mulatto puppet. Shot partly in the Colombian seaport Cartagena. (See *Deeper into Movies*.)

Butch Cassidy and the Sundance Kid (1969)—Paul Newman and Robert Redford are charming people to watch on the screen, even when the vehicle doesn't do them justice. George Roy Hill directed this enormously popular, overblown, frolicsome Western from William Goldman's script. With Katharine Ross; cinematography by Conrad Hall. The song "Raindrops Keep Fallin' on My Head" is by Burt Bacharach and Hal David. 20th Century-Fox. color (See *Deeper into Movies*.)

The Buttercup Chain (1970)—British bathos about the unhappy overprivileged. Hywel Bennett and Jane Asher, who love each other, are the children of identical twins; Sven-Bertil Taube is a Swede who swims nude; and Leigh Taylor-Young is an American girl who drives on the wrong side of some very fancy roads. Robert Ellis Miller directed, from Peter Draper's adaptation of Janice Elliott's novel. With Clive Revill and Roy Dotrice. color

Butterfield 8 (1960)—The John O'Hara novel that seemed perfect for the movies, plus the role that seemed perfect for Elizabeth Taylor—and this is the garish mess it became. Daniel Mann's direction is maybe even worse than the Charles Schnee–John Michael Hayes script. With Laurence Harvey; Dina Merrill, doing a noble wife to end all noble wives; and a vacuum on the screen that is said to be Eddie Fisher. M-G-M. color

By Design (1982)—A buoyant, quirky sex comedy directed by the Canadian Claude Jutra, who has a light, understated approach to slapstick. His sensibility suggests a mingling of Tati and Truffaut; he never makes a fuss about anything. His two heroines are curly-red-haired Angie (Sara Botsford), who is tall and has a hell raiser's smile, and serious little Helen (Patty Duke Astin). They're in love, and they live and work together happily—they run their own fashion business in

Vancouver. When these two face the camera, we're confronted by four bright-blue eyes and a quandary: Helen yearns to be a mother. As they explore the possibilities open to them, Jutra takes a look around the whole modern supermarket of sex. The script, by Joe Wiesenfeld, Jutra, and David Eames, seems to skip along from one incident to the next. What holds the movie together is the bond between the two women, who couldn't be more unlike. At the start, Jutra's matter-of-fact style may take a little getting used to, and there's a bewildering display of the heroines' fashions (which are garish). But then things get going, and the central sequence of crosscutting between two couples in bed is near to being irresistibly funny and, finally, it's romantic. This picture isn't exactly bubbly while you're watching it, but it effervesces when you think it over. It's like a Lubitsch sex comedy stripped of the glamour but not of the fun. With Saul Rubinek as a girl chaser; Clare Coulter as an intense young social worker; Sonia Zimmer as Suzie the model; Alan Duruisseau as a dimply Swede; and Jeannie Elias as the cowgirl teenybopper. Music by Chico Hamilton; cinematography by Jean Boffety. color (See *Taking It All In.*)

Bye Bye Birdie (1963)—The Michael Stewart satirical musical about a rock 'n' roll idol who gets drafted, with its parodistic Charles Strouse and Lee Adams score, sounds like a good movie idea, but the central character (played by Jesse Pearson) has been softened, the sit-com plotting is tedious, and the film aims for cornball zest rather than wit. Ann-Margret, playing a brassy 16-year-old with a hyperactive rear end, takes over the picture; slick, enamelled, and appalling as she is, she's an undeniable presence. The cast, which performs erratically, includes Dick Van Dyke, Janet Leigh, Maureen Stapleton, Paul Lynde, and Bobby Rydell. Directed by George Sidney. Columbia. color

Bye Bye Braverman (1968)—Sidney Lumet takes Wallace Markfield's mean-spirited satirical novel, *To an Early Grave*, and turns the material into a crudely affectionate comic romp. The movie is often gross and it's sloppily thrown together, but the characters' rhetoric has some juice in it. No one is ever likely to say that he was put to sleep by Sidney Lumet's good taste. Besides, there may never be another movie on the highly specialized subject of the comic failure of New York Jewish intellectuals. When Braverman, a minor literary figure, suddenly dies, his four literary friends gather in Greenwich Village, pile into a Volkswagen, set out to attend the funeral service in Brooklyn, and get lost. It's a low-comedy situation played for emotional wallowing as well as for laughs. Jewish actors playing Jews have a tendency to overdo it, as if they thought they might be taken for Gentiles if they behaved normally, and Lumet appears to have encouraged this; you keep wishing the camera would back away a bit. With George Segal; Jack Warden (miscast as a poet); Sorrell Booke, who has some wonderful mad movements of his head, as a fussy little book reviewer; Joseph Wiseman, whose cold, bitter characterization is very effective. Also with Alan King, Phyllis Newman, Jessica Walter, Anthony Holland, Zohra Lampert (whose voice seems disembodied), and Godfrey Cambridge, who picks up the pace and brings the movie a welcome contrast. The screenplay is by Herbert Sargent; cinematography by Boris Kaufman. Shot in New York. Warner–Seven Arts. color (See *Going Steady.*)

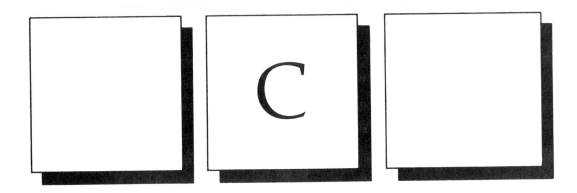

Cabaret (1972)—A great movie musical. Taking its form from political cabaret, it's a satire of temptations. In a prodigious balancing act, Bob Fosse, the choreographer-director, keeps the period—Berlin, 1931—at a cool distance. We see the decadence as garish and sleazy; yet we also see the animal energy in it—everything seems to become sexualized. The movie does not exploit decadence; rather, it gives it its due. With Joel Grey as our devil-doll host—the master of ceremonies—and Liza Minnelli (in her first singing role on the screen) as exuberant, corruptible Sally Bowles, chasing after the life of a headliner no matter what; Minnelli has such gaiety and electricity that she becomes a star before our eyes. From Christopher Isherwood's *Goodbye to Berlin* stories, via the play and movie of *I Am a Camera*, and the Broadway musical *Cabaret*, which has been adapted for the screen by Jay Presson Allen, with the assistance of Hugh Wheeler. The metallic songs, by John Kander and Fred Ebb, have a distinctive acrid flavor. With Michael York, Helmut Griem, Marisa Berenson, and Fritz Wepper. Shot in West Germany; cinematography by Geoffrey Unsworth. Produced by Cy Feuer, for Allied Artists release. color (See *Deeper into Movies*.)

Cabin in the Cotton (1932)—Bette Davis in her first wickedly sexy role, trying to tempt Richard Barthelmess away from virtue (Dorothy Jordan). The melodrama about the cheating Southern planters is naïvely socially conscious, but Davis has a lot of fresh impact. Michael Curtiz directed; with Henry B. Walthall, Clarence Muse, Hardie Albright, David Landau, Tully Marshall, and oily, villainous Berton Churchill. The script by Paul Green was adapted from H. H. Knoll's novel; produced by Hal B. Wallis, for Warners. b & w

Cabin in the Sky (1943)—This was the first film Vincente Minnelli directed and his approach was fresh and enthusiastic. It's a joyful, stylized treatment of *faux-naïf* Negro folklore, with an all-black cast, and it's one of the best musicals ever made in this country. It becomes even better with the years: now, it's easier to ignore the weaknesses in the script, because it's so exciting to see legendary artists, such as Ethel Waters, Lena Horne, Louis Armstrong, and Bubbles (John William Sublett), as they were in the 40s. The slinky dancing of Bubbles (to the song "Shine") is a high point; so is Ethel Waters singing "Happiness Is Just a Thing Called

Joe," and so is Lena Horne on "Honey in the Honeycomb." The cast includes Eddie "Rochester" Anderson, Rex Ingram, Kenneth Spencer, Mantan Moreland, Willie Best, Duke Ellington and his orchestra, and the Hall Johnson Choir. The script by Joseph Schrank is based on the stage musical, with book by Lynn Root, lyrics by John Latouche, and music by Vernon Duke. Only three of the songs in the movie are from the original score; the others are from a variety of sources. Produced by Arthur Freed, for M-G-M. Made in sepia.

The Cabinet of Dr. Caligari *Das Kabinett des Dr. Caligari* (1919)—The audience, confined in the madman's universe, sees what the madman sees: distorted perspectives, eerie painted lights and shadows, an angular, warped world of fears and menace. The sets are used expressionistically to convey the madman's thoughts, to intensify the characters' emotions, and to emphasize the meanings of the action. This film is so entrenched in the "masterpiece" classification that a few cautionary remarks should be added, lest your initial reaction be disappointment: you may be delighted that the flats express something, because most of the actors don't; you may find that the decor, which is highly experimental in terms of space and distance but is derivative from the stage use of Expressionism, is a monotonous zigzag (too many hooks and no fish). *Caligari*, the most complete essay in the decor of delirium, is one of the most famous films of all time, and it was considered a radical advance in film technique, yet it is rarely imitated—and you'll know why. Werner Krauss is the nightmare image of a psychoanalyst—the hypnotist Caligari—with, in his cabinet, the somnambulist Cesare, played by the extraordinary tall, thin, young Conrad Veidt. The cast includes Lil Dagover, and Friedrich Feher as the student-inmate. Produced by Erich Pommer; directed by Robert Wiene. The scenario by Carl Mayer and Hans Janowitz was originally intended as an attack on irrational authority, but the meanings got turned around; the art direction is the work of three painters—Hermann Warm, Walter Reiman, and Walter Röhrig. The Nazis labelled the film "degenerate art." Eisenstein, who, in his own way, agreed, called it "this barbaric carnival of the destruction of the healthy human infancy of our art." (A 1962 American film used the same title, but has no other connection with the original.) Silent. b & w

Cactus Flower (1969)—A movie adaptation of the kind of Broadway play that drives you to the movies. Full of forced, unnaturally fast quips that one might, in a state of extreme exhaustion, find fairly funny. With Walter Matthau as a dentist, Ingrid Bergman as his assistant, and Goldie Hawn, whom God must have sent to us. But why didn't He provide her with better material? (She plays the dentist's mistress.) Also with Jack Weston and Irene Hervey. Directed by Gene Saks, from I.A.L. Diamond's script, based on Abe Burrows' play, which was adapted from a French play, which . . . Columbia. color

Caddie (1976)—The reserved, aloof Caddie (played by the lovely, toothy Helen Morse) is a young Australian housewife who, in 1925, leaves her husband, taking their two small children with her; penniless, she goes to work as a barmaid. The picture often has the charm of photographs of the past, but that's all it has. Taken from a woman's pseudonymous autobiography, the movie doesn't dramatize Caddie's life; she just stays on her treadmill, and we never learn anything of how she feels. The audience has every reason to think, Why was a movie made about her? Every time we get interested in someone who crosses Caddie's path—the snappy barmaid Josie (Jacki Weaver), the brash, flippant bookie Ted (Jack Thompson, who gives the film a burst of energy), the shy peddler Sonny (Drew Forsythe)—and some interaction seems possible, the character promptly drops out of the picture, never to return. With Takis Emmanuel as the boring, gentlemanly Greek. Directed by Donald Crombie, from Joan Long's adaptation. color (See *Taking It All In*.)

Caesar and Cleopatra (1946)—Despite its resonant title, Shaw's play is a minor comedy—a slight, sly conceit—and it was blown up out of proportion in this extravagant, Shaw-adoring version directed by Gabriel Pascal, from Shaw's script. The pomp overpowers the parody and the playfulness. Vivien Leigh romps about as the cruel, deceiving kitten who is to become a passionate, tragic queen, while Claude Rains—as her lover and mentor, the amused, dispassionate Caesar—displays a world-weary wisdom that is more smugly shallow than Shaw could have intended. When Rains played a small part he sometimes gave the impression that he was carrying a movie, but here his equanimity and his impish grin aren't enough. It's lucky that Leigh has such an amusing dingaling quality—she lightens portions of this overstaged production. With an entertaining celebrity-show cast that includes Flora Robson, Stewart Granger, Francis L. Sullivan, Basil Sydney, Michael Rennie, Cecil Parker, Stanley Holloway, Leo Genn, Anthony Harvey, Jean Simmons, Esmé Percy, and the invaluable Ernest Thesiger. Music by Georges Auric; cinematography by Freddie Young, Robert Krasker, Jack Hildyard, and Jack Cardiff; decor and costumes by Oliver Messel and sets by John Bryan. color

La Cage aux folles II (1980)—The return of Albin (Michel Serrault) and Renato (Ugo Tognazzi). This picture isn't as original as the first, but it gives the actors more range, and it's more smoothly directed (by Edouard Molinaro, who also did the first). A thriller plot serves as a pretext to get the two middle-aged homosexuals out of their apartment and into the straight world. The movie is most inventive when they're in Italy and Albin, dressed as a peasant woman, is toiling in the fields among the women; he looks youthful and radiantly fulfilled—he really believes that he is one of them. Albin doesn't see what we can see: wherever he is and however he's dressed, he's so far into his fantasy that he looks like no one else. This film has nothing to do with the art of movies, but it has a great deal to do with the craft and art of acting, and the pleasures of farce. Serrault gives a superb comic performance—his Albin is a wildly fanciful creation. And maybe it's only in this exaggerated form that a movie about the ridiculousness and the tenderness of married love can be widely accepted now. With Marcel Bozzufi. In French. color (See *Taking It All In*.)

La Caida, see *The Fall*

Calamity Jane (1953)—Doris Day is at her friendliest and most likable as the tomboy heroine of this big, bouncy Western musical about Jane's romance with Wild Bill Hickok (easygoing Howard Keel). The script, by James O'Hanlon, is ingenious (until the last 15 minutes or so); the framework allows for some singing and dancing by the charming Allyn McLerie, and a good drag act. The score by Sammy Fain and Paul Francis Webster is just fine, except that Day's main ballad "Secret Love" (or at least the way it's staged) is out of character and doesn't seem to belong in the film. Directed by David Butler. With Phil Carey, Dick Wesson, Paul Harvey, Chubby Johnson, and Gale Robbins. Warners. color

Calcutta (1969)—In the late 1960s, Louis Malle, fed up, he said, with "actors, studios, fiction, and Paris," took off for India for a period of "total improvising." Working with a minimal crew (a cameraman and a soundman), he shot the footage out of which he made the 92-minute *Calcutta* and the 7-part *Phantom India*—masterful personal documentaries. Malle himself narrates in English, and his soft, cultivated voice and observations are integral to this film, which fuses squalor, death, and beauty. It's an incomparable vision of the poetic insanity of India. color

California Suite (1978)—Neil Simon's four battling-couples playlets set in the Beverly Hills Hotel have been intercut, and the director, Herbert Ross, has bleached the space around the pairs of combatants to get rid of it as tastefully as possible. This look of sun-struck swank is appropriate to the two mawkish, bittersweet Wasp playlets (Jane Fonda and Alan Alda, Maggie Smith and Michael Caine), in which gallant people use bitchy wisecracks to conceal their breaking hearts. The third playlet (low-comedy Jewish, with Walter Matthau as a husband caught with a hooker by his wife, Elaine May) is directed apathetically, and the fourth (slapstick black, with Richard Pryor and Bill Cosby as vacationing doctors from Chicago) is a disaster, and not only because it has no comic rhythm. When the black doctors stumble around a flooded hotel room, crash into each other, and step on broken glass, and Cosby bites Pryor's nose, the sequences have horrifying racist overtones. (Inadvertently, the movie seems to be saying that while these black men may be educated, they're still savages.) The audience doesn't get restless, because the pairs of actors keep whacking each other with insults; at the end, there's always the loneliness, the fear, and the reconciliation. Simon and Ross turn vaudeville into mush. Pro-

duced by Ray Stark. Columbia. color (See *When the Lights Go Down*.)

Call Me Madam (1953)—Ethel Merman gets more elbowroom than usual in Howard Lindsay and Russel Crouse's topical satire on the activities of a wealthy Washington hostess whom Harry Truman appoints ambassador to the sort of country where people are poor but love to yodel, and where the chorus hops around in what are alleged to be peasant dances. Merman has tedious telephone conversations with Truman about his daughter's troubles in her singing career, but the Irving Berlin score has a few songs good enough to make the whole apparatus tolerable. Chief among them is the duet "You're Just in Love," sung by Merman with Donald O'Connor, who works surprisingly well with her—he's so ingratiating he lightens her a bit. (He also gets in some dancing.) George Sanders, in one of his rare singing roles, has a voice and personality weighty enough to make him a fit romantic partner for the lady. With Vera-Ellen (dubbed) as a princess who's anxious to marry O'Connor, quite clearly a commoner; and Walter Slezak, Billy De Wolfe, Helmut Dantine, Lilia Skala, Steven Geray, and Ludwig Stossel. Directed by Walter Lang; adapted by Arthur Sheekman; choreography by Robert Alton. 20th Century-Fox. color

Calmos, see *Femmes fatales*

Camelot (1967)—One of Hollywood's colossal financial disasters. The film of the Lerner and Loewe musical (from T. H. White's *The Once and Future King*) got so expensively big that it went out of control; the sets and people and costumes seem to be sitting there on the screen, waiting for the unifying magic that never happens. The picture wavers in tone, but it does have good bits tucked in among the elaborate mistakes. It has a fascination;

C ——————————————————————————————

it's like a huge ruin that makes one wonder what the blueprints could possibly have indicated. It's hard to guess what the director, Joshua Logan, was aiming at. Richard Harris's King Arthur is eccentric and unfathomable in the first half, but he achieves some powerful moments later on; Vanessa Redgrave, flying high—sometimes lyrically, sometimes satirically—is a puzzling yet spectacular Guenevere. With David Hemmings as Mordred, Franco Nero as Lancelot, Laurence Naismith as Merlyn, and Estelle Winwood and Lionel Jeffries. Cinematography by Richard H. Kline. (181 minutes.) Warners. color

Camille (1937)—Like parents crowing over Baby's first steps, M-G-M announced "Garbo talks!" (for *Anna Christie*) and "Garbo laughs!" (for *Ninotchka*), but they missed out on this one, when they should have crowed "Garbo acts!" Under George Cukor's direction, she gives a warm yet ironic performance that is possibly her finest. Her Camille is too intelligent for her frivolous life, too generous for her circumstances; actually Garbo is inconceivable as a whore—her Camille is a divinity trying to succeed as a whore. (No movie has ever presented a more romantic view of a courtesan.) With the exception of Henry Daniell, as Baron de Varville, the rest of the cast does not rise to the occasion. As Armand, Robert Taylor is inept but not completely unforgivable: he had, at least, a romantic profile. As M. Duval, Lionel Barrymore *is* unforgivable. (Both of them are irredeemably American.) The slow, solemn production is luxuriant in its vulgarity; it achieves that glamour which M-G-M traditionally mistook for style. But, in spite of M-G-M, Garbo's artistry triumphs, and the tearjerker *Camille* is transformed into the "classic" the studio claimed it to be. With Lenore Ulric as Olympe, Laura Hope Crews as Prudence, and Elizabeth Allan, Jessie Ralph, Rex O'Malley, and E. E. Clive. From the novel by Alexandre Dumas, adapted by Frances Marion, James Hilton, and Zoë Akins. b & w

Le Camion, see *The Truck*

The Canary Murder Case (1929)—Philo Vance, the cultured amateur-detective hero of S. S. Van Dine's mystery novels, speaks so ornately, with such paralyzing erudition, that his unravelling a crime often seems more trouble than it's worth. He is far more sleek and entertaining as William Powell plays him in this early Paramount talkie. This was the first of the many Philo Vance cases to be filmed (published in 1927, it was the second—and best—of the books). The story is about the murder of a blackmailing musical-comedy star, who is played by the dazzling flapper Louise Brooks, with her short straight hair and bangs; from the way she looks (she seems to incarnate Art Deco), the men she has mistreated were lucky. With Jean Arthur, James Hall, Gustav von Seyffertitz, Eugene Pallette, Lawrence Grant, Ned Sparks, Louis John Bartels, E. H. Calvert, and Charles Lane. Directed by Malcolm St. Clair; the writers were S. S. Van Dine, Herman J. Mankiewicz, Florence Ryerson, and Albert S. LeVino. (William Powell went on to play Philo Vance three more times; Basil Rathbone had a shot at it, and then Warren William, Paul Lukas, Edmund Lowe, and many others.) b & w

Cancel My Reservation (1972)—A shameful low for Bob Hope. As a TV personality caught in a murder case, he delivers a steady string of sour, wheezing one-liners. Eva Marie Saint is mired in this one, along with Chief Dan George and Keenan Wynn. The cast includes Ralph Bellamy, Forrest Tucker, Anne Archer, and Doodles Weaver, with guest appearances by John Wayne, Flip Wilson, Bing Crosby, and Johnny Carson. Directed by Paul

Bogart (who also plays Dr. Kaufman), from a script by Arthur Marx and Robert Fisher, taken from the Louis L'Amour novel *The Broken Gun*. Produced by Bob Hope; released by Warners. color

Candy (1968)—Though it sticks fairly closely to Terry Southern's and Mason Hoffenberg's book, which was an erotic satire, it isn't erotic. It's a shambles, and the idea of Candide as a teen-age American girl who believes what men tell her—she's a born dupe whose innocence serves as an aphrodisiac—wears down fast. But there are funny sections: Marlon Brando's Grindl the Guru episode (especially under the covers), Richard Burton's parody of Dylan Thomas (though it does go on), and the bloody hospital sequence with James Coburn as Dr. Krankeit. This spoof of surgery is a bad sick joke and you know you should want it to end, because it's wicked and crude, but you're laughing helplessly. As Candide, Ewa Aulin lacks the necessary dewy freshness and isn't, and can't act, American; she sounds rather like Peter Lorre in his pussycat roles. With Walter Matthau, John Astin, and John Huston. There are also appearances by Charles Aznavour, Ringo Starr, and Elsa Martinelli who seem to be looking for a friend to tell them what they're supposed to do. There was a director—Christian Marquand—but the movie doesn't look directed; one has visions of the editor holding his head—his brain slipping through his fingers—as he tried to figure out how to put this stuff together. Adapted by Buck Henry; the cinematography is by Giuseppe Rotunno. color (See *Going Steady*.)

O Cangaceiro *The Bandit* (1953)—The raw murderousness of this Brazilian film contrasts with its smooth technical proficiency (it is rather like a handsome American Western directed by a sadist). The bandit (Milton Ribeiro) and his band of outlaws sack a village, brand the women, and carry off the schoolmistress. Violence then breaks out over her fate. The plot is not especially original, and the dialogue is often creaky, but the cinematography, the music (it's an unusually powerful score), and the atmosphere of eroticism and cruelty give the film a fetid fascination. The director, Lima Barreto, with the help of expert European technicians, demonstrated that the infant Brazilian film industry could be corrupt in the course of taking its first baby steps. In Portuguese. b & w

Can't Help Singing (1944)—The grown-up Deanna Durbin in a musical Western in which she gets to sing "Californ-i-ay." Unexciting, despite the songs by Jerome Kern and E. Y. Harburg. With Akim Tamiroff, Leonid Kinskey, and some colorless, forgettable leading men; Frank Ryan directed. Universal. color

The Canterville Ghost (1944)—In this heavy whimsey taken from an Oscar Wilde story, Charles Laughton is atrociously coy and florid. As the ghost of a man who was a coward, he's doomed to flutter about until his descendant, Robert Young, proves himself brave. With Margaret O'Brien in a prominent part, and Peter Lawford, Una O'Connor, Mike Mazurki, Rags Ragland, and William Gargan. Directed by Jules Dassin, who clearly lacks the requisite light, comic tone; was some executive punishing him? From a script by Edwin Blum. M-G-M. b & w

Captain Blood (1935)—The 25-year-old Errol Flynn has the smile and dash to shout "All right my hearties, follow me!" as he leaps from his pirate ship to an enemy vessel. As young Dr. Peter Blood, who is sent into slavery for treating a wounded rebel, he speaks with an Irish lilt and draws his sword against Basil Rathbone on a Caribbean beach. This happy swashbuckler, based on a Rafael Sabatini novel, was adapted by Casey Robinson and directed by Michael Curtiz. (The exteriors were actually Corona, Laguna Beach, and Palm Canyon near Palm Springs.) The cast includes Olivia de Havilland, Ross Alexander, Lionel Atwill, Guy Kibbee, Henry Stephenson, Robert Barrat, Hobart Cavanaugh, Donald Meek, David Torrence, Pedro de Cordoba, Jessie Ralph, J. Carrol Naish, E. E. Clive, Halliwell Hobbes, and Holmes Herbert. The cinematography is by Hal Mohr. A Cosmopolitan Production, for Warners. b & w

Captains Courageous (1937)—One of M-G-M's powerhouse moralizing "family" entertainments, it's beefy and rousing, with almost guaranteed tears and laughter for children. Freddie Bartholomew plays the rich brat who learns about life from the fishermen of the Gloucester fleet, especially from Spencer Tracy (as a Portuguese) and with a little help from Mickey Rooney. Victor Fleming keeps the handsome production in motion; the Kipling novel was reworked—sugared— by experienced hands: John Lee Mahin, Marc Connelly, and Dale Van Every. (The film can leave kids upset, though: the father figure dies.) With Melvyn Douglas, the inevitable Lionel Barrymore, John Carradine, Charley Grapewin, Leo G. Carroll, and Jack La Rue, cast against type as a priest; the score is by Franz Waxman. Academy Award for Best Actor (Tracy). (The entire picture was shot on a sound stage, and it looks it.) b & w

The Captain's Paradise (1953)—Alec Guinness leads a double life, and acts out one of the most common fantasies of Western man: as the captain of a ferry steamer, he alternates nights between a cozy middle-class cottage with homebody wife Celia Johnson on the Gibraltar end, and a torrid, opulent apartment with passionately exuberant wife Yvonne De Carlo on the Morocco end. "Two women," he says, "each with half of the things a man wants," and happily split between two lives and two wives, he doesn't realize that he is satisfying only half of each wife's desires. This comedy never quite finds its style, but the two wives are better than any man (or the film) deserves. With Charles Goldner, Miles Malleson, Bill Fraser. Directed by Anthony Kimmins, written by Alec Coppel and Nicholas Phipps. b & w

Car Wash (1976)—A junk-food mixture of poetry, black anger, bathroom humor, routines that have come through the sit-com mill, and worn-to-the-stump faggot jokes. The action is centered on one workday in an L.A. car wash that is white-owned but staffed mostly by blacks. The film's specialty is yanking laughs by having adult blacks do dirtier versions of the standard pranks that naughty kids used to do in comedies. Michael Schultz directed, from a script by Joel Schumacher; the editing (by Christopher Holmes) to the music (by Norman Whitfield) was probably a big factor in the film's box-office success. With Franklyn Ajaye, Lauren Jones, Tracy Reed, Melanie Mayron, Ivan Dixon, Bill Duke, Sully Boyar, Garrett Morris, Clarence Muse, Lorraine Gary, Antonio Fargas, Jack Kehoe, and brief appearances by Richard Pryor, George Carlin, Prof. Irwin Corey, and the Pointer Sisters. Cinematography by Frank Stanley. An Art Linson Production, for Universal. color (See *When the Lights Go Down.*)

Les Carabiniers (1963)—Jean-Luc Godard's film about two blank-faced conscripts who go off to war thinking it a great opportunity to get rich is oddly distanced and pedagogical, and it stumbles along—in a deliberately uninvolving style—for its first hour. But when the men return with their loot, in the form of picture postcards, the sequence is conceived with great wit and is brilliantly prolonged; this huge joke seems to be what everything else was heading toward. For a viewer, the elation of this sequence can make the whole experience seem original and exciting. From a script by Godard, Jean Gruault, and Roberto Rossellini, based on the play *I Carabinieri* by Benjamino Joppolo. In French. b & w

The Card, see *The Promoter*

Carefree (1938)—Fred Astaire plays a psychiatrist who was psychoanalyzed out of thinking he wanted to be a dancer; his friend, Ralph Bellamy, is in love with Ginger Rogers, who's in show business. Ralph, who can't get anywhere with Ginger, sends her to see Fred on a professional basis—to be cured of her indifference to him. Ginger begins to fall for Fred, but he hypnotizes her so that she'll love Ralph; then Fred discovers that he's in love with her himself. It sounds promising, in a chaotic sort of way, but this is one of the least scintillating of the Astaire-Rogers pictures; there's too much plot and too much leaden comedy between the dances. It doesn't have the spirit of their best films, or the Art Deco furnishings, either—the production numbers are performed in an ugly, cluttered country-club set. Fred's profession allows for the lovely, hypnotic "Change Partners" dance when Ginger is in a trance—it's probably the film's high point. Ginger is wackily sexy-funny in some of the dance scenes, and she gets to wear big halo hats, but her timing is off, or maybe the timing of the director, Mark Sandrich, is off, because there's a lot of footage of her trying to be chipper and charming yet coming across as awfully dumb. It may be that nobody could work up much conviction in the material, written by Allan Scott, Ernest Pagano, Dudley Nichols, and Hagar Wilde. The supporting cast is also less than luminous. As

Ginger's aunt, Luella Gear seems numbly confused by her feeble lines. Also with Jack Carson, Franklin Pangborn, Hattie McDaniel, Walter Kingsford, Tom Tully, Kay Sutton, and Clarence Kolb. The Irving Berlin score includes "The Yam." Technically, this was the next to last of the Astaire-Rogers R K O series, which had begun in 1933, with *Flying Down to Rio,* but actually it marked the end of an era; their last R K O picture, *The Story of Vernon and Irene Castle,* wasn't a contemporary musical comedy—it was a period piece, a biographical extravaganza. Produced by Pandro S. Berman, for R K O. b & w

Carmen Jones (1954)—The setting of Bizet's *Carmen* has been changed from Mérimée's Spain to Jacksonville, Florida, and Meilhac's and Halévy's libretto has been rewritten by Oscar Hammerstein II, who provides colloquial, rather basic lyrics, but the music retains much of its excitement in this flamboyant version with an all-black cast. Dorothy Dandridge is a marvellous-looking Carmen—fiery and petulant, with whiplash hips in a hot-pink skirt. (Her singing is dubbed by Marilyn Horne.) The man Carmen destroys is played by Harry Belafonte, who seems miscast and miserable (he's also dubbed). It's somewhat frustrating to watch performers who *can* sing but aren't allowed to; of the principals, only Pearl Bailey sings in her own voice—she comes up with a whacking rendition of the Gypsy Song. She's pure comic energy up there in the center of the screen, and the director, Otto Preminger, seems to just stand back, enjoying her, like the rest of us. Made from a hit Broadway musical, this movie is terribly uneven—best when it's gaudy and electric, worst in its more realistically staged melodramatic moments, especially toward the end. Overall, it's an entertaining show, choreographed by Herbert Ross, featuring the dancers Carmen de Lavallade and Archie Savage, and with a cast that includes Diahann Carroll, Olga James, Joe Adams, Nick Stewart, and Brock Peters, who plays Sgt. Brown and also dubs the singing voice of Rum, played by Roy Glenn. Adapted to the screen by Harry Kleiner; art direction by Edward L. Ilou. 20th Century-Fox. color

Carnal Knowledge (1971)—Jules Feiffer, who wrote the screenplay, had what sounds like a promising idea: to take two college roommates in the mid-1940s and follow their sexual attitudes and activities through to their middle age in the early 70s. But Feiffer rigged the case and wrote a grimly purposeful tract on depersonalization and how we use each other sexually as objects, and, in the director Mike Nichols' cold, slick style, the movie is like a neon sign spelling out the soullessness of neon. Glowering Jack Nicholson (who becomes a tax lawyer) is a jock with a big-breast fixation, and we watch him over the years yelling at his mistress, Ann-Margret, and exploding in frustration as he becomes more and more impotent, until finally he's being lied to and serviced by a prostitute (Rita Moreno). Arthur Garfunkel (who becomes a doctor) is a mild drip who goes from a dull, proper marriage with Candice Bergen to an affair with a snooty bitch (Cynthia O'Neal) and winds up with a curly-haired, teen-age hippie (Carol Kane). It's a parallel history of dissatisfaction and emptiness, and as the men age the picture scores off them repeatedly and never lets them win a round. In the film's politicized morality, if well-heeled Americans have sex it must be vile, because how could they possibly know anything about love? As Mike Nichols has directed the material, the effects are almost all achieved through the line readings, and the cleverness is unpleasant—it's all surface and whacking emphasis. This surefire, hit-it-on-the-button comedy style has about the same relationship to humor that belting has to singing. An Avco Embassy–Joseph E. Levine Production. color (See *Deeper into Movies*.)

Un Carnet de bal (1937)—An episodic, star-studded film, directed by Julien Duvivier, that had a great success here in the emerging foreign film theatres and was widely imitated in Hollywood and Europe. A wealthy, nostalgic widow (Marie Bell) goes in search of what might have been. She sets out to find the men listed on the dance program of her first ball, 20 years before, and manages to locate many of the most famous French actors of the day: Harry Baur, who has become a monk; Raimu, a town mayor; Louis Jouvet, a crook; Pierre Blanchar, a shady doctor; Fernandel, a hairdresser; Pierre-Richard Willm, an Alpine guide. The performances form an astonishing catalogue of acting styles. Even Françoise Rosay turns up. People who saw this movie in their youth still talk about its big scene—the revelation of the discrepancy between what the widow remembered as her first great ball and the poor little provincial dance it actually was. And they tend to have the same kind of nostalgia toward *Un Carnet de bal*—which despite its stars and its awards is a little tawdry, too. As a work of romantic entertainment it doesn't compare with Duvivier's other 1937 film, *Pépé Le Moko*. But it's redolent of the 30s, and it could serve as a text on the varieties of French acting. Music by Maurice Jaubert; the five writers included Henri Jeanson and Duvivier. In French. b & w

Les Carnets du Major Thompson, see *The French They Are a Funny Race*

Carnival in Flanders *La Kermesse héroïque* (1935)—It is a day in 1616; a Spanish regiment comes to a town in occupied Flanders. The cowardly burghers hide, but their charming ladies meet the challenge, and in the morning the Spaniards depart, poorer in worldly

C

goods, richer in experience. Jacques Feyder directed this classic comedy in the styles of Bruegel and Boccaccio, and it's almost too close to perfect; it's so archly classic that it isn't really very funny. From a script by Charles Spaak. With Françoise Rosay, Louis Jouvet, Jean Murat, Alerme, Micheline Cheirel. Designed by Lazare Meerson; cinematography by Harry Stradling. (This much-honored film's sophisticated approach to sexual collaboration would, of course, have been impossible in the 40s.) In French. b & w

Carny (1980)—As the teen-age small-town girl looking for excitement who joins up with a carnival that's travelling through, Jodie Foster has a marvellous sexy bravado. With her long legs and knowledgeable eyes, this blooming young actress gives the picture a toehold on recognizable human experience. But the carny partners she hooks up with are played by Gary Busey and Robbie Robertson, and it's hard to know what they think they're doing. Busey is the carnival's hostile, sadistic bozo (who manipulates customers by insulting them), yet we can't see what his meanness comes out of—he seems to be an open-faced farm boy. And the heavy-lidded Robertson, who was so remarkable as himself in *The Last Waltz*, Scorsese's concert film about The Band, acts like a burnt-out dowager here. His twitches and druggy, Garbo-esque expressions don't connect with anything. The lowlife carny world has been shot for funky exoticism, and the director, Robert Kaylor, overdoes it—the images are too grotesque, too ominous, too garish, and the music (by Alex North) is too insistent. There isn't enough humor and there isn't enough clarity about how things work; it doesn't help to have a carny hand say to somebody, "You still don't get it, do you?" when we don't either. There's an authentically eerie scene of Harold the 600-pound Fat Man (George Emerson) singing, and an even

eerier moment when he goes out into the rain—presumably the only shower big enough for him. The dialogue, from Thomas Baum's screenplay, is often colorful, but the picture is heavy. The minute Elisha Cook, Jr., turns up as an endearing crazy, it's obvious he's going to be bumped off, and there's an ugly sequence with Jodie Foster apparently trapped by a sexual psychopath. With Meg Foster, who gives off a lot of energy, though she has nothing to do, and Kenneth McMillan and Bert Remsen. Cinematography by Harry Stradling, Jr. A Lorimar film; released by United Artists. color

The Carpetbaggers (1964)—In the tawdry, lavish *roman-à-clef* genre, but of its kind fairly energetic, and the pop psychology is self-serious enough to be funny. The source is a Harold Robbins novel with a thinly disguised Howard Hughes for its playboy-hero—spoiled-rotten, rich Jonas Cord, Jr. (George Peppard). (Robert Ryan gave a far more compelling performance based on Hughes in the Max Ophuls film *Caught*, but Peppard is just right for this picture.) The characters, synthesized from old scandal sheets, are impersonated by Alan Ladd (it was his last film), Carroll Baker, Lew Ayres, Martha Hyer, Elizabeth Ashley, Leif Erickson, Audrey Totter, Martin Balsam, Archie Moore, and Robert Cummings. Directed by Edward Dmytryk; written by John Michael Hayes; produced by Joseph E. Levine, for Paramount. color

Carrie (1952)—William Wyler's version of Theodore Dreiser's *Sister Carrie* is graced by one of Laurence Olivier's finest screen performances. Olivier has always given credit to Wyler for teaching him how to act in the movies when they did *Wuthering Heights* together, but it's in *Carrie* that he showed how much he had learned. As George Hurstwood, the manager of an elegant Chicago grog-and-steak house, who ruins himself for a pretty

121

face (Jennifer Jones), Olivier is so impassioned and so painfully touching that everything else in the movie, including the girl whose story it's meant to be, fades into insignificance. With Miriam Hopkins as the rigidly unforgiving Mrs. Hurstwood, and Eddie Albert as a dry-goods salesman. Adapted by Ruth and Augustus Goetz. Paramount. b & w

Carrie (1976)—The best scary-funny movie since *Jaws*—a teasing, terrifying, lyrical shocker, directed by Brian De Palma, who has the wickedest baroque sensibility at large in American movies. Pale, gravel-voiced Sissy Spacek gives a classic chameleon performance as a repressed high-school senior whose energy is released only telekinetically, and Piper Laurie plays her deep-voiced, sexy fundamentalist mother. With John Travolta, Nancy Allen, Amy Irving, and William Katt. United Artists. color (See *When the Lights Go Down*.)

Cartouche (1962)—Philippe de Broca's lush comedy extravaganza, full of brocades and brawls—a travesty of cape-and-sword romances that actually outdoes most of them in romanticism. Jean-Paul Belmondo is a goodhearted acrobatic thief (in the Fairbanks-Flynn tradition) operating in 18th-century Paris. He hooks up with a gypsy pickpocket named Venus (Claudia Cardinale), overthrows the nasty leader (Marcel Dalio) of the pickpocket gang, turns it into a crime syndicate, and embarks on a series of Robin Hoodish adventures, giving to the poor the fancy baubles of the rich. The film's high spirits and occasional grand gestures almost make up for its insistently antic tone. With Odile Versois, Jean Rochefort, Noël Roquevert, and Jess Hahn. In French. (A dubbed, English-language version was released under the title *The Thundering Sword*.) color

Casablanca (1942)—Ingrid Bergman became a popular favorite when Humphrey Bogart, as Rick, the most famous saloonkeeper in screen history, treated her like a whore. Although their romance was certified by a collection of Academy Awards, they didn't press their luck and never appeared together again. In the role of the cynic redeemed by love, Bogart became the great adventurer-lover of the screen during the war years. In this film he established the figure of the rebellious hero—the lone wolf who hates and defies officialdom (and in the movies he fulfilled a universal fantasy: he got away with it). Questioned about his purpose and motives, he informs the police: "I came to Casablanca for the waters." "Waters? What waters? We're in the desert." "I was misinformed." It's far from a great film, but it has a special appealingly schlocky romanticism, and you're never really pressed to take its melodramatic twists and turns seriously. The international cast includes Paul Henreid, Conrad Veidt, Sydney Greenstreet, Claude Rains, Peter Lorre, Marcel Dalio, Helmut Dantine, S. Z. Sakall, Joy Page, Leonid Kinskey, Curt Bois, Dan Seymour, Ludwig Stossel, Ilka Gruning, Frank Puglia, Madeleine LeBeau, John Qualen, and, memorably, Dooley Wilson singing "As Time Goes By." Academy Awards: Best Picture; Director (Michael Curtiz); Screenplay (Julius J. and Philip G. Epstein and Howard Koch). And the Thalberg Memorial Award went to the producer, Hal B. Wallis. Based on the play *Everybody Comes to Rick's*, by Murray Burnett and Joan Alison. Warners. b & w

The Casino Murder Case (1935)—One in the Philo Vance series, but with Paul Lukas taking over the role created by William Powell, and which Basil Rathbone and Warren William had also appeared in. Lukas is smooth, though his Magyar accent blurs some of his *mots*; he's obviously battling with the English language. M-G-M surrounded him with an unusually bright supporting cast, headed by the rising young Rosalind Russell, and including Alison Skipworth, Louise Fazenda, Eric Blore, Ted Healy, Leo G. Carroll, Donald Cook, Arthur Byron, Leslie Fenton, Purnell Pratt, Isabel Jewell, and Claudelle Kaye. The plot, which involves a rich family of neurotics, is short on mystery, but Florence Ryerson and Edgar Allan Woolf, who adapted the S. S. Van Dine novel, supplied an amiable, wisecracking script. Directed by Edwin L. Marin; score by Dmitri Tiomkin. b & w

Casino Royale (1967)—This Charles K. Feldman production, an all-star send-up of the Bond films, with multiple Bonds and multiple directors, has some laughs, but it makes one terribly conscious of wastefulness. Jokes and plots and possibilities are thrown away along with huge, extravagant sets, and famous performers go spinning by. The best excuse for seeing it is that toward the end Woody Allen (in a dual role as Jimmy Bond and as the head of F.A.N.G.) has his best moments yet on film. The directors included Joe McGrath, Robert Parrish, Val Guest, Ken Hughes, and John Huston, who also acted in it; the writers possibly included Wolf Mankowitz, Ben Hecht, Terry Southern, and Billy Wilder. With Peter Sellers, David Niven, Peter O'Toole, Orson Welles, Charles Boyer, William Holden, George Raft, Jean-Paul Belmondo, Vladek Sheybal, Ursula Andress, Deborah Kerr, Jacqueline Bisset, Daliah Lavi, and Joanna Pettet. Columbia. color

Casque d'or (1952)—Simone Signoret had her finest role (until *Room at the Top*) as a gigolette with a glorious helmet of golden hair in Jacques Becker's sultry, poetic account of the Paris underworld in 1900. Her performance is a triumph of sensuality: faintly smiling, she is so intensely, ripely physical that she takes command of the screen. Becker introduces a world of cutthroats, apaches, and gun molls, and then subtly evokes an atmosphere that gives meaning and passion—and an overdose of doom—to their rivalries and intrigues. The love scenes between Signoret and Serge Reggiani are unusually simple and tender; perhaps because of this, the grim conclusion is almost insupportably painful. The movie is beautifully made, yet there's something touristy about its view of lowlife—"Look, *they* have feelings, too." With Claude Dauphin as the gang leader, Raymond Bussières, and Gaston Modot. Written by Becker and Jacques Companeez; art direction by Jean d'Eaubonne. In French. b & w

Cast a Giant Shadow (1966)—Melville Shavelson wrote and directed this big biographical action picture about Colonel "Mickey" Marcus (Kirk Douglas), a West Point graduate and an adviser to President Roosevelt during the Second World War, who, at the request of the Israelis, went to Israel in the late 40s to re-organize the army. In this account, based on a book by Ted Berkman, Mickey Marcus is the master strategist who leads the Israelis to victory in the war with the Arabs. Shavelson admires him too much to make him human; he doesn't become a myth—he's a blank. And Shavelson is so eager to please the public that he throws in guest stars, such as Frank Sinatra and Yul Brynner, and agonizes over Mickey's moral conflict between Angie Dickinson, the wife he leaves at home in the U.S., and Senta Berger, the female warrior he takes up with. Even those willing to accept the hours of incoherence and banality may recoil at the obscenity of being asked to experience the horrors of Dachau as reflected in John Wayne's bleary eyes. With Topol, who, briefly, revitalizes the audience, and Michael Hordern, James Donald, Stathis Giallelis, Ruth White, Gordon Jackson, Luther Adler, Gary Merrill, and Jeremy Kemp.

Cinematography by Aldo Tonti. Released by United Artists. color

Casualties of War (1989)—A great, intense movie about war and rape, based on a Vietnam incident of 1966 that was reported in *The New Yorker*, October 18, 1969, by the late Daniel Lang. He gave an emotionally devastating account of the actions of a squad of five American soldiers who kidnapped a Vietnamese village girl, raped her, and then covered up their crime by killing her. One of the five men refused to take part in the rape, and, despite threats and attempts on his life, forced the Army to bring the other four to trial. He's the one who suffers from guilt: he can't forgive himself for his inability to save the girl's life. Directed by Brian De Palma, the movie is the culmination of his best work. Sean Penn gives a daring performance as the squad's 20-year-old leader; Michael J. Fox is impressive as the soldier who can't keep quiet; Thuy Thu Le is the dazed, battered girl who haunts the movie long before she's dead. Also with Erik King as Brownie, John Leguizamo as Diaz, John C. Reilly as Hatcher, Don Harvey as Clark, Ving Rhames as Lieutenant Reilly, and Sam Robards as the chaplain. The adaptation (too explicit in a few places) is by David Rabe; the cinematography is by Stephen H. Burum; the music is by Ennio Morricone. Columbia. color (See *Movie Love*.)

A Cat and Two Women *Neko to Shozo to Futari no Onna* (1956)—A wry psychological comedy about a man who prefers his cat to his two wives. The tart flavor of the film derives from the familial nastiness: one can't like any of them, one can't even really like the cat. Some of the most famous Japanese players are the leads: the first wife is the legendary Isuzu Yamada (she was in over 300 movies between 1929 and 1956, had been married six times, and was still playing romantic roles); Kyoko Kagawa, usually a demure heroine, plays the unsympathetic second wife; Hisaya Morishige is the indolent, cat-loving husband; the character actress Cheiko Naniwa plays his mother. The manner in which these four scheme for affection and power, using the cat as a decoy, is a perverse object lesson in Japanese mores. The story (by Junichiro Tanizaki) is set among shopkeepers at a small seaside town near Osaka, in the Kansai district. The director, Shiro Toyoda, is more traditional than is usually the case with Japanese directors whose films reach this country, and the narrative construction is a bit trying for American moviegoers, but the film is distinctive enough to be worth the small effort of adjustment. (Japanese movies are notorious for badly selected, derivative music; this one is an exception.) In Japanese. b & w

Cat Ballou (1965)—A self-consciously cute parody Western about a girl (Jane Fonda) who turns train robber, a lovable old drunken wreck of a gunfighter (Lee Marvin), two gun-shy young cattle rustlers (Michael Callan, Dwayne Hickman), a bronco-busting Indian (Tom Nardini), and assorted robberies, killings, and wisecracks. There are occasional good lines and some nice things: Nat King Cole singing "They'll Never Make Her Cry"; Lee Marvin's ritual preparations for a gunfight; Marvin mistaking funeral candles for a birthday celebration. But mainly it's full of sort-of-funny and trying-to-be-funny ideas. The director Elliot Silverstein's spoofy tone is ineptitude, coyly disguised. Adapted from Roy Chanslor's novel, by Walter Newman and Frank R. Pierson. With Stubby Kaye, John Marley, Bruce Cabot, J. C. Flippen, and Reginald Denny. Columbia. color (See *Kiss Kiss Bang Bang*.)

Cat on a Hot Tin Roof (1958)—The Tennessee Williams play about the girl (Elizabeth Taylor) whose husband (Paul Newman)

doesn't want to have sex with her. Much hocus-pocus about the reasons; when the "true" reason is revealed it sounds the hokiest. But Taylor looks very desirable, and the cast is full of actors whooping it up with Southern accents (Burl Ives, Judith Anderson, Madeleine Sherwood). Directed by Richard Brooks. M-G-M. CinemaScope, color

Cat People (1942)—The psychoanalyst (Tom Conway) calmly explains to his patient (Simone Simon) that her idea that she is turning into a member of the cat family is a fantasy; she silences him with fang and talon. Val Lewton made his name as a producer with this ironic horror film, produced for R K O on a minuscule budget. While other B-budget horror producers were still using gorillas, haunted houses, and disembodied arms, Lewton and the director, Jacques Tourneur, employed suggestion, creepy sound effects, and inventive camera angles, leaving everything to the viewers' fear-filled imagination. Lewton pictures aren't really very good, but they're so much more imaginative than most of the horror films that other producers were grinding out at the time that his ingenuity seemed practically revolutionary. Some of the sequences, such as the scare at the swimming pool, are in their own way classic. The acting of most of the cast isn't up to the effects; with Kent Smith as the Cat Woman's husband, Jane Randolph, Jack Holt, and Alan Napier. Written by DeWitt Bodeen; cinematography by Nicholas Musuraca; editing by Mark Robson. b & w

Cat People (1982)—Working with his team—the visual consultant Ferdinando Scarfiotti, the cinematographer John Bailey, and the composer Giorgio Moroder—the director Paul Schrader is perfecting an apocalyptic swank. Each shot looks like an album cover for records you don't ever want to play. The picture (it's set in New Orleans) is meant

to be poetic and "legendary." It has all the furnishings for a religious narrative about Eros and Thanatos, but what's going on is that Nastassia Kinski and Malcolm McDowell—the sister and brother with black leopards inside them—are jumping out of their skins and leaving little puddles of guck behind. The obscure proceedings are often ludicrous (especially in the orange-colored primal-dream sequences), yet you don't get to pass the time by laughing, because it's all so queasy and so confusingly put together that you feel shut out. Just when a scene begins to hold some interest, Schrader cuts away from it; the crucial things seem to be happening between the scenes. The film is comatose; you're brought into it only by the camera tricks or the special-effects horrors, or, perhaps, the nude scenes. With John Heard, Annette O'Toole, Ruby Dee, and Ed Begley, Jr. From a script by Alan Ormsby that's a total reworking of the much simpler 1942 film of the same title. Universal. color (See *Taking It All In*.)

Catch-22 (1970)—Mike Nichols' third picture was this hugely ambitious failure. He gave Joseph Heller's World War II novel—a black comedy about the insanity of military life— a grandiloquent staging, with Terry Southern–style caricatures out of *Dr. Strangelove* and Fellini-style episodes set in Rome, and the picture got so heavy and messagey that the ironies were buried. There's a beautiful flight-tower sequence early on, and there are startling effects and good revue touches here and there, but the picture goes on and on, as if it were determined to impress us. It goes on so long that it cancels itself out, even out of people's memories; it was long awaited and then forgotten almost instantly. With Alan Arkin as Yossarian, Jon Voight, Richard Benjamin, Art Garfunkel, Buck Henry (who also wrote the script), Martin Balsam, Orson Welles, Bob Balaban, Paula Prentiss, Martin

Sheen, Jack Gilford, Peter Bonerz, Charles Grodin, Tony Perkins, Bob Newhart, and, in a particularly offensive scene, Marcel Dalio. The acting of some of the high-ranking officers is so gross that at times one thinks the moral must be that as soon as your rank reaches major, you're a monster. Cinematography by David Watkin. Paramount. color

Catch Us If You Can, see *Having a Wild Weekend*

The Catered Affair (1956)—Forgettable. Paddy Chayefsky's TV drama, adapted by Gore Vidal, of whom there is no detectable trace. A Bronx cab-driver (Ernest Borgnine) and his shrewish, socially ambitious wife (Bette Davis) wrangle about whether their daughter (Debbie Reynolds) should have a big wedding or a simple ceremony, in which case the father could invest his money in a new taxi. The wife's leprechaun brother (Barry Fitzgerald)—full of Gaelic shenanigans—gets into this drab argument. Richard Brooks directed. With Rod Taylor, Madge Kennedy, and Dorothy Stickney. M-G-M. b & w

Cattle Annie and Little Britches (1980)—An unusual Western with a tip-top cast. The movie is based on the lives of two adolescent girls in the late 19th century who became infatuated with the outlaw heroes they'd read about in Ned Buntline's stories and ran off to join them. The girls (Amanda Plummer, who is excitingly, weirdly lyric in her movie début, and the fastidious young actress Diane Lane) find the mangy, demoralized remnants of the Doolin-Dalton gang, led by the aging Bill Doolin (Burt Lancaster), and try to inspire them to live up to the legend created by Buntline. Scott Glenn, in long sideburns and a mustache, is Bill Dalton, and the gang also includes John Savage. The director, Lamont

Johnson, has a warm, honest touch that the actors respond to. He even manages to hold down Rod Steiger, who plays the beady-eyed U.S. marshal chasing Doolin, and the result is one of Steiger's best performances in years. Though the script, by David Eyre and Robert Ward, from Ward's book, doesn't seem to build, and the film isn't as explosively funny as it should be, most of the incidents have a neat, dry humor, and Burt Lancaster's Doolin is a magnificent, sagging old buffalo—a charmer. The cinematography (with crisp, intense color) is by Larry Pizer. A King-Hitzig Production; Universal. color (See *Taking It All In*.)

Caught (1948)—This movie, with its portrait of Howard Hughes, is probably the most American of Max Ophuls' American movies. Ophuls had suffered at Hughes' hands—had wasted time on worthless projects and been referred to as "the oaf." In this movie, a vicious, half-mad millionaire (Robert Ryan) marries a young innocent (Barbara Bel Geddes) in order to spite his analyst. The movie centers on the desperate predicament of the girl when, pregnant, she realizes that she is just a cynical joke to her husband. James Mason plays the doctor who tries to help her. Curt Bois appears as the millionaire's slimy pimp—a worm who finally turns. This well-acted, little-publicized melodrama was a financial failure, but it's emotionally complex and has strong undercurrents. Robert Ryan is very convincingly scary. The script, by Arthur Laurents, was ostensibly based on the novel *Wild Calendar*, by Libby Block, which Enterprise Pictures had hired Ophuls to do, but which he had no interest in. Actually, Laurents built the script on stories that Ophuls told him about Hughes, and on the accounts given by one of Hughes' girls. Cinematography by Lee Garmes; music by Frederick Hollander. M-G-M. b & w

Cavalcade (1933)—An orgy of British self-congratulation in the restrained, clipped style of Noël Coward, with the added know-how of an American producer (Winfield Sheehan) and a Hollywood director (Frank Lloyd). Americans doted on this gilded tearjerker that begins with Clive Brook and his wife, Diana Wynyard, toasting the advent of the 20th century, and follows the fortunes of their son (Frank Lawton) and their servants (Herbert Mundin and Una O'Connor) up to the present—i.e., when the picture was made. The self-conscious good taste of it all creaks, but Noël Coward knows plenty of tricks, and the performers know how to get the most out of his lines. The cast includes Ursula Jeans, Billy Bevan, Beryl Mercer, and John Warburton and Margaret Lindsay honeymooning on the Titanic. Adaptation of Noël Coward's play by Reginald Berkeley; William Cameron Menzies worked on the war scenes. Fox. b & w

Caveman (1981)—A funky, buoyant farce, in which Ringo Starr plays Atouk, a peewee caveman who, in order to win the beautiful Lana (Barbara Bach), learns to stand upright and, in one great day, discovers fire and then cooking. That night, he and his group, sitting around the first campfire, discover musical instruments; in about 10 seconds, they're chanting and singing, and 30 seconds later they have moved on to syncopation, and Atouk has become a rock drummer. Making his début as a movie director, Carl Gottlieb (a comedy actor and a co-writer on *Jaws*, and *Jaws II*, and *The Jerk*), gets crack timing from the whole cast and never lets a routine go on too long. The picture doesn't have the dirt or meanness or malice to make you explode with laughter, but it's consistently enjoyable. With John Matuszak, Dennis Quaid, Shelley Long, Jack Gilford, Avery Schreiber, and four dinosaurs. (Created by highly sophisticated animation techniques, they're domesticated, parody versions of the scary monsters in sci-fi horror films.) Written by Gottlieb and Rudy DeLuca, who devised a 15-word language for the cave people; it's indebted about equally to comic-strip balloonese and Yiddish. Shot in Mexico; with a satiric musical score by Lalo Schifrin. United Artists. color (See *Taking It All In*.)

C. C. and Company (1970)—A tame sort of porno-wheeler with Joe Namath saving high-fashion writer Ann-Margret from rape by his outlaw-motorcycle gang, led by Moon (William Smith). Namath has a light, high voice, and he's generally mild and camera-shy—he's rather sweet, in the manner of sub-teen favorites. There's no explanation for what this clean-cut fellow is doing among the crude pack. The film has its visual quirks: the gang's girls make the sexual overtures to the men, and these bouts lead to quick dissolves, but when Namath lands hard-to-get Ann-Margret they roll and roll while the camera makes lyrical hay. The movie is too silly to be offensive; it contains ads for pleasures such as Kraft Cheese and the Flamingo Hotel in Las Vegas. Directed by Seymour Robbie (in extenuation, it's his first); produced by Allen Carr and the scenarist Roger Smith. Avco-Embassy. color

Celui qui doit mourir, see *He Who Must Die*

C'Era una Volta, see *More Than a Miracle*

César (1936)—The last film of the Marcel Pagnol trilogy (after *Marius* and *Fanny*) is named for the pivotal character, played by Raimu. César, the proprietor of a waterfront bar—and the soul of the trilogy—is the father of Marius (Pierre Fresnay), who runs off to sea, leaving his fiancée, Fanny (Orane Démazis), pregnant. She marries the kind, middle-aged sailmaker, Panisse (Charpin). In this concluding film—the only one of the three actually directed by Pagnol—Marius and Fanny are, at last, reunited. Pagnol wrote the story for the stage in the 20s, and, despite the Marseilles setting, the films are very literal-minded and constricted. But the actors redeem much of the pedestrian filmmaking. After Raimu's death, J. B. Priestley wrote, "We can magically command him to return out of those flat tins of film, and show us again his rich humanity and massive, deliberate art. . . . The French should erect a monument to the memory of this player, who reminded us that France had known a Rabelais, a Molière, a Balzac." (There was a 1938 American version, *Port of Seven Seas*, with Wallace Beery at his most offensively "human" as César, and a Broadway musical, *Fanny*, which compressed the trilogy, was filmed in 1961, retaining the score only as background music and with a miscast Charles Boyer as César.) In French. b & w

César and Rosalie (1972)—Yves Montand, in a jovial, parodistic performance as César, a scrap-metal tycoon—a super-confident self-made man who enjoys being No. 1 in work and in play. He adores Rosalie (Romy Schneider), and there are no obstacles to their happiness; they have everything—yet almost inexplicably, before our eyes, it evaporates. An old love of Rosalie's—an eminent cartoonist (the wan, elegantly despondent Sami Frey)—turns up, and when she sees him again, her feelings about César change. Nobody's fault—just bad luck; it's as if César were cuckolded by a moonbeam. Whenever you think the relationships are going to be stabilized into formulas, the picture wiggles free. It's a fluky, wry ode on the imperfect, haphazard nature of romantic love. What sustains it is that it never takes its three subjects too solemnly; the movie's essential frivolousness makes its melancholy tone ac-

ceptable: we can laugh at the characters' self-centered sorrows. Directed by Claude Sautet, the film suggests a *chanson*. The script is by Sautet and Jean-Loup Dabadie; the whirling, soft-color cinematography is by Jean Boffety. With Umberto Orsini and Isabelle Huppert. In French. (See *Reeling*.)

Cet Obscur Objet du désir, see *That Obscure Object of Desire*

Chained (1934)—Joan Crawford and Clark Gable and a superabundance of M-G-M's big, turgid, melodramatic emotions. It's all somewhere between camp and plod, but with a strong enough sexual current between Crawford and Gable to make it a hit. She plays a woman who's going with a married man (Otto Kruger) when she meets Gable. Clarence Brown directed; the cast includes Stuart Erwin, Akim Tamiroff, Una O'Connor, Marjorie Gateson, and Mickey Rooney. The script by John Lee Mahin was based on an Edgar Selwyn story. b & w

The Champ (1931)—Jackie Cooper, who had just scored in the good-natured *Skippy*, was asked to carry this soggy load of heartbreaking melodrama on his all-too-valiant little shoulders. He plays the pathetic son of an alcoholic ex-prizefighter (Wallace Beery, who pulled out more than a few stops and won the Academy Award for best actor) in a tedious story devised by Frances Marion (she got an Academy Award, too)—something about Tia Juana and horse racing and boxing. King Vidor directed. M-G-M. b & w

The Champagne Murders *Le Scandale* (1968)—Odd, sardonic murder mystery, directed by Claude Chabrol, released here in an English-language version that never sounds quite right. The characters are affluent, bored, and ambivalent; Chabrol himself seems rather ambivalent about the whole handsome, hollow project. With Maurice Ronet, Tony Perkins, Stéphane Audran, and Yvonne Furneaux. Cinematography by Jean Rabier. Universal. color

The Chant of Jimmie Blacksmith (1978)— This great Australian film was taken from Thomas Keneally's novel, which is like Nat Turner's story as a lusty ironist—an Irish Nabokov, perhaps—might have written it. The director, Fred Schepisi, dramatizes the inability of the displaced Europeans at the turn of the century (scrabbling tightwads who got where they are by self-denial) to understand the aborigines who live in the remnants of a tribal society with an elaborate structure of claims: men are obliged to give a share of their earnings to their kin, even if their kin are drunken and diseased and want the money only to go on a binge. And men offer their wives to visiting kin as a form of hospitality. To the whites, giving money away is unfathomable laxity, and since the black women are so easily available the white men treat the aboriginal settlements as brothels. Jimmie Blacksmith is a product of one of these visits to a tin shanty: a half-caste who is taught by a Methodist minister, he grows up determined to escape the debased existence of aborigines in their hovels by working hard, buying land, and, as the minister's wife has advised him, marrying a nice white girl off a farm, so his children will be only a quarter black and the next generation scarcely black at all. The film is the grotesque, explosive comedy-tragedy of what happens to this young man; trying to improve himself, he's like a hair-raisingly foolish cross between Jude the Obscure and Gunga Din. When he rebels, it isn't out of conscious militancy or a demand for political justice, it's out of helplessness and frustration. It's as if he had let his unconscious take over. He says he has declared war, but he doesn't wage war directly against the men; he attacks the men's

most prized possessions—their robust, well-fed women, their pink-and-white children. With Tommy Lewis as Jimmie, and Freddy Reynolds as laughing Mort, his aborigine half-brother, a loyal, easygoing bum in ragged tweeds who makes us understand what the Europeans have destroyed. This is a large-scale film—a visually impassioned epic. color (See *Taking It All In*.)

Chaos, see *Kaos*

Un Chapeau de paille d'Italie, see *The Italian Straw Hat*

The Chapman Report (1962)—If you want to see how entertaining a trashy American movie can sometimes be, this is a nifty example. It's adapted from an Irving Wallace novel that takes off from *The Kinsey Report*. Chapman (Andrew Duggan) is doing a study of women's sex behavior in a suburb. This silly, opportunistic premise allows for some stunning performances. The 24-year-old Jane Fonda, brittle and skittish in a broad-brimmed hat, proves herself a skillfully naughty comedienne. The comic veteran Glynis Johns is as deft here as she was in 1952, in *The Promoter*, when she explained to Alec Guinness about the death of her rich, old husband on their honeymoon—"The doctor said it was over-exertion." And the greatest surprise is Claire Bloom: as the nympho, she's thin, beautiful, exhibitionistic, and quite brilliant. The movie is burdened with Efrem Zimbalist, Jr., but to balance that it has Henry Daniell, and it has color design by Hoyningen-Huené and some amusing dialogue, by Wyatt Cooper and Don M. Mankiewicz. Directed by George Cukor, the picture was initially reputed to be even more of a kick than it is now; Cukor said his version was recut by Darryl F. Zanuck. The cast includes Shelley Winters, Ray Danton, Cloris Leachman, Ty Hardin, Harold J. Stone, John

Dehner, Jack Cassidy, Corey Allen, Grady Sutton, and Chad Everett. Warners.

Chappaqua (1967)—Conrad Rooks stars himself in this hokey phantasmagorical-autobiographical account of a spoiled rich boy's drug visions and his attempted cure at a sanatorium in Paris; Jean-Louis Barrault is the attending physician. Eugen Schüfftan started as the cameraman, then was replaced by Robert Frank, who shot most of the startlingly elegant footage, which has been stunningly edited; the sound is also often experimental. But Rooks is at his peak when he shuffles around in his nightie, blinking sleepily; when he tries to act, he's hopeless. He financed the film and takes credit as both director and writer, but there is little evidence of either function. The film seems auto-erotic, in a pre-sexual way; it's put together as a psychedelic turn-on, mostly about the fun and glamour of addiction, with a score by Ravi Shankar, who also appears in the film, as do William S. Burroughs, Allen Ginsberg, Ornette Coleman, Paula Pritchett, Swami Satchidananda, Moondog, and the Fugs. color

Charade (1963)—A debonair macabre thriller—romantic, scary, satisfying. "How do you shave in there?" Audrey Hepburn asks, putting her finger up to the cleft in Cary Grant's chin. (She's trying to seduce a legend.) This piece of high-style kitsch, directed by Stanley Donen, from a smooth, smart script by Peter Stone and Marc Behm, is as enjoyable in its way as *The Big Sleep*. (Yet it was widely panned when it came out; the mixed tones of comedy and grisliness seemed to offend the press.) The setting is Paris. Hepburn is a young widow who is stalked by the mourners at her husband's funeral. With Walter Matthau, and James Coburn, George Kennedy, and Ned Glass as scheming thugs. The score is by Henry Mancini; the cinema-tography is by Charles Lang, Jr.; Hepburn's clothes are by Givenchy. Universal. color

The Charge of the Light Brigade (1936)—In this Michael Curtiz version—a military swashbuckler—the foreground story is conventional nonsense about two brothers (Errol Flynn and Patric Knowles), Lancers in India, who have quarreled over a girl (Olivia de Havilland). In historical terms the film is simply a bad joke, yet the patriotic inanities serve a rousing melodramatic function and when the charge comes it is so spectacularly staged and choreographed that it takes over the movie, and it is really all that one remembers. This sequence is a testament to the virtuosity of the second unit. A Warner Brothers production, from a screenplay by Michael Jacoby and Rowland Leigh, with a Max Steiner score. With Nigel Bruce, Donald Crisp, David Niven, C. Aubrey Smith, Spring Byington, Henry Stephenson, and C. Henry Gordon and J. Carrol Naish, E. E. Clive, Robert Barrat, and Lumsden Hare. b & w

The Charge of the Light Brigade (1968)—Tony Richardson's quasi-absurdist vaudeville-epic—a view of the Crimean War with modern revue humor. It's composed of Victorian vignettes, with fragments of dialogue, mostly a few lines leading to a snapper. It's extravagantly pretty (David Watkin shot it); some of it is very funny (especially John Gielgud as the whimsical, doddering supreme commander of the British forces, and an undressing sequence with Trevor Howard and Jill Bennett). And at times, the satire of political platitudes is excruciatingly entertaining. But Richardson and his scenarist, Charles Wood, seem to shrink everything they touch. This epic has so little feeling for the courage that went with the idiocies of the past that it diminishes itself along with its targets. And at the end what should be the military debacle is instead a debacle of staging—you can't figure out what went wrong or who is responsible. With David Hemmings and Vanessa Redgrave. The interpolated animation (by Richard Williams), which provides the only clear exposition of what's going on in the movie, is remarkably witty and effective. color (See *Going Steady*.)

Charlie Bubbles (1968)—Albert Finney as a rich, incredibly famous writer (from a working-class background) who feels alienated. The details are well written (by Shelagh Delaney), and the movie is photographed by Peter Suschitzky in an extremely complicated style that attempts to produce for us the flat unreality of how things look to Charlie—the world with some vital dimension omitted. There is talent in the movie, but a larger dose of irritation. The dreariness of Charlie's life, though deliberate and stylized, alienates the audience, too. With Liza Minnelli and Billie Whitelaw—she's wonderful as Charlie's ex-wife. Finney directed. Universal. color (See *Going Steady*.)

Chariots of Fire (1981)—The story of the courage and the triumph of two young runners who represented Britain in the 1924 Olympics, held in Paris. The runners—Harold Abrahams (Ben Cross), a wealthy Jewish boy who is a student at Cambridge, and Eric Liddell (Ian Charleson), a Scottish divinity student—win because they have something to run for. The unbelievably self-possessed Abrahams runs against anti-Semitic snobbery and prejudices, represented here, rather grandly, by Lindsay Anderson and John Gielgud, as a pair of gargoyles—masters at Cambridge. The devout Liddell runs in an ecstatic state, because "when I run, I feel His pleasure," and the film is structured so that its big crisis comes when Liddell's qualifying heat is scheduled for a Sunday and he refuses to take part. The picture is a piece of technological lyricism held together by the glue

of simpleminded heroic sentiment; basically, its appeal is in watching a couple of guys win their races. One good scene: a charming flirtation between Abrahams and a young D'Oyly Carte singer-actress, played by Alice Krige, whose cooing, artificial style is a little reminiscent of Joan Greenwood's purring. Produced by David Puttnam; directed by Hugh Hudson (it's his début film); cinematography by David Watkin. With Ian Holm, Cheryl Campbell, Dennis Christopher, Brad Davis, Nigel Havers, Nicholas Farrell, Nigel Davenport, Patrick Magee, and David Yelland as the Prince of Wales. Academy Awards: Best Picture, Original Screenplay (Colin Welland), Score (Vangelis), Costume Design. color (See *Taking It All In*.)

Charley Varrick (1973)—Walter Matthau as a droll, wily bank robber who discovers he has stolen Mafia money, and outsmarts the police and the Mafia, too. He's presented as an underdog figure, an old-timey hood David against the Mafia Goliaths; he traps everyone who stands in his way to freedom, and gets everyone killed. It's noisy and brutal, with sentimental flourishes. The director, Don Siegel, slogs along from scene to scene. This picture's idea of characterization is to have the Mafia man (Joe Don Baker) a boorish racist who says "nigra," and the bland, smooth Mafia-connected banker (John Vernon) an anti-Semite. You may feel sordid watching a scene in which a drunken, cowardly lout (Andy Robinson) slobbers while he's being kicked and butchered. And when the gruesome sequences need suspense, Lalo Schifrin's music beats your ears. With Sheree North, Felicia Farr, and Norman Fell. The script, by Howard Rodman and Dean Riesner, is based on John Reese's novel *The Looters*. Universal. color (See *Reeling*.)

Charly (1968)—Sometimes mawkish pictures (like *David and Lisa* and *To Sir, with Love* and this one) catch on with the public and are taken seriously; characteristically naïve, "sincere," and pitifully clumsy in execution, they are usually based on material that experienced directors are too knowing to attempt. *Charly*, which had already been a heavily anthologized short story ("Flowers for Algernon," by Daniel Keyes), a TV play, and a novel, has the kind of terrible idea that makes what is often called "a classic"—really a stunted perennial. In the movie, directed by Ralph Nelson and adapted by Stirling Silliphant, Charly (Cliff Robertson), the mentally retarded adult whose teacher (Claire Bloom) helps him get brain surgery, tries to rape her as soon as he gets some book learning. Rejected, he becomes a hippie and a Hell's Angel, but he soon goes back to his books and becomes a fantastic, computer-sharp supergenius, and he and the teacher have an affair. The scheming scientists didn't tell him, though: his genius is only temporary—he must go back to being a dummy. This cheap fantasy with its built-in sobs also takes the booby prize for the worst use (yet) of the split screen; it's a slovenly piece of moviemaking and it's full of howlers. *Charly* may represent the unity of schlock form and schlock content—true schlock art. Cliff Robertson's performance won him the Academy Award for Best Actor. With Lilia Skala, Ruth White, Leon Janney, Barney Martin, and Dick Van Patten. Music by Ravi Shankar. Produced by Selmur Pictures, a subsidiary of ABC. color (See *Going Steady*.)

Le Charme discret de la bourgeoisie, see *The Discreet Charm of the Bourgeoisie*

The Chase (1966)—Marlon Brando as the sheriff of a corrupt, blood-lusting Texas town in the mythical America of liberal sadomasochistic fantasies. Lillian Hellman wrote the screenplay (from Horton Foote's material), and the little foxes really took over. Our vines have no tender grapes left in this hellhole of wife-swapping, nigger-hating, and nigger-lover-hating, where people are motivated by dirty sex or big money, and you can tell which as soon as they say their first lines. Many people all over the world blame Texas for the assassination of Kennedy—as if the murder had boiled up out of the unconscious of the people there—and the film exploits and confirms this hysterical view, going so far as to provide a facsimile of Jack Ruby's shooting of Oswald, with a racist, who is, of course, a white, Gentile Southerner, as a substitute for Ruby, and a totally innocent hero (Robert Redford) as a substitute for Oswald. The producer, Sam Spiegel, said that it was about "the consequences of affluence," and it does suggest *La Dolce Vita* on the range. Lillian Hellman publicly expressed her dissatisfaction with the results, and it was generally acknowledged that the director, Arthur Penn (who tried to set things on fire with the old Elia Kazan bazooka), didn't have artistic control over the production. But the picture affects some people very strongly, and it has a considerable reputation, especially in Europe. With Jane Fonda, Angie Dickinson, Miriam Hopkins, E. G. Marshall, Robert Duvall, Janice Rule, James Fox, and Henry Hull. Columbia. color (See *Kiss Kiss Bang Bang*.)

Un Chien andalou (1928)—Even if you're prepared for the famous shock image of the sliced eye, Luis Buñuel's and Salvador Dali's short silent film has the hallucinatory and incendiary effect they sought. Some of the images have great poetic force, and at times they have an erotic humor that one has difficulty explaining, even to oneself. With Pierre Batcheff as the cyclist, Dali as the priest, and Buñuel as the man with the razor. b & w

The Childhood of Maxim Gorky *Detsvo Gorkovo* (1938)—This is the first film of the justly celebrated trilogy directed by Mark

Donskoi, based on the memoirs of Maxim Gorky and dealing with the early experiences that turned him into a writer. (The second film is *My Apprenticeship* and the third is *My Universities*.) The trilogy is episodic and uneven, but it's charged with a lyric, revolutionary romanticism; it is also believed to be fair and exact in its portrait of czarist Russia. This first film has a wonderful spaciousness; the landscapes are vast and serene, as the boy Alexei (played by Alexei Lyarsky) observes the grandparents who are raising him. The grandfather (Mark Troyanovski) is brutal and authoritarian, and is wasting the family's resources, but the grandmother (Varvara Massalitinova) is a wonder—she has the understanding that her husband lacks. Though the characters are fully realized, it's the expressiveness of the images of the Volga that stays with you. The visual beauty seems to be what holds the episodes together. Donskoi and I. Gruzdev did the unusually faithful adaptation for all three films. In Russian. b & w

The Children Are Watching Us *I Bambini ci Guardano* (1942)—In this film, Vittorio De Sica found his writer, Cesare Zavattini, and his theme—the destruction of innocence. As in his later works, the enemy is human injustice—not intentional injustice, but what people are driven to do to each other. This is one of those rare movies that are so finely felt that they're too painful and too intransigent ever to reach a large audience. Like De Sica's *Umberto D.*, it is a picture of loneliness, but at the other end of the life-span. Umberto has little time left; Prico, the 4-year-old, has his whole ruined life ahead. His mother, sensually drawn to her lover, hasn't the strength to cling to the child; his ego-shattered father kills himself. Prico is left, agonized and inarticulate, walking the corridors of a boarding school. Except for *Forbidden Games* there has probably never been such a clear view of the antagonism and desolation that separate adult and child life. In Italian. b & w

Children of Paradise *Les Enfants du Paradis* (1945)—This lushly romantic creation, directed by Marcel Carné and written by Jacques Prévert, is a one-of-a-kind film, a sumptuous epic about the relations between theatre and life. At first, it may seem a romance set in the Paris of Balzac; it turns into a comparison of dramatic modes—it includes at least five kinds of theatrical performance. And, encompassing these, it is a film poem on the nature and varieties of love—sacred and profane, selfless and possessive. It was made during the Occupation, and it is said that the starving extras made away with some of the banquets before they could be photographed. With Jean-Louis Barrault as the soulful mime Deburau (the Pierrot—Barrault sucks in his cheeks so much that he sometimes suggests Dietrich); the incomparable Arletty as Garance; Pierre Brasseur as the Shakespearean actor Lemaître (the Harlequin); Louis Salou as the count; Marcel Herrand as the philosophical murderer; Pierre Renoir as the ragpicker-informer; and Maria Casarès, who has the unrewarding role of the theatre manager's daughter, who marries Deburau and becomes the mother of an abominable offspring. (The child is pure Hollywood.) In French. b & w

The Children's Hour (1961)—William Wyler, who in 1936 had made *These Three*, a bowdlerized yet very fine version of the Lillian Hellman play *The Children's Hour*, returned to the material in 1961 and, in the freer atmosphere of that period, remade it, with the charge of sexual deviation restored—that is, with the two schoolmistress heroines (Audrey Hepburn and Shirley MacLaine) accused of lesbianism by one of their pupils. The result is too self-conscious, though; the cinematography, by Franz Planer, may sometimes evoke Balthus, but the atmosphere is heavy and lugubrious. There were complaints at the time that the studio had hacked out the center of the film—which is a bit like complaining that a corpse has had a vital organ removed. With Miriam Hopkins, who had been one of the young teachers in the 1936 version, as the aunt; Fay Bainter as the rich old villainess; and James Garner. Hellman, who did the adaptation, is so rough on the Fay Bainter character (when the woman realizes her error and begs forgiveness, it is denied) that one develops a perverse sympathy for her. United Artists. b & w

Child's Play (1972)—Diabolism on the loose in a Catholic boarding school for boys. The boys indulge in decidedly uncharming mutilations, while two rival teachers (the hated pedant James Mason and the popular Robert Preston) quarrel about who is responsible, and a new teacher (Beau Bridges) tries to puzzle matters out. Unpleasantly tense melodrama, with noisy rattles on the soundtrack to alert the audience to lurking depravity. Mason's fine performance is marred by an excess of abrupt, badly cropped closeups. Sidney Lumet directed; from the Robert Marasco play, adapted by Leon Prochnik. Produced by David Merrick, for Paramount. color (See *Reeling*.)

Chimes at Midnight, see *Falstaff*

China Is Near *La Cina è Vicina* (1968)—A witty, subtly freakish modern comedy about sex and politics, directed by the prodigiously talented 27-year-old Marco Bellocchio in a fluid style that is full of surprises. Bellocchio's characters are as much a private zoo as Buñuel's; the five principals, who are so awful they're funny, use one another in every way they can, with the film structured like a classic comic opera. (It has the intricacy and the boudoir complications.) Among the five are a pair of working-class lovers—a secretary and a Socialist functionary—who scheme to marry into the rich landed gentry. Their targets are a pot-bellied professor (Glauco Mauri), who is running for municipal office on the Socialist ticket, and his sister (Elda Tattoli), a great lady who lets every man in town climb on top of her but won't marry because socially they're all beneath her. The fifth is the younger brother in the rich household—a prissy, sneering 17-year-old Maoist (who provides the title when he scrawls "China Is Near" on the walls of his brother's campaign headquarters). As the pairs of lovers combine and recombine and the five become one big, ghastly family (with a yapping little house pet as an emblem of domesticity), Bellocchio makes it all rhyme. The camera glides in and out and around the action; it moves as simply and with as much apparent ease as if it were attached to the director's forehead. The script is by Bellocchio and Elda Tattoli (she was also the art director); cinematography by Tonino Delli Colli; music by Ennio Morricone; produced by Franco Cristaldi. In Italian. b & w (See *Going Steady*.)

China Seas (1935)—Classy-lady Rosalind Russell and Jean Harlow, as tough, hard-drinking "China Doll," compete for the affections of ship's officer Clark Gable. Russell can't compete, of course, 'cause that common girl is *funny*. Sleazy but likable M-G-M shipboard melodrama based on the formula that had proved a big hit in 1932 in *Red Dust*. With Wallace Beery, in his likable-villain period, and Lewis Stone, in his noble-sufferer period, Robert Benchley as a drunk, and Dudley Digges, C. Aubrey Smith, Akim Tamiroff, Donald Meek, and Edward Brophy. Directed by Tay Garnett, from a wisecracking, sexy screenplay by Jules Furthman and James K. McGuinness, based on a novel by Crosbie Garstin. b & w

Chinatown (1974)—Set in the 30s, this nostalgic thriller, in the style of Hammett and Chandler, draws on the history of Los Angeles, specifically the water-rights and real-estate swindles. You can feel the conflict between the temperaments of the scriptwriter, Robert Towne, and the director, Roman Polanski. In Towne's conception, the audience discovers the depth of the corruption along with the romantic-damn-fool detective J. J. Gittes (Jack Nicholson). Polanski, whose movies don't leave you anything to hang on to, turns the material into an extension of his world view: he makes the L.A. atmosphere gothic and creepy from the word go. The film holds you, in a suffocating way. Polanski never lets the story tell itself. It's all over-deliberate, mauve, nightmarish; everyone is yellow-lacquered, and evil runs rampant. You don't care who is hurt, since everything is blighted. And yet the nastiness has a look, and a fascination. There's a celebrated background story to the film. The script had originally ended after Gittes realizes what horrors the woman he loved, the twitchy liar Evelyn Mulwray (Faye Dunaway), had been through. And then she kills her incestuous, baronial father (John Huston) in order to save her daughter from him, and Gittes helps the young girl get to Mexico. But Polanski, an absurdist, seals the picture with his gargoyle grin. He ends it with the death of Evelyn Mulwray and the triumph of the Huston character, who had raped the land, raped his daughter, and would now proceed to corrupt the daughter's daughter. Polanski's temperament dominates (and he seems indifferent to some of the plot points). Yet Towne's temperament comes through, too, especially in Nicholson's Jake Gittes, the vulgarian hero who gives the picture much of its comedy: Gittes gets to tell wittily inane, backslapping jokes, and to show the romanticism inside his street shrewdness. With Polanski as the vicious "midget" hood who takes his knife

and slits open Gittes' nose, Burt Young as the man looking at pictures of his faithless wife, John Hillerman, Perry Lopez, Joe Mantell, and Diane Ladd. Cinematography by John A. Alonzo; production design by Richard Sylbert; editing by Sam O'Steen; music by Jerry Goldsmith. (A sequel, *The Two Jakes*, was released in 1990.) Robert Evans produced, for Paramount. color

La Chinoise (1967)—The writer-director Jean-Luc Godard's fast, clever political comedy (and elegy) about the late-60s incorporation of revolutionary heroes and ideas into Pop. The film is made in a new, semi-satirical shorthand; it centers on the terrorist actions of a group of young French Maoists—naïve, forlorn little ideologues who live out a Pop version of *The Possessed*. Anne Wiazemsky (married at the time to Godard) plays the affectless killer Véronique, a teen-age philosophy student; she and the four other members of her Maoist group share the apartment where most of the movie takes place. They study Marxism-Leninism and chant Chairman Mao's sayings from the little red book like nursery rhymes. Godard's hard-edge visual style is stripped down for speed and wit; he wants you to be able to read the whole picture (and the words) at once. He uses words here in more ways than any other filmmaker has: they're in the dialogue and on the walls, on book jackets and in headlines; they're recited, chanted, shouted, written, broken down; they're in commentaries, quotations, interviews, narration; they're in slogans and emblems and signs. Those who dislike verbal allusions will be irritated, and those who want only straightforward action may be driven wild by Godard's neo-Brechtian displacement devices (his voice on the soundtrack, a cut to Raoul Coutard at the camera) and by his almost novelistic love of digression—his inclusion of anecdotes, of speculations about movie art, and of direct-to-the-camera interviews. In a section toward the end Godard brings in Francis Jeanson playing himself—an older radical from a humane tradition; Jeanson asks Véronique the political questions that resonate through the movie—questions about the consequences of terrorism. The movie is like a speed-freak's anticipatory vision of the political horrors to come; it's amazing. With Jean-Pierre Léaud, Juliette Berto, Michel Sémianko, Lex de Bruijn as Kirilov, and Omar Diop as Comrade X. In French. color (See *Going Steady*.)

Chloe in the Afternoon *L'Amour, l'après-midi* (1972)—Will the squeamish, married hero (Bernard Verley) break down and go to bed with bohemian Chloe (Zouzou), or won't he? The author-director, Eric Rohmer, a specialist in the eroticism of non-sexual affairs, is a lapidary craftsman who works on a very small scale. This movie is, in its way, just about perfect, but it's minor, and so polished that it practically evaporates a half hour after it's over. In French. color (See *Reeling*.)

Choose Me (1984)—Written and directed by Alan Rudolph, this romantic comedy-fantasy is about a group of lovers whose madnesses and illusions interlock, and it's giddy in a magical, pseudo-sultry way—it seems to be set in a poet's dream of a red-light district. Teddy Pendergrass is on the soundtrack, and the entire movie has a lilting, loose, choreographic flow. And though you can't always tell the intentional humor from the unintentional, this low-budget picture has a marvellous cast, headed by Lesley Ann Warren, Geneviève Bujold, Rae Dawn Chong, and Keith Carradine. Also with John Larroquette, Ed Ruscha, and Patrick Bauchau as the brutal racketeer. The swoony cinematography is by Jan Kiesser. color (See *State of the Art*.)

Christmas Holiday (1944)—The screenwriter, Herman J. Mankiewicz, took Somerset Maugham's novel of the same name, changed the setting from France to New Orleans, and turned it into a vehicle for Deanna Durbin, who had outgrown her singing adolescent heyday. Though a bit chubby-cheeked (maturing child stars are rarely lucky in their bone structure), she's not too objectionable in the role of a young singer from Vermont who marries a no-good charmer (Gene Kelly), scion of an old Creole family. Just about everything is sodden and unconvincing, though. The husband murders a bookmaker, and the wife blames herself for not having been a stronger influence on him. The director, Robert Siodmak—so astute in many of his other films—seems stuck and has to take these sentiments unduly seriously. (This film was made in the days of the Code, and when the wife is forced to perform in a dive we have to accept her word that she is leading a degraded life, since what we see is peachy clean.) Durbin sings "Always" and "Spring Will Be a Little Late This Year"; Kelly neither sings nor dances, and he hasn't much more luck with the weakling role than actors generally do. With Richard Whorf, Gladys George, Gale Sondergaard, and David Bruce. Universal. b & w

Christmas in July (1940)—Preston Sturges wrote and directed this little slapstick romance when he was just warming up as a director. Dick Powell and Ellen Drew are the young couple whose luck turns when he thinks he has won $25,000 in a slogan contest. It's agreeable enough—it's rather sweet, actually—but it lacks the full-fledged Sturges lunacy. Paramount. b & w

Christopher Strong (1933)—An arch, high-strung, sickeningly noble Katharine Hepburn movie, but one of the rare movies told from a woman's sexual point of view. Directed by Dorothy Arzner from a screenplay by Zoë Akins, it's the story of a record-breaking English aviatrix who falls in love with a distinguished political figure (Colin Clive). As soon as they go to bed together, he insists—late on the very first night—that she not fly in the contest she is entered in. It's the intelligent woman's primal post-coital scene. In movies up to the 70s, this primal scene was never played out satisfactorily; the woman always gave in, either in the paste-up screwball style that provided the fake resolutions of the 40s, or, as in this picture, fatally. (The heroine commits suicide.) The directing seems enervated and the film was a flop, but it's not one that independent-minded women can easily forget. Hepburn is exquisitely gaunt and boyish in her sleek, high-fashion gowns, including one that she says makes her look like a moth. It does; the movie is a moth-and-flame story. With Billie Burke, Ralph Forbes, Helen Chandler, and Jack La Rue. From a novel by Gilbert Frankau; music by Max Steiner. Produced by Pandro S. Berman, for R K O. b & w

Chronicle of a Summer *Chronique d'un été* (1960)—A pioneer work of *cinéma vérité* on which the anthropologist-filmmaker Jean Rouch and the sociologist–film critic Edgar Morin collaborated. A Negro student, a factory worker, a girl survivor of the concentration camps, and others are interviewed; later they discuss whether they "acted." Some revealing moments, though the confessional atmosphere gets a bit thick. In French. b & w

Chronique d'un été, see *Chronicle of a Summer*

A Chump at Oxford (1940)—Laurel and Hardy, in pretty good form, in a feature with a story line that makes it possible for them to do a retrospective of their own careers—brief re-enactments of routines from several of their earlier shorts. (There are bits that recall *Another Fine Mess, The Second Hundred Years, Wrong Again,* and *Towed in a Hole.*) As a reward for catching a bank robber (actually, he slips on a banana skin they have dropped), Stan and Ollie are sent to Oxford for an education. The bank that rewards them is called the Finlayson National Bank, in tribute, no doubt, to James Finlayson, who once again appears with them. Alfred Goulding directed; Harry Langdon was one of the scriptwriters. The cast includes Peter Cushing as one of the Oxford students. A Hal Roach Production; released by United Artists. b & w

Le Ciel et la boue, see *The Sky Above, The Mud Below*

Cimarron (1931)—One of Edna Ferber's heartfelt, numbskull treks through the hardships and glories of the American heritage. Swaggering Yancey Cravat (Richard Dix), a gallant braggart afflicted with wanderlust, marries fragile Irene Dunne, and they head out for the Oklahoma land rush. The film covers 40 years of their lives—a long, trying saga, especially after Irene Dunne, deserted by her husband, learns to carry on valiantly, editing the local paper in his place and becoming a congresswoman. It would be more fun if the audience could go off to the Cherokee Strip with Richard Dix and forget about the indomitable Irene Dunne. With Edna May Oliver and Estelle Taylor, who enliven some episodes, and with George E. Stone, Nance O'Neil, William Collier, Jr., and Roscoe Ates as a stuttering printer. Wesley Ruggles directed; adapted by Howard Estabrook. The picture was a huge success and was taken very seriously by a great many people. (That was not the case with the 1961 remake, in color and CinemaScope, starring Glenn Ford and Maria Schell.) R K O. b & w

La Cina è Vicina, see *China Is Near*

Cinderella Liberty (1973)—A sordid, messy affair between a Baptist sailor (James Caan)

and a beat-out whore (Marsha Mason), combined with a high-minded interracial big-brother story. (Caan can't save Mason, but her little part-black son—Kirk Calloway—stirs his paternal impulses.) The Mark Rydell picture, taken from Darryl Ponicsan's script, based on his novel, wants to jerk tears but just doesn't have the knack. Some of the acting is fine, but the film is a swampy experience; you feel as if you're wading through. With Eli Wallach and Allyn Ann McLerie. Shot in Seattle. Cinematography by Vilmos Zsigmond; music by John Williams. 20th Century-Fox. color (See *Reeling*.)

La Ciociara, see *Two Women*

Cisco Pike (1971)—Though it was Kris Kristofferson's first picture, he's at his ease. What the movie tries to get at is the romantic quest—almost the romantic *instinct*—of someone who no longer knows what he's after. Cisco is both mellow and desperate; his dreams have failed him. A former pop idol, he hangs around the L.A. music business trying to find the comeback trail, but after two convictions for dealing, he knows the bottom, too. Gene Hackman plays a narcotics agent; enraged and cracking up, he confiscates 100 kilos of top-grade marijuana and blackmails Cisco into dealing it in 2½ days. As Cisco looks up his contacts in the music world to unload the stuff on them, the picture catches the high-risk glee and the sense of invulnerability of dealers who get high on dealing itself. Cisco's scroungy little transactions turn him on as if he'd just sold the world to the highest bidder; he digs his triumphs—the excitement brings him to life. This was one of the best of the dealer-user pictures of the period, but (like *Born to Win*) it came at the tail end of the cycle and was all but buried. Bill L. Norton, the 27-year-old writer-director, wrote an original script for his directing début, then got some help; Rob-

ert Towne did a major rewrite. (The film has some similarities to *Shampoo*.) Karen Black plays Cisco's girl, and does it straight, without a wasted motion; Viva, looking like a stoned, weirdly benign bird of prey, plays a rich girl he encounters while he's crashing around the city. Also with Joy Bang, Harry Dean Stanton, Roscoe Lee Browne, Severn Darden, Antonio Fargas, and Allan Arbus. Produced by Gerald Ayres, for Columbia. color

The Citadel (1938)—A. J. Cronin's best-sellers lack literary distinction, and their seriousness shades into oppressive sobriety; still, there's some substance in his high-minded, commonplace approach. You can feel the director, King Vidor, straining to give the theme—doctors' struggles with their consciences—prestige-picture importance, but he holds one's interest. He does especially well in the early scenes, when the hero, Robert Donat, is working among the Welsh miners, and then he slacks off during the passages about the Harley Street phonies. Fortunately, there are actors to watch when the preachiness gets thick; Rex Harrison, Ralph Richardson, Rosalind Russell, and Emlyn Williams all have major roles. M-G-M. b & w

Citizen Kane (1941)—The Orson Welles film is generally considered the greatest American film of the sound period, and it may be more fun than any other great movie. Based on the life of William Randolph Hearst, it's an exuberant, muckraking attack on an archetypal economic baron. With Welles, of course, and Joseph Cotten, Dorothy Comingore, Agnes Moorehead, Everett Sloane, George Coulouris, Ruth Warrick, Ray Collins, Erskine Sanford, William Alland, Paul Stewart, Fortunio Bonanova, Gus Schilling, and Philip Van Zandt. Screenplay by Herman J. Mankiewicz and Welles; cinematography by

C

Gregg Toland; editing by Robert Wise and
Mark Robson; music by Bernard Herrmann;
art direction by Van Nest Polglase and Perry
Ferguson. R K O. b & w (See *The Citizen Kane
Book*.)

Citizens Band Also known as *Handle with
Care*. (1977)—A high-spirited, elegantly
deadpan comedy, with a mellow, light touch.
Paul Brickman, who wrote the screenplay,
had an idea worthy of Preston Sturges: that
the psychology of those who operate CB
radio units might be like the psychology of
crank phone callers and breathers and obscene phone callers, too—that as disembodied voices, with identities borrowed from pop
fantasies, and signal names to confirm their
new self-image, people could live another life
on the public airwaves. In the film, the CB
users are secret celebrities, eloquent on the
air, or, more often, aimlessly loquacious. But
they dry up when they actually meet. CB
functions as an authorized madness; it allows
the characters to release their inhibitions
while keeping one foot on the ground. The
story is about the people in a Southwestern
town and the collisions of their free-floating
ids. Paul Le Mat is the hero—a small-town
Boy Scout who never grew up. Marcia Rodd
is a trucker's hard-bitten wife, and Ann
Wedgeworth is a trucker's softheaded wife;
these two become a tearstained running gag
when it turns out that they're both married
to the same trucker. Jonathan Demme directed, in a soft, subdued style—the film is
lyrical and wiggy at the same time. It has the
consistent vision of a classic comedy; it undercuts the characters' illusions without a
breath of ill will. With jutting-jawed Charles
Napier as the impulsive, generous bigamist,
Alix Elias as the plump, giggly hooker whose
CB name is Hot Coffee, Roberts Blossom as
the hero's father, Candy Clark, Bruce McGill,
Richard Bright, and Michael Rothman as
Cochise, Harry Northup as The Red Baron,

Leila Smith as Grandma Breaker, Ed Begley,
Jr., as The Priest, and Will Seltzer as Warlock.
Cinematography by Jordan Cronenweth; titles by Pablo Ferro; music by Bill Conti. Paramount. color (See *When the Lights Go Down*.)

City of Gold (1957)—This 23-minute film
from Canada, a reconstruction of the Yukon
gold rush from period photographs, shows
the men who left all ties behind in the quest
for gold and glory; the film provides more
sense of what gold fever is, and of what these
people were actually like and what they were
after, than all the dozens of Hollywood epics
on the theme. One marvellous photograph
shows the climb through Chilkoot Pass—the
climb re-created by Chaplin in *The Gold Rush*.
And there are photographs of the Dawson
City girls who actually entertained the men
of the Yukon: fat, plain, lewd, they don't look
much like the dance-hall girls in Hollywood
Westerns. But the young men have a beauty
and an air of excitement that Hollywood has
never been able to reproduce. Narrated by
Pierre Berton. Directed by Colin Low and
Wolf Koenig; written by Roman Kroiter; produced and edited by Tom Daly. b & w

City Streets (1931)—A love story in a gangster setting which got carried away into so
much fancy expressionism and symbolism
that it seems stylized out of all relationship
to the actual world. The director, Rouben Mamoulian, appears to be the culprit; he's so
busy with his camera arabesques he forgets
to tell the story, and then, at the end, tries
to save the movie with a big chase. Gary
Cooper is the honest, gaunt young hero from
the world of the circus who gets into the beer
racket and starts wearing coats with fur collars; Sylvia Sidney is the sacrificing heroine
who goes to jail for her father (Guy Kibbee).
With Wynne Gibson, Paul Lukas, Stanley
Fields, and William Boyd—sometimes called
William (Stage) Boyd to differentiate him

from the actor who eventually played Hop-along Cassidy. The script is based on a story by Dashiell Hammett; Lee Garmes did the elaborate cinematography. Paramount. b & w

Claire's Knee *Le Genou de Claire* (1970)—The air is thick with summer and leisure in Eric Rohmer's serene story of a vacationing diplomat (Jean-Claude Brialy) who says he is interested only in women's minds and then has an "undefined desire" to stroke a young girl's knee. There's a rather enigmatic woman novelist who stands in for the director and makes ponderous remarks, but Rohmer's quiet, complacent movie-novel game is pleasing, and a captivatingly gawky teen-age actress, Béatrice Romand, who plays a subsidiary role, looks like a Pisanello princess. With Laurence De Monaghan as Claire, and Aurora Cornu as the novelist. Cinematography by Nestor Almendros. In French. color (See *Deeper into Movies*.)

Clash by Night (1952)—This Fritz Lang version of a Clifford Odets melodrama about jealousy never quite comes together; the stylized Odets dialogue seems bizarrely out of place in the setting of a fishing village. But it's a handsome black-and-white production, and though Barbara Stanwyck (as the adulteress) and Paul Douglas (as the betrayed husband) suffer rather too strenuously, Robert Ryan (as the wife's lover, a projectionist in a movie theatre) is so intensely sexual that the film momentarily achieves real, even if stagey, power. And as a good-natured girl, full of animal high spirits, Marilyn Monroe is appealing in an unmannered style that's very different from her later acting. With Keith Andes and J. Carrol Naish. Adapted by Alfred Hayes; cinematography by Nicholas Musuraca. R K O.

Claudine (1939)—A light, poetic study of adolescence, based on Colette's first novels (the Claudine series), and dealing with her schooldays at the turn of the century—or, at least, her version of them. It has a charming innocent naughtiness. With Blanchette Brunoy and Pierre Brasseur. Directed by Serge de Poligny. In French. b & w

Clean Slate, see *Coup de torchon*

Cleo from 5 to 7 *Cléo de 5 à 7* (1962)—One of the few films directed by a woman in which the viewer can sense a difference. The story is about the moods of a beautiful, chic popular singer (Corinne Marchand) during the two hours she waits to find out if she has cancer. Childish and fearful, she consults her horoscope and goes to a fortuneteller; she buys a hat; she rehearses a song; she cries. And throughout, the writer-director, Agnès Varda, sustains an unsentimental yet subjective tone that is almost unique in the history of movies. Cinematography by Jean Rabier; editing by Janine Verneau; music by Michel Legrand (who also plays a part). With Antoine Bourseiller, Dorothée Blanck, and Dominique Davray. In French. b & w

Cleopatra (1934)—The dialogue sounds like gossip over backyard clotheslines, with occasional Shakespearean overtones—flattened, of course. ("Her infinite variety" becomes "She's always new.") In this De Mille version, the actors' diction provides such dividends as Caesar (Warren William) saying "Nope" to the senators, and Antony (big, solid Henry Wilcoxon) mumbling "I'm dying, Egypt, dying" in the inflection of "I gotta pain." The extravaganza is moderate, with too much Rome and too little Egypt and the usual Roman holidays, processions, and atrium orgies. Cleopatra (Claudette Colbert) wiggles her slim hips and wonders if her dress is becoming. It is, and the big bash aboard her barge has its own dreamy chic. A netful of beautiful adagio dancers are hauled out of the sea, which certainly beats popping out of a giant cake. Like the later, longer Elizabeth Taylor version, it's terrible and yet compulsively watchable. With Gertrude Michael, Joseph Schildkraut, Ian Keith, C. Aubrey Smith, Arthur Hohl, Irving Pichel, little Ferdinand Gottschalk, and John Carradine. Written by Waldemar Young and Vincent Lawrence. Paramount. b & w

Cleopatra Jones (1973)—The first swashbuckler to star a fighting superwoman. Beautiful black Amazon Tamara Dobson, who doesn't take herself any more seriously than Errol Flynn used to, plays a cross between James Bond and Robin Hood. A 6-foot-2-inch C.I.A. narcotics agent, Cleopatra is out to get the dope dealers who are preying on blacks; the leader of the international dope ring, which operates out of Los Angeles, is "Mommy" (Shelley Winters, in blazing wigs). The movie is brightly colored and energetic, and there's a comic strip grossness (yet good-naturedness) about the continuous mayhem. The whole thing suggests a Pop art racial and sexual spoof—Mommy's chief aide, the black "Doodlebug" (Antonio Fargas), has an English chauffeur, and at the climax, two black brothers named Melvin and Matthew use kung fu to destroy Mommy and her gang. Directed by Jack Starrett, with lowbrow gusto; written by Max Julien and Sheldon Keller; cinematography by David Walsh. With the ravishing Brenda Sykes as Tiffany, Bernie Casey as Cleopatra's love object, and Bill McKinney, Dan Frazer, Esther Rolle, Stafford Morgan, Mike Warren, and Caro Kenyatta (Melvin) and Albert Popwell (Matthew). Warners. color

The Clock (1945)—A sweetly charming, if maybe too irresistible, Second World War romance, featuring Judy Garland and Robert Walker. There's a very shrewd, very wet script—Robert Nathan, working with Joseph Schrank, spread his trembling sensitivities upon the already shaky story by Paul and Pauline Gallico. Fortunately, the director, Vincente Minnelli (this was his first job of straight—non-musical—direction), gave it a very distinctive innocent quality, so that it doesn't seem intolerably calculated. Robert Walker plays a gentle country boy, a corporal with two days of leave in New York before going overseas. He meets Judy Garland, a New York office worker, in Pennsylvania Station and they go sightseeing together. They're separated in a crowded subway and each is panicked by the fear of never seeing the other again; when they find each other, they decide to get married—immediately. The film has a love-hate relationship with New York City. It makes each of the young lovers feel alone and frightened. Yet together they can enjoy it. Amazingly, this picture was all shot in the studio, using street sets and back projection; even the old Penn Station, where so much of the action takes place, is a set. The film is beautifully rhythmed and it isn't all romance: the edges are filled with comic characters—Keenan Wynn and Moyna MacGill are the most memorable. Also with James Gleason, Lucille Gleason, Ruth Brady, Marshall Thompson and fleeting appearances by Arthur Freed (who produced), Robert Nathan, and Roger Edens. (Minnelli and Garland were married shortly after the film's completion.) M-G-M. b & w

A Clockwork Orange (1971)—This Stanley Kubrick film might be the work of a strict and exacting German professor who set out to make a porno-violent sci-fi comedy. The movie is adapted from Anthony Burgess's 1962 novel, which is set in a vaguely socialist future of the late 70s or early 80s—a dreary, routinized England that roving gangs of teenage thugs terrorize at night. In this dehumanizing society, there seems to be no way for the boys to release their energies except in vandalism and crime. The protagonist, Alex (Malcolm McDowell), is the leader of one of these gangs; he's a conscienceless schoolboy sadist who enjoys stealing, stomping, raping, and destroying, until he kills a woman and is sent to prison. There he is conditioned into a moral robot who becomes nauseated by thoughts of sex and violence. Burgess wrote an ironic fable about a future in which men lose their capacity for moral choice. Kubrick, however, gives us an Alex who is more alive than anybody else in the movie, and younger and more attractive, and McDowell plays him exuberantly, with power and slyness. So at the end, when Alex's bold, aggressive, punk's nature is restored to him, it seems not a joke on all of us (as it does in the book) but, rather, a victory in which we share, and Kubrick takes an exultant tone. Along the way, Alex has been set apart as the hero by making his victims less human than he; the picture plays with violence in an intellectually seductive way— Alex's victims are twisted and incapable of suffering. Kubrick carefully estranges us from these victims so that we can *enjoy* the rapes and beatings. Alex alone suffers. And how he suffers! He's a male Little Nell— screaming in a strait jacket during the brainwashing; sweet and helpless when rejected by his parents; alone, weeping, on a bridge; beaten, bleeding, lost in a rainstorm; pounding his head on a floor and crying for death. Kubrick pours on the hearts and flowers; what is done to Alex is far worse than what Alex has done, so society itself can be felt to justify Alex's hoodlumism. With Patrick Magee and Adrienne Corri; score by Walter Carlos. Produced by Kubrick, for Warners. color (See *Deeper into Movies*.)

Close Encounters of the Third Kind (1977)— This celebration of the wonders up there in the skies is the best-humored of all technological-marvel fantasies. It has visionary magic and a childlike comic spirit, along with a love of surprises and a skeptical, let's-try-it-on spirit. It sends you out in a state of blissful satisfaction. Written and directed by Steven Spielberg. With Richard Dreyfuss, François Truffaut, Teri Garr, Melinda Dillon, Bob Balaban, and Cary Guffey. Columbia. color (See *When the Lights Go Down*.)

Close Encounters of the Third Kind, the Special Edition (1980)—Steven Spielberg re-edited the 1977 film—he made some trims, put in some outtakes, and shot a few new bits. The action is swifter, and the central character, played by Richard Dreyfuss, is easier to understand, but you may miss some of the scenes that have been cut, and find that the outtakes that Spielberg has substituted for the scenes you remember keep jarring you. (See *Taking It All In*.)

Closely Watched Trains *Ostre Sledovane Vlaky* (1966)—A wryly tender Czech film about how a shy, scared young man, who comes from a long line of patsies and fools, succeeds in bed but loses his life. This first film directed by Jiří Menzel is based on the well-known ironic novel by Bohumil Hrabal, who collaborated with Menzel on the scenario. It's set during the Second World War, and most of it takes place at a village railway station; it's fairly simple—the modest sort of film that shows human concern and decency but isn't very stimulating, and that sometimes takes the Academy Award for Best Foreign Film (as this one did). But it's also a sophisticated, elliptical folk tale, with quirky moments of small-town passion, and a funny sequence in which an assistant station-master rubber-stamps a girl telegrapher's buttocks. In Czech. b & w

Clouds Over Europe, see *Q Planes*

Cluny Brown (1946)—A girl with a passion for plumbing is terribly repugnant to stuffy people who don't want to admit that they have drains. This wonderfully suggestive idea is at the center of Ernst Lubitsch's mischievous satire on English propriety, set in contemporary rural England. Jennifer Jones is Cluny (it's her lightest, funniest performance, rivalled only by her dippy blonde in *Beat the Devil*) and Charles Boyer is a debonair scrounger—a displaced European sophisticate who encourages her to flout social conventions. These two are surrounded by a prime collection of English class and mass types—the wheezy Richard Haydn, Una O'Connor as his mother, Reginald Owen, Margaret Bannerman, Peter Lawford, Helen Walker, Ernest Cossart, Sara Allgood, Florence Bates, Reginald Gardiner, C. Aubrey Smith, Queenie Leonard, Billy Bevan, Whit Bissell, and many others. It's a lovely, easygoing comedy, full of small surprising touches. Based on Margery Sharp's novel, adapted by Samuel Hoffenstein and Elizabeth Reinhardt. 20th Century-Fox. b & w

Club Paradise (1986)—A pleasantly offhand resort-club comedy that's like those giddy, casual farces that Paramount turned out in the 30s—pictures like *We're Not Dressing*, in which Burns and Allen, Bing Crosby, Carole Lombard, and Ethel Merman goofed around on an island. The uninhibited Andrea Martin is like a funkier Gracie Allen; the fire of adventure lights her saucer eyes. She and tall, gloomy Steven Kampmann appear as a vacationing couple hoping to put new zest into their fading marriage. Robin Williams is the club's social director; Twiggy is his girlfriend; Eugene Levy and Rick Moranis are businessmen guests, both named Barry, who are obsessed by the idea of scoring with women; Peter O'Toole is the governor general of this British flyspeck—the mythical Caribbean island of St. Nicholas; Joanna Cassidy is a tough redhead who writes about resorts for *The New York Times*; and Joe Flaherty, Brian Doyle-Murray, Adolph Caesar, Robin Duke, and Mary Gross all turn up. Jimmy Cliff appears as the owner of the club and the leader of its reggae band. His songs have a relaxing, rolling rhythm that matches the lazy surf; they don't come charging into your skull, and the movie itself doesn't pound or strain to impress you, either. Directed by Harold Ramis, from a script he wrote with Doyle-Murray that at least two other sets of writers had a share in earlier. Members of the cast were encouraged to come up with gags and dialogue of their own (as long as they didn't improvise on camera). The island scenes were shot in Port Antonio, on the Jamaican coast. Warners. color (See *Hooked*.)

Cobra Woman (1944)—Camp classic, with Maria Montez as voluptuous twins. She's the good Tollea, a South Seas girl who is kidnapped just as she's about to marry Jon Hall (who smiles his moony, Mona Lisa smile and looks as boneheaded as ever), and she's the evil High Priestess Nadja, who rules a tribe of snake worshippers on Cobra Island. The impeccably lifeless cast includes Sabu, Edgar Barrier, Lon Chaney, Jr., Lois Collier, Mary Nash, Samuel S. Hinds, and Moroni Olsen. Among the exotic treats: a rumbling volcano, a pet chimp, ominous gong sounds, forest-glade love scenes, human sacrifices, Nadja's handmaidens in their high-heeled pumps, her imperious writhing during what is supposed to be a demonic dance, and the good Tollea's plea for the symbol of the power that is rightfully hers, "Gif me the cobra jool!" Produced by George Waggner for Universal, and directed by that playful wit Robert Siodmak (on sets that are often parodistic), from a script by Gene Lewis and Richard Brooks, based on a story by W. Scott Darling. This heavenly absurdity has been an inspiration to Charles Ludlam, of the Ridiculous Theatrical Company, and Gore Vidal (*Myra Breck-inridge, Myron*). color

The Cobweb (1955)—By the mid-50s, nobody was surprised that the new variant of *Grand Hotel* was an expensive, exclusive loony bin (inspired by Austin Riggs Center, at Stockbridge). Plots and subplots tangle and untangle as the staff and patients rush through their intrigues and affairs. Charles Boyer is the weary director of the asylum: when things start to go to hell, he flees, bottle in hand, to a motel. Richard Widmark, tense and fairly unconvincing as the "dynamic" new psychoanalyst, shuttles between his petulant wife (Gloria Grahame), who makes trouble for everybody, and an idealized occupational therapist (Lauren Bacall), who is having an affair with him. John Kerr and Susan Strasberg are young, sick, and in love. The prize comic maniac is Oscar Levant—shown at one point under a restraining sheet, in a continuous warm bath, gulping sedatives and singing "Mother." Vincente Minnelli directed, and, to his credit, most of the confusion is calculated—and enjoyable, in an almost campy bad-movie way. With Lillian Gish, who comes closest to being the star, even though her part is small; Fay Wray (in wonderful shape, considering the way King Kong used to squeeze her); Paul Stewart; Adele Jergens; and Tommy Rettig. Based on William Gibson's novel, adapted by John Paxton; music by Leonard Rosenman; produced by John Houseman, for M-G-M. color.

The Cocoanuts (1929)—The Marx Brothers' first feature, shot in Paramount's Astoria Studios on Long Island, is a somewhat cumbersome transcription of their Broadway musical-comedy hit about the Florida land boom. Most of the action takes place in a hotel lobby; the characters walk on and off, as if they were in a stage play, and they do stage business. The material hasn't been paced for the screen; there are dead spots (without even background music), but there are also a lot of funny verbal routines and a musical burlesque of *Carmen*, and Harpo, as a fiendish pickpocket, is much faster (and less aesthetic and self-conscious and innocent) than in the Brothers' later comedies. With Kay Francis in her then daring mannish hairdo as Penelope, a jewel thief; Margaret Dumont in lace dresses and floppy hats as the rich Mrs. Potter, the possessor of a valuable necklace; and a pair of forgettable singing lovers (Mary Eaton and Oscar Shaw). Based on the musical play by George S. Kaufman and Morrie Ryskind, with music and lyrics by Irving Berlin, adapted by Ryskind, and directed by Joseph Santley and Robert Florey. With the Berlin song "When My Dreams Come True." The cast includes Basil Ruysdael and Cyril Ring. b & w

Cocoon (1985)—A science-fantasy sit-com, in which the old people from a St. Petersburg, Florida, retirement community go off to the planet Antares, a Shangri-La in space. If audiences enjoy the movie, it's largely because of the elderly actors and the affection that the young director, Ron Howard, shows for them. Wilford Brimley, with his walrus mustache and friendly belly, brings an ornery impudence to his role, and Don Ameche is amusing as a vain, natty old sheik. But Ron Howard overworks his ecumenical niceness—his attempt to provide something for all age groups and all faiths—and he keeps trying to extract tender emotions from scenes that could get by only as slapstick. Things get pretty cloying. With Hume Cronyn, Jack Gilford, Maureen Stapleton, Gwen Verdon, Jessica Tandy, Herta Ware, Steve Guttenberg, Barret Oliver, and Brian Dennehy as the leader of the Antareans, who include Tahnee Welch and Tyrone Power, Jr. The script, by Tom Benedek, is based on a novel by David Saperstein. The special effects by Industrial

Light & Magic are warmed-over versions of the basic imagery of *Close Encounters of the Third Kind*. A Zanuck-Brown Production, for 20th Century-Fox. color (See *Hooked*.)

A Cold Wind in August (1961)—When people who work in the movie industry get together they often talk about the small, offbeat pictures made outside the studio system, and this shrewdly conceived and well-acted piece of what might be called tawdry but frank eroticism almost always comes up. It's about a stripper in her late 30s who amuses herself by seducing a 17-year-old boy and discovers greater sexual gratification than she has ever before experienced. The boy finds out she's a stripper, is disgusted and leaves her (to play around at his own age level), and she's left in despair. That's all there is to it—or that's all there might be except for the intensity Lola Albright brings to the stripper's role. Unquestionably the movie was made as a low-budget exploitation film—an American ersatz version of Radiguet's *Devil in the Flesh* and Colette's *The Game of Love*—but it doesn't pretend to be set on a high plane, and it's saved by the honesty and clarity of its low intentions. Regrettably, in order to point up the boy's indifference to the meaning the affair has for her, he has been made too simple and callow, and although the actor (Scott Marlowe) manages to convey an emotional nature without overdoing it, Joe De Santis, who plays his good Italian papa, seems far more attractive. At least he does until the writer, Burton Wohl, who adapted his own novel, and the director, Alexander Singer, load him down with a preposterous piece of business. Papa delivers quiet words of wisdom and decency—good counsel—to his son and then sits back to read his well-thumbed leatherbound volume. It was hard to concentrate on the next scene: What *could* that book be? You never find out. Apart from Albright's arousing performance, the movie's chief strength is the economical script, which is also its weakness. If you set out to be a flesh merchant, you should offer more than a skeleton of material. With Herschel Bernardi; cinematography by Floyd Crosby. b & w

The Colditz Story (1955)—This English movie about the Second World War is based on P. R. Reid's account of his experiences in Colditz Castle, the "impregnable" fortress in Saxony to which the German High Command sent the Allied officers who were considered veteran escapees—i.e., men who couldn't be contained in conventional prison camps. These escape artists—English, French, Dutch, and Poles—are so prodigal of ideas that the senior British officer (Eric Portman) forms a four-power committee to coordinate all the escape plots. The movie is proficient, but it doesn't live up to the subject. With John Mills as Reid, Ian Carmichael as Robin, Frederick Valk as the Kommandant, Christopher Rhodes as the Scottish lieutenant, Theodore Bikel as the Dutch prisoner, and Bryan Forbes, Lionel Jeffries, and Anton Diffring. Directed (and co-adapted) by Guy Hamilton. b & w

The Collector (1965)—Terence Stamp is the young London bank clerk who collects butterflies; when he wins a fortune in a sports pool he stalks an iridescent butterfly of a girl (Samantha Eggar), captures her, and keeps her locked up in a cellar. Stanley Mann's banal script does no great service to John Fowles' novel, but the William Wyler production has an inexorable, compulsive drive. It's a handsome, though too dignified, movie—it doesn't have enough psychological weight to support its rich, classical style. We never really feel our way into the collector's scary obsession; Stamp works at his role (he suggests a young Charles Laughton), but the whole idea seems a shallow, literary device. With Mona Washbourne and Maurice

Dallimore. Music by Maurice Jarre; made in the U.S. and England, with cinematography by Robert L. Surtees and Robert Krasker. Columbia. color

College (1927)—A beautiful little comedy. Buster Keaton is a bookworm, working his way through college and determined to become a star athlete. The story line isn't as miraculously fresh as in a couple of his films, but it allows for some of his most startlingly inventive stunts. Despite the many pilferings from this film (it has been a gold mine for other comedians), the routines are executed so precisely and with such an air of confident innocence that they are charged with surprise—and probably will be forever. Silent. b & w

The Color of Money (1986)—This Martin Scorsese film takes up Paul Newman as Fast Eddie Felson 25 years after the close of the 1961 Robert Rossen film *The Hustler*, in which Eddie, the new poolroom champion, quit the game rather than spoil it by truckling to the crooked manager who had staked him. Now he's a silver-haired Chicago liquor salesman who drives a white Cadillac and wears a neat mustache and natty duds, a likable cynical sharpie who himself stakes young hustlers (for 60 per cent of their winnings). When he sees the raw, cocky upstart Vincent (Tom Cruise), he makes a deal to train the kid. Newman brings off some beautiful smiling deviltry. The kick he gets out of acting is inseparable from Eddie's con artistry, and, with the help of pungent lowlife dialogue by Richard Price, who wrote the script, he carries the action along. The picture might have been a pop classic if it had stayed near the level of impudence that it reaches at its best. But about midway Fast Eddie has a crisis of conscience, or something, and when Eddie locks his jaw and sets forth to become a purified

man of integrity the joy goes out of Newman's performance, which (despite the efforts of a lot of good actors) is the only life in the movie, except for a brief, startling performance by the 25-year-old black actor Forest Whitaker as a pool shark called Amos. With Mary Elizabeth Mastrantonio, Helen Shaver, John Turturro, and Bill Cobbs. Cinematography by Michael Ballhaus; score by Robbie Robertson; production design by Boris Leven; editing by Thelma Schoonmaker. Academy Award for Best Actor (Newman). Touchstone (Disney). color (See *Hooked*.)

The Color Purple (1985)—The popular novel by Alice Walker is about the bonding of Southern black women in the first half of the century. The women are generous, hardworking, artistically gifted, and understanding; the men are lazy, lecherous oppressors. Probably the book gets by with its rampant female chauvinism because the story is put in the mouth of the battered 14-year-old heroine Celie; it's written in a raw, cadenced dialect and it has a joyous emotional swing to it. Steven Spielberg, who directed the movie version, appears to have taken the novel seriously—inspirational tone, pop-folk religiosity, triumph of the human spirit, and all—and been intimidated by it. It's not just that he can't give this 30-year family saga the push of that earthy folk style of Walker's; it's that he filters everything through movies and sees rural Georgia in 1909 the way a European director might. The picture seems to be taking place in a made-up, faraway kingdom. With Desreta Jackson as the young Celie and Whoopi Goldberg taking over the role, Danny Glover as Celie's brute of a husband, Willard Pugh as her stepson, Margaret Avery as the woman she falls in love with, Oprah Winfrey as the powerhouse Sofia, whose mighty punch at a white man lands her in jail for 12 years, and Adolph Caesar, Rae Dawn Chong, Akosua Busia, and Dana Ivey. The cinematography is by Allen Daviau; the script is by Menno Meyjes; the gooey score is by Quincy Jones; the production design is by J. Michael Riva; the editing is by Michael Kahn. Tata Vega dubbed Margaret Avery's songs. Shot in North Carolina and Kenya. Warners. color (See *Hooked*.)

Colors (1988)—This muckraking melodrama about L.A.'s two most powerful confederations of drug-trafficking youth gangs—the Bloods, who wear red, and the Crips, who wear blue—is deadened by standard cop-movie ploys. The veteran cop (Robert Duvall), who is due for retirement, and his new partner, the young fireball (Sean Penn) who likes to rough up suspects, are the only characters we get to know, and we already know them. The director, Dennis Hopper, and the cinematographer, Haskell Wexler, try for vividness, with the camera hightailing after the fast-moving gang members, and they catch images of the random violence of boys who are high on crack or PCP, and have arsenals of assault rifles and submachine guns. But despite the film's kinetic style it feels slow and long and tame. We're turned into passive voyeurs: we get a look at gang violence without being asked to become emotionally involved. Hopper isn't inside the material, except for his identification with its nihilistic view that the cops' activities are purposeless and that life doesn't make any sense. He's a visual aesthete—less a director than an artistic arranger of people in the frame. He takes us on an art tour of the graffiti-covered walls in the ghettos and barrios. With Maria Conchita Alonso, Trinidad Silva, and a cast that includes a dozen or so actual gang members. The script, by Michael Schiffer, is based on the story he devised with Richard DiLello;

music by Herbie Hancock. Orion. color (See *Hooked*.)

Coma (1978)—Geneviève Bujold as a surgical resident in a Boston hospital. After her closest woman friend (Lois Chiles) goes into an irreversible coma during an abortion, she discovers that large numbers of young, healthy patients have gone into comas while undergoing minor surgery, and then, vegetablized, have been packed off to a facility—the grim, fortresslike Jefferson Institute—that provides long-term life-support systems. Single-handed, she begins to investigate. When the action moves from the hospital to the Institute, the story shades off from a factual, realistic view of modern hospital practices to sci-fi fantasy, without any change in the film's tone. *Coma* is so cleanly made, with such an impersonal, detached feeling, that it looks untouched by human hands. Even the actors seem disinfected of any traces of personality. But not Bujold. There's no way to sanitize this actress. She's like a soft furry animal and she's irreducibly curious; she snuggles deep inside the shallow material. Thin-skinned, touchy, she seems almost to sniff out fakery. And as she goes from one dangerous situation to the next, the narrative trap tightens; you fear for her safety and the suspense gets you in the stomach and maybe the chest, too. But *Coma* doesn't give you a lift. Directed by Michael Crichton, who did the adaptation of Robin Cook's novel, the picture is all plot, and it glides along smoothly, as if computer-operated. The scenes inside the Institute have a chill, spectral beauty, yet the spookiness doesn't explode. The movie seems a little too cultivated, too cautious; Crichton probably accepts impersonality as part of technological advance—he doesn't satirize it. With Michael Douglas, Richard Widmark, Rip Torn, Elizabeth Ashley, and

Lance Le Gault. M-G-M. color (See *When the Lights Go Down*.)

Come Back, Africa (1960)—Semi-documentary on what it's like to be black in South Africa. Lionel Rogosin's film centers on a man who has left his farm and is trying to make a living in Johannesburg. Clumsy, but some rarely seen material. b & w

Come Back, Little Sheba (1952)—Lola mourns her losses—youth, beauty, love, and Little Sheba, the dog that ran away. As Lola, Shirley Booth is the essence of all those dreamy, slatternly, gabby, sentimental women who move one to pity by their harmlessness and to disgust by their vacuity. As Lola's husband, Doc, Burt Lancaster scores A for effort but just passes on performance. Daniel Mann directed the adaptation (by Ketti Frings) of William Inge's tragicomedy; it's not much of a movie—it's just a setting for Shirley Booth, who won the Academy Award as Best Actress and also the Best Actress award at Cannes. With Terry Moore and Richard Jaeckel. Produced by Hal B. Wallis, for Paramount. b & w

Come Back to the 5 & Dime Jimmy Dean, Jimmy Dean (1982)—It's doubtful if a major film director has ever before voluntarily taken on as thoroughgoing a piece of drivel as this one—a play by Ed Graczyk set in a Texas small-town 5 & Dime and centering on the reunion of a James Dean fan club on the 20th anniversary of his death. The movie version shouldn't work, but it does. When Robert Altman gives a project everything he's got, his skills are such that he can make poetry out of fake poetry and magic out of fake magic. Moving in apparent freedom, the principal actresses—Sandy Dennis, Cher, Karen Black, and, in a smaller part, Marta Heflin—go at their roles so creatively that they find some kind of acting truth in what

they're doing. They bring conviction to their looneytunes characters. Also with Sudie Bond, Kathy Bates, and, in the only male role, Mark Patton. The airy and lyrical cinematography is by Pierre Mignot. Released by Cinecom International. color (See *Taking It All In*.)

Comes a Horseman (1978)—This Western, set during the Second World War and starring Jane Fonda and James Caan, and Jason Robards as an evil cattle baron, is so self-conscious about its themes that nothing in the storytelling occurs naturally. Basically, the story is a variant of the evil land-grabber who is determined to take the land of the honest, hardworking rancher: now the honest rancher is a woman. But it's a film of few words (and about a quarter of them mangled by the sound recording), and the melodrama is smothered under sullen, overcast skies—how can you get involved in the conflict between the good guys and the bad guys if you can't even see them? Has the director, Alan J. Pakula, become perversely artistic, or is it that he let his cinematographer, Gordon Willis, get carried away? The film's dark, overblown pictorial style works against the exhilaration possible in the Western genre. Caan gives his lines wryly humorous readings, but Fonda's acting is disappointingly constricted, though she looks great in her tan weather-beaten makeup and tight jeans. With Richard Farnsworth, in a likable performance as an old cowhand, and George Grizzard as a banker. From a script by Dennis Lynton Clark. United Artists. color (See *When the Lights Go Down*.)

Comfort and Joy (1984)—The Scottish writer-director Bill Forsyth made this film in Glasgow, his native city. It's the story of what happens to Alan Bird (Bill Paterson), the disc-jockey host of the local early-morning radio show, after his girl, Maddy (Eleanor David), walks out on him, a few days before Christmas. Forsyth is probably trying to get down under his comic tone and do something deeper than he did in his earlier pictures—something like *McCabe & Mrs. Miller*. The visual scheme is warm and cool—amber and fluorescent blue—and it's stark raving gorgeous. (The cinematography is by Chris Menges.) Forsyth sets up a plot in which the disc jockey tries to mediate a war over turf and price between two groups of Italian ice-cream venders, but the venders, who seem meant to represent freedom and passion and irrationality, are presented as petty buffoons and that throws the movie off. Yet the failed plot doesn't wreck the movie. What's best is the hero's daily routines: the ordinary, rather fussy Alan undergoes a magical transformation when he's at his job, helping his listeners get through the blur of sleep and into the new day. Everyday life is an idyll in this movie. With Patrick Malahide as Alan's doctor friend, Claire Grogan as Charlotte, Alex Norton as Trevor, and Roberto Bernardi as Mr. McCool. color (See *State of the Art*.)

The Comic (1969)—The life of a silent-film comedian is a potentially great subject, and, as Billy Bright, Dick Van Dyke has the true manic feeling for the silent-comedy routines, and Mickey Rooney, as his teammate, Cockeye, creates a character out of almost nothing and lives it on the screen so convincingly that you fully expect to see him again after the movie is over. But Carl Reiner, who directed and was the co-writer and co-producer (with Aaron Ruben), uses his subject in the way TV writers use subjects—as a peg to pin some jokes on. Reiner tickles us, but he seems terrified of trying anything that might have any depth. His movies are as thin as skits. He's prodigiously facile, though, and his inventive re-creations of silent routines help to compensate for the dedication and the story development that are missing. With Michele

Lee, who's charming, and the likable Pert Kelton, at the end of her career, and Steve Allen, Cornel Wilde, and Reiner. Columbia. color (See *Deeper into Movies*.)

Coming Apart (1969)—A psychiatrist (Rip Torn) who has taken the name Glassman cracks up, and you get to see it all reflected in a mirror. This movie is fun, at first, when the idea just seems a put-on and an excuse for some amusing sexual encounters. But then the writer-director, Milton Moses Ginsberg, begins to take the theme seriously, and it all becomes a lot of whimpering and screaming and shattered glass. With Sally Kirkland and Viveca Lindfors. (See *Deeper into Movies*.)

Coming Home (1978)—Allowing for the differences in the wars, this may be one of the post-Vietnam equivalents of the post–Second World War movie *The Best Years of Our Lives*, which also dealt with returning veterans in smooth, popular terms. Throughout, there's a strong element of self-admiration in the film's anti-Vietnam attitude. The time is 1968; the place is Los Angeles. Jane Fonda plays the proper, repressed wife of a hawkish Marine captain (Bruce Dern); after her husband leaves for Vietnam she volunteers for work in a veterans' hospital and meets a paraplegic (Jon Voight), who is in a rage of helplessness. Then the movie, which started out to be about how the Vietnam war changed Americans, turns into a movie about a woman who has her first orgasm when she goes to bed with a paraplegic, and the porny romanticism of this affair has a morbid kick to it. The musical prelude to the sex is reverential—moviemakers haven't found a slicker way of combining purity and eroticism since Marlene Dietrich unknowingly married a runaway monk (Charles Boyer). Hal Ashby directed this intuitive yet amorphous movie, which falls apart when he resorts to melodramatic crosscutting. Though it was shot by Haskell Wexler, a wizard of fast-moving strong graphics, it has a Waspy glaze to it— a soft pastel innocuousness, as if all those involved were so concerned to get their blandly humanitarian message across without offending anyone that they fogged themselves in. With Robert Carradine and Penelope Milford. Those involved in the writing were Nancy Dowd, Waldo Salt, and Robert C. Jones; produced by Jerome Hellman. Academy Awards: Best Actor (Voight), Actress (Fonda), Screenplay. Released by United Artists. color (See *When the Lights Go Down*.)

The Competition (1980)—Amy Irving and Richard Dreyfuss are two of the six finalists in an international piano competition being held in San Francisco. When they fall in love, will Amy, who is rich, sure of herself, and only 21, throw the contest to Richard, who is poor, distraught because of the financial strain he has caused his dying father, and almost 30? And if Amy doesn't, and *she* wins, will she lose Richard? The picture doesn't rise above this daytime-soap-opera level, and between them Irving and Dreyfuss have acquired enough bad acting habits for a different kind of competition. Her voice suggests that she's in a thick, muggy haze, and she drawls affectedly. He scrunches up his face, claps his hand to the back of his neck, and turns away; trying to act a sensitive musician under a terrible strain, he comes across as a throbbing, shuddering wreck. As Irving's teacher, Lee Remick delivers some stunted, pathetic little howlers about life and art; as the vain, lecherous, silver-haired maestro of the symphony orchestra that performs with the finalists, Sam Wanamaker (who looks startlingly like Leonard Bernstein here) gives a polished, old-pro's satirical performance, and struts away with the picture. Directed by Joel Oliansky, from his own screenplay (based on a story he conceived with the producer, William Sackheim). Released by Columbia. color (See *Taking It All In*.)

Compromising Positions (1985)—Susan Isaacs wrote the screenplay adapted from her likably crafted 1978 detective novel, set on Long Island, and her fresh dialogue rhythms give you a lift. Directed by Frank Perry, the movie provides a batch of actresses with a chance to show some comic verve. Susan Sarandon does inspired double-takes—just letting her beautiful dark eyes pop. She's the heroine, whose unquenchable curiosity saves her from the doldrums of affluence in the suburbs with a lawyer husband; when her smiley-eyed, lecherous dentist (Joe Mantegna) is murdered in his snazzy office, she can't resist poking into the case, because it reveals so much about what has been going on around her which she has been unaware of. (Her spontaneous, impetuous fixation on the murder is charmingly irrational; you can feel that something is bubbling up from way down inside her.) Judith Ivey is in top form as the heroine's best friend and opposite number—a frisky cynic who seems to have been wised up from birth. And Deborah Rush is startlingly poignant as a tarty, uneducated blonde, with scars on her tummy and frightened eyes. The cast includes Raul Julia as the police investigator, Anne DeSalvo as the widow, Mary Beth Hurt, Josh Mostel, Joan Allen, and Edward Herrmann, who, as the heroine's husband, starts out as a lively, friendly fellow, and then is turned into her oppressor. That's the plot development that pulls this pleasant, light entertainment down to banality in its second half. Cinematography (with an inexplicable emphasis on ceilings) by Barry Sonnenfeld. Paramount. color (See *Hooked*.)

Compulsion (1959)—Based on the famous case of two Chicago Raskolnikovs—Loeb and Leopold, brilliant students but miserably sloppy murderers. The movie has a stylish, jazz-age format, but the script can't make up its little bit of mind—is it an exploitation of thrills and decadence, or a piece of crime research, or an attack on capital punishment? The three principals—Dean Stockwell, Bradford Dillman, and Orson Welles as their lawyer—were jointly given the Best Actor Award at Cannes, but there's only one remarkable performance—Stockwell's as Judd Steiner (i.e., Nathan Leopold). It's always great to see Welles, but as a spokesman for humanity and humility, he's a terrible humbug, and the oration he's called upon to deliver is just blather. (Clarence Darrow's two-day summation is reduced to 12 minutes of spongy sentiment.) There are all kinds of possibilities in the material, but the movie settles for all-purpose generalities. With Diane Varsi, Richard Anderson, E. G. Marshall, and Martin Milner as the student-reporter (if the murderers had really been the aesthetes they were said to be, he would have been the victim). Richard Fleischer directed, from Richard Murphy's script, based on Meyer Levin's play; cinematography by William C. Mellor. 20th Century-Fox. b & w

Un Condamné à mort s'est échappé, see *A Man Escaped*

Conduct Unbecoming (1975)—Michael Anderson directed this film version of Barry England's contrived courtroom play, set in a cavalry outpost in India in 1878. James Faulkner plays the junior officer accused of sexual assault on a regimental widow (Susannah York), and Michael York is the officer who defends him. The material has no real point or logic, though every now and then a line of dialogue pushes a button marked "Military

Hypocrisy," or "Corruption of Colonialism," or "Subterranean Sex Perversion." The big-name cast includes Trevor Howard, Christopher Plummer, Stacy Keach, and Richard Attenborough. color (See *When the Lights Go Down*.)

The Confession *L'Aveu* (1970)—Costa-Gavras's beautifully detailed demonstration of how the prisoners at the Stalinist show trials in Czechoslovakia in 1952 were made to confess to imaginary crimes. A great, neglected movie subject, intelligently presented. Yves Montand gives a fine non-egotistic performance; with Simone Signoret, Gabriele Ferzetti, Michel Vitold, and Jean Bouise. Screenplay by Jorge Semprun, based on an autobiographical story by Lise and Artur London; cinematography by Raoul Coutard. Produced by Robert Dorfman and Bertrand Javal. In French. color (See *Deeper into Movies*.)

The Confessions of Felix Krull (1957)—Thomas Mann's last novel (a debonair expansion of his early short story) is a lively account of a cherubic young confidence man who uses his natural endowments in a variety of heterosexual and homosexual liaisons. Fox-eyed Horst Buchholz plays the role as if born to it. Kurt Hoffmann made the film in Germany, Paris, and Lisbon, and—like the book—it bounces along from affair to affair. Among Felix's admirers are Liselotte Pulver as Zaza, Ingrid Andree as Zouzou, Susi Nicoletti as Madame Houpfle (who tears off Felix's clothes, forces him to steal from her, and then cries, "Oh, how delightfully you debase me!"), and Walter Rilla as Lord Killmarnoch (who wants to adopt Felix). The fun isn't sustained, but the first part of the picture has considerable charm. The screenplay was written by Robert Thoeren in cooperation with Erika Mann, who appears in the bit part of an English governess. In German. b & w

Confidential Agent (1945)—A tired, aging Spanish Loyalist (tired, aging Charles Boyer, giving an extraordinarily realistic and intense performance) starts out by trying to prevent a Fascist business deal in England, and is variously chased, beaten, and framed by some of the most unsavory characters who ever conspired. The cast includes Peter Lorre, Katina Paxinou, Victor Francen, George Coulouris, Wanda Hendrix, John Warburton, Miles Mander, and George Zucco. It also includes Lauren Bacall; she was elegantly feline in *To Have and Have Not*, which preceded this film, and in *The Big Sleep*, which followed it, but she is clumsy and self-conscious here. Despite the unusual cast and the possibilities in the material (from a Graham Greene novel, adapted by Robert Buckner), the movie is pedestrian, and it marked the end of the screen career of the director, Herman Shumlin, the well-known stage producer. Those unfamiliar with the melodramas of the 40s may be shocked at the brutalities that sneaked by under cover of the anti-Fascist theme. Cinematography by James Wong Howe. Warners. b & w

The Conformist *Il Conformista* (1970)—Bernardo Bertolucci wrote and directed this extraordinarily rich adaptation of the Alberto Moravia novel about an upper-class follower of Mussolini. It's set principally in 1938. Bertolucci's view isn't so much a reconstruction of the past as an infusion from it; the film cost only $750,000—Bertolucci brought together the decor and architecture surviving from that modernistic period and gave it all unity. Jean-Louis Trintignant, who conveys the mechanisms of thought through tension, the way Bogart did, is the aristocratic Fascist—an intelligent coward who sacrifices everything he cares about because he wants

the safety of normality. Stefania Sandrelli is his deliciously corrupt, empty-headed wife, and Dominique Sanda, with her swollen lips and tiger eyes, is the lesbian he would like to run away with. The film succeeds least with its psychosexual approach to the Fascist protagonist, but if the ideas don't touch the imagination, the film's sensuous texture does. It's a triumph of feeling and of style—lyrical, flowing, velvety style, so operatic that you come away with sequences in your head like arias. With Pierre Clémenti as the chauffeur, Gastone Moschin as Manganiello, and Enzo Tarascio as the anti-Fascist professor (who resembles Godard). Cinematography by Vittorio Storaro. In Italian. color (See *Deeper into Movies*.)

A Connecticut Yankee in King Arthur's Court (1949)—This version of the Mark Twain story has none of the Rodgers and Hart songs of the Broadway musical and is devoid of the Will Rogers aw-shucks wit that was so effective in the 1931 movie. Bing Crosby is effortlessly amiable as the Hartford handyman who gets a thump on the head, circa 1905, and is transported to Camelot, but the score (by Johnny Burke and Jimmy Van Heusen) is a series of duds, and the tricks by which Crosby proves himself a magician (such as lighting a fire by focussing the sun's rays through a watch crystal) become a little tiresome. The tacky pageantry is more suited to the opening of a West Coast supermarket than to an English court in the 6th century. Tay Garnett directed, from Edmund Beloin's script; with Cedric Hardwicke, Rhonda Fleming, and William Bendix. (There was a silent version in 1921.) Paramount. color

The Connection (1961)—Adapted by Jack Gelber from his play, and directed by Shirley Clarke, the film became famous because of its four-letter-word censorship troubles. A group of addicts in a New York flat wait for the pusher, Cowboy (Carl Lee), their "connection." There's also a more experimental and more ambitious aspect to the situation: a documentary-film director (William Redfield) and his cameraman are also in the apartment, making a film of the addicts, and thus *The Connection* tries to be a comment on the relationship of artist and subject, as well as on addiction. It's painfully obvious that the dialogue is dramatic writing, and this doesn't jibe too well with the conceit of the documentary's being made. And there are characters (such as a Salvation Army sister) who carry a whiff of antique dramaturgy. With Warren Finnerty, Roscoe Lee Browne, Garry Goodrow, and Jerome Raphel. The music includes Charlie Parker's recording of "Marmaduke" and jazz by Freddie Redd, who is on camera, along with his group, among the addicts. b & w

Conquest (1937)—Greta Garbo as Napoleon's mistress, Countess Marie Walewska, who bore him a son, and Charles Boyer as Napoleon, who, it appears, loved Marie intensely, but briefly. The M-G-M picture cost $3 million and was the fourth most expensive movie made up to that date; it's ornate, unexpectedly tasteful, carefully detailed—and lifeless. There is some literate writing in it, but the various scenarists—Samuel Hoffenstein, Salka Viertel, and S. N. Behrman—working from Helen Jerome's version of a Polish play, don't seem too sure of what the movie is about, or where its center should be. They don't allow Marie Walewska enough shadings or enough strength; her tenderness—which is about all she *is* allowed—becomes tedious. Garbo is stunningly costumed (by Adrian), but her interpretation is muffled. This is one of the rare occasions when her melancholy beauty didn't dominate a film; there's skill but no poetry in her performance. Boyer takes over, by the force of his talent, and because Napoleon (treated less

sympathetically by the writers) has more sides to him. Padded to look pudgy and with his romantic handsomeness de-emphasized (he's even slightly bald), Boyer gives the picture traces of irony and tension. Directed by Clarence Brown, who, failing inspiration, could perhaps have used a little vulgarity, or some speed; the pacing is measured. With Maria Ouspenskaya, Dame May Whitty, Reginald Owen, Alan Marshal, Henry Stephenson, Leif Erickson, C. Henry Gordon, Vladimir Sokoloff, George Zucco, and Scotty Beckett. Cinematography by Karl Freund; art direction by Cedric Gibbons (the retreat from Moscow in the snow was staged in the studio, with painted backdrops). b & w

Conrack (1974)—Jon Voight's features look larger, and the anxious, staring eyes that seemed so close together when he was Joe Buck in *Midnight Cowboy* are bright and confident; he seems to have come strappingly alive. He plays a ribald, freewheeling teacher who tries to wake up a bunch of whipped black kids and wakes up the school authorities, who fire him. Based on *The Water Is Wide*, by Pat Conroy, a young Southerner's account of what he went through in his year of teaching on an island off the South Carolina coast, the picture takes its mood from Voight's roller-coaster performance. It has the airy feeling of the teacher's improvising nature; it has his gusto. The director, Martin Ritt, and the cinematographer, John Alonzo, work in a clear and spacious style; the script is by Irving Ravetch and Harriet Frank, Jr. With Madge Sinclair, who plays a black principal with a slave-overseer mentality; she's so strong and unyielding that she's like an obstinate natural force. Also with Hume Cronyn (this virtuoso of the show-them-what-an-actor-you-are school just can't tone down his slimy villainy for the camera), Ruth Attaway, Paul Winfield, Tina Andrews, and

Antonio Fargas. 20th Century-Fox. color (See *Reeling*.)

Continental Divide (1981)—John Belushi plays a muckraking Chicago reporter so famous that everyone on the streets knows him, and Blair Brown is a saintly ornithologist who lives on a mountaintop in Colorado studying the American bald eagle. Then the scriptwriter, Lawrence Kasdan, is at an impasse: How can he get these two together in marriage without taking either away from a dedicated endeavor at one particular site? Kasdan has eliminated all the conflicting interests and the psychological impediments to a happy marriage, leaving the physical separation as the only obstacle. There's nothing left for the movie to be about except how the hero and the heroine can conquer space. (And at the end, the picture fudges even this.) The characters' mild quandary drags on and on, while the director, Michael Apted, tries to create a little texture out of the void. What the movie never even whispers (because it would be bad sexual politics) is the simple fact that neither of these people cares enough about the other to give up anything. With Tony Ganios, Allen Goorwitz, Carlin Glynn, and Val Avery. Universal. color (See *Taking It All In*.)

Conversation Piece *Gruppo di Famiglia in un Interno* (1975)—The theme is *Death in Venice* all over again, with Burt Lancaster playing Aschenbach to Helmut Berger's Konrad (a garish, grown-up Tadzio). But the director, Luchino Visconti, is in a jovial mood, and the dignified older man—a retired American professor—isn't destroyed; on the contrary, he is recalled to life. Visconti pictures have often had an undercurrent of silliness, and in this one the silliness is very close to the surface; however, there's grandeur in the director's follies and in his allowing his sexual and political obsessions to be displayed so openly.

As Konrad, who moves into an apartment in the professor's house, Berger flaunts the mannerisms that many other actors avoid. A petulant little nymph, Konrad is being kept by a venemous, tantrummy Countess (Silvana Mangano), but he's also supposed to be a revolutionary. In Visconti's view, Konrad is a victim of those to whom he sells his favors, and at the end he stands revealed as a saint. It's an idiosyncratic film, it's cuckoo—an old man's film (partly directed from a wheelchair)—but it's very likable. With Claudia Marsani and Stefano Patrizi, and brief appearances by Dominique Sanda and Claudia Cardinale. Written by Suso Cecchi D'Amico, Enrico Medioli, and Visconti. In Italian. color (See *When the Lights Go Down*.)

Convoy (1978)—Sam Peckinpah's happy-go-lucky ode to the truckers on the road—a sunny, enjoyable picture with only ketchup being splattered (in a mock fight in a diner). The setting is the American Southwest (with lighting that suggests J.M.W. Turner), and the theme is the pettiness of men's quarrels contrasted with the spaciousness of the land. The script fails to dramatize this disparity, and the film, which barely introduces its characters, seems silly at times. However, the trucks give real performances: Peckinpah uses the big rigs anthropomorphically, and while watching this picture, you recover the feelings you had as a child about the power and size and noise of trucks, and their bright, distinctive colors. Graeme Clifford's editing provides fast, hypnotic rhythms, and sequences with the trucks low in the frame and most of the image given over to skies with brilliant white clouds are poetic gestures, like passages in Dovzhenko. As a horny trucker, Kris Kristofferson lacks the common touch that might have given the movie some centrifugal force, though he's as majestic-looking as the big trucks. With the infuriating Ali MacGraw exercising her nostrils, J. D. Kane as Big Nasty, Ernest Borgnine as a vindictive lawman, Cassie Yates as a sad-eyed waitress, and Franklyn Ajaye, Burt Young, Madge Sinclair, Seymour Cassel, and a glimpse of Peckinpah. The B.W.L. Norton script was based on the hit song by C. W. McCall. Cinematography by Harry Stradling, Jr. An E.M.I. production. color (See *When the Lights Go Down.*)

The Cool World (1964)—Shirley Clarke's documentary-style film, based on Warren Miller's novel and the play by Miller and Robert Rossen. Hampton Clanton plays Duke, the 14-year-old Harlem boy who is trying to get a gun from a racketeer (Carl Lee) so he can be leader of his gang, the Royal Pythons. The footage, shot by Baird Bryant, is often fine in itself (and it's far superior to the juvenile-gang story), but it's used for a facile cry of social outrage and for "art," rather than being integrated with the story. The film tries to encompass too much: you get the feeling that the director thought she could use everything good that she caught. There are beautiful bits, but they don't come together. Dizzy Gillespie, James Moody, Mal Waldron, and others are on the jazz and rock 'n' roll track. The cast includes Gloria Foster and Clarence Williams III. Screen adaptation by Shirley Clarke and Carl Lee; produced by Fred Wiseman. b & w

Le Corbeau *The Raven* (1943)—Henri-Georges Clouzot's gall-and-wormwood thriller about a town terrorized by a series of vicious poison-pen letters that drive various townspeople to crime and suicide. The plot— tracking down the blackmailer—is rather mechanical, but Clouzot can give an audience the cold creeps. At the time, the depravity and political corruption revealed in this slice of provincial life were nastily shocking; there's not a likable person in the entire film, and, since it was released during the Occu-

pation, it was thought to serve the interests of the Nazis. When France was liberated, both Clouzot and the picture's star, Pierre Fresnay, were accused of unpatriotic activity. With Ginette Leclerc as the lame girl. (Remade in 1951, by Otto Preminger, as *The 13th Letter.*) In French. b & w

The Corn Is Green (1945)—Bette Davis was only 36 when she played Miss Moffat, the aging spinster schoolteacher of Emlyn Williams' play. (Ethel Barrymore had done it on the stage in the U.S., Sybil Thorndike in England.) Lacking the moral authority of age and the solidity, Davis substituted an air of pedantic refinement that is too thin-spirited for the material. The film lingers in the memory anyway. It's on the side of all our angels: education, liberalism, generosity of spirit— and in an emotionally affecting way. Miss Moffat, an Englishwoman, comes to teach school in an illiterate Welsh mining town in 1890, and discovers that one of her students, a young miner (John Dall), has unusual promise—genius, perhaps. It's a shame that the miner is importuned to become the savior of his country; it's also very apparent that Hollywood isn't Wales. But the director, Irving Rapper, rose to the occasion, and the supporting players—Joan Lorring, Rosalind Ivan, Rhys Williams, Nigel Bruce, Arthur Shields, Mildred Dunnock—have stronger personalities than in most Davis films. Adapted by Casey Robinson and Frank Cavett; music by Max Steiner. Warners. b & w

Corvette Summer (1978)—This film, which marked the directorial début of Matthew Robbins (and which he wrote with his partner, Hal Barwood, who was the producer), was released without much publicity, and very few people saw it. It's about a Southern California boy's love for an automobile: Kenny (Mark Hamill) scrounges parts from an automobile graveyard, and he and his high-school shop class build a shiny Corvette Stingray. On the night the class takes the car out for a trial run, it is stolen. The rest of the picture is Kenny's obsessive pursuit of the car, which he tracks to Las Vegas; the movie doesn't ridicule this quest and doesn't romanticize it—it treats Kenny's passion with gentle respect. The picture doesn't have a snappy enough rhythm, and the repartee is often too slow, and the story takes a bad turn just past midway by making a melodramatic villain out of a likable character. But until then it's generally fresh, and it has a lovely soft visual quality, with unusually pleasing camera placement. (The cinematography is by Frank Stanley.) As the hero, Hamill takes a little getting used to: this picture was made between *Star Wars* and *The Empire Strikes Back*, after the car accident which disfigured him, and he also seems unsure of himself vocally; however, this disturbing element dwindles in importance when Annie Potts enters the story. As a teen-ager who's on her way to Vegas to become a hooker, she's charmingly funny in her distinctive, stylized way until the last 10 minutes, when she is turned into a dingbat. The picture has other lapses of judgment—a gay chief villain, mushy music, and an overeagerness to make banal points about corruption. Yet a radiant lyricism comes through it all. With Eugene Roche, Kim Milford, and Philip Bruns. United Artists. color

The Cotton Club (1984)—The dark, lacquered visual style doesn't come out of the material; it's a fashionable style that's imposed, like the visual formats of videos, and the only goal of the director, Francis Coppola, seems to be to keep the imagery rushing by—for dazzle, for spectacle. The action is centered on the famous Harlem late-night supper club—a speakeasy with a great floor show, in which "colored" headliners and the "tall, tan, and terrific" Cotton Club Girls per-

formed for a white clientele. There's so much going on you can't take your eyes off it, but none of it means anything. The staccato imagery fragments the musical numbers, and knocks the life out of the performers; the sound is disembodied, and so are the dancers. The tall, sinuous Lonette McKee, with her long, expressive arms upraised, actually gets to complete a number (the torchy "Ill Wind"), Richard Gere flashes a pretty smile and is more agreeable than usual, and a few of the actors playing mobsters—Julian Beck, Bob Hoskins, and Fred Gwynne—seem to be invincible. But from the way Coppola directs the cast here, people exist to reflect light. With Nicolas Cage, Gregory and Maurice Hines, Diane Lane, James Remar, Gwen Verdon, Honi Coles, Novella Nelson, Larry Fishburne, and Joe Dallesandro as Lucky Luciano. Screenplay by Coppola and William Kennedy; cinematography by Stephen Goldblatt; production design by Richard Sylbert. A Zoetrope Production, released by Orion. color (See *State of the Art*.)

Counsellor-at-Law (1933)—John Barrymore seems an unlikely choice for the ghetto-born lawyer of Elmer Rice's play, but this is one of the few screen roles that reveal his measure as an actor. His "presence" is apparent in every scene; so are his restraint, his humor, and his zest. The material is success-story-with-heartbreak—a typical American well-made play of the period: energetic, naïve, melodramatic, goodhearted, and full of gold-diggers, social climbers, and dedicated radicals. The director, William Wyler, sticks close to the play and tells the story in a simple, unadorned way, which has the advantage for us now of preserving the theatrical style of the time. With Bebe Daniels, Melvyn Douglas, Doris Kenyon, Mayo Methot, Thelma Todd, Onslow Stevens, Isabel Jewell, John Qualen, Vincent Sherman, and, as the horrid stepson, Richard Quine. The adaptation is by

Rice; cinematography by Norbert Brodine. Universal. b & w

The Count of Monte Cristo (1934)—A beautifully made Napoleonic era swashbuckler, telling a story that spans 20 years and moves back and forth among Elba, Marseilles, Paris, and Rome by the fluid use of short, pithy scenes and fade outs. Its greatest asset is the handsome young English actor Robert Donat who had a beautiful triste (asthmatic) voice and something elusively sympathetic about him. His Edmund Dantes, the innocent sea captain who is caught in a political trap, locked in a fortress, and certified dead, stands out among all Hollywood's adventurer heroes. Dantes is saved from the darkness by another prisoner, the Abbé Faria (O. P. Heggie), who has inscribed the world's knowledge on his dungeon walls. And the Abbé endows Dantes with the fabulous wealth that enables him to seek justice for the treacherous three men—now eminent—who incarcerated him (Louis Calhern, Sidney Blackmer, Raymond Walburn). As Mercedes, the woman Dantes loves, Elissa Landi tries a little too hard to be spirited but improves with age. Also with Georgia Caine as her mother, Douglas Walton as her son, and Mitchell Lewis, Luis Alberni, and Clarence Muse as the smugglers, and Irene Hervey, Holmes Herbert, and William Farnum. A fine job of directing by Rowland V. Lee, from a script by Philip Dunne, Dan Totheroh, and Lee himself, based on the (often filmed) novel by Alexandre Dumas. The cinematography is by Peverell J. Marley; the less than inspired music is by Alfred Newman. A Reliance Picture, released by United Artists. b & w

Country (1984)—This film, which stars Jessica Lange, who conceived it and had a hand in producing it, is trying to be a feminist *The Grapes of Wrath*. Lange isn't playing a character—she's playing a set of virtues that she associates with her idea of an "ordinary" luminous Midwestern woman, a contemporary Ma Joad. When the Farmers Home Administration moves to foreclose on the 180-acre farm that has been in the heroine's family for over a hundred years, and her husband (Sam Shepard) and her father (Wilford Brimley) fall apart, she's firm in her resolve and she holds on to the land. Working from a script by William D. Wittliff, the director, Richard Pearce, gives us standard hokey melodrama, but he doles it out as if it were full of integrity. Every frame is planned to be a work of American art. Essentially, this is a movie about Jessica Lange's spirit-of-the-prairie face. With Levi L. Knebel, who gives a fresh, affecting performance as Lange and Shepard's teen-age son, and Matt Clark and Sandra Seacat. The cinematography is by David M. Walsh. Touchstone (Disney). color (See *State of the Art*.)

The Country Girl (1954)—This rather odd movie, derived from a Clifford Odets play, features the least broken-down of actors, Bing Crosby, as a broken-down actor—a weak-willed, alcoholic heel who lives on the strength of his wife, Grace Kelly. William Holden is the Broadway director who misinterprets the tangle of dependencies and tries to free the husband from the wife. Rather inexplicably, this sadomasochistic morass was one of the biggest box-office hits of its year, and somewhat inexplicably also, Academy Awards were presented to Grace Kelly as Best Actress and to the director, George Seaton, for his uneven and incoherent screenplay. The film has virtues, however—Holden's performance, good backstage dialogue, and Anthony Ross in a small role. With Gene Reynolds; songs by Ira Gershwin and Harold Arlen. Produced by William Perlberg, for Paramount. b & w

Coup de foudre, see *Entre nous*

Coup de grâce (1976)—This Franco-German film version of Marguerite Yourcenar's novel is so gray and bleak and wintry that it's like a classic made in the Soviet Union 25 years ago and played intensively on PBS. It's by no means bad; the director, Volker Schlöndorff, is highly skilled. But the emotions don't fully emerge, and even after it's over one isn't certain what it was about—though probably we're meant to see that the proud Countess Sophie (Margarethe von Trotta) has been so deeply wounded because Erich, the Prussian officer she loves (Matthias Habich, a heel-clicking Richard Harris), doesn't love her that she throws her life away. Her self-destructive passion is only one element in a movie which has a few too many sexual, historical, and political crosscurrents; some of them, such as Erich's sexual involvement with Sophie's brother, Konrad (Rudiger Kirschstein), are presented so elliptically they're like blurred memories of a dream. (Schlöndorff's artistry gets in the viewer's way.) The story takes place in 1919 in the Baltic area (which had just been divided into Latvia, Lithuania, and Estonia) during the sporadic fighting among various factions that continued after the official end of the First World War. Sophie, who is struggling to emancipate herself, is involved with the Communist cause, while Erich is fighting against Red Army units and mopping up Bolshevik guerrillas. Eventually, she is killed by the man she loves, as in the spy melodramas of 30 years ago—only this time there are more layers of ambiguity about their feelings. The legendary cabaret artist Valeska Gert (she played the procuress who brought Greta Garbo into the brothel in Pabst's 1925 *Joyless Street*) appears as Sophie's half-crazed aunt and is utterly bizarre: shrivelled, yet more intensely alive than anyone else in the movie. The screenplay is by Schlöndorff and by von Trotta (his wife). In French and German. b & w

Coup de torchon *Clean Slate* (1981)—Bertrand Tavernier's film is set in some sort of French colonial Dogpatch in Africa, in 1938, just before the start of the Second World War, and it stars Philippe Noiret as a cuckolded weakling who is jeered at by the pimps and the other brutal white men who exploit the natives. He is also the only officer of the law in the area, and he secretly kills off the exploiters, using his reputation for being cowardly and ineffectual as a cover. The movie is torpid even in the early sequences that aim at sly farce, and its thesis is that even such drastic and half-mad cleanup jobs are hopeless. For a while it's a *Dirty Harry* revenge fantasy for liberals; then the officer lets us know that he thinks he is Christ returned and the picture shifts into Christ mythology. Tavernier may think he's bringing out the rage behind despair, but all he brings out is his sense of futility. He's saying horrible, senseless, inexplicable things (such as the whopper that killing on a small scale is less immoral than killing on a big scale). The film chokes on its own unresolvable ambiguities. With Isabelle Huppert, who frisks about nakedly and amusingly, and Jean-Pierre Marielle, Stéphane Audran, Guy Marchand, Eddy Mitchell as Nono, Samba Mane as Friday, Abdoulaye Diop as Fête Nat, and Irene Skobline as the schoolteacher. The script, by Jean Aurenche and Tavernier, is based on the American pulp novel *Pop. 1280*, by Jim Thompson, which was set in the American South. In French. color (See *Taking It All In*.)

Cousin, Cousine (1975)—The success of this rhythmless, mediocre piece of moviemaking may be in part attributable to its winsome heroine (Marie-Christine Barrault, who is sexy in a fleshy, smiling-nun way) and in part to its silliness. With its wholesome carnality, this film about a big family is so pro-life that it treats sex like breakfast cereal. It features adultery without dirt—adultery as carefree nonconformity—and the way the chorus of understanding kids applauds the parents' displays of innocent happy sensuality, it could be the first Disney True Life Adventure about people. With Victor Lanoux and Marie-France Pisier, who gives the liveliest performance. Written and directed by Jean-Claude Tacchella. In French. color

The Cousins *Les Cousins* (1959)—Claude Chabrol's subtle, glittering film about a naïve, plodding country cousin (Gérard Blain) who destroys his gifted, bohemian city cousin (the suave Jean-Claude Brialy). Perhaps that country boy is not really as honest as he seems: his diligence, his sobriety, all his antique virtues may be just a self-deceiving defense against the facts of modern life. The heroine (Juliette Mayniel), who almost thinks she loves him, realizes that this is just an intellectual and aesthetic response; she would like to be able to believe in a pure, sweet, and enduring love. One of the major New Wave films, it now has added interest for its portrait of the French student life of the 50s. In French. b & w (See *I Lost it at the Movies.*)

Cousins (1989)—Bland, dreamy effervescence is what's being sold in this canny Americanization of the celebrated French makeout movie *Cousin, Cousine* (1975). Set in the Pacific Northwest, it starts with a wedding that links Italian and Polish families. As the picture goes on and on, and you get its box-office formula—sex without messiness, family without oppressive closeness—you may begin to feel as if you were in a carefree pink padded cell, or as if you were back in a Doris Day comedy, except that this film isn't so insistently bright, and it's more woodlandsy, more radiant and idyllic. As honest, free-spirited adulterers, Isabella Rossellini

and Ted Danson are at the still center, smiling serenely while the others in the cast busily bang away at their joie de vivre. Rossellini's unforced expressiveness has a grace—it's as if she were too friendly and sensible to do what we think of as "acting." Joel Schumacher directed; Stephen Metcalfe did the adaptation. With William L. Petersen, Sean Young, Norma Aleandro, George Coe, Lloyd Bridges, Keith Coogan, and Gina DeAngelis. Shot in British Columbia. Paramount. color (See *Movie Love.*)

Cover Girl (1944)—The wartime plot about hoofers and models is a shambles, and there's a prolonged flashback to the Gay Nineties that is almost ruinous, but this big, flashy, Technicolor musical has a lot to recommend it: Rita Hayworth, Gene Kelly, Phil Silvers, and songs by Ira Gershwin and Jerome Kern, including "Put Me to the Test," and the slurpy but affecting "Long Ago and Far Away." Kelly and Silvers are a livelier team than Kelly and Hayworth, though she does look sumptuous, and her big smile could be the emblem of the period. The cast includes Lee Bowman, Otto Kruger, Eve Arden, Edward Brophy, Jinx Falkenburg, and dozens of celebrated models. Charles Vidor directed; Virginia Van Upp wrote the script; Stanley Donen, Kelly, Seymour Felix, and Jack Cole staged the dances; Nan Wynn dubbed Hayworth's singing. Arthur Schwartz produced, for Columbia.

The Cowboys (1972)—Blood and homilies on one of the most torpid cattle drives since the invention of motion pictures. Eleven boys, aged 9 to 15, are so well trained by their surrogate big daddy, John Wayne, that when he is shot by a rustler (a cringing cur of the old school, played by Bruce Dern) they wipe out the whole 17-man gang. The point of view of the movie is that killing makes them men. When the rotten Dern is trapped under his horse and pleads for help, a boy cuts one strap loose and fires a gun to frighten the horse, and the whole troupe watches impassively as the horse runs, dragging the man screaming to his death. The obscenely complacent movie invites us to identify with these good little men and to be proud of them. Mark Rydell directed this pious muck. With Roscoe Lee Browne, who does his charming, urbane number as the cook on the drive, Leora Dana as Wayne's gruff, understanding wife, Colleen Dewhurst as a madam, and Slim Pickens. The script by Irving Ravetch and Harriet Frank, Jr., and William Dale Jennings is based on Jennings' novel; music by John Williams. Warners. color (See *Deeper into Movies*.)

Cracked Nuts (1931)—Vaudevillians and Ziegfeld stars of the 20s, Bert Wheeler and Robert Woolsey carried over their stage routines and became a popular R K O comedy team in the early 30s. It was often impossible to decide if they were wonderfully terrible or just plain terrible, but they were totally unpretentious. Round-faced Wheeler was the teary, innocent, eternal juvenile; skinny, bespectacled Woolsey was the con man, nibbling on a long cigar and spitting out quips. The story here is about their efforts to seize the throne of the kingdom of Eldorania; the villains include Boris Karloff and Stanley Fields. The cast also includes Edna May Oliver as the aunt of the pert straight-girl heroine, Dorothy Lee, an actress of such bright-eyed, dizzying incompetence that she wins you over. Memorable bit: Ben Turpin as an aerial bomber. His cockeyes are in closeup when he assures his boss (Karloff) that he'll hit his target. Edward Cline directed; Al Boasberg and Ralph Spence did the writing. b & w

The Cranes Are Flying *Letyat Zhuravli* (1957)—The Mikhail Kalatozov film was made during the de-Stalinization period of the late 50s; set during the Second World War, it deals with a beautiful Moscow girl (the lovely Tatiana Samoilova) who is trapped in a loveless marriage with an unpatriotic and hence decadent pianist after her fiancé (Alexei Batalov) goes to the front. Somewhat silly, but with fine sequences, and Miss Samoilova, a grandniece of Stanislavsky, does him honor. In Russian. b & w

Crazy Love, see *Love Is a Dog from Hell*

The Crazy Quilt (1965)—The story "The Illusionless Man and the Visionary Maid" by the psychoanalyst Allen Wheelis provided the basis for John Korty's first feature, filmed in and around Stinson Beach, near San Francisco, with Tom Rosqui as the practical, down-to-earth husband, and Ina Mela as Lorabelle, the always romantic, ever hopeful wife. It's a lightly told comedy-fable on sex differences, on attitudes to life, and on marriage itself. Korty's lack of facility makes it a little bumpy, and the adaptation which he did doesn't have the subtlety of the story. Korty, who also photographed the film and edited it, is a more skillful cinematographer than writer. His next film, *Funnyman*, was considerably more craftsmanlike, but this is a pleasantly amateurish start. It was made for less than $100,000. Narration by Burgess Meredith; music by David and Peter Schickele. b & w

The Creature from the Black Lagoon (1954)—The amusingly slimy monster—a sort of rubbery, leering frog that stands upright, like a man—has obscene intentions toward the fainting heroine (Julia Adams). This low-grade horror film from Universal came out in 3-D, and kids seemed to adore the amphibious villain. (There were two sequels.) William Alland produced; Jack Arnold directed, from a script by Harry Essex and Arthur Ross. With Richard Carlson, Richard Denning, Antonio Moreno, Nestor Paiva, Whit Bissell, and Ben Chapman and Ricou Browning as the monster. b & w

Les Créatures (1966)—Michel Piccoli plays a writer with a pregnant wife (Catherine Deneuve, looking inhumanly beautiful) who has lost the power of speech; they're in an island house where he plans to work on a novel. Complicated, full of gamesmanship and some seven subplots and mystical sci-fi, and maybe only for those who like to play chess—if for them. (The film features a magical chessboard with live chessmen.) Agnès Varda wrote and directed. With Eva Dahlbeck, Jacques Charrier, and Nino Castelnuovo. Produced by Mag Bodard; a French-Swedish co-production. In French. b & w and color

Cries and Whispers *Viskningar och Rop* (1972)—Ingmar Bergman's dream play is set in a manor house at the turn of the century where a spinster in her late 30s (Harriet Andersson) is dying. Her two sisters (Ingrid Thulin and Liv Ullmann) have come to attend her, and they watch and wait, along with a peasant servant (Kari Sylwan). The movie is built out of a series of emotionally charged images that express inner stress, and Bergman handles them with the fluidity of a master. Superbly photographed by Sven Nykvist in a style suggesting Edvard Munch, and with blood-red backgrounds, the film is smooth and hypnotic; it has oracular power and the pull of a dream. Yet there's a 19th-century dullness at the heart of it. Each sister represents a different aspect of woman—woman viewed as the Other—and the film mingles didacticism with erotic mystery.

With Erland Josephson as the doctor, and Anders Ek as Isak. In Swedish. color (See *Reeling.*)

Crime and Punishment (1935)—There's almost everything you can think of the matter with this Hollywood version, directed by Josef von Sternberg, but it has got a great Raskolnikov: Peter Lorre. He had only three roles that tapped his full talent—the child-murderer in *M*, the hero in *The Face Behind the Mask*, and this remarkably suggestive and witty Raskolnikov. Stolid Edward Arnold is embarrassingly miscast as Inspector Porfiry; if Harry Baur, who did the role in the French version, had played opposite Lorre, the film might have caught fire. As the pawnbroker, Mrs. Patrick Campbell adds some distinction, but not much can be said for the Madonna lighting given to Marian Marsh's placid Sonya, or for the standard Hollywood performances of Elisabeth Risdon as Raskolnikov's mother, Tala Birell as his sister, and Gene Lockhart, Robert Allen, and Douglass Dumbrille. There's nothing Russian about them but the long-winded names by which they address each other. Lucien Ballard did the cinematography, in the stylized von Sternberg manner. Columbia. b & w

Crime and Punishment *Crime et châtiment* (1935)—Marcel Aymé's adaptation has clarity and power; the director, Pierre Chenal, uses the controversial, rather stagey technique of conveying the characters' dissociation from their environment by a slight distortion in the settings. As Raskolnikov, Pierre Blanchar is older, more eccentric than one expects: he emphasizes the tortured isolation, the near madness, of the character. It is in Harry Baur's performance as Inspector Porfiry that the film achieves its stature; Graham Greene long ago described the performance as "the finest in the cinema this year, with his tortoise movements, his streak of cruelty, his terrible good humor"—it is one of the great performances of any year. In French. b & w

Crime et châtiment, see *Crime and Punishment*

Crime Without Passion (1934)—Ben Hecht and Charles MacArthur devised a tricky plot about a devilishly unscrupulous lawyer (Claude Rains), who looks for a perfect alibi to conceal a murder. They also produced and directed, and they got very fancy; their pseudo-stream-of-consciousness story is dolled up with a lot of symbolism and dated avant-garde novelties. The film, which emphasizes nightclub life, was produced at the Astoria Studios in New York; Lee Garmes was the cinematographer and associate director, and the famous Slavko Vorkapich designed two montage sequences. The one with the Furies being unleashed is a true period piece; this is an entertainingly terrible movie. The blond Whitney Bourne is the lawyer's new love, and the brunette Margo his old love and his victim. With Esther Dale, and a fleeting appearance by Helen Hayes in a hotel lobby. Paramount. b & w

Crimes and Misdemeanors (1989)—Written and directed by Woody Allen, it's a sad, censuring look at an eminent ophthalmologist (Martin Landau) and other crooks in high places who (in Allen's view) have convinced themselves that they can do anything, because they don't think God is watching. Allen is making the film equivalent of a play of ideas, and the ideas have no excitement. He's telling us not just what we already know but what we've already rejected. Woody Allen himself plays a little, grubbing-for-a-living documentary filmmaker who falls in love but can't compete for the woman (Mia Farrow) against a darling of the media, a tall, egomaniacal TV producer played with a wonderfully smug, screwy abandon by Alan

Alda. Except for Alda, and Landau (when he's showing nervous impatience), and Jerry Orbach, who plays the ophthalmologist's shady brother, most of the large cast is proficient yet brittle and dull. With Sam Waterston (as a rabbi who's going blind), Anjelica Huston, Claire Bloom, Joanna Gleason, Caroline Aaron, Nora Ephron in a bit, and Daryl Hannah—uncredited, but looking so luscious she almost stops the show. The bland cinematography is by Sven Nykvist. Orion. color (See *Movie Love.*)

Crimes of the Heart (1986)—Diane Keaton, Jessica Lange, and Sissy Spacek playing sisters and sparking off each other are something to see. The play, by Beth Henley—a comedy about wacked-out normality, set in Hazlehurst, Mississippi—has its goofy charm; it's thin material, though, and her screen adaptation is just the usual "opening out." But the three actresses put so much faith in their roles that they carry the movie, triumphantly. They take the play's borderline pathos about heartbreakingly screwed-up lives—it's a mixture of looniness and lyricism—and give it real vitality. These are inspired performances. With Sam Shepard, Tess Harper, David Carpenter, and Hurd Hatfield. Directed by Bruce Beresford. De Laurentiis. color (see *Hooked.*)

The Criminal Life of Archibaldo de la Cruz *Ensayo de un Crimen* (1955)—Only intermittently amusing black comedy, made in Mexico by Luis Buñuel. Directed rather indifferently, though the story has a Buñuelian perversity—perhaps a little more giddy than usual. It has a wonderful start: Archibaldo finds a music box which reawakens his memories of a childhood experience. His governess had found him dressed up in his mother's clothes, and while she was bawling him out for it, a stray bullet from the revolution going on outside had killed her. This gratification of his desires gave him ecstasy. Later, Archibaldo keeps trying to recapture that sexual pleasure, but his attempts to commit murder are continually frustrated by the deaths of his intended victims. With Ernesto Alonso as the smiling dilettante and fantasist, Archibaldo, and Miroslava Stern as the amoral Lavinia. The script, by Buñuel and Eduardo Ugarte, is based on a story by Rodolfo Usigli. In Spanish. b & w

The Crimson Pirate (1952)—This wonderful travesty of the buccaneer film has the physical exuberance of the early Douglas Fairbanks, Sr., pictures. Burt Lancaster and his old circus partner Nick Cravat tumble and jump with exhilarating grace. They charge the film with physical sensations, and if you wanted to dance after seeing the Rogers-Astaire musicals, you'll want to get in condition after experiencing the acrobatics here. Robert Siodmak's direction is lively; Roland Kibbee's script is bright and improvisatory (much of the film's wit derives from a series of casual anachronisms). With James Hayter as a wildly improbable inventor who looks like Benjamin Franklin, and Eva Bartok, Torin Thatcher, and Margot Grahame. Cinematography by Otto Heller; music by William Alwyn. A Hecht-Lancaster Production; Warners. color

Crin blanc, see *White Mane*

Il Cristo Proibito *Strange Deception* (1951)—Curzio Malaparte's only film is a visually exciting but emotionally upsetting allegory of justice, guilt, and expiation. Malaparte, author of *Kaputt* and *The Skin*, stopped at many stations—Fascist, Communist, pro-American—and in this somewhat ludicrous semi-Christian lament for man's inability to solve his moral problems, he finds his strongest image in the masked, robed procession for the Game of the Cross.

The hero, Raf Vallone, returns to his Italian village after the war and tries to hunt down the man who caused his brother's death. The villagers, sick of blood and vengeance, refuse to tell him anything; to put an end to the search, his best friend (Alain Cuny) falsely confesses that he was the betrayer. The movie was condemned by the Catholic Church, attacked by the Communists, and ignored by the public. Perhaps there is a kind of writer's moviemaking that, despite talent and originality, despite "art," is too self-serious and is doomed at the box office. *Il Cristo Proibito* has similarities to Pasolini's *Accatone*. They are boring, fascinating, maddening movies. In Italian. b & w

Cromwell (1970)—Was there ever a period of history when the clothes were less photogenic? The actors waddle around in their Puritan barrels and bloomers, then stand still to make speeches at each other. Richard Harris, of the hangdog expression, delivers his lines in a cracked, rasping voice with no music in it. He plays Cromwell as a sullen prig who hates power; the movie never explains how he got it. Alec Guinness barely wiggles a few facial muscles and manages to make an acting showcase out of his restrained performance as King Charles I. But Shakespeare spoiled us for this sort of thing: we wait for great speeches and witty remarks, for rage and poetry, and we get dedicated stodginess. Ken Hughes wrote and directed this English production. With Robert Morley, Dorothy Tutin, Timothy Dalton, Michael Jayston, Frank Finlay, Patrick Wymark, Charles Gray, and Patrick Magee. Cinematography by Geoffrey Unsworth. color (See *Deeper into Movies*.)

Cross Creek (1983)—Very loosely based on Marjorie Kinnan Rawlings' semi-autobiographical tales of her years in an orange grove in the Florida swamps, this movie, directed by Martin Ritt, suggests a child's storybook version of women's liberation. Everything is lighted to look holy, and whenever the score isn't shimmering and burnishing, nature is twittering. It's all pearly and languid, and more than a little twerpy—it's one long cue for "Oh, What a Beautiful Mornin'." The heroine is envisioned as a muted, passive artist who soaks up the local color, and the audience is left to watch her soak. As Mrs. Rawlings, Mary Steenburgen is withdrawn; she has a tight, little-girl voice, and she seems to count to ten before she speaks—she comes across as a lyrical stiff. The movie is lulling, in a semi-stupefying way. Most of it is sun-coated and sugar-cured. But Rip Torn plays a Cracker on a grand scale; he's too powerful for sweetening. And Ritt shows his flair for melodrama in his handling of the hyper-emotional entanglement between Torn and Dana Hill, who plays his daughter; the two work together with what looks like spontaneous frenzy. The Cracker's emotions rear up very large, and he simply discharges them—when he's bashing chairs or tables, it's like brushing a tear away. It's a rampaging role, but Rip Torn doesn't seem to be afraid of anything, and he gives a demonstration of a wild-man actor's art. The picture would be stone cold without it. With Alfre Woodard as Geechee, and Peter Coyote—he has a Jiminy Cricket charm as Norton Baskin, who becomes Mrs. Rawlings' second husband. Also with Malcolm McDowell as Maxwell Perkins (who just happens to be in the neighborhood because he has been visiting "Ernest in Key West"), Cary Guffey, Joanna Miles, John Hammond, and Toni Hudson. The script is by Dalene Young; the cinematography is by John A. Alonzo. Produced by Robert B. Radnitz; Universal. color (See *State of the Art.*)

Crossfire (1947)—Psychological depths are sounded, though not deeply: the murder victim is a Jew, the murderer an anti-Semite. (The depths in the original novel, *The Brick Foxhole*, by Richard Brooks were a little different: the victim was a homosexual.) This tense, well-acted thriller was made by the producer Adrian Scott, the director Edward Dmytryk, and the writer John Paxton. Robert Ryan brings his considerable talent for portraying obsessive, isolated individuals to the role of the sly, anti-Semitic ex-sergeant. With Robert Mitchum, Gloria Grahame, Robert Young, Sam Levene, and Paul Kelly. There are condescending little messages on the evils of race prejudice that make you squirm; this is the patina of 40s melodrama. R K O. b & w

Crossroads (1986)—It takes its title from the legend that the Mississippi Delta guitarist and singer Robert Johnson—perhaps the finest bluesman who has ever lived—sold his eternal soul to the Devil at a lonely crossroads. The movie gives Johnson a fictional friend, the harmonica player and singer Willie Brown (Joe Seneca) who went to the crossroads a few years later. Now 80, and in a prison nursing home in Harlem, Willie cons a white teen-age Juilliard student (Ralph Macchio), who's trying to find a lost Robert Johnson song, into helping him escape and get back to Mississippi. The first three-quarters of an hour—with the grizzled old hipster Willie snarling at the boy's softness, his musical pretensions, his wanting to follow in the footsteps of other whites who have ripped off black music—is junkily entertaining. But when they're on the road in the South, Willie turns into a curmudgeonly guardian angel, the boy starts learning lessons about life, and the picture is contemptible. In *The Karate Kid*, the bland, toneless-voiced Macchio was taught the martial arts by an elderly Japanese and defeated opponents twice his size; that picture was a box-office hit, so this time he engages in a musical variant of the big fight—battling guitars with the Devil's top musician (and winning the match with the assistance of Mozart). Sticking to the script by John (one-piece-of-information-per-scene) Fusco, the director, Walter Hill, shows little of his flair. It would be easy to quarrel with Ry Cooder's blues numbers, but at least they're dramatic—they have a twangy intensity. With Jami Gertz (not very pleasing as the boy's love interest), Robert Judd as Scratch, Joe Morton as Scratch's assistant, and Allan Arbus, Dennis Lipscomb, Gretchen Palmer, and Steve Vai as the boy's adversary in the final contest. There's some fine harmonica work by Sonny Terry. The cinematography is by John Bailey. Columbia. color (See *Hooked.*)

The Crusades (1935)—Maybe the most ludicrous of all the De Mille epics—possibly because it's more romantic and less spectacular. Loretta Young, in rope-like blond hair as Berengaria, has excruciatingly colloquial diction that blights her attempts at Middle Ages winsomeness; she is formally married to Richard the Lion-Hearted's sword. When the stalwart Henry Wilcoxon, as the King, finally meets her, he has to take a deep breath and freeze his facial muscles before delivering simple lines such as ''I love you, Berengaria.'' Your heart goes out to him. This glorious schlock pageant will be even more enjoyable for those who take a few minutes beforehand to bone up on the historical data; they'll be able to appreciate how willfully and gratuitously De Mille garbled every single historical character and incident. It isn't that he improved on them: he simply had to make them his own. Charles Ludlam, of the Ridiculous Theatrical Company, could hardly improve on this one. With Ian Keith as the likable infidel, Saladin, who takes Berengaria prisoner; Katherine De Mille as the woman spurned by Richard; and Joseph Schildkraut, Alan Hale, C. Henry Gordon, Jason Robards, Sr., Montagu Love, George Barbier, Hobart

Bosworth, Lumsden Hare, William Farnum, and Mischa Auer. Paramount. b & w

Crusoe (1989)—In this variation on the famous story, Aidan Quinn is a Tidewater Virginia slave trader whose eagerness for profits leads him, in 1808, to charter a ship in the dangerous autumn months. The story has been re-imagined so that when the ship is wrecked and the immature, unfeeling money-grubber is swept onto an island, what follows is not a wilderness test of survival—it's an enforced spiritual retreat. Directed by Caleb Deschanel, from a script by Walon Green, this version is spare and evocative; it tends toward wordlessness and suggests a haiku movie. Essentially, it's all images of entrapment and freedom—it's about Crusoe's learning to revere freedom, after he has twice been saved from death by a native warrior (Adé Sapara). Deschanel's lack of narrative skill is frank and deliberate; his emotionality and his feeling for atmosphere can carry a viewer along. He has a style; it comes out of the meekness in the way he works. And slim, curly-topped Aidan Quinn, with his dazed voice and his fixated blue eyes, is Crusoe as a hippie Christ figure—a young man finding his way to be gentle. Open, receptive, a New Age Montgomery Clift, he's the right actor for Deschanel's conception. The movie suggests a revised *Tempest*, in which Prospero and Caliban find out they're brothers. With a wonderful scrawny, predominantly Airedale mutt. Shot mostly on the Seychelles Islands. Island Pictures. color (See *Movie Love.*)

Cry Freedom (1987)—The producer-director Richard Attenborough attempts to use the martyrdom of the young South African Stephen Biko (Denzel Washington), the leader of the Black Consciousness Movement, to arouse the audience to the tragic injustice of apartheid. This epic collapses before midpoint when Biko is badly beaten while in the custody of the Security Police and dies, in September, 1977, of brain injuries. The story then shifts to the efforts of Donald Woods (Kevin Kline), a white newspaper editor, to escape with his wife and five children, taking with him the manuscript of a book he has written about his friend Biko. When Attenborough starts crosscutting from the escape to Woods' flashback memories (with bursts of choral music), the movie is dumbfounding. It looks as if Attenborough staged scenes and then didn't know what to do with them, so he stuck them in by having the escaping Woods think back. And every time Biko appears in a flashback our interest quickens; this man with fire in his eyes commands the screen—Denzel Washington is the star by right of talent. When the movie cuts back to the grayish, undefined Woods, the family escape story recalls *The Sound of Music*. And we're painfully aware that despite the movie's hopes of raising the white audience's consciousness, we whites are assumed to need a white man to identify with. Screenplay by John Briley, based on Woods' books *Biko* and *Asking for Trouble*. There are performers who seem exactly right: the rich-voiced Juanita Waterman as Biko's wife; Kate Hardie as the Woods' adolescent daughter; John Matshikiza as a black reporter; Gerald Sim as a police doctor, frightened when he sees Biko's injuries; and John Thaw as the duplicitous Minister of Police. Cinematography by Ronnie Taylor; shot mostly in Zimbabwe. Released by Universal. (157 minutes.) color (See *Hooked*.)

A Cry in the Dark (1988)—The director, Fred Schepisi, attempts an epic dissection of how superstitions can spread, and how false the public perception (based on the media) can be. He uses the case of Lindy Chamberlain (Meryl Streep), the wife of a Seventh Day Adventist minister, who was tried for murder and convicted, to ask why Australians cynically rejected her account of seeing a dingo (the Australian wild dog) slink off from the tent her 9-week-old daughter was in. Perhaps the thing that made her the most hated woman in Australia was that TV had accustomed people to grieving mothers who showed their frailty and their naked pathos, and here was Lindy on TV—stoic, matter-of-fact, and bluntly impatient at the endless dumb questions. Streep has seen that Lindy's hardness saves a part of her from the quizzing and prying of journalists and lawyers—that she needs her impersonal manner to keep herself intact. (From time to time, Streep suggests the strong emotions that Lindy hides in public, and we feel a bond with her—we feel joined to her privacy.) There are wonderful night scenes of the search for the baby in the blackness around Ayers Rock, in the Outback, and the movie is never less than gripping. But Schepisi, who worked on the script with Robert Caswell (it's based on John Bryson's study of the case, *Evil Angels*), put together more elements than he could develop. The film is like an expanded, beautifully made TV "Movie of the Week." Streep seems to be playing a person in a documentary. This is also true of the accomplished Sam Neill, though he seems faultlessly right as Lindy's husband, who becomes incoherent during the trial and loses his faith. You come out moved—even shaken—yet not quite certain what you've been watching. Cinematography by Ian Baker. Released by Warners. color (See *Movie Love*.)

The Curse of the Cat People (1944)—Val Lewton produced this sequel to his famous low-budget thriller, the hard-to-forget *Cat People*, in which Simone Simon tried to convince her husband (Kent Smith) that she would turn into a panther if he tried to consummate the marriage. He sent her to a psychiatrist who attempted to make love to her and was mauled to death, after fatally wounding her. In the misbegotten sequel, Kent Smith, who has remarried, fears that his small daughter, Amy (Ann Carter), is under the influence of his first wife, and by his repressiveness he drives the lonely, imaginative child to invent a friend, who is indeed the first wife (played once again by Simone Simon). The film is a true oddity, since Lewton perversely refused to give the studio the feline shocker it wanted, and instead tried to make a poetic film about a lonely child's need for an imaginary friend. The film is a clumsy mixture of unrealized ideas, gothic effects, and stiff, dull acting, but it has some unusual qualities; David Riesman devotes several pages to it in *The Lonely Crowd*. Directed by Gunther Von Fritsch and Robert Wise. R K O. b & w

Curtain Up (1952)—Two of England's top performers match wits. Robert Morley plays the strutting director of a seedy stock company, Margaret Rutherford the spinster dramatist determined to keep every line of her play intact. The idea is more tantalizing than the movie; still, it has a bit of theatrical flavor. With Kay Kendall, Olive Sloane, Joan Rice, and Michael Medwin. Directed by Ralph Smart, from the screenplay by Michael Pertwee and Jack Davies, based on the play *On Monday Next* by Philip King. Rank. b & w

Cutter and Bone, see *Cutter's Way*

Cutter's Way (1981)—Its original title, *Cutter and Bone*, is also the name of Newton Thornburg's 1976 novel, on which it's based. This moody fantasia on post-Vietnam bitterness is set in Santa Barbara and other parts of Southern California; it has an odd, hallucinatory lyricism—the atmosphere is never less than absorbing. John Heard is Cutter, a mutilated veteran whose conversation is a series of twisted, rasped-out gibes; Jeff Bridges is lover-boy Bone, an Ivy League beach bum who lives on his suntanned amiability. When these two friends become involved in trying to expose and/or shake down an oil tycoon who they believe is also a sexual psychopath, the film suggests a counterculture version of the anti-Fascist thrillers of the 40s. Directed by Ivan Passer, from a much too literary script by Jeffrey Alan Fiskin, the film is an attempt to get at something that—if it were arrived at—might turn out to be less subtle than all the ambiguous reaching and groping suggests. Writers who aren't forcibly restrained love to go for "mordant" protagonists, and actors love to play them. Heard gives a stylized performance of a man full of self-lacerating energy; Cutter isn't a character—he's a one-eyed, one-legged literary conceit. As his burnt-out wife, Mo, Lisa Eichhorn carries a load of existential sorrow and honesty—she's wound up tight, like an American Glenda Jackson, but without Jackson's shaping and style. The film is packed with symbolic gestures, though they're not quite as effective as the ghostly fiesta scene behind the opening titles, with señoritas dancing to music that's different from the music we hear, and castanets silently clicking. With Stephen Elliott as J. J. Cord, and Ann Dusenberry, Arthur Rosenberg, and Nina Van Pallandt. The cinematography is by Jordan Cronenweth; the music is by Jack Nitzsche. Produced by Paul R. Gurian; United Artists. color

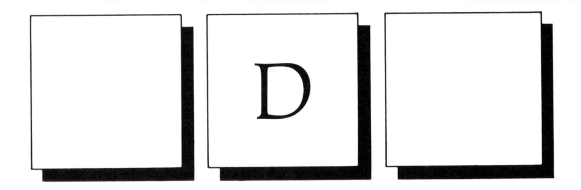

D

Dad (1989)—Making his first movie, Gary David Goldberg, the "creator" of the TV series "Family Ties," has attempted to open his sit-com sensibility to real life; he's filled *Dad* with therapeutic lore about old age and hospital care, as if moviemaking were a form of community service. Now 78 and retired from his blue-collar job, Dad (Jack Lemmon) is dominated by his wife (Olympia Dukakis), who does everything for him, enfeebling him. But when his wife has a heart attack and is hospitalized, his Wall Street investment-banker son (Ted Danson) arrives, moves in with him, and stirs him to action: the helpless old coot comes alive. That's only the beginning; the movie keeps going through permutations until, finally, the banker hero's devotion to Dad helps him reach out to his own (estranged, college-age) son, played by Ethan Hawke. This is a saga: three (television) generations. At the start, Lemmon has vanished almost totally into his role, but soon he's so insufferably perky and boyish and obliging that you feel he deserves the puling lines that Goldberg gives him. With Kathy Baker, Kevin Spacey, Zakes Mokae, and J. T. Walsh. Based on the William Wharton novel. Amblin Entertainment, for Universal. color (See *Movie Love*.)

Daddy Long Legs (1955)—This story of a May-December romance between an adorable orphan and her benefactor was published in 1912; it became a 1914 play starring Ruth Chatterton, a 1919 silent movie with Mary Pickford, and a 1931 talkie with Janet Gaynor. By the time Leslie Caron and Fred Astaire made this musical version, the accumulated adorableness was overpowering. Everybody involved seems to be trying to compensate for the dated sentimental material. Astaire doesn't look comfortable in the balletic "Guardian Angel" dance he does with Caron, and her healthy gamine charm calls attention to the age difference between them. He was about 56, she perhaps 24, and when he tries to looked charmed by her, his smiles appear forced, even pained. These two don't connect. There's one lively number—"Slue-foot"—but the two overdressed ballets choreographed by Roland Petit seem endless. Johnny Mercer did come through with a new song, "Something's Gotta Give." With Thelma Ritter, Fred Clark, Larry Keating, and Terry Moore. 20th Century-Fox. Cinema-Scope, color

The Damned (1969)—Luchino Visconti's view of the depravity in the Third Reich—

grandiose, lurid, sluggish. The Nazis are rotten, scheming degenerates; green lights play on their faces and they look like werewolves talking politics. When the young hero's impersonation of Marlene Dietrich is interrupted by the news that "in Berlin, the Reichstag is burning," he goes into a snit. Visconti is grimly serious about all this curling-lip-and-thin-eyebrow decadence. The centerpiece is the orgy and massacre of Roehm's homosexual Brown Shirts, with gorgeous naked boys in black lace panties; he doesn't seem sure what attitude to take and he stages it immaculately, reverentially. Ingrid Thulin is the fag-hag mother, a Krupp-Borgia baroness who turns her son (Helmut Berger) into a dope-addicted transvestite; he molests little girls and eventually beds down with mother—which is too much even for her and turns her into a zombie. It's really a story about a good boy who loves his wicked mother, and how she emasculates him and makes him decadent—the basic mother-son romance of homoerotic literature, dressed up in Nazi drag. With Dirk Bogarde, Helmut Griem, Charlotte Rampling, Florinda Bolkan, and Umberto Orsini. Though some of the actors speak their own English, this version of *The Damned* has all the disadvantages of a dubbed movie—everything sounds stilted and slightly off. The characters talk in a language that belongs to no period or country and sounds like translated subtitles. color (See *Deeper into Movies*.)

The Damned Don't Cry (1950)—A rigid-faced Joan Crawford, in a role that would make sense only if played by a ravishing young beauty. She's twice too old for it, and her acting is grim and masklike. She plays a woman from a drab background who wants money and power, and thinks she'll do anything to get them; she leaves her husband and takes up with gangsters. Steve Cochran, who's one of them, has the only appealing role; he has some energy and freshness, and the picture dies when he's killed off. With Kent Smith, David Brian, Selena Royle, and Richard Egan. Directed (unexcitingly) by Vincent Sherman, from a script by Harold Medford and Jerome Weidman, based on Gertrude Walker's novel *Case History*. Warners. b & w

Dance Fools Dance (1931)—Rich playgirl Joan Crawford goes to work as a reporter after her father is wiped out in the stock-market crash; her weak brother (William Bakewell) gets involved with gangsters. Turgid, forgettable melodrama, with Crawford proving what a great girl she is and winning a millionaire (Lester Vail). Redeeming features: Clark Gable, before his starring days, as a wicked gangland boss, and Cliff Edwards as a reporter. Harry Beaumont directed. M-G-M. b & w

Dance, Girl, Dance (1940)—The R K O B-movie plot undermines the attempts of the director, Dorothy Arzner, and the writers, Tess Slesinger and Frank Davis, to work in modern, liberated-woman attitudes. Maureen O'Hara plays a hardworking ballet dancer and Lucille Ball, also a dancer, is "Bubbles," a tough, generous-hearted gold-digger who gets a job in burlesque. Friends, they both become entangled with a millionaire playboy (a disastrously stilted performance by Louis Hayward), and it seems to take forever for O'Hara to discover that her future lies with Ralph Bellamy, the head of a ballet company. Lucille Ball gives the flabby film some bounce when she does her long-legged semi-burlesque numbers, and, as a club owner, Harold Huber has a nifty scene of reacting to O'Hara's dancing (mildly, appreciatively) and then reacting to Ball's strutting (with shiny-eyed fervor). With Maria Ouspenskaya as a former Russian ballerina now teaching in New York, Virginia Field,

Katharine Alexander, Mary Carlisle, Edward Brophy, Walter Abel, Sidney Blackmer, Emma Dunn, Ernest Truex, and Chester Clute. Based on a Vicki Baum story. Handsomely designed and shot, in b & w.

Dance With a Stranger (1985)—Set in London in 1954 and 1955, and featuring Miranda Richardson as Ruth Ellis, the demi-prostitute who put a few slugs in her weakling young lover (played by Rupert Everett), and was the last woman in England to be sent to the gallows, this English film might be described as kitchen-sink *film noir*. Working from a no-nonsense script by Shelagh Delaney, the director, Mike Newell, doesn't give you a minute's relief. He's obviously biting off a serious theme—he might be chewing on tinfoil. Trying for an unsentimental look at England's cold hypocrisy about class and sex, he seems mortally afraid of light. He shoots in dim, smoky interiors, in a color range from olive-drab to gray. The picture is assaultingly cramped and monotonous; it's all style—style used to show us the shabbiness of the characters' lives and how they're all trapped, doing what's inevitable. Miranda Richardson's hard-edged, snippy performance took a lot of technique, and you see it all. She acts as if every cell in her body were overstimulated; she can't stop acting, even when a viewer is begging her to, hoping for a glimpse of something besides white-knuckled control. With Ian Holm and Jane Bertish. Cinematography by Peter Hannan. (See *Hooked.*)

Dancing Mothers (1926)—Clara Bow, Alice Joyce, and Conway Tearle are the stars in this flapper period piece—a scandalous success in its day. The clothes of the 20s are worn triumphantly by the alarmingly active Miss Bow and the languidly patrician Miss Joyce. The sentiments are frightfully noble, though the serviceable theme—mother-daughter competition—was later used for less noble

(and less amusing) effects in movies such as *Mildred Pierce.* Glittering sheaths enclose Elsie Lawson, Dorothy Cumming, and Leila Hyams, while Norman Trevor is an impeccable figure in white tie and tails. Herbert Brenon directed, from a play by Edgar Selwyn and Edmund Goulding. Silent. b & w

A Dandy in Aspic (1968)—The sorrows of espionage. Laurence Harvey is the homesick Russian spy who finds solace in the emaciated arms of Mia Farrow, a product of Western decadence. But not for long: a double agent, he's given orders by the British to assassinate himself. An overproduced, glossily self-important thriller that promises more ingenuity than it delivers—maybe because the director, Anthony Mann, died during the shooting. (Harvey completed the film.) Derek Marlowe, who wrote the novel, also did the screenplay; the elegant cinematography is by Christopher Challis. With Tom Courtenay, Per Oscarsson, Lionel Stander, Peter Cook, and Harry Andrews. Set in London and Berlin. An English production, released by Columbia. color

Dangerous (1935)—Bette Davis is such an eerie stimulant in this movie that you can see why some people loved her and others hated her, while still others were split. This is the mawkish, trashy movie for which she won her first Academy Award; the award was generally considered to be belated recognition of her work the year before in *Of Human Bondage*, but terrible as *Dangerous* is, she hypes it with an intensity that frequently makes you sit up and stare. She plays Joyce Heath, a self-destructive, hard-drinking actress (possibly modelled on Jeanne Eagels) who is convinced that she jinxes the people she gets involved with. Davis is remarkable in her gone-to-the-dogs barroom scene, and she can be tough and surly, as in her scene with Alison Skipworth ("I don't want any of your greasy food; give me a drink"), but nobody could do much with the sequences in which she's required to renounce her true love, an architect (Franchot Tone), and sacrifice herself to the mealy-mouthed husband (John Eldredge) who is crippled for life as a result of her enraged, suicidal driving. (He's such a crawly masochist that she seems to have done him a favor by mutilating him.) Alfred E. Green directed, without much control over the tone, so that certain scenes seemed ludicrous even when the picture first came out. Written by Laird Doyle; with Margaret Lindsay, Dick Foran, and Richard Carle. Warners. b & w

Dangerous Liaisons (1988)—One of the least static costume films ever made, and what costumes! The women—Glenn Close, Michelle Pfeiffer, Uma Thurman, Swoosie Kurtz, Mildred Natwick—look as if they'd been dressed by Gainsborough. (Actually, it was James Acheson, who also dressed *The Last Emperor*.) Principally about the erotic power games played by the Marquise de Merteuil (Glenn Close) and the Vicomte de Valmont (John Malkovich), who were once lovers but are now allies and co-conspirators, this first-rate piece of work by the daring and agile director Stephen Frears is alive in a way that movies of classics rarely are. The paradisially beautiful Pfeiffer is wonderfully affecting as the pawn of the debauchers' final game. The screenwriter, Christopher Hampton, reworked his 1985 theatrical version of the 1782 novel by Choderlos de Laclos; cinematography by Philippe Rousselot. Filmed in France. Warners. color (See *Movie Love*.)

Dangerous Moves *La Diagonale du fou* (1984)—This Swiss picture is about a world-championship chess match held in Geneva between the longtime titleholder (Michel Piccoli), a courtly and cagey gray-bearded Russian Jew from the Soviet Union, and his

former pupil, the handsome, high-strung challenger (Alexander Arbatt), a young Lithuanian who defected from the Soviet Union and now lives in France. At first, the young man's flamboyance and the older man's seething anger put us in an expectant mood, but the film turns into an uninspired account of the psychological pressures laid on the contestants, who are both being manipulated by the Soviet bureaucracy. And after the arrival of the young man's wife (Liv Ullmann), who is sent from a psychiatric hospital in Moscow to Geneva to upset him, the picture caves in on itself. Even Piccoli, who gives a cunning, authoritative performance, has no chance to wing past the pedantry of the conception. Written by Richard Dembo, who makes his début as a director; the cinematography is by Raoul Coutard. With Leslie Caron in the dismal role of Piccoli's earnest, devoted wife, and Bernhard Wicki as the monitor. In French. color (See *State of the Art*.)

Daniel (1983)—Sidney Lumet directed, from E. L. Doctorow's script, based on his 1971 novel *The Book of Daniel*. The quasi-modernist novel is a personal fantasy that plugs into the persecution fears that the Rosenberg case stirred up. Doctorow went right for the torn, bleeding heart of the matter: the emotions of the two young children orphaned by the electric chair. It's a mussy, mixed-up, passionate book—demagogic and harrowing. The movie is all those things, too, except it's not passionate, and so it doesn't carry you along. When Lumet gets into one of his chronicles of agonized morality, it seems as if his normally high energy level sinks, and the melodramatic materials he's working with thicken and become clotted. The action here jumps back and forth among four decades shot in slightly different color ranges, and nothing takes hold now or then or in between. Timothy Hutton is Daniel, the son of the "Isaacsons," who is searching for the meaning of his dead parents' lives, and Amanda Plummer is his driven-mad younger sister; Lindsay Crouse and Mandy Patinkin are the parents. The cast includes Ellen Barkin, Ed Asner, Carmen Matthews, John Rubinstein, Maria Tucci, Julie Bovasso, Tovah Feldshuh, and many other well-known players; some of them must have flinched when they saw their performances here. Paul Robeson's voice rolls across the soundtrack during perhaps half a dozen sequences. Paramount. (See *State of the Art*.)

Dark Eyes *Otchi Tchornyia* (1987)—Directed by Nikita Mikhalkov and shot in Italy and the Soviet Union, it amalgamates several short stories by Chekhov and is the kind of movie that is referred to as a "broad tapestry," or, as *Variety* put it, "a joyful sleighride through the turn of the century." It features obviousness and mugging—each in almost unprecedented amounts. Everything in it is overacted, is too slow and too close. And everything—the peasant merrymaking, the bands of gypsies who sing, the servants who are humiliated, the decadent rich who go to spas and take mud baths—provides us with a moral lesson. Marcello Mastroianni is the weak, self-hating Romano who tells the story of his wasted life: how he became the spoiled pet of his rich wife (Silvana Mangano), took mistresses (Marthe Keller is one of them), and at a spa was touched by the seriousness of Anna (Elena Sofonova)—Chekhov's woman with the little dog—and, on the pretext of opening a factory, followed her to Russia. At this point, the film turns into a satire of bureaucracy in Imperial Russia as he goes from ministry to ministry trying to get the necessary permit. Mastroianni won the best-actor award at Cannes in this massive hunk of Italo-Russian kitsch. When he's Romano, it's as if he were putting on a classroom exhibition of how to turn yourself into another person—he shows the class every bit of cal-

culation. It's exemplary; it's horrible. (He's like Paul Muni in *Juarez* and *The Life of Émile Zola*.) The cast includes Vsevolod Larionov as the beaming Pavel and Innokenti Smoktunovski as Anna's husband. The script is by Alexander Adabachian and Mikhalkov, with the collaboration of Suso Cecchi D'Amico. In Italian. color (See *Hooked*.)

Dark Habits *Entre Tinieblas* (1983)—This amusingly erratic convent farce by the Spanish writer-director Pedro Almodóvar shows us his naughty-Catholic-schoolboy side. (Here, and in his later movies, he uses Catholic fetishism as camp.) Cristina S. Pascual plays Yolanda, a Madrid nightclub singer, who hides out from the police in a convent that specializes in the salvation of murderesses, prostitutes, and junkies. The Mother Superior (Julieta Serrano) is so avid to recruit sinners that she'll shoot them up with heroin and supply anything else they want. (She's a junkie herself.) The jokes are sometimes labored; still, Almodóvar already had the disreputable sensuality that links him to early De Palma. And he catches something very appealing in the musical numbers, especially at the convent party where three singing nuns (including Carmen Maura on the bongos) serve as backup singers for Yolanda. Maura is a dadaist clown—which, of course, is what Almodóvar himself is; we're witnessing the director and his star finding each other. In Spanish. color (See *Hooked*.)

Dark Passage (1947)—"Dark" in a movie title generally seems to be an attempt to give some sinister allure to opacity and confusion, as in *The Dark Corner*, *Dark Waters*, *The Dark Mirror*. And this Bogart-Bacall bummer is no exception. Throughout most of the miserably plotted picture, Bogart, accused of murder, hides out in Bacall's fashionable San Francisco apartment while recovering from plastic surgery; with his head bandaged, he can't do much except nod appreciatively while Bacall feeds him through a glass straw. In moments of stress, she dilates her nostrils; he's so trussed up he can't even do that. The picture is an almost total drag, though Agnes Moorehead, as the villainess, has a sensational exit through plate-glass windows. Written and directed by Delmer Daves, from a David Goodis story. Warners. b & w

Dark Victory (1939)—Bette Davis in a kitsch classic, playing a rich doomed-to-die girl who throws herself away on meaningless pleasures and then finds redemption in unselfish love—for her doctor, George Brent. A gooey collection of clichés, but Davis slams her way through them in her nerviest style. The steals from all over include a Lawrentian stable groom, played by Humphrey Bogart. Ronald Reagan is among the heroine's swains, and Geraldine Fitzgerald is her best friend. Edmund Goulding directed. Warners. b & w

Darling (1965)—Written by Frederic Raphael and directed by John Schlesinger, this English film was one of the big hits of the 60s. The key sequence invites us to laugh at documentary footage of boobish "little" people in the street answering a television interviewer (played by Dirk Bogarde) who is asking "What is wrong with England?" The film itself presents an answer just as silly and badly thought out as theirs. The darling, played by Julie Christie, drifts upward. She casually models, has a bit part in a movie, leaves a husband, deceives a lover, goes to new ones; after such tribulations as an abortion, an orgy, and a religious conversion, she winds up unhappily married to a prince. We know what we're *supposed* to think: that this girl has no direction in life. We can see that she's supposed to be as bored and as jealous of what she doesn't understand as Mildred in *Of Human Bondage*: there she is screaming, "I hate books," as she throws them off the shelves. We can see that she's supposed to be as empty and lonely and loveless as *The Goddess*: there she is in her palace not enjoying her finery one little bit. We can see that she's as starved for playful companionship as Jo in *A Taste of Honey*: there she is saying to a homosexual photographer, "We could do without sex. I don't really like it that much." She even spells it all out for us: "If I could just feel complete." What is *Darling* saying beyond such decorative jabs as showing overstuffed rich people being served by little black boys in livery and powdered wigs while they listen to an appeal for funds to fight hunger? It's saying that the boobs on the street are taken in by this girl and believe that she's an ideal success story, while we in the audience are being taught better. We are prodded to see that this bitch is a child of our times. But is this mod movie any different from, or more profound than, the "inside-story" magazines and columns which also show how dirty the lives of celebrities *really* are? Since the girl was empty and pushing at the beginning and is still empty at the end, all we can really feel is, "Well, if she's going to be unhappy, rich is better." The film's chief distinction is Julie Christie; she's extraordinary—petulant, sullen, and very beautiful. With Laurence Harvey; cinematography by Ken Higgins; music by Johnny Dankworth. (In the English TV series "The Glittering Prizes," which was written by Raphael, he has a thinly disguised version of his achieving success with this film.) b & w (See *Kiss Kiss Bang Bang*.)

A Date with Judy (1948)—A Joe Pasternak–M-G-M musical intended for the whole family; deliberately corny, shiny clean, and cheery, but with some redeeming energy. Elizabeth Taylor and Jane Powell are the ingenues, and Robert Stack, looking like a Greek god, junior division, is the juvenile. Tolerable score, with one especially pleasing number ("It's a Most Unusual Day"); Richard Thorpe directed. With Wallace Beery, Carmen Miranda, and Xavier Cugat and his orchestra. color

David and Lisa (1962)—This awkward movie about two disturbed adolescents (Keir Dullea and Janet Margolin) in an institution is an attempt to do something in decent, understanding terms, but, lacking toughness of mind, it becomes sickly sweet. It's like a 50s television program sponsored by a psychiatric association. What emerges as the theme is that love conquers mental illness, and audiences seemed to believe it. (They even seemed willing to believe that earnestness conquers art.) Made independently, on a small budget, the film was a surprise success—perhaps because the amateurishness of the director, Frank Perry, was perceived as fidelity to life. (Perry repeatedly shows us the psychiatrist—Howard Da Silva—thinking out his kind, humane thoughts before he delivers them. Those words must be loaded with wisdom, they take so long getting out.) Redeeming feature: Dullea's fine performance. With Neva Patterson and Clifton James. Written by Eleanor Perry, based on a book by Theodore Isaac Rubin. Produced by Paul M. Heller. b & w

Dawn of the Dead (1979)—The recently deceased rise from their graves; they're insatiably hungry, and they cannibalize the living, chomping on anyone they can grab. The chomped, in turn, become ghouls. This idea had already served the director George A. Romero as the subject of his 1968 *Night of the Living Dead*, a cheaply made, gray and grainy, truly frightening movie, but this time he did it in shining, comic-book color, and on an epic scale. The four central characters hole up in a suburban shopping mall and are besieged there, and for most of the film's 2 hours and 6 minutes the audience watches

as, one by one, heads splatter and drip in bright, gory reds. You're supposed to need a strong stomach to sit through this one, but it's so stupefyingly obvious and repetitive that you begin to laugh with relief that you're not being emotionally affected; it's just a gross-out. With Scott Reiniger, Ken Foree, Gaylen Ross, and David Emge. Made in the Pittsburgh area. A Laurel Group Production. (See *Taking It All In*.)

The Dawn Patrol (1938)—Edmund Goulding is the director and Errol Flynn the star of this remake of the famous 1930 Howard Hawks film. With its flying scenes, the continual din of the big guns, the bad nerves at headquarters, and schoolboy aviators being sent up to be shot down by a vicious German ace, the film was generally lauded as a stirring attack on the futility of war, though the Hawks version, made in peacetime, was far more pointed in its disillusionment, and this Goulding version, made on the eve of the Second World War, turned the plot to patriotic purposes. The most perceptive movie critic of the day dismantled the pacifist claims made for it; see *Graham Greene on Film*. With David Niven, Basil Rathbone, Donald Crisp, Melville Cooper, Barry Fitzgerald, and Carl Esmond. Warners. b & w

A Day at the Races (1937)—The Marx Brothers in a sort of morning-after to *A Night at the Opera*. It has something to do with a sanatorium, a group of bankers, a blond siren, and a steeplechase. Groucho is Hugo Z. Hackenbush, a horse doctor posing as a fashionable neurologist. ("Either this man is dead or my watch has stopped.") He shuffles off with the picture. (Groucho's rendezvous with a big, beautiful blonde—Esther Muir—is interrupted by paperhangers. "This is the worst insult I've ever had in my life," she announces. "Well, it's only eight o'clock," replies Groucho.) The total effect is that of highly satisfying derangement; it's not up to *Opera* or *Duck Soup*, but it's better than just about everything else they did—though *A Night in Casablanca* has its moments. The Brothers are fortified by Margaret Dumont; the cast includes Maureen O'Sullivan, Allan Jones, Douglass Dumbrille, and Sig Rumann; the teen-age Dorothy Dandridge may be glimpsed among the kids in the "All God's Chillun Got Rhythm" number, and the singer is Ivie Anderson. Directed by Sam Wood, from the script by Robert Pirosh, George Seaton, and George Oppenheimer. Two songs— "I'm Dr. Hackenbush" and "I've Got a Message from the Man in the Moon"—were cut after the film's opening, before the general release; the footage was later destroyed. M-G-M. b & w

Day Dreams (1928)—Silent slapstick comedy rarely encompassed visual elegance, but in England an oddly assembled group—the director Ivor Montagu (known to film scholars as the translator of Pudovkin), the writer H. G. Wells, and the heroine Elsa Lanchester, assisted by pudgy young Charles Laughton as the mock villain, and absurdly lean Harold Warrender as the mock hero—produced this little (23-minute) triumph of "advanced" editing and Art Nouveau decor, within the slapstick form. Wells' story—a servant girl fantasizes herself in the throes of aristocratic passions, as a great actress, as a leader of fashion, etc.—has more sly wit than the later, more labored variations on the same theme. *Day Dreams* is the sort of inventive, playful use of the medium that makes you want to go right out with your friends and make a movie. b & w

Day for Night *La Nuit américaine* (1973)— François Truffaut made this tribute to the conventional movies that once gave him pleasure, and apparently still do. He himself plays a director who is shooting an American-financed film called "Meet Pamela," with Jean-Pierre Léaud, Jean-Pierre Aumont, Jacqueline Bisset, and Valentina Cortese. *Day for Night*, unfortunately ordinary in its approach to character, is very childlike—filled with a deeply innocent love of the magic of moviemaking. There's not much to it, though it's graceful. In French. color (See *Reeling*.)

A Day in the Country *Une Partie de campagne* (1937)—Jean Renoir's 37-minute film from a de Maupassant story is one of the two or three greatest short-story films ever made—a lyric tragedy that ranks with his finest work. Visually, it recaptures the Impressionist period; in tone, it accomplishes a transformation from light nostalgic comedy to despair. In the late 1800s a merchant (Gabriello) takes his family for an outing on the banks of the Marne; there, his wife (Jeanne Marken) and his innocent young daughter (Sylvia Bataille) are seduced—the one delightedly, the other tremblingly, like a captured bird. Renoir himself plays the role of an innkeeper. Cinematography by Claude Renoir and Jean Bourgoin; music by Kosma. Originally this film was part of the three-part picture *Ways of Love*. In French. b & w

The Day of the Dolphin (1973)—The most expensive Rin Tin Tin picture ever made, with a gimmick the Rin Tin Tin pictures never stooped to: the dolphins here are dubbed with plaintive, childish voices and speak in English. Mike Nichols directed this elaborate exercise in anthropomorphic tearjerking, which turns the dolphins into fishy human babies. George C. Scott is the godlike dolphin trainer, whom they call Pa. The movie is about a plot to assassinate the President by using the dolphins Scott has trained as bomb carriers; the star dolphins—Alpha and Beta—foil this attempt, just as Rin Tin Tin would have done. But this isn't a happy movie: Nichols and the writer, Buck Henry,

D

who adapted the Robert Merle novel, exploit Watergate and the political assassinations of recent decades for a despairing attitude toward corruption. The picture ends with the bawling-baby Alpha protesting love for Pa while Scott tells the pair that they must trust no man, and forces the whimpering babies to leave their home forever. The moviemakers who put out the Rin Tin Tin pictures didn't take themselves so seriously that they felt the need to break kids' hearts—this movie sends kids out destroyed. It's preposterously ill-conceived. With Trish Van Devere, Fritz Weaver, and Paul Sorvino. Cinematography by William A. Fraker; music by Georges Delerue. Avco-Embassy. color (See *Reeling*.)

The Day of the Locust (1975)—John Schlesinger's overblown version of Nathanael West's novel is a mosaic that never comes together. Waldo Salt attempted the next-to-impossible job of adapting the novel—an aesthete's view of society, set in Los Angeles in the 30s, in which the culturally debased people bring on the apocalypse. There wouldn't be much to remember from the movie if it weren't for a few of the performers—Burgess Meredith as an old vaudevillian, Billy Barty as a macho dwarf, and William Atherton in the thankless role of the artist Tod. With Karen Black, Donald Sutherland, Geraldine Page, Lelia Goldoni, Richard A. Dysart, and Bo Hopkins. Cinematography by Conrad Hall; production design by Richard MacDonald. Paramount. color (See *Reeling*.)

Day of Wrath *Vredens Dag* (1943)—It has been said that Carl Dreyer's art begins to unfold just at the point where most directors give up, and this psychological masterpiece, suggesting a fusion of Hawthorne and Kafka, is proof. In 1623, the young second wife of an austere pastor desires his death because of her love for his son; when she tells the pastor of her feelings, he suffers a stroke and dies. Accused of witchcraft, she becomes what she and her accusers believe a witch to be, and as she is trapped, and all possibility of hope is stripped away from her, the viewer's identification with her fear becomes unbearable; then Dreyer dissolves our terror as she is purified beyond even fear. The most intense, powerful film ever made on the subject of witchcraft, it explores the erotic tensions of the "'witch" and her accusers. With Lisbeth Movin as the wife and Anna Svierkier as Marthe, the old woman who is arrested and burned at the stake in the great early sequences. Based on the play *Anne Pedersdotter* by Wiers Jensen; the musical arrangements of the "Dies Irae" (which gives the film its title) and the other fateful hymns are by Poul Schierbeck. Not shown outside Denmark until after the war; opened in the U.S. in 1948. In Danish. b & w

Daybreak, see *Le Jour se lève*

Days and Nights in the Forest *Aranyer din Ratri* (1969)—On the surface, this Satyajit Ray film is a lyrical romantic comedy about four educated young men from Calcutta, driving together for a few days in the country, and the women they meet. The subtext is perhaps the subtlest, most plangent study of the cultural tragedy of imperialism; the young men are self-parodies—clowns who ape the worst snobberies of the British. A major film by one of the great film artists, starring Soumitra Chatterji and the incomparably graceful Sharmila Tagore. In Bengali. b & w (See *Reeling*.)

Days of Heaven (1978)—Terrence Malick wrote and directed this story of adultery, set principally in the wheat fields of the Texas Panhandle just before America entered the First World War. It's both a nostalgic and an anti-nostalgic vision of the American past. The landscapes are vast and lonely, with the space in the images strained and the figures tilted; the characters are monosyllabic—near-mute. What is unspoken in this picture weighs heavily on us, but we're not quite sure what it is. The film is an empty Christmas tree: you can hang all your dumb metaphors on it. Richard Gere plays Bill, who works in a blast furnace in Chicago; he gets into a brawl with the foreman and heads south, taking his girl, Abby (Brooke Adams), and his 12-year-old sister, Linda (Linda Manz), with him. They find work in the fields of a wealthy young farmer (Sam Shepard), who falls in love with Abby. When Bill learns that the farmer may be dying, he encourages Abby to marry him—so that she can soon be a rich widow. The movie is oblique, except for the narration, which is by Linda; she's a little-girl wise guy, and all the humor in the film comes from her laconic remarks, but she's also precociously full of the wisdom of the ages, and at times her illiterate poetry is drenched in wistfulness and heartbreak. Shot by Nestor Almendros, with additional photography by Haskell Wexler, the film is a series of pictorial effects—some of them, such as a train passing over a lacework bridge, extraordinary—but the overpowering images seem unrelated, pieced together. The movie suffers from too many touches, too many ideas that don't grow out of anything organic. It's an epic pastiche. Though the irregularly handsome, slightly snaggle-toothed Shepard has almost no lines, he makes a strong impression; he seems authentically an American of an earlier era. But Gere, with his post-50s acting style and the associations it carries of Brando and Dean and Clift and all the others who shrugged and scowled and acted with their shoulders, is anachronistic. Shot in Alberta, Canada. Released by Paramount. color

The Dead (1987)—Working in a mood of tranquil exuberance, the 80-year-old John Huston made a great warm, funny movie out of the great story that James Joyce wrote at 25. Huston never before blended his actors so intuitively, so musically. The party that the Morkan sisters and their fortyish niece give in their Dublin town house on January 6, 1904, the Feast of the Epiphany, suggests the Chekhov production of your dreams, or maybe one of Satyajit Ray's triumphs. The cast is glorious: Donal McCann is Gabriel; Anjelica Huston is Gabriel's wife, Gretta; Donal Donnelly is Freddy; Marie Kean is Freddy's mother; Cathleen Delany is Aunt Julia; Helena Carroll is Aunt Kate; Ingrid Craigie is Mary Jane; Dan O'Herlihy is the Protestant Mr. Browne; and Frank Patterson is the tenor who sings "The Lass of Aughrim." Screenplay by Tony Huston; cinematography by Fred Murphy; score by Alex North. Vestron. color (See *Hooked*.)

Dead End (1937)—The setting of Sidney Kingsley's once celebrated play is a dead-end street on the East River, where an expensive apartment house towers over the slums; the play is about the confrontations of rich and poor, and it features a gang of street-wise kids and a gangster, bred there, who comes back for a visit. (The film was advertised as "Dead End, Cradle of Crime.") The movie has the ambiance of Broadway social consciousness of the 30s, which, like the beautifully engineered plot, is highly entertaining. Humphrey Bogart is the gangster—Baby Face Martin—with Allen Jenkins as his sidekick, Claire Trevor as his old girlfriend who has turned whore, and Marjorie Main (before her Ma Kettle days) as his mother. The contrasting characters of the poor and honest lovers are played by Sylvia Sidney and Joel McCrea (who is almost tempted away by Wendy Barrie). And the thieves who steal the picture are the Dead End Kids: Gabriel Dell, Leo Gorcey, Huntz Hall, Billy Halop, Bobby Jordan, and Bernard Punsley. Directed by

William Wyler; cinematography by Gregg Toland; screenplay by Lillian Hellman. A Samuel Goldwyn Production; released by United Artists. b & w

Dead Men Don't Wear Plaid (1982)—Steve Martin stars, as a private eye, in this spoof of detective movies; it splices together footage of Martin and footage from films of the 40s, such as *White Heat* and *The Glass Key* and *Double Indemnity*—putting him right into scenes from the movie past. The director, Carl Reiner, worked with dedicated craftsmen and achieved a smooth composite; even the sound levels were carefully matched. Reiner and the others must have become so proud of their workmanship that they didn't register what a monotonous, droning feat they were engaged in. They smoothed out their one big chance for comic friction—the contrast between old and new. Martin has a few good silly gags, but you may find yourself fighting to stay awake and losing. With Rachel Ward as the curvy, low-voiced femme fatale, and Reni Santoni. Written by Reiner (who also appears), George Gipe, and Martin. The cinematography is by Michael Chapman; the production design is by John De Cuir. The costumes are by Edith Head; it was her final film. Universal. b & w (to match the old movies), but the prints are processed by Technicolor.

Dead of Night (1945)—Michael Redgrave plays a schizophrenic ventriloquist tormented by his dummy, and his overpowering performance—a small work of art—lifts this five-part English production above the elegant, sophisticated entertainment it aspired to be. The individual stories are meant to accumulate in intensity, until the trap closes in the surreal climax—an encompassing ghost story. When the film was first shown in this country, two of the stories were omitted, and though these were the weakest

sequences, the omission made the climax partly unintelligible. The complete version begins with Mervyn Johns's arrival at a country house and proceeds through these five episodes: Antony Baird and Miles Malleson in "room for one more"; Sally Ann Howes in the murdered child sequence (good material poorly done); Googie Withers and Ralph Michael in the story of the mirror that reflects the crime of an earlier century; Basil Radford and Naunton Wayne in the golfers' story told by Roland Culver (which is pretty awful); Michael Redgrave as the ventriloquist, with Hartley Power as his rival and Frederick Valk as the psychoanalyst; then the nightmarish summation. John Baines and Angus Mac-Phail did the screenplay, using stories by H. G. Wells, E. F. Benson, and themselves; the master writer of English film comedy, T. E. B. Clarke, did the additional dialogue. Directed by Robert Hamer (the mirror story), Basil Dearden, Charles Crichton, and Alberto Cavalcanti (the ventriloquist sequence). Score by Georges Auric. b & w

Dead Poets Society (1989)—Robin Williams gives an astonishingly empathic performance as an eager, dedicated prep-school teacher in the late 50s. This teacher talks to his boys about the passions expressed in poetry and helps them release their creative impulses. But the movie shifts from one genre to another: the dedicated teacher gives way to the sensitive, misunderstood kid. The link is that one of the boys, soaring on his new confidence, lacks the shrewdness and courage to deal with his rigid, uncomprehending father, and makes a disastrous move. The shift in genres sidelines the one performer who sparks the viewer's imagination and substitutes a familiar figure: the usual romantic victim to identify with. Directed by Peter Weir, from a script by Tom Schulman, the picture is an example of conservative craftsmanship: it draws out the obvious and turns itself into a classic with a gold ribbon attached to it. Despite the film's elegiac tone the perception of reality here is the black and white of pulp fiction. The young actors are presentable—even admirable—but they're all so camera-angled and director-controlled that they don't have a zit they can call their own. With Robert Sean Leonard, Ethan Hawke, Josh Charles, Gale Hansen, and Kurtwood Smith and Norman Lloyd. Touchstone (Disney). color (See *Movie Love*.)

Dead Reckoning (1947)—A forgettable Bogart melodrama that was already familiar when it came out; it had been synthesized from several of his hits, with Lizabeth Scott's role processed out of Mary Astor and Lauren Bacall routines. Scott double-crosses a friend of Bogart's, and as he takes her to the authorities he snarls, "You're going to fry." "Ah," she says yearningly, flaring her nostrils, "can't we put this behind us? Don't you love me?" He sneers heavily, though you can see that deep down under he loves her. She fries. John Cromwell directed; with Morris Carnovsky, Wallace Ford, and William Prince. Columbia. b & w

The Deadly Invention *Vynalez Zkazy* Also known as *The Fabulous World of Jules Verne*. (1958)—Among Georges Méliès' most popular creations was his 1902 version of Jules Verne's *A Trip to the Moon* (which was used at the beginning of Michael Todd's production of *Around the World in Eighty Days*). Another great movie magician, the Czech Karel Zeman, also turning to Jules Verne for inspiration, made this wonderful giddy science fantasy. (It's based on *Facing the Flag* and other works.) Like Méliès, Zeman employs almost every conceivable trick, combining live action, animation, puppets, and painted sets that are a triumph of sophisticated primitivism. The variety of tricks and superimpositions seems infinite; as soon as you have

one effect figured out another image comes on to baffle you. For example, you see a drawing of half a dozen sailors in a boat on stormy seas; the sailors in their little striped outfits are foreshortened by what appears to be the hand of a primitive artist. Then the waves move, the boat rises on the water, and when it lands, the little sailors—who are live actors—walk off, still foreshortened. There are underwater scenes in which the fishes swimming about are as rigidly patterned as in a child's drawing (yet they are also perfectly accurate drawings). There are more stripes, more patterns on the clothing, the decor, and on the image itself than a sane person can easily imagine. The film creates the atmosphere of the Jules Verne books which is associated in readers' minds with the steel engravings by Bennet and Riou; it's designed to look like this world-that-never-was come to life, and Zeman retains the antique, make-believe quality by the witty use of faint horizontal lines over some of the images. He sustains the Victorian tone, with its delight in the magic of science, that makes Verne seem so playfully archaic. Released in the U.S. with narration and dialogue in English. b & w

Deadly Is the Female, see *Gun Crazy*

Dealing: or the Berkeley-to-Boston Forty-Brick Lost-Bag Blues (1972)—A good idea for a comedy-thriller, gone slack. Michael and Douglas Crichton's glib, clever novel about educated young hustlers in the collegiate marijuana-dealing business is treated with droopy solemnity by the director, Paul Williams. More than half an hour passes before the plot mechanism is set in motion, and the movie never recovers from this initial lassitude. Robert F. Lyons (Elliott Gould's crazy buddy in *Getting Straight*) is engaging as a sallow, runty Harvard law student (he's best when he follows a girl—Barbara Hershey—and almost walks into a door), and John Lithgow is a cherubic rich boy who has become a new-style mobster. The Harvard-Boston scene is mostly dubbed by Toronto. Warners. color

Death in Venice (1971)—The beginning—with the boat carrying the weary, over-disciplined Aschenbach (Dirk Bogarde) to Venice—is magnificent. It's like a series of views by Boudin, only more voluptuous. But sometimes a picture's triumphs work against it more than its failures do: How can the director, Luchino Visconti, surpass this long virtuoso opening—how can he organize the movie so that it has balance and proportion? Once Aschenbach falls in love with the androgynous 14-year-old boy Tadzio (Bjorn Andresen) and dyes his hair and rouges his cheeks, the picture seems to end over and over again. In the Thomas Mann short novel, Aschenbach (who was based on Mahler) was made a writer; Visconti (and his co-writer Nicola Badalucco) turn him into a composer, and use Mahler's Third and Fifth Symphonies on the soundtrack. That works well, but Visconti over-elaborates the story, adding flashbacks with discussions about art and adding a character (Alfred, played by Mark Burns), who's a disastrous intrusion. After a while the languor experienced by Aschenbach is experienced by the audience as plain pokiness. And though it isn't Bogarde's fault, this English actor (made up to suggest Mann) diminishes the whole conception; he's not a stiff, overworked German—he just seems dull and prissy, and there's no real horror in his painted face or his ridiculous behavior. There are superb visual contributions by the cinematographer Pasqualino De Santis, the art director Ferdinando Scarfiotti, and the costume designer Piero Tosi. (The time is 1911.) The cast includes the sumptuously turned out Silvana Mangano as Tadzio's mother, and Franco Fabrizi, Romolo Valli, Marisa Berenson, and the ravishing Carol

Andre as the whore Esmeralda. Some of the post-synching is very poor. Released by Warners. color

Death Kiss (1932)—The ultimate in forgettable murder mysteries. The cast (Bela Lugosi, Mona Maris, David Manners, Adrienne Ames, Vince Barnett) makes it sound promising, and so does the setting for the murder (a movie studio). But the script is a bummer, the direction by Edwin L. Marin is dismal, and Lugosi is given nothing to do. He just glowers. From a novel by Madelon St. Dennis. b & w

Death of a Cyclist *Muerte de un Ciclista* Also known as *Age of Infidelity.* (1955)—The bored young wife of a wealthy industrialist and her university-professor lover run down a bicyclist, and, fearing exposure of their relationship, leave the victim to die. In the aftermath, the hit-and-run accident destroys them both. This attack on the Spanish upper classes, which was condemned in the Falangist press, took the Critics' Award at Cannes and the director, Juan Bardem, became the hero of Spanish students. Bardem uses his melodramatic story as a way of showing the rich at their cocktail parties and racetracks and cabarets, and showing their indolence and greed and moral emptiness. His editing is rather too flashy, in an out-to-outdo Orson Welles manner, but what really weakens the movie is that Bardem seems unable to endow his actors with distinct personalities. The beautiful Lucia Bose doesn't seem to have enough imagination to commit adultery, and you can't tell her husband and her lover apart. In Spanish. b & w

Death on the Nile (1978)—Anthony Shaffer's adaptation of Agatha Christie's 1937 novel has wit and edge and structure—too much structure, as it turns out, for the methodical pacing of the director, John Guillermin. The movie is fatally perfunctory about emotion, atmosphere, suspense. But if the overall effect is disappointing, from moment to moment the details are never less than engaging, and are often knobby and funny. The steamer, full of victims and suspects, has a passenger list that includes Maggie Smith, in a triumphantly mannered performance, as a spinsterish nurse-companion, and Angela Lansbury, in a superlative caricature, as a wreck of a vamp. (She's all curves, satin turbans, amber beads that hang to her crotch, and drizzling clouds of chiffon and fringe; she's whooping it up one moment and sagging from booze the next.) Peter Ustinov is an ideal fatuous, vain Hercule Poirot. With Mia Farrow, whose pale-pink eerie sprite face takes the light as delicately as any face in movies, and Bette Davis, I. S. Johar as the Indian manager of the cruise ship, Simon MacCorkindale, Jon Finch, Jack Warden, David Niven, Olivia Hussey, Harry Andrews, Jane Birkin, and, regrettably, the inexpressive Lois Chiles (who sounds dubbed or vaguely ventriloquial, like a transsexual) and George Kennedy (who gives his usual blustering, overscaled performance). Paramount. color (See *When the Lights Go Down.*)

Death Race 2000 (1975)—Low-budget sci-fi, from an often amusing suspense script by Robert Thom and Charles B. Griffith, directed by Paul Bartel in his ingratiatingly tacky, sophomoric manner. Bartel seems to have an instinctive kinky comic-book style; the picture zips along, and there's a flip craziness about it—it's an ideal drive-in movie. In the role of a legendary driver in a killer race—points are scored for every pedestrian run down—David Carradine has star presence, and his easy, confident manner gives the film some class; he's very elegant in his black leather clothes and black leather cape. Sylvester Stallone is rather funny as the slobbish, stupid villain, who's always expostulating in

anger or disgust. With Louisa Moritz as the crude dumb blonde, and Simone Griffith. Produced by Roger Corman. color

Deathtrap (1982)—This movie is for people who dream of seeing *Sleuth* again—there must be at least one or two of them. It's set in the East Hampton home of a once successful playwright (Michael Caine) who specializes in thrillers; he plans to murder a former student (Christopher Reeve) and steal his flawless play *Deathtrap.* Ira Levin's wisecracking whodunit, which was a hit on Broadway, is all twists and reversals, and it's designed to be played frivolously and artificially, by slick, easy actors. But the director, Sidney Lumet, and the screenwriter, Jay Presson Allen, have decided to make the movie version as realistic as possible. What this comes down to is a broad, obvious movie that looks like an ugly play and appears to be a vile vision of life, and, at the end, the staging and editing are so quick and muddled that you can't be sure what's happening. Except for the shouting, which has become *de rigueur* in a Lumet film, the actors don't disgrace themselves. But their skill gives one no pleasure. With Dyan Cannon, Irene Worth, and Henry Jones. Warners. color (See *Taking It All In.*)

The Début *Naciala* (1971)—A Soviet film about a plain girl who is desperately determined to become an actress and is selected to star in a movie about Joan of Arc. She seems to be the stuff actresses are made of—actresses like Helen Hayes and Julie Harris, who are transformed onstage, some by will and energy, others by will and talent. But, as the story turns out, she isn't meant to be that appealing-mouse kind of actress—she's meant to be a sad-sack factory girl deluded about her talent. The movie declines into implausible, none too lucid ironies, but as the girl Inna Churikova is spellbinding; her face tells you everything and yet is mysteriously closed, and her toothy, gummy smile is peculiarly mirthless. Not a particularly good picture, and it's padded out with footage of the Joan of Arc spectacles, but it holds you. Directed by Gleb Panfilov. In Russian. b & w (See *Deeper into Movies.*)

Deception (1946)—Blissfully foolish—a camp classic. Alex Hollenius (Claude Rains) is the greatest composer in the United States; his febrile mistress (Bette Davis) can escape him only by shooting him. Considering that he has set her up in the finest apartment in Manhattan, swaddled her in ermine, drenched her in champagne, and taught her to play the piano with a skill approximating that of Arthur Rubinstein, some might regard this as rank ingratitude. But he's a venomous genius, and an epicure besides, and given to wearing velvet jackets. He treats the cellist (Paul Henreid) whom she loves very shabbily—badgering him until he gets so nervous that he can hardly handle a bow. Irving Rapper, who had directed this trio in *Now, Voyager*, let them run rampant this time, especially the leering Rains, who outdoes Davis in bravura. (She doesn't look young or glamorous, either; she's a rather puffy-faced femme fatale.) John Abbott and Benson Fong are also in the cast. Erich Wolfgang Korngold did the music, with Shura Cherkassky dubbing Davis's "Appassionata." John Collier and Joseph Than adapted the Louis Verneuil play *Monsieur Lamberthier*, which had been filmed in 1929, as *Jealousy*, with Jeanne Eagels and Fredric March. Warners. b & w

La Decima Vittima, see *The 10th Victim*

La Declin de l'empire américain, see *The Decline of the American Empire*

The Decline of the American Empire *Le Declin de l'empire américain* (1986)—The French-Canadian writer-director Denys Arcand takes on the subject of sex in a period of social change, without the binding ties of family and religion or strong commitment to the future. The eight principal characters—aging middle-class intellectuals connected with the History Department of a Montreal university—no longer believe in postponing pleasure. On this Friday afternoon in autumn, the women, who need to keep in shape in order to appeal to men, work out together at a gym in the city while the men, gathered at a lakeside cottage, prepare trout coulibiac for a festive dinner. Both groups talk about sex, and when they're together in the long evening they go on talking about sex, but more discreetly—with less bawdiness and bravura. Arcand isn't out to expose these people as spiritually empty; he's trying to present a truthful look at how they live. And he's a highly skilled filmmaker: he slips in flashbacks without breaking the flow of talk or jostling the ravishing natural changes in the light at the lake. There's nothing weighty in his approach; it's a lovely, very unassuming picture, yet there is enough drama so that by the end a subtle shift in all the relationships is necessary. And the foreground action and the flashbacks that had been providing the background begin to merge. The film is structured like a concerto for nine instruments. (A ninth character, an outsider, joins the group at the dinner table.) With Dominique Michel, Dorothée Berryman, Louise Portal, Geneviève Rioux, Pierre Curzi, Rémy Girard, Yves Jacques, Daniel Brière, and Gabriel Arcand. Cinematography by Guy Dufaux. In French. color (See *Hooked.*)

The Deer Hunter (1978)—A romantic adolescent-boy's view of friendship, with the Vietnam War seen in the Victorian terms of such movies as *Lives of a Bengal Lancer* and *Four Feathers*—as a test of men's courage. This is the fullest screen treatment so far of the mystic bond of male comradeship. Without sharing the film's implicit God-and-country, flag-on-the-door political assumptions, one can see that, even with its pulp components and its superman hero (Robert De Niro, as a Pennsylvania steelworker), it is not merely trying to move people by pandering to their prejudices. It is also caught in its own obsessions. And because the director, Michael Cimino, plays them out on such a vast canvas, the film has an inchoate, stirring quality. It has no more moral intelligence than the Clint Eastwood action pictures, yet it's an astonishing piece of work, an uneasy mixture of violent pulp and grandiosity, with an enraptured view of common life—poetry of the commonplace. With Christopher Walken, Meryl Streep, John Cazale, John Savage, George Dzundza, Chuck Aspegren, Shirley Stoler, Rutanya Alda, and Amy Wright. Screenplay by Deric Washburn; story by Cimino, Washburn, and others; music by Stanley Myers; cinematography by Vilmos Zsigmond. Academy Awards: Best Picture, Director, Supporting Actor (Walken), Sound, Editing (Peter Zinner). Universal. color (See *When the Lights Go Down.*)

Defense of the Realm (1985)—An English political thriller—quick, hushed, intelligent, complicated. An amoral young Fleet Street journalist (Gabriel Byrne) goes after a scoop, gets some hot tips, and writes stories that destroy the career of an Opposition leader, a Labour M.P. (Ian Bannen). Then he discovers that the tips he acted on were phonies, engineered by the Tory government. The movie is just about all plot, and you don't have time to think about what's going on—you're locked into just finding out what it is. Though the story is fictional, the picture is probably the closest English equivalent to *All the President's Men,* but the atmosphere is much darker and more oppressive. This is a new-style acrid thriller, an Orwellian coffee jag

rather than a Graham Greene entertainment. An example of paranoiac realism, it infuses *cinéma-vérité* shooting with a spirit of grim fantasy. It has everything but the basic story-telling astuteness to give you a good time; after a while, you feel charred. Directed by David Drury, from a script by Martin Stellman; cinematography by Roger Deakins. With Denholm Elliott, Greta Scacchi, Bill Paterson, Robbie Coltrane, and Fulton Mackay. color (See *Hooked.*)

Le Déjeuner sur l'herbe, see *Picnic on the Grass*

Le Dernier Milliardaire, see *The Last Millionaire*

Dernier Tango à Paris, see *Last Tango in Paris*

Il Deserto Rosso, see *Red Desert*

Desire (1936)—Marlene Dietrich, with her pencil-line arched eyebrows, as the most elegantly amusing international jewel thief ever. She steals a pearl necklace in Paris and speeds toward Spain; on her way she has a series of encounters with Gary Cooper, a motor engineer from Detroit who is on holiday. Produced by Ernst Lubitsch, for Paramount, and directed by Frank Borzage, this is a polished light comedy in the "continental" style—a sophisticated romantic trifle, with Dietrich more chic and modern than in her von Sternberg pictures. When she eyes Cooper she's so captivating, you almost feel sorry for him; there's an image of her standing against French doors that is simply peerlessly sexy. But you can also see why this European sophisticate longs for the American innocent. Cooper is a bit coy and rambunctious in his Americanness, but wearing narrow-tailored suits and with his hair sleek he's the ideal Art Deco hero. And he's great when he leans close to Dietrich and says, dreamily, "All I know about you is you stole my car and I'm insane about you." When he's being threatened by her crooked associate (John Halliday), who remarks, tauntingly, "One mustn't underestimate America—it's a big country," he bends forward and says, "Six foot three." With William Frawley, Ernest Cossart, Alan Mowbray, Zeffie Tilbury, Akim Tamiroff, and Marc Lawrence. The script by Edwin Justus Mayer, Waldemar Young, and Samuel Hoffenstein is based on a play by Hans Szekely and R. A. Stemmle; cinematography by Charles Lang. Dietrich sings "Awake in a Dream" by Leo Robin and Frederick Hollander. b & w

Désirée (1954)—A ridiculously simpleminded costume picture—ten-ton romantic fluff, with some campily enjoyable scenes. With his nose built up and his hair plastered down in bangs, Marlon Brando is an amused Napoleon; he speaks in a hoarse whisper, his enunciation an odd, crisp parody of an Englishman's. (It might be a takeoff on Claude Rains in *Caesar and Cleopatra*.) Jean Simmons is the pensive Désirée whom he keeps yearning for. The two stars play together with conspiratorial charm; doubtless they knew they were trapped in a joke and tried to have as good a time as possible. Brando makes one laugh out loud when his Napoleon elevates his sisters to royal rank by rapping them on their heads—hard. And he's quite funny when he grabs the crown and crowns himself. With Merle Oberon as Josephine, Michael Rennie as Bernadotte, Elizabeth Sellars, Cathleen Nesbitt, Evelyn Varden, Isobel Elsom, John Hoyt, Carolyn Jones, and Alan Napier. The director, Henry Koster, and the scenarist, Daniel Taradash, didn't earn any prizes. 20th Century-Fox. CinemaScope, color

Desk Set (1957)—The eighth of the films that co-starred Spencer Tracy and Katharine Hepburn; it was one of their bummers. He's a wizard engineer. She's in charge of a TV-network research department, and, misunderstanding his intentions, she thinks he means to put her group out of work by installing an electronic brain called Emmy. Gig Young and Joan Blondell help out, but it's a dispirited, straining-for-laughs sit-com. Tracy looks bulky, and Hepburn looks scraggy and cheerless; both seem overage for their roles. Walter Lang directed; Henry and Phoebe Ephron adapted William Marchant's 1955 Broadway play. With Dina Merrill and Neva Patterson. 20th Century-Fox. color

Desperately Seeking Susan (1985)—Set in the punk world, it's a mistaken-identity fantasy about doe-eyed Roberta (Rosanna Arquette), a suburban housewife in New Jersey, who becomes fixated on a drifter named Susan (played by the rock star Madonna). This attempt at screwball charm was directed by Susan Seidelman, who wipes out her actors. All their responsiveness is cut off—there's nothing going on in them. No subtext—nothing. This flatness can make your jaw fall open, but it seems to be accepted by the audience as New Wave postmodernism. Nobody comes through except Madonna, who comes through as Madonna (she moves regally, an indolent, trampy goddess), and the cinematographer Edward Lachman, whose lighting gives the East Village shops and streets a funky prettiness—like an Expressionist painting of neon squalor and lollipops. The transactions between the people on the screen are stupefying (and often in woozy slow-motion, like a rock video going poetic). The script is by Leora Barish. The cast includes Robert Joy, Aidan Quinn, Mark Blum, Laurie Metcalf, Will Patton, and the comedian Steven Wright; there are also glimpses of Richard Hell, Anne Carlisle, Richard Edson, Ann Magnuson, John Lurie, Shirley Stoler, Rockets Redglare (as a taxi-driver), and other "inside" celebrities. Orion. color (See *State of the Art.*)

Destination Moon (1950)—George Pal produced this relatively inexpensive rocket trip to the moon; the set designs are ingenious, and the movie has a realistic look (which helped to make it a big hit). But the acting and the direction (by Irving Pichel) are earthbound. The actors have names (Warner Anderson, John Archer, Tom Powers, and Dick Wesson), but they're truly anonymous. Released by Eagle Lion. color

Destry Rides Again (1939)—"Marlene Dietrich! . . . When you wear feathers, and furs, and plumes, you wear them as the birds and animals wear them, as though they belonged to your body."—Jean Cocteau. "She possesses the rarest of civilized virtues, irony."—Kenneth Tynan. These two gifts were combined in her classic comedy role as Frenchy, the quixotic harlot of a frontier saloon. George Marshall directed this satiric revitalization of a 1932 Tom Mix Western, based on a Max Brand novel. By taking her spangles and feathers into the Old West and dropping her sultry voice to a howling baritone, Dietrich revitalized her own career. James Stewart is charming and even a little bit sexy as the mild-mannered Destry. With a large group of people who all contribute to the flavor, some in good-sized parts—Mischa Auer, Brian Donlevy, Charles Winninger, Una Merkel, Samuel Hinds—and in lesser parts—Jack Carson, Allen Jenkins, Irene Hervey, Warren Hymer, and Billy Gilbert. Script by Felix Jackson, Gertrude Purcell, and Henry Myers. Dietrich sings "Li'l Joe the Wrangler," "You've Got That Look That Leaves Me Weak," and "The Boys in the Back Room"—

all by Frank Loesser and Frederick Hollander. (Marshall remade the film in 1954 as *Destry*, starring Audie Murphy and Mari Blanchard; there was also a partial remake in 1950, called *Frenchie* and starring Joel McCrea and Shelley Winters.) Universal. b & w

The Detective Known as *Father Brown* in England. (1954)—Father Brown, the detective priest of G. K. Chesterton's stories, is perhaps too facile a role for Alec Guinness, and he shows a hitherto unsuspected tendency toward endearing, owlish coyness. But the film is an amusing series of chases, well directed by Robert Hamer (*Kind Hearts and Coronets*). Peter Finch is the connoisseur-thief who steals beautiful things simply to round out his collection of objets d'art; when he makes off with the cross once owned by Saint Augustine, Father Brown goes after him. Joan Greenwood plays a rich, pious widow; Cecil Parker is Father Brown's bishop; the exquisitely desiccated Ernest Thesiger is a librarian. With Marne Maitland, Sidney James, and Bernard Lee. From the story "The Blue Cross," adapted by Thelma Schnee; music by Georges Auric. b & w

The Detective (1968)—Frank Sinatra as a New York City police detective. He doesn't give much hint of his sometime ability as an actor in this brutal thriller that's meant to be cool and tough and gamy. Homosexuality, police corruption, and race relations are exploited in the moralistic "outspoken" style of the screenwriter Abby Mann, while the director, Gordon Douglas, keeps pounding away. With Lee Remick, Jacqueline Bisset, Jack Klugman, Al Freeman, Jr., Robert Duvall, William Windom, Tony Musante, and Ralph Meeker. From a novel by Roderick Thorp; music by Jerry Goldsmith. 20th Century-Fox. color

Detective Story (1951)—The brash, hyperactive Sidney Kingsley melodrama set in a precinct station-house, directed by William Wyler. The action is stagey, but there's certainly enough going on. Kirk Douglas plays a brutal detective, full of hatred for the offenders who cross his path, and Eleanor Parker is his wife. When he learns that she once had an affair with a gangster, he can't forgive her, and then can't live with himself. That's only one of the interrelated stories, which involve Lee Grant as a flirtatious shoplifter and Joseph Wiseman as a seasoned burglar (playing roles they'd already scored in on the stage), as well as George Macready, William Bendix, Horace McMahon, Bert Freed, Frank Faylen, Gerald Mohr, Cathy O'Donnell, and Warner Anderson. Cinematography by Lee Garmes. Paramount. b & w

Detsvo Gorkovo, see *The Childhood of Maxim Gorky*

Les Deux Anglaises et le continent, see *Two English Girls*

Devi (1962)—Satyajit Ray's dreamily sensual, ironic film about Indian superstitiousness was originally banned from export until Nehru interceded. The story, about a wealthy man who convinces his son's bride (Sharmila Tagore) that she is an incarnation of the goddess Kali, has startling Freudian undertones. Ray's feeling for the intoxicating beauty within the disintegrating way of life of the 19th-century landowning class makes this one of the rare, honest films about decadence. With Soumitra Chatterji and Chhabi Biswas. In Bengali. b & w

The Devil and Miss Jones (1941)—This ambitious but obvious comedy has a reputation because it's (vaguely) about the relation of capital and labor. Charles Coburn plays "the richest man in the world," a stuffy old grouch who goes to work as a shoe clerk in a department store he happens to own in order to do a little spying on the employees, who are joining a union. This being a Hollywood romance, he comes to share the employees' grievances, and is humanized so rapidly that he goes on strike against himself. Jean Arthur is appealing enough as the working-girl heroine, but her antics seem forced, and she's not at her best (who is?) with Robert Cummings; he plays her boyfriend, the union organizer. With Edmund Gwenn as a nasty department head, Spring Byington, William Demarest, and S. Z. Sakall. Directed by Sam Wood, from a script by Norman Krasna; the production was designed by William Cameron Menzies. Produced by Frank Ross (then married to Jean Arthur), for R K O. b & w

The Devil Doll (1936)—Creepy. Some bits are fairly certain to return in nightmares. Lionel Barrymore, a fugitive convict masquerading as an old lady, sells dolls to his enemies. The dolls are miniaturized people (Grace Ford and Arthur Hohl) who steal and kill. Tod Browning directed this adaptation of Abraham Merritt's novel *Burn, Witch, Burn!* With Maureen O'Sullivan, Frank Lawton, Rafaela Ottiano, and Henry B. Walthall. M-G-M. b & w

Devil in the Flesh *Le Diable au corps* (1947)—Raymond Radiguet, a prodigy and now a legend, wrote the novel when he was 17; at 20 he was dead. But his account of the clandestine love affair between an adolescent schoolboy and the discontented wife of a soldier hounded the woman who was his model all her tragic life (she insisted that the precocious Radiguet had invented the sexual aspects of their relationship). Claude Autant-Lara re-created this story of the First World War with nostalgic tenderness. His dramatization treats the affair with such delicacy that many critics consider the love scenes to be among the most beautiful ever photographed. *Devil in the Flesh* is perhaps the kind of wartime love story that people hoped to see when they went to *A Farewell to Arms*: it has the beauty and despair of lovers attempting to save something for themselves in a period of hopeless confusion. It isn't really as good a movie as people want to believe it is, but the young Gérard Philipe was so extraordinary a camera subject that despite the dozens of roles which followed, he is best known for his incarnation of the passionate, egocentric schoolboy. Micheline Presle is the woman. With Denise Grey and Jean Debucourt. The script is by Jean Aurenche and Pierre Bost. In French. b & w

The Devil Is a Woman (1935)—Directed by Josef von Sternberg and starring Marlene Dietrich, this is the most famous version of *La Femme et le pantin*, Pierre Louÿs' short novel about a femme fatale, published in 1898. It was filmed earlier with Geraldine Farrar (1920) and with Conchita Montenegro (1929), and after the von Sternberg movie it was filmed in 1958, by Julien Duvivier, under the title *A Woman Like Satan*, starring Brigitte Bardot, and then in 1977 by Buñuel, as *That Obscure Object of Desire*, with two actresses playing the leading role. It's a story of obsessive love, and von Sternberg's version is certainly obsessive. There's a slightly crazy daringness about his approach to the mythic. (You're never invited into the heroine's state of mind.) The film's near-abstract decorative quality has the fascination of a folly. With Lionel Atwill, Cesar Romero, Alison Skipworth, Edward Everett Horton, Don Alvarado, Hank Mann, and Edwin Maxwell. Von Sternberg was credited as both director and photographer, with Lucien Ballard as assistant photographer; John Dos Passos and S. K. Winston were the scenarists; Hans Dreier was the art director. Paramount. b & w

The Devil Strikes at Night *Nachts, Wenn der Teufel Kam* (1958)—Robert Siodmak's Hollywood films, such as *The Spiral Staircase, The Suspect, Phantom Lady, The Killers,* and *The Crimson Pirate,* are much better known than he is—perhaps because his films are often mistakenly attributed to other directors or to highly publicized producers. In the 20s in Berlin he directed *People on Sunday* (with a crew that included Billy Wilder and Fred Zinnemann); in France he directed films with Harry Baur and Maurice Chevalier; and after many years in Hollywood he returned to Germany where he made this thriller based on the Bruno Luedke case. Luedke was a half-witted mass murderer who killed about 80 women; Hitler tried to suppress all information about him, because the Nazis had been publicizing the trial of a French murderer to demonstrate the degeneracy of France, and the idiot-maniac Luedke was not a foreigner or a Jew or a hereditary misfit—he was a "pure Aryan." Then, too, in the midst of the Nazi genocide, Luedke's individual initiative in mass murder might, if publicized, have seemed almost a parody of the government's policies. The film is more interesting in the ideas and ironies it suggests than in itself. As a thriller it doesn't achieve a satisfactory unity or style, but it sends one out arguing about the characters and the possible courses of action; it's a movie that nags at the mind. With Mario Adorf as Bruno, Hannes Messemer as the SS officer Rossdorf, Claus Holm as the "good" police officer, Werner Peters as the Nazi fall guy Willi Keun. In German. b & w

The Devil's Disciple (1959)—The Shaw play, not too well directed by Guy Hamilton, but Laurence Olivier is an irresistible General Burgoyne. As an English critic remarked, he administers "such a drubbing to his American co-stars that Burgoyne's military defeats are triumphantly avenged." With Kirk Douglas, Eva Le Gallienne, Burt Lancaster (who has one great scene), and Janette Scott. United Artists. b & w

The Devil's Envoys, see *Les Visiteurs du soir*

The Devil's General   *Des Teufels General* (1955)—The devil takes his reckoning of a gallant Luftwaffe general (based on the famous ace Ernst Udet, who was so popular he used to make guest appearances in movies— as in *The White Hell of Pitz Palu*). The general works for Hitler because he loves his air force; he is a man of conscience who becomes aware of what he is doing, and "can't eat as much as I want to vomit." Though the film is a melodrama of conscience, it derives much of its impact from the sexual assurance of Curt Jurgens in the leading role. Helmut Käutner's direction is not imaginative, but for a solid story, well-told, about characters and obstacles, it doesn't need to be: the film has the necessary pulse and excitement. From Carl Zuckmayer's play—which was the biggest stage success of postwar Germany up to that time. With Marianne Koch and Victor de Kowa. In German. b & w

The Devil's Playground (1976)—The Marist Brothers at the Catholic seminary around which most of the film is set seem to be looking into themselves, puzzled and deeply disappointed by their own physicality. And the pubescent boys gaze with thunderstruck eyes at the eruptions of their bodies. This semi-autobiographical first feature by the Australian writer-director Fred Schepisi is always on the borderline of comedy, because they have all—monks and seminarians alike—been taught that "an undisciplined mind is the Devil's playground," yet they can't get their minds off their bodies. This isn't an anti-Catholic movie. Far from it. Schepisi loves these tormented comedians. But he looks at them with humorous pagan eyes. His pas-

sionate feelings are expressed visually—in his thematic use of water imagery and in the vibrancy of his color, which eroticizes the environment. He's a great filmmaker, with his own softly rhythmed style. You feel he's got the whole thing right. With the novelist Thomas Keneally as the bald and bewhiskered Father Marshall, Arthur Dignam as Brother Francine, who dreams of being underwater, surrounded by beautiful naked nymphs, and Nick Tate as Brother Victor, who goes into the city wearing civvies, picks up two women and flirts and teases right up to the verge of actual sex, and then escapes, gasping, "They nearly had me." (See *Taking It All In*.)

Le Diable au corps, see *Devil in the Flesh*

Diabolique (1955)—The setting is a French provincial school for boys; the headmaster's wife (Vera Clouzot) and mistress (Simone Signoret) conspire to murder him. It sounds simple, but the characters seem fearfully knowing, and there are undertones of strange, tainted pleasures and punishments. According to the director, Henri-Georges Clouzot, "I sought only to amuse myself and the little child who sleeps in all our hearts— the child who hides her head under the bedcovers and begs, 'Daddy, Daddy, frighten me.'" Clouzot does it, all right; his Grand Guignol techniques are so calculatedly grisly that they seem silly, yet they succeed in making one feel queasy and sordid and scared. (Some people may feel too queasy to find the film really pleasurable.) With Paul Meurisse as the malignant headmaster, and Charles Vanel, Noel Roquevert, and Michel Serrault. From a novel by Boileau and Narcejac. In French. b & w

La Diagonale du fou, see *Dangerous Moves*

Dial M for Murder (1954)—Those who like drawing-room murder and cold, literate, gentlemanly skulduggery will find this ingenious and almost entertaining. Ray Milland is the suitably suave husband who hires unsavory, penny-dreadful Anthony Dawson to kill his rich, unfaithful wife, Grace Kelly; he then calmly goes out for the evening with her lover, Robert Cummings. The unexpected happens: the wife dispatches her would-be assassin with scissors, so the determined husband goes to work to make the murder look premeditated. All this is related with Alfred Hitchcock's ghoulish chic, but everyone in it seems to be walking around with tired blood. Amusingly, John Williams, as the inspector who unravels the case, is so wryly, archly dexterous that he makes everybody else's underplaying look positively boisterous. (A mystery darker than any propounded in the film: Why did Hitchcock persist in using actors as unattractively untalented as Robert Cummings?) Grace Kelly is very beautiful here, in a special, pampered way. From Frederick Knott's play, just slightly adapted by the author; music by Dmitri Tiomkin. (Made in 3-D, but generally released in conventional form; the 3-D version was reissued in 1980.) Warners. color

Diamonds Are Forever (1971)—Unimaginative Bond picture (it was the seventh) that is often noisy when it means to be exciting. It lacks elegance and visual opulence, but it has got Sean Connery (he didn't appear in the otherwise topnotch sixth, *On Her Majesty's Secret Service*). Connery's Bond is less lecherous than before and less foppish—and he's better this way. In this one, Bond is attacked by two Amazons named Bambi and Thumper. With Charles Gray as Blofeld, Jill St. John as Tiffany Case, Jimmy Dean as a Howard Hughes–like character, and Bruce Cabot as Saxby. Directed by Guy Hamilton. Produced by Albert R. Broccoli and Harry Saltzman. color

The Diary of a Chambermaid (1945)—Jean Renoir parodies historical romances in this wildly improbable divertissement. Chambermaid Paulette Goddard loves gloomy master Hurd Hatfield (fresh from *The Picture of Dorian Gray*), but his Freudianized mama, Judith Anderson, and a whole lot of other people get in the way. The screenplay is by Burgess Meredith from a novel by Octave Mirbeau; Meredith also contrived to find a part for himself, as a demented gent who eats his way through a rose garden. Francis Lederer, meant to be a menacing servant, is the most elegantly turned-out actor in the movie; probably he just couldn't resist looking his best. It's slightly crazy but highly entertaining. United Artists. b & w

The Diary of a Country Priest *Le Journal d'un curé de campagne* (1950)—Robert Bresson's masterly adaptation of the Georges Bernanos novel about the suffering of a young priest (Claude Laydu) whose faith is neither understood nor accepted by his parishioners. A film of great purity and, at the end, a Bach-like intensity. The dialogue and the passages read from the diary are taken directly from the novel, though while you're watching you feel as if you were seeing a silent movie. (It's the effect of the expressive images and the general austerity.) This is one of the few modern works in any art form that help one to understand the religious life—which for this useless young man is a terrible one, yet with moments of holiness. If there is a flaw in the film it's the rhythm—you feel you're dying with the priest. The film may raise a question in your mind: Does Bresson know what a pain this young man is? The priest's austere spirituality may give the community the same sort of pain that Bresson's later movies give some of us in the audience. With Nicole Maurey and Nicole Ladmiral. The music is by Jean-Jacques Grünenwald; the beautiful bleak cinematography is by L.-H. Burel. In French. b & w

Les Dimanches de Ville d'Avray, see *Sundays and Cybèle*

Diner (1982)—A wonderful movie, set in Baltimore, around Christmas of 1959. A fluctuating group of five or six young men in their early 20s hang out together; they've known each other since high school, and though they're moving in different directions, they still cling to their late-night bull sessions at the diner—where, magically, they always seem to have plenty to talk about. It's like a comedy club—they take off from each other, and their conversations are all overlapping jokes that are funny without punch lines. Conversations may roll on all night, and they can sound worldly and sharp, but when these boys are out with girls, they're nervous, constricted, fraudulent, half crazy. Written and directed by Barry Levinson, *Diner* provides a look at middle-class relations between the sexes just before the sexual revolution, at a time when people still laughed (albeit uneasily) at the gulf between men and women. It isn't remarkable visually but it features some of the best young actors in the country: Mickey Rourke, Ellen Barkin, Daniel Stern, Kevin Bacon, Steve Guttenberg, Paul Reiser, and Timothy Daly. M-G-M. color (See *Taking It All In*.)

Dinner at Eight (1933)—Jean Harlow, with her bee-stung pucker and her tinny voice, at her comic best. George Cukor directed this witty, much improved version of the Edna Ferber–George S. Kaufman play, with a big-gun cast that includes Marie Dressler, John Barrymore, Lee Tracy, Wallace Beery, and Edmund Lowe. Among the people who toned up the dialogue were Herman J. Mankiewicz and Donald Ogden Stewart. M-G-M. b & w

Dirty Dancing (1987)—Set in a Catskills resort in the summer of 1963, this bright dance musical is about the role that dancing had in the embryonic counterculture. It's also a girl's version of that old phony: the-summer-I-grew-up-and-everything-changed. In the boys' version, the hero typically came down to earth with a jolt. But this is a girl's coming-of-age fantasy: the 17-year-old heroine, Baby (Jennifer Grey), ascends to spiritual and sensual perfection. For Baby, a doctor's daughter, the change occurs as the result of self-discovery through dancing and then through her sexual initiation and her full and open commitment to the resort's working-class dance instructor, Johnny (Patrick Swayze). He has been treated as nothing and he has come to believe he's nothing; Baby the fearless changes all that. Too many life lessons are learned in this bubbleheaded, retro vision of growing up in the 60s, and its wish-fulfillment aspect makes Baby and Johnny and all their dirty-dancing friends pure of heart—it defuses any possible explosiveness in the material. But the director, Emile Ardolino, and the choreographer, Kenny Ortega, use the dancing to bring out the sensual dreaminess of the songs, and the screenwriter, Eleanor Bergstein, writes light, rumpled dialogue that helps you over the hooey. You come out of the theatre giggling happily. (The movie has echoes of the 1938 *Having Wonderful Time* and the 1958 *Marjorie Morningstar*.) With Cynthia Rhodes, Jack Weston, Jerry Orbach, Honi Coles, Lonny Price, Kelly Bishop, and Jane Brucker. Vestron. color (See *Hooked*.)

Dirty Hands *Les Mains sales* (1951)—Sartre did the adaptation of his play, and so the drama is still in the political conflict between the intransigence of the young Communist Hugo (Daniel Gélin) and the compromises of the seasoned, disillusioned Hoederer (Pierre Brasseur). This isn't any great shakes as moviemaking but it's absorbing—it's probably the only film that has ever captured the meaning and spirit of the battles within modern revolutionary parties. Fernand Rivers directed. In French. b & w

Dirty Harry (1971)—This right-wing fantasy about the San Francisco police force as a helpless group (emasculated by the unrealistic liberals) propagandizes for para-legal police power and vigilante justice. The only way that the courageous cop Dirty Harry Callahan (Clint Eastwood) can protect the city against the mad hippie killer (Andy Robinson) who terrorizes women and children is by taking the law into his own hands. Harry, who knows what justice is and how to carry it out, is the best there is, a Camelot cop; he got his nickname because he's the dedicated troubleshooter who draws the dirtiest assignments. He is our martyr—stained on our behalf. As suspense craftsmanship, the picture is trim, brutal, and exciting; it was directed in the sleekest style by the veteran urban-action director Don Siegel, and Lalo Schifrin's pulsating, jazzy electronic trickery drives the picture forward. It's also a remarkably single-minded attack on liberal values, with each prejudicial detail in place—a kind of hardhat *The Fountainhead.* Harry's hippie adversary is pure evil: sniper, rapist, kidnapper, torturer, defiler of all human values. This monster—who wears a peace symbol—stands for everything the audience fears and loathes. The action genre has always had a fascist potential, and it surfaces in this movie. It was a big success, and Eastwood played Harry again in three sequels: *Magnum Force* (1973), *The Enforcer* (1976), and *Sudden Impact* (1983). With Reni Santoni, Harry Guardino, and John Vernon. Written by Harry Fink and his wife, R. M. Fink, Dean Riesner, and also John Milius (uncredited). Warners. color (See *Deeper into Movies.*)

Dirty Rotten Scoundrels (1988)—Michael Caine and Steve Martin as con men on the Côte d'Azur, in a remake of the 1964 *Bedtime Story.* Caine is the slick, discreet continental who operates by plan and fleeces middle-aged rich American women. Martin is a happy-go-lucky American spaz in wrinkled baggy pants; he's an improviser, a vagabond who chases after the most attractive young women he spots, and shamelessly, in a loud, whiny voice, cadges meals and a few bucks off them. The movie is mildly pleasant; it has amusing moments and a sunny sheen. The director, Frank Oz, takes such a square approach, though, that the action doesn't absorb your full attention. (Couldn't the women at least have been smart and lusty?) Caine and Martin preen beautifully. At their best, they're like a vaudeville team zapping each other and doing a soft-shoe. But the script, by Dale Launer, who reworked the 1964 script, by Stanley Shapiro and Paul Henning, is such a lazy ripoff of the past that there's not much juice in the roles: we seem to be watching the last pressing of the grapes. With Glenne Headly, Barbara Harris, Dana Ivey, Anton Rodgers, and Ian McDiarmid. Cinematography by Michael Ballhaus. Orion. color (See *Movie Love.*)

The Discreet Charm of the Bourgeoisie *Le Charme discret de la bourgeoisie* (1972)—Luis Buñuel's most frivolously witty movie, directed (at the age of 72) with exhilarating ease. It's a cosmic vaudeville show—an Old Master's mischief. He is no longer savage about the hypocrisy and inanity of the privileged classes; he has grown almost fond of their follies—the way one can grow fond of the snarls and the silliness of vicious pets. This episodic story is about a group of six friends—discreetly charming amoral beasts—whose attempts to have dinner together are always being interrupted: food, that ritual center of bourgeois well-being, keeps eluding them. Buñuel takes an off-hand, prankish approach to the medium; he keeps tweaking us, catching us up in an anecdote or a spooky death joke, and then dropping it. With Stéphane Audran, Julien Bertheau (who plays a bishop with supreme finesse), Fernando Rey, Delphine Seyrig, Jean-Pierre Cassel, Paul Frankeur, Bulle Ogier, Milena Vukotić, Claude Piéplu, and Michel Piccoli. Written by Buñuel and Jean-Claude Carrière. In French. color (See *Reeling.*)

Dishonored (1931)—The dullest of the Marlene Dietrich films directed by Josef von Sternberg. He wrote the story (which was a mistake) and then the scenario was prepared by Daniel Rubin (another mistake). Dietrich plays a "woman of the streets" who is given the chance of spiritual redemption by serving her country; she becomes the glamorous spy X-27, but falls in love with an enemy agent (Victor McLaglen). McLaglen is the really hopeless mistake. He's meant to be dashing, but he lacks style and physical grace—he's a grinning buffoon, with zero sex appeal. Dietrich goes through her repertory of teases, lowering her eyelids demurely and raising them amusingly; she's charming, but she's playing all alone. (At times she might as well be doing eye exercises.) In a few sequences (especially the ones in which she impersonates a peasant hotel maid) she's clearly having a good time, and, when she poses with a cat, she's sleekly, still youthfully, beautiful (she was born 27 December 1901); the mask of mysterious remoteness and agelessness is just beginning to form. Her ironic, spacey gallantry—the way she keeps her firing squad waiting while she takes out her lipstick and touches up her mouth—is the only real entertainment in this lamely directed movie; the lines are so stiffly paced that they're like failed epigrams. (You wince.) With Lew Cody, Gustav von Seyffertitz, Warner Oland,

Barry Norton, and, in a small part, Bill Powell. (Every one of them seems more desirable than McLaglen.) Cinematography by Lee Garmes. Paramount. b & w

Distant Thunder *Ashani Sanket* (1973)—Satyajit Ray sets this film in a torpid Bengali village in the early 1940s. Soumitra Chatterji, Ray's one-man stock company, who played the passionately romantic Apu in *The World of Apu,* is cast as a newly arrived Brahmin, the only educated man for miles around. "You are the jewel in our crown," the ignorant villagers tell him, and he agrees. But the faraway Second World War causes the price of rice to soar, the traditions that bind the community are eroded, and the condescending Brahmin is no longer treated as a jewel. This isn't one of Ray's greatest films; it's forced and riddled with flaws. Yet it's still a Satyajit Ray film, full of feeling and astonishingly beautiful; the women are conceived as in a dream of the past—moving in their thin, clinging saris, they create sensuous waves of color in the steamy air. In Bengali. (See *When the Lights Go Down.*)

Diva (1981)—An up-to-the-minute glittering toy of a movie, a romantic thriller from France, made by a new director, Jean-Jacques Beineix, who has a fabulous camera technique and understands the pleasures to be had from a picture that doesn't take itself too seriously—the whole high-tech incandescence of the film is played for humor. The diva is an awesomely beautiful black American soprano (Wilhelmenia Fernandez) who refuses to make recordings. Frédéric Andrei is the wide-eyed 18-year-old postal messenger who adores her; he sneaks his Nagra tape machine into her concert in Paris so he'll be able to listen to her at home—and all hell breaks loose around him. He's pursued by two baroque thugs: one is tall and Latin and chews gum with the jaws of a hippopotamus;

the other (Dominique Pinon) is small, with spiky blond hair and sunglasses, and an earplug so he can listen to a transistor radio while he's on his murderous errands—he's so dissociated he's practically a mutant. The unfazable heroine (the 14-year-old Thuy An Luu) is a post-Godardian tootsie—in her short-short skirts and transparent plastic coat, she's a lollipop wrapped in cellophane. A man named Gorodish (Richard Bohringer), a Mr. Cool in a white suit and a white Citroën, comes to the aid of the besieged messenger. The film may remind you of Welles' *Touch of Evil*; it's Welles romanticized, packaged. It's a mixture of style and chic hanky-panky, but it's genuinely sparkling. The screenplay by Beineix and Jean Van Hamme is based on a novel by Delacorta (a pseudonym for Daniel Odier, who also writes under his own name); the cinematography is by Philippe Rousselot; the art direction is by Hilton McConnico. In French. color (See *Taking It All In*.)

The Divided Heart (1954)—In 1952 *Life* devoted its first eight pages to a legal case that had become an international incident. Someone had to make a decision, although everyone understood that either of the two possible decisions would be a cruel injustice. A Yugoslav family had been broken up by Hitler's soldiers—the husband shot, the wife separated from her 20-month-old son and sent to Auschwitz. She returned in 1945 and spent 5 years trying to locate the boy. Meanwhile a German woman in Sudetenland, childless for 10 years, had adopted the baby from an orphanage, and, after her husband was sent to a Soviet prison camp and she and the baby were expelled from their home, she had found work as a seamstress in order to take care of the child. The conflicting claims of these two mothers (Cornell Borchers and Yvonne Mitchell) are dramatized in this English film, directed by Charles Crichton. It's

far from great, but better than you might expect. You do get a feeling of the chaos, and of how the lives of both women are centered on this one little boy. With Michel Ray, Alexander Knox, Armin Dahlen, Liam Redmond, Eddie Byrne, and Geoffrey Keen. Written by Jack Whittingham; cinematography by Otto Heller; music by Georges Auric. b & w

Divine Madness (1980)—Essentially a one-woman show: Bette Midler is alone on the stage with her backup trio, the Harlettes, but like Craig Russell in *Outrageous!*, she seems to have a whole troupe of people inside. In this film, shot on three successive nights at the Pasadena Civic Auditorium, she tells jokes (she may be better at bawdiness than any other woman entertainer alive) and she sings. She really gives a song a workout—she may swing it, wail it, shout it, rock it, and throw in some scat, gospel, funk, and punk. She's an emotional whirligig, and the film is hugely entertaining, though the best numbers come at the beginning; the last quarter—when Midler comes on as a boozing bag lady who is trying to capture the bird of happiness—has a sodden inspirational quality. Directed by Michael Ritchie; cinematography by William A. Fraker. Released by Warners. color (See *Taking It All In*.)

The Divorce of Lady X (1937)—Expensively produced attempt at a sophisticated romantic comedy; it's rather foolish and a little draggy, and is mainly of interest because of the cast—Laurence Olivier, Merle Oberon, Ralph Richardson, Binnie Barnes. They don't do much in the way of acting, but their arch romping is, at least, a curiosity. Alexander Korda produced; Tim Whelan directed. color.

The Divorcée (1930)—Norma Shearer and the double standard. Her husband (Chester Morris) is unfaithful, but she isn't allowed to be; they split. This being intended as a sizzling, daring movie, she turns to Robert Montgomery and Conrad Nagel before reconciling (on New Year's Eve, of course) with her ex-husband. Shearer's specialty was sexy suffering in satin gowns by Adrian; here, she always seems to want to abandon herself to naughtiness, but one damned thing after another stops her. With Florence Eldridge. Robert Z. Leonard directed, from an adaptation of Ursula Parrott's novel *Ex-Wife*. M-G-M. b & w

Dr. Cyclops (1940)—As Dr. Cyclops, Albert Dekker is a nutty biologist in a South American jungle who miniaturizes people to doll size; they get so small that the giant alligators down there can snap them up like beads of caviar. The color gives this lavish horror film an unintended prettiness, and Ernest B. Schoedsack's direction lacks sinister overtones. The picture didn't make it into the horror big time; the moviemakers don't seem to be cooking with the right recipe. With Victor Kilian and Janice Logan. From a script by Tom Kilpatrick; produced by Merian C. Cooper. Paramount.

Doctor Faustus (1967)—By the time Richard Burton was in a position to star in a movie of Marlowe's *Doctor Faustus*, further dealing with the Devil probably had become anticlimactic. It wouldn't be hard to overlook the visual redundancies (if Faustus says "gold" or "pearls," the screen shows gold or pearls), the ominous, funereal music, the Technicolored beauties parading like the Goldwyn Girls. What can't be overlooked is that Burton gives a dead, muffled reading. And so, despite an imposing young Mephistopheles (Andreas Teuber), this production, with Elizabeth Taylor as Helen of Troy, is the dullest episode in the Burton and Taylor great-lovers-of-history series that started with *Cleopatra*. Eventually, Burton gets to the speech that begins "Was this the face that launched a thousand ships" and ends "And none but thou shalt be my paramour!" By then, it's clear that Faustus and Helen are just Dick and Liz. Co-directed by Burton and Nevill Coghill. Released in the U.S. by Columbia. color

Dr. Jekyll and Mr. Hyde (1932)—Fredric March goes in for hilarious makeup that includes a change in the shape of his skull and an alarming number of huge teeth, and his rampaging Hyde is so exuberantly athletic he seems to be modelled on Douglas Fairbanks, Sr. The director, Rouben Mamoulian, rather overdoes the pseudo-science at the beginning, but at some levels this story seems to work in every version, and this one, set in a starched mid-Victorian environment, suggests the lust that has to come out—and the attraction of the gutter. With Miriam Hopkins, shiny-eyed with sexual mischief, as the trollop, and Rose Hobart. Paramount. b & w

Dr. Knock *Knock* (1931)—Louis Jouvet had a special talent for the role of a happy hypocrite. Jules Romains provided the perfect vehicle with *Dr. Knock, le triomphe de la médecine*, in which Jouvet played the high priest of medical pseudo-science. The role of the quack who reduces a whole healthy village to imaginary sickness became his greatest stage success. This medical entrepreneur builds a hospital and puts the entire local population in it. Jouvet filmed it twice—once in 1931 and again in 1950. The 1931 version is much better—fresher and looser. In French. b & w

Dr. X (1932)—A famous chiller about a series of murders committed during the full moon in the vicinity of a medical college. It's the source of many of the most delirious clichés of the mad-scientist genre, and the first of Fay Wray's horror films (she gets to scream in her very first scene). But the pacing is very deliberate and it's a little tedious, especially in the wisecracking comedy-relief scenes with Lee Tracy as the reporter-hero; Tracy's vocal tricks and stylized gestures fall flat here. (One wouldn't guess how funny he would be that same year in *Blessed Event*, or the year after in *Bombshell*.) The title role, Dr. Xavier, is played by Lionel Atwill, an expert at polished menace; he can be wonderful in the way he examines a corpse while commenting "Strangely enough, only the left deltoid has been severed." His suavity is heavy, though, and he weighs this picture down a bit. The director, Michael Curtiz, plays things too straight; he doesn't have the perverse comic sense of a James Whale. (There are bits—such as talk of cannibalism, and a doctor unscrewing his artificial arm—that cry out for the sort of twist Whale would have given them.) With Preston Foster, Arthur Edmund Carewe, Willard Robertson, Robert Warwick, Mae Busch, Leila Bennett, George Rosener, John Wray, and Tom Dugan. The script, by Earl Baldwin and Robert Tasker, is adapted from the play by Howard Comstock and Allen C. Miller. First National. Originally in a Technicolor process, though black-and-white prints were shipped to smaller cities.

Doctor Zhivago (1965)—The pure-souled poet-doctor Zhivago (Omar Sharif, with wet, dark eyes) is at the center of the scenarist Robert Bolt's poetic enigma, and the director David Lean surrounds him with enormous historical reconstructions of the Russian Revolution. Neither the contemplative Zhivago nor the flux of events is intelligible, and what is worse, they seem unrelated to each other. (It's hard to know what kind of hero or even what kind of group of people *could* hold these events together.) And in this movie, so full of '"realism," nothing really grows—not the performances, not the ideas, not even the daffodils, which are also so "real" they have obviously been planted for us, just as the buildings have been built for us. After the first half hour you don't expect the picture to breathe and live; you just sit there. It isn't shoddy (except for the balalaika music, which is so repetitive you could kill the composer); it's stately, respectable, and dead. Though not in itself a disgraceful failure, it does have one disgraceful effect: the final shot of a rainbow over the huge dam where Zhivago's lost daughter is working. This banal suggestion that the suffering has all been for the best and that tomorrow will be brighter is not only an insult to the audience, it is a coarse gesture of condescension and appeasement to the Russians. Would Lean and Bolt place a rainbow over the future of England? With Julie Christie, who does have some life as Lara, and Rod Steiger, who brings something powerful, many-sided, and sexual to the role of Komarovsky, and Geraldine Chaplin, Alec Guinness, Tom Courtenay, Siobhan McKenna, Jack MacGowran, Rita Tushingham, Ralph Richardson, Adrienne Corri, Geoffrey Keen, Noel Willman, and Klaus Kinski, with his eyes popping and huge veins bulging out of his forehead, as the nihilist who declares, "I am the only free man on this train." From the novel by Boris Pasternak; cinematography by Freddie Young; production design by the aptly named John Box; produced by Carlo Ponti, for M-G-M. (193 minutes.) color (See *Kiss Kiss Bang Bang*.)

Doctors' Wives (1971)—A Jacobean soap opera—bloody surgery is thrown in at regular intervals, like the sex acts in a porny picture. Dyan Cannon plays the husband-poaching chief bitch and she's a great sexpot-tease. How could Mike Frankovich, who produced, and George Schaefer, who directed, and Daniel Taradash, who wrote the script, make the mistake of killing her off in the first reel, leaving us with nothing but Richard Crenna and a troupe of bland surgeons with sexually distraught wives? Sex here is some sort of hysterical affliction that attacks only

D

women. Janice Rule writhes in drug-induced lust; Diana Sands plays her big scene in a see-through blouse; Rachel Roberts, in closeup, confesses to a lesbian affair that began when the seductress removed a cinder from her eye. . . . The picture is just a major studio (Columbia) making a bid for the skin-flick trade. With John Colicos, Gene Hackman, Carroll O'Connor, Ralph Bellamy, Cara Williams, and Richard Anderson. From Frank G. Slaughter's novel. color (See *Deeper into Movies*.)

Dodsworth (1936)—While other writers were turning out novels ridiculing American materialism and glorifying the expatriate existence, Sinclair Lewis conceived a businessman-hero and showed him to be a true dreamer, while his culture-mad wife, longing to be enriched by life in Europe, was a foolish horror. Sidney Howard made a play of Lewis's novel, and Walter Huston gave a legendary performance as the hero. He also stars in the movie version, which was produced by Sam Goldwyn with great care and taste; William Wyler is the director. There's only one trouble, really, but it's central: Sidney Howard also did the screenplay, and the movie follows the stage version too closely. It looks programmed and underpopulated, though in an elegantly stylized way. (Rudolph Maté was the cinematographer.) Ruth Chatterton plays the wife; Mary Astor is the woman who appreciates Dodsworth's real value; and the cast includes Maria Ouspenskaya (she's Viennese this time), Paul Lukas, David Niven, Odette Myrtil, Spring Byington, and John Payne. b & w

Dog Day Afternoon (1975)—One of the best ''New York'' movies ever made. Sidney Lumet directed this fictional re-creation of an unusual bank robbery on a 97-degree day in August, 1972, working from Frank R. Pierson's very fine script. Sonny (Al Pacino), who is trapped in the middle of robbing a bank, with a crowd gathering in the street outside, is a married working-class man; he got into this robbery mess by trying to raise money for his lover Leon (Chris Sarandon) to have a sex-change operation. The most touching element in the film is Sonny's inability to handle all the responsibilities he has assumed. Though he is half-crazed by his situation, he is trying to do the right thing by everybody—his wife and children, the suicidal Leon, the hostages in the bank. In the sequence in which Sonny dictates his will, we can see that inside this bungling robber there's a complicatedly unhappy man, operating out of a sense of noblesse oblige. Pacino has a telephone conversation with Sarandon that by ordinary dramatic standards goes on too long, but this willingness to violate ordinary practice permits the two actors to go further and further emotionally. Lumet keeps so much low comedy and crazy melodrama going on in the bank, on the street, among the police, that he can risk the long, quiet scenes that draw us in. (He doesn't even use a musical track.) Pacino's Sonny, grandstanding to the crowds who cheer him on, brings just the right urban craziness to the situation. The contrast between the small, frightened nutty robbers inside the bank and the huge apparatus of police, F.B.I., and news media outside adds to the lunacy. And Sarandon gives one of the finest homosexual performances ever seen in a movie; he's true to Leon's anguish in a remarkably pure way—he makes no appeal for sympathy. There are structural problems and there are gross, static scenes involving Sonny's relatives, but there are also surprising, wonderful things from such actors as John Cazale, who plays Sonny's partner in the robbery with a despairing burnt-out face, and Charles Durning as a police detective who becomes irascible and begins shouting like Sonny. The cast, which is huge and of highly variable quality, includes

Penny Allen, Carol Kane, Gary Springer, James Broderick, Judith Malina, Susan Peretz, and Sully Boyar. (Sonny is based on John Wojtowicz, who was serving a 20-year sentence when the film was released.) Produced by Martin Bregman and Martin Elfand. Warners. color

The Dogs of War (1981)—A crisp, tough-minded action film about an international group of mercenaries who stage a coup in a small, decaying West African country run by an Idi Amin–Papa Doc-style despot. The casting of Christopher Walken as Shannon, the leader of the group, gives the film the fuse it needs. Walken, with his pale, flat-faced mask of pain, his glaring eyes and lithe movements, suggests a restless anger. We aren't asked to like the mercenaries, and Shannon kills a spy (set on him by his own employer, who doesn't trust him) in such a horrifying way that we really couldn't like him. But we do want to watch him. This is the first feature film by John Irvin, an English documentarian and TV director ("Tinker, Tailor, Soldier, Spy"); he has studied a master—during the actual raid, some of the most feral images are almost direct quotations from Peckinpah's *The Wild Bunch*. With Colin Blakely as a TV journalist who's tenacious about following a story, and Tom Berenger, Paul Freeman, and Jean-François Stevenin. Cinematography by Jack Cardiff; freely adapted from Frederick Forsyth's best-seller by Gary DeVore and George Malko. A Norman Jewison–Patrick Palmer Production; released by United Artists. color (See *Taking It All In*.)

$ (1971)—Bank heist in Hamburg, masterminded by Warren Beatty, assisted by Goldie Hawn as a kook hooker. For the first 20 minutes, it's impossible to know what's going on; after that, there are so many camera setups and such noisy, overextended chases that the whole thing becomes hectic and exhausting.

Overwritten and overdirected by Richard Brooks. With Gert Fröbe. Columbia. color

Domicile conjugal, see *Bed and Board*

Don Quixote (1934)—An international artistic collaboration of rather overwhelming proportions: under the direction of G. W. Pabst (a German) the Russian basso Feodor Chaliapin appeared in three different language versions of the Cervantes novel, with three supporting casts. The French version (which is sometimes shown in the U.S.) features Dorville as Sancho Panza; in the English version, George Robey plays the part. The film is not completely satisfying—Jacques Ibert's music is undistinguished and, despite remarkable cinematography and a stunning windmill sequence, the treatment seems rather cold. But if the film fails as *Don Quixote* it allows us to be in the presence of a great performer who is already a legend. Chaliapin was one of the rare great singers who was also a great actor. (There's a suggestion of John Barrymore in his self-awareness.) He isn't just a singer photographed: the voice is part of the actor's equipment. He's magnificent—a master of gesture who seems born to the camera. b & w

La Donna della Domenica, see *Sunday Woman*

The Donskoi Trilogy, see *The Childhood of Maxim Gorky, My Apprenticeship,* and *My Universities*

Don't Bother to Knock (1952)—Marilyn Monroe as a psychotic babysitter. She wasn't yet a box-office star, but her unformed—almost blobby—quality is very creepy, and she dominated this melodrama. In other respects, it's standard, though the New York hotel setting helps, and also the young Anne Bancroft, as a singer who works in the hotel.

Roy Baker directed fairly efficiently, from Daniel Taradash's screenplay, based on Charlotte Armstrong's novel. With Richard Widmark as the airline-pilot hero, Donna Corcoran, Elisha Cook, Jr., Jim Backus, Don Beddoe, Jeanne Cagney, and Lurene Tuttle. Cinematography by Lucien Ballard. 20th Century-Fox. b & w

Don't Look Now (1973)—A Daphne du Maurier story of the occult, presented in fast, splintered, almost subliminal imagery. Julie Christie and Donald Sutherland team up wonderfully as parents whose drowned daughter may or may not be sending them messages. The meanings are on a simple Hitchcock level, but the unnerving cold ominousness of the environment (mostly Venice, deserted at the end of the season) says that things are not what they seem. Life is treated as a puzzle and the clues are in references that go by in split seconds. This is the fanciest, most carefully assembled enigma yet put on the screen. Nicolas Roeg is a chillingly chic director; the picture is an example of high-fashion gothic sensibility. It seems to say what Joseph Losey never dared to but what the audience for Losey's films was always responding to: that decay among the rich and beautiful is sexy. Venice, the labyrinthine city of pleasure, with its crumbling, leering gargoyles, is obscurely, frighteningly sensual here, and an early sex sequence with Christie and Sutherland nude in bed, intercut with their post-coital mood as they dress to go out together, has an extraordinary erotic glitter. Dressing is splintered and sensualized, like fear and death. Using du Maurier as a base, Roeg comes closer to getting Borges on the screen than those who have tried it directly, but there's a distasteful clamminess about the picture. Roeg's style is in love with disintegration. color (See *Reeling*.)

Double Indemnity (1944)—Every turn and twist is exactly calculated and achieves its effect with the simplest of means; this shrewd, smoothly tawdry thriller is one of the high points of 40s films. The director, Billy Wilder, collaborated with Raymond Chandler in adapting James M. Cain's story (from his book *Three of a Kind*), and it's a tribute to them that one is likely to remember the names of the principal characters. Barbara Stanwyck's Phyllis Dietrichson—a platinum blonde who wears tight white sweaters, an anklet, and sleazy-kinky shoes—is perhaps the best acted and the most fixating of all the slutty, cold-blooded femmes fatales of the *film-noir* genre. With her bold stare, her sneering, over-lipsticked, thick-looking mouth, and her strategically displayed legs, she's a living entrapment device. Fred MacMurray's Walter Neff, an insurance salesman, is the patsy she ensnares in a plot to kill her businessman-husband and collect on the double-indemnity clause in his policy; MacMurray's slightly opaque, regular-guy, macho Americanness is perfectly used here (he has never had better audience empathy). And as Keyes, the claims investigator for the insurance company, Edward G. Robinson handles his sympathetic role with an easy mastery that gives the film some realistic underpinnings. It needs them, because despite the fine use of realistic sets—a cheerless middle-class home, a supermarket, offices—Chandler's dialogue is in his heightened laconic mode, and the narration (Walter Neff tells the story) is often so gaudy and terse that it seems an emblem of 40s hard-boiled attitudes. This defect may be integral to the film's taut structure. Another, lesser defect isn't: except for the three stars, the cast is just barely adequate. With Jean Heather, Porter Hall, Tom Powers, Byron Barr, Richard Gaines, and Fortunio Bonanova. Art direction by Hans Dreier and Hal Pereira; cinematography by John Seitz; score by Miklós Rózsa. Paramount. b & w

A Double Life (1947)—The Ruth Gordon–Garson Kanin script takes off from the professional hazard of actors: living their parts offstage. Usually this hazard is treated satirically, but the Kanins do it in a souped-up, portentously melodramatic version. Ronald Colman is the actor who starts hearing bells in his ears and loud keening noises during his run in *Othello*. His friends stare at him, puzzled, until after he has smothered a harmless blond waitress (Shelley Winters) and tried to kill a press agent (Edmond O'Brien) whom he suspects of having designs on his Desdemona—his actress wife, played by Signe Hasso. Colman is not at his best, and the role of Othello is so far out of his range that he's gentlemanly and dispassionate when he means to be fiery hot, but he got the Academy Award for Best Actor, anyway. The theatrical milieu doesn't help this picture much, though the theatre scenes were shot in the famous Empire, which was demolished in 1953. George Cukor directed; with Millard Mitchell, Philip Loeb, Ray Collins, Fay Kanin, and Frederic Worlock. Music by Miklós Rózsa. Universal. b & w

Down and Out in Beverly Hills (1986)—Jokes you can't explain may be the best kind, and the director Paul Mazursky is a master of them. When he gets rolling here, you're not responding to single jokes—it's the whole gestalt of the movie that's funny. Taking off from Renoir's 1931 film *Boudu Saved from Drowning* (which was based on a play by René Fauchois), Mazursky and his writing partner, Leon Capetanos, set you down in a bastion of the new rich, and the cinematographer, Don McAlpine, gives you a vision of the sensuousness of money wrapped in sunshine. Nick Nolte plays the shaggy, smelly drifter who attempts suicide and is rescued by a self-made millionaire (Richard Dreyfuss). Taken into the millionaire's guest cabaña, the bum is decked out in silk lounging robes; he's soon lord of the sunshine manor. Lean now, Dreyfuss is more precise and agile than he used to be, and he uses his slightness for comic effects vis-à-vis the deep-voiced Nolte, who towers over him. As Dreyfuss's creamy-skinned, pampered wife, Bette Midler is more seductive than in her earlier screen roles, and she has a warped charm rather like that of Teri Garr, but riper, juicier; she trots through the halls of her mansion jiggling in her frilly dresses and making tippy-taps with her high heels. Her eyes are pixilated; she's ready for anything. As a record-producer neighbor, Little Richard uses the maniacal energy that went into his singing; he has a bursting presence—you look at him and laugh. Peppy and pleasurable, this is one of the most sheerly beautiful comedies ever shot. Mazursky isn't afraid of uproarious silliness: there are some dizzying slapstick routines that reach their peak when a small black-and-white Border collie takes over. The cast includes Elizabeth Peña as a sulky, hot maid with a bedroom mouth, Tracy Nelson, Evan Richards, Donald F. Muhich as a dog psychiatrist, and Mazursky himself as a curly-haired accountant. Touchstone (Disney). color (See *Hooked*.)

Down Argentine Way (1940)—20th Century-Fox 40s-musical camp, so outrageous that it's hard to believe it isn't at least partly intentional—but why would anybody make this picture on purpose? The queen of these excruciating extravaganzas was Alice Faye, but she had become ill, and Betty Grable, a featured player for a decade, got her big chance. Unbelievably, this picture made her a star. With stolid Don Ameche, smiling his pained, hardworking smile, just as he always had for Alice; Charlotte Greenwood, the high-kicker who had seen better days before she started playing chaperones; and Carmen Miranda, the "Brazilian Bombshell" in her manic début. When she stands on her nine-inch heels and sings "Mama Yo Quiero," she is so frenetically irresistible that there's no use trying to fight it, though some people have been hiding under seats for decades. Irving Cummings directed. color.

Down by Law (1986)—Jim Jarmusch's follow-up to his 1984 *Stranger Than Paradise* is also a low-key minimalist comedy about American anomie shot in black-and-white—this time by Robby Müller. The setting is New Orleans, where two deadbeats—Jack, an ineffectual pimp (John Lurie), and Zack, an itinerant disk jockey (Tom Waits)—become the victims of frameups and are put in the same prison cell, where they vegetate in hostile silence. And the moviemaking itself shares in their lethargy; that's what gives the film a cachet of modernism. Everything changes when a little, life-loving Italian, Roberto (Roberto Benigni), is put in with them; the three become pals, grinning and talking together. And, eventually, Roberto devises an escape plan. Jarmusch's passive style has its wit, but the style is deadening here until he brings in Roberto—a character out of folk humor. And without the boredom of the first three-quarters of an hour Roberto wouldn't be so funny. The best scene in the movie is the least characteristic of Jarmusch: it comes almost at the start, when Ellen Barkin, as Zack's girlfriend, throws a tantrum, quiets down, then gets sore again, and—wham-wham-wham!—his possessions land in the street. That's the most active the movie ever gets. With Billie Neal, Nicoletta Braschi, Rockets Redglare, and Vernel Bagneris. The music is by Lurie, the songs are by Waits. An Island Pictures Release. (See *Hooked*.)

Down to Earth (1947)—Celestial-whimsey musical, with arch acting and a dull score. Rita Hayworth is the goddess Terpsichore, who descends from Heaven in order to make a Broadway show called "Swinging the Muses" less offensive and more authentic. This was an attempt to cash in on the box-office success of *Here Comes Mr. Jordan*, and it used the same director (Alexander Hall) and some of the same characters—Max Corkle and the Heavenly Messenger, played by the same actors, James Gleason and Edward Everett Horton. Mr. Jordan, a high executive on the Other Side, turns up in it, too, with Roland Culver replacing Claude Rains in the role. Larry Parks is the producer of the offending show; he does his own singing here, which jarred the sensibilities of viewers who had seen him in *The Jolson Story*, dubbed by Jolson. (His own voice is much less convincingly his.) But it all balances out, since Hayworth's singing is dubbed by Anita Ellis. James Gleason does what he can, but his part is threadbare. With Marc Platt and George Macready. Written by Edwin Blum and Don Hartman. Columbia. color

Down to the Sea in Ships (1949)—Life aboard a New Bedford whaler, as seen by a young boy (Dean Stockwell). The conflicts between the hard-bitten old skipper (Lionel Barrymore), who has no use for book learning, and his cultured, true-blue mate (Richard Widmark) make for dismally pat situations, but when the film sweeps out to sea it's fairly lively, what with whale chases, a whaleboat disappearing in a fog, and the whaler eventually coming up heavily against an iceberg while sailing around the Horn. The director, Henry Hathaway, gets a lot of pictorial effectiveness out of the sea; it's too bad he didn't hack away some of the blubbery dialogue. With Cecil Kellaway, Gene Lockhart, Harry Davenport, Fuzzy Knight, and Jay C. Flippen. Written by John Lee Mahin and Sy Bartlett; cinematography by Joe MacDonald; music by Alfred Newman. This large-scale adventure film, designed to attract children as well as their parents, is a remake of the 1922 film success. 20th Century-Fox. b & w

Dracula (1931)—It begins well, wandering around the crypt of Dracula's castle in the Carpathian Mountains as the vampires get up from their coffins. But this first American version, directed by Tod Browning, was adapted from a play based on the Bram Stoker novel, rather than from the novel itself, and it becomes too stagey. It was a tremendous popular success, however (it was advertised as "The Strangest Love Story of All"), and spawned many sequels. As Count Dracula, Bela Lugosi is the courtly personification of evil. He had played the role on Broadway in 1927 and had toured in it for years, and he seemed inside it in a wonderfully hammy, slightly demented way; his stilted manner and his ripe Hungarian accent have been imitated and parodied by subsequent Draculas. With pale Helen Chandler, who seems too anemic to attract a vampire, David Manners, Frances Dade, Edward Van Sloan, and the peerlessly degraded Dwight Frye, always looking for insects to munch on. Cinematography by Karl Freund; script by Garrett Fort, with dialogue by Dudley Murphy; play by Hamilton Deane and John L. Balderston. Universal. b & w

Dragon Seed (1944)—If M-G-M had a sense of shame, this abomination wouldn't have been released. Based on a novel by Pearl S. Buck, it is about the effects of war on a Chinese family, but it was made in a California-built China, and the Chinese simplefolk characters are played by Katharine Hepburn, Turhan Bey, Walter Huston, Agnes Moorehead, Hurd Hatfield, Akim Tamiroff, Aline MacMahon, and Henry Travers. It's a howler all right, but so drearily, patronizingly high-minded that there aren't many laughs. Directed by Jack Conway and Harold S. Bucquet, from a script by Marguerite Roberts and Jane Murfin; with a particularly offensive "ethnic" score, devised by Herbert Stothart. b & w

Dragonslayer (1981)—It's like reading a fairy tale that has the mixture of happiness and trauma to set your imagination whirling; the fire-breathing dragon—scaly, winged, huge—is more mysterious, probably, than any we could have imagined for ourselves. The setting is Britain during the Dark Ages. Ralph Richardson is Ulrich the Sorcerer, who receives a delegation from the remote Kingdom of Urland, which has been ravaged by the monster. The sorcerer's apprentice (Peter MacNicol) goes forth to face the dragon, but he's just a kid who's in over his head. Ulrich and the dragon are the two great antagonists in this movie—probably the only movie in which Richardson shows the full, magnificent balminess that has marked his recent stage appearances. In the terms this film sets, it's almost completely successful. The producer, Hal Barwood, and the director, Matthew Robbins, wrote the script. The cinematography is by Derek Vanlint; the score is by Alex North; the production design is by Elliot Scott. All of them understand that the film has one purpose: to be magical. With Caitlin Clarke as Valerian, Peter Eyre as the King, Chloe Salaman as the princess, John Hallam as Tyrian, and Sydney Bromley as Old Hodge. Paramount and Disney. color (See *Taking It All In*.)

A Drama of Jealousy, see *The Pizza Triangle*

Dramma della Gelosia, see *The Pizza Triangle*

The Draughtsman's Contract (1983)—Set on an English estate in the summer of 1694, this formalist tease by the writer-director Peter Greenaway is a fantasia of conceits about perspective, and about the relationship between the artist, his art, and the world. It's also a victimization fantasy: the draughtsman (Anthony Higgins), a lover of landscape, is attacked and destroyed by those who love only property. The film is mannered and idiosyncratic; the speeches are so arch and twitty they seem to be pitched higher than a dog whistle, and the people talking are popinjays in perukes shaped as geometrically as the shrubs at Marienbad. This impishness congeals, because there's no dramatic motor in the sequences. For Greenaway, a movie is a set of theorems to be demonstrated by tableaux. His mind may be active but his camera is dead. With Janet Suzman and Anne Louise Lambert. color (See *State of the Art.*)

The Dream Team (1989)—As a wisecracking, intermittently violent lunatic, Michael Keaton electrifies this quirky farce; in a restaurant scene, he's like a James Cagney character—doing something he knows he shouldn't while his face tells us how thoroughly he's enjoying it. Keaton, Peter Boyle (he has some of his best moments since *Young Frankenstein*), Christopher Lloyd, and Stephen Furst are patients in a mental hospital who are taken on an excursion and then stranded in an unstructured loony bin, New York City. Directed by the (erratic) slapstick specialist Howard Zieff, from a script by Jon Connolly and David Loucka, the film isn't the knockout it might have been if it had a few big wild routines. And, yes, it's sentimental. But the sentimentality isn't overplayed, and Keaton's fast rap cauterizes much of it. He's a cross between a mouth and a moonbeam. With Dennis Boutsikaris, Lorraine Bracco, Jack Duffy as the shopkeeper in the army-navy store, and Larry Pine as the advertising executive, and Milo O'Shea, Philip Bosco, and James Remar. Universal. color (See *Movie Love.*)

Dreamchild (1985)—Coral Browne plays Lewis Carroll's Alice in 1932, just before her 80th birthday, when she sails to New York to speak at the Lewis Carroll centenary celebration at Columbia University. Disoriented by the voyage and exhilarated by New York City, she experiences a second childhood; her mind wanders back to 1862, when the young Reverend Charles Dodgson (Ian Holm), Lecturer in Mathematics at Christ Church, Oxford, where her father was the Dean, had attempted to entertain her and her sisters by spinning his nonsense tale. It's only now, at the commemoration, and with her own death close at hand, that the elderly Alice grasps how deeply tormented he was and that he loved her. And with New York jogging her out of her confining Victorian primness, she sees how narrow her life has been. Written by Dennis Potter and directed by Gavin Millar, the picture suggests a literate TV show rather than a movie; but it's very enjoyable, and in some scenes it achieves levels of feeling that movies rarely get near. The elderly Alice's Potteresque adventures in the Art Deco New York wonderland wobble in tone, yet the picture is magically smooth, and it's full of felicities. Nothing in Coral Browne's other screen performances suggests the frailty and beauty she brings to her Alice, and Ian Holm's performance is wonderful—sneaky-dirty in its recessiveness, funny and painful at the same moments. With Amelia Shankley as the forthright little Alice at 10, Jane Asher as her mother, Peter Gallagher and Nicola Cowper as young lovers, and six Lewis Carroll–Tenniel creatures, from Jim Henson's Creature Shop. Billy Williams' cinematography has a glowing dreaminess; his lighting helps us over the transitions between 1932 and 1862, and into the glimpses of the world inhabited by these eerie critters. color (See *Hooked.*)

Dreaming Lips (1937)—That extraordinary chameleon Elisabeth Bergner, who could be alternately a drab little mouse or an astonishingly sophisticated sensual animal, had a triumph in this English production. As the wife of one artist (Romney Brent) and the mistress of another (Raymond Massey), she moves like a starved cat, *talks* on tiptoe, and ever so cleverly breaks your heart. Henri Bernstein, the greatest boudoir dramatist of them all, wrote the play (*Melo*). Carl Mayer adapted it, and Paul Czinner directed. This film is one of the best examples of a genre that has all but disappeared: the bittersweet conflict of desire versus responsibility—pure romance. b & w

Dreams *Kvinnodröm* (1954)—Ingmar Bergman on the sex wars, with Eva Dahlbeck as a fashion editor and Harriet Andersson as a young model. The editor visits a former lover (Ulf Palme); the model gives an old goat (Gunnar Björnstrand) a run for his money. Bergman's source material seems to be the M-G-M women's pictures of the previous decade. In Swedish. b & w

Dreamscape (1984)—Joseph Ruben, the young director of this tight, clever thriller, starts off with a cocky swagger and he can sustain it, because he has the bedrock of a script, by David Loughery, Chuck Russell, and himself, that has real development and structure. Dennis Quaid plays a young psychic who has been having a fine time hanging out at the racetrack picking winners and making out with girls; then Max von Sydow, a research scientist working for the government, sends for him, and pretty soon he's involved in some of the funniest, most audacious dream sequences since the 1962 *The Manchurian Candidate*. Quaid's slightly mocking free-and-easy manner makes it possible for him to hold his own against David Patrick Kelly, who might otherwise have walked away with the picture—his performance as a psycho psychic gives the political assassination plot the primal terror it needs. Ruben has a light, happy touch with the actors, who include Kate Capshaw, Christopher Plummer, George Wendt, and Eddie

Albert as the President—tan and fit-looking but racked by nightmares. Released by 20th Century-Fox. color (See *State of the Art*.)

Dressed to Kill (1980)—One of the most sheerly enjoyable films of recent years, this sophisticated horror comedy, written and directed by Brian De Palma, is permeated with the distilled essence of impure thoughts. Set in Manhattan, it's about sex and fear; De Palma presents extreme fantasies and pulls the audience into them with such apparent ease that the pleasure of the suspense becomes aphrodisiacal. Angie Dickinson shows a much warmer expressive range than might be expected as a beautiful, aging golden blonde, married yet frustrated, and longing to be made love to; Michael Caine brings fine, precise shadings of ambiguity to the role of her analyst; the breezy comedienne Nancy Allen is a pretty, investment-minded hooker, who witnesses a murder; Keith Gordon is Dickinson's teen-age prodigy son, who builds computers; and Dennis Franz is a brash police detective. The music is by Pino Donaggio, the cinematography is by Ralf D. Bode, and the editing is by Jerry Greenberg. Filmways. color (See *Taking It All In*.)

The Dresser (1983)—Almost everything in this screen version of Ronald Harwood's 1980 play is good except what relates to its theme: the symbiotic relationship between an old Shakespearean actor-manager (Albert Finney)—a knight of the theatre who is touring the provinces with his dilapidated company during the Second World War—and his dresser (Tom Courtenay). The material is conceived as a tribute to the flyweight dresser, who cajoles and teases and mothers the old trouper, and keeps him going. In the film's view, great actors are incorrigible, demented children; they need these dedicated nannies hopping about and fussing over them. Courtenay played the dresser on the stage, and his performance is too practiced; it's all dried up. Finney, however, is juicy, with a thundering voice and wonderful false humility. Peter Yates directed, and he provides some fond, light moments. Lockwood West, Edward Fox, and Cathryn Harrison shine in smaller roles; Eileen Atkins is the stage manager and Zena Walker is the old star's "Lady Wife." color (See *State of the Art*.)

The Dressmaker (1988)—The whole cast rises to the occasion—a chance to appear in John McGrath's fine adaptation of the 1973 Beryl Bainbridge novel (published in the U.S. in 1974 as *The Secret Glass*). Joan Plowright as Nellie, the prudish unmarried dressmaker, and Billie Whitelaw as Margo, the widow with a roving eye who works in a munitions factory, are sisters. The setting is Liverpool in 1944, and the plot centers on what happens when sallow, skinny Rita (Jane Horrocks), the 17-year-old niece they have raised, falls in love with Wesley (Tim Ransom), a Yank from Mississippi, but is frightened of his hands on her and keeps slapping him away. There's a tinge of comedy in the situation, but there's also a tinge of queasy horror. This good, inexpensive British movie is about morbid respectability, and the director, Jim O'Brien, makes it possible for the actors to create a maze of claustrophobic subtexts. It's doubtful if either Plowright or Whitelaw has ever before been this scarily effective on-screen; Whitelaw's sky-blue eyes stab you—she seems to have become the nakedest of performers. With Peter Postlethwaite, Pippa Hinchley, and Rosemary Martin. color (See *Movie Love*.)

The Driver (1978)—This gangster picture, which failed commercially here and is also an aesthetic failure, was Walter Hill's second film as a writer-director. (It was made after *Hard Times* and before *The Warriors*.) Hill attempted to stylize gangster characters and conventions, and although he succeeded in the action sequences, which have a near-abstract visual power, the stylized characters, with their uninflected personalities, flatten the movie out. In trying to purify the gangster film, he lost the very element that has made gangster movies so enjoyable: the colorful lowlifes and braggarts, with their own slang. (Instead, the characters stare at each other in silence.) And in exalting "professionalism"— in setting forth a neo-Hemingway elitist attitude for judging people on the basis of their grace and courage—Hill shows such a limited perspective that the film is comic-book cops-and-robbers existentialism. Ryan O'Neal, with his soft voice, gives the central role a strange, callow quality that's very effective, but as his adversary in the police department, Bruce Dern is at his mannered worst. As a woman of mystery, Isabelle Adjani drops her voice down to a Dietrich level and never varies it—or her expression: she's as blank-faced as a figure at Mme. Tussaud's. With Ronee Blakley, who looks more vividly alive than anyone else but gets killed off fast, and Joseph Walsh. Cinematography by Philip Lathrop. 20th Century-Fox. color

Driving Miss Daisy (1989)—Alfred Uhry's adaptation of his much honored play is still full of manipulative bits—it's virtually all manipulative bits—but the director, Bruce Beresford, understands how to work them while cutting down on their obviousness. Set in Atlanta, starting in 1948, the movie is the story of the companionship that develops between stubborn, suspicious Miss Daisy (Jessica Tandy), a wealthy Jewish widow of 72, and her resilient chauffeur, Hoke (Morgan Freeman), a widower about a decade younger than she is. Essentially, it's about how he changes her. He's made upright, considerate, humane—he's made perfect—so that nothing will disturb our appreciation of the gentle, bittersweet reverie we're watching.

But it's acted (and directed) eloquently. Tandy and Freeman achieve a beautiful equilibrium. And Dan Aykroyd comes through with a fine performance as Miss Daisy's good-ol'-boy son. With Esther Rolle and Patti LuPone. Cinematography by Peter James. Academy Awards: Best Picture, Actress (Tandy), Adapted Screenplay, Makeup. Warners. color (See *Movie Love*.)

Drôle de drame, see *Bizarre, Bizarre*

Drugstore Cowboy (1989)—Nihilistic humor rarely bubbles up in a movie as freely as it does here. Set in Portland, Oregon, in 1971, the story is about two couples who live together and travel around the Pacific Northwest robbing hospitals and pharmacies, grabbing fistfuls of pills and capsules. They're like a junkie version of Clyde Barrow's gang. The director, Gus Van Sant, takes us inside a lot of underground attitudes: the druggies are monomaniacal about leading an aimless existence—they see themselves as romantic figures. They're comic, but they're not put down for being comic. The picture keeps you laughing because it's so nonjudgmental. Van Sant is half in and half out of the desire of adolescents to remain kids forever. As the gang's 26-year-old leader, Matt Dillon brings the role a light self-mockery that helps set the tone of the film, and Kelly Lynch is strikingly effective as his wife. Also with James Le Gross, Heather Graham, James Remar, Max Perlich, Beah Richards, Grace Zabriskie, and William Burroughs. The script, by the director and Daniel Yost, was based on a then unpublished novel by James Fogle, who's in prison for drug-related robberies. Avenue Pictures. color (See *Movie Love*.)

Drums Along the Mohawk (1939)—One of John Ford's less inspired epics, this lavish color version of the Walter D. Edmonds novel never seems to get going. No one appears to know why the picture is being made, or what its point is, exactly. Claudette Colbert and Henry Fonda are the young couple who go to the Mohawk Valley of upstate New York and are caught up in the Revolutionary War; there are scraps with Indians and various upheavals, but one gets more involved in Colbert's spotless gowns—a tribute to pioneer laundering—and the fussy, dainty interiors, full of Early American decorator touches. Script by Lamar Trotti and Sonya Levien; the enormous cast includes Edna May Oliver, John Carradine, Ward Bond, Dorris Bowdon, Jessie Ralph, Arthur Shields, Robert Lowery, and Mae Marsh. 20th Century-Fox.

A Dry White Season (1989)—In Johannesburg, a naïve white schoolmaster (Donald Sutherland) has his eyes opened to the police brutality involved in the death of his black gardener, and imagines he can obtain justice for the man's family. Marlon Brando is airily light and masterly as the veteran anti-apartheid barrister who takes the case even though he knows that he can't get anywhere with the rigged court. The romantic in Brando must have responded to the old rebel's romantic gesture: he saves the picture for the (short) time he's onscreen. But the director, Euzhan Palcy, seems lost; her work is heavy-handed, and the script (by Colin Welland and the director, from a novel by André Brink) is earnest and didactic. Performers such as Susan Sarandon, Jürgen Prochnow, Winston Ntshona, Janet Suzman, Michael Gambon, and Zakes Mokae sink into the obviousness of their roles and leave no trace. (Poor, uninspired, virtuous Sutherland is out of it; his characterization is one long whimper.) M-G-M. color (See *Movie Love*.)

Du Rififi chez les hommes, see *Rififi*

Duck Soup (1933)—The Marx Brothers in their greatest movie—a semi-surrealist farce about war. With Margaret Dumont, Edgar Kennedy, and Louis Calhern. The unsentimental screenplay is by Bert Kalmar and Harry Ruby, who also did the songs. Directed by Leo McCarey. Paramount. b & w

Due Soldi di Speranza, see *Two Cents Worth of Hope*

Duel in the Sun (1946)—Hilariously florid—sometimes referred to as "Lust in the Dust." This Wagnerian Western features Gregory Peck and Jennifer Jones as lovers so passionate they kill each other. She's Pearl Chavez, a half-breed wench, and so, by Hollywood convention, uncontrollably sexy, and Peck actually manages to bestir himself enough to play a hunk of egotistic hot stuff—maybe the name Lewt McCanles got to him, or maybe the producer, David O. Selznick, used electric prods. Peck clangs his spurs and leers, while Jones tosses her hair and heaves her chest; when they kiss, lightning blazes. Set in Texas, it's a lavish, sensual spectacle, so heightened it becomes a cartoon of passion; the director, King Vidor, gives much of it a galloping bravura excitement, and the hokum is irresistibly entertaining. With Walter Huston having a roaring good time as a hellfire preacher, Butterfly McQueen going even further with the character she created in *Gone with the Wind*, and Joseph Cotten, Charles Bickford, Lillian Gish, Herbert Marshall, Lionel Barrymore, Harry Carey, Sidney Blackmer, Joan Tetzel, Otto Kruger, Tilly Losch, and other well-known performers. The cinematographers include Lee Garmes and Hal Rosson; Dmitri Tiomkin perpetrated the score. The movie was "suggested" by the Niven Busch novel, and Selznick himself takes the screenplay credit. He also directed some scenes and Josef von Sternberg, William Dieterle, Otto Brower, B. Reeves Eason, and others had a hand in it. (138 minutes.) color

The Duellists (1978)—An adaptation of Joseph Conrad's Napoleonic-period story "The Duel," about a cavalry officer's sudden flare-up of rage over a trifling, imagined insult by another officer, which grows into a private war. The hussars (Harvey Keitel and Keith Carradine) go on fighting for over 15 years, and the origin of the quarrel becomes lost in legend, like the causes of the larger wars that they're both fighting in. This English production—a first film by the director Ridley Scott—is consistently entertaining and eerily beautiful. Its special quality is in its Géricault-like compositions; what keeps them from palling is that they have a graphic power of their own, and they're coolly impassioned—a story of obsessive enmity is being told by way of these ravishing yet unsettling images. The mixed American and British cast includes Cristina Raines, Albert Finney, Alan Webb, Edward Fox, Diana Quick, Jenny Runacre, Robert Stephens, Tom Conti, and Meg Wynn Owen. color (See *When the Lights Go Down.*)

Duet for Cannibals (1969)—Written and directed by Susan Sontag, who made this hermetic, guess-what's-real movie in Sweden. It's about two couples and the games they play, which would be more entertaining if we could figure out the rules or discover if there is anything at stake. Adriana Asti acts mysterious and neurotic, and the other performers (Gösta Ekman, Lars Ekborg, and Agneta Ekmanner) seem to be stranded on the screen, trying to fill in the slack of the dry, expository dialogue and looking for clues to what's wanted of them. There's a good bit—a psychotic old man eating in a restaurant and making everybody nervous. In Swedish. b & w

Dulces Horas, see *Sweet Hours*

Dune (1984)—David Lynch directed, and he did the adaptation of Frank Herbert's ecological sci-fi fantasy, but he doesn't make the story his own. Basically, this isn't a David Lynch movie—it's *Dune.* He lays out Herbert's grandiose vision of a galactic system, with hordes of characters parcelled out over four planets, and a messiah who is preordained to lead the righteous in a holy war. And he brings on the giant man-eating worms that produce the consciousness-altering spice that holds this universe together. The movie is heavy on exposition, and the story isn't dramatized—it's merely acted out (and hurried through), in a series of scenes that are like illustrations. And despite the care that has gone into the sets and costumes and the staging, the editing rhythms are limp and choppy. Lynch's best work is in the comedy scenes that involve Kenneth McMillan,

Sting, Brad Dourif, Linda Hunt, Leonardo Cimino, and the creepy 8-year-old Alicia Roanne Witt. The cast includes Sian Phillips, Max von Sydow, Francesca Annis, José Ferrer, Freddie Jones, Richard Jordan, Virginia Madsen, Everett McGill, Dean Stockwell, Sean Young, Silvana Mangano, Jürgen Prochnow, Paul L. Smith, Jack Nance (of *Eraserhead*), and Kyle MacLachlan as the warrior messiah. Cinematography by Freddie Francis; production design by Anthony Masters; and creatures by Carlo Rambaldi. Produced by Raffaella De Laurentiis; a Dino De Laurentiis film, released by Universal. color (See *State of the Art.*)

Dwaj Ludzie z Szafa, see *Two Men and a Wardrobe*

Each Dawn I Die (1939)—The title of this prison picture is superb; convicts have often said that the title describes their feelings exactly. But nothing in the melodrama lives up to it. James Cagney plays an honest, muckraking reporter who is framed and sent up by a crooked D.A.; on his way to prison, he meets George Raft (slick and crooked as usual—which is welcome here). Cagney's virtuous suffering grows tedious, and the script (full of double crosses and jailbreaks) isn't persuasive. The director, William Keighley, brings off some moderately forceful scenes, but toward the end of the 30s, the Warners underworld pictures began to get hazy and high-minded, and in this one the pre–Second World War spiritual irradiation blurs the conventions of the prison genre. With Jane Bryan as Cagney's girl, George Bancroft as the warden, Slapsie Maxie Rosenbloom as an amiable con, and Alan Baxter, Victor Jory, and Stanley Ridges. b & w

The Eagle with Two Heads *L'Aigle à deux têtes* (1948)—The structure is similar to that of *Beauty and the Beast* but with inversions—this time it is the Queen (Edwige Feuillère) who is awakened from her trance by the revolutionary poet (Jean Marais), who has come to assassinate her. And, while the Beast addressed Beauty with only a few simple words, here the Queen dunks her Angel of Death in a torrent of elegant language. This is a sweepingly romantic picture—a beautiful trifle. Feuillère has a sense of gesture that almost any actress might envy, and Marais demonstrates once again that despite his almost comical square-headed handsomeness he can act. Jean Cocteau adapted his own play, and directed. It's the least-known of the few films that he actually did direct; a dozen or so are falsely advertised as his. (Antonioni made a video color version of the play in 1979, under the title *The Oberwald Mystery*.) In French. b & w

The Earrings of Madame De . . . *Madame de . . .* (1953)—Perfection. This tragedy of love, which begins in narcissistic flirtation and passes from romance to passion to desperation, is set, ironically, in aristocratic circles that seem too superficial to take love tragically. The very beauty of Max Ophuls' film is sometimes used against it: the gliding, sensuous camerawork, the extraordinary romantic atmosphere, the gowns, the balls, the chandeliers, the nuances of language, and the sense of honor are regarded as evidence of lack of substance. But Ophuls loved Mozart and Stendhal, and he also calls up a third master: the opera sequence that gives the film its musical theme is Gluck's *Orfeo*. The performances by Danielle Darrieux as Madame de, by Charles Boyer as her husband, Monsieur de, a general, and by Vittorio De Sica as her lover, the Baron, are quite likely the finest each has given. Ophuls' lush, decorative style, his re-creation of a vanished elegance, and his darting, swirling camera are used to evoke the protection that style and manners and wealth provide, and to demonstrate that passion can destroy it all. Even the fashionable and secure become rash, make fools of themselves. Boyer, the general, attempting to use military discipline to cure his wife of her unseemly displays of emotion, is as helpless as she is. Anna Karenina gets her lover but she finds her life shallow and empty; Madame de's life has been so shallow and empty that she cannot keep her lover. She is destroyed, finally, by the fact that women do not have the same sense of honor that men do, or the same sense of pride. When she lies to the Baron, how could she know that he would take her lies as proof that she did not really love him? What he thinks dishonorable is merely unimportant to her. She places love before honor (what woman does not?) and neither her husband nor her lover can forgive her. With Jean Debucourt as the jeweler, and Lia de Lea as the general's mistress. Based on Louise de Vilmorin's novella *Madame de . . .* , which is far more astringent than the film; the script is by Marcel Achard, Annette Wademant, and Ophuls. Cinematography by Christian Matras; sets by Jean d'Eaubonne. In French. b & w

Earth *Zemlya* Also known as *Soil.* (1930)—The specific subject is collectivization, but Dovzhenko's masterwork is a passionate lyric on the continuity of man, death, and nature. The theme is perhaps most startlingly expressed in a sequence about a man who has just celebrated the arrival of a tractor. He starts to dance—for sheer love of life—on his way home, and as he dances in the middle of the moonlit road he is suddenly struck by a bullet. (In the 50s, it was voted one of the 10 greatest films of all time by an international group of critics.) Silent. b & w

Earthquake (1974)—L.A. gets it. The picture is swill, but it isn't a cheat; it's an entertaining marathon of Grade-A destruction effects, with B-picture stock characters spinning through it. Among them are Ava Gardner, the grimly resolute Charlton Heston, and Geneviève Bujold, whose witty style gives the picture its only touch of class. The cast also includes Lorne Greene, Marjoe Gortner, Gabriel Dell, Barry Sullivan, George Kennedy, Richard Roundtree, and Walter Matthau. Directed by Mark Robson; screenplay by George Fox and Mario Puzo. Universal. color (See *Reeling.*)

East of Eden (1955)—An amazingly highstrung, feverishly poetic movie about Cain and Abel as American brothers living on a lettuce farm in California in the years just before the First World War. Elia Kazan directed this adaptation of Steinbeck's novel, and it's like seeing a series of teasers: violent moments and charged scenes without much coherence. As the romantic, alienated young hero, James Dean is decorated with all sorts of charming gaucheries; he's sensitive, defenseless, hurting. Maybe his father (Raymond Massey) doesn't love him, but the camera does, and we're supposed to; we're thrust into upsetting angles, caught in infatuated closeups, and prodded—"Look at all that beautiful desperation." When this Cain strikes his brother (Richard Davalos), the soundtrack amplifies the blow as if worlds were colliding; a short, heavy dose of Expressionism may be followed by a pastoral romp or an elaborate bit of Americana; an actor may suddenly assume a psychotic stance and another actor shatter a train window with his head. It's far from a dull movie, but it's certainly a very strange one; it's an enshrinement of the mixed-up kid. Here and in *Rebel Without a Cause*, Dean seems to go just about as far as anybody can in acting misunderstood. With Julie Harris, who gives a memorably lyric performance, and Burl Ives, Jo Van Fleet, Albert Dekker, Lois Smith, Barbara Baxley, Timothy Carey, Jonathan Haze, Mario Siletti, Harold Gordon, Lonny Chapman, and Nick Dennis. Script by Paul Osborn; cinematography by Ted McCord; music by Leonard Rosenman. Warners. CinemaScope, color (See *I Lost it at the Movies*.)

Easter Parade (1948)—There's not much comedy and not much invention in this oversize M-G-M musical, but Fred Astaire and Judy Garland finally get to their great number, "A Couple of Swells." With Ann Miller and Peter Lawford; Lola Albright may be glimpsed as a hat model. Charles Walters directed; the score, by Irving Berlin, includes "It Only Happens When I Dance with You." color

Easy Living (1937)—One of the most pleasurable of the romantic slapstick comedies of the 30s, and full of surprises. Jean Arthur is the working girl whose life is completely changed when a sable coat, thrown out a millionaire's window, lands on her head. The movie is a wonderful fluke: the script by Preston Sturges is in his manic, everybody-with-something-to-say style; the director, Mitchell Leisen (once De Mille's art director), tempered it with smooth takes and elegant clothes and sets, including a lily-shaped bathtub. The film has impish, sweet moments (such as the half-asleep heroine's delayed reaction after a kiss from the hero—Ray Mil-

land) and at least one classic slapstick sequence (the little glass doors in an Automat fly open and people lunge for the free food). With Edward Arnold (a little louder than necessary—that was always his vice), and Mary Nash, William Demarest, Luis Alberni, Franklin Pangborn, Esther Dale. From a story by Vera Caspary. Paramount. b & w

Easy Rider (1969)—Two pothead bikers—Wyatt (Peter Fonda), who refers to himself as Captain America, and Billy (Dennis Hopper)—collect their money for a drug deal and set off on a crosscountry quest for freedom, the freedom to "do your own thing." Hopper directed, Fonda produced, and they wrote the script, with Terry Southern. The picture—a road movie that's also a pop-mythology ballad movie—expressed the primitive religious element in the hippie movement. Wyatt and Billy (for Wyatt Earp and Billy the Kid) are long-haired Christ figures, and trigger-happy squares are out to get them. The two encounter a Southern lawyer (Jack Nicholson), a lush with the grin of a kid who hasn't grown up, and they introduce him to pot, but he doesn't get to enjoy it for long. The movie's sentimental paranoia obviously rang true to a large young audience's vision. In the late 60s, it was cool to feel that you couldn't win, that everything was rigged and hopeless. The film was infused with an elegiac sense of American failure, and it had a psychedelic pull to it. The idea grew out of the A.I.P. Westerns on motorcycles such as *The Wild Angels*, but this time everything was seen from the point of view of the bikers. The landscapes had dazzling textures; the terrific music by Jimi Hendrix and groups such as The Band and The Byrds gave the sluggish scenes a pulse; and Fonda, with his air of saintly noblesse oblige, died for American sins. The film became a ritual experience. It was the downer that young audiences wanted; they puffed away at it. Hopper became a culture hero; Nicholson, who's very funny in it, became a star. With Karen Black, Warren Finnerty, Robert Walker (Jr.), Luana Anders, and Phil Spector as the connection. Cinematography by Laszlo Kovacs. Released by Columbia. color (See *Deeper into Movies*.)

Eat the Peach (1987)—Whimsical, with an element of desperation underneath. The setting is an Irish village just a few miles across the border from Northern Ireland. Thrown out of work when the local Japanese computer factory closes down, Vinnie (Stephen Brennan) and his brother-in-law, Arthur (Eamon Morrissey), watch a cassette of Elvis Presley in the 1964 *Roustabout* and see a motorcyclist ride in a carnival Wall of Death—a round, wide, high, barrel-like track where centrifugal force keeps the rider up in the air circling. Soon they're building their own Wall of Death. This engaging, informal movie—it's loose, with a lot of humor—is about the deep-seated eccentricity of a man like Vinnie, who doesn't use his problem-solving ingenuity in order to make a living or to provide decent quarters for the wife and child he loves. He's an impractical man who solves only those problems that tease his imagination. Building the Wall keeps his brains and hopes from rotting. The director, Peter Ormrod, and the producer, John Kelleher, wrote the script together; they tell the story (which is based on actual events) as if it were a simple one, taking care to let it expand in our minds. This is not like any other film you've seen; at times you may feel a little tuned out, but then the vision comes together. When Vinnie's little daughter, her face as determined as his, rides her tricycle along the Wall, trying to climb it, there's nothing coy about the kid. And when she wakes up one night and rushes out, her hair streaming back from her head, she's the soul of Ireland, the way Sara Allgood was when she played in *Juno and the*

Paycock. With Catherine Byrne as Nora, Niall Toibin as Boots, and Bernadette O'Neill as the blond barmaid. Channel Four and the Irish production company Strongbow. color (See *Hooked*.)

Eating Raoul (1982)—The director, Paul Bartel, and his 5-foot-11 star, the innately kinky Mary Woronov, play a couple of prissy squares—the Blands, of Los Angeles—who consider sex disgusting and want to open a nice, clean country restaurant. They raise the money they need by murdering swinging singles; in their eyes these swingers deserve to be punished. This spoofy black comedy is thin-textured and it's sedated; it doesn't have enough going on in it—not even enough to look at. The nothingness of the movie is supposed to be its droll point, but viewers may experience sensory deprivation. With Richard Beltran, who brings some energy to the role of Raoul, Garry Goodrow, and Buck Henry. Written by Richard Blackburn and Bartel. color

The Eclipse *L'Eclisse* (1962)—Some like it cold. Michelangelo Antonioni on alienation, this time with Alain Delon and, of course, Monica Vitti. Even she looks as if she has given up in this one. In Italian. b & w

L'Eclisse, see *The Eclipse*

Ecstasy *Extase* (1933)—The once scandalous Czech film, directed by Gustav Machaty, and starring the very young Hedy Lamarr. It was originally intended to be called "Symphony of Love"; along with some explicit sexual sequences, there is symbolic erotic imagery that is romantic, poetic, and, despite its innocent absurdity, sensuous and exciting. The picture was banned and then released and then withdrawn and finally reissued, in so many different versions that everyone who talks about it appears to have seen (or imagined) different sex acts. (In the 50s, there were versions in which someone had decided to prolong the ecstasy by printing the climactic scenes over and over.) Still, whichever *Ecstasy* one sees, it's delicately, tenderly erotic. The theme is Lawrentian, as Henry Miller pointed out in the definitive essay on the film, "Reflections on Extasy." In German. b & w

Edge of the City Also known as *A Man Is Ten Feet Tall.* (1957)—Sidney Poitier is startlingly good as an intelligent, easygoing foreman on the docks who is destroyed by his friendship with a weak, unstable white man (John Cassavetes). Martin Ritt, directing his first movie, sustains the tension with great skill but can't resist clinching the case with gratuitous violence, and the author, Robert Alan Aurthur (adapting his own television play), works with such precision that he reduces his subject to pat melodrama. However, it's a solid, often powerful movie. With Jack Warden and Ruby Dee. The music is by Leonard Rosenman; when he completed the score, he must have cut another notch on his gun—he's certainly out to slaughter the audience. M-G-M. b & w

Educating Rita (1983)—It's no more than a two-character play—a duet—"opened up" a bit for the screen, but the lines have surprise and wit. Michael Caine plays a dispirited, burnt-out slob of a college professor who tries to conceal his mediocrity by carrying on as if he were Dylan Thomas. Rita, played by Julie Walters, is a street-smart young hairdresser in Liverpool who signs up for literature tutorials in the Open University and is assigned to him. She wants the education that he, with his doctorate and his fancy turns of speech, has decided is worthless. Julie Walters' performance may be too "set" for the camera (she played the role on the London stage), but her inflections are funny in unexpected

ways. Rita is Julie Walters' role in the way that Billie Dawn in *Born Yesterday* was Judy Holliday's role. The material isn't sustained—Rita, like Billie Dawn, is inevitably less entertaining after she's transformed—but Caine gives a master film actor's performance. You can see the professor's impotence in his pink-rimmed, blurry eyes; he's crumbling from within. Caine lets nothing get between you and the character. You don't observe his acting; you just experience the character's emotions. You feel his smirking terror. Directed by Lewis Gilbert; Willy Russell adapted his own play. color (See *State of the Art.*)

The Effect of Gamma Rays on Man-in-the-Moon Marigolds (1972)—Beatrice (Joanne Woodward), also known as Betty the Loon, is a rampaging jokester-mother who is frustrated and lost; she inflicts her misery on her two daughters (Nell Potts and Roberta Wallach). Although Paul Newman's direction is sensitive and well balanced, the Paul Zindel play is essentially a camp version of the mood-memory plays of Tennessee Williams and William Inge. Woodward has the right sashaying toughness for the role, but it's pretty hard to bring conviction to Betty the Loon's vengeful meanness. Released by 20th Century-Fox. color (See *Reeling.*)

8½ (1963)—Fellini's celebrated autobiographical phantasmagoria. Guido (Marcello Mastroianni), the director-hero, is the center of the film's universe, the creator on whose word everything waits, the man sought after by everyone. He can do anything, and the possibilities confuse him. Just as *La Dolce Vita* confirmed popular suspicions about the depravity of the rich and gifted, 8½ confirms the popular view of the life of a *successful* genius. We see Guido's conflicts between his love for his wife, his desire for his mistress, his ideal of innocence, and his dreams of a harem, and we are given to understand that he must come to grips with himself as a precondition to "creation." The multi-ringed circus of *8½* is such a luxuriously externalized version of an artist's inner life that it's more like the fantasy of someone who wishes that he were a movie director—someone who has soaked up those movie versions of an artist's life, in which in the midst of a carnival or a ball the hero receives inspiration and dashes away to transmute life into art. It's a deluxe glorification of creative crisis, visually arresting (the dark and light contrasts are extraordinary, magical) but in some essential way conventional-minded. The cast includes Anouk Aimée, Sandra Milo, Claudia Cardinale, Rossella Falk, Barbara Steele, Madeleine Lebeau, Guido Alberti as the producer, Jean Rougeul as the critic, Annibale Ninchi as Guido's father, and Edra Gale as La Saraghina. The cinematography is by Gianni Di Venanzo; the score is by Nino Rota; the script is by Fellini, Ennio Flaiano, and others. In Italian. b & w (See *I Lost it at the Movies*.)

8 Million Ways to Die (1986)—A macho fantasy about cops and robbers, coke and hookers. Jeff Bridges plays Scudder, a narcotics detective for the L.A. County Sheriff's Department, and the film, directed by Hal Ashby, has an overlush pictorial exoticism, as if being coked out comes with the territory. The script, credited to Oliver Stone and David Lee Henry (other hands were also involved), is pulpy, tawdry stuff, but it suggests more hardboiled narrative drive than Ashby delivers. The film is permeated with druggy dissociation: plot points don't connect, as though they don't matter, the actors often sound as if they're making up their lines, and Ashby seems less interested in the thriller aspect of the material than in men in a semi-stupor challenging each other. The crazy confusion of these macho shouting matches is halfway amusing—you don't know what's going on, or if the director does, either. Violence and dreaminess are blended. The story involves a bright-eyed, coke-snorting young hooker called Sunny (Alexandra Paul); when she's murdered, Scudder's suspicions settle on a sleek Colombian-American racketeer, played by Andy Garcia, who does Latino sleaze and volatility to hammy perfection, flashing his eyes like semaphores, and giving the picture a shot of energy. With Rosanna Arquette and Randy Brooks. From Lawrence Block's mystery novels featuring Matthew Scudder. The cinematography is by Stephen H. Burum. Tri-Star. color (See *Hooked*.)

El Literally, "He," but in this country it has sometimes been called *This Strange Passion*. (1952)—Working in Mexico, Luis Buñuel made this mocking study of irrational love and jealousy—a film with suggestions of Freud and the Marquis de Sade. Francisco (Arturo de Cordova), a wealthy Catholic, marries Gloria (Delia Garcés), and the symptoms begin on their honeymoon: imagining that her former fiancé is in the next room spying on them, he thrusts a knitting needle through the keyhole. As the symptoms mount in an absurd but frightening crescendo, Buñuel makes his own thrusts at the Church, and by carrying the Spanish male's obsession with female chastity to paranoia, he exposes the insanity that's inherent in it. (One critic described the film as "an *Othello* with the hero as his own Iago.") By the time Francisco takes needle and thread to his wife, one is still not convinced that the movie isn't ludicrous, but in the final scene, when Francisco has gone to a monastery and we see his crooked little steps (they are like the movements of his thoughts), Buñuel's daring is fully apparent. Except for the well-edited anticlerical sequences, however, one must be prepared to enjoy this daring (which usually takes the form of bizarre jokes) despite the careless, cheaply made look of the film. In Spanish. b & w

El Dorado (1967)—John Wayne and Robert Mitchum, parodying themselves while looking exhausted. When the movie starts, you have the sense of having come in on a late episode of a TV series. Mitchum plays a drunken old sheriff, and there are home remedies for alcoholism, vomiting scenes that are supposed to be hilarious, and one of those girls who hide their curls under cowboy hats and are mistaken for boys until the heroes start to wrestle with them. Wayne has a beautiful horse, but when he's hoisted onto it and you hear the thud you don't know whether to feel sorrier for man or beast. Except for a few opening shots, this Howard Hawks Western was made in a studio. Wayne and James Caan help the sheriff pull himself together and fight the bad guys. With Arthur Hunnicutt, Charlene Holt, and Ed Asner. Script by Leigh Brackett, based on Harry Brown's novel *The Stars in Their Courses*. Produced by Wayne's production company, Batjac, for Paramount. color (See *Kiss Kiss Bang Bang*.)

Electra (1962)—The Greek director Michael Cacoyannis has filmed his own adaptation of the Euripides tragedy in an outdoor setting, with an authentic solemn grandeur, and with the handsome young Irene Papas as his heroine. Still, trying to show how vividly modern this classic is, he produces discomfort: we're neither quite here nor quite back there. With Aleka Catselli as Clytemnestra, Yannis Fertis as Orestes, and Manos Katrakis as the tutor. Cinematography by Walter Lassally; music by Mikis Theodorakis. In Greek. b & w

Eléna et les hommes (1956)—Jean Renoir made this love-carnival film, set in France in the 1880s, in color and with an expensive international cast—Ingrid Bergman, Mel Ferrer, and Jean Marais. The first American audiences couldn't judge it properly, because it was released here in a botched, dubbed version called *Paris Does Strange Things*; Marais spoke in a gravelly baritone so far from his own voice that people laughed. Ferrer seemed weak even for Ferrer, and the picture had little besides Bergman's astonishing, ripe beauty to recommend it. The French version has considerably more, although it is far from a success. With Pierre Bertin, Elina Labourdette, Magali Noel, Jean Richard, and Juliette Greco. Cinematography by Claude Renoir; music by Joseph Kosma. In French.

Eleni (1985)—This epic-scaled film, based on the Nicholas Gage book and directed by Peter Yates, tells the story of how Nick, who left Greece as a child in 1948, went back 30-odd years later to track down the men who had killed his mother. A peasant in a remote mountain village, she was executed by the Communist guerrilla army; her crime was that she defied the order to turn over her children (who were to be sent to neighboring Communist countries), and packed them off at night to start the journey to America. The disastrous script, by Steve Tesich, turns the story into a piece of anti-Communist, pro-motherhood poster art; Eleni (Kate Nelligan), who dies with her fists flung up high as she cries out in exaltation, "My children!," is the answer to the Reds. And though the constant cutting between what happened in the 40s and what happens in the 80s, as Nick (John Malkovich) puts the facts together, is meant to build suspense, it does just the opposite; it dissipates whatever momentum develops. The two starring roles seem virtually unplayable (Malkovich is like a wraith wandering through the picture); cast as Communist vipers, Oliver Cotton and Ronald Pickup give off the only energy. With Linda Hunt. Cinematography by Billy Williams; music by

Bruce Smeaton. A CBS Production, released by Warners. color (See *Hooked*.)

The Elephant Man (1980)—A very pleasurable surprise. The by now well-known story of John Merrick, the grievously eminent Victorian who is sometimes said to have been the ugliest man who ever lived, is told by the young director, David Lynch, with such grace and imagination that it becomes a tale of a terrible enchantment. Inside Merrick's misshapen body is an astonishingly sweet-souled gentleman of his era. There's something indefinably erotic going on here; it's submerged in the film's rhythm and in the director's whole way of seeing. Scene by scene, you don't know what to expect; you're seeing something new—subconscious material stirring within the format of a conventional narrative. John Hurt plays Merrick, and Anthony Hopkins is Frederick Treves, the doctor who rescues him from the world of sideshows. With John Gielgud, Wendy Hiller, and Hannah Gordon, and less effective performances by Anne Bancroft as the actress Mrs. Kendal, and Freddie Jones as the drunken Bytes. Lighted by Freddie Francis, this film is perhaps the most beautiful example of black-and-white cinematography in about 15 years. Script by Christopher De-Vore, Eric Bergren, and Lynch. Paramount. (See *Taking It All In*.)

Elevator to the Gallows *Ascenseur pour l'échafaud*—Also known as *Frantic*. (1957)—Louis Malle's first film—a thriller about an attempt at a perfect crime, made in a tense yet velvety style. Jeanne Moreau, who was to become famous the next year in Malle's second film, *The Lovers*, is less expansive here; her sullen, sensual mask is just right for this limited but absorbing *policier*, set to Miles Davis's music. The film has an unusual sense of control and style, considering that the plot itself is third-rate; the black-and-

white cinematography is by Henri Decaë. With Maurice Ronet, Lino Ventura, and Georges Poujouly. In French.

11 Harrowhouse (1974)—An awkward, harmless, small-time American (Charles Grodin) tries to rob the international diamond syndicate, based in London and headed by John Gielgud. This lackadaisical caper comedy is inoffensive, but the comic ideas don't build or erupt, and since the director, Aram Avakian, fails to get any suspense going, it becomes a bumbling and stupid romp. The cast includes Candice Bergen at her most beautiful (she's so consistently gorgeous that she looks like a science-fiction creation); Trevor Howard, waving his arms a lot in a helpless attempt to earn his salary; Helen Cherry; and James Mason, who provides the only two good scenes in the movie. Playing an underling of Gielgud's, he shows the sly, almost dirty sense of farce that he demonstrated in *Lolita*. 20th Century-Fox. color (See *Reeling*.)

Elmer Gantry (1960)—Burt Lancaster and Jean Simmons as Bible Belt evangelists in the 20s, in a loud, striking, big-scale melodrama based on the Sinclair Lewis novel about con artists, adapted and directed by Richard Brooks. The movie cheats on the issues and it's overloaded with gigantic sets, enormous crowds, fires, riots, and human stampedes. But it's coarsely compelling and—though exhausting—never boring. When Lancaster plays a kinetic, broadly exaggerated character like the lecher Gantry, you can't take your eyes off him, and Simmons is one of the most quietly commanding actresses Hollywood has ever trashed. With Shirley Jones as Lulu Bains, Edward Andrews as George Babbitt, and Arthur Kennedy, Dean Jagger, Patti Page, John McIntire, Rex Ingram, Hugh Marlowe, and Philip Ober. Academy Awards: Best Actor (Lancaster), Supporting Actress

(Jones), and Screenplay (Brooks). United Artists. color

Elvira Madigan (1967)—Thommy Berggren gives a skillful, sensitive performance as the handsome young cavalry officer who falls fatally in love with a circus girl (Pia Degermark, who is so exquisitely fresh that she doesn't need to act) in Bo Widerberg's lushly beautiful movie about romantic insanity, set in the late 19th century. The lovers, who live only for each other, cut themselves off from society, and prefer to die rather than risk growing apart. Based on an actual double suicide; Widerberg wrote the script, directed, and also edited. Cinematography by Jorgen Persson; the music is Mozart's Piano Concerto No. 21, played by Geza Anda. In Swedish. color

The Emerald Forest (1985)—John Boorman's theme is that civilized man, having lost tribal man's magic unity with nature, spreads his brutal, nature-destroying sickness. To put this across, Boorman sets his story in Brazil, where the 7-year-old son of an American engineer (played by Powers Boothe) is abducted by an Amazon rain forest tribe called the Invisible People. For 10 years, the father searches for the boy in whatever time he can take off from his job of building a giant dam. When, at last, he locates his 17-year-old son (played by the director's son, Charley Boorman), he realizes that the boy's consciousness surpasses his own and that the boy's life is superior to anything civilization has to offer. And soon the father realizes that the dam is destroying the boy's tribe. The film touches on all sorts of major themes, especially the fate of the rain forests, but mostly it attempts to reëstablish the myth of the noble savage by imbuing it with hallucinogenic romanticism—trance visions, out-of-body travel, and all. It's a puerile movie. The faults that have plagued Boorman's films—

his lack of interest in character, his rather lordly failure to dramatize the issues that excite him the most, his wacko ear for dialogue—really pile up this time, and he doesn't seem able to get any kind of seductive flow going. With Rui Polonah (as the shaman-chief), Meg Foster, Dira Paes, and Eduardo Conde. From a script by Rosco Pallenberg; cinematography by Philippe Rousselot. Boorman published a good account of making the movie, *The Emerald Forest Diary*. Released by Embassy Pictures. color (See *Hooked.*)

The Emigrants *Utvandrarna* (1971)—Jan Troell's broad-backed nature epic on the mid-19th-century Swedish emigration to this country. A bursting, resonant work, it covers the grim farm life, under a hierarchy of masters, that drove a group to emigrate, the brutal sea voyage, and then the landing of the survivors and their trip by train, by Mississippi paddleboat, and on foot until they staked out a claim in Minnesota. Troell's achievement is prodigious. (He is his own cinematographer and editor, and he collaborated on the writing.) The story is concluded in a second film, *The New Land*. Both with Liv Ullmann and Max von Sydow. Adapted from the novels of Vilhelm Moberg. *The Emigrants* ran 190 minutes in Sweden; Troell had to cut it to 150 minutes for the American distributors, Warners. In Swedish. color (See *Reeling.*)

Emitai (1971)—A film by the Senegalese writer-filmmaker Ousmane Sembène about black villagers who are pushed closer and closer to resistance by the inhuman demands of a colonial power (the French, during the Second World War). Yet they delay. Even after their women and children are rounded up and put in the sun, the men postpone taking action; they make sacrifices to their gods, hoping to learn what to do—but the gods are silent. (Emitai is the Master of Thunder.) The film deals with the interrelationships in the village between the men and the women, and between the men and their gods—and in both cases they turn out to be complex, ironic, puzzling. Ousmane Sembène's approach is thoughtful and almost reticent; the viewer contemplates a series of tragic dilemmas. Yet for all its intelligence, the movie isn't memorable—partly because the last section is unsatisfying. In Wolof, an African language. color

The Emperor Jones (1933)—Eugene O'Neill's play about a black man's disintegration was conceived in a semi-Expressionist style, and it was filmed in that style by Dudley Murphy, from a screenplay by Dubose Heyward. Murphy, a director with ideas but almost no technique, used painted sets, exaggerated decor, and an artificial jungle; the effects are sometimes powerful, sometimes ridiculous. O'Neill's violent emotions are accurately rendered by Paul Robeson and Dudley Digges, though they seem to be acting on a stage. United Artists. b & w

Empire of the Sun (1987)—At the outset, this Steven Spielberg epic is so big and majestic you want to laugh in pleasure, and it stays that way for about 45 minutes—Spielberg takes over Shanghai, and makes it his city. But then, first in brief patches and then in longer ones, his directing goes terribly wrong. The story, taken from J. G. Ballard's autobiographical novel, is set at the outbreak of the Second World War, and it's about Jim (Christian Bale), an 11-year-old British schoolboy, who is separated from his parents when the Japanese Army invades the city, on December 8, 1941, and how he changes in order to survive three years of starving in a prison camp. It isn't told straightforwardly, though. Spielberg throws himself into bravura passages, lingers over them trying to

give them a poetic obsessiveness, and loses his grasp of the narrative. For the sake of emotion—to have something to say, to give the picture some meaning—he pumps it full of false emotion. (That's what his poetry is.) The picture is a combination of craftsmanship and almost unbelievable tastelessness. Every time Spielberg tries to make a humanitarian statement, he falls flat on his face—not just because his statements are so naïve but because they go against the grain of Ballard's material. John Williams' editorializing music swells and swooshes, trying to make you feel that something religious is going on. Christian Bale is a fine performer, directed superlatively; also with John Malkovich, Miranda Richardson, Nigel Havers, and Joe Pantoliano. The adaptation is credited to Tom Stoppard (it was also worked on by Menno Meyjes); the cinematography is by Allen Daviau. Spielberg had permission to shoot in Shanghai for only three weeks; the settings were matched up and constructed in Spain and London. Warners. (153 minutes.) color (See *Hooked*.)

The Empire Strikes Back (1980)—By far the most imaginative part of the *Star Wars* trilogy. This middle, bridging film is chained to an unresolved plot and doesn't have the leaping comic-book hedonism of the 1977 *Star Wars*, but you can feel the love of movie magic that went into its cascading imagery. George Lucas kept the first movie hopping by cutting it into short, choppy scenes; Irvin Kershner, who directed this one, is a master of visual flow, and, joining his own kinks and obsessions to Lucas's, he gave *Empire* a splendiferousness that may even have transcended what Lucas had in mind. When Han Solo (Harrison Ford) is frozen into sculpture—his face protruding from a bas-relief, the mouth open as if calling out in pain—the scene has a terrifying grandeur. The characters in this fairy-tale cliff-hanger show more depth of feeling than they had in the first film, and the music—John Williams' variations on the *Star Wars* theme—seems to saturate and enrich the intensely clear images. Scenes linger in the mind: the light playing on Darth Vader's gleaming surfaces as this metal man, who's like a giant armored insect, fills the screen; Han Solo saving Luke's life on the ice planet Hoth by slashing open a snow camel and warming him inside; Luke's hand being lopped off, and his seemingly endless fall through space; Chewbacca, the Wookie, yowling in grief or in comic fear, his sounds so hyper-human you couldn't help laughing at them; the big-eared green elf Yoda, with shining ancient eyes, who pontifically instructs Luke in how to grow up wise—Yoda looks like a wonton and talks like a fortune cookie. With Mark Hamill, Carrie Fisher, Billy Dee Williams, and Alec Guinness. The story is by Lucas; the script is by Leigh Brackett and Lawrence Kasdan. The cinematography is by Peter Suschitzky; the editing is by Paul Hirsch. Lucasfilm, released by 20th Century-Fox. color

The Enchanted Cottage (1945)—A fantasy about a horribly scarred war veteran (Robert Young), hiding from the world, and a plainer-than-plain spinster (Dorothy McGuire), who are transformed by love and look miraculously beautiful to each other in their New England cottage. The DeWitt Bodeen and Herman J. Mankiewicz updating of the Pinero play was given the full solemnly sensitive treatment by the director, John Cromwell, which only seems to add to the painful ickiness of the material. The pathos and sloshy uplift can make one squirm with embarrassment mixed with anger. With Herbert Marshall as a blind composer who tries to explain the inexplicable, and Mildred Natwick, Spring Byington, and Hillary Brooke. (A 1924 silent version starred Richard Barthelmess.) R K O. b & w

End as a Man, see *The Strange One*

End of the Road (1970)—The John Barth 1958 novel is about a triangle in an academic setting, and the film's best scenes are the quiet ones that are closest to the spirit of the book. But most of the time the director, Aram Avakian, and his co-screenwriters, Dennis McGuire and Terry Southern, feverishly pound us with shock effects and heavyweight messages. The cinematography by Gordon Willis is often beautiful, the optical effects are sometimes elegant, and the sets and details are often remarkably fine, but the absurdist point of view has too self-congratulatory a tone. Guns and American flags are the running shticks of the movie, and the performers (Stacy Keach as the catatonic hero, Dorothy Tristan, Harris Yulin, James Earl Jones, James Coco, Grayson Hall, and Ray Brock) are intercut with mushroom clouds, atrocities, and the moon shot. Allied Artists. color (See *Deeper into Movies*.)

The End of the World in Our Usual Bed in a Night Full of Rain (1978)—Except for flashbacks this Lina Wertmüller film made in English takes place during one very wet night. A Communist Italian journalist (Giancarlo Giannini) and a rich American feminist photojournalist (Candice Bergen) have been married 10 years, and in all that time they've been having sexual intercourse only in the missionary position. On this night, she suggests that she'd like to try something else, and there's much dishevelment, hysteria, shrieking, and running out into the rain—and the marriage collapses. The entire film has a tutti-frutti romanticism, and parts of it rank with such kitschfests as *Youngblood Hawke* and *The Barefoot Contessa*. The couple live in a lavish apartment that is gorged with objets d'art, family mementos going back hundreds of years, a photograph of Coppola and Fidel Castro, a basset hound, a de Chirico; it represents Europe, or maybe history, or civilization. There's a Greek chorus that talks directly to the camera, often in leering closeups, and it materializes whenever the two need ideological prompting in their male-female warfare. Cinematography by Giuseppe Rotunno. A Liberty Film Production, for Warners release. color (See *When the Lights Go Down.*)

Endless Love (1981)—A predictable fiasco—still it's considerably worse than you might have expected. Directed by Franco Zeffirelli, from Judith Rascoe's adaptation of Scott Spencer's novel about a teen-age boy's single-minded love for his young girlfriend, the movie is an icky, shapeless mess. The novel was a purplish glorification of the hero's masochism, and it was purplish in a violent way. The love that was endless was a physical addiction. The two kids fornicated furiously and just about constantly; they went at each other like battle-scarred veterans of the sex wars. And the boy's passionate love resulted in his being sent to an insane asylum. Even in the 50s when movies were full of misunderstood young heroes, no boy ever suffered so much for love. Zeffirelli has turned this passion into tender, gentle romance, with the scenes of intercourse so "tastefully" rendered that nothing in the movie makes much sense, not even the graceful sexual position of the two young actors—Martin Hewitt as David and Brooke Shields as Jade. If people's early encounters were this refined, sex wouldn't have got a bad name. Maybe teen-agers will be touched by the sensitivity and devotion of the pair; adults may go a little giggly-crazy, especially since the parents are a quartet of leches and bores—reminiscent of the parents in *Splendor in the Grass*, where a passionate *girl* (Natalie Wood) was packed off to a loony bin. Shirley Knight, who acts by smacking her lips, is Jade's mother; Don Murray, who even at first sight seems viciously deranged, is her father; and, as David's parents, Beatrice Straight and Richard Kiley are a left-wing Maggie and Jiggs. This may be the silliest-looking movie ever lighted by a first-class cinematographer (David Watkin); it's all bathed in a Zeffirellian golden glow. When David and Jade are at the Planetarium and he says, "I'm going to name a star after you," a voice in the theatre piped up, "Brooke Shields is already a star." Also with Penelope Milford. A Keith Barish–Dyson Lovell Production, for PolyGram; released by Universal. color

Enemies: A Love Story (1989)—Emotionally overwhelming. Adapted from Isaac Bashevis Singer's New York City novel, set in 1949—a post-Holocaust sex farce in which three passionately jealous women are in love with a guilt-ridden, self-effacing man. The director, Paul Mazursky, has gathered a superbly balanced cast and kept the action so smooth that the viewer is carried along on a tide of mystical slyness. Ron Silver is the Polish-Jewish intellectual who survived the Final Solution by hiding in a hayloft. Margaret Sophie Stein is the Gentile peasant (now his wife) who risked her life to take care of him. Lena Olin is his diabolically willful mistress, a survivor of the camps. Anjelica Huston is the wife (with an erotic aura) he thought was killed by the Nazis. This richly satisfying movie is restrained, yet it has its own deeply crazy turmoil. Mazursky pulls the rug out from under us, and we drop through the farce. With Alan King, Judith Malina, Phil Leeds, and Mazursky. The cinematography is by Fred Murphy; the script is by Roger L. Simon and the director. The soundtrack features a klezmer band. 20th Century-Fox. color (See *Movie Love.*)

The Enemy Below (1957)—A duel of nerves, instincts, intelligence, and seamanship is fought by Curt Jurgens as the captain of a

German submarine and Robert Mitchum as the captain of an American destroyer. Dick Powell's direction of this Second World War action-adventure picture is clean and professional; everything is well-done, but nothing surprises you and nothing thrills you, either. With Theodore Bikel and Kurt Kreuger. The script by Wendell Mayes is based on a book by Commander D. A. Rayner. 20th Century-Fox. CinemaScope, color

Les Enfants du Paradis, see *Children of Paradise*

Les Enfants terribles Also known as *The Strange Ones*. (1949)—The director, Jean-Pierre Melville, expands Cocteau's novel about the shared disorder and confused narcissism of a brother and sister into a baroque tragicomedy. The movie glides along, gathering intensity, as the characters move—compulsively, as in a dream—toward self-destruction. With Nicole Stéphane, fiercely elegant as the dominating Elisabeth; Edouard Dermithe as Paul; Renée Cosima as Dargelos and Agatha; Jacques Bernard as Gérard. Almost voluptuous in its evocation of temperament and atmosphere, this film was shot, on a shoestring, in "real" settings—the director's flat, the lobby of the *Petit Journal*, the stage of the Théâtre Pigalle. When Melville was ill, Cocteau directed the summer beach scene in Montmorency, under snow. Cocteau also provides cryptic, emblematic narration. The score (Bach-Vivaldi) is one of the rare effective film usages of great music. (Melville appeared in *Breathless* as the celebrity being interviewed.) Cinematography by Henri Decaë. In French. b & w

The Enforcer (1950)—This crime melodrama, inspired by newspaper accounts of the organization of killers-for-hire known as Murder, Inc., has a good, tense opening sequence, set at night, with Humphrey Bogart as a D.A. trying to protect the gangster (Ted de Corsia) who is scheduled to be his witness in the morning. But as the D.A. goes back over the case, in flashback, the suspense gradually seeps away. The narrative keeps moving along, but it doesn't build and the flashbacks aren't ingeniously pieced together—they're not fun. Bogart, who seems to be the police investigator as well as the prosecutor, walks through his colorless part; he's far less entertaining than the hoods—a collection of brutish misfits who pick on each other. De Corsia, with his sinister accent and his humorlessness and impersonal anger, takes over as the star. Others in the cast include Zero Mostel as Big Babe, Lawrence (later Michael) Tolan as Duke, Don Beddoe as O'Hara, who's sodden on muscatel, and Jack Lambert, Robert Steele, John Kellogg, King Donovan, Roy Roberts, Tito Vuolo, and Mario Siletti; despite the crude writing (the script is by Martin Rackin) each of these men makes a distinct impression. Only Everett Sloane as the mastermind, Mendoza, is a disappointment—he's smoothly actorish and outclasses his amoral-killer role. The women (Adelaide Klein, Pat Joiner, and Susan Cabot) are treated negligently, as mere accessories to the story. The film is well-shot (by Robert Burks) and astutely designed, though it seems to have been made on the cheap; there's almost no one on the screen who isn't directly related to the case. A puzzling omission: we never learn how Murder, Inc., actually worked; how did potential customers find out how to get in touch with the murder ring? Directed by Bretaigne Windust; produced by Milton Sperling, for an independent company. Released by Warners. b & w

The Enforcer (1976)—Clint Eastwood once again as Dirty Harry, the San Francisco police inspector who is a law unto himself; by now Eastwood appears to be taking Harry's saintliness so seriously that he hisses his lines angrily, his mouth pulled thin by righteousness. Directed by James Fargo, this third in the series doesn't have the savvy to be as sadistic as its predecessors (*Dirty Harry*, *Magnum Force*); it's just limp. The script by Stirling Silliphant and Dean Riesner is no more than scaffolding; its strategy is simply to set up a collection of villains—the Revolutionary Strike Force—so disgustingly cruel and inhuman that Eastwood can spend the rest of the movie killing them with a perfect conscience. These revolutionaries who are imperilling the city (which is run by the usual contingent of liberal twits) are thrill-seeking mercenaries, led by vicious homosexuals. The staging is so lackadaisical, though, that jowly revolutionaries shoot with one eye on the time clock. The film's only distinction is Tyne Daly's warm performance as the policewoman assigned to work with Harry: deliberately unglamorous, she manages to show some believably human expressions of confusion and discomfort. With Bradford Dillman, Harry Guardino, John Mitchum, DeVeren Bookwalter, and John Crawford. The story is by G. M. Hickman and S. W. Schurr. Produced by Eastwood's company, for Warners. color (See *When the Lights Go Down*.)

England Made Me (1972)—Very slight, but it has a hushed, becalmed quality that is pleasing—and peculiar, too, for a film set in Germany during the early 30s. The halcyon atmosphere is creepily ambiguous, to say the least. Adapted from a Graham Greene novel published in 1935, it's about an amiable, giddy young Englishman (Michael York)—a schoolboy at heart—at loose among the Nazis. Hildegard Neil plays his sister, the mistress of a humorless swindler-financier (Peter Finch), and Michael Hordern turns up as a mildewed old newspaperman. Understated and rarefied, the movie often seems more Noël Coward than Graham Greene, but

that's partly because Greene in 1935 wasn't yet quite Greene. The plot and characters are very close to his originals, and the dialogue is almost verbatim; the lines are spoken with the snap that good actors bring to good lines, like fish rising to live bait. It's far from great, but it's not bad, and York gives one of his best performances. With Joss Ackland and Tessa Wyatt. An English production, directed by Peter Duffell, who wrote the script with Desmond Cory. Cinematography by Ray Parslow; shot in Yugoslavia. color (See *Reeling*.)

Ensayo de un Crimen, see *The Criminal Life of Archibaldo de la Cruz*

Enter the Dragon (1973)—Bruce Lee and John Saxon in a kung-fu movie that's a good-natured example of the pleasures of schlock art. There's so much going on that the whole history of movies seems to be recapitulated in scrambled form. It could be billed as the movie with a thousand climaxes. But it's not all schlock: the slender, swift Bruce Lee was the Fred Astaire of martial arts, and many of the fights that could be merely brutal come across as lightning-fast choreography. With Jim Kelly as Williams, Ahna Capri as Tania, Bob Wall as Oharra, Shih Ken as Han, Angela Mao Ying as Su-Lin, Yang Sze as Bolo, Betty Chung as the secret agent, Mei Ling, Geoffrey Weeks as Braithwaite, and Peter Archer as the New Zealander, Parsons. Directed by Robert Clouse; written by Michael Allin; music by Lalo Schifrin; produced by Fred Weintraub and Paul Heller, for Warners. color

The Entertainer (1960)—The John Osborne play, set during the Suez crisis of 1956, was staged by Tony Richardson in 1957, starring Laurence Olivier as Archie Rice; it was his greatest contemporary role, and he appears in this film version, again directed by Richardson. The play is a lewd, tragic vaudeville about the life of a bankrupt pursued by creditors, a crapulent song-and-dance man whose emotions break through onstage in stale blue jokes as he ogles the half-naked chorus girls and razzes the orchestra leader. ''Don't clap too hard—it's a very old building,'' he jeers at the patrons, who are sitting on their hands. And if there's mincing hatred in his tone, and the desperate self-disgust of a performer who can't get a response there's also a trace of affection for the run-down theatre, which suggests dilapidated, crumbling England. The action shifts between the music-hall stage and the rooms that Archie and his wife, Phoebe (Brenda de Banzie), share with his father, Billy Rice (Roger Livesey), who was a headliner in his day but now, in his seventies, is retired to a life of mildewed gentility. Old Billy—''Granddad'' to Archie's three grown-up children—wears ancient, carefully preserved smart clothes and conducts himself with the rakish dignity of an Edwardian gentleman. Billy was a great performer, part of a living tradition; Archie, still hanging on at 50, has never had the purity that his father had—he refers to himself as ''old Archie, dead behind the eyes.'' He's obscenely angry as he lashes out at us, the audience, in frustration at his own mediocrity. Osborne is a master of invective. He can't bring Archie's principled, observant daughter, Jean (Joan Plowright), to life, but when it comes to a character like Archie—a man who does so much to make you hate him that you can't— he gives him a Shakespearean fury. The film errs in many ways, and at times the editing seems glaringly poor, but Olivier's performance gives it venomous excitement. Adapted by Osborne and Nigel Kneale; cinematography by Oswald Morris. With Albert Finney, Alan Bates, Shirley Anne Field, Daniel Massey, and Thora Hird. (An American TV version, starring Jack Lemmon, was made in 1976.) b & w (See *When the Lights Go Down*.)

Entre nous Also known as *Coup de foudre*. (1983)—The French actress-turned-filmmaker Diane Kurys tells the story of two young married women in the 1950s who don't recognize how unfulfilled they have been in their marriages until they meet each other. The two women (Isabelle Huppert and Miou-Miou) are lighted and posed so that they are two heroic profiles, with taut neck tendons and beautiful chins. Kurys lets us see their self-preoccupation and their unresponsiveness to their children, but this is all pushed to the side; it isn't given any weight. The women are romanticized and politicized as soul mates; they're turned into feminist precursors, while the husbands (Guy Marchand and Jean-Pierre Bacri), who always seem to need a shave, are treated as lumps, as part of the common herd. Kurys tells us that the characters played by Huppert and Marchand are her parents, and Marchand, who plays his role superbly, is the only one a viewer is likely to have any feeling for. But Kurys has made a very peculiar kind of memory film: its psychology goes in one direction, its sexual politics take it in another. And the construction is lackadaisical and flabby. Apparently we're supposed to think that whether or not the women are lovers is irrelevant to the changes in consciousness they bring out in each other. Yet the picture keeps teetering on the verge of a seduction scene, and that teasing possibility gives many of the scenes their only tension. This is a movie about two women not having a lesbian affair. The only thing that's distinctive about it is its veneer of post-feminism. Written by the director and Alain Le Henry. In French. color (See *State of the Art*.)

Entre Tinieblas, see *Dark Habits*

The Epic That Never Was (1965)—Bill Duncalf's documentary, made for the BBC, about the circumstances that caused the 1937 Alexander Korda production of *I, Claudius,* based on Robert Graves' *I, Claudius* and *Claudius the God,* to be abandoned midway. The temperamental problems between the star, Charles Laughton, and the director, Josef von Sternberg, were clearly enormous, and the production was hit by a series of disasters; however, from the look of the footage which is included, the world did not lose a masterpiece. The interviews with survivors of the debacle (such as Merle Oberon, who was supposed to play Messalina) are very entertaining. This is probably the only film ever made about an abandoned film.

Equus (1977)—Careful, unimaginative version of Peter Shaffer's play, directed by Sidney Lumet. The sensitive-important-picture pacing is like a black armband. As the tormented psychiatrist, Richard Burton has eight long soliloquies in which he does his elocutionary thing, sitting at his desk and talking right to us. Burton can't be accused of slacking off; he's intense as all getout. He turns his lines into tongue twisters to rush us to the big ironies, squinching his eyes in pain. The case that has upset the doctor is that of a teen-ager (Peter Firth), a part-time stablehand who has blinded six horses. Investigating the crime, the doctor discovers that the boy comes from a repressive background in which religion is a pressure point between the boy's anti-religious father (Colin Blakely) and his devout mother (Joan Plowright), and that the boy has transformed her Christ worship into equine worship. Burton assembles all this (dubious) Oedipal data at a slow crawl, and there's all this *acting.* Each character has to reveal his sore spots, his tensions, and his basic decency. And when the picture finally moves on, it's back to Burton at his lectern, linking the boy's case to ancient Greece and to Dionysian mysteries. The film sets Peter Shaffer's worst ideas on a pedestal. With Harry Andrews, Eileen Atkins, Jenny Agutter, and Kate Reid. Cinematography by Oswald Morris; music by Richard Rodney Bennett; produced by Lester Persky and Elliott Kastner. United Artists. color (See *When the Lights Go Down.*)

Eraserhead (1977)—David Lynch, who had made short films during his student days at the Pennsylvania Academy of Fine Arts, worked for five years in Los Angeles to complete this first feature, which was shot (mostly at night) in 35-mm black and white. He was the writer, the director, and the set designer, and was also responsible for the wonderfully grubby special effects. He seems to have reinvented the experimental-film movement; watching this daringly irrational movie, with its interest in dream logic, you almost feel that you're seeing a European avant-garde gothic of the 20s or early 30s. There are images that recall Fritz Lang's *M* and Cocteau's *Blood of a Poet* and Buñuel's *Un Chien andalou,* and yet there is a completely new sensibility at work. Lynch pulls you inside wormy states of anxiety. Time seems completely still while the hero, Henry (John Nance), whose hair stands on end, as if permanently shocked, in an Afro pompadour that's squared off—it suggests an eraser on the head of a pencil—moves through streets reminiscent of the ones Peter Lorre sidled through in *M.* Henry appears to come out of the viewer's subconscious; he experiences a man's worst fears of courtship and marriage and fatherhood (to a whimpering monster). The slow, strange rhythm is very unsettling and takes some getting used to, but it's an altogether amazing, sensuous film; it even has an element of science fiction and some creepy musical numbers, and the soundtrack is as original and peculiar as the imagery. There is perhaps nothing else in contemporary films that is as eerily erotic as the moment when Henry commits adultery with the girl from across the hall and the two lovers deliquesce into their bed—disappearing in the fluid, with only the woman's hair left floating on top. The sound man was Alan R. Splet (who later won an Academy Award for his work on *The Black Stallion*); the cast includes Judith Roberts, Charlotte Stewart, Laurel Near, and Jack Fisk as the deus ex machina. (The monsters in the 1979 *Prophecy* were clearly based on Henry's babe.)

Eréndira (1983)—Moderately amusing in the surreal-picaresque mode, it was written by Gabriel García Márquez but seems more like the work of someone faking Gabriel García Márquez. The Brazilian director Ruy Guerra seems too earnest for the task at hand; he puts the García Márquez touches in place, but they have no hallucinatory tingle—the only resonance they have is that they remind us of García Márquez's other writing. A mad old witch (Irene Papas) forces her virginal 14-year-old granddaughter Eréndira (Claudia Ohana) to work for her as a whore. Dressed in the ensembles of a regal ragpicker, the witch is carried in a sedan chair as she and Eréndira travel through the desert (the film was made in Mexico), setting up shop wherever they go. And before long the witch is festooned in gold ingots. Little Claudia Ohana is lovely, and the scene of Eréndira's sexual initiation—by rape—is affecting in a semi-prurient way. And Papas is marvellous; she isn't fake anything—she's an original. The old bawd blows out the candles on her birthday cake in one quick, impatient gust, sinks her hand into the cake (which is full of rat poison), eats it gluttonously, and burps with pleasure. Roaring with laughter and giggling on top of it, she survives one attempt on her life after another. Papas's merriment is gargantuan. With Michel Lonsdale, Rufus, Pierre Vaneck, and Oliver Wehe as the duped angel. A Mexican-French co-production. In Spanish. color (See *State of the Art*.)

Escape (1940)—An utterly unconvincing anti-Nazi picture starring Norma Shearer and Robert Taylor. He plays the American-born son of an imprisoned German woman (Alla Nazimova, implausible as a German but a pleasure to see in any role). The director, Mervyn LeRoy, takes forever to set up the maneuvers by which Taylor rescues his mother, and the villain, Conrad Veidt, is so much more attractive than the hero that the whole thing turns into a feeble, overproduced joke. With Philip Dorn, Bonita Granville, Albert Basserman, and Felix Bressart. For the script, Arch Oboler and Marguerite Roberts are the culprits; Ethel Vance wrote the novel. M-G-M. b & w

The Escape Artist (1982)—The husky-voiced Griffin O'Neal is a great-looking gamin daredevil as Danny, the teen-age magician, who believes that his dead father was "the greatest escape artist in the world, after Houdini." The setting is a small Midwestern city (the exteriors are Cleveland) in an indeterminate time in the past. And, with the young director Caleb Deschanel guiding him, O'Neal lets you see the calculations that are going on in Danny's mind as he attempts to perform the tricks that his father did—even the one that may have caused his father's death. But the movie seems to lose its way when Raul Julia turns up as the half-mad son of the crooked Mayor (the senior Desi Arnaz), and the plot begins to revolve around the Mayor's stolen wallet, which contains graft money. (The narrative slackens even though Julia and Arnaz are quite funny together.) There are lapses in the continuity, and the picture is pushed toward a ready-made, theatre-of-the-absurd melodrama—the kind of instant fantasy that filled *One from the Heart*. With Jackie Coogan as the owner of a magic shop, Elizabeth Daily as the girl Danny courts so that he can persuade her to be sawed in half, and Joan Hackett, Gabriel Dell, and Teri Garr. Script by

Melissa Mathison and Stephen Zito, from David Wagoner's novel. A Zoetrope Studios Production; an Orion release through Warners. color (See *Taking It All In*.)

Et mourir de plaisir, see *Blood and Roses*

E.T. The Extra-Terrestrial (1982)—Steven Spielberg's movie is bathed in warmth and it seems to clear all the bad thoughts out of your head. It's the story of a 10-year-old boy, Elliott, who feels fatherless and lost because his parents have separated, and who finds a miraculous friend—an alien inadvertently left on Earth by a visiting spaceship. This fusion of science fiction and mythology is emotionally rounded and complete; it reminds you of the goofiest dreams you had as a kid, and rehabilitates them. It puts a spell on the audience; it's genuinely entrancing. The stars are Henry Thomas, as Elliott, and E.T., who was designed by Carlo Rambaldi. With Drew Barrymore, Robert Macnaughton, Dee Wallace, and Peter Coyote. The script is by Melissa Mathison. Universal. color (See *Taking It All In*.)

The Eternal Husband *L'Homme au chapeau rond* (1946)—There were glimpses of Dostoevski's complexity in Harry Baur's performance as Porfiry in the French *Crime and Punishment*, in Peter Lorre's Raskolnikov in the American production, and in Edwige Feuillère's role in *The Idiot*. But none of these films has ever communicated Dostoevski in more than flashes. Maybe because it copes with a smaller work—a short novel—this movie is more sustained. (It lacks texture, though.) It was the last screen appearance of Raimu, for decades the tragicomic spirit of French films. His performance is a startling climax to his career: the warm, forgiving cuckold of *The Baker's Wife* is gone, and in his place is an icy, bitter cuckold. Raimu is Trusotsky, ridiculous on the surface, but spiri-

tually dead—he hates the child he knows is not his own and hates the lover (Aimé Clariond) of his dead wife. It's a masterly performance. Directed by Pierre Billon. In French. b & w

The Eternal Return *L'Eternel Retour* (1943)—Jean Delannoy directed Jean Cocteau's modern-dress adaptation of the Tristan and Isolde legend. Jean Marais, in a celebrated medieval-looking pullover sweater, and the straight-silk-haired, snow-blond Madeleine Sologne are absurdly glamorous lovers; though the film has the decorative look of ballet and is heavy and stilted, they became the rage of Paris. With Yvonne de Bray and the dwarf Piéral. The cinematographer, Roger Hubert, does occasionally succeed in capturing a misty, mythic atmosphere, and Marais is accompanied by a great dog (his own). Music by Georges Auric. In French. b & w

L'Eternel Retour, see *The Eternal Return*

Evelyn Prentice (1934)—William Powell and Myrna Loy as husband and wife, but this isn't a comedy; it's a refined, high-minded courtroom drama. Powell is a prominent attorney, engrossed in his work. He becomes involved with a woman whom he has defended in a manslaughter case, and the neglected Myrna turns her attention to a poet who wanders by. How could she know that the poet's fancy would turn to thoughts of blackmail? The most solemnly awful portions of the movie take place in a nursery: between bouts of genteel adultery, Powell and Loy keep racing back to their infant's crib for a good cry. After the lawyer defends his wife on a murder charge, they forgive each other; by then you're forgiving no one. William Howard directed, from a screenplay by Lenore Coffee, based on a novel by W. E. Woodward. With Rosalind Russell, Una Merkel, Harvey Stephens, Edward Brophy, and Isabel Jewell. M-G-M. b & w

Evergreen (1935)—In the 30s, the English Jessie Matthews, with her big, rabbity smile, her satin pajamas, and her famous long-legged high kicks, was the closest female equivalent to Fred Astaire. Musical-comedy lovers used to dream of a pairing of the two, but, except for Ginger, he was likely to be stuck dragging girls like Joan Leslie through their paces, while Jessie Matthews stayed in England and had to carry her movies by solos, or by comic turns with Sonnie Hale. Here (with Sonnie Hale) she dances exquisitely in a classic British musical—i.e., charming but a little extended, and less snappy, noisy, and brash than American musicals of the same period. She plays a double role—mother and daughter. Victor Saville directed, from an often witty script by Emlyn Williams and Marjorie Gaffney, based on Benn W. Levy's play. The songs, including "Over My Shoulder Goes One Care" and "Dancing on the Ceiling," are by Rodgers and Hart, and Harry M. Woods. (Matthews had her greatest success in the stage version, which opened in London in 1930.) b & w

Every Man for Himself *Sauve qui peut/La Vie* (1979)—This picture, which Jean-Luc Godard calls his "second first film," was widely hailed as a return to his great, innovative work of the 60s. It's wonderful to feel the pull of Godard's images again, but the movie may also make you feel empty. The setting is a nameless Swiss city, where the lives of the three main characters are loosely intertwined—Jacques Dutronc is a video filmmaker, Nathalie Baye is the woman who is leaving him, and Isabelle Huppert is a practical-minded prostitute. It's about money and people selling themselves—their minds or their bodies. Godard's political extremism

has been replaced by a broader extremism—total contempt, colored by masochism. He's saying, "Everything is for sale." It's simplistic cynicism, like that of the barroom pundit who tells you that every man has his price. The look of the picture isn't inhuman, even though what it's saying is; that's its poignancy. Godard shows us the soft shadings of what might have been. He also tickles the audience with a variety of jokes about the joylessness of sex, but he's too despairing to be really funny. In French. color (See *Taking It All In*.)

Every Man for Himself and God Against All, see *The Mystery of Kaspar Hauser*

Every Night at Eight (1935)—Moderately pleasant program picture from Paramount about a band-leader and three girl singers, with Alice Faye, Frances Langford, Patsy Kelly, and George Raft. (He was certainly a star, but why?) Unusually good songs, including "I'm in the Mood for Love" and "I Feel a Song Coming On," by Dorothy Fields and Jimmy McHugh, and also the nifty torch song "Then You've Never Been Blue." Directed by Raoul Walsh, from the story "Three on a Mike," by Stanley Garvey, adapted by Gene Towne and Graham Baker. Also with Harry Barris, Herman Bing, and Walter Catlett. Produced by Walter Wanger. b & w

Everybody Wins (1990)—This Karel Reisz *film noir*, from an Arthur Miller screenplay, was opened without press screenings and was generally taken for a dud. It's reminiscent of well-constructed problem plays (it demonstrates that "the system" is corrupt), but it also has an idiosyncratic hallucinatory quality and wonderful performances. The setting is a (fictional) small, decaying industrial city in New England; a prominent doctor has been murdered and a young man has been convicted for the crime. Claiming that the youth is innocent and that "everybody" knows who the real killer is, a seductive sometime hooker named Angela (Debra Winger) persuades a private investigator, an outsider (played by Nick Nolte), to look into the case. The movie isn't about good triumphing over evil; it asks, What's going on? Why have the town officials conspired to convict the wrong man? The mood-swinging Angela is the chief mystery: What does she know? Why does she behave in such contradictory ways? Can anything she says be believed? Angela isn't a simple liar. She's something new in thrillers: a schizophrenic femme fatale, and Winger throws herself into the role and makes Angela's irrationality passionately real. You can see why the investigator becomes her lover and her patsy. Winger's Angela is soft and boneless and appealingly whory. (The director seems to let the actress set the film's rhythms.) Winger warms up her voice; it's less husky, more maternal. (There's no hype in her sexiness, and her switches of personality seem simply natural.) Nolte, playing a lapsed Catholic, has bangs, like a Richard Burton priest. Angela is as anxious and bewildering as Marilyn Monroe; the investigator, drawn into an erotic fantasy, always catches on to her emotions too late. For a brief period in the late 60s and early 70s, moviegoers seemed willing to be guided through a movie by their intuitions and imagination; if this slyly funny picture had been released then, it might have been considered a minor classic. (Arthur Miller put together his *An Enemy of the People* consciousness and his Marilyn Monroe problem.) With Kathleen Wilhoite as the stoned Amy and Frank Military as the imprisoned kid, and Judith Ivey, Frank Converse, Jack Warden, and Will Patton. The fresh-looking cinematography is by Ian Baker; Leon Redbone's singing on the investigator's tape deck gives the movie a shaggy, ironic framework. The exteriors were shot in Norwich, Connecticut. Orion. color. (See *Movie Love*.)

Excalibur (1981)—John Boorman's retelling of the Arthurian legends is a serious, R-rated fairy tale. Boorman plunges into the Dark Ages, smiting us with raging battles, balls of flame, mists of dragon's breath, knights with horns and tusks jutting out of their armored heads, and battle-axes that hack off limbs, which seem to ricochet off the armor. The dialogue is pedantic, we hardly have a chance to meet the characters before they're off and running, and the whole film is soaked in Jung, but it has its own crazy integrity. The imagery is impassioned and has a hypnotic quality. The film is like Flaubert's more exotic fantasies—one lush, enraptured scene after another. As Merlin, Nicol Williamson (who affects a touch of the Gaelic and makes wonderful lilting and growling sounds) is the presiding spirit; he stands in for Jung, and he informs us of the meaning of what we're seeing. The film spans three generations—first Uther Pendragon and his feuding with the other Celtic lords, then his son Arthur's reign with the Knights of the Round Table gathered at Camelot, and finally, the challenge to Arthur's power by *his* son, the demonic Mordred. The characters aren't scaled heroically enough for the myths built on their adventures, so we don't experience the elation that we have come to expect at the end of a heroic story, but the film gives us a different kind of elation. It's as if Boorman were guiding us down a magic corridor and kept parting the curtains in front of us. With Nigel Terry as Arthur, Paul Geoffrey as Perceval, Cherie Lunghi as hot little Guenevere, Helen Mirren as Morgana, and Nicholas Clay as Lancelot. Script by Rosco Pallenberg and Boorman; cinematography by Alex Thomson; production design by Anthony Pratt;

Trevor Jones prepared the score (which uses themes from Wagner and from Carl Orff's "Carmina Burana") and conducted it. Made in Ireland. An Orion release, through Warners. color (See *Taking It All In*.)

Executive Action (1973)—Feeble, insensitive fictionalization of how President Kennedy might have been the victim of a large-scale right-wing plot. It's a dodo-bird of a movie, the winner of the *Tora! Tora! Tora!* prize—in miniature. With matchlessly dull performances from a cast that includes Burt Lancaster, Robert Ryan, and Will Geer. The script by Dalton Trumbo is based on a story by Donald Freed and Mark Lane; directed by David Miller. National General. color (See *Reeling*.)

The Exile (1947)—The title is all too apropos: Max Ophuls had many sad days in Hollywood, and this piece of costume theatrics, set in the period just before the reign of Charles II, filled a number of them. Douglas Fairbanks, Jr., was the producer, the writer, and the gymnastic star, and Maria Montez, Paule Croset, Henry Daniell, Robert Coote, and Nigel Bruce are in the cast. The cinematographer, Franz Planer, had worked with Ophuls in happier times. From the novel *His Majesty, the King*, by Cosmo Hamilton. Universal. sepia

The Exiles (1961)—American Indians were granted citizenship in 1924, given civil rights in 1934. Since then many have left the reservations; dispersed, they are strangers—exiles—within the big American cities. It seems to be the same in each city: many of the Indians live "communally"—sponging off each other, drinking, brawling, working for a few days, perhaps committing petty thefts. And in each city there is a gathering place—a hill, a park, a beach, where, late at night, they gather to sing tribal songs, beat the drums, and dance. This documentary follows a group in Los Angeles through a day and a night of eating, drinking, and fighting, and to the hill where, high above the lights of the city, they sing and dance until dawn. The movie was made over a period of several years by a group of young U.S.C. film school graduates, headed by Kent Mackenzie; the group's convictions about moviemaking were strong enough to impress some two dozen people into financing it. The picture shows you things going on around you that you've been only dimly aware of, and it's made with skill and imagination. But it's very doubtful that the investors ever got their money back. b & w

The Exorcist (1973)—The demonic possession of a child, treated with shallow seriousness. The picture is designed to scare people, and it does so by mechanical means: levitations, swivelling heads, vomit being spewed in people's faces. A viewer can become glumly anesthetized by the brackish color and the senseless ugliness of the conception. Neither the producer-writer, William Peter Blatty, nor the director, William Friedkin, shows any feeling for the little girl's helplessness and suffering, or for her mother's. It would be sheer insanity to take children. With Linda Blair, Ellen Burstyn, Max von Sydow, and Jason Miller. A huge box-office success. Warners. color (See *Reeling*.)

Exorcist II: The Heretic (1977)—Directed by John Boorman, this picture has a visionary crazy grandeur (like that of Fritz Lang's loony *Metropolis*). Some of its telepathic sequences are golden-toned and lyrical, and the film has a swirling, hallucinogenic, apocalyptic quality; it might have been a horror classic if it had had a simpler, less ritzy script. But, along with flying demons and theology inspired by Teilhard de Chardin, the movie has Richard Burton, with his precise diction, helplessly and inevitably turning his lines into camp, just as the cultivated, stage-trained actors in early-30s horror films did. Like them, Burton has no conviction in what he's doing, so he can't get beyond staginess and artificial phrasing. The film is too cadenced and exotic and too deliriously complicated to succeed with most audiences (and when it opened, there were accounts of people in theatres who threw things at the screen). But it's winged camp—a horror fairy tale gone wild, another in the long history of moviemakers' king-size follies. There's enough visual magic in it for a dozen good movies; what it lacks is judgment—the first casualty of the moviemaking obsession. With Linda Blair, four year older than in the first film and going into therapy because of her nightmares, Louise Fletcher as the therapist, and Max von Sydow, Kitty Winn, Ned Beatty, Paul Henreid, and James Earl Jones as Pazuzu. The script is credited to William Goodhart; the cinematography is by William Fraker; the production designer was Richard MacDonald; the music is by Ennio Morricone. Warners. color

Expresso Bongo (1959)—This very funny, very distinctive musical satire accepts its targets with good-natured incredulity. An English production, it opens with the camera roving around the teen-age haunts and entertainment palaces of London. The film is written in a brash theatrical idiom with a Yiddish flavor; it's like the language in *Sweet Smell of Success*, but it's used much more affectionately. In *A Kid for Two Farthings* the writer Wolf Mankowitz performed the remarkable feat of turning a narcissistic weightlifter into a fairy-tale character; here he lifts a segment of the modern world to the level of fantasy, by stylizing theatrical sentimentality and vulgarity. In the role of a glib Soho talent agent who's scrounging for a living, Laurence Harvey gives perhaps his most likable performance; he has some very deft

bits—this agent has the amusing theatrical habit of adapting his speech to the accents of the people he talks to. He owns 50 per cent of a young, bewildered rock 'n' roll singer, played by Cliff Richard. The singer is childlike and withdrawn and opportunistic; he tells his juvenile fans that he is a "deeply religious boy," and he sings a song about mom and home called "The Shrine on the Second Floor." With Sylvia Syms, Yolande Donlan, Hermione Baddeley, Ambrosine Philpotts, Avis Bunnage, Kenneth Griffith, Susan Hampshire, Eric Pohlmann, Wilfrid Lawson, and Gilbert Harding as himself, and Meier Tzelniker, re-creating his stage role as the record manufacturer, who describes his product in a song called "Nausea." Mankowitz first wrote the material as a short story, then as a musical play, and then as a film. Val Guest directed. With choreography by Kenneth MacMillan. b & w

Extase, see *Ecstasy*

An Eye for an Eye *Oeil pour oeil* (1957)—The early sequences, in which Curt Jurgens, as a successful, sophisticated European doctor, is stranded in a remote, corrupt Arab settlement where he can communicate with no one, have the fascination and humor of a Paul Bowles story. But the director, André Cayatte, destroys his own best effects, and he winds up with his two principal characters in an apparently endless desert—which is what the movie also turns into. The plot is one of those terrible trick ideas that sometimes work on the screen. When it collapses here, you've got nothing except atmosphere. That's not a total loss. Christian Matras' cinematography may have you convinced that you're in strange Levantine byways, within walking distance of Damascus. (The picture was actually shot in southern Spain.) With Folco Lulli, Lea Padovani, and Pascale Audret. In French. color

Eyes of Laura Mars (1978)—This New York–set thriller operates on mood and atmosphere and moves so fast, with such delicate changes of rhythm, that its excitement has a subterranean sexiness. Faye Dunaway, with long, thick, dark-red hair, is Laura Mars, a celebrity fashion photographer who specializes in the chic and pungency of sadism; the pictures she shoots have a furtive charge—we can see why they sell. Directed by Irvin Kershner, the film has a few shocking fast cuts, but it also has scabrous elegance and a surprising amount of humor. Laura's scruffy, wild-eyed driver (Brad Dourif) epitomizes New York's crazed, hostile flunkies; he's so wound up he seems to have the tensions of the whole city in his gut. Her manager (René Auberjonois) is tense and ambivalent about Laura—about everything. Her models (Lisa Taylor and Darlanne Fluegel), who in their poses look wickedly decadent, are really just fun-loving dingalings. As for Dunaway, constantly kneeling or sprawling to take photographs, her legs, especially her thighs, are far more important to her performance than her eyes; her flesh gives off heat. Tommy Lee Jones is the police lieutenant who represents old-fashioned morality, and when the neurotically vulnerable Laura, who has become telepathic about violence, falls in love with him, they're a very creepy pair. With the help of the editor, Michael Kahn, Kershner glides over the gaps in the very uneven script (by John Carpenter and David Z. Goodman, with an assist from Julian Barry). The cast includes Raul Julia, Rose Gregorio, Meg Mundy, and Bill Boggs (as himself). Columbia. color (See *When the Lights Go Down*.)

Eyes Without a Face *Les Yeux sans visage* (1959)—This famous film by Georges Franju opened in this country on double bills in a dubbed version called *The Horror Chamber of Dr. Faustus*, but it's perhaps the most austerely elegant horror film ever made. Franju called it "a poetic fantasy," and it's a symbolist attack on the ethics of scientists. Though in its way it's as simpleminded as the usual romantic young poet's denunciations of war or commerce, it has a vague, floating, lyric sense of dread which goes beyond the simpler effects of horror movies that don't make intellectual claims. Franju's approach is almost as purified and as mystic as Bresson's. The story is about a surgeon (Pierre Brasseur) who, in systematic experiments, removes the faces of beautiful young kidnapped women and tries to graft them onto the ruined head of his daughter (Edith Scob). He keeps failing, the girls are destroyed, yet he persists, in a terrible parody of the scientific method. In the end, the daughter—still only eyes without a face—liberates the baying hounds on which he has also been experimenting, and they tear off *his* head. The film is both bizarrely sophisticated (with Alida Valli as the mad surgeon's mistress, doing the kidnapping in a black leather coat) and ridiculously naïve (in its plot elements). With Juliette Mayniel as Edna, and François Guérin as Jacques, and Claude Brasseur. The cinematography is by the great Eugen Schüfftan; the music is by Maurice Jarre; the superb gowns are by Givenchy. From Jean Redon's novel; Claude Sautet was one of Franju's troupe of co-writers. In French. b & w (See *I Lost it at the Movies*.)

Eyewitness (1981)—The director Peter Yates and the writer Steve Tesich try to make a new, more meaningful version of a 40s melodrama, but their Manhattan-set thriller bogs down in a tangle of plot. The hero must be a first for a Hollywood hero; he's a janitor in an office building. William Hurt (who plays this janitor) has an entertaining flirtation with Sigourney Weaver, as a TV reporter who comes to film a news item about a murder in the building. In order to pique her interest, he suggests that he may have been an eye-witness, and this fib of his makes the two of them targets for the killers, for those who seek to avenge the killing, for the police, and—it begins to seem—for every passerby. Maybe because of the moviemakers' failure to adapt and modernize 40s conventions, something berserk happens: Weaver, Irene Worth, and Christopher Plummer, who are all playing Jews, play them like Nazis. They're intense, drawn, haggard, rich, and highly cultured—a stiff and sinister bunch. The movie is punctuated with frequent, inept

cuts to a couple of Vietnamese thugs who sneak around eavesdropping, following people, and boding ill. There are good, funny moments, though, with Hurt, with Weaver (before she gets too pinched), with Morgan Freeman and Steven Hill as a cynical, griping team of police lieutenants, with Pamela Reed as the janitor's old girlfriend, and with Kenneth McMillan as the janitor's father. The cast includes James Woods and Albert Paulsen. Cinematography by Matthew F. Leonetti. Released by 20th Century-Fox. color (See *Taking It All In*.)

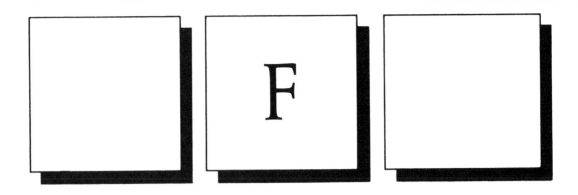

F

The Fabulous Baker Boys (1989)—Two lounge pianists (brothers, played by Beau and Jeff Bridges) add a vocalist (Michelle Pfeiffer) to their act, and she changes their lives. This romantic fantasy has a 40s-movie sultriness and an 80s movie-struck melancholy. Put them together and you have a movie in which 80s glamour is being defined. The young writer-director Steve Kloves trips off your bluesy, narcissistic feelings about popular music and commercial-movie emotions; he invites you to laugh if you want to. (You feel the heat even if you're laughing.) The three stars seem perfect at what they're doing—newly minted icons. When Pfeiffer (who does her own singing) delivers ''Makin' Whoopee,'' while crawling over a grand piano like a long-legged kitty-cat, she rivals Rita Hayworth in *Gilda*. With Jennifer Tilly as Monica. Cinematography by Michael Ballhaus. 20th Century-Fox. color (See *Movie Love*.)

The Fabulous World of Jules Verne, see *The Deadly Invention*

A Face in the Crowd (1957)—Andy Griffith as a hillbilly guitarist who rises to dangerous prominence on television in Elia Kazan's blast at the fascist potential in American mass culture. Some exciting scenes in the first half, but the later developments are frenetic, and by the end the film is a loud and discordant mess. With Patricia Neal, Walter Matthau, and Anthony Franciosa. They could all use a good cold shower. Lee Remick, making her film début, is an amazingly sexy young baton-twirler. Budd Schulberg wrote the script; the music is by Tom Glazer. Warners. b & w

Face to Face, see *The Bride Comes to Yellow Sky* and *The Secret Sharer*

Faces (1968)—John Cassavetes' semi-documentary method is peculiar in that its triumphs and its failures are not merely inseparable from the method but often truly hard to separate from each other. The acting that is so bad it's embarrassing sometimes seems also to have revealed something, so we're forced to reconsider our notions of good and bad acting. But working out of themselves (as his actors do), they can't create characters. Their performances don't have enough range, so we tend to tire of them before the movie is finished. Still, a lot of people found this psychodrama agonizingly true and beautiful. It's about the meaning-lessness of life for the well-heeled middle-aged; the deliberately raw material is about affluence and apathy, the importance of sex, and the miseries of marriage. With John Marley, Gena Rowlands, Lynn Carlin, and Seymour Cassel. b & w (See *Going Steady*.)

Fahrenheit 451 (1966)—Ray Bradbury's story about a future society in which books are forbidden was filmed in England by François Truffaut, with Julie Christie and Oskar Werner. The idea has an almost irresistible appeal, but Truffaut doesn't exploit the obvious possibilities. He barely dramatizes the material at all, and though there are charming, childlike moments, the performers seem listless, and the whole enterprise is a little drab. color (See *Kiss Kiss Bang Bang*.)

The Falcon and the Snowman (1985)—As it was reported in the press in the late 70s, the story of the intelligent Chris Boyce and his coked-up buddy, Daulton Lee, the two boys from well-heeled, conservative Southern California backgrounds who sold key documents about U.S. surveillance satellites to the Russians, had everything—bravado, black humor, and a kind of all-American kinkiness. The movie version isn't really interested in what the boys did or in why they did it, either. The director, John Schlesinger, wants to shock the hell out of us by justifying Boyce, making the point that his actions weren't the traitorous ones—the C.I.A.'s were. The sumptuousness of Schlesinger's style is impressive. There's something lordly (and a little bored) in this director's command of the medium. While he gives you the feeling that he knows what he's doing, he has no staying power—he doesn't develop any of the ideas he tosses in. Timothy Hutton, who plays Boyce, makes you respond to the freak hidden inside the proper manners, and the flickers of subversive life under his clean-cut,

regular-featured handsomeness suggest where the drama in the story is. But Schlesinger treats all this glancingly, and does his ritual song and dance, showing us how we are really the guilty ones. And the attention shifts to Sean Penn's whiny, strung-out Daulton Lee—an attention-getting bummer of a performance. (You feel as if the artist has disappeared and you were left watching a twerp playing a twerp.) With David Suchet as Alex, the K.G.B. man, and Dorian Harewood, Lori Singer, Pat Hingle, Boris Leskin, and Joyce Van Patten. The (disjointed) screenplay, by Steven Zaillian, is based on the book by Robert Lindsey; cinematography by Allen Daviau. Orion. color (See *State of the Art*.)

The Falcon Takes Over (1942)—George Sanders played the Falcon (the suave, lighthearted detective created by Michael Arlen) four times, before turning the role over to his brother, Tom Conway. This was the third in the Sanders series—all brief, B-budget films scheduled for the lower half of double bills but still engaging. Its special interest is that the Michael Arlen character is placed inside the plot of Raymond Chandler's *Farewell, My Lovely* (which was filmed again in 1945 as *Murder, My Sweet*, and again in 1976 under Chandler's original title). Lynn Root and Frank Fenton did the adaptation and Irving Reis directed. With James Gleason, Lynn Bari, Anne Revere, Allen Jenkins, and Ward Bond as Moose. R K O. b & w

The Fall *La Caida* (1961)—The films of the Argentine director Leopoldo Torre Nilsson are very distinctive—atmospheric and sensitive, yet fragile, self-conscious, and not quite satisfying; they always promise more than they deliver. In this one, Elsa Daniel is a lonely young university student who takes a room with a fatherless family. The sickly, neurotic mother seems frightened of her callous, dreamy children; the family hero is an uncle, to whom the student is attracted. Banality sets in just when you hope for excitement. From a novel by the director's wife, Beatriz Guido. In Spanish. b & w

Fallen Angel (1945)—There was a brief period when Otto Preminger made well-paced, engaging melodramas, and this is one of them; it isn't in the class of his *Laura*, but it's tolerable, in a tawdry sort of way. Dana Andrews arrives in a small California town with a dollar to his name, gets an itch for a money-loving waitress (Linda Darnell, so it's easy to sympathize with him), and marries the local rich girl (Alice Faye) to get the dough to win the waitress. But his sordid plan misfires: the waitress is murdered, and he becomes the prime suspect. Dana Andrews is saturnine and convincing, and although Alice Faye isn't altogether comfortable playing Brahms on a church organ and poring over Proust, the good cast includes Charles Bickford, Bruce Cabot, Jimmy Conlin, John Carradine, Anne Revere, and Percy Kilbride. Harry Kleiner adapted Marty Holland's novel. 20th Century-Fox. b & w

The Fallen Idol (1948)—Carol Reed and Graham Greene collaborated on this tricky, highly original thriller. It's about the muddled attempt of an 8-year-old boy (Bobby Henrey), the son of the French ambassador to England, to protect the embassy butler, Baines (Ralph Richardson), whom he idolizes, from a charge of murder. The plot is just about perfect, and there are two wonderful parallel episodes, when the child attempts to impart vital information, which two sets of adults ignore because they think he's just prattling nonsense. There are terrifying, tense moments, too; the whole movie is very cleverly worked out. Maybe it's too deliberate, though, with its stylized lighting and its rigid pacing—you wait an extra beat between the low-key lines of dialogue. It's too delib-erate and too hushed to be much fun. It's a polite thriller—which is close to a contradiction in terms. And the key characters—the decent Baines and the typist (Michèle Morgan) whom he loves—are too ordinary, too controlled, too nice. They're unexciting people. The child actor, however, is wonderfully jittery and intelligent. (Carol Reed had a way with child performers.) And as the unhappy Mrs. Baines, the embassy housekeeper who's a malignant disciplinarian with the child, Sonia Dresdel is really good at evil; she brings the film something out of the ordinary—something clammy and horrible. Greene based the screenplay on his short story "The Basement Room"; cinematography by Georges Périnal. b & w

Falling in Love (1984)— A piece of big-star packaging in which Robert De Niro and Meryl Streep play two prosperous Westchester commuters, each married to someone else, in marriages that have become empty. It's pleasant to see these two in a picture where they're not carrying all the sins of mankind on their shoulders, but they've gone too far in the opposite direction—they're not carrying anything. The picture has been called an 80s *Brief Encounter*, but it's interminable, and in some ways it's more like an East Coast *Tender Mercies*—it's about two anomics who inch their way to spiritual rebirth. Directed by Ulu Grosbard, from a vacuous, would-be-romantic script by Michael Cristofer. Peter Suschitzky's cinematography has a vibrancy that makes you feel hopeful, and Michael Kahn's editing has an elating precision, but after a while the pleasures of technical proficiency shrivel. With Jane Kaczmarek (who's lively in her first scenes), Harvey Keitel, George Martin, Dianne Wiest, and David Clennon. The music by Dave Grusin is ultra-mediocre. Paramount. color (See *State of the Art*.)

Falstaff Also known as *Chimes at Midnight*. (1967)—One of Orson Welles' best and least-seen movies. It is damaged by technical problems resulting from lack of funds, and during the first 20 minutes viewers may want to walk out, because although Shakespeare's words on the soundtrack are intelligible, the sound doesn't match the images, and often we can't be sure who is supposed to be talking. But then despite everything—the use of doubles in long shots, the editing that distracts us when we need to concentrate on the dialogue—the movie begins to be great. Welles brought together the pieces of Falstaff that Shakespeare had strewn over the two parts of *Henry IV* and *The Merry Wives of Windsor*, with cuttings from *Henry V* and *Richard II*, and fastened them into place with narration from Holinshed's *Chronicles* (read by Ralph Richardson). Those of us who resisted our teachers' best efforts to make us appreciate the comic genius of Shakespeare's fools and buffoons will not be surprised that Welles wasn't able to make Falstaff very funny; he's a great conception of a character, but the charades and practical jokes and the carousing and roistering seem meant to be funnier than they are. The movie does have a great Shakespearean comic moment, though: garrulous Falstaff sitting with Shallow (Alan Webb) and Silence (Walter Chiari), rolling his eyes in irritation and impatience at Silence's stammer. Though Welles' performance as Falstaff is short on comedy, it's very rich, very full. Oddly, we never really see the friendship of Falstaff and Prince Hal—played extraordinarily well by Keith Baxter—but John Gielgud's refined, monkish Henry IV gives the film the austerity it needs for the conflict within Hal to be dramatized. The film is a near-masterpiece. Welles' direction of the battle of Shrewsbury is unlike anything he has ever done—indeed, unlike any battle ever done on the screen before. It ranks with the finest of Griffith, John Ford, Eisenstein, Kurosawa. The compositions suggest Uccello, and the chilling, ironic music is a death knell for all men in battle. The soldiers, plastered by the mud they fall in, are already monuments. It's the most brutally sombre battle ever filmed, and it does justice to Hotspur's great "O, Harry, thou hast robbed me of my youth." With Margaret Rutherford, Jeanne Moreau, Marina Vlady, Norman Rodway, Fernando Rey, Tony Beckley, and Beatrice Welles as the page boy. Shot on Spanish locations, which are photographically stylized—to suggest a slightly unrealistic world. b & w (See *Kiss Kiss Bang Bang*.)

Fame Is the Spur (1948)—A study of human weakness and social pressures, with Michael Redgrave as a man from the working class who sheds his socialist ideals as he rises to power and eminence. The material suggests the career of Ramsay MacDonald, yet except for a few good scenes there's no real illumination, and the picture doesn't stay in your mind. With Rosamund John, Anthony Wager, Carla Lehmann, and Bernard Miles. From the Howard Spring novel; Nigel Balchin did the adaptation. John and Roy Boulting produced and directed. b & w

Family Life, see *Wednesday's Child*

Fanfan la tulipe *Fanfan the Tulip* (1951)—This is a sort of Louis XV Western and its humor is of the type that can best be described as "irrepressible" or "roguish." Fanfan (Gérard Philipe) is a handsome peasant lout with good physical equipment and no excess weight of mind or morals; his agility in bed and battlefield provides a light burlesque on the arts of love and war. Gina Lollobrigida is his most decorative playmate; other ladies bursting their bodices include Geneviève Page as La Pompadour and Sylvie Pelayo as Henriette de France. With Marcel Herrand as the king, and Noël Roquevert.

F

Christian-Jaque directed—as usual, he seems to mistake archness for style. Cinematography by Christian Matras. In French. b & w

Fanny (1932)—Though the three films of the Marcel Pagnol trilogy are interrelated, each is complete in itself. This second one was directed by Marc Allégret (and Pierre Prévert), with the same cast as the first, *Marius*. After Marius (Pierre Fresnay) goes to sea, his pregnant fiancée, Fanny (Orane Démazis), marries the sailmaker (Charpin); Marius's father, César (the great Raimu), acts as godfather to his grandson. César's dominating, expansive character is the central force of the film. When Marius returns, he finds that his leaving was an irremediable mistake—that the sailmaker is acknowledged as the father of his son and that there is no place for him (until the concluding film, *César*). You need a lot of tolerance for warm comic invention; it drags fearfully. In French. b & w

Fanny and Alexander *Fanny och Alexander* (1983)—Ingmar Bergman's festive and full-bodied dream play—a vision of family life as a gifted boy might have perfected it, replacing his strict family (Bergman's father was a clergyman) with a generous-hearted theatrical clan. In what Bergman says is his final movie, his obsessions are turned into stories, and he tells them to us—he makes us a beribboned present of his Freudian-gothic dream world. The movie is scaled big; it runs for 3 hours and 10 minutes, and its lovingly placed warm gingerbreading is enormously enjoyable. But the conventionality of the thinking in the film is rather shocking. It's as if Bergman's neuroses had been tormenting him for so long that he cut them off and went sprinting back to Victorian health and domesticity. With Gunn Wållgren, Ewa Fröling, Jan Malmsjö, Erland Josephson, Pernilla Wållgren, Harriet Andersson, Jarl Kulle, Allan Edwall, Gunnar Björnstrand, Börje Ahlstedt,

Mona Malm, Christina Schollin, and Bertil Guve as Alexander and Pernilla Allwin as Fanny. Cinematography by Sven Nykvist. Academy Awards: Best Foreign-Language Film, Art Direction, Cinematography, Costume Design. In Swedish. color (See *Taking It All In*.)

Fantasia (1940)—Disney enlisted an odd assortment of collaborators (among them Stokowski, who did it voluntarily, and Stravinsky, who was brought in involuntarily), and this grab bag of ambitious animated shorts—an attempt to combine high art and mass culture—was publicized as if it were an artistic landmark. Disney's animators provided visual interpretations of Bach's "Toccata and Fugue in D Minor" (in Stokowski's transcription, which is a precursor of the musical processing in *2001*) and of hyped-up excerpts from "The Nutcracker Suite," "The Sorcerer's Apprentice," "The Rite of Spring," the "Pastoral Symphony," "The Dance of the Hours," and "A Night on Bald Mountain" (which somehow leads into the "Ave Maria"). Volcanoes erupt and dinosaurs battle during "The Rite of Spring"; garlanded girl centaurs cavort during Beethoven's "Pastoral." Initially, the film was a box-office failure, but it proved successful in revivals, especially in the early 70s, when it became a popular head film, because of such ingredients as the abstract first section, the mushroom dance during "The Nutcracker" (one of the liveliest sequences), and the overly bright—somewhat psychedelic—color. "The Sorcerer's Apprentice," featuring Mickey Mouse, and parts of other sequences are first-rate Disney, but the total effect is grotesquely kitschy.

Fantastic Voyage (1966)—The sci-fi idea is ingenious, promising both poetry and excitement: a medical team is miniaturized so it can go into the bloodstream of a scientist to destroy a blood clot on his brain; the team has only sixty minutes for the journey and operation and getting out. But there's the usual little argument about whether to take the heroine, Raquel Welch, along ("A woman has no place on a mission like this"), and we know who the villainous saboteur is as soon as we hear one of the scientists spouting atheism. The body entered looks pretty, shiny clean, and expensive, like a new refrigerator, and the adventures inside are no more mysterious than a trip through Disneyland. (The action doesn't go below the waist.) Stephen Boyd is the stout-hearted hero; with Edmond O'Brien, Donald Pleasence, Arthur Kennedy, William Redfield, Arthur O'Connell, and a lot of bubbly special effects. The process shots are so clumsy that the actors look as if a child has cut them out with a blunt scissors—an effect that might be witty in a different context. It isn't terrible, just disappointing. Directed by Richard Fleischer, from Harry Kleiner's script. (The script was novelized by Isaac Asimov.) Produced by Saul David, for 20th Century-Fox. CinemaScope, color (See *Kiss Kiss Bang Bang*.)

Le Fantôme de la liberté (1974)—Buñuel's theme is freedom, in the sense of chance: the picture is a random series of anecdotes and paradoxes, and they miss as often as they connect. Buñuel has a great spare, tonic style, but the domesticated surrealism of this picture has no sting and no after-effect. The film drifts out of your head before it's over. The actors come on in relays: the cast includes Monica Vitti, Jean-Claude Brialy, and Adriana Asti. In French. color (See *Reeling*.)

Far From the Madding Crowd (1967)—John Schlesinger's misconceived attempt to bring the great Hardy novel to the screen is in some ways a very beautiful film. It's a botch, but you can feel that it was made with love. With Julie Christie, Alan Bates, Terence Stamp,

and Peter Finch. The script is by Frederic Raphael; the cinematography is by Nicolas Roeg; the music is by Richard Rodney Bennett; the production design is by Richard MacDonald. Dorset stands in for Wessex. Released in the U.S. by M-G-M. color

Le Farceur, see *The Joker*

Farewell, My Lovely see *Murder, My Sweet*

Farewell Uncle Tom (1972)—In this Italian pseudo-documentary about the horrors of black slavery, the Italian moviemakers Gualtiero Jacopetti and Franco Prosperi (whose previous films include *Mondo Cane*) claim to show exactly what slavery was like, from slave ship to plantation life. They feature scenes such as a slave-breeding farm, Southern white women rolling in the hay with their young slaves, and blacks in cages used for mad scientific experiments. And all this prurience and voyeuristic hypocrisy is thrown together with scenes on board a slave ship which can't help affecting you; your emotions get all tangled up, caught in Jacopetti and Prosperi's porno fantasies. Set in the United States but shot mostly in Haiti. Released by Cannon. color (See *Reeling*.)

The Farmer's Daughter (1947)—This political comedy was enormously popular—maybe because of its smooth, bland, apolitical cheerfulness, which some people considered fresh. It's amiable but unrelentingly clean and nice. With blond braids wound in clusters over her ears, and turning *j*'s into *y*'s, Loretta Young plays a Swedish housemaid who finds a job in the home of a patrician, politically influential family (dominated by Ethel Barrymore), and gets to be a congresswoman. With Joseph Cotten, Charles Bickford, Rose Hobart, Rhys Williams, Harry Davenport, Lex Barker, Don Beddoe, and

Jason Robards (père). Directed by H. C. Potter, from a screenplay by Allen Rivkin and his partner-wife, Laura Kerr. R K O. b & w

Fashions of 1934—Bette Davis at her blondest as a fashion artist professionally and romantically involved with suave, shady promoter William Powell. Elaborate piffle, directed by William Dieterle; it mixes fashions and show business in the sort of bewildering combination that used to come off the Hollywood assembly line. With Hugh Herbert, Henry O'Neill, and Frank McHugh (as Snap), Verree Teasdale (as the Duchess), and Reginald Owen (as Baroque). Written by F. Hugh Herbert and Carl Brickson; choreography by Busby Berkeley; songs by Sammy Fain and Irving Kahal. Warners. b & w

Fast Times at Ridgemont High (1982)—Not bad. It may fall into the general category of youth-exploitation movies, but it isn't assaultive. The young director, Amy Heckerling, making her feature-film début, has a light hand. If the film has a theme, it's sexual embarrassment, but there are no big crises; the story follows the course of several kids' lives by means of vignettes and gags, and when the scenes miss they don't thud. In this movie, a gag's working or not working hardly matters—everything has a quick, makeshift feeling. If you're eating a bowl of Rice Krispies and some of them don't pop, that's O.K., because the bowlful has a nice, poppy feeling. The friendship of the two girls—Jennifer Jason Leigh as the 15-year-old Stacy who is eager to learn about sex and Phoebe Cates as the jaded Valley Girl Linda who shares what she knows—has a lovely matter-of-factness. With Sean Penn as the surfer-doper Spicoli— the most amiable stoned kid imaginable. Penn inhabits the role totally; the part isn't big but he comes across as a star. Also with Robert Romanus, Judge Reinhold, Brian Backer, and Ray Walston. The script, by

Cameron Crowe, was adapted from his book about the year he spent at a California high school, impersonating an adolescent. The music—a collection of some 19 pop songs— doesn't underline things; it's just always there when it's needed. Universal. color (See *Taking It All In*.)

Fat City (1972)—Set and shot in Stockton, California, this John Huston movie about boxing is almost a really memorable movie, but it suffers from a central piece of miscasting. Stacy Keach is catatonically drab as Tully, the boxer on the skids. The film is beautifully acted and directed around the edges, but it also suffers from a tragic tone that has a blurring, antiquing effect. You watch all these losers losing, and you don't know why they're losing or why you're watching them. Their losing appears to be a plot necessity for the sake of a faded idea of classical structure. In the role of a nice, dumb young fighter, Jeff Bridges helps to compensate for the missing center. He doesn't have much chance for characterization, but the way he moves is so unobtrusively natural and right that you feel you know the kid and understand him. Curtis Cokes, a fighter who had never acted before, is remarkable as Earl. Also with the flamboyant Susan Tyrrell as the drunken Oma, and Candy Clark, Art Aragon, and Nicholas Colosanto. The screenplay, by Leonard Gardner, is adapted from his novel; the cinematography is by Conrad Hall. With the song "Help Me Make It Through the Night," by Kris Kristofferson. Produced by Ray Stark; he later acknowledged he'd made a mistake in rejecting Huston's choice for Tully—Marlon Brando, who wanted to play the part. Columbia. color

Fat Man and Little Boy (1989)—It's about how the collaboration of General Leslie R. Groves (Paul Newman) and J. Robert Oppenheimer (Dwight Schultz) resulted in the two atomic bombs' being dropped on Japan. The director, Roland Joffé, and his co-screenwriter, Bruce Robinson, took this inherently dramatic subject and got lost in it; the script is a shambles. Newman, though miscast, is still too smooth to be matched by Schultz—he isn't a forceful enough actor to suggest Oppenheimer's Joan of Arc presence, which kept the collection of scientists together. In this version, both men are diminished: Oppenheimer is just an arrogant, ivory-tower idealist, and the gruff, deceitful Groves seems to pick him for his weakness. With John Cusack, Laura Dern, Natasha Richardson, Bonnie Bedelia, Gerald Hiken, John C. McGinley, and Fred Dalton Thompson. Music by Ennio Morricone. (The TV docudrama *Day One*, featuring Brian Dennehy as Groves and David Strathairn as Oppenheimer, shows how the Manhattan Project developed its own momentum; it has the complexity and drive that Joffé's version lacks.) Paramount. color (See *Movie Love*.)

Fatal Attraction (1987)—A primer on the bad things that can happen if a man cheats on his wife. There's sometimes a fine line between sexiness and craziness, and the hero (Michael Douglas), a Manhattan corporate lawyer—a settled married man—isn't hip enough to catch the danger signals when he lets a woman book editor (Glenn Close) talk him into going with her to her loft. Once this woman begins behaving as if she had a right to a share in the lawyer's life, she becomes the dreaded lunatic of horror movies. But with a difference: she parrots the aggressively angry, self-righteous statements that have become commonplaces of feminist fiction, and they're so inappropriate to the circumstances that they're proof she's loco. They're also the director Adrian Lyne's and the screenwriter James Dearden's hostile version of feminism. The film is about men seeing feminists as witches, and the way the facts

are presented here, the woman *is* a witch. Brandishing a kitchen knife, she terrorizes the lawyer and his family. Basically this is a gross-out slasher movie in a glossy format. It's made with swank and precision, yet it's gripping in an unpleasant, mechanical way. The violence that breaks loose doesn't have anything to do with the characters who have been set up; it has to do with the formula they're shoved into. The picture enforces conventional morality (in the era of AIDS) by piling on paranoiac fear. With Anne Archer as the beautiful homebody wife, Ellen Hamilton Latzen as the bright little daughter, and Stuart Pankin as the clowning pal. Tip-top editing by Michael Kahn and Peter E. Berger. (Dearden's script is an expansion of the 42-minute film *Diversion*, which he wrote and directed in England in 1979.) Paramount. color (See *Hooked*.)

The Fatal Glass of Beer (1933)—This is the wildest of W. C. Fields' 2-reelers, and the best. It also has the easiest-to-remember title and a great punch line—"It ain't a fit night out for man or beast." b & w

Father Brown, see *The Detective*

Father Goose (1964)—An imitation of *The African Queen*. This time it's Cary Grant who's a scroungy unshaven sot. (When the Cary Grant voice comes out of this stumblebum, the performance seems like a masquerade.) Alone, on an island in the South Seas during the Second World War, this air observer for the Australian navy is suddenly stuck with six or seven little girls and Leslie Caron, who's out to reform him and hides his booze, so he won't be a bad example to the kids. This dismal confection was directed by Ralph Nelson, from a script by Peter Stone and Frank Tarloff. The cast includes Trevor Howard. Universal. color

Father of the Bride (1950)—Deeply conventional, plushly middle-class view of normal romance and marriage, seen from the point of view of the banker-father (Spencer Tracy) of the bride (Elizabeth Taylor, still in her teens). Albert Hackett and Frances Goodrich wrote this comedy with an eye to the father's misgivings about the groom and his Oedipal fixation on his daughter; it's an archetypal sit-com situation. Vincente Minnelli directed very simply and skillfully, keeping us at a discreet distance; we look on at the follies of sensible, prosperous people in their clean, comfortable, Waspy homes. Within its own terms the picture is sensitive and very well done, but it's also tiresomely fraudulent—an idealization of a safe, shuttered existence, the good life according to M-G-M, 24-karat complacency. Tracy, at the center of things, gives his basic sturdy-clod performance, somewhat better modulated than usual. Elizabeth Taylor is gentle and soft-toned, and Minnelli uses her sparingly, resisting the temptation to feast on her in closeup; she and Joan Bennett, who plays her mother, match up together neatly. Don Taylor as the groom is a mistake, though; he lacks solidity—he's so nice-boy lightweight he's like an updated David Manners. With Leo G. Carroll, Melville Cooper, Billie Burke, Moroni Olsen, and Russ (then Rusty) Tamblyn. From the book by Edward Streeter; produced by Pandro S. Berman. b & w

Fellini Satyricon (1970)—Fellini's big pagan ball, with the debauchery of the pre-Christian Roman world at the time of Nero as an analogue of the modern post-Christian period. In *La Dolce Vita*, he used the orgies of modern Rome as a parallel to ancient Rome, and now he reverses the analogy to make the same point—that man without a belief in God is a lecherous beast. The film is full of cautionary images of depravity that seem to come out of the imagination of a Catholic schoolboy: an unconscionable number of performers stick out their evil tongues at us, and there are leering cripples, fat freaks with hideous grins, and so on. Fellini draws upon his master-entertainer's feelings for the daydreams of the audience, and many people find this film eerie, spellbinding, and even profound. Essentially, though, it's just a hip version of De Mille's *The Sign of the Cross* (also a photogenic demonstration of the highly dubious proposition that godlessness is lawlessness), and it's less entertaining than De Mille's kitsch—maybe because no one is given a role to play; Fellini is the only star. He uses Petronius and other classic sources as the basis for a movie that is one long orgy of eating, drinking, cruelty, and copulation. We seem to be at a stoned circus, where the performers go on and on whether we care or not, and, for a work that is visual if it is anything, the film leaves disappointingly few visual impressions. The fresco effect becomes monotonous; we anticipate the end a dozen times. There's a charming episode with a beautiful slave girl (Hylette Adolphe) in a deserted house, and some of Danilo Donati's set designs (a ship like a sea serpent, a building with many floors and no front wall) have a hypnotic quality. With Max Born as Gitone, Martin Potter as Encolpius, and Hiram Keller as Ascyltus; Mario Romagnoli as Trimalchio, Magali Noel, Alain Cuny, Capucine, Lucia Bose. Written by Fellini and Bernardino Zapponi. In Italian. color (See *Deeper into Movies*.)

Fellini's Casanova (1976)—Fellini has done something no one else in screen history ever has: he has made an epic about his own alienation. And perhaps this can't be done successfully—not with all this pageantry, anyway. When an artist moves inward yet deals with his own spiritual crises on a spectacular and lavish scale, there is a conflict in form. Something goes rotten. With Donald

Sutherland, who is used as a deliberately unfunny caricature of Casanova. color

Fellini's Roma (1972)—It's an imperial gesture at documentary: a sketchbook about the city of Fellini's imagination, that love-hate dream-nightmare city which is more familiar to us by now than Rome itself. This autobiographical fantasy includes extras painted up as voracious citizens, a high-camp ecclesiastical fashion show, and a mock excavation in a subway which uncovers a Roman villa. Designed by Danilo Donati, who is a magician, and shot by the great Giuseppe Rotunno, the film is like a funeral ode to an imaginary city under purplish, poisoned skies. Some of the images are magisterial and marvellous, like a series of stormy Turners, but whenever there's dialogue or *thought*, the movie is fatuous. Fellini is at the center of the film, played as a young man fresh from the provinces by a toothsome, lusciously handsome actor (dimply Peter Gonzales, from Texas), and then by himself, speaking in English—most of it dubbed—in this version. He interacts with no one; he is the star, our guide, and like many another guide he often miscalculates our reactions, especially to his arch, mirthless anticlerical jokes. The ambiance is least oppressive when he stages a 40s vaudeville show—a return to the world of his early movies. The picture reaches its nadir when he goes celebrity-chasing and interviews Gore Vidal, who informs us that Rome is as good a place as any to wait for the end of the world. Fellini appears to see himself as official greeter for the apocalypse. In English and Italian. color (See *Reeling*.)

La Femme du boulanger, see *The Baker's Wife*

La Femme infidèle (1969)—This Claude Chabrol film is an exquisitely detailed, impeccably acted, stunningly directed suspense story about adultery and passion among the bourgeoisie. Yet there isn't a breath of life in it. You observe Michel Bouquet's foxy little performance as the cuckold, the glossy beauty of Stéphane Audran (she looks like a rich, chic Jeanne Hébuterne) as the wife, and Maurice Ronet's assured professionalism as the seducer, and you see the points being made about the hidden violence of overcivilized people. But the expertise is so tired, so masterly and perfectly slick, that the film looks as if Chabrol polished it until he ran out of spit. With Michel Duchaussoy. Chabrol wrote the script; cinematography by Jean Rabier. In French. color (See *Deeper into Movies*.)

Une Femme mariée, see *A Married Woman*

Femmes fatales Also known as *Calmos*. (1976)—The first half hour of this sexual extravaganza by the highly original French writer-director Bertrand Blier is a peerless dirty-boy romp. The heroes (Jean-Pierre Marielle and Jean Rochefort) are two 40-year-old Parisian boulevardiers who look like wax grooms on a stale wedding cake. Marielle is a gynecologist who can't bear to inspect women's genitals anymore, and Rochefort is a baby-blue-eyed pimp who is exhausted by women's sexual demands. They run away to the countryside, to a village where they eat and drink and wear old clothes and begin to stink. Calm, that's what they want. Up to this point, the film is an inspired exploitation-porno fantasy, with Claude Renoir's Panavision images and Georges Delerue's music providing a feeling of grandeur and folly. But then the story takes a science-fiction turn. It shifts from the lunacy and regressions of these two men to the sexual revulsion felt by men en masse, and Blier and his co-scriptwriter (Philippe Dumarcay) lose the flavor and the characters. Yet no one but Blier has matched such raunchiness with such beauty;

you have to have a true respect for raunchiness to do that. With Brigitte Fossey, who's like sensual porcelain, as the doctor's blond cat of a wife. In French. color (See *When the Lights Go Down*.)

La Fête à Henriette, see *Holiday for Henrietta*

Fiddler on the Roof (1971)—This joyously square musical succeeds in telling one of the root stories of American life. Tevye, the shtetl dairyman pulling his wagon, is a myth-sized version of a limited, slightly stupid Common Man. As Tevye's daughters marry and disperse, and the broken family is driven off its land and starts the long trek to America, his story becomes the story of the Jewish people who came to America at the turn of the century—what they left behind and what they brought with them. The movie offers the pleasures of big, bold strokes; it's American folk opera, commercial style. It's not a celebration of Jewishness; it's a celebration of the sensual pleasures of staying alive and of trying to hang on to a bit of ceremony, too. Isaac Stern plays the theme (as he does in the solo parts throughout the movie) with startling brio and attack, and Topol's Tevye has the same vitality and sweetness and gaiety as Stern's music; he's a rough presence, masculine, with burly, raw strength. Directed by Norman Jewison, from Joseph Stein's play, based on Sholom Aleichem's stories. The music is by Jerry Bock, the functional, uninspired lyrics by Sheldon Harnick. With Leonard Frey, Rosalind Harris, Paul Mann, Molly Picon, Neva Small, Michele Marsh, Norma Crane, Paul Michael Glaser, and Raymond Lovelock. The picture was originally 3 hours long and was run in two parts, with an intermission; then it was trimmed, and then trimmed again when it was reissued in 1979. Altogether, it lost 32 minutes. (In 1939 a Yiddish film, *Tevye*, starring Maurice Schwartz, was adapted from the same sto-

ries.) United Artists. color (See *Deeper into Movies*.)

Field of Dreams (1989)—Kevin Costner, a New Age farmer in Iowa, longs to be reconciled with his dead father, a minor-league baseball player whose outlook he had rejected in the 60s. He hears a whispered command to build a baseball field, and when he obeys the command the spirits of Shoeless Joe Jackson (Ray Liotta) and the other White Sox who were barred from baseball for life after the 1919 World Series scandal arrive and play regularly. This is only the beginning of the hero's mystical encounters. The writer-director, Phil Alden Robinson (who adapted W. P. Kinsella's 1982 novel, *Shoeless Joe*), may treat us as if our brains were mush, but he'd just about have to be sincere to work so methodically, putting each new miracle in its narrative slot, and providing this doggerel emotion, these corn-fed epiphanies. That the film is sincere doesn't mean it's not manipulative; when the weepers in the audience start up, you may feel like a pariah if you're not moved. With Amy Madigan, James Earl Jones, Burt Lancaster, Dwier Brown as the father, and Gaby Hoffman. Universal. color (See *Movie Love*.)

The Fighting 69th (1940)—James Cagney and the patriotic gamut. He plays a First World War coward—a mean, loudmouth runt from Brooklyn who turns yellow in his first charge over the top, screaming in panic and drawing the fire of the Germans upon his regiment. He reforms, of course (the picture was made during the Second World War), and becomes a hero of the Argonne, losing his life willingly. Cagney is an expert in the jangled rotten-nerves department, but you have to be doggedly devoted to him to watch a picture like this voluntarily. You really have to be a masochist, considering that the humor is of the sentimental, fighting-

Irish variety, and that Pat O'Brien plays a priest and Jeffrey Lynn is Joyce Kilmer dreaming up *Trees*. It's sometimes forgotten that Warners was just as high on patriotic nobility in the 40s as it was on social protest in the 30s. With George Brent, Frank McHugh, Guinn Williams, Alan Hale, William Lundigan, Henry O'Neill, John Litel, and Dick Foran. Directed by William Keighley; written by Norman Reilly Raine, Fred Niblo, Jr., and Dean Franklin; produced by Hal B. Wallis. b & w

The File on Thelma Jordon (1950)—Did any other actress—even Joan Crawford—get herself into as much heavy melodramatic trouble as Barbara Stanwyck? This time, she's on trial for murder, and the assistant district attorney (Wendell Corey) falls in love with her and deliberately loses the case. Robert Siodmak directed very efficiently (there's a sequence with the camera following Stanwyck from her jail cell to the courthouse which is a model of film craft), and Ketti Frings's script has some sharp dialogue (Stanwyck has a first-rate last line). But the movie is unexciting, and despite Stanwyck's professionalism we don't much care whether or not Thelma Jordon is a killer, or whether she's purified by love, either. This may be because of the plot contrivances (from a story by Marty Holland) and also because the male actors aren't in Stanwyck's league. Corey demonstrates innate goodness by being blankly wide-eyed, and the bad guy in Thelma's life—played by Richard Rober—has no sexual threat in his nastiness. With Stanley Ridges, Joan Tetzel, Paul Kelly, and Minor Watson. Cinematography by George Barnes; music by Victor Young. Produced by Hal B. Wallis, for Paramount. b & w

La Fille du puisatier, see *The Well-Digger's Daughter*

Film ohne Titel, see *Film Without a Name*

Film Without a Name *Film ohne Titel* (1947)—This is one of the most original and nonchalant comedies of the immediate postwar period—a satirical improvisation on the theme that there are no movie themes in the German shambles. The star is Hildegarde Neff, the hungry-voiced, alluringly sad-eyed actress who at the time seemed more or less the female equivalent of Curt Jurgens. Neff (that's how Knef spelled it then) is joined by Willy Fritsch and Hans Sohnker as they act out a group of romantic episodes, including a succulent little parody of *The Blue Angel*, and do a routine on the actors' pox—vanity. Helmut Käutner, Ellen Fechner, and Rudolf Jugert wrote the script; Jugert directed. Made in the British Zone. In German. b & w

The Final Test (1953)—Robert Morley—a famous aesthete and man of letters—doesn't enter until the scene has been so thoroughly prepared that he can trundle off with the rest of the picture. Terence Rattigan did the adaptation of his own television play and Anthony Asquith directed. Jack Warner is the aging cricket batsman who is going to the wicket for the last time; Ray Jackson is his poet son, who is blithely indifferent and, on the great day, goes to visit the literary eminence. We Americans are clued in to what's going on: there's a visiting American senator, who cannot understand what cricket is all about, and a superbly contemptuous Englishman who explains the game to him. Rattigan has cleverly underlined the meaning of the game by having it apply to the movie itself—and by extension, to English humor and character. There's something too snug about this kind of affectionate English comedy, yet the picture is so cleverly done that you enjoy it in spite of yourself. With Valentine Dyall in a pseudo-Greek play, George Relph and

Adrianne Allen, and a collection of famous cricketers. b & w

A Fine Madness (1966)—Sean Connery brings ravenous energy to the role of a New York poet who's engaged in the daily battle to express himself. He falls into the hands of a group of psychiatrists who are appalled by his nonconformist impulses. He cuckolds one of them (Patrick O'Neal), who decides to have him lobotomized (i.e., castrated). Directed by Irvin Kershner, from a script by Elliott Baker, based on his novel, the movie suggests a farcical cross between Joyce Cary's *The Horse's Mouth* and Shaw's *The Doctor's Dilemma*. There's a well-substantiated Hollywood story that Jack Warner suddenly got the point of the picture, discovered that it was "antisocial," and ordered it recut. What's left is uneven and it has unresolved areas, but it also has a 60s charge to it. Connery walks across a bridge in a way that tells you the world is his. (Women, though, may be puzzled about why the poet's socking his wife—Joanne Woodward—is meant to be hilarious.) The film has a great look (it was shot by Ted McCord) and an amazing cast: Jean Seberg, Colleen Dewhurst, Zohra Lampert, Sorrell Booke, Jackie Coogan, Clive Revill, Harry Bellaver, Kay Medford, Gerald S. O'Loughlin, Bibi Osterwald, Mabel Albertson, and Sue Ane Langdon. The music is by John Addison. Produced by Jerome Hellman, for Warners. color

Finian's Rainbow (1968)—Some of the whimsey in this message operetta is hard to take, but, considering the moldering ponderousness of the whole project, the young Francis Ford Coppola did his best to keep things moving in a carefree, relaxing way. (But the filtered, gauzy lyrical effects are so soft that the occasional hard-focus closeup of the principals is really brutal.) Coppola is helped by Petula Clark, Al Freeman, Jr., and Keenan Wynn; however, Fred Astaire is miscast, and, as the Puckish leprechaun, Tommy Steele doesn't know how to scale down his thumping stage personality, and probably no matter who played it the Susan the Silent routine would be beyond sufferance. With Avon Long, Roy Glenn, and Jester Hairston as the Passion Pilgrim Gospeleers. Warner–Seven Arts. color (See *Going Steady*.)

Fingers (1978)—Directing his first film, the writer James Toback seems to be playing the literary-adolescent's game of wanting to go crazy so he can watch his own reactions. Because he doesn't censor his masculine racial fantasies, his foolishness and his terrible ideas pour out freely. The protagonist (Harvey Keitel) is an artist with the soul of a violent hood. Toback doesn't just risk self-parody—he falls into it. Yet the film never seems ridiculous, because he's got true moviemaking fever. With Jim Brown, Tisa Farrow, and Michael V. Gazzo. Produced by George Barrie; a Brut release. color (See *When the Lights Go Down*.)

Fire Over England (1937)—The Armada is a toy fleet, but the actors are full-scale and stirring—a young daredevil Laurence Olivier leaps about the battle scenes and makes love to an incredibly pretty Vivien Leigh, while Flora Robson plays a great-hearted Queen Elizabeth, and Raymond Massey is Philip II of Spain. It's swashbuckling nonsense (and slow to get under way), but with a fine spirit. Alexander Korda produced, William K. Howard directed, James Wong Howe was the cinematographer. b & w

The Firefly (1937)—Jeanette MacDonald partnered with Allan Jones in a long and lavish costume operetta, set in the early 19th century, during the war between France and Spain. She's a Spanish spy (in disguise) and sings wearing a Napoleon hat. (She's very hard to take.) Strictly for those who are prepared to listen to such songs as "Love Is Like a Firefly" and "He Who Loves and Runs Away" and "When a Maid Comes Knocking at Your Heart"—and, of course, Allan Jones going at "The Donkey Serenade" energetically. (He's alive in a way that Nelson Eddy never was.) Rudolf Friml dominates the music department; the movie is based on his 1912 Broadway show, sans the original libretto. The script is credited to Frances Goodrich, Albert Hackett, and Ogden Nash. With Henry Daniell, Warren William, George Zucco, Douglass Dumbrille, and Billy Gilbert. Directed by Robert Z. Leonard. M-G-M. b & w

Fires on the Plain *Nobi* (1959)—Based on the book by Shohei Ooka, which is said to be the greatest Japanese novel to have come out of the Second World War, this film, set on Leyte, is an obsessive cry of disgust. It's an appalling picture; it's also a work of epic poetry. The subject is modern man as a cannibal, and after a few minutes this subject doesn't seem at all strange or bizarre: it seems, rather, to be basic. Tamura, the hero, is one of the stragglers of the disintegrating retreating Japanese army—terrified of the Americans, the Filipinos, and of each other. Tamura walks across the plain unharmed because he is already a dead man: he is tubercular—no one wants his flesh. In the middle of this desolation, there are bonfires—ambiguous flames in the distance that kindle hope. (Perhaps they are signal fires? Perhaps Filipino farmers are burning corn husks? Perhaps there is still some normal life going on?) At the end Tamura approaches the flames and his last illusion is dispelled. Like the novel, which, as its translator, Ivan Morris, said, draws a shocking analogy between "the cannibalism of the starving soldiers . . . and the Christian doctrine of the Mass,"the film is very simple. The passion that informs the character of Tamura is so intense that he

seems both painfully close to us and remote—detached from what is ordinarily thought of as emotion. The atmosphere of the film is also remote from our ordinary world: there is nothing banal, nothing extraneous to the single-minded view of man *in extremis*. Directed by Kon Ichikawa; the script is by his wife, Natto Wada. It's a masterpiece. In Japanese. b & w (See *I Lost it at the Movies*.)

The First Circle (1972)—Alexander Ford, once head of the Polish film industry, made this version of the Alexander Solzhenitsyn novel in Denmark. It's not a great film, but it's good enough to raise the issue of the moral and intellectual choices left open when political freedom is gone. Gunther Malzacher plays Nerzhin-Solzhenitsyn—the lean, ironic gadfly-hero who is sent to Siberia to starve and die but who feels morally triumphant. Because the Scandinavian, Polish, and German actors spoke in accented English, nonaccented voices have been dubbed in for them. Under the circumstances, this seems a sensible solution, and the somewhat impersonal voices make the argument of the film easy to follow. color (See *Reeling.*)

First Love (1939)—The high moment comes at a Cinderella ball. Cinderella Deanna Durbin, in her first party dress, meets her Prince Charming (Robert Stack), sings to him, and at midnight bolts down the stairs, her slipper left behind. Working for the producer Joe Pasternak, the director, Henry Koster, patented a kind of toothsome niceness that some people used to take for wonderful entertainment. With Eugene Pallette. The script is by Bruce Manning and Lionel Houser. Universal. b & w

First Love (1970)—Nymphomania and motheaten passion and decadence poured on top of a fine Turgenev novella about an adolescent boy's crush on his father's mistress.

With the English John Moulder Brown as the boy, the French Dominique Sanda as the mistress, and the Austrian Maximilian Schell, the Italian Valentina Cortese, and assorted actors like Marius Goring and John Osborne—all playing Russians. The movie is elaborately and cleverly dubbed and post-synchronized; you're never really certain whether the slightly disembodied voices are issuing from the people you're looking at. At times, as when John Osborne, in a big black hat, recites "How Do I Love Thee?" to a gathering of sows, you may prefer to think you're not looking at the real person, either. In between the poetry readings, people visit a crypt or play with daggers and shriek and laugh. At the end, when what should have been the theme is summed up by the narrator in Turgenev's own words, the precise intelligence of what his story was about comes as a complete surprise. Schell, who directed this mélange, has a penchant for enigmatic passions and he confuses mystification with lyricism, but the film was superbly photographed by Sven Nykvist (though edited by a butcher's helper). Adapted by Schell and John Gould. color (See *Deeper into Movies*.)

First Name: Carmen *Prenom: Carmen* (1983)—In this modern-day version of the Carmen story, the director, Jean-Luc Godard, looks at the performers with the eyes of an apathetic stranger. From the way the movie is put together, it appears that he is resigned to having to tell some sort of story, but he feels it's an imposition on him—an irritation, or worse. He displaces the sensuality that people expect from a Carmen movie onto images that have no specific relation to her story—waves breaking against rocks, Paris traffic at dusk, views of a string quartet that is practicing and (sometimes) performing the Beethoven we hear on the soundtrack. Godard keeps all his sets of images in motion: he's the rare case of an artist whose command of his medium becomes more assured as his interests dry up. Working with Raoul Coutard as cinematographer, he gives you the feeling that he can do almost anything and you'll keep watching it, mesmerized by the rhythms of sound and image. The picture is Godardian in a dissociated way that is sometimes amusing but makes us condescend to it, fondly—and, after a while, not so fondly. Godard himself plays Uncle Jean, a dotty, broken-down filmmaker who mutters spacey epigrams and whacks himself in the face; his slapstick self-parody makes more connection with the audience than anything else in the shallow, withdrawn movie. Godard gives the impression that maybe he'd rather sit around listening to Beethoven quartets than make movies. He wryly (and ambivalently, of course) celebrates being out of it. The basic feel of this *Carmen* is "What's the use?" Uncle Jean's niece Carmen is played by a very pretty young Dutch actress, Maruschka Detmers; Joseph is played by Jacques Bonaffé. The script (which uses no more than a few familiar signposts of the femme-fatale genre) was adapted by Godard and/or his collaborator, Anne-Marie Miéville, from Prosper Mérimée's brief novel that became famous because of Bizet's opera. In French. color (See *State of the Art*.)

Fists in the Pocket *I Pugni in Tasca* (1966)—This first film by Marco Bellocchio must surely be one of the most astonishing directorial débuts in the history of movies, yet it is hard to know how to react to it. The direction is exhilaratingly cool and assured, and the whole movie is charged with temperament, but the material is wild. It's about a bourgeois family of diseased monsters; epileptic fits multiply between bouts of matricide, fratricide, and incest. The material is so savage that the movie often seems intended to be funny, but *why* it was so intended isn't clear.

It features the best strange-brother-and-sister act since *Les Enfants terribles*: Lou Castel, with his pug-dog manner, and Paola Pitagora, looking like a debauched gazelle. Cinematography by Alberto Marrama; music by Ennio Morricone. In Italian. b & w

Fitzcarraldo (1982)—The biggest disappointment in this epic written and directed by Werner Herzog is Peru. After a visually promising beginning, Herzog seems to lose interest in the external world (and no one in this movie has much of an internal world, either). Though the shots are lovely, they're held too long and they don't have the ghostly, kinky expressiveness of the great images that sustain one through the dragginess of *Aguirre, the Wrath of God*. Set in the 1890s, the film is about a 320-ton steamboat being dragged over a mountain that separates one tributary of the Amazon from another. At times, the ship slowly climbing the mountain seems rather magical, but 2 hours and 37 minutes is a long sit, and the deliberateness of Herzog's pacing can put you in a stupor. The sight that we wait for turns out to be a bust: when the ship is poised at the very top, it looks like a big toy. The hero, played by Klaus Kinski, is trying to get rich in the rubber trade so that he can build an opera house in the jungle and bring Caruso to sing in it. He seems meant to be a lovable loser, but it's hard to know quite what Kinski's Fitzcarraldo is because he's not like anyone else in the world—except maybe Bette Davis playing Rutger Hauer. As Molly, the whorehouse madam, Claudia Cardinale is ripely alive in this asexual movie. (For an account of its making, see the documentary *Burden of Dreams*.) In German. color (See *Taking It All In*.)

The Five-Day Lover *L'Amant de cinq jours* (1961)—In the arms of her lover, the dreamy, role-playing little nymphomaniac (Jean Se-berg) looks out over the rooftops of Paris (a scene that inevitably recalls René Clair) and rhapsodizes, "all those cells for love." She feels no bitterness at the end of an affair—"Love's a lie, a bubble," she says; "when it touches earth, it's over." Philippe de Broca's lyric boudoir comedy stays aloft in its own sphere; his originality is in his use of incongruities. Jean-Pierre Cassel (he has a witty face) is the lover; François Périer is the scholarly husband; and Micheline Presle—like a younger Tallulah Bankhead—is Cassel's couturière-mistress who pays the bills. These four are joined in a network of romance and deceit; the threads move and snap, and suddenly we see the people from different angles, here a feeling exposed, there a dream dissolved. The dialogue is graceful and often inexplicably touching: Périer, the bustling little cuckold, puts the children to bed and explains their mother's absence, "You're wondering why Mummy's late. It's because she wears high heels and they're difficult to walk on." With a lovely score by Georges Delerue. In French. b & w

Five Fingers (1952)—The spy Cicero (James Mason), a valet at the British Embassy in Ankara, sells the Germans the plans for the Normandy invasion, but the Germans think the documents are false. This suspense thriller, directed by Joseph L. Mankiewicz, sticks closely to the facts of one of the great ironic spy stories of the Second World War, yet it isn't very exciting. Something seems missing—maybe from the character of Cicero himself; we don't have much involvement with him, or with anybody else. With Danielle Darrieux, Michael Rennie, Walter Hampden, Oscar Karlweis, Herbert Berghof, and Michael Pate. The script is by Michael Wilson, based on the book *Operation Cicero*, by L. C. Moyzich; cinematography by Norbert Brodine. 20th Century-Fox. b & w

Five Graves to Cairo (1943)—Erich von Stroheim struts his stuff as Field Marshal Erwin Rommel in an ingeniously plotted melodrama about why the Germans lost at El Alamein. Billy Wilder, who directed and, with Charles Brackett, also wrote the script, based on a play by Lajos Biro, must have had something a little grander in mind; the cleverness lacks luster. With Franchot Tone, Anne Baxter, Peter Van Eyck, Akim Tamiroff, Miles Mander, Ian Keith, and Konstantin Shayne. Paramount. b & w

The Five Thousand Fingers of Dr. T. (1953)—This was cut shortly after its first disastrous showings, but later became available in its original form. The movie is mostly the nightmare-fantasy of a little boy who doesn't understand why his mother insists on his practicing the piano, and who hates his music teacher, Dr. Terwilliker. You can see why: Hans Conried is Dr. T., and he's the slimiest villain since W. C. Fields slipped the gin in Baby LeRoy's bottle. In Dr. T.'s castle, 500 boys with their 5,000 fingers are trapped at a mile-long double-decker piano. Unfortunately, good, progressive parents knowing that this was a Stanley Kramer production, from a script by Dr. Seuss, took their children to see it, and thus heard their kids scream with fear and excitement. (The kids didn't take their parents with them when they went to see *Psycho*.) With Tommy Rettig, Peter Lind Hayes, and Mary Healy. Directed by Roy Rowland; choreography by Eugene Loring; cinematography by Franz Planer; music by Frederick Hollander; Allan Scott worked on the script with Dr. Seuss (Theodore Geisel). Columbia. color

The Fixer (1968)—Borrowed grandeur can make a movie look fairly seedy, and in the Bernard Malamud book the grandeur was maybe already a little tattered. The story is about a Jew (Alan Bates) falsely accused of a crime in prerevolutionary Russia, and his refusal to confess. John Frankenheimer's version crawls along on its exalted intentions, and the Dalton Trumbo script, out of the dignity-and-indomitable-spirit-of-man school of screenwriting, is as flat as unleavened bread. You might think that Frankenheimer, who was confined to a cell for *Bird Man of Alcatraz*, would avoid being trapped again, but he's more heavily shackled than his hero. If the script and the direction had given Alan Bates some help, he might almost have carried the picture by sheer intelligence and determination; he has some promising scenes with Dirk Bogarde as a decent, melancholy magistrate—but then the magistrate dies. The cast includes Ian Holm, David Warner, Jack Gilford, Georgia Brown, Hugh Griffith, Elizabeth Hartman, Carol White, and Murray Melvin. Shot in Hungary. M-G-M. color (See *Going Steady*.)

The Flame of New Orleans (1941)—The first of the four amiable, far from great features René Clair directed in this country, and not the best (which was the 1943 *It Happened Tomorrow*). This one is a harmlessly empty-headed romantic melodrama written by Norman Krasna and set in the antebellum South. Marlene Dietrich is Claire, a good-bad girl posing as a countess while she cruises the rich men of the bayous. Roland Young is an eligible bachelor, but Bruce Cabot is the handsome sailor who makes her eyes light up. Dietrich needs more than that brief spark: these were the years when Hollywood didn't know how to use her. She's charming here, even droll, but the sensual mystery is gone. With Mischa Auer, Laura Hope Crews, Franklin Pangborn, Andy Devine, Frank Jenks, and Eddie Quillan. Cinematography by Rudolph Maté; produced by Joe Pasternak. Universal. b & w

Flamenco (1954)—The Spanish dancer Antonio (once a member of the team of Antonio and Rosario) was already a legend; he was known as one of the most intense and exciting dancers who had ever lived. In this documentary made in Spain, he performs the classical bolero against the background of the Escorial, and gypsy dances against cliffs and crumbling Moorish towers. There are 14 numbers by some of Spain's leading dancers (Pilar Lopez, Maria Luz with the Ballet Español), and by little-known village performers. There are celebrated singers and guitarists, and Juan Belmonte appears in a bullfight sequence. Directed by Edgar Neville; English titles by Walter Terry. color

The Flamingo Kid (1984)—It's the summer of 1963, and Matt Dillon is the Brooklyn kid who gets a job parking cars at El Flamingo, a beach club on Long Island. He plans to go to Columbia in the fall, but when he's taken up by the club's gin-rummy champ, Brody (Richard Crenna), a foreign-car dealer who wears silk shirts and sports a sapphire on his pinkie, he begins to think college would be a waste of time. Of course, by the end of Labor Day weekend he has got himself straightened out: he sees through Brody's flash, and learns to appreciate the fact that his own father (Hector Elizondo) is an honest man—a hardworking plumber who gives value for money. The movie is a crude, convivial sit-com about disillusionment as a rite of passage. The director, Garry Marshall, pushes you around, but in an amiable way, and he gets his laughs, though nothing carries over and the gags (along with the pop songs on the track) turn into a blur. Watching this slapped-together comedy, a viewer may begin to feel that Brody directed it. Some of the film's junkiness is enjoyable, but there's also an unenjoyable cultural fundamentalism at work. Marshall is telling us that the complications of the last two decades are unimportant. He's saying that what matters is: Listen to your honest old man and don't sell out. And he squeezes the good plumber's scenes so that they show "humanity." The moviemakers must have wanted to take advantage of the ripe possibilities for caricature in a Long Island Jewish club, but not wanted to limit their "universal" theme—so the characters' names don't provide much clue to their backgrounds. Marshall gives us ethnic humor without ethnics. With Jessica Walter, Janet Jones, Carole R. Davis, and Bronson Pinchot. The screenplay by Neal Marshall (not related to the director) was first optioned in 1972; he later revised it, and then it was rewritten by Bo Goldman, who had his name removed after the director reworked it. 20th Century-Fox. color (See *State of the Art.*)

Flamingo Road (1949)—The screen's supreme masochist—Joan Crawford—at it again. This time, she's a carnival hootchy-kootchy dancer stranded in a small town; she gets involved with a weakling—Zachary Scott, the same heel who betrayed her in *Mildred Pierce*—and she's implicated in murder again, and with the same director, Michael Curtiz, and the same producer, Jerry Wald. But the script lacks the mythic, overwrought James M. Cainisms of the earlier film. It's just garishly overwrought. The ostentatious miscasting of Sydney Greenstreet as a sheriff gives the picture a campy charm; he's a mean villain, persecuting the brave, suffering heroine—framing her, running her out of town, railroading her into prison. David Brian is the local political boss who falls in love with her; he seems not to see what we do—that she's rigid, monstrous. With Gladys George, Gertrude Michael, Tito Vuolo, and Fred Clark. Robert Wilder's script is based on a play he wrote with Sally Wilder; additional dialogue by Edmund H. North.

Music by Max Steiner; cinematography by Ted McCord. Warners. b & w

Flash Gordon (1980)—It's like a fairy tale set in a discothèque in the clouds. Up there, the arch-fiend Ming the Merciless (Max von Sydow) toys with Earth until three Earthlings—Dr. Zarkov (Topol), the golden-haired Flash Gordon (Sam J. Jones), and the cuddly Dale Arden (Melody Anderson)—go up in a rocket and crash-land at Ming's palace in Mongo. This picture has some of the knowing, pleasurable giddiness of the fast-moving Bonds. The images are flooded with the primary colors of comic strips—blue and, especially, red at its most blazing; the designer, Danilo Donati, and the cinematographer, Gil Taylor, make the colors so ripely intense that they're near-psychedelic. Ming's daughter, the tiny, voluptuous Princess Aura (Ornella Muti), wiggles and slinks through the palace wearing a shimmering scarlet jump suit; she's a flaming nympho and a perfect little emblem of camp. There's a wonderful, fairy-tale form of Russian roulette, when Flash and Timothy Dalton (as the dashing Prince Barin) take turns putting a hand into the crevices of a gnarled tree trunk, risking the fatal bite of the resident monster. The director, Mike Hodges, gets right into comic-strip sensibility and pacing. With Brian Blessed as Prince Vultan, the leader of the hawk men (who have huge wings), and Mariangela Melato and John Osborne. From a script by Lorenzo Semple, Jr.; produced by Dino De Laurentiis; music by the rock group Queen. Released by Universal. (See *Taking It All In.*)

Flashdance (1983)—A lulling, narcotizing musical, it sells the kind of romantic story that was laughed off the screen 30 years ago, and then made a comeback with *Rocky I, II,* and *III,* and it's like a sleazo putting the make on you. The 18-year-old working-class Catholic heroine (dewy-eyed face and darling smile by Jennifer Beals, dancing by Marine Jahan) is a welder by day, and a dancer in a bar at night. In her dreams, she's a ballerina, handed bouquets, like a princess. The music throughout is synthesizer pop—some of Giorgio Moroder's throbbing specials along with bits of other whiplash disco songs; basically the movie is a series of rock videos. It has Vegas sound, thumping, thumping; the whole damn thing throbs, and it gives a hard sell even to the heroine's confessions to her priest. The dancing doesn't go the way a body goes; the dancing goes the way an eggbeater goes. Richard Colon, one of a group of black "breakers," who do the only real dancing in the movie, is so fast that he isn't subjected to the chop-chop editing—he's allowed to perform in his own time. Directed by Adrian Lyne, from a script by Tom Hedley and Joe Eszterhas. Paramount. color (See *State of the Art.*)

Flatliners (1990)—This head trip about life after death is staged and shot in a baroque, hallucinatory style, and it moves, but it's unbearably preachy. It's like a small-time Sunday school lesson conducted in a vast haunted cathedral. Kiefer Sutherland, Julia Roberts, Kevin Bacon, William Baldwin, and Oliver Platt are the Chicago medical students who take part in experiments—stopping and then restarting their hearts—and learn that in the afterlife they must do penance for the bad things they've done in this one. The picture doesn't even show a sense of humor about Baldwin's sins: videotaping his sexual exploits without getting the women's consent. (Oliver Platt's line readings provide the only entertainment.) The director, Joel Schumacher, seems too gifted (visually) to be working with this soggy screenplay, by Peter Filardi, and this swelling score, by James Newton Howard. The cinematography—heavy on fire and steam and cadavers—is by

Jan De Bont; the production design is by Eugenio Zanetti. Columbia. color

Flesh and Fantasy (1943)—Three spooky stories by Oscar Wilde, Laslo Vadnay, and Ellis St. Joseph are linked together by a device involving Robert Benchley as a pragmatic type who doesn't believe in the supernatural. Produced by Charles Boyer and the director, Julien Duvivier, the film has somewhat more flair and ingenuity than Duvivier's other American trick omnibus film, *Tales of Manhattan*, but it still suffers from the overexplicit Hollywood style of the 40s, and it lacks the ease and believability of Duvivier's earlier French films. There are a few neat plot twists, though, and in addition to Boyer as a tightrope walker, the cast includes Barbara Stanwyck, Edward G. Robinson, Thomas Mitchell, Dame May Whitty, Edgar Barrier, C. Aubrey Smith, and Betty Field as a girl who has got it in her head that she isn't pretty enough to attract—hold it—blobby Robert Cummings. Universal. b & w

Flesh and the Devil (1927)—Greta Garbo, with pencil-line eyebrows above sex-drugged lids, plays a bored, sensual, wicked woman in a story about sacred and profane love, derived from a novel by Hermann Sudermann. It's far from a work of art, but Garbo was a blissfully beautiful 21 at the time, and no other actress went at the bodies of her leading men the way she did. This time John Gilbert and Lars Hanson each go a round with her. Clarence Brown directed; with Barbara Kent as the good girl. Silent. M-G-M. b & w

Fletch (1985)—Chevy Chase does some of his smoothest, most polished underplaying in this low-key, investigative-reporter-as-private-eye comedy, directed by Michael Ritchie, from a script by Andrew Bergman. (It's based on a novel by Gregory McDonald.) It's a lightweight, breezy movie with no pretense of realism. The setting is L.A., where Chase's wisecracking Fletch, who's researching an exposé on the drug scene at the beach and also trying to figure out a murder that's about to take place, wears a series of disguises. (They're tomfoolery: at 6 feet 5 inches Chase is fairly easy to spot.) It's too bad that the crime plot doesn't come to enough (nothing ever seems to be at stake) and that some of the supporting players—Richard Libertini and Geena Davis, in particular—are wasted in stock roles. Although Joe Don Baker, as a dimply, crooked police chief, has a good moment or two, the movie is really nothing but a star turn for Chase, who is required to be laid-back, deft, and, regrettably, more clever than anybody else. His line readings are beautifully timed, but smart-aleck facetiousness and smugness are built into the conception of the character; Fletch is the narrator, and even when he's talking to someone, most of the time he's putting that person on and joking directly to us. Ritchie gets everything he can out of Bergman's dialogue; he keeps the picture moving along, and its casual tone might be likable and diverting on television. In the theatre, it isn't enough, the casualness doesn't pay off, and the picture just drifts by. With Dana Wheeler-Nicholson, M. Emmet Walsh, George Wendt, Larry Flash Jenkins, Kenneth Mars, Tim Matheson, and Kareem Abdul-Jabbar as himself. Universal. color

The Flight of the Eagle *Ingenjör Andrées Luftfärd* (1982)—Jan Troell's account of the 1897 North Pole expedition by balloon undertaken by the Swedish engineer S. A. Andrée and two colleagues—all of them pitifully inexperienced aeronauts. When the balloon falls, the movie takes off, and it has the emotionally devastating effect of a major novel. (There's a heft to Troell's sensibility.) This is an epic about the suppressed hysteria and the male obsession with proving oneself by great, daring achievements which we associate with Victorianism. Troell's moviemaking here is a one-of-a-kind mixture of stolidity and lyricism, with a touch of the uncanny. He is both the cinematographer and the director, as he was on his two-part epic *The Emigrants* and *The New Land*, and also, once again, the film editor and one of the collaborators on the script. (It's based on the 1967 book by Per Olof Sundman.) With Max von Sydow as Andrée; Göran Stangertz as Nils; huge, burly Sverre Anker Ousdal as Knut; and Clément Harari as Lachambre, the balloon manufacturer. In Swedish. color (See *Taking It All In*.)

Flower Drum Song (1961)—Pseudo-Oriental Rodgers and Hammerstein musical about a Chinese girl who smuggles herself into San Francisco as a "picture bride" under contract to marry a young man she has never seen; back of the dragonish false front are such plain ancestors as *Abie's Irish Rose* and *The Jazz Singer*. If you think Joseph Fields, who wrote the screenplay, has been able to resist such wisecracks as "You got egg foo yung all over your face," you're a dreamer. Practically all the actors are of Far Eastern ancestry, which somehow heightens one's sense of disbelief instead of lessening it; Nancy Kwan, James Shigeta, Miyoshi Umeki, Juanita Hall, Benson Fong, and Jack Soo are the hardest workers. Songs can sometimes redeem a musical, but here the songs themselves are beyond redemption. Henry Koster directed, in his cloying kindergarten manner; the choreography is by Hermes Pan. Universal. color

The Fly (1958)—James Clavell—not yet a popular novelist—wrote the script for this tacky low-budget picture about a scientist whose carelessness gets him into a tragic pickle. It became a considerable box-office success. Maybe the idea of a man's head being reduced in size so that it fit onto the body of a fly was just so silly that it was rather

tantalizing. Or maybe audiences couldn't resist the final sequence: caught in a spider's web, with the spider bearing down on him, the man-fly squeaks "Help me!" in the tiniest of voices. With Vincent Price, Herbert Marshall, Patricia Owens, Kathleen Freeman, and Al (later David) Hedison as the unlucky fellow. The draggy direction is by Kurt Neumann; based on a short story by George Langelaan. (There were two less popular sequels—*The Return of the Fly* in 1959, and *The Curse of the Fly* in 1965—before the 1986 reworking of the original by David Cronenberg.) 20th Century-Fox. CinemaScope, color

The Fly (1986)—Jeff Goldblum is the brilliant loner scientist Seth Brundle who turns into Brundlefly, in David Cronenberg's remake of the 1958 horror film. Cronenberg gives the B-picture material new weight, and for what this version is it's very well done. In the opening half, Brundle and a science reporter, played by Geena Davis, become lovers, and their scenes have a romantic-comedy edge. But Cronenberg narrows the film down to one man's decaying body, and concentrates your attention on one stage after another of poor Brundle's becoming bent over double and deformed. Cronenberg wants to drive you to revulsion; that's his aim. And if the movie has a power, it's simply in our somewhat prurient fixation on watching a man rot until finally he's pleading for a coup de grâce. So, despite Goldblum's terrific performance and despite the graceful teamwork between him and Geena Davis, moviegoers may not feel that they're having such a great time. Shot in Toronto, with John Getz as the science-magazine editor and Cronenberg as the gynecologist. Based on a short story by George Langelaan; the script, by Charles Edward Pogue, was reshaped by Cronenberg. Cinematography by Stuart Cornfeld. Released by 20th Century-Fox. color (See *Hooked*.)

Flying Down to Rio (1933)—The romantic leads in this R K O musical were the dark-eyed, incomparably beautiful Dolores Del Rio as a Brazilian aristocrat, the ultra-blond Gene Raymond as an American dance-orchestra leader who's smitten by her, and soulful Raul Roulien as her Brazilian fiancé. But it's famous for being the movie in which Ginger met Fred; they were intended for comic relief. Dazzlingly slender, sexy Ginger was the brash, good-natured vocalist for Raymond's band, and Fred was the accordionist. But when they cut loose on the dance floor and did the Carioca, the glamorous triangle became an obstruction. (You begin to notice how many times Del Rio flashes her eyes haughtily.) The picture—which is almost surreally entertaining—is also famous for its madcap choreography: chorus girls dancing on the wings of planes, to the title song. In another gigantic number, people tango in mass formations to "When Orchids Bloom in the Moonlight." The black singer Etta Moten does a twinkly, flirtatious version of the "Carioca," and a troupe of black dancers are featured. The film has a bright, stylized Art Moderne look, though the pacing is ragged. With Eric Blore, Franklin Pangborn, Paul Porcasi, Luis Alberni, Clarence Muse, Roy D'Arcy, and, in a bit, Betty Furness. Directed by Thornton Freeland, from a screenplay, by Louis Brock, that's based on a play by Anne Caldwell; the dances were staged by Dave Gould. The exhilarating score, by Vincent Youmans, Edward Eliscu, and Gus Kahn, includes "Music Makes Me." The flying scenes were filmed over Malibu Beach, with backgrounds shot in Rio de Janeiro. b & w

Fog Over Frisco (1934)—One of the routine Warners gangster pictures that Bette Davis was tossed into. She's a dissolute heiress, out for thrills; her socializing with the mob lands her, at last, curled up in a rumble seat, nastily dead. It moves along but everything is stamped "synthetic," and there's time wasted on Donald Woods as a smart-aleck reporter with deadline troubles. Davis gives it that nervy flash of hers; she doesn't get much help from the likes of prissy-voiced Margaret Lindsay, or from Lyle Talbot, either. Directed by William Dieterle, from Robert N. Lee's script, based on a novel by George Dyer. With Arthur Byron, Irving Pichel, Hugh Herbert, Douglass Dumbrille, Alan Hale, Robert Barrat, and Henry O'Neill. (A 1942 remake was called *Spy Ship*.) b & w

Folies-Bergère (1935)—Maurice Chevalier, in a dual role as a famous sporting baron who's a devil with the ladies and a Folies-Bergère entertainer whose most popular number is an impersonation of the baron. Inevitably, the baron hires the entertainer to take his place, and the entertainer winds up in the boudoir of the baroness (Merle Oberon). The baroness flirts with the false baron, allowing him to think she thinks he's the real baron, and then she succumbs to the real baron, allowing him to think she believes him to be the false baron. This elaborate coquetry may sound tedious but it's surprisingly effective as a framework for slightly risqué comedy, and the plot was used again for two more musicals—for Don Ameche and Alice Faye in the 1941 *That Night in Rio*, and for Danny Kaye and Gene Tierney in the 1951 *On the Riviera*. This first film version is a sumptuous entertainment, and it was very popular. It features some lovely songs, including "You Took the Words Right Out of My Heart," "I Don't Stand a Ghost of a Chance with You," and "Rhythm of the Rain"—during this one, the chorus girls are loaded down with umbrellas and dance glumly in several inches of water. In the film's finale, those same poor girls wear straw hats, hide under large straw hats, and dance on straw hats of epic proportions. With Ann Sothern and Eric Blore. Roy Del Ruth directed. The choreography is by Dave Gould; the script by Bess Meredyth and Hal Long is based on the play *The Red Cat*, by Rudolph Lothar and Hans Adler. A 20th Century Picture; released by United Artists. b & w

Follow the Boys (1944)—When it came to putting together all-star revues (in the name of the war effort), Universal wasn't really in the same league as the major studios with their rosters of contract players, but the producer Charles K. Feldman managed to pull in a motley collection of stars. Orson Welles does his magic act and saws Marlene Dietrich in half, Zorina has a big dance number, and Jeanette MacDonald, Dinah Shore, W. C. Fields, Carmen Amaya, the Andrews Sisters, Donald O'Connor, Peggy Ryan, Arthur Rubinstein, Ted Lewis, Freddie Slack, Charlie Spivak, Louis Jordan, Lon Chaney, the Delta Rhythm Boys, and Sophie Tucker make appearances. There are scattered pleasures, such as "Is You Is or Is You Ain't My Baby?" You have to slog your way through the linking story though; it's by Lou Breslow and Gertrude Purcell, and it's about how the stars entertain the troops. Also with George Raft, George Macready, Grace McDonald, Maxie Rosenbloom, Maria Montez, and a couple dozen other well-known performers. Directed by Eddie Sutherland. b & w

Follow the Fleet (1936)—Astaire and Rogers at their most buoyant. In this one, Astaire and Randolph Scott are (implausible) shipmates, and Rogers and Harriet Hilliard are (implausible) sisters. (From Hilliard's enervated performance, one would never guess that she would go on to become a TV star and spawn a dynasty.) The material, derived from the 1922 play *Shore Leave* (which had earlier become the musical *Hit the Deck*), had grown a bit of moss. The characters aren't as rich and sophisticated as in the best-known

Astaire-Rogers movies but the corniness is alive. Astaire—chewing gum rhythmically—looks great in his bell-bottoms and he does a lot of snappy hoofing. (He's less balletic than usual here.) The numbers are mostly playful and fresh, and the Irving Berlin score includes "Let Yourself Go," "I'm Putting All My Eggs in One Basket," and the big finale, "Let's Face the Music and Dance." The cast includes Astrid Allwyn as the predatory bitch, and Betty Grable, Lucille Ball, Frank Jenks, and Tony Martin. Directed by Mark Sandrich; the script is by Dwight Taylor; the choreography is by Astaire and Hermes Pan. Produced by Pandro S. Berman, for R K O. b & w

Folly to Be Wise (1952)—This English comedy is in the nature of an anecdote—it's an unusual one because it seems to get funnier the longer it's spun out. Alastair Sim is the chaplain assigned as entertainment officer to an army camp. He decides to stage a quiz show and innocently gathers together a panel of experts that includes some rather sophisticated people—Martita Hunt, Miles Malleson, and Edward Chapman are reasonably safe, but Roland Culver, Elizabeth Allan, and Colin Gordon are, unfortunately, husband, wife, and lover. Once the question is asked, "Is marriage a good idea?" everything gets out of the flustered chaplain's control. Directed by Frank Launder, from the adaptation he and John Dighton did of James Bridie's play *It Depends What You Mean*. Cinematography by Jack Hildyard. Produced by Launder and Sidney Gilliat. b & w

Fool for Love (1985)—You'd think that if anybody could film Sam Shepard's 1983 play and keep it metaphorical and rowdy and sexually charged it would be the intuitive Robert Altman, but the material seems to congeal on the screen, and congealed rambunctiousness is not a pretty sight. The play—a carnal (and existential) screwball comedy—is about the no-exit tormented sex relationship between Eddie, a broken-down rodeo cowboy (Shepard), and his half sister, May (Kim Basinger), who lives in a cheap motel "on the edge of the Mojave Desert." It's counterculture macho (circa *Easy Rider*) gone mythic. Though this stuff isn't much, it might get by if it were just faster and more kinetic, if there were less mood and atmosphere, and Eddie and May were ferociously passionate and excitable. But Sam Shepard's adaptation opens out the play and the steam escapes. And Altman directs this adaptation almost reverently, as a series of near-static pictures. As Eddie, Shepard is a feeble presence; when he delivers Eddie's lines they have no visceral force. Kim Basinger works hard and she has a flushed, smeary-faced, wounded quality, yet she lacks spirit. Randy Quaid gives the role of Martin, May's gentleman caller, a solid, hick doggedness (and Shepard does his best acting in his hipster-outlaw gamesmanship with Quaid). As the Old Man, the lovers' father, Harry Dean Stanton has the right tequila-swigging grunginess though he doesn't seem to have any idea what he should be doing. With Sura Cox as the teen-age May, and Martha Crawford as May's mother. The cinematography is by Pierre Mignot; the country songs were written and performed by Sandy Rogers. Cannon Films. color (See *Hooked*.)

Foolish Wives (1922)—This was the first time Erich von Stroheim lost control of a film he wrote and directed; Universal cut it by about a third. What's left is still fairly overpowering: a thick mixture of fetishistic sophistication and sentimentality. It's just about impossible to sort out one's responses. Has any other filmmaker made carnal desire so revolting? This time von Stroheim is the corrupt lecher Count Karamzin, and he goes after the wife of the American ambassador to Monaco. With Mae Busch, Miss Dupont, Ce-

sare Gravina, Dale Fuller, and Maude George. Silent. b & w

Footlight Parade (1933)—This came out the same year as two other celebrated Warners musicals—*42nd Street* and *Gold Diggers of 1933*—and it has some silly, yet irresistibly wonderful examples of Busby Berkeley's pinwheel choreography. Based, possibly, on Berkeley himself, it's about a young director, played by James Cagney, who whips up ideas for the musical "prologues" which first-run movie palaces used to put on and stages them. In the latter part of this lopsided movie we get to see three of the finished products; they're built around the songs "Honeymoon Hotel," "By a Waterfall," and "Shanghai Lil." Cagney gives the picture some snap; he dances (in his amazing early-vaudeville style) and rushes around and shows off his Olivier-like eyes; Joan Blondell is tough and honest; Dick Powell sings; and Ruby Keeler dances while bending down anxiously to watch her leaden feet. Also with Guy Kibbee, Billy Barty, Hugh Herbert, Frank McHugh, Ruth Donnelly, Claire Dodd, Herman Bing, Dave O'Brien, Hobart Cavanaugh, and Jimmy Conlin. Directed by Lloyd Bacon; the script is by Manuel Seff and James Seymour; the music is by Harry Warren and Al Dubin, and Sammy Fain and Irving Kahal. b & w

Footloose (1984)—High-school kids in a mythical Midwestern community that bans rock 'n' roll and dancing—a piece of neo–Andy Hardyism, with plot elements from *Rebel Without a Cause* and dance numbers chopped to pieces in the rock-video manner of *Flashdance*. (Footloose is what they're not.) The director, Herbert Ross, and the writer, Dean Pitchford, exhaust one bad idea after another, and build up to a letdown: you don't get the climactic dance you expect. This will probably be the only rock musical ever made in which every single character is white Protestant. With Kevin Bacon as the new boy in town who challenges the bans and fights for the right of the students to have a senior prom; John Lithgow as the glum Reverend (of the town's only church); Lori Singer as the Reverend's spitfire daughter, Christopher Penn as a sluggish hayseed, and Jim Youngs, Sarah Jessica Parker, and Dianne Wiest. There's an exhilarating title sequence, a good brief scene with a little boy asleep in church, and an entertaining passage in which Bacon teaches Penn to dance. And despite the retrograde material, Lori Singer has a startling radiance, and Penn manages to be funny and appealing. Edited by Paul Hirsch. Paramount. color (See *State of the Art*.)

For Me and My Gal (1942)—Fresh from his Broadway success in *Pal Joey*, Gene Kelly made his movie début here as a good-bad guy, playing opposite Judy Garland. They are a vaudeville team who are just getting their big break when Kelly is inducted (the period is the First World War); he deliberately injures his hand so he won't have to fight and—the movie having been made during the Second World War—he must then reform and become a gallant hero. The story is naïvely patriotic and sentimental, but Kelly is amazingly fresh; his grin could melt stone, and he and Garland are a magical pair (especially when they're singing "The bells are ringing for me and my gal"). The songs include "Ballin' the Jack," "Smiles," and "After You've Gone," and there are some nifty comedy routines featuring Kelly and Ben Blue. Produced by Arthur Freed and directed by Busby Berkeley; with George Murphy, Horace (later Stephen) McNally, Richard Quine, Keenan Wynn, and Marta Eggerth. The writers were Fred Finklehoffe, Sid Silvers, Richard Sherman, and Howard Emmett Rogers. M-G-M. b & w

For Whom the Bell Tolls (1943)—Everybody concerned must have thought they were making a classic out of the Hemingway novel, but what with the typical Hollywood compromises, plus the political pressures from Spain and from Catholics—or the fears of such pressures—the whole thing became amorphous and confused. Paramount did rather better by the romance than the politics: Ingrid Bergman is lovely and affecting as Maria. (It's one of her best performances.) Hand-picked by Hemingway to be his hero, Gary Cooper does well, though occasionally he falls into his simpering and, at times, he seems to fade into the background. The film is populated with other famous actors who stand out too much, and most of them go wrong in one scene or another. They include Katina Paxinou, Akim Tamiroff, Arturo de Cordova, Vladimir Sokoloff, Mikhail Rasumny, George Coulouris, Joseph Calleia, Alexander Granach, and many others—even Yvonne De Carlo. The director, Sam Wood, seems to have his hands too full. Dudley Nichols did the screenplay. Paramount. color

For Your Eyes Only (1981)—The 12th James Bond film goes through the motions, but not only are we tired of them, the actors are tired of them—even the machines are tired. It has got to the point where if the machines do something they haven't done before, we've seen it before anyway. Roger Moore is Bond again, and his idea of Bond's imperturbable cool is the same as playing dead. The producers have made the mistake of deciding on a simpler, more realistic package, without dazzling sets or a big, mad supervillain. The heroine (Carole Bouquet) is a lovely tall brunette who photographs like a goddess but has no more animation than the hero; the only jazziness in the movie comes from Lynn-Holly Johnson, playing a teen-age trollop who's a champion ice skater. With Topol, Julian Glover, Jill Bennett, Cassandra Harris, and Janet Brown as the Prime Minister. Directed by John Glen; written by Richard Maibaum and Michael Wilson. Produced by Albert R. Broccoli. United Artists. color

Forbidden (1932)—Movies about women who sacrifice everything for their married lovers or their illegitimate babies were big box office in the 20s and 30s, but they were generally concocted by masters of the tearjerking craft, as in *Back Street*, *Madame X*, *Stella Dallas*, *The Sin of Madelon Claudet*. The director, Frank Capra, wrote this story himself, and he just didn't have the knack. The heroine is unbelievably sacrificial over a span of twenty years, and despite Barbara Stanwyck's amazingly unaffected, straightforward performance, most of the picture is lifeless. As the lover, Adolphe Menjou has the self-possession of a man with power; you can understand the heroine's attraction to him. But that's as far as plausibility goes. She gives up her baby girl to this lover, to be raised by his childless wife; she marries a nasty newspaperman (Ralph Bellamy) in order to further the lover's political career; she shoots her husband when he threatens to expose the liaison. Even after she's been in prison, she's still protecting her lover's good name. Jo Swerling's dialogue doesn't help: early on, when the heroine arrives late at her secretarial job and her boss asks if she realizes what time it is, she replies, "It is springtime." And there are such unfortunate lines as Menjou's casual, chatty remark to her (when she's already pregnant): "I meant to tell you before that I was married." Capra doesn't dwell on the sad scenes; the picture moves along so efficiently that it doesn't seem maudlin. It just seems a little crazy. Joseph Walker was the cinematographer; with Dorothy Peterson, Charlotte V. Henry, and Myrna Fresholt. Columbia. b & w

Forbidden Games *Jeux interdits* (1952)—René Clément's beautiful, lacerating film on the themes of innocence, Christianity, war, and death. It is perhaps the greatest war film since *La Grande Illusion*. (Neither deals with actual warfare.) On a crowded highway outside Paris in 1940, a delicate 5-year-old girl wanders away from the strafed bodies of her parents, clutching her dead puppy in her arms. She and an 11-year-old peasant boy become playmates: their game—their passion—is to collect dead animals for their private cemetery, and for this game they steal crosses from churches and graveyards. Clément's method of presentation—a series of harsh contrasts, with on the one side the intuitive, lyric understanding between the two children and on the other the ludicrous comedy of the quarrelsome, ignorant peasant adults—is perhaps unfair to the adults. But it's an act of kindness to the audience: without this element of gross caricature, we might dissolve in tears. This classic of the French postwar period was a commercial failure until it won the grand prize at Venice; it went on to international success. With Brigitte Fossey and Georges Poujouly. From the novel by François Boyer. In French. b & w (See *I Lost it at the Movies*.)

Forbidden Planet (1956)—The best of the science-fiction interstellar productions of the 50s lifted its plot and atmosphere from Shakespeare: the magical island of *The Tempest* becomes the planet Altair-4, where the sky is green and the sand is pink and there are two moons. The magician Prospero becomes the mad scientist Morbius (Walter Pidgeon); Prospero's daughter Miranda, who knows no man except her father, is Altaira (Anne Francis); and (though this is less clear) the sprite Ariel becomes Robby, the friendly robot. Caliban has become a marvellously flamboyant monster out of Freud—pure id. It's a pity the film, directed by Fred Wilcox, didn't lift some of Shakespeare's dialogue: it's hard to believe you're in the heavens when the diction of the hero (Leslie Nielsen) and his spaceshipmates flattens you down to Kansas. (More serviceable than one might suspect, *The Tempest* in the 40s had been set in a ghost town at the edge of a desert in *Yellow Sky*, and with a humor frequently indulged in under cover of the Western genre, Miranda became Anne Baxter's Mike.) M-G-M. CinemaScope, color

Forced March (1989)—Chris Sarandon plays an American television star, of Hungarian-Jewish parentage, who leaves his Beverly Hills swimming pool and goes to Europe to star in a fact-based film about Miklos Radnoti, the famous Hungarian-Jewish poet—he was killed near the end of the Second World War, during a forced march from a labor camp in Yugoslavia to Hungary. Directed by Rick King, from a script by Dick Atkins and Charles K. Bardosh, the American-Hungarian co-production is about the effect on the "spoiled" TV star of playing an authentic, suffering artist of the past. There's an idea here, but the moviemakers don't seem sure what to do with it. The material never comes to enough—it's serious (in a slightly affected way), well paced, and utterly uninspired. It simply isn't as deep as it wants to be. With Josef Sommer, Renée Soutendijk, and John Seitz as the sadistic director of the film within a film. color

A Foreign Affair (1948)—This deliberately cynical political farce by the team of Charles Brackett (producer) and Billy Wilder (director) often seems on the verge of being funny, but the humor is too clumsily forced. (The next picture Brackett and Wilder made was *Sunset Boulevard*; the jump was enormous.) As Phoebe Frost, a spinster congresswoman from Iowa investigating the morale of the American forces in Occupied Berlin, Jean Ar-

thur looks far from her best; she hasn't much to do but act primly shocked at corruption, and then, turning womanly, get into a glittering evening gown, put a flower in her hair, and go after an Army captain—lacklustre John Lund. It's a formula that suited her better some years earlier, and so Marlene Dietrich, as Phoebe's rival—worldly-wise Erika von Schlutow, former mistress of a high-ranking Nazi and now a singer in a cellar called the Lorelei—comes off rather better, though her songs (by Frederick Hollander) are not memorable. With Millard Mitchell, and, in a bit part, Freddie Steele. Written by Brackett, Wilder, Richard Breen, and Robert Harari. Paramount. b & w

Foreign Correspondent (1940)—Hitchcock appears to have concocted this spy thriller out of all the breathtaking climaxes he'd been hoarding; there's the assassination with the gun concealed by a newsman's camera, the Dutch windmill going against the wind, and a tremendous finale aboard a transatlantic plane from London on the very day war is declared. The plot that links all this is barely functional, and the jaunty reporter-hero (Joel McCrea) is held down a bit when he has to attend to the ever-busy heroine (Laraine Day), but the movie is intermittently first-rate, and the topnotch supporting cast includes George Sanders, Albert Basserman, Herbert Marshall, Edmund Gwenn, Martin Kosleck, Eduardo Ciannelli, Barbara Pepper, and Robert Benchley, who also had a hand in the dialogue. The script was by Charles Bennett and Joan Harrison. Produced by Walter Wanger; released by United Artists. b & w

Forever Amber (1947)—This bowdlerization follows Kathleen Winsor's novel as if her narrative line had been carved in sacred stone; maybe the literalness is what does it in, despite the efforts of the director, Otto Preminger, to be colorful and gamy. In this view of the Restoration, all males are so sex-starved that a sudden glance from a female reduces them to gibbering lust. Linda Darnell is rounded and enticing but she doesn't have the flash or variety to carry off the starring role. With Cornel Wilde, Richard Greene, George Sanders as Charles II, Richard Haydn, Jessica Tandy, Glenn Langan, Anne Revere, Leo G. Carroll, and Robert Coote. Music by David Raksin; the less than scintillating script is by Philip Dunne and Ring Lardner, Jr. 20th Century-Fox. color

Forsaking All Others (1934)—Joan Crawford's 30s melodramas are such tinselled toys that they can be completely unconvincing and still be hypnotic. Swathed in Adrian dresses here, and flanked by Clark Gable and Robert Montgomery, she stares at us solemnly, directly—as if challenging us to come to terms with her overwrought modern-woman's problems. In this role, which Tallulah Bankhead had played on Broadway, she's deserted at the altar by Montgomery, then meets Gable and goes on to give Montgomery the same treatment he gave her. In manner, Crawford is somewhere between the lively flapper excitement that made her a star (she could still look sexed to the gills) and the agonized, toothachy concentration that became her style for dramatic acting in the 40s. W. S. Van Dyke directed from Joseph L. Mankiewicz's adaptation of the play by E. B. Roberts and F. M. Cavett. With Rosalind Russell, Billie Burke, Charles Butterworth, Frances Drake, and Arthur Treacher. M-G-M. b & w

Fort Apache (1948)—Henry Fonda, as an imperious, wrong-headed lieutenant colonel whose men are massacred because they obey him; the John Ford film, set after the Civil War, never suggests that they should defy him, though he's practically a certifiable maniac. This is one of Ford's beautiful but irritating epic Westerns. The fights and dances and other big scenes are triumphs of staging, but the coy love interest (Shirley Temple and John Agar) and the Irish horseplay are infantile. And the whole picture is bathed in a special form of patriotic sentimentality: scenes are held so that we cannot fail to appreciate the beauty of the American past. With John Wayne, Ward Bond, Anna Lee, Victor McLaglen, Pedro Armendariz, Mae Marsh, Irene Rich, and George O'Brien. The screenplay by Frank S. Nugent was suggested by the story "Massacre" by James Warner Bellah. R K O. b & w

Fort Apache, the Bronx (1981)—It takes a long time for an actor to develop the assurance that the trim, silver-haired Paul Newman has acquired, and there's a bloom on everything he does in the role of Murphy, the veteran of 18 years on the New York police force, who has spent most of those years in the rotting 41st Precinct, in the South Bronx—the most shattered, crime-ridden section of the city. Murphy and his young partner, Corelli (dark-haired, loose-limbed Ken Wahl), do the best they can in dealing with muggers, arsonists, pimps, pushers, and killers—one of them a fellow-officer, Morgan (Danny Aiello), who throws a Puerto Rican teen-ager off a roof. The film is an attempt to show urban crisis *in extremis*, and it's an expression of disgust at racism. But the director, Daniel Petrie, glides over the action, levelling things out, shooting on the hellhole Bronx locations as if he were making a travelogue. Heywood Gould's script, which is based on the accounts of two policemen (Thomas Mulhearn and Pete Tessitore), is an intricately designed mixture of street vaudeville and drama of conscience. The film has many of the ingredients of a shocking, memorable movie, but it's shallow and earnest. Its point is that Murphy's faith in the police is undermined by Morgan's racist action; Murphy can't understand how a cop could do such a horrible thing. For the movie to be really good he would have to understand all too well. It's a mess, with glimmerings of talent and with Newman's near-great performance. The cast includes Rachel Ticotin as a Hispanic nurse, Pam Grier as a stoned hooker, Ed Asner in the tired role of the martinet who takes over as commanding officer at the precinct, Miguel Piñero as a drug dealer, and Kathleen Beller as Corelli's girlfriend. A Time-Life Production; released by 20th Century-Fox. color (See *Taking It All In*.)

The Fortune (1975)—Charmless slapstick farce set in the 20s, with Warren Beatty as a larcenous sheik and Jack Nicholson as a gleaming-eyed lowlifer and freaky coward. These two play mercenary clowns who fumble in their attempts to kill a plump-cheeked heiress (Stockard Channing). Mike Nichols directed, from a screenplay by Adrien Joyce (a pseudonym for Carol Eastman). The tone is too playful, too bright. Is the heiress herself meant to be a treasure? Is she meant to be charmingly klutzy? You can't tell. The whole thing seems to exist in a frame of reference that rules out feeling, but then the heiress's mascara is smeared at the end; this suggests that she's capable of suffering, though she has never been permitted a human emotion, such as believing in the two men. Some vital element seems to be missing from the film— affection, maybe, or confidence in the insulated, cloud-cuckoo-land atmosphere (which may remind you of Elaine May's much friendlier *A New Leaf*). Nicholson, with his sparse hair frizzed out in all directions, comes through the best; at moments he lifts himself single-handed into slapstick, like a demented Laurel & Hardy in one. With Scatman Crothers, Richard B. Shull, Dub Taylor, Ian Wolfe, and Florence Stanley. Columbia. color

The Fortune Cookie (1966)—A sour, visually ugly comedy from director Billy Wilder and his co-writer, I. A. L. Diamond, which gets worse as it goes along—more cynical and more sanctimonious. Jack Lemmon plays a TV cameraman who is accidentally knocked unconscious in the course of covering a football game; Walter Matthau (the only possible excuse for seeing the picture) is Whiplash Willie, Lemmon's venomous, shyster-lawyer brother-in-law, who hatches a plot to bilk the insurance companies. By the time that Ron Rich, the decent, heartsick black football player who knocked Lemmon down, arrives to take care of him, and they become loving buddies, only Leslie ("Come back to the raft ag'in, Huck honey") Fiedler could care. With Cliff Osmond, Judi West, Lurene Tuttle, Les Tremayne, Ann Shoemaker, Ned Glass, Archie Moore, and Sig Rumann. United Artists. b & w

40 Carats (1973)—The sort of strained, wisecracking frivolity that can be a hit on Broadway but all too often congeals on the screen. The affair of the 40-year-old Liv Ullmann and the 22-year-old Edward Albert is meant to be romantic and slightly daring, but the miscast Ullmann doesn't have the dryness for comedy. She's much too touching and anxious for her superficial role, and she and the wet-lipped young Albert are a dismaying pair. At this point Ullmann's English was heavily accented, and she articulates her colloquial lines with considerable difficulty. You sympathize with her instead of laughing. Directed by Milton Katselas, from Leonard Gershe's adaptation of the Broadway play by Jay Presson Allen, based on a Parisian success by Pierre Barillet and J. C. Gredy. With Gene Kelly, who looks too old to be Ullmann's ex-husband but has a few likable bits and one inventive moment when he kicks an imaginary child, and Binnie Barnes, Deborah

Raffin, Nancy Walker, Rosemary Murphy, Natalie Schaefer, Billy Green Bush, and Don Porter. Columbia. color

48 Hrs. (1982)—Walter Hill's fast and brutal action comedy is a roller coaster that hurtles along. Nick Nolte plays a San Francisco police detective and Eddie Murphy (making his movie début) is a young hipster thief who outsmarts him by his hustler's verbal finesse and his black man's sense of irony. The detective has been turned into a rabid honkie so that the sleek 21-year-old Murphy can be the underdog hero and deliver the zingers. The two set out as brawling and cursing enemies and, of course, become guffawing pals; the racial infighting is what gives the film its charge. You're probably meant to think that this paranoid fantasy of race relations is what the TV shows with black and white buddies don't have the guts to let you see. It's as false as they are but in a hip way. It's like *The French Connection*, *Dirty Harry*, *Butch Cassidy and the Sundance Kid*, and a half-dozen other films all put in a compactor, smashed, and pressed into cartoon form. Hill loads some of the scenes with style because they have no other weight. With Annette O'Toole, Frank McRae, James Remar, Sonny Landham, Brion James, Olivia Brown, David Patrick Kelly, and the Busboys. The script is by Roger Spottiswoode, Hill, Larry Gross, and Steven E. de Souza; the cinematography is by Ric Waite. (A sequel, *Another 48 Hrs.*, was released in 1990.) Paramount. color (See *Taking It All In*.)

The Forty-First *Sorok Pervyi* (1956)—Visually, this Soviet film is extraordinary—magnificent scenes in the Asian desert, storms at sea in exquisite silvery blues. The content is a "tragic" love story set in the civil war period. The point of the film is supposed to be that the Red Army girl, who has killed 40

men, falls in love with a White officer, but learns that class conflicts are stronger than love—and he becomes her 41st. This is not likely to be what you'll make of it, though. It runs along rather like an entertaining Hollywood action movie of an earlier era, and the decadent Cossack is so much more attractive than the good Red Army men that you may begin to wonder if sex appeal is a right-wing deviation. The Cossack's suggestion that he and the girl get the hell out of Russia seems remarkably sensible, and when the rather monolithic heroine shoots him down, you're very likely to take the politically frivolous view that she's simpleminded—where would she find another man like that? This was the first film directed by Grigori Chukrai, fresh out of the State Institute of Cinematography. (It was a remake of a 1927 Russian film, based on a novel by Boris Lavrenyov.) In Russian. color

42nd Street (1933)—This big, cheerful Warners musical was based on a novel by Bradford Ropes but was also an unofficial remake of the 1929 *On with the Show*; it gave new life to the clichés that have kept parodists happy—what's surprising is how organic the clichés once were. The backstage story is pleasantly tawdry and corny. Warner Baxter is the great Broadway producer-director (with heart trouble) who makes the memorable (and much lampooned) speech: "Miss Sawyer, you listen to me . . . and you listen hard. Two hundred people, 200 jobs, $200,000, five weeks of grind and blood and sweat depend upon you! It's the lives of all these people who've worked with you. You've got to go on and you've got to give, and give and give! They've got to like you, got to. You understand? You can't fall down, you can't. Because your future's in it, my future and everything all of us have is staked on you. All right now, I'm through. But you keep your feet on the ground and your head on those shoulders of yours, and, Sawyer, you're going out a youngster, but you've got to come back a star!'' Peggy Sawyer, the understudy who has to go on for the star, is Ruby Keeler, who wears little puffed sleeves (for innocence) even in her rehearsal clothes; training her for the opening, the tough Baxter never tells her to stop looking at her feet—and neither, apparently, did the film's choreographer, Busby Berkeley. It's hard to decide which is klunkier—her dancing or her line readings—but it's just about impossible not to like her. (She had to play the nice girl—what else could she play?) Bebe Daniels is the fading star (in fox furs) who breaks her ankle; George Brent is her lover; Dick Powell is the singing and smiling twerpy juvenile; Ginger Rogers is the gold-digging chorine known as the ''countess''; Guy Kibbee is a sugar daddy; Una Merkel and Toby Wing are in the chorus. Also with Ned Sparks, Allen Jenkins, George E. Stone, Robert McWade, Eddie Nugent, and Henry B. Walthall. The songs by Harry Warren and Al Dubin (who make brief appearances) include ''Shuffle Off to Buffalo,'' ''You're Getting to Be a Habit with Me,'' ''Young and Healthy,'' and, of course, ''42nd Street.'' Lloyd Bacon directed; the screenplay is by Rian James and James Seymour; cinematography by Sol Polito. It may be noted that there's no penetrable internal logic for the variations in Busby Berkeley's kaleidoscopic dance numbers. (That's part of their surreal charm; so is his indifference to the dancing—he's interested only in the patterns.) And they have no external logic, either—what conceivable story-line Broadway show could they fit into? Apparently Berkeley devised his choreographic spectacles on his own, without reference to the script, and without worrying about whether they would pass as parts of one musical. The director and the editors couldn't figure out how to insert them strategically, and so at the end, there are three big numbers, one right after another. b & w

The Fountainhead (1949)—A little delirious and definitely skewed. Can people who see this picture ever forget the sight of the silvery-blond columnist Dominique (Patricia Neal) galloping up on her black horse and slashing her riding crop across the face of the tall, mocking stranger who had looked at her impertinently while he was using a pneumatic drill in the quarry? He's the genius architect Howard Roark (Gary Cooper). When his design for a public-housing project is altered, he dynamites the building; put on trial, he justifies his action with an attack on collectivism and the parasites of the left. Ayn Rand wrote the screenplay, based on her 1943 novel, and true to her hero's principles, she wouldn't permit any changes in her (megalomaniac, comic-book) dialogue. King Vidor directed this paean to the individualism of ''superior'' people, made in a sleek, hollow, Expressionist style that owes a lot to *film noir*. It's an extravaganza of romantic, right-wing camp, with the hyper-articulate superman Roark standing in the wind on top of a phallic skyscraper, and the fierce, passionate Dominique rising in an open elevator to join him there. Despite Rand's denials, Roark was said to be based on Frank Lloyd Wright, and Vidor wanted Wright to design Roark's buildings, but had to settle for some bland imitations. The futurist structures are often obvious models and painted backgrounds. With Raymond Massey as the newspaper tycoon; Kent Smith as the mediocre architect; Robert Douglas as the despicable architecture critic; Henry Hull as Roark's Louis Sullivan–like teacher; and Ray Collins and Jerome Cowan. Warners. b & w

Four Bags Full *La Traversée de Paris* (1957)—When Marcel Aymé's long short story was published in *Partisan Review*, it was called simply "Crossing Paris"; this explosively funny movie version, directed by Claude Autant-Lara, was known in England as *Pig Across Paris*; in the U.S. it was called *Four Bags Full*, but was unknown under any title. Somehow it never caught on here. (It had won the award for best film of the year in France.) The period is the German Occupation: a petty, anxious black marketeer (Bourvil) hires a helper (Jean Gabin) for a night's work—transporting a slaughtered pig across Paris to a butcher in Montmartre. The helper, a famous painter who has taken on the job for the hell of it, has an uproarious night, teasing his dull companion, outwitting both the French police and the German soldiers. Bourvil was selected best actor at Venice for his performance, but the star of the film is Gabin, lusty and powerful as the man who enjoys life so much he can play games with it. In the middle of sordid little perils, the artist devises quick-witted solutions, and then howls with delight, "This pig's making a genius of me!" The contrast between him and the terrified, sweating fellow at his side makes you know you're watching a fable, but Autant-Lara shows class—he doesn't tie it with a ribbon and hand it to you. Screenplay by Jean Aurenche and Pierre Bost. In French.

Four Daughters (1938)—This picture was hugely popular, and you can still feel why. It sets up a happy small-town family—a widowed doctor of music (Claude Rains) and his four musical daughters (Priscilla, Rosemary, and Lola Lane and Gale Page) whose interplay gives off some sparks. All four of the girls are dazzled by a handsome, confident young composer (Jeffrey Lynn), but he brings in a piano player he has hired to do the orchestration on his new composition, and this big-city musician—a cynical loser who claims that the fates have always been against him—disrupts the apparent harmony of the all-American household. This loser was the first important film role for John Garfield, and he's more original and surprising than he was ever to be again. It's as if an Odets depression hero—ethnic and resentful, with a quizzical eyebrow and a hefty chip on his shoulder—had stormed into the Waspy decorum of the 1933 *Little Women*. Garfield's negativism energizes the movie: you see the birth of a new kind of star. (Later, his loser number got stylized.) Directed by Michael Curtiz, from a lively script, by Julius Epstein and Lenore Coffee, that's based on Fannie Hurst's novel *Sister Act*, the movie is very shrewdly conceived, even though Rains is allowed to mug and there's a lot of over-obvious acting. Fannie Hurst's sentimental realism—it has a heartless, practical side—is something you can't fight off. (There's a good piece of editing when one of the sisters announces her engagement to the composer, and the other girls' suddenly stricken expressions give way to their announcements of plans.) With May Robson, Frank McHugh, and Dick Foran. (Remade, in 1955, as *Young at Heart*, with Frank Sinatra in the Garfield role.) Warners. b & w

The Four Feathers (1929)—The A.E.W. Mason novel, one of the kitsch classics of British colonial gallantry, was first filmed in 1921, and again, after this version, in 1939 and 1955, and then as a made-for-TV movie. Here, Richard Arlen is the young officer who shows a streak of cowardice; before he can redeem himself by becoming the bravest of the brave, his beautiful fiancée (Fay Wray) throws him over, and his comrades (Clive Brook, William Powell, and Theodore Von Eltz) break with him. It's Paramount mid-Victorian, with the hero, at the climax, trapped in an outpost in the Sudan that is besieged by "fuzzy-wuzzies"; the sight of the British relief column is meant to stir the audience's patriotic emotions. But the directors, Merian C. Cooper, Ernest B. Schoedsack, and Lothar

Mendes, tip us off about where their real feelings are: a sequence of baboon families in flight from a jungle fire and crossing a river is far and away the finest footage in the film. There's a standard sub-theme in the colonial movies: a native child or bearer, befriended by the hero, is loyal to him to the death; in this movie, the hero's friendship with a black child is far more tender than his relationship with his fiancée. With Noah Beery, Noble Johnson, George Fawcett, Zack Williams, Harold Hightower, and Philippe De Lacy as Arlen as a child. The script is by Howard Estabrook. The African footage was shot on location. Silent, except for a musical score and sound effects. b & w

Four Friends (1981)—Arthur Penn goes laboriously, painfully wrong in this story about the friendship of three boys and the girl each of them loves at some time—a friendship that spans the American social changes of the 60s, and takes the four through adolescence (in Indiana) to maturity. The script is a semi-autobiographical account by Steve Tesich of the arrival in this country of a Yugoslavian working-class youth, Danilo, who comes with a big, heavy symbolic trunk—it seems to be full of solid values. There's a wholesome, beefy moralism in Tesich's writing, particularly in his sense of humor, and Penn, trying for a large-scale social vision, brings out its hearty bouquet. The film combines the worst of the Freudianism and self-pity of the William Inge–Elia Kazan *Splendor in the Grass* with the worst of the big, immigrant theme of Kazan's *America America*, and in order to accommodate a whole catalogue of symbolic events of the 60s—everything from a race riot to the landing on the moon—the plot bounces along exhaustingly. The characters are always learning life's important lessons. In a key sequence we get crosscutting between Danilo folk-dancing in the sunshine with his immigrant-worker friends and the

girl with her soul-sick druggie-hippie pals at a strobe-lighted psychedelic revel that features acid and a suicide in flames. It's health versus sickness, life versus death. And the movie carefully spells out which side it's on. The colorless quartet is made up of Craig Wasson as Danilo, Jodi Thelen as the girl, Jim Metzler, and Michael Huddleston. Also with Miklos Simon, Reed Birney, Julia Murray, James Leo Herlihy as a rotten-rich swine, and Lois Smith as his wife—she gets to let out a yelping sound that's like the grandmommy of a scream. So may you. Filmways. color (See *Taking It All In*.)

The Four Musketeers (The Revenge of Milady), see *The Three Musketeers (The Queen's Diamonds)*

Four Nights of a Dreamer *Quatre Nuits d'un rêveur* (1971)—Robert Bresson used to postpone emotion deliberately; here he postpones it indefinitely. Expressionlessly, the non-actors talk of love in this adaptation of the same early Dostoevski story, "White Nights," that Visconti filmed in 1957. Bresson sets it in modern Paris, in color, and with pop music on the track, but the Paris his characters live in might be a crypt. The mixture of the director's famed austerity with this sort of facetiousness is a mistake: the picture borders on deadpan absurdity. With Isabelle Weingarten, Guillaume Des Forets, and Jean-Maurice Monnoyer. In French.

The 4th Man *De Vierde Man* (1982)—The dialogue is slangy and pungent. The Dutch director Paul Verhoeven and his usual scenarist, Gerard Soeteman, are out to give us a shockingly good time in this thriller about a homosexual writer (Jeroen Krabbé) who allows himself to be pampered by a rich blond widow (Renée Soutendijk), because he has a passionate yen for her longtime lover. The film's comic tone depends on our being tickled by the writer's arrogance and mean-spiritedness. When he sneakily maneuvers the widow into inviting her lover for a visit, he's reminiscent of James Mason's Humbert Humbert in Kubrick's *Lolita*, courting Mrs. Haze while he can't wait to get his hands on her daughter. At a literary gathering that recalls the one in *The Third Man*, the writer explains that he takes incidents from life and embroiders them, and all through the movie we see glimpses of his embroideries. They're not conscious, they're involuntary imaginings—omens, forebodings, warnings. Some of these dream glimpses relate to Ingmar Bergman movies, some of them to religious symbolism (the writer is a Catholic), and some to his phobia about women. In his visions, the widow is a deadly spider and castrater—a witch. What keeps the movie from being any more than a tongue-in-cheek homoerotic fantasy is that the widow, who needs to be a teasingly ambiguous figure—so that we can't tell if the writer is deluding himself that she's a killer who has already dispatched three husbands, or if his hyperactive imagination is alerting him to the truth—is disappointingly placid, a blank. But the film is amusing, and the talented Jeroen Krabbé plays worminess exuberantly. Adapted from a novel by the Netherlands writer Gerard Reve, who lends the writer-protagonist his own name. A Spectrafilm release. In Dutch. color (See *State of the Art*.)

The Fox (1968)—This is D. H. Lawrence's 1923 novella stripped of its subtlety, Freudianized, and turned into something resembling Lillian Hellman's *The Children's Hour*, but in a woodsy setting. It's now a story about two young women—sickly, chattering, ultra-feminine Jill (Sandy Dennis) and dark, quiet, strong March (Anne Heywood)—who are trying, rather hopelessly, to run a chicken farm in Canada. There is some symbolism about a fox that has been raiding the hen coop, and along comes a marauding male (Keir Dullea, with his voice lowered to indicate masculine strength), who kills the fox, puts the farm in order, and proposes to March, thus awakening the lesbianism dormant in the women. In making the movie sexually explicit, the adapters, Lewis John Carlino and Howard Koch, and the director, Mark Rydell, have diminished the material—have made it tamely "sexy" and brightly colored and "healthy." You have to go back to Lawrence to see how much more powerful and frightening the repressed sexuality that he was writing about was. Warners. (See *Going Steady*.)

Frankenstein (1931)—Probably the most famous of all horror films, and one of the best. It was not the first version of the Mary Shelley novel (there had been a *Frankenstein* as early as 1910), but this version, directed by James Whale, with Boris Karloff as the sad, lumbering Monster and Colin Clive as the high-strung, tormented Dr. Frankenstein, caught the imagination of a large public—and has held it for decades. With Mae Clarke, John Boles, Edward Van Sloan, and Dwight Frye as the Monster's first victim. Universal. (A few of the original prints were tinted an eerie green—"the color of fear.") b & w

Frantic (1957), see *Elevator to the Gallows*

Frantic (1988)—It begins promisingly, with Harrison Ford as a San Francisco heart surgeon who comes to Paris with his wife (Betty Buckley); they arrive at their hotel and while he takes a shower she disappears. The director, Roman Polanski, shows his guile and wit, but a thriller needs more than an occasional perverse undertone; it needs some design, some shapeliness. This thing grinds on without ever being able to compensate for its pathetic plot and its unwritten characters. It involves mixed-up suitcases and a couple of nightclubs and rooftops, and dope dealers and Arabs and a childlike, amoral tootsie (Emmanuelle Seigner). The script is credited to Polanski and Gérard Brach; the cinematography is by Witold Sobocinski; the music is by Ennio Morricone. With brief appearances by Alexandra Stewart and David Huddleston. Warners. color (See *Hooked*.)

Freaks (1932)—The original ads quoted Louella Parsons, who said, "For pure sensationalism *Freaks* tops any picture yet produced." She wasn't far off, and it's still a shocker. Though this circus story, directed by Tod Browning, is superficially sympathetic to the maimed and the mindless that it features, it uses images of physical deformity for their enormous potential of horror, and at the end, when the pinheads and the armless and legless creatures scurry about to revenge themselves on a normal woman (Olga Baclanova), the film becomes a true nightmare. If this film were a silent it might be harder to shake off, but the naïve, sentimental talk helps us keep our distance. With Leila Hyams, Wallace Ford, Harry and Daisy Earles, Johnny Eck (who had half a torso), Randion (known as the Living Torso), the Siamese twins Daisy and Violet Hilton, Roscoe Ates, Edward Brophy, and Henry Victor as the strong man. Adapted from the story "Spurs," by Tod Robbins. M-G-M. b & w

A Free Soul (1931)—This wheezing melodrama was a sensational success. Adela Rogers St. John, the daughter of a lawyer, wrote the story about a brilliant alcoholic lawyer (Lionel Barrymore) whose independent, "free" daughter (Norma Shearer) had a hot affair with a man whom her father had got acquitted on a murder charge—a racketeer known as Ace (Clark Gable). Shearer's acting is dreadful (she seems to be working hard to show *poise*), but she was in her bold-indiscreet-modern-woman period and looks sexily undressed in her silky Adrian gowns. Gable had erotic menace in his villainous role, and he gives the picture its only charge. (This was the performance that made him a star.) Things get pitifully maudlin when highminded Leslie Howard, Shearer's former fiancé, shoots Gable and is defended by Barrymore, and Barrymore hams fearfully (he got an Academy Award for it); the father's courtroom plea for Howard is that the whole mess is really *his* fault—that he didn't give his daughter firm enough guidelines. (He finishes his overwrought summation and drops dead.) This is a vintage fraudulently "daring" movie in the glossy-hokey M-G-M style. Clarence Brown directed, from John Meehan's script. With James Gleason. b & w

Freebie and the Bean (1974)—James Caan mugs and Alan Arkin, deadfaced and overcontrolled, relies on vocal tricks—hesitation humor, mostly—to do his acting. They're playing cop-buddies in San Franciso, and they swallow so many of their lines that it could be they're ashamed to say them. There's a beating or a killing or, at least, a yelling scene every couple of minutes in this spoofy slapstick farce, directed by Richard Rush and written by Robert Kaufman (a déclassé George Axelrod). It was conceived in the pre-Watergate Nixon era, and the heroes seem to have a license to maim and slaughter people. The film's *Dirty Harry* spirit combined with its primitive sense of comedy make it a crowd-pleaser, though at one point, when a supposedly funny, carefree car chase goes through a girls' marching band, strewing bodies all over the street, the audience seems to experience a slight discomfort. However, the picture has one big-laugh car stunt: the heroes in their car dive off a bridge ramp into a third-floor apartment, and audiences seem willing to forgive it everything else, even its brutal murder sequences—one in a men's lavatory and one (with porno overtones) in a ladies' lavatory. With Valerie Harper, Loretta Swit, Linda Marsh, Jack Kruschen, Mike Kellin, Alex Rocco, and Christopher Morley as a transvestite. Warners. color

The French Connection (1971)—Tracking down a shipment of heroin in New York City. A hugely successful slam-bang thriller that zaps the audience with noise, speed, and brutality. It's certainly exciting, but that excitement isn't necessarily a pleasure. The ominous music keeps tightening the screws and heating things up; the movie is like an aggravated case of New York. It proceeds through chases, pistol-whippings, slashings, murders, snipings, and more chases for close to two hours. This is what's meant to give you a charge. There are no good guys. Gene Hackman plays the lowlife police detective who cracks the case; porkpie-hatted and lewd and boorish, he's also a sadist. With Fernando Rey, Roy Scheider, Tony LoBianco, and Marcel Bozzufi. Music by Don Ellis; cinematography by Owen Roizman. The script, by Ernest Tidyman, was based on the supposedly factual account by Robin Moore in a book about the largest narcotics haul in New York police history up to that time. William Friedkin directed. Academy Awards: Best Picture, Director, Actor (Hackman), Screenplay. 20th Century-Fox. color (See *Deeper into Movies*.)

The French Conspiracy *L'Attentat* (1973)— The stars in this political thriller bring so many associations from other political thrillers (better ones) that it's almost a satire. But this movie, based on the Ben Barka kidnapping, isn't satire; it isn't anything. No thrills and no political content, just a lot of stars— Gian Maria Volonte talking heroic hogwash as Ben Barka, while Jean-Louis Trintignant, Michel Piccoli, Michel Bouquet, and Philippe Noiret connive and intrigue, and Jean Seberg

worries. All the film's energy must have gone into meeting the payroll. Yves Boisset directed. In French. color

The French Lieutenant's Woman (1981)— Meryl Streep gives an immaculate, technically accomplished performance as Sarah Woodruff, the romantic mystery woman of John Fowles' novel, but she isn't mysterious. We're not fascinated by Sarah; she's so distanced from us that all we can do is observe how meticulous Streep—and everything else about the movie—is. Harold Pinter, the famed compressor who did the adaptation, has emptied out the story, and the director, Karel Reisz, has scrupulously filled in the space with "art": every vocal inflection is exact, the 1867 settings seem flawless, and the cinematographer Freddie Francis's camera movements and muted colors are superbly elegant. The result is overblown spareness. It's all so controlled that everything seems to be happening punctually, even in the interpolated modern story about the actors who are performing in a movie version of the Fowles book. There are some lovely moments, and a few have magical overtones, but most of the picture might be taking place in a glass case. With Jeremy Irons, Lynsey Baxter, Hilton McRae, Leo McKern, Patience Collier, Charlotte Mitchell, Penelope Wilton, and David Warner. (In the modern scenes Streep wears a short, straight hairdo—the most disfiguring star coiffure since Mia Farrow's thick wig in *The Great Gatsby*.) Production design by Assheton Gorton. Made at Twickenham Studios, London, and on location in England. United Artists. color (See *Taking It All In*.)

French Provincial *Souvenirs d'en France* (1975)—A gifted young romantic wit, André Téchiné, has turned parody into something so emotionally charged that the meanings radiate every which way. The story spans several decades, contrasting the lives of two brides—Jeanne Moreau, as Berthe the no-nonsense seamstress, and Marie-France Pisier, as Régina the rapacious bourgeois dreamer—who are both too much for their husbands. Scenes take you back through so many layers of film history that you can't sort out all the influences, but this rich impasto is essentially new. The picture is effective on the most sophisticated level but naïve and scatterbrained on some of the simplest levels—such as that of telling a coherent story. Written by Téchiné and Marilyn Goldin; cinematography by Bruno Nuytten. With Michel Auclair, Orane Démazis, Julien Guiomar, Françoise Lebrun, Claude Mann, Aram Stephan, Marc Chapiteau, and Michele Moretti. In French. color (See *When the Lights Go Down*.)

The French They Are a Funny Race (1957)—Released in France as *Les Carnets du Major Thompson*, in 1956. A film based on a collection of minor essays has, at the outset, a certain skittishness; the essays themselves formed *The Notebooks of Major Thompson*, which was written, not by Major Thompson, but by Pierre Daninos, and it was a Frenchman's idea of an Englishman's account of French life. The American writer-director Preston Sturges, an expatriate in the late 50s, turned all this into an amusing series of wheezes—a kind of literate vaudeville. Maybe you can no longer laugh at anecdotes like the British mother's wedding-night advice to her daughter ("My dear, it's utterly unbearable, but just close your eyes and think of England") but acted out, this sort of thing acquires a fresh insanity. There is one routine that is Sturges at his best: an English courtship on horseback, and there are divertissements on French bureaucracy, English body-fitness, and so on. Jack Buchanan is the Major, Catherine Boyl his English wife, Martine Carol his French wife, Noël-Noël his French friend.

Die Freudlose Gasse, see *The Joyless Street*

Friendly Persuasion (1956)—Taken from Jessamyn West's stories, this William Wyler film is disappointing but far from shameful. It's about a group of Quakers in Indiana at the time of the Civil War; they try to hold onto their belief in nonviolence despite the actions of Confederate raiders. The presentation is too gently bucolic; the head of the house (Gary Cooper) races a neighbor to Sunday meeting in the family buggy, and buys an organ, which his wife (Dorothy McGuire) regards as an instrument far too profane to install in a proper home. Meanwhile, their daughter (Phyllis Love) is swooning over the boy next door and their older son (Anthony Perkins) considers pouring lead into the first Rebel who turns up in the neighborhood. This was one of the first of Perkins' confused, canny, emotional characters; his mood shifts hadn't yet become ticky, and he's marvellously likable as he imitates Cooper's lanky movements—he's a very convincing son. The film was actually shot in California and the acreage looks so manicured that one half expects a station wagon to come into view; still, it was an attempt to deal with an offbeat subject, and Wyler's work shows care and taste. With Marjorie Main, Richard Eyer, Robert Middleton, and Walter Catlett. The script is by Michael Wilson; the cinematography is by Ellsworth Fredericks; the music is by Dmitri Tiomkin. Allied Artists. color

Friends for Life, see *Amici per la Pelle*

The Friends of Eddie Coyle (1973)—Boston Irish crooks and cops. Robert Mitchum is the aging hood, Eddie Coyle, who is slipping a little information to a smart, treacherous narcotics officer (Richard Jordan), in order to stay out of jail. Peter Boyle, a bartender, handles murder contracts and ruthlessly plays all sides against each other. Based on the novel by George V. Higgins, former assistant attorney general in Massachusetts, this movie should be better; the plot and the dialogue are first-rate. The elements are all there, and Mitchum, looking appropriately square-headed, tries hard and has some good scenes. But you get the impression that the dialogue is moving faster than the action. Probably this picture, directed by the English Peter Yates, needed an American director with an instinctive feeling for the milieu; the movie is shallow and a little mechanical, with noise and loud music used to build up excitement. The police and the gangsters have no roots, and intertwined roots are what the story is meant to be about. Jordan, acting chillingly pleasant, gives the most effective performance, and Steven Keats, as a dealer in guns, gives the showiest one. With Alex Rocco, Joe Santos, Helena Carroll, Mitchell Ryan, and Jack Kehoe. Adaptation by Paul Monash, who also produced, for Paramount. color

From Here to Eternity (1953)—Prewitt, the bugler-hero of James Jones' Dreiserian novel about Army life in Hawaii before Pearl Harbor, is a soldier who loves the Army (he's committed to be a 30-year man), yet he believes that "if a man don't go his own way, he's nothin'." The conflict between his status and his determination to have his rights is the mainspring of the action. Jones' bulky book does such an honest job of storytelling that it triumphs over its pedestrian prose; the movie succeeds by the smooth efficiency of Fred Zinnemann's lean, intelligent direction, and by the superlative casting. Montgomery Clift's bony, irregularly handsome Prewitt is a hardhead, a limited man with a one-track

mind, who's intensely appealing; Clift has the control to charm—almost to seduce—an audience without ever stepping outside his inflexible, none-too-smart character. Burt Lancaster has a role that's just about perfectly in his range as Sergeant Warden, the man's man who's also a ladies' man (the lady is Deborah Kerr); Frank Sinatra, in his first straight acting part, surprised audiences with a softly modulated, likable performance as Maggio, who loses his life because of his high spirits; Ernest Borgnine is the smiling, innocently murderous Fatso; Donna Reed is the respectable prostitute. This was the movie of its year, as *On the Waterfront* was to be the next year, and not just because each swept the Academy Awards, but because these films brought new attitudes to the screen that touched a social nerve; they weren't the same kind of winner as *Ben-Hur*. Yet a displacement occurs in the course of the action here: Prewitt's fate gets buried in the commotion of the Japanese attack on Pearl Harbor. And Clift's innovative performance was buried in the public praise for Sinatra and Lancaster. It was almost as if the public wanted to forget Prewitt's troublesome presence. The remarkably compact screenplay is by Daniel Taradash. Produced by Buddy Adler, for Columbia; cinematography by Burnett Guffey. With Philip Ober, Harry Bellaver, and Mickey Shaughnessy. b & w

From Noon Till Three (1977)—Charles Bronson plays a desperado in the Old West, who takes refuge for three hours with a romantic widow (Jill Ireland) in her Victorian mansion; afterward, she thinks he has been killed and she churns out a popular book— her fantasy version of their time together. When he returns, he is so much less than the creature of her imagination that she doesn't recognize him. This is essentially the plot gimmick of the Douglas Fairbanks, Sr., *The*

Private Life of Don Juan—a dud film of 1934. After an ingenious dream-sequence opening, this Western, written and directed by Frank Gilroy, is a dud, too. The faults are in Gilroy's uninspired writing (he treats us like children), in his pedestrian directing, and in Jill Ireland's performance. It is really a star vehicle for her, and though she is an adequate actress—she has voice and control and carriage—she has no excitement, and no audience empathy whatever. With Douglas Fowley as a grizzled old outlaw. United Artists. color

From Russia with Love (1963)—The second in the James Bond series—exciting, handsomely staged, and campy—with Sean Connery pitted against a blond Robert Shaw and Lotte Lenya with a dagger in her shoe. Also with Pedro Armendariz, Daniela Bianchi, Vladek Sheybal, and the regulars—Bernard Lee, Lois Maxwell, and Desmond Llewelyn. Directed by Terence Young, from a script by Richard Maibaum and Joanna Harwood, based on Ian Fleming's novel. The score is by John Barry. United Artists. color

The Front (1976)—The writer, Walter Bernstein, had a nifty comedy idea—to make a movie about the blacklisting in the entertainment industry during the McCarthy era, centering on a political innocent who fronts for blacklisted writers—but he didn't develop its comic potential. Woody Allen gives the film its only spark. He plays Howie, a restaurant cashier and small-time bookie who becomes a front; the funniest, most original scenes show the stirrings of literary vanity within this non-writer. The bulk of the film, though, is set up like a wartime anti-Nazi melodrama; it's the good guys versus the bad guys, and Howie becomes the Everyman who has to learn to choose sides. The pacing of the director, Martin Ritt, is off, the sequences don't

flow, and the film seems sterile, unpopulated, and flat. With Zero Mostel in a major role, and Michael Murphy, Herschel Bernardi, Remak Ramsey, and the dark, solemnly woebegone Andrea Marcovicci. Columbia. color (See *When the Lights Go Down.*)

The Front Page (1974)—Ben Hecht and Charles MacArthur's rowdy dream of newspaper life, first produced on the stage in 1928, seems to be foolproof, and the structure still stands up in this version, directed by Billy Wilder. But something singular and marvellous has been diminished to the sloppy ordinary. Wilder and his co-scenarist, I.A.L. Diamond, think that the way to make a dialogue comedy work for modern audiences is to convert the dialogue into noise; their version is a harsh, scrambling-for-laughs gag comedy. Walter Matthau, who gets a chance at a really classy American character—Walter Burns, the funny, mean, egomaniac editor—plays him like a whistle-stop Bear Bryant. Matthau, however, still gets his laughs. Jack Lemmon doesn't; his Hildy Johnson—the best reporter in Chicago—is like a mortuary assistant having a wild fling. There's only one freshly felt performance—Austin Pendleton's as Earl Williams, the fuddled anarchist concealed in the famous rolltop desk; speaking softly but hurriedly, the words tumbling together in a slight and affecting stammer, Pendleton provides the only touch of innocence in this loud production. With Carol Burnett, Susan Sarandon, David Wayne, Vincent Gardenia, Allen Garfield, Charles Durning, and Herbert Edelman. (The play was also filmed in 1931, and in 1940 as *His Girl Friday.*) Universal. color (See *Reeling.*)

Full Metal Jacket (1987)—Stanley Kubrick's Vietnam film stays reasonably close to its source, Gustav Hasford's compressed, white-hot novel *The Short-Timers*, yet the novel has an accumulating force of horror and the movie doesn't. The first three-quarters of an hour is basic training in the Marines stripped down to a cartoonish horrorshow; it's military s & m, and the pounding compulsiveness can easily be taken for the work of a master director. After that, the movie becomes dispersed, and you can't get an emotional reading on it. Kubrick probably believes he's numbing us by the power of his vision, but he's actually numbing us by its emptiness. Here's a director who has been insulated from American life for more than two decades, and he proceeds to define the American crisis of the century. He does it by lingering for a near-pornographic eternity over a young Vietnamese woman who is in pain and pleads "Shoot me! Shoot me!" This is James M. Cain in Vietnam. The script is by Kubrick, Michael Herr, and Hasford. Shot in England, with Matthew Modine as Private Joker, who wears a peace symbol; Vincent D'Onofrio as poor, doughy-faced Pyle; Lee Ermey as the gunnery sergeant; and Arliss Howard, Dorian Harewood, and Adam Baldwin. Released by Warners. color (See *Hooked*.)

Fun with Dick and Jane (1977)—A nitwit mixture of counterculture politics and madcap comedy, with a bit of toilet humor thrown in. George Segal and Jane Fonda are Dick and Jane of the children's primers, grown up, married, and living beyond their means in L.A. in a suburban-palatial dream house; when Dick loses his executive job they turn to robbery. What kind of political comedy can you have with a director like Ted Kotcheff who makes practically every employee of every institution—every janitor or clerk—look stupid? When Kotcheff puts the Bach Magnificat on the soundtrack while a street crowd scrambles for money that's been tossed out of a car, we're supposed to see the contrast between man's possibilities and what men have become. The director doesn't even have the grace to indicate that some of these people may need the money. They're just swine heading for slops. The picture was based on Gerald Gaiser's screenplay for a serious film, which was turned into a lampoon by David Giler, then reworked by Jerry Belson, and finally, sent to Mordecai Richler for a fast (three-week) shuffle. With Ed McMahon as Dick's employer. Produced by Peter Bart and Max Palevsky. Columbia. color (See *When the Lights Go Down*.)

Funny Face (1957)—Fred Astaire as an Avedonish fashion photographer who discovers Audrey Hepburn working in a bookshop and takes her to Paris to model clothes for a *Vogue*-like magazine. The Givenchy clothes are lovely; the sequences (which Avedon supervised) of Astaire taking photos are often amusingly, romantically misty; best of all, the George and Ira Gershwin score has some of the fresh spriteliness it must have had when it served the original *Funny Face* on Broadway 30 years before (also with Astaire). This big Stanley Donen musical isn't all it should be, though. You keep wanting it to turn into wonderful romantic fluff, but it's only spottily successful. The Leonard Gershe script (which has no relation to the earlier show) is weak, particularly in Astaire's role, and the movie emphasizes Astaire's age by trying to ignore it. And it's a sour idea to use a Sartre-like thinker (Michel Auclair) as the villain, a philandering phony. Hepburn's rescue from European sex-mad intellectualism by clean-minded, all-American-boy Astaire is so cheap and false a plot development that the picture's sophistication sinks into a very unphotogenic miasma. Still, Hepburn is a charming sidekick for Astaire, and the satirist Kay Thompson is agreeable as the rangy, hardboiled fashion editor. With Suzy Parker, Ruta Lee, and Robert Flemyng. Produced by Roger Edens, for Paramount; Eugene Loring assisted Donen and Astaire on the choreography. color

Funny Girl (1968)—A bravura performance by Barbra Streisand. As Fanny Brice, she has the wittiest comic inflections since the comediennes of the 30s; she makes written dialogue sound like inspired improvisation. As the shady gambler Nicky Arnstein, phlegmatic Omar Sharif appears to be some sort of visiting royalty, with a pained professional smile to put the common people at their ease. But Streisand's triumphant talent rides right over the film's weaknesses. William Wyler directed, with musical sequences staged by Herbert Ross. With Walter Pidgeon, Kay Medford, and Anne Francis. Screenplay by Isobel Lennart, from her play; songs by Jule Styne and Bob Merrill; production designed by Gene Callahan. Produced by Ray Stark, for Columbia. color (See *Going Steady.*)

Funny Lady (1975)—The moviemakers weren't just going to make a sequel to *Funny Girl*—they were going to kill us. (And they wanted to outdo *Cabaret*, besides.) Again as Fanny Brice, Barbra Streisand is no longer human; she's like a bitchy female impersonator imitating Barbra Streisand. She's in beautiful voice, but her singing is too terrific—strident overdramatization turns a song into a big number. The picture is overproduced and badly edited, with a 40s-movie-heartbreak plot. A great deal of talent has been badly used, though James Caan has some good scenes as scrubby, anxious Billy Rose, and Streisand is charming in the wittily staged "I Found a Million Dollar Baby in a Five and Ten Cent Store." Ray Stark produced; Herbert Ross directed. The new songs are by Kander and Ebb. Columbia. color (See *Reeling.*)

A Funny Thing Happened on the Way to the Forum (1966)—Richard Lester's short-term camera magic keeps cutting into and away from the comedians (Phil Silvers, Zero Mostel, Jack Gilford, and Michael Hordern), who never get a chance to develop a routine or to bring off a number. They're rushed pell-mell through this fractured version of the wonderful musical farce by Burt Shevelove, Larry Gelbart, and Stephen Sondheim, taken from Plautus (and set in ancient Rome). We get the sense that Lester thinks it would be too banal just to let us see a dance or a pair of burlesque clowns singing a duet. He trashes the men, even old Buster Keaton, and the women are blank-faced bodies or witless viragos. Some of the best effects are the least doctored: Hordern's vocal inflections, a satirical entrance song by Leon Greene. And Lester's fracturing technique is sometimes successful—as in the parody recap of the love duet, which has lyrical wit, like the song in the snow in *Help!* Mostly, Lester's visual gags seem just pointless agitation. He proceeds by fits and starts and leaves jokes suspended in midair; it's as if he'd forgotten what it's all for. And for an audience the experience becomes one of impatience and irritation—like coitus interruptus going on forever. With Michael Crawford, Annette Andre, Patricia Jessel, and Beatrix Lehmann. Cinematography by Nicolas Roeg; sets and costumes designed by Tony Walton; script by Melvin Frank (who was the producer) and Michael Pertwee. Released by United Artists. color (See *Kiss Kiss Bang Bang.*)

Funnyman (1967)— John Korty's loose, unlabored style was probably at its best in this fresh and original film about a young comedian (Peter Bonerz) who gets tired of "improvising" the same material for hundreds of nights as a member of The Committee, the improvisational-revue troupe in San Francisco. He's wry and self-conscious, and automatically turns whatever situation he's in into a put-on—his "life situations" have the rhythm of revue acts, and vice versa. Korty doesn't make a big thing of his funnyman hero; the movie just skips along, and in places (especially in the second half) dawdles along—but without solemnity. Even when it goes flat it has a pleasant soft-edge quality, and the characters have air to breathe. The script is by Korty and Bonerz; the music is by Peter Schickele; Korty was the cinematographer and also did the animation. With Carol Androsky, Sandra Archer, Larry Hankin, Marshall Efron, Barbara Hiken, Jane House, Gerald Hiken, Alan Myerson, Jerry Mander, and Budd Steinhilber as the animator working on insecticide commercials. b & w and color

Fury (1936)—When this melodrama about an orgy of mob violence against an innocent man—it was Fritz Lang's first American movie—opened in London, Graham Greene said in his review that it was "the only film I know to which I have wanted to attach the epithet of 'great.' " Though Americans may rate it high, they are unlikely to go that far. Spencer Tracy (as the victim) and Sylvia Sidney are very fine, and the picture has so much vitality that it's easy to make allowances for the tacky ending, which doesn't jibe with Lang's sensibility and style. But the sensibility and style are themselves hurdles. The schematic view of fate, the lighting and design, the stylized movements of the lynchers all relate to the theatrical wing of the German Expressionist movement; Lang brings a heavy battery of advanced stagecraft to the small-town American Southern setting. Joseph L. Mankiewicz produced; Norman Krasna did the story; Bartlett Cormack and Lang did the screenplay. With Edward Ellis, Walter Brennan, Bruce Cabot, Frank Albert-

son, and Walter Abel. Cinematography by Joseph Ruttenberg. M-G-M. b & w

The Fury (1978)—Brian De Palma's visionary, science-fiction thriller is the reverse side of the coin of Spielberg's *Close Encounters.* With Spielberg, what happens is so much better than you dared hope that you have to laugh; with De Palma, it's so much worse than you feared that you have to laugh. The script (John Farris's adaptation of his novel) is cheap gothic espionage occultism involving two superior beings—spiritual twins (Andrew Stevens and Amy Irving) who have met only telepathically. But the film is so visually compelling that a viewer seems to have entered a mythic night world; no Hitchcock thriller was ever so intense, went so far, or had so many "classic" sequences. With Kirk Douglas, Carrie Snodgress, John Cassavetes, Daryl Hannah, Dennis Franz, and Charles Durning. 20th Century-Fox. color (See *When the Lights Go Down.*)

Der Fussgänger, see *The Pedestrian*

F/X (1986)—Robert Mandel directed this ingenious suspense film about a movie special-effects wizard (Bryan Brown), based in New York, who lets himself be bamboozled by a couple of men from the Justice Department's Witness Relocation Program; they hire him to stage the fake assassination of a Mafia boss (Jerry Orbach), so that this gangster can give evidence against his associates and be relocated without fear of reprisals. Bryan Brown underplays niftily, and he's joined by a second hero—swaggering Brian Dennehy, built like a barn and sporting a big, messy mustache, as a rogue cop. He grabs the movie in his choppers and shakes it up. This picture loses something when it takes a turn toward acceptance of corruption, but the script, by

Robert T. Megginson and Gregory Fleeman, gives Dennehy some sharp tough-guy lines, and he sends them home like a master comedian. He's so enthusiastically overscaled that he fills the screen. Despite the film's high body count, it's not the kind of thriller that leaves a viewer feeling debauched; Mandel's work is clean and brisk. The cinematographer, Miroslav Ondříček, gives the city a rich, dark glint. With Diane Venora as the wizard's actress-girlfriend, Joe Grifasi, Jossie deGuzman, Cliff DeYoung, Mason Adams, and a few weak scenes with Martha Gehman. Orion. color (See *Hooked*.)

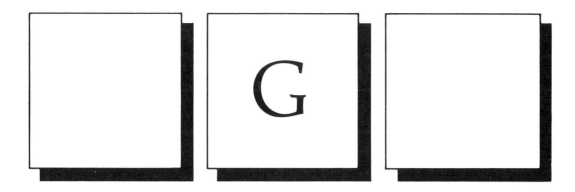

G

Gable and Lombard (1976)—Limply raunchy, meaningless picture, with nothing to say about the movies, about love, or about stardom. The moviemakers couldn't come up with any subject but the sex drive of its hero and heroine, who keep hopping on each other like deranged rabbits. One of the most famous quotes in Hollywood history is Lombard's "My God, you know I love Pa, but I can't say he's a hell of a lay." Their love affair must have had a great many things going for it besides sex, but this movie can't imagine what they might be. Barry Sandler wrote the trivializing, falsifying script, and Sidney J. Furie directed, with James Brolin and Jill Clayburgh in the leads, and Allen Garfield, Red Buttons, and Melanie Mayron. Cinematography by Jordan Cronenweth. Universal. color (See *When the Lights Go Down.*)

Le Gai Savoir (1968)—*Weekend* (made earlier this same year) was the culmination of Jean-Luc Godard's great, rampaging, innovative career, and after it he seemed to be back at Square One, trying to found a new Maoist political cinema. *Le Gai Savoir* was the first of his monotonous, didactic experiments, and it's just about impossible to sit through. Juliet Berto (as the daughter of Lumumba) and Jean-Pierre Léaud (as Rousseau's great-great-grandson) begin on a course of study; there's not much to look at, and since the soundtrack is full of bleeps to cover the obscenities, there's nothing to do but read the subtitles as the two of them talk. In French. color

Gaily, Gaily (1969)—Ben Hecht's reminiscences and fantasies about his early years as a Chicago newspaperman are marvellous movie material—evocative, good-humored, full of life. The promising subject and not too bad a script (by Abram S. Ginnes) are mostly lost, however, in this overproduced period re-creation, which is only moderately entertaining. The director, Norman Jewison, just doesn't have the feeling for Hecht's Chicago; he uses huge mobs and big locations, and the joyous comedy of our corrupt past is turned into picturesque (non-denominational) Americana—too embellished, overplayed, and almost always off target. As the young Candide-Ben, Beau Bridges has a smiling, engaging presence, and, as the older reporter, Brian Keith is splendid; the best reason to see the picture is for his timing, and for the way he can deliver an epithet like "You quack!" But the scenes of Carl Sandburg reciting a poem and the young hero

G

screaming about political power are really inexcusable. With Melina Mercouri, who, as the madam of a bordello that looks as big as the Ritz, acts like a tempestuous female impersonator, and Hume Cronyn, who is at his worst in a condescending performance as a politician. A noteworthy anacronistic howler: the 1910 demonstrators who gather outside the Chicago Board of Trade carry placards calling for "Love." United Artists. color (See *Deeper into Movies*.)

Gallipoli (1981)—An exemplary academic film about the waste of war—two young Australian runners, played by (dark-haired) Mel Gibson and (blond) Mark Lee, are slaughtered. (They and other Australians are sacrificed in an ill-conceived First World War maneuver designed to protect the British.) It's an "artistic" film, full of familiar pathos and irony—a tragic buddy-buddy movie directed by Peter Weir. His widescreen staging is very elegant; his weakness is in his habit of stereotyping villains (in this case they're mostly the British). There's also a larger weakness; there's no discernible reason for him to have made the picture except to bring off a "classic." Gibson gives a fresh and impressive performance, but Lee does a very ordinary acting job and his character is much too gallant and good and brave. With Bill Kerr, a fine, bald-headed actor with a great voice, as Uncle Jack, who reads aloud to the children. The script is by David Williamson; the cinematography is by Russell Boyd. color

Gambit (1966)—It wants to be a jaunty heist-caper movie, like *Topkapi*, of 1964, but it's of quintessential mediocrity: not hip enough to sustain interest, not dreary enough to walk out on. The opening idea (lifted from Preston Sturges's *Unfaithfully Yours*) is promising, but the writers (Jack Davies, Alvin Sargent) and the director (Ronald Neame) kill it. As a cock-

ney thief, Michael Caine, still new to movies, isn't secure enough to waltz through. And as his Eurasian confederate, Shirley MacLaine needs help—she can't keep her timing from slipping. With Herbert Lom (the cut-rate Charles Boyer of so many English melodramas) as the potentate to be robbed, and John Abbott and Arnold Moss. Universal. color

The Gambler (1974)—The gambler here is a brilliant young Jewish prince, professor of literature to ghetto blacks, and potential great novelist. The conflicts in his psyche are spelled out in his discussions of will and Dostoevski with his students at City University. He's as flamboyantly superior as Norman Mailer's Rojack, and the prevailing tone of the film is Mailerian dread, abetted by Jerry Fielding's elegantly oppressive score, based on Mahler's Symphony No. 1. The script, by James Toback, is a grandiloquent, egocentric novel written as a film; it spells everything out, and the director Karel Reisz's literal-minded, proficient style calls attention to how airless and schematic it is. The big difference between Robert Altman's gambling film *California Split* and this one is not just that Altman's allusiveness is vastly entertaining while *The Gambler* seeks to impress us, but that *California Split* invites us into the world of its characters, while *The Gambler* hands us a wrapped package and closes us out. In *Bay of the Angels*, as in *California Split*, we shared in the highs and lows of gambling; for those of us who aren't gamblers it was a heady sensation, like entering a foreign culture. Here, we're trapped at a maniacal lecture on gambling as existential expression. The picture isn't at all dull, though—it has a self-conscious flash. As the hero, James Caan stays clenched, the bit in his teeth; it's a commanding performance but not a convincing one. With Lauren Hutton, Burt Young, Morris Carnovsky, Jacqueline Brookes, and Paul Sorvino. Paramount. color (See *Reeling*.)

The Game of Love *Le Blé en herbe* (1954)—
Claude Autant-Lara's film version of the Colette story treats the theme with beautiful
simplicity. The 16-year-old boy (Pierre-
Michel Beck) and the 15-year-old girl (Nicole
Berger) are disturbed by the emotions and
impulses developing in them; it isn't until the
boy is initiated by an older woman (Edwige
Feuillère) that the two adolescents get together—he passes on what he has learned.
Feuillère conveys the painful and degrading
position of the older woman with infinite tact
(though not to the reviewer of one newspaper, who described her as a black widow spider searching for prey). In French. b & w

Games (1967)—A Manhattan-set thriller,
with James Caan as a cold-blooded, fortune-
hunter husband, Katharine Ross as his rich,
bewildered wife, and Simone Signoret as a
mysterious woman in black, fond of gazing
into her crystal ball. Corpses are encased in
plaster to resemble sculpture by George
Segal, and the ambiance is meant to be chic
and modern, but the story is uninvolving, the
plot twists don't do as much for us as they
need to, and Curtis Harrington's directing
lacks pace. This tedious movie is handsomely
got up, however, and the good cast includes
Don Stroud, Estelle Winwood, George Furth,
Florence Marly, and Kent Smith. The script
is by Gene Kearney; the cinematography is
by William Fraker; the music is by Samuel
Matlovsky. Universal. color

Gandhi (1982)—A biographical epic, directed by Richard Attenborough, whose sensibility is conventional. Spanning 55 years,
the picture covers some of the principal
events in Gandhi's public life and tidies up
his rather kinky domestic relations. Gandhi
goes by in a cloud of serenity, and everyone
who sees him knuckles under (with the exception of a few misguided fellows, of
course). Ben Kingsley, who plays the Ma-
hatma, looks the part, has a fine, quiet presence, and conveys Gandhi's shrewdness.
Kingsley is impressive; the picture isn't. The
first half builds up considerable interest in
Gandhi; the second half is scattered—as if it
had been added to or subtracted from at random. And Kingsley can't give his role a core,
because it has been written completely from
the outside. A viewer's reaction: "I felt as if
I had attended the funeral of someone I didn't
know." From a script by John Briley. With
Edward Fox, John Gielgud, Trevor Howard,
Martin Sheen, John Mills, Ian Charleson,
Candice Bergen, Ian Bannen, John Clements,
Michael Hordern, Richard Griffiths, and with
Rohini Hattangady as Kasturba Gandhi,
Athol Fugard as General Smuts, Saeed Jaffrey
as Sardar Patel, Geraldine James as Mira-
behn, Alyque Padamsee as Mohamed Ali Jin-
nah, and Roshan Seth as Pandit Nehru. (3
hours and 8 minutes.) Academy Awards:
Best Picture, Director, Actor (Kingsley), Orig-
inal Screenplay, Art Direction, Cinematog-
raphy, Costume Design, Film Editing.
Released by Columbia. color (See *Taking It All
In.*)

The Gang That Couldn't Shoot Straight
(1971)—When farce isn't expertly played and
directed, it becomes just stupid, and that's
what happens to this Mafia farce, from the
Jimmy Breslin book. Lionel Stander, Jo Van
Fleet, and Jerry Orbach are among the clownish crooks who are impaled by the camera;
molestable Leigh Taylor-Young and the
buoyant (and very funny) Robert De Niro are
the romantic leads. Directed by James Gold-
stone; the script is by Waldo Salt. Also with
Hervé Villechaize and Joe Santos. M-G-M.
color

The Gang's All Here (1943)—Busby Berkeley's own special brand of kaleidoscopic fantasy, turned into psychedelic surrealism by
the electric reds and greens of 20th Century-

Fox's color processing. Those who consider Berkeley a master consider this film his masterpiece. It is his maddest film: chorus girls dissolve into artichokes; there's a banana xylophone; and, for the song "The Lady in the Tutti-Frutti Hat," Carmen Miranda appears in platform wedgies on an avenue of giant strawberries. Alice Faye sings the torch song "No Love, No Nothing," and also introduces the "Polka-Dot Polka" ballet, which, as a piece of staging, passes description. With Benny Goodman and his orchestra, and Charlotte Greenwood, James Ellison, Edward Everett Horton, Sheila Ryan, Eugene Pallette, and Phil Baker. The songs are by Leo Robin and Harry Warren, except that polka, which is David Raksin's. Screenplay by Walter Bullock, from a story concocted by three other fellows.

The Garden Murder Case (1936)—S.S. Van Dine's supersleuth Philo Vance (Edmund Lowe) is called in when a man is killed during a steeplechase. William Powell was a more amusing Philo Vance earlier in the series, but the backup actors are the same here—Nat Pendleton as the lummox Heath, and Etienne Girardot as the minuscule coroner, Dr. Doremus. Not much stays in the mind from this one except Frieda Inescort being pushed from a double-decker bus. Virginia Bruce and Benita Hume are as lovely as ever. Directed by Edwin L. Marin. M-G-M. b & w

The Garden of Allah (1936)—Heavenly romantic kitsch, panting with eternal love, a moment's happiness, and spiritual anguish. Marlene Dietrich is the lonely, rich Domini, dressed in swirling chiffon as she seeks truth in the African desert. She meets Charles Boyer (whose eyes have never been darker or more liquid) and marries him. Then, right at the purple start of their desert honeymoon, his conscience and a Trappist liqueur combine to ruin everything, for he is a Trappist monk who has bolted the monastery and violated his vow of silence. Back he must go to repent. Taken from Robert Hichens' old squash pie of a novel, it's the juiciest tale of woe ever, and David O. Selznick produced it in poshly lurid color, with a Max Steiner score poured on top. Richard Boleslawski directed; with Tilly Losch, who has a wild minute as an entertainer in an Algerian hot spot, and Basil Rathbone, John Carradine, Joseph Schildkraut, C. Aubrey Smith, and Lucile Watson. Just about perfection of its insanely goopy type. Adapted by W. P. Lipscomb and Lynn Riggs. Released through United Artists.

The Garden of Delights *El Jardín de las Delicias* (1971)—Carlos Saura's comedy about upper-middle-class greed is the story of an amnesiac industrialist (J. L. López Vásquez) whose relatives act out grotesque psychodramas from his childhood, trying to shock him into remembering and telling them the number of his Swiss bank account. The film is elegant in a dark, heavy-lidded sort of way, but Saura has a maddening habit of cutting away from a sequence just when we've got interested in where it's going, and the film lacks impetus. Saura works in a sedate, measured style; he isn't an instinctual Surrealist, and, given the nature and drive of Surrealism, that's the only authentic kind. He's an academic Surrealist: his images don't come from the hidden and unadmitted—they're impeccably planned to be Surreal. There's one brief gloriously redemptive sequence: when the voluptuous Lina Canalejas enters the industrialist's Art Deco bedroom, opens the French windows, and lets the breeze waft through the curtains and her chiffon gown, the film has a trace of magical reminiscence— she brings back all the sexy, elusive movie stars who ever wafted through our imaginations. Written by Rafael Azcona and Saura. In Spanish. color (See *Deeper into Movies*.)

The Garden of the Finzi-Continis *Il Giardino dei Finzi-Contini* (1970)—Vittorio De Sica's lyric evocation of a vanished group of people (the cultivated, aristocratic Jewish-Italian landowners) and a vanished mood. Based on Giorgio Bassani's semi-autobiographical novel, the film records how Giorgio, a middle-class outsider (Lino Capolicchio), is drawn into the decaying, enchanted world of the Finzi-Continis by the imperious, contrary Micòl (Dominique Sanda); she and her languid brother (Helmut Berger) are spoiled, beautiful people without the will to save themselves. This extraordinary film, with its melancholy glamour, is perhaps the only one that records the halfhearted anti-Jewish measures of the Mussolini period—which were, however, sufficient to wipe out the Finzi-Continis and all they represented. In Italian. color (See *Deeper into Movies*.)

Gardens of Stone (1987)—The period of this Francis Coppola film is 1968 and 1969, and the title refers to Arlington National Cemetery; most of the characters serve in the Old Guard, the Army's official ceremonial unit, and take part in the burials of up to 15 young men a day. The film is far from being a seamless work of art, but it probably comes closer to the confused attitudes that Americans had toward the Vietnam war than any other film has come, and so its messiness seems honorable. James Caan gives a sturdy, hypermasculine performance as the sergeant who loves the Army but doesn't believe the war can be won. The movie is too wet when it deals with his fatherly efforts to wise up an eager, gullible young trainee (D. B. Sweeney), but when Caan and James Earl Jones, as the sergeant major who's his best friend, express their profane disgust with the war and the Army bureaucracy they're great together, overacting joyously. (Jones' strange gray eyes have a dancing wit.) Coppola stages some terrific scenes. When the ser-

geant is giving a dinner party to impress the woman he has just met, a *Washington Post* reporter (played by Anjelica Huston), and the sergeant major is there with his steady woman friend, a senator's aide (played by Lonette McKee), the conversational crosscurrents are explosively funny. At other times, the film is pulpy, and its energies are dispersed. With the magical, humorous Dean Stockwell, and Mary Stuart Masterson, Dick Anthony Williams, Casey Siemaszko, and, in a scene that's an embarrassment, Bill Graham. The screenplay, by Ronald Bass, was adapted from Nicholas Proffitt's novel; cinematography by Jordan Cronenweth. Tri-Star. color (See *Hooked*.)

Gaslight (1944)—Ingrid Bergman is the cherubic bride who is terrorized by the grisly, dirty tricks of her husband, Charles Boyer. She runs the gamut from antimacassar to antimacassar, and it's good scary fun all the way (with a prize at the end—the Academy Award for Best Actress). This pseudo-Victorian thriller is rather more enjoyable than one might expect, and Bergman is, intermittently, genuinely moving. (Though at times you may suspect that she is feeling rather than acting, her hysteria in the musicale sequence is a good demonstration of how hard it sometimes is to tell the difference.) Boyer is expert, and the cast includes Joseph Cotten, Dame May Whitty, and Angela Lansbury (only in her teens, but you couldn't guess it). Patrick Hamilton's play has been toned up with smooth dialogue by John van Druten, Walter Reisch, and John Balderston, and the full-dress production is directed by George Cukor. When you watch a picture like this one, you're so aware of how expensively careful it is that you can't help being a little impressed and maybe more than a little depressed. (In this case, the expense included the cost of suppressing the 1940 English ver-

G

sion by Thorold Dickinson, with Diana Wynyard and Anton Walbrook.) M-G-M. b & w

Gate of Hell *Jigokumon* (1954)—Famed for its use of color, this exquisitely stylized tragedy of passion tells a subtle story (which resembles *The Rape of Lucrece*) of a warrior's desire for a married noblewoman and her way of defeating him. It's as if the director, Teinosuke Kinugasa, had read those critics who compare every Japanese movie to a Japanese print and had decided to give them more pictorial effects than they could handle—delicately choreographed battles, the flow and texture of garments, and everywhere grace of movement and composition. The setting is 12th-century Kyoto, where the abstract patterns of interiors and architecture suggest that modern decor has a long way to go to catch up with medieval Japan. With Machiko Kyo as the Lady Kesa and Kazuo Hasegawa as the demonic warrior Moritoh. In Japanese.

Gates of Paris, see *Porte des lilas*

Il Gattopardo, see *The Leopard*

The Gauntlet (1977)—Clint Eastwood, as a slow-witted cop, and Sondra Locke, as the fast-witted hooker he's bringing back from Las Vegas to testify in a trial in Phoenix, are always in movement. They use a police car, a motorcycle, a train, a bus. A mere whisper of a plot serves as a pretext for shoot-'em-ups with thousands of rounds of ammunition going into whatever buildings or vehicles the cop and the hooker are in or on. At times the whole world seems to be firing at them; buildings and cars are turned to lace. You look at the screen even though there's nothing to occupy your mind—the way you sometimes sit in front of the TV, numbly, because you can't rouse yourself for the effort it takes to go to bed. Eastwood directed; the script is by

Michael Butler and Dennis Shryack. With Pat Hingle and William Prince. A Malpaso Production, for Warners. color (See *When the Lights Go Down*.)

The Gay Desperado (1936)—Rouben Mamoulian was in a playful kooky mood when he put together this satirical farce that's also a parody of an operetta. Leo Carrillo is the Mexican bandit chief who's enraptured by the racketeering methods he sees in American movies; soon, his men are doing their damnedest to behave like Chicago mobsters. The movie kids the clichés of several genres. The chief is a music-lover, and he kidnaps a tenor (Nino Martini) to sing to him. This has the unfortunate result of forcing us to listen to some over-familiar arias and a song, "The World Is Mine Tonight," that's particularly hard to take. Luckily the tenor becomes romantically involved with a gang hostage, who is played with great zest by the young Ida Lupino. This deliberately artificial comedy was shot on stylized "picturesque" sets that feature giant cacti, giant sombreros, and archways and cathedrals—it's all a takeoff of Eisenstein's Mexican footage. (Peons pose in ponchos.) The pacing is often too slow for the silly, semi-surreal jokes, but there are a lot of compensations. With Mischa Auer, Harold Huber, Stanley Fields, James Blakeley, Paul Hurst, Frank Puglia, and Chris-Pin Martin. The script by Wallace Smith is based on a story by Leo Birinski; the cinematography is by Lucien Andriot. Produced by Pickford-Lasky. b & w

The Gay Divorcée (1934)—Fred Astaire and Ginger Rogers appeared together in *Flying Down to Rio* in 1933, but this was their first co-starring film. The plot is trivial French farce (about mistaken identities), but the dances are among the wittiest and the most lyrical expressions of American romanticism on the screen. It may be accurate to say that no one who saw them do "The Continental" or watched the great, tense, seductive dance they perform to Cole Porter's "Night and Day" has ever quite forgotten *The Gay Divorcée*—even if he thinks he has. With Alice Brady, Edward Everett Horton, Eric Blore, Erik Rhodes, E. E. Clive, Lillian Miles, Paul Porcasi, and Betty Grable—a cuddly pixie in satin pajamas dancing "Let's K-nock K-neez." Directed by Mark Sandrich; adapted from the stage musical *The Gay Divorce*. R K O. b & w

The General (1926)—One of Buster Keaton's most celebrated comedies. It's a classic and many people swear by it, although it isn't funny in the freely inventive way of his *Steamboat Bill, Jr.* (1927). Its humor is too drawn out for laughter. And yet it has a beauty: it has the shape of comedy. The time is the Civil War. Keaton plays a shy railroad engineer on a steam engine called The General. He wrote the script and directed, in collaboration with Clyde Bruckman. The girl is Marion Mack. Silent. b & w

General della Rovere *Il Generale della Rovere* (1959)—Vittorio De Sica has perhaps his greatest role in this otherwise mediocre film, directed by Roberto Rossellini. It is set in Genoa in 1943. De Sica is a small-time swindler with a classic con man's grand manner; the Germans induce him to impersonate a Resistance general whom they have inadvertently shot, and send him to a political prison, where he is supposed to ferret out information for them. But the petty, self-loathing crook, experiencing for the first time the respect and admiration—even the awe—of other men, becomes as courageous as the fighter he impersonates. The mask has molded the man, and the Nazis must destroy their own creation. De Sica is superb; we watch his evolution from worm to Il Generale with utter astonishment and delight. At its

most original, the film is a shockingly funny black comedy: the con man, battered and bleeding from torture, weeps sentimentally over a photograph of the real Generale's children—a scene as excruciatingly comic as the surreal torture scenes in *Bend Sinister*, Nabokov's novel about the Nazis. But this film, made on a slender budget and shot and edited in six weeks, is—surprisingly—too long; the director doesn't seem to have discovered his best material until it was too late to pull the story together. The compositions, the groupings of actors, the ideas, and the milieu are like a reprise of the neo-realist *Open City* (1945). The rawness and immediacy are gone, though; the faces are actorish, and the sets are obviously sets. With Hannes Messemer, Sandra Milo, Giovanna Ralli, Anne Vernon. From a script by Sergio Amidei, Diego Fabbri, Indro Montanelli, and Rossellini. In Italian. b & w

Il Generale della Rovere, see *General della Rovere*

Generals Without Buttons, see *La Guerre des boutons*

Genevieve (1953)—Genevieve is a venerable motor vehicle, a 1904 Darracq; this English film is a venerable little vehicle in its own right. John Gregson and Dinah Sheridan race the Darracq against Kenneth More and Kay Kendall in a 1904 Spyker. That the two men should be testing their masculine prowess in these antiques gives the comedy a double edge. Kenneth More is wonderfully smug and infuriating as an advertising man; Kay Kendall had perhaps her happiest (and most irresistible) role as the trumpet-playing model. Written by William Rose, directed by Henry Cornelius, harmonica music by Larry Adler, cinematography by Christopher Challis. Also with Joyce Grenfell and Geoffrey Keen. Everything about this movie seems to

G

go right, and it looks relaxed and effortless. color

Le Genou de Claire, see *Claire's Knee*

Gentleman Jim (1942)—As the young James J. Corbett, a chipper showoff bank clerk in San Francisco who's loyal to his family and friends, Errol Flynn plays in the quick-witted, cool, and cocky style that he was best at. Narrow-hipped and long-legged, he's fast on his feet; he looks as if he might be able to lick his opponents, or, at least, outdance them. The film, which covers Corbett's transition from amateur boxer to professional, is well paced and has considerable charm, though the Corbett clan, headed by Alan Hale as Jim's father, is Warners lovable Irish, with hot tempers and wobbly brogues. As a young society woman who develops a love-hate relationship with Jim, Alexis Smith wears her hair in a thick roll swept up from her forehead, and goofy high hats; she looks like a ship in full sail, but she's quite entertaining. With Ward Bond, as the magnetic John L. Sullivan, and Jack Carson, William Frawley, John Loder, Rhys Williams, Madeleine Le-Beau, and Lon McAllister. Directed by Raoul Walsh; one of the scriptwriters was Horace McCoy. (The film straightens out Corbett's life—his marriages have been divided by three.) b & w

Geordie, see *Wee Geordie*

Georgy Girl (1966)—A glib little farce that tickled a lot of people. Georgy (Lynn Redgrave) is a brontosaurus of a girl who's childlike and "natural" and artistic, and the picture is determinedly heartwarming and kinky and on the side of youth. We're supposed to like Georgy because she acts out her ludicrous and self-pitying impulses, and doesn't think too much about it afterward. She has all the blessings of affect and affect-lessness. Georgy gets a baby to mother only to have the authorities take it away. (Underneath all the 60s nonconformity gear are the crooked little skeletons of old Shirley Temple pictures.) In those years, young men identified with the gorilla hero of *Morgan!* and a surprising number of young women identified with the misfit Georgy. With James Mason, Charlotte Rampling, Alan Bates, and Rachel Kempson. Directed by Silvio Narizzano, from the script by Margaret Forster and Peter Nichols, based on Forster's novel. Released in U.S. by Columbia. b & w (See *Kiss Kiss Bang Bang*.)

Gervaise (1956)—A painstaking and rich evocation of mid-19th-century Paris, photographed to suggest Daguerre. René Clément's rather heavy-going film deals with the spiritual destruction of Gervaise (Maria Schell)—a destruction accomplished by her lover, who deserts her, and her gentle husband, who becomes an uncontrollable drunkard (a memorable performance by François Périer). Gervaise Macquart, for those who find Zola overpoweringly uninviting, is the heroine of *L'Assommoir*, one of the 20 novels in the Rougon-Macquart series, and the mother of that corrupt little Nana who figures in a later volume (and many a movie). With Suzy Delair as Virginie, except for the scene in which Virginie gets paddled; at that moment, a dubber known as Rita Cadillac offers her bottom to the camera. Music by Georges Auric. In French. b & w

Get Carter (1971)—There's nobody to root for but the smartly dressed sexual athlete and professional killer (Michael Caine) in this English gangland picture, which is so calculatedly cool and soulless and nastily erotic that it seems to belong to a new genre of virtuoso viciousness. What makes the movie unusual is the metallic elegance and the single-minded proficiency with which it adheres to its sadism-for-the-connoisseur formula. With John Osborne, Britt Ekland, and Ian Hendry. Directed by Mike Hodges, who also wrote the fashionably fragmented script, based on the novel *Jack's Return Home*, by Ted Lewis; the cinematography is by Wolfgang Suschitzky. Shot in Newcastle. color

Get Out Your Handkerchiefs *Préparez vos mouchoirs* (1978)—This sex comedy by the writer-director Bertrand Blier is flagrantly funny in a slangy, buoyant, unpredictable way. Feelings are expressed that hadn't come out in movies before, yet it's all reassuringly quiet; the film's texture is soft and sensual, and there's a velvety underlayer to the scenes. Blier's slapstick poetic logic is so coolly, lyrically sustained that nothing that happens seems shocking. Like his earlier *Going Places*, it's about two pals (played by Gérard Depardieu and Patrick Dewaere) who don't really understand women, and their not understanding women is part of their bond. This time, the two aren't roughnecks; they're polite, respectable men, for whom women are like another species. Seeing this film, a woman enters a man's fantasy universe stripped of hypocrisy. With the lovely, dark Carole Laure as Depardieu's wife and Dewaere's mistress, Michel Serrault as the neighbor, and Riton as the Mozartian prodigy. Cinematography by Jean Penzer; music by Mozart, by Georges Delerue (writing in the spirit of Mozart), and by Schubert. In French. color (See *When the Lights Go Down*.)

The Getaway (1972)—Another bank heist, and the wholesome, clean-cut robber pair (Steve McQueen and Ali MacGraw) take forever to make it across the Mexican border with their loot. The audience hoots her line readings and applauds when he smacks her around; maybe this audience participation helps to explain the film's success. Sam Peckinpah directed in imitation of Sam Peckinpah;

it's a mechanical job, embellished with a vicious, erotic subplot involving Al Lettieri and Sally Struthers. The cast includes Slim Pickens and Ben Johnson. The script, by Walter Hill, is based on Jim Thompson's novel; cinematography by Lucien Ballard; music by Quincy Jones. First Artists. color (See *Reeling*.)

The Getting of Wisdom (1977)—A minor post-Victorian autobiographical novel about an Australian girl's coming-of-age, re-created for the screen in its own terms—or, rather, in what the re-creators think are its own terms. At 13, an impoverished girl (Susannah Fowle) from the back country who is highly precocious and a gifted musician comes to Melbourne, and she spends five years there at the Presbyterian Ladies College, a select school for the daughters of the wealthy, where the teachers sneer at her because her mother runs a post office in the bush, and the girls are harpies. She almost succumbs to snobbery, but she has her brains and her talent and her intrepid nature to see her through. This self-infatuated fantasy is presented in the guise of harsh realism, and the faithful, meticulous period re-creation makes it hard for us to connect with the heroine or with anything else. Directed by Bruce Beresford, whose attitude toward the material is cold and literal, as if we were in need of a muckraking exposé of the Victorian education of ladies. From a script by Eleanor Witcombe; cinematography by Don McAlpine. color (See *Taking It All In*.)

Ghare-Baire, see *The Home and the World*

The Ghost and Mrs. Muir (1947)—The dashing Rex Harrison is the ghost of a sea captain and Gene Tierney is the widowed Mrs. Muir, who falls in love with him. Joseph L. Mankiewicz directed this somewhat too gentle and whimsical diversion; it's on the sleepy side—partly because it has all been designed and staged to show "class." The script, by Philip Dunne, is taken from a novel by R. A. Dick. The music is by Bernard Herrmann. The cast includes Edna Best, George Sanders, Natalie Wood, Vanessa Brown, Anna Lee, and Robert Coote. 20th Century-Fox. b & w

The Ghost Goes West (1935)—A rich American (Eugene Pallette) buys Glourie castle in Scotland, complete with its unhappy ghost, has it dismantled, shipped across the ocean, and reconstructed in Sunnymede, Florida, with modern plumbing. This crude, painfully frolicsome satire on America was written by Robert E. Sherwood and directed by René Clair. The movie is lucky in its star: Robert Donat brings elegance and his melancholy face and voice to the dual role of Donald Glourie and his phantom ancestor, Murdoch Glourie. Intermittently, he redeems the action. With Elsa Lanchester and Jean Parker. Americans loved the barbs thrust at them in this picture; it was very popular. b & w

Ghostbusters (1984)—A scare comedy, with Bill Murray, Dan Aykroyd, and Harold Ramis as parapsychologists who try to save New York City from an influx of spooks. Murray is the film's comic mechanism: the more supernatural the situation, the more jaded his reaction. But nobody else has much in the way of material, and since there's almost no give-and-take among the three men, Murray's lines fall on dead air. The film cost roughly $32 million, and the producer-director Ivan Reitman may have been overwhelmed by the scale of the sets and special effects; his work here is amateurish, with kids-movie pacing. Audiences respond to the picture, though, and their laughter helps to fill the dead spots. The movie does have some things going for it. Playing opposite Murray, Sigourney Weaver is a living zinger; when she stands talking to Murray, she's eye to eye

with him and she looks vivid and indestructible. When he asks her for a date, he rises in the viewer's estimation. (And in his own, too—after she agrees to go out with him, he lifts his arms toward heaven and twirls.) The cast includes Annie Potts, who uses her wonderful self-enclosed quality, and Rick Moranis, Ernie Hudson, William Atherton, and David Margulies. The script is by Aykroyd and Ramis; the cinematography is by Laszlo Kovacs. The images have a heavy, overdeliberate look—they're too rigid for comedy. Columbia. color (See *State of the Art.*)

Ghostbusters II (1989)—Surprisingly, it's more enjoyable than the first *Ghostbusters*. It's a big comedy, but it's light on its feet, and the throwaway jokes are weightless—they *ping*! and dissolve in the air. You can't remember what you're laughing at, but you feel great. The script, by Harold Ramis and Dan Aykroyd, is a floating crap game, like the scripts for the Hope and Crosby *Road* pictures. Bill Murray holds it together, and assorted comedians—Sigourney Weaver, Rick Moranis, Annie Potts, Ernie Hudson, Peter MacNicol, Cheech Marin, Harris Yulin, Ramis and Aykroyd—come in and out of the scenes, dropping one-liners. The comic premise is that the collective angry energy of Manhattanites is feeding an underground river of boiling slime, which is swelling; our bad vibes are literally destroying the city. Directed by Ivan Reitman; cinematography by Michael Chapman. Columbia. color (See *Movie Love.*)

Giant (1956)—George Stevens directed this handsomely designed, big, glossy version of the profoundly second-rate Edna Ferber novel about a couple of generations of a Texas cattle-ranching family, and James Dean (in a supporting role) ran away with it. This was the last film in his brief, meteoric career, and he was dead when it was released. His appearance here is particularly startling, because he plays his misfit role in the twitchy, self-conscious, "modern" manner of the 50s, while the rest of the movie is in the conventional heavy-going style that had always been deemed appropriate for sprawling family sagas. (This one sprawls for 3 hours and 18 minutes.) It's an example of commercial filmmaking straining for prestige, and the performers can't blink an eye without announcing that they're acting—and acting, what's more, to live up to the scale of the production. Yet Stevens' craftsmanship is effective at an unsubtle level, and the movie is often entertaining, with the narrative push that Ferber was so skilled at. Elizabeth Taylor and Rock Hudson are the leads; with Carroll Baker, Dennis Hopper, Rod Taylor, Mercedes McCambridge, Judith Evelyn, Sal Mineo, Jane Withers, Chill Wills, Alexander Scourby, and Earl Holliman. Screenplay by Fred Guiol and Ivan Moffat; music by Dmitri Tiomkin; cinematography by William C. Mellor; designed by Boris Leven, with Ralph Hurst. (Stills of the huge gothic house standing in a vast bare stretch of ground call up the movie as surely as the mention of "Rosebud" calls up *Citizen Kane*.) Warners. color

Il Giardino dei Finzi-Contini, see *The Garden of the Finzi-Continis*

La Gifle, see *The Slap*

Gigi (1950)—Danièle Delorme as Colette's Gigi—offspring of a long line of courtesans. Gigi's grandmother (Yvonne de Bray) and her great-aunt (Gaby Morlay), both retired from active service, attempt to train her to carry on the tradition, but the virtuous Gigi violates the rules. A pleasant, unexciting movie, with Frank Villard and Jean Tissier. Directed by Jacqueline Audry. In French. b & w

Gigi (1958)—A plushy, cheerful, musical version of the Colette story, with Leslie

Caron as the adolescent girl who is tutored to be a courtesan but is so enchantingly innocent and eager that she winds up the betrothed of the richest, handsomest young man in Paris. Vincente Minnelli directed, in a confident, confectionery style that carries all—or almost all—before it. The elderly Maurice Chevalier singing "Thank Heaven for Little Girls" may give one pause. With Louis Jourdan as Gigi's catch, and Hermione Gingold, Isabel Jeans, John Abbott, Eva Gabor, Jacques Bergerac, and Monique Van Vooren. Produced by Arthur Freed, book and lyrics by Alan Jay Lerner, music by Frederick Loewe, and costumes by Cecil Beaton. Ten Academy Awards, including Best Picture and Director. M-G-M. CinemaScope, color

Gilda (1946)—The story is turgid, melodramatic nonsense, but Rita Hayworth is at her most sexy-masochistic, and does a knockout of a fully dressed striptease as she sings "Put the Blame on Mame." (It's Anita Ellis's voice we hear.) With Glenn Ford and George Macready. Directed by Charles Vidor. Columbia. b & w

Ginger and Fred *Ginger e Fred* (1986)—The title of this Fellini movie is alluring, but the picture isn't about those two tapping, twirling icons. It's about two mediocre dancers (played by Giulietta Masina and Marcello Mastroianni)—small-timers, curiosities—who, in the 1940s, entertained Italian vaudeville audiences by imitating the Astaire-Rogers numbers. Now they are being reunited, in Rome, for an appearance on a Christmas TV special. This situation (which is reminiscent of Neil Simon's *The Sunshine Boys*) serves as a pretext for Fellini to vent his disgust at TV. He "flashes" his spoofs of TV programs and commercials as if they were obscene images, and he means them to be obscene. They're images of piggy abundance—oral and infantile. But Fellini has no zest to energize these skits, or the rest of the material, either. This is a cranky, wobbling movie. Fellini appears to be condemning TV for being a green slime that's absorbing everything, and denouncing it, too, for passing him by. The film treats Masina's character with an element of condescension, and Mastroianni is playing the Maestro's view of himself as an aging, crumbling tower of a man—a drunken bum. With Franco Fabrizi as host for the special and Frederick Ledebur as the old admiral. The score, by Nicola Piovani, has a lovely finesse; the script is by Fellini, Tonino Guerra, and Tullio Pinelli. In Italian. An Italian–French–West German film, produced by Alberto Grimaldi. color (See *Hooked*.)

Una Giornata Particolare, see *A Special Day*

Girl Crazy (1943)—This popular, second movie version of the 1930 Broadway musical with the score by George and Ira Gershwin stars Judy Garland and Mickey Rooney; it's more freely adapted than the first, a 1932 R K O film that starred Wheeler and Woolsey. This time the company is M-G-M, and the cast includes June Allyson and Nancy Walker, with Tommy Dorsey and his orchestra and nine Gershwin songs, including "Embraceable You" and the great, masochistic "But Not for Me." Norman Taurog directed; Busby Berkeley staged the song-and-dance sequences, including the killer finale, "I Got Rhythm," with Garland in white buckskins. (It had been Ethel Merman's big number in the original show.) With Guy Kibbee, Rags Ragland, Frances Rafferty, and Henry O'Neill. The script by Fred Finklehoffe, based on the play by Guy Bolton and Jack McGowan, has to do with the girl-crazy Rooney being sent to a boys' college in Arizona; he saves the school by staging a musical rodeo. In its own terms, the movie—the eighth Garland and Rooney had made together—is just

about irresistible. (A less buoyant, 1965 M-G-M version, with Connie Francis and Harve Presnell, was called *When the Boys Meet the Girls*.) b & w

A Girl in Black *Koritsi me ta Mavra* (1955)—The heroine is the classic beauty Ellie Lambetti, whose thoughtful, passionate Mediterranean face is one of the glories of Greek films. Here she plays the shy daughter of an impoverished, once-genteel family—a family that has become the victim of the meanness, the pettiness, and the harsh sexual standards of the villagers. She's trapped on an island where everyone knows everyone else and where throngs of children call out the news of her widowed mother's latest fornication. The young writer-director, Michael Cacoyannis, made *A Girl in Black* on the island of Hydra on a budget of approximately $60,000, with a single camera in the hands of Walter Lassally. It's a strongly individual work—the camera moves fluidly over the dark expressive faces and the narrow streets; the Greek sunlight hits the white houses and the whole island seems exposed. Cacoyannis's script is much smoother than in his earlier *Stella*, but there is no adequate preparation for the startling last sequence, which may give you the uncomfortable feeling that a group of children are drowned in order to strengthen the character of the hero—a weak Athenian writer (intelligently played by Dimitri Horn). The film has a vibrant simplicity, though, and its defects are, at least, Cacoyannis's—they're not the results of compromises and studio edicts. With Georges Foundas as a handsome, loutish fisherman; Notis Pergialis as the writer's friend; Eleni Zafiriou as the widow; and Anestis Vlachos as her son. In Greek. b & w

A Girl in the Mist *Kiri no Naka no Shojo* (1955)—One of the most artless and most charming Japanese films ever to reach the

West, Hideo Suzuki's 44-minute pastoral comedy is about a college student who has returned to her small-town home for the summer vacation and is visited by her Tokyo boyfriend. She, her younger sister, and the boy are three of the most radiant people ever seen on the screen. At times, they're so unlike the usual characters in movies that you forget this is a film, and a foreign one, at that. You may feel as if you were watching country neighbors and eavesdropping as the mother and father argue, the grandmother drinks, the adolescent sister worries about propriety. And it appears that intellectual college students have the same gaucherie and pretentiousness the world over. In Japanese. b & w

The Girl Was Young, see *Young and Innocent*

Giulietta degli Spiriti, see *Juliet of the Spirits*

Give a Girl a Break (1953)—An unusual M-G-M musical in that it is modest, but it is so modest that it has no particular flavor or distinction, despite the efforts of some talented people. Stanley Donen directed, and the cast includes Marge and Gower Champion, Bob Fosse, Debbie Reynolds, Kurt Kasznar, Helen Wood, Larry Keating, and Richard Anderson. The songs by Ira Gershwin and Burton Lane are remarkably uninspired; the choreography by Donen and Gower Champion is pleasant but not memorable. Frances Goodrich and Albert Hackett wrote the negligible script—a backstage story. It all reeks of niceness. color

The Glass Key (1942)—Alan Ladd, Veronica Lake, and Brian Donlevy in a not particularly memorable, though reasonably faithful, version of the Dashiell Hammett novel. Stuart Heisler directed, from Jonathan Latimer's screenplay. Paramount. b & w

The Glass Slipper (1955)—Leslie Caron as an elfin sweater-girl Cinderella, in a musical whimsey concocted by Helen Deutsch and directed by Charles Walters. This follow-up to their box-office hit *Lili* doesn't find a tone; the viewer can't help knowing that he's watching a flop. With Estelle Winwood as a loony kleptomaniac fairy godmother, Elsa Lanchester as the evil stepmother, Michael Wilding as the prince, Barry Jones his father, and Keenan Wynn his confidant. Also with Liliane Montevecchi, Amanda Blake, and Lurene Tuttle. There are a couple of ballets choreographed by Roland Petit. M-G-M. color

The Glenn Miller Story (1954)—Blandly dull big bio, with James Stewart as a pedantic Glenn Miller; with Miller trying to discover "his own sound," it's like a Hollywood version of the life of an inventor. June Allyson plays the all-American square Miller marries; right after the ceremony, she is taken up to Harlem, where Gene Krupa and Louis Armstrong get into a jam session (they do "Basin Street Blues"), and it's typical of the family-films format that we're expected to identify with her getting tired and sleepy. Most of the music in this film does have a soporific quality. Miller's famous numbers, such as "Tuxedo Junction" and "Little Brown Jug," have been re-created (Joe Yukl dubs Stewart on the trombone), and they don't quite swing. The director, Anthony Mann, seems out of his element. With Henry (later Harry) Morgan, Sig Rumann, George Tobias, Charles Drake, Carleton Young, Frances Langford (as a blonde), and the Modernaires, the Archie Savage Dancers, and the Mello-Men. The script is by Valentine Davies and Oscar Brodney. Universal. color

Glorifying the American Girl (1929)—The rise of a young girl (Mary Eaton) from the sheet-music department of a big store, through the dilemmas of small-town vaudeville, to her ultimate glorification in the Ziegfeld Follies, where, finally, we get glimpses of Helen Morgan, Rudy Vallee, and Eddie Cantor, as well as Ziegfeld himself (who also supervised the production), and such celebrities as Mayor Jimmy Walker, Ring Lardner, Texas Guinan, Johnny Weissmuller, Otto Kahn, and Adolph Zukor. Along her interminable way, the heroine renounces love (Edward Crandall) for the headdresses and bangles of a showgirl; the moral is that you pay a price for applause. Meanwhile, the moviegoer who wants to see how musical numbers were staged in Ziegfeld's day pays heavily for a few minutes of pleasure. The songs include "At Sundown," "Blue Skies," "What Wouldn't I Do for That Man," and "I'm Just a Vagabond Lover." Millard Webb directed; Ted Shawn choreographed the ballets. The Follies sequences were originally in Technicolor. Paramount Famous Lasky.

Glory (1989)—This Civil War epic, based on fiery, spirit-stirring material that had never before been tapped for the movies, is emotionally moving even when the scenes falter. It's about the 54th Regiment of Massachusetts Volunteer Infantry, the first black fighting unit to be formed in the North. Robert Gould Shaw, the 25-year-old son of abolitionists, was the colonel in charge; he was to carry out the visionary plan of proving that black men had the discipline and valor to stand up against the enemy. As the shy idealist Shaw, Matthew Broderick shows us the misery of a softhearted commanding officer who is determined to prepare his men for what's ahead; it's a lovely performance, as remote and touching as a daguerreotype. The more flamboyant performances are given by Denzel Washington as an ornery, troublemaking runaway slave, Morgan Freeman as a former gravedigger, and Andre Braugher as a bookish recruit. They're performers of such skill that they're vivid, and almost persuasive, as

enlistees who bicker and quarrel before they shape up and become fine soldiers. (The actors perform these roles as if they've never been played before.) Although the script is a conventional melodrama, the director, Edward Zwick, has made something more thoughtful than that. He doesn't have the instinct for images that would burst the written framework, but he's made a good film on a great subject. With Jihmi Kennedy, who is quietly impressive as a backcountry recruit, and Cary Elwes as a white officer. The screenplay, based partly on Shaw's letters, is by Kevin Jarre. The cinematography is by Freddie Francis, and the score, which features the Boys Choir of Harlem, is by James Horner. Tri-Star. color (See *Movie Love.*)

Go Into Your Dance (1935)—Al Jolson and Ruby Keeler have a terrific number together ("About a Quarter to Nine"), and when he sings "She's a Latin from Manhattan," you get a sense of how magnetic he must have been on the stage. The movie isn't topnotch, though; the script (by Earl Baldwin, from a story by Bradford Ropes) is dreary and things don't quite come together. But the cast includes Helen Morgan, Glenda Farrell, Patsy Kelly, Akim Tamiroff, Benny Rubin, Phil Regan, Sharon Lynne, and Barton MacLane; the songwriters Al Dubin and Harry Warren also appear. Ruby Keeler had been in many musicals before this one, but she retains her peculiarly appealing (and baffling) amateurishness. Archie Mayo directed, for Warners. b & w

Go West (1925)—Not one of the great Buster Keaton comedies. It's perhaps unique among his films in that it aims for intense pathos; however, it's sad and funny at the same time—which wasn't true of Chaplin's pathos. Keaton plays Friendless—a lonely, buffeted, uncomplaining drifter without home, country, or dime. Having found the city's heart cold, he hides in a freight train going to Arizona, and there among the cacti he finds his first and only comfort and fellowship in a sad-eyed cow. Together they weather it through storm and sunshine. (The cow has a lot of personality—she may remind you of Daisy, Gene Wilder's beloved sheep, in Woody Allen's *Everything You Always Wanted to Know About Sex*.) Keaton is so unembarrassed and so unself-consciously stoic in adversity that the pathos is never offensive—not even when a dog he tries to pat moves away from him. It's a strange movie, directed and partly written by Keaton right after the breakup of the team he had been working with since his 2-reeler days. There's an amazing finale, in which Friendless and Brown Eyes the Cow round up hundreds of steers that are bellowing through the streets of Los Angeles. Silent. M-G-M. b & w

Go West (1941)—The Marx Brothers in what is, arguably, their worst picture; *Love Happy* is possibly even worse. This one—set in the Old West—has a good opening sequence and not much else. The cast includes John Carroll, Walter Woolf King, and Iris Adrian; Edward Buzzell directed; and the script can be blamed on Irving Brecher. M-G-M. b & w

The Goddess (1958)—Paddy Chayefsky's attack on the American dream of stardom centers on an unloved child in the South who grows up incapable of loving and becomes a big empty wreck of a Marilyn Monroe–type star. (It's a kind of clinical sentimentality.) The film takes a psychiatric and sociological view of her career: she's a pathetic creature who has been deceived by false values and is destroyed by the bitch-goddess Success. Chayefsky is so concerned with the heroine's pitifully unformed character that he fails to suggest what would make her stand out from all the other poor, deceived girls—what

would make her a star. This is a conscientious, ambitious bad movie, with Chayefsky's famous ear for dialogue in full cauliflower. John Cromwell directed the high-powered cast. The intense Kim Stanley is in the central role (her compelling overnon-acting makes the bum writing rather painful). Patty Duke plays the heroine as the lonely child with no one to praise her; she informs her cat, "Kitty, I got promoted today"—a line which became a camp favorite. Betty Lou Holland is the star's mother. Steven Hill is the star's first husband; he's called upon to deliver the author's prophetic insights—i.e., the lines that should have been cut. Lloyd Bridges gives a fine performance as the prizefighter husband, who feels shut out by his wife's misery. And Elizabeth Wilson is the final, gorgonlike attendant. The score is by Virgil Thomson. (Collectors of errata may note that Chayefsky has the heroine say she was in *Stage Door* by "Moss Hart and George S. Kaufman.") Columbia. b & w

The Godfather (1972)—A wide, startlingly vivid view of a Mafia dynasty, in which organized crime becomes an obscene nightmare image of American free enterprise. The movie is a popular melodrama with its roots in the gangster films of the 30s, but it expresses a new tragic realism, and it's altogether extraordinary. Francis Ford Coppola directed. Marlon Brando is Don Vito Corleone, with Al Pacino, John Cazale, James Caan, and Talia Shire as his children. The cast includes Robert Duvall, Richard Castellano as Clemenza, Diane Keaton, John Marley, Lenny Montana, Richard Conte, Sterling Hayden, Abe Vigoda, Al Lettieri, Alex Rocco, Richard Bright, Simonetta Stefanelli as Apollonia, Gianni Russo, and Al Martino. The script, credited to Mario Puzo and Coppola, is based on Puzo's best-seller. (The film runs just under 3 hours; the period is 1945 to the mid-50s.) Cinematography by Gordon Willis;

production design by Dean Tavoularis; music by Nino Rota. Paramount. color (See *Deeper into Movies*.)

The Godfather Part II (1974)—The daring of *Part II* is that it enlarges the scope and deepens the meaning of the first film. Visually, *Part II* is far more complexly beautiful than the first, just as it's thematically richer, more shadowed, fuller. The completed work, contrasting the early manhood of Vito (Robert De Niro) with the life of Michael, his inheritor (Al Pacino), is an epic vision of the corruption of America. (The 3 hours and 20 minutes of *Part II* span almost 70 years.) Directed by Francis Ford Coppola. The script is credited to Coppola and Mario Puzo, from Puzo's novel. The cast includes Robert Duvall, John Cazale, Lee Strasberg, Michael V. Gazzo, Talia Shire, Troy Donahue, Gianni Russo, Diane Keaton, G. D. Spradlin, Morgana King, Harry Dean Stanton, Joe Spinell, Fay Spain, Danny Aiello, Richard Bright, Gaston Moschin as Fanucci, Abe Vigoda, Tom Rosqui, B. Kirby, Jr., Leopoldo Trieste, and a brief appearance by James Caan, and appearances by Phil Feldman, Roger Corman, and William Bowers as United States senators. Cinematography by Gordon Willis; production design by Dean Tavoularis; music by Nino Rota, conducted by Carmine Coppola. Paramount. color (See *Reeling*.)

Goin' Down the Road (1970)—There is scarcely a false touch. The Canadian Don Shebib is so good at blending actors into locations that one has to remind oneself that this is an acted film and not a documentary. Shebib has a delicate feeling for the nuances not of traditional "class" but of the class tones that come from different educations, and he uses this gift to put in social perspective the lives of two totally unhip boys from Nova Scotia (Doug McGrath and Paul Bradley) who come to Toronto for the legendary opportu-

nities of the big city. Perceptively acted, though the story is too familiar and the film turns out to be a somewhat hollow triumph of craft. In color (sensitively shot) and blown up from 16 mm; the total cost was $82,000. (See *Deeper into Movies*.)

Goin' South (1978)—Jack Nicholson directed and plays a cackling, scratching, horny, mangy slob in this barnyard comedy set in the Old West. He's about to be strung up, but the Texas border town he's in has an unusual ordinance: a condemned outlaw can escape the noose if a woman of property agrees to marry him. A virginal young Miss Muffet type (Mary Steenburgen), who needs a man to work her gold mine, claims him, and the film is about their squabblings and misunderstandings until they find love—it's a mixture of *Blazing Saddles* and *The African Queen*. Nicholson's fatuous leering performance dominates the movie, and because his prankishness also comes out in the casting and directing, the movie hasn't any stabilizing force; there's nothing to balance what he's doing—no one with a strait jacket. An actor-director who prances about the screen manically can easily fool himself into thinking that his film is jumping; Nicholson jumps, all right, but the movie is inert. With Veronica Cartwright, John Belushi (in his movie début), Christopher Lloyd, Richard Bradford, Luana Anders, Danny DeVito, and Ed Begley, Jr. Cinematography by Nestor Almendros; script by an assortment of writers. Paramount. color (See *When the Lights Go Down*.)

Going Places *Les Valseuses* (1974)—Bertrand Blier's explosively funny erotic farce is both a celebration and a satire of men's daydreams. It makes you laugh at things that shock you, and some people find its gusto revolting in much the same way that the bursting comic force of the sexual hyperbole in Henry Miller's book *Tropic of Cancer* was thought revolting. The crude energy of the two young roughneck protagonists (Gérard Depardieu and Patrick Dewaere) is overwhelming, grungy, joyous. They're outsiders without jobs or money who want to satisfy their appetites. So they snatch purses, steal cars, swipe things from shops, and make passes at almost every woman they get near. It takes a half hour or so before a viewer grasps that the two pals are guileless raw innocents and that almost everything they do backfires on them. They're cavemen who give women what in their exuberant male fantasies women want. Brutal, lyrical slapstick connections get made in this movie. With Brigitte Fossey as the nursing mother on the train; Miou-Miou as the scraggly blond waif; Jeanne Moreau as the middle-aged woman who, after 10 years in prison, emerges sex-starved; and Isabelle Huppert as the teen-ager. The screenplay, by Blier and Philippe Dumarcay, is based on Blier's novel. The cinematography is by Bruno Nuytten; the jazz violin score is by Stephane Grappelli. In French. b & w (See *When the Lights Go Down*.)

Gold (1974)—A recycling of the old straightforward adventure films: the musty plot is about an international syndicate that floods a South African mine in order to drive up the price of gold. The picture is mindlessly passable, largely because it was shot on location in South African mines and in and around Johannesburg. The director, Peter Hunt, can't be much more than efficient with this material, but at least he doesn't try to squeeze us emotionally on behalf of the stock characters, played by bland, dimply Roger Moore, and Simon Sabela, Susannah York, Bradford Dillman, John Gielgud, and Ray Milland, who manages to inject the only note of personality. The script is by Wilbur Smith

and Stanley Price. Allied Artists. color (See *Reeling*.)

Gold Diggers of 1933—A funny, good-natured backstage musical, and a Depression period piece as well. It sums up what is meant by the phrase "pure thirties." Ginger Rogers wears a costume made of big coins and sings "We're in the Money" in pig Latin, and 60 electrically wired chorus girls, singing "In the shadows let me come and sing to you" while waltzing and playing violins, merge to form one great big neon fiddle. Warners advertised that this film would "surpass the glories of *42nd Street*" (which had come out earlier in the year) and the geometric choreographer Busby Berkeley and the songwriters Harry Warren and Al Dubin all tried to top themselves. Mervyn LeRoy directed this time, and the plot is something about Dick Powell as a blueblood songwriter trying to raise money for a show he has written. The cast is a Who's Who of Warners types: the prim, awesomely untalented Ruby Keeler, and Joan Blondell, Warren William, Aline MacMahon, Ned Sparks, Guy Kibbee, Sterling Holloway, Ferdinand Gottschalk, and Billy Barty as the infant who winks at Dick Powell and hands him a can opener to use on Ruby Keeler's shiny tin costume, in the "Pettin' in the Park" sequence. Busby Berkeley appears in a bit part as the backstage call-boy (can this really be the correct term?) shouting such directions as "On stage for the Forgotten Man number!" The black singer in this number is Etta Moten. The script by Erwin Gelsey and James Seymour is based on an Avery Hopwood play; cinematography by Sol Polito. b & w

Gold Diggers of 1935—Dick Powell is hired by Alice Brady to escort her daughter, Gloria Stuart, while Gloria's fiancé, Hugh Herbert, completes his book on snuffboxes. Guess what happens. The score is good, even though the picture is terrible—in a pleasant sort of way. Busby Berkeley, who usually only choreographed, did the directing, too, and everything seems labored. With Glenda Farrell, Wini Shaw, Adolphe Menjou, Frank McHugh, and Grant Mitchell. The songs by Al Dubin and Harry Warren include "The Lullaby of Broadway" and "The Words Are in My Heart." Script by Manuel Seff, Peter Milne, and the producer, Robert Lord; cinematography by George Barnes. First National. b & w

The Gold of Naples *L'Oro di Napoli* (1956)—Vittorio De Sica directed this collection of Neapolitan episodes, featuring Totò as a little clown imposed on by a bullying racketeer, Silvana Mangano as a prostitute, Sophia Loren in her celebrated comic turn as a pizza seller, and De Sica himself as a gambler—which the whole world knows he was. He was also a director who could combine melancholy and wit. It's an uneven film, but Loren walking and De Sica gambling are works of art. In Italian. b & w

The Gold Rush (1925)—He enters, "pursued by a bear"—the man who for generations of filmgoers has been the embodiment of "the little fellow": humanity. In this extraordinarily sweet and graceful comedy, Chaplin is the weak and helpless perfect gentleman in the Klondike world of bears and brutes; yet his gallantry wins him the gold and the girl, too. In 1958 an international jury at Brussels selected this work as the second greatest film of all time (after *Potemkin*). With Mack Swain as Big Jim, Georgia Hale, Tom Murray, and Henry Bergman. Produced, written, and directed by Chaplin; the assisting directors were Charles Riesner and H. d'Abbadie d'Arrast; the cinematographer was Rollie Totheroh. (The snowy exteriors were filmed in Nevada.) Silent; Chaplin later added music and a narration. b & w

The Golden Age of Comedy (1957)—These sequences from Mack Sennett and Hal Roach 2-reelers made between 1923 and 1928 show off the talents of Ben Turpin, Harry Langdon, Will Rogers, the Keystone Cops, the Sennett Bathing Beauties, etc., and best of all, they exhibit Stan Laurel and Oliver Hardy in several classics of demolition-style silent comedy. Their custard pie sequence is perhaps the high point of the collection—a demonstration that throwing a pie can be both art and science. In *The Cosmological Eye* Henry Miller called it "the ultimate in burlesque" and "the greatest comic film ever made—because it brought pie-throwing to apotheosis." Their paintbrush routine is a beauty, and there is also a methodical, fatalistic car-wrecking ritual. Jean Harlow makes a stunning appearance in black teddies, but Carole Lombard is, unfortunately, not at her best. Robert Youngson compiled these clips (the original directors include Frank Capra, Leo McCarey, and George Stevens); Youngson added a tireless narrator who lards the clips with a layer of sentiment about how "beloved" these players were, and what "tragic" fates they met, and explanations of gags that are perfectly clear to the eye. But the irritations are minor when you are looking at what is possibly the best collection of sight gags ever brought together. b & w

Golden Boy (1939)—William Holden—young, sensitive, and handsome—as the violinist turned prizefighter, in an only semi-reprehensible version of the Clifford Odets play, directed by Rouben Mamoulian. The role of Lorna Moon was built up to be large enough for Barbara Stanwyck, and the play was softened, rearranged, and wrenched around to provide for a happy ending. Yet the Odets material still has its dramatic pull, and Lee J. Cobb as the boy's father, Sam Levene as his taxi-driver brother-in-law, and Joseph Calleia as the slimy gangster out to corrupt him bring back some of the ambiance of the New York theatre in Odets' impassioned heyday. Adolphe Menjou plays the prizefight manager; with Don Beddoe, Edward S. Brophy, Frank Jenks, and Clinton Rosemond. Cinematography by Nicholas Musuraca and Karl Freund. Produced by William Perlberg, for Columbia. b & w

The Golden Coach (1953)—At his greatest, Jean Renoir expressed the beauty in our common humanity; that's what Anna Magnani at *her* greatest expressed. This movie—his tribute to the commedia dell'arte—is also a tribute to her fabulous gifts, and she gives the film its gusto. We see her here not only as a sensual, earthy "woman of the people" but as an artist who exhausts her resources in creating the illusion of volcanic reality. Though Renoir has taken Prosper Mérimée's vehicle and shaped it for her, it will be forever debatable whether it contains her or she explodes it. But as this puzzle is parallel with the theme—a Pirandellian confusion of theatre and everyday life—it adds another layer to the ironic comedy. The film is set in a dusty frontier in Renaissance Peru: a band of Italian strolling players is attempting to bring art to South America. The movie has been compared to *Così Fan Tutte*—it is light and serious, cynical and beautiful, a blend of color, wit, and Vivaldi music. Though Magnani, in her first English-speaking role, is vocally magnificent, some of the other actors speak in dreary tones and some of the minor characters appear to be dubbed. Duncan Lamont, as the Spanish viceroy, and Riccardo Rioli, as the bullfighter, are just fine, but Paul Campbell, as the Castilian nobleman, is inept and his scenes go limp. This was Renoir's second color film (after *The River*), and his directorial rhythm seems to falter in his work in color, but in the glow and warmth of *The Golden Coach* this defect, like the others, is trifling.

The cinematography is by Claude Renoir. (See *I Lost it at the Movies*.)

The Good Earth (1937)—Having purchased Pearl S. Buck's prestigious Chinese-family saga, M-G-M sent an expedition to China which brought back two million feet of atmospheric shots and 18 tons of costumes, native animals, dismantled farmhouses, and a village shrine. Then 500 California acres were landscaped and terraced to simulate a Chinese farm, locusts were rented for a scourge, and Occidentals were chosen for the leads, with Orientals in the supporting roles, and as the babies. Luise Rainer, who had taken an Academy Award for her Anna Held in *The Great Ziegfeld*, won another for her monotonous yet affecting performance as the stoic O-Lan, the wife of the peasant Wang (Paul Muni); during the looting of a manor house, she picks up the jewels which raise her family out of starvation into prosperity. But spoiled by wealth, Wang loses contact with the good earth; he becomes infatuated with Lotus, the dancer (Tilly Losch, who does a lot of finger-twirling), and takes her as his second wife, and his lust almost destroys the family. The locust plague brings him to his senses. It's a melodramatic sermon—a glorification of the passive, selfless, suffering mother, O-Lan. (There isn't a shred of sympathy for Lotus, who is bought and sold.) The film domesticates exoticism: it's as predictable as an Andy Hardy picture, but much more sober, and much, much longer. With Walter Connolly as the scoundrelly uncle, Charley Grapewin as the family patriarch, Keye Luke and Roland Lui as the sons, Jessie Ralph, and Harold Huber. The script by Talbot Jennings, Tess Slesinger, and Claudine West was partly based on a stage version by Owen and Donald Davis. This film, which was four years in the making, is dedicated to its producer, Irving Thalberg, who died in 1936; his associate, Albert Lewin, completed it. The first director, George Hill, who had supervised shooting the background footage in China, committed suicide, and the project was taken over by Sidney Franklin, who directed with his usual lack of imagination, individuality, style. He was the M-G-M heavyweight champ. Herbert Stothart was in charge of the music; the montage work is by Slavko Vorkapich; Arnold Gillespie headed the special effects department that produced the visually exciting locust attack. The cinematographer was the great Karl Freund. In sepia.

The Good Fairy (1935)—Hired to sanitize one of Ferenc Molnár's lesser plays, Preston Sturges embroidered the whimsical comedy until it was almost worthy of the talents of Margaret Sullavan. (He also managed to work in one of the movie-within-a-movie scenes that later bacame one of his trademarks.) Sullavan plays a naïve, unworldly orphan who becomes an usher in a movie theatre; she's so helplessly innocent that various men (Herbert Marshall, Frank Morgan, Reginald Owen) come to her aid, and their lives get turned upside down. William Wyler, who directed, has told the story of how he quarrelled with Margaret Sullavan at first, and the tension between them made her look nervous and strained in the rushes. In order to improve her appearance he took her out to dinner to make peace, and was so successful that they were married two weeks before the picture was finished. With Cesar Romero, Alan Hale, Beulah Bondi, Eric Blore, and Hugh O'Connell. Cinematography by Norbert Brodine. Universal. b & w

The Good Father (1986)—Directed by Mike Newell, it has the festering gloom and dissatisfied-with-itself hatefulness that seem to be the mid-80s English badge of integrity. Anthony Hopkins plays Bill Hooper, who was once a college radical and aspiring writer, and is now a grimy-souled marketing executive with a publishing house. He came of age in the 60s, believing in equal rights for women; he's still pro-feminist but when he thinks of the wife he has left he hears himself muttering "Bloody bitch." (And he has horrible, guilty dreams of murdering his tiny son.) Based on the 1983 novel by Peter Prince, this is an attempt to get at the new complications in the sex wars and perhaps at the whole modern English muddle. There are glimmers of truth in this movie, and it holds you, yet everything seems blue and damp and constricted. If Newell has a goal, it seems to be to leave you with a sense of impacted bleakness. You never see Bill Hooper (or the director) take pleasure in anything. Newell keeps showing you what lice Englishmen are. (Englishwomen seem exempt from the moral pollution—they've been made a shade too tender and decent.) With Jim Broadbent, Fanny Viner, Harriet Walter, and bravura turns by Simon Callow as a beady-eyed little devil of a barrister and Miriam Margolyes as a feminist lawyer up against a reactionary judge. Screenplay by Christopher Hampton. Financed by British television (Group Four). Released in the U.S. by Skouras Pictures. color (See *Hooked*.)

Good Morning, Babylon (1987)—The first film made in English by the Taviani brothers tells the story of two teen-age Tuscan workmen (Vincent Spano and Joaquim de Almeida), from a family of church builders and restorers, who go off to seek their fortune in the New World. Eventually they find jobs as plasterers in San Francisco, working on the Italian Pavilion of the 1915 Panama-Pacific Exposition, and then in Hollywood, working for D. W. Griffith (Charles Dance), building the elephants for the Babylonian set of *Intolerance*. But it takes them too dismally long to get to the West Coast: the film's poetic, storybook style slumps into masochism during their hardships in this country, when they work at bizarre, humiliating jobs along the way. And even after they reach L.A. and meet the people associated with Griffith they seem pitiable, and it takes forever (and more humiliation) before the great man gives them the nod. There are some lovely effects, but the attempt to show that the magic of movies comes out of anonymous, egalitarian teamwork makes your tongue feel coated. With Greta Scacchi, Desiree Becker, Omero Antonutti, and Margarita Lozano. Based on an idea by Lloyd Fonvielle, the screenplay is by the Tavianis and Tonino Guerra. The music is by Nicola Piovani; the cinematography is by Giuseppe Lanci. Early L.A. was re-created in Italy and the Grand Canyon sequence was shot in Spain. (The Tavianis don't speak English.) An Italian-French-U.S. production. color (See *Hooked*.)

Good Morning, Vietnam (1987)—It sounded like a first-rate idea: Robin Williams doing his manic free-association comedy as a disc jockey, Adrian Cronauer, on Armed Forces Radio in Saigon in 1965. But the picture makes the character out to be a vulnerable, compassionate, respectful-of-the-Vietnamese wonderful guy, and the director, Barry Levinson, has a numbing sense of rhythm. Williams' riffs are chopped short, and the film keeps cutting to soldiers breaking up over his spiel before it's out of his mouth. There is an Adrian Cronauer, and the movie is very loosely based on his exploits, but the way the story line (from the script by Mitch Markowitz) has been directed it's a clumsier version of the plots of 50s musicals. With Forest Whitaker, Bruno Kirby, J. T. Walsh, Uikey Kuay as the elderly student of English, and Richard Edson. (People who want to see Williams running wild within a character ought to take a look at the 1983 *The Survivors* or the 1986 *The Best of Times*.) Touchstone (Disney). color (See *Hooked*.)

The Good Mother (1988)—When Anna (Diane Keaton), the divorced mother of a 6-year-old daughter, discovers sexual pleasure with an Irish sculptor (Liam Neeson) and begins to live a more bohemian existence, her ex-husband sues for the child's custody. The director, Leonard Nimoy, and the screenwriter, Michael Bortman, who adapted the 1986 Sue Miller novel, ask us to see Anna as a victim of generations of patriarchal domination. She has been recklessly happy with the Irishman, but now she goes limp. For the sake of her child, she accepts the limited role in her daughter's future which the court grants her. She learns to live with her loss. And though this is what her character has been rigged to do from the start, it's a let-down for the audience. Since the movie is the story of Anna's meek, uncomprehending acceptance of defeat and her effort to make the best of it, women can feel it's saying, "That's how it is, folks. Resign yourselves." The big clinker in this victimization fantasy (losing her child is the price a woman pays for an orgasm) is that it's a few decades too late. You sit in the audience thinking that a different judge would have made all the difference, or that the case might have been won by an attorney less hidebound than the fogey she hires—Jason Robards, in a gloomy brown office that seems to say "All hope abandon." And so the whole structure seems shaky; it provides an inevitability that you can't accept. The movie has a sickly passivity. (Elmer Bernstein provides oozing, sad music.) But Neeson comes through strongly, the child is well played by Asia Vieira, and Diane Keaton, whose daring is in her spontaneity, has a gift for making even closed-in characters like Anna transparent. She's extraordinary. With Joe Morton, Tracy Griffith, and shamefully poorly directed performances by Ralph Bellamy, Teresa Wright, and James Naughton. Touchstone (Disney). color (See *Movie Love*.)

G

Good News (1947)—One of the best of the lighthearted rah-rah collegiate musicals. The affable young Peter Lawford and goofy, blithe June Allyson are the leads and do the number "The French Lesson," by Comden and Green and Roger Edens, and Joan McCracken, with a gleeful look in her eyes, dances and sings the memorable novelty "Pass That Peace Pipe," by Edens and Ralph Blane and Hugh Martin. The rest of the score, including "The Varsity Drag," "Lucky in Love," and "The Best Things in Life Are Free," is from the original 1927 Broadway show by DeSylva, Brown, and Henderson (which was filmed once before, in 1930). This was the first film directed by the choreographer Charles Walters, and the first movie script by Comden and Green. The cast includes Mel Tormé, Ray McDonald, Patricia Marshall, Donald MacBride, Clinton Sundberg, Morris Ankrum, Tom Dugan, and Connie Gilchrist. Produced by Arthur Freed, for M-G-M. color

The Good, the Bad and the Ugly *Il Buono il Brutto il Cattivo* (1966)—In this Sergio Leone spaghetti Western, if a man crosses a street in Santa Fe, the street looks half a mile wide; a farmer's hut has rooms opening into rooms into the distance, like the Metropolitan Museum; a cowtown hotel has a plush lobby big enough for a political convention. The movie is like *High Noon* and *The Ox-Bow Incident* and a dozen others all scrambled together and playing in a giant echo chamber. The bad men are enormously, preposterously evil—larger-than-life parodies—and each wound they inflict is insanely garish. The change of scale is rather fascinating. This Western, set in our Civil War period but shot in Spain, looks more foreign to us than an ordinary Italian film. With Clint Eastwood, Eli Wallach, and Lee Van Cleef. Score by Ennio Morricone. color

Goodbye, Children, see *Au revoir les enfants*

The Goodbye Girl (1977)—The prolific Neil Simon at it again; this time it's a tearful comedy that he wrote directly for the screen, and for Marsha Mason and Richard Dreyfuss. She's a 30ish former chorus girl who has been deserted by an actor husband and then by an actor lover, and has become so defensive that she's hostile toward a new actor (Dreyfuss) who, through elaborately contrived circumstances, comes to share the apartment she and her 10-year-old daughter (Quinn Cummings) live in. So she says gratuitously abrasive things to him, and he prisses his lips and tells her off. The forced snappiness of the exchanges suggests two woodpeckers clicking at each other's heads. Irritability provides the rhythm in Neil Simon's universe. The only relief comes when Dreyfuss is rehearsing in *Richard III*—Shakespeare's dialogue is a blessed sound. Simon's idea of depth is a tug at your heartstrings, and Marsha Mason's chin keeps quivering—her face is either squinched up to cry or crinkled up to laugh. This may be the bravest, teariest, most crumpled-face performance since the days of Janet Gaynor. Another hit. Herbert Ross directed; the cast includes Paul Benedict, Barbara Rhoades, Theresa Merritt, and Marilyn Sokol. (Dreyfuss won the Academy Award for Best Actor.) Produced by Ray Stark; Warners. color (See *When the Lights Go Down*.)

Goodbye, Mr. Chips (1939)—James Hilton's gentle tribute to his schoolmaster father became an American best-seller when that old sentimentalist Alexander Woollcott touted it on the radio. M-G-M bought the novel and sent Sam Wood to England to film it. Robert Donat's portrait of the frightened young junior master, rigid and forbidding in his twenties, who is humanized by marriage and mellowed by 60 years of contact with youth, won him the Academy Award for Best Actor.

Greer Garson, in her screen début, played his warm and gracious wife. An overripe little boy named Terry Kilburn played the ubiquitous Little Colley. It's an ingratiating, bittersweet record of a good life, though the movie clogs the nose more than necessary. b & w

Goodbye, Mr. Chips (1969)—An overblown version of James Hilton's tearstained little gold mine of a book, with songs where they are not needed (and Leslie Bricusse's songs are never needed), yet there's still charm in the story, and Peter O'Toole gives a romantic performance of great distinction as the schoolmaster whose life is transformed by the Cinderella touch of an actress, played now by Petula Clark. (She isn't good at the beginning but she has a lovely glow in the Second World War period of the film.) Terence Rattigan, who did the new adaptation, has added a character—an actress named Ursula Mossbank; as played by Sian Phillips she's a witty Beardsley vamp who gives her scenes an edge. This new picture is far from being a good one, and every time a music cue starts up your heart may sink, but the first-time director, Herbert Ross (who was formerly a choreographer), has managed to keep parts of it fairly buoyant. And O'Toole's performance may help sustain you through the songs, though there are 11 of them, as distinct one from another as sections of beige wall-to-wall carpet, and while they're being sung, mostly offscreen, you're treated to "mood" visuals—providing enough redundancy to pad the movie out to 2 hours and 31 minutes. M-G-M. color (See *Deeper into Movies*.)

GoodFellas (1990)—The director, Martin Scorsese, gives you a lift. He loves the Brooklyn organized-crime milieu, because it's where distortion, hyperbole, and exuberance all commingle. His mobsters are high on having a wad of cash in their pockets. The movie is about being cock of the walk, with banners flying and crowds cheering. Based on Nicholas Pileggi's non-fiction book *Wiseguy*, it's a triumphant piece of filmmaking—journalism and sociology presented with the brio of drama. But the three major hoods, played by Ray Liotta, Robert De Niro, and Joe Pesci, don't have a strong enough presence, and the movie lacks the juice and richness that come with major performances. (It's like the Howard Hawks *Scarface* without Scarface.) What you respond to is Scorsese's bravura: the filmmaking process becomes the subject of the movie. Watching it is like getting strung out on pure sensation. Paul Sorvino as Paulie and Lorraine Bracco as Karen both come through, and Tony Darrow as a restaurant owner, Welker White as a drug courier who needs her lucky hat to make a coke delivery, and other performers in minor roles give the movie a frenzied, funny texture. Christopher Serrone plays the boy who turns into Liotta. The screenplay is by Pileggi and Scorsese; the cinematography is by Michael Ballhaus; the editing is by Thelma Schoonmaker. Warners. color (See *Movie Love*.)

The Goonies (1985)—A group of kids in a seaport town in Oregon search in the caves along the coast, looking for the buried treasure left by One-Eyed Willie, a 17th-century pirate, and find his ship floating in an underground lagoon. With its echoes of *Peter Pan* and *Treasure Island* and Tom Sawyer and Becky caught in the caves, this adventure comedy should be wonderful fun. Produced by Steven Spielberg, who also wrote the story, it's full of slapstick cliff-hangers, like a junior edition of *1941* and *Indiana Jones and the Temple of Doom*, and some of the sets designed by J. Michael Riva have a magical aura. But it was directed by Richard Donner, who doesn't invite the audience in or shape the scenes—there's all this stuff going on and none of it stands out. And with the kids' constant jabbering, the clutter, the hyperexcited rushing about, and the many scenes shot in the claustrophobic darkness of the caves, the movie can really give you a case of the heebie-jeebies. With Ke Huy Quan as Data, who devises contraptions, Sean Astin as Mikey, Josh Brolin as Brand, Jeff Cohen as Chunk, Corey Feldman as Mouth, Martha Plimpton as Stef, Kerri Green as Andy, and Anne Ramsey as Mama Fratelli, Robert Davi as her son Jake, Joe Pantoliano as her son Francis, and John Matuszak as the amiable monster Sloth. The script is by Chris Columbus; the cinematography is by Nick McLean. Warners. color

The Gorgeous Hussy (1936)—The title is deceptive. The film is about Andrew Jackson (Lionel Barrymore) and his Presidential problems. Specifically, it deals with his dissolving his Cabinet because the wives of the members had cut a certain Mrs. Eaton (Joan Crawford). Something like this actually happened, though the picture will never convince anyone of it. Beulah Bondi smokes a corncob with the assurance befitting a First Lady, Melvyn Douglas plays dreary, gentlemanly John Randolph, and Robert Taylor and Franchot Tone are the handsome young men. Clarence Brown directed. M-G-M. b & w

Gorillas in the Mist (1988)—Sigourney Weaver as the anthropologist Dian Fossey, in what seems meant to be a triumphant epic about an activist heroine who made a difference. (A title at the close tells us that Fossey saved the mountain gorillas from extinction.) Weaver's physical strength alone is inspiring here, and there's a new freedom in her acting. She's so vivid that you immediately feel Fossey's will and drive. But Michael Apted, who directed, has an indeterminate approach to some of the key incidents; he doesn't locate a dramatic core in Anna Hamilton Phelan's

script. The movie is reasonably faithful to Fossey's ruthless, half-crazed side and it's quite watchable, but it's disappointing. It belongs to the past of movies rather than to the modern era. The Maurice Jarre music is a definite negative factor; another is the use of the head tracker as the symbolic dignity and conscience of Africa. Despite the subject, the movie can't be taken seriously. It's a feminist version of *King Kong*—now it's the gorillas who do the screaming. With Bryan Brown, Julie Harris, John Omirah Miluwi as the tracker, and Iain Cuthbertson, who's casual and rather humorous as Dr. Louis Leakey. Released by Warners and Universal. color (See *Movie Love*.)

The Gospel According to St. Matthew *Il Vangelo Secondo Matteo* (1964)—Pier Paolo Pasolini's interpretation features the rocky settings of Southern Italy, an eclectic score, and a rigid Jesus who demands obedience. Some find the slow rhythm fascinating, others think it punishing. (There's a funny description of the film in the opening pages of Iris Owens' novel *After Claude*.) In Italian. b & w

The Gracie Allen Murder Case (1939)—S. S. Van Dine, the author of the Philo Vance detective novels, wrote Gracie into one of them, and Paramount very sensibly decided to film it. (George Burns figured in the story, but he was dropped in the film version and Gracie thus made her first solo movie appearance.) It's a casual, entertaining absurdity; Gracie's peculiarly uncorseted mind is a wonderful corrective to Warren William's usual stuffiness as Philo Vance; he hardly gets a word in edgewise. Alfred E. Green directed a good cast, including Donald MacBride, Kent Taylor, Ellen Drew, H. B. Warner, Horace McMahon, and William Demarest. b & w

The Graduate (1967)—One of the most talked about hits of the 60s, it was a formative influence on the counterculture, and it was the movie that made Dustin Hoffman a star. He plays Benjamin Braddock, who returns to his swank L.A. home after graduating from college, and feels alienated from his insensitive, self-indulgent parents and their whole set of lewd, money-making friends. As Mrs. Robinson (whose name was used for the title of one of the Simon and Garfunkel songs on the soundtrack), Anne Bancroft is tremendous fun, at first. She's the amusingly voracious middle-aged woman who seduces the naïve Benjamin, and when he's in bed with her and wants to talk about art, the comic moments click along with the rhythm of a hit Broadway show. But then the movie deliberately undercuts its own hip expertise and begins to pander to youth. Benjamin falls in love with Mrs. Robinson's fresh, wide-eyed daughter (Katharine Ross), and the mother is turned into a vindictive witch. (And the comedy turns into melodrama.) Commercially, this worked: the rejection of upper-middle-class values had a special appeal for upper-middle-class college students. The inarticulate Benjamin became a romantic hero for the audience to project onto. The movie functioned as a psychodrama: the graduate stood for truth; the older people stood for sham and for corrupt sexuality. And this "generation-gap" view of youth and age entered the national bloodstream; many moviegoers went to see the picture over and over again. Mike Nichols directed, from a script by Calder Willingham and Buck Henry, based on the novel by Charles Webb. With William Daniels and Elizabeth Wilson as Benjamin's parents, and Murray Hamilton as Mr. Robinson. Buck Henry is the hotel clerk. The cinematography is by Robert Surtees; the production design is by Richard Sylbert. Academy Award for Best Director. Embassy. color (See *Going Steady*.)

Grand Hotel (1932)—From her first line, "I have never been so tired in my life," Greta Garbo sets the movie in vibration with her extraordinary sensual presence. ("Mademoiselle Hamlet," Alice B. Toklas called her.) Garbo plays a *première danseuse* whose career is fading—a weary, disillusioned woman briefly reconciled to life by a passion for a shady nobleman: John Barrymore. Garbo was only 26 when she played this role (Barrymore was 50), but the fatigue, the despair, seem genuine. There is every reason to reject *Grand Hotel* as an elaborate chunk of artifice; there are no redeeming qualities in Vicki Baum's excruciating concepts of character and fate, and anyone who goes to see this movie expecting an intelligent script, or even "good acting," should have his head examined. Most of the players give impossibly bad performances—they chew up the camera. But if you want to see what screen glamour used to be, and what, originally, "stars" were, this is perhaps the best example of all time. *Grand Hotel* is still entertaining because of the same factor that made it a huge hit in its day (it even won the Academy Award as Best Picture): the force of the personalities involved in the omnibus story. As a secretary working in the hotel, there is a startlingly sexy minx named Joan Crawford, who bears only a slight resemblance to the later zombie of that name; at about 26 also, she still connected with other actors, and her scenes with Lionel Barrymore (in one of his rare likable performances: he's a dying man spending his life savings on a last fling) show a real rapport. The fifth star is Wallace Beery, as a brutal, crooked tycoon; he overacts mightily and charmlessly. Also in the cast are Lewis Stone, Jean Hersholt, Rafaela Ottiano, Ferdinand Gottschalk, Frank Conroy, Tully Marshall, Purnell Pratt, Morgan Wallace, Robert McWade, and Edwin Maxwell. Striding through it all is a living legend of the screen: Garbo, in her chinchilla polo coat, with her drawn face and wrinkled forehead and her anguished "I want to be alone." (Her clothes seem to get in her way, and there's a ridiculous little bobby pin that keeps her hair firmly in place during her big love scenes with Barrymore.) Directed by Edmund Goulding, from William A. Drake's adaptation of Vicki Baum's *Menschen im Hotel;* cinematography by William Daniels; art direction by Cedric Gibbons; gowns by Adrian. (A 1945 remake was called *Weekend at the Waldorf.*) M-G-M. b & w

The Grand Maneuver *Les Grandes Manoeuvres* (1956)—As the director René Clair described it, what begins as a comedy of seduction ends as a tragedy of love. Just before the outbreak of war in 1914, a bored young cavalry officer (Gérard Philipe), stationed in a provincial town, bets his fellow officers that within a month he can seduce any woman in the town. They draw a name out of a hat and it turns out to be a milliner from Paris (Michèle Morgan). She resists and resists, but she falls in love with him and he with her. Her resistance is almost at an end when she learns of the bet. The soldiers are leaving to go on maneuvers: if she forgives him she will open her window. But he leaves and the window remains closed. Whether Clair failed to resolve his conception, or whether his conception is simply too cold for the audience to accept, the film (which was much praised in the press) has tended to alienate people. To Clair it's an illustration of "the disadvantages of the human condition," and certainly it's an elegant expression of the triumph of pride over love, but the film's tone—dry, forlorn, disenchanted—isn't very pleasing. In French. color

La Grande Illusion (1937)—In form, *La Grande Illusion* is an escape story; yet who would think of it in this way? It's like saying that *Oedipus Rex* is a detective story. Among

other things, this film is a study of human needs and the subtle barriers of class among a group of prisoners and their captors during the First World War. The two aristocrats—the German prison commander von Rauffenstein (Erich von Stroheim) and his prisoner the French officer de Boeldieu (Pierre Fresnay)—share a common world of memories and sentiments. Though their class is doomed by the changes that produced the war, they must act out the rituals of noblesse oblige and serve a nationalism they don't believe in. The Frenchman sacrifices his life for men he doesn't really approve of—the plebeian Maréchal (Jean Gabin) and the Jew Rosenthal (Marcel Dalio). Jean Renoir directed this elegy for the death of the old European aristocracy, and it is one of the true masterpieces of the screen. Von Rauffenstein and de Boeldieu are in a great romantic tradition; Cyrano has his plume, they draw on their white gloves. Maréchal, the mechanic who has become an officer, is uneasy in the presence of urbanity and polish, but he has natural gallantry, and he's the one with survival power. The performances of von Stroheim, Fresnay, and Gabin are in three different styles of acting, and they illuminate one another. With Gabin, you're not aware of any performance; with von Stroheim and Fresnay, you *are*—and you should be: they represent a way of life that is dedicated to superbly controlled outer appearances. With Dita Parlo, Gaston Modot, Julien Carette, Jean Dasté, Georges Péclet, and Jacques Becker (who was the assistant director). Written by Charles Spaak and Renoir; the music is by Kosma; the camerawork is by Christian Matras and Claude Renoir. In French, with the German and English characters speaking in their own languages. b & w (see *I Lost it at the Movies.*)

Les Grandes Manoeuvres, see *The Grand Maneuver*

The Grapes of Wrath (1940)—In the years right after the worst of the Depression, the John Steinbeck book was compared with *Uncle Tom's Cabin* and *Les Misérables* and widely, if not very astutely, regarded as the greatest novel ever written by an American. It deals with the Joads, a family of sharecroppers who leave their eroded, dust-bowl farm in Oklahoma and come to the promised land of California, where they become the lowest of the low—migratory farm laborers. The movie version is full of the "They can't keep us down, we're the people" sort of thing, and a viewer's outrage at the terrible social injustices the film deals with is blurred by its gross sentimentality. This famous film, high on most lists of the great films of all time, seems all wrong—phony when it should ring true. Yet, because of the material, it is often moving in spite of the acting, the directing, and the pseudo-Biblical pore-people talk. In some externals, the production is as authentic as a documentary; the cast includes Henry Fonda as Tom, John Carradine as Casey, Charley Grapewin as Grampa, John Qualen as Muley, Eddie Quillan as Connie, Dorris Bowdon as Rosasharn, Russell Simpson as Pa, Zeffie Tilbury as Granma, Darryl Hickman as Winfield, and Ward Bond, Grant Mitchell, Joe Sawyer, Frank Faylen. Screenplay by Nunnally Johnson; cinematography by Gregg Toland. Academy Awards: Best Director—John Ford; Best Supporting Actress—Jane Darwell as Ma Joad. She's impossibly fraudulent, though there's a memorable scene with Ma burning her old postcards. 20th Century-Fox. b & w

The Great Adventure *Det Stora Äventyret* (1953)—One of the handful of great nature films, Arne Sucksdorff's feature-length documentary is a sensuous mixture of beauty and cruelty. Refusing, as he says, "to rape reality," Sucksdorff waits until he gets the shot he wants—lynx and otter, fox and wood grouse, framed in dazzling compositions. In Swedish. b & w

The Great Bank Robbery (1969)—A haphazard mixture of two genres—the big heist and the Western spoof. It isn't as funny as the people engaged in it try to convince you it is: you keep remembering earlier movies that did these jokes better. Hy Averback directed, from William Peter Blatty's script, based on a novel by Frank O'Rourke. With Zero Mostel, Kim Novak, Clint Walker (who's not bad), Akim Tamiroff, Ruth Warrick, Sam Jaffe, Claude Akins, Larry Storch, and Elisha Cook, Jr. Warners. color

Great Expectations (1946)—David Lean directed this handsome British production from J. Arthur Rank; it takes us back to that period in English letters when heroes had nice manners, a story had sweep and flourish, and all the stray subplots were gathered up and "rhymed." The rather creamy look (like an expensive gift edition of a classic) is not particularly appropriate to Dickens, but the film has a strong style that is very different from Lean's earlier work. He seems finally to have let go—to have pulled out all the stops. The film is emotional, exciting, full of action; sequences are planned in terms of heightened dramatic contrasts and sudden, scary tensions. This hyperbolic style rushes us past the awkward bits of staging and the slight dissatisfaction we may feel about the boy Pip (Anthony Wager) turning into John Mills, who plays his role very tentatively— almost as if he were trying out for it. Jean Simmons is the young girl, Estella, and then Valerie Hobson takes over the part, though it's inconceivable that one could grow into the other, and despite Hobson's dignity and beauty something seems to be lost. The rest of the cast, though, is close to miraculous: Alec Guinness is Herbert Pocket; Finlay Currie is Magwitch; Martita Hunt is Miss Havisham; Bernard Miles is Joe Gargery; Freda Jackson is Mrs. Gargery; Ivor Barnard is Wemmick; Torin Thatcher is Bentley Drummle; Eileen Erskine is Biddy; O. B. Clarence is The Aged Parent; and Francis L. Sullivan (who had played the same role in the 1934 Hollywood version) is that most alarming upholder of the law Jaggers. The producer, Ronald Neame, collaborated with Lean on the adaptation. Guy Green took the Academy Award for Best Black-and-White Cinematography; John Bryan and Wilfred Shingleton also won for Black-and-White Art Direction and Set Decoration.

The Great Gabbo (1929)—After the picture he was directing—*Queen Kelly*—was cancelled, Erich von Stroheim turned to acting and had a popular success as a megalomaniac ventriloquist who expresses his sensitive feelings only through his grotesque little dummy, Otto. Directed by James Cruze, from a Ben Hecht story, the film is effective only in a few bits. When the ventriloquist gets into the Follies, his story gets lost between mediocre musical-comedy numbers (which were originally in color). With the talented Betty Compson. b & w

The Great McGinty (1940)—After writing a series of successful pictures, Preston Sturges offered Paramount this script (which was to win an Academy Award) for peanuts, on condition that he be allowed to direct it. Given a three-week shooting schedule and a budget of less than $350,000, he made his début as a director (thus preparing the way for other writer-directors, such as John Huston and Billy Wilder). In this satire of American political corruption, the lowlife hero (Brian Donlevy) gets in solid with the local boss (Akim Tamiroff) by voting 37 times in one day. He rises to be alderman, then mayor, and, finally, governor, but having fallen in love, he tries to go straight, and his career is wrecked.

Not up to the classic Sturges comedies that followed, partly because of Donlevy's lack of personality (the viewer can't see what would attract the competent, worldly woman—played by Muriel Angelus—who marries him), and partly because of the uneven pacing. There are wonderful patches, though, with the slapstick reversals on Horatio Alger success themes that became the Sturges specialty, and Akim Tamiroff peps up every scene he's in. With Allyn Joslyn, William Demarest, Libby Taylor, Thurston Hall, Arthur Hoyt, Steffi Duna, Esther Howard, Jimmy Conlin, Harry Rosenthal, Robert Warwick, Frank C. Moran, and Dewey Robinson; many of them were to become members of the Sturges "stock company." b & w

The Great Man (1956)—"The great man," a popular and influential radio-television personality, has died; it is the task of a commentator (José Ferrer) to prepare a memorial broadcast. If it is successful, he may become the great man's replacement. Though the outcome of the research is predictable, the further step in the plot is so efficiently cynical that the venality we have explored appears to be merely a childish prelude to a new venality. These inside-story ironies are too neat, though—the film has no resonance. But Ferrer, who directed, holds to a good, even pace and a suspenseful tone, and the picture is almost over before one realizes how bare and shallow it is. Structurally, it's mostly a series of two-person sequences, as the commentator (*Citizen Kane*–style) interviews the people closest to the dead man; this series might have been very mechanical if the director-star hadn't been so generous and tactful in the way he presents each of the other actors. The most memorable of them is Ed Wynn, playing a kind, thoughtful man who knows that he appears to be ridiculous; Wynn brought off his six-minute scene, which is virtually a monologue, in a single take, and it was reported that when he finished, the technicians applauded and the director wept. Momentarily, Ed Wynn gives the picture something close to a soul. And his son Keenan Wynn, playing a despicably soulless character, momentarily provides some uncouth ruthlessness and energy; he stirs things up. With Julie London as a boozing, second-rate singer, and Dean Jagger, Joanne Gilbert, Russ Morgan, Jim Backus, Henny Backus, and Lyle Talbot. From the novel by Al Morgan, who wrote the script, with Ferrer. (The picture failed commercially; Ferrer tried again, in 1958, with *The High Cost of Loving*, which also failed.) Universal. b & w

The Great Profile (1940)—In his later years, the boozing John Barrymore kept his career going by buffoonery and self-caricature. A lot of people found this film's exploitation of his fallen reputation offensive, but his antics and his wordplay are very funny. This cynical burlesque (in which he performs with a troupe of acrobats) has some low, wild moments. He *enjoys* horsing around. Directed by Walter Lang, from a script by Milton Sperling and Hilary Lynn. With Mary Beth Hughes, Anne Baxter, Gregory Ratoff, John Payne, Lionel Atwill, Willie Fung, and Edward Brophy. 20th Century-Fox. b & w

The Great Santini Also known as *The Ace*. (1980)—This slice-of-family-life melodrama features Robert Duvall as the military-psychopath father and Michael O'Keefe as the sensitive, thoughtful teen-age son. There's a sequence that is a strong metaphor for the ugly competitiveness inside a father's determination to toughen up a son: a one-on-one basketball game between them. Refusing to accept his defeat, the father follows the boy inside the house and demands another game; walking up the stairs right behind the boy, he tries to goad him by bouncing the ball, hard, off the boy's head and calling him "my sweetest little girl." This is the only sequence that hits home, though. Adapted from Pat Conroy's autobiographical novel *The Great Santini*, the movie is set in 1962 in Beaufort, South Carolina, where Conroy grew up, but (as written for the screen and directed by Lewis John Carlino) it takes place in the TV land of predictability—that plain of dowdy realism where a boy finds his manhood by developing the courage to stick to his principles and stand up to his father. Almost inevitably, since this is the South, the principles involve friendship with a saintly black (Stan Shaw), who is crippled and has a stammer, or at least a hesitation, and is martyred by redneck stupidity and cruelty. With Blythe Danner, who comes close to creating a believable woman out of an idealized mother figure, and brings in shadings that help to suggest a real family, though she doesn't have a single scene that is really hers. Also with Lisa Jane Persky as the family comic, Theresa Merritt as the housekeeper, David Keith as the redneck so mean he shoots the black's dawg, and Paul Mantee. Music by Elmer Bernstein. A Bing Crosby Production; released by Orion Pictures. color (See *Taking It All In*.)

The Great Train Robbery (1979)—Handsome re-creations of mid-Victorian England. The year is 1855, and Sean Connery plays a thief who masquerades as a wealthy businessman in order to plan the theft of gold bullion that is being shipped by train to pay the British troops in the Crimea; the film is a fictionalized version of what, according to Michael Crichton, who directed, and adapted from his own novel, was the first train robbery. There's a total absence of personal obsession—even moviemaking obsession—in the way Crichton works; he never excites us emotionally or imaginatively, but the film has a satisfying, tame luxuriousness, like a super episode of "Masterpiece Theatre." With Lesley-Anne Down, Donald Sutherland, Alan Webb, Gabrielle Lloyd as his daughter, Malcolm Terris as a bank manager, Robert Lang as a Scotland Yard inspector, Pamela Salem, and Wayne Sleep. Cinematography by Geoffrey Unsworth. color (See *When the Lights Go Down*.)

The Great Waldo Pepper (1975)—100% pure-plastic adolescent male fantasy. It's set in the 20s, with Robert Redford as a First World War aviator who spends time barnstorming in the Midwest and then goes to Hollywood, where he lives out his dream of fighting the No. 1 Imperial German ace. Scene after scene ends with a snapper. William Goldman's cold-hearted, clever script and the cool, fresh-painted storytelling of the director, George Roy Hill, almost amount to a style: total inauthenticity. With Susan Sarandon, Bo Svenson, Bo Brundin, Geoffrey Lewis, Margot Kidder, Edward Herrmann, Philip Bruns, and Roderick Cook. Cinematography by Robert Surtees. Universal. color (See *Reeling*.)

The Great Waltz (1938)—The passion of Johann Strauss according to M-G-M. Fernand Gravet—talented enough in French films— seems horror-stricken and depressed as Strauss, and Luise Rainer, as his sniffling, suffering wife, and the soprano Miliza Korjus, as the other woman, are not exactly cures for melancholia. A big, overdressed bore, directed by Julien Duvivier, with musical arrangements by Dmitri Tiomkin. There's a great howler of a sequence in which Strauss, riding in a carriage with Korjus, hears the *clip-clop* of the horses' hooves, hunters' horns, and the chirping of the birds, and he composes "Tales from the Vienna Woods," which she proceeds to sing. The cast includes Lionel Atwill, Herman Bing, Hugh Herbert, Minna Gombell, Henry Hull, and Curt Bois. The script is by Walter Reisch and Samuel Hofenstein, from Gottfried Reinhardt's story. b & w

The Great Waltz (1972)—Written and directed by Andrew L. Stone, the foremost primitive at work in the musical form. (This is not a compliment.) An atrocity, with Horst Buchholz as Johann Strauss. Also with Mary Costa, Rossano Brazzi, Yvonne Mitchell, and Nigel Patrick. The choreography is by Onna White. M-G-M. color

The Great White Hope (1970)—How a black prizefighter (James Earl Jones) is brought down because of white men's fear of the strength of blacks. Martin Ritt's big, noisy production clunks along like a disjointed play; it defeats Jones, and along the way it also inadvertently exposes the clobber-them-with-guilt tactics of the dramatist, Howard Sackler. When it was done on the stage did audiences really accept the beware-the-ides-of-March doom crier and the rag-doll-Ophelia finish of the heroine? In the movie, all this grandiosity makes you squirm. Based on the life of Jack Johnson (called Jack Jefferson here). With Jane Alexander and Lou Gilbert. 20th Century-Fox. color (See *Deeper into Movies*.)

The Great Ziegfeld (1936)—William Powell plays Ziegfeld, and the two Mrs. Ziegfelds are played by Myrna Loy, as Billie Burke, and Luise Rainer, as Anna Held. Fanny Brice is herself, though she isn't on screen enough to vitalize this lavish, tedious musical biography; it goes on for a whopping 3 hours, but through some insane editing decision she's cut off in the middle of singing "My Man." Inexplicably, this thing won the Academy Award for Best Picture, and Rainer, who did her heartbreak specialty—smiling through tears and looking irresistibly fragile—was given the Best Actress award. With Ray Bolger, who has a few redemptive moments, and Gilda Gray, Harriet Hoctor, Frank Morgan, Reginald Owen, William Demarest, Leon Errol, Stanley Morner (who became the singing star Dennis Morgan, though here his "Pretty Girl Is Like a Melody" is dubbed by Allan Jones), and Virginia Bruce, who gets glorified to the tune of "You Never Looked So Beautiful Before." Directed by Robert Z. Leonard, from a script by William Anthony McGuire, who had worked for Ziegfeld, as had the set designer, John Harkrider, and the choreographer, Seymour Felix. Produced by Hunt Stromberg, for M-G-M. b & w

The Greatest Question (1919)—Lillian Gish has said that she can't remember working on this one, and probably D. W. Griffith wanted to forget it, too. The rural surroundings are lovely, but the story is about Miss Gish's being saved from rape, with Robert Harron coming to the rescue this time, and there are also a mother communicating with her son after his death, a ghost appearing at midnight in answer to a prayer, and, as the capper, the discovery of oil—provided by a kind Lord. Griffith seems to have got into this potboiling mess because of the interest in spiritualism that Sir Oliver Lodge had just stirred up. Silent. b & w

The Greatest Show on Earth (1952)—A huge, mawkish, trite circus movie directed by Cecil B. De Mille in a neo-Biblical style. It suggests that the rivalry and love affairs of a couple of trapeze artists (Betty Hutton and Cornel Wilde), an assistant (Gloria Grahame) to an elephant trainer, the circus manager (Charlton Heston), and a clown (James Stewart) are awesome. Life under this particular big top is also awesomely clean and awesomely melodramatic; Stewart isn't just a clown—he's a doctor who has disguised himself as a clown. Also with Dorothy Lamour, Lyle Bettger, Henry Wilcoxon, Lawrence Tierney, Emmett Kelly, and John Ringling North. This cornball enterprise won the Academy Award for Best Picture. Paramount. color

The Greeks Had a Word for Them Also known as *Three Broadway Girls*. (1932)—An enormously likable sophisticated comedy about three gold-diggers, played by Madge Evans, Joan Blondell, and the great sophisticate herself—Ina Claire. This is one of the few movies in which she was able to show some of the tricky high style that made her the most fashionable stage comedienne of her time. The three actresses play contrasting types: Madge Evans is the elegant and tasteful one; Joan Blondell is, of course, good-humored and wisecracking; and Ina Claire is naughty and determined—she sets out to tantalize a man by going out in a fur coat with nothing worn under it. With David Manners, and Lowell Sherman, who also directed. Sidney Howard wrote the adaptation of Zoë Akins' play, *The Greeks Had a Word for It*. Produced by Samuel Goldwyn, for United Artists. b & w

Green Dolphin Street (1947)—The actors in this stupefyingly flimsy epic seem to be in competition for booby prizes. Richard Hart is the New Zealander who gets stewed and doesn't remember whether the girl who took his fancy on an island off the Newfoundland coast was named Marianne or Marguerite. He writes to Marianne (Lana Turner), proposing marriage, although it was her sister, Marguerite (Donna Reed), he wanted; when Marianne arrives he marries her, and Marguerite, naturally upset, hies off to a nunnery. The married couple raise sheep, reproduce, go through a fierce earthquake, and almost get killed when the Maoris go on an anti-Caucasian rampage; fortunately the couple have an influential pal (Van Heflin) who sees to it that the aborigines keep their distance. Adapted from a piece of unleavened dough kneaded into a best-selling novel by Elizabeth Goudge, and directed by Victor Saville, from Samson Raphaelson's script. Also with Edmund Gwenn. M-G-M. b & w

Green for Danger (1946)—Alastair Sim, as Inspector Cockrill of Scotland Yard, uses humor, ingenuity, and skill to solve a batch of murders among a group of doctors and nurses. This suspense comedy is almost a classic of its pleasant, minor genre: you meet the characters, learn that one of them is going to kill two of the others, and you spend an hour and a half guessing. The director, Sidney Gilliat, shows a neat light touch. With Trevor Howard, Leo Genn, Rosamund John, and Sally Gray. From Christianna Brand's novel, adapted by Gilliat and Claude Guerney; produced by Launder and Gilliat. b & w

The Green Light (1937)—An inspirational movie, based on a Lloyd C. Douglas novel. As a man of God, Cedric Hardwicke wears white hair and pious expressions; he dominates the film by the sheer awfulness of his performance. The hero, Errol Flynn, is so noble that only Anita Louise could play opposite him. (Nobody else would look pure enough.) He's a doctor who is inspired by the spirituality of a dying patient (Spring Byington); he risks everything to develop a serum to combat spotted fever. The director, Frank Borzage, actually got by with this sickly uplift. With Margaret Lindsay, Henry O'Neill, Walter Abel, and Erin O'Brien-Moore. The script is by Milton Krims; the music is by Max Steiner. Hal B. Wallis produced, for Cosmopolitan Productions; released by Warners. b & w

The Green Man (1956)—Alastair Sim is so limpid of eye, so arch in speech, and so gentle, unctuous, and tragic of demeanor, that he suggests the modern epitome of agonized courtesy: the undertaker. In this ma-

cabre farce, he is cast just one jump away: as an assassin with the soul of an aesthete. It's unlikely that anybody in the history of movies has ever matched Sim's peculiar feat of flipping expressions from benign innocence to bloodcurdling menace in one devastating instant. As the assassin, he dispatches an assortment of expendable types: headmasters, businessmen, dictators, et al., but gets snarled up while trying to liquidate a distasteful cabinet minister. The picture isn't genteel: it has the virtues of English comedy combined with the more energetic style of satirical American comedy—it makes you laugh out loud. With George Cole, Terry-Thomas, Jill Adams, Dora Bryan, Raymond Huntley, and a string trio of ladies right out of a George Price cartoon. Written by the producers, Frank Launder and Sidney Gilliat, from their play, *Meet a Body*; directed by Robert Day. b & w

The Green Pastures (1936)—The Angel Gabriel calls, "Gangway for de Lawd God Jehovah!" and then, more humbly, "Ten cent seegar, Lawd?" In this pop-folk fantasy of the Old Testament stories as a Negro child in the South (of an earlier period) might imagine them, Southern idiom, delicious fish fries, and naïve theology are fused with awe and wonder. Marc Connelly's adaptation of Roark Bradford's stories was perhaps the most famous and most popular of Negro stage productions; the screen version (which was also successful) was directed by William Keighley and Connelly, with Rex Ingram as De Lawd, Eddie "Rochester" Anderson, and Oscar Polk; the music is by Erich Wolfgang Korngold. Warners. b & w

The Greene Murder Case (1929)—William Powell again as Philo Vance, in the second of the films based on S. S. Van Dine mysteries; it's tolerably enjoyable, which puts it way ahead of the book (published in 1928). The

Greenes are an unlucky, hateful family who live in a big mansion on the East River; despite Philo Vance's best efforts, there are fewer of them at the end of the picture than there were at the start. With Jean Arthur, Florence Eldridge, Eugene Pallette, E. H. Calvert, Gertrude Norman, Ullrich Haupt, Lowell Drew, Brandon Hurst, and Shep Camp. Directed by Frank Tuttle; the writers were Louise Long, Bartlett Cormack, and Richard H. Digges. Paramount. b & w

The Greengage Summer, see *Loss of Innocence*

Greetings (1968)—A pleasantly tawdry mixture of an underground film, a skin-flick, and a college revue, with a draft-evader hero and good-humored, casually obscene performances from a whole gallery of talented actors, including Robert De Niro, Jonathan Warden, Gerrit Graham, and Allen Garfield. Directed, edited, and co-written by Brian De Palma, who made it on a shoestring of less than $40,000, and in color. The other writer was Charles Hirsch, who was also the producer; cinematography by Robert Fiore.

Gremlins (1984)—The director Joe Dante has the sensibility of a freaked-out greeting-card poet. This whimsical pop shocker is set in a sleepy small town at Christmastime. The hero Billy (Zach Galligan), a young bank teller, is given a mogwai—a tiny creature who nests in a box and makes gentle cooing sounds; when the instructions that Billy is given for its care are inadvertently disobeyed, the mogwai multiplies, and its progeny turn into greedy, demonic little gargoyles. The picture is a black humorist's parody of Steven Spielberg's *E.T.*—a demonstration that the underside of E.T. is like the monster in Ridley Scott's *Alien*. Billy's mogwai is a good child; the other mogwai are its aggressively vulgar, beer-guzzling brothers—children of the night. When one of them blows his snout on a drape, he's like Jean Renoir's Boudu expressing his contempt for bourgeois life by wiping his shoes on a bedspread. These demons are like bad pets making messes. The movie never comes together, but Dante is a genuine eccentric talent with a flair for malice, and it's certainly clear why Spielberg, whose production company made the film, believes in him—there are some crack sequences. At one point the lewd hipster dragons take over the town movie theatre, where *Snow White and the Seven Dwarfs* is playing; they pad up and down the aisles, eating, laughing, tearing up the place. And when the Seven Dwarfs on the screen start to sing "Heigh-Ho," they join in the singing. In their enthusiasm, they spin around on the projectors, and rip the screen to shreds. It's a delirious, kitschy travesty—a kiddy matinée in Hell. With Frances Lee McCain as Billy's mother, Polly Holliday as the town's Wicked Witch–Scrooge, Dick Miller as the town drunk, and Phoebe Cates, Hoyt Axton, Keye Luke, Glynn Turman, Judge Reinhold, Edward Andrews, and Chuck Jones as Mr. Jones. Written by Chris Columbus; the critters were designed by Chris Walas. (A sequel, *Gremlins 2: The New Batch*, was released in 1990.) Warners. color (See *State of the Art*.)

The Grey Fox (1983)—The story of a legendary gentleman bandit, Bill Miner (Richard Farnsworth), who served 33 years in San Quentin for robbing stagecoaches and then, when he got out, took up robbing trains. There may never have been photographs of trains more exultant than the shots here of the old Northern Pacific steaming through mountain forests. This first feature, directed by the Canadian Phillip Borsos at 27, after a number of highly regarded documentaries, has spectacular work by the British cinematographer Frank Tidy; the images are dense and ceremonious, and the picture has the most lovingly photographed rain since

McCabe & Mrs. Miller. Farnsworth is a superb camera subject, with a lulling sexual presence, and he and Jackie Burroughs, who plays a red-haired suffragette, do some highly photogenic flirting. The movie is like the book *Wisconsin Death Trip* with a romantic bandit at its center. Robbery here is the only honorable profession for a man with Bill Miner's courtliness and sense of style. Borsos appears to have a dandy's approach to crime and social injustice, but he's an inspired image-maker, and the film manages to be an art Western without making you hate it. Based on a script by John Hunter that stays fairly close to the historical accounts and leaves a lot of gaps—we never find out how Miner, who'd been in prison most of his life, became a civilized, sensitive man and a lover who admired a flamboyant, free-thinking woman. With Wayne Robson as the little boozer Shorty. color (See *State of the Art*.)

Greystoke: The Legend of Tarzan, Lord of the Apes (1984)—The director Hugh Hudson brings his unique mixture of pomposity and ineptitude to this expensively mounted version of the Edgar Rice Burroughs material. The first half, in the jungle, is fairly absorbing; the actors playing the apes are very well made up (so that each has distinguishing features), and they comport themselves convincingly. But it's unlikely that anyone will ever congratulate Hudson for seamless moviemaking. When he sets something up, chances are there won't be any follow-through. Men who look like villains appear and are never seen again; the hero is given portentous advice that never has any application. After a while you lose that sense of expectation which is one of the glories of big adventure films. And Hudson has his child Tarzan experiencing so much physical torment and humiliation—the apes are constantly batting him around—that young kids are likely to be horrified. From infancy to adulthood, this Tarzan is more sufferer than hero. The young Frenchman Christopher Lambert, who plays the adult, has a fine physique—muscular yet graceful—but he's a charmless, unmagnetic Tarzan; he's never allowed to be playful. The only performer who clearly enjoys himself is that old prankster, Ralph Richardson, in his last screen appearance, as Tarzan's grandfather, Lord Greystoke; he comes up with one emotional flourish after another. In the film's second half, Hudson twists the story into knots in order to deliver his "statement" that apes are more civilized than people; the movie simply loses its mind, and dribbles to a pathetically indecisive conclusion. Andie MacDowell is a softly enticing Jane, and Nigel Davenport makes a strong visual impression as a gun-happy British major. Also with Ian Holm, James Fox, Ian Charleson, Paul Geoffrey, and Cheryl Campbell. The first script, by Robert Towne, was trimmed and rewritten by Michael Austin. (Towne uses a pseudonym in the credits—P. H. Vazak, the kennel name of the dog he loved, who died.) The cinematography is by John Alcott. Warners. color (See *State of the Art*.)

Il Grido (1957)—Just before his international breakthrough with *L'Avventura*, Antonioni made this flawed yet affecting, mournful, wintry film about the neurotic apathy of a working-class man. It's poetic without being believable. The American actor Steve Cochran plays Aldo, a skilled worker in a sugar refinery; when the woman he has been living with (Alida Valli) no longer wants him, he falls into a numb despair and wanders around with his small daughter. He meets other women, but they don't make enough impression on him for him to get a grip on life. Without the moneyed decadence of the characters in Antonioni's later films, the atmospheric gloom seems less chic, more purely depressive. Set in the muddy Po Valley. With Betsy Blair, Dorian Gray, and Lyn Shaw. In Italian. b & w

The Groove Tube (1974)—Inoffensively scatological revue, lampooning TV, Kubrick's *2001*, and American culture. About half of the grungy, manic skits are very funny; the others might have been funny, too, if their timing had been better. At the end, the talented director and star, Ken Shapiro, does a lovely, flaked-out dance through rush-hour crowds along Park Avenue. With Chevy Chase, Richard Belzer, Buzzy Linhart, Christine Nazareth; and Lane Sarasohn, who also wrote the material, with Shapiro; animation by Linda Taylor and Pat O'Neill. Made for $400,000; it started as a video-theatre entertainment. color

The Group (1966)—Sidney Lumet turns Mary McCarthy's novel about the Vassar girls of '33 into a carelessly busy, likable, energetic film. In the big cast are Joan Hackett, Shirley Knight, Joanna Pettet, Elizabeth Hartman, Candice Bergen, Kathleen Widdoes, Mary-Robin Redd, Carrie Nye, James Broderick, Larry Hagman, Richard Mulligan, Robert Emhardt, and Hal Holbrook. The script is by Sidney Buchman; cinematography by Boris Kaufman. United Artists. color (See *Kiss Kiss Bang Bang*.)

Groupies (1970)—The baby rock-band molls here are a spooky bunch of junior hookers and hardened name-droppers. Because of their extreme youth, brazen parasitism, and specialized shallowness, they're fascinating; they're gutsy little girls, but like all hangers-on, they're depressing. The subject is so good that this documentary holds one's speculative interest even though the crew didn't bring much skill or depth to the project. Directed by Ron Dorfman and Peter Nevard. color (See *Deeper into Movies*.)

Gruppo di Famiglia in un Interno, see *Conversation Piece*

The Guardsman (1931)—More like a photographed play than a movie adaptation, but a memento of Alfred Lunt and Lynn Fontanne at work; they appear to be having a wonderful time mugging and grinning. They play an acting couple, and for a good part of the film the jealous husband (in disguise from his flirtatious wife) wears something stuck under his lower lip, which gives him a beefy, puffed-out-jaw that is irresistibly ridiculous. Sidney Franklin directed this early-talkie version of the Ferenc Molnár play, which Lunt and Fontanne had done on Broadway in 1924. (In 1941 it was turned into a movie musical, *The Chocolate Soldier*.) The cast includes Roland Young as a critic, Ann Dvorak as a fan, ZaSu Pitts, Maude Eburne, and Herman Bing. The adaptation is by Ernest Vajda and Claudine West. M-G-M. b & w

La Guerre des boutons *Generals Without Buttons* (1938)—This polished little parable on man's folly used to be considered a film classic, but it's the sort of classic that makes you yawn. The children of Longeverne pray for rain to ripen their cabbages; their neighbors, the children of Valrans, pray for sunshine to ripen their grapes. The dispute is bitter and the children organize for battle, with heroes, sacrifices, and all the accoutrements of war except the longed-for buttons of real generals. Jacques Daroy directed, using a mixture of professional and non-professional children, as well as Jean Murat and Saturnin Fabre. From the novel by Louis Pergand. (Remade by Yves Robert in 1961.) In French. b & w

La Guerre est finie (1966)—Yves Montand as the Spaniard Diego, a professional (i.e., paid) revolutionary, a courier in the Communist underground, who goes on stoically carrying out policies he knows are futile. Alain Resnais directed this attempt at an elegy on the themes of exile and of living on old ideals—living in the past. The courier is like a weary commuter who has been through it all so many times that he can see what's coming; past and future are one. It's easy to satirize force of habit—as W. C. Fields demonstrated when he blew the head off an ice-cream soda. But Resnais, although he allows most of Diego's associates to appear ridiculous, protects Diego very tenderly. He isn't presented as a Party hack or a tool—he's noble. His melancholy is glamourized, and when he goes to bed with his mistress (Ingrid Thulin) he has such high-quality sex that we actually hear the soprano vocalizing of a heavenly choir. The film, from a script by Jorge Semprun, is ambivalent and smooth and chic, with an overexposed semi-abstract sex scene between Diego and a pouting kitten (Geneviève Bujold) and anticipatory flash-forwards. The political material has been subjected to the French equivalent of Hollywoodization; it's soaked in romantic defeatism, in existentialism used decoratively to make a hero of a numb, apathetic man. With Michel Piccoli, Jean Dasté, Bernard Fresson, and Jean Bouise. In French. b & w (See *Kiss Kiss Bang Bang*.)

A Guide for the Married Man (1967)—A series of dumb skits on how to cheat on your wife. It's hard to know what's more tiresome about this picture: the camera's fixation on bottoms (and on bosoms that look like bottoms), or the this-movie-is-moral-after-all finish, with the common man at the higher income level (Walter Matthau) deciding he loves his wife too much to be unfaithful after all. There are a few pleasant pantomime bits by Art Carney and Ben Blue. Directed by Gene Kelly, from a script by Frank Tarloff. The cast includes Robert Morse, Lucille Ball,

Phil Silvers, Carl Reiner, Jack Benny, Inger Stevens, Sid Caesar, Terry-Thomas, Wally Cox, Jayne Mansfield, Sue Ane Langdon, and many others; what they do is no more memorable than the plugs for brand-name products that are scattered throughout. 20th Century-Fox. color

Gun Crazy Originally called *Deadly Is the Female*. (1949)—Peggy Cummins and John Dall in a tawdry version of the Bonnie and Clyde story. Cummins is a really mean broad, whose partner is her desperately eager victim. In its B-picture way, it has a fascinating crumminess. With Morris Carnovsky, Berry Kroeger, Annabel Shaw, and Don Beddoe. Directed by Joseph H. Lewis, from a screenplay based on MacKinlay Kantor's *SatEvePost* story, and credited to Kantor and Millard Kaufman. Dalton Trumbo, who was blacklisted at the time, later revealed that he wrote the script and persuaded Kaufman to let his name be used. Produced by Frank and Maurice King; released by United Artists. b & w

Gunga Din (1939)—One of the most enjoyable nonsense-adventure movies of all time—full of slapstick and heroism and high spirits. R K O intended to make one of those trouble-in-the-colonies films, and it was supposedly to be "inspired" by the Rudyard Kipling poem. Howard Hawks was set to direct; he brought in Hecht and MacArthur, who stole the plot of their own *The Front Page* and threw some wonderful hokum together. Then Hawks brought in William Faulkner for some rewriting. R K O soon decided that the project was becoming too expensive, got rid of Hawks, and put George Stevens, who was under contract, in charge. Stevens brought in Fred Guiol, a gagwriting buddy from Stevens' Laurel & Hardy days, and at some point Joel Sayre also did some rewriting. The result of these combined labors is a unique pastiche—exhilarating in an unself-consciously happy, silly way. The stars are a rousing trio: Cary Grant, having the time of his life as a clowning roughneck; the dapper, gentlemanly Douglas Fairbanks, Jr.; and the eternal vulgarian, Victor McLaglen. Who has forgotten Eduardo Ciannelli in dark makeup as some sort of mad high priest, or Sam Jaffe as Gunga Din, the essence, the soul of loyalty? Who remembers Joan Fontaine as the pallid and proper heroine? With Abner Biberman, Montagu Love, Cecil Kellaway, Lumsden Hare, and Robert Coote. The superb cinematography is by Joseph H. August; the art direction is by Van Nest Polglase; the music is by Alfred Newman. b & w (See *When the Lights Go Down*).

Guns of the Magnificent Seven (1969)—The third of three cowboys-and-bandits movies based on Kurosawa's *The Seven Samurai*; the other two—*The Magnificent Seven* of 1960 and *Return of the Seven* of 1966—starred Yul Brynner as Chris. This time George Kennedy, normally and literally a heavy, is the noble Chris. Trying to play a nice fellow seems way beyond his range here, and his attempts at athleticism make the John Wayne of *True Grit* seem a model of agility. The miscasting is only the first mistake of this movie: from there you can take your pick of watching people being trampled to death or twitching to death. Paul Wendkos directed this shambles, set in Mexico, shot in Spain. With James Whitmore, Monte Markham, Bernie Casey, Reni Santoni, Joe Don Baker, and Frank Silvera. United Artists. color

Guys and Dolls (1955)—Samuel Goldwyn's big, beribboned version of the Broadway musical which Jo Swerling and Abe Burrows took from Damon Runyon's stories about lovable lowlifes, with a score by Frank Loesser. The director-scenarist Joseph L. Mankiewicz seems to have fallen in love with Damon Runyon's cute, stilted locutions; the camera stands still while the actors mince through lines like "This is no way for a gentleman to act and could lead to irritation on the part of Harry the Horse." Frank Sinatra is the crapgame proprietor who bets Marlon Brando that he can't lure straitlaced Jean Simmons, a mission worker, into going to Havana with him. Sinatra sings pleasantly, and Brando and Simmons are ingratiatingly uneasy when they burst into song and dance, but the movie is extended and rather tedious. The Broadway version is legendary; the movie provides no clue as to why. With Vivian Blaine, Stubby Kaye, Sheldon Leonard, and the Goldwyn Girls. Michael Kidd did the choreography, Oliver Smith the self-conscious sets. M-G-M. color

Gycklarnas Afton, see *The Naked Night*

Gypsy (1962)—An extremely unpleasant version of the Broadway musical based on Gypsy Rose Lee's memoirs. Rosalind Russell is the psychopathic stage mother who uses and destroys everyone within reach of her excruciatingly loud voice. Natalie Wood (almost pitifully miscast) is the daughter Russell rants at, and Karl Malden gets it, too. Jule Styne and Stephen Sondheim wrote the songs. Mervyn LeRoy's direction is heavy and coarse, and the script (by Leonard Spiegelgass, from the Arthur Laurents play) and the other credits match. With Ann Jillian as Baby June, and an unbilled appearance by Jack Benny. (Rosalind Russell's songs were partially dubbed by Lisa Kirk.) Warners. color

Gypsy Wildcat (1944)—One more celebration of the wriggling topography of Maria Montez and the manly opacity of Jon Hall. In earlier pairings, Montez and Hall made contact at the bottom of a swimming pool and on a desert; this time they snuggle in a Transylvanian forest. She is the gypsy dancer,

Carla, taken captive by the lewd villain, Douglass Dumbrille, before being restored to her rightful title (Countess) and her castle. The picture tries hard but it never rises to the wild camp of her *Cobra Woman* earlier that year; it's just *opéra bouffe* without music. With Gale Sondergaard, Leo Carrillo, Curt Bois, and Nigel Bruce. Directed by Roy William Neill, from a script that James M. Cain had a hand in. Produced by George Waggner. (Neill and Waggner were given parody homage in the 1981 *The Howling*.) Universal. color

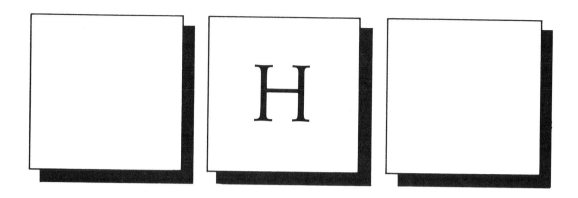

Hail the Conquering Hero (1944)—If you've never seen one of Preston Sturges's classic comedies, you may not quite know what hit you. He uses verbal slapstick as well as visual slapstick, and his timing is so quirkily effective that the dialogue keeps popping off, like a string of firecrackers. In this satire on hero worship, patriotism, and mother love, Eddie Bracken, son of his town's biggest First World War hero, joins the Marines in the Second World War and is discharged for hay fever. Ashamed, he writes his mother that he's been sent overseas, and thinking he can never return home, tells his girl (Ella Raines) that he doesn't love her anymore. But one night he's out drinking with six Marines, and one of them, known as Bugsy, for good reason, tells him he should go home and see his beautiful mother; the sergeant agrees, and the upshot is that they drag him home, claiming that he's a war hero. The town goes mad. With Freddie Steele, once middleweight boxing champion of the world, as Bugsy, William Demarest as the sergeant, and Raymond Walburn, Esther Howard, Elizabeth Patterson, Jimmy Conlin, Franklin Pangborn, Chester Conklin, Paul Porcasi, Dewey Robinson, and Arthur Hoyt. Sturges wrote and directed. Paramount. b & w

Hairspray (1988)—The writer-director John Waters treats the message movie as a genre to be parodied, just like the teenpic. Combining the two, he comes up with a pop dadaist musical comedy, set in Baltimore in 1962. Waters loves narrative, and he has half a dozen plots crisscrossing each other. In the middle are the spherical Mrs. Edna Turnblad (played by the male actor Divine) and her baby-blimp daughter, Tracy (Ricki Lake); they wear matching mother-and-daughter outfits. Tracy, who's the newest teen-age dancer on "The Corny Collins Show," discovers that black kids aren't allowed to take part and she becomes a leader in the fight for integration. Meanwhile, Divine watches over Tracy and preens like a mother hen. There's a what-the-hell quality to Divine's acting which the film needs; it would be too close to a real teenpic without it. When Divine's Edna Turnblad is onscreen in the sleeveless dresses she's partial to, the movie has something like the lunacy of a W. C. Fields in drag. With Colleen Fitzpatrick as Tracy's bitchy rival Amber, Leslie Ann Powers as shy Penny, and Michael St. Gerard, Clayton Prince, Ruth Brown, Debbie Harry, Sonny Bono, Jerry Stiller, Shawn Thompson, Ric Ocasek, Pia Zadora, Jo Ann Havrilla, and

Waters himself as a sicko psychiatrist. Released by New Line Cinema. color (See *Hooked*.)

Hakuchi, see *The Idiot* (1951)

Hallelujah, I'm a Bum (1933)—This graceful romantic comedy, shot in sepia tones in imaginative Art Deco sets, and with a Richard Rodgers and Lorenz Hart score, failed when it came out, and it has never attracted much of an audience. Maybe that's because its star is Al Jolson, and people just didn't expect him to be in a stylized, sophisticated, lyrical movie. He's very good in it, though; he doesn't wear blackface or get on his knees to sing. Directed by Lewis Milestone, he just takes it easy, and we can enjoy his finesse. The whimsical script was written by S. N. Behrman and Ben Hecht, and Rodgers and Hart provided a recitative in rhyming couplets. The time is the Depression. Wearing a white suit and hat and a dark shirt, Jolson is Bumper, the "mayor" of a group of hobos who hang out in Central Park—happy-go-lucky 30s versions of beatniks. When Bumper meets an amnesiac girl (Madge Evans) and falls in love with her, he gets a job in order to take care of her; then she regains her memory. . . . The film is uneven, but it has some of the rhythm and charm of the early-30s René Clair musicals (especially *À nous la liberté*), and it has the lovely song "You Are Too Beautiful." With Harry Langdon as Jolson's crony, Egghead; Frank Morgan as the dapper, Jimmy Walker–like Mayor of New York City; Chester Conklin as Sunday; and the black actor Edgar Connor as Acorn. When Bumper and Acorn go to work and get paid, Bumper is delighted to have the money but Acorn complains that you have to waste so much time to get it. The clothes show the most elegant side of 30s fashion; the art direction was by Richard Day. United Artists.

Hallelujah the Hills (1963)—Adolfas Mekas and a troupe of friends made this prankish improvisational movie in Vermont; they parody other movies and frisk about in the snow, or in the autumn woods, or in an old cabin, and the hero, Peter H. Beard, slides off roofs and out of trees. Except for a mock battle in a cemetery, the picture fades from memory very fast. Cinematography by Ed Emshwiller; produced by David C. Stone. b & w

Halloween (1978)—John Carpenter, who made this low-budget scare picture, has a visual sense of menace, but he isn't very gifted with actors, and he doesn't seem to have any feeling at all for motivation or for plot logic. An escaped lunatic wielding a kitchen knife stalks people in a small Midwestern town, and that's about it. There's no indication of why he selects any particular target; he's the bogeyman—pure evil—and he wants to kill. The film is largely just a matter of the camera tracking subjectively, from the mad killer's point of view, leading you to expect something awful to happen. But the camera also tracks subjectively when he isn't around at all; in fact, there's so much subjective tracking you begin to think everybody in the movie has his own camera. *Halloween* keeps you nervous and jumpy rather than pleasurably excited. Yet it has been a huge box-office success and a lot of people seem to be convinced that it's a classic. Maybe when a horror film is stripped of everything but nightmarish dumb scariness and sudden shocks it satisfies part of the audience in a more basic, childish way than sophisticated horror pictures do. With Donald Pleasence, Jamie Lee Curtis, P. J. Soles, Nancy Loomis, and Tony Moran as the monster. Music by Carpenter; he also wrote the screenplay, with the producer, Debra Hill. Shot in Los Angeles. color (See *When the Lights Go Down*.)

Hamburger Hill (1987)—It tells the story of a squad of 14 American soldiers who, in Vietnam, in 1969, are ordered to take a hill. The men keep going up the hill and being driven back by enemy fire; when it rains, they slide down the mud while the North Vietnamese throw grenades at them. After 10 days they're in control of the hill, but most of the squad have given their lives to it. This film doesn't provide the viewer with the shelter of melodrama. It's a straightforward, unblinking account of the interrelationships of these young men—most of them boys of 19. Almost inevitably, the hill comes to represent Vietnam, but it does so without histrionics. Most of the power of this scrupulously honest memorial isn't in the talk; it's in the terror and the foreignness—the far-from-homeness—of the imagery. Directed by John Irvin, the film has great decency; it joins together terror and thoughtfulness. The script, by Jim Carabatsos, merely touches the appropriate points to achieve a balanced view. Cinematography by Peter MacDonald; editing by Peter Tanner. With Dylan McDermott, M. A. Nickles, Courtney B. Vance, Tegan West, and Steven Weber. An R K O picture, released by Paramount. color (See *Hooked*.)

Hamlet (1948)—Laurence Olivier produced and directed this fluid, handsome, satisfyingly paced version, and he himself is a witty and active platinum-blond Hamlet. It's a tribute to Shakespeare's passionate immediacy that everyone has his own idea of the play, and many will find much to quarrel with in this film. (For example, the soliloquies have been turned into interior monologues, which diminishes them.) But even if you feel that certain scenes should be done differently, when has the rest of the play been done so well? Whatever the omissions, the mutilations, the mistakes, this is very likely the most exciting and most alive production of *Hamlet* you will ever see on the screen. It's never dull, and if characters such as Fortinbras and Rosencrantz and Guildenstern have been sacrificed, it's remarkable how little they are missed. With Jean Simmons as Ophelia, Basil Sydney as the King, Eileen Herlie as the Queen, Stanley Holloway as the Grave Digger, Felix Aylmer as Polonius, Norman Wooland as Horatio, Terence Morgan as Laertes, Esmond Knight as Bernardo, Anthony Quayle as Marcellus, Harcourt Williams as First Player, and John Laurie as Francisco. The adaptation is by Alan Dent, and the music is by William Walton. b & w

Hamlet (1969)—Bearded, and with a nasal twang, Nicol Williamson is a surly Hamlet, deliberately, wretchedly unattractive. Williamson's acting is all pathos and vituperation, snarls and tantrums, and he stares so much that he's in danger of wearing out his eyeballs. The tension is gone, because this Hamlet is not a man who is destroyed by the events we see and by his own divided feelings; he is weak at the outset. The play collapses not only as drama but as poetic drama—Hamlet's speeches, as Williamson delivers them, lack beauty. This movie, directed by Tony Richardson, isn't a reinterpretation of *Hamlet* but an exploitation of what's worst in Nicol Williamson as an actor; it isn't tragic or absurdist—it's just cheap Jacobean-Mod, sexed up whenever possible. Shot in the Round House, the old London engine shed converted into a theatre, where Richardson also staged the play, the film is done almost completely in oppressive close-ups. There are a few fine moments: Roger Livesey's entrance with the players provides a touch of humanity; he is in beautiful cracked voice and fine music-hall spirit. And Anthony Hopkins is an appealing though very young Claudius—one rather wishes he were left in peace to rule the country, since

Hamlet is obviously unfit. With Marianne Faithfull as Ophelia, Judy Parfitt as Gertrude, Gordon Jackson as Horatio, Mark Dignam as Polonius, and Michael Pennington as Laertes. Cinematography by Gerry Fisher. color (See *Deeper into Movies*.)

Handle with Care, see *Citizens Band*

Der Händler der Vier Jahreszeiten, see *The Merchant of Four Seasons*

Hands Across the Table (1935)—Carole Lombard as a manicurist on the lookout for a wealthy husband meets Fred MacMurray, a fellow who grew up rich but is now broke and intends to marry an heiress. Cynical about romance, these two hang out together while waiting to land their prospective mates. Hers is to be a kindly millionaire (dreary Ralph Bellamy); his is the pineapple king's daughter (Astrid Allwyn). But what you expect to happen happens. As the manicurist puts it, in blunt, archetypal 30s terms— "Hardboiled Hannah was going to fall in love with a bankroll! You can't run away from love." This isn't one of the first-string slapstick romances of its period, but it's a pretty fair example of the second string. Basically uninspired, it's determinedly irreverent. You can see the jokes being set up; when the payoff comes, you're already tired. But MacMurray knows how to read a good line when he gets one, and though he isn't the subtlest of farceurs, that works just fine with Lombard because of her gift for uninhibited comedy. Lombard is the rare performer whose enjoyment of her own jokes adds to the audience's pleasure. Mitchell Leisen, directing his first comedy, had Ernst Lubitsch, the production chief at Paramount, guiding him. With William Demarest, Ruth Donnelly, Marie Prevost, and Edward Gargan. From a Viña Delmar story, adapted by Norman Krasna, Vincent Lawrence, and Herbert Fields. Cinematography by Ted Tetzlaff. b & w

Hannah and Her Sisters (1986)—A minor, agreeably skillful movie by Woody Allen, a new canto in his ongoing poem to love and New York City which includes *Annie Hall* and *Manhattan*. It's likable, but you wish there were more to like. The principal characters are members of a show-business family, with the stable, dependable Hannah (Mia Farrow), a successful actress who manages a career and children with equal serenity, as the pivotal figure, and Barbara Hershey and Dianne Wiest as her sisters. Hannah's parents are played by Maureen O'Sullivan and Lloyd Nolan, her financial-consultant husband by Michael Caine, and her TV writer-producer ex-husband by Allen himself. The picture would be lifeless without him; the other roles are so thin that there's nobody else to draw us into the story. All the vital vulgarity of Woody Allen's early movies has been drained away here, as it was in *Interiors*, but this time he's made the picture halfway human. (People can laugh and feel morally uplifted at the same time.) The willed sterility of his style is terrifying to think about; the picture is all tasteful touches, and there's an element of cultural self-approval in its tone, and a trace of smugness in its narrow concern for family and friends. He uses style to blot out the rest of New York City. It's a form of repression, and, from the look of the movie, repression is what's romantic to him. With Max von Sydow as Barbara Hershey's gloomy, rigidly intellectual lover, Julie Kavner as Allen's TV-partner, and Carrie Fisher, Daniel Stern, Sam Waterston and Tony Roberts (both uncredited), and Bobby Short as himself. The cinematography is by Carlo Di Palma. Orion. color (See *Hooked*.)

Hans Christian Andersen (1952)—Lavish, cloying, pseudo-whimsical monstrosity, contrived by Moss Hart and directed by Charles Vidor, under the aegis of Samuel Goldwyn. It's the conceit of the movie to make Andersen (Danny Kaye) a simpleton bordering on active idiocy. With Zizi Jeanmaire, Roland Petit, Erik Bruhn, Joey Walsh, Farley Granger, and John Qualen. The drippy songs are by Frank Loesser. R K O. color

The Happening (1967)—George Maharis has a couple of funny scenes. That's just about all that can be said for this Elliot Silverstein comedy, though there's a good idea (about a kidnap victim discovering no one wants to ransom him) buried in it. (It's the same O. Henry idea that was buried in the 1958 English comedy *Too Many Crooks*.) The kidnappers here are four hippies, and the movie means to be very 60s, but the biggest laugh comes when the kidnap victim (Anthony Quinn) says, ''When you can't go to the bathroom, that's *trouble!*'' It isn't right to give a movie's jokes away, but if you miss *The Happening*, this should help you appreciate what you're missing. With Faye Dunaway (it was her first film), Michael Parks, Robert Walker (Jr.), Milton Berle, Oscar Homolka, Martha Hyer, and Jack Kruschen. The script is by Frank R. Pierson, James D. Buchanan, and Ronald Austin. Columbia. color

The Happiest Days of Your Life (1950)—If you are the helpless victim of English comedy, you have probably had the dismaying experience of trying to share this taste with someone who has been stonily impervious while you were breaking up. The disease simply isn't communicable—either you get it or you don't, and a plot synopsis of a movie like this one would be no inducement and would probably result in the charge of supreme silliness. But for those who need no inducement: through a bureaucratic error, a boys' school is billeted with a girls' school; there is spinster-grandmother-sergeant Margaret

Rutherford as headmistress of St. Swithin's, feuding with soulful-eyed Alastair Sim as headmaster of Nutbourne; there is gangly, gurgling Joyce Grenfell, the undermistress, with her copy of *The New Statesman*; and there are troops of boys and girls with oaths, sports, mottoes, Grecian dances, and all the hideous paraphernalia of pubescent youth. Frank Launder directed, from John Dighton's play. Ronald Searle provided the drawings for the titles. b & w

Happy Birthday, Wanda June (1971)—Rod Steiger as a sexist big-game hunter, in Kurt Vonnegut's screen adaptation of his 1970 off-Broadway play—an attempt at a Shavian drama of ideas about the end of the bullish dominating male. Steiger's tragedy is that he sounds like Rod Steiger; his familiar vocal rhythms push Vonnegut's florid lines over the cliff, and they splash when they land. The director, Mark Robson, tried for a theatrically stylized tone, and the results are calamitous, though it's not certain that any other directorial approach would have worked much better. With Susannah York, who is miscast but comes through as an able farceur anyway, and Pamelyn Ferdin, who has a few funny moments as Wanda June, and Don Murray, George Grizzard, Steven Paul, and William Hickey. Columbia. color

The Happy Ending (1969)—Richard Brooks wrote and directed this flamboyantly misconceived story of a Denver lawyer's wife (Jean Simmons) who has gone on pills and booze because her life is empty. It's a sort of female version of *The Arrangement*, and it's meant to be a message movie for women's liberation, but this kind of movie never liberated anyone. With John Forsythe, Shirley Jones, and Nanette Fabray. Cinematography by Conrad Hall; music by Michel Legrand. United Artists. color

H

The Happy Time (1952)—Charles Boyer and Louis Jourdan illustrate the French approach to love in this surprisingly tolerable comedy, set in the 20s. It's about the Canadian split between the relaxed French and the prudish Anglo-Saxons. With Kurt Kasznar, Marcel Dalio, Marsha Hunt, Bobby Driscoll, Linda Christian, and Jeanette Nolan. Produced by Stanley Kramer; directed by Richard Fleischer; from Samuel Taylor's play, adapted by Earl Felton. Columbia. b & w

Hard Times (1975)—Spacious, leisurely, and with elaborate period re-creations of Louisiana in the 30s, this first feature directed by the young screenwriter Walter Hill is unusually effective pulp, perhaps even great pulp. The hero (Charles Bronson) rides into town on the rails, looking like an authentic Depression worker—a cap on his head, his face worn, narrow slits of hurting eyes. This aging itinerant never speaks of his past; he hooks up with a gambler (James Coburn) and fights—bare-fisted, no-holds-barred—for gambling stakes. By using Bronson with superb calculation, so that he is the underdog in every situation, Hill gets our hearts pounding in fear that our hero will be hurt or vanquished; the big fight sequence, with Bronson pitted against a boulder of flesh (Robert Tessier), makes you feel the way you did as a kid at the movies. You don't resent the film's grip on you, because Hill respects the loner-underdog myth. Shot on locations in and around New Orleans; with Strother Martin as a hophead medic, and Jill Ireland. Written by Hill, Bryan Gindorff, and Bruce Henstell. Columbia. color (See *When the Lights Go Down*.)

The Hard Way (1943)—Sharply observed and well acted; it doesn't rise to any heights, but it moves along and holds one's attention. Ida Lupino plays a classic stage-mother role, except it's her younger sister (Joan Leslie) whose career she's pushing, as a way of lifting them both out of grimy, Pennsylvania mill-town poverty. Daniel Fuchs and Peter Viertel wrote the script, from a story by Jerry Wald (who also produced), and it has unusual authenticity and vitality for two thirds of the way; then the film gets lost in a series of compromises. It was essential to establish the fresh-faced younger sister's complicity in Lupino's ruthless scheming and sleeping with anyone who could be useful, but (perhaps on orders from the Warners brass?) Joan Leslie is given a pure, outdoor-life romance, and the picture goes flabby. Ida Lupino's English accent comes through at times but she gives one of the best of her intense, hyper-aware, overcontrolled performances (she seemed to relax only in comedy); the conception here justifies much of her tightness, and she suggests desperate, self-pitying layers under the calculation. The male leads, Jack Carson and Dennis Morgan, who play small-time vaudeville hoofers, are very well directed by Vincent Sherman; as a dumb lug who lets the two women walk all over him, Carson is surprisingly touching and convincing. With Gladys George as a beat-out, trampy actress, singing in a whiskey alto, and Paul Cavanagh, Roman Bohnen, Faye Emerson, Julie Bishop, Joan Woodbury, Ann Doran, and Leona Maricle. Well shot (especially the first sequences in the mill town) by James Wong Howe. (Inexplicably, both sisters frequently wear fancy little over-one-eye hats, like papier-mâché cream puffs.) b & w

Hardcore (1979)—George C. Scott is the Calvinist father from Grand Rapids who searches for his runaway teen-age daughter in the porno-prostitution world of California. The father feels no temptation, so there's no contest; he's above sex, and he hates porno the way John Wayne hates rustlers and Commies. The writer-director, Paul Schrader, sets up the picture as a demonstration of the superiority of fundamentalist moral values over pornographic laxness—as if there were nothing in between. It's a detached, opaque, affectionless movie; since it doesn't regard the young prostitutes as human, there's no horror in their dehumanization—only frigid sensationalism. With Peter Boyle and Season Hubley. Columbia. color (See *When the Lights Go Down*.)

The Harder They Come (1973)—Jimmy Cliff, the reggae singer, has the verve of an instinctive actor. In this crude but sensual Jamaican film, he plays a country boy who wants to become a pop star and who achieves his ambition only by becoming a famous killer; he reaches the top of the hit-record charts when he's on the Most Wanted posters. The film, directed by Perry Henzell, is feverish and haphazard, but the music redeems much of it, and the rhythmic swing of the Jamaican speech is hypnotic. color (See *Reeling*.)

Harlan County, U.S.A. (1977)—A documentary with a great subject, and with the taste and sensitivity not to betray it. The director, Barbara Kopple, went to live among the coal miners of Harlan County, Kentucky, when they went out on strike in 1973. This film is about an underdog group with its own folk culture, based on the unending struggle with "the owners." color (See *When the Lights Go Down*.)

Harlow (1965)—There is not a single line in the Joseph E. Levine production *Harlow*, starring Carroll Baker, that sounds as if the speaker felt it or thought it, or could possibly have said it. The falseness is total: from "Oh, Mama, all they want is my body" to "She died of life. She gave it to everyone else and there wasn't enought left for her." Even the title is false; what we see should be called "Landau." It's about this wonderful agent,

Landau (Red Buttons), who wanted to bring this beautiful talent to the world—a story which seems to parallel Levine's faith in Carroll Baker. She's about as talented as Harlow but in different ways. When Landau says to her, "You have the body of a woman and the emotions of a child," we can see it's just the reverse. The script is loaded with such choice epigrams as: "A bedroom with only one person in it is the loneliest place in the world." Surely not lonelier than theatres playing *Harlow*? Directed by Gordon Douglas. With Raf Vallone, Angela Lansbury, and Peter Lawford. Released by Paramount. color

Harold and Maude (1971)—Bud Cort is Harold, a rich, suicidal introvert with a soft, unformed face—he's 19 but looks younger. Ruth Gordon is poor but spunky Maude, the wizened 79-year-old woman who's like a cheerleader for Life. She lives in a railway car, would like to change into a sunflower, frets over how to save an ailing tree, prankishly steals vehicles and drives crazily; she advises Harold to "reach out." In this satirical-whimsical romantic comedy, directed by Hal Ashby from a script by Colin Higgins, Harold reaches out by falling in love with Maude, and their love is consummated on the eve of her 80th birthday. Many young moviegoers have returned to this eccentric film repeatedly (in 1974, one 22-year-old claimed to have seen it 138 times); maybe this is partly because of its mixture of the maudlin and the highly sophisticated. The message is not very different from that of *Hello, Dolly!* or *Mame*, but Harold's flaccid asexuality (he's like a sickly infant, a limp, earthbound Peter Pan) and Maude's advanced stage of pixiness give that message a special freaky quality. And the film has been made with considerable wit and skill. The early scenes, in which Harold tries out various gruesome methods of suicide without scaring his unflappable mother (Vivian Pickles), have a stylized humor.

But Ashby has *directed* eccentrically. The actors are often seen at a great distance and the dialogue reaches us from a distance, too; the sound level varies so much that we keep losing the voices, and Harold's lines often fade away. With Cyril Cusack, Ellen Geer, and Charles Tyner. Music by Cat Stevens, with mush-minded lyrics. Paramount. color

Harper (1966)—Paul Newman in a bungled attempt to recapture the Bogart private-eye world of *The Big Sleep.* In mitigation of his mugging: what can an actor do with a role that calls for him to be half-drowned and beaten to a bloody pulp—all of which merely serves him as an aphrodisiac? Shelley Winters gives the picture artificial respiration for a few minutes, but it soon relapses. Lauren Bacall appears in an in-joke: not in her old role in *The Big Sleep* but as the rich old paralytic in the wheelchair. Funny like a crutch. The big-name cast includes Julie Harris, Janet Leigh, Pamela Tiffin, Robert Wagner, Strother Martin, Robert Webber, and Arthur Hill. Directed by Jack Smight; adapted from Ross Macdonald's *The Moving Target* by William Goldman; cinematography by Conrad Hall. A private-eye movie without sophistication and style is ignominious. Nevertheless, *Harper* was a hit. Warners. color (See *Kiss Kiss Bang Bang.*)

Harry & Tonto (1974)—Paul Mazursky's old-man-on-the-road comedy, with Art Carney, is the most difficult kind of comedy to bring off, because it comes directly from the moviemaker's feelings about life. It has a kind of transparency; that's why someone in the audience can say, "I don't know why I'm crying—this is such a silly movie." Harry is a widowed retired teacher. Evicted from his Upper West Side apartment because the building is being demolished, he tries suburban life in Riverdale with his businessman son (Phil Bruns). Rejecting that, he sets out

with his cat Tonto to visit his daughter (Ellen Burstyn), a bookstore owner in Chicago, and his other son (Larry Hagman), who's hanging on by his teeth in Southern California. Uneven and often clumsy, yet with a distinctive satirical charm, the picture is full of misfits and faddists and social casualties. The celebrated acting teacher Herbert Berghof appears as Harry's New York friend, an aged radical. Joshua Mostel is Harry's grandson who has taken a vow of silence. Harry meets a young girl, played by Melanie Mayron, and shares a jail cell with a medicine man, played by Chief Dan George. In a less felicitous episode he visits his first love, Geraldine Fitzgerald. Carney, who was actually 55, plays 72 without overdoing it (and without going lovable on us); Burstyn's charcter is alone and bitter in ways that impress themselves on one's memory; and Larry Hagman is simply amazing. Sally Marr (Lenny Bruce's mother) plays the friendly old broad at the end who suggests to Harry that they get together. Screenplay by Mazursky (who turns up for a flash, cruising Hagman) and Josh Greenfield. Academy Award for Best Actor (Carney). 20th Century-Fox. color

Harvest *Regain* (1937)—One of the true and essential French film classics. Jean Giono's novel—a love story set in an abandoned village that the lovers bring to life—was made in Provence by Marcel Pagnol. With a superb cast, including the young Fernandel as the itinerant tinker who sells his slavey mistress, Orane Démazis (the Fanny of the Pagnol trilogy), to the hunter, Gabriel Gabrio, and with Marguerite Moreno, Delmont, and Le Vigan. Music by Arthur Honegger. In French. b & w

The Harvey Girls (1946)—In this lavish, high-spirited M-G-M period musical, Judy Garland leads the forces of respectability (the clean, starched waitresses who serve travellers food only), and Angela Lansbury is the wicked, glittering dance-hall queen whose girls provide God-knows-what illicit pleasures. The central conceit of glorifying progress and moral uplift in a musical comedy set in New Mexico in the 1880s is certainly a strange one, but it worked out surprisingly well—though the charm is mostly heavy. With John Hodiak (an ill-chosen romantic partner for Judy Garland) and Ray Bolger, Cyd Charisse, Marjorie Main, Kenny Baker, Virginia O'Brien, Chill Wills, Selena Royle, and Preston Foster. There is, of course, the deservedly famous classic number "On the Atchison, Topeka, and the Santa Fe"—it's one of the triumphant sequences in screen-musical history—as well as a batch of other Johnny Mercer and Harry Warren songs, including "The Wild, Wild West" and "It's a Great Big World." George Sidney directed. color

The Haunting (1963)—An elegantly sinister scare movie, literate and expensive (though basically a traditional ghost story), with those two fine actresses Claire Bloom and Julie Harris. As a Greenwich Village lesbian, Bloom plays a female variant of the role that would once have been assigned to Dwight Frye; Julie Harris is the chaste heroine, a post-Freudian version of those anemic virgins Helen Chandler used to play. This "old dark house" movie is set in a marvellous Victorian gothic pile in New England, and it's good fun. With Richard Johnson, Russ Tamblyn, Fay Compton, Valentine Dyall, Rosalie Crutchley, and Lois Maxwell. The director, Robert Wise, hadn't done a simple amusement like this since his youth; Nelson Gidding did the adaptation of the Shirley Jackson novel *The Haunting of Hill House*. M-G-M. b & w

Having a Wild Weekend Also known as *Catch Us If You Can*. (1965)—Directed by John Boorman, from a script by Peter Nichols, this English movie featuring the Dave Clark Five and Barbara Ferris is partly a reaction against the pop world. Its tone is uneven, its style is faltering and somewhat confused, but it's trying to get at something. It's trying to be a success and to question the meaning of success—and inevitably fails on both counts. At the beginning, the musicians are involved in filming a commercial, but then, as if the inanity of the project overwhelmed them, the hero and heroine try to escape their advertising milieu. They don't want to be turned into products, they don't want to be sold. They begin to look at various escape routes from modern commercialism: drugs, antique collecting, yearning for an island. They encounter middle-aged failures when they're picked up by a dreadful yet sympathetic couple (Robin Bailey and Yootha Joyce), who suggest the Almans—the horribly bickering pair from *Wild Strawberries* (she with her hysteria, he with his Catholicism). The movie seems to discover tentatively, with regret and bewilderment, that the cures are illusory, are only more symptoms. It's as if Pop art had discovered Chekhov—the Three Sisters finally set off for Moscow and along the way discover that there isn't any Moscow. The young refugees from urban corruption look for pastoral innocence and solitude, and find that the corruption has infected the countryside. It is total. And the island the girl dreamed of turns out—at low tide—to be attached to the mainland. The pair were drawn together by the quest; when they are defeated, they split. This movie has an aftertaste. It's bittersweet—which is an old-fashioned word with connotations of sadness, of nostalgia, and perhaps of something one might call truth. It is one of those films that linger in the memory. (Additional irony:

it's said that the Dave Clark Five were dubbed.) b & w

Having Wonderful Time (1938)—Those who had seen Arthur Kober's stage comedy about life in a Catskills resort complained of the dilution of the humor in this de-Jewished movie version, starring Ginger Rogers as the stenographer on vacation and Douglas Fairbanks, Jr., as a law student working as a waiter, but it's a lively, wisecracking film with a good cast and a pleasant romantic flavor. With a very young Red Skelton (billed as Richard Skelton) as the camp's desperate-to-please director of entertainment, and Lee Bowman, Lucille Ball, Eve Arden, Ann Miller, Jack Carson, Donald Meek, Grady Sutton, Inez Courtney, and Dean Jagger. Alfred Santell directed, from Kober's own adaptation. R K O. b & w

Hawaii (1966)—It's an epic in the tradition of best-seller adaptations, with love and rape and incest and childbirth and storms at sea and battles and fires and epidemics; it's based on an 1,130-page book (by James A. Michener) with 8 extra pages of genealogical charts. During the seven years that the film was in various stages of preparation, it wore out a succession of screenwriters and directors. All this may make it appear to be a stinker, and by formal aesthetic standards it is, but it's surprisingly absorbing just the same. It opens in 1819, roughly 40 years after Captain Cook landed, and covers the influx of missionaries and land grabbers. At the center of the action (and, luckily, he is rarely offscreen) is Max von Sydow; he plays an insufferable, tactless Calvinist minister who antagonizes everybody—a racist who believes in the superiority of his God, his skin, his traditions. Von Sydow carries this movie. He accomplishes the almost impossible: he makes us give this scarecrow of a minister our grudging admi-

ration. As the minister's wife, Julie Andrews, pleasing enough in her early scenes, doesn't have the range or depth to develop the character, but Richard Harris, in the role of a swashbuckling sea captain, provides great romantic strength, and, as the native queen, a Tahitian woman, Jocelyne La Garde, is near sublime. The final director, George Roy Hill, develops characters that succeed in binding the material, despite the awkward, crude action scenes. The screenplay credit went to Dalton Trumbo and Daniel Taradash. The huge cast includes Torin Thatcher, Carroll O'Connor, Gene Hackman, John Cullum, George Rose, Lou Antonio, and Dorothy Jeakins (who did the costumes) appears as Hepzibah Hale. A Walter Mirisch Production, for United Artists. color (See *Kiss Kiss Bang Bang*.)

He, see *Le Rosier de Madame Husson*

He Married His Wife (1940)—John O'Hara and the other writers (Sam Hellman, Darrell Ware, Lynn Starling) come up with flippant surprises. At times, this slapstick romance about serial marriage and divorce is almost as mad and good as *Bringing Up Baby*. It features a cow horn and a wonderfully foolish weekend house party at a place called Duck Point. Joel McCrea is the man who loses his wife (Nancy Kelly) because he can't stay away from the racetrack. This was Nancy Kelly in happier days, before she became the mother of *The Bad Seed* (1956). With Mary Boland, Roland Young, Cesar Romero, Elisha Cook, Jr., Mary Healy, Lyle Talbot, and Spencer Charters as the mayor. Directed by Roy Del Ruth; the original story was by Erna Lazarus and Scott Darling. 20th Century-Fox. b & w

He Who Must Die *Celui qui doit mourir* (1958)—This French film, based on Nikos Kazantzakis' *The Greek Passion*, was made by the American (political) expatriate, Jules Dassin, on Crete. It's set in 1921, when the Cretan villagers, living under the traditionally decadent Turkish Agha (Grégoire Aslan makes him a dear, cynical old pederast), are about to stage their annual passion play. The survivors of another village, burned out by the Turks, come to ask for refuge; the town brass (including the head of the local church) drive them out, but the shepherd chosen to play Christ rallies his disciples to their aid. You get the idea. It's about oppressors and oppressed, those who believe in the forms of Christianity and those who believe in the spirit. Christ gets crucified, and the militant oppressed wind up at the barricades. (To turn the other cheek?) You may be left with the uncomfortable feeling that Christ is being claimed for the underdogs in much the same terms that Abe Lincoln and Tom Paine were in the 40s. This big, emotionally overwrought film was very popular at American art houses. With Pierre Vaneck, Melina Mercouri, Jean Servais, Roger Hanin, Fernand Ledoux, Gert Fröbe, Maurice Ronet, and Nicole Berger. Screenplay by Ben Barzman and Dassin; music by Georges Auric. In French. CinemaScope, b & w

Head (1968)—Before the producer, Bert Schneider, and the director, Bob Rafelson, collaborated on *Five Easy Pieces*, they had made their names on TV with "The Monkees," and this first film they did together was an attempt to do for the Monkees what Richard Lester's *A Hard Day's Night* had done for the Beatles. The film tosses in old jokes, blackout routines, documentary footage of the suffering and horror of war, plus the Monkees, and tries to sell it all as a mind-blowing, psychedelic collage. With Annette Funicello, Timothy Carey, and Abraham So-

faer. Written by Rafelson and Jack Nicholson. Released by Columbia. color

Heart Like a Wheel (1983)—A friendly movie with a cold center, this biographical film is about what it cost the drag racer Shirley Muldowney—who has won the National Hot Rod Association World Championship three times—to win out over men in what was previously considered the domain of macho daredevils. Hoyt Axton plays Shirley's earthy and congenial father, the honky-tonk singer Tex Roque, who has gusto in his canny eyes and grinning face; Leo Rossi plays the mechanic-husband who tools up the cars she races; and Beau Bridges brings his marvellous radiance to the role of the impulsive, rowdy Connie Kalitta, who becomes Shirley's partner. Beau Bridges' Connie, who lives on his instincts, makes sense as a drag racer; Shirley doesn't. Bonnie Bedelia, who plays Shirley from 16 to 40, gives a tightly controlled starring performance; she's compelling and she brings the role a dry and precise irony. But her Shirley is a planner and a pusher who thinks everything out—the thrill sport of drag racing is a fulfillment of nothing visible in her character. Directed by Jonathan Kaplan from a script by Ken Friedman, the movie has a B-picture sensibility. It has plenty of action sequences (of the kind that action-film enthusiasts call "existential" and "cinematic"), and it avoids dramatic climaxes (of the kind that these enthusiasts disparage as "theatrical"). And this can make a movie seem honest and authentically American—none of your highbrow stuff. Shirley's hardness is presented simply as what happens to a woman who bucks a sexist society, and the movie expects us to sympathize with her bitterness about not getting the recognition that women in more genteel sports do. When Shirley staggers out of a crash in flames, and her son (Anthony Edwards) runs out to her and looks into her charred helmet, the scene exposes the superficiality of most of the film's treatment of her determination to be the fastest hot-rodder of them all. With Paul Bartel, Dean Paul Martin, and Dick Miller. Released by 20th Century-Fox. color (See *State of the Art*.)

Heartaches (1981)—In this relaxed, enjoyable film, directed by Don Shebib, Rita (Margot Kidder) and Bonnie (Annie Potts) meet on a bus headed for Toronto, and when the harried bus driver is outraged by Rita's language and throws them both out onto the highway, they have no alternative but to become friends. The movie is about this friendship, and about the romantic nature that Rita—a frowzy bleached blonde—hides under her hard-bitten exterior. Rita dresses like a bad dream, and she moves with her head and arms thrust out, as if she were ready to take a swing at the world; she's tough, all right. Dark-haired, big-eyed Bonnie, who's pregnant, is running away from her husband. She seems woozy and remote; she whines like a cuddly puppy with a stomach ache—she sounds so forlorn she's funny. Shebib has his own loose style of Canadian picaresque; you find yourself looking at his characters' messy lives with smiling good will. And Margot Kidder's brazen Rita is a full performance, with the depth that was missing from her earlier roles. Rita is one of those characters—like Barbara Stanwyck's Stella Dallas—who are coarse yet sensitive. They're preposterous creations—sentimental, gutsy, possibly even tearjerking—yet they're played with so much honest emotion that they become intensely likable. With Robert Carradine and Winston Rekert; from a script by Terence Heffernan. color (See *Taking It All In*.)

The Heartbreak Kid (1972)—The director Elaine May finds her comic tone and scores a first besides—no other American woman has ever directed her daughter in a leading role on the screen. Jeannie Berlin is her mother's surrogate here, and she plays the Elaine May addled nymph even better than her mother does. As Lila, she's a middle-class Jewish peasant, her ripe lusciousness a cartoon of sensuality. You can read her life story in her gypsy-red dresses. Lila is the voluptuously giddy bride, whose groom (Charles Grodin) falls in love with a cool American dream girl (Cybill Shepherd) three days after the wedding. Elaine May is a satirist whose malice isn't cutting; something in the woozy atmosphere she creates keeps it mild—yet mild in a thoroughly demented way, mild as if impervious to sanity. All apologies, she has a knack for defusing the pain without killing the joke. From Neil Simon's script, based on Bruce Jay Friedman's short story "A Change of Plan." With Eddie Albert, Audra Lindley, and William Prince. 20th Century-Fox. color (See *Reeling*.)

Heartbreak Ridge (1986)—It's well known that many people have strong feelings about anal intercourse, but it's doubtful if a whole movie had ever been devoted to the expression of those feelings until this one. Clint Eastwood, who directed, plays (so to speak) a Medal of Honor winner from the Korean war and a decorated Vietnam vet—a Marine gunnery sergeant whose abhorrence of being put in a passive sexual position seems to be what makes him super-tough and manly. The marines in his platoon stand waiting while Old Gunny wraps his jowls around witless scurrilous insults, all involving what he's going to shove up their orifices. This should be the portrait of a pathetic vulgarian militarist with terrible anal-aggressive problems, but Eastwood presents him as a great fighting man, a relic of a time when men were men. And, in the last half hour, the film presents proof of what Gunny's training does for his platoon: it celebrates Grenada as a victory that evens the score, after a tie in Korea and a loss in Vietnam. This movie is offensive on just about every level. The script is credited to James Carabatsos; with Marsha Mason, Mario Van Peebles, Everett McGill, Moses Gunn, Eileen Heckart, Bo Svenson, Boyd Gaines, and Arlen Dean Snyder. A Malpaso Production, for Warners. color (See *Hooked*.)

Heartbreakers (1984)—Set in L.A., this is about what's underneath the buddy relationship of the prosperous, darkly handsome Eli (Nick Mancuso), who takes over his father's business, and the tall, boyish Blue (Peter Coyote), a driven, unsuccessful painter, always broke. The writer-director Bobby Roth gets at the unresolved feelings that go into making them friends and rivals. Women— Carole Laure, Kathryn Harrold, and Carol Wayne—are their battlefield. The film is all moods and moments; Roth may not go deep enough, but his work has temperament. He succeeds in using the two men as a way into the American culture of sex, circa the mid-80s, and he captures something of West Coast bohemianism. The picture becomes more involving as it goes on, and when it's over, you feel you've seen something (even if you're not quite sure what). With Max Gail, Jamie Rose, George Morfogen, and James Laurenson. Cinematography by Michael Ballhaus; music by Tangerine Dream. Orion. color (See *State of the Art*.)

Heartburn (1986)—Directed by Mike Nichols, and written by Nora Ephron, who adapted her own 1983 novel (a jokey, fictionalized version of her marriage to Carl Bernstein), the film is rich in fillips—smart little taps and strokes. But after a while you start asking yourself, "What is this movie about?" (You're still asking when it's over.) Mike Nichols takes much of the cheapness out of the material, but the gossipy kick has gone out, too. Working with the cinematographer Nestor Almendros, he shoots the story (of the husband's infidelity and the pregnant wife's rage) in a tight, airless, neutral style. And with the heroine's life no longer treated as rowdy comedy, and the "pain" brought to the surface, the effect is like a weak mixture of *Carnal Knowledge* and a Woody Allen picture and Robert Benton's *Kramer vs. Kramer*. With Meryl Streep and Jack Nicholson, arguably miscast in the leads, and Stockard Channing, Richard Masur, Catherine O'Hara, Maureen Stapleton, Steven Hill, and John Wood—all in top form. Also with Jeff Daniels, Miloš Forman, Aida Linares, and Karen Akers. Music by Carly Simon. Paramount. color (See *Hooked*.)

Hearts of the West (1975)—Jeff Bridges is just the right actor to play Lewis Tater, an Iowa farm boy who writes Western stories and aspires to be like his idol, Zane Grey. Lewis leaves home in 1929, heads toward the land of his purple-prose dreams, and stumbles into a job as a stuntman in Western pictures directed by a penny-pinching hysteric played by Alan Arkin. This nostalgia comedy has an eccentric enchantment to it. The troupe of cowboy actors, headed by Andy Griffith, is the most engaging ensemble since the Dead End Kids, and the heroine, a script girl, is played by wide-eyed Blythe Danner, who is reminiscent of both Margaret Sullavan and Jean Arthur. The people and the atmosphere are so good that one wants more of them; the rinky-dink chase plot isn't needed at all, and there are also unnecessary complications involving Herbert Edelman, as a movie producer, and Donald Pleasence, as a Western-pulp publisher. But it's a film that plays on in the mind. Howard Zieff directed, from Rob Thompson's script. M-G-M. color (See *When the Lights Go Down*.)

Heartworn Highways (1981)—An informal documentary, shot and directed by James Szalapski, about performers such as Guy Clark, David Allan Coe, Townes Van Zandt, and Steve Young—part of the 70s "outlaw" generation of country music (outlaw because it wasn't sanctioned by the recording companies in Nashville). Szalapski shot most of the footage in six weeks around Christmas of 1975, and then spent three or four years, off and on, trying to get the movie distributed. There's very little in the film that isn't friendly or funny or really soul-stirring. It's disorganized, though—it's like being at a good party, but you don't know how you got there, and you never quite catch the last names of the assorted celebrities telling tall tales and singing lovely sad songs. color (See *Taking It All In.*)

Heat (1972)—A slack, depressive Paul Morrissey version of *Sunset Boulevard*, with Joe Dallesandro as a stud hustler and Sylvia Miles as the predatory star in the big mansion. It's meant to be a funny exploitation movie, but the comic moments are rare. Produced by Andy Warhol. color

Heathers (1989)—Westerburg High's three rich beauties who make life hell for those less gilded are all named Heather. Their reluctant associate, Veronica (Winona Ryder), confides in her diary that she dreams of "a world without Heather," and a psychotically fearless juvenile delinquent, J.D. (Christian Slater), materializes, and goads her to become his accomplice in making her dream come true. The script, by Daniel Waters, has a lot of prankish, spiky dialogue and some good rowdy slapstick nastiness, such as Veronica and J.D.'s killing two football heroes and arranging their deaths to suggest that they were lovers in a suicide pact; the script promises that the picture will lift off into the junior division of Blue Velvetland. But layers of didacticism weigh it down, and the young, inexperienced director, Michael Lehmann (who uses hyper-bright colors for a facetious artificial effect), doesn't find the right moods for the gags. About a half hour from the end, Waters and Lehmann pull back from their sadistic gaudiness. Veronica represents their we-don't-really-mean-it side—we don't want to hurt anybody's feelings. Where's the sting? With Kim Walker as tall, blond Heather Chandler. New World Pictures. color (See *Movie Love.*)

Heaven Can Wait (1943)—Ernst Lubitsch produced and directed this whimsical, uneven, yet generally disarming comedy of manners (it lightly satirizes social and sexual conventions), from a screenplay by his frequent collaborator Samson Raphaelson. Perhaps it isn't well known because it stars the rather drab Don Ameche, who appeared in many forced and charmless routine pictures, but here (as in *Midnight*) he's reasonably engaging. He plays a well-born New Yorker, Henry Van Cleve—a lifetime dandy and stage-door Johnny—who thinks that his sexual improprieties are sinful and qualify him for Hell, but as he applies to Satan and tells his story we see his life in flashbacks and see his essential generosity and innocence. Gene Tierney plays the Kansas girl he steals from his stuffy cousin (Allyn Joslyn). With Charles Coburn, Marjorie Main, Laird Cregar, Spring Byington, Florence Bates, Eugene Pallette, Louis Calhern, Clarence Muse, Adele Jurgens, Clara Blandick, and Scotty Beckett and Dickie Moore as Henry at 7 and 15, Signe Hasso as the French maid, and Anita Bolster as Mrs. Cooper-Cooper. Loosely based on the Hungarian play *Birthdays*, by Laszlo Bus-Fekete. This film has no connection with Warren Beatty's 1978 *Heaven Can Wait*, which is a remake of the 1941 *Here Comes Mr. Jordan*, which was taken from an American play called *Heaven Can Wait*, by Harry Segall. 20th Century-Fox. Lubitsch's first film in color.

The Heiress (1949)—This William Wyler production is very likely the best film adaptation of Henry James, with the possible exception of *The Innocents*. The screenplay, by Ruth and Augustus Goetz, is based on their stage version of James's *Washington Square*, and at first the period settings and clothes may make the movie seem a little heavy and stagey, but then Wyler's mastery of the psychological nuances can have you drawing deep breaths. It's a peerless, super-controlled movie, in the same mode as Wyler's 1952 *Carrie*, though more fully sustained. Wyler's greatness here is that he can hold the elements of the film in his palm without constricting the actors. He frees them. Montgomery Clift is just about perfect as James's fortune hunter Morris Townsend and Olivia de Havilland does her finest work ever as the heiress Catherine Sloper. With Ralph Richardson, Miriam Hopkins, Vanessa Brown, Betty Linley, Ray Collins, Selena Royle, and Mona Freeman. Music by Aaron Copland; art direction by John Meehan and Harry Horner. Academy Award for Best Actress (de Havilland). Paramount. b & w

Hell in the Pacific (1969)—Lee Marvin and Toshiro Mifune are the stars and there's nobody else in the movie—just this American soldier and this Japanese soldier stranded on a Pacific island during the Second World War, and neither speaking a word of the other's language. Haven't you always longed for a movie full of Toshiro Mifune grunting and Lee Marvin muttering to himself? Actually Marvin is rather funny talking to himself, but the theme is—you guessed it—brotherhood. The director, John Boorman, and the cinematographer, Conrad Hall, get so glittering flashy that they make the Pacific island a pile

of sequins, and Lalo Schifrin's score sparkles like the purest ersatz. Cinerama color

Heller in Pink Tights (1960)—Sophia Loren, as a blond international actress, tours the Far West with Anthony Quinn's theatrical troupe, in George Cukor's only Western. The best parts are the theatrical performances of *Mazeppa* and *La Belle Hélène*, and some interchanges between Margaret O'Brien and Eileen Heckart, who play a stage mother-and-daughter team. The film is handsomely made, but the material is flat in an inoffensive sort of way, and Cukor dawdles; the final edit was not his, and he was unhappy with it. Adapted from a Louis L'Amour novel by Dudley Nichols and Walter Bernstein. With Ramon Novarro, Edmund Lowe, and Steve Forrest. Hoyningen-Huené was the color consultant. Paramount.

Hello, Dolly! (1969)—The whole archaic big-musical circus here surrounds a Happening—Barbra Streisand—and it's all worth seeing in order to see her. Directed by Gene Kelly. 20th Century-Fox. color (See *Deeper into Movies*.)

Hello, Frisco, Hello (1943)—The Barbary Coast, again. Mediocrity enshrined. A musical from 20th Century-Fox, with Alice Faye, John Payne, Jack Oakie, Laird Cregar, June Havoc, Lynn Bari, Ward Bond, George Barbier, and Aubrey Mather. The paste-up score ranges from "You'll Never Know" and "Hello Ma Baby" to such lethal jobs as "It's Tulip Time in Holland." Bruce Humberstone directed. color

Hell's Angels (1930)—The aviation footage is still something to see, with great shots of zeppelin warfare; toward the end of the first half, a zeppelin looms through the clouds, which part at moments to show London below. And the dogfight sequences, with a camera mounted on the front of a plane, still have a kinetic immediacy. There are experts who believe that this spectacular footage, which Howard Hughes worked out on blackboards and with model planes before he staged it, contains scenes that have never been surpassed. But the First World War story, involving two brothers, Oxford men who join the Royal Flying Corps (Ben Lyon and James Hall), and Jean Harlow, as the smoldering woman they both love, is plain awful. Written by Howard Estabrook and Harry Behn, the movie, which started shooting in 1927, was planned as a silent. Hughes, still in his early twenties, financed and produced, and he also directed, after disputes with a couple of directors whom he had hired. He lost money on the film because he spent so much to get the effects he wanted; the sequence of the zeppelin's flaming descent cost several times as much as a conventional movie of the day. After the film was previewed, he decided to add sound. That's when Harlow was hired (replacing Greta Nissen, who had a Norwegian accent). Hughes also hired Joseph Moncure March to write the dialogue scenes and James Whale to direct them, and after 31 months in production and an expenditure of almost $4 million, the film opened. And, of course, audiences howled at the corny story and at Harlow's ludicrous wriggling and slinking. Reactions to the film have always been divided—it inspires admiration and laughter. b & w, with color sequences

Henry V (1944)—Shakespeare's *Henry V* is the story of the playboy Plantagenet who grew up to become a great leader and, at 27, defeated the armies of France at Agincourt. There, at the last major stand of medieval chivalry, the English archers, outnumbered five to one, cut down the fatally encumbered knights of France. Laurence Olivier once said that it was the sort of juvenile role that you can't play when you're a juvenile—"When you are young, you are too bashful to play a hero; you debunk it. It isn't until you're older that you can understand the pictorial beauty of heroism." He came to it at the right time. His production—it was his first time out as a film director—is a triumph of color, music, spectacle, and soaring heroic poetry, and, as actor, he brings lungs, exultation, and a guileful wit to the role. The film has true charm. With Renee Asherson as Princess Katherine, Leslie Banks as Chorus, George Robey as Falstaff, Esmond Knight as Fluellen, Leo Genn as the Constable of France, Felix Aylmer as the Archbishop of Canterbury, Niall MacGinnis as MacMorris, Robert Newton as Ancient Pistol, Harcourt Williams as Charles VI, Max Adrian as the Dauphin, Robert Helpmann as the Bishop of Ely, and Ernest Thesiger as the Duke of Berri. The music is by William Walton; the cinematography is by Robert Krasker and Jack Hildyard. (2 hours and 14 minutes.) color

Henry V (1989)—This fast-paced version, adapted and directed by its young star, Kenneth Branagh, isn't exultant, like the version made 45 years earlier by Laurence Olivier. Branagh emphasizes the price paid for war: the bloodshed. And, in keeping with his generation's supposed disillusion with war, he minimizes the play's glorification of the English fighting man. His conception of how to film the play is to look closely at the conniving, the misgivings, the ego wars. (This epic *noir* doesn't indicate why the French lost at Agincourt.) Branagh is not an overnight great moviemaker; his attempts at spectacular effects strain his inventiveness. But as an actor he has something of James Cagney's confident Irishness; he's intensely likable, with a beautiful, expressive voice, and a straightforwardness that drives the whole film ahead. He and the other performers are so up that you feel their pride in working on true dramatic poetry. It's a company of stars: Paul Scofield as the melancholy French king whose face foretells the doom of his army, Christopher Ravenscroft as the herald Mountjoy, Derek Jacobi as the Chorus, Judi Dench as Mistress Quickly, Robbie Coltrane as Falstaff, Brian Blessed as Exeter, Richard Briers as Bardolph, Richard Easton as the Constable of France, Alec McCowen as Ely, Robert Stephens as Pistol, Emma Thompson as Katherine, Geraldine McEwan as Alice, Christian Bale as Falstaff's boy, and best of all, perhaps, Ian Holm as the chattering Welshman Fluellen. Released by the Samuel Goldwyn Company. color (See *Movie Love*.)

Her Cardboard Lover (1942)—A mistake that Norma Shearer made when she was old enough to know better. Her companions in this overstuffed whimsey that turns into sheer misery are Robert Taylor and George Sanders. George Cukor is listed as the director; it's up to him to refute the charge. With Frank McHugh, Elizabeth Patterson, and Chill Wills. From a Jacques Deval play that had been filmed in 1928 with Marion Davies, and in 1932, as *The Passionate Plumber*, with Buster Keaton; the adaptors (John Collier and Anthony Veiller were among them) must have hidden even from their families. J. Walter Ruben produced, for M-G-M. b & w

Here Comes Mr. Jordan (1941)—In this scatterbrained fantasy, the soul of Joe Pendleton (Robert Montgomery), a contender for the heavyweight championship, arrives in the hereafter fifty years before the appointed time through the overzealousness of a Heavenly Messenger (Edward Everett Horton) who has snatched Pendleton from an airplane crash that he was supposed to survive. The problem of getting Joe back into mortal flesh so that he can win the championship is so acute that it's taken over by Mr. Jordan (Claude Rains), a high executive on the Other Side. The slickly hammy Rains gives Mr. Jordan a sinister gloss, as if he were involved in some heavenly racket, like smuggling Chinese; James Gleason has the contrastingly gruff-voiced role of the fighter's manager. There's too much metaphysical gabbing and a labored boy-gets-girl romance, but audiences loved this chunk of whimsey. With Evelyn Keyes, Rita Johnson, John Emery, Donald MacBride, Halliwell Hobbes, and Benny Rubin. Alexander Hall directed; Sidney Buchman and Seton I. Miller adapted Harry Segall's play *Heaven Can Wait*. (Remade as *Heaven Can Wait* by Warren Beatty in 1978.) Columbia. b & w

L'Héritier, see *The Inheritor*

Hester Street (1975)—A modest comedy about the assimilation process among a group of Russian-Jewish immigrants living on the lower East Side in 1896. Independently made, this first feature by the writer-director Joan Micklin Silver begins lamely, but it wins one over. Carol Kane is lovely as the timid, pious, rejected wife of a sweatshop worker who has broken away from the Old World traditions that she represents. Mel Howard plays Bernstein, the scholarly boarder who loves her. The weaknesses are in the casting and the handling of the aggressive characters, and in the thin, audience-pleasing attitudes toward the Americanization process. With Steven Keats and Dorrie Kavanaugh; adapted from a story by Abraham Cohan. b & w (See *When the Lights Go Down*.)

Hets, see *Torment*

Hi, Mom! (1970)—Robert De Niro is at his most spontaneous in this amazing, freewheeling comedy, written and directed by Brian De Palma, from a story he concocted with his young producer, Charles Hirsch. It was made in a cabaret style, taking on one societal target after another. De Niro—very boyish, with thick, shiny brown hair—does some great, fast double-talk routines with Allen Garfield; they rattle on together in a fixed frame. (The camera doesn't move—*they* move around in the frame.) De Palma uses a lot of camera gags in this film—he keeps you conscious of the film medium by playing Buster Keaton–like games with it. De Niro is a Vietnam vet who's trying to make out with girls. At first, he wants to shoot Peep Art films (the windows he peeps into become fixed frames); then he begins to see himself with the cuties in those frames, so he goes up, knocks on the doors, talks his way into the pictures, and lives his fantasies. Next he joins a mostly black theatre-of-cruelty-and-revolt troupe that stages an audience-participation play—"Be Black, Baby." The black actors appear in whiteface and they daub black paint on the faces of the white liberals who attend, telling them that they are going to experience what it means to be black. Then they proceed to beat them and rob and rape them. This sequence becomes rather overpowering; conceptually it's satire, but it's too wild and chaotic to be very funny. However, when the liberals call for the police to help them and De Niro comes on as a cop and refuses to believe their stories, the insane comic tone is restored. (Eventually the guilt-ridden masochistic audience convinces itself that it has had a worthwhile experience.) When the actors become bored with theatrical approaches to revolution, they become urban guerrillas, and our hero comes closer to his dream of "total involvement" by setting bombs. De Niro does quirky parody numbers all the way through; when he's a guerrilla living in disguise as a middle-class insurance salesman, he becomes a Harold Lloyd type. He has long scenes with several of the other performers in which he and his partners set the rhythm as they would on a stage (the camera is motionless), and the results are cra-

zily likable timing. The cast includes Jennifer Salt as the dumpling in one of the windows, and Lara Parker, Gerrit Graham, and Ruth Alda. This underground vaudeville show may have been too hip even for 1970; it didn't have the success it deserved. De Palma's dialogue may be the best that he has ever had to work with. Edited by Paul Hirsch. color

High and Dry Also known as *The Maggie*. (1953)—A piece of American folklore—the innocent American vanquishing the wicked, experienced Europeans—is set bottomside up. The bullishly efficient American millionaire (Paul Douglas) is no match for a group of Scots with fiendishly winning ways. He wants to get a cargo of plumbing to an island he has bought; they fleece him by transporting it on a condemned barge. When he jettisons his valuable plumbing to preserve their worthless barge, the desperate desire of the American to do the right thing in a world of traditions he cannot comprehend is given its most humane, satirical treatment. The materialistic American, it turns out, is the sentimental sucker, full of empathy for everybody. This comic parable of the postwar American in Europe was directed by Alexander Mackendrick, from a script by William Rose; it should be livelier—it's poky in places. b & w

High Anxiety (1977)—Mel Brooks' rehash of some of Hitchcock's most famous thriller effects. This is a child's idea of satire—imitations, with a funny hat and a leer. Brooks plays Dr. Thorndyke, a Nobel Prize–winning psychiatrist who is the new director of a Los Angeles asylum—the previous one having died suddenly. He leaves this *Spellbound* situation and goes up to San Francisco for a psychiatrists' convention and into locations that recall *Vertigo*. There isn't a whisper of suspense, and there are few earned laughs; all Brooks does is let us know he has seen some of the same movies we have. When he forgets about Hitchcock, he has a couple of buoyant sequences: he does a terrific parody of Frank Sinatra's hyper-nonchalant singing style, breaking up words into sizzling syllables and tossing the mike cord from side to side and snapping it like a whip; and he and the heroine, Madeline Kahn, do an old-Jewish-couple vaudeville-patter number in the San Francisco airport. With Cloris Leachman, Harvey Korman, Ron Carey, Dick Van Patten, Howard Morris, Jack Riley, Charlie Callas, and Albert J. Whitlock, who also did the special effects, and Rudy DeLuca, Ron Clark, and Barry Levinson, who also collaborated with Brooks on the script. 20th Century-Fox. color (See *When the Lights Go Down*.)

The High Cost of Loving (1958)—This satirical comedy about organization men has a feeling for the everyday inadequacies and anxieties that you laugh at out of the wrong side of your face. And it has a very funny opening sequence, with the happily married lowly business executive (José Ferrer) and his wife (Gena Rowlands, in her film début) getting up and preparing to go to their jobs without a word to each other. The picture, which Ferrer directed, isn't really much (the writing is weak, the subject is small), but it moves along and it was one of the few even passable comedies of its year. Yet (like Ferrer's earlier picture, *The Great Man*) it failed at the box office and Ferrer didn't direct any more chance-taking movies, though his work here shows that he was just beginning to enjoy the craft and see the possibilities. With Jim Backus, Werner Klemperer, Joanne Gilbert, Philip Ober, Edward Platt, and Bobby Troup. Script by a writer with the unlikely name of Rip Van Ronkel. M-G-M. b & w

High Hopes (1988)—Mike Leigh's wacked-out comedy-drama about life in Thatcherland features three couples: the rich twits (David Bamber and Lesley Manville as a young champagne dealer and his cool socialite wife); the pushy Yups (Philip Jackson and Heather Tobias as a boorish car salesman and his shrill, social-climber wife); the working poor (bearded Philip Davis and dark-eyed Ruth Sheen as a pot-smoking Marxist who scrapes by as a motorcycle messenger and his companion of ten years, who likes to grow things). This may sound like a liberal-left horror, but the English delight in extreme, preposterous silliness hasn't died even among the serious left: the characters keep turning into absurdist cartoons. As the twitty nymph Laetitia, Lesley Manville is a cutup, like Andrea Martin or Catherine O'Hara. It's an exuberantly likable movie—not always satisfying but never drab, never ordinary. With Edna Doré as the messenger's forgetful old mum; the cinematography is by Roger Pratt. color (See *Movie Love*.)

High Noon (1952)—The Western form is used for a sneak civics lesson. Gary Cooper is the marshal who fights alone for law and order when his cowtown is paralyzed by fear. Much has been made of the film's structure (it runs from 10:40 A.M. to high noon, coinciding with the running time of the film); of the stark settings and the long shadows; of the screenwriter Carl Foreman's psychological insight and his buildup of suspense. When the film came out, there were actually people who said it was a poem of force comparable to *The Iliad*. But its insights are primer sociology, and the demonstration of the town's cowardice is Q.E.D. It's a tight piece of work, though—well directed by Fred Zinnemann. With Grace Kelly, Katy Jurado, Lee Van Cleef, Thomas Mitchell, Lloyd Bridges, Henry Morgan, Lon Chaney, Jr., and Otto Kruger. The script is based on the story "The Tin Star" by John W. Cunningham; the cinematography is by Floyd Crosby; and the score is by Dmitri Tiomkin (who took an

Academy Award for it). Cooper also won the Best Actor award, and the editors were also honored. Produced by Stanley Kramer, for United Artists. b & w

High School (1969)—What we see in Fred Wiseman's documentary, shot in a high school in a large Eastern city, is so familiar and so extraordinarily evocative that a feeling of empathy with the students floods over us. How did we live through it? How did we keep any spirit? b & w (See *Deeper into Movies*.)

High Season (1988)—Clare Peploe's first feature is a high comedy set on the Greek island of Rhodes, and it has some of the yumminess of a picture like *Shampoo*. It's about the relations of expatriates, tourists, and the natives, with Jacqueline Bisset giving a warm, juicy performance in the pivotal role of an English photographer who is broke and may have to sell her house and leave this island she loves. Irene Papas plays the Englishwoman's widowed friend—weather-beaten, deeply goofy, and as much a part of the magnificence of the place as the honking donkeys; she regards the tourists as enemies—as an army of occupation, like the Nazis. These two women are both scenic wonders, and so is Sebastian Shaw, who plays an elderly art historian. Shaw—he was born in 1905—was a handsome leading man in British films of the 30s and he's still handsome; his face opens to the sunlight and the camera. The whole movie is superbly cast. The wizardly young Kenneth Branagh plays a practical-minded Englishman, who shares a moonlight dip with Bisset and imagines himself in love. Lesley Manville is his romantic wife, who discovers Byron's poetry; James Fox is Bisset's estranged husband; Ruby Baker is her 13-year-old daughter; Paris Tselios is Papas's son; and Robert Stephens is an obscenely rich Greek-American. The script is by the director and her brother

Mark; the meltingly beautiful cinematography is by Chris Menges. color (See *Hooked*.)

High Sierra (1941)—This Humphrey Bogart picture, directed by Raoul Walsh, set a new style in gangster movies—the aging outlaw as an anachronism in a changing world. Bogart's performance as the weary Dillinger-like ex-convict—the man who just wants to pull off one more job so he can get out of what has become just a dirty business—is a classic. The film romanticizes this last-of-a-breed figure, but it's smart enough to romanticize him in a hard-edged realistic way, and Bogart is convincingly—often excitingly—tense and tired. About half the movie is definitive; the other half is sunk in a maudlin subplot about the outlaw's love for a lame girl (Joan Leslie, maddeningly fresh-faced). With Ida Lupino, Alan Curtis, Arthur Kennedy, Henry Hull, Barton MacLane, Cornel Wilde, Henry Travers, Jerome Cowan, Minna Gombell, Donald MacBride, Willie Best, Isabel Jewell, Elisabeth Risdon, and George Meeker. (Remade by Walsh in 1949 as *Colorado Territory*, starring Joel McCrea; it was also remade in 1955 by Stuart Heisler as *I Died a Thousand Times*.) Warners. b & w

High Spirits (1988)—A busload of American tourists arrive at a castle that's advertised as the most haunted place in Ireland. The producers may have been hoping for something on the order of National Lampoon's Irish Vacation with a jigger of *Ghostbusters*; they whacked away at the film, removing between 15 and 25 per cent of the footage, but it's still clear that what the writer-director, Neil Jordan (best known for his 1986 *Mona Lisa*), was trying for was an Irish phantasmagoria—a *Midsummer Night's Dream*, with love swaps and ghostly transformations. And once you get past the clumsily antic early scenes, the moody texture can take hold of your imagination. At its best, the film is a soft Irish kiss.

There may never have been a movie ghost who was as sexy and ethereal a love object as Daryl Hannah is here, and as a rich, tough American, Beverly D'Angelo has her own walloping gorgeousness. Peter O'Toole is the owner of the castle; Liam Neeson is Hannah's ghostly bridegroom; Steve Guttenberg is a love-struck ninny. Also with Peter Gallagher, Jennifer Tilly, Liz Smith, Donal McCann, and Martin Ferrero. The cinematography is by Alex Thomson; the satisfyingly spooky special effects are by Meddings Magic Camera Company. Tri-Star. color (See *Movie Love*.)

High Tide (1987)—A great many young women are likely to feel that this is the movie they've wanted to make. It's a woman's picture in the way that *Stella Dallas* was—it's about the mother-daughter bond. But it's also a woman's picture in a new way: the Australian director Gillian Armstrong has the technique and the assurance to put a woman's fluid, not fully articulated emotions right onto the screen. And she has an actress—Judy Davis—who's a genius at moods. As one of three backup singers for a touring Elvis imitator, Judy Davis is contemptuous of the cruddy act, contemptuous of herself. Feeling put down, the dumb-lug Elvis fires her, and she's left alone at the beginning of winter in a ramshackle beach town on the magnificent, windswept coast of New South Wales. There she encounters her lonely teen-age daughter (Claudia Karvan), whom she'd given up to her confident, belligerent mother-in-law (Jan Adele) 13 years earlier. The film's emotional suggestiveness makes it almost a primal woman's picture: Judy Davis has been compared with Jeanne Moreau, and that's apt, but she's Moreau without the cultural swank, the high-fashion gloss. She speaks to us more directly. The script is by Laura Jones; the superb cinematography is by Russell Boyd, who was also the camera operator; the stunningly effective editing is by Nick Beauman. With Colin Friels, Bob Purtell, John Clayton, and Mark Hembrow. color (See *Hooked*.)

High, Wide, and Handsome (1937)—Irene Dunne (in musicals, the Julie Andrews of her day) at her cornball primmest, singing alongside a farm horse, when Randolph Scott isn't around. This long, lavish, musical Western, set in the mid-19th century, was written by Oscar Hammerstein II and has music by Jerome Kern, which is, however, of widely varying quality and is sung mostly by the ever-noble Miss Dunne. (Her demonstration of how to belt out beer-hall songs is surely on a par with José Iturbi's demonstrations of how to play boogie-woogie.) Dorothy Lamour has a few numbers, and the cast includes Ben Blue, Akim Tamiroff, Charles Bickford, Elizabeth Patterson, Alan Hale, Raymond Walburn, William Frawley, Irving Pichel, and Lucien Littlefield. The director was Rouben Mamoulian. Paramount. b & w

Der Himmel über Berlin, see *Wings of Desire*

The Hindenburg (1975)—On May 6, 1937, the giant transatlantic zeppelin, the Hindenburg—filled with explosive hydrogen, because the United States wouldn't sell Nazi Germany non-explosive helium—blew up while coming down for a landing at Lakehurst, New Jersey, with 97 people on board. 13 passengers and 22 members of the crew were killed. Since there were newsreel cameramen waiting there to photograph the arrival, they recorded the disaster, and millions of people saw it in theatres. In 34 seconds, the great luxury airship, longer than two football fields, became a mass of flames, and its aluminum-alloy skeleton was exposed as it crashed. The movie is a fictional version of what happened on its last flight, culminating in the actual newsreel footage. It's obvious that the logistics of the production were a real killer, and Albert Whitlock's matte effects are very fine trompe-l'oeil. But the picture is so dry that you begin to feel dehydrated and your mind goes on the fritz. Anne Bancroft plays the blasé doper Ursula, a sneering German countess whose hair has been coiffed to be so authentically 30s that it looks like black potato chips stuck to her head; as soon as she speaks with her familiar New York intonation, her hauteur crumbles, though her eyebrows remain elevated. When she uses her classy allure on George C. Scott—a disillusioned Luftwaffe colonel—those eyebrows waggle like Groucho's. Perfectly good actors like William Atherton, Burgess Meredith, and Charles Durning all hang in there while the director, Robert Wise, and his scenarist, Nelson Gidding, shuffle the subplots in order to create the impression of action. Wise directs with lame good taste; there's none of the blissful trippiness of being carried in the belly of a zeppelin, and none of the carnival vulgarity that can pep up a disaster thriller. Wise turns his disaster picture into an anti-Nazi disaster picture, and he brings all his flatulent seriousness to the endeavor. One gasbag meets another. With Gig Young, Roy Thinnes, Richard A. Dysart, René Auberjonois, Robert Clary, Peter Donat, Stephen Elliott, Katherine Helmond, and Joanna Moore. Music by David Shire; based on the book by Michael M. Mooney; Richard Levinson and William Link prepared the screen story. Universal. color (See *When the Lights Go Down*.)

Hiroshima, mon amour (1959)—Hushed and hypnotic, it makes you so conscious of its artistry that you may feel as if you're in church and need to giggle. This first full-length film by Alain Resnais has a script by Marguerite Duras that features musical, incantatory dialogue, and a crucial line, "They make movies to sell soap, why not a movie to sell peace?" The movie, which opens with the intertwined nude bodies of a French movie actress (Emmanuèle Riva) and a Japanese architect (Eiji Okada), was taken as powerful propaganda against the atom bomb. The lovers are covered in symbolic ash, and when the woman says that she has seen everything in Hiroshima the man tells her she has seen nothing in Hiroshima; then they say the same things over again, and again, and perhaps again. As the film goes on, the woman tells him about her first experience of love: it was with a German soldier, who was killed on the last day of fighting. She was dragged away and her head shaved; she went mad and was hidden in a cellar by her shamed parents. Her lyric, masochistic account lingers in the air. With its doomed romance in the past and its tortured affair in the present, this is a woman's picture in the most derogatory sense of the term, but with a high-cultural tone. Riva gives a remarkably fine performance. Eiji Okada says no more than an analyst might; he is simply a sounding board. And if, being Japanese, he is supposed to represent the world conscience, he brings an unsuitably bland, professionally sympathetic, and upper-class manner to the function. The images of the two in bed are intercut with what is supposed to be documentary footage of the effect of the bomb on Hiroshima, but some of the footage is from a fictional atrocity movie. In French. b & w (See *I Lost it at the Movies*.)

His Double Life (1933)—One of several movie versions of Arnold Bennett's *Buried Alive*. This time, that nimble actor Roland Young is the shy, world-famous artist who is delighted to be thought dead in order to escape the annoyances of fame and settle down with genteel, middle-class Lillian Gish. The whimsey palls. Directed by Arthur Hopkins. (A much livelier 1943 version—*Holy Matrimony*—stars Monty Woolley and Gracie Fields.) Paramount. b & w

His Girl Friday (1940)—In 1928 Ben Hecht and Charles MacArthur wrote *The Front Page*, the greatest newspaper comedy of them all; Howard Hawks directed this version of it— a spastic explosion of dialogue, adapted by Charles Lederer, and starring Cary Grant as the domineering editor Walter Burns and Rosalind Russell as Hildy Johnson, the unscrupulous crime reporter with printer's ink in her veins. (In the play Hildy Johnson is a man.) Overlapping dialogue carries the movie along at breakneck speed; word gags take the place of the sight gags of silent comedy, as this race of brittle, cynical, childish people rush around on corrupt errands. Russell is at her comedy peak here—she wears a striped suit, uses her long-legged body for ungainly, unladylike effects, and rasps out her lines. And, as Walter Burns, Grant raises mugging to a joyful art. Burns' callousness and unscrupulousness are expressed in some of the best farce lines ever written in this country, and Grant hits those lines with a smack. He uses the same stiff-neck, cocked-head stance that he did in *Gunga Din*: it's his position for all-out, unsubtle farce. He snorts and whoops. His Burns is a strong-arm performance, defiantly self-centered and funny. The reporters—a fine crew—are Ernest Truex, Cliff Edwards, Porter Hall, Roscoe Karns, Frank Jenks, Regis Toomey; also with Gene Lockhart as the sheriff, Billy Gilbert as the messenger, John Qualen, Helen Mack, and Ralph Bellamy as chief stooge—a respectable businessman—and Alma Kruger as his mother. Columbia. b & w (See *The Citizen Kane Book*.)

L'Histoire d'Adèle H., see *The Story of Adèle H.*

History Is Made at Night (1937)—The plot is so preposterously arbitrary that it's as if several scripts had been chopped up and stuck together, yet the director, Frank Borzage, plunges ahead until an ocean liner (with most of the cast aboard) crashes into an iceberg and brings the madness to a halt. Jean Arthur plays a woman in distress. Trying to escape from her rich, powerful, mad husband (Colin Clive), she meets a gallant gentleman (Charles Boyer), who turns out to be a headwaiter. The husband tries to frame the headwaiter for a crime he himself committed. Leo Carrillo and Ivan Lebedeff are also mixed up in this silly melodrama, which is so souped up with demonic passions and tender glances and elegant photography (by Gregg Toland) that it's really quite entertaining. Walter Wanger produced, for United Artists; the scenario is credited to Gene Towne and Graham Baker. b & w

History of the World—Part I (1981)—An all-out assault on taste and taboo. Mel Brooks is the writer, the director, and the star of this series of bawdy sketches. It's a floating burlesque show that travels from one era to the next, lampooning the particular infamies of each age. Brooks' staging is often flaccid and disorderly, and even when he and the dozens of other comics in the cast are racing about, the movie feels static. It's powered by its performers, though, and their way with a joke; some of the routines are golden shtick. Brooks is Moses, a singing and dancing Torquemada, Louis XVI, and Comicus, a stand-up philosopher who performs for Nero— played by Dom DeLuise, embracing rottenness with blissful abandon. Also with Gregory Hines, Bea Arthur, Madeline Kahn, Paul Mazursky, Ron Carey, Sid Caesar, Cloris Leachman, Harvey Korman, Spike Milligan, and John Hurt. The graceful painted vistas are by the special-effects wizard Albert J. Whitlock. 20th Century-Fox. color (See *Taking It All In.*)

Hobson's Choice (1953)—Charles Laughton is superbly vulgar in this whack at the backside of Victorianism. He makes a great vaudeville turn out of the role of an egocentric scoundrel, the prosperous bootmaker who doesn't want to part with his three marriageable daughters because they are too useful as unpaid labor. As the oldest daughter, the spinster in spite of herself, Brenda de Banzie is so "right" that when she marries her father's best workman and puts belching, drunken old Dad out of business, one feels the good old-fashioned impulse to applaud. John Mills is the fortunate young man whom she overpowers. David Lean directed this English comedy, based on the Harold Brighouse play. Cinematography by Jack Hildyard. b & w

Hold Your Man (1933)—Jean Harlow and Clark Gable in a mixture of farce and melodrama that begins in Brooklyn and ends in jail. Anita Loos concocted some raucous bits, and Harlow goes around smacking and swatting people—she has a wonderful left. There's less fun when she shows signs of budding maidenliness and things go lofty in the women's reformatory. Sam Wood directed, and the cast includes Stuart Erwin and Dorothy Burgess. M-G-M. b & w

Holiday (1938)—In the 30s, Katharine Hepburn's wit and nonconformity made ordinary heroines seem mushy, and her angular beauty made the round-faced ingenues look piggy and stupid. Here she is in her archetypal role, as the rich tomboy Linda in Philip Barry's romantic comedy. She had understudied the role in 1928 on Broadway and had used it for her screen test, and she was the moving force behind this graceful film version, which Donald Ogden Stewart and Sidney Buchman tailored for her and which George Cukor directed. In the pivotal role of a man who wants a holiday in order to discover his values, Cary Grant manages to make a likable and plausible character out of

a dramatist's stratagem. With Edward Everett Horton and Jean Dixon as the man's friends; Lew Ayres as Linda's brother; Henry Kolker as her father; Doris Nolan as her stuffy, patrician sister; and Henry Daniell and Binnie Barnes among her obnoxious relatives. (A 1930 film version starred Ann Harding, with Mary Astor as her sister.) Columbia. b & w

Holiday for Henrietta *La Fête à Henriette* (1952)—The scenarists, Julien Duvivier and Henri Jeanson, parody the various film personalities they have worked with in a story about making a movie in Paris on the July 14 holiday. The movie within the movie includes such divertissements as a circus equestrienne, a thief posing as an airline pilot, etc. This picture is unassuming and featherweight—a holiday for moviemakers. Duvivier directed. With Dany Robin, Hildegarde Neff, and Michel Auclair. Music by Georges Auric. (Remade in 1963 as *Paris When It Sizzles*.) In French. b & w

Hollywood Canteen (1944)—One of those shameless testimonials to its own patriotism that Hollywood turned out during the Second World War. This one is from Warners and features what used to be called the Warners stable: Bette Davis, John Garfield, Ida Lupino, Dennis Morgan, Sydney Greenstreet, Alexis Smith, Peter Lorre, and so on, as well as Eddie Cantor, Jack Benny, Joe E. Brown, Joan Crawford, Barbara Stanwyck, the ineffable Andrews Sisters, the superb dancers Antonio and Rosario, Jimmy Dorsey and his band, and on and on. This loosely held together musical revue takes one back to an era when "Yank" was meant to be a cheery word and patriotic songs were bouncy ("Gettin' Corns for My Country"). Written and directed by Delmer Daves. b & w

Hollywood Party (1934)—Plunked down right in the middle of this M-G-M musical revue is a Disney cartoon about some chocolate soldiers who melt in the sun; the cartoon is introduced by Mickey Mouse, an uninvited guest at the Hollywood Party. Who were the hosts? The picture doesn't carry producer or director credits; the entire extravaganza is hit-or-miss casual, as if the brass at M-G-M didn't want to admit having committed themselves to make the thing, and the big M-G-M stars never show up. Instead, you get Jimmy Durante in a Tarzan takeoff and singing a song about reincarnation, as well as Polly Moran as an oil tycoon's wife, Charles Butterworth and Ted Healy, and June Clyde, Jack Pearl, and Lupe Velez, who join Laurel & Hardy in an egg-breaking routine. Some fairly funny moments, and a pleasant score. The writing was probably by Howard Dietz and Arthur Kober, the directing by Richard Boleslawski, Allan Dwan, and Roy Rowland. b & w and color

The Hollywood Revue (1929)—M-G-M put this lavish revue together (it originally had Technicolor sequences) and threw in their biggest stars. Conrad Nagel (always pallid but considered full of prestige) and Jack Benny are the masters of ceremony; Joan Crawford sings; Marie Dressler and Polly Moran do a skit; Marion Davies sings and taps; Norma Shearer and John Gilbert do a flapper *Romeo and Juliet*; and so on, with minstrel choruses and the Albertina Rasch Ballet. The quality is extremely variable, but it contains so much of the history of popular theatre that it's invaluable. Charles Reisner directed.

Holy Matrimony (1943)—That expert at literate comedy, Monty Woolley, plays Arnold Bennett's painter who lets his valet be buried in Westminster Abbey and then tries to live the valet's life. With Gracie Fields as the wonderfully sensible woman he marries, Laird Cregar, and Melville Cooper. John Stahl di-

rected, from Nunnally Johnson's screenplay. (Made in 1933 as *His Double Life*.) 20th Century-Fox. b & w

The Home and the World   *Ghare-Baire* (1984)—Victor Banerjee is a maharajah in Bengal with a Western education and liberal views. His wife (Swatilekha Chatterjee) is content to live in the women's quarters of his palace and be visible to no man except him. But he loves her and wants her to be a modern woman, able to move in the world. She first saw him at their wedding: how will he ever know whether she really loves him if she doesn't have the opportunity to choose him—to prefer him to other men? He persuades her to leave the incense and silks, the Arabian Nights cushions and the English bric-a-brac of the women's quarters, and she immediately becomes enthralled by the cocksure masculinity of a fiery radical (Soumitra Chatterjee). This Satyajit Ray movie, adapted from a Rabindranath Tagore novel, is in deep, glowing colors; the main characters talk, and the camera just stays on them and waits until they finish, yet these conversations in golden light and shadows have their own kind of voltage. You watch the graceful people in draped garments in their lethargic, patterned decor, and everything in the country seems draped, hanging, defeated—and hectic, too. Set in 1907, this marvellous film is about the destruction of the marriage, and the riots and bloodshed caused by the radical's terrorist supporters. Ray wrote the screenplay and also the music. In Bengali. (See *State of the Art*.)

Home Before Dark (1958)—Jean Simmons gives a reserved, beautifully modulated performance that is so much better than the material that at times her exquisite reading of the rather mediocre lines seems a more tragic waste than her character's wrecked life. The script starts with a good idea. A professor

(Dan O'Herlihy) commits his young wife to a state mental hospital; she returns home after a year, exhausted from eight rounds of shock treatment, her hair gray, but feeling cured—reasonable and happy, rid of her former delusions. Then as she slowly discovers that the delusions the doctors were shocking out of her were actually the truth, she loses her bearings and begins to go mad. Unfortunately, the script makes the heroine too sympathetic, and it has an edge of fashionable, self-congratulatory virtue—the "one must be more understanding toward discharged mental patients" attitude, and Mervyn LeRoy directs in a glossy, uninspired style that drags the material out at least half an hour too long. With Efrem Zimbalist, Jr., and Rhonda Fleming. Warners. b & w

The Homecoming (1973)—Harold Pinter's mannered, floating ominousness has been used to tone up many movies (it was at its most effective in his script for *Accident*), but his own plays—*The Caretaker*, *The Birthday Party*, and *The Homecoming*, too—transfer to film badly. When this play is presented on the stage, the tensions bounce around, and one can respond to the actors' relish in their roles, but on the screen the material is so lethally *set* that Pinter sounds Pinteresque. The movie seems cheaply theatrical, with cryptic reversals of attitude, and sudden outbreaks of violence and sex, plus a coronary and some unspecified sort of seizure. And the attitudes are cheap; Michael Jayston, smiling a tiny, tight smile, plays the philosophy professor who, accompanied by his wife, Ruth (Vivien Merchant), returns from America to visit his Cockney family; the role is none other than that old standby of middlebrow theatre—the prissy, unfeeling, vaguely impotent intellectual. Stoic Ruth, the one woman in this archetypal-rancorous-family play, is mother-wife-whore and, of course, is sphinxlike—the ultimate, controlling mystery of life. The suggestiveness of the play remains, along with some of its charge, and so does Pinter's idiom, with its wit, though in the movie the language sounds crisped—overcalibrated. With Paul Rogers as the domineering butcher-father, Cyril Cusack as the weak uncle, Ian Holm as the satanic pimp son, and Terence Rigby as the thick-headed son; they are all playing so high they cancel out each other's performances. Directed by Peter Hall; cinematography by David Watkin; music by Thelonious Monk. Produced by Ely Landau, for American Film Theatre. color (See *Reeling*.)

L'Homme au chapeau rond, see *The Eternal Husband*

L'Homme de Rio, see *That Man from Rio*

Un Homme et une femme, see *A Man and a Woman*

L'Homme qui aimait les femmes, see *The Man Who Loved Women*

Honey (1930)—Paramount in its frivolous, popular-musical-comedy glory, when it was raiding Broadway and the Algonquin. The original material was by Alice Duer Miller and A. E. Thomas; Herman J. Mankiewicz did the adaptation; and the star is Nancy Carroll, as the aristocratic young Southern girl who rents her family mansion to rich New Yorkers and takes the job of cook, while her brother (Skeets Gallagher) plays butler. A great hit, it was followed by dozens of movies that aped its characters and situations; television sit-coms finally exhausted them. (The picture itself looks very tired.) The cast includes Lillian Roth, Mitzi Green, ZaSu Pitts, Harry Green, and Jobyna Howland; Wesley Ruggles directed. The musical numbers include "Sing You Sinners." b & w

The Honey Pot (1967)—Joseph L. Mankiewicz wrote and directed this movie, based on Frederick Knott's play *Mr. Fox of Venice*, which was adapted from Thomas Sterling's novel *The Evil of the Day*, which was based on Ben Jonson's *Volpone*. And the movie feels at that far a remove from the play (which was filmed by Maurice Tourneur in French in 1939, starring Harry Baur and Louis Jouvet). In this overcomplicated, talk-infested Mankiewicz version, set in the present day, Rex Harrison is Cecil Fox, reputedly a millionaire, who lives in Venice. After attending a performance of *Volpone*, he decides to trick three of his ex-mistresses (Edie Adams, Capucine, and Susan Hayward) into believing he's dying. The story then plunges into conventional 20th-century mystery, complete with a corpse, a bungling detective, misleading clues, locked attic rooms, and flickering electric lights. Even Mankiewicz may have wondered how he was going to get out of the whole damn thing. Maggie Smith is also around, and Cliff Robertson, Adolfo Celi, and Herschel Bernardi. Originally it ran 150 minutes, but it was cut to 131 minutes; count your blessings. Cinematography by Gianni Di Venanzo. A Charles K. Feldman Production, released through United Artists. color

The Honeymoon Killers (1970)—Based on the lives of the multiple murderers Martha Beck and Raymond Fernandez, who met their victims through Lonely Hearts clubs, and who were put to death at Sing Sing in 1951. This low-budget black-and-white movie is so literal-minded that it resembles a *True Detective* account of the case; it's as if someone re-created the Grade-Z pictures of the 40s and did so in absolute seriousness. The movie goes through the chronicle of the Beck-Fernandez crimes with pedestrian relentlessness; it's paced as if the actors were walking in lockstep. After the almost incredible lack of depth of the first half-hour, the film begins to acquire a fascination *because* of its total superficiality—it becomes something resembling Minimal art. The writer-director, Leonard Kastle, whose first (and thus far only) picture this was, keeps the images so brightly lighted and so exactly planned and worked out that every ugly detail is in place—the hammer blow on the head, the trickle of blood, the ludicrous tongues sticking out of dead faces. As the 200-pound Martha Beck, Shirley Stoler is much too shrill at the start but quiets down and improves as the movie plods on; as the sleazy charmer Ray Fernandez, Tony LoBianco is alarmingly authentic to the pulpy genre. The women victims include Marilyn Chris, Barbara Cason, and Mary Jane Higby. Produced by Warren Steibel; the film uses music by Gustav Mahler. (See *Deeper into Movies*.)

Honeysuckle Rose (1980)—The film seems color-coordinated to Willie Nelson's hippie-Indian earth-tone clothing; he plays Buck Bonham, a country-and-Western singer, a regional idol who has never quite attained national success. Buck loves travelling in his tour bus with his backup band; life on the road is the answer to his restlessness. As Buck's wife of 15 years, Dyan Cannon (who sings in a good torchy blues voice) is so full of energy and humor and knowingness that she gives the audience hope: if this is maturity, then life looks pretty good. Having stumbled onto this affirmation, the director, Jerry Schatzberg, knows what he's got and doesn't overplay his hand and wreck it. The songs (by Nelson, Kris Kristofferson, Leon Russell, and others) have a lot of energy, and the music and the imagery move together. The film has no big dramatic conflicts, but in its loose, non-linear way it has more going on than most movies, though what's going on is understated and sometimes a little screwed up, with story points undeveloped or left dangling. The story is *Intermezzo* out

West, with Amy Irving as the young musician who is in love with Buck. (Willie Nelson has a calm, rascally sexual magnetism.) The film is very sensual in its color, in the looks that the two central women characters exchange with Buck, and in the music itself. Also with Slim Pickens, who has come to sound even more endearingly hoarse and scratchy than Andy Devine, and Charles Levin, Joey Floyd, Priscilla Pointer, and a guest appearance by Emmylou Harris. Most of the musicians are members of Nelson's actual backup band, and the byplay among them is unforced and funny. Cinematography by Robby Müller; music supervised by Richard Baskin; the almost nonexistent script is credited to three writers; many others reportedly worked on it, too. Released by Warners. (See *Taking It All In*.)

Honky Tonk (1941)—Practically indistinguishable from several other Clark Gable pictures featuring sheriffs, cardsharps, and girls in net stockings and feather boas, but a bigger hit. The lush, 21-year-old Lana Turner is a New England lady out West to catch up with her father (Frank Morgan); she speedily becomes entangled with the town's good-bad man (Gable), gets him drunk, and marries him. That's only the start of the picture; from then on it's turgidly predictable. Jack Conway directed, from a script by Marguerite Roberts and John Sanford; with Claire Trevor, Marjorie Main, Chill Wills, Albert Dekker, Esther Muir, Betty Blythe, and Veda Ann Borg. M-G-M. b & w

Hope and Glory (1987)—A great comedy about the blitz. In this autobiographical film, the writer-director John Boorman has had the inspiration to desentimentalize wartime England and show us the Second World War the way he saw it as an 8-year-old—as a party that kept going day after day, night after night. The movie has a beautiful pop clarity.

He doesn't deny the war its terrors, but it also destroys much of what the genteel poor like the Rohans have barely been able to acknowledge they wanted destroyed. Boorman lets his characters say the previously unsayable. Bored with crouching indoors during the nightly raids by the Luftwaffe, the dimply blond 15-year-old Dawn (Sammi Davis), the eldest of the three Rohan children, runs outside, watches the firefighters at work on a blazing house, and dances in the Rohans' postage-stamp-size front garden. "It's lovely!" she calls out. The movie is wonderfully free of bellyaching; it's a large-scale comic vision, with 90-foot barrage balloons as part of the party atmosphere. The large cast includes Sebastian Rice Edwards as the 8-year-old Bill, Geraldine Muir as his little sister, Sarah Miles as his mother, David Hayman as his father, Ian Bannen as his grandfather, and Susan Wooldridge, Derrick O'Connor, and Jean-Marc Barr as the Canadian jokester. Released by Columbia. color (See *Hooked*.)

A Hora da Estrela, see *The Hour of the Star*

La Hora de los Hornos, see *The Hour of the Furnaces*

The Horror Chamber of Dr. Faustus, see *Eyes Without a Face*

Horse Feathers (1932)—The Marx Brothers in one of their niftiest corny-surreal comedies; it isn't in the class of their *Duck Soup* but then what else is? The setting is academic, with emphasis on football; Groucho is Professor Wagstaff, the new president of Huxley College, who explains his policy in the song "Whatever It Is, I'm Against It," and Thelma Todd is the college widow to whom all four brothers make overtures. So there's some naughty sense to it when Groucho sings the picture's theme song to her, "Everyone Says

'I Love You!' " Norman McLeod directed, for Paramount, from a screenplay by Bert Kalmar and Harry Ruby (who also wrote the songs) and S. J. Perelman and Will B. Johnstone. Produced by Herman J. Mankiewicz; with Robert Greig as the solemn-voiced biology professor, David Landau as the villain, and Nat Pendleton. b & w

The Horse's Mouth (1958)—Joyce Cary's painter-hero, Gulley Jimson, is a fabulous, lewd creation: the modern artist as a scruffy, dirty little bum. Gulley's antic self-destructiveness is partly based on the behavior of Cary's friend Dylan Thomas, and his approach as a painter is derived from the tradition of William Blake. Alec Guinness's sly, likable Gulley isn't all that one might hope for (Guinness lacks passion and innocence and the real fire of insolence), and the movie is too literal-minded—it's a conformist movie about nonconformity—but, with that said and out of the way, let's admit how marvellously enjoyable it is. Set in London. With Ernest Thesiger as Hickson; Renée Houston as wily old Sara; Kay Walsh (less successful) as Coker, the conscience-ridden barmaid; and Michael Gough (wretched) as the sculptor. Ronald Neame directed Guinness's adaptation; Gulley's paintings were done by John Bratby. The score is adapted from Prokofiev. color

The Hospital (1971)—That great spangled ham George C. Scott in Paddy Chayefsky's farce about the killing incompetence in a modern big-city hospital. The picture strains for seriousness now and then, but even when it makes a fool of itself it's still funny. Arthur Hiller directed. With Diana Rigg, Barnard Hughes, Nancy Marchand, and Richard Dysart. United Artists. color (See *Deeper into Movies*.)

Höstsonaten, see *Autumn Sonata*

The Hot Rock (1972)—A cheerful caper movie set around New York City. The dialogue is often painfully hip-cute, but the actors manage to be funny anyway. Ron Leibman plays a demonic getaway driver, George Segal is a panicky lock picker, Paul Sand is a spaced-out bomb wizard, and Robert Redford is the straight-man leader of the gang. Peter Yates directed, from William Goldman's screenplay. Music by Quincy Jones. 20th Century-Fox. color (See *Deeper into Movies*.)

Hotel (1967)—In his novel, Arthur Hailey used the same omnibus formula that he was to use for *Airport*, but this production, directed by Richard Quine, isn't as paralyzing. Quine manages to wring a little humor out of the collection of junk passing for a plot. With Rod Taylor, Melvyn Douglas, Karl Malden, Merle Oberon, Catherine Spaak, Richard Conte, Michael Rennie, and Kevin McCarthy, and with Carmen McRae playing the Dooley Wilson role from *Casablanca*. The script is by Wendell Mayes. Warners. color

The Hound of the Baskervilles (1939)— "Murder, my dear Watson," Holmes announces, with undisguised satisfaction, in this handsome, gripping, semi-serious version of the Conan Doyle story—the first appearance of Basil Rathbone as Sherlock Holmes. Immaculately right in the role, Rathbone played Holmes suavely (though with diminishing wit) for the next eight years, always with Nigel Bruce as his bumbling Dr. Watson. Here, among the moors and mists, Holmes investigates the mystery involving "the footprints of a gigantic hound," and at the end he actually says, "Quick, Watson, the needle." The cast includes fatuously dimpled Richard Greene, and Lionel Atwill, Wendy Barrie, John Carradine, E. E. Clive, Beryl Mercer, and Ralph Forbes. Sidney Lanfield directed. 20th Century-Fox. b & w

H

The Hour of the Furnaces *La Hora de los Hornos* (1968)—An attempt to use film as a revolutionary weapon. A didactic, explosive semi-documentary on Peronism and the necessity to create national consciousness in Argentina and other Latin-American countries. By the Argentine director Fernando Solanas. (4 hours and 20 minutes.) In Spanish. b & w (See *Deeper into Movies*.)

The Hour of the Star *A Hora da Estrela* (1985)—A lot of the scenes don't quite work, but something numinous happens when you watch this first feature by the Brazilian Suzana Amaral, the mother of nine, who, at the age of 52, shot it in four weeks on a budget of $150,000. It's as if the characters' souls became magically visible. Working from a script adapted from the novella by Clarice Lispector, Amaral tells the story of Macabéa (Marcelia Cartaxo), a 19-year-old orphan from the northeast, a girl without skills or education or even training in keeping herself clean, who comes south to São Paulo, a city of 14 million. Macabéa smiles serenely as she celebrates her Sunday by taking a ride on the subway, and her terrible aloneness gets to you. Like De Sica's *Umberto D.*, this film has moments of uncanny humor and painful intuition, but it goes from neorealism to magic realism. The hallucinatory effect seems somewhat alien to Amaral's temperament; she's better at the plain, level scenes—they have a truer magic. Still, this Latin-American mash of dreams and reality and American advertising art and images from the movies has an awkward, mystic sanctity. It's contrived, yet affecting. With José Dumont as Olimpico and Fernanda Montenegro as the *macumbeira*. The script is by the director and Alfredo Oroz; the cinematography is by Edgar Moura. In Portuguese. color (See *Hooked*.)

The House of Lovers, see *Pot-Bouille*

Housekeeping (1987)—Marilynne Robinson's novel about two orphaned sisters and the nature-loving, itinerant aunt who arrives to keep house for them has a wonderful representation of a psychological state: Aunt Sylvie seems to spend her life falling into a nonverbal world—staring at nothingness. But the novel also has a bag-lady mystique—a poetic view of vagrancy. The idea seems to be that if you give up conventional values and material things you can wander the earth and lead a magical life. Bill Forsyth, who adapted and directed the movie version, was perhaps too respectful of the internalized and estranged nature of Robinson's vision. (It's all subtext.) He doesn't make the material his own; he doesn't find his own rhythms. The early scenes are whimsical and promising, but the later ones have a clammy, awkward lyricism. Since Sylvie is always remote and has to wake up out of her basic trance to respond to a situation, Christine Lahti, who plays the part, can't call on her full resourcefulness. Gaunt here, and with her curly hair and huge, curlicue dimples, she suggests a pioneer woman who's been bopped on the head. Sara Walker and Andrea Burchill are the sisters; with Margot Pinvidic, Anne Pitoniak, and Barbara Reese. Cinematography by Michael Coulter. Shot in Nelson, British Columbia (the mountain town used in *Roxanne*). Columbia. color (See *Hooked*.)

How Green Was My Valley (1941)—John Ford's much-honored movie about the decline of a Welsh mining family is moving and impressive in a big-Hollywood-picture way. Roddy McDowall and Walter Pidgeon are the leads, and the cast includes Maureen O'Hara, Sara Allgood, Barry Fitzgerald, and many other Irish actors (though the singers are really Welsh). 20th Century-Fox. b & w

How I Won the War (1967)—Richard Lester's big try that failed disastrously—an anti-war black comedy, from a script by Charles Wood, and with ideas and techniques from the Theatres of Cruelty and the Absurd. Similar to the film of *Catch-22*, though more British in subject and tone. At first, it seems daring for Lester and Wood to have picked the Second World War—the war that many people consider a just war—for an attack on war. But the film concentrates on the class hatreds of British officers and men, who aren't engaged in defending London or in bombing Germany—they're dying in the course of building an officers' cricket pitch in Africa. The surreal vaudeville is painfully flat. With Michael Crawford as a modern Candide and bespectacled John Lennon as a Cockney soldier, and Roy Kinnear, Jack MacGowran, Michael Hordern, and Alexander Knox. Based on a novel by Patrick Ryan; cinematography by David Watkin. color

How the West Was Won (1963)—"How the West Was Lost" would be a more appropriate title for this dud epic, since, as conceived by the writer, James R. Webb, the pioneers seem to be dimwitted bunglers who can't do anything right. The film is in segments, directed by John Ford, Henry Hathaway, and George Marshall, and the cast includes John Wayne, Gregory Peck, James Stewart, Spencer Tracy, Debbie Reynolds, Eli Wallach, Thelma Ritter, Carroll Baker, Richard Widmark, Karl Malden, Robert Preston, Lee J. Cobb, George Peppard, and Raymond Massey as Lincoln, and Henry Fonda, in a walrus mustache, as a buffalo hunter. M-G-M. Cinerama, color

How to Steal a Million (1966)—An expensive cast in an anemic suspense comedy-romance. Audrey Hepburn is the devoted daughter of a vain, roguish art forger (Hugh Griffith): in order to save him from jail, she persuades a detective (Peter O'Toole) to help her steal a bogus Cellini "Venus" that her father has exhibited in a Paris museum. William Wyler directed, from a rather tired screenplay by Harry Kurnitz. The picture isn't offensive, and it's handsome enough, but it's just blah. With Charles Boyer, Eli Wallach, Marcel Dalio, and Fernand Gravet. 20th Century-Fox. color

The Howards of Virginia (1940)—Cary Grant, miscast as a rough-hewn surveyor at the time of the American Revolution. Costume pictures were never his forte, and he gives one of his rare really bad performances in this one. Martha Scott is the highborn woman he courts; Cedric Hardwicke is her proud, aristocratic brother. The script, by Sidney Buchman, from Elizabeth Page's novel *The Tree of Liberty*, also saddles Grant with a crippled son, whom he rejects until the maudlin end, when his son's bravery wins him over. Glimpses of Jefferson (Richard Carlson), Washington (George Houston), and Patrick Henry (Richard Gaines) provide a cultural note without adding much to the party. Frank Lloyd directed; some scenes were filmed in Williamsburg. Columbia. b & w

The Howling (1981)—This werewolves-in-California movie has a spoofy erotic tone and isn't afraid of being silly—which is its chief charm. The director, Joe Dante, seems a mixture—in just about equal parts—of talent, amateurishness, style, and flake. You're entertained continuously, though you don't feel the queasy, childish dread that is part of the dirty kick of the horror genre. There are no embarrassments in the cast, which includes Patrick Macnee as a plump, bland psychiatrist; Dee Wallace as a pretty blond TV newscaster; Dick Miller as a gabby bookshop owner; Elisabeth Brooks as a fiery slut; and Christopher Stone, John Carradine, Kevin McCarthy, Slim Pickens, and Dennis Dugan. When the characters turn into werewolves they transform on camera: you see the stages they go through—growing fur and fangs, their chests expanding and their teeth yellowing—and you see each long snout shoot out of the face like a locomotive. It's a funny, elegant effect, devised by Rob Bottin. John Sayles, who rewrote the Terence H. Winkless script (based on the novel by Gary Brandner), appears as an attendant at the morgue; Roger Corman, for whom Dante, Sayles, Bottin, and the editor, Mark Goldblatt, all worked together on the 1978 *Piranha*, turns up waiting outside a phone booth. Released by Avco Embassy. color (See *Taking It All In*.)

Hud (1963)—Hugely entertaining contemporary Western, set in the Texas of Cadillacs and cattle, crickets and transistor radios; handsomely designed, and shot in black-and-white (by James Wong Howe), it's visually simple and precise and unadorned. The film is schizoid: it tells you to condemn the nihilistic heel Hud (Paul Newman), who represents modern "materialism," but casting Newman as a mean materialist is like writing a manifesto against the banking system while juggling your investments to make a fortune. Newman has energy and wit and his physique and "them there eyes," while his clean-old-man father (Melvyn Douglas), who stands for high moral principles, is a pious fuddy-duddy—inhuman, except for a brief sequence when he's at the local movie house and he follows the bouncing ball and sings "Clementine." The plot involves Hud's wanting to sell off a herd that is possibly infected with hoof-and-mouth disease, and his father's rectitude in having the cattle slaughtered. As the ranch housekeeper, Patricia Neal, full-bodied and likable, has an easy, raunchy good humor, and talks seductively, in a deep-toned Texas twang; the sexual byplay between her and Newman has just the right summertime temperature—this is some of the best work the director, Martin Ritt, has

ever done. The script is by Irving Ravetch and Harriet Frank, Jr., from Larry McMurtry's novel *Horseman, Pass By*. As Hud's nephew—our observer—Brandon deWilde is a less appealing, adolescent version of the boy he played in *Shane*. With Whit Bissell as the vet. Paramount. (See *I Lost it at the Movies*.)

Humain, trop humain (1975)—A study of assembly-line work. Louis Malle shot this 77-minute documentary in the Citroën assembly plant in Rennes and at the 1972 Automobile Show in Paris. The film is not a confirmation of the typical movie view of factory labor as dehumanizing, nor does it make any large claims about the workers' being happy. Malle's film is so open and neutral a look at the work process that although one may feel that it gets beyond the usual bromides, it still doesn't seem to go very deep. The surfaces of the auto industry are very photogenic, but there are no revelations in this film. In French. color

The Human Beast, see *La Bête humaine*

The Human Comedy (1943)—William Saroyan wrote the script for this deliberately unsensational wartime family story set in a small town, and his love and woozy high spirits come pouring through. You can fight it, but part of the time you lose—especially when freckled 5-year-old Jackie (Butch) Jenkins waves hopefully at passing trains. Mickey Rooney plays Jackie's older brother, and Van Johnson is his oldest brother, who's in the Army. Fay Bainter is the impossibly lofty mother of this brood. Saroyan and the director, Clarence Brown, were trying for something—and the film is worth seeing—but there's also a cloying M-G-M shininess to it. With Donna Reed, Barry Nelson, Marsha Hunt, James Craig, Alan Baxter, Ray Collins, and Darryl Hickman. b & w

Human Desire (1954)—Fritz Lang's melodramatic Hollywood version of Zola's novel about blind instinct, *La Bête humaine*, which had been turned into a classic film by Jean Renoir in 1938. There's nothing very special about this updated version, set in America, and starring Glenn Ford, Gloria Grahame as a ruthless, taunting wife, and Broderick Crawford as her jealous husband. Lang didn't want to make the film but was contractually forced into it by Columbia, which hoped for a success comparable to his *The Big Heat* of the year before, also with Grahame and Ford. With lots of high angles and night scenes, and also Edgar Buchanan and Dan Seymour. b & w

Humoresque (1946)—In this second version of Fannie Hurst's hokey weeper, the heroine (Joan Crawford) is myopic, dipsomaniacal, dissatisfied with her husband (Paul Cavanagh), older than her ghetto-born violinist lover (John Garfield), and given to brooding heavily about the futility of a life devoid of everything but sables, limousines, Napoleon brandy, town houses, seashore estates, and enough liquid assets to make a Morgan partner's eyes widen. She bears her burdens gallantly, and when she realizes that her career as a social butterfly has not prepared her adequately to be the helpmate of her violinist she bravely wades out into the ocean and gurgles to her doom, wreathed in seaweed and clamshells. (The music that accompanies her demise is the "Liebestod" from *Tristan und Isolde*.) Clifford Odets worked on the update, and some of the dialogue is sharp-witted, but with frequent interruptions for big yeasty passages on the meaning of life and art. If Carol Burnett were to step in and take over, she'd hardly have to change a thing. Garfield saws away impressively while Isaac Stern is heard playing several violin concertos, and there are lines to treasure,

such as Cavanagh's remark about the music: "It has fire—rather like what you'd feel in a van Gogh painting." Jean Negulesco directed. (Possibly Odets was called in because he'd used a violinist hero in his 1937 play *Golden Boy*.) As the hero's old neighborhood pal, Oscar Levant plays the piano and makes jokes; with J. Carrol Naish, Craig Stevens, Ruth Nelson, John Abbott, Fritz Leiber, and Robert (then Bobby) Blake. Warners. b & w

The Hunchback of Notre Dame (1939)—Playing Quasimodo (Lon Chaney's old role), Charles Laughton seems determined to outdo Chaney's horrifying makeup. With only one eye and a hump so big his head seems to be in the middle of his chest, this Quasimodo is so distorted and misshapen that little of the human being, much less of the actor, survives. It's an appallingly masochistic performance. The adaptation of the Victor Hugo novel (by Sonya Levien and Bruno Frank) seems rather perfunctory, but the film, directed by William Dieterle, is an elaborate, well-photographed mixture of historical spectacle and Grand Guignol. Maureen O'Hara is a ravishing Esmeralda, and the cast includes Edmond O'Brien (in his film début), Cedric Hardwicke, Thomas Mitchell, George Zucco, Alan Marshal, Walter Hampden, Minna Gombell, Fritz Leiber, Etienne Girardot, and Harry Davenport as Louis XI. R K O. b & w

Hunger *Sult* (1966)—Per Oscarsson plays a starving young writer—a performance with brilliant, glinting variations on self-mockery and paranoia. Henning Carlsen has transcribed the Knut Hamsun novel to the screen with amazing fidelity. It's an intense and remarkable movie—a classic of the starving-young-artist genre. With Gunnel Lindblom. In Swedish. b & w

Hunters of the Deep (1955)—Unlike the mystic and didactic film excursions into life undersea in which each gelatinous blob reveals God's purpose, this film is not weighted down with messages and interpretation. Curiosity and aesthetic sense are its unpretentious tools. The camera follows the antique creatures of the sea: lolling sea elephants, gloomy mantas, giant groupers—and captures the iridescence and opulence of an inexplicably beautiful universe. Produced by Allan Dowling; narrated by Dan O'Herlihy. color

The Hurricane (1937)—Handsome and exciting adventure film, directed by John Ford, with some exteriors shot in Samoa. The tallcorn story seems to enhance this particular movie; Dorothy Lamour, in her sarong, is the native girl, and chesty Jon Hall is her sweetheart, who is unjustly sentenced to prison by a vicious European governor (Raymond Massey). With Mary Astor, Thomas Mitchell, Jerome Cowan, John Carradine, and C. Aubrey Smith. The hurricane itself is a knockout. Dudley Nichols did the screenplay, from Oliver H. P. Garrett's adaptation of the Nordhoff and Hall novel; Samuel Goldwyn produced, lavishly. Music by Alfred Newman. (A 1979 remake, directed by Jan Troell, was a disaster of large proportions.) Released by United Artists. b & w

Husbands (1970)—Three actors (John Cassavetes, Peter Falk, and Ben Gazzara) playing three suburban husbands in a semi-improvised movie directed by Cassavetes. The actors have occasional intense and affecting moments, going through emotions that they set off in each other, but Cassavetes is the sort of man who is dedicated to stripping people of their pretenses and laying bare their souls. Inevitably, the results are agonizingly banal. Columbia. color (See *Deeper into Movies*.)

Hush . . . Hush, Sweet Charlotte (1965)—Bette Davis in a Grand Guignol melodrama directed by Robert Aldrich—an attempt to reproduce the box-office success of their camp gothic *What Ever Happened to Baby Jane?*, in which Davis's co-star was Joan Crawford. Crawford was to have appeared in this one also, but became ill and was replaced by Olivia de Havilland. Davis is a rich, dotty recluse living in a moldy mansion in Louisiana; she wanders about the shadowy rooms in streaming hair and billowing nighties, whispering telepathic endearments to her long-dead daddy. De Havilland is her treacherous cousin, Agnes Moorehead the witchlike housekeeper, and Joseph Cotten the family doctor. The story, redolent of mutilation and assorted horrors, is from a novel by Henry Farrell, who also was the source of the earlier film. A lot of people seemed to enjoy the spectacle of Davis crawling and howling and looking wildly repulsive. With Victor Buono, Mary Astor, Bruce Dern, George Kennedy, and Cecil Kellaway. 20th Century-Fox. b & w

Hustle (1975)—As a Los Angeles police officer, Burt Reynolds despairs over the American loss of innocence and, since the system is rigged on the side of the rich, he takes the law into his own hands. He's a romantic-liberal Dirty Harry in this sloshy melodrama, which is caught between the pulpy weltschmerz of the writer, Steve Shagan, and the harshness of the director, Robert Aldrich. When Aldrich tries for tenderness, it turns to sleaze. With Paul Winfield, Catherine Deneuve, and Eddie Albert. Paramount. color (See *When the Lights Go Down*.)

The Hustler (1961)—The test of what a man has inside him—the basic Hemingway-style masculine story that's frequently set in the bullring or, in this country, in the world of sports, especially among prizefighters—is set here in the world of pool sharks. Paul Newman is the young contender, Fast Eddie Felson, and Jackie Gleason is the old champ, Minnesota Fats. But Hemingway would cut out extraneous material, thereby raising the simple, unadorned test to the level of myth; the director Robert Rossen and his co-writer, Sidney Carroll, surround the test with an extra 40 minutes or so of flabby "poetry." The dialogue comes out of the 30s and borrows heavily from Clifford Odets. A character does not ask a simple question like "Are you his manager?" He asks, "Are you his manager? His friend? His stooge?" And there's a tortured, crippled girl (Piper Laurie) who speaks the truth: she's a female practitioner of the Socratic method who is continually drinking her hemlock. The picture is swollen with windy thoughts and murky notions of perversions, and as Eddie's manager the magnetic young George C. Scott seems to be a Satan figure, but it has strength and conviction, and Newman gives a fine, emotional performance. You can see all the picture's faults and still love it. It's the most vital and likable of Rossen's movies. With Murray Hamilton, Myron McCormick (who is stuck with the worst pseudo-Odets role), Michael Constantine, Stefan Gierasch, and Vincent Gardenia. Based on the Walter Tevis novel; cinematography by Eugen Schüfftan; production design by Harry Horner; music by Kenyon Hopkins; editing by Dede Allen. (In 1965, the theme was adapted to poker, in *The Cincinnati Kid*; in 1986, Paul Newman appeared in the sequel to *The Hustler—The Color of Money*.) 20th Century-Fox. CinemaScope, b & w

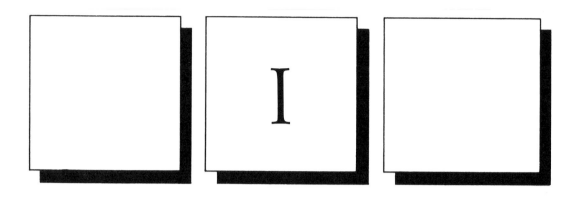

I **Am a Camera** (1955)—Derived from the same Christopher Isherwood Berlin stories that were later used in *Cabaret*, but aimed at a simpler, frothy, madcap quality. Julie Harris is Sally ("Shall we have a drink first or shall we go right to bed?") Bowles, and Laurence Harvey is Isherwood, with Shelley Winters and Anton Diffring in the subplot. Henry Cornelius (who directed *Genevieve*) did this erratic version from John Collier's adaptation of the John van Druten play. b & w

I **Am a Fugitive from a Chain Gang** (1932)— One of the best of the social-protest films— naïve, heavy, artless, but a straightforward, unadorned story with moments that haunted a generation, such as the hungry hero (Paul Muni) trying to pawn his Congressional Medal of Honor. And there is one of the great closing scenes in the history of film: the hero is asked how he lives and he answers, "I steal." Those involved in making the movie hoped it might help to ameliorate the condition of convicts, but it did more to ameliorate financial conditions at Warners and was a factor in making it the "socially conscious" studio. With Glenda Farrell, Helen Vinson, Preston Foster, Edward Ellis, Allen Jenkins, and Berton Churchill. Directed by

Mervyn LeRoy, from an autobiographical story by Robert E. Burns; produced by Hal B. Wallis. b & w

I **Am Curious—Yellow** *Jag Ar Nyfiken* (1967)—In her search for political commitment, the angry young heroine, Lena Nyman, goes around as an inquiring reporter questioning people about non-violence, the labor movement, socialism, and so on. The picture improves when sex and politics mix; there are some free—and very funny—sequences of simulated copulation. The film caused a great stir here because the U.S. Customs Office seized the first print that the distributor (Grove Press) imported; by the time the ban was lifted, people expected something really sizzling. Written and directed by Vilgot Sjöman, who also appears as the director. With Anders Ek as the Instructor and Holger Löwenadler as the King, and also Martin Luther King, Olof Palme, and Yevgeni Yevtushenko. (The second part of Sjöman's material was released as *I Am Curious—Blue*.) In Swedish. b & w

I **Confess** (1953)—A priest with a past (Montgomery Clift) caught in a trap; either he must betray the secrets of a murderer's confession or he himself will be convicted of the murder. The premise of this Hitchcock thriller is promising, but the movie, set in Quebec and partly shot there, is so reticent it's mostly dull. Clift seems determined not to move more than the tiniest facial muscles. With a miscast Anne Baxter, and Brian Aherne, O. E. Hasse, Karl Malden, and Dolly Haas. From a play by Paul Anthelme, adapted by George Tabori and William Archibald. Warners. b & w

I Could Go On Singing (1963)—Dreadful, but often fascinating: Judy Garland in the sort of movie that is usually made about a performer long after the events, and with someone else playing the lead. Her face puffy, her manner distressed, she goes through a sort of *Madame X* version of a selfish singer's life, in which she belts out numbers at the Palladium. Made in England and directed by Ronald Neame. With Dirk Bogarde, Jack Klugman, and Aline MacMahon. United Artists. color

I Cover the Waterfront (1933)—Up front, this is a commonplace romantic melodrama about a wisecracking, hard-drinking reporter (Ben Lyon) who exploits his love affair (with Claudette Colbert) in order to get a good story for his paper, but the background is far from commonplace. Colbert's father (played by Ernest Torrence) is a huge wreck of a sea captain who smuggles Chinese to the West Coast; he's a moody, illiterate mercenary who throws his passengers overboard tied to anchor chains when the Coast Guard approaches. There are several strong, memorable scenes, and such unusual moments as the heroine's passing the time of day with the madam of a brothel while waiting to take her boozed-up father home. James Cruze directed; from Max Miller's book. United Artists. b & w

I Dood It (1943)—Red Skelton's best movie musical. It's a lavish M-G-M production with a comedy-of-errors story about a pants presser who is mistaken for a millionaire, and it features Lena Horne and Eleanor Powell, and Hazel Scott at the piano and singing in the extraordinarily intense "Jericho" number—which is in the hot, revivalist, jazzy style of 20s theatre. The direction is credited to Vincente Minnelli, but he took over after someone else had started shooting—he didn't direct the battleship number or the rope-twirling scene. With Butterfly McQueen, Sam Levene, Richard Ainley, Thurston Hall, and Lee Young on drums, Jimmy Dorsey and his orchestra, Helen O'Connell, and Bob Eberle. Script by Sig Herzig and Fred Saidy, loosely derived from the 1929 Buster Keaton film *Spite Marriage*. The songs include "So Long Sarah Jane" and "Taking a Chance on Love." b & w

I Know Where I'm Going (1945)—This romance is set in large part during a gale in the Western Isles of Scotland. It features dense fog, a squall, and a huge, roaring whirlpool. It also features Art Deco images of the young Wendy Hiller as an assured, impudent working girl who is scheduled to marry a rotten-rich, middle-aged tycoon, until she's caught in that storm. She meets a kind-faced naval officer (Roger Livesey); he's the impoverished Laird of Kiloran, and after a few days and nights of his gentle Gaelic voice she's thoroughly confused. Written, produced, and directed by Michael Powell and Emeric Pressburger, this is a charmer of a movie. In a party sequence, everything else stops while we listen to the rapid group singing of the Highlanders: it's a soul-satisfying interlude. The cinematography is by Erwin Hillier; the art direction is by Alfred Junge. With Pamela Brown, Finlay Currie, Nancy Price, Jean Cadell, Catherine Lacey, Valentine Dyall, George Carney, Margot Fitzsimmons, John Laurie, and Petula Clark. (In his autobiography, Powell explained that Livesey couldn't get out of his role in a London play, and a double filled in for him in the exterior scenes; Livesey "never came within 500 miles of the Western Isles.") The Archers. b & w

I Love You, Alice B. Toklas! (1968)—A giddy, slapdash, entertainingly inconsequential comedy, written by Paul Mazursky and Larry Tucker, and starring Peter Sellers as a Los Angeles Jewish lawyer who turns hippie. With Joyce Van Patten as his anxious fiancée, and Leigh Taylor-Young, Jo Van Fleet, David Arkin, Herbert Edelman, Salem Ludwig, Edra Gale, Lou Gottlieb, and Grady Sutton. The picture makes you laugh surprisingly often. Directed by Hy Averback. Warners. color (See *Going Steady*.)

I Love You to Death (1990)—When Joey (Kevin Kline), the self-admiring pizzeria owner, walks down the street, his little rump is alert to everything. That's what gets him into trouble: he's surrounded by opportunities for seduction, and he's a practiced master of the art. Easing into conversation with a young beauty (Phoebe Cates) at a bar, he skillfully convinces her that the man she's with isn't worthy of her, and she apologizes for being with such a second-rate guy. You can't dislike the narcissistic Italian-American Joey; he's essentially innocent. That's why it takes so long for his loving wife (Tracey Ullman) to see what's going on. When her eyes are opened, she gives in to her hardbitten Yugoslavian mother (Joan Plowright) who arranges to have Joey killed. Directed by Lawrence Kasdan, from John Kostmayer's script, this amiably slack screwball farce is based on an actual case in which five botched attempts were made on an errant husband's life. The picture is often on the verge of being really funny, but it doesn't have much energy, and

it lacks comic precision until (near the end) the wildly gifted Miriam Margolyes, who plays Joey's mother, whacks him on his bandaged head; her explosive timing lifts the scene sky-high. Kevin Kline is a little too conscious of his deadpan style, but Keanu Reeves and William Hurt are a fine pair of dopeheads who hire on as hit men. (Reeves shows a flair for spaced-out clowning.) Plowright has a few near-inspired routines, and River Phoenix, playing a busboy, comes through as a giddy comedian. Watching the cast you may feel tolerant, the way you do watching a bunch of boisterous pros enjoying themselves in a sloppy summer-stock production. With Victoria Jackson and Heather Graham. Set in Tacoma, Washington. Tri-Star. color

I Married a Witch (1942)—Moderately amusing romantic fantasy, with Veronica Lake at her prettiest (and getting the full star treatment) as a witch burned in Puritan days who comes back in modern times and discovers that "love is stronger than witchcraft." René Clair directed, and the cast includes Fredric March, Robert Benchley, Cecil Kellaway as a warlock, and Susan Hayward as a bitch. From Thorne Smith's *The Passionate Witch*. United Artists. b & w

I Married an Angel (1942)—Rodgers and Hart's sophisticated musical comedy was purchased for Jeanette MacDonald and Nelson Eddy when their popularity in stale-whipped-cream operetta was waning, but then M-G-M became nervous, removed the sophistication, and turned the musical comedy into something as bland as operetta but without its energy. This disaster was MacDonald and Eddy's last film together. Directed by W. S. Van Dyke. With Binnie Barnes, Janis Carter, Mona Maris, and Edward Everett Horton. b & w

I Met Him in Paris (1937)—Claudette Colbert escapes her department-store job and her prig of a fiancé (Lee Bowman). She picks up Melvyn Douglas and Robert Young in Paris, travels to Switzerland with them, and falls in love with the wrong one. Simple-minded, predictable romantic comedy, with Colbert panicking on skis and getting tossed into snowbanks. (The Alpine scenes were shot in Sun Valley.) Wesley Ruggles directed; Claude Binyon wrote the screenplay, based on a story by Helen Meinardi. With Mona Barrie. Paramount. b & w

I Never Sang for My Father (1970)—Bargain-basement dramaturgy is used to surprisingly powerful effect in this account of a middle-aged man's unresolved relationship with his father. The dramatist, Robert Anderson, who adapted his own play, keeps things on that truthful level where no solutions are really satisfactory, and the director, Gilbert Cates, doesn't cheat—he accepts the risks of being solidly obvious. And by its decency in not pulling sloppy feelings out of us, the film develops valid emotion. Gene Hackman and Melvyn Douglas perform unsentimentally and intelligently as the son and the self-righteous father. With Estelle Parsons and Dorothy Stickney. Columbia. color (See *Deeper into Movies*.)

I Remember Mama (1948)—Kathryn Forbes' novel about her Norwegian family in San Francisco is used as the framework for a mother image of formidable proportions. This image is held to with the serene nostalgia that we reserve for our very best fantasies—Mama (Irene Dunne) is tall and beautiful, wise and omniscient. Except for a few gooey lapses (the worst is a bathetic hospital scene), George Stevens directed with warmth and intelligence; it's not a bad movie, though it has a too careful look, with meticulous reconstructions of San Francisco streets circa 1905–10. Philip Dorn is Papa, and Barbara Bel Geddes does well as daughter Katrin. As the rakehell Uncle Chris, Oscar Homolka goes in for too many flourishes and loiters too long on his deathbed; Edgar Bergen is the timid undertaker who marries Mama's sister. The movie seems hemmed in, maybe because DeWitt Bodeen's script sticks too closely to the stage adaptation by John van Druten. Also with Cedric Hardwicke, Rudy Vallee, Barbara O'Neil, Florence Bates, Peggy McIntyre, June Hedin, and Steve Brown. Cinematography by Nicholas Musuraca. R K O. b & w

I See a Dark Stranger Originally released in the U.S. as *The Adventuress*. (1945)—A romantic suspense comedy, with Deborah Kerr as an Irish girl, fed on anti-British folklore by her father. On her 21st birthday she goes off to Dublin, hoping to join the I.R.A., but becomes involved in a different kind of anti-British activity: spying for the Nazis. Frank Launder and Sidney Gilliat, who produced, with Launder also directing, had written Hitchcock's *The Lady Vanishes* and Carol Reed's *Night Train to Munich* and other witty thrillers; this script, which they wrote with Wolfgang Wilhelm, has the same basic ingredients. But without a Hitchcock or a Carol Reed to supply style and terror, the results seem too consciously clever. The musical score and the attitudes are a little arch, a little condescending. It's pleasant enough, but unexciting; its only spark is from Kerr, who's fresh and lovely, with full pouty young lips. The hero, Trevor Howard, has nothing to do but follow her around, adoringly; Raymond Huntley plays the Nazi who recruits her. b & w

I Walk the Line (1970)—This John Frankenheimer picture has gone so far in deglamourizing everything that it forgets to give you a reason for watching it. Gregory Peck, a weather-beaten, gaunt-faced Tennessee sheriff, married to well-meaning Estelle Parsons, gets tragically involved with a young girl (Tuesday Weld), the daughter of a moonshiner (Ralph Meeker). The dirt-poor people look at each other expressionlessly, hopelessly, and talk in hillbilly dialect, with a pause after every line so you'll know their lives are arid. This is the kind of rural-elemental movie in which a slobbering bully forces himself on the lovely young heroine and shoots the dog who's guarding her. The screenplay by Alvin Sargent is based on the novel *An Exile*, by Madison Jones. Columbia. color (See *Deeper into Movies*.)

I Was a Male War Bride (1949)—Somebody must have thought it would be funny to put Cary Grant in skirts and a horsehair wig. The whole thing is one of those awful transvestite jokes that never has the grace to go off-color; it all stays at the chortling wholesome-family-picture level. Ann Sheridan plays the WAC lieutenant whom Grant (a French Army captain) marries; the gimmick is that she's stationed in Occupied Germany (where the film was made) and the only Army regulation under which he can accompany her back to the U.S. is the one concerning the immigration of war brides. The conception requires Sheridan to be bossy and butch (it's one of her least pleasant performances) and Grant is never so beefy and clumsy as when he's in drag; he doesn't play a woman, he threatens to—flirting with the idea and giggling over it. Howard Hawks directed, but his pacing is off and everything seems forced. The screenplay is by Charles Lederer, Leonard Spigelgass, and Hagar Wilde, from a book by Henri Rochard (Grant plays Henri Rochard). There are no subsidiary roles of any consequence; with Ken Tobey, Robert Stevenson, and William Neff. 20th Century-Fox. b & w

I Will, I Will . . . For Now (1976)—The worst. Combines the most simperingly forced elements of 50s mistaken-identity farces with a mushy soft-core version of the sex-clinic pornos. The hero, who suffers from premature ejaculation, and the heroine, who is frigid, go to a Santa Barbara clinic where "Nothing Is Unnatural" is emblazoned in neon in the patients' cottages. The message is false: swallowing this movie is an unnatural act for any person of average intelligence. Elliott Gould is fairly thoroughly trashed, but Diane Keaton manages to save face despite what's going on around her. Norman Panama directed, from a script he and Albert E. Lewin devised. With Madge Sinclair, Robert Alda, and Paul Sorvino. 20th Century-Fox. color (See *When the Lights Go Down*.)

Ice (1970)—Made during the Vietnam war, this film by Robert Kramer is set in an indefinite near future, when Vietnam has been superseded by a war in Mexico. The picture is an extension of the late-60s urban-guerrilla attitudes and activities, and it is made in a hazy, semi-documentary style, as if a stoned anthropologist were examining his own tribe and were so indifferent to the filmmaking process that he hadn't learned how to read a light meter or bothered to work out a continuity. It's a film about political commitment that is made not only without any commitment to film as an art form but without any enthusiasm for its own political commitment. Yet this gray, grainy, painfully stagnant movie is a revealing account of the anomalies in the urban-guerrilla movement. Though it cost only $12,000 (from the American Film Institute), it has a cast of 250. b & w (See *Deeper into Movies*.)

Ice Follies of 1939—For necrophiliacs. This grotesque M-G-M musical died the day it was released. It stars Joan Crawford, with James Stewart and Lew Ayres, and the forgettable score includes such gems as "Loveland in the Wintertime." The unlucky Reinhold Schunzel directed; produced by Harry Rapf. With Lionel Stander, Lewis Stone, and the International Ice Follies. b & w, with color sequences

Iceman (1984)—John Lone is awe-inspiring in the way he stirs our empathy with the hero—the prehistoric man who has been asleep inside glacial ice for 40,000 years. The Iceman is thawed out in a sequence that is comparable in creepiness and fascination to the famous laboratory scene in James Whale's 1931 *Frankenstein*, in which the monster comes to life. But the tone here is altogether different: the water dripping from the icy casket suggests weeping. Uncouth as this Neanderthal may look, he has a full range of feeling in his eyes. He's unmistakably human, and he's confused about where he is; he thinks he has been enchanted and that he's being punished. It's a strange, elating movie with the Iceman at its emotional center; his mystical fervor takes hold. The director, Fred Schepisi, is working with a weak script, yet he and his two longtime collaborators, the composer Bruce Smeaton and the cinematographer Ian Baker, achieve that special and overwhelming fusion of the arts which great visual moviemaking can give us. With Timothy Hutton, Lindsay Crouse, Josef Sommer, and David Strathairn. Written by Chip Proser and John Drimmer, from Drimmer's story; a Norman Jewison and Patrick Palmer Production, for Universal. color (See *State of the Art.*)

The Iceman Cometh (1973)—Eugene O'Neill's great, heavy, simplistic, mechanical, beautiful play has been given a straightforward, faithful production in handsome,

dark-toned color. A filmed play like this one doesn't offer the sensual excitement that movies *can* offer, but you don't go to it for that; you go to it for O'Neill's crude, prosaic virtuosity, which is also pure American poetry, and for the kind of cast that rarely gathers for a stage production. The characters are drunken bums and whores who have found sanctuary in Harry Hope's flophouse saloon; each has a "pipe dream" that sustains him until Hickey, the salesman—the "iceman"—who attempts to free them all by stripping them of their lies and guilt, takes the life out of them. The play is essentially an argument between Larry, an aging anarchist (Robert Ryan), and Hickey (Lee Marvin); Larry speaks for pity and the necessity of illusions, Hickey for the curative power of truth. They're the two poles of consciousness that O'Neill himself is split between. Larry, a self-hating alcoholic, is a weak man and a windbag, but Ryan brings so much understanding to Larry's weakness that the play achieves new dimensions. Ryan becomes O'Neill for us; he has O'Neill's famous "tragic handsomeness" and the broken-man jowls, too, and at the end, when Larry is permanently "iced"—that is, stripped of illusion—we can see that this is the author's fantasy of himself: he alone is above the illusions that the others fall back on. He is tragic, while the others, with their restored illusions, have become comic. Yes, it's sophomoric to see yourself as the one who is doomed to live without illusions, yet what O'Neill does with this sophomoric conception is masterly. And Ryan (who died shortly after) got right to the boozy, gnarled soul of the play. The film is marred by the central miscasting of Lee Marvin (he's thick, somehow, and irrelevantly vigorous, and his big monologue doesn't register at all), but it isn't destroyed. Though the characters are devised for a thesis and we never lose our awareness of that, they are nevertheless marvellously playable. Fredric March interprets Harry Hope with so much quiet tenderness that when Harry regains his illusions and we see March's muscles tone up we don't know whether to smile for the character or the actor. And there are Jeff Bridges as Parritt, Bradford Dillman as Willie (you can almost taste his joy in the role), and Martyn Green, George Voskovec, Sorrell Booke, Moses Gunn, Tom Pedi, and John McLiam as Jimmy Tomorrow. Directed by John Frankenheimer—tactfully but not very probingly. Produced by Ely Landau. (See *Reeling*.)

The Idiot (1946)—The young Gérard Philipe is an extraordinarily sensitive Prince Myshkin, and Edwige Feuillère, that remarkable mistress of the language of gesture, is a spectacular Nastasya in this emotional, surprisingly effective version of the Dostoevski novel. Directed by Georges Lampin. In French. b & w

The Idiot *Hakuchi* (1951)—Kurosawa made this version of the Dostoevski novel right after *Rashomon*, using the same two men— Masayuki Mori (the husband in *Rashomon*) as Prince Myshkin, and Toshiro Mifune (the bandit in *Rashomon*) as Rogozhin. It's a long, uneven, fascinating film, with such curiosities as a Nastasya Filipovna (Setsuko Hara) modelled on Maria Casarès in Cocteau's *Orpheus*. In Japanese. b & w

The Idiot *Nastasia Filipovna* (1958)—The first half of a planned two-part film; the second half was never shot. Yuri Yakovlev's Prince Myshkin doesn't make anything like the impression that Gérard Philipe's Prince did in the 1946 French version, but the film shows the considerable intelligence of the director, Ivan Pyriev, who also did the adaptation. He experimented with a theatrical style, using single sets for long sequences. In Russian. color

Idiot's Delight (1939)—Robert Sherwood's high reputation as a dramatist was always a little mystifying and never more so than when his windy intellectuality was recorded on film. This allegorical comedy from M-G-M has Clark Gable as a hoofer and Norma Shearer as a fake Russian countess (the roles made famous on Broadway by Lunt and Fontanne). It's set in an Alpine wintersports hotel high above a world about to be engulfed in war. The characters include a leftist, a pair of honeymooners, and so forth; and there's got to be an anti-war message in it somewhere. Gable isn't bad (he does a deliberately clunky, bedraggled dance to "Puttin' On the Ritz"), but oh, that Shearer. With Burgess Meredith, Edward Arnold, Charles Coburn, Joseph Schildkraut, Skeets Gallagher, Laura Hope Crews, Pat Paterson, Virginia Grey, Joan Marsh, Bernadene Hayes, and Fritz Feld. Directed by Clarence Brown, who struggles hopelessly trying to give this stagey material some style and impudence. Sherwood did the adaptation himself, providing early scenes to establish that the hoofer and the "countess" had had an affair years before (when they were both in vaudeville), and a new, upbeat ending. b & w

The Idolmaker (1980)—A likable first feature by the director Taylor Hackford; it has verve and snap, despite a rickety script and a sloshy finish. Ray Sharkey plays a brash young songwriter from the Bronx who becomes a hype artist. He takes a baby-faced, boozing pillhead (Paul Land) and turns him into a rock idol for teen-agers, and then finds a swarthy, 16-year-old busboy (Peter Gallagher) whose eyes and mouth are impossibly—foolishly—large and saturates the country with publicity, pre-selling the kid as an idol before the public even hears his voice. The picture keeps moving, and the satirical musical numbers are cheerful and impudent. The script by Edward Di Lorenzo was suggested by the life of the rock impresario Bob Marcucci, who promoted Frankie Avalon and Fabian. With Kenneth O'Brien as the corrupt disc jockey, Jimmy Carter as the jiggling blond singer, and Tovah Feldshuh (a dreary, smirky performance). Produced by Gene Kirkwood and Howard W. Koch, Jr.; released by United Artists. color (See *Taking It All In*.)

If . . . (1969)—At first, and for a considerable stretch, this Lindsay Anderson film appears to be a clinical exposé of the horrible organized bedlam inflicted on English boys in the name of a gentleman's education. The movie is especially fixated on the cruelties that the students perpetrate against each other, with lingering attention to scenes of juvenile sadism and flogging and nasty homoeroticism. Then it turns into an epic on student revolt. You can read the signals all right—the poster of Ché and the student-hero's forbidden mustache and his playing the "Missa Luba." But the style of the film is constricted and charged with ambivalent feelings. Can it be meant to be a story of the revolutionary spirit of the young when it's so full of bile about youth? Anderson devotes most of his energy to the meanness of the students. And it's really not a rebellion of the young that he shows us but a rebellion of a self-chosen few—three boys (and a girl picked up along the way) who set fire to the school on Speech Day and start sniping at those who flee the fire, including the rest of the young. Their way of destroying the prison is to kill the inmates. The conspirators are cleaning out the whole mess, apparently—killing everybody, because nobody's fit to live. The last shot is a glamorous and apparently approving closeup of the hero as he fires away, like Robert Taylor aiming at "the Japs" at the end of *Bataan*. There are so many muddy undercurrents in this film that even the best sequences are often baffling, and the ways in which Anderson tries to il-

lustrate the desire for freedom don't carry any conviction. With Malcolm McDowell. Written by David Sherwin; cinematography by Miroslav Ondříček. b & w and color (See *Going Steady*.)

If I Had a Million (1932)—Perhaps the best of the American all-star episode films of its era. Each brief story has a different comic flavor. The cast includes W. C. Fields, Alison Skipworth, Charles Laughton, Gary Cooper, Mary Boland, Jack Oakie, George Raft, and Wynne Gibson as the prostitute who, given a million dollars, goes to bed alone. Directed by Ernst Lubitsch, among others. Paramount. b & w

If I Were King (1938)—Lively costume romance. Ronald Colman smiles with mocking charm as the braggart poet François Villon, quick-witted with epigrams and swords. Fortunately, the script is by Preston Sturges. Frances Dee is the frosty great lady whom the poet melts (or thaws, anyway), and Ellen Drew is the warmer number, Huguette, an unkempt wench who hangs around the fellows in the wine cellars. With Basil Rathbone as a sly, wily Louis XI, and a first-rate cast, including Henry Wilcoxon, Bruce Lester, Alma Lloyd, Sidney Toler, Ralph Forbes, Montagu Love, and William Farnum. Frank Lloyd directed this version of Justin McCarthy's play, first filmed in 1920 staring William Farnum, then in 1926 starring John Barrymore, then in a musical version in 1930 starring Dennis King and Jeanette MacDonald, and again (unsuccessfully this time) in 1955 starring Oreste Kirkop and Kathryn Grayson. Paramount. b & w

If It's Tuesday, This Must Be Belgium (1969)—Said to be the first cartoon caption ever made into a full-length movie. Suzanne Pleshette and Mildred Natwick are among the stereotyped American tourists; Ian Mc-

Shane is their guide. The director, Mel Stuart, keeps everything moving cheerfully, and there are a few passable one-liners, but you feel as if you've seen the picture before—on television. The script is by David Shaw; with Peggy Cass, Marty Ingels, Murray Hamilton, Pamela Britton, Michael Constantine, Sandy Baron, and Norman Fell. A Wolper Production; United Artists. color

If You Could Only Cook (1935)—This eminently watchable romantic comedy has a neatly contrived 30s-style opening. An automobile engineer and tycoon (Herbert Marshall) becomes impatient with his board of directors and walks out on them. He goes to the park to cool off and meets a girl (Jean Arthur) who's perusing the want ads. She thinks that he's unemployed, too, and proposes that they hire out as cook and butler. There are also some gracefully conceived sequences: the test on the use of garlic that she has to pass at the home of a gourmet (Leo Carrillo), a retired racketeer; the tycoon asking his own butler tricks of the butling trade. There are also some silly melodramatic moments, but the film is remarkably good-natured and fresh. Jean Arthur brings out the best in Marshall—or maybe the director, William Seiter, livened him up. (He smiles—almost broadly—now and then.) With Lionel Stander and cello-voiced Frieda Inescort. The script by Gertrude Purcell and Howard J. Green is based on F. Hugh Herbert's screen story. Columbia. b & w

Ikiru (1952)—The last days of a Japanese Everyman (Takashi Shimura) doomed by cancer, as he explores the ways of confronting death. It's extremely uneven—there are slick and sentimental passages and some that are impenetrable. But there are also emotional revelations and there's a superb sequence—almost an epiphany—when the dying man, who has accomplished what he hoped to, sits in a swing in the snow and hums a little song. Directed by Akira Kurosawa. In Japanese. b & w

I'll Be Seeing You (1945)—This Selznick project originated in a radio play (by Charles Martin), and it may have *sounded* like a good movie idea. But oh, my! Ginger Rogers is the young woman doing a six-year prison stretch for having killed a man in the course of defending her honor. Midway in her sentence, she's allowed to return home for three weeks to visit her family—an aunt (Spring Byington), an uncle (Tom Tully), and their daughter (Shirley Temple). They are a tactless bunch, so compulsively drawn to the subject of her penal servitude that one imagines that she'd have preferred to remain in the jug. But she meets a shell-shocked sergeant (Joseph Cotten) on furlough from an Army hospital; he is being harassed by the local people's insistence on talking to him about the war. Having the same problem brings them together, and at the close they return to their separate institutions, planning to reunite forever. Doesn't it reek of radio drama? On the screen, as directed by William Dieterle from a script by Marion Parsonnet, it's damned close to intolerable. Released by United Artists. b & w

I'll Cry Tomorrow (1955)—This maudlin M-G-M bio-pic, based on Lillian Roth's book (written with Mike Connolly and Gerold Frank) about how she rose to fame as a singer-actress and then drank her way to shame, has a low-grade, sordid, masochistic appeal. Susan Hayward was close to 40 when she played the part, and her scenes as the teen-age Lillian lack the necessary eagerness and vividness. Hayward deepens her speaking voice, and, though it is said that she did her own singing, the big, low, rather toneless voice doesn't seem to emanate from her, and when she stands with her chest pushed out and imitates the movements Roth made when she sang, there's no drive behind what she's doing—nothing to suggest what made Lillian Roth a headliner. There's very little left to suggest what made Hayward a star, either; she falls back on tired technique and flaccid, self-pitying nobility. (You have to see her in something like *Deadline at Dawn* of 1946 to get an idea of how much she'd slipped.) Eddie Albert gives the booby-prize performance; as the Alcoholics Anonymous man who brings about Lillian's spiritual rebirth, he keeps his square jaw tilted upward—humility lifts his every thought to heaven. Considering the feeble script (by Helen Deutsch and Jay Richard Kennedy) it's surprising that the director Daniel Mann managed to hold viewers at all, but he doesn't establish a sense of period or of locale or of the passage of time. The only scenes that have any energy are those with Richard Conte as Lillian's sadistic husband; the viewer feels a queasy curiosity and dread. There's a classic pulp ending: the heroine walks forward to the stage for a "This Is Your Life" show, her face bathed in heavenly light. With Jo Van Fleet as Lillian's monomaniacal stage mother, Ray Danton, Don Taylor, Margo, Virginia Gregg, and Don Barry; the little girl who plays Lillian at 8 is uncannily like both Roth *and* Hayward. b & w

Illicit Interlude, see *Summer Interlude*

I'm All Right, Jack (1960)—This isn't one of those gentle English comedies with glancing bits of social spoofery; it's a cynical and raucous slapstick farce—the one really funny film satire of the labor-management conflicts. Its view of the philosophy of the citizens of the welfare state is summed up in the title, derived from the English armed-forces catch phrase: "—— you, I'm all right, Jack." The big businessmen are the villains in the plot, but the film also shows the trade unionists

as smug and self-centered, and though the satire of union practices is much more affectionate, it is so accurately aimed—and we are so unused to it—that it comes off much the better. As the shop steward, Peter Sellers is avid to protect the workers' rights—he's earnest, he's monstrously self-serious. He wears a little Hitler mustache—that mustache was always an oddly lower-middle-class adornment on Hitler—and while this shop steward is certainly lower middle class in his habits, he's a fanatical proletarian in theory, and he speaks in a jargon that derives from political pamphlets. The movie parodies this beady-eyed little stuffed shirt and the featherbedding practices of his union. The cast includes Terry-Thomas as an Army officer turned personnel manager; Ian Carmichael as an innocent from Oxford who wants to become a business executive; Dennis Price and Richard Attenborough as capitalist tricksters; and Margaret Rutherford, Miles Malleson, Irene Handl, Marne Maitland, Liz Fraser, Raymond Huntley, and Malcolm Muggeridge—as himself, of course. Produced and directed by Roy and John Boulting; from the novel by Alan Hackney, adapted by John Boulting, Frank Harvey, and Hackney. b & w (See *I Lost it at the Movies*.)

I'm No Angel (1933)—Mae West as a lion tamer, Cary Grant as a society lion, lots of adenoidal innuendo, and some good honky-tonk songs ("That Dallas Man," et al.). Arguably West's best film, certainly one of her funniest. When she isn't wiggling in her corsets and driving men wild she's sashaying around and camping it up for her plump black maids (Gertrude Howard, Libby Taylor). With Edward Arnold, Gregory Ratoff, Kent Taylor, Ralf Harolde, Gertrude Michael, Nat Pendleton, Dennis O'Keefe, Irving Pichel, and Dorothy Peterson. Directed by Wesley Ruggles; the story, screenplay, and dialogue are by Mae West, with continuity by Harlan Thompson. Paramount. b & w

Images (1972)—Robert Altman's modern variant of the *Caligari* ploy—the world as seen through a mad person's eyes. A classy schizo (Susannah York) duplicates herself, confuses the living with the dead, and can't tell her husband (René Auberjonois) from her lovers (Marcel Bozzufi, Hugh Millais). Her madness seems to be a matter of tinkling wind chimes, slivers of glass, windows, lenses, mirrors—"images." To be effective, the movie needs to draw us in to identify with her hallucinations, but the cold shine of the surfaces doesn't do it. The imagery itself fails to stir the imagination, though the cinematographer, Vilmos Zsigmond, shot some unusual landscapes, inhumanly clear and visible at a great distance, and there are some ravishing pastoral scenes. It's a hollow puzzle movie despite the seductive editing rhythms and the many inventive moments. From a screenplay by Altman, with improvisations; in this ornamental setting, with so much care given to twirling glassy baubles, the occasional flat improvised lines are like peanut shells stuck in jewelry. Susannah York is the author of "In Search of Unicorns," the stupefyingly high-flown story for children, which the heroine narrates. With Cathryn Harrison. Made in Ireland. Columbia. color (See *Reeling*.)

Imitation of Life (1934)—Classic, compulsively watchable rags-to-riches-and-heartbreak weeper, from a novel by Fannie Hurst. Claudette Colbert and Louise Beavers are the white and black women who go into business together, and Rochelle Hudson and Fredi Washington are their daughters. Ross Hunter produced a remake in 1959 which pulled out all the stops; in both versions you want to laugh at yourself for choking up, but, at least, the original is simpler and the sobs aren't torn out of your throat. With Warren William, Ned Sparks, Alan Hale, Franklin Pangborn, Noel Francis, Hazel Washington, Madame Sul-Te-Wan (the black actress who worked with D. W. Griffith), Hattie McDaniel, Henry Armetta, and Henry Kolker. Directed by John Stahl. Universal. b & w

The Importance of Being Earnest (1952)—Oscar Wilde's deliriously convoluted, perfect comedy—the most preposterous work of art ever written. Wit cascades through the play in a natural flow. Considered too effete for general consumption, it was never filmed until this production, directed by Anthony Asquith, who also did the adaptation and left the play alone as much as possible. The film is stagey, but highly enjoyable; Wilde's multiple-entendres about love and money are delivered in the required high, dry style by an extraordinary cast. Michael Redgrave is Jack Worthing; Edith Evans is triumphantly larger than life as Lady Bracknell; Joan Greenwood is the Hon. Gwendolen Fairfax; Michael Denison is Algernon Moncrieff; Dorothy Tutin is a wonderful, twittering Cecily Cardew; Margaret Rutherford, her great jaw wobbling with emotion, is Miss Prism; and Miles Malleson is Reverend Chasuble. People who have seen this movie have been known to giggle with pleasure years later as they recall the timbre and phrasing that Edith Evans gives to such lines as "Prism! Where is that baby?" color

In a Lonely Place (1950)—Humphrey Bogart, as a cynical, tired Hollywood screenwriter named Dixon Steele, in an atmospheric but disappointingly hollow murder melodrama directed by Nicholas Ray. In talking to a hat-check girl, Steele discovers that she has read the book he is supposed to adapt to the screen; not wanting the bother of reading it himself, he invites her to his place so he can grill her about it. When the girl is murdered, the police think he did it. Steele is in love with Gloria Grahame (who lives in the same complex of courtyard apartments), but he's under so much pressure because of the police that he almost strangles her in a jealous rage. That makes her queasily fearful, and he knows he's lost her. Ray doesn't seem to have an adequate budget or enough ideas to play with; he keeps the thing going and uses the courtyard setting for a special L.A. feeling, but the dialogue is no more than functional, and there's not much of a supporting cast— Frank Lovejoy, Carl Benton Reid, Jeff Donnell, Art Smith, Robert Warwick, Steven Geray, and Hadda Brooks as the singer in the nightclub sequence. (Some people have interpreted the film's murky undertones in terms of the breakup of Ray's marriage to Gloria Grahame; they split when the picture was finished.) From a novel by Dorothy B. Hughes, adapted by Edmund H. North and Andrew Solt; cinematography by Burnett Guffey; music by George Antheil. Columbia. b & w

In Caliente (1935)—Mediocre but tolerable foolishness—an inexpensive, makeshift musical from First National with one memorable number: sultry Wini Shaw singing "The Lady in Red." The plot is some nonsense about a dancer (Dolores Del Rio) falling in love with a critic who gave her a bad review. The cast includes Pat O'Brien, Glenda Farrell, Leo Carrillo, Phil Regan, Judy Canova, Luis Alberni, Herman Bing, and Edward Everett Horton; Lloyd Bacon directed, from a screenplay by Jerry Wald and Julius Epstein, based on a story by a couple of other fellows. There is an appalling song called "Muchacha." b & w

In Like Flint (1967)—This sequel to *Our Man Flint* (1966) has just one memorable bit. Told that the President (Andrew Duggan) has been kidnapped and is being impersonated by an actor, agent Flint (James Coburn) cries out, "An actor the President of the United States!" Directed by Gordon Douglas, from a script by Hal Fimberg. With Lee J. Cobb and Anna Lee. 20th Century-Fox. CinemaScope, color

In Name Only (1939)—Slinky Kay Francis is the cold-hearted wife in name only. All she wants of her husband, Cary Grant, is his wealth and social position, while he is so desperate for a divorce in order to marry the companionable Carole Lombard, a young widow with a small daughter, that he becomes ill and almost dies of pneumonia. This is one of the rare movies in which the robust Grant actually has sickbed scenes. John Cromwell directed this "mature" (*Dodsworth* influenced) view of marital incompatibility, which emphasizes the wife's shrewdness in manipulating her in-laws. It's a solemn, soapy picture, but with unusually good performances. With Charles Coburn as Grant's father, and Helen Vinson, Peggy Ann Garner, Katharine Alexander, Alan Baxter, Maurice Moscovitch, and Nella Walker. Adapted by Richard Sherman, from Bessie Breuer's novel *Memory of Love*. R K O. b & w

In Old Chicago (1938)—Alice Brady has a few miraculous scenes as Mrs. O'Leary, whose cow kicks over a lamp and starts the big blaze. The remainder of the film, which features Don Ameche as her goody-boy son and Tyrone Power as her shrewd, black-sheep scamp, is on a different level altogether. It's a mediocre, though jolly, quasi-historical melodrama involving brawls, riots, capricious temperaments, police squads, café ladies, gaudy saloons, and Alice Faye smiling that great open smile of hers that makes it possible to forgive her acting and to bask in her mellow-voiced numbers. (Ameche is so fatuous here he's almost likable.) Henry King directed, from the screenplay by Lamar Trotti

I

and Sonya Levien, based on Niven Busch's *We the O'Learys*; the more immediate inspiration for the film was the box-office success of M-G-M's 1936 *San Francisco*. With Gene Reynolds, Phyllis Brooks, Tom Brown, Andy Devine, Sidney Blackmer, Brian Donlevy, Berton Churchill, and Paul Hurst. b & w

In the Heat of the Night (1967)—A comedy-thriller with Sidney Poitier as a quick-witted police officer from the North and Rod Steiger as a blundering Southern chief of police. Fast and enjoyable, with Poitier's color used for comedy. He's like a black Sherlock Holmes in a Tom-and-Jerry cartoon of reversals. For once it's funny (instead of embarrassing) that he's superior to everybody else. In the final joke, Steiger plays redcap to him. With Lee Grant, Warren Oates, Beah Richards, Scott Wilson, Peter Masterson, Matt Clark, Peter Whitney, James Patterson, and Larry Gates. The cinematography by Haskell Wexler has an exciting, alive quality, and the good Quincy Jones score includes a title song sung by Ray Charles. Directed by Norman Jewison, from a script by Stirling Silliphant based on a novel by John Ball. Academy Awards: Best Picture, Actor (Steiger), Screenplay, and Editing (Hal Ashby). United Artists. color (See *Going Steady*.)

In the Year of the Pig (1969)—Emile de Antonio assembled news footage and interviews from many sources for this overview of the background and issues of the Vietnam war. There are some almost forgotten faces, like Emperor Bao Dai's and Madame Nhu's, and some American speeches we might like to forget. The film makes sense out of what was going on, even if this sense isn't the only sense to be made of it. De Antonio is overly fond of schoolboy tricks—loaded, crude bits of satire. But in the main line of the narrative he plays a highly sophisticated game: he presents the American leaders and American

policy as Hanoi might see them, and he's done it out of our own mouths. (See *Deeper into Movies*.)

In Which We Serve (1942)—During the Second World War, Noël Coward and David Lean co-directed this skillful, discreetly realistic film about the courage and sacrifice of the British Navy, specifically the men on a destroyer. Coward himself plays the ship's commander; he also wrote and scored the movie and produced it. Coward's ability to package emotions and to break the audience's heart without relaxing his upper lip is more perplexing here than elsewhere. The restraint of his proud patriotism may seem a much worse con than rampant jingoism, but he'a a wizard at this English game. The cast includes Celia Johnson, John Mills, Kay Walsh, Michael Wilding, and Richard Attenborough. b & w

Les Inconnus dans la maison, see *Strangers in the House*

The Incredible Sarah (1976)—An aberration. The staccato, wrenchingly modern Glenda Jackson plays the lyrical, incandescent Sarah Bernhardt. Written by Ruth Wolff and directed by Richard Fleischer, this picture is in the stupefying tradition of *Song of Norway*. With Daniel Massey as Sardou and Yvonne Mitchell as Mam'selle. Produced by Helen M. Strauss, for Reader's Digest. color (See *When the Lights Go Down*.)

The Incredible Shrinking Man (1957)—B-budget science-fiction and simple stuff, but with more consistency and logic than usual, and with some rather amusing trick photography. And after all these years of the hero escaping every kind of disaster and atomic monster, it's fun to have him wind up as a twinkle in God's eye. With Grant Williams.

360

Directed by Jack Arnold, from a script by Richard Matheson. Universal. b & w

The Incredible Shrinking Woman (1981)— An amiable, sloppy, light satirical fantasy starring Lily Tomlin as Pat, a sweetly loony happy housewife in a pretty-poison dream world. The film is an idyll of consumerism. Everything in the suburban development where Pat lives with her advertising-man husband (Charles Grodin) and their two children has a muted artificiality; the style is Necco Deco—a sort of plastic lyricism. The whole family is a little benumbed—like the people in TV commercials, who don't react to anything that doesn't roll on or come in an aerosol can or make the floor shine. Then Pat starts to shrink (because of exposure to the chemicals in the products that the family delights in). Directed by Joel Schumacher, from a script by Jane Wagner (which retains only a few incidents from the Richard Matheson novel that was the basis of the 1957 sci-fi film *The Incredible Shrinking Man*), the picture loses much of its stylized originality when it sets up a good-guys-versus-bad-guys conflict in order to give us a rooting interest in the outcome. But even when it turns into a gimcrack farce it's offhand and likable. Pat, imprisoned in a hamster's cage, finds a friend in a zonked lab technician (Mark Blankfield), and she becomes the beloved of a gorilla named Sidney (played by Rick Baker). It should be a great movie for kids; it's full of toys. With Ned Beatty, Henry Gibson, Elizabeth Wilson, and John Glover. Universal. color (See *Taking It All In*.)

Indagine su un Cittadino al di sopra di Ogni Sospetto, see *Investigation of a Citizen Above Suspicion*

Independence Day (1983)—A fine, quiet movie about the small-town youth of a woman artist whose desperation takes the form of affectations and pretensions. Kathleen Quinlan plays the part with a delicate fierceness—this heroine challenges herself to become what she's *almost* sure she could be. The script is by the novelist Alice Hoffman, who has shaped the story around the risk-taking heroine and her boyfriend's sister (Dianne Wiest), a battered wife, clammy with fear, who revenges herself on her husband in the grand manner. It's a funny thing about Wiest's performance—you keep expecting it to turn into something trite, but pretty soon you're forced to admit you've never seen anything like it. Wiest has hold of an original character and plays her to the scary hilt. Directing his first movie, Robert Mandel keeps the whole cast interacting satisfyingly. With David Keith as the boyfriend, Josef Sommer, Frances Sternhagen, Cliff DeYoung, Richard Farnsworth, Brooke Alderson, and Bert Remsen. Designed by Stewart Campbell; cinematography by Charles Rosher; music by Charles Bernstein. Warners. color (See *State of the Art*.)

Indiana Jones and the Last Crusade (1989)— This mediocre third film in the Indiana Jones trilogy—a reprise of the first, *Raiders of the Lost Ark*—is a mixture of cliff-hanger and anti-Nazi thriller and religious spectacle. It's enjoyable, but familiar, and the action lacks the exhilarating, leaping precision that the director, Steven Spielberg, is famous for. The only real spin is in the slapstick teamwork of Harrison Ford as the archeologist-adventurer Indy and Sean Connery as Indy's father, a medievalist who's too engrossed in his studies to pay much attention to his daredevil son's triumphs. The Ford-Connery clowning can distract you from the doldrums of punches and chases and plot explication (this time the Nazis are after the Holy Grail, which, in this account, confers everlasting life). With River Phoenix playing Indy as a boy, Alison Doody, Denholm Elliott, John

Rhys-Davies, and Julian Glover. The screenplay, by Jeffrey Boam, is based on a story devised by the producer George Lucas and Menno Meyjes. Paramount. color (See *Movie Love*.)

Indiana Jones and the Temple of Doom (1984)—In this follow-up to *Raiders of the Lost Ark*, Steven Spielberg creates an atmosphere of happy disbelief: the more breathtaking and exhilarating the stunts are, the funnier they are. Nobody has ever fused thrills and laughter in quite the way that he does here. Momentum has often been the true—even if not fully acknowledged—subject of movies. Here it's not merely acknowledged, it's gloried in. The picture has an exuberant, hurtling-along spirit. Spielberg starts off at full charge in the opening sequence and just keeps going, yet he seems relaxed, and he doesn't push things to frighten us. The movie relates to Americans' love of getting in the car and taking off—it's a breeze. Harrison Ford is the archeologist-adventurer hero; Ke Huy Quan plays his child sidekick Short Round; and Kate Capshaw is the gold-digger heroine. The plot involves them with an odious boy maharajah and with Mola Ram (an anagram for Malomar), the high priest of a cult of Kali worshippers who come right out of the 1939 adventure comedy *Gunga Din*. This is one of the most sheerly pleasurable physical comedies ever made. A Lucasfilm Production, from a story idea by George Lucas, and a script by Willard Huyck and Gloria Katz. The score by John Williams is too heavy for the tone of the film, and it's too loud. With Amrish Puri as Mola Ram, and Dan Aykroyd in a half-second joke. Paramount. color (See *State of the Art*.)

Indiscreet (1958)—Rather tired. One of those would-be fluffy comedies written by Norman Krasna. Cary Grant, an American diplomat abroad, pretends to be married so

that Ingrid Bergman, an actress with whom he's having an affair, won't get matrimonial ambitions. Of course, he's found out, and the wheels grind on to a happy ending. Stanley Donen directed; Cecil Parker and Phyllis Calvert round out the cast of people who are a little overage for the childish pranks. Released by Warners. color

Indiscretion of an American Wife (1954)—The clashing temperaments of the producer, David Selznick; the director, Vittorio De Sica; and the stars, Jennifer Jones (at the time Mrs. Selznick) and Montgomery Clift, resulted in a very odd (and commercially unsuccessful) love drama, which was shot between many a midnight and dawn at Rome's railway station. De Sica had wanted to film a small-scale Cesare Zavattini story about a love affair that doesn't work out, but agreed to set it in the then new $35 million colossal railway station to satisfy Selznick's desire for grandeur. The film is remarkable chiefly for the way De Sica used Clift: something weak-willed—almost oozingly soft—came through in his performance, and it is impossible to tell how much of this was intended by the actor or the director. It is unlike Clift's work in any other movie. With Richard Beymer and Gino Cervi. Truman Capote worked on the dialogue. b & w

The Informer (1935)—Victor McLaglen in his Academy Award–winning role as Gypo Nolan, the Dublin drunkard who turns stool pigeon and betrays his friend (Wallace Ford) to the police for the reward. The period is 1922, during the Sinn Fein rebellion. This John Ford film, taken from Liam O'Flaherty's fine novel, is perhaps too pure and diagrammatic for modern tastes—Gypo's frenetic, desperate squandering of the reward money, his spasms of fury, of pleasure, of terror, are more clarified than we require now. But if the scenarist, Dudley Nichols, and the director clinched their points, they also had the discipline to keep the work all of a piece—naïve yet powerful. (They also won Academy Awards.) It is part of Hollywood legend that Ford got McLaglen boozed up so that he was bewildered and couldn't do his usual brand of acting—and it's probably true. With Preston Foster, Heather Angel, Una O'Connor, Margot Grahame, Joe Sawyer, and J. M. Kerrigan. The score is by Max Steiner. (Remade, with a black cast, as *Up Tight* in 1968 by Jules Dassin.) R K O. b & w

Ingenjör Andrées Luftfärd, see *The Flight of the Eagle*

Inherit the Wind (1960)—In 1925, in Dayton, Tennessee, a young high-school biology teacher named John T. Scopes instructed his class in Darwin's theory of evolution in order to test a state law forbidding the teaching of anything that "denies the divine creation of man as taught in the Bible." At his trial—the famous Monkey Trial—the great orator William Jennings Bryan, a Bible-thumping fundamentalist who had three times been a candidate for the U.S. Presidency, served as prosecutor; the famous criminal lawyer and agnostic, Clarence Darrow, represented the defense; H. L. Mencken reported the case. This semi-fictionalized version of the events was adapted from the Broadway play by Jerome Lawrence and Robert E. Lee, and produced and directed by Stanley Kramer, for United Artists release. Padded and heavily made up, Fredric March does an embarrassingly hollow imitation of the portly Bryan. Spencer Tracy, whose girth made him the more likely candidate for the role, is cast instead as the lean Darrow, and he plays the part in his patented wise, humane, meant-to-be-irresistible manner. Scopes (Dick York) is portrayed as a man torn between his principles and his love for the local preacher's daughter (Donna Anderson). The movie pre-sents the fundamentalists as foolish bigots, then turns around and tries to make peace with them by coming out against Mencken's satirical outlook (which is equated with cynicism). This Mencken (Gene Kelly) is a brash, hollow, lip-curling villain and Bryan and Darrow join forces to denounce him—"Where will your loneliness lead you? No one will come to your funeral!" The case itself had so many dramatic elements that the movie can't help holding our attention, but it's a very crude piece of work, totally lacking in subtlety; what is meant to be a courtroom drama of ideas comes out as a caricature of a drama of ideas, and, maddeningly, while watching we can't be sure what is based on historical fact and what is invention. With Florence Eldridge, Harry Morgan, and Norman Fell. b & w

The Inheritor *L'Héritier* (1973)—There's so much going on in this talky thriller—flashbacks and crosscutting, plus gadgetry and split-second cityscapes—that you're never allowed any peace. It's a traffic jam of a movie. The director, Philippe Labro, has flash and expertise, but the story (centering on Jean-Paul Belmondo as the inheritor of steel factories and a weekly newsmagazine) is just a glamour fantasy, synthesized from the Bond pictures and the Costa-Gavras political melodramas. It's more exhausting than entertaining. With Carla Gravina, Jean Rochefort, and Charles Denner. Cinematography by Jean Penzer. In French. color

Innerspace (1987)—With Dennis Quaid as a germ-size Navy test pilot floating around inside the bloodstream of a fretful hypochondriac supermarket clerk, played by Martin Short, this sci-fi buddy-buddy comedy sounds stupid-crazy-funky, and at its best that's what it is. But mostly it gets by on being good-natured enough for you to accept its being clumsy and padded and only borderline entertaining. The director, Joe Dante, made his reputation by the subversion of cuddly themes. Here, working from a script by Jeffrey Boam (and Chip Proser) that's a synthesis of the 1966 *Fantastic Voyage* and the 1984 *All of Me*, he seems to be slogging through pages of plot, dutifully trying to set up the mechanics for the gags to pay off. And a lot of the time he's setting up the emotional apparatus to give the movie "heart." Luckily, Quaid comes through even though it's an almost totally encapsulated performance; he may be the only actor who can be infectiously free and breezy while scrunched up inside a pod. The blitheness of Meg Ryan, who's the heroine, gives the picture a lift. And Short has a drunken dance scene in which he's like an insect in convulsive ecstasy. With a large cast that includes Robert Picardo, Wendy Schaal, and Ken Tobey. A Steven Spielberg Production, for Warners. color (See *Hooked*.)

The Innocent *L'Innocente* (1976)—For its first half, this Visconti film, based on the 1892 D'Annunzio novel, is a steamy comedy of manners that seems an almost perfect preparation for a tragicomedy of jealousy, and Visconti's work is masterly in its expressive turn-of-the-century decor, and in its control. Tullio (Giancarlo Giannini), an aristocratic liberal, has become sexually indifferent to his innocent, round-cheeked, country-mousy wife (Laura Antonelli), and has turned to a liaison with an ardent, glittering countess (Jennifer O'Neill). But when this gentle wife becomes interested in another man, he falls passionately in love with her. In the second half, the picture runs out of steam and turns into a ponderous melodrama. Giannini is far from ideally cast, but he seems acceptable until he remembers to act; toward the end he's all over the place acting. Antonelli gives the picture some amusing sexual suspense. At first, she's like a placid ingenue, except that she has furtive yearnings—naughty thoughts. When she's finally nude, in bed, and aroused, she heaves and writhes so prodigiously she's like a storm-tossed sea. It's the kind of passion you learn in a circus: she's a horizontal belly dancer. Visconti had finished shooting this film when he died in 1976, but he did not complete the editing, and perhaps the maundering second half is partly the fault of others. With Marie Dubois as the Princess, Marc Porel as the novelist, Rina Morelli as Tullio's mother, Claude Mann as the Prince, and Massimo Girotti and Didier Haudepin. From a script by Suso Cecchi d'Amico, Enrico Medioli, and Visconti; cinematography by Pasqualino De Santis; art direction by Mario Garbuglai; costumes by Piero Tosi. In Italian. color (See *When the Lights Go Down*.)

Innocent Bystanders (1973)—Misleading title; it's a labyrinthine spy thriller and a revolting example of the constant use of brutality (plus a dash of sexual sadism) to rouse the audience from the apathy brought on by the familiarity of the material. The massively built Stanley Baker is impressive as the tired British secret agent, but he can't save this picture; it's just one noisy beating after another. The major resource of the director, Peter Collinson, appears to be loud karate chops. The members of the M.P.A.A. Rating Board who gave it a PG must have grown calluses on their brains. With Geraldine Chaplin, Dana Andrews, Vladek Sheybal, and Donald Pleasence, who is probably as weary of playing an icy bastard as the audience is weary of watching him. Screenplay by James Mitchell, based on the novel by James Munro. color

L'Innocente, see *The Innocent*

The Innocents (1961)—Directed by Jack Clayton and photographed by Freddie Francis (in CinemaScope, in black and white), this version of Henry James's *The Turn of the Screw*

is one of the most elegantly beautiful ghost movies ever made. It features a scary, intense performance by Deborah Kerr, as the governess who sees demonic spectres and forces one of her two charges—the little boy Miles (Martin Stephens)—to confront them. Both Kerr and Michael Redgrave, as the gentleman who hires her, have just the right note of suppressed hysteria in their voices. The settings—the house, the park, the lake—are magnificent, and the script by William Archibald, Truman Capote, and John Mortimer offers the pleasures of literacy. The filmmakers concentrate on the virtuoso possibilities in the material, and the beauty of the images raises our terror to a higher plane than the simple fears of most ghost stories. There are great sequences (like one in a schoolroom) that work on the viewer's imagination and remain teasingly ambiguous. With Pamela Franklin, Megs Jenkins, Peter Wyngarde, and Clytie Jessop. Music by Georges Auric. Released in the U.S. by 20th Century-Fox. (See *I Lost it at the Movies*.)

Inserts (1976)—The script, by the young writer-director John Byrum, is a long one-act play, reminiscent of Michael McClure's *The Beard*. The action takes place on one set, which represents a house in Hollywood around 1930, where The Boy Wonder (Richard Dreyfuss), a once-famous director whose genius burned out, now shoots stag movies. The picture should be more fun than it is; the plot devices don't add up to much, and Byrum likes his own worst lines so much that they're repeated. He falls back on absurdism by necessity. With Jessica Harper, Bob Hoskins, and, as the stag-movie star, Veronica Cartwright, who flings herself into her role in the dissolute, romantic manner of Jeanne Eagels. She's a grown-up talent in a kid's show. Produced by Davina Belling and Clive Parsons. United Artists. color (See *When the Lights Go Down*.)

Inside Daisy Clover (1966)—Natalie Wood plays the heroine, a teen-age singing movie star (fill in Judy Garland, Deanna Durbin, et al.), in Robert Mulligan's film, based on Gavin Lambert's adaptation of his own novel. The people who make Daisy a star seem to have some terrible secret that we're never let in on; the movie is full of lurking evil that seems unrelated to anything. It's an inside-Hollywood movie with a gothic atmosphere. It's short on characters, detail, activity, dialogue, even music; it's so determined to be stylish and knowing that, rather than risk banality, it eliminates almost everything. What's left are sinister, funereal pauses and a few ghoulish people, such as the head of the studio (Christopher Plummer, whose performance mightn't be so maddening if it were just speeded up). Even the showy recording-room sequence, with the heroine breaking down while post-synching a song with her image on a large screen, doesn't work right—it's *too* showy. The film seems to be working against itself—cynical yet sentimental, it rarely achieves a satisfying emotional tone. Natalie Wood's way of acting teen-age is to be like a brassy Tom Sawyer. As the young star's no-good, vaguely homosexual husband (one of the most cryptic roles ever written), Robert Redford gives the only fresh performance. With Ruth Gordon as Daisy's mother, and Katharine Bard, Roddy McDowall, and Harold Gould. Produced by Alan J. Pakula; choreography by Herbert Ross; art direction by Robert Clatworthy; music and songs by André Previn, with lyrics by Dory Previn. Warners. color

Interiors (1978)—The people in this serious Woody Allen film are destroyed by the repressiveness of good taste, and so is the picture. It's a puzzle movie, constructed like a well-made play from the American past (such as *Craig's Wife*), and given the beautiful, solemn visual clarity of a Bergman film, without, however, the eroticism of Bergman. *Interiors* looks like a masterpiece and has a super-banal metaphysical theme (death versus life). The problem for the family in the film is the towering figure of the disciplined, manipulative, inner-directed mother (Geraldine Page). She is such a perfectionist that she cannot enjoy anything, and the standards of taste and achievement that she imposes on her three daughters (Diane Keaton, Mary Beth Hurt, and Kristin Griffith) tie them in such knots that they all consider themselves failures. (Alvy Singer, the role Woody Allen played in *Annie Hall*, was just such a compulsive, judgmental spoilsport, and Allen's original title for that film was *Anhedonia*—the lack of the capacity for experiencing pleasure.) The mother's impoverished conception of good taste is sustained in the style of the film. It's a handbook of art-film mannerisms; it's so austere and studied that it might have been directed by that icy mother herself—from the grave. Woody Allen's idea of artistic achievement (for himself, at least) may always be something death-ridden, spare, perfectly structured—something that talks of the higher things. People who watch this movie are almost inevitably going to ask themselves, How can Woody Allen present in a measured, lugubriously straight manner the same sorts of tinny anxiety discourse that he generally parodies? With E. G. Marshall, Maureen Stapleton, Richard Jordan, and Sam Waterston. Cinematography by Gordon Willis. United Artists. color (See *When the Lights Go Down*.)

Intermezzo: A Love Story (1939)—David O. Selznick, who arranged this début for Ingrid Bergman in English-speaking films, wasn't going to take any chances; it's a remake of a picture she'd already had a hit with in Sweden, in 1936. Selznick even retained the same slurpy "haunting" theme music. Leslie Howard is the wan and renowned violin virtuoso, afflicted with the boredom of fame and of domestic bliss with his beloved, understanding wife (Edna Best). He falls in love with Bergman, his daughter's piano teacher. Handsome and eager, she's a brilliant young pianist who becomes his accompanist. On a tour of the concert halls of Europe, the two combine business with passion, though at last the finer overtones of conscience separate them. The crisis occurs in a picturesque Mediterranean village—Selznick saw to it that the romantic upheavals of such artistic people got the smartest settings—and there are snacks of Brahms, Liszt, and Grieg to fill out the plump cultural tone. The film's only real claim on anyone's attention is Bergman, whose natural look (full eyebrows, and even a shine on her nose) seemed revolutionary at the time. The first director, William Wyler, was replaced by Gregory Ratoff, and the first cinematographer, Harry Stradling, was replaced by Gregg Toland. With John Halliday, Cecil Kellaway, Enid Bennett, Ann Todd, and Douglas Scott. The script by George O'Neil was based on the Swedish script by Gösta Stevens and Gustaf Molander; the virtuoso violin work was dubbed by Toscha Seidel, the piano work by Norma Drury. (This drippy thing was remade again in 1968 with Oskar Werner, and in 1980 it was loosely adapted for the film *Honeysuckle Rose*.) b & w

Internal Affairs (1989)—Bad fun. This sophisticated variant of the L.A. cops-and-coke-and-art-world thrillers has a creepy, rhythmic quality that sucks you in and keeps you amused. (You may find yourself breaking into a grin when you recommend it to friends.) The subtext is ingeniously nasty: it's a dirty, sexy twist on the Iago-Othello relationship. The Iago is a prosperous veteran cop, played by Richard Gere, who's being investigated by two officers from the Police Department's internal-affairs division: a righteous, ramrod-straight Latino (Andy Garcia) with a beautiful blond wife, and his sane, honest partner (Laurie Metcalf). Gere slithers through the picture very dexterously. He torments the stiff-backed Othello (Garcia), boasting of his adulterous conquest of the blond wife (Nancy Travis), and manipulates him into a jealous rage. Garcia gives a one-note, glaring-eyed performance: except for his key, violent explosions (which are terrific), he's so rigid he's barely human. As Garcia's partner, a lesbian who doesn't try to ingratiate herself with anybody, Metcalf gives a strong, contained performance. Directed by Mike Figgis, whose previous feature was the 1988 *Stormy Monday*. The smart script is by Henry Bean. Paramount. color (See *Movie Love*.)

Intimate Lighting *Intimní Osvětlení* (1965)— A satirical folk comedy about a young cellist with the Prague symphony who takes his big-city girlfriend with him when he goes to visit a friend from his days at the Conservatoire. The musician from Prague is to be the soloist at a concert of the small-town orchestra that the friend now conducts. The director, Ivan Passer, is witty in tiny, match-flare-size details; he shows us lives that have become a negotiation of small irritants. Day-to-day living in the town is like a prolonged silent-movie comedy. (How can a man's drunken friend help him get through double doors after he's got his head stuck?) The people are frustrated in petty ways and they're so fidgety that it's no wonder they make a botch of the music; everything in their lives is the opposite of the music they try to play. You find yourself doing small double-takes as you watch this movie. It builds to a freeze-frame closing gag that's so funny and so completely dotty that you're not likely to forget it. Cinematography by J. Ondříček and J. Strecha; written by V. Šašek, J. Papoušek, and Passer. In Czech. b & w

Intimní Osvětlení, see *Intimate Lighting*

Intolerance (1916)—D. W. Griffith's epic celebration of the potentialities of the film medium—perhaps the greatest movie ever made and the greatest folly in movie history. It is charged with visionary excitement about the power of movies to combine music, dance, narrative, drama, painting, and photography—to do alone what all the other arts together had done. In this extravaganza one can see the source of most of the major traditions of the screen—the methods of Eisenstein and von Stroheim, the Germans and the Scandinavians, and, when it's bad, De Mille. It combines extraordinary lyric passages, realism, and psychological details with nonsense, vulgarity, and painful sentimentality. Four stories set in different historical periods are told by crosscutting, and they reach simultaneous climaxes. The cast includes Lillian Gish in the linking device; Mae Marsh and Robert Harron in the modern story, "The Mother and the Law"; Bessie Love in the Biblical story, "The Nazarene"; Margery Wilson and Eugene Pallette in "The Medieval Story," which includes the St. Bartholomew's Day Massacre of the Huguenots in 1572; Constance Talmadge, Elmo Lincoln, Seena Owen, Alfred Paget, and Tully Marshall in "The Fall of Babylon." Cinematography by Billy Bitzer and Karl Brown; Griffith's assistants included W. S. Van Dyke, Tod Browning, and von Stroheim. Silent. The prints were originally dyed in several hues, and crews of girls added extra color frame by frame; the projectionists were also instructed to throw beams of red and blue light to intensify the effects.

Intruder in the Dust (1949)—Lucas Beauchamp, the "stubborn and insufferable" hero of William Faulkner's novel, is a black man who enrages the white people in his corner of Mississippi by his refusal to play nigger for them. The director, Clarence Brown, shot this movie in Faulkner's home town—Oxford, Mississippi—with the inhabitants in bit parts and in the crowd scenes. "All in all, I think it is a good movie," Faulkner said at the première, and it *is* a good movie—straightforward, tense, and assured. (It is perhaps Brown's finest picture.) As in the novel, inflexible Lucas (Juano Hernández), who refuses to accept condescension or patronage, is conceived as a focus of white ambivalence. The other major character is Chick (Claude Jarman, Jr.), a white boy who has made the stupid mistake of offering Lucas money as payment for hospitality and is humiliated by Lucas's stony refusal. When Lucas is arrested for murder and the townspeople get their chance to turn him into a nigger, Chick finds his opportunity to discharge his debt—by saving Lucas's life. At the very end, a false note is struck by Chick's uncle (David Brian): "It will be all right, as long as some of us are willing to fight—even one of us," and the ultimate cliché, "Lucas wasn't in trouble; *we* were in trouble." It's the movie that gets in trouble. But Juano Hernández's Lucas has the intensity and humor to transcend these Northern liberal platitudes. We can see that, as Faulkner put it, Lucas is "now tyrant over the whole county's white conscience." Two character actors perform with great skill: Porter Hall as the murdered man's father and Elizabeth Patterson as the little old lady who believes in doing what's right. Also with Will Geer and Charles Kemper. The screenplay is by Ben Maddow, with some tinkering by Faulkner (who also helped scout locations); cinematography by Robert Surtees. M-G-M. b & w (See *Kiss Kiss Bang Bang.*)

The Invasion of the Body Snatchers (1956)—A B-picture classic. This plain and inexpensive piece of science fiction employs few of the resources of the cinema (to put it mildly),

but it has an idea that confirms everyone's suspicions. People are being turned into vegetables—and who can tell the difference? Kevin McCarthy and Dana Wynter, who try to cling to their animality and individuality, seem inexplicably backward to the rest of the townspeople. Some of the best lines of dialogue are voice-overs—the chatter of the dehumanized. Directed by Don Siegel, for Allied Artists. With Carolyn Jones, Larry Gates, and Sam Peckinpah (who worked on the script) in a few bits. Based on a *Collier's* serial by Jack Finney; the adaptation is credited to Daniel Mainwaring. Cinematography by Ellsworth Fredericks. b & w

Invasion of the Body Snatchers (1978)—Undiluted pleasure and excitement. The scriptwriter, W. D. (Rick) Richter, supplies some funny lines, and the director, Phil Kaufman, provides such confident professionalism that you sit back in the assurance that every spooky nuance you're catching is just what was intended. This set of variations on the low-budget classic of 1956 has its own macabre originality. Set in San Francisco. With Brooke Adams, Veronica Cartwright, Jeff Goldblum, Donald Sutherland, Art Hindle, Lelia Goldoni, Leonard Nimoy, Kevin McCarthy, Don Siegel, and Robert Duvall, in an uncredited bit. Music by Denny Zeitlin; cinematography by Michael Chapman. United Artists. color (See *When the Lights Go Down.*)

Investigation of a Citizen Above Suspicion *Indagine su un Cittadino al di sopra di Ogni Sospetto* (1970)—Elio Petri's indirect way of telling a story—which gradually takes the form of a paranoid fantasy—makes the viewer apprehensive. His purpose is ostensibly political, but sometimes he becomes so sophisticated and nasty and perverse that you don't trust his purposes. Here, starting with Kafka's cryptic "He is a servant of the law and eludes judgment," he sets out to demonstrate that those in authority are above the law they are supposed to serve. He chooses for his demonstration the megalomaniac chief of Rome's homicide squad (Gian Maria Volonte), who believes he has a license to kill, and has just been promoted to a new post, in which he is to deal with political dissidents. The queasy, tense atmosphere derives not from the horror of the proposition itself but from the kinkiness of the details, such as Ennio Morricone's jangly music when the cop slits the throat of his mistress (Florinda Bolkan). The film is extremely dislikable. Petri is a highly skilled director but he doesn't use suspense pleasurably; he doesn't resolve the tensions, and so you're left in a rather foul mood. In Italian. color (See *Deeper into Movies*.)

The Invisible Man (1933)—James Whale, the director of *Frankenstein*, made this handsomely tricked-up version of H. G. Wells' fantasy, from a well-written adaptation by R. C. Sherriff (and Philip Wylie, though he's not credited); the dialogue is unusually important, since the star (Claude Rains) is disembodied during most of the movie and has to do all his acting with his voice. Rains plays a scientist who experiments with a drug that, while making him invisible, also turns him into a megalomaniac murderer. A little poky but impressively well done, with witty special effects (by John P. Fulton) and traces of the Whale humor that enlivened his *Old Dark House* and *The Bride of Frankenstein*. With blond, bosomy Gloria Stuart—a fleshy heroine for a fleshless hero—and Dudley Digges, Una O'Connor, William Harrigan, Henry Travers, and E. E. Clive. Universal. b & w

The Invisible Man Returns (1940)—Vincent Price and Cedric Hardwicke star in Universal's attempt to repeat the success of James Whale's 1933 picture; Hardwicke is a mur-

derer who contrives that the blame for his crime be put on his victim's brother, and Price is the brother, who escapes from the death cell by means of a chemical that makes him invisible. John P. Fulton is once again in charge of special effects, but this time the director is Joe May, working from a script by Curt Siodmak and Lester Cole. Though the film has its bright moments, and some weird ones, too, the first freshness is gone. Even the effects seem repetitive. With Nan Grey as Price's relentlessly devoted fiancée, and Cecil Kellaway, John Sutton, and Alan Napier. b & w

Invitation to Happiness (1939)—Irene Dunne as a mournful heiress, and Fred MacMurray as a heavyweight boxer whom she marries. They have a nasty little snob of a child, and their marriage seems to be a groan from the start—an uninspired and very long groan. Wesley Ruggles directed, from Claude Binyon's screenplay. With Charles Ruggles. Paramount. b & w

Invitation to the Dance (1956)—This picture bollixed the career of Gene Kelly, who directed and choreographed it, and probably broke his heart as well: practically nobody saw it. The film consists of three ballets, with some pantomime and also some animated-cartoon work. "Circus," set to Jacques Ibert music, features Igor Youskevitch as a high-wire artist, Claire Sombert as a bareback rider in love with him, and Kelly as a clown in love with her; "Ring Around the Rosy," about a bracelet that goes through various hands, has an André Previn score, and the dancers include Youskevitch, Tamara Toumanova, Tommy Rall, and Kelly; "Sinbad the Sailor" features Carol Haney as Scheherazade and Kelly as Sinbad. The film was beset by difficulties. It had to be made in England because that's where M-G-M had frozen funds, and, with interruptions for Kelly to do other jobs, the work spread over three years. He was further hampered by front-office directives—for example, the second ballet was danced to a score that the M-G-M brass didn't like, so Previn had to write a new score to the already filmed dancing. Then the studio put the film on the shelf for another year. There should be an ironic kicker: the picture should be a neglected marvel. But it isn't. Kelly's choreography had always seemed weakest when he became balletic; this picture is set right in his area of least originality. Produced by Arthur Freed. color

The Ipcress File (1965)—Michael Caine as a myopic spy, in Sidney J. Furie's overwrought (and rather silly) version of a Len Deighton novel. This film was a big box-office hit; Caine must have been the chief reason. With Nigel Green. color

Iphigenia (1977)—There's fervor and dedication in Michael Cacoyannis's version of Euripides' *Iphigenia in Aulis*; what's missing is the excitement of a new interpretation. And was there a little too much Arthur Miller in Euripides? (The arguments have an ideological ring.) But Costa Kazakos's robust, irresolute Agamemnon is very fine, and if Irene Papas's performance as Clytemnestra is overscaled, her Clytemnestra certainly makes you believe in the vengeance she will take on Agamemnon. The role suffers from a topical flaw; Clytemnestra's female rage sounds too much like what we heard in the 70s. She has become a precursor, and less of a character. There's also a problem of style: the film is all rocks and scrub brush and Clytemnestra swelling with wrath and Menelaus (Costa Carras) expostulating. Performed this way, *Iphigenia* is like a wildlife film about rhinoceroses—everybody's snorting at each other. With Tatiana Papamoskou as the young heroine. In Greek. color (See *When the Lights Go Down*.)

Irene (1940)—This pre-camp version of the musical comedy (by James H. Montgomery, with music and lyrics by Harry Tierney and Joseph McCarthy) tries to be innocuously charming, and the effort is all too evident. The English director Herbert Wilcox and his star, Anna Neagle (who later became his wife), made a series of costume pictures (*Peg of Old Drury*, *Victoria the Great*, *Nurse Edith Cavell*, etc.), and a series of musicals (*Irene*; *Sunny*; *No, No, Nanette*) based on sweet, safe, dated shows. This one surrounded its star with Ray Milland, Roland Young, May Robson, Arthur Treacher, Billie Burke, and Alan Marshal, and it was the biggest hit R K O had that year, but it dismally lacks vivacity, and when Anna Neagle sings "Sweet Little Alice Blue Gown," she is not the pretty young comedienne of one's musical-comedy dreams. The screenplay is by Alice Duer Miller. b & w and color

Irma la Douce (1963)—Abominable, inexplicably popular sex farce, adapted from a stage musical comedy, but with the score omitted. Billy Wilder, the producer-director, and his co-scenarist, I.A.L. Diamond, hit us over the head with the old rotten jest that prostitution is a petit-bourgeois way of life like any other. Shirley MacLaine and Jack Lemmon, vivid and gifted comics, wrestle painfully with the gross dialogue. Sample: MacLaine, showing Lemmon her attic apartment, explains that it once belonged to an artist who cut off his ear. "Oh," says Lemmon. "Was his name van Gogh?" "No," says MacLaine, "Schwartz." With Lou Jacobi and Herschel Bernardi. United Artists. color

Ironweed (1987)—The director, Hector Babenco, treats William Kennedy's Albany novel, set in 1938, as a joyless classic; the movie has no momentum—the running time (144 minutes) is like a death sentence. As Francis Phelan, the alcoholic hobo hero who is torn by guilt over the family he deserted 22 years ago and sees the phantoms of men he has done violence to, Jack Nicholson seems to be in a slow-motion dream. He drops his voice down so heroically low he even has to talk slowly. And Meryl Streep, who is Francis's hobo crony Helen, forces her voice down deep, too. The only moments of reprieve from all the sombre artistry come when Streep sings "He's Me Pal" in the all-out, sentimental-Irish manner of a balladeer of a decade or two earlier; it's a spectacular re-creation of the old technique for "selling a song." Tom Waits, Hy Anzell, and Margaret Whitton provide brief changes of mood and emotion. Also with Carroll Baker, Fred Gwynne, Diane Venora, Michael O'Keefe, Laura Esterman, Priscilla Smith, and Black-Eyed Susan. The screenplay is by Kennedy. Released by Tri-Star. color (See *Hooked*.)

Is There Sex After Death? (1971)—Porno-spoof with the usual sex scenes and the usual sex jokes. And the usual fatigue factor, because the gags in films of this type are repetitive and interchangeable. However, this one has some funnier-than-usual skits involving Buck Henry, Jim Moran, and Marshall Efron. At times it's like a college revue gone wild, and partly because of its photographic quality and the use of pastels you don't get that depressed, crummy feeling that usually settles in with the first shots of a porny picture. Written, directed, and produced by Jeanne and Alan Abel. color (See *Deeper into Movies*.)

Isabel (1968)—The setting is the Gaspé coast of Canada. Geneviève Bujold with her hair cropped is a sensitive young girl haunted by the mysterious violent deaths in her family. It turns out that she is probably the daughter of her mother's brother, and in the omens-of-doom dramaturgy of the Canadian writer-director Paul Almond, this is sufficient excuse

for her to "give herself" to a man who resembles her brother. Not a movie for the tough-minded. With Mark Strange, who also wrote the songs. color

Ishtar (1987)—Written and directed by Elaine May, this must have started out to be a casual, tacky *Road to* comedy about two aging nonentities—singer-songwriters (Warren Beatty and Dustin Hoffman) who can only be booked into faraway night spots. Dreaming of show-business success, they arrive in the Middle East and get caught up in revolutionary politics they don't know a thing about. Though determinedly inconsequential, the picture was made on authentic locations and in a glamorous romantic style; it gets stalled in exposition and in the sand of the Sahara. It isn't dislikable, but it has no comic energy. May's directing is limp, passive; she doesn't do the obvious, but sometimes she doesn't do anything else, either. And when Beatty and Hoffman play small-timers it's a reverse conceit, a form of affectation. Besides, they don't have the kind of sketch-humor savvy to goof off gracefully. They do have a great desert scene with a troupe of unusually handsome, well-groomed vultures. And there are performers who bring some charge with them: Jack Weston, as the team's two-bit hustling agent; Rose Arrick, in a tiny role as Hoffman's mother. And, as the C.I.A. villain, Charles Grodin manages to be fairly amusing because of his bland, whiny *lack* of charge. With Isabelle Adjani, whose pure, childlike face peeps out of the dark Moroccan clothes she's swathed in; she seems hidden in the picture. Also with Tess Harper, Carol Kane, Aharon Ipalé, and Herb Gardner. Cinematography by Vittorio Storaro. Columbia. color (See *Hooked*.)

The Island (1961)—A ponderously simple Japanese film by Kaneto Shindo that aims at universality by stripping away all the particularities—which are considered to be the nonessentials of civilization and personality. The result is something so barren that those who acclaim it as a masterpiece seem to be asserting proof of virtue. It's about a family living on an island without fresh water: the family members' life is a succession of trips to the mainland for water, which they then carry by shoulder yoke up steep paths to pour over their crops. The film is made without dialogue, and this silence of the characters has been widely commended as the perfect use of silence—the demonstration that the family gives all its energy to the effort to stay alive and has no need for idle talk. We are supposed to regard this preverbal existence and the silent struggle with elemental forces as more basic, more "true to nature," and hence greater than our talky superficial lives. (If the members of this island family—so sure of their relationships to each other and to the earth and water and plants that they have nothing to say—ever figure out how to get a pipeline in from the mainland, they'll be liberated from that primal struggle with the elements and soon they'll be on their path to conversation and what—in Kaneto Shindo's view—is probably sophistication, corruption, and decadence.) Though we are spared the kind of uplifting film conversation that filmmakers with this approach usually provide (the lean, true words of real people), the images are saturated with a musical score of prodigious monotony. *The Island* was made on a small budget, and its pictorial qualities have been highly praised. It's pictorial, all right. b & w

Islands in the Stream (1977)—The implacable stodginess of this Franklin J. Schaffner version of Hemingway's posthumous novel is stupefying yet impressive. It's fascinating to see Hemingway's themes placed in this huge glass jar for our inspection. George C. Scott gives a scrupulous performance as the fisherman-artist hero living in the Bahamas at the outbreak of the Second World War, who is visited by his three sons from two broken marriages, and then by his first wife (Claire Bloom). By being respectful and dedicated, and incompetent at action, Schaffner and his scenarist, Denne Bart Petitclerc, bring out the worst in Hemingway—his mystique. Scott's features are totally unlike Hemingway's, but with a crew cut, a grizzled gray-white beard, neatly clipped, the chestiness, and the familiar Hemingway shirts and shorts and bush jackets, Scott suggests Hemingway as he looked on the *Time* cover in 1954, when he won the Nobel Prize—reflective, slightly withdrawn. Scott's artist-hero, a titan with slate-blue eyes, a crumbled nose, and a booze-busted, I've-been-through-hell voice, is terribly grand. Everyone else in the movie is a child compared with him. With Julius Harris, David Hemmings, Gilbert Roland, Hart Bochner, Brad Savage, and Michael-James Wixted as the middle boy, Davy. Paramount. color (See *When the Lights Go Down*.)

Isle of the Dead (1945)—Val Lewton produced, but except for a few touches, it's a mess—something about demons on a plague-ridden Greek island, involving premature burial and evil possession of the resurrected body. Boris Karloff and Katherine Emery are the leads; she comes out of her crypt and starts stabbing people with a trident. With Ellen Drew, Alan Napier, and Jason Robards, Sr., in a surprisingly poor performance. Mark Robson directed. R K O. b & w

It Happened One Night (1934)—No one has ever fully explained what gives this basically slight romantic comedy its particular—and enormous—charm. It's no more than the story of a runaway heiress (Claudette Colbert) and a fired newspaperman (Clark Gable) who meet on a long-distance night bus and fall in love. Yet the film (which neither of its stars wanted to appear in) caught on with the public and made audiences happy in a way that only a few films in each era do; in the mid-30s, the Colbert and the Gable of this film became Americans' idealized view of themselves—breezy, likable, sexy, gallant, and maybe just a little harebrained. (It was the *Annie Hall* of its day—before the invention of anxiety.) It has a special American Depression-era on-the-road humor and an open, episodic form, with oddball mashers and crooks turning up. There's a classic singing sequence (the passengers on the bus join together for "The Man on the Flying Trapeze") and a classic demonstration of hitchhikers' techniques for stopping cars—Gable's thumb versus Colbert's legs. The two stars interact with easy, on-the-button timing; Gable has a gift for seeming virile even at his most foolish, and when things go wrong Colbert manages to look starry-eyed and blankly depressed at the same time. Frank Capra directed, from Robert Riskin's script, based on Samuel Hopkins Adams' short story "Night Bus." With Walter Connolly, Roscoe Karns, Alan Hale, Ward Bond, Arthur Hoyt, and as the jilted bridegroom, Jameson Thomas. Five Academy Awards: Picture, Director, Actor, Actress, Script. (Remade in 1956 as *You Can't Run Away from It.*) Columbia. b & w

It Should Happen to You (1954)—Judy Holliday in a pleasantly erratic satirical comedy; the targets—advertising, TV, and urban gullibility—are rather easily pinked, but the scenarist, Garson Kanin, and the director, George Cukor, don't loiter over them for long. (Still, the film runs down.) The heroine, who yearns for celebrity, takes her life savings and places her name—Gladys Glover—in giant letters across a billboard in Columbus Circle. Before long, she is as inescapably in the public eye as one of the Gabors. She also tosses about in romantic indecision: Should she give her heart to an honest documentary filmmaker (Jack Lemmon, in his Hollywood début) and say farewell to the big time, or should she surrender herself to the sudsy embraces of a soap manufacturer (Peter Lawford)? With Connie Gilchrist, Melville Cooper, and Michael O'Shea, who is particularly funny as a seedy entrepreneur. There are also appearances by Constance Bennett, Ilka Chase, and Wendy Barrie as themselves. Columbia. b & w

It Started with Eve (1941)—Deanna Durbin as a waif who gets involved with the family of a saintly old millionaire (Charles Laughton). He plays Cupid and schemes to have his grandson marry her. And you need the stomach of a saint to sit through it. Joe Pasternak produced, Henry Koster directed, and Norman Krasna was one of the writers. (Durbin does only some incidental singing.) Universal. b & w

The Italian Straw Hat *Un Chapeau de paille d'Italie* (1927)—René Clair took the Eugène Labiche and Marc Michel play that Bergson used to illustrate his theory of comedy and turned it into a model of visual wit. This silent satire on middle-class pretension is so expertly timed and so elegantly directed that farce becomes ballet. With Albert Préjean as the bridegroom. Designed by Lazare Meerson. b & w

It's a Wonderful Life (1946)—Frank Capra's most relentless lump-in-the-throat movie. The hero (James Stewart) is a self-sacrificial good man who runs a small-town building-and-loan association that is threatened by the local ogre, the wickedly selfish Lionel Barrymore. Thinking he has no resources left, the hero is on the brink of suicide when he is given a vision of what life would be like for his family and his town if he had never been born. Donna Reed plays his wife, Gloria Grahame is the town "fast" girl, and the excruciatingly familiar cast includes Thomas Mitchell, Henry Travers, Beulah Bondi, Ward Bond, H. B. Warner, and Samuel S. Hinds. In its own slurpy, bittersweet way, the picture is well done. But it's fairly humorless, and, what with all the hero's virtuous suffering, it didn't catch on with the public. Capra takes a serious tone here though there's no basis for the seriousness; this is doggerel trying to pass as art. It's not just that it didn't match the post–Second World War mood—it might have seemed patronizing even in the post–First World War period. This picture developed a considerable—if bewildering—reputation, based largely on television viewing, about three decades later. (Marlo Thomas played the suffering protagonist in the 1977 TV-movie remake, *It Happened One Christmas*.) R K O. b & w

It's a Wonderful World (1939)—The title presses the point, and so does the lunatic comedy-mystery. In the role of a tough-minded, devil-may-care poet, Claudette Colbert is forced to strain for laughs; the gag-filled script, by Ben Hecht and Herman J. Mankiewicz involves her with crooks, cops, amateur actors, and Boy Scouts, and requires her to knock a man out. James Stewart plays opposite her as a detective. With Guy Kibbee, who gets whacked a lot; Ernest Truex, who is almost electrocuted; and Nat Pendleton and Edgar Kennedy. Directed by W. S. Van Dyke. It's fast-paced but far from memorable. M-G-M. b & w

It's Always Fair Weather (1955)—The title is a misnomer. Comden and Green's tart follow-up to *On the Town*, and directed by the same team (Gene Kelly and Stanley Donen), is like a delayed hangover. The three buddies are now Kelly, Dan Dailey, and Michael Kidd; at war's end they swear eternal friendship and promise to meet in ten years. At their reunion, they discover that they hate each other and themselves, and go looking for the hopes they abandoned. The film's mixture of parody, cynicism, and song and dance is perhaps a little sour; though the numbers are exhilarating and the movie is really much more fun than the wildly overrated *On the Town*, it doesn't sell exuberance in that big, toothy way, and it was a box-office failure. As the sickened advertising man, Dan Dailey has the best routine in the film—a Chaplinesque, drunken satire of "advertising-wise" jargon. (To a great extent this is Dailey's movie.) Dolores Gray's role (as a TV star) is too broadly written, but her smooth, glib style is refreshingly brassy and she has a dazzling number—"Thanks a lot but no thanks"; Cyd Charisse is beautiful and benumbed until she unhinges her legs in the Stillman's Gym number. Produced by Arthur Freed, for M-G-M. CinemaScope, color

It's Love I'm After (1937)—A light farce in which Leslie Howard and Bette Davis play a shallow, vanity-ridden matinée idol and his hot-tempered leading lady, and relish every hammy, slapstick minute of it. They are surrounded by the millionaires (George Barbier), valets and butlers (Eric Blore, E. E. Clive), and silly heiresses (Olivia de Havilland) who were at one time as much of a convention in American comedy as the fops of Restoration theatre. Casey Robinson's script (from a story written for the screen by Maurice Hanline) is musty and Archie Mayo's direction is sluggish, but the movie is pleasantly bad. It begins with a burlesque of the tomb scene from *Romeo and Juliet* and proceeds like a somewhat deranged *Taming of the Shrew*. With Bonita Granville, Patric Knowles, and Spring Byington. Warners. b & w

Ivan the Terrible, Parts I and II *Ivan Grosny* (1944–46)—Eisenstein's two-part extravaganza on the evils of tyranny is obviously a magnificent work and it imposes its style on the viewer, yet it's so lacking in human dimensions that you may stare at it in a kind of outrage. True, every frame in it looks great—it's a brilliant collection of stills—but as a movie, it's static, grandiose, and frequently ludicrous, with elaborately angled, overcomposed photography, and overwrought, eyeball-rolling performers slipping in and out of the walls, dragging their shadows behind them. The city of Alma Ata was rebuilt full scale in Central Asia with lumber imported from Siberia, and millions of rubles worth of sets, beards, and brocades went into it—it's a heavy dose of decor. In *Part I*, released in 1945, Ivan is crowned, and then because of the opposition of the boyars (or nobles) who, among their evil deeds, poison his wife, he is forced to abdicate. *Part II*, which Eisenstein called *The Boyars' Plot*, was his last film. Made in 1945–46, censured by the Central Committee and suppressed, it was not released until five years after Stalin's death (the director, still in disgrace, had died in 1948). In *Part II* the boyars strike again. Ivan has been restored to power with the help of "the people," but, under the leadership of Ivan's ratty old aunt Efrosinia, who hopes to put her (crazy? homosexual? both?) son on the throne, the boyars plot to assassinate Ivan. He outwits them and destroys their power in a big, bloody purge. All this may suggest a libretto. The movie *is* operatic—and opera without singers is a peculiar form. Something momentous seems about to be imparted to us in each great frozen composition; it's almost as if the aria were about to begin. (In one of the most satisfying moments in *Part I* there *is* a song.) Overpowering in style, the movie resembles a gigantic Expressionist mural. The figures are like giant spiders and rodents: as in science fiction, some horrible mutation seems to have taken place. The conflict in Ivan is between the good man dedicated to the welfare of his people and the power-mad despot (and, given when it was made, it's easy to see a parallel to Stalin). Oddly, the makeup that Nikolai Cherkassov uses as Ivan seems to be based on Conrad Veidt's makeup in Paul Leni's 1924 film *Waxworks*, in which Ivan was used simply as a horror figure (the decor and camera work also recall *Waxworks*). And as James Agee pointed out, Eisenstein gave Cherkassov "a chin and cranium which becomes ever more pointed, like John Barrymore as Mr. Hyde." In some ways the film *is* close to the horror genre. It's as mysterious to the American eye and mind as Kabuki, to which it is often compared. Music by Prokofiev; cinematography by Edward Tisse, assisted by Andrei Moskvin on *Part II*. In Russian. b & w, with one long sequence in *Part II* in rich, experimental color

Ivanhoe (1952)—What a ruckus! Everybody in 12th-century England is fighting everybody else—lunging at one another with long lances while on horseback, or throwing rocks off the parapets of keeps, or raising and lowering drawbridges over moats and plunging shouting, screaming men into the water below. In between, barbecue pits are made ready for human roasts and stakes are erected for the purpose of burning beautiful young women. The Normans, who have pledged their allegiance to Prince John (Guy Rolfe), are at war with the Saxons, who are committed to Richard the Lion-Hearted (Norman Wooland), and the Saxon hero Wilfred of Ivanhoe (Robert Taylor) is trying to raise the ransom money to free Richard from his foreign captors. Ivanhoe is also attentive to the fair Rowena (Joan Fontaine) and to the dark, sensitive Jewish outcast Rebecca (Elizabeth

Taylor). Elizabeth Taylor, just turned 20, is so eerily beautiful that Fontaine, ordinarily a great beauty in her own right, seems pallid and smarmy. The big clash between Ivanhoe and the villain (George Sanders) is unaccountably brutal—they go at each other with axes and heavy spiked balls attached to chains. No one could say this wasn't a rousing movie. It's also romantic, big, commercial, and slick, in the M-G-M grand manner.

Produced by Pandro S. Berman, directed by Richard Thorpe, and made in England, it was shot by Freddie Young (who was later to do *Lawrence of Arabia*). With Emlyn Williams, Finlay Currie, Felix Aylmer, Basil Sydney, Robert Douglas, Harold Warrender, Sebastian Cabot, and Valentine Dyall. Screenplay by Noel Langley, from the Walter Scott novel; art direction by Alfred Junge; score by Miklós Rózsa. color

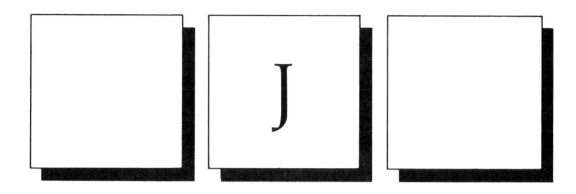

Jag Ar Nyfiken, see *I am Curious—Yellow*

Jagged Edge (1985)—This thriller doesn't offer the pleasures of style, but it does its job. It catches you in a vise—it's scary, and when it's over you feel a little shaken. Jeff Bridges plays the San Francisco newspaper publisher-editor who is tried for the murder of his rich wife, who owned the paper; Peter Coyote is the D.A. prosecuting him; and Glenn Close is the radiantly blond woman lawyer who defends him, and falls in love with him. She's the star of the movie; we feel an immediate, empathic connection with her excitement. Good thrillers have an electric current running through them; here it runs through her performance, and then charges the film's last section. Working from a script by Joe Eszterhas that's smart, pared down, and efficient, the director, Richard Marquand, sets up the situations and delivers the payoffs; he doesn't show much in the way of imagination or devotion to craft, but he gets distinctively pungent performances. Bridges is marvellously hooded; you can't read his emotions. (This is some of the best work he has done.) And Coyote's D.A. has a suggestion of something rancid and vindictive. As the profane, hard-drinking private investigator who tracks down witnesses for the defense, Robert Loggia provides a few puckish curlicues and walks off with his scenes. Also with Leigh Taylor-Young, Marshall Colt, and, as a final surprise witness, Karen Austin, in an intense scene that has a porno queasiness about it. Columbia. color (See *Hooked*.)

Jailhouse Rock (1957)—Elvis Presley, convicted of manslaughter and shorn by a jailhouse haircut, sings and plays the guitar to entertain the prison inmates. At one point, he strips to the waist and the guards flog him, though not for his singing. Richard Thorpe directed this package, shrewdly designed to give satisfaction to the new raunchy rock generation. The story ends happily, and the movie made millions, though Presley never begins to suggest the vitality that he showed in documentary footage. With Judy Tyler, Dean Jones, and Mickey Shaughnessy. Script by Guy Trosper, from a story by Ned Young. M-G-M. b & w

Jalsaghar, see *The Music Room*

Jamaica Inn (1939)—A forgettable, generally forgotten Hitchcock gothic, from a Daphne du Maurier novel, full of Cornwall shipwrecks and smuggling and murder in the time of good King George IV. The picture is dominated by Charles Laughton (with a false beak) as an evil, bound-to-go-mad rake; his flamboyant ghoulishness appears to have paralyzed Hitchcock, whose staging of the wild flights from assassins, the midnight escapes, the prowlings up and down corridors, over roofs, through barnyards, and over moors is almost shockingly uninspired. With Maureen O'Hara, who is a very dim heroine here, Emlyn Williams enjoying himself playing a sinister scamp, and Leslie Banks, Robert Newton, and Marie Ney. The picture was produced (by Erich Pommer) on a large scale; the Regency costumes seem to overpower the performers and the inn is packed with crowds of actors impersonating violent, hard-drinking louts—Graham Greene said that they were "reminiscent of the noisier characters in Shakespeare acted at a girls' school." Written by Sidney Gilliat, Joan Harrison, and J. B. Priestley. b & w

El Jardín de las Delicias, see *The Garden of Delights*

Jaws (1975)—It may be the most cheerfully perverse scare movie ever made. Even while you're convulsed with laughter you're still apprehensive, because the editing rhythms are very tricky, and the shock images loom up huge, right on top of you. The film belongs to the pulpiest sci-fi monster-movie tradition, yet it stands some of the old conventions on their head. Though *Jaws* has more zest than an early Woody Allen picture, and a lot more electricity, it's funny in a Woody Allen way. When the three protagonists are in their tiny boat, trying to find the shark that has been devouring people, you feel that Robert Shaw, the malevolent old shark hunter, is so manly that he wants to get them all killed; he's so manly he's hom-

icidal. When Shaw begins showing off his wounds, the bookish ichthyologist, Richard Dreyfuss, strings along with him at first, and matches him scar for scar. But when the ichthyologist is outclassed in the number of scars he can exhibit, he opens his shirt, looks down at his hairy chest, and with a put-on artist's grin says, "You see that? Right there? That was Mary Ellen Moffit—she broke my heart." Shaw squeezes an empty beer can flat; Dreyfuss satirizes him by crumpling a Styrofoam cup. The director, Steven Spielberg, sets up bare-chested heroism as a joke and scores off it all through the movie. The third protagonist, acted by Roy Scheider, is a former New York City policeman who has just escaped the city dangers and found a haven as chief of police in the island community that is losing its swimmers; he doesn't know one end of a boat from the other. But the fool on board isn't the chief of police, or the bookman, either. It's Shaw, the obsessively masculine fisherman, who thinks he's got to prove himself by fighting the shark practically single-handed. The high point of the film's humor is in our seeing Shaw get it; this nut Ahab, with his hypermasculine basso-profundo speeches, stands in for all the men who have to show they're tougher than anybody. The shark's cavernous jaws demonstrate how little his toughness finally adds up to. This primal-terror comedy quickly became one of the top-grossing films of all time. With Lorraine Gary; Murray Hamilton; Carl Gottlieb, who co-wrote the (uneven) script with Peter Benchley, as Meadows; and Benchley, whose best-seller novel the script was based on, as an interviewer. Cinematography by Bill Butler; editing by Verna Fields; music by John Williams. Produced by Richard D. Zanuck and David Brown, for Universal. (Spielberg didn't direct the sequels—the 1978 *Jaws 2*, the 1983 *Jaws 3-D*, and the 1987 *Jaws the Revenge*.) color (See *When the Lights Go Down*.)

Jazz on a Summer's Day (1960)—The 1958 Newport Jazz Festival, with Anita O'Day, Big Maybelle, Dinah Washington, Gerry Mulligan, Thelonious Monk, Chico Hamilton, Louis Armstrong and Jack Teagarden, and other joys. Bert Stern's camera style infectiously conveys the festival's happy, lazy-day atmosphere; the America's Cup observation trials, which are also going on, are an unstressed part of the film's visual texture. In the evening, when Mahalia Jackson, with her majestic chest tones, sings the word "soul," she defines it for all time. This is one of the most pleasurable of all concert films. Aram Avakian edited. color

Jean de Florette (1987)—The setting is Provence in the early 1920s. As the hunchback Jean de Florette, an educated, nature-loving city fellow who has learned about farming from books, Gérard Depardieu wears "GOOD MAN" in capital letters across his wide brow; in smaller letters we can read "He has poetry in his soul." Jean has a devoted wife (Elisabeth Depardieu), who used to sing in opera, and a delicate little daughter named Manon. And for slightly over two hours we watch him trudge across the land he has inherited hauling two barrels of water that are fastened across his hump. When there's no rain, his plants shrivel and his rabbits die, and it's agonizing for us, because we know that there's a spring of fresh mountain water on the land. His neighbors—the prosperous, greedy old peasant César Soubeyran (Yves Montand) and César's dull-witted nephew, Ugolin (Daniel Auteuil)—have hidden the spring under a load of cement, so that Jean will be forced to sell out to them. Adapted from the first volume of Marcel Pagnol's two-part novel *The Water of the Hills*, published in 1963 (it was derived from a picture he made in 1952), *Jean de Florette* was followed by *Manon of the Spring*. The director, Claude Berri, who did the adaptation with Gérard Brach, aimed for fidelity to the novel; he said that it was his task to give the material "a cinematic rhythm," but "there was no need for imagination." That's what *he* thinks. The widescreen cinematography is by Bruno Nuytten. In French. color (See *Hooked*.)

Jeannie (1942)—This English comedy is a small joy, and it doesn't turn up nearly often enough. Barbara Mullen gives a lovely, delicately toned performance as the Scottish peasant who might have been a prim, lonely spinster forever if she hadn't come into an inheritance and taken a trip to prewar Vienna. The surrounding material isn't in a class with Mullen (who was actually American-born), but it's inoffensive, with Michael Redgrave, ingratiating as a British businessman, Albert Lieven as a rotter of a count, Wilfrid Lawson, Googie Withers, and Kay Hammond. Directed by Harold French, from a play by Aimee Stuart. b & w

Jeder für Sich und Gott Gegen Alle, see *The Mystery of Kaspar Hauser*

Jenny Lamour, see *Quai des Orfèvres*

Jeremiah Johnson (1972)—Robert Redford doing a self-consciously cool version of a strong, silent Western loner. The movie crawls through the wilderness at a snail's pace and is stretched out with ponderous lore. It celebrates tooth-and-claw revenge while featuring the kind of pithy dialogue that produces bellyache: "Keep your nose to the wind and your eye to the skyline." Directed by Sydney Pollack; written by John Milius and Edward Anhalt. With Will Geer and Allyn McLerie. Warners. color (See *Reeling*.)

Les Jeux de l'amour, see *The Love Game*

Jeux interdits, see *Forbidden Games*

Jezebel (1938)—A dazzling romantic melodrama. Bette Davis is impulsive, complex Julie, the Southern belle who destroys her chances for happiness by perversely flouting convention. William Wyler produced and directed this sumptuous, moss-hung evocation of pre–Civil War New Orleans, with its great balls where tradition decreed that unmarried ladies dress in white—and where Julie's red dress wrecks her life. It's hard to know which is Davis's "big scene" in the movie—the painful, flamboyant error of her appearance in red, or the breathtaking moment of her apology in white. The material was already dated but was brought out of mothballs and refurbished because of the popularity of the novel *Gone with the Wind*, which the production beat to the screen; without the zing Davis gave it, it would have looked very mossy indeed. She took the Academy Award as Best Actress. With Henry Fonda, George Brent, Margaret Lindsay, Richard Cromwell, John Litel, Donald Crisp, Spring Byington, Eddie Anderson, Henry O'Neill, Irving Pichel, and Fay Bainter (Best Supporting Actress). The script by Clements Ripley, Abem Finkel, and John Huston (based on a play by Owen Davis, Sr.) has some remarkable passages. Cinematography by Ernest Haller; music by Max Steiner. Warners. b & w

Jigokumon, see *Gate of Hell*

The Jinx (1953)—Luigi Zampa directed this 16-minute film adapted from Pirandello's *La Patente*, a satirical comedy about a man who tries to capitalize on his own bad luck. It stars the great clown Totò, who died in 1967. Off stage and screen he was Antonio, Prince De Curtis, and his titles included Prince of Byzantium, Cilicia, Macedonia, Thessaly, and Ponte; Duke of Cyprus and Epirus; Count of Drivasto and Durazzo, Noble Knight of the Holy Roman Empire. No wonder he looked at us with those tired eyes that had seen everything. Here, he is Don Rosario, who tries to be officially certified as the local jinx, so that people will pay him to stay away from them, and he is a world and a style unto himself. In Italian. b & w

Jinxed! (1982)—Bette Midler rates better material than this frazzled screwball romance. Even the movies it was lifted from (such as *The Only Game in Town*) are bad. Midler is a great mischief, and she turns even moderately amusing lines into zingers, but the situations don't go anywhere. She plays an entertainer in the casinos at Lake Tahoe and Reno who lives with a sadistic gambler (Rip Torn)—he likes to beat her up. Though Midler has her spandex pants and her wiggle-walk and the lewd twinkle in her eyes, the character has been so thinly conceived that all she can do is play comic mannerisms. She invents like a crazy dynamo and she turns the movie into a one-woman comedy show, but you can see what the effort is costing her and she carries only part of it. There's a good frantic routine: between the stanzas of a rowdy medley that she's singing onstage, she bumps and grinds her way to the wings where her new lover (Ken Wahl), a young blackjack dealer, is standing, and without losing her rhythm she hisses out the procedures of a plan to murder the hateful sadist. Ken Wahl doesn't prosper in this picture; the camera seems to zero in on his handsome, clear-eyed face just when he's pleading for the director's help. He has been turned into a TV-style hunk. And Midler's platinum hairdo bleaches out her rosiness and her radiance. Don Siegel directed, from a script by Bert Blessing (a pseudonym for Frank Gilroy, who wrote *The Only Game in Town*), which was then reworked by David Newman; it suggests a sprinkling of James M. Cain novels. With Val Avery, Jack Elam, and Benson Fong. M-G-M/United Artists. color (See *Taking It All In*.)

Jo Jo Dancer, Your Life Is Calling (1986)—Richard Pryor produced, directed, and is the star of this semi-autobiographical movie, which opens with Jo Jo the cokehead comedy star preparing to freebase and bursting into flame. Then, as he lies swathed in bandages in the burn ward, he thinks back over how he got there. But Pryor doesn't have the skills to tell his story in this form. As a standup entertainer, he sees the crazy side of his sorrows; he transforms pain and chaos into comedy. As a moviemaker, he's a novice presenting us with clumps of unformed experience. It isn't even raw; the juice has been drained away. He was himself—demons, genius, and all—in *Richard Pryor Live in Concert* and, though to a lesser extent, in *Richard Pryor Live on the Sunset Strip*. Here, trying to be sincere, he's less than himself. With E'lon Cox as the 8-year-old Jo Jo, Carmen McRae as his grandmother, Diahnne Abbott as his mother, Scoey Mitchlll as his father, Paula Kelly and Billy Eckstine as the grown-up Jo Jo's friends, Fay Hauser, Barbara Williams, Debbie Allen, and Tanya Boyd as his wives, and Art Evans, Wings Hauser, Marlene Warfield, and J. J. Barry. The script was written by Rocco Urbisci, Paul Mooney, and Pryor. Cinematography by John Alonzo; production design by John De Cuir. Columbia. color (See *Hooked*.)

Joe Hill (1971)—The Swedish writer-director Bo Widerberg (*Elvira Madigan, Adalen 31*) made this life of the Swedish emigrant to America—a troubadour—who became a member of the Industrial Workers of the World and was convicted of murder and executed. There are some pretty period re-creations here, but it's a sadly shallow movie. It looks exactly like Widerberg's Swedish films, and the dreamy, pastoral look seems all wrong for the subject; the imagery has no strength or moral outrage—everything is subtly off. Widerberg doesn't catch the Wob- blies' spirit or humor; the U.S. here is an idyllic fascist country. Thommy Berggren plays the young hero-martyr who was celebrated in the ballad by Alfred Hayes and Earl Robinson. Many of the American locations had to be faked in Sweden; the dialogue is mainly in English. Released by Paramount. color

John and Mary (1969)—Dustin Hoffman picks up Mia Farrow at a singles bar. It's meant to be a magical modern romance; there's no magic but it's clever and dexterous, in a wispy sort of way. It leaves a bad aftertaste, though, because you can feel the presence of regiments of technicians hiding behind the butterfly's wing and trying to make it iridescent. John has a block—not a sexual one but reservations about opening his life to feeling; the understanding little Mary sticks around until the block is overcome. Remember when that man in *The Graduate* told Hoffman to go into plastics? Well, he did when he made this one. With Michael Tolan and Tyne Daly. Directed by Peter Yates, from John Mortimer's script, based on a novel by Mervyn Jones; music by Quincy Jones. 20th Century-Fox. color (See *Deeper into Movies*.)

Johnny Belinda (1948)—Jane Wyman, previously known as a giddy second-string blonde, surprised audiences with her touching performance as the brunette deaf-mute Belinda and won an Academy Award. The setting is an island off Nova Scotia, where a poor, proud farmer, appropriately named McDonald (Charles Bickford), lives with his acidulous sister (Agnes Moorehead) and his afflicted daughter, who is generally regarded as an idiot. Along comes a kindly young doctor (Lew Ayres), who teaches her sign language and encourages her to comb her hair, and she becomes presentable enough to attract a leering local bully (Stephen McNally, better known as Horace McNally), who rapes her. She has a baby—Johnny Belinda. This

J ————————————————————————————

Jerry Wald production might have been as exasperating as the Broadway play by Elmer Harris that it's based on, but the director, Jean Negulesco, managed to provide an atmosphere in which the hokey, tearjerking elements are used for more than mere pathos—an example of technique over subject matter. With Jan Sterling as an unscrupulous tart, Rosalind Ivan, Dan Seymour (sometimes mistaken for Zero Mostel), and Mabel Paige. Cinematography by Ted McCord. Warners. b & w

Johnny Eager (1942)—Lana Turner, in her dimpled prime, as the débutante who falls in love with a handsome, arrogant racketeer (the uniquely unconvincing Robert Taylor, with a mustache). Turner does her usual highly emotional, mannered substitute for acting; she's almost as stylized a bad actress as Crawford but much softer, more infantile. Taylor looks tired; his face seems tight and he's less handsome than we're supposed to think. This glossy, full-dress gangster melodrama from M-G-M doesn't add up to anything much, but it can be watched without pain. Best known for Van Heflin's ingratiating, picture-stealing performance as Taylor's friend; actually, he's more like Taylor's pet—a weak but lovable puppy dog. With Barry Nelson, Edward Arnold, Robert Sterling, Diana Lewis, Paul Stewart, Connie Gilchrist, Henry O'Neill, Charles Dingle, and Glenda Farrell. Directed by Mervyn LeRoy, from a script by James Edward Grant and John Lee Mahin. b & w

Johnny Handsome (1989)—Walter Hill directed this hog-wild revenge melodrama, in which Mickey Rourke plays a hoodlum Elephant Man—a deformed boy mocked by the world and forced into a life of crime. Ellen Barkin, in a cartoon performance, is the degenerate slut who jeers the loudest. The only

sanity here is in some of the acting. Rourke does a fine, competent job, but the movie is stolen clear away by Morgan Freeman and Forest Whitaker as antagonists—a tough-minded veteran police detective and a warm, idealistic prison doctor. Whitaker believes that if he performs plastic surgery on the kid and makes him handsome he'll go straight. Freeman listens to Whitaker and grins in wonder: how can anyone be this innocent? It's tickling to see the two together; their scenes crackle. Other moments are redeemed by Elizabeth McGovern as a working-class girl, Scott Wilson as Rourke's only buddy, David Schramm as a money launderer, and Raynor Scheine as a gun dealer. Ken Friedman's screenplay (which is based on a novel by John Godey) is a tortuous reworking of Joan Crawford's 1941 vehicle *A Woman's Face* (which was a remake of a Swedish film with Ingrid Bergman); the big change is that the new film's slant is cruelly kinky. (It's as if *A Woman's Face* were redone, with the Crawford character once again surgically transformed and all—only now in the last scene somebody throws acid at her.) Set in New Orleans. Tri-Star. color (See *Movie Love*.)

The Joker *Le Farceur* (1961)—Philippe de Broca's idiosyncratic little comedy begins by showing us a dreamy, eccentric family, and the whimsey is too soft-headed, but the film gets better (and more subtle than one expects) as it goes along. The lyric and lustful young hero, Jean-Pierre Cassel, pursues the glamorous Anouk Aimée, and when he catches her discovers how dreary she is. Still in his 20s when he made this film (it was preceded by *The Love Game*), de Broca has a deft, balletic style; the film is sprightly, but in an inoffensive way. With Georges Wilson and Geneviève Cluny. Written by de Broca and Daniel Boulanger; music by Georges Delerue. In French. b & w

Le Joli Mai (1963)—In May, 1962, the month the war ended in Algeria, the French documentarian Chris Marker recorded a series of casual, impromptu interviews with Parisians and discovered that they would rather think of anything but politics. This Anglo-American version of his film is marred by a commentary spoken in almost mockingly accented English by Simone Signoret, but Marker's distinctively lyric and generous approach to his subject keeps the picture afloat—though just barely.

Jonah Who Will Be 25 in the Year 2000 *Jonas qui aura 25 ans en l'an 2000* (1976)—A whirling political comedy about the 70s' lunatic fringe of people in their 20s and 30s, each with his own answers to the problems of society. This film, a play of ideas with the laconic irony of Renoir's *Boudu Saved from Drowning* and Buñuel's *The Discreet Charm of the Bourgeoisie*, stays suspended in the air, spinning—a marvellous toy, weightless, yet precise and controlled. The director, Alain Tanner, and his co-writer, John Berger, are willing to entertain possibilities for social rebirth even if they're cracked or pickled. It's a romantic, mystic, utopian comedy—an Easter fable, with a dialectical bunny. Set in Geneva (the birthplace of Rousseau); with Miou-Miou, Jean-Luc Bideau, and Raymond Bussières. In French. color (See *When the Lights Go Down*.)

Jour de fête (1950)—As a director, Jacques Tati has a spare, quick, improvisatory touch. As a comedian, buoyancy and impersonal eccentricity in the face of disaster are his special style. In this film, shot in the village of Sainte-Sévère-sur-Indre, with villagers playing many of the parts, the tall, ungainly Tati is the postman who attends the village fair and sees a documentary on the advanced, mechanized American postal system. He is overcome with enthusiasm for speed, and though

he has no helicopter, he has his bicycle. He takes off, and what happens is unpredictable, even if you've already seen the movie—it's all so odd you forget it. Still, the film's melancholy humor is probably a little too mild or quaint for most American tastes. Written by Tati and Henri Marquet. It's not silent (it has sound effects and music), but it's not in French, either; Tati has devised a kind of unintelligible yet expressive gibberish. It's like the talk of robots who've got fouled up. b & w

Le Jour se lève *Daybreak* (1939)—The director, Marcel Carné, and the writer, Jacques Prévert, collaborated on this justly famous film about a decent sort of man (Jean Gabin) who is forced to become a murderer by the masochistic trickery of the man he kills, played by Jules Berry (who had had a warmup for this role in Renoir's 1935 *The Crime of Monsieur Lange*, also from a script by Prévert). Perhaps the finest of the French poetic melodramas, it's a definitive example of sensuous, atmospheric moviemaking—you feel that you're breathing the air that Gabin breathes. With Arletty and Jacqueline Laurent, and a good score by Maurice Jaubert. (Remade in the U.S. in 1947, by Anatole Litvak, as *The Long Night*, with Henry Fonda in the Gabin role.) In French. b & w

Le Journal d'un curé de campagne, see *The Diary of a Country Priest*

Journey into Fear (1943)—This labyrinthine spy story about smuggling munitions out of Turkey is loaded down with terror hocus-pocus and high-toned conversations. It's a halfhearted—almost fey—film, with a lot of dark atmosphere and unusual camera angles that don't amount to much; the pacing is uncertain, and the suspense doesn't build. Orson Welles, who appears as the Turkish police chief Colonel Haki, is credited, along with Joseph Cotten, for the rather eccentric adaptation of the Eric Ambler novel. Welles also supervised the making of this Mercury Production, though it was at least partly directed by Norman Foster. The cast includes Cotten, Dolores Del Rio, Everett Sloane, Agnes Moorehead, Edgar Barrier, Jack Moss, Ruth Warrick, Richard Bennett as the ship's captain, and Hans Conried as the magician. Cinematography by Karl Strüss; editing by Mark Robson. R K O. b & w

The Joyless Street *Die Freudlose Gasse* Also known as *The Street of Sorrow.* (1925)—Set in Vienna (and filmed entirely in the studio, in Germany), this erotic view of the breakdown of postwar society made the ravishing young Greta Garbo (in the flimsiest of evening gowns) internationally famous, although the star of the film is the great, strange Asta Nielsen, as a kept woman. G. W. Pabst directed this extraordinary triumph of cinematography and Expressionist design; the movie is like a big novel in the way that the characters' lives are interwoven, and it has its weak, dull parts, but it makes a very strong visual impression. With Valeska Gert as the procuress, Werner Krauss as a butcher, and Einar Hanson as an American. Willy Haas wrote the script, from the novel by Hugo Bettauer. Silent. b & w

Juarez (1939)—The time is the 1860s. Paul Muni is the straight, stern President of Mexico, with bowed, heavy shoulders and a rigid profile. Brian Aherne, in blond sideburns and chin whiskers, is the gentle, ineffectual Hapsburg Archduke Maximilian, who becomes a puppet Emperor, and Bette Davis, huge-eyed and wearing a black wig, is the barren, doomed Empress Carlota. She looks both fragile and tempestuous, and gets a chance to show off her best violent spasms when she pleads for help at the Tuileries and frightens the Empress Eugénie (Gale Sondergaard, who doesn't frighten easy). It's a lumpy big movie; Muni's big-star solemn righteousness is like a dose of medicine. But there are incidental diversions: John Garfield, as Diaz, gives a blue-ribbon bad performance, and Claude Rains, Joseph Calleia, Gilbert Roland, Henry O'Neill, Donald Crisp, and Harry Davenport all stomp around in fancy costumes. William Dieterle directed. John Huston and Franz Werfel were among the writers. Warners. b & w

Judge Priest (1934)—Some Irvin S. Cobb stories, brought to the screen by John Ford. Viewed now, this piece of Americana about a trial in a Kentucky town in 1890 is also a slice of old Hollywood: the cast includes Will Rogers, Anita Louise, Rochelle Hudson, Hattie McDaniel, and that much maligned comedian, Stepin Fetchit. Fox. b & w

Judgment at Nuremberg (1961)—Stanley Kramer's version of the meaning of the Nuremberg trials, from a script by Abby Mann. Gavin Lambert summed it up: "An all-star concentration-camp drama, with special guest-victim appearances." Spencer Tracy is the simple, humane superjudge, a Yankee version of Tolstoy's clean old peasant, and the cast includes Burt Lancaster, Richard Widmark, Maximilian Schell, Marlene Dietrich, William Shatner, Werner Klemperer, and Alan Baxter. With Judy Garland and Montgomery Clift as the guests. When Mann's screenplay won the Academy Award, he accepted it, with excruciating humility, not only for himself "but for all intellectuals." (190 minutes.) United Artists. b & w (See *Kiss Kiss Bang Bang*.)

Judith of Bethulia (1913)—Seen now, this D. W. Griffith 4-reeler (which was one of the first 4-reel films made in America) appears to be a warmup for the splendors of his *Intol-*

erance. Judith of Bethulia is not an altogether likable picture, but it has its heavy pseudo-Oriental charms. Blanche Sweet is the plump and pious Jewish widow who decks herself out as a courtesan and gains entrance to the camp of the Assyrian general Holofernes (Henry B. Walthall). Mae Marsh and Robert Harron are young lovers, and Lillian Gish, in a grand coup of unlikely casting, plays a young Jewish mother. Silent. b & w

Juggernaut (1974)—Fast, crackerjack entertainment by Richard Lester; he demonstrates what a sophisticated director with flair can do on a routine big-action project. (The plot is about a bomb wizard who has planted seven whoppers on a luxury liner carrying 1200 passengers.) The genre may be that of *The Poseidon Adventure*, but the tone isn't—it's jaunty, cynical slapstick. With Richard Harris, Shirley Knight, Omar Sharif, David Hemmings, Anthony Hopkins, and Roy Kinnear. United Artists. color (See *Reeling*.)

Jules and Jim *Jules et Jim* (1962)—François Truffaut's celebration of bohemian life in France and Germany in the years of artistic ferment between the First World War and the Second. The Austrian, Jules (Oskar Werner), and the Frenchman, Jim (Henri Serre)—the sort of young artists who grow up into something else—have a peaceful friendship. But when they are with Catherine (Jeanne Moreau), they feel alive; anything may happen. She's the catalyst, the troublemaker, the source of despair as well as the source of joy; an enchantress, she's also a fanatic, an absolutist, and a little crazy. Determined to live as fully as a man, she claims equality while using every feminine wile to increase her power position. She's the independent, intellectual modern woman satirized by Strindberg (who also adored her). Catherine marries Jules, who can't hold her, and, in despair, he encourages Jim's interest in her—

"That way she'll still be *ours*." She insists on her freedom to leave men, but if they leave her (as Jim does), she is as devastated and as helpless as any clinging vine (perhaps *more* devastated—she can't even ask for sympathy). Elliptical, full of wit and radiance, this is the best movie ever made about what most of us think of as the Scott Fitzgerald period (though the film begins much earlier); Truffaut doesn't linger—nothing is held too long, nothing is overstated, or even *stated*. He explores the medium and plays with it. He overlaps scenes; uses fast cutting, in the manner of *Breathless*, and leaping continuity, in the manner of *Zero for Conduct*; changes the size and shape of the images, as Griffith did; pauses for Jeanne Moreau to sing a song (Boris Bassiak's "Le Tourbillon"). Throughout, Georges Delerue's music is part of the atmosphere; it's so evocative that if you listen to it on the phonograph, it brings back the emotions and images—such as Jim and Catherine's daughter rolling on a hill. Adapted by Truffaut and Jean Gruault from Henri-Pierre Roché's autobiographical novel, with some additional material from his later work *Les Deux Anglaises et le continent* (which Truffaut filmed in 1972). Cinematography by Raoul Coutard. With Marie Dubois as Thérèse, who smokes like a steam engine, and Bassiak as Albert. Condemned when it opened in the U.S. by the Catholic Legion of Decency. In French. b & w (See *I Lost it at the Movies*.)

Julia (1977)—Jane Fonda as Lillian Hellman, Jason Robards as Dashiell Hammett, and Vanessa Redgrave as Julia in the film version of Hellman's story about her smuggling bribe money into Nazi Germany, from her book of memoirs *Pentimento*. Directed by Fred Zinnemann, from a script by Alvin Sargent, it has been made in conservative—classical humanist—style. After a while, it becomes apparent that Zinnemann and Sargent are trafficking in too many quotations and flashbacks because they can't find the core of the material. The film's constraint is frustrating, because Jane Fonda has the power and invention to go further in the character; she could crack the cautious, contemplative surface and take us places we've never been to. With Rosemary Murphy and Hal Holbrook as Dorothy Parker and Alan Campbell, and Meryl Streep, John Glover, Cathleen Nesbitt, Maximilian Schell, Maurice Denham, and Susan Jones as the young Lillian and Lisa Pelikan as the young Julia. Cinematography by Douglas Slocombe; music by Georges Delerue; produced by Richard Roth. Academy Awards: Supporting Actor (Robards), Supporting Actress (Redgrave), and Screenplay. Released by 20th Century-Fox. color (See *When the Lights Go Down*.)

Juliet of the Spirits *Giulietta degli Spiriti* (1965)—Federico Fellini looks at a mousy wife's fantasy life; her unconscious seems to be stuffed with leftover decor from M-G-M musicals. A peculiarly ungallant film. With Giulietta Masina, and Sandra Milo, Valeska Gert, Lou Gilbert, José-Luis de Villalonga, Sylva Koscina, Valentina Cortese, and Friedrich Ledebur. Cinematography by Gianni Di Venanzo; music by Nino Rota. Written by Fellini, Ennio Flaiano, Tullio Pinelli, and Brunello Rondi. In Italian. color

June Bride (1948)—One of those straining-to-be-bright 40s comedies in which the supercompetent career woman (in this case Bette Davis, as the editor of a woman's magazine called "Home Life") behaves like a prison matron and battles with a male (Robert Montgomery, as her assistant and former lover) before succumbing to him and giving up her job. In this one, the wrangling pair are covering a wedding in Indiana. Montgomery wears his hat brim turned up to show he's a reporter and keeps snapping off electric lights

to put Davis in a soft, loving mood; one couldn't guess from this performance that a few years earlier he had been the best romantic comedian on the screen. One couldn't guess that Davis had much stature, either. The director, Bretaigne Windust, keeps the dialogue tight and stagey. Ranald MacDougall adapted the play *Feature for June*, by June Tighe and Graeme Lorimer. With Fay Bainter, Betty Lynn, Jerome Cowan, Barbara Bates, Tom Tully, and, in a small part, Debbie Reynolds. Warners. b & w

Jungle Book (1942)—Sabu appears to have a very good time as Mowgli, the child adopted by the wolves who lives among the wild beasts as one of them; he swings from tree to tree like a nursery Tarzan. In the dark-green jungles of this lush, handsome Alexander Korda production, directed by Zoltán Korda, Mowgli has more to do with human folk than in the Kipling book—Joseph Calleia is around, and also little Patricia O'Rourke, for a suggestion of precocious romance. Laurence Stallings, who wrote the screenplay, may wander a bit from Kipling, but the plot about a treasure, a python, and a ruined city are entertaining enough. Children will probably still love the movie—and adults will have a better time than they expect. Released by United Artists. color

Just Between Friends (1986)—A homemaker/husband/career-woman triangle, with everything spelled out, according to accepted TV procedures by the writer-director Allan Burns. The star is Mary Tyler Moore as a California wife and mother of two teen-agers, with Ted Danson as her seismologist husband and Christine Lahti as her best friend, a TV newscaster. Ostensibly, the movie is about how the timid-mouse wife must become self-reliant after her husband is killed in a car accident, and how the friendship between the two women is sustained after the wife learns that her friend was having an affair with her husband and is pregnant by him. But the subtext, which is tied in to the exercise class where the women first meet, dominates the movie. For two hours, we're invited to admire what terrific shape Mary Tyler Moore is in. There are so many shots of her tight, trim rear end in leotards as she gyrates for the camera that the film begins to seem a vanity production. She looks agonizingly ill at ease about her age, and this exhibition of her beautiful state of preservation makes her seem much older than she is. Lahti walks off with the picture; her voice has a witty dryness, with deep resonance, and she plays the sophisticated newscaster like a new, more plangent version of Rosalind Russell at her peak, in *His Girl Friday*. With Sam Waterston (engaging as a sheepish friend of the family), Salome Jens (amusing as Helga, the head of the exercise studio), and Jane Greer. An MTM Enterprises Production, for Orion. color (See *Hooked*.)

Just Imagine (1930)—Perhaps the only sci-fi musical comedy ever made, this is set in New York 50 years in the future—1980. It's a lighthearted, cheerfully foolish view of scientific progress: papier-mâché skyscrapers soar into the painted heavens, stop-and-go signs refer to the traffic of airplanes, J-21 (John Garrick) is a suitor for the hand in marriage of LN-18 (Maureen O'Sullivan), and he and his pal RT-42 (Frank Albertson) pilot a rocket ship to Mars. What helped to make it a hit were the broad antics of the Swedish-accented yokel comic El Brendel in the role of Single-O, a Rip van Winkle character who had died in 1930 and was revived in 1980; he's a stowaway on the Mars expedition. The script and the songs are by Lew Brown, B. G. DeSylva, and Ray Henderson; David Butler directed for Fox; Seymour Felix choreographed. With Mischa Auer, Marjorie White, and Hobart Bosworth. b & w

Just Tell Me What You Want (1980)—There are a lot of funny scenes in this satirical romantic farce about Max Herschel, an economic baron (who shares a number of characteristics with the movie mogul Ray Stark). The head of a New York–based conglomerate, who makes big deals for the joy and excitement of it, Max (Alan King) can't accept losing anything. When his young mistress (Ali MacGraw) tells him that she just got married, he's a suave good sport while she's in the room; as soon as she has gone, he cries out to his secretary (Myrna Loy) with Old Testament fervor—"I'm a dead Jew." The movie is about Max's ruthless finagling to teach the girl he has lost a lesson: his methods include buying a play by the pure, incorruptible writer she has married and hiring him to adapt it to the movies. The charm of the movie is in the pleasure it takes (which we share) in the sacred monster Max—tantrumy, shrewd, obsessed with his own health and longevity. Alan King revels in his role, and Ali MacGraw is a lot better than she has ever been before. The second half is too choppy—it feels as if it might have been cut. But there's some real gusto in this satire of power games (and modern movie business), and the director, Sidney Lumet, gets juicy performances from most of the cast. Keenan Wynn plays an ancient movie magnate, a white-bearded shrewdie who affects an old-world courtliness while maneuvering to make his homosexual grandson (Tony Roberts) head of a studio; Dina Merrill is Max's alcoholic Wasp wife; Joseph Maher is her doctor-lover; Peter Weller is the pure-prig writer. Also with Sara Truslow as Cathy, and Judy Kaye as Baby. (The movie opened and closed almost simultaneously.) From Jay Presson Allen's screenplay, based on her own novel.

She and Lumet co-produced. Cinematography by Oswald Morris; production design by Tony Walton. Warners. color

Justice est faite, see *Justice Is Done*

Justice Is Done   *Justice est faite* (1950)—André Cayatte examines the private lives of the seven jurors sitting in judgment on a woman doctor (Claude Nollier) who admits to the mercy killing of her lover. A fine cast, including Valentine Tessier, Jean Debucourt, Noel Roquevert, and Michel Auclair, acts out the ironic message of the title. Cayatte gives you the impression that he feels he's giving you something to think about; there's a solemn righteousness inside all the melodrama. Screenplay by Charles Spaak and Cayatte; cinematography by Jean Bourgoin. In French. b & w

Juvenile Court (1973)—In his early documentaries, each time Fred Wiseman examines an institution, he seems to uncover a whole new world, and in each of these worlds he finds people—those in authority and those caught in the wheels of authority—struggling with perversely funny, insurmountable, tragic everyday problems. This 2½-hour film was made in the Memphis Juvenile Court. The characters include an 11-year-old prostitute; a boy babysitter charged with assaulting the child in his care; the child's mother, who is obsessed with what seems to have been a minor feeling-up incident; a teen-age girl who slashes her wrist and says her stepfather made advances to her; and an intelligent judge trying to serve justice in impossible situations. Watching the film is like seeing the underbelly of TV soap operas; the faces cut against clichés the way the faces in the televised Watergate hearings did. When the children plead for themselves, their voices have a familiar terror. It's the same sound that middle-class children make when they claim their parents have been unjust to them, but here, whether the prisoners are innocent or guilty of the specific charge, the injustice seems cosmic. They're trapped by everything. Wiseman's open-eyed approach to the stories of their lives is perhaps motivated less by reforming zeal than by his own sense of the mystery of those lives. b & w

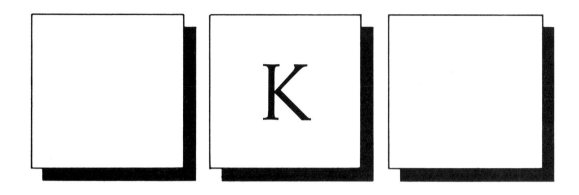

K

Das Kabinett des Dr. Caligari, see *The Cabinet of Dr. Caligari*

Kagemusha *The Shadow Warrior* (1980)—Warfare is treated dispassionately in this epic film in color by Kurosawa, which is set during the wars of the clans in 16th-century Japan (the period just before the country was unified). Kurosawa seems to be saying that wisdom dictates caution, security, stasis, but that to be alive is to be subject to impulse, to chaos. The film's style is ceremonial rather than dramatic; it's not battle that Kurosawa is interested in here but formations in battle regalia. He appears to see war as part of the turmoil of life, and he asks us simply to observe what he shows us. Perhaps he thinks that this way the horror will reach us at a deeper level. But he's also in love with the aesthetics of warfare—he's a schoolboy setting up armies of perfect little soldiers and smiling at the patterns he has devised. These two sets of feelings may have neutralized *Kagemusha*—put it at a remove and made it somewhat abstract. The film seems fixated on mountains, triangles, and threes. Tatsuya Nakadai plays the warlord known as The Mountain, and he also plays the thieving peasant who has been condemned to death but whose life is spared so that he can serve as the lord's double. Written by Kurosawa and Masato Ide. In Japanese. (See *Taking It All In*.)

Kagi *The Key* Also known as *Odd Obsession*. (1959)—Perverse in the best sense of the word. As a treatment of sexual opportunism it's a bit reminiscent of *Double Indemnity*, but it's infinitely more complex. At the start, a young doctor, sensual and handsome, smug with sexual prowess, tells us that his patient, an aging man, is losing his virility. And the old man bends over and bares his buttocks—to take an injection. But the old man doesn't get enough charge from the injection, so he induces the young doctor, who is his daughter's suitor, to make love to his wife. By observing them, by artificially making himself jealous, the old man is able to raise his spirits a bit. The comedy, of course, is that the wife, superbly played by Machiko Kyo, is the traditional, obedient Japanese woman—and she cooperates in her husband's plan. She is so cooperative that, once aroused by the young doctor, she literally kills her old husband with kindness—she excites him to death. (It's both a perfect suicide and a perfect murder.) The title—the key—

fits the Tanizaki novel that the film is based on, but the film might better be called the keyhole. Everybody is spying on everybody else, and although each one conceals his motives and actions, nobody is fooled. The screen is *our* keyhole, and we are the voyeurs who can see them all peeking at each other. When the old man takes obscene pictures of his wife, he gives them to the young man to develop. The young man shows them to his fiancée, the daughter, whose reaction is that she can do anything her mother can do. A further layer of irony is that she can't—the film is also a withering satire on the Westernized modern Japanese girl. As the mother, Machiko Kyo, with her soft, sloping shoulders and her rhythmic padding walk, is like some ancient erotic fantasy. Directed by Kon Ichikawa, this film about pornography would be just about perfect if it didn't have a stupid tacked-on ending (that isn't in the novel). In Japanese. color (See *I Lost it at the Movies*.)

Kameradschaft (1931)—Based on an actual incident in which German miners crossed the border to go to the assistance of French miners trapped by an explosion, G. W. Pabst's study of disaster and rescue is a powerful and imaginative re-creation of a high moment in human comradeship. The socialist-pacifist implications which Pabst sees in the episode had tremendous international impact in the days when people were more idealistic. In the early 30s it was still possible for large audiences to believe in the symbolic revolutionary meaning of smashing through artificial frontiers for the sake of natural brotherhood. This movie belongs to a genre that has disappeared. Technically a brilliant achievement, *Kameradschaft* is famous among film craftsmen for the experimental use of sound, and for magnificent creative editing. The subterranean scenes have a nightmarish authenticity. The cast of French and German

players includes Alexander Granach and Elizabeth Wendt. In German. b & w

Kanchenjungha (1962)—Satyajit Ray made this ambitious film in color on location in Darjeeling in 1961 (though it didn't open in the U.S. until 1966). Under the primitive working circumstances, the story about love and ambition and the collision of cultures was perhaps too complex, but the setting and the beautiful women help to compensate for the awkwardness and naïveté. With Chhabi Biswas. In Bengali.

Kaos Also known as *Chaos*. (1984)—Partly financed by Italian television, this film by Paolo and Vittorio Taviani is composed of adaptations of four folkloric Pirandello stories set in Sicily, plus a prologue and an epilogue. It was intended to be shown on TV, in four installments, as well as in theatres, and when foreign distributors bought the rights to present it theatrically the Tavianis suggested that they should cut one story or another—the one least likely to appeal to their country's tastes. The American distributor decided to run the film in toto. That might be called exemplary, but the result is a mixed blessing. At 3 hours and 8 minutes it's too much movie, and too much harsh beauty. The panoramic grandeur wears you down. You feel emotionally filled by the first and second stories, which are about fate and have superb moments. During the third and fourth, which are about trickery, you feel surfeited. They're hardly worth sitting through, but they take you to the revivifying epilogue, which is a full-fledged epiphany and sends you out dazed and happy. There's greatness in this movie, but it's wise to be prepared for the passages that are clumsy and tedious; don't get angry and leave, or you'll lose the rapturous beauty of the epilogue. With the magnificent Margarita Lozano as the madwoman of the first story, and, in the final moments,

Omero Antonutti as Pirandello. Tonino Guerra collaborated with the Tavianis on the script; the marvellous score is by Nicola Piovani; the cinematography is by Giuseppe Lanci. In Italian. Released by M-G-M/United Artists Classics. color (See *Hooked*.)

Keeper of the Flame (1943)—Tracy and Hepburn, but not a comedy, and not good, either. She plays the widow of a "great American"; Tracy is a journalist admirer of the dead man who wants to write the definitive biography. The widow won't cooperate with him and puts obstacles in his path because she's trying to conceal the fact that her husband was the secret head of a traitorous Fascist organization. The screenwriter, Donald Ogden Stewart, had become very political during the war years, and he seems to have felt it incumbent on him to stuff the script (based on I.A.R. Wylie's novel) with anti-Fascism. Tracy is monotonous, and Hepburn looks beautiful but suffers all over the place and speaks mournfully, like a spiritualist's medium. It's a gothic wet blanket of a movie, directed by George Cukor, with an impressive, wasted cast—Richard Whorf, Frank Craven, Margaret Wycherly, Horace McNally, Donald Meek, Howard Da Silva, Percy Kilbride, and Audrey Christie. M-G-M. b & w

The Kennel Murder Case (1933)—One of the pleasanter films in the series starring the suave comedian William Powell as S. S. Van Dine's detective Philo Vance. The plot involves some lively Scotties and a handsome Doberman, as well as that sinister figure, the connoisseur of Oriental objects of art. (In the 30s, Ming and murder always seemed to go together.) Mary Astor, at an in-between stage in her career, has a conventional role that doesn't much suit her; however, most of the other players are cast so inevitably to type that the film is like a demonstration of the principles of running a stock company. The

group includes snake-hipped Helen Vinson, wicked Jack La Rue, tedious Ralph Morgan, and Paul Cavanagh, Etienne Girardot, Robert Barrat, Eugene Pallette, Frank Conroy, Arthur Hohl, Henry O'Neill, and Robert McWade. Directed by Michael Curtiz. Warners. b & w

Kentucky Kernels (1934)—One of the better-made Wheeler and Woolsey comedies, and also one of the most popular. George Stevens directed, and Bert Kalmar and Harry Ruby did the story and provided the song "One Little Kiss." Wheeler and Woolsey adopt a child (Spanky McFarland), go down to the South to claim his inheritance, and get caught in a feud between families headed by Noah Beery and Lucille LaVerne. With Mary Carlisle, Willie Best, and Margaret Dumont. R K O. b & w

La Kermesse héroïque, see *Carnival in Flanders*.

The Key, see *Kagi*

Key Largo (1948)—The soporific Maxwell Anderson play is an unlikely subject for John Huston but he steers a shrewd course, bailing Anderson out in order to stay afloat. What the play was supposed to be about—which was dim enough in the original—is even more obscure in the script that he and Richard Brooks (then a screenwriter) prepared, but the movie is so confidently and entertainingly directed that nobody is likely to complain. Huston fills the rancid atmosphere of the setting—a hotel in the Florida Keys—with suspense, ambiguous motives, and some hilariously hammy bits, and the cast all go at it as if the nonsense about gangsters and human dignity were high drama. Humphrey Bogart plays a Second World War veteran—a major who goes to the hotel, which is run by the widow (Lauren Bacall) and father (Lionel Barrymore) of one of his men. The major has become disillusioned about the value of fighting, but when gangsters (who are symbols of reaction, corruption, Hitlerism) take over the hotel and start killing people, he is forced into action. Bogart wins Bacall, who looks wonderful but gives a stiff, amateurish performance. The most memorable image is that of Edward G. Robinson, as the head racketeer, chomping on a cigar while soaking in a bathtub; he has, as Huston said, "the look of a crustacean with its shell off." For diversion, this home-grown Hitler humiliates his aging, drunken mistress, played by Claire Trevor, who packed such a load of pathos into her role that she won the Academy Award for Best Supporting Actress. Thomas Gomez, as one of the hoods, and Barrymore do their usual overacting. With Marc Lawrence, Dan Seymour, Monte Blue, Jay Silverheels, Harry Lewis, John Rodney, and Rodric Redwing. The handsome, airy cinematography is by Karl Freund; the music is by Max Steiner. Produced by Jerry Wald for Warners. b & w

The Keys of the Kingdom (1944)—Hollywood at its most virtuous. This account of the adventurous life of a 19th-century Scottish priest—a missionary in China—is like an ad for piety. The humble hero keeps telling people what an uninteresting sort of man he is, and with Gregory Peck in the role we believe it. His saintliness comes across as lack of imagination—utter sterility. How did Joseph L. Mankiewicz and Nunnally Johnson get trapped into writing the script, which is based on A. J. Cronin's novel? (You couldn't find two writers less suited, by temperament, to inspirational moviemaking.) The director, John M. Stahl, sets a slow, sanctimonious pace and holds to it, with Peck's beautiful, uncharismatic face lighted "from within." (He glows, hollowly.) This is perhaps the most dignified and sexless performance ever

given by a rising young male star. With Cedric Hardwicke, Edmund Gwenn, Thomas Mitchell, Peggy Ann Garner, Roddy McDowall, Rose Stradner, Anne Revere, Ruth Nelson, Benson Fong, James Gleason, Sara Allgood, Edith Barrett, Abner Biberman, Vincent Price, Ruth Ford, Richard Loo, and Arthur Shields. Music by Alfred Newman. Mankiewicz produced, for 20th Century-Fox. b & w

The Kid (1921)—The most enchantingly Victorian of Chaplin's features, and perhaps because of the way his sentimentality (which was often awkward, and even mawkish, later) fits the subject, this film seems remarkably innocent and pure. Edna Purviance is the destitute young mother who abandons her infant; Charlie, the tramp, takes the child to his garret, and five years later the child (Jackie Coogan) smashes windows, which Charlie, now a glazier and wearing glass on his back like angel wings, repairs. The story is about the love between these two street waifs and about Charlie's fight to keep the child out of the hands of the authorities. A little girl named Lita Grey (known as Lolita), later to be Chaplin's wife, appears in a dream sequence set in Heaven. Silent. b & w

A Kid for Two Farthings (1955)—Wolf Mankowitz takes the language of the East End of London and uses it as a poetic idiom. And he transforms his characters into creatures of fantasy and fable. Directed by Carol Reed, this film has some of the same verbal magic that Mankowitz gave to *The Bespoke Overcoat* and *Expresso Bongo*, and many of the characters could step in and out of any of these films. In this one, a boy looks for the unicorn that can work miracles and finds a sick goat with one horn. Reed achieves enough small miracles to lift the film to an unfamiliar realm, but he can't quite solve the problem of *how* to tell the story. The success of this type of fantasy depends on the contrast between the child's world and the adult's: in *The Rocking Horse Winner*, for example, the director stays outside the child's world and we view what goes on inside with terror and apprehension; in *White Mane*, Albert Lamorisse helps us to enter the child's domain. Here we are caught in a fairy tale set somewhere in between. The East End is made so fascinating that reality and fantasy are inseparable, and though a child may well apprehend them this way, the fabulous reality confuses the point for us. With Jonathan Ashmore, David Kossoff, Celia Johnson, Brenda de Banzie, Sidney James, Alfie Bass, Vera Day, Diana Dors, Joe Robinson, and Primo Carnera as the ogre. color

The Kid from Spain (1932)—Sam Goldwyn put a million dollars into this Eddie Cantor musical, and a fair number of them must have gone into the Busby Berkeley dance numbers. Berkeley stages a Spanish-café routine with the Goldwyn Girls forming a human tortilla, and an aquatic sequence with the Girls showing a lot of buxom wet flesh. (Some of the most attractive smiles belong to Lucille Ball, Betty Grable, Paulette Goddard, and Virginia Bruce.) Cantor and Robert Young play college boys who are innocently involved in a robbery; they escape to Mexico, where Cantor is mistaken for a matador and is forced to fight in the ring. The film has everything that money could buy—which does not include comic inspiration, though the final bullfight is fairly inventive. It's Cantor himself who doesn't wear well—maybe because he always retained his stage timing and delivery, which are too slow and broad for the camera. Leo McCarey directed, and Bert Kalmar and Harry Ruby wrote reasonably pleasant songs and also worked on the script. The cast includes Lyda Roberti, grinning with perverse vivacity, and Ruth Hall, Noah Beery, John Miljan, J. Carrol Naish, Stanley Fields, and

the matador Sidney Franklin. Cinematography by Gregg Toland. A Samuel Goldwyn Production. b & w

Kid Galahad (1937)—By 1937, Bette Davis had earned something better than the role of Fluff, girlfriend to a fight manager (Edward G. Robinson), but the movie was directed by Michael Curtiz, and though it has few dimensions it has pace and "entertainment value." Wayne Morris is the bellhop turned fighter, whom Fluff christens Kid Galahad; Humphrey Bogart is the bad guy; and Jane Bryan plays Robinson's sister. With Harry Carey, the ineffable Veda Ann Borg as the Redhead, and, for the finale, a Warners' operatic shootout in which Robinson and Bogart kill each other. (Remade in 1941, as *Wagons Roll at Night*, and in 1962, starring Elvis Presley.) b & w

Kidnapped (1971)—Jack Pulman has drawn a trim, craftsmanlike screenplay from Robert Louis Stevenson's *Kidnapped* and its sequel, *David Balfour*. The director, Delbert Mann, keeps everything comprehensible, though he doesn't seem to know how to make the narrative stirring. Fortunately, Michael Caine acts Alan Breck with a mixture of swagger and intelligence that keeps the movie alive. Caine is assisted by Trevor Howard as the Lord Advocate, Lawrence Douglas as David, and Donald Pleasence as old Ebenezer, a Scrooge if ever there was one. Not as exciting as the best swashbuckling adventure movies, but the feeling behind the whole production is so decent and affectionate that viewers may forgive the deficiencies. The exteriors were shot in Scotland. color

The Killer Elite (1975)—Sam Peckinpah's poetic, corkscrew vision of the modern world, claustrophobically exciting. The somewhat incoherent story is about a professional killer (James Caan) who turns against his employers—a company with C.I.A. connections—but the energy and the humor appear to derive from Peckinpah's own desire for revenge against his movie-business employers. With Gig Young, Robert Duvall, Burt Young, Bo Hopkins, and Arthur Hill. From a script by Marc Norman and Stirling Silliphant. United Artists. color (See *When the Lights Go Down*.)

The Killers (1946)—Ernest Hemingway's short story about the man who doesn't try to escape his killers is acted out tensely and accurately, and, for once, the gangster-thriller material added to it is not just padding but is shrewdly conceived (by Anthony Veiller and the uncredited John Huston) to show why the man didn't care enough about life to run away. Under the expert direction of Robert Siodmak, Burt Lancaster gives his first screen performance (and is startlingly effective), and Siodmak also does wonders with Ava Gardner. With Charles McGraw and William Conrad in the opening sequence, and Edmond O'Brien, Albert Dekker, Sam Levene, Donald MacBride, Vince Barnett, and Jeff Corey. (A 1964 version starring Lee Marvin and directed by Don Siegel was intended to be a TV movie but was considered too brutal and was released in theatres instead; the cast includes Angie Dickinson, John Cassavetes, and Ronald Reagan, at the end of his movie career, as a tough crook.) Universal. b & w

Killer's Kiss (1955)—Stanley Kubrick's second feature (after *Fear and Desire*, in 1953) is a poorly written New York–set thriller that culminates in a fight in a mannequin factory. It has vivid feeling for the tawdry milieu but not much else; it's conceived in flashy sequences rather than as a believable story, and the guiding sensibility still seems light years away from Kubrick's third feature, *The Killing*, in 1956. With Frank Silvera. Kubrick also

shot the picture and did the writing and editing. United Artists. b & w

The Killing (1956)—Stanley Kubrick had made two pictures before this one, but they were juvenilia; this shrewdly worked out suspense film, which he made at the age of 27, is the real beginning of his career. Centering on a racetrack robbery, it has fast, incisive cutting; a nervous, edgy style; and furtive little touches of characterization. The cast includes many familiar second-string actors, but they go through enough unfamiliar movements to keep one in an agreeable state of anxious expectation. Sterling Hayden is impressive as the ex-convict who plans the crime (there's a slight melancholy about him). With Elisha Cook, Jr., and fierce, tight Marie Windsor as his mismate; the generally underrated fine actress Coleen Gray; Jay C. Flippen; Timothy Carey as the sharpshooter; Ted de Corsia; Joe Sawyer; Vince Edwards; and Kola Kwarian as the chess-playing wrestler. Adapted by the director, from Lionel White's novel *Clean Break*; cinematography by Lucien Ballard. Independently produced by Harris-Kubrick; released through United Artists. b & w

The Killing Fields (1984)—Based on Sydney Schanberg's 1980 *New York Times Magazine* article "The Death and Life of Dith Pran," the British film shows us the Khmer Rouge transforming Cambodia into a nationwide gulag, and the scenes of this genocidal revolution have the breadth and terror of something deeply imagined. Like the article, the film tells the story of how Schanberg (Sam Waterston), who was the *Times* correspondent in Cambodia from 1972 to 1975, was separated from his interpreter and assistant, Pran (Haing S. Ngor), and of his remorse and general anguish until the wily, resourceful Pran, after four years of slave labor and hiding, made his way into Thailand, late in 1979, and got word to him. It's an ambitious movie made with an inept, sometimes sly, and very often equivocal script (by Bruce Robinson); it's written like a TV docudrama and it bogs down in the crosscutting between Pran's experiences of the atrocities in Cambodia and Schanberg's guilt and misery in various settings in the U.S. At times, it's almost as if Cambodia only existed to make Waterston's Schanberg suffer and soliloquize, endlessly asking, "Did I do what was right?" But it's by no means a negligible movie. Roland Joffé, making his début as a movie director, and the cinematographer, Chris Menges, give us imagery that suggests the work of a macabre lyric poet, and there are accomplished performances—most notably by John Malkovich, Bill Paterson, and Athol Fugard. The score, by Mike Oldfield, mars some of the finest scenes; it insists on hyping death. The cast includes Craig T. Nelson, Spalding Gray, and Julian Sands. Produced by David Puttnam; released by Warners. color (See *State of the Art*.)

Kind Hearts and Coronets (1949)—This tart black comedy on the craving for social position and the art of murder has a brittle wit that came as a bit of a shock: such amoral lines were not generally spoken in 40s movies. The film is heartless, and that is the secret of its elegance. Ninth in line to inherit a dukedom, the insouciant young hero (Dennis Price) systematically eliminates the intervening eight—a snob, a general, a photographer, an admiral, a suffragette, a clergyman, a banker, and the duke—all, by a casting stroke of genius, played by Alec Guinness. Secure in the knowledge that Guinness will return in another form, the audience suffers no regret as each abominable D'Ascoyne is coolly dispatched. And as the murderer takes us further into his confidence with each foul deed, we positively look forward to his next success. With purring little Joan Greenwood

as the minx-nemesis Sybilla, Valerie Hobson as the high-minded Edith, Miles Malleson as the poetasting executioner. Based on the 1907 novel *Israel Rank*, by Roy Horniman, adapted by Robert Hamer and John Dighton. Hamer directed. b & w

A King in New York (1957)—Maybe the saddest (and worst) movie ever made by a celebrated film artist. Chaplin mugs archly as King Shadhov, a deposed Ruritanian monarch who becomes a TV celebrity in New York. With Dawn Addams, Harry Green, and young Michael Chaplin, from whom his father coaxed a grotesque performance. b & w

King Kong (1976)—The greatest misfit in movie history makes a comeback in this new version. Monster, pet, misunderstood kid, unrequited lover, all in one grotesquely oversized body, the innocent ape is martyred once again. The movie is a romantic adventure fantasy—colossal, silly, touching, a marvellous Classics Comics movie (and for the whole family). This new *Kong* doesn't have the magical primeval imagery of the first *King Kong*, in 1933, and it doesn't have the Gustave Doré fable atmosphere, but it's a happier, livelier entertainment. The first *Kong* was a stunt film that was trying to awe you, and its lewd underlay had a carnival hucksterism that made you feel a little queasy. This new *Kong* isn't a horror movie—it's an absurdist love story. When the 40-foot Kong stands bleeding and besieged at the top of the World Trade Center, and his blonde (Jessica Lange) pleads with him to pick her up, so that the helicopters won't shoot at him, even Wagner's dreams seem paltry. We might snicker at a human movie hero who felt such passion for a woman that he'd rather die than risk harming her, but who can jeer a martyr-ape? This film can stand in one's affections right next to the original version. John Guillermin directed, from Lorenzo Semple, Jr.'s, script;

with Jeff Bridges, Charles Grodin, John Randolph, Ed Lauter, Julius Harris, René Auberjonois, and John Agar. Cinematography by Richard H. Kline; music by John Barry; produced by Dino De Laurentiis. Paramount. color (See *When the Lights Go Down*.)

King Lear (1971)—Blindness and nothingness are the controlling metaphors in this gray, cold Peter Brook production. Brook has a unified vision and never lets go of the reins; there are no accidental pleasures in the movie—and no deliberate ones, either. This *Lear* is made essentially plotless not by removing the plot (that is practically all that *remains* of the play) but by using the plot as a diagram for movement abstracted from psychological and dramatic meaning. By the time you've seized the outline, the cutting has become jaggedly mannered, with sudden shifts from one angle to another and from long shots to closeups, often while someone is speaking, and then your eyes are punished by blinding flashes that are like exploding bombs. The cutting seems designed as an alienation device, but who wants to be alienated from Shakespeare's play and given the drear far side of the moon instead? Though Paul Scofield's stage appearances as Lear are world-famous, he gives a freezing performance here. Only Alan Webb's Gloucester has a sneaking humanity that occasionally flickers through the stylized acting. b & w (See *Deeper into Movies*.)

The King of Comedy (1983)—Robert De Niro plays Rupert Pupkin, a grossly insensitive, cold-hearted deadhead who is determined to become a TV star like his idol, the comic Jerry Langford, played by Jerry Lewis. The director, Martin Scorsese, must have decided to give us the cold creeps; the shots are held so long that we look for more in them than is there. Scorsese designs his own form of alienation in this mistimed, empty movie,

which seems to teeter between jokiness and hate. It's *The Day of the Locust* in the age of television, but with a druggy vacuousness that suggests the Warhol productions of the 60s. With Sandra Bernhard as the hysterical Masha, who helps Pupkin kidnap Langford. (Pupkin's ransom demand is a 10-minute guest appearance on Langford's late-night talk show.) Also with Diahnne Abbott as the bartender Rita and Shelley Hack as a secretary. From a script by Paul Zimmerman. Released by 20th Century-Fox. color (See *Taking It All In*.)

The King of Marvin Gardens (1972)—Indecipherable, dark-toned movie about brothers and spurious goals and the American Dream. Set in the decaying playground of Atlantic City, in the gray, wintry off-season, it keeps declaring its alienation. Bruce Dern works hard trying to be charismatic as the promoter brother who fronts for black gangsters (Scatman Crothers is the big boss). Jack Nicholson is the artist brother. He does monologues on late-night FM radio, with such pronouncements as "Goodby, written word" and, referring to his own life, "Tragedy isn't Top Forty—which is just as well." Trying to act intellectual Nicholson wears a prissy expression, huddles in his overcoat, and gives a dim, ploddingly serious performance. (If the roles had been reversed the film might have had a *little* energy.) As Dern's aging, rejected mistress, who is being replaced in his affections by her own stepdaughter, Ellen Burstyn works valiantly, but her role is a series of florid gestures—it's like all of Claire Trevor's biggest scenes put together. This is an unqualified disaster of the type that only talented people have; the producer-director, Bob Rafelson, and the scriptwriter, Jacob Brackman, seem to be saying "Let them eat metaphors." With Julia Anne Robinson as the stepdaughter, Charles Lavine as the brothers' grandfather, and Garry

Goodrow, Sully Boyar, and Josh Mostel. Cinematography by Laszlo Kovacs; a BBS Production, released by Columbia. color

King Solomon's Mines (1950)—A smashing kitsch entertainment—H. Rider Haggard's 1886 pulp adventure novel about a search for legendary African diamond mines, given the full M-G-M Technicolor treatment, and with an additional romance between an English lady on safari (Deborah Kerr) and the valiant white guide (Stewart Granger) provided by the scenarist, Helen Deutsch. You have to be prepared to put part of your mind to sleep, so that you don't get too outraged by the colonialist underpinnings of this sort of fiction; the noblest character is the loyal black servant Umbopa (played by Siriaque, a Watusi), who turns out to be the Mashona chief. (In the 1937 British version, Paul Robeson was a magnificent smiling Umbopa.) But one can enjoy this picture for its superb showmanship (and the Watusi dances and the stunning native fabrics). The film was shot in the African highlands—at Murchison Falls and Mount Kenya—and the elephants and mandrills and leopards and cobras are all startlingly clear and close. It's one exciting incident after another, and there's even a suggestion of sex, when Kerr and Granger wake after a night of hiding high in a tree and look passionately at each other. (An incident early on, when an elephant tramples a native, may frighten small children, but children generally love the rest of the film.) Produced by Sam Zimbalist; directed by Compton Bennett and Andrew Marton; cinematography by Robert Surtees, who won the Academy Award for it. With Richard Carlson, Hugo Haas, and Lowell Gilmore. Also with Kimursi, of the Kipsigi tribe, and Sekaryongo and Baziga, of the Watusi tribe; the Africans take all the acting honors. (A cut-rate sequel, *Watusi*, in 1959 had a script by James Clavell.)

The King Steps Out (1936)—Those with merciful memories blocked this one out long ago. Josef von Sternberg asked that the film not be included in retrospectives of his work, but he really did make the damned thing. It's a monstrously overstaged version of Fritz Kreisler's operetta *Cissy*, with Grace Moore and Franchot Tone struggling through the scenery playing Princess Elizabeth of Bavaria and the young Emperor Franz Josef. Columbia. b & w

Kings Row (1942)—The typical nostalgic view of American small-town life turned inside out: instead of sweetness and health we get fear, sanctimoniousness, sadism, and insanity. Tranquilly accepting the many varieties of psychopathic behavior as the simple facts of life, this film has its own kind of sentimental glow, yet the melodramatic incidents are surprisingly compelling. The time is the beginning of the 20th century, and the hero (Robert Cummings) is interested in the new ideas of Sigmund Freud. (Which is unfortunate: when Cummings, eyes lighted with idealism, mouths naïve views on Freud, almost any contemporary audience is bound to break up.) The director, Sam Wood, gets some remarkably well-defined performances from others, though: Ann Sheridan is radiant in the role of a girl from the wrong side of the tracks, and Betty Field's frightened, passionate Cassie is a memorable vignette. Charles Coburn and Claude Rains are the town's doctors; Coburn likes to perform amputations without anesthetics (his special victim is Ronald Reagan), and Rains keeps his daughter locked up in his house. The cast also includes Judith Anderson, Maria Ouspenskaya, Nancy Coleman, and Kaaren Verne. Casey Robinson adapted Henry Bellamann's best-seller; James Wong Howe was the cinematographer; and William Cameron Menzies was the production designer. Warners. b & w

Kipps (1941)—Carol Reed directed this genial, endearingly noiseless version of the H.G. Wells novel, with Michael Redgrave as the orphan who works in a draper's shop and becomes a whiz of a bourgeois success. It's a very satisfying movie—observant without fuss, sly yet substantial. (The story was later inflated to the point of unintelligibility in the musical *Half a Sixpence*.) With Diana Wynyard, Phyllis Calvert, Max Adrian, Michael Wilding, Helen Haye, Edward Rigby, Hermione Baddeley, and the famous music hall artist Arthur Riscoe as Chitterlow. The script is by Frank Launder and Sidney Gilliat; the costumes are by Cecil Beaton. b & w

Kiri no Naka no Shojo, see *A Girl in the Mist*

Kismet (1944)—Ronald Colman and Marlene Dietrich look blithe and take it easy. She dances in the court of the Grand Vizier of Baghdad wearing half a pail of gilt paint, and as the rogue-hero he fusses with sleight-of-hand tricks involving handkerchiefs and knives. This version of Edward Knoblock's durable kitsch (it opened on Broadway in 1911) comes with a harem swimming pool, and it's less strenuous than most costume films of the period. Edward Arnold is the villainous Vizier who smiles craftily throughout; when Colman stabs him in that harem pool, he drops his smile—that's as subtle a nuance of the actor's art as you'll find in *Kismet*. Joy Ann Page plays Colman's daughter, with James Craig opposite her. William Dieterle directed; Harburg and Arlen provided a couple of songs. M-G-M. color

Kismet (1955)—This time, it was Vincente Minnelli who tried his hand with the familiar material, in a Hollywood-doctored version of the Broadway show that featured music derived from Borodin (including "A Stranger in Paradise" and the ubiquitous "Baubles, Bangles, and Beads"). Despite Howard Keel's relaxed, strong voice and Dolores Gray's low-down wiles, it didn't work the way it had on the stage—it had lost its sensual power. This is a fruity, kitschy production—a studio film in the worst sense of the term—and defeat seems to hover over the players' heads. Jack Cole staged the dances; the cast includes Ann Blyth, Vic Damone, Monty Woolley, and Sebastian Cabot. Produced by Arthur Freed, for M-G-M. color.

Kiss Me Kate (1953)—A backstage farce set during the staging of a musical version of *The Taming of the Shrew*, with Kathryn Grayson and Howard Keel as the warring stars. Grayson's trilling is something to contend with, and so is her busy, amateurish performance, and there's a lot of badly placed rambunctious comedy from just about everybody. But there's also a marvellous Cole Porter score, with such songs as "Where Is the Life That Late I Led?," "Why Can't You Behave?," "Too Darn Hot," "I've Come to Wive It Wealthily in Padua," and "Always True to You in My Fashion." And there is Howard Keel, with his strong baritone and his good-hearted leering; a dark goatee gives him more chin and, with his great height, he looks hilarious in Petruchio's striped pants. And there is the dancing of Bob Fosse, Tommy Rall, and Bobby Van—their "From This Moment On" number, choreographed by Fosse, is one of the high points of movie-musical history; in its speed and showmanship one can see the Fosse style in its earliest film realization. This sequence more than balances out the grossly embarrassing moments, such as the one when Keel tells Grayson, who is about to quit acting and go off with a Texan (Willard Parker), that she belongs in the theatre. Maybe because Grayson looks so uncomfortable—so aware of her shortcomings as an actress—Ann Miller, who obviously enjoys performing, comes off as lively and amusing; she doesn't just do her usual tick-tock tapping, because she's working with those three leaping male dancers, and with Carol Haney, too. Produced by Jack Cummings and directed by George Sidney, with dances staged by Hermes Pan. The cast includes Keenan Wynn and James Whitmore, who try (and fail) to be delightful clowns, and Jeanne Coyne, Ron Randell, Kurt Kasznar, Claude Allister, and Dave O'Brien. The Cole Porter Broadway show, with a book by Samuel and Bella Spewack, was adapted to M-G-M's requirements by Dorothy Kingsley—i.e., it was cleaned up and overtamed. (Filmed in 3-D.) color

Kiss Me, Stupid (1964)—This Billy Wilder box-office failure isn't more grating than some of his hits—it's just more insecure. Essentially, it's an old-fashioned boulevard farce, but it was generally panned as "coarse and smutty" and "repellent," and it was condemned by the Catholic Legion of Decency (the first such condemnation of a major-studio production since *Baby Doll*, in 1956). United Artists, uneasy about public criticism, sent it out under the label of Lopert Pictures, a subsidiary that usually distributed foreign films. Bad luck plagued this marital-mixup comedy from the start: Peter Sellers, who had been cast as the central character (a composer stuck teaching piano in the desert town of Climax, Nevada), had a heart attack a few weeks into shooting and was replaced by Ray Walston, who is singularly charmless in the role. The plot has the composer attempting to sell his songs to a lecherous star, Dino (Dean Martin), who happens to be passing through town, but he's so fearful that Dino will seduce his wife (Felicia Farr) that he sends her away overnight and brings in the local B-girl, Polly the Pistol (Kim Novak), to pose as his wife. The central miscasting is compounded by the chortling tone, the overemphatic double-entendres, and the drab look of the film, but there's something going

on in it. Maybe because of all the dumb leering, Kim Novak is touching in her dreamy-floozy, Marilyn Monroe–like role. Her clothes are so tight she seems to be wearing her dresses under her skin; she seems exposed, humiliated. Her lostness holds the film together. With Henry Gibson, Cliff Osmond, Alice Pearce, Doro Merande, Barbara Pepper, and Mel Blanc. Script by Wilder and I. A. L. Diamond, suggested by a play by Anna Bonacci. b & w

Kiss of Death (1947)—A tense, terrifying New York crime melodrama, with an unusually authentic seamy atmosphere; the director, Henry Hathaway, brought his crew in from Hollywood and shot the entire film on location, in such places as a Harlem nightclub, a house in Queens, the Criminal Courts Building, the Tombs, Sing Sing. Victor Mature gives an unexpectedly subdued, convincing performance as a hoodlum convict who, for the sake of his children (their mother has committed suicide), agrees to work with the police as an informer. Richard Widmark, in his film début, created a sensation; he's a giggling, sadistic gunman with homicidal mania in his voice, and when he grins his white teeth are more alarming than fangs. Ben Hecht and Charles Lederer wrote the script, from a story by Eleazar Lipsky. With the talented, refreshingly unactressy Coleen Gray as the hero's new wife, and Brian Donlevy, Taylor Holmes, Karl Malden, Anthony Ross, Mildred Dunnock, Millard Mitchell, Robert Keith, and Harry Bellaver. Cinematography by Norbert Brodine; in the nightclub sequence, it's Jo Jones on drums. (Remade in 1958 as *The Fiend Who Walked the West*.) 20th Century-Fox. b & w

Kiss of the Spider Woman (1985)—Set in a nameless South American country, Hector Babenco's film version of Manuel Puig's famous novel is about a homosexual window dresser, Molina (William Hurt), and a revolutionary, Valentín (Raul Julia), who share a prison cell. Molina tries to comfort Valentín and help him forget his pain and misery by telling him the stories of old movies. Hurt is just about the only thing to look at; he's very likable in the scenes where Molina reveals his tenderness and warmth and humor, and the picture can work on audiences in the way that *Midnight Cowboy* did back in 1969. (The times having changed, it can make explicit what was potential in that earlier relationship.) But it's a slack piece of moviemaking, and as sentimental as the 40s screen romances that Molina is infatuated with; that is to say, it moves an audience at the obvious points. The novel is a sly celebration of the seductive, consoling power of movies; Babenco reaches for something larger, something aggressively moral. Valentín, a Marxist prig and a puritan about pleasure, learns humility and becomes more of a man through his close friendship with the sweetly maternal Molina. And Molina is transfigured through the power of love and happiness and a new self-respect. This Brazilian production, made in English, was shot in São Paulo; the screenplay is by Leonard Schrader, the cinematography by Rodolfo Sanchez. With Sonia Braga. Academy Award for Best Actor (Hurt). Island Pictures. color (See *Hooked*.)

Kitty Foyle (1940)—Ginger Rogers won the Academy Award for Best Actress for her "serious" performance as a white-collar girl whose baby dies. In a long career of giving pleasure, this is one of the few occasions when she failed; it isn't her worst acting (that's probably in *Tender Comrade*) but there's nothing in the soggy material to release the distinctive Ginger Rogers sense of fun. Dalton Trumbo and Donald Ogden Stewart adapted Christopher Morley's novel; Sam Wood directed. With Dennis Morgan, James Craig, Gladys Cooper, Florence Bates, Eduardo Ciannelli, Cecil Cunningham, and Nella Walker. R K O. b & w

Klondike Annie (1936)—Mae West and Victor McLaglen. They don't bring out the best in each other. With Phillip Reed, Esther Howard, Harold Huber, and Helen Jerome Eddy. Directed by Raoul Walsh. Paramount. b & w

Klute (1971)—Jane Fonda in possibly her finest dramatic performance, as Bree, an intelligent, high-bracket call girl, in Alan J. Pakula's murder-melodrama. The picture is reminiscent of the good detective mysteries of the 40s—it has the lurking figures, the withheld information, the standard gimmick of getting the heroine to go off alone so she can be menaced (in this case, it's by a bigshot sadistic sex fiend), and so on. And there's no conviction in Pakula's use of those devices; they're hokum—the shadows and crazy camera angles are as silly as a fright wig. But at the center is a study of Bree's temperament and drives, and here the picture is modern. The life surrounding Bree's profession frightens her, but the work itself has peculiar compensations—she enjoys her power over her customers. She's maternal and provocative with them, confident and contemptuously cool. She's a different girl alone—huddled in bed in her disorderly room. The suspense plot involves the ways in which prostitutes attract the forces that destroy them. Bree's knowledge that as a prostitute she has nowhere to go but down and her mixed-up efforts to escape make her one of the strongest women characters to reach the screen. And Fonda is very exciting to watch: the closest closeup never reveals a false thought and, seen on the movie streets a block away, she's Bree, not Jane Fonda, walking toward us. With Donald Sutherland, Charles Cioffi, Roy Scheider, Dorothy Tristan, Rita Gam, Richard Shull, and Anthony Holland. Written by Andy and Dave Lewis;

cinematography by Gordon Willis; edited by Carl Lerner; music by Michael Small. Warners. color (See *Deeper into Movies*.)

The Knack . . . And How to Get It (1965)—In Richard Lester's version of the Ann Jellicoe play (as adapted by Charles Wood), the jokes whiz by so fast that the ingenuity becomes exhausting. The gags don't go anywhere. Lester gets caught up in surface agitation and loses track of what it's all for. The story (which is just his jumping-off place) is about three men (Michael Crawford, Ray Brooks, Donal Donnelly) who live in the same London House; Rita Tushingham, a country girl just come to the big city, also moves in. The assured Brooks has a knack for attracting women, and the shy, frightened Crawford desperately wants that knack. The dreamlike David Watkin photography often seems too brilliantly sun-bleached and the film's spirit is too anarchistically chic and on the side of larky youth. It's a fashionable, professionally youthful treatment of 60s underground attitudes; the content seems to be the same as the content of TV commercials, and by the time you're outside the theatre, you've already forgotten the movie. The more spurious the spontaneity around them, the more flat the performers seem, though somehow Donnelly's fevered leprechaun quality comes through. b & w (See *Kiss Kiss Bang Bang*.)

Knave of Hearts, see *Monsieur Ripois*

Knightriders (1981)—George A. Romero wrote and directed this Arthurian wheeler: the motorcyclists wear medieval-looking helmets with plumes, and they joust on their bikes at the Renaissance tournaments that they stage. They're a travelling Camelot, with a king, Billy (Ed Harris), who administers a code that is supposed to keep them safe from the hucksterism of the outside world. Possibly, Romero had in mind both the big

M-G-M *Ivanhoe* (1952) and Tom Laughlin's *Billy Jack* (1971), with its mystical man-of-action hero. The picture isn't offensive; it's simpleminded, though, inept, and long (2 hours and 26 minutes). Romero keeps his stunt men whirring by, crashing, flying through the air, but there's no kinetic drama in the hurtling bodies. Most of the time, we don't even see the weapons hit the riders and unseat them, and the way that the contests are photographed, there's no physical grace in the bikers' athleticism. With Tom Savini as Morgan, Brother Blue as Merlin, Ken Hixon as Steve the lawyer, Warner Shook as Pippin, Amy Ingersoll as the queen, Gary Lahti as Alan (the Lancelot figure), Christine Forrest as the grease monkey, Patricia Tallman as the teenage groupie, and the horror novelist Stephen King as a beer-swilling rube. Made in the Pittsburgh area. A Laurel Group Production; released by United Artists. color (See *Taking It All In*.)

Knock, see *Dr. Knock*

Knock on Any Door (1949)—John Derek as a young delinquent on trial for killing a policeman, and Humphrey Bogart as the lawyer defending him. As the lawyer talks, we see the boy's grim past in flashback; his father died in prison, he was sent to reform school, his child wife committed suicide. Making this solemn sociological case for him, Bogart is so wearing that you wish he'd stop orating and get out his own rod again. Nicholas Ray directed. Columbia. b & w

Knock on Wood (1954)—This Danny Kaye comedy was fairly universally certified as a howl, but some few of us may hear ourselves moaning. Kaye's talents are violently evident, but they're sunk in the mud of "family entertainment." He plays a ventriloquist who can't control his dummy (the plot resemblance to the Redgrave episode in *Dead of*

Night may not be wholly coincidental) and Mai Zetterling is his analyst. The tiresome, naïve young man occasionally breaks out into frenzied satire, but more frequently he just pushes his way through some clumsy routines (if he uses that Irish impersonation again, even the infants may crawl out for a cigarette). Norman Panama and Melvin Frank wrote and directed. Michael Kidd did the choreography; the music and lyrics are by Sylvia Fine. With Abner Biberman, Steven Geray, Torin Thatcher, and Gavin Gordon. Paramount. color

Koritsi me ta Mavra, see *A Girl in Black*

Kotch (1971)—Hopelessly warm and coy. With Walter Matthau as a clean old man who is mistaken for a dirty old man. If the gimmick had been reversed, the picture might have had something. With Felicia Farr, Deborah Watts, and Charles Aidman. Directed by Jack Lemmon, from John Paxton's adaptation of a Katherine Topkins novel. color

The Koumiko Mystery *Le Mystère Koumiko* (1966)—This lovely hour-long documentary about a modern Japanese girl was shot by a Frenchman, Chris Marker, in Tokyo during the Olympics. The mystery is the mystery of human individuality, and Marker's approach is personal, lyrical. Earlier, he made the short *La Jetée*, which is very possibly the greatest science-fiction movie yet made. His Tokyo has something of science fiction, too: it looks as if it were built the day after tomorrow, and it's almost inconceivable that it was ever intended to endure. Koumiko, with her archaic Oriental beauty, walks through this transient World's Fair atmosphere, seeing herself as an outsider in modern Japan. The movie expresses a new mood—the acceptance of estrangement. In French. color

Kriemhild's Revenge, see *Nibelungen Saga*

Kumonosu-jo, see *The Throne of Blood*

Kvinnodröm, see *Dreams*

Kvinnors Väntan, see *Secrets of Women*

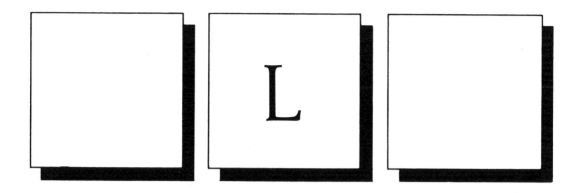

Lacombe, Lucien (1974)—About a boy who has an empty space where feelings beyond the purely instinctual are expected to be. The time is 1944, and the boy—a French peasant—goes to work each day hunting down and torturing people for the Gestapo. The director, Louis Malle, casts as Lucien a teenage country boy (Pierre Blaise) who can respond to events with his own innocence, apathy, and animal shrewdness. Malle's gamble is that the cameras will discover what the artist's imagination can't, and, steadily, startlingly, the gamble pays off. Without ever mentioning the subject of innocence and guilt, this extraordinary film, in its calm, dispassionate way, addresses it on a very deep level. With Aurore Clément as a Parisian Jewish girl; Holger Löwenadler as her punctilious, cultivated father; Thérèse Giehse as her grandmother; Gilberte Rivet as the boy's mother; Stephane Bouy; and Jacques Rispal. The script is by Malle and Patrick Modiano. In French. color (See *Reeling*.)

Ladies in Retirement (1941)—An entertainingly hokey murder chiller on the stage, but not very successfully adapted to the screen. With Charles Vidor directing, this lonely-rural-cottage gothic seems to take itself too seriously, as if it were really a psychological study. Ida Lupino works hard as a severe, plain-faced murderess, Isobel Elsom sips her wine and nibbles her bonbons as the woman who innocently befriends her, and Elsa Lanchester and Edith Barrett are Lupino's loony sisters, who stuff their neat rooms with their collections of crows' feathers, dead birds, and underbrush. From the play by Reginald Denham and Edward Percy; with Louis Hayward. Columbia. b & w

Ladies of Leisure (1930)—Though she came from the theatre, Barbara Stanwyck seemed to have an intuitive understanding of the fluid physical movements that work best on camera; perhaps she had been an unusually "natural" actress even onstage. This was her first big hit in the movies. Under Frank Capra's direction, she plays a tough "party" girl (euphemism for call girl) who poses for a wealthy young artist (Ralph Graves); he sees in her the spirituality that she attempts to deny. The story is a museum piece of early-talkies sentimentality, but, in a way, that only emphasizes Stanwyck's remarkable modernism. With Marie Prevost, Lowell Sherman, Juliette Compton, and Nance O'Neil. Beautifully lighted by the cinematographer, Joseph Walker. Columbia. b & w

Ladri di Biciclette, see *The Bicycle Thief*

Lady Be Good (1941)—A dispensable plot about the tribulations of a married song-writing team, but some classic numbers by the Gershwins ("Fascinating Rhythm," "Hang on to Me," and the great title song) and by Arthur Freed and Roger Edens ("You'll Never Know") as well as the slightly sickening Oscar Hammerstein II and Jerome Kern effort, "The Last Time I Saw Paris." The cast includes Red Skelton, Ann Sothern, Eleanor Powell, Virginia O'Brien, Robert Young, Dan Dailey, Phil Silvers, Lionel Barrymore, and Jimmy Dorsey and his orchestra. Norman Z. McLeod directed; the choreography is by Busby Berkeley. Based (very remotely) on a 1924 Broadway show. M-G-M. b & w

Lady Caroline Lamb (1973)—Robert Bolt, directing for the first time, thrashes about from one style and point of view to another. The film seems to have been made by a square Ken Russell; Bolt tries for romantic excess, but he can't get anything warmed up. His Caroline Lamb is an hysterical fool but also a misunderstood free spirit struggling against a hypocritical society—a sort of Regency Zelda. Sarah Miles acts like a dizzy shopgirl dreaming of being a great lady, and falling flat even in her dreams; as Byron, Richard Chamberlain scowls and sneers. With Jon Finch as Lamb; Margaret Leighton as his mother; Laurence Olivier as Wellington; and Ralph Richardson as the King. color (See *Reeling*.)

The Lady Eve (1941)—A frivolous masterpiece. Like *Bringing Up Baby, The Lady Eve* is a mixture of visual and verbal slapstick, and of high artifice and pratfalls. Barbara Stanwyck keeps sticking out a sensational leg, and Henry Fonda keeps tripping over it. She's a cardsharp, and he's a millionaire scientist who knows more about snakes than about women; neither performer has ever been funnier. The film, based on a story by Monckton Hoffe, and with screenplay and direction by Preston Sturges, is full of classic moments and classic lines; it represents the dizzy high point of Sturges's comedy writing. With Charles Coburn, Eugene Pallette, William Demarest, and Eric Blore. (Remade as a musical in 1956—*The Birds and the Bees*.) Paramount. b & w

Lady in the Dark (1944)—Monstrously overproduced musical about the Oedipal hangups and sexual frustrations of a fashion-magazine editor (Ginger Rogers), whose problems are solved when she stops wearing the pants—i.e., gives up her job to a man (Ray Milland). The content is insulting to women; the form is insulting to audiences of both sexes. It's a real botch. Directed by Mitchell Leisen; adapted from Moss Hart's Broadway show, with music by Kurt Weill and lyrics by Ira Gershwin. With Jon Hall, Warner Baxter, Mischa Auer, Barry Sullivan, Mary Philips, and Don Loper. Paramount. color

Lady in the Lake (1947)—A Raymond Chandler murder mystery with the camera functioning as the Private Eye—that is, as the eyes of Philip Marlowe, the narrator-protagonist (Robert Montgomery), who is seen in his entirety only when his reflection is caught in mirrors. This novelty is a nuisance, and is frustrating besides, since Montgomery (who also directed) is the only star; the plot isn't involving enough to compensate for the absence of star byplay. At one point, the face of Audrey Totter, the feminine lead, comes swimming out at you, lips ajar, as if to honor you with a great big kiss; then she's lost in shadows. That's about as close as you get to any fun. With Lloyd Nolan, Leon Ames, and Jayne Meadows. M-G-M. b & w

Lady in White (1988)—This ghost movie has an overcomplicated plot, but it has a poetic feeling that makes up for much of the clutter. And its amateurishness often adds to its effectiveness—gives the movie a naïve power. It's a piece of Catholic Americana with a Disney-Spielberg ingenuousness and shafts of horror. Lukas Haas plays the 9-year-old Frankie Scarlatti, who dreams of his dead mother; on Halloween, 1962, he's locked in the school cloakroom and sees the ghost of a little girl who was murdered by a serial killer. The editing is patchy, and the writer-director Frank LaLoggia, who also composed the score, lingers on actors in a way that exposes their limitations (and his inexperience), but little Lukas Haas has no problem. He loves acting so much that when he's miming spooked terror he's tickled to be doing it. As he plays Frankie, the boy's rapt belief in his visions lends credibility to the events. You get a sense that the horrors that beset him relate to his mother's having died—that the story has (underdeveloped) psychological roots. And there are visual and nostalgic touches that charm you. The location shooting was done in the upstate New York town of Lyons, near Rochester, where LaLoggia was born. With Jason Presson, who's amiable as the older brother, and Alex Rocco, Len Cariou, Katherine Helmond, and Jared Rushton. color (See *Hooked*.)

The Lady Is Willing (1942)—Marlene Dietrich, excruciatingly miscast, as an actress who adopts a baby and marries a pediatrician (Fred MacMurray); the baby has a mastoid operation just as she is opening in a new show. Hatted by John-Frederics, Dietrich simpers and suffers; every nuance is inane. Mitchell Leisen directed, in a spirit of hopelessness, from a script by James Edward

Grant and Albert McCleery. With Aline MacMahon, Arline Judge, and Stanley Ridges. Columbia. b & w

Lady of Burlesque (1943)—Gypsy Rose Lee's murder-mystery novel, *The G-String Murders,* cleaned up, and burlesque as an institution considerably tamed. The movie has scenes in which burlesque audiences are stimulated into raucous excitement by the sight of girls clothed practically to the stifling point. Barbara Stanwyck's bumps and grinds are communicated via her face and a few percussion sounds, but she acts with a hard realism that suggests something of the milieu, and Michael O'Shea, who plays opposite her, has a relaxed show-biz authenticity. With J. Edward Bromberg, Iris Adrian, Marion Martin, Gloria Dickson, Pinky Lee, Frank Conroy, and Frank Fenton. Considering how few of Gypsy Rose Lee's racy bits are actually left, the director, William Wellman, does a good job of simulating raciness. United Artists. b & w

Lady on a Train (1945)—Ugh. A murder mystery that starts from a Leslie Charteris story but never gets anyplace you'd want to go to. Made in the period when the former child star Deanna Durbin was turning into a fairly substantial young matron, the film casts her as a girl who witnesses a murder from a train that is nearing Grand Central and who becomes involved with the friends and relatives of the victim, as well as with a mystery-story writer. (Has that gimmick ever worked?) The film betrays an obvious uncertainty about how the public wants to see its Deanna. One minute she is just a little girl in pigtails lost in a great big raincoat, and the next minute she is a many-curved siren crooning "Give Me a Little Kiss, Will You, Huh?" in a strange, guttural manner evidently intended to suggest that passion has got a stranglehold on her. The cameraman photographs her from so many angles that at any particular moment it's hard to know whether she's standing up or lying down. Charles David directed; with Ralph Bellamy, Edward Everett Horton, George Coulouris, Dan Duryea, David Bruce, Allen Jenkins, and Patricia Morison. The script is by Edmund Beloin and Robert O'Brien. Universal. b & w

Lady Sings the Blues (1972)—The chemistry of pop vulgarization is all-powerful here; factually, this life of Billie Holiday is a fraud, but emotionally it delivers. That great, dizzy imp Diana Ross gives herself to the role with an all-out physicality that wins the audience over. Regrettably, she sings too much like Billie Holiday, and the songs blur one's memories. Sidney J. Furie directed. With Richard Pryor as Piano Man, and Billy Dee Williams. Released by Paramount. color (See *Reeling*.)

The Lady Vanishes (1938)—Alfred Hitchcock's murder mystery about a fussy, jolly old lady who boards a train and disappears on it is directed with such skill and velocity that it has come to represent the quintessence of screen suspense. It provides some of the finest examples of Hitchcock touches—little shocks and perversities of editing and detail. The hero is played by a tall, callow young man making his first major film appearance— Michael Redgrave; the heroine is Margaret Lockwood, and the lady is Dame May Whitty. With Paul Lukas, Cecil Parker, Margaretta Scott, Catherine Lacey, Mary Clare, Linden Travers, Googie Withers, and the team of Naunton Wayne and Basil Radford doing a parody of the "jolly-good-show" type of Britisher. Screenplay by Sidney Gilliat, Frank Launder, and Alma Reville, based on the novel *The Wheel Spins* by Ethel Lina White. (A 1979 remake with Elliott Gould, Cybill Shepherd, and Angela Lansbury is good-natured but totally flat; the director, Anthony

Page, doesn't seem to have an instinct for the thriller form.) b & w

Ladyhawke (1985)—Set in the Middle Ages, it's about the romance between Princess Isabeau (Michelle Pfeiffer) and the noble Navarre (Rutger Hauer), which is cursed by an evil sorcerer-bishop (John Wood). Each sunrise, Isabeau turns into a hawk; each sundown, Navarre turns into a black wolf. The settings and accoutrements have grandeur; just about everything connected with the movie is big except the storytelling instinct of its director, Richard Donner. At almost every point where we might expect a little ping of surprise or mystery, Donner lets us down. It's a limp and dreary movie. The lovers are helped by a boy thief, played by Matthew Broderick, who is like a contemporary urban-American adolescent placed in medieval France—the effect is something like putting, say, a boy Woody Allen at Robert Taylor's elbow in *Ivanhoe*. The device doesn't feel integral and the boy is made too endearing and impish, yet even when Broderick's lines are irritating, this happy, ingenious young actor isn't. Put up on the screen for comic relief, he has more of a fairy-tale quality than anyone else. With Leo McKern as the swillbelly priest, and Ken Hutchinson. The overly fastidious script, which lifts its climax from Mark Twain's *A Connecticut Yankee in King Arthur's Court,* is by Edward Khmara, Michael Thomas, and Tom Mankiewicz; the cinematography is by Vittorio Storaro; the disco-medieval music is by Andrew Powell. Warners. color (See *State of the Art*.)

The Ladykillers (1956)—This sinister black comedy of murder accelerates until it becomes a grotesque fantasy of murder. The actors seem to be having a boisterous good time getting themselves knocked off. Alec Guinness, almost done in by great, hideous teeth—so enormous they give him master-criminal status—is the leader of a horrendous gang that includes Peter Sellers as Harry, the plump, awkward teddy boy. Katie Johnson is the cheerful old lady who upsets their fiendish plans simply by living in a world of her own. As her victims are, in some ways, even less real than she (she, at least, is as real as a good fairy), the disasters that befall them are extravagantly funny. With Cecil Parker, Herbert Lom, Danny Green, Jack Warner, and Frankie Howerd as the barrow boy. Directed by Alexander Mackendrick; written by William Rose. color

A Lady's Morals (1930)—Originally called *The Soul Kiss*; neither title indicates what a big, heavy-spirited M-G-M musical tearjerker this is. Grace Moore plays Jenny Lind, who loses her voice while singing in *Norma*, and Reginald Denny is a young composer who loves her but goes blind. Wallace Beery turns up as P. T. Barnum. Sidney Franklin directed, and Adrian draped Miss Moore, who moved a little less than gracefully. With Jobyna Howland, George F. Marion, Paul Porcasi, Gilbert Emery, and Bodil Rosing. b & w

The Landlord (1970)—Hal Ashby's début film as a director is one of his best. Based on the novel by Kristin Hunter, a black woman, and adapted by another black writer, William Gunn, it's about an affable, rich blond bachelor (Beau Bridges) who gets in over his head when he buys a house in a black ghetto, intending to throw out the tenants and turn it into his own handsome townhouse. The tenants include Pearl Bailey, and Diana Sands in probably her finest screen performance—when she becomes sexually and emotionally involved with the new landlord, he starts learning something about passion and terror. The dialogue is crisp and often quite startling, and though the editing may be a little too showy and jumpy, the picture has originality and depth, and it's full of sharp, absurdist

humor. Lee Grant is particularly funny as Beau Bridges' ditsy mother and Lou Gossett, Jr., is fairly amazing as Diana Sands' axe-wielding husband. Also with Mel Stewart, Susan Anspach, Marki Bey, Grover Dale, Bob Klein, Walter Brooke, and Douglas Grant. Produced by Norman Jewison; cinematography by Gordon Willis; music by Al Kooper. The distributors may have been frightened off by the tense, interracial byplay—or perhaps the public was; relatively few people saw the picture and it's rarely revived. United Artists. color

Lasky Jedne Plavovlasky, see *Loves of a Blonde*

The Last American Hero (1973)—Jeff Bridges stars in Lamont Johnson's fine, scrupulous film based on Tom Wolfe's article about Junior Johnson, the moonshiner's son who learned to drive by running his daddy's whiskey on back roads at night, and who, as a racer, beat the expensive cars sponsored by Detroit. The casting, the acting, and the milieu seem effortlessly, inexplicably right. This movie transcends its genre; it isn't only about stock-car racing, any more than *The Hustler* was only about shooting pool. With Art Lund, Geraldine Fitzgerald, Ed Lauter, Valerie Perrine, and Gary Busey. Written by William Roberts and the uncredited William Kerby. 20th Century-Fox. color (See *Reeling*.)

The Last Days of Dolwyn, see *Woman of Dolwyn*

The Last Detail (1974)—After 14 years in the Navy, Buddusky (Jack Nicholson), the tattooed signalman, lives on ingrained resentment, quick anger, and booze. The screenwriter, Robert Towne, shaped the role to Nicholson's gift for extremes, and it was the best full-scale part he'd had up to that time. (Some think it's the best part he's ever had.) The movie is the record of the beer-

L

soaked journey that Buddusky and a gunner's mate (Otis Young) take when they're assigned to escort a morose 18-year-old seaman (Randy Quaid) from the brig in Norfolk, Virginia, to the naval prison in Portsmouth, New Hampshire. The film is distinguished by the fine performances of Nicholson and Quaid, and by remarkably well-orchestrated profane dialogue. It's often very funny. It's programmed to wrench your heart, though—it's about the blasted lives of people who discover their humanity too late. Hal Ashby directed. With Michael Moriarty, Carol Kane, Luana Anders, Clifton James, Nancy Allen, and Gilda Radner. Cinematography (grainy and gloomy) by Michael Chapman. Adapted from Darryl Ponicsan's book. Columbia. color (See *Reeling*.)

The Last Emperor (1987)—Bernardo Bertolucci tells the story of Pu Yi, who was not quite 3 when, in 1908, he was set on the Dragon Throne in Peking's Forbidden City and became the titular ruler of a third of the people on earth. After being deposed and then enthroned again in Japanese-occupied Manchuria, he was in Soviet custody for 5 years, and then spent 10 years being "re-educated" in a Chinese war-criminals prison. The movie doesn't have the juicy absurdity that seems to pour right out of the historical story. And it suppresses the drama. But it has pictorial grace and a dull fascination. Bertolucci presents Pu Yi (John Lone) as a man without will or backbone who lives his life as spectacle—who watches his life go by. And so we're given a historical pageant without a protagonist. There's an idea here, but it's a dippy idea—it results in a passive movie. This epic is meant to be an attack on privilege (and at times it's like a replay of *The Conformist* in Manchuria). Bertolucci and Mark Peploe, who wrote the script with his assistance, want us to believe that Pu Yi became a model citizen through the ministrations of the kindly prison governor (Ying Ruocheng), and that in his later years, when he worked as an under-gardener, he experienced freedom for the first time. They want us to believe that what some might disparage as Communist brainwashing actually cleaned away his decadence and healed him. With the gifted Joan Chen as the empress, the likable Wu Jun Mimei as the No. 2 wife, Peter O'Toole as Pu Yi's tutor, and Maggie Han as the lesbian spy. Cinematography by Vittorio Storaro; sets by Ferdinando Scarfiotti; costumes by James Acheson; music by Ryuichi Sakamoto, David Byrne, and Cong Su. (The film shows the palaces and courtyards of the 250-acre Forbidden City.) Academy Awards: Best Picture, Director, Adapted Screenplay, Art Direction, Cinematography, Costume Design, Film Editing, Score, Sound. Released by Columbia. (166 minutes.) color (*See Hooked.*)

Last Holiday (1950)—This lovely ironic comedy—an almost perfect "little" picture—stars Alec Guinness as an ordinary sort of fellow who is told that he has only six weeks to live; liberated from anxieties about the future, he finds in that time all the opportunities for wealth, fame, and happiness that he had never found before. The dexterity—the impeccable "rightness"—of J. B. Priestley's screenplay is close to infuriating: within the genteel, socialist-mystic limits that he has set, he is an unerring master. The film is rounded and complete—in the contentedly banal way of an O. Henry story. With Kay Walsh, Wilfrid Hyde-White, Beatrice Campbell, Grégoire Aslan, Bernard Lee, David McCallum as the blind violinist, Sidney James, and that great asset of English comedy Ernest Thesiger. Henry Cass directed. b & w

The Last Hurrah (1958)—John Ford turned into a sentimental faker whenever he got near the Blarney stone, and Edwin O'Connor's novel about the final campaign and last days of Frank Skeffington, an old-style Boston mayor (Spencer Tracy), gave him an opportunity he couldn't resist. The subject is richly comic, and the picture has its moments despite the sprightly foolery, but Skeffington is so full of the milk of human kindness that he almost moos. The extraordinary cast includes James Gleason, Pat O'Brien, Ricardo Cortez, Edmund Lowe, John Carradine, Basil Rathbone, Jeffrey Hunter, Donald Crisp, Anna Lee, and Jane Darwell. Columbia. b & w

The Last Laugh *Der Letzte Mann* (1924)—A breathtaking achievement in silent-film technique, from the German studio UFA. Emil Jannings is the man whose self-esteem and position in society depend on his uniform, in F. W. Murnau's masterpiece of design and cinematography. The scenario is by Carl Mayer; the camerawork is by Karl Freund. With added musical track. b & w

The Last Millionaire *Le Dernier Milliardaire* (1934)—The queen of the bankrupt mythical kingdom of Casinario, which is modelled somewhat on Monaco and bears a resemblance to the Marx Brothers' kingdom in *Duck Soup,* invites the world's richest banker (Max Dearly) to run things. He becomes dictator, is hit on the head and lapses into childish ways, and the people go on taking his idiotic edicts as signs of genius. Chairs, hats, and cravats are banned, and the new system of barter results in transactions such as a customer who has paid his café bill with a hen and received two chicks and an egg in change leaving the egg as a tip. When the picture came out, the political atmosphere in Europe was so sensitive that this light satirical comedy by René Clair (not quite at his best) was banned in Italy and Germany, and was such a scandalous failure in France that its writer-director left the country. With Raymond Cordy and Annabella. Cinematography by

Rudolph Maté and Louis Née; music by Maurice Jaubert. In French. b & w

The Last Movie (1971)—Dennis Hopper directed this put-on, knockabout tragedy, in which he stars as a stunt man with an American film company in Peru who becomes a Christ figure when the natives imitate film-making. The movie grinds to a painful halt right at the start; it is visually beautiful, but the editing is so self-destructive that it's as if Hopper had slashed his own canvases. Cinematography by Laszlo Kovacs; screenplay by Stewart Stern. With Julie Adams, Tomas Milian, Samuel Fuller, Sylvia Miles, Rod Cameron, Severn Darden, Peter Fonda, Henry Jaglom, Kris Kristofferson, John Phillip Law, Michelle Phillips, Dean Stockwell, and Russ Tamblyn. Universal. color (See *Deeper into Movies.*)

The Last Picture Show (1971)—This straightforward, involving, narrative picture about growing up in a small town in Texas in the early 50s was Peter Bogdanovich's first great success. It's plain and uncondescending in its re-creation of what it means to be a high-school athlete, of what a country dance hall is like, of the necking in cars and movie houses, and of the desolation that follows high-school graduation. Concerned with adolescent experience seen in terms of flatlands anomie—loneliness, ignorance about sex, confusion about one's aims in life—the movie has a basic decency of feeling, with people relating to one another, sometimes on very simple levels, and becoming miserable when they can't relate. Robert Surtees's stylized cinematography is in black and white, and the frequent silhouetting—so that we seem to be looking at a map of life as it was—helps to clarify the subject matter. The film badly needs this stylization, because, of course, its shallow overview of town life is dangerously close to TV, and especially to the "Peyton Place" series. The movie suggests what TV soap opera would be if it looked at ordinary experience in a non-exploitative way, if it had observation and humor. This is perhaps an *ideal* TV show. From Larry McMurtry's novel, adapted by McMurtry together with the director. With Timothy Bottoms, Jeff Bridges, Ellen Burstyn, Cybill Shepherd, Ben Johnson, Eileen Brennan, and Cloris Leachman. (A sequel, *Texasville*, also directed by Bogdanovich, was released in 1990.) Columbia. (See *Deeper into Movies*.)

The Last Run (1971)—A picture that closed so fast (deservedly) that few knew it had ever opened. It's mostly fast driving over European roads and George C. Scott in a cool, Bogartian role that is exactly wrong for his febrile talents. Scott needs antagonists to taunt and jeer at, needs situations in which he can smolder. Here, as an aging gangster who comes out of retirement for one last job, he never finds a character. The script, by Alan Sharp, is pseudo-Hemingway; the direction, by Richard Fleischer, is so bland and mechanical that even Sven Nykvist's cinematography doesn't help much. With Tony Musante as a hood, Trish Van Devere miscast as a moll, and Colleen Dewhurst stupefyingly miscast as a whore in a Mediterranean village. M-G-M. color

Last Tango in Paris *Ultimo Tango a Parigi Dernier Tango à Paris* (1972)—Exploitation films had been supplying mechanized sex—sex as physical stimulant but without passion or emotional violence. Then, in this film, Bernardo Bertolucci used sex to express the characters' drives. Marlon Brando, as the aging American, Paul, is working out his aggression on the young bourgeois French girl, Jeanne (Maria Schneider), and the physical menace of sexuality that is emotionally charged is such a departure from everything that audiences had come to expect at the movies that the film created a sensation. It's a bold and imaginative work—a great work. When Brando improvises within Bertolucci's structure, his full art is realized; his performance is intuitive, rapt, princely. Working with Brando, Bertolucci achieves realism with the terror of actual experience still alive on the screen. With Jean-Pierre Léaud, Massimo Girotti, Catherine Allegret, and Maria Michi. Script by Bertolucci and the editor, Franco Arcalli; cinematography by Vittorio Storaro; music by Gato Barbieri; production design by Ferdinando Scarfiotti; produced by Alberto Grimaldi. (The film has been subjected to many varieties of legal prosecution, particularly in Italy. The version circulated in the U.S. with an R rating is severely cut.) In French and English. color (See *Reeling*.)

The Last Ten Days *Der Letzte Akt* (1955)—G. W. Pabst, who directed this account of the last 10 days in Hitler's headquarters, employs a restrained style that makes the collapse of discipline and the final disintegration seem like an enveloping nightmare. Erich Maria Remarque's script, based on Judge Michael A. Musmanno's chronicle *Ten Days to Die*, perhaps errs in systematically constructing little episodes to illuminate chaos; the atmosphere is so compelling that these vignettes seem trite and unnecessary. Albin Skoda's Hitler is an intelligent approach to a terribly difficult part; Oskar Werner's heroic role as a liaison officer from one of the Army corps is a flamboyant invention, and he gives it a fine flourish. Surrounding Hitler are Lotte Tobisch as Eva Braun, Willi Krause as Goebbels, and, of course, the generals of all kinds and attitudes: General Krebs, for example, who asks if God exists, and General Burgdorf, who replies, "If He did, we wouldn't." Whatever your judgment of the picture's value as historical interpretation, it is an experience to spend two hours in this claustrophobic bunker with Pabst and his actors. Made in Austria. In German. b & w

The Last Tycoon (1976)—Harold Pinter adapted Fitzgerald's unfinished novel about Hollywood, and Elia Kazan directed the picture, which was produced by Sam Spiegel and stars Robert De Niro as the artist-businessman Monroe Stahr. The result is so enervated that it's like a vampire movie after the vampires have left. De Niro gives an authentic interpretation of a New York–Jewish Hollywood intellectual giant of the 30s, but he might be acting under a blanket. He stands around waiting while Ingrid Boulting, who plays Kathleen, loiters over inane remarks. (Of all Fitzgerald's implausible heroines, Kathleen—the runaway mistress of a European king—is the most vaporous.) Probably the first mistake was to approach the book cap in hand, and the next was to hire Pinter; the film needed a writer who would fill in what's missing—Pinter's art is the art of taking away. With Jack Nicholson, Robert Mitchum, Jeanne Moreau, Ray Milland, Donald Pleasence, Theresa Russell, Dana Andrews, and Tony Curtis—the only one who shows any vitality. Paramount. color (See *When the Lights Go Down*.)

The Last Valley (1971)—Michael Caine as an intelligent man of action in a large-scale historical adventure story set in Germany during the Thirty Years War. He leads his band of brutal mercenaries into a hidden valley; it's as if the men from Kurosawa's *The Seven Samurai* had discovered Shangri-La. The director, James Clavell, is a good storyteller, and the film, which looks at the conflicts in the world outside the valley and at the quality of the life of fat burghers and bigots inside the valley, has a core of feeling. With Omar Sharif, Florinda Bolkan, Nigel Davenport, Per Oscarsson, and Arthur O'Connell, who is unmistakably an actor in makeup, even at a

distance in a crowd. Written and produced by Clavell. The picture deserves a simpler score than the thick, rich musical sludge dredged up by John Barry. color (See *Deeper into Movies*.)

The Last Waltz (1978)—Arguably, the best of all rock-concert documentaries. Martin Scorsese's film of The Band's Thanksgiving, 1976, performance in San Francisco is even-tempered and intensely satisfying. Scorsese, who shot it while he was still working on *New York, New York*, seems in complete control of his talent and of the material. Visually, it's dark-toned and rich and classically simple. The sound (if one has the good luck to catch it in a theatre equipped with a Dolby system) is so clear that the instruments have the distinctness that one hears on the most craftsmanlike recordings. And the casual interviews have a musical, rhythmic ease; Scorsese's conversations with the men give us a sense of the pressures that strain their feelings of community. With Band members—Robbie Robertson, Levon Helm, Garth Hudson, Richard Manuel, and Rick Danko. Also with performers who represent the different styles of rock and the traditions that have fueled it—Joni Mitchell, Bob Dylan, Van Morrison, Eric Clapton, Muddy Waters, Neil Young, Ronnie Hawkins, Dr. John, the Staples, Ringo Starr, Paul Butterfield, Emmylou Harris, Neil Diamond, and others. It's a relief to see a rock film without whizzing-around, catch-as-catch-can cinematography; Scorsese planned the camera cues like a general deploying his troops, and Michael Chapman, Vilmos Zsigmond, Laszlo Kovacs, David Myers, and several other cinematographers are responsible for the serene imagery and its inner excitement. United Artists. color

The Last Wave (1977)—The plot of this Australian film is a throwback to the B-movies of the 30s and early 40s, and the dialogue—by the young director Peter Weir and his two co-scriptwriters, Tony Morphett and Peter Popescu—is vintage R K O and Universal. Weir provides apparitions holding sacred stones, frog noises in the night, shadows in slow motion, and the kind of haunted-house acting that many of us have a certain affection for. But it's hokum without the fun of hokum; despite all the scare-movie apparatus, this film fairly aches to be called profound. The occult manifestations are linked to the white Australians' guilt over their treatment of the aborigines. The decadent white race is represented by a sickly paleface corporate lawyer (Richard Chamberlain), and the aborigines by a lithe, graceful young man (Gulpilil) and a dignified wily shaman (Nandjiwarra Amagula). The aborigine actors, with their deep-set eyes, are by far the most vital element, yet they're kept on the margins and used as supernatural forces. Weir, who has apparently studied Nicolas Roeg's films, knows how to create an allusive, ominous atmosphere. But the film is overdeliberate and sluggish, and Chamberlain can't stop quivering his lips to connote sensitivity and contracting his nostrils for apprehensiveness and pulling in his cheek muscles for ineffable sorrow. He keeps us conscious that he's acting all the time. His toes act in his shoes. With Olivia Hamnett as the lawyer's wife. color (See *When the Lights Go Down*.)

Last Year at Marienbad *L'Année dernière à Marienbad* (1961)—The characters, or rather figures, in this Alain Resnais movie are a tony variant of the undead of vampire movies—"We live as in coffins frozen side by side in a garden." This high-fashion puzzle movie, written by Alain Robbe-Grillet, is set in what is described to us as an "enormous, luxurious, baroque, lugubrious hotel—where corridors succeed endless corridors." The mood is set by climaxes of organ music and this distended narration; it's all solemn and ex-pectant—like High Mass. The dialogue about whether the characters met the year before is like a parody of wealthy indolence. The settings and costumes seem to be waiting for a high romantic theme or fantasy; the people, pawns who are manipulated into shifting positions, seem to be placed for wit, or for irony. But all we get are pretty pictures. Robbe-Grillet says that the film is a pure construction, an object without reference to anything outside itself, and that the existence of the two characters begins when the film begins and ends 93 minutes later. It has a hypnotic effect on some people; others may be tempted to end it sooner. With Delphine Seyrig, Sacha Pitoëff, and Giorgio Albertazzi. The cinematography is by Sacha Vierny. The exteriors were shot at the chateaus of Nymphenburg, Schleissheim, and at other Munich locations; the interiors were shot in a Paris studio. In French. Distributed in the U.S. by Astor Pictures. b & w (See *I Lost it at the Movies*.)

The Late Show (1977)—The writer-director, Robert Benton, has followed the rules of the detective-movie genre, but he's also added something: the detective (Art Carney) is overweight, old, and scared. None of this prevents the heroine (Lily Tomlin), who hires him, from perceiving that he's different from the other men she knows. This one-of-a-kind murder mystery pays off in atmosphere, spooking us by the flip, greedy ordinariness of evil. Eugene Roche is a fence who loves his stolen goodies; Bill Macy is a scrounging bartender; Joanna Cassidy is a lying, cheating charmer; Howard Duff is a penny-ante detective who dies muttering about the money he's going to make; and John Considine is a sleekly handsome strong-arm man. They're all originals. Warners. color (See *When the Lights Go Down*.)

The Laughing Policeman (1973)—Standard, gory imitation of *Dirty Harry*, *The French Con-*

nection, and *Bullitt*. There isn't much acting honor to be had from it, but Walter Matthau, playing a black-haired police detective, loses what little there is to Bruce Dern, who plays his partner. Matthau does the ancient obvious, while Dern's contentious, muffled manner is the latest in fey one-upmanship. The choppy film makes practically no sense; Stuart Rosenberg's direction features massacres, cadavers, and close inspection of wounds. Adapted from the popular Stockholm-set novel by Maj Sjöwall and Per Wahlöö and moved to San Francisco. (Once again the mad mass murderer is some implausible sort of fancy homosexual.) With Joanna Cassidy, Louis Gossett, Jr., and Anthony Zerbe. 20th Century-Fox. color

Laughter (1930)—Just before his death, Herman J. Mankiewicz, who produced this film, said that of all the movies he'd worked on, it was his favorite. A lovely, sophisticated comedy, an ode to impracticality, it failed commercially but its attitudes and spirit influenced the screwball hits of the 30s. (Even the famous Bogart exchange with Claude Rains about coming to Casablanca for the waters is paraphrased from *Laughter*.) Fredric March is the composer-hero who returns to New York after some expatriate years in Paris; he finds that the Follies beauty (Nancy Carroll) whom he loved has married for money and lost her gift of laughter. The pacing of the director, H. d'Abbadie d'Arrast, is a little leisurely, and he dawdles just when he should move faster, but he has visual style, especially when he works in interiors or in deliberately artificial sets. (Nature throws him off balance.) The Art Deco sets here are elegant, and the enchanting Nancy Carroll wears perhaps the best clothes ever seen on the screen (with the *possible* exception of Garbo's in *A Woman of Affairs*). And there's a simple scene with March at the piano and Carroll and another girl (Diane Ellis) jazz

dancing that is one of the loveliest, happiest moments in the movies of the period. The writing was mostly by Donald Ogden Stewart, though d'Abbadie d'Arrast and Douglas Doty had a share in it, and Mankiewicz probably set the tone; the script bogs down a little in conventional melodrama. With Frank Morgan as the beauty's millionaire husband and Glenn Anders in the boggy subplot. Paramount. b & w

Laughter in Paradise (1951)—A charming, neatly contrived English comedy. An old prankster (Hugh Griffith) dies, leaving a will that outlines the tasks his relatives must complete before receiving their inheritance— such tasks as robbery, marriage, etc. Alastair Sim has a classic comic sequence trying to get arrested, and a classic fiancée—Joyce Grenfell, a W.A.A.F. whom he describes as "an officer and lady." Mario Zampi's direction is not all it should be, but the cast is so good it hardly matters: George Cole, A. E. Matthews, Beatrice Campbell, John Laurie, Fay Compton, Guy Middleton, Ernest Thesiger, Anthony Steel, and, in a tiny role, Audrey Hepburn. The ingenious script is by Michael Pertwee and Jack Davies. b & w

Laura (1944)—Everybody's favorite chic murder mystery. Gene Tierney is the dead girl who ends up as the heroine; Clifton Webb and Vincent Price are her suitors; Dana Andrews is the charmingly necrophiliac detective; and Judith Anderson is modishly contemptible. (Speaking of Price, she says, "He's no good, but he's what I want. I'm not a nice person, neither is he. . . . We're both weak and can't seem to help it.") Produced and directed by Otto Preminger; adapted from the novel by Vera Caspary; script credited to Jay Dratler, Samuel Hoffenstein, and Betty Reinhardt—but it was Hoffenstein's work that saved it. With Dorothy Adams as

Bessie. Music by David Raksin. 20th Century-Fox. b & w

The Lavender Hill Mob (1951)—As the prim, innocuous civil servant with a hidden spark of nonconformity, Alec Guinness carries out a dream of larcenous glory: robbing the Bank of England. A man who steals three million in gold bullion may be permitted to coin a word: Guinness describes his gleaming-eyed, bowler-hatted little man as the "fubsy" type, and he's an image of Everyman. T.E.B. Clarke's script, Charles Crichton's direction, and Georges Auric's music contribute to what is probably the most nearly perfect fubsy comedy of all time. It's a minor classic, a charmer. Stanley Holloway is the genteel, artistic accomplice; Alfie Bass and Sidney James the professional assistants, and one of the beneficiaries of Guinness's wrongdoing is a bit player, Audrey Hepburn. b & w

Law and Disorder (1974)—While you're watching this comedy about the frustrations and foul-ups of New Yorkers Carroll O'Connor and Ernest Borgnine as they try to protect their families by organizing an auxiliary-police unit, you can tell how the scenes were meant to play and why they don't. You can see that the gifted Czech director, Ivan Passer, doesn't have the unconscious equipment for the look and feel of ordinary American life, and that he is trying to strike a compromise between his feelings and the demands of the American marketing system—and satisfying neither. O'Connor has some fine restrained moments, and Allan Arbus contributes an entertaining bit as a gooney-bird psychologist (in a tight whiny voice he gives a lecture on how to prevent rape), but the film is a painful failure—lumpish and crude. Passer is trying to do the sort of thing that gets louder laughs than his own kind of comedy, and he doesn't really know how. With

Ann Wedgeworth, Karen Black, Jack Kehoe, Pat Corley, Anita Dangler, David Spielberg, and Joseph Ragno. Produced by William Richert; screenplay by Passer, Richert, and Kenneth Harris Fishman. Columbia. color (See *Reeling*.)

Law of Desire *La Ley del Deseo* (1987)—This flamboyantly glamorous homosexual fantasy by Madrid's gagster-artist Pedro Almodóvar is satirical, romantic, metaphorical; it has wonderful jokes and the exaggerated plot of an absurdist Hollywood melodrama. It doesn't disguise its narcissism; it turns it into bright-colored tragicomedy. And even when it loses its beat (after a murder) there's always something happening. Carmen Maura, a powerful actress in the manner of the early Anna Magnani, with the trippiness and self-mockery of Bette Midler, plays Tina, a transsexual who has a hot, roiling temperament. Tina's celebrity brother Pablo (Eusebio Poncela) directs classy homoerotic films. One night, Pablo takes home Antonio (Antonio Banderas), a government minister's son, who has been stalking him; by morning, Antonio loves him, is determined to possess him completely, and refuses to get out of his life. This is one of the rare movies that's sensually exciting at the same time that it's funny. With Miguel Molina as Pablo's true love, Manuela Velasco as little Ada, and the male transvestite Bibi Andersen as Tina's lesbian ex-lover. Cinematography by Ángel Luis Fernández. Released by Cinevista. In Spanish. color (See *Hooked*.)

Lawrence of Arabia (1962)—If you went to see it under the delusion that it was going to be about T. E. Lawrence, you probably stayed to enjoy the vastness of the desert and the pleasures of the senses that a huge movie epic can provide. Directed by David Lean, from a script by Robert Bolt, loosely based on Lawrence's *Seven Pillars of Wisdom*, this picture fails to give an acceptable interpretation of Lawrence, or to keep its action intelligible, but it is one of the most literate and tasteful and exciting of expensive spectacles. The central figure is played quite stunningly by Peter O'Toole, though he seems to be doing *Lord Jim*—which he was cast in a couple of years later (and then it looked as if he were doing Lawrence all over again). Bolt and Lean turn the hero into such a flamboyant poetic enigma that he is displaced in the film by a simpler hero—Omar Sharif's Ali, a handsome sheik with liquid brown eyes and conventionally sympathetic lines to speak. Ali, an old-fashioned movie hero, was more at home in what, despite the literacy, was a big action movie. And as it became apparent that most people in the audience hadn't the remotest idea of what the Arabs and the Turks were doing in the First World War, or which was which, or why the English cared, the question raised by the movie was: can complicated historical events and a complex hero really get across in a spectacle? Fortunately for this particular spectacle, audiences seemed to be satisfied with the explanation that the Turks were more cruel than the Arabs, and although the movie's Lawrence became cruel, too, there was warmhearted Ali to take over. (When Bolt and Lean cast Sharif as their poetic enigma in their next film, *Dr. Zhivago*, they forgot to provide a simpler fellow as a standby.) With Alec Guinness, José Ferrer, Anthony Quinn, Arthur Kennedy, Jack Hawkins, Claude Rains, Anthony Quayle, and Donald Wolfit. Cinematography by Freddie Young; music by Maurice Jarre; produced by Sam Spiegel. (221 minutes.) color (See *Kiss Kiss Bang Bang*.)

Leap Into the Void *Salto Nel Vuoto* (1979)—The Italian director Marco Bellocchio (*Fists in the Pocket, China Is Near*) has a feral sense of the ridiculous and a snake charmer's style. This film is poised between farce and trag-edy, and he keeps it in slippery chiaroscuro—it all might be taking place in a dark dream. Michel Piccoli gives a mesmerizing performance as an Italian judge who's a worm—a spoiled worm wriggling in its comfortable nest; he's a craven fraud—a distant cousin to the characters W. C. Fields used to play. Anouk Aimée is the judge's older sister, a menopausal virgin who has spent her life keeping the nest cozy for him; now she has begun to rebel—she has been having fits of hysteria. This film about family entanglements and the functions of madness is perverse, horrifying, and funny. Bellocchio is probably the only director (with the big exception of Buñuel) whose morbidity is exhilarating. With Michele Placido, as a dashing bearded outlaw (and sociopath), and the director's small son, Piergiorgio. Written by Bellocchio, Piero Natoli, and Vincenzo Cerami. In Italian. color (See *Taking It All In*.)

Leave Her to Heaven (1945)—Gothic pyschologizing melodrama, so preposterously full-blown and straight-faced that it's a juicy entertainment. Evil, beautiful Ellen (Gene Tierney) hoards her father's ashes and has a penchant for eliminating people who clutter up her life. There are scenes to cherish: Ellen impassively watching her brother-in-law drown; Ellen flinging herself down a flight of stairs to terminate an annoying pregnancy; Ellen going lickety-split on a charger, tossing father's remains around the Technicolored New Mexico landscape; Ellen's long-suffering writer-husband (Cornel Wilde) remarking, "While I was watching you, exotic words drifted across the mirror of my mind as summer clouds drift across the sky." John M. Stahl directed; Jo Swerling did the adaptation of the Ben Ames Williams best-seller. With Jeanne Crain, Vincent Price, Ray Collins, Gene Lockhart, Reed Hadley, Mary Philips, and Chill Wills. 20th Century-Fox.

Léda Also known as *Web of Passion* and *À double tour*. (1959)—This ingenious thriller by Claude Chabrol was made directly after *The Cousins*. Shot by Henri Decaë and featuring peacocks and fields of scarlet poppies, as well as a murderer who conducts Berlioz, it is perhaps the most richly detailed and overripe of Chabrol's films. With Jean-Paul Belmondo, Madeleine Robinson, Bernadette Lafont, Jeanne Valerie, and—as Léda—Antonella Lualdi. In French. color

The Left Handed Gun (1958)—Arthur Penn's first film, adapted by Leslie Stevens from a television play by Gore Vidal, has some of the violent, legendary, nostalgic qualities of his later *Bonnie and Clyde*. A young, great-looking Paul Newman plays Billy the Kid as an ignorant boy in the sex-starved Old West. There's a foreshadowing of the sensibility that shaped *Bonnie and Clyde* when Billy's shotgun blasts a man right out of one of his boots. The man falls in the street, but his boot remains upright; a little girl starts to giggle at the boot and doesn't get very far—her mother slaps her, and that slap is the seal of the awareness of horror. It says that even children must learn that some things that look funny are not only funny. It says that only idiots would laugh at pain and death. The slap is itself funny, and yet we suck in our breath; we don't dare to laugh. With Hurd Hatfield, Lita Milan, John Dehner, Denver Pyle, Nestor Paiva, John Dierkes, and James Congdon. Warners. b & w

Legal Eagles (1986)—As a New York assistant district attorney, Robert Redford bestirs himself more than he did in *The Natural* and *Out of Africa*, and he reminds you of what made him a star—but his affable performance is no more than a reminder. Debra Winger is confined in the prim, tailored-suit role of a dedicated young defense lawer; she has glimmers of humor, but the part is an emotional strait jacket, and she's practically deadpan. And Daryl Hannah, who is charged with stealing one of her dead artist father's paintings, and then with murder, has no character to play—she goes through the movie pouting, her long blond hair flowing, her eyes blank. Except for David Clennon as a bug-eyed assistant D.A. who's a complete stinker, everybody is unformed or only partly formed. The cast includes Terence Stamp (more assured every year and looking great), Brian Dennehy, Roscoe Lee Browne, Christine Baranski, Sara Botsford, Steven Hill, and many other gifted performers who flit on-screen and off, with nothing to do but push the engine-less plot uphill. Directed by Ivan Reitman, from a script credited to Jim Cash and Jack Epps, Jr., the movie, which is set in the art world, seems to have taken the scandal of how Mark Rothko's estate was managed and scrambled it up with pieces of romantic comedy-thrillers such as *Charade* and courtroom comedies such as *Adam's Rib*. It's all plot, and the plot is all holes; it's not just that it doesn't add up right—most of the episodes don't quite make sense. About all that carries the movie along is the functional—and occasionally smooth, bright—dialogue. This was the wrong kind of movie for Ivan Reitman to have attempted; it needed a director with style. Reitman endows it with the visual excitement of a Rotary Club lunch, and the most you can say for the square cinematography (by Laszlo Kovacs) is that it's instantly scannable. Also with John McMartin and Jennie Dundas. Story by Reitman, Cash, and Epps. Universal. color (See *Hooked*.)

The Legend of Lylah Clare (1968)—Heavy-handed camp about Hollywood—an attempt to fuse *Sunset Boulevard*, *Vertigo*, *The Barefoot Contessa*, and *What Ever Happened to Baby Jane?* Peter Finch plays a Svengali-like movie director. His great star, the glamorous foreigner Lylah Clare, died mysteriously a few hours after marrying him, and now he is turning a young American actress (Kim Novak) into Lylah. The stale, gaudy script (from a teleplay by Robert Thom and Edward De Blasio) provides roles for Coral Browne as a bitch columnist, Rossella Falk as a predatory European lesbian, and Valentina Cortese as a designer. Maybe an amusing macabre pastiche could have been made of it if the director, Robert Aldrich, hadn't been so clumsy; it's a static piece of filmmaking. With Michael Murphy, George Kennedy, and Ernest Borgnine, who has rarely been worse—he demonstrates his shouting range. Cinematography by Joseph Biroc; adaptation by Hugo Butler and Jean Rouverol. M-G-M. color

En Lektion i Kärlek, see *A Lesson in Love*

Lenny (1974)—This earnest Bob Fosse film starring Dustin Hoffman is for those who want to believe that Lenny Bruce was a saintly gadfly who was martyred only because he lived before *their* time. Working from a weak script by Julian Barry, Fosse accepts the view that Bruce's motivating force was to cleanse society of hypocrisy, and, having swallowed that, he can only defuse Bruce's humor. So when you hear Hoffman doing Bruce's shticks you don't even feel like laughing. Despite the fluent editing and the close-in documentary techniques and the sophisticated graphics, the picture is a later version of the one-to-one correlation of an artist's life and his art which we used to get in movies about painters and songwriters. Hoffman makes a serious, honorable try, but his Lenny is a nice boy. Lenny Bruce was uncompromisingly not nice; the movie turns a teasing, seductive hipster into a putz. As Honey, Valerie Perrine does a dazzling strip and gives an affecting, if limited, perfor-

mance. With Gary Morton, Jan Miner, and Stanley Beck. United Artists. b & w (See *Reeling.*)

The Leopard *Il Gattopardo* (1963)—It had been cut to 2 hours and 41 minutes when it opened in the U.S., in a dubbed-into-English version that didn't always seem in sync, and with the color brightened in highly variable and disorienting ways. The new version, not released here until September, 1983, is in Italian, with subtitles, and at its full length—3 hours and 5 minutes. And it's magnificent—a sweeping popular epic, with obvious similarities to *Gone with the Wind,* and with an almost Chekhovian sensibility. Based on the novel by Giuseppe Tomasi di Lampedusa, an impoverished Sicilian prince, it has a hero on a grand scale—Don Fabrizio, Prince of Salina, played superlatively by Burt Lancaster, who has acknowledged that he modelled his performance on the nobleman director, Luchino Visconti. The film is set in the 1860s, when Italy was in the middle of a revolution, but it's essentially about the Prince himself—the aging Leopard—and how he reacts to the social changes. We couldn't be any closer to Lancaster's Prince if we were inside his skin—which in a way we are. We see what he sees, feel what he feels, and, in the last hour, set at a splendid ball that marks the aristocrats' acceptance of the Mafia-dominated parvenus who are taking over their wealth and power, we're inside his mind as he relives his life, experiences regret, and accepts the dying of his class and his own death. It's one of the greatest of all passages in movies. With Alain Delon as the Prince's sly nephew; Claudia Cardinale as a shrewd, sensual heiress; Paolo Stoppa as her beady-eyed, land-grabbing father; Rina Morelli as the Prince's repressed, whimpering wife; and Romolo Valli, Serge Reggiani, Leslie French, and Pierre Clémenti. (Both Paolo Stoppa and Rina Morelli give superb performances; Alain

Delon is perhaps too airy for his role.) The score is by Nino Rota; the cinematography is by the justly celebrated Giuseppe Rotunno. (See *State of the Art*.)

Les Girls (1957)—George Cukor directed this backstage-story musical (it's about a lawsuit over a former showgirl's memoirs), and the color consultant, George Hoyningen-Huené, gave it a classy look, but, with one exception, nobody connected with it was really at his best—not Gene Kelly, who was the star, or the scenarist, John Patrick, and certainly not the choreographer, Jack Cole. (He hit rock bottom, with horrible quasi-cultured numbers.) Even the Cole Porter score is weak, and the whole picture is overproduced. The exception is the tall, blithe, and beautiful comedienne Kay Kendall, who does a funny, drunk "La Habanera" and has a number with Kelly in which she seems to be outdancing him and having an easy, amused time of it. Her role isn't large enough, though. The cast includes Henry Daniell, Taina Elg, Jacques Bergerac, Patrick Macnee, Leslie Phillips, and a bane of 50s movie musicals—the movie executives' idea of "adorable"—Mitzi Gaynor. From a story by Vera Caspary. M-G-M.

A Lesson in Love *En Lektion i Kärlek* (1953)—The burnt-out marriage of Eva Dahlbeck and Gunnar Björnstrand is rekindled when he becomes jealous of her. This is a rather more middle-class marital comedy than one expects from Ingmar Bergman. (He wrote and directed.) With Harriet Andersson. In Swedish. b & w

Let's Do It Again (1975)—This innocent, cheerful farce about an Atlanta milkman (Sidney Poitier) and a factory worker (Bill Cosby) who go to New Orleans and pull off a great scam is like a black child's version of *The Sting*. The con involves hypnotizing a spindly

prizefighter, played by Jimmie Walker, of TV's "Good Times," in his first screen role. Cosby looks spaced out on his own innocent amiability, and he floats away with the show; Poitier, who directed, plays straight man to him and gives an embarrassed, unfunny performance. It's crude slapstick, but the people on the screen are very likable. The cast includes Ossie Davis, Julius Harris, Mel Stewart, John Amos, Lee Chamberlin, Denise Nicholas, and Calvin Lockhart. Warners. color (See *When the Lights Go Down*.)

Let's Get Lost (1988)—This documentary, by Bruce Weber, isn't primarily about Chet Baker the jazz trumpeter and singer: it's about Chet Baker the love object, the fetish. And maybe because Weber, despite his lifelong fixation on this charmer, knew him only as a battered, treacherous wreck, in the two years before his death, it's one of the most suggestive (and unresolved) films ever made. The soundtrack is made up of Baker recordings that span more than three decades—the idealized essence of the man. The 16 mm black-and-white cinematography (by Jeff Preiss) is reticent yet expressive, impassioned; the film has a great look. (See *Movie Love*.)

The Letter (1940)—Bette Davis's 43rd movie; it marked her 10th year in films, and it is one of her few good vehicles. Somerset Maugham's melodrama (generally believed to be based on an actual incident) had been a Broadway success for Katharine Cornell and was filmed—memorably—in 1929 with Jeanne Eagels. (Those blessed with movie-loving parents may still retain images of Eagels' corrupt beauty, and of her frenzied big scene when the heroine tells off her husband.) The central figure is the wife of a rubber-plantation owner—a woman of such unimpeachable respectability that she can empty a gun into her lover and get away with it (in the courts, at least, because in Singapore the white ruling class must stick together). Davis gives what is very likely the best study of female sexual hypocrisy in film history. Cold and proper, she yet manages to suggest the passion of a woman who'd kill a man for trying to leave her. She is helped by an excellent script (by Howard Koch) and by two unusually charged performances—James Stephenson as her lawyer and Herbert Marshall as her husband. The cast also includes two formidable women—Frieda Inescort, who seems ineffably absurd as the lawyer's wife, and Gale Sondergaard, whose performance as the Eurasian woman was actually taken very seriously by many people. With Bruce Lester, Cecil Kellaway, Victor Sen Yung, Willie Fung, Tetsu Komai, and Doris Lloyd. The insistent music is pure, adulterated Max Steiner. It demeans William Wyler's clear, taut direction and the erotic awareness he brings to the material. Warners. b & w

Letter from an Unknown Woman (1948)— Joan Fontaine suffers and suffers, but so *exquisitely* in this romantic evocation of late-19th-century Vienna that one doesn't know whether to clobber the poor, wronged creature or to give in and weep. Max Ophuls made this film in Hollywood but its Vienna is as romantically stylized and as beautifully textured as his European work. His theme (it was almost always his theme) is the difference in approaches to love. A pianist, Louis Jourdan, seduces the impressionable adolescent Joan and promptly forgets her; years later he meets her again, and, thinking her a fresh conquest, seduces her again. But in the intervening years she has borne him a child and remained hopelessly in love with him. This ironic love story, which is probably the toniest "woman's picture" ever made, is based on Stefan Zweig's "Brief Einer Unbekannten" and was written for the screen by Howard Koch. With Mady Christians. Cin-

ematography by Franz Planer; art direction by Alexander Golitzen; produced by John Houseman, for Universal. b & w

A Letter to Jane (1972)—A 45-minute-long lecture demonstration that is a movie only in a marginal sense. A single news photograph appears on the screen; it is of tall Jane Fonda towering above some Vietnamese, and on the track Jean-Luc Godard and Jean-Pierre Gorin discuss the implications of the photograph. Their talk is didactic, condescending, and offensively inhuman. In French.

A Letter to Three Wives (1949)—Joseph L. Mankiewicz won Academy Awards for Best Screenplay and Best Director for this satirical comedy on American social and marital conventions. The letter is from the town seductress informing the three wives that she has taken away one of their husbands: as each threatened wife reviews her marriage, we get, at best, a sharp, frequently hilarious look at suburbia, and, at worst, a slick series of bright remarks. Mankiewicz coaxed good performances out of Jeanne Crain and Linda Darnell, and the others certainly didn't need coaxing—Paul Douglas is pretty close to magnificent, and Ann Sothern, Kirk Douglas, Florence Bates, Thelma Ritter, and Connie Gilchrist are first-rate. Also with Barbara Lawrence, Jeffrey Lynn, and Hobart Cavanaugh, and narration by Celeste Holm. From a story by John Klempner. 20th Century-Fox. b & w

Letyat Zhuravli, see *The Cranes Are Flying*

Der Letzte Akt, see *The Last Ten Days*

Der Letzte Mann, see *The Last Laugh*

La Ley del Deseo, see *Law of Desire*

Les Liaisons dangereuses (1959)—Valmont and Juliette, the 18th-century characters in the Laclos novel, are former lovers who, writing to each other about their strategies, targets, and fresh conquests, turn love into something as studied and calculated as war. They take the love out of love. Modernizing the story, the director Roger Vadim ties things up rather neatly by having Valmont (in a tired, too-sweet performance by Gérard Philipe—his last) and Juliette (Jeanne Moreau at her ravaged best) married. In Laclos the pleasure seems to be in carrying out the plan, achieving the victory—a triumph of austere, rational conquest; in Vadim's version a sensuous aura surrounds and permeates the objects. The first scene of Marianne (Annette Stroyberg) in the snow, her mouth open in laughter for a romantic eternity, isn't on a much higher level than the *Playboy* bunnies of the month; Vadim also uses jazz and Negroes and sex all mixed together in a cheap and sensational way that was probably exotic for the French in the 50s. But, using these elements, he attempts to give them a rhythm and feeling that are, at least, unusually high-class commercialism. Vadim's erotic cleverness is so transparent and shoddy that it verges on the comic; yet the snowflower lyric innocence about Marianne does have pathos and there's a suggestion of spirituality to Valmont's feeling for her. It is Juliette's independence when Valmont wants to halt their activities that gives the film its character. She is not, then, pursuing this life of conquest merely to hold her husband: she has developed a passion that, once he has softened and reneged, can only destroy them both. When Valmont and Juliette declare their war on each other, the film becomes less corrupt, more interesting. Though it is he who wants to give up the game, it is she who breaks the rules by using his letters against him. They were both talented at long, drawn-out military maneuvers, but when it comes to the passions of war, they finish each other off as viciously and destructively as if they had

never heard of finesse. (If you've read the novel, in which Juliette, at the end, is disfigured by smallpox, you may get a turn when you see the vaccination mark on Moreau's arm.) With Jeanne Valerie, Jean-Louis Trintignant, and Simone Renant. Background music by Thelonious Monk; party music by Art Blakey and the Jazz Messengers, with Kenny Clarke. In French. b & w

Libeled Lady (1936)—A wisecracking newspaper comedy, from M-G-M, with Spencer Tracy as the editor whose paper is being sued for libel, Jean Harlow as his fiancée, Myrna Loy as the maligned heiress who is suing, and William Powell as the man Tracy hires to put Loy in a compromising position, so she'll drop the suit. And, in order to give Powell the married status necessary for the plan, he asks Harlow to marry Powell—just for a few weeks. That's only the beginning of the complications. The director, Jack Conway, keeps up the fast pace by a lot of shouting and busywork—people are always rushing in and out, and practically every line is meant to be funny. Some of them are, and the others are, at least, perky. The picture isn't bad—it's enjoyable, but it's rather charmless. It's constructed like a 70s sit-com, and it has the same kind of forced atmosphere of hilarity; it looks and sounds factory-made. The stars (and the supporting players, too) do their patented characters—the ones they'd invented some years earlier. (Almost nothing seems to be happening for the first time.) Loy is assured and levelheaded; Harlow is a tough cookie—loud and shrill but sentimental at heart; Tracy is a solid man's man; Powell is a suave ladies' man. With Charley Grapewin as the owner of the paper (he gives perhaps the best performance, but there isn't enough of it); Walter Connolly as Loy's father; Cora Witherspoon; George Chandler in a bit; and E. E. Clive as a fishing specialist. (Powell has a fly-fishing scene that

Howard Hawks must have liked, because in 1964 he did his version of it in *Man's Favorite Sport?*) Written by Maurine Watkins, Howard Emmett Rogers, and George Oppenheimer. b & w

The Life and Times of Judge Roy Bean (1972)—Nihilism plus sentimentality about the rugged-individualist hero—Paul Newman. A mock-epic Western that cannibalizes old movies and mixes an enthusiasm for slaughter with a tacky geniality. John Huston directed this logy, thick-skinned movie from a brutal, jokey script by John Milius, whose imagination appears to have been fed by John Ford, Kurosawa, and a heavy dose of Jodorowsky's *El Topo*. The big scenes don't grow out of anything, and there are no characters—just mannerisms. Newman, his voice lowered to a gruff, non-musical level, sounds like Huston; hiding in a beard throughout, he goes in for a lot of beer-drinking. With Stacy Keach, who has a funny bit as a wild albino, and Ava Gardner as Lily Langtry, and Jacqueline Bisset, Roddy McDowall, Anthony Perkins, Tab Hunter, Victoria Principal, Ned Beatty, Anthony Zerbe, and Huston. (The 1940 Gary Cooper movie *The Westerner* also dealt with Roy Bean, who was played by Walter Brennan.) A First Artists Production. color (See *Reeling*.)

Life with Father (1947)—The director, Michael Curtiz, seems to be totally out of his element in this careful, deadly version of the celebrated, long-running Broadway comedy—a piece of starched Americana—by Howard Lindsay and Russel Crouse, based on Clarence Day's stories. William Powell plays the crotchety head of a large, tumultuous upper-middle-class New York household in the 1880s; this must have seemed like a plum of a role, yet Powell's timing (usually impeccable) is way off, and the comic expressions freeze on his face. Everybody seems to

be trying too hard. With Irene Dunne, Elizabeth Taylor, Edmund Gwenn, ZaSu Pitts, Jimmy Lydon, Monte Blue, Emma Dunn, and Martin Milner. The script is by Donald Ogden Stewart. Warners. color

Lifeboat (1944)—Ham-handed, wartime Hitchcock, highly regarded by many, and a big hit. John Steinbeck and Jo Swerling concocted the symbol-laden script about the ordeal of a group of survivors of a torpedoed ship; the script's chief virtue is that it provides a raucous opportunity for Tallulah Bankhead to strut her comic sexiness. The picture made her, for the first time, a popular movie star. She plays a famous mink-coated journalist who develops a yen for John Hodiak, an oiler from the ship's engine room. Others aboard the small boat include Canada Lee as a pickpocket, Henry Hull as a millionaire manufacturer, Heather Angel as a simpleton mother with a new baby, Mary Anderson as a nurse, Hume Cronyn as the ship's radio operator, and regrettably, in terms of the didactic uses they are put to, Walter Slezak as the U-boat captain, and William Bendix as a wounded seaman. 20th Century-Fox. b & w

Lifeguard (1976)—A low-key account of the life of a Southern California star high-school athlete (Sam Elliott) who goes on working as a lifeguard, clinging to the pleasures of adolescence rather than joining the money-grubbing world of his old classmates. Well thought out and with a feeling for ordinary American talk, but too mechanical, too blandly sensitive, too cool to be popular; it's the sort of small-scale picture that's a drag in a theatre but shines on Home Box Office. The athlete happens to meet his high-school sweetheart (Anne Archer) of 15 years before and they have a fling. (That must be the fulfillment of a widespread male fantasy.) Kathleen Quinlan gives an unusually appealing unconventional performance as a teen-ager drawn to the overage lifeguard. Directed by Daniel Petrie, from Ron Koslow's script. With Parker Stevenson. Paramount. color

The Light That Failed (1940)—This faithful adaptation of the Kipling novel jerks cultured tears. Ronald Colman plays Heldar, the great painter, who is injured by a spear in the Sudan and later goes blind, so he doesn't know that his masterpiece has been destroyed—splashed with turpentine—by his spiteful Cockney model, Bessie Broke (Ida Lupino). When he learns the truth, he goes back to the Sudan, bent on suicide. The director, William Wellman, said of Colman, "He didn't like me; I didn't like him—the only two things we agreed fully on." Fortunately, Wellman seems to have got along well with Lupino (it was her big entry in the Bette Davis–slut sweepstakes) and Walter Huston, who plays the painter's friend. With Muriel Angelus, Dudley Digges, and Ernest Cossart. Paramount. b & w

Lili (1953)—Millions of schoolchildren chirruped "Hi-Lili, Hi-Lo" when this sickly musical whimsey from M-G-M was released. Mel Ferrer smiles his narcissistic, masochistic smiles as the crippled puppeteer who can speak his love to the 16-year-old orphan girl Lili (Leslie Caron) only through his marionettes. Caron is much too good for him, but the movie doesn't know it. With Jean-Pierre Aumont, Zsa Zsa Gabor, and Kurt Kasznar. Charles Walters choreographed and directed, from Helen Deutsch's script, based on a Paul Gallico novel. Bronislau Kaper was given an Academy Award for that infernal score; Hollywood is shameless. color

Lilith (1964)—Jean Seberg is the demonic, corrupt Lilith, a patient in an elegant Maryland asylum who wants to "leave the mark of her desire on every living creature in the world"; Warren Beatty is the trainee therapist who finds her madness seductive. This high-toned, humorless attempt to create a mystic enigma was the last work of Robert Rossen, who adapted the J. P. Salamanca novel and directed; it's an unusual sort of disaster—full of symbols, chitchat about schizophrenic spiders, and exquisite cinematography (by Eugen Schüfftan), and utterly lacking in energy and depth. Beatty gives his most irritating performance: he broods over each bit of dialogue for an eternity, his heavy eyelids flickering. With Peter Fonda, Kim Hunter, Gene Hackman, Jessica Walter, Anne Meacham, and René Auberjonois; the score is by Kenyon Hopkins. Columbia. b & w

Lillian Russell (1940)—Alice Faye, overblown to vacuous perfection, and likable despite it all, wears gigantic hats; the headgear is about the only connection this scrubbed-up bio has with the actual Lillian Russell. In this heavily mounted version, the child Lillian is overheard singing by Tony Pastor (Leo Carrillo), a fatherly type in theatre business; he immediately makes her a star, and she becomes the rage of London and New York. All sorts of generous people—Diamond Jim Brady (Edward Arnold) among them—just keep sending her diamonds and emeralds. Love comes into her life when Henry Fonda rescues her and her Grandma (Helen Westley) from a team of runaway horses. This is the sort of movie in which Lillian the celebrity can never think of Grandma without getting tears in her eyes. A mixture of musical numbers; with Weber and Fields as themselves, Eddie Foy, Jr., as Eddie Foy, Sr. (who, one hopes, was better). 20th Century-Fox. b & w

Limelight (1952)—Chaplin's sentimental and high-minded view of theatre and himself. His exhortations about life, courage, consciousness, and "truth" are set in a self-pitying, self-glorifying story. As Calvero the old, impoverished English clown, he appears at a gala benefit and shows the unbelievers who think him finished that he is still the greatest, and then dies in the wings as the applause fades; this is surely the richest hunk of self-gratification since Huck and Tom attended their own funeral—and Chaplin serves it up straight. The mediocrity of Calvero's stage routines may be the result of Chaplin's aiming at greatness. At one point Calvero awaits a young ballerina (acted with considerable charm by Claire Bloom, and danced with authority by Melissa Hayden). In the darkened theatre after she has performed, he says to her, "My dear, you are a true artist, a true artist," and the emphasis is on *his* eyes, *his* depth of feeling. And is it because Chaplin didn't talk on screen until late in his career that he doesn't seem to have a dramatic instinct for language? (He talks high-mindedly and incessantly.) With Sydney Chaplin, Nigel Bruce, Norman Lloyd, André Eglevsky, and, all too briefly, Buster Keaton. United Artists. b & w

The Lion in Winter (1968)—Imitation wit and imitation poetry at the 12th-century court of the Plantagenets. Anthony Harvey directed James Goldman's adaptation of his own 1966 play. On the Broadway stage this play seemed to be an entertaining melodrama about the Plantagenets as a family of monsters playing Freudian games of sex and power, but it was brought to the screen as if it were poetic drama of a very high order, and the point of view is too limited and anachronistic to justify all this howling and sobbing and carrying on. Peter O'Toole is in great voice and good spirits as Henry II—he's so robust he almost carries the role off. Not a small feat when you have to deliver lines such as "Well, what shall we hang? The holly or each other?" and "The sky is pocked with stars." Goldman's dialogue can't bear the weight of the film's aspirations to grandeur,

and, as Eleanor of Acquitaine, Katharine Hepburn does a gallant-ravaged-great-lady number. She draws upon our feelings for *her*, not for the character she's playing, and the self-exploitation is hard to take. With Timothy Dalton as King Philip of France, Anthony Hopkins as Prince Richard, and Jane Merrow, John Castle, Nigel Stock, Kenneth Griffith, and Nigel Terry. The cinematography is by Douglas Slocombe; the music was composed and conducted by John Barry; the costumes are by Margaret Furse. This British production has some location scenes but was mostly shot at Ardmore Studios in Dublin. Martin Poll was the producer. color (See *Going Steady*.)

Lions Love (1969)—Agnès Varda is probably the finest technician among women movie directors and her first American feature (financed independently, it cost less than a quarter of a million dollars) is pleasantly loose, and with a sunny, lyrical quality. But it's short of substance—and what there is makes you regret that there's any. Set in Los Angeles, it's about make-believe and would-be movie stars (Viva, the wilted flower of the underground, and Gerome Ragni and James Rado, the authors of *Hair*). They play house, cuddle in bed, watch the television coverage of Robert Kennedy's death, and murmur inanities. The film is occasionally funny but it lacks a sense of the fitness of things: we don't want to hear Viva make vacuous little remarks about how sorry she feels for the orphaned Kennedy children. With Shirley Clarke. color (See *Deeper into Movies*.)

The List of Adrian Messenger (1963)—This detective-story film has many of the pleasures of the genre—phonetic clues, some fancy murder methods, a fox hunt, a war-hero detective. The leading roles are played by George C. Scott and Kirk Douglas, and there are several guest stars who appear, or were advertised as appearing, in disguise (Tony Curtis, Frank Sinatra, Robert Mitchum, and Burt Lancaster). They're rather like those maddening suspicious characters in detective novels who seem to be introduced for the sole purpose of throwing dust in our eyes; the stardust is slightly irritating—you find yourself trying to clear up the incidental mystery and losing track of the action. Still, it's a fairly sophisticated diversion. There's a joker in the disguised pack: Mitchum, who defies makeup—when he peels off the layers, the wonder is that he could be wearing so much to so little purpose. There was also a hoax on the audience: Lancaster and Sinatra were seen stripping off their disguises at the end, but other performers played their roles. John Huston directed, from Anthony Veiller's screenplay, based on Philip MacDonald's novel. The cast includes Clive Brook, Gladys Cooper, Marcel Dalio, Dana Wynter, Jacques Roux, John Merivale, Herbert Marshall, Bernard Archard, Noel Purcell, and a couple of Hustons. Cinematography by Joe MacDonald. Universal. b & w

Lisztomania (1975)—In a couple of sequences, it erupts successfully with a wholehearted, controlled comic-strip craziness, but, for all his lashing himself into a slapstick fury, the director, Ken Russell, can't seem to pull the elements of filmmaking together. Roger Daltrey is Liszt, Paul Nicholas and Veronica Quilligan are Richard and Cosima Wagner, and Sara Kestelman is Princess Carolyne SaynWittgenstein. color (See *When the Lights Go Down.*)

Little Big Man (1970)—Thomas Berger's comic, picaresque novel about the events that led up to Custer's Last Stand was brought to the screen by Arthur Penn during the anti–Vietnam war period, and he put white murderousness and racism at the center of the narrative. Dustin Hoffman has the leading role of Jack Crabb, an American Candide whose adventures take him back and forth between the red man's culture and the white man's culture. For roughly an hour, the comic tone is pleasantly askew, and throughout the film amusing characters turn up and disappear and turn up again. They include Faye Dunaway as a preacher's wife, Jeff Corey as Wild Bill Hickok, Martin Balsam as a swindler getting cheerfully dismantled limb by limb, and Chief Dan George as an Indian chief who is part patriarch, part Jewish mother. But after the first hour the massacres start coming, and the speeches, too. Thomas Berger suggested that the Indians looked like Orientals, but when you notice that Jack Crabb's lovely Indian bride looks Vietnamese you start waiting uneasily for more slaughter. And long before you get to Custer's Last Stand you've heard the little click in your brain that says, "Enough." For a tall tale to function as an epic form, the violence must be wry and only half believable—insane, as it is in the book, and not conventionally bloody like this. To be successful, the picture should deepen by comic means, and when Penn goes for seriousness he collapses the form of the movie. It proceeds from hip to straight, and one cancels the other out. In scenes such as a raid on the Indians with one of the leaders of the raid leering with genocidal delight as he goes in for the killing, Penn loses any claim to sensitivity: this is just crude, ideological filmmaking. With Richard Mulligan as General Custer, Carol Androsky as Caroline, Amy Eccles, and Thayer David. Script by Calder Willingham; cinematography by Harry Stradling, Jr.; production design by Dean Tavoularis; edited by Dede Allen. Produced by Stuart Millar, for Cinema Center Films. (2½ hours.) color (See *Deeper into Movies.*)

Little Boy Lost (1953)—This postwar story of an American journalist's efforts to determine whether the child he locates in a French orphanage is his lost son is drawn out and lacklustre, yet the material isn't easily forgotten. Bing Crosby is inoffensive in the lead, though he lacks an actor's tension; he's colorlessly "natural." And the director, George Seaton, who adapted Marghanita Laski's novel, is also rather gray and low-key. The movie is relentlessly worthy and life-affirming; the script is full of lessons. And there are peculiarities: speaking in English, the great Gabrielle Dorziat overdoes her role—her elocutionary style is too grand for a woman who runs a convent orphanage. And Claude Dauphin and Nicole Maurey don't contribute a great deal. Perhaps the picture is as effective as it is partly because the little boy (Christian Fourcade) is so totally unlike American children that we can see how Crosby would find it impossible to believe that this was his son. And there is a heartbreaker of a gimmick to effect the father's acceptance of the boy. Maybe George Seaton's lack of slickness helps. It should be a stinker and it isn't, quite—the movie's lameness and dullness seem to make it more touching. Paramount. b & w

Little Caesar (1930)—Edward G. Robinson's Rico is one of the major prototypes of the movie gangster, but Mervyn LeRoy's direction is sluggish, and the actors seem to be transfixed by the microphone. With Douglas Fairbanks, Jr., Glenda Farrell, George E. Stone, Sidney Blackmer, William Collier, Jr., and Stanley Fields. From a novel by W. R. Burnett, adapted by Francis Faragoh.

The Little Drummer Girl (1984)—Directed by George Roy Hill, this suspense movie, based on John le Carré's novel, is set in 1981 during a rash of Palestinian terrorist bombings of Israeli institutions around the world. The tragedy of these two peoples, killing each other because each has just claims to the same plot of ground, is presented with efficient, impersonal evenhandedness, so that we care about neither of them. The film centers on Charlie (Diane Keaton), an American actress working in a small, third-rate repertory company in England; a left-wing pro-Palestinian, she is recruited by an Israeli intelligence unit that turns her thinking around and uses her to infiltrate the Palestinians and trap their chief terrorist (Sami Frey, who gives the film a bit of bravura). The conception of Charlie is a modern cliché: she's an actress looking for a role to play that will make her feel "real." But Keaton takes this conception so far that she gives it a painful, shrill validity; initially off-putting, she leaps right over likability and crowd-pleasing—she's out there all alone doing something daring. It's maddening that this performance can't carry the dead weight put on it. With Klaus Kinski as Kurtz, Yorgo Voyagis as Joseph, Moti Shirin as Michel, Michael Cristofer as Tayeh, and Anna Massey as the chairlady. The screenplay is by Loring Mandel. Warners. color (See *State of the Art*.)

Little Fauss and Big Halsy (1970)—As buddy-buddy motorcycle racers, Michael J. Pollard does an extended version of his runty, nasal pixie bit and Robert Redford makes the mistake of acting raunchy. He's symbolically wounded, and has a great big scar running down his spine to prove it. The scar is much in evidence, because Redford, playing a swaggering oaf, rarely wears a shirt. (This will not, however, do as much for his career as it did for Paul Newman's.) Redford can't seem to keep his pants up, either, and he's constantly fiddling with his zipper and juggling his genitals (on one occasion, in what is possibly a movie first, in a close shot).

He also flashes his teeth, keeps a toothbrush stuck in his mouth, wears funny hats, and wiggles his behind. The heroine, Lauren Hutton, enters naked, running toward the camera for no particular reason. Sidney J. Furie directed, from a script by Charles Eastman that's trying to tell us about people's quests for something or other—it isn't clear what. Big Halsy Redford appears to be the stud as loser. The picture is truly terrible; Johnny Cash is on the soundtrack with messages such as "It takes nerve to take a curve." With Lucille Benson and Noah Beery. Produced by Albert S. Ruddy; the racing leathers were designed by Pierre Cardin. Paramount. color (See *Deeper into Movies*.)

The Little Foxes (1941)—Bette Davis's tight, dry performance was probably a mistake; her Regina is so villainous that this version of Lillian Hellman's play about a Southern family of predators doesn't have the temperament and drive that Tallulah Bankhead gave it on the stage. But it's a handsome movie melodrama, well contrived and showily acted. William Wyler directed; with Herbert Marshall, Teresa Wright, Patricia Collinge, Richard Carlson, Charles Dingle, and Dan Duryea, overdoing the whinnying weakling. A Samuel Goldwyn Production; released by R K O. b & w

The Little Mermaid (1989)—Disney-style kitsch. It's technologically sophisticated, but with just about all the simpering old Disney values in place. They're just slightly updated: the Little Mermaid—a teen-age tootsie in a flirty seashell bra—is like Sleeping Beauty plus tomboy spunk. The film does have a cheerful calypso number ("Under the Sea," by Howard Ashman and Alan Menken), and the color is bright—at least, until the mermaid goes on land, when everything seems to dull out. Pat Carroll provides the voice of Ursula, the Sea Witch; Samuel E. Wright provides the voice of Sebastian. (See *Movie Love*.)

The Little Minister (1934)—This R K O picture was one of the movies that helped make Katharine Hepburn box-office poison in the mid-30s. Five writers are credited with adapting the James M. Barrie material (which probably means that at least 25 worked on it), and there's no consistency to the results, but for about a third of the picture Hepburn pretends to be a wild gypsy girl, and she's enchanting in this section. The rest is barely tolerable. Richard Wallace directed. John Beal is the hero; with Donald Crisp, Andy Clyde, and Beryl Mercer. b & w

Little Miss Marker (1934)—People hadn't seen anything like it; that doesn't mean they needed to. Tiny tot Shirley Temple is left as a "marker" with a bunch of gambler-racketeers, who talk in the coy Broadway lowlife argot invented by Damon Runyon, on whose story the film is based. Adolphe Menjou is the head hoodlum; he and the others bedeck themselves as King Arthur's knights in order to please wee Shirley, and at her instigation he also recites "Now I lay me." No one can deny that the infant Shirley Temple was a trouper; she delivers her lines with a killer instinct, and she sings, natch. Alexander Hall directed this exceedingly popular whimsey. With Charles Bickford, Dorothy Dell, and Lynne Overman. (Remade as *Sorrowful Jones* in 1949, reworked as *40 Pounds of Trouble* in 1962, and remade with the original title in 1980.) Paramount. b & w

Little Murders (1971)—Jules Feiffer's 1967 play was a wisp of a satirical comedy about the American adjustment to random violence—to assassinations on the national level and on the level of local snipers. In this movie version, which Feiffer also wrote, and which was directed by Alan Arkin, the dialogue has comic authority, and there are some strong scenes of rabid farce, yet things keep going out of kilter and the humor slides into something ugly and slightly rancid. The film seems to be a collection of ideological points—it's pious about its anti-Establishment attitudes. With Elliott Gould as the catatonic hero—a saintly dropout; and Marcia Rodd, Vincent Gardenia, Elizabeth Wilson, Lou Jacobi, Jon Korkes, Doris Roberts, John Randolph, and Arkin, and Donald Sutherland in a funny turn as an all-accepting minister. Cinematography by Gordon Willis; produced by Jack Brodsky. 20th Century-Fox. color (See *Deeper into Movies*.)

A Little Night Music (1978)—You know what you're in for near the beginning, when the hero (Len Cariou) is greeted with "Good afternoon, Lawyer Egerman." This film is a cut above *Song of Norway* and *The Blue Bird*, but it's in that general sylvan-settings category. It's an adaptation of the Broadway show, which was a reworking, with music and lyrics by Stephen Sondheim and a book by Hugh Wheeler, of Ingmar Bergman's *Smiles of a Summer Night*. What was lyrical farce in the Bergman film has now become clodhopping operetta. This picture has been made as if the director (Harold Prince) had never *seen* a movie. With Diana Rigg and Lesley-Anne Down, who manage to get a performance rhythm going in some of their scenes, and with Elizabeth Taylor. New World. color (See *When the Lights Go Down*.)

The Little Prince (1974)—The Saint-Exupéry book, the first of the modern mystic-quest books to become a pop hit, is a distillation of melancholy, and it comes close to being self-glorifying, masochistic mush. Possibly something might have been made of the material if Alan Jay Lerner, who wrote the movie script, along with the lyrics for Frederick Loewe's music, had a more delicate feeling

for spiritual yearning. The director, Stanley Donen, is handicapped by the intractably graceless writing and by the Big Broadway sound of the Lerner-Loewe score. Bob Fosse's snake-in-the-grass dance number is the film's high spot, and Gene Wilder, as a red fox, triumphs over some of his material. As the child Prince, Steven Warner holds the screen affectingly; as the author-aviator, Richard Kiley is pleasant enough but colorless. Paramount. color (See *Reeling*.)

The Little Shop of Horrors (1960)—Amateurish yet funny, in a gross way. A simpleton (Jonathan Haze) who works in a florist shop has a prize plant that becomes a voracious, blood-seeking man-eater. It cries, "Feed me! Feed me!" The film is notable for the performance that Jack Nicholson gives in a minor role; as a pain freak who is in ecstasy in a dentist's chair, he shows the comic intensity that later made him a star. Produced and directed by Roger Corman, from a script by Charles B. Griffith. b & w

Little Shop of Horrors (1986)—Jivey, senseless fun. This musical is taken from the off-Broadway show that was based on Roger Corman's 1960 quickie—a junky travesty of sci-fi genetic-mutation pictures (from a script that Charles B. Griffith threw together). Rick Moranis plays Seymour, the assistant in a skid-row flower shop, circa 1960, who tends the ravenous little flowering cactus that he names after the sexpot clerk Audrey (Ellen Greene). Her steady date is a sadistic biker-dentist (Steve Martin), and Bill Murray plays this brute's pain-freak patient. The Martin-Murray sequence is a classic encounter: a piece of transcendent slapstick. Levi Stubbs provides the deep, rumbling basso of Audrey II, and Tichina Arnold, Tisha Campbell, and Michelle Weeks are the streetwise teen-age girl group who serve as a Greek chorus, commenting on the action. Also with Vincent

Gardenia, John Candy, Christopher Guest, and James Belushi. The director, Frank Oz, keeps the action right smack in front of your face and the movie is nothing but blown-up cartoon-style friskiness, but it makes you feel as inexplicably sappy and contented as a kid used to feel on Sunday morning lying on his stomach reading the funnies. Only, this is bigger, brasher, with its own kind of higgledy-piggledy ecstasy. The script and the lyrics are by Howard Ashman; the music is by Alan Menken. Produced by the Geffen Company; released by Warners. color (See *Hooked*.)

Little Women (1933)—There are small flaws—a few naïve and cloying scenes, some obvious dramatic contrivances—but it's a lovely, graceful film, and surprisingly faithful to the atmosphere, the Victorian sentiments, and the Victorian strengths of the Louisa May Alcott novel. Katharine Hepburn gives an inspired performance as willful Jo; she has a joyous tomboy abandon when she first enters Laurie's mansionlike home, and cries out, "What richness!" She strikes absurdly romantic poses, and they're enchanting. Joan Bennett is very amusing as vain, selfish, pretentious Amy; Frances Dee is Meg (she's charmingly funny when she's being proposed to by John Lodge, as the tutor); Edna May Oliver is Aunt March; Douglass Montgomery is Laurie (at times, full face, he resembles John Updike; too bad his bright lipstick makes his teeth look an uncanny white); Paul Lukas is the gentle, older man who courts Jo. The cast also includes Henry Stephenson, Samuel Hinds, Mabel Colcord as Hannah, and Nydia Westman. Directed by George Cukor, for the most part imaginatively and with unusual delicacy (the sequence with the play that Jo stages is particularly fine), and produced by David O. Selznick, for R K O. The dismal score is by Max Steiner, and Spring Byington as Marmee is sugary and sacrificial (she's a pain), and Jean Parker, as frail Beth, is not the world's greatest actress—she simpers a lot, though she's very touching when she goes to thank her gruff benefactor (Stephenson) for the piano he has sent her. Screenplay by Sarah Y. Mason and Victor Heerman. (Remade in 1949, at M-G-M.) b & w

The Little World of Don Camillo *Le Retour de Don Camillo* (1953)—In a village in North Italy, an ingenuously devout and militant priest, Fernandel, and a godless Communist mayor, Gino Cervi, battle it out with guile, charm, words, and fists. Julien Duvivier directed this popular version of Giovanni Guareschi's novel; it was a big art-house success. In French. b & w

The Lives of a Bengal Lancer (1935)—Sticks were driven under Gary Cooper's fingernails and set on fire, but he wouldn't betray his comrades-at-arms. This was one of the movies that put audiences into a Victorian boys'-adventure, rites-of-manhood universe where war and military service are a test of a man's courage. We're supposed to feel pride in the imperial British gallantry of the Lancers (as they put down an uprising on the Indian frontier), and at some level we do, despite our more knowledgeable, disgusted selves. The adolescent boys' fantasy atmosphere is very powerful; the director, Henry Hathaway, gives us an empathic identification with all the high-minded stuff that's going on inside Cooper and his buddy, Franchot Tone. At the same time, part of the picture's romantic charge is its underlying homoeroticism, which comes out in Cooper and Tone's comic camaraderie. And the film works on an adolescent's fear of showing cowardice by supplying a weakling character (Richard Cromwell). But if the movie is morally repugnant, it's also a terrific piece of Hollywood Victoriana. With Sir Guy Standing,

C. Aubrey Smith, Douglass Dumbrille, Akim Tamiroff, Monte Blue, Kathleen Burke, Noble Johnson, J. Carrol Naish, and Leonid Kinskey. Five writers are credited; the source is a book by Francis Yeats-Brown. The cinematography is by Charles Lang, with Indian location footage shot by Ernest B. Schoedsack. Paramount. b & w

The Lizards *I Basilischi* (1963)—Earlier in the year Lina Wertmüller worked as an assistant to Fellini; then she wrote and directed this film, in which she observes the loves of three aimless young men in a Southern Italian town; it's like a feminine view of the over-age "adolescents" who were the subject of Fellini's *I Vitelloni*. It's very sensitive (especially in the fragmentary scenes that show the lives of the women) and if it doesn't come to quite enough (it lacks depth and excitement), it is still a remarkably poised and intelligent début film (beautifully shot by Gianni Di Venanzo). Despite the smooth technique, this film isn't at all commercial. It gives promise of something very different from the noisy, slam-bang theatricality Wertmüller became famous for in the 70s. Music by Ennio Morricone. In Italian. b & w

Local Hero (1983)—A magical comedy by the Scottish writer-director Bill Forsyth, who observes the people in the movie as if they were one-of-a-kind creatures in a peculiarly haphazard zoo. The story (which involves a rabbit that doesn't turn into anything but a dinner) is about an American mergers-and-acquisitions executive—played by Peter Riegert—who is sent to Scotland to buy a fishing village and experiences something new to him, happiness. He never formulates his infatuation with the villagers, the crescent of beach, the glistening bay, the starlight, and the good, dark beer; we see the effect it all has on him in his wistful, stupefied face. Forsyth is rarely explicit about anything—the

picture is like one of those lovely Elizabethan songs that are full of tra-la-la-la-la-las. Denis Lawson—the most relaxed actor of a large, relaxed cast—is Gordon, the village innkeeper, pub owner, accountant, unofficial mayor, and great lover, and he makes each of Gordon's functions funny in a suavely different high style. (Each has its own form of self-satisfaction.) Burt Lancaster brings an imperial, romantic aura to the role of Riegert's boss—an oil tycoon whose penthouse includes a private planetarium. Also with Peter Capaldi as Danny, Jenny Seagrove as the marine biologist who seems to live in the water and has a hint of iridescence about her, Fulton Mackay as the hermit, Chris Rozyki as the Russian, and Jennifer Black as Gordon's bride. The opening sequence, set in a Houston skyscraper, is heavy-handed and coy, and most of the other Houston scenes falter, but the rest of the film has an original, feathery charm. The score is by Mark Knopfler. Produced by David Puttnam, for Goldcrest; released by Warners. color (See *Taking It All In*.)

Lola (1961)—This first film by Jacques Demy is like an adolescent's dream of romance, formed from old movies. Lola (Anouk Aimée) is simple and open, an untalented and not too bright cabaret dancer, a vulnerable, sentimental girl. The film gives us life rose-tinted—a lovely, quirky mixture of French-movie worldliness circa 1939 and the innocent cheerfulness of the Gene Kelly–Frank Sinatra M-G-M musicals of the 40s (*Anchors Aweigh*, *On the Town*), with their generous, shy sailors, kind to kids and looking for love. Demy gently mocks romantic movie effects, which he employs more romantically than ever. Characters suddenly get rich or are stranded on an island, and Lola's dreams come true—and not just her dreams but her illusions. This is a poetic world in which illusions are vindicated. Lola, abandoned by her sailor lover, brings up their son in the best sentimental, goodhearted-bad-girl movie tradition, believing all the time that her man will return, and, because she sustains her faith in this illusion, he does return, fabulously rich and still in love with her, and they drive off into a bright future as the other cabaret girls weep in unison at the soul-satisfying beauty of it all. Lola, in top hat and boa for her nightclub act, is herself a quotation—an homage to Dietrich's "Lola Lola" of *The Blue Angel*, but only to the effervescent and harmless half. (In Demy's 1964 *The Umbrellas of Cherbourg*, the melancholy diamond merchant who sings "Once, I Loved a Woman Named Lola" is played by the actor who was the young drifter who loved her and lost her in this film, and Demy continued the story of Lola in his 1969 American film *Model Shop*.) With Marc Michel and Elina Labourdette; cinematography by Raoul Coutard; score by Michel Legrand. In French. b & w

Lola Montès (1955)—This ambitious phantasmagorical treatment of the scandalous life of the 19th-century courtesan and dancer Lola Montès is a reflection on the ephemeral nature of fame, beauty, and pleasure. It was the last film completed by Max Ophuls; as he lay dying, his producers were shortening and re-editing his version (it was cut from 140 minutes to 110 to 90) in the hope of recouping their investment, which had been large. (The film was shot in CinemaScope and color and was made on an opulent scale.) But even in a restored form, it's disappointing—poorly acted and too shallow for its melancholy tone and its rich decor and elaborate structure. Lola (Martine Carol), far past her prime, is seen being exhibited and humiliated in a circus in New Orleans; the ringmaster—Peter Ustinov—tells the audience that it will see Lola's life story, and her early conquests and adventures are shown in flashbacks. Regrettably, Martine Carol couldn't manage to look young enough for Lola's radiant early days, and she was too bad a dancer even to play a bad dancer—she was a non-dancer. There is nothing unusual about her Lola—nothing that would explain why men are going mad over her. The center of the movie seems to be missing, and this isn't just the fault of the actress. The swirling, rococo camera movement at the circus is surprisingly elegant (though presumably the circus is meant to be tawdry). The movement suggests that this rather dumpy little woman has had an extraordinary emotional life, yet nothing seems to happen in those flashbacks—which don't gain in depth from our knowing what Lola has come down to. And she loiters so long with the king in Bavaria that one wants to give her carriage a push. What makes this folly so poignant and so painful to watch is that its virtuoso director didn't allow himself any middle ground: the film had to be his greatest masterpiece to be any good at all. According to his script girl, he died knowing he had failed. (The film was also one of the worst box-office disasters of its era.) With Anton Walbrook as King Ludwig I, Oskar Werner, Ivan Desny, and Will Quadflieg as Liszt. Ophuls and three others worked on the shockingly empty script, adapted from a French best-seller by Cecil St. Laurent. Sets by Jean d'Eaubonne and Willy Schatz; costumes by Georges Annekov; cinematography by Christian Matras; music by Georges Auric. In French.

Lolita (1962)—Wild, marvellously enjoyable comedy, adapted from Nabokov's novel. James Mason is the lover of little girls, the smiling, obsequious, phony Humbert Humbert; Shelley Winters is Charlotte Haze, the culture vulture rampant; Sue Lyon is her sexy daughter, Lolita; and Peter Sellers (at his most inspired) is Quilty, Humbert Humbert's walking paranoia. Stanley Kubrick directed. M-G-M. b & w (See *I Lost it at the Movies*.)

The Lonely Guy (1984)—Thrown out by his girlfriend, Steve Martin falls into a subculture of Lonely Guys, a secret society of men who recognize each other. (It's like the closeted gay subculture of the 50s.) Adapted from Bruce Jay Friedman's 1978 *The Lonely Guy's Book of Life*, this comedy has some wonderful gags and a lot of other good ideas for gags, but it was directed by Arthur Hiller, who is the opposite of a perfectionist, and it makes you feel as if you were watching television. Steve Martin has his moments, though, and he and Charles Grodin (as a veteran Lonely Guy) do a series of partly improvised sketches; they're a great manic-depressive team—Martin is starry-eyed and hopeful, Grodin is droopy and negative. With Judith Ivey, Steve Lawrence, Robyn Douglass, and pointless guest appearances by Loni Anderson, Merv Griffin, and Dr. Joyce Brothers. The adaptation is by Neil Simon; the script is by Ed Weinberger and Stan Daniels. The atrocious cinematography is by Victor J. Kemper. Universal. color (See *State of the Art*.)

Lonely Hearts (1982)—This movie is very casually strung together. It's an Australian variant of the comfy-cozy Ealing comedies of the 50s, but it doesn't have their precise construction—it moves from one small slapstick diversion to the next. As the timid, sexually repressed heroine, Wendy Hughes is lovely in the standard fine-actress-playing-dowdy-aging-virgin performance. As the piano tuner who courts her, Norman Kaye has a furtive, childlike prankishness, and that's what keeps the movie alive. The core idea is moist, but the film's humor is dry and sometimes darting and sneaky. Directed by Paul Cox, who wrote the script with John Clarke, the film has a cheerless look and dreary, crabbed cinematography. You have to settle for the fly-speck jokes, and the acting; it's all mildly satirical, mildly romantic, and mildly engaging. With Jonathan Hardy as the piano tu-ner's amiable, innocent brother-in-law and Jon Finlayson as the flamboyant director of an amateur theatrical group. color (See *State of the Art*.)

The Lonely Passion of Judith Hearne (1987)—A spinster in spite of her sensual nature, Judy Hearne, who lives in Dublin, is all pretension. Everybody sees through her, and she knows it, but she can't get rid of her own mealymouthed phoniness: it's ingrained in her. Maggie Smith, who plays the part, lets you read every shade of feeling in Judy's face; she makes you feel the ghastliness of knowing you're a figure of fun. Taken from Brian Moore's novel (a work of surpassing empathy written in 1955, when he was only 27), the movie, directed by Jack Clayton, is a phenomenal piece of work. It's about Judy's misunderstanding the attentions of her landlady's brother (Bob Hoskins) and thinking herself to be in the midst of a romance; it's about her isolation, her secret drinking, and her rage against the Church for her wasted life. There has probably never been another movie in which a woman rejected the Church fathers' ready-made answers. Maggie Smith and Wendy Hiller (who plays Judy's tyrannical aunt) are magnificent together, and the cast includes Ian McNeice, who, as the landlady's son, gives the film a baroque touch that helps offset the shallow, virtuous ending, Marie Kean as the landlady, and Rudi Davies as a young slavey. The adaptation is by Peter Nelson. color (See *Hooked*.)

Long Ago, Tomorrow (1971)—Doomed love between paraplegics, who must go through considerable wheelchair wiggling even to kiss. For people who want to be turned on by the sadness of it. With Malcolm McDowell and Nanette Newman; directed by Bryan Forbes. color (See *Deeper into Movies*.)

L

Long Day's Journey Into Night (1962)—This portrait of the artist as an Irish-American has the worst American failings: it's obvious, sprawling, yet crabbed. But if you respond at all, you may go all the way to exaltation. Perhaps just because of its naked familiarity, its grinding, ludicrous wrestling with expressiveness, *Journey* is, at last, an American family classic; the usual embarrassments are transcended, and the family theme is raised to mythic heights. This is the best film ever made from an O'Neill play (and it's O'Neill's greatest play). Katharine Hepburn, Ralph Richardson, Jason Robards, Jr., and Dean Stockwell are the quartet. Hepburn's transitions here—the way she can look 18 or 80 at will—seem iridescent. She surpasses herself: the most beautiful screen comedienne of the 30s and 40s becomes our greatest screen tragedienne. Sidney Lumet directed; Boris Kaufman did the cinematography. The complete film runs 170 minutes; frequently, a version 34 minutes shorter is shown, which seriously damages the structure and omits several of Robards' finest scenes. Produced by Ely Landau; released by Embassy Pictures. b & w

The Long Goodbye (1973)—In his novel, set in 1953, Raymond Chandler situated his incorruptible knight Philip Marlowe in Los Angeles, the city famed as the place where you go to sell out. And Chandler wrote to his agent that what he cared about in this book was "how any man who tried to be honest looks in the end either sentimental or plain foolish." Chandler's sentimental foolishness is the taking-off place for Robert Altman's heady, whirling sideshow of a movie, set in the early 70s L.A. of the stoned sensibility. Marlowe (Elliott Gould) is a wryly forlorn knight, just slogging along; still driving a 1948 Lincoln Continental and trying to behave like Bogart, he's the gallant fool in a corrupt world—the innocent eye. Even the police know more about the case he's involved in than he does. Yet he's the only one who *cares*. Altman kisses off the private-eye form as gracefully as *Beat the Devil* parodied the international-intrigue thriller. Less accidental than *Beat the Devil*, this picture is just about as funny, though quicker-witted and dreamier, in soft, mellow color and volatile images. Altman tells a detective story all right, but he does it through a spree—a high-flying rap on Chandler and the movies and L.A. The film drives you a little crazy, turns you on the way some musicals (*Singin' in the Rain, Cabaret*) and some comedies (*M*A*S*H*, parts of *Bananas* and *Everything You Always Wanted to Know About Sex*) do. Gould gives a loose and woolly, strikingly original performance. With Nina Van Pallandt, Sterling Hayden, Mark Rydell, Jim Bouton, Henry Gibson, Jack Riley, and Ken Sansom. Vilmos Zsigmond is responsible for the offhand visual pyrotechnics (the imagery has great vitality); John Williams' score is a witty series of variations on the title song; the script is credited to Leigh Brackett, but when you hear the Altman-style improvisatory dialogue you know you can't take that too literally. United Artists. (See *Reeling*.)

The Long, Hot Summer (1958)—This amalgam of Faulkner's stories "Barn Burning" and "Spotted Horses" (which is part of his novel *The Hamlet*) turned out to be highly commercial and hugely entertaining. The setting is a Mississippi town run by Will Varner (Orson Welles); Paul Newman plays Ben Quick, the stud drifter who comes into town and makes a deal with Varner to marry his tough-minded, virgin schoolteacher daughter (Joanne Woodward). Ben Quick is one of those arrogant-on-the-outside, vulnerable-on-the-inside roles that Newman could do better than any other movie actor, and he and Woodward have some electric, strong scenes together. Martin Ritt directed from a crackerjack popular screenplay by Irving Ravetch and his wife, Harriet Frank, Jr. (In 1945 Faulkner had worked on a screen treatment of "Barn Burning" but nothing came of it.) With Angela Lansbury, Lee Remick, Anthony Franciosa, and Richard Anderson. 20th Century-Fox. CinemaScope, color

Long Pants (1927)—This Harry Langdon comedy, directed by Frank Capra, wasn't up to *The Strong Man* of the year before; it has its dull side, but it has some inventive moments. Langdon, with his ineffectual, fluttering gestures, is a creepy mixture of the infantile and the effete. He isn't funny, exactly—he's fixating. Here, he plays a meek small-town adolescent who yearns for romance and finds it with his first pair of long pants. When he sees the scheming dame he falls for, she's sitting in an open car, and he circles around her on his bicycle, helplessly infatuated and trying to impress her by trick riding. He leaves his family and the girl next door and follows this vamp (Alma Bennett) to the city. (She turns out to be nothing less than a murderer.) Frankie Darro plays Harry as a small boy. Written by Arthur Ripley. Distributed by First National. Silent. b & w, with (originally) a dream sequence in color

The Long Voyage Home (1940)—One of the finest of all the movies that deal with life at sea, and one of the most successful of all attempts to put Eugene O'Neill on film—perhaps because the director, John Ford, and the adaptor, Dudley Nichols, were so free in their approach to O'Neill's material. The young Mildred Natwick has a memorable scene in a café with John Wayne, and Barry Fitzgerald's return to the ship (shrunken and chastened) is a truly great moment. Gregg Toland did the cinematography (which includes some early experiments in deep focus); with Thomas Mitchell, Wilfrid Lawson, Ward Bond, John Qualen, and Joe Sawyer. Produced by Walter Wanger; released by United Artists. b & w

The Longest Yard (1974)—Burt Reynolds, as a sellout quarterback turned superstud gigolo, lands in prison; he rediscovers his manhood through helping a bunch of convicts fight for theirs. The picture is a brutal bash, but the laughter at the brutality has no meanness in it; everybody knows that the blood isn't real. Robert Aldrich directed this comic fantasy, centering on a football game between crazily ruthless convicts and crazily ruthless guards; for all its bone-crunching collisions, it's almost irresistibly good-natured and funny. With Ed Lauter, Eddie Albert, and Bernadette Peters. Paramount. color (See *Reeling*.)

Look After Amelia, see *Oh, Amelia!*

Look Back in Anger (1959)—The English "angry young man" bursts onto the screen—an intellectual "wild one" and "rebel without a cause"—delivering some of the most electrifying dialogue of the era. Jimmy Porter (Richard Burton) is a blazingly articulate hero with passion and power, and no place in life, or cause or goal. He is an artist with no art to practice. As rancorous as Hamlet, he rages at his pale, zombie-like wife (Mary Ure), at his foxy mistress (Claire Bloom), at his good friend (Gary Raymond), and at all the dismal English life around him. The movie is uneven, and, at the end, damp and foggy as a postwar *Winterset*. But it has fire. Jimmy paces like a tiger caged in the welfare state, and even if you think that the movie is basically incoherent and that he's an exhibitionist whose scorn of the heritage of the previous generation is infantile ranting, you'll have to admit that he has a voice—his abusive shouts and epigrams have the authentic ring of drama. British understatement is gone; the case is marvellously overstated.

And Claire Bloom gives a wickedly smart performance; in her own way she's as sensual and knowing as Simone Signoret is in her much more sympathetic role in *Room at the Top*. Also with Edith Evans, George Devine, and Donald Pleasence. Directed by Tony Richardson, from Nigel Kneale's adaptation of the landmark play by John Osborne, it's something of a mess, but this mess—and *The Entertainer*, also a mess—are possibly the most exciting films to have come out of England in this period. Cinematography by Oswald Morris. b & w (See *I Lost it at the Movies*.)

Looker (1981)—Pseudo-scientific piffle about the machinations of the head of a conglomerate, played by James Coburn in the desiccated-amoral-old-bastard manner of John Huston. This rascal's laboratories are developing computer-generated images to make hypnotic TV commercials for political as well as economic use. To the rescue of civilization as we know it comes Albert Finney, like a lame tortoise; boredom seems to have seeped into Finney's muscles and cells—he's sinking under the weight of it, and the only part of him still alert is his wiry hair. He plays an eminent plastic surgeon who has "perfected" several women models according to mathematically correct specifications supplied by Coburn's lab; a couple of them come to mystifying violent ends—which are, unfortunately, still mystifying when the picture is over. (We never learn why the models were marked for destruction.) Written and directed by Michael Crichton in his untouched-by-human-hands style. The picture seems ingenious at the start, but Crichton can't write people, and he directs like a technocrat. This is the emptiest of his pictures to date. With Susan Dey, Dorian Harewood, Leigh Taylor-Young, Terri Welles, Darryl Hickman, and Terrence McNally. A Ladd Company Release, for Warners. color (See *Taking It All In*.)

Looking for Mr. Goodbar (1977)—Diane Keaton as Theresa Dunn, the teacher who cruises singles bars and is murdered by a man she picks up. Richard Brooks, who adapted the novel by Judith Rossner and directed, has laid a windy jeremiad about our permissive society on top of fractured film syntax. He's lost the erotic, pulpy morbidity that made the novel a compulsive read; the film is splintered, moralistic, tedious. With Tuesday Weld, William Atherton, Richard Kiley, Alan Feinstein, Richard Gere, and Tom Berenger. Cinematography by William A. Fraker. Paramount. color (See *When the Lights Go Down*.)

Lord Jim (1964)—Peter O'Toole, looking pale-blue eyed and pale-pink skinned, is the only Englishman among the officers of the Patna who save themselves, leaving the passengers (400 Moslems) to drown. But the ship survives, and Jim, devoured by the shame of his cowardice, faces an investigation. Written and directed by Richard Brooks, this adaptation of Joseph Conrad's novel is hugely ambitious and almost totally unrealized. Brooks didn't find a way to dramatize the themes; the narration tells us what the movie is meant to be about, and the characters (such as the ones played by Curt Jurgens and Eli Wallach) discuss their own character defects, and have literary-sounding exchanges. Trying to be a saint in order to expiate his guilt, Jim seems weak when he should be strong. O'Toole's wide-eyed stare is too mannered, and he has a special problem: he already played Lord Jim when he did *Lawrence of Arabia*, so this seems repetitive. (After a stretch, though, you do begin to feel for his Jim.) The talk of destiny and fate seems a mistake (it always seems a mistake). The film is most effective as a simple adventure story—the account of a revolutionary uprising by hideously mistreated natives. With James Mason, whose well-paced delivery and sheer professionalism help his scenes, and Jack Hawkins, Paul

Lukas, Akim Tamiroff, Daliah Lavi, Marne Maitland, Christian Marquand, and many others. Cinematography by Freddie Young; music by Bronislau Kaper. Columbia. color

Lord Love a Duck (1966)—This satire on teen-age culture, modern education, psychoanalysis, and what have you was the best American comedy of its year, and yet it's mostly terrible. The picture is bright and inventive, but it's also a hate letter to America that selects the easiest, most grotesque targets and keeps screaming at us to enjoy how funny-awful everything is. Finally we're preached at for our tiny minds and our family spray deodorants. Tuesday Weld has a wonderful blank, childlike quality as a Los Angeles high-school student who lusts after cashmere sweaters and wants everybody to love her. The director, George Axelrod, drew upon the novel *Candy*, which he beat to the movie post, as well as *What's New, Pussycat?* and the Richard Lester movies; there is eating à la *Tom Jones* and there are other tidbits from all over, even from *Nights of Cabiria*. Roddy McDowall plays a genie; Lola Albright is spectacularly effective as Tuesday's cocktail-waitress mother; and Ruth Gordon does her special brand of dementia. Several of the other performers—Max Showalter (sometimes known as Casey Adams), Sarah Marshall, Martin West—are in good form until they're made to slaver and shout. Also with Harvey Korman, Lynn Carey, Martin Gabel, and Joseph Mell. From Al Hine's novel, adapted by Larry H. Johnson and Axelrod. United Artists. b & w

Lord Mountdrago (1954)—(Originally one of the three unrelated stories in the English film *Three Cases of Murder*.) Orson Welles, when he was a magnificent figure and playing at his top flamboyant form. Nobody seems to enjoy the sheer physical pleasure of acting as much as he does in roles like this. As the proud, brilliant Foreign Secretary of the Somerset Maugham story, he's neatly matched against Alan Badel as Owen, a lowborn member of the opposition. There's a supernatural element here that sneaks up on you so cleverly that the analyst (André Morell) chatters along smugly and very convincingly until you realize that his explanations explain nothing. George More O'Ferrall directed this skillful mixture of comedy and horror; the cinematography is by Georges Périnal. With Helen Cherry as Lady Mountdrago and Zena Marshall as the blonde in the nightclub scene. b & w

Lords of the Forest Also known as *Masters of the Congo Jungle*. (1959)—This elegant record of the interrelations of man, animal, bird, and volcano was made by an international group of cameramen and scientists (international is a euphemism for German) under the sponsorship of Leopold of Belgium. The finest African documentary of its period, it has one truly superb sequence—young Watutsi girls performing a ritual dance in imitation of the courtship of the Crowned Cranes. The film could do with more facts and fewer of the poetic legends that Orson Welles and William Warfield narrate. color

Loss of Innocence (1961)—The original English title, *The Greengage Summer*, is the title of the 1958 Rumer Godden novel it's based on. The remarkable 22-year-old Susannah York plays a well-brought-up (i.e., inexperienced) 16-year-old English girl who sets out with her mother and the three younger children for a summer holiday at a *pension* in the country; the mother takes ill and is hospitalized and the girl seems to grow up before our eyes, as she practices her wiles on a shady, dashing boarder (Kenneth More), who plays uncle to the delighted children. The film takes for granted, without any heavy breathing, the lesbian relationship of two Frenchwomen—Claude Nollier and Danielle Darrieux, the mistress of the establishment, who also has a close relationship with her star boarder, More. The girl goes from her experimental flirtation to situations that she can't control; jealous and piqued, she betrays More to the police. The director, Lewis Gilbert, handles the children skillfully (the little boy is so beautiful he brings tears of delight to the eyes), and the camera is up close to the girl, revealing her confused shades of feeling so that she seems both mysterious and stripped bare. The whole thing doesn't quite come off, though, and we're always too aware of the sensitive qualities it's aiming at. It's a reasonably good picture that misses being a really memorable one. But York, Darrieux, and More are everything they should be. With Maurice Denham, Jane Asher, and David Saire. Adapted by Howard Koch; cinematography by Freddie Young. color

Lost Horizon (1937)—The orginal version of the James Hilton novel, directed by Frank Capra, from Robert Riskin's script—part popular adventure and part prissy, high-flown cracker-barrel sentimentality. The early trip through the icy waste is exciting, and Ronald Colman speaks in his charmingly cadenced manner, but Shangri-La, the genteel Himalayan utopia of peace, health, and eternal life, resembles, as Graham Greene pointed out, a film star's luxurious estate in Beverly Hills. With Sam Jaffe as the High Lama, Edward Everett Horton, Thomas Mitchell, Isabel Jewell, H. B. Warner, John Howard, Margo, and Jane Wyatt. Score by Dmitri Tiomkin. Columbia. b & w

Lost Horizon (1973)—This version, produced by Ross Hunter and directed by Charles Jarrott, is in color and is padded out with a wan operetta score by Burt Bacharach and Hal David. It retains James Hilton's inspired gimmick—longevity—and his invin-

cibly banal ideas, but it was a box-office fiasco. You can't help laughing at it—its Shangri-La, a cheery-goody haven where you can live indefinitely, lounging and puttering about for hundreds of years, is about as alluring as Forest Lawn. Inhabitants might be driven to slide down the mountains to the nearest Sin City. The leads—Peter Finch and Liv Ullmann—are pitilessly miscast. Finch's shrouded performance consists of a series of sickly, noble little smiles, as if to reassure himself and his fellow actors that this role, too, will pass. The generally embarrassed residents include Charles Boyer, John Gielgud, Michael York, Sally Kellerman, Olivia Hussey, Bobby Van, James Shigeta, and George Kennedy. The narrative has no energy, and the pauses for the pedagogic songs are so awkward you may feel that the director's wheelchair needs oiling. The script is by Larry Kramer; the musical numbers were staged by Hermes Pan. Columbia. (See *Reeling*.)

Lost in America (1985)—Original and pleasantly snappy. It lacks the fullness of a major comedy, but Albert Brooks, who stars in it and directed, is on to something: satirizing the upper middle class from within, he shows the nagging terror along with the complacency. And he keeps you laughing fairly steadily. As David, an L.A. advertising whiz, he's an only slightly exaggerated specimen of a large number of rising young businessmen and professional men—the insecure successes, the swollen-headed worriers. He's an anxious wreck who tortures himself and his wife over every detail of his existence. With her little-girl breathiness and her look of panic, Julie Hagerty is an ideal choice for the timid, depressed woman who puts up with him. The picture is about what happens when these two buy a luxury motor home, and, with the security of a nest egg of roughly $145,000, set out to find themselves and get in touch with the real America. With Garry Marshall as the pit boss of the Desert Inn Casino, and Art Frankel and Michael Greene. The script is by Brooks and Monica Johnson. Warners. color (See *State of the Art*.)

The Lost Weekend (1945)—Charles Jackson's novel about a well-brought-up, frustrated, dipsomaniacal writer who goes on a five-day binge that lands him in Bellevue was turned into an unusually daring popular melodrama by the writing team of Charles Brackett (who produced) and Billy Wilder (who directed). As the star, Ray Milland, reprieved from his usual lightweight leading-man roles, surprised the public with his tautness and irony. The picture lacks fluidity, and the slowly paced scenes seem overcalculated, with each colorful character and tense vignette standing out too sharply; everything is nailed down to a meaning for us. The whole thing is short on imaginative resonance; what it has is the Brackett-and-Wilder specialty—a distinctive cruel (and sometimes cruelly funny) edge. And there are some famous sequences: the hero's lust for a drink during "Libiamo," the opening aria of *La Traviata*; his long, plodding walk along Third Avenue in an attempt to hawk his typewriter when the pawnshops are closed for Yom Kippur. With Frank Faylen as a spiteful, supercilious male nurse, Howard Da Silva as a harsh-voiced bartender, Jane Wyman as a *Time* researcher, Doris Dowling as the girl who says "natch," Phillip Terry as the hero's brother, Clarence Muse, and Lillian Fontaine. Filmed partly on locations in New York, such as Bellevue. Academy Awards: Best Picture, Actor, Screenplay. Paramount. b & w

Lot in Sodom (1933)—This avant-garde effort (by Dr. James S. Watson and Melville Webber) certainly didn't point movies in any direction that sensible people wanted to follow, but it keeps coming back, so perhaps it has attained some sort of classic status. It's a symbolic interpretation of the Biblical story, with bodies writhing and swaying in poetic debauchery. 2 reels. b & w

Love and Anarchy *D'Amore e d'Anarchia* 1973)—Lina Wertmüller's large, epic film is set mostly in a 30s brothel; there, a young country bumpkin (Giancarlo Giannini, looking like a freckled young chicken), who intends to assassinate Mussolini, falls in love and botches his plans. The movie is uneven; it often seems like a silent film, and sometimes it is extravagant and operatic. But when Wertmüller concentrates on the whores' faces and attitudes it can be very beautiful. With Mariangela Melato, Lina Polito, Elena Fiore, and Eros Pagni. Cinematography by Giuseppe Rotunno; music by Nino Rota. In Italian. color

Love at First Bite (1979)—A rowdy burlesque of the Dracula movies, set in Manhattan, with dilapidated stuffed bats and a large assortment of gags; some of them are funny in a low-grade, moldy way, and some are even stupidly racist, but many are weirdly hip, with a true flaky wit. The scriptwriter, Robert Kaufman, will never be called a man of fine discrimination: he takes equal—almost obscene—relish in them all. Yet it's this relish—which the director, Stan Dragoti, seems to share—that fuels the movie, and, except for a wearying chase sequence toward the end, it bumps along entertainingly. As Count Dracula, George Hamilton uses the self-parody he first demonstrated in *Once Is Not Enough*; his Dracula is a swooningly romantic, ingenuously prurient gigolo with an indeterminate Transylvanian accent—his declaration of love sounds like "I lob you." His lady is a famous model, played by Susan Saint James; she isn't well photographed, but she has such great inflections that she hits her lines for every nuance of wacked-out comedy that's in them. And in the Van Helsing role, Richard Benjamin has some good silly moments as the model's whiny-voiced psychiatrist. With Dick Shawn as a cop, Arte Johnson as Renfield, and Ronnie Schell in a bit. Score by Charles Bernstein; from a story by Kaufman and Mark Gindes; produced by Joel Freeman, with Kaufman and Hamilton as the executive producers. A Melvin Simon Production, released by A.I.P. color

Love Finds Andy Hardy (1938)—Immensely entertaining. The fourth and perhaps the most charming of the Andy Hardy series, Louis B. Mayer's make-believe vision of Middle America. There's a sweet sly joke: Judy Garland, saying softly and tentatively to Mickey Rooney, "I sing, you know." In addition to Judy (who sings "In-Between"), the girls in Mickey's life include the teen-aged Lana Turner, and Ann Rutherford and Cecilia Parker, as his sister. Lewis Stone is Judge Hardy, and Fay Holden his wife. George B. Seitz directed, from William Ludwig's script. The songs include "It Never Rains But It Pours." With Gene Reynolds and Raymond Hatton. M-G-M. b & w

Love from a Stranger (1937)—A neat little thriller, featuring Basil Rathbone as a cold-eyed killer with charming drawing-room manners. This variation on the Landru theme is taken from Frank Vosper's play, based on Agatha Christie's *Philomel Cottage*. The opening is stage-bound and too leisurely, but by the time the killer's bride (Ann Harding) realizes what she has married, and sits down to dinner with her husband knowing that the servant has been sent off, the doors are locked, and they are alone together in a remote cottage, it is very scary. Made in England, with Rowland V. Lee directing. (A remake in 1947 featured John Hodiak.) b & w

The Love Game *Les Jeux de l'amour* (1960)—Philippe de Broca's wayward, featherweight comedy, one of the rare carefree films that came out of the early French New Wave, and blessedly trivial. Geneviève Cluny, who provided the story idea, is the girl who wants to get married; the spinning, dancing actor Jean-Pierre Cassel is the man trying to keep his freedom. They're so frivolous that at first they appear almost ridiculous, but they know how to seize the joys of the world about them, and in their hands small pleasures come to seem enormous. De Broca's style has a choreographic bounce, and the film is full of surprises and casual incongruities. With Jean-Louis Maury as the slavishly proper friend of the "family," and Claude Chabrol in a bit part. (This is the film that Godard used as the basis for *A Woman Is a Woman*, but the original has more charm.) In French. b & w

Love in the Afternoon (1957)—Wide-eyed Audrey Hepburn as the Parisian schoolgirl whom Elisabeth Bergner played in *Ariane*. A student of the cello, this Ariane falls in love with an aging American roué ensconced in the Paris Ritz—Gary Cooper, looking as if he knows how unappealing he is in the role. The director, Billy Wilder, and his co-scenarist, I.A.L. Diamond, have made her the daughter of a detective (Maurice Chevalier), who is then hired by Cooper to investigate her. It's all meant to be airy and bubbly, but it's obvious, overextended (2 hours plus), and overproduced. It was shot in France, and much of it is location work, but the art director, Alexander Trauner, built the first floor of the Paris Conservatoire in a studio, as well as the second floor of the Ritz full-scale, with actual, operating elevators. For the performance of *Tristan and Isolde*, Wilder engaged 960 extras in full evening dress. At the end, there's a fine view of a smoking, chugging locomotive in a splendid, vaulted railroad station—and for a moment one wonders if this, too, is a set. Allied Artists. b & w

Love Is a Dog from Hell Also known as *Crazy Love*. (1987)—A low-key sexual reverie from Belgium about young Harry, who loves women but is rejected by them, and is able to show his tenderness only to a corpse. Adapted from Charles Bukowski's tales, principally "The Copulating Mermaid of Venice, California," this is a Flemish-language art film with its own erotic tone—faintly ironic, faintly queasy. Its softness gets to you. The 31-year-old director, Dominique Deruddere, made the final episode, which is set in 1976, as a half-hour short, and then (with his co-writer, Marc Didden) worked up the two episodes of Harry's earlier life, set in 1955 and 1962, in order to make a feature—his first. The final necrophiliac section is too poetic—it's just a few tones away from being a parody of an adolescent fantasy. (It might work better without the prehistory that explains it so neatly.) But the middle episode—Harry's high-school graduation dance and his torment over being covered with acne and boils and pustules—has a masochistic potency, and some humor and rage. The band plays American pop tunes, such as "Love Hurts," and the girl vocalist has a wonderfully vacuous, self-absorbed sexiness. This is a movie for people with a perverse sense of humor or a persistent sexual acne. With Geert Hunaerts as Harry at 12, and Josse De Pauw as Harry at 19 (a bit like the young Alec Guinness) and at 33 (a bit like Nicol Williamson). color (See *Hooked*.)

Love Me Forever (1935)—Far from sophisticated, but this Grace Moore hit has a sprightly good humor that helps to redeem the tale of a racketeer (Leo Carrillo) who has a passion for music and falls in love with a poor, unknown soprano; builds a café ("La Margerita") in her honor; and eventually ar-

ranges for her to sing *La Bohème* at the Met. The movie drips a few too many tears, but it features such curiosities as a mockup of the old Met, an impersonation of Gatti-Casazza, and the quartet from *Rigoletto* expanded for 40 voices. Victor Schertzinger wrote the story, directed, and had a big hand in the music. With Luis Alberni, Douglass Dumbrille, and Spring Byington. Columbia. b & w

Love Me or Leave Me (1955)—Doris Day as Ruth Etting. A lot of people were deeply impressed with this melodramatic, musical bio, which tries for an authentic show-business tawdriness; it's certainly better than most movie bios of popular entertainers, but that's not saying all that much. Doris Day is a little less butch than usual, though you can't tell what makes her Ruth Etting a star. (From the evidence of her movie appearances and her records, the young, soft, and sensual Ruth Etting was just about the opposite of this cold woman.) The script by Daniel Fuchs and Isobel Lennart is several notches above the usual, and James Cagney brings frightening strength to his role as the singer's vicious lover. Their relationship is horrifying, yet your sympathy may go out to the scummy little guy beating her up. Some good songs, including "Mean to Me" and "Ten Cents a Dance." With Cameron Mitchell, Robert Keith, Tom Tully, Harry Bellaver, and Richard Gaines. Directed by Charles Vidor; produced by Joe Pasternak, for M-G-M. CinemaScope, color

Love on the Run (1936)—One of the big-star pictures nobody ever talks about. Not for the first time, Joan Crawford appears as an heiress. Clark Gable and Franchot Tone are antic reporters pursuing her, and there are international spies. The whole movie is on the run—London, the Riviera, Fontainebleau, Continental trains, and airplanes. Joseph L.

Mankiewicz produced and W. S. Van Dyke directed, from a script that John Lee Mahin and others worked on. You can see how hard everybody is trying to make this a slick sexy hit. With Mona Barrie, Ivan Lebedeff, William Demarest, and Reginald Owen. M-G-M. b & w

The Loved One (1965)—In 1947 Evelyn Waugh went to Hollywood to clear up censorial objections to the script for his *Brideshead Revisited;* after seven weeks he simply withdrew the book and went back to England. Out of his experiences he wrote the essay "Death in Hollywood" on Forest Lawn Memorial Park, and in 1948, *The Loved One,* a short satirical novel about one of the last outposts of empire—the British colony in the movie business and its renegade poet who goes to work in a cemetery for pets. Bought for the movies, the novel became a Hollywood legend through the efforts of various writers (including Luis Buñuel and Elaine May) to get an acceptable film script out of material that was considered too naughty and macabre for the screen. By the time Tony Richardson was signed to direct the film, from Christopher Isherwood's script, movies had changed so much that Terry Southern was brought in to juice the material up. (Waugh tried, but was unable, to withdraw *The Loved One.*) From the look of the film Richardson shot every plausible idea that came to him, and then, as the footage had no flow, no development, he choppd it up and slapped it together hard, trying to use overlapping sound to plug up the holes. But it's funny anyway. Although the picture has lost its center (the poet—played by Robert Morse—has become as quirky and crazy as everybody else), some of the fragments are good and jagged. This botched picture is a triumphant disaster—a sinking ship that makes it to port because everybody on board is too giddy to panic. Milton Berle and Mar-

garet Leighton—who might seem the world's most unlikely married couple—are quite amazing together; Rod Steiger is an embalmer; Ayllene Gibbons is his bedridden fat mother (who has orgasms from looking at the food in TV commercials); Jonathan Winters is a charlatan; and Liberace is a casket salesman. Also with James Coburn, John Gielgud, Robert Morley, Roddy McDowall, Anjanette Comer, Tab Hunter, Lionel Stander, and Paul Williams, as a child scientist. Cinematography by Haskell Wexler. (*Brideshead Revisited* was finally turned into an 11-part TV series in England, in 1981.) M-G-M. b & w

Lovers and Thieves *Assassins et voleurs* (1957)—In the year he died, Sacha Guitry, who was 72, made a couple of films. This sly detective comedy, which he wrote and then directed from a wheelchair, is one of them. The old master of casual, ironic wit had intended to play the leading role himself, but old age had at last caught up with him, and he appeared only in a bit part. In 1936, in Guitry's *The Story of a Cheat,* the narrator provided a cynical and witty counterpoint to the action. (The technique was to become familiar to a later generation through the English comedy *Kind Hearts and Coronets.*) This approach, to which Guitry returned in *Lovers and Thieves,* permitted him to treat the film medium with nonchalant intimacy—there are freakish interruptions, changes of subject and pace. He teases the classic unities as well as the classic virtues: in his offhand way, he seems to say, "Look how easy it is to make a movie—one just begins and then improvises." He directed an extended romantic sequence that is one of the most impudent ever filmed: Magali Noel, the enchanting, stylish murder victim, loathes her husband so much that she and her lover make love all over Paris, so that everyone will know the husband is a cuckold. The lover, who is also the narrator (Jean Poiret), inadvertently commits a murder for which an innocent thief (Michel Serrault) is sent to prison. Conscience-stricken, the lover takes over the occupation of the thief. But all this is only the loose framework; Guitry makes a sortie into a great loony bin, provides an audacious painting theft, and stops everything while a mad beatnik (Darry Cowl) addresses a courtroom. It's a fresh, lovely movie. Clément Duhour helped on the directing. (Jean Poiret later wrote the play *La Cage aux folles* and Michel Serrault appeared in it as the female impersonator, on the stage and in the movie.) In French. b & w

Lover Come Back (1962)—Broadly played, in the 50s telegraphing-every-thought comic style. It was a big hit. Doris Day is an ethical advertising woman; Rock Hudson is a smart, unscrupulous advertising man—a roué. He knows how to manipulate dumb-broad sexpots, such as a Southern-belle redhead (Edie Adams, bulging like Marilyn Monroe) and he knows how to goad Day, who's a virgin. As Hudson's neurotic ad-agency boss, Tony Randall uses a lot of vocal tricks, and gives the movie some energy. Also with Jack Oakie in a cameo as a tycoon who plays the bull fiddle, and Jack Kruschen and Jack Albertson. Directed by Delbert Mann, from a script by Stanley Shapiro and Paul Henning. Universal. color

Lovers of Paris, see *Pot-Bouille*

The Lovers of Teruel *Les Amants de Teruel* (1962)—An elaborate ballet-drama of romantic tragedy. Ludmilla Tcherina dances the role of a doomed, demented girl, and then finds that life has cast her in the same role. More than a bit much, with dialogue such as "What good is my body if you cannot have my soul?" (Especially silly, because Miss Tcherina isn't much of a dancer but has a sensational body.) The director, Raymond

Rouleau, is in love with colored lights. Cinematography by Claude Renoir; music by Mikis Theodorakis. In French. color

Lovers of Verona *Les Amants de Vérone* (1948)—Two young understudies for the stars making a film of *Romeo and Juliet* fall in love and, as star-crossed as Shakespeare's lovers, they re-enact the drama. The film's sensuous, poetic elegance contrasts with the seamy elements it encompasses (the aging film stars, the young girl's decadent, fascistic family). You may feel you've been made too aware of the film's artistic intentions, and the romanticism can drive you a little nuts. Serge Reggiani and Anouk Aimée are the lovers. Directed by André Cayatte; screenplay by Jacques Prévert. With Martine Carol, Pierre Brasseur, Marcel Dalio, Marianne Oswald, and Louis Salou. Photographed in Verona and Venice by Henri Alekan. In French. b & w

Loves of a Blonde *Lasky Jedne Plavovlasky* Also known as *A Blonde in Love.* (1965)—A dreamily romantic young girl who is depressed and lost in her regimented factory milieu mistakes the casual interest of a young musician for a serious interest, and follows him to his home. The Miloš Forman picture is a comedy, and yet it's too painful and desolate to be funny; it reveals a horribly petty middle-class world within the Socialist economy. With Hana Brejchova and Vladimir Pucholt. In Czech. b & w

Lovesick (1983)—Among the many psychoanalyst characters are the hero Dudley Moore, his crony Wallace Shawn, and Selma Diamond, John Huston, Alan King, Stefan Schnabel, Richard B. Shull, and Alec Guinness (as the shade of a trim, urbane Sigmund Freud). The writer-director, Marshall Brickman, has a dapper, weird precision of tone that's funny, and he starts with a promising (if flimsy) situation: Moore inherits a patient, a young playwright (Elizabeth McGovern), from Shawn, who has fallen in love with her and died of guilt; of course, Moore falls in love with her, too. But Brickman's attention seems to wander away, and the dramatic tension dribbles out. The film's tasteful sprightliness keeps it from being about anything, but there are some terrific comedy performances by Anne DeSalvo, Kent Broadhurst, David Strathairn, Gene Saks, and Renée Taylor. Also with the painter Larry Rivers, his great-bird head held high, as a painter, and Ron Silver as a Hollywood star (who resembles Al Pacino). A Ladd Company Release, through Warners. color (See *Taking It All In*.)

Loving (1970)—A beautifully sustained piece of moviemaking by Irvin Kershner. It's an unusual American movie in that it has the sensibility and humor and feeling for character generally associated with Czech films or prewar French films. It looks at the failures of middle-class life without despising the people; it understands that they already despise themselves. There's a decency—almost a tenderness—in the way that Kershner is fair to everyone; he never allows us to feel superior to the characters. George Segal is a free-lance illustrator who makes good money but never makes enough money; he wriggles this way and that because he doesn't like his life. He's trying to do right by his wife (Eva Marie Saint) and his children, and still keep the possibility open that he could yet be a dashing, gifted artist. The new girl he longs to run away with is not very different from his wife—only younger, and not bound down by his children. Eva Marie Saint gives a stunning performance as a tough, gallant woman who doesn't have many illusions about her husband or herself, and Segal has a loose, informal sense of irony—he radiates likable human weakness. There are some wonderful scenes: the couple going to see a

house that has come on the market because of a divorce, Segal just standing and looking at his two daughters through the window of a suburban dress shop—children who are simultaneously alien to their father's life and at the center of it. With Keenan Wynn, Sterling Hayden, Nancie Phillips, Janis Young, Andrew Duncan, Sherry Lansing, and Roy Scheider. Produced and written by Don Devlin, from J. M. Ryan's novel *Brooks Wilson, Ltd.* Cinematography by Gordon Willis; music by Bernardo Segall. Columbia. color (See *Deeper into Movies*.)

The Lower Depths *Les Bas-Fonds* (1936)—Jean Renoir's version of the Maxim Gorky play features those two magnetic poles of French acting—Louis Jouvet as the gambling baron who sinks to living in a flophouse, and Jean Gabin as the thief trying to climb up to a different life. Their scenes together are gems of the French film tradition. The fine cast includes Le Vigan as an actor, Jany Holt as a prostitute with aspirations toward love with sentiment, and Junie Astor, Suzy Prim, and Vladimir Sokoloff. This movie has one of those emblematic moments that people talk about for years afterward: Jouvet, having lost everything, comes away from the gaming tables and can't light his cigarette. This scene was, for the 30s, what Belmondo rubbing his lips in *Breathless* was for the 60s. In French. b & w

Luci del Varietà, see *Variety Lights*

Lucky Lady (1975)—Liza Minnelli is a blond floozy-singer, and Gene Hackman and Burt Reynolds are her competing lovers; they're all rumrunners in the early 30s, and meant to be adorable. This is a big, expensive movie for people who don't mind being treated like hicks: the audience is expected to shudder with delight every time it hears an obscenity or sees a big movie-star grin. Hackman keeps a low profile and comes off better than the others, but it's not much of a contest. Reynolds does his simp act; he's willing to play a twit, but he plays it a little cute, so you'll know Burt Reynolds could never be convincing as a twit. There's nothing to be done with the role anyway, and he isn't obstreperously offensive. What is is the way Liza Minnelli is presented as a strident, selfish bitch, and is then sentimentalized, as if her viciousness and rasping out at everything were really delightful. The film specializes in fancy destruction scenes—boats exploding, burning, sinking, people shot up, blown to bits. Directed by Stanley Donen, from a script by Willard Huyck and Gloria Katz. 20th Century-Fox. color (See *When the Lights Go Down*.)

Lucky Partners (1940)—Sacha Guitry's film *Bonne Chance*, adapted by Allan Scott and John van Druten, provides a moderately naughty script for Ginger Rogers and Ronald Colman. Colman plays an artist who makes a deal with a businessman (Jack Carson) to substitute for him on his honeymoon (with Rogers, of course). The first two-thirds of the film rank with the good, lively Hollywood comedies; though the last third is too arch the spirit is still genial. With Harry Davenport, Spring Byington, and Cecilia Loftus. Directed by Lewis Milestone. R K O. b & w

Ludwig (1973)—The Luchino Visconti film has been trimmed since its opening, but it's still footage in search of a style. The continuity is a splatter of choppy, confused scenes, and the relationships of the characters are never made clear. As Ludwig II of Bavaria, the supreme childish fantasist among kings, Helmut Berger is a tense, prissy-mouthed, gloomy cuckoo, and it isn't until he begins to lose his teeth (from overindulgence in sweets) that the picture becomes fitfully amusing. With Romy

Schneider, Trevor Howard, and Silvana Mangano. color (See *Reeling*.)

Lumière (1976)—Jeanne Moreau wrote, directed, and stars in this elevated daydream about the life of an actress. The picture is delicately dissociated; it nibbles around the edges of its subject. And it shares a weakness of many other high-flown junk movies: it is less interested in pace than in culture. With Francine Racette, Bruno Ganz, François Simon, Caroline Cartier, and Lucia Bose. In French. color (See *When the Lights Go Down*.)

La Lune dans le caniveau, see *The Moon in the Gutter*

Lust for Life (1956)—Unlike the usual Hollywood lives of artists, this biographical movie about Vincent van Gogh (Kirk Douglas) and his loneliness and frustrated attempt at friendship with Gauguin (Anthony Quinn) is thoughtful, ambitious in a dedicated way, and remarkably free of howlers. Perhaps just because it is so concerned with fidelity to the facts it's less exciting than one might hope; something seems to be missing (a unifying dramatic idea, perhaps), but it's far from a disgrace, and the performers are never an embarrassment. The cast includes James Donald as Theo, Pamela Brown, Henry Daniell, Lionel Jeffries, Jill Bennett, Everett Sloane, Niall MacGinnis, Isobel Elsom, Laurence Naismith, Madge Kennedy, and Noel Purcell. The team of art directors worked out locations (in France and Holland) and interiors that relate to the paintings, many of which are shown. Vincente Minnelli directed for M-G-M, in CinemaScope and color; John Houseman produced; Norman Corwin adapted Irving Stone's best-selling biography; Freddie Young and Russell Harlan were the cinematographers; Miklós Rózsa did the music. Quinn took the Academy Award for Best Supporting Actor.

M (1931)—Fritz Lang's first sound film has visual excitement, pace, brilliance of surface, and feeling for detail. Above all, it has, caught in a manhunt, a small, fat man, sweating in his uncomfortable clothes—the sexual psychopath who murders little girls—interpreted by Peter Lorre with a spark of genius. It is Lorre's triumph that he makes us understand the terrified, suffering human being who murders. The film is based on the case of the Düsseldorf murderer: the police, in trying to track him down, disturbed the normal criminal activities of the city, and the underworld organized to find him, so that crime could go on as usual. Lang turns the movie into a melodramatic thriller by centering on this ironic chase—actually, on the two converging chases of the police and the underworld. The structure is so mechanical it's almost pulpy, and the film reaches for other easy effects—it's similar to *The Threepenny Opera* in its satirical use of beggars and criminals. But there's nothing facile about Lorre: trapped by the underworld, he screams, "I can't help myself!" Our identification with him as a psychopath is so complete it's hard to believe that while appearing before Fritz Lang's cameras in the daytime, he was, at night, acting as a comedian in a farce. With Gustaf Gründgens and Otto Wernicke; cinematography by Fritz Arno Wagner; script by Thea von Harbou and others. (The tune Lorre whistles is the theme from Grieg's *Peer Gynt*.) In German. b & w

Macbeth (1971)—Slaughter is the star; Shakespeare's offstage corpses and murders are added to the onstage ones, and they so dominate the material that it's difficult to pay attention to the poetry. The director, Roman Polanski, shows such literal horror—and always a shade faster than you expect, so you're not prepared—that there is no horror left to imagine. He treats the play not as a great cautionary nightmare but as an illustration of how power normally changes hands. The film says that nothing is possible but horror and more horror, and, at the end, the cycle of bloodletting is about to begin again. It's well-acted, but it reduces Shakespeare's meanings to the banal "life is a jungle." With Jon Finch, Francesca Annis, Martin Shaw, Nicholas Selby, and John Stride. The screenplay is by Polanski and Kenneth Tynan. Playboy Productions and Columbia. color (See *Deeper into Movies*.)

McCabe & Mrs. Miller (1971)—A beautiful pipe dream of a movie: Robert Altman's fleeting vision of what frontier life might have been, with Warren Beatty as a cocky small-time gambler and Julie Christie as an ambitious madam in the turn-of-the-century Northwest. Delicate, richly textured, and unusually understated, this modern classic is not like any other film. Altman builds a Western town as one might build a castle in the air—and it's inhabited. His stock company of actors turn up quietly in the new location, as if they were part of a floating crap game, and he creates an atmosphere of living interrelationships. With Keith Carradine, Shelley Duvall, René Auberjonois, John Schuck, Bert Remsen, Michael Murphy, Anthony Holland, Corey Fischer, Hugh Millais, Manfred Schulz, Jack Riley, Robert Fortier, and, in the one sequence that doesn't really work, William Devane as a blowhard lawyer. The script by Altman and Brian McKay is based on the novel *McCabe* by Edmund Naughton; the cinematography is by Vilmos Zsigmond; the production design and costume supervision are by Leon Ericksen; the songs are by Leonard Cohen; and Lou Lombardo is credited as the second unit director. Filmed in West Vancouver, British Columbia. Warners. color (See *Deeper into Movies*.)

McQ (1974)—Prostratingly dull. John Wayne, eager at the time to change his image, plays a tough cop, modelled on Clint Eastwood's Harry Callahan. As a member of the Seattle police force, Wayne clutches a little gun in gnarled hands the size of cattle hocks. John Sturges directed, at a funereal pace. With Eddie Albert and Colleen Dewhurst. Warners. color (See *Reeling*.)

Mad Love (1935)—Karl Freund, the famous UFA cinematographer, directed this version of the horror story *The Hands of Orlac* for M-G-M, starring Peter Lorre, with Gregg Toland (who was later to shoot *Citizen Kane*) in the camera crew. Freund's direction is disappointingly static, but the film has a distinctive Grand Guignol style and it's of considerable visual and historical interest. Peter Lorre's mad doctor (who grafts the hands of a knife-wielding murderer onto the sensitive pianist, Orlac, played by Colin Clive) might almost be an early sketch for Orson Welles' performance as the elderly Kane; the gothic sets of the two pictures have many similarities, and a white cockatoo turns up in both of them. With Frances Drake, Ted Healy, Edward Brophy, Sara Haden, Keye Luke, Cora Sue Collins, Henry Kolker, and Harold Huber. Guy Endore, John L. Balderston, and P. J. Wolfson adapted the Maurice Renard novel, which Robert Wiene filmed as a silent in Germany, with Conrad Veidt as Orlac. b & w (See *The Citizen Kane Book*.)

Mad Max 2, see *The Road Warrior*

The Mad Miss Manton (1938)—Something ground out by people in a desperate mood. Barbara Stanwyck, miscast as a dizzy débutante, is one of a covey of Junior League girls in fox capes; she walks her dog at three in the morning after a costume ball and finds a corpse in a deserted house. Inspirited by the spectacle, she immediately corrals her flighty friends; in their best party dresses, they scurry about the scene of the crime, squealing and looking for clues. This is the kind of movie that helped kill the screwball genre. Henry Fonda is the hero; the cast includes Sam Levene, Hattie McDaniel, Stanley Ridges, Miles Mander, and Whitney Bourne. Directed by Leigh Jason, from Philip G. Epstein's script. Produced by Pandro S. Berman, for R K O. b & w

Madame Bovary (1934)—Flaubert's Emma Bovary has usually been a role for screen beauties—Lila Lee in 1932, Pola Negri in 1937, and Jennifer Jones in 1949—but in this version, adapted and directed by Jean Renoir, Emma is played by Valentine Tessier as an anomalous creature, half swan, half goose. This large woman is not at all what one expects, yet she's surprisingly effective. The sunlight and the spaciousness emphasize Emma's loneliness; she's a middle-class woman with an ample figure, drifting along on romantic daydreams. When she's at the opera she's fatuously carried away from the emptiness of provincial life. Renoir's film ran 3½ hours; the backers cut it to 2 hours and had a commercial disaster, anyway. Early viewers who saw the full version pronounced it a masterpiece; what's left is like a Renoir nature essay on Flaubertian themes. It lacks Flaubert's intensity, but it has fine, unstressed images and scenes that stay with one. The director's brother, Pierre Renoir, plays the uncomprehending philistine Charles Bovary, Max Dearly is M. Homais, and Robert Le Vigan is Lheureux. In French. b & w

Madame Bovary (1949)—Fancy-dress version, starring Jennifer Jones. If you hadn't read the book, you really couldn't guess what it was about from this film, though the scriptwriter, Robert Ardrey, uses the framing device of Flaubert (James Mason) on trial for corrupting morals. This M-G-M production was advertised with the slogan "Whatever it is that French women have, Madame Bovary has more of it!", and Jennifer Jones' Emma is surfeited with clothes and handsome leading men—Louis Jourdan and Alf Kjellin (who appears here under the name Christopher Kent) among them, while Van Heflin plays her dull husband. The director, Vincente Minnelli, stages an impressive romantic ball, but the whole movie is hopelessly overscaled.

With Gladys Cooper, Paul Cavanagh, Eduard Franz, Gene Lockhart, George Zucco, and John Abbott. b & w

Madame Butterfly (1932)—Is there someone out there who has always wanted to know what the opera is about, without being distracted from the plot by the music? Sylvia Sidney, got up in fancy kimonos, mournfully smiles through tears, and a not yet suave Cary Grant is the rotten-hearted Occidental who deserts her. Based on a stage version that David Belasco had co-written, it's every bit as bad as you might expect. Marion Gering directed; the cast includes Charlie Ruggles, Helen Jerome Eddy, Irving Pichel, and Sandor Kallay. Paramount. b & w

Madame Curie (1943)—Mrs. Miniver (Greer Garson) returns as the famous scientist, with Mr. Miniver (Walter Pidgeon, sporting a beard now) in attendance as her partner-in-science husband, Pierre Curie. Greer Garson is an actress who turns restraint into a cover for obscene self-assurance; when she discusses laboratory formulas she manages to invest every syllable with sanctity. Adapted from Eve Curie's biography of her mother, the movie is a product of simplification, distortion, and dullness of mind. The Curies are scoffed at by the authorities, surmount insurmountable obstacles, and, finally—bang!—they isolate radium. Directed by Mervyn LeRoy for M-G-M, with James Hilton serving as narrator. The enormous cast includes Robert Walker, Dame May Whitty, Van Johnson, Albert and Elsa Basserman, Margaret O'Brien, Victor Francen, Reginald Owen, Henry Travers, and C. Aubrey Smith. Written by Paul Osborn and Paul H. Rameau. b & w

Madame de . . . , see *The Earrings of Madame de . . .*

Madame Satan (1930)—A hodgepodge by Cecil B. De Mille, culminating in an extravagant masked ball, costumed by Adrian, aboard an enormous dirigible. The party entertainment is an electrical ballet; the dancers are dressed with such motifs as sparkplugs and lightning streaks. God is angered, of course, and the festivities are interrupted by a real bolt of lightning. Some of the passengers are saved by their parachutes; the parachuteless hero, Reginald Denny, jumps to safety in the Central Park Reservoir—a stunt that the movies have never repeated. Lillian Roth, buxom and dimpled before she boozed and repented and told all (*I'll Cry Tomorrow*), is the wildly energetic showgirl Trixie; Kay Johnson is the heroine—the wife who disguises herself as Madame Satan in order to win her husband back. Also with Roland Young and Martha Sleeper. You have to wait so long for the dirigible climax that you may be too exhausted to enjoy its lunacy. Written by Jeanie Macpherson. M-G-M. b & w

Madame Sousatzka (1988)—As a flamboyant, grande-dame piano teacher of Russian lineage, Shirley MacLaine seems to have entered the Simone Signoret sweepstakes, but she doesn't project Signoret's generosity—she doesn't spill over emotionally. This is, arguably, MacLaine's worst performance. She has flurries of physical mannerisms, but she's tight and held in; she's a wacky witch with frizzy red hair—she could be Norma Desmond's small-town spinster sister. Sousatzka lives in London (in an Edwardian house that is to be demolished) and devotes her energies and her hopes to the most prodigious of her students, a 15-year-old Indian boy raised in England—a role played with intelligence and poise by Navin Chowdhry. The blindingly derivative movie is about the boy's breaking free of her, though he knows he'll remain in her debt forever. Directed by John Schlesinger, this is a handsomely mounted production, and the musical community may regard it as a treasure—as the *Red Shoes* of the keyboard. With Peggy Ashcroft, Shabana Azmi, Geoffrey Bayldon, Leigh Lawson, and an appealingly understated performance by Twiggy. The script, by Ruth Prawer Jhabvala and Schlesinger, is based on the 1962 novel by Bernice Rubens. Cineplex Odeon Films. color (See *Movie Love.*)

Madame X (1966)—A woman is forced to abandon her baby and years later, having committed a murder, is defended by . . . her very own son, who does not know that . . . *she is his very own mother!* Alexandre Bisson's courtroom melodrama melted hearts in silent-movie houses in 1916 and again in 1920; Ruth Chatterton had a personal triumph in the first talkie version, in 1929; and in 1937 Gladys George gave it the benefit of her gin-and-tears voice. It requires an actress who knows how to get some mileage out of it, but in this Ross Hunter production, spiritually dedicated to the glossy woman's-picture style of the 1940s, Lana Turner hasn't the power or the technique—she isn't Madame X, she's Brand X. At the start, Turner is supposed to be a ravishing young newlywed, and the production is designed like a cocoon to protect her. There isn't a young actress in the cast, not even among the bit players. This *Madame X* isn't about mother love; it's about mummy love. Ross Hunter was addicted to lavish wardrobes, and so the outcast heroine keeps changing her clothes, and to compensate for all those swell dresses, she keeps suffering: not one moment of fun in twenty years. With almost every line a howler, this is a camp special. David Lowell Rich directed. With Constance Bennett (in her last film appearance), Keir Dullea, John Forsythe, Ricardo Montalban, Burgess Meredith, Kaaren Verne, Virginia Grey, and Joe De Santis. Universal. color (See *Kiss Kiss Bang Bang.*)

Mädchen in Uniform (1932)—A willowy young girl (Herthe Thiele) in a fashionable school is unhappy under the harsh, Prussian discipline; she flowers when a sympathetic, understanding teacher (Dorothea Wieck) gives her special consideration. This consideration is ambiguous and certainly sensual. The teacher is not viewed as decadent, or even naughty; she appears to be on the side of the liberal, humanitarian angels, yet she seems unmistakably lesbian. This legendary film, temporarily obstructed by U.S. censors, was later voted the best film of the year by the New York press. It was directed by Leontine Sagan from Christa Winsloe's play *Yesterday and Today*—one of the few occasions in film history when a woman writer's material has also been directed by a woman. The picture is always described as sensitive, and it is; it's also a rather loaded piece of special pleading. In German. b & w

Das Mädchen Rosemarie, see *Rosemary*

Made for Each Other (1939)—Carole Lombard and James Stewart as plain, ordinary struggling young married folk in New York, having money troubles. The film, written by Jo Swerling and directed by John Cromwell, manages to jack up a little excitement when the couple's baby gets sick and serum must be flown from Utah. The mercy plane goes through a storm, gales, blizzards, thunder, and lightning. You'll be relieved to know that the serum arrives in the very nick of time, and the husband gets a promotion. With Charles Coburn, Lucile Watson, Harry Davenport, Eddie Quillan, Esther Dale, and Louise Beavers. Produced by David O. Selznick; released by United Artists. b & w

Made for Each Other (1971)—Renée Taylor and her husband, Joseph Bologna, wrote and star in this original, romantic comedy about a knocked-out, bleached-blond failed actress and a grubby misfit who meet in an encounter group. The movie believes there is a Kingdom of Heaven that you can get to if you help each other be vulnerable and open. It's Frank Capra updated by ethnic humor and simplified Freudianism, but it's so skillfully worked out that it's emotionally pleasing, and Renée Taylor's performance gives the film depth and conviction. Robert B. Bean directed. 20th Century-Fox. color (See *Deeper into Movies*.)

Made in Heaven (1987)—It's about finding perfect love, losing it, and stumblingly trying to recover it—in another life. Timothy Hutton and Kelly McGillis have a love literally made in Heaven; when their souls are returned to earth in newborn babes, they have a spiritual need to find each other, though they don't remember the love they shared. This whimsey might have been semi-appealing if it had been worked out more ingeniously—if the scenes took some shape, if they didn't dither and sag. And if McGillis, who's meant to be the sort of lyrical, ethereal creature that Jennifer Jones used to play, weren't pure granite. The director, Alan Rudolph, is reported to have had differences with the producers; there were three—Raynold Gideon, Bruce A. Evans, and David Blocker—and since Gideon and Evans wrote the script he may not be fully responsible for the film's randomness. A batch of smart performers give it some flavor around the edges: Mare Winningham, Ann Wedgeworth, James Gammon, Maureen Stapleton, David Rasche, and Amanda Plummer. And Hutton has a nice, cowlicky quality in the comedy scenes. With two uncredited performances: Ellen Barkin as a Luciferian temptress (it's a mistake), and Debra Winger (then married to Hutton), almost unrecognizable in a red punk hairdo, with pasty makeup and a deep, hoarse voice, as Emmett, the fellow who manages things in Heaven. Hutton clearly has more rapport with this weirdly androgynous Emmett than he has with McGillis. (Heaven is actually Charleston, S.C., with some special effects.) Also with Timothy Daly, Don Murray, Willard Pugh, and John Considine. A number of celebrities show up in bit parts: the singer and songwriter Neil Young as a truck driver, the novelist Tom Robbins as a toymaker, the cartoonist Gary Larson as a guitarist, the rock star Tom Petty as the owner of a roadhouse, the rock star Ric Ocasek, of the Cars, as a mechanic. They don't have any presence, but this movie can use all the quirky drop-ins it can get. Lorimar. color (See *Hooked*.)

Madeleine (1950)—British film based on the news accounts and court records of the case of a young woman in Victorian Glasgow who was accused of murdering her French lover. The verdict at Madeleine Smith's trial was neither guilty or innocent; it was "not proven"—and we are left in the same uncertainty. The director, David Lean, has shaped the whole movie for this enigmatic uncertainty, yet the effect is unsatisfying— in fact, numbing—and Lean's moviemaking techniques are so stiff they seem Victorian, too. In the title role Ann Todd (Mrs. Lean at the time) deliberately emphasizes her own glacial reserve. But she's so rigidly made up that her face looks about to crack. It's an unappealing performance; she was already past 40 and too austerely controlled to play the scenes of Madeleine's passionate abandon to the blackmailing Frenchman (Ivan Desny, who's like a foreign-voiced young Orson Welles). With Leslie Banks, Norman Wooland, André Morell, Elizabeth Sellars, Jean Cadell, and Ivor Barnard as the druggist who sells Madeleine arsenic. The humorless script

is by Stanley Haynes and Nicholas Phipps. b & w

Mademoiselle Gobette (1955)—A girl who can't keep her clothes on may seem like a subject for low-grade entertainment, but suppose that her foible is used to ridicule the conventions of respectable society? This neat little farce begins with a judge investigating charges that a theatrical performer (Silvana Pampanini) is too scantily dressed; she proceeds to scandalize a number of overdressed people, and ends up happily ensconced with the Minister of Justice. The cast and the director (Pietro Germi) are Italian, but the source is a French play (by Maurice Hennequin and Pierre Weber), and the whole thing somehow got itself into French with English subtitles—presumably on the basis that boudoir comedy would do better in French in the American sex-art houses of the 50s. The boudoir is used as a vantage point for some very deft horseplay. Even the strapping Pampanini shows a relaxed, inventive comedy style. b & w

Mado (1976)—The French director Claude Sautet is a master of modulation; he doesn't labor anything—not even the defeats of his characters. (They shrug, painfully, and move on.) This is a superlatively crafted story about the moral—and sexual—complexities of a real-estate swindle. The crime involves a group of middle-aged businessmen and young working-class dissidents who are linked by Mado (Ottavia Piccolo), a whore with red-gold hair, creamy pink skin, and a natural pout—she's like a softer young Lana Turner. The film never quite makes a leap to greatness, but it's consistently intelligent and has moments of surprising feeling—particularly in a sequence featuring Romy Schneider as a woman whose whole emotional life centers on a man (Michel Piccoli) who doesn't care about her. Piccoli probably does as fine a job at suggesting a shallow man's range of dissatisfaction with his existence as any actor who ever lived. With Jacques Dutronc, Julien Guiomar, Charles Denner, Jean-Denis Robert, Michel Aumont, Bernard Fresson, and Claude Dauphin. From a script by Sautet and Claude Neron; the expressive, fluid cinematography is by Jean Boffety (when the characters leave Paris and go to the country, the compositions often recall Auguste Renoir). In French. color

The Madwoman of Chaillot (1969)—The remnants of Jean Giraudoux's slight, whimsical play can still be perceived in Edward Anhalt's vile modernization and a lot of famous actors can be recognized even in the performances they give here. Bryan Forbes directed. The cast includes Katharine Hepburn (an extremely sane madwoman), Margaret Leighton, Edith Evans, Giulietta Masina, Charles Boyer, Yul Brynner, Donald Pleasence, Danny Kaye, John Gavin, Nanette Newman, Oscar Homolka, Claude Dauphin, Richard Chamberlain, Paul Henreid, and Fernand Gravet. Cinematography by Claude Renoir and Burnett Guffey. An Ely Landau–Bryan Forbes Production; released by Warners. color (See *Deeper into Movies*.)

The Maggie, see *High and Dry*

Magic (1978)—It's intended to be a thriller, but there's little suspense and almost no fun in this account of a schizophrenic ventriloquist (Anthony Hopkins), adapted by William Goldman from his novel, and directed by Richard Attenborough. Since Hopkins has no light or happy range and doesn't show a capacity for joy, there's nothing at stake when things go wrong for him. This Welshman is bewilderingly miscast as Corky, a Borscht Belt vaudevillian; the gloomily withdrawn Hopkins has no vulgarity in his soul—

nothing that suggests any connection with the world of entertainment. The picture grinds along, as we watch most of the tiny cast being eliminated. It depends just about completely on the morbid visual effect of the devil-doll dummy. With Ann-Margret, Burgess Meredith, and Ed Lauter. A Joseph E. Levine Production, for 20th Century-Fox. color (See *When the Lights Go Down*.)

The Magic Christian (1970)—Terry Southern's satirical novel, in a sloppy British version, directed by Joseph McGrath, that never quite seems on target. There are funny moments, but they don't add up to enough. With Peter Sellers, Ringo Starr, Laurence Harvey, Spike Milligan, Raquel Welch, Leonard Frey, Christopher Lee, John Cleese, Graham Chapman, Dennis Price, Patrick Cargill, Roman Polanski, and Wilfrid Hyde-White. color

The Magic Flute *Trollflöjten* (1975)—Ingmar Bergman said that making this film "was the best time of my life: you can't imagine what it is like to have Mozart's music in the studio every day." Actually, watching the movie, one can. He has treated Mozart's peerlessly silly masterpiece with elegance and supreme affection. He emphasizes the theatricality of the piece, using space as stage space but with the camera coming in close. We get the pixilated feeling that we're near enough to touch the person who is singing; we might be dreamers sailing invisibly among the guests at a cloud-borne party. The English translation of Bergman's adaptation (he clarifies the text) has considerable grace, and the titles are unusually well placed in the frame; the story comes across even more directly than when you hear the opera sung in English. Cinematography by Sven Nykvist. In Swedish. color (See *When the Lights Go Down*.)

The Magician *Ansiktet*, which means "The Face." (1958)—This Ingmar Bergman film isn't a masterwork, or even a very good movie, but it is clearly a film made by a master. It has a fairy-tale atmosphere of expectation, like those stories that begin "We started out to see the King, and along the way we met. . . . " Then it becomes confused and argumentative. But the mysterious images of Max von Sydow as the 19th-century mesmerist, Vogler, and Ingrid Thulin as his assistant, Aman (Vogler's wife, Manda, in male disguise), carry so much latent charge of meaning that they dominate the loosely thrown-together material. Bergman labels the film a comedy, though audiences may not agree. It's a metaphysical gothic tale, with some low-comedy scenes and some grisly jokes involving an eyeball and a hand. The theme—magic versus rationalism or, if one prefers, faith versus scepticism, or art versus science, or illusion versus reality—is treated too theatrically to sustain such heavy-breathing dialogue as "I always longed for a knife to cut away my tongue and my sex—to cut away all impurities." There are times when one would be happy to hand Bergman that knife. He uses a 19th-century setting for the clichés of the 20th-century—the man of science (Gunnar Björnstrand as Vergérus, the physician) is cold and sadistic, etc. Those who worry about the supposed division between emotion and intellect never leave one in doubt about which side they're on. With Bibi Andersson as Sara, Erland Josephson as Egerman, Gertrude Fridh as Mrs. Egerman, Naima Wifstrand as Vogler's sorceress grandmother, Bengt Ekerot as the actor Spegel, and Åke Fridell as Tubal. Photographed by Gunnar Fischer. In Swedish. b & w

The Magnet (1950)—A likable, quirky English joke at the expense of grown-ups for their tendency to oversentimentalize children, with a stuffy young psychoanalyst as one of the butts. Directed by Charles Frend, from an original script by T. E. B. Clarke. With Stephen Murray, Kay Walsh, William (later James) Fox, and Thora Hird. b & w

The Magnificent Ambersons (1942)—Orson Welles' second film has greater depth than *Citizen Kane*, though it doesn't have the driving force that might have held it together. Working from the Booth Tarkington novel, Welles achieved some great sequences of family life—intense, harrowing squabbles. Tim Holt plays the arrogant mother-fixated son who falls from the American aristocracy to the working class; Dolores Costello, the fragile blond beauty of the silent era, is his soft, yielding mother; and as the nervous, bitter hysterical-spinster aunt, Agnes Moorehead is uncannily powerful, in a hyper-realistic way. (It's a classic performance.) With the amazing old Richard Bennett as the family patriarch, Joseph Cotten, Anne Baxter, and Ray Collins. The film wasn't completed in the form that Welles originally intended, and there are pictorial effects that seem scaled for a much fuller work, but even in this truncated form it's amazing and memorable. Cinematography by Stanley Cortez; editing by Robert Wise. R K O. b & w

Magnificent Obsession (1935)—This first version of the inspirational Lloyd C. Douglas novel—starring Irene Dunne as the virtuous widow and Robert Taylor as the drunk driver who was responsible for her husband's death—should certainly have been the last, but the woebegone trickeries of the material made the movie a four-handkerchief hit, and damned if Ross Hunter didn't produce another version in 1954 (with Jane Wyman and Rock Hudson), and the slop made money all over again. Irene Dunne spends a lot of time in the hospital and is at her most infuriatingly gallant and womanly; Sara Haden and Theodore Von Eltz don't help much. Directed by

John M. Stahl, not known for his sense of humor, though Charles Butterworth manages a funny scene or two. Universal. b & w

The Magnificent Seven (1954), see *The Seven Samurai*

The Magnificent Seven (1960)—The first of several Westerns based on Kurosawa's *The Seven Samurai*, and fairly rousing for about two thirds of the way. The setting is now Mexico. John Sturges directed a good cast: Yul Brynner in the lead, with Steve McQueen, James Coburn, Horst Buchholz, Charles Bronson, Eli Wallach, Robert Vaughn, and Vladimir Sokoloff. Ragged when it tries for philosophical importance, but it's fun to see so many stars at an early stage in their careers. You can certainly tell why they became stars. Written by William Roberts; music by Elmer Bernstein. United Artists. color

Magnum Force (1973)—The bloody, brutal sequel to *Dirty Harry*. This time, Clint Eastwood doesn't speak for vigilante justice, and he slaughters those who do. But he's the same emotionless hero, who lives and kills as affectlessly as a psychopathic personality. The setting is San Francisco, but, as in the spaghetti Westerns, Eastwood's gun power makes him the hero of a totally nihilistic dream world. Ted Post's direction is mediocre; the script by John Milius and Michael Cimino is cheaply effective. The villains this time are a Nazi-style elite cadre of clean-cut, dedicated cops (with a prim Führer—Hal Holbrook) who have taken the law into their own hands and are assassinating the labor racketeers, the drug dealers, and the gangsters. The movie is full of what in a moral landscape would be sickening scenes of death—for example, a huge metal girder smashes right into a man's face. Here, the audience is meant not to empathize but to say "Wow!" The ugliest scene: a black pimp's murder of a black whore, which is staged for a turn-on erotic effect. With Felton Perry, Mitchell Ryan, Adele Yoshioka, and, as the young neo-Nazis, David Soul, Tim Matheson, Robert Urich, and Kip Niven. Warners. color (See *Reeling*.)

The Magus (1968)—Probably the only movie in which one will ever see a copy of Empson's *The Seven Types of Ambiguity*. That's a few too many types for this elaborate, trashy literary conceit, which should be eerie fun but isn't. It's certainly deluxe, though, with Michael Caine, Anthony Quinn, Anna Karina, and Candice Bergen all being enigmatic on Majorca. Guy Green directed; John Fowles adapted his own novel. 20th Century-Fox. color

Mahanagar *The Big City* (1963)—The city is Calcutta, and Satyajit Ray's heroine, a young married woman, takes a job in order to supplement her husband's income (which must support them, their child, his teen-age sister, and his parents). The movie deals with the wife's discovery of life outside the home, and her changed relations with each member of the family. Madhabi Mukherjee is lovely as the gentle but strong wife, and there are telling portraits of her cruddy, hustling boss, and of an Anglo-Indian girl (Vicky Redwood) who is the victim of his discrimination. The film does what it sets out to do, and it's perceptive and revealing; it stays with one. Yet it is very quiet and rather thin; it lacks the depths and richness and creative imagery of the best of Satyajit Ray. In Bengali and English. b & w

Mahogany (1975)—Diana Ross is a garish, garbled black version of outmoded white kitsch. As a secretary from the South Side of Chicago, who becomes the first black model to crack the color bar and goes on to be a whirling international celebrity as well as a terrific haute-couture designer, and then gives it all up to help her black lover (Billy Dee Williams) fight to improve conditions at home, she has an overachiever debauch. The decadent whites who paw her or bitch at her include Tony Perkins, Nina Foch, Marisa Mell, and Jean-Pierre Aumont. Berry Gordy directed this setback to Ross's talent; he seems to have worked from a do-it-yourself kit. With Beah Richards. The script by John Byrum is based on a story by Toni Amber. A Motown Production; released by Paramount. color (See *When the Lights Go Down*.)

Maid of Salem (1937)—Accusations of witchcraft in an only so-so, sometimes pompous picture directed by Frank Lloyd for Paramount. Claudette Colbert is alluring in the prim garb of a Puritan maid, with a severe frill at her neck and a wicked bonnet that dooms her to Bonita Granville's accusation, but Colbert's performance suggests that she would rather have been in another period, in a different picture. Something similar could be said of Fred MacMurray's performance as her suitor, but then it could really be said of almost any of his performances. (He rarely seemed to fit in right.) Edward Ellis makes a strong appearance, and the black actress Madame Sul-Te-Wan has a fascinating episode. b & w

Maidstone (1971)—As a movie director, Norman Mailer didn't have much to retrogress from, but he managed. To the degree that there is any hero involved in this sad enterprise, it is Rip Torn, who, perceiving that there was no movie unless *something* happened, attacked the star (and director) with a small hammer. color

Les Mains sales, see *Dirty Hands*

The Major and the Minor (1942)—Determinedly sassy wartime comedy, in which

Ginger Rogers, as a New York career girl down on her luck, without enough money to return home to Iowa, dresses up as a twelve-year-old and buys a half-fare railroad ticket. On the train, she meets Ray Milland, an Army major stationed at a military school for boys, and he is bewildered by his attraction to the overgrown tyke. The Major's fiancée (Rita Johnson) becomes suspicious, so the heroine is forced to keep up her charade, even while fending off lecherous youngsters at the school. The farce situations are pushed too broadly, and have a sanctimonious patriotic veneer, but this first American film directed by Billy Wilder was a box-office hit. With Robert Benchley, Frankie Thomas, Diana Lynn as the kid who sees through the heroine's masquerade, and Lela Rogers, Ginger's mother, who plays her mother. The script, by Charles Brackett and Wilder, seems to have been concocted after the title, but it's actually derived from disparate sources—the play *Connie Goes Home* by E. C. Carpenter and the story "Sunny Goes Home" by Fannie Kilbourne. Paramount. (Remade in 1955 as *You're Never Too Young*, with Dean Martin and Jerry Lewis.) b & w

Major Barbara (1941)—Terrible, but bearable; there's a fascination to its clunkiness. Shaw had allowed *Pygmalion* to be cut and adapted for the screen, and it was a great success, but he got stubborn on this one and hung on to his dialogue; Gabriel Pascal, who had produced *Pygmalion*, had also been spoiled by its success and decided to direct this time. Their failings were compounded: the actors posture and talk, and the movie goes on and on until whatever it's meant to be about no longer seems to matter. It's too cheerful to be really boring, however. The cast includes Rex Harrison (in a role based on Gilbert Murray), Wendy Hiller, Robert Morley, Sybil Thorndike, Robert Newton, Emlyn Williams, Deborah Kerr, and Stanley

Holloway. William Walton did the score, Cecil Beaton the costumes. b & w

The Makioka Sisters *Sasame Yuki* (1983)— This Kon Ichikawa film has a triumphant simplicity about it. You don't just watch the film—you coast on its rhythms and glide past the precipitous spots. Ichikawa celebrates the delicate beauty of the four Makioka sisters— the four heiresses of an aristocratic Osaka family, who move as if always conscious that they must be visual poetry—and at the same time he makes you feel that there's something amusingly perverse in their poise and their politesse. Set in 1938, the film is based on Junichiro Tanizaki's novel, orginally titled *A Light Snowfall,* and it's like a succession of evanescent revelations; the images are stylized and formal, yet the quick cutting melts them away. The venerable Ichikawa is doing what so many younger directors have claimed to be doing: he's making visual music. And he's doing it without turning the actors into zombies, and without losing his sense of how corruption and beauty and humor are all rolled up together. The themes are worked out in shades of pearl and ivory for the interiors and bursts of color outside— cherry and maple and red-veined burgundy. With Sayuri Yoshinaga as Yukiko, who keeps saying no to her suitors, Keiko Kishi as Tsuruko, the oldest, Yoshiko Sakuma as Sachiko, the next oldest, and Yuko Kotegawa as Taeko, the youngest. Also with Juzo Itami. Cinematography by Kiyoshi Hasegawa; screenplay by Shinya Hidaka and Ichikawa. The musical theme is from Handel. (Two earlier versions were filmed under the title *A Light Snowfall*—in 1950, by Yutaka Abe, and in 1959, by Koji Shima.) In Japanese. (140 minutes.) (See *State of the Art.*)

Mala Noche *Bad Night* (1986)—This first feature made in Portland, Oregon, by Gus Van Sant (his second was the 1989 *Drugstore Cowboy*) is a story of romantic obsession, shot in 16 mm, mostly in black and white, and completed for $25,000. It's the story of Walt (Tim Streeter), a young clerk in a skid-row convenience store, who falls hopelessly in love with a Mexican boy, a tease who accepts handouts from him but derides him as a "stupid faggot." Based on a short novel by the Oregon poet Walt Curtis, the movie has a wonderful fluid, grainy look—expressionist yet with an improvised feel. It has an authentic grungy beauty; at moments, it's reminiscent of Jean Genet's short film masterpiece *Un Chant d'amour.* The tease, Johnny, is played by Doug Cooeyate, an American Indian who doesn't speak Spanish. (His lines were dubbed.) The screenplay is by Van Sant; the (often hand-held) cinematography is by John Campbell.

The Maltese Falcon (1941)—Humphrey Bogart's most exciting role was Sam Spade, that ambiguous mixture of avarice and honor, sexuality and fear, who gave new dimension to the detective genre. This film, the first directed by John Huston, is an almost perfect visual equivalent of the Dashiell Hammett thriller. Huston used Hammett's plot design and economic dialogue in a hard, precise directorial style that brings out the full viciousness of characters so ruthless and greedy that they become comic. It is (and this is rare in American films) a work of entertainment that is yet so skillfully constructed that after many years and many viewings it has the same brittle explosiveness—and even some of the same surprise—that it had in its first run. Bogart is backed by an impeccably "right" cast: Mary Astor as Brigid O'Shaughnessy, Sydney Greenstreet as Casper Gutman, Peter Lorre as Joel Cairo, Gladys George as Iva, Elisha Cook, Jr., as Wilmer the gunsel, Jerome Cowan as Miles Archer, Lee Patrick as

Effie, Ward Bond and Barton MacLane as the cops, and the director's father, Walter Huston (uncredited), as Captain Jacoby. The young Huston was a good enough screenwriter to see that Hammett had already written the scenario, and he didn't soften Sam Spade's character. Bogart played him as written by Hammett, and Hammett was not sentimental about detectives: they were cops who were going it alone, i.e., who had smartened up and become more openly mercenary and crooked. Bogart's Spade is a loner who uses nice, simple people. He's a man who's constantly testing himself, who doesn't want to be touched, who's obsessively anti-homosexual—he enjoys hitting Joel Cairo and humiliating Wilmer. A flaw: the appalling Warners music (by Adolph Deutsch), rising and swelling to call our attention to the big "I won't because all of me wants to" speech at the end, almost kills the scene. And a regret: that Huston didn't (or couldn't) retain Hammett's final twist—Effie's realization of what a bastard Spade is. But perhaps its absence is part of what made the movie a hit: Huston, by shooting the material from Spade's point of view, makes it possible for the audience to enjoy Spade's petty, sadistic victories and his sense of triumph as he proves he's tougher than anybody. Spade was left a romantic figure, though he's only a few steps away from the psychopathic "Nobody ever put anything over on Fred C. Dobbs" of *The Treasure of the Sierra Madre* (1948), which was a box-office failure—perhaps because the audience was forced to see what was inside the hero. Warners had already got its money's worth out of *The Maltese Falcon*—in 1931, with Ricardo Cortez and Bebe Daniels, and again in 1936, as *Satan Met a Lady*, with Warren William and Bette Davis. b & w

La Maman et la putain, see *The Mother and the Whore*

Mame (1974)—Too terrible to be boring; you can get fixated staring at it and wondering what exactly Lucille Ball thinks she's doing. When that sound comes out—it's somewhere between a bark, a croak, and a quaver—does she think she's singing? When she throws up her arms, in their red giant-batwing sleeves, and cries out "Listen, everybody!" does she really think she's a fun person? Onna White choreographs like mad, with bodies hurtling over and around the near-stationary star (Lucille Ball was well into her 60s at the time), and the director, Gene Saks, tries to wring a little humor out of the frayed old skits that serve as the story line. The material, which is about how the sophisticated, generous-hearted Mame raises her nephew, and shows him (and everyone else) a good time, originated in the Patrick Dennis book, *Auntie Mame,* and persisted on stage and screen. Mame is a camp heroine—a female impersonator's dream woman: constantly changing her wigs and her gowns and her decor, basking in jewels and bitchy repartee. The 1958 film version, *Auntie Mame,* which starred Rosalind Russell, was stale and squawking; subsequently the material was turned into the Broadway musical *Mame* and then into this hippopotamic slapstick musical. About 10 minutes of this film, featuring Beatrice Arthur as Mame's bosom buddy, Vera Charles—she's like a coquettish tank—are genuinely satirical, and Jane Connell as a sweetly wan Agnes Gooch and Robert Preston as Mame's sturdy, relaxed suitor, Beauregard, are in there working and doing better than might be expected. Screenplay by Paul Zindel; music and lyrics by Jerry Herman. With Bruce Davison, Joyce Van Patten, Don Porter, John McGiver, Audrey Christie, and a little boy named Kirby Furlong who twinkles and delivers lines such as "Would you take a kiss on account?" Warners. color (See *Reeling.*)

A Man and A Woman *Un Homme et une femme* (1966)— Probably the most efficacious make-out movie of the swinging 60s. The young cinematographer-director Claude Lelouch conveys tender love by cutting to gamboling lovers among gamboling horses and then lambs and then dogs. The characters have exciting, photogenic occupations: stunt man, script girl, racing-car driver. They take their kids on photogenic boats or for walks on wintry beaches. The actors don't have to do anything because the camera—shooting through rain and snow and ice and into sunsets—supplies the moods for them. Anouk Aimée is blankly mysterious and glamorous; Jean-Louis Trintignant and Pierre Barouh are like a teen-age girl's dream boyfriends— daredevils to the world but gentle and sweet with her. Lelouch blurs for romantic softness and he tints for mood and variety; he throws a nimbus of mist around everything. The score is by Francis Lai; the script is by Lelouch and Pierre Uytterhoeven. In French. color

The Man Between (1953)—The title of this English thriller, directed by Carol Reed, refers to James Mason as a man caught between the East and West in postwar Berlin, but he really seems to be halfway between the character he played in Reed's *Odd Man Out* and the character Orson Welles played in Reed's *The Third Man.* Mason is cast as a disenchanted, opportunistic victim of the war who is engaged in some fancy double-dealing, Claire Bloom is an English girl who innocently gets involved with Mason; the most exciting person in the film, however, is Hildegarde Neff (later Knef), in a world-weary, war-ravaged, Garboesque performance that is much too brief. Reed's love of photogenic corruption, his technical finesse, and his feeling for atmospheric intrigue almost make something really good out of Harry Kurnitz' synthetic script. The sogginess overpowers him, though. b & w

A Man Escaped *Un Condamné à mort s'est échappé* (1956)—In this country, escape is a theme for action movies, but the French director Robert Bresson is famous for his uncompromising methods, and having been a prisoner of the Nazis himself, he is not disposed to treat his material—André Devigny's account of his escape from the Montluc fortress prison—lightly. Bresson's hero's ascetic, single-minded dedication to escape is almost mystic, and the fortress constitutes a world as impersonal and as isolated as Kafka's. The movie was shot at Montluc with fanatic authenticity; the photography, by Léonce-Henry Burel, is austerely beautiful. François Leterrier, a Sorbonne philosophy student, is the lead. The music is Mozart's Mass in C Minor. All this makes it sound terribly pretentious, yet sometimes even the worst ideas can be made to work. It's a marvellous movie. In French. b & w

A Man for All Seasons (1966)—The director, Fred Zinnemann, places himself at the service of Robert Bolt's play about the moral tug of war between Sir Thomas More (Paul Scofield) and Henry VIII (Robert Shaw), and the results are tasteful and moderately enjoyable. The weakness is that though Bolt's dialogue is crisp, lucid, and well-spoken, his presentation of More's martyrdom is so one-sided we don't even get to understand *that* side. More is the only man of honor in the movie, and he's got all the good lines; he's the kind of hero we used to read about in biographies of great men written for 12-year-olds, and Scofield is so refined, so controlled, so dignified, so obviously "subtle" he's like a man of conscience in a school play. With Orson Welles as Wolsey, Leo McKern as Cromwell, and Susannah York, Wendy Hiller, Nigel

Davenport, John Hurt, and Corin Redgrave. Columbia. color (See *Kiss Kiss Bang Bang*.)

Man Hunt (1941)—Fritz Lang directed the Dudley Nichols adaptation of Geoffrey Household's *Rogue Male*—an anti-Nazi thriller about a broad-shouldered British big-game hunter (Walter Pidgeon) stalking Hitler at Berchtesgaden. It's ingenious, all right, but the direction is too insistent and the plot too tangled for a first-rate entertainment. Joan Bennett plays the streetwalker heroine, whom the studio turned into a "seamstress" to get past the Hays office. With George Sanders, John Carradine, Roddy McDowall, and Ludwig Stossel. Produced by Kenneth MacGowan, for 20th Century-Fox. b & w

The Man I Killed, see *Broken Lullaby*

The Man I Love (1947)—Of its kind, not bad at all. Warner Brothers, combining two genres in the hope of snaring a double audience, put together several of these musical melodramas, and this one, directed by Raoul Walsh, is one of the smoothest. Ida Lupino starred, as a singer, with Bruce Bennett as a jazz musician (one of his few good roles), Robert Alda, Andrea King, Martha Vickers, Alan Hale, Dolores Moran, and some talented dubbers. The score includes a whole raft of classics—"The Man I Love," of course, and "Body and Soul," "Bill," "Liza," "Why Was I Born?," "If I Could Be With You One Hour Tonight." b & w

The Man in the White Suit (1951)—Alec Guinness has often been at his comic best in the role of an ordinary man with an obsession, and who can be as ordinary and obsessed as an inventor? In this film, he plays a quirky, idealistic scientist who lives in the modern economy of quick obsolescence yet is fixated on the long-range benefits to hu-

manity of a cloth that will stay clean and last forever. Guinness's bland monomaniacal scientist is beautifully matched by Joan Greenwood, who is all guile and scorn and perversity, without any real aim or purpose. Alexander Mackendrick directed this deft capital-science-labor comedy. With Cecil Parker, and Ernest Thesiger as a half-dead industrialist. Screenplay by Roger MacDougall, John Dighton, and Mackendrick. (Item for collectors of movie memorabilia: the gurgling, bubbling squirts and drips of the hero's experimental apparatus were joined to a rhythm and issued by Coral Records as "The White Suit Samba.") b & w

Man in the Wilderness (1971)—Richard Harris is mauled by a grizzly bear at the gory beginning and spends the rest of the movie dragging himself across iridescent landscapes while flashbacks reveal his past life. He gives a cheerlessly powerful performance in this mystical, superstition-laden survival fantasy set in the early 19th century. Directed by Richard C. Sarafian; the dazzling cinematography is by Gerry Fisher. With John Huston, Prunella Ransome, Ben Carruthers, and Henry Wilcoxon. The self-conscious script is by Jack DeWitt. Warners. color (See *Deeper into Movies*.)

A Man Is Ten Feet Tall, see *Edge of the City*

Man of a Thousand Faces (1957)—Unappetizing bio of the turmoiled, forbidding Lon Chaney, with James Cagney giving the role more conviction than the viewer really wants; the script and conception are so maudlin and degrading that Cagney's high dedication becomes somewhat oppressive. He discards his mannerisms and his usual bravado, and acts out the Chaney characters—the hunchback of Notre Dame, the mad organist of the Paris Opéra, the cripple of *The Miracle Man*, etc., giving them a gruesome tenderness that is almost as upsetting as Chaney's own brand of compassion. With Dorothy Malone as Chaney's lackadaisical first wife, and Jane Greer, cast wildly against type, as the fine, upstanding chorus girl who becomes his perfect second wife. Joseph Pevney's direction is at its worst with these two; he's a little more comfortable with Celia Lovsky as Chaney's deaf-mute mother. The cast includes Marjorie Rambeau, Jim Backus, Jack Albertson, Jeanne Cagney, Hank Mann, Snub Pollard, and Robert Evans as Irving Thalberg. Written by R. Wright Campbell, Ivan Goff, and Ben Roberts. Universal. CinemaScope, b & w

Man of Aran (1934)—Robert Flaherty gave two years of his life to making this film and left the Aran Islands with a truly exalted work—the greatest film tribute to man's struggle against hostile nature. The Atlantic, which sweeps in all the way from America, lashes the cliffs of Aran with an almost malignant ferocity; it is considered the most horrible sea in the world. Only 30 miles from Galway, civilized people live on islands of rock so bare that they must gather seaweed to plant their potatoes in. Perhaps because of the mixture of extreme courage and extreme simplicity in the lives of these people, who act out incidents based on past occurrences, the film achieves a true epic quality—a celebration of heroic traditions. b & w

Man of La Mancha (1972)—The lyrics still sound as if they had been translated from Esperanto, and it's a slow haul to a sentimental haven, but toward the middle, Peter O'Toole, looking like an elongated Alec Guinness, is so wafer-thin and stylized, and his woefulness is so deeply silly, that the contrast between his Don Quixote and the full-bodied, realistic Aldonza of Sophia Loren becomes affecting. Loren, with her great, sorrowing green-brown eyes, is magnificently sensual and spiritual; she brings the soul of Italian opera to this Broadway bastardization, which combines Cervantes' life with his novel. With James Coco, Harry Andrews, and Brian Blessed. Directed by Arthur Hiller; the script by Dale Wasserman is based on his bewilderingly successful play (the movie, however, was a box-office failure). The cinematography is by Giuseppe Rotunno. Released by United Artists. color (See *Reeling*.)

Man on a Swing (1974)—Irritatingly pointless. Frank Perry's pseudo-documentary murder mystery is based on the unsolved crime that an Ohio reporter, William A. Clark, wrote about in *The Girl on the Volkswagen Floor*—a crime that became complicated when a man who claimed to be clairvoyant got involved in trying to solve it. If the movie had stuck to the facts, it might have been effective; if the scriptwriter, David Zelag Goodman, had fictionalized the case and given it a solution, that might also have been effective. But the movie is a murky jumble of both (with echoes of *Laura* besides), and in changing the central character, the reporter, to a chief of police (Cliff Robertson), Goodman failed to restructure the reporter's activities. So one keeps wondering who's running the police department while Robertson wanders off investigating parapsychology. Robertson's acting is far from inspired; his eyes are so bright and alert that he's staring even when he isn't, and his mouth is fixed in a semi-sneer. The picture's only interest is a creepy, volatile performance by Joel Grey, as the man who says he's clairvoyant; Grey is so intense you can't take your eyes off him, and you don't want to. With Dorothy Tristan, Peter Masterson, Dianne Hull, George Voskovec, Elizabeth Wilson, and Christopher Allport. Paramount. color

The Man on the Eiffel Tower (1948)—A nasty thriller with some fancy degenerate aspects, and some imaginative photography and trial and error work with color that put it in a special class—it might even be called an experimental thriller. Burgess Meredith directed this peculiar (and not particularly enjoyable) manhunt, with himself as one of the hunted. Franchot Tone makes a cunning psychopathic killer—the really horrid kind that tries to put the noose on an innocent neck—and Charles Laughton is Inspector Maigret. The Simenon novel *A Battle of Nerves* was adapted by Harry Brown. With Robert Hutton, Belita, Patricia Roc, Jean Wallace, and Wilfrid Hyde-White. Shot in Paris; Stanley Cortez was the cinematographer.

Man on the Flying Trapeze (1935)—From their titles, it's hard to tell the W. C. Fields movies apart; as John Mosher observed, "Fields is Fields, a rose is a rose." For the record, in this one Fields is Ambrose Wolfinger, and he and his daughter (Mary Brian) are the defenseless victims of his new wife (Kathleen Howard) and her sponging relatives (the worst is Grady Sutton). Directed by Clyde Bruckman. Paramount. b & w

The Man Who Came to Dinner (1942)—In the 30s, the unctuous, sentimental Alexander Woollcott was loved by millions of radio listeners; Woollcott the outrageous master of euphonious insults was loved and hated by a small circle. Two members of this circle, George S. Kaufman and Moss Hart, made him the hero and the target of their 1939 Broadway hit—a cheerful spoof on celebrity in that period. In this film version, the devastatingly adroit Monty Woolley (a former professor of drama at Yale) plays the arrogant, infantile Sheridan Whiteside, who goes on a lecture tour and breaks his hip while attending a dinner in his honor at the home of boring, worshipful fans. Stuck in that

home until his hip mends, he takes it over and orders the residents around. Woolley has a wonderful way of looking at these hick fans with compassionate contempt—he feels sorry for them because they're too obtuse to appreciate how brilliant he is. The play, however, was built on topical jokes and a series of vaudeville turns, and in this version the jokes are flat and the turns seemed forced and not very funny. With Bette Davis as Whiteside's secretary, Reginald Gardiner impersonating Noël Coward, Jimmy Durante in the role based on Harpo Marx, Ann Sheridan as the sexpot actress, and Billie Burke, Richard Travis, George Barbier, and Grant Mitchell. Directed by William Keighley; the script, by the Epstein brothers, changed only a few lines. Warners. b & w

The Man Who Could Work Miracles (1937)—This version of H. G. Wells' comic fantasy is one of the most touching and good-natured of all the films that employ "supernatural" tricks and illusions. It's also one of the few with any real point. With Roland Young, as the mild, bewildered miracle-maker, Ralph Richardson as the militarist whose swords are turned into plowshares, Ernest Thesiger (who never disappoints), Joan Gardner, George Zucco, Torin Thatcher, and, in a tiny part as a god, young George Sanders. Alexander Korda produced; Wells did the script, with Lajos Biro; Lothar Mendes directed, with Vincent Korda designing the production. b & w

The Man Who Fell to Earth (1976)—Nicolas Roeg has a talent for eerily soft, ambiguous sex—for the sexiness of passivity. In this movie, the forlorn, limp hero—David Bowie—a stranger on earth, doesn't have a human sex drive. He isn't even equipped for it: naked, he's as devoid of sex differentiation as a child in sleepers. When he splashes down in a lake in the Southwest and drinks water like a vampire gulping down his life-blood, one is drawn in, fascinated by the obliqueness and by the promise of an erotic sci-fi story. It is and it isn't. The stranger has come to earth to obtain the water that will save his people, who are dying from drought, but he is corrupted, and then is so damaged that he can't return. Although Roeg and his screenwriter, Paul Mayersberg, pack in layers of tragic political allegory, none of the layers is very strong, or even very clear. The plot, about big-business machinations, is so un-involving that one watches Bowie traipsing around—looking like Katharine Hepburn in her transvestite role in *Sylvia Scarlett*—and either tunes out or allows the film, with its perverse pathos, to become a sci-fi frame-work for a sex-role-confusion fantasy. The wilted stranger can be said to represent everyone who feels misunderstood, every-one who feels sexually immature or "differ-ent," everyone who has lost his way, and so the film is a gigantic launching pad for any-thing that viewers want to drift to. Roeg can charge a desolate landscape so that it seems ominously alive and he photographs sky-scrapers with such lyric glitter that the U.S. (where the movie was shot) seems to be showing off for him. And his cutting can cre-ate a magical feeling of waste and evil. But the unease and the sense of disconnectedness between characters also disconnect *us*. Roeg's effects become off-puttingly abstract, and his lyricism goes sentimental—as most other Christ movies do. With Buck Henry, Candy Clark, Bernie Casey, and Rip Torn as a sci-entist—perhaps his least convincing role. Based on the novel by Walter Tevis. Pro-duced by Michael Deeley and Barry Spikings. color (See *When the Lights Go Down.*)

The Man Who Knew Too Much (1934)— This Hitchcock thriller about a kidnapping and an attempted political assassination fea-tures Leslie Banks, Edna Best, Pierre Fresnay, Nova Pilbeam as the kidnapped child, and Peter Lorre (it was Lorre's début in English-language films), and it has the director's in-genuity and flair and sneaky wit. The best scenes—especially an assassination attempt at Royal Albert Hall—are stunning, but Hitchcock seems sloppily unconcerned about the unconvincing material in between the tricks and jokes (a fault that persisted in the later, stodgier version, which he made in 1955, in color with James Stewart and Doris Day). b & w

The Man Who Laughs (1928)—No one who saw this silent movie as a child is likely to have forgotten it. The Victor Hugo story is about fairly conventional 17th-century En-glish court intrigues, except for one detail about the hero, Gwynplaine (Conrad Veidt). The heir to an earldom, he was kidnapped as a child and, at the orders of the king, a political enemy of his father, he was muti-lated—his face carved into a perpetual grin. He had no choice but to become a clown. Produced by Universal on a lavish scale, the film is by no means a cheap horror story. The German-born director Paul Leni had a true gift for macabre decor, and the film's ambi-tious mixture of morbidity and historical melodrama is very effective, even with its heavy sentimentality. With the physically el-egant Veidt as the hero, the picture has a romantic center that it would not have had with Lon Chaney. (John Barrymore played Gwynplaine on the stage.) Mary Philbin is beautiful, though sticky, as a blind girl who loves the clown; Olga Baclanova is a rowdy, loose duchess who is drawn to him. b & w

The Man Who Loved Women *L'Homme qui aimait les femmes* (1977)—The dedicated skirt-chaser of François Truffaut's film is meant to be irresistibly charming, but his compulsion looks to be about as exciting as building a two-foot replica of the Pentagon with toothpicks. In its gross flippancy, this film resembles Truffaut's *Such a Gorgeous Kid Like Me*—it may be even worse, because of the mixture of evasiveness and obviousness. With Charles Denner, Nelly Borgeaud, Brigitte Fossey, and Leslie Caron. Cinematography by Nestor Almendros; music by Maurice Jaubert. In French. (Remade in 1983 by Blake Edwards.) color (See *When the Lights Go Down*.)

The Man Who Shot Liberty Valance (1962)— The reputation of this John Ford Western is undeservedly high: it's a heavy-spirited piece of nostalgia. John Wayne is in his flamboyant element, but James Stewart is too old for the role of an idealistic young Eastern lawyer who is robbed on the way West, goes to work in the town of Shinbone as a dishwasher, and learns about Western life. Opposite him, Vera Miles is as proficient and colorless as ever. There's not much of the outdoors; the action takes place mainly in Shinbone, and even a stagecoach robbery was filmed on a sound stage. With Lee Marvin as the villainous Liberty Valance, Edmond O'Brien as the newspaper editor, and Andy Devine, John Carradine, Woody Strode, and Strother Martin. Paramount. b & w

The Man Who Would Be King (1975)—John Huston's exhilarating farfetched adventure fantasy, based on the Rudyard Kipling short story, is about two roughneck con men, Danny and Peachy (Sean Connery and Michael Caine), in Victoria's England, who decide to conquer a barbarous land for themselves, and set out for Kafiristan, a region which was once ruled by Alexander the Great. This ironic fable about imperialism has some of the pleasures of *Gunga Din*; it's a wonderfully full and satisfying movie, with superb performances by Connery and Caine and also by Saeed Jaffrey, who plays Billy

Fish. The role of Kipling is played by Christopher Plummer, and Roxanne is played by Shakira Caine. The script is by Huston and Gladys Hill; the cinematographer was Oswald Morris; the music is by Maurice Jarre; the production design is by Alexander Trauner. Allied Artists. color (See *When the Lights Go Down*.)

Man with a Million The English title, *The Million Pound Note*, is the title of the Mark Twain story on which the movie is based. (1954)—There is something wonderfully satisfying about watching a shabby young man dine in a restaurant and then casually hand over a million pound banknote, while murmuring, "I'm awfully sorry, but I don't have anything smaller." Mark Twain's little satire on attitudes toward money and on English mores posits a perfect practical joke: a young American (Gregory Peck), stranded in London, is given an authentic million pound note; but he cannot cash it, he can only flash it. The question is, Can a penniless man live for a month by this display? This ingratiating English comedy failed completely in this country; Americans may have assumed from the author's name that the film (which is set in Twain's period) was a dull classic. The cast includes Jane Griffith, such distinguished old charmers as Ronald Squire and A. E. Matthews, and also Bryan Forbes, Joyce Grenfell, Hartley Power, and Wilfrid Hyde-White. Directed by Ronald Neame, from Jill Craigie's screenplay; cinematography by Geoffrey Unsworth. color

The Man with the Golden Arm (1955)— Frank Sinatra's performance is pure gold, but the director, Otto Preminger, goes for sensationalism; the film is effective, but in a garish, hyperbolic, and dated way. It's a lot more entertaining than the other pictures about dope addiction in that period, though. The others tended to treat it very gingerly, with edifying explanations of childhood traumata, or a slice-of-life view of the addict's environment. (In the 1957 *A Hatful of Rain* the real problem seemed to be the drab low-cost housing.) Here, the emphasis is on excitement. The film is based on Nelson Algren's Chicago-set novel about the hot poker dealer and addict Frankie. Sinatra's performance is rhythmic, tense, and instinctive, yet beautifully controlled, and of course, he has a performer's presence. Eleanor Parker's Zosh is somehow out of context, but in its own terms it has some appeal. The young Kim Novak's Molly has a dumb, suffering beauty that's very touching. With Arnold Stang as Sparrow, Darren McGavin as Louie, Robert Strauss as Schwiefka, Doro Merande, Leonid Kinskey, Emile Meyer, and George E. Stone. Adapted by Walter Newman and Lewis Meltzer; cinematography by Sam Leavitt; titles by Saul Bass; music by Elmer Bernstein, with jazz sequences in which Shorty Rogers and Shelly Manne appear, along with Bud Shank, Ralph Pena, and others. (Shelly Manne also served as "tutor" for Sinatra.) United Artists. b & w

The Man with the Golden Gun (1974)—Set in the Orient, this is the ninth—and one of the more dispirited—of the James Bond series. The production is a little snappier than in the preceding voodoo one (*Live and Let Die*), and this time Guy Hamilton's direction isn't quite as crude, but the script lacks satiric insolence, and the picture grinds on humorlessly. The villain Christopher Lee's fanged smile is the only attraction. With that iceberg Roger Moore as Bond, Britt Ekland, Maud Adams, Hervé Villechaize, Clifton James, Bernard Lee, Lois Maxwell, Desmond Llewelyn, Marne Maitland, Richard Loo, and Marc Lawrence. Written by Richard Maibaum and Tom Mankiewicz. color.

The Man with Two Brains (1983)—As the world's greatest brain surgeon, Steve Martin is an exuberantly dirty-minded kid; sunny, grinning, lewd, Martin is wired up for the whole movie—a slapstick burlesque that moves along enjoyably. The surgeon perceives himself as a man of the world, but he's a guileless innocent compared with the flirty, dimply sadist (Kathleen Turner) who marries him for her convenience and coos with pleasure as she frustrates him. With David Warner as a soft-spoken mad doctor who keeps live human brains in candy jars before putting them into gorillas, Paul Benedict as his butler, and George Furth. There's at least one inspired love scene (between Martin and a brain, in a rowboat). This movie has the kind of maniacal situations that are so dumb they make you laugh, and since much of what children find hilarious has this same giddiness, they'd probably like the film a lot. But it also has the kind of raunchiness that may worry their parents (though it will probably just make the kids giggle). Directed (more gracefully than usual) by Carl Reiner; written by Reiner, Martin, and George Gipe. The cinematography, by Michael Chapman, has a graphic vitality that's unusual in a comedy. Warners. color (See *State of the Art*.)

The Manchurian Candidate (1962)—A daring, funny, and far-out thriller about political extremists. George Axelrod adapted the Richard Condon novel, and John Frankenheimer came to life as a director. This picture plays some wonderful, crazy games about the Right and the Left; although it's a thriller, it may be the most sophisticated political satire ever made in Hollywood. With Angela Lansbury, Frank Sinatra, Laurence Harvey, Janet Leigh, James Gregory, John McGiver, Henry Silva, Madame Spivy, Whit Bissell, James Edwards, Leslie Parrish, Khigh Dhiegh, and Albert Paulsen. United Artists. b & w

Manhattan Melodrama (1934)—The film made famous when Public Enemy No. 1, John Dillinger, went to see Clark Gable in it (as Blackie, a gangster who strode to the electric chair with a smile on his face) and was shot down as he emerged. It's a deluxe melodrama. Gable and William Powell play boyhood friends from the slums who grow up on what Hollywood writers used to call "opposite sides of the law." In the climax, Powell, the District Attorney, must prosecute his old friend, who gallantly dies rather than allow Powell to jeopardize his career. Despite the heavy moralizing tone, the picture holds one's interest; Powell manages to get his conflicting emotions across, and he has an unusual rapport with Myrna Loy, the woman both men love. (Powell and Loy were then teamed and made *The Thin Man* later that year.) Produced by David O. Selznick and directed by W. S. Van Dyke, it was originally released by M-G-M as one of their Cosmopolitan Productions (which meant a William Randolph Hearst production), but after the Dillinger shooting, Hearst, who was sensitive to any hint of scandal or notoriety, had the Cosmopolitan credit deleted. The cast includes Leo Carrillo, Isabel Jewell, the one-man goon squad Nat Pendleton, Leonid Kinsky playing a Trotskyite, and Mickey Rooney playing Clark Gable as a 12-year-old. The screenplay involved at least four writers (Oliver H. P. Garrett, Rowland Brown, Joseph L. Mankiewicz, Pete Smith), working from Arthur Caesar's Academy Award–winnign screen story. Cinematography by James Wong Howe; Shirley Ross appears in a set that is meant to represent the Cotton Club, singing "The Bad in Every Man"—a song by Rodgers and Hart that later got new lyrics and became "Blue Moon." b & w

The Manhattan Project (1986)—The writer-director Marshall Brickman and his co-writer, Thomas Baum, have a knack for capturing the way brainy people talk to each other, and how ridiculous and touching they can be. And the actors—John Lithgow, especially—seem overjoyed to be speaking such good satirical dialogue. Lithgow plays a beaming, self-conscious nuclear scientist, the director of a new, secret government research center in Ithaca, New York. He courts a woman (Jill Eikenberry) whose prankish 17-year-old son (Christopher Collet), a scientific wizard, is miffed—the boy swipes plutonium from the center and builds a homemade nuclear bomb to enter in the competition of high-school students at the National Science Fair in Manhattan. The title is from the Second World War Manhattan Project, where the first atom bomb was devised, by largely apolitical scientists, such as Oppenheimer, Teller, and Fermi, and the movie is about how the boy's folly forces the man to shed the illusion that he's apolitical and face up to his responsibilities. When this bland moral rectitude takes over, the film's comedy spirit withers. But there are a lot of enjoyable things: Lithgow's warming presence, and the way he has of turning his lines into boomerangs; Cynthia Nixon's cool self-possession—she plays the boy's pretty blond girl friend who helps him sneak into the center; the break-in itself, which is a series of ingenious, silent slapstick tricks; Warren Manzi as the courtly day attendant at the center; Sully Boyar's puzzled routine as the night guard—it's like a sober variation on a Barry Fitzgerald drunk routine; and the kids at the Science Fair whose projects take you back to the looniest absorbing interests you ever had. The cast includes John Mahoney as the hardheaded colonel. Bran Ferren designed the laboratory effects; the cinematography is by Billy Williams; the editing is by Nina Feinberg; the music is by Philippe Sarde. 20th Century-Fox. color (See *Hooked.*)

Mannequin (1938)—A star vehicle in which the star—Joan Crawford—is a lyric talker and so solemnly noble that you want to strangle her. Poetic flights are her specialty as she rises from Hester Street to penthouses, suffering from emotional conflicts every step of the way. Alan Curtis, a corner loafer with a mean slant to his fedora, is the bad egg whom she marries and stays loyal to, even after she meets Spencer Tracy, a self-made shipping tycoon, who has been looking all his life for her kind of nobility. As the picture drags along from one crisis to another, the self-righteousness in Crawford's voice seems to get throatier and more grating. The director, Frank Borzage, gives some care to the tenement sequences, but he's perfunctory when the locales become swanky. The unconvincing script (from a Katherine Brush story) is no more than an excuse for M-G-M gloss and glamour; a simple statement of the truth would solve the heroine's wracking problems. With Mary Philips as the heroine's nononsense friend, and Leo Gorcey, Ralph Morgan, and Elisabeth Risdon. b & w

Männer . . . , see *Men . . .*

Manpower (1941)—This is one of those roughneck melodramas about two men friends who both fall for the same woman. Marlene Dietrich comes out of prison after serving a year for theft and gets involved with Edward G. Robinson and his buddy, George Raft, who are Los Angeles light-and-power-company linemen; the hackneyed situation isn't improved by a tragic ending—Robinson attacks Raft on a high-tension tower during a storm. Dietrich has never seemed more foolishly miscast than in her bungalow apron, baking biscuits for good, honest Robinson. She's so thin she's wraithlike, and her face is a cold, bored mask; Robinson doesn't give a bad performance, but he's playing a crippled, overeager, goodhearted

fellow—the sort of virtuous character nobody wants to watch. Raoul Walsh directed; Richard Macaulay and Jerry Wald concocted the script—obviously out of such films as the 1932 *Tiger Shark* (also with Robinson) and the many versions of *They Knew What They Wanted.* With Alan Hale, Eve Arden, Ward Bond, Frank McHugh, Faye Emerson, Barton MacLane, Joyce Compton, Walter Catlett, Anthony Quinn, and Barbara Pepper. Warners. b & w

A Man's Castle (1933)—Spencer Tracy and the lovely, big-eyed Loretta Young in a Depression idyll about an independent-minded man who takes in a homeless waif and falls in love with her—one of Frank Borzage's heavily sentimental yet magically romantic movies. With Glenda Farrell, Marjorie Rambeau, Walter Connolly, Arthur Hohl, and Dickie Moore. The script is by Jo Swerling, the cinematography by Joseph August. Columbia. b & w

Marathon Man (1976)—William Goldman's book—a visceral thriller about a Nazi ring of thieves in New York—seemed a lead-pipe cinch to make audiences almost sick with excitement (the way *The French Connection* did); it's *Death Wish* with a lone Jewish student (played by Dustin Hoffman) getting his own back from the Nazis. But the director, John Schlesinger, opts for so much frazzled cross-cutting that there isn't the clarity needed for suspense. The only emotion one is likely to feel is revulsion at the brutality and general unpleasantness. With Laurence Olivier, Roy Scheider, Marthe Keller, William Devane, and Fritz Weaver; cinematography by Conrad Hall. Paramount. color (See *When the Lights Go Down.*)

Marie (1985)—Sissy Spacek stars in what is advertised as the true story of Marie Ragghianti, who, in 1976, became the first woman to head Tennessee's Board of Pardons and Paroles, and discovered that she was expected to rubber-stamp the deals of the state officials who were selling pardons. Directed by Roger Donaldson, the movie tells Marie's story clearly and briskly in political-thriller style, ending in courtroom drama after she sues the governor for firing her. Yet the picture is weightless, and the story it tells doesn't add up right. The script, by John Briley, gives us too much about Marie's early hardships, but skitters over such matters as what she thought she was getting into when she took the job. The Marie it presents is unbelievably naïve and good. And fine, magnetic actress though she is, Spacek doesn't appear to have any way of communicating experience, maturity, womanhood. (It isn't her tininess that limits her; it's the girlish, small-voiced acting style that she developed because of it.) With Jeff Daniels, who, as the governor's legal counsel and toady, suggests the scary side of Southern chivalry—he's Marie's protector, but only for as long as she does just what he tells her to; and Fred Thompson, the lawyer who represented Marie Ragghianti in court, playing himself. Also with Keith Szarabajka as Kevin, and Morgan Freeman and John Cullum. Cinematography by Chris Menges; music by Francis Lai. Based on *Marie: A True Story* by Peter Maas. A Dino De Laurentiis Production, released by M-G-M/United Artists. color (See *Hooked*.)

Marie Antoinette (1938)—A resplendent bore. M-G-M built a grand ballroom that was several feet longer than the original at Versailles, and Adrian designed 1,250 gowns, as well as costumes for two poodles. The effort to create a sympathetic interpretation of Marie that would be suitable for Norma Shearer—M-G-M's "first lady" and, as Irving Thalberg's widow, a large stockholder—resulted in a lugubriously noble central character. Since King Louis XVI (Robert Morley) wasn't much of a love interest, Shearer was given Tyrone Power (as a Swedish count) for a bit of romance; meant for leavening, this doomed affair only adds to the sodden weight. W. S. Van Dyke directed; with John Barrymore, Gladys George, Anita Louise, and Joseph Schildkraut. b & w

La Marie du port (1949)—In the 30s, that durable representative of simple, hardworking humanity, Jean Gabin, was the favorite hero of Jean Renoir (*La Bête humaine, La Grande Illusion, Les Bas-Fonds*) and Marcel Carné (*Quai des brumes, Le Jour se lève*). Here he is seen weathered and aged; the passions of his early roles have given way to worldly-wise scepticism. Directed once again by Carné, he plays a successful restaurant and theatre owner who discovers how susceptible he is to the natural wiles of an inexperienced teenage girl (Nicole Courcel). A highly civilized film, simple in theme yet meant to be subtle in the great French tradition. But the ordinariness of the characters and their emotions becomes oppressive, rather than illuminating. With Blanchette Brunoy and Julien Carette. Cinematography by Henri Alekan; music by Joseph Kosma. From the novel by Georges Simenon. In French. b & w

Marius (1931)—The first film of the celebrated Marcel Pagnol trilogy. Static and visually unimaginative (Alexander Korda directed) but famous for its dialogue and characterization, and for the rich humanity Raimu brought to the role of César, the Marseilles café owner. In the film, the life along the harbor centers on this café. The story involves César's son, Marius (the elegant Pierre Fresnay, oddly miscast), who longs to go to sea, though he loves Fanny (Orane Démazis). Produced and written by Pagnol. In French. b & w

Mark of the Vampire (1935)—This is a failed effort of Tod Browning's, though it's handsomely staged and well photographed (by James Wong Howe). The cast includes Carol Borland as an amusing female vampire who flies on huge bat wings, Lionel Barrymore, Bela Lugosi, Lionel Atwill, and Elizabeth Allan. (It's a remake of Browning's 1927 *London After Midnight,* with Lon Chaney.) M-G-M. b & w

The Mark of Zorro (1940)—Tyrone Power, wanly miscast, stars in this lavish and inoffensive yet somewhat tiresome remake of Douglas Fairbanks, Sr.'s, innocent, buoyant swashbuckler. The often imitated material had been squeezed dry by the time this version was made, and there are so many leisurely quaint conversations among Linda Darnell, Basil Rathbone, Gale Sondergaard, and Eugene Pallette that the swordplay, fast riding, and holdups seem like interpolated spasms of activity. Rouben Mamoulian directed; with Montagu Love, Janet Beecher, and J. Edward Bromberg. 20th Century-Fox. b & w

Marked Woman (1937)—As the smart, lively young "clip-joint hostess" who turns police informer, Bette Davis is the embodiment of the sensational side of 30s movies. The closest later equivalent was Jeanne Moreau in *Bay of the Angels,* but Moreau is different, more purely conceptual; she's never as vibrantly, coarsely *there* as Davis, swinging her hips in her beaded-fringe dress. This racketeering melodrama is based on the career of Lucky Luciano, who lived high at the Waldorf-Astoria on the proceeds of a thousand prostitutes. In the film, Eduardo Ciannelli plays the role, with Humphrey Bogart (never at his best when cast on the side of officialdom—but then, who is?) taking over Thomas E. Dewey's function as prosecutor. One of the prostitutes Dewey persuaded to testify was branded—"marked"—as Davis is here. The film has the tawdry simplicities of many of the 30s movies that were built out of headline stories, but it also has more impact than most of the melodramas played out in more elevated surroundings, and when Davis tells Luciano-Ciannelli, "I'll get you even if I have to crawl back from my grave to do it," you believe it. At the time, the presence of Allen Jenkins in the cast certified the film as Warners contemporary. Talented young Jane Bryan plays the heroine's sister, and there are the whores of the Club Intime—Mayo Methot, Lola Lane, Isabel Jewell, Rosalind Marquis—who negate the euphemism "hostesses." Lloyd Bacon directed; Robert Rossen and Abem Finkel wrote the screenplay. b & w

Marlowe (1969)—As Raymond Chandler's detective, in this adaptation of *The Little Sister,* James Garner doesn't disgrace himself, but the film, directed by Paul Bogart, doesn't stay with you in the way that most of the Philip Marlowe pictures do. It just doesn't have much personality. The script by Stirling Silliphant is no help. With Gayle Hunnicutt, Carroll O'Connor, Rita Moreno, Bruce Lee, Sharon Farrell, William Daniels, and Jackie Coogan. M-G-M. color

Marnie (1964)—Hitchcock scraping bottom. Marnie (Tippi Hedren) is a frigid kleptomaniac; Sean Connery, looking pale and beleaguered, plays the man scheduled to cure her on both counts. It hardly seems worth the trouble. With Diane Baker, Martin Gabel, Louise Latham, and Bruce Dern. Screenplay by Jay Presson Allen, based on a novel by Winston Graham; music by Bernard Herrmann. Universal. color

Marooned (1969)—A space epic with a horse-and-buggy script. It's dull out there in space, though not as depressing as listening to the astronauts' wives back home. John Sturges directed, in his sleep. The actors playing Mr. Nice include Gregory Peck, James Franciscus, Richard Crenna, and David Janssen. Columbia. color (See *Deeper into Movies*.)

The Marquise of O. . . . *Die Marquise von O. . . .* (1976)—Eric Rohmer's word-for-word, gesture-for-gesture transcription of the 1808 Heinrich von Kleist novella manages to miss the spirit just about completely. A bold, funny story becomes a formal, tame film—it's like a historical work recreated for educational television. Edith Clever is skilled and likable as the Marquise, but the droopy Bruno Ganz is miscast as the rapist Count. With Edda Seippel as the Marquise's mother. Cinematography by Nestor Almendros. In German. color (See *When the Lights Go Down.*)

A Married Woman *Une Femme mariée* (1964)—Jean-Luc Godard wrote and directed this peculiarly abstract treatment of a young married woman (Macha Méril), her dissatisfactions, her patterns as a consumer, and her infidelities. There are witty bits, but they don't add up to much. Godard doesn't seem involved with the woman; he doesn't seem to care about her. With Bernard Noël, Philippe Leroy, and Roger Leenhardt as himself. In French. b & w

The Marrying Kind (1952)—In the early 50s, Hollywood wasn't making very many movies about the troubled lives of average couples, and so some people took this uneven, serious sit-com, directed by George Cukor from a script by Ruth Gordon and Garson Kanin, to be highly commendable. As the couple whose marriage is breaking up, Judy Holliday (of the friendly brass lungs) and Aldo Ray (with his lightweight cracked-gravel croak) have a surprising rapport. But there's nothing to this movie except the expertly contrived misunderstandings of simple "little" people. It's warm; at times it's likeable. But does anybody believe a minute of it? With Madge Kennedy as a judge, and Peggy Cass and Phyllis Povah. Columbia. b & w

Marty (1955)—It was the first American film to take the Golden Palm at Cannes; then it became a huge success at home and went on to rack up four Academy Awards: Best Picture, Actor—Ernest Borgnine, Director—Delbert Mann, Screenplay—Paddy Chayefsky. Borgnine is the shy, fat Bronx butcher who goes to a dance hall and meets a lonely high-school teacher (Betsy Blair). You have to have considerable tolerance to make it through Chayefsky's repetitive dialogue, his insistence on the humanity of "little" people, and his attempt to create poetry out of humble, drab conversations. With Esther Minciotti as Borgnine's Italian mother; Augusta Ciolli as his aunt; Joe Mantell as Angie, the image of the futile male; and Jerry Paris and Karen Steele. This small-scale, overly celebrated film began life as a television play. (On TV it starred Rod Steiger). United Artists. b & w

Mary of Scotland (1936)—Not a vintage year for Katharine Hepburn films; this was one of her three box-office duds, and it deserved to fail. The picture drips prestige. John Ford directed, and Dudley Nichols adapted the Maxwell Anderson play. And poor Fredric March was enlisted to play the fighting Scotsman Bothwell, who loved Mary and proved to be her undoing. The film is performed in a horribly high-flown style, with everybody posing against the fake-looking backgrounds and reciting lines that are so bad there's no way to say them without sounding affected. March also tries to manage an accent; it's probably Scottish, but all you can be sure of is that it's a mistake. Hepburn tries for an exalted, romantic manner of speech, and she goes in for a lot of openmouthed radiance and fluttering eyelashes. (You can see why she became box-office poison for a while.) With Florence Eldridge, who plays Queen Elizabeth as a wicked witch (she laughs heh heh heh), and Donald Crisp, John Carradine, Robert Barrat, Monte Blue, Alan Mowbray, Moroni Olsen, Frieda Inescort, and Douglas Walton. Produced by Pandro S. Berman, for R K O. b & w

Mary, Queen of Scots (1971)—Periods of history "fraught with intrigue"—as they used to say—don't film well. Mary's "tragic destiny" has always been a movie flop. There's no motivating idea visible in this version, produced abroad by Hal B. Wallis, and the leaden script, by John Hale, lacks romantic spirit and dramatic sense. We're offered primer polarities: Mary is a woman before she's a queen and Elizabeth vice versa. The banner lines on the ads were: "Mary, Queen of Scots, who ruled with the heart of a woman" and "Elizabeth, Queen of England, who reigned with the power of a man." In other words, Mary the loser was a real woman. (Elizabeth didn't reign with the power of a man but with the power of a queen.) Vanessa Redgrave brings a tremulous, romantic-goddess quality to Mary; Glenda Jackson, likable but as contemporary in this version as Bette Davis, gives Elizabeth a sort of camp humor. Her red wigs seem almost prankishly terrible, as if designed to subvert the imposing production. (She looks like a ragpicker hag dressed by Klimt.) The director, Charles Jarrott, struggles to give it all a little lift, but without a better script Hercules couldn't raise this story off the ground. With Trevor Howard, Timothy Dalton, Ian Holm, Patrick McGoohan, Daniel Massey, and Nigel Davenport. Cinematography by Christopher Challis. Universal. color

La Maschera del Demonio, see *Black Sunday*

Masculin-féminin, see *Masculine Feminine*

Masculine Feminine *Masculin-féminin* (1965)—Jean-Luc Godard's graceful, intuitive examination of the courtship rites of "the children of Marx and Coca-Cola." The boy, a pop revolutionary (Jean-Pierre Léaud), is full of doubts and questions. The girl (Chantal Goya) is a yé-yé singer with a thin, reedy little voice; her face is haunting just because it's so empty—she seems alive only when she's looking in the mirror toying with her hair. The film—a combination of journalistic sketches, love lyrics, and satire—is about the differing attitudes of the sexes toward love and war in an atmosphere of total and easy disbelief, when government policies are accepted with the same contempt as TV commercials. The two lovers and their friends are united by their disdain for the world of adults, and by the pop culture which they love. The film includes informal boy-to-boy conversations about women and politics; there is a phenomenal six-minute single-take parody interview conducted by the hero with a Miss Nineteen; and there are two boy-girl sessions which define the contemporary meaning of masculine and feminine. Godard captures the awkwardnesses that reveal—the pauses, the pretensions, the mannerisms. He gets at the differences in the way girls are with each other and with boys, and boys with each other and with girls. Not just what they do, but how they smile and look away. In French. b & w

M*A*S*H (1970)—Robert Altman's marvellously unstable comedy—a tough, funny, and sophisticated burlesque of military attitudes that is at the same time a tale of chivalry. It's an episodic film, full of the pleasures of the unexpected, and it keeps you busy listening to some of the best overlapping comic dialogue ever recorded. The title letters stand for Mobile Army Surgical Hospital; the heroes, played by Donald Sutherland and Elliott Gould, are combat surgeons patching up casualties a few miles from the front during the Korean war. They do their surgery in style, with humor; they're hip Galahads, saving lives while ragging the military bureaucracy. They're quick to react to bull—and in startling, unpredictable ways. The movie's chief charm is a free-for-all, throwaway attitude. It combines traditional roustabout comedy with modern attitudes. It's hip but it isn't hopeless. A surgical hospital where the doctors' hands are lost in chests and guts is certainly an unlikely subject for a comedy, but M*A*S*H is probably the sanest American movie of its era. With Tom Skerritt, Sally Kellerman, Robert Duvall, René Auberjonois, Jo Ann Pflug, Gary Burghof, Fred Williamson, Roger Bowen, David Arkin, Michael Murphy, John Schuck, Kim Atwood, Bud Cort, Carl Gottlieb, and Corey Fischer. The semi-improvised material takes off from a script by Ring Lardner, Jr., based on the novel by Richard Hooker (a doctor's pseudonym). Cinematography by Harold E. Stine. Produced by Ingo Preminger; the associate producer was Leon Ericksen. (The movie provided the basis for the long-running TV series starring Alan Alda.) 20th Century-Fox. color (See *Deeper into Movies*.)

The Mask of Dimitrios (1944)—This glossy "international" thriller, based on an Eric Ambler novel, seems modest because there are no stars in it, only featured players. In the days when studios had stars under contract, it didn't cost the company anything to toss them into a movie, so this starless picture was considered a real oddity. Peter Lorre is—surprise—the good guy. This doesn't turn out to be such a hot idea: when Lorre isn't being a degenerate, sly pussycat he's plump and pleasant, but colorless. He is cast as a Dutch novelist who tries to track down the background of the corpse, Dimitrios (Zachary

Scott). The trail leads to strange places (Istanbul, Smyrna, Sofia, Belgrade, etc.) and to familiar people—Sydney Greenstreet, Victor Francen, Faye Emerson, Eduardo Ciannelli, Florence Bates, Monte Blue, Steven Geray, and John Abbott (you could hardly have a tale of dark intrigue without him). Directed by Jean Negulesco, the picture has more mood than excitement. The screenplay is by Frank Gruber. Warners. b & w

The Mask of Fu Manchu (1932)—Fortunately, Boris Karloff doesn't seem to take his Oriental accoutrements too seriously. As the sinister Dr. Fu Manchu's daughter, Myrna Loy isn't as archly bemused as Karloff, but she's fun to see in her slinky getup. A tolerable, campy entertainment, with Karen Morley, Lewis Stone, Jean Hersholt, and, in the juvenile lead, Charles Starrett, who has a perfect profile and is a perfectly deadly actor. Charles Brabin and Charles Vidor directed; from the Sax Rohmer story. M-G-M. b & w

Maskerade, see *Masquerade in Vienna*

Masquerade (1988)—A tranquil, sophisticated thriller set in the Hamptons. The orphan heroine (Meg Tilly) belongs to the old rich; her money—about $200 million—has a patina. The men who circle around her are Rob Lowe as a hired-hand yachting captain, John Glover as the last of her mother's many husbands, and Doug Savant as a new police officer. Thin as the picture is, it has an odd, subterranean pull. Murders take place, but the narrative just keeps unfolding effortlessly, and you're drawn along, wanting to understand the pattern of deceit. Bob Swaim directed, from a crafty and even-toned script by Dick Wolf; the cinematography, by David Watkin, gives the life of the rich a luxuriance—makes it palpably desirable. With

Dana Delany, Kim Cattrall, and Erik Holland. M-G-M. color (See *Hooked*.)

Masquerade in Vienna *Maskerade* (1934)— Anton Walbrook, young and elegant, plays the artist who sketches the wife of a prominent Viennese surgeon in nothing but a mask and a muff, and then is forced to invent a model. Paula Wessely is the girl he invents. Walter Reisch's light, romantic screenplay is an almost perfect example of writing for the screen. Directed by Willi Forst; cinematography by Franz Planer. In German. b & w

Masters of the Congo Jungle, see *Lords of the Forest*

Mat', see *Mother*

Matador (1986)—Directed by Pedro Almodóvar (just before he made the 1987 *Law of Desire*), this comedy is all lush, clownish excess. Everything is eroticized—the colors, the violence. The opening (horrible, slasher images on a VCR—crimes against women— that a retired, gored bullfighter masturbates to) stuns you for a few seconds before it makes you laugh. The characters in this movie act out their wildest fantasies, or, like the handsome, wealthy young virgin Ángel (Antonio Banderas), try to act them out, and embarrass themselves. Ángel is training to be a bullfighter, but he faints at the sight of blood. He's such a supreme fantasist that he hallucinates and sees what happened in a recent series of murders. Unluckily, he's fantasist enough to think that he committed them. The images are sumptuously sick and funny, with hair ornaments used as daggers, tall women in swirling cloaks, and love rites performed on the matador's hot-pink cape spread fanlike on the floor. This trashiness has its own poetry and bravura. Assumpta Serna plays a culmination of the scarlet-woman tradition of Joan Crawford, Rita Hay-worth, Ava Gardner, and Anouk Aimée—all those flaming man-killers with their too vibrant smiles. And Almodóvar himself appears as a mad-genius couturier who messes up his curly hair before he appears in public. Also with Nacho Martínez as the matador, Eusebio Poncela as the police inspector, Carmen Maura as the psychiatrist, and Eva Cobo, Julieta Serrano, and Chus Lampreave. Written by the director and Jesús Ferrero; cinematography by Ángel Luis Fernández. In Spanish. color (See *Hooked*.)

A Matter of Time (1976)—The romantic story, taken from Maurice Druon's novel *Film of Memory,* is about a peasant girl (Liza Minnelli) who gets a job as a maid in a Roman hotel. A contessa (Ingrid Bergman) who lives there was once a great demimondaine; she talks about her romantic adventures, and the maid visualizes herself living through the events. But the film has been mangled: the producers took it away from the director, Vincente Minnelli, shifted scenes around, cut others, and even added stock footage. The result exposes Liza Minnelli, in particular, to ridicule; however, though Ingrid Bergman's performance has no rhythm left, Bergman herself is assured enough to do much of the role in statuesque repose, and she has a glamour beyond anything she's had before on-screen. With Charles Boyer and Isabella Rossellini; cinematography by Geoffrey Unsworth. Released by A.I.P. color (See *When the Lights Go Down*.)

Maurice (1987)—The director, James Ivory, painstakingly reproduces the limp, drawn-out construction of E. M. Forster's novel, written in 1913 and 1914, but not published until 1971, a year after his death. It's about a young man's struggle to come to terms with his homosexuality. Forster wants to show that homosexuality is natural, and so Maurice (pronounced Morris) is an average Edwardian stockbroker who lives in the suburbs—a proper hale-and-hearty fellow, narrow-minded and snobbish, like others of his (middle) class. And then Forster tries to demonstrate that Maurice's full physical commitment to his homosexual drives is his redemption—that it burns away his snobbery and turns him into a more perceptive man, a better man. The trap for both the novel and the film is Maurice's blandness; the actor who plays him—tall, blond James Wilby—comes across as passive and slow. (You'd think being a gay man was tantamount to being retarded.) Ivory has a fine, trained eye for light and composition, but when it comes to capturing the feel of repression and of bursting desire he isn't there. The movie is suffocatingly discreet, with classical music in the clinches. Hugh Grant plays Maurice's upper-class Cambridge friend Clive Durham, with whom he experiences three years of platonic frustration, and Rupert Graves is Durham's under-gamekeeper Scudder, with whom Maurice finally experiences physical love. Also with Billie Whitelaw as Maurice's mother, Judy Parfitt as Durham's mother, and Peter Eyre, Denholm Elliott, Ben Kingsley, Simon Callow, and Helena Michell and Kitty Aldridge as Maurice's sisters. The screenplay is by Kit Hesketh-Harvey and Ivory; the dark-toned cinematography is by Pierre Lhomme. A Merchant-Ivory Production, made in England. color (See *Hooked.*)

Mayerling (1936)—This beautifully made version of the legendary tragic love of Archduke Rudolf, heir apparent to the Hapsburg Empire, for the young Maria Vetsera is one of the most memorable of all French romantic movies. (Several less effective versions followed.) Anatole Litvak directed with far more delicacy than he showed in his later work, and the doomed lovers are played by Charles Boyer and Danielle Darrieux. Boyer hangs a cigarette on his Hapsburg lip and grabs a girl's leg and the movie takes off. In this account Rudolf is a dissolute voluptuary redeemed by his love for the innocent Vetsera—and the young Darrieux is so sexy and lovely in the role that you can just about believe it all. The affair ended abruptly in 1889, at Mayerling, the royal hunting lodge in the Vienna woods; the first movie about these lovers was probably the one produced in Russia in 1915. In French. b & w

Mayerling (1969)—Omar Sharif, in stunning uniforms, as Rudolf, the Hapsburg crown prince, tragically in love with Catherine Deneuve—pallid and demure as Maria Vetsera. It's fortunate for other stars that Sharif is around to play these noble noodles, or the others might get stuck with them. Sharif's accent may be unaccountable here, since his parents are James Mason and Ava Gardner, but this movie is not to listen to but to swoon over. If you can get in the right mood maybe you won't notice that Sharif plays moments of passion as if he were straightening his collar. He is the least dashing and explosive of romantic stars; there is nothing bottled up in him, not even a hint of repressed emotion. He is so placid an actor that he seems to ruminate before he speaks. Yet his handsome, soulful face is a token of all romantic heroism, and his pained little smile an emblem of doomed romance. In keeping with the 60s, Rudolf is now a morphine addict who is in love with his mother, and he's also a secret revolutionary—he is introduced to us among the students arrested during a demonstration. (He is incognito, of course.) Sharif's eyes don't sparkle the way they did in *Lawrence of Arabia*, but they make tears beautifully. And, dull as he is—with his sucked-in cheeks for "spirituality," and the greenish tinge to his skin—he is the perfect royal loser. Rudolf seems the part he was born to; that he can't *play* it is almost beside the point, he is so perfectly cast. Directed and written by

M

Terence Young (with additional dialogue by other hands), this lavish French-British co-production is swathed in lovely decor, and Sharif is surrounded by actors of such over-powering passivity that he almost passes for energetic. No one speaks above a murmur; it's as if the film had been shot in a public-library reading room. The choice of Ava Gardner—a star famous for beauty and un-deracting—to play Sharif's mother, the em-press, seems inspired. They even resemble each other, and one would have to work hard to dislike either of them. With James Robert-son Justice, Geneviève Page, Ivan Desny, Moustache, Jacques Berthier, and the Grand Ballet Classique de France—which gives the film its only intense moments. The cinema-tography is by Henri Alekan; the production design is by Georges Wakhévitch; the cos-tumes are by Marcel Escoffier. color (See *Going Steady*.)

Maytime (1937)—Jeanette MacDonald and Nelson Eddy in one of their lavish musicals that is enjoyable for more than camp reasons. The picture is too drawn out, the framing story is pitiably artificial, the staging is often suffocating (with MacDonald dressed in acres of ruffles and flounces), and the score rots your brain, but John Barrymore brings a bitter edge to the role of MacDonald's husband, and the atmosphere of thwarted passion is compelling. Robert Z. Leonard directed, replacing Edmund Goulding, after the pro-ducer, Irving Thalberg, died; Hunt Strom-berg took over as producer. The huge cast includes Herman Bing, Billy Gilbert, Tom Brown, Lynne Carver, Rafaela Ottiano, Paul Porcasi, Sig Rumann, Harry Davenport, Ivan Lebedeff, and Leonid Kinskey. The montages are by Slavko Vorkapich. The script by Noel Langley is loosely based on the 1917 operetta (with music by Sigmund Romberg), which was based on a 1914 German play. (There was a silent film version in 1923.) M-G-M. b & w,

with sepia-tinted sequences in the original prints

Me and My Brother (1969)—The photogra-pher Robert Frank made this film about Julius Orlovsky, a catatonic boy released from a state institution, and how he is taken care of by his brother, Peter Orlovsky, and Allen Ginsberg. Julius appears in the film and is also acted in some sequences by Joseph Chai-kin. Frank tries to investigate insanity, meth-ods of treatment, the nature of acting, the nature of what one records on film, and so on; he tries to do too much, and the viewer doesn't get a chance to sort out his own re-actions. color and b & w

Me and My Gal (1932)—Joan Bennett is lively as a wisecracking, gum-chewing wait-ress; Spencer Tracy is her policeman boy-friend. The Irish humor is spread on thick, but every once in a while Arthur Kober, who did the script, gets off a good one. The melo-dramatic plot revolves around Bennett's bru-nette sister (Marion Burns), who is in love with a gangster. Raoul Walsh directed this naïve, pasted-together yet rather pleasing picture. With Henry B. Walthall as a man who has lost the power of speech, George Chandler as his foolish, good-natured son, and J. Farrell MacDonald. Fox. b & w

The Mean Season (1985)—It starts out huff-ing and puffing about opportunistic journal-ism, but it turns out to be nothing more than an inept thriller about a Miami reporter (Kurt Russell) who gets hot tips from a serial mur-derer about where to look for fresh corpses. And it has an unintentional, bottomless source of hilarity: the reporter's school-teacher girlfriend, who screams helplessly in emergencies, is played by the 6-footer Mariel Hemingway. The director, Phillip Borsos, and the cinematographer, Frank Tidy, sus-tain a lively, stormy gothic atmosphere, and most of the cast is good, but the script, based on John Katzenbach's *In the Heat of the Summer*, and credited to the pseudonymous Leon Piedmont, is hopelessly moralistic and self-important. The film is at its worst when the heroine scolds the hero (she even scolds the killer), and it's at its near worst when the hero and heroine play scare pranks on each other while the Lalo Schifrin score builds ominously. It's at its best when Richard Jordan is onscreen as an insanely clever sociopathic killer. Jordan has put on some heft, and the fleshiness makes his smoothly handsome baby face more imposing; he has a Brando-like look about him here—with his pampered quality and his big, deep voice, he has finally become *weird*. With Andy Garcia (he's quietly effective as Martinez), Richard Masur, Joe Pantoliano, and Richard Bradford. Orion. color (See *State of the Art.*)

Mean Streets (1973)—A true original, and a triumph of personal filmmaking. This picture about the experience of growing up in New York's Little Italy has an unsettling, episodic rhythm and it's dizzyingly sensual. The director, Martin Scorsese, shows us a thicker-textured rot than we have ever had in an American movie, and a riper sense of evil. With Harvey Keitel as Charlie, Robert De Niro as Johnny Boy, and Richard Romanus, David Proval, Harry Northup, George Memmoli, Amy Robinson, Cesare Danova, and, in bits, David Carradine, Robert Carradine, and the director—he's the gunman in the car. Script by Scorsese and Mardik Martin; cinematography by Kent Wakeford; produced by Jonathan Taplin. (Most of the film was actually shot in Los Angeles.) Warners. color (See *Reeling.*)

The Medium (1951)—With the technical assistance of Alexander Hammid, Gian-Carlo Menotti directed this film version of his opera; it is still the only opera ever put on film by its composer. Menotti had written the libretto in English, so there was no problem of translation, and the movie, made in Rome, doesn't have that deadly air of compromise which poisons attempts to "popularize" opera. *The Medium* was, of course, popular from the start, and never labored under what—in movie terms—can be the mixed blessings of greatness. The story is a Grand Guignol thriller about a swindling charlatan of a medium who, in the middle of a fake séance, feels a ghostly hand on her throat; visually menacing, it's like an extended episode from *Dead of Night* with music. The roles are expertly handled by the American contralto Marie Powers as the shrewd, blowsy brute of a woman, the 14-year-old Italian coloratura Anna Maria Alberghetti, and Leo Coleman as the mute gypsy. b & w

Meet John Doe (1941)—An odd, socially conscious picture, directed by Frank Capra and starring Gary Cooper and Barbara Stanwyck, about a man who tries to commit suicide in order to call attention to a right-wing plot. For the sake of a happy ending that would keep Gary Cooper alive, the meanings were so distorted that the original authors sued. The picture starts out in the confident Capra manner, but with a darker tone; by the end, you feel puzzled and cheated. The script is credited to Robert Riskin; with Edward Arnold, Walter Brennan, James Gleason, Regis Toomey, Spring Byington, Gene Lockhart, Ann Doran, Warren Hymer, Rod La Rocque, and Andrew Tombes. Released by Warners. b & w

Meet Nero Wolfe (1936)—Edward Arnold enjoying himself as the illustrious Nero Wolfe, Rex Stout's omniscient, bullying detective who can trace a killer and his method without leaving the house where he keeps his fine orchids and his special brew of beer. This is one of those thrillers that depend too much upon a lot of things that happened years before to a lot of people whom you can't sort out. You may never be entirely clear about what stirred up the crowd of Barstows and Kimballs some 15 years ago down in South America, or about how that led to the murder at hand. Herbert Biberman directed. With Rita Hayworth, Lionel Stander, Victor Jory, Joan Perry, Nana Bryant, and John Qualen. Columbia. b & w

Melvin and Howard (1980)—This lyrical comedy, directed by Jonathan Demme, from a script by Bo Goldman, is an almost flawless act of sympathetic imagination. Demme and Goldman have entered into the soul of American blue-collar suckerdom; they have taken for their hero a chucklehead who is hooked on TV game shows, and they have made us understand how it was that when something big—something legendary—touched his life, nobody could believe it. Paul Le Mat plays big, beefy Melvin Dummar, a sometime milkman, sometime worker at a magnesium plant, sometime gas-station operator, and hopeful songwriter—the representative debt-ridden American for whom game shows were created. Jason Robards plays Howard Hughes, who is lying in the freezing desert at night when Melvin spots him—a pile of rags and bones, with a dirty beard and straggly long gray hair. Melvin, thinking him a desert rat, helps him into his pickup truck but is bothered by his mean expression; in order to cheer him up (and give himself some company), he insists that the old geezer sing with him or get out and walk. When Robards' Howard Hughes responds to Melvin's amiable prodding and begins to enjoy himself on a simple level and sings "Bye, Bye, Blackbird," it's a great moment. Hughes' eyes are an old man's eyes—faded into the past, shiny and glazed by recollections—yet intense. You feel that his grungy paranoia has melted away, that he has been healed. With Mary Steenburgen, who has a pearly aura as Melvin's go-go-dancer wife, Lynda; Pamela Reed as Melvin's down-to-earth second wife; Elizabeth Cheshire as the child Darcy; Jack Kehoe as the dairy foreman; and the real Melvin Dummar as the lunch counterman at the Reno bus depot. This picture has the same beautiful dippy warmth as its characters; it's what might have happened if Jean Renoir had directed a comedy script by Preston Sturges. Cinematography by Tak Fujimoto. Universal. color (See *Taking It All In.*)

The Member of the Wedding (1952)—The Carson McCullers dialogue is one of the high points of literacy in American films—sharp and full of wit, yet lyrical. Scrawny, cracked-voiced Julie Harris (she was 26 at the time) plays Frankie, the motherless, fiercely lonely 12-year-old tomboy, caught between childhood and adolescence, and fighting them both. Ethel Waters plays Berenice, the cook who looks after her, and Brandon deWilde is Frankie's owlish little playmate and whipping boy. The setting is a small Georgia town; the time is the summer when these three characters, who have been clinging to each other, are torn apart. Adapted from McCullers' 1950 stage success (with the same cast), the film is weak when it tries to "open up" the material, but fortunately Fred Zinnemann's direction respects Carson McCullers' intensity and humor. This remarkable film failed commercially, perhaps for want of a conventional "story"; it is said that in some towns viewers didn't understand the material and, for most of the film, thought that Frankie was a boy. The movie company then cut a crucial 20-minute segment (which included Ethel Waters' finest scene) and tossed the film into the lower half of double bills; in the 70s the footage was restored in some prints. b & w

The Memory of Justice (1975)—Centering on the definitions of war crimes formulated at the Nuremberg Trials, Marcel Ophuls examines the atrocities committed in Vietnam and other places; he attempts nothing less than an investigation of the nature of war guilt, and the film runs 4 hours and 38 minutes. Striving for complexity, Ophuls extends his inquiry in so many directions that he loses his subject; despite some remarkable footage, the film is chaotic, plodding, and excessively self-conscious. Released by Paramount. color and b & w (See *When the Lights Go Down.*)

The Men (1950)—Marlon Brando made his first screen appearance as the paraplegic Second World War hero, rebelling furiously and helplessly against his condition; paradoxically, Brando gives an overpoweringly physical performance. He's amazingly sensitive and intense—no one before him who smoldered on screen ever gave off so much heat. Fred Zinnemann directed, with sureness and tact, using the paraplegic patients in a California veterans' hospital as part of the cast. With Jack Webb, Teresa Wright, and Everett Sloane. Produced by Stanley Kramer; conventional melodramatic banalities mar the Carl Foreman script, but it's an economical, vivid narrative. Released by United Artists. b & w

Men . . . *Männer . . .* (1985)—This West German comedy was written and directed by the 31-year-old Doris Dörrie, and people go to it hoping to see men through a woman's eyes. The disappointment is not just that you don't see men through a woman's eyes. Dörrie's characters have no substance; they're not quite human—you don't see anybody through anybody's eyes. When the handsome self-centered Julius (Heiner Lauterbach), a Munich advertising executive, discovers that his wife (Ulrike Kriener) has been having an affair with the oafish Stefan (Uwe Ochsenknecht), a long-haired bohemian, he wants to know what Stefan's attraction is, so he assumes a false name and moves in with him. Julius takes some kind of revenge by turning Stefan into an orderly bourgeois with a regular job; while that happens, whimsical gags are tossed together with a jocular feminist exposé of men's attitudes toward women. The picture is harmless and insipid, in the mode of French farces such as *Cousin, Cousine*; it sags in the middle and then collapses in an absurdist ending. In German. color (See *Hooked.*)

Men in War (1957)—This film came and went quietly and too quickly. A platoon in the Korean war is surrounded by the enemy; the attempt to get back to its own lines is the substance of the film. Under Anthony Mann's direction and with the performances of Robert Ryan, Aldo Ray, and Robert Keith, this attempt is charged with desperate anxiety. As *Time* put it, " . . . there comes a moment when any averagely sensitive person will begin to get that cold sensation along his spine, and to realize a little how a fighting man feels when he is buying a Section Eight." Written by Philip Yordan. Released by United Artists. b & w

Men in White (1934)—Clark Gable seldom suggests the high-strung and brilliant young surgeon-hero of the Sidney Kingsley Pulitzer Prize–winning play—the man whose idealism overrides any financial or romantic considerations. Nor is Myrna Loy exactly at her best when she is called upon to contemplate "Humanity." The director, Richard Boleslawski, is engrossed in the pictorial aspects of the wards and laboratories and internes' rooms; he loves the shadow of a microscope on a wall, the barred lights from venetian blinds across a sickbed, the glint of knives and pincers in the operating room. The characters don't fare so well, but then their problems are fearfully strained and prestigious anyway. With Jean Hersholt, Elizabeth Allan, Otto Kruger, and Wallace Ford. Adaptation by Waldemar Young; cinematography by George Folsey. M-G-M. b & w

Ménage *Tenue de soirée* (1986)—The first half hour of this sex farce is wonderfully brisk and slam-bang provocative: the writer-director Bertrand Blier violates old formulas and experiments with ideas of subversion and chaos. Gérard Depardieu, huge, and with the belly of a bear, is the burglar who, at night in a café, overhears a callous bitchy wife, Miou-Miou, bawling out her loving husband, Michel Blanc—a wisp of a man, meek, sad-eyed, and bald—because he can't make enough money to please her. Enamored of the mousy husband, Depardieu slugs the wife, throws a mess of money at her, and then takes the two along on his surreally easy burglaries and showers the loot on them, waiting for his chance to bed the man. During the house break-ins, Blier has a comic inspiration: the rich victims are so bored that they love the excitement of being robbed. But he drops this and concentrates on Depardieu's seduction of Blanc, which is only briefly amusing. It's the first step in Blier's screwball-fable demonstration of how arbitrary sex preferences are. By the time that Miou-Miou has been sold to a pimp and the two men are in drag, working as prostitutes, Blier is trying so hard to be outrageous that he loses the beat; the outrageousness comes to seem another kind of bondage to formula. Depardieu has learned how to push everybody around and take over the screen; he's an accomplished clown (and that jaw of his is hilarious when you first see him made up as a woman), but his other qualities aren't in evidence here. With Bruno Cremer. In French. color

Menilmontant (1924)—Dmitri Kirsanov, a young Russian emigré who worked as a violinist in a Paris moviehouse, made one of the greatest of all experimental films—an exquisite, poetic 40-minute movie that is one of the least known masterpieces of the screen. Working by himself, apart from even the experimental filmmakers of the period, he developed a technique that suggests the movement known in painting as Futurism. The extraordinary editing is, at first, confusing and upsetting, and, finally, dazzling. The story is of two sisters who are both betrayed by the same man; the performance by Nadia Sibirskaya as the younger of the two is surpassingly beautiful. In one scene she is seated on a park bench next to an old man who surreptitiously shares his food with her—it's as great as anything in Chaplin. Silent. b & w

Mephisto (1981)—István Szabó's indictment of a soulless actor, Hendrik Höfgen (played by Klaus Maria Brandauer), who, because he wants to go on performing, truckles to those in power and becomes the leading actor in Nazi Germany. (Hendrik Höfgen is based on Gustaf Gründgens, who was married during his early years to Thomas Mann's daughter Erika; the movie is loosely adapted from the 1936 novel *Mephisto*, by her brother Klaus Mann, who is believed to have been Gründgens' lover.) Szabó sets up the willful, unpredictable Höfgen as a symbolic actor—a man who has no substance, who is merely the sum of the roles he plays offstage and on, and at the outset Brandauer, who has gleaming cat eyes and a seductive, impish smile, suggests an *enfant terrible*, a baby-faced killer-genius, like the young Orson Welles. Höfgen isn't allowed to be a great actor, though, and he seems too small for the epic scale of the attack. The picture is like *Citizen Kane* with somebody like John Dean at its center. The film is gripping but its stern air of rectitude produces discomfort; essentially Szabó seems to be condemning Höfgen for being an actor. With Rolf Hoppe as the General, a Göring-like figure, and the superb, feline Karin Boyd as Höfgen's dancer mistress, and a multinational cast—some of them dubbed. The script is by Szabó and Péter Dobai. This West German–Hungarian co-production was originally 2 hours and 40 minutes long; the version that opened in the U.S. runs 2 hours and 16 minutes. Academy Award for Best Foreign-Language Film. In German. color (See *Taking It All In*.)

The Merchant of Four Seasons *Der Händler der Vier Jahreszeiten* (1971)—A measured, distanced study of a victim (Hans Hirschmuller)—a rejected son of a middle-class family—and how he loses the will to live. The film is considered by many to be a masterpiece, but the style of the director, Rainer Werner Fassbinder, doesn't have enough authority; an American viewer may be uncertain how to react to the distancing devices, and how to react to the masochism and the misogyny and the view of women as cold-hearted betrayers. When is Fassbinder being sardonic, and when is the degradation and futility meant to be taken straight? The picture, which has some conceptual resemblances to the later films of Robert Bresson and to Dreyer's *Gertrud*, and some psychological resemblances to such Emil Jannings films as *Variety*, is an art thing, all right, but perhaps not a work of art. And most important of all, it isn't likable. With Irm Hermann and Hanna Schygulla. In German. color

Metropolis (1926)—H. G. Wells called this German silent "quite the silliest film"; Hitler was so impressed by the conception that many years later he tried (unsuccessfully) to persuade its director, Fritz Lang, to make Nazi movies. Lang's prophetic city of the 21st century (suggested by his first view of New York) has two levels: one for the rich and pleasure-loving, another—labyrinthine, underground—for the slave-workers who tend the machines. The industrialist-tyrant who runs Metropolis plots to incite riots so that he can crush the workers' rebelliousness. His son has gone down to the workers and fallen in love with the saintly firebrand Maria (Brigitte Helm). The tyrant plots with an inventor, Rotwang (a mad, medieval type like Dr. Caligari and, with his mechanical arm, father to Dr. Strangelove), who, in a phenomenal science-fiction laboratory sequence, creates a steel double for Maria—the false Maria, who leads the masses to revolt. But the destruction gets out of hand, the children of the workers are about to be caught in a flood, and all of Metropolis would be destroyed were it not for the final alliance of the industrialist, his son, the true Maria, and the workers. One of the last examples of the imaginative—but often monstrous—grandeur of the Golden Period of the German film, *Metropolis* is a spectacular example of Expressionist design (grouped human beings are used architecturally), with moments of almost incredible beauty and power (the visionary sequence about the Tower of Babel), absurd ineptitudes (the lovesick hero in his preposterous knickerbockers), and oddities that defy analysis (the robot vamp's bizarre, lewd wink). It's a wonderful, stupefying folly. With Alfred Abel as the industrialist, Gustav Fröhlich as his son, Rudolf Klein-Rogge, Fritz Rasp, and Heinrich George. Script by Thea von Harbou (who did go to work for the Nazis); cinematography by Karl Freund and Gunther Rittau, with Eugen Schüfftan shooting the special effects. b & w Note: In 1984, Giorgio Moroder did a "reconstructed" version, with tinting that (supposedly) attempts to follow Lang's original specifications; he has gone in for a lot of hocus-pocus with the footage, and put on a pop score—it includes contributions by Loverboy, Pat Benatar, Adam Ant, Billy Squier, and Bonnie Tyler.

Mexicali Rose (1929)—Barbara Stanwyck called the film "an abortion," and she wasn't being too rough on it. Though she had an impressive stage reputation, she was still a novice in movies (she had appeared in a silent in 1927, and then had made her first talkie earlier in 1929), and this picture, in which she's cast as a hip-wiggling tart, almost finished her career. (Her next, Frank Capra's *Ladies of Leisure*, was to make her a star.) With Sam Hardy and William Janney. Directed by Erle Kenton. Columbia. b & w

Micki & Maude (1984)—A light screwball farce with Dudley Moore as a TV reporter who becomes a bigamist through his tender regard for the feelings of two pregnant women—the blazing Ann Reinking and the pearly Amy Irving. The director, Blake Edwards, working from a screenplay by Jonathan Reynolds, brings out the bigamist's living-in-the-moment hopefulness. He's convinced that everything will come out all right because he doesn't feel he's done anything wrong. And the audience is put in the position of sharing his loony optimism. The movie may seem insipid to people who want something substantial, but there's a special delight about the timing of actors who make fools of themselves as personably and airily as Dudley Moore and Amy Irving do here. He's romantic in the silken, self-effacing manner of Cary Grant, and her acting is a form of heavenly flirtation. There are a couple of slapstick sequences in which Edwards shows some of his love of free-for-all lunacy, and Moore turns into a comic projectile hurtling into walls. With the deep-voiced Richard Mulligan, Lu Leonard, H. B. Haggerty, George Gaynes, Wallace Shawn, John Pleshette, Priscilla Pointer, Robert Symonds, and

George Coe. Columbia. color (See *State of the Art*.)

Midnight (1939)—Rapturous fun. Slim-hipped, wide-eyed Claudette Colbert, stranded in Paris in an evening gown, gets involved with rich, aristocratic John Barrymore, who is trying to regain the affections of his straying wife, Mary Astor, who is hooked on dapper gigolo Francis Lederer. This romantic comedy, directed by Mitchell Leisen for Paramount, from a script by Charles Brackett and Billy Wilder, is one of the authentic delights of the 30s. The cast includes Hedda Hopper, Monty Woolley, Elaine Barrie, Rex O'Malley, and Don Ameche. Actually, Ameche has an important role; he isn't bad—for Ameche. Based on a story written for the screen by Edwin Justus Mayer and Franz Schultz. b & w

Midnight Cowboy (1969)—Jon Voight as Joe Buck, a dishwasher from a small town in Texas, who hopes to make a living in New York by servicing rich women, and Dustin Hoffman as Ratso Rizzo, the crippled petty thief and con man he meets. The director, John Schlesinger, uses fast cutting and tricky camerawork to provide a satirical background as enrichment of the story, but the satire is offensively inaccurate—it cheapens the story and gives it a veneer of almost hysterical cleverness. The point of the movie must be to offer us some insight into the two derelicts—two of the many kinds of dreamers and failures in the city. But Schlesinger keeps pounding away at America, determined to expose how horrible the people are—he dehumanizes the people Joe Buck and Ratso are part of. If he could extend the same sympathy to the other Americans that he extends to them, the picture might make better sense. His spray of venom is just about overpowering, yet the two actors and the simple *Of Mice and Men* kind of relationship at the heart of the story save the picture. Hoffman's raspy voice and jumpy walk and Jon Voight's pallor and blue eyes and hurt, bewildered stare provide a core of feeling. With Brenda Vaccaro, Sylvia Miles, John McGiver, Barnard Hughes, Ruth White, Gil Rankin, Jennifer Salt, Anthony Holland, Bob Balaban, Viva, Taylor Mead, Paul Morrissey, Ultra Violet, Paul Jabara, and International Velvet. From James Leo Herlihy's novel, adapted by Waldo Salt; cinematography by Adam Holender. Produced by Jerome Hellman; United Artists. color

Midnight Express (1978)—Puts the squeeze on us right from the start. It's single-minded in its manipulation of the audience: this is a clear-cut case of film technique split off from any artistic impulse. The film is based on the story of Billy Hayes, a vacationing American college student who was caught smuggling two kilos of hashish out of Turkey and imprisoned. But its juiciest episodes are inventions; the screenwriter, Oliver Stone, and the director, Alan Parker, have subjected their Billy (Brad Davis) to the most photogenic sadomasochistic brutalization that they could dream up. The film is like a porno fantasy about the sacrifice of a virgin. It rushes from torment to torment, treating Billy's ordeals hyponotically in soft colors—muted squalor—with a disco beat in the background. The prison itself is more like a brothel than a prison. All of this is packaged as social protest. With John Hurt as Max, Randy Quaid as Jimmy, Bo Hopkins as Tex, Paolo Bonacelli as Rifki, Mike Kellin as Billy's father, and Paul Smith as the Turkish head guard, Hamidou, who looks like a Picasso bull. Music by Giorgio Moroder; shot in Malta. Released by Columbia. color (See *When the Lights Go Down*.)

A Midsummer Night's Sex Comedy (1982)— Woody Allen's overrefined reworking of Bergman's *Smiles of a Summer Night*; it has a meticulous art atmosphere and Mendelssohn on the track. This time, it's an American weekend in the country, early in the century, and Woody Allen is the host; he works on Wall Street but dabbles in inventions—small, winged contraptions for flying, and mystical devices such as a "spirit ball" for getting through to the other, unseen world. Mary Steenburgen plays his wife, and the guests are José Ferrer, a pompous genius professor who is a free thinker in sexual matters but is contemptuous of psychic research; Mia Farrow, the prof's glamorous young fiancée; Tony Roberts, a lecherous doctor; and Julie Hagerty as a nurse who's the most trusting and gullible of all human creatures, and is avid for sex (she's the best thing in the movie). The group is rather amusing, but the talk seems somnambulistic and nothing really develops. Woody Allen is trying to please, but his heart isn't in it, and his talent isn't, either. He is so much a man of our time that his comedy seems denatured in this classy, period setting. Written and directed by Allen; cinematography by Gordon Willis. Orion. color (See *Taking It All In*.)

Mighty Joe Young (1949)—King Kong domesticized and turned into a children's pet. Terry Moore plays an orphan girl, raised in Africa, who buys a sweet, docile gorilla, Joe, who adores her; Robert Armstrong (who discovered King Kong) finds them and transports them to a Hollywood nightclub. Joe, a 10-footer, holds Terry and a grand piano up in the air on a platform while she beats out "Beautiful Dreamer." But Joe turns out to be a moralist who disapproves of drinking and carrying on, and eventually he wrecks the nightclub in an impressive fury. He engages in a pretty funny tug-of-war with a team composed of Man Mountain Dean, Primo Carnera, and some other oversize types. Ernest Schoedsack directed this nonsense; it has some spectacular effects, but a wretched script. With Ben Johnson, Frank McHugh, and Douglas Fowley. R K O. b & w

The Mikado (1939)—Malice, Victorian style, with decor of the finest counterfeit Japanese—the D'Oyly Carte performers bounce through Gilbert & Sullivan's lyrical parody of the institutions of love and justice. Martyn Green's giddy Lord High Executioner and Sydney Granville's thunderous Pooh-Bah are just about perfect, and even anti–Gilbert & Sullivanites will have a hard time resisting the hirsute charms of Katisha. As box-office lure, Kenny Baker was tossed in as Nanki-Poo; he is quite passable. Directed by Victor Schertzinger. color

Mike's Murder (1984)—Debra Winger, in a superb full-scale starring performance, as a radiantly sane young bank teller in L.A. who has an affair with a curly-haired clear-faced young tennis instructor called Mike (Mark Keyloun). It's a wobbly affair: she hears from him randomly over the course of two years—whenever the mood hits him, he phones her. One night, he's supposed to come over late, but he doesn't show. When she gets a call telling her he's dead, it's abrupt, bewildering. She can't let go of him so quickly, and she tries to find out everything she can. Winger has thick, long, loose hair and a deep, sensual beauty in this movie. James Bridges, who directed, wrote the role for her after directing her in *Urban Cowboy*, and her performance suggests what Antonioni seemed to be trying to get from Jeanne Moreau in *La Notte*, only it really works with Winger—maybe because there's nothing sullen or closed about her. The picture is atmospheric yet underpopulated; at times, it feels thin, and it turns into overheated melodrama in a sequence featuring Darrell Larson. But its view of the cocaine subculture (or culture) of L.A. is probably Bridges' most original and daring effort, and it has a brief, intense appearance by Paul

Winfield (as the record producer who brought Mike to L.A.) that's right up there with Winger's acting. With Brooke Alderson, Robert Crosson as Sam, and Daniel Shor as Richard, the performance artist. The Warner executives refused to release the picture until Bridges made some cuts and changes, and they probably breathed a few sighs of relief as they buried it. color (See *Hooked*.)

Mildred Pierce (1945)—Joan Crawford rises from poverty to affluence and then suffers glamorously in beach house, roadhouse, and mansion from the nasty semi-incestuous goings on of her cad husband (Zachary Scott) and her spoiled daughter (Ann Blyth). Miss Crawford's heavy breathing was certified as acting when she won an Academy Award for her performance here. Michael Curtiz directed this glossy adaptation of the James M. Cain novel. With Jack Carson and Eve Arden. Warners. b & w

Milestones (1975)—An acted-out cross-section view of what the young radicals of the 60s are doing in the 70s—how they're trying to find a revolutionary way of life. It's so long (195 minutes) and so miserably structured that the viewer can't tell who is living with whom, or where, or what the economic base of any of the groups is. The directors, Robert Kramer and John Douglas (who also wrote and edited the film), cut back and forth among people living in communes and burned-out apartments and on the road, who talk about their feelings, and the need to be open about those feelings, in banal, strangely indirect, and abstract terms. It's all so maundering and haphazard that it looks like an after-apocalypse movie; this is certainly part of the point, but we never get to understand what the directors' principles of selection were. With Douglas playing a blind potter, Grace Paley playing a filmmaker, and David C. Stone as Joe, of Joe's Bar. color

The Milky Way *La Voie lactée* (1968)—This Luis Buñuel film concerns two pilgrim-tramps and their encounters with the Devil, the Virgin Mary, people who are arguing about Catholic doctrine, and assorted religious zealots. It's all genial enough, and the tone of cool irony is charming and very distinctive, but an awful lot of Buñuel's little jokes are clerical and enigmatic. At times, the film seems to be a Catholic-college revue, full of dud barbs and daring seminary humor. It looks beautiful, though (the cinematography is by Christian Matras), and it moves along in a masterly way that is specifically, characteristically Buñuelian; it's all very simple—just one episode after another, with past and present joined without effort or fuss, and with occasional (and very odd) animal sounds on the track. Screenplay by Buñuel and Jean-Claude Carrière. The cast includes such well-known performers as Julien Bertheau, Alain Cuny, Edith Scob, Michel Piccoli, Paul Frankeur, Laurent Terzieff, Claudio Brook, Delphine Seyrig, and Pierre Clémenti (as the Devil), yet no one leaves a very distinct impression. In French. color (See *Deeper into Movies*.)

Le Million (1931)—René Clair at his exquisite best; no one else has ever been able to make a comedy move with such delicate, dreamlike inevitability. René Lefèvre plays the poor young painter who has a winning lottery ticket—only he hasn't quite got it; it was in the pocket of a coat that got sold to a secondhand shop. The entire film, which Clair adapted from a stage musical, is the hero's chase after the ticket, with his creditors, his girl (Annabella), his friends, and the police chasing after him. (The sequence in the opera house is clearly the inspiration for a sequence in *A Night at the Opera*.) This movie is lyrical, choreographic, giddy—it's the best French musical of its period. The cinematog-

raphy is by Georges Périnal; the art direction is by Lazare Meerson. In French. b & w

Million Dollar Legs (1932)—One of the silliest and funniest pictures ever made: a lunatic musical satire on the Olympics, with W. C. Fields, Jack Oakie, Andy Clyde, Ben Turpin, and Lyda Roberti singing ''It's Terrific.'' The Mankiewicz brothers (Herman J. and Joseph L.) worked together on this one, and Edward Cline directed. Paramount. b & w

Million Dollar Mermaid (1952)—Esther Williams was a great advertisement for the one-piece bathing suit; still, centering a story on the invention of the thing leaves a lot of dead space in a movie that goes on for 115 minutes. The director, Mervyn LeRoy, is not known for his sense of pace. In this M-G-M musical splasher, Esther Williams plays Annette Kellerman, the Australian swimming champ who went into show business. Walter Pidgeon plays her father, Maria Tallchief plays Anna Pavlova, and Victor Mature is the American promotor who discovers first Annette and then Rin Tin Tin. The picture's only claim on one's attention is in the two sequences staged by Busby Berkeley, which were excerpted for *That's Entertainment!* Berkeley used smoke pots and sparklers, and put Williams, wearing a chain-mail bathing suit made of thousands of gold flakes, at the top of a geyser. color.

The Million Pound Note, see *Man with a Million*

Millionaires of Naples *Napoli Milionaria* (1952)—Totò plays a black marketeer, nouveau riche, in Eduardo de Filippo's film adaptation of his own play, and de Filippo, one of the most important figures in Italian theatre at the time, co-stars and directs. He has a great lived-in face, and his acting lives up to the descriptions of his stage performances. Rechristened *Side Street Story* by a capricious American distributor, this fine comedy passed almost unnoticed in this country. In Italian. b & w

Mimi (1935)—Gertrude Lawrence seems miscast as the heroine of this British-made version of *La Vie de Bohème* (the story but not the opera). Her artifice doesn't photograph well, and her Mimi is singularly unmagical; however, Douglas Fairbanks, Jr., is exuberantly romantic as the lover. The director, Paul L. Stein, didn't do much with the material, but even in this pokey, unimaginative version, the heartbreak and melodrama have a compulsive interest—rather like the appeal Edna Ferber built into *Show Boat*. b & w

The Mind of Mr. Soames (1970)—Science fiction and educational polemics, from England, and dreary. Can a young man (Terence Stamp) recently awakened from a 30-year coma find happiness with Nigel Davenport (strict structural educator) or Robert Vaughn (permissive educator)? With Donal Donnelly. Directed by Alan Cooke. color

Ministry of Fear (1944)—Very little of Graham Greene's mystery novel survives in this unmemorable Paramount picture, directed by Fritz Lang. As melodramas of the period go, however, this one is better made than most. Ray Milland has just been released from an insane asylum, where he was confined for murdering his wife, when he is drawn into a plot by a gang of German spies who are after defense plans. The heroine is the unimposing Marjorie Reynolds; the villain is that falsetto cutthroat Dan Duryea. b & w

Minnie and Moskowitz (1971)—John Cassavetes built this movie on a small conceit—a love affair between two people who are wildly unsuited to each other—and it doesn't work. The picture drivels on about the joys of spontaneity, while Gena Rowlands and Seymour Cassel remain embarrassingly wrong for each other. Universal. color

Miquette et sa mère (1950)—A mad, freewheeling satire of early movies, by Henri-Georges Clouzot. Louis Jouvet plays an outrageously bad actor; Danièle Delorme is the ingenue; Bourvil is the virtuous juvenile; Saturnin Fabre, the aristocratic lecher; Mireille Perrey, the mother who looks after the lecher. In French; the English subtitles purify Clouzot's dialogue. b & w

The Miracle *Il Miracolo* (1948)—This Roberto Rossellini film is itself a miracle: brief (43 minutes), utterly simple in its means, and perhaps the most fully achieved—and most sensual—of all his movies. Anna Magnani stars as the peasant woman who is convinced that the child in her belly is a new Christ child, and Federico Fellini (who also wrote the story) plays the man who put the baby there. This is the film that was the subject of a censorship case that was fought all the way up to the Supreme Court. The screenplay is by Tullio Pinelli and Rossellini; the cinematography is by Aldo Tonti. In Italian. b & w

Miracle in Milan *Miracolo a Milano* (1951)—Part social satire, part fantasy, this Vittorio De Sica film suggests a childlike view of Dostoevski's *The Idiot*. A fun-loving old lady finds a newborn baby in a cabbage patch. The baby becomes Toto the Good, the happy man who loves everyone; when he is frustrated in his desire to help people, the old lady, now an angel, comes down and gives him the power to work miracles. Toto the hero, naïve and full of love, organizes a hobo shantytown into an ideal community, but the social contradictions are ludicrously hopeless—not even magic powers can resolve them. The failure of innocence here is touchingly absurd; the film is stylized poetry, and it is like nothing else that De Sica ever did. Francesco Golissano is perfect as Toto; the heroine, Brunella Bovo, is what Chaplin's heroines should have been but weren't. The film provides a beautiful role for that great, almost legendary lady of the Italian theatre, Emma Gramatica (many, many years before, she had taken over Duse's roles and acted under the direction of D'Annunzio); as the supremely silly old woman of De Sica's fairy tale, she is as yielding and permissive as his Umberto D. is proud and stubborn. With Paolo Stoppa as the unhappy man. Cesare Zavattini adapted his own novel, *Toto Il Buono.* In Italian. b & w

The Miracle of Morgan's Creek (1944)—It's wartime, and Betty Hutton is the overenthusiastic girl who dates a soldier and produces sextuplets. This is one of Preston Sturges's surreal-slapstick-satire-conniption-fit comedies, and part of our great crude heritage. The picture was held up a year because of censorship problems, and you'll know why. With Eddie Bracken, Diana Lynn, William Demarest, Porter Hall, Esther Howard, J. Farrell MacDonald as the Sheriff, Jimmy Conlin as the Mayor, and, carried over from *The Great McGinty,* Brian Donlevy as the Governor, and Akim Tamiroff as the Boss. (Remade as *Rock-A-Bye Baby* in 1958.) Paramount. b & w

The Miracle Woman (1931)—Barbara Stanwyck gives a peerless performance as a young evangelist—a girl from a religious background who is taken over by a carny promoter (Sam Hardy) and is developed into a big-time shear-the-sheep phenomenon, with her own church. Frank Capra directed this fictionalized version of the life of Aimee Semple McPherson. It was softened by a mawkish love story: the heroine is redeemed through her unselfish love for a blind aviator (David Manners, God help us all). But it's still a beauty, well staged and handsomely lighted (Joseph Walker was the cinematographer), and with some intermittent good writing; the screenplay is by Jo Swerling, from the play *Bless You Sister,* by John Meehan and Robert Riskin. With Beryl Mercer and Russell Hopton. Columbia. b & w

The Miracle Worker (1962)— Arthur Penn, who had directed the Broadway version of William Gibson's play about Annie Sullivan and her pupil, Helen Keller, brought his two chief players with him—Anne Bancroft and Patty Duke. The play has some weaknesses, and they come through all too glaringly in the performances of Victor Jory and Inga Swenson as Helen's parents, but the dramatic force of the pitched battle between the strong-willed Annie and the equally strong, animal-willed Helen carries everything before it. Truffaut's *The Wild Child* is a more beautifully conceived picture on the same theme, but even with its imperfections and staginess this early Penn film is extraordinary. Anne Bancroft won the Academy Award as Best Actress, Patty Duke as Best Supporting Actress. United Artists. b & w

Il Miracolo, see *The Miracle*

Miracolo a Milano, see *Miracle in Milan*

The Mischief-Makers, see *Les Mistons*

Les Misérables (1935)—There are at least 10 screen versions of the Victor Hugo novel; this stuffy Hollywood production is perhaps the best known, though Richard Boleslawski, who directed, can't seem to get the plot moving. Charles Laughton's Inspector Javert is so pathologically dedicated to the strictest interpretation of the law that he fills you with fear. You can see that he feels more than fatherly love for Cosette (Rochelle Hudson) and that his persecution of Jean Valjean (Fredric March) is compulsive. Laughton plays Javert as a sadistic, repressed homosexual, a suffering man, and because of him the movie holds you (in a ghastly, masochistic way). But the look of the other actors, their makeup, and their manner of speaking are all howlingly wrong. The endlessly victimized Valjean is not very compelling: in the early scenes March wears a scraggly beard and seems to be imitating both John and Lionel Barrymore; after Valjean's spiritual rebirth, March acts impossibly virtuous, and his light voice makes it hard to take him seriously. And Cedric Hardwicke is so saintly as the Bishop who gives Valjean the silver candlesticks that you wish Valjean had bopped him over the head with them. The pacing improves as the film goes on, but not enough, and the musical score is a killer. Maybe all that needs to be said about the tone of the movie is that Valjean hears bits of the "Ave Maria" after the Bishop is kind to him. With John Beal, Frances Drake, Florence Eldridge, Jessie Ralph, John Carradine, Ferdinand Gottschalk, and Leonid Kinskey. (The child actress who plays Cosette as a little girl gives memorably awful coquettish line readings.) The screenplay is by W. P. Lipscomb; the cinematography is by Gregg Toland. United Artists. b & w

The Misfits (1961)—An erratic, sometimes personal in the wrong way, and generally unlucky picture that is often affecting. Arthur Miller wrote the screenplay (from a story he'd published in *Esquire*) about contemporary cowboys—"misfits" in the film's symbolism—who hunt down wild horses and sell them to be butchered for dog food. Marilyn Monroe is a lonely, emotionally unstable divorcée who is deeply upset by the men's determination to capture the horses. Monroe had never worked her vulnerability so ful-

somely before; the film has an uncomfortable element of fake psychodrama—she's pushy about her own sensitivity. Clark Gable plays an aging cowhand who falls in love with her, and Montgomery Clift is particularly engaging in the smaller role of a cowhand–rodeo rider with mother troubles. If there is a right tone in which to play the Miller script, the director, John Huston, doesn't find it. Much publicity attended the making of the film (in Nevada); it was plagued by delays caused by Monroe's psychiatric disorders and these delays, the heat, and the arduous actions required of Gable are widely believed to have caused his heart attack and death, just after shooting was finished. At a final cost of $4 million, it was one of the most expensive black-and-white movies made up to that time. The score is by Alex North; the cinematography is by Russell Metty. With Eli Wallach, Thelma Ritter, Kevin McCarthy, Marietta Tree, James Barton, and Estelle Winwood. United Artists–Seven Arts.

Miss Firecracker (1989)—Adapted by the fey, witty playwright Beth Henley from her 1984 play, *The Miss Firecracker Contest*, it's a farce about Southern eccentrics that's at the same time (and here's the death knell) a loving tribute to the indomitability of screwed-up, lonely dreamers. Holly Hunter is the waif Carnelle (in Yazoo City, Mississippi), who thinks that if she can just win this year's 4th of July beauty pageant—the Miss Firecracker Contest—she'll be respected. Thomas Schlamme, directing his first feature, tried for vividness, and the movie is never plain boring, but its comic pathos and Southern-gothic cuteness can grate on you. He force-feeds the audience Carnelle's desperation, her courage, and her heartbreaking pint-size gallantry. (So it's just about impossible to laugh at her.) The only element that really makes the movie worth seeing is the wild sense of fun in Tim Robbins' performance as Carnelle's courtly, impulsive cousin. (The role is a baroque contraption, and that's what Henley is good at.) Robbins and Mary Steenburgen, who plays his patrician sister, have a tingling love-hate intimacy; they're marvellous together. And he and Alfre Woodard are nuttily harmonious as love-struck clowns. Also with Ann Wedgeworth, Trey Wilson, Angela Turner, Amy Wright, and Scott Glenn. (Filmed on location in Yazoo City.) Corsair Pictures. color (See *Movie Love*.)

Miss Julie (1950)—Strindberg's passionate, relentless drama of sexual debasement, directed by Alf Sjöberg. Anita Björk is the fragile, capricious, feudal aristocrat who encourages her father's valet to seduce her; she sustains the demanding role with intensity and grace. As the valet, Ulf Palme matches her performance with a surly, sly arrogance that makes his conquest of her a true degradation. The expansion of the play over considerable lyric acreage and preceding generations is ill-advised; it tends to dissipate the confined, harrowing drama. But the performances make this a powerful version, nevertheless. In Swedish. b & w

Miss Sadie Thompson (1953)—Somerset Maugham's story "Miss Thompson" was adapted to the stage as *Rain* and opened in 1922, starring Jeanne Eagels. A movie version came out in 1928, starring Gloria Swanson as the sinner-heroine, and another in 1932, with Joan Crawford. Sadie Thompson was the prototype of many of the shady ladies in exotic locales played by Jean Harlow, Marlene Dietrich, Hedy Lamarr, Mae West, Ann Sheridan, Ava Gardner, and dozens of others. But by the 50s Maugham's durable vehicle, in which the conflict is between Sadie the honest whore and the wrathful, hypocritical Reverend Davidson, had run into Production Code censorship troubles, so in this updated-to-the-Second World War version Sadie (Rita

Hayworth) just seems a naturally high-spirited girl who likes to sing and dance and scamper about with small children. She's wandering from one island to another because she's looking for a nightclub engagement, and Davidson (José Ferrer) isn't even allowed to be a clergyman. He appears to be an insomniac spoilsport who wants her to stop entertaining the troops so he can get a night's sleep in the South Pacific hostel that shelters him, Sadie, a batch of Marines, and the sergeant (Aldo Ray) who falls in love with her. Rita Hayworth seems physically overblown, and, attempting to be sincere, she's rather dull (though she works hard to be scorching when she sings). There are several musical numbers in this Columbia Technicolor version, written by Harry Kleiner and directed by Curtis Bernhardt; in its initial showing in New York it was in 3-D, but that was dropped for the national release.

Missing (1982)—Making his first American movie, Costa-Gavras uses the same approach that American directors have often used when they wanted to teach us something: he has given his accusatory political thriller a soft, warm-and-human center. As the businessman Ed Horman, the father of a young American who has disappeared in Chile during the days after the military coup that overthrew Allende, Jack Lemmon is playing a variant of the role that Jane Fonda played in films such as *Coming Home* and *The China Syndrome*: he's the naïve, protected, non-political conservative who is radicalized (or, at least, re-educated) by what he learns. And Lemmon is so eager to have depth that he looks on a serious role as a chance for redemption; Ed arrives in Santiago to look for his son and we are stuck, observing each step in the calibrated process of his learning to distrust American and Chilean officials and coming closer to the counterculture values of his son's wife (Sissy Spacek, who's fresh and natural). Costa-Gavras's antipathy to Americans appears to be so deep-seated that he can't create American characters. The only real filmmaking is in the backgrounds: in the anxious, ominous atmosphere of a city under martial law—the sirens, the tanks, the helicopters, the feeling of abnormal silences and of random terror. With John Shea as the son, Charles (seen in flashbacks), and Melanie Mayron, Janice Rule, and Charles Cioffi. Based on the book (about an actual disappearance) by Thomas Hauser; script by the director, and Donald Stewart, and the uncredited John Nichols. Shot in Mexico. Produced by Edward and Mildred Lewis, for Universal. color (See *Taking It All In*.)

Mississippi Burning (1988)—Set in Mississippi in the summer of 1964, it opens with a fictionalized re-creation of the murder of the three civil-rights workers—James Chaney, Andrew Goodman, and Michael Schwerner—but it isn't really about the civil-rights movement. The director, Alan Parker, treats Southerners the way he treated the Turks 10 years before in *Midnight Express*. And he twists facts here as he did there, with the same apparent objective: to come up with garish forms of violence. Two F.B.I. men (Gene Hackman and Willem Dafoe) arrive to find out what happened to the three activists, and a huge manhunt is initiated. The movie hinges on the ploy that the F.B.I. men can't stop the K.K.K. from its terrorism against blacks until they swing over to vigilante tactics. And we're put in the position of applauding the F.B.I.'s dirtiest forms of intimidation. This cheap gimmick undercuts the whole civil-rights subject; it validates the terrorist methods of the Klan. Hackman is superb, and there's impressive work by Frances McDormand, Brad Dourif, Park Overall, Stephen Tobolowsky, and others. But the film is morally repugnant. The script is credited to Chris Gerolmo (Parker

says he rewrote it). Cinematography by Peter Biziou; the pulsating score that's designed to work you up for the violence is by Trevor Jones. Orion. color (See *Movie Love*.)

Mrs. Miniver (1942)—M-G-M's wartime salute to gallant England, engineered to make the audience choke up. The theme is the gentry under fire, with, at the same time, some regard for the old nobility and a smile for the quaint antics of the servants under stress. Greer Garson is the excruciatingly proper paragon-heroine, courteous and controlled in every crisis, and Walter Pidgeon is her husband. William Wyler directed this generally offensive picture, adapted from a novel by Jan Struther; shamelessly, it ends with the heroic characters singing "Onward Christian Soldiers" in a partially destroyed church. With Dame May Whitty, Richard Ney, Henry Wilcoxon, Helmut Dantine, Reginald Owen, and Peter Lawford. One of the most scandalously smug of all Academy Award winners, it took Best Picture, Director, Actress (Garson), Supporting Actress (Teresa Wright), and Cinematography (Joseph Ruttenberg). b & w

Mrs. Soffel (1984)—This love story with a Victorian madwoman heroine is based on an actual case that goes back to 1902, when the wife of the warden of the Allegheny County Jail in Pittsburgh helped two prisoners—the Biddle brothers—escape from Murderers' Row, and ran off with them. Diane Keaton has some startling moments as the sickly, frustrated, unstable Kate Soffel; Mel Gibson is superb as the passionate opportunist Ed Biddle, and Matthew Modine is very fine as his younger brother Jack. Working from a script by Ron Nyswaner, the young Australian director Gillian Armstrong doesn't lay out the reasons for what happens; she evokes them partially, suggestively. The themes don't fully emerge, but there isn't a single image that looks ordinary or stale, and the movie builds an excitement that has something to do with the fact that the flight of the Biddles with Kate in tow is deranged. (They're killing each other by staying together.) With Edward Herrmann as Soffel, Trini Alvarado, Jennie Dundas, Danny Corkill, and Harley Cross as the Soffel children, and Paula Trueman and Les Rubie as the elderly couple. Cinematography by Russell Boyd; production design by Luciana Arrighi. The prison is the one from which the trio actually fled into the night. M-G-M. color (See *State of the Art*.)

Mr. Buddwing (1966)—You can have a better time cleaning closets than watching this thing. Periodically the director Delbert Mann expiates his box-office successes (*Lover Come Back*, *That Touch of Mink*) with earnest endeavors. This one is full of TV-style clichés about how people feel when they've Sold Out. James Garner is the amnesiac hero searching for his identity, and he's not just an amnesiac—he's Everyman. Jean Simmons and Angela Lansbury are sunk in this morass; Suzanne Pleshette manages to stay afloat for a few scenes; then she, too, is submerged. Also with Jack Gilford, Katharine Ross, Raymond St. Jacques, and George Voskovec. The script, by Dale Wasserman, is based on Evan Hunter's novel *Buddwing*. M-G-M. b & w

Mr. Deeds Goes to Town (1936)—Frank Capra–style folk humor is better in slightly shorter doses (this runs almost two hours and the pace could be quicker), but there's no use fighting one's enjoyment of this homey fantasy demonstrating the triumph of small-town values over big-city cynicism. Gary Cooper is Longfellow Deeds, the sincere greeting-card poet from New England who comes to New York; Jean Arthur is the wise-acre newspaperwoman who starts out by making a public joke of him and then falls in

love with him. The film culminates in a courtroom sequence that introduced the word "pixilated" to just about every American home, and set people to examining each other's casual scribbles or sketches—their "doodles." Robert Riskin adapted the Clarence Budington Kelland *SatEvePost* story, "Opera Hat." The cast includes George Bancroft, Lionel Stander, Douglass Dumbrille, Ruth Donnelly, Emma Dunn, Raymond Walburn, Warren Hymer, Walter Catlett, Mayo Methot, and Jameson Thomas as the twitcher. Capra took the Academy Award for Best Director. Columbia. b & w

Mr. Hulot's Holiday *Les Vacances de Monsieur Hulot* (1953)—People are at their most desperate when they are working at enjoying themselves; it is Jacques Tati's peculiar comic triumph to have caught the ghastliness of a summer vacation at the beach. Fortunately, his technique is light and dry slapstick; the chronicle of human foibles and frustrations never sinks to the moist or the lovable. As director, co-author, and star, Tati is sparse, eccentric, quick. It is not until afterward—with the sweet, nostalgic music lingering—that these misadventures may take on a certain depth and poignancy. The Golden Palm, Cannes. In French. b & w

Mr. Klein (1977)—The title may sound like a Jewish detergent, but nothing gets washed away in this unsatisfying French quasi-thriller, set in Paris in 1942, during the Occupation. It's about a fashionable art dealer (Alain Delon), an Aryan, who buys up treasures from fleeing Jews and then, through what may or may not be a bureaucratic mistake, becomes confused with another Mr. Klein, a non-Aryan. Written by Franco Solinas, this is the kind of parable-thriller that has to be tight to be effective, but the director, Joseph Losey, keeps it going for over two hours. It's a classic example of his weighty emptiness; the atmosphere is heavily pregnant, with no delivery. Delon gives a serious, deliberately charmless performance; as Klein, he's stiff, almost military in bearing, with a dollar-signs-for-eyes look. We watch as this lacklustre, repellent man, with a void where his soul should be, suffers the nervous, embarrassed anxiety of trying to prove he's not Jewish; the scenes are so pointed that they poke you in the eye. (This is a solemn, medicinal variant on *Gentleman's Agreement*.) With Jeanne Moreau, Michel Lonsdale, and Juliet Berto. Cinematography by Gerry Fisher. In French. color (See *When the Lights Go Down*.)

Mr. Lucky (1943)—A wartime comedy-melodrama, with Cary Grant as a draft-dodging gambler out to bilk a charity organization. He meets a wholesome society girl (Laraine Day) and reforms. It's meant to be breezy, and Grant does get a chance to use Cockney rhyming slang, but the script is gimmicky. He looks uncomfortable in the role of a brash heel, and his mugging doesn't help. H. C. Potter directed competently; the cast includes Florence Bates, Charles Bickford, Kay Johnson, Paul Stewart, and Vladimir Sokoloff. Written by Milton Holmes and Adrian Scott. R K O. b & w

Mr. Moto Takes a Vacation (1939)—From 1937 to 1939 there were eight of these ingratiating, mildly amusing B-pictures starring Peter Lorre as the smiling, super-polite, super-smart Oriental detective with a bunny-rabbit smile. (This likable fellow—the Columbo of his day—had been thought up by John P. Marquand.) The films were scheduled on the lower half of double bills, but were frequently the better half. This is the last of the batch; in this one Mr. Moto perceives, from an examination of footprints, that a man who is taken for lame is faking. Norman Foster directed; with Joseph Schild-kraut, Lionel Atwill, and Virginia Field. 20th Century-Fox. b & w

Mr. Peabody and the Mermaid (1948)—William Powell fantasizing a romance and Ann Blyth with a lot of scales on her dress. So-so, and that's putting it generously. Audiences loved the idea, though. Irving Pichel directed; the cast includes Irene Hervey, Andrea King, and Clinton Sundberg. Based on a novel by Guy and Constance Jones; the script is by Nunnally Johnson, who was also the producer. Universal. b & w

Mister Roberts (1955)—The comic and heroic spirit went out of the famous stage success by Thomas Heggen and Joshua Logan when the play was transferred to the screen; it's a miserable piece of moviemaking—poorly paced and tearjerking. Henry Fonda recreates his stage role as the ideal modest, quietly strong American—a Second World War lieutenant who is frustrated by the petty boredom of life on a rear-line Navy cargo ship and wants to get into action. Those on board include James Cagney as the tyrannical captain, William Powell as the weary-eyed ship's doctor, and Jack Lemmon, who provides a few enlivening moments, as the laundry officer—the jokester on board. Also with Betsy Palmer, Ward Bond, and Nick Adams. Two directors were involved: John Ford and Mervyn LeRoy. Adapted by Frank Nugent and Logan; produced by Leland Hayward, for Warners. color

Mr. Smith Goes to Washington (1939)—Frank Capra's attempt to repeat the country-boy-defeating-the-city-slickers formula of *Mr. Deeds* succeeded commercially, but the picture has more of the heartfelt in it than is good for the stomach, and it goes on for over two hours. James Stewart is the naïve small-town hero sent to the Senate; Jean Arthur (whose voice is as teasing as it was in *Mr.*

Deeds) is the knowing secretary who is at first horrified by his simplicity. When the young Senator's illusions are shattered, he stages a filibuster, defeats the villains, and reëstablishes the whole government on a firm and honorable basis. No one else can balance the ups and downs of wistful sentiment and corny humor the way Capra can—but if anyone else should learn to, kill him. Sidney Buchman wrote the screenplay, from a story by Lewis R. Foster. The cast includes Claude Rains as a corrupt senator, Guy Kibbee as a venal governor, Beulah Bondi as Ma Smith, and Edward Arnold, Thomas Mitchell, Ruth Donnelly, Harry Carey, H. B. Warner, Porter Hall, Astrid Allwyn, and Eugene Pallette, who gets stuck in a phone booth. Members of the U.S. Senate were so outraged about the picture (and for the wrong reasons) that there was actually talk of a retaliatory bill against the movie interests; the storm blew over when it became apparent that the public loved the film. Music by Dmitri Tiomkin; montage by Slavko Vorkapich. Columbia. b & w

Les Mistons *The Mischief-Makers* (1957)—In this 27-minute film, five little French boys seek to become members of a courtship: they follow the lovers (Gérard Blain and Bernadette Lafont), spy on them, jeer at them. François Truffaut's first feature film, the 1959 *The 400 Blows*, is a child's cry of protest against a world black with adult injustice; this earlier film is a poetic reverie: the children look at the adult world greedily but contemptuously, and the adult world pays no heed. For an experimental work, it shows a marvellous command of sensual image and atmosphere (the opening bicycle ride, for example), but to Americans the total conception may seem fearfully sensitive and precious. The English commentary is full of high-flown romantic nostalgia for the first confused stirrings of sexual desire—"the fate and the priv-

ilege of the flesh" sort of thing—with references to mythology, rites, divinity, etc. Based on the short story "Virginales" by Maurice Pons. b & w

Mitsou (1957)—Proust wrote Colette that he had wept a little over her love story, *Mitsou*; the film version, directed by Jacqueline Audry, achieves some of the story's absurdly touching quality. The milieu is the grotesquely patriotic music-hall life of World War I, where Mitsou (Danièle Delorme) performs happily, under the protection of a financier, Fernand Gravet, until she meets a snobbish young officer (François Guérin). Gaby Morlay plays Mitsou's mother, and guest stars, such as Gabrielle Dorziat, are sprinkled through the production. In French. color

Moby Dick (1930)—John Barrymore's second Ahab; he had also appeared in a silent version called *The Sea Beast*, with Dolores Costello as the beautiful girl waiting on shore. In this talkie remake, directed by Lloyd Bacon, the girl is played by Joan Bennett. (Dolores Costello had become Mrs. Barrymore and was pregnant.) It should be explained that in both these versions Ahab's driven character is accounted for by the existence of a beautiful girl who really did love him but whom he misunderstood. The first version was, at least, excitingly romantic; this talkie is much less so—Barrymore is 48 and isn't wildly in love with his leading lady (as he quite clearly was in the first), and he's working with a whale that resembles a vast mattress. J. Grubb Alexander did the (very loose) adaptation from Melville. With Lloyd Hughes. Warners. b & w

Moby Dick (1956)—It's an impressive attempt to be faithful to Melville, and the battles with the elements (and the whale) were so difficult to stage that the footage was shot over a two-year period, while the cost of the production rose to almost $5 million. Yet for all his dedication to this ambitious project, the director, John Huston, must not have been able to keep up his energy level; at times, his work seems surprisingly perfunctory. The film begins imaginatively, with Richard Basehart as Ishmael going down to the shore, and has all kinds of stirring things in it—Orson Welles' reading of Father Mapple's wonderful sermon about Jonah; finely textured cinematography by Oswald Morris, which has the look of steel engravings and calls up suggestions of Coleridge; exciting sequences; some great rhetoric; and a general display of Huston's pyrotechnics. But Gregory Peck—the least demonic of leading men—is a disastrous Ahab; bearded, he looks like a stock-company Lincoln. And the movie doesn't add up to anything approaching the novel; it lacks the unity, the rhythm, the poetry, the mind at work. There are still more than enough reasons to see it. Ray Bradbury and Huston wrote the screenplay. With Leo Genn as Starbuck, Friedrich Ledebur as Queequeg, Royal Dano as Elijah, and Bernard Miles, James Robertson Justice, Harry Andrews, and Mervyn Johns. Shot off the coasts of Wales and the Canary Islands, and on location in Ireland, as well as in a London studio. (This was the third version; both earlier ones—1926 and 1930—starred John Barrymore.) Warners. color

The Model and the Marriage Broker (1951)—George Cukor directed this New York–set comedy the year after he had his big success with *Born Yesterday* but practically no one went to see it. The dumb-sounding title may have scared people off. Also there's nothing terribly new or original about the story, and no dominating, star performances—nothing to get the picture talked about. It's entertaining, though. Thelma Ritter, who plays the marriage broker, doesn't show any new sides, but she's awfully good at her hard-bitten specialty, and Jeanne Crain is very likable as the model. With Scott Brady, Michael O'Shea, Zero Mostel, Dennie Moore, Frank Fontaine, and Jay C. Flippen. Written by Charles Brackett, Walter Reisch, and Richard Breen. Produced by Brackett, for 20th Century-Fox. b & w

Model Shop (1969)—Making his first American movie, Jacques Demy takes the heroine of his first film, *Lola*, and brings her to Los Angeles. Lola is again played by Anouk Aimée, and Demy indicates that she's the same woman at a later stage of her life, but she has an entirely different character. The young Lola was an open-hearted, effervescent cabaret dancer; the new Lola is imperious and refined, and Anouk Aimée is glamorously dull. Supposedly stranded in L.A. and working in a "model shop" (i.e., posing for men who take "dirty" pictures), she appears in stunning, simple white and drives a long white car, and she has become a high priestess of wisdom. The young architect-hero (Gary Lockwood), who yearns to be creative, needs the will to go on; he obtains it from this mysterious *dea ex machina* in white. There's something ingratiating about Demy's romantic and lyrical approach to L.A., but his way of looking at American youth is inane. He doesn't have the toughness of mind to see anything funny in the hero's girlfriend who wants him to commit himself to life by letting her have a baby, or to see anything ironic in the rock musicians' casting themselves and selling themselves in the life style of sweet Jesus. The movie is very pretty, but numbingly superficial. With Alexandra Hay, Carol Cole, and Severn Darden. Cinematography by Michel Hugo; music direction by Marty Paich. Written by Demy, with English dialogue by Adrien Joyce (Carol Eastman). color (See *Going Steady*.)

Modern Times (1936)—After *City Lights*, which was silent, with a musical accompaniment and sound effects, Charlie Chaplin was absent from the screen for five years; he returned in triumph with this rambunctious comedy in which he still doesn't speak, although he uses background sounds and, as a singing waiter in a crowded cabaret, he does a wonderful jabberwocky patter song that you can't get out of your head. (It is, of course, a demonstration of how unnecessary words are.) Influenced by René Clair's *À nous la liberté*, Chaplin opens the film with a satire on the dehumanizing effects of technology (the machines speak—they whir and pound and screech), but Chaplin is far more basic and sadistic than Clair. As a worker on an assembly line, Charlie the tramp is run through the gears of a huge machine and is force-fed by an experimental, time-saving contraption that splashes soup in his face and shoves corn on the cob into his mouth. He can't take a second off work to scratch himself without turning the whole plant into chaos; after a long stretch of tightening screws, he becomes a robot who runs to tighten the buttons he sees on women. The picture is about the social disorders of the 30s, and there are clashes between the unemployed and the police, and a gag about a Communist demonstration, yet it's one of the happiest and most lighthearted of the Chaplin pictures—partly because his new leading lady, Paulette Goddard, playing a character listed as "a Gamin," has a beautiful grin and a bouncy, outgoing personality. And with the use of more sound, Chaplin seems to drop some of his pathos; this picture doesn't pull at your heartstrings—it has the spirit of a good vaudeville show, and the tramp doesn't lose out at the end (he gets his gamin). Produced, written, and directed by Chaplin, who also takes credit for the music. With Henry Bergman as the café proprietor, Chester Conklin as the mechanic, and Hank Mann as one of the burglars. Released through United Artists. b & w

Mogambo (1953)—Clark Gable as a mighty hunter in Africa, in a remake of *Red Dust*, which he'd starred in 21 years before; Ava Gardner plays the old Jean Harlow role—the wisecracking, tough broad—and Grace Kelly does her hot-ice bit as a ladylike prig (the old Mary Astor role). Gable certainly doesn't have the animal magnetism he had in the earlier version, but when Gardner and Kelly bitch at each other, doing battle for him, they're vastly entertaining anyway. (Gardner has never seemed happier.) The director, John Ford, got a little carried away with African wildlife (*Red Dust* was faster and funnier), but this sexual melodrama never takes itself too seriously. John Lee Mahin revamped his earlier script; the color cinematography is by Robert Surtees and Freddie Young. With Donald Sinden, Denis O'Dea, and Laurence Naismith. M-G-M.

Moi Universiteti, see *My Universities*

The Molly Maguires (1970)—Sean Connery, Richard Harris, and Samantha Eggar in an elegiac movie about labor violence among the Irish immigrant coal miners in Pennsylvania in the 1870s. It was clearly a labor of love for the director, Martin Ritt. The cinematography, by James Wong Howe, which stresses abstract and geometric values, is integral to the stylized plan, and the handsome use of space gives the movie an imposing solidity. But we never get any explanation of the strategy of the miners who are dynamiting the trains carrying the coal they have just mined; how will this sabotage get them the living wage they need? Instead, we see them martyred after their secret organization has been infiltrated by a company spy. Playing this wily, smart, weak man, Richard Harris has a volatile edginess that draws us into the spy's divided spirit and contributes most of the suspense. Connery gives a sure and intelligent performance as the leader of the saboteurs, even though it's an almost unwritten role and we never discover what's in his head or how he thinks his explosions will feed his family. Samantha Eggar is surprisingly forceful as the girl who becomes the fiancée of the stool pigeon. Ritt takes his time in building the atmosphere and introducing the people, and lets an image stay on the screen until we take it in. The movie is impressive yet lifeless, and there are some very bad scenes (Frank Finlay, as a sadistic cop, talking to Harris; the Judas routine at the end). The script by Walter Bernstein isn't up to the look of the film, and the music by Henry Mancini is so repetitive that by the second hour his few themes are an assault. With Anthony Zerbe, Bethel Leslie, Art Lund, Philip Bourneuf, Frances Heflin, and Malachy McCourt. Paramount. color (See *Deeper into Movies*.)

The Moment of Truth *Il Momento della Verità* (1965)—The Italian director Francesco Rosi's working title for this superb, angry film was simply *Spain*. He takes the conventional *Blood and Sand* story and stripping it of romance and sentiment and melodrama, makes it the classic organic story of Spanish society, and part of the great neo-realist theme of migration from rural poverty to urban poverty, dislocation, and corruption. A boy leaves the Andalusian farm so that he won't have to live an animal's life like his father, but the city is no better. The lure of bullfighting is the money to be made at it: "For a million I'd wait for the bull with open arms." Those who talk about "sacred art" are just bull-slingers; it's an "art" like prizefighting for an ambitious American black with no capital but his body and nerve, and what's "sacred" about it is the risk of death. The bravado of "courage" is your trade, it's the self you sell. What you keep for yourself is fear. Rosi and his great cinematographer, Gianni Di Venanzo, used documentary techniques, following the young bullfighter Miguelin from city to city, shooting silent with hand-held cameras, in color. The approach is a kind of dramatic journalism: the footage has looseness and freedom and immediacy. Near the end there is an image of Miguelin alone on the screen with the large head of a bull: it's like a time between wars. With Linda Christian. In Italian. (See *Kiss Kiss Bang Bang*.)

Il Momento della Verità, see *The Moment of Truth*

Mommie Dearest (1981)—The best that can be said about this jumbled scrapbook of Joan Crawford's life from her middle years to the end is that it doesn't seem to get in the way of its star, Faye Dunaway, who gives a startling, ferocious performance. It's deeper than an impersonation; she turns herself into Joan Crawford, all right, but she's more Faye Dunaway than ever. Her performance is extravagant—it's operatic and full of primal anger. She invests the role with so much power and suffering that the camp horror scenes—the nocturnal rampages—transcend camp. (These destruction orgies were the most talked-about episodes in the book by Crawford's adopted daughter, Christina, on which the movie is based.) Alone and self-mesmerized, Dunaway plays the entire film on emotion. With Mara Hobel, Diana Scarwid, Steve Forrest, Howard Da Silva, Rutanya Alda, Jocelyn Brando, Harry Goz, Michael Edwards, Priscilla Pointer, and Belita Moreno. Produced by Frank Yablans; directed by Frank Perry; the screenplay is credited to Yablans, Perry, Tracy Hotchner, and Robert Getchell. Paramount. color (See *Taking It All In*.)

Mon Oncle (1958)—One often appreciates what Jacques Tati is trying to do more than what he actually brings off. His target is the depersonalization of modern life—not so much the mechanization that René Clair satirized in *À nous la liberté* and Chaplin in *Modern Times*, but the sterile, tasteless tedium that modern hygienic design has produced. There are genuinely inventive moments: the little boys gambling on whether passers-by will fall into their lamp-post trap; the old man directing a chauffeur who is trying to park an inordinately long car; the willful garage doors; the wonderful use of the modern functional house as a cartooned face, so that heads at the circular windows become eyes looking out. But the moments are intermittent, and a fundamental miscasting confuses the issues: shouldn't the unemotional, gawky, butterfingered Tati be playing the plastics manufacturer rather than the warm, friendly uncle? With Jean-Pierre Zola, Lucien Frégis, and Alain Bécourt. In French. color

Mon Oncle Antoine, see *My Uncle Antoine*

Mona Lisa (1986)—Directed by the Irish novelist turned moviemaker Neil Jordan, the whole movie has some of the potency of cheap music that's represented by the title song (in Nat King Cole's 1950 recording). The short, chunky Bob Hoskins is tremendous as a onetime petty crook, just emerged from prison, who's a decent, simple guy; given the job of chauffeuring a black call girl (Cathy Tyson) on her nightly rounds, he falls in love with her. Haughty, uncommunicative, and a head taller than he, she sets him to searching for a friend she's worried about—a blond 15-year-old heroin addict. As he makes his way through the strip joints and whores' hangouts, he's sickened by the way the girls are mistreated, and he sees that his old boss (Michael Caine) is in the rotten thick of it. The movie is lurid in a beautiful way. Most of it was shot on location in London and Brighton, but they don't look merely realistic; Jordan

shows a gift for making the emotional atmosphere visual, and vice versa. And the way he uses baroque touches and the clichés of old thrillers they become part of a fluid, enjoyable texture, a melodramatic impasto with an expressive power of its own—a romanticism that pulls you along. Making her film début in the title role, the lovely young Tyson is as mysteriously stirring to us as she is to the chauffeur. Caine gives a brilliantly scary performance; he's believably rotten, just as Hoskins' little mug is believably kind yet violent. With Robbie Coltrane as Hoskins' burly old pal, Clarke Peters as the sadistic black pimp, and Zoe Nathenson as Hoskins' daughter. Script by Jordan and David Leland; cinematography by Roger Pratt; score by Michael Kamen. A HandMade Films Release through Island Pictures. color (See *Hooked*.)

Mondo Cane (1963)—The Italian documentary-maker Gualtiero Jacopetti and his associates are actually documentary fakers: they set out to demonstrate how uncivilized the world is, and then fake the proofs. There's no shortage of available evidence, but they prefer titillating, shocking frauds. The grossness of the picture works to the advantage of the filmmakers, since it seems almost naïve to attack it. color.

Monkey Business (1931)—The four Marx Brothers as anarchic stowaways on an ocean liner who get involved with bootleggers and Thelma Todd. The first of their films written directly for the screen (by S. J. Perelman, Will B. Johnstone, and Arthur Sheekman). Norman McLeod directed this heavenly, corny nonsense, which features such songs as "You Brought a New Kind of Love to Me" and "When I Take My Sugar to Tea." Paramount. b & w

Monkey Business (1952)—Grating screwball farce. As a middle-aged professor who drinks a rejuvenating potion, Cary Grant is required to act frolicsomely juvenile; it's painful to see him playing cowboys and Indians with a bunch of kids. As his wife, who also swigs the potion, Ginger Rogers is reduced to thumb-sucking infantilism, and she gives a nightmarishly busy performance. This boisterous, labored whimsey, which also features Marilyn Monroe and Charles Coburn, was scripted by Ben Hecht, I. A. L. Diamond, and Charles Lederer from a story by Harry Segall, and was directed by Howard Hawks, for 20th Century-Fox. With Hugh Marlowe, Larry Keating, Esther Dale, and George Winslow, the little boy with the foghorn voice. b & w

Monsieur Ripois Also known as *Knave of Hearts.* (1954)—René Clément's original and amusing study of a compulsive seducer, a Frenchman (Gérard Philipe) at work in London on a succession of English girls, was made in two versions—French and English. *Knave of Hearts* so incensed the English that "nasty" and "disgusting" appeared in almost all reviews. (*The Daily Mirror* cried, "a story about a French wolf who comes to prey on our girls.") The reason for this hostility is the satiric treatment of English morals: the shallow French roué has a knack for spotting women's weaknesses, and he seduces the English girls (who take themselves fairly seriously) by appealing to each one's aspirations and fantasies. The English may also have resented the photographic invasion of their urban ugliness by Oswald Morris's concealed cameras; the movie catches the pubs, restaurants, busses, and rush hours of a gray and grubby city which was not visible in English movies until later films like *Room at the Top*, *Look Back in Anger*, and *Saturday Night and Sunday Morning* broke down English reserve. Roman Vlad contributes a witty score with a little theme for each mistress (Joan Greenwood, Margaret Johnston, Valerie Hobson, Natasha Parry, et al.). The script (by

Raymond Queneau and others) provides some subtle mockery of the Don Juan type; expert at playing roles to please women, the Frenchman cannot win love in his own character. (In the U.S., the film was cut and released under two titles—*Lovers, Happy Lovers* and *Lover Boy*.) b & w

Monsieur Verdoux (1947)—Chaplin as a Parisian bank clerk—a dapper Bluebeard—in a comedy with attempted Shavian ironies. This private entrepreneur who charms rich widows and murders them for their money feels guiltless, and contrasts what he does with what governments do in war. "Numbers sanctify," he says. Chaplin is more talented at carrying out his pantomime bits than in the talky, anti-war passages, which are meant to be complexly unsettling and come across as dubious and even rather lamebrained. There are also static sentimental interludes about Verdoux's devotion to his virtuous wife (Mady Correll). The casting is not all it might be, with the glorious exception of Martha Raye as Annabella, who is so full of low-comedy life that, despite all Verdoux's calculations, and one attempt after another, he fails to kill her. With Isobel Elsom, Marilyn Nash, William Frawley, Virginia Brissac, Robert Lewis, Fritz Leiber, and a glimpse of Edna Purviance. Produced, written, and directed by Chaplin, with Robert Florey and Wheeler Dryden as his assistant directors. United Artists. b & w

Monsieur Vincent (1947)—Pierre Fresnay's performance as the desperately compassionate Vincent de Paul gives extraordinary feeling to Jean Anouilh's sensitive, lucid scenario. Though de Paul's very considerable intellectual gifts are minimized, this diminution is preferable to the usual solution of having an actor mutter platitudes while the other actors gasp, How brilliant! The character is simplified, but the emotions—the revulsion and horror at poverty, misery, cruelty—come through without mawkishness. Directed by Maurice Cloche; cinematography by Claude Renoir. The cast includes Aimé Clariond, Jean Debucourt, and Gabrielle Dorziat. In French. b & w

Monte Walsh (1970)—Taciturn, funereal Western, with Lee Marvin, Jeanne Moreau, Mitch Ryan, and Jack Palance starving and suffering. It's so solemn about the bygone days of the cowboys that the elegiac intentions are not polluted by suspense and the characters are given almost nothing to say. A melancholy hour passes before you discover that there's actually going to be some sort of story, and then all the principal characters die off except Monte (Marvin), who is left a senile derelict, talking to his horse. Bo Hopkins, G. D. Spradlin, Matt Clark, Allyn Ann McLerie, John McLiam, and Jim Davis are among the actors stranded in this one. William A. Fraker directed, from a screenplay by Lukas Heller and David Z. Goodman, based on the novel by Jack Schaefer. The handsome cinematography is by David M. Walsh; the music is by John Barry. National General. color (See *Deeper into Movies*.)

The Moon in the Gutter *La Lune dans le caniveau* (1983)—Coming right after Jean-Jacques Beineix's sparkling, gift-wrapped *Diva*, this oppressive romantic tragedy, in which Gérard Depardieu plays a stevedore obsessed with memories of his dead sister, may be a shock, but it's the kind of excruciatingly silly movie that only a talented director can make. (Hacks don't leave common sense this far behind.) Beineix is celebrating the poetry of the movies, which for him is the poetry of artificiality. Nastassia Kinski is posed like Hedy Lamarr in *Algiers*; she's the unattainable—the moon that shines on poor Depardieu down there in his Brando T-shirt in the *film-noir* gutter. The actors are helpless,

because the movie isn't about their characters' emotions—it's about Beineix's swooning response to the earlier movie stars that they're standing in for. Beineix can sometimes engage us by his visual flourishes—abstractions of men at work, blood that's like spilled fingernail polish, a cathedral like a witch's palace. But it's a suffocating, empty movie in thick, nocturnal color, and with glamour music that's an exaggeration of Hollywood's old soaring and slurping scores—the kind that make you wince during revival showings. With Victoria Abril as hot little Bella, who's like a parody of generations of sensual, jealous spitfires, and Bertice Reading, Dominique Pinon, Vittorio Mezzogiorno, and Milena Vukotić. Based on the 1953 American novel by David Goodis; cinematography by Philippe Rousselot; art direction by Hilton McConnico. In French. (See *State of the Art*.)

Moonraker (1979)—The previous James Bond film (*The Spy Who Loved Me*, 1977) had been a triumph of design, choreographed action, and self-parody; this one doesn't look too bad, but it has no snap, no tension. It's an exhausted movie; maybe the director, Lewis Gilbert, and the production designer, Ken Adam, just couldn't work up the charge they gave to the earlier film. Roger Moore is dutiful and passive as Bond; his clothes are neatly pressed and he shows up for work, like an office manager who is turning into dead wood but hanging on to collect his pension. As the scientist-heroine, Lois Chiles is so enervated she barely reacts to the threat of the end of the world. And as Drax the industrialist, a neo-Hitler with a city in outer space and plans to create his own master race, Michel Lonsdale walks through impassively. The only zest is shown by Richard Kiel, who returns as Jaws; this time, he falls in love. The picture is big, though. (It cost more than twice as much as its predecessor—

and even allowing for inflation, that still means a huge rise in expenditure.) And it was extremely successful. The script is by Christopher Wood; the cinematography is by Jean Tournier. With Desmond Llewelyn as "Q," Corinne Clery, and Blanche Ravalec as Dolly. Produced by Albert R. Broccoli; United Artists. color

The Moon's Our Home (1936)—A thoroughly frivolous farce. Those who've seen it aren't likely to have forgotten the gag of the wedding night when the groom (Henry Fonda) has a violent reaction to the perfume that his bride (Margaret Sullavan) has doused herself with. Fonda plays a celebrity explorer-author; Sullavan plays a socialite movie star, high-strung, and hot-tempered. The film's premise is that these two world-famous (and self-infatuated) people meet and marry without either knowing who the other is. This may seem like the worst kind of madcap comedy (it's taken from a *Cosmopolitan Magazine* novel by Faith Baldwin), but after a script was written (by Isabel Dawn and Boyce DeGaw), Dorothy Parker and her husband Alan Campbell were called in to do a rewrite, and they did some near-ribald improvisation. There's something else that works to the picture's advantage: Fonda and Sullavan had actually been married and divorced. When they fight in the movie, you feel you're hearing their real battling rhythms. And when they're romantic, that has a real pulse to it, too. They look great: his long coats emphasize his height; her sleek dresses and fur pieces emphasize her tiny waist and narrow hips. (At times she seems to be parodying Katharine Hepburn.) Charles Butterworth is wonderfully mild as Sullavan's high-society suitor, and the other featured players have some good pungent scenes, because most of the characters surrounding the celebrities are wise to their narcissistic games. With Margaret Hamilton, Walter Brennan, Beulah

Bondi, Henrietta Crosman, Dorothy Stickney, and Lucien Littlefield. Directed by William A. Seiter; produced by Walter Wanger, for Paramount. b & w

Moonstruck (1987)—A rose-tinted black comedy, with its own special lushness. Cher is devastatingly funny and sinuous and beautiful as a widowed bookkeeper who lives with her Italian-American family in a big old brownstone in Brooklyn. When the bookkeeper and her fiancé's brother, a baker (Nicolas Cage), start lusting for one another, a fairy-tale full moon lights up the movie. And when you see that the whole cast of family members are involved in libidinal confusions the opera-buffa structure can make you feel close to deliriously happy. Cage is a wonderful romantic clown: he can look stupefied while he smolders. And the director, Norman Jewison, working from John Patrick Shanley's script, stylizes the ethnic performances given by the husky-voiced Olympia Dukakis, the great, leering Julie Bovasso, Vincent Gardenia, Danny Aiello, John Mahoney, Anita Gillette, Louis Guss, Feodor Chaliapin, and Nada Despotovich. The picture is slender, but it's an original: its mockery is a giddy homage to our desire for grand passion. Cinematography by David Watkin; musical score by Dick Hyman; editing by Lou Lombardo. Shot in Brooklyn, Manhattan, and Toronto. Academy Awards: Best Actress (Cher), Supporting Actress (Dukakis), Original Screenplay. M-G-M. color (See *Hooked*.)

More Than a Miracle *C'Era una Volta* Literally "Once Upon a Time." (1967)— Francesco Rosi's romantic fairy-tale fantasy starring Sophia Loren and Omar Sharif has some of the magical silliness and sweetness of De Sica's *Miracle in Milan* and the Alexander Korda production of *The Thief of Bagdad*. It's set in 17th-century Southern Italy (dominated by the Spanish), where a Prince (Sharif), refusing to marry one of the seven eligible princesses, goes forth on his white stallion and finds a lusciously ripe peasant girl (Loren). This splashy and beautiful comic tale is set in forests and yellow fields and at locations that include the 14th-century monastery of San Lorenzo at Padula, the 15th-century town of Bracciano, and the ruins of the 4th-century Circus of Maxentius. With Dolores Del Rio as Sharif's mother, Georges Wilson as the palace chef, and Leslie French as the flying monk, Brother Joseph. An Italian-French co-production, released here in English; the dubbing is often both funny and charming, especially when the warty old witches speak in voices that seem to come from another planet. (Some of them were actually Italian peasant men dressed as women, and some were elderly English actresses.) Written by Rosi, Tonino Guerra, and others, based on a story by Guerra; cinematography by Pasqualino De Santis. Produced by Carlo Ponti; released by M-G-M. color

The More the Merrier (1943)—It has a memorable, summer-night love scene: the very proper government-worker heroine (Jean Arthur) reluctantly sits down on the front steps of her apartment building with the inventor-hero (Joel McCrea); they begin to neck, and she's embarrassed by what she feels. It's lovely: sexy and funny. The film is set in Washington, D.C., during the Second World War; the housing shortage results in their becoming part of an innocent *ménage à trois* with Charles Coburn, an elderly businessman who enjoys playing Cupid. Directed by George Stevens, this hit comedy is lively and well paced, but the fun is too often forced, and Jean Arthur overdoes her adorably prim act. McCrea, though, makes it all look easy; he's casually sophisticated, and as usual, he serves his co-stars, gets his laughs, and never hogs attention. Written by many hands (Rob-

ert Russell, Frank Ross, Richard Flournoy, Lewis R. Foster); with Bruce Bennett and Richard Gaines. Columbia. (Remade in 1966 as *Walk, Don't Run*, with Cary Grant in the Coburn role.) b & w

Morgan! Called *Morgan—A Suitable Case for Treatment* in England. (1966)—Morgan (David Warner) is a slightly crazy left-wing artist who is losing his beautiful, well-heeled wife (Vanessa Redgrave). In his fantasy life, he is King Kong. So when he's frustrated and upset he wears a gorilla suit; it's symbolic, of course—Morgan is the misfit as hero, and he's a childlike romantic rebel, anarchist, outsider, nonconformist. Directed by Karel Reisz, from David Mercer's adaptation of his own TV play, this satirical tragicomedy often seems to be out of control as it teeters along, sometimes presenting its hero as cute and funny, other times as tragic and in pain. The film's grotesque and discordant elements seemed to touch a nerve for American college students in the late 60s: Morgan was mad in a pop way—it was madness as the ultimate irresponsibility for the rebel, the only sanity for those who see what the "responsible" people supposedly did to the world. The picture came out just when these attitudes were becoming popular—when the counterculture was taking shape. With Robert Stephens and Irene Handl. Music by Johnny Dankworth. b & w

The Morning After (1986)—Jane Fonda gives a raucous-voiced, down-in-the-dirty performance that has some of the charge of her Bree in *Klute*, back in 1971. As Alex, a former screen actress whose career blew up in scandal, she still has her face and her figure, but she has a hard, tortured look under her fluffy blond hair, and she drinks so much she has blackouts. (Fonda has said that she modelled the character on the starlet Gail Russell, who, at 36, was found dead in her apartment, among empty liquor bottles.) In the opening scene, Alex wakes up in bed Thanksgiving morning with a man she can't remember even meeting; he has a knife sticking out of his heart. The director, Sidney Lumet, keeps things efficiently paced, but he coasts for too long on Fonda's work and on the polished bitchiness of the dialogue; he doesn't build the thriller elements that would give the film the kick it needs, and he fails to establish a couple of the important characters (played by Raul Julia and Diane Salinger, both miscast). The solid Jeff Bridges, who plays opposite Fonda, could be a good foil for her flare-ups, and if the relationship had been developed maybe the two would be more vivid and resonate a little, and would survive what was happening around them. But all the forced, phony elements come together at the end and bring the picture down. The script is attributed to James Hicks (a pseudonym for James Cresson); others who worked on it include David Rayfiel and Jay Presson Allen. 20th Century-Fox. color (See *Hooked*.)

Morning Glory (1933)—Katharine Hepburn got her first Academy Award for her performance as "Eva Lovelace"—the name taken by a girl who comes to New York obsessively determined to become a great actress. It's a strange, ambivalent study of that lying-cheating kind of determination, taken from a play by Zoë Akins and directed by Lowell Sherman. With Douglas Fairbanks, Jr., and Adolphe Menjou. (The picture was remade in 1957 as *Stage Struck*, starring Susan Strasberg.) R K O. b & w

Morocco (1930)—Marlene Dietrich's first Hollywood film, and perhaps Josef von Sternberg's most effective piece of romantic mythmaking. It's enchantingly silly, full of soulful grand passions, drifting cigarette smoke, and a few too many pictorial shots of the Foreign Legion marching this way and that. Dietrich is Amy Jolly, a mysterious woman, with a past she won't talk about, who arrives in Morocco and gets a job singing in a rough café. You feel that she's a real performer here: when she comes out to sing, her energy level soars. For her first number, she appears in top hat, white tie, and tails; a Legionnaire (Gary Cooper) shushes the raucous, jeering crowd. She sings, in a deep, harsh voice, and then, in perhaps the most daring moment in all of her pictures, she eyes a woman at a table, takes a flower from her, kisses the startled woman on the mouth, and turning, tosses the flower to Cooper. When, in a feather boa and a short leotard that show off her long sleek legs, she sings "What am I bid for my apples?", the Legionnaire knows just what to offer. Dietrich is at the peak of her naughty perfection—cool effrontery and a hint of amusement. The contrast of her high, rounded forehead and Madonna-like face with her low, uncouth voice provides an extraordinary sexual charge; her torso is sturdier than in her later movies, and her upper arms look full and strong, yet her face seems more ethereal than perhaps at any other time. Still the German Dietrich—not the almost abstract, international Dietrich she later became—she's charming throughout, and she and Cooper look great together. This is the movie with the classically giddy, ridiculously satisfying romantic finish: she says goodbye to the rich, kind, worldly Adolphe Menjou, who loves her, kicks off her high heels, and follows Cooper and the departing Legionnaires into the desert. With Juliette Compton, Ullrich Haupt, and Eve Southern; one could do with less of the eavesdropping café owner (Paul Porcasi). Jules Furthman wrote the script, based on the novel *Amy Jolly*, by Benno Vigny. The cinematography is by Lee Garmes, with additional work by Lucien Ballard; the songs are by Leo Robin and Karl Hajos. Paramount. b & w

Moscow on the Hudson (1984)—Robin Williams as a Russian sax player who defects, in Paul Mazursky's wonderful comedy about a tragedy—about going away forever, about not being able to go home. The defection takes place in a sound-stage version of Bloomingdale's, and the plot radiates from this temple of the mouth-watering temptations of capitalist decadence. It doesn't take long before the sax player discovers the isolation and paranoia of living in New York. The brutality of the city confuses him; in Russia, he says, he knew who the enemy was. Imaginative and mellow, this movie displays Mazursky's distinctive funky lyricism at its best. With Maria Conchita Alonso, a beauty who's an unself-conscious cutup, and Alejandro Rey as a Cuban lawyer, Cleavant Derricks as a security guard, Elya Baskin as a Russian circus clown, and Mazursky himself as a Florida tourist named Dave. The film's comic rhythm (though not its mood) falters in the last third. The script is by the director and Leon Capetanos; the cinematography is by Don McAlpine. Columbia. color (See *State of the Art*.)

The Most Dangerous Game (1932)—An amusing classic suspense melodrama; the plot was used several times, but this version, directed by Irving Pichel and Ernest Schoedsack, is the most entertaining. Leslie Banks (with his schizoid face—one half suave Englishman, the other half twisted and with suggestions of exotic evil) is the mad hunter who stalks human prey, and Joel McCrea is is target. Fay Wray does her usual charming terrified heroine. R K O. b & w

Mother *Mat'* (1926)—Frequently selected by critics as one of the greatest films of all time. Pudovkin's masterpiece, based on Maxim Gorky's novel, which is set during the 1905 revolution, is not overtly political; it gives an epic sense of that revolution through the emotions of the participants, and sweeps one along by its fervor and a brilliant and varied use of the medium. Vera Baranovskaya plays the mother who is tricked by the police into betraying her son (Nikolai Batalov). Pudovkin (unusual among the great Russian directors for his interest in acting) himself plays the officer who interrogates her. Silent. b & w

The Mother and the Whore *La Maman et la putain* (1973)—This controversial 3-hour-and-30-minute film, produced, written, and directed by Jean Eustache, is about the aging young of the Left Bank, who live in an atmosphere of apocalyptic narcissism. It is about the disaffection of those who are stranded in a confusion of personal freedom and social hopelessness. Eustache's method resembles the static randomness of the Warhol-Morrissey pictures, but the randomness here is not a matter of indifference; it's a conscious goal. The actors—Jean-Pierre Léaud, Bernadette Lafont, Françoise Lebrun, Isabelle Weingarten, and Jacques Renard—were not allowed to deviate from the script, yet Eustache wants the look of chance. He tries to push viewers beyond patience—to rub our noses in his view of reality. Implicitly, he is saying, "I'm going to show you more of the tormented soul than anybody has ever shown you before." This soul belongs to a poor young nurse named Veronika, and the picture stands or falls on the viewer's attitude toward her recital of her sexual humiliations and her loathing of sex without love. In French. b & w (See *Reeling*.)

Mouchette (1966)—Robert Bresson has made several films of such sobriety that while some people find them awesomely beautiful, other people find sitting through them like taking a whipping and watching every stroke coming. *Mouchette*, from a Bernanos novel, is about a lonely, mistreated 14-year-old girl who commits suicide. Cinematography by Ghislain Cloquet. In French. b & w

Moulin Rouge (1953)—It's hard to believe this was made by the John Huston who made *The Maltese Falcon*. That was lean; this is fatty (and soft at the center). It's a biography of Toulouse-Lautrec (José Ferrer, standing on his knees in tricky boots), with visual re-creations that are often extraordinary. But the script, by Anthony Veiller and Huston, based on Pierre LaMure's book, has been conceived in a deluxe style and takes itself very seriously. It's a pompous movie. Ferrer speaks with a weird, rolling accent and recites his epigrams and his over-written lines as if they were well memorized. With Colette Marchand, Suzanne Flon, and Zsa Zsa Gabor as Jane Avril, singing the famous Georges Auric theme song in a dubbed voice. (Gabor is radiantly pretty, though her gestures while she pretends to sing are idiotic.) Ferrer also plays Lautrec's father—a tall, unfeeling aristocrat. And the cast includes Katherine Kath as La Goulue, Christopher Lee as Gauguin, and Claude Nollier, Muriel Smith, Mary Clare, Jill Bennett, and Peter Cushing. Oswald Morris was the cinematographer; Eliot Elisofon was the color consultant; Paul Sheriff was the art director; the costumes are by Marcel Vertès. Filmed in France. A Romulus Films Production, released by United Artists.

Mourir à Madrid, see *To Die in Madrid*

Mourir d'aimer, see *To Die of Love*

Mourning Becomes Electra (1947)—O'Neill's 6-hour Freudian-American Greek tragedy accumulates power on the stage, but it merely becomes oppressive in the nearly 3 hours of this painstaking yet static version, written and directed by Dudley Nichols. Rosalind Russell is the Electra, Katina Paxinou her adulterous mother, Raymond Massey her father, and Michael Redgrave her brother. (It is apparent from their accents that they have only recently become a family.) With Kirk Douglas and Leo Genn. R K O. b & w

The Mouse That Roared (1959)—This is the English comedy in which Peter Sellers—playing a field marshal, an imposingly big-bosomed grand duchess, and the Prime Minister of Grand Fenwick—made his first big impression on American moviegoers. It's about a minuscule mythical country that declares war on the United States, expecting to be quickly defeated and thus eligible for the cash benefits of rehabilitation. Twenty Grand Fenwickians, dressed in armor and toting bows and arrows, set sail for New York in a ramshackle tug. That's about as far as the comedy gets. The film abandons its small, amusing idea and goes off on a wearying tangent about a scientist (David Kossoff) with a big bomb and an ingenue-daughter (Jean Seberg), but it was hugely and inexplicably popular. Leo McKern and William Hartnell are in the cast. Jack Arnold directed; from a novel by Leonard Wibberley, adapted by Roger MacDougall and Stanley Mann. color

Movie Movie (1978)—It's better than the dum-dum title would suggest: it's a pair of skillful parodies of early 30s movies, written by Larry Gelbart and Sheldon Keller, and directed by Stanley Donen. The two "features," which give chances to a lot of new people, have some of the zest that the brash, intrepid performers fresh from the stage brought to early talkies. The star of both is George C. Scott, who seems to preside. In the first—a black-and-white spoof of Warners fight pictures—he's a white-haired old geezer, a manager-trainer to a young boxer. And in the second—a color parody of backstage musicals, principally based on *42nd Street*—he's slick-haired Spats Baxter, a Broadway impresario. As the night-school law student with the knockout punch, Harry Hamlin makes an agreeable début, and as the wriggling nightclub performer who corrupts him, Ann Reinking out-Ann-Margrets Ann-Margret. In the second, Barry Bostwick, who plays the singer-composer hero, has that wonderful Dick Powell candied-yam cheerfulness, and there's 6 feet 4 of him falling all over himself; Rebecca York is his saucer-eyed true-blue Ruby Keeler. With Kathleen Beller, Michael Kidd, Jocelyn Brando, Eli Wallach, Red Buttons, and Trish Van Devere, who has a tickling charm in the first but is totally miscast in the second. The film is too tame and too dependent on mismatched metaphors, and the second "feature" sags, but it's generally friendly and enjoyable. There's an expendable introduction by George Burns. Warners. (See *When the Lights Go Down*.)

Muerte de un Ciclista, see *Death of a Cyclist*

Mujeres al Borde de un Ataque de Nervios, see *Women on the Verge of a Nervous Breakdown*

The Mummy (1932)—When Karl Freund, the great UFA cinematographer, came to the U.S. he shot both *Dracula* and *Murders in the Rue Morgue* for Universal, and then the studio offered him the chance to direct *The Mummy*. What he did was so elegant and uncommercial that he got only one other chance to direct (*Mad Love* in 1935) and that was for a different studio, and in a far more obvious macabre style. *The Mummy* unnerves one because instead of fast chills there are long, quiet, ominous scenes; the lighting is so masterly and the moods are so effectively sustained that the pictures gives one prickly sensations. Boris Karloff is the 3000-year-old mummy brought back to life, and the dark, arresting Zita Johann is the English girl whom he stalks in the streets of Cairo because she is the incarnation of the princess he loved. It's silly but it's also disturbingly beautiful. No other

horror film has ever achieved so many emotional effects by lighting; this inexpensively made film has a languorous, poetic feeling, and the eroticism that lives on under Karloff's wrinkled parchment skin is like a bad dream of undying love. With Bramwell Fletcher, David Manners, Arthur Byron, Noble Johnson, Leonard Mudie, and the inevitable Edward Van Sloan. The screenplay by John L. Balderston is based on a story by Nina Wilcox Putnam and Richard Schayer; the cinematography is credited to Charles Stumar. Universal. b & w

Munro (1961)—A classic satire of the military. Jules Feiffer's character Munro is a 4-year-old who is drafted into the U.S. Army. This 8-minute animated cartoon was directed by Gene Deitch. color

Murder (1930)—A carefully designed early Hitchcock whodunit set among theatre people. It's more languidly paced than his mid-30s work, and the dialogue is spoken in stage rhythms, but there are inventive moments. Herbert Marshall, dryly amiable in his first talking picture, plays an eminent actor—a knight serving on a jury. Convinced of the innocence of the young actress (Norah Baring) who is on trial for murder, he tries to solve the case in order to save her life. There's an experiment with a stream-of-consciousness monologue, there's an odd, perhaps partly improvised comedy scene involving some children invading Marshall's bedroom, and there's also a tricky sequence in which he listens to *Tristan* on the radio while he shaves. The actual murderer turns out to be a transvestite—daring at the time. It's a very class-conscious film, but in a somewhat snobbish way; we seem to be expected to identify with Marshall's stylish courtliness and to see the "lower orders" through his eyes. With Miles Mander, Esmé Percy, Donald Calthrop, Edward Chapman and Phyllis Konstam as the couple in the breakfast scene, and a glimpse of Hitchcock on a street. The screenplay, by Alma Reville, is taken from the stage version of Clemence Dane's novel *Enter Sir John*. b & w

Murder at the Vanities (1934)—A backstage musical with a murderer loose in the theatre—an unusual mixture of thriller and musical that is moderately effective both ways, though the doubling of the 30s conventions makes it plot-heavy and doubly antiqued. The star is the dimpled international idol Carl Brisson (who sings "Cocktails for Two"); with Jack Oakie, Kitty Carlisle, Victor McLaglen, Gail Patrick, Dorothy Stickney, Gertrude Michael (who sings "Marahuana"), and some sumptuous footage of Duke Ellington and his orchestra. Directed by Mitchell Leisen; written by Carey Wilson, Joseph Gollomb, and Sam Hellman. Paramount. b & w

Murder by Contract (1958)—A cleanly constructed low-budget suspense picture about a hired killer (Vince Edwards). Shot in just eight days, it was directed by Irving Lerner, who was better known as an editor. The material is thin, but it has been worked out in visual terms, and the movie is often taut and exciting. Some high-contrast sequences are models of black-and-white atmospheric storytelling. With Herschel Bernardi, Michael Granger, Joseph Mell, and Caprice Toriel as the killer's elusive target. From a screenplay by Ben Simcoe; score by Perry Botkin; cinematography by Lucien Ballard.

Murder by Decree (1979)—A newly written Sherlock Holmes story, set in Victorian London. Directed by Bob Clark, this handsome Anglo-Canadian production features fine Whistler-like dockside scenes and many beautiful, ghoulish gothic-movie touches, but the modern political attitudes expressed by the writer, John Hopkins, misshape the picture. The mellifluous-voiced Christopher Plummer makes a good-looking Holmes, but, as usual, Plummer, though accomplished, is totally unconvincing. And, as the role is written, Holmes seems less a master of deduction than a wet-eyed saintly firebrand trying (ineffectively) to save mankind from the corruption of those in power. This Holmes also patronizes the common man, in the form of Dr. Watson, with whom he lives in an "odd couple" relationship that is the film's best comic resource. James Mason is a superb Dr. Watson—silly, querulous, innately good; it's a small-scale but great performance. With Geneviève Bujold, who does one of her finest child-woman numbers, and Donald Sutherland, John Gielgud, David Hemmings, Susan Clark, Frank Finlay, and the bland, tedious-as-usual Anthony Quayle. The dialogue is fairly lively, though the plot is impenetrable. color

Murder, He Says (1945)—In the same native cornball-surreal black-comedy mode as *Arsenic and Old Lace* but much looser, sillier, funnier. Fred MacMurray is the insurance agent who stumbles into the house of a family of homicidal hillbillies; Mabel Paige is the unloved grandma, Marjorie Main is the yowling, whipcracking mother, Porter Hall the mousy meek father, and Peter Whitney the half-witted twin sons—one of whom suffers from a crick in his back. Mother's cooking features a poison that glows in the dark, and in the climactic sequence the assembled characters keep turning off the lights and spinning the lazy-Susan table to avoid the poison. (There has probably never been anything like this sequence in other farces; it's a classic of slapstick craziness.) The work of the director, George Marshall, is square at times; it isn't up to the madness and invention of Lou Breslow's screenplay (based on Jack Moffitt's story). With Helen Walker, Jean Heather, and Barbara Pepper. Paramount. b & w

Murder, My Sweet (1945)—Philip Marlowe (Dick Powell) is employed by Moose Malloy (Mike Mazurki), a murderous, cretinous giant, to find the sweetheart he lost while doing a stretch in the jug; two beautiful women (Claire Trevor and Anne Shirley) periodically embrace Marlowe—a not especially perceptive detective—for the purpose of pulling his own gun on him. There was a time when Raymond Chandler regarded this movie, based on his *Farewell, My Lovely*, as the most successful film adaptation of his novels, and thought that Dick Powell came closest to his conception of Marlowe. The author's judgment seems shaky: the movie is energetic enough, but its crumminess can't all be explained by fidelity to the material. Edward Dmytryk directed, in the brutal, fast style popular in the war years; the screenplay is by John Paxton. With Esther Howard, Otto Kruger, Miles Mander, and Ralf Harolde. (The 1945 version is, however, much livelier than a 1975 remake that returned to Chandler's title, *Farewell, My Lovely*; it was directed by Dick Richards and stars Robert Mitchum as a Marlowe who keeps telling us what's going on, using embarrassingly ornate tough-guy phrases concocted by the scenarist, David Z. Goodman.) R K O. b & w

Murder on the Orient Express (1974)—This all-star version of an Agatha Christie antiquity promises to be a sumptuous spread, and so it is, but not as tasty as one had hoped. When the train stops—it's snowbound throughout the murder investigation—the picture loses its impetus. Vanessa Redgrave, Rachel Roberts, and Ingrid Bergman are standouts in a cast that includes John Gielgud, Lauren Bacall, Wendy Hiller, Jacqueline Bisset, Sean Connery, Richard Widmark, Tony Perkins, Michael York, Jean-Pierre Cas-

sel, Martin Balsam, George Coulouris, Colin Blakely, Denis Quilley, and Albert Finney as Hercule Poirot. Sidney Lumet directed, from Paul Dehn's script. The percussively edited pre-title montage is by that wizard of film shorthand, Richard Williams; the film proper, shot by Geoffrey Unsworth, reaches its visual peak in the railway station, at the opening. Production design by Tony Walton. Paramount. color (See *Reeling*.)

Le Mure di Malapurga, see *The Walls of Malapaga*

Murmur of the Heart *La Souffle au coeur* (1971)—Louis Malle's exhilarating high comedy about French bourgeois life. He looks into his own backyard—the film is set in Dijon in 1954 at the time of Dien Bien Phu, and it's about the sex education of the 14-year-old Laurent (Benoit Ferreux), the youngest, brightest son of a successful gynecologist (Daniel Gélin) and his Italian-born wife (Léa Massari). Malle sees not only the prudent, punctilious surface but the volatile and slovenly life underneath. His bourgeois bestiary is funny and appalling and also—surprisingly—hardy and happy. This is perhaps the first time on film that anyone has shown us the bourgeoisie enjoying its privileges. Though the movie itself reveals the sources of Malle's humor, this story probably wouldn't have been nearly so funny or, perhaps, so affectionate if Malle had told it 15 years earlier. Massari is superb as Clara, the carelessly sensual mother; Clara is shamelessly loose and free, and she's loved by her sons because of her indifference to the bourgeois forms, which they nevertheless accept—on the surface, that is. The story moves toward its supremely logical yet imaginative conclusion so stealthily that the kicker joke is perfect. With Michel Lonsdale as Father Henri. The script is by Malle. In French. color (See *Deeper into Movies*.)

Music Box (1989)—When the cast and the script are right for Costa-Gavras—as they are here—he can give a courtroom melodrama the pull and excitement of a thriller. Jessica Lange is the Chicago lawyer defending her retired steelworker father (Armin Mueller-Stahl) against deportation to Hungary, where the Communist government is waiting to try him for war crimes. The emotional core of the movie is that during the trial, as the Second World War victims give their accounts, the daughter begins to lose faith in her father's innocence. There are no flashbacks; there's no shock apparatus. We simply take in what they're saying, and we watch her take it in. Lange verges on the astounding. Costa-Gavras provides a low-key, controlled atmosphere, and she fills it with passion. The final plot developments feel fake, but this is an unusually lucid piece of storytelling. The script is by Joe Eszterhas; with Frederic Forrest, Donald Moffat, Lukas Haas, Michael Rooker, and Sol Frieder as the bald old man with the goatee, and Elzbieta Czyzewska as the precise, closed-faced woman who describes how she was raped. Tri-Star. color (See *Movie Love*.)

The Music Lovers (1971)—Ken Russell seems to have invented a new genre of pornobiography. This time, Tchaikovsky (Richard Chamberlain) is the chief victim of Russell's baroque vulgarity. For much of the movie, the characters slide in and out of fantasies that seem not so much theirs as Russell's. Whose fantasy are we in when Glenda Jackson, as Nina, Tchaikovsky's wife, writhes in torment in a blue-green madhouse and, in one sequence, is seen deliberately lying across a grating, spread-eagled, while the madmen locked below reach up under her skirt? It's unlikely to be Tchaikovsky's fantasy, because his wife (whom he lived with for only a few weeks) wasn't confined in bedlam until three years after his death.

The central plot mechanism—Tchaikovsky's patroness throws him out when his castoff lover reveals that he is homosexual, and so he is forced to become a conductor to support himself—is a concoction. When the facts were falsified in the old Hollywood bios, it was to soften and simplify, to please the audience. Russell makes everything frenzied and violent and sadistic, as a form of stimulus for the audience, and possibly even more for himself. Everything is caught *in flagrante delicto*. The film is homoerotic in style, and yet in dramatic content it's bizarrely anti-homosexual. There are a few really good moments, such as Glenda Jackson's self-conscious grin when she first goes to meet Tchaikovsky, and this part of the film has some suspense; later, her role comes dangerously close to self-caricature. With Max Adrian, Christopher Gable, and Kenneth Colley. The screenplay is credited to Melvyn Bragg, based on the book *Beloved Friend* by Catherine Drinker Bowen; cinematography by Douglas Slocombe. United Artists. color (See *Deeper into Movies*.)

The Music Man (1962)—A heavy-footed version of the Broadway musical by Meredith Willson and Franklin Lacey—a cheerful, broad piece of Americana about a silver-tongued con man, who drifts into an Iowa town and persuades the gullible residents that the children need to organize a fine big marching band. Morton DaCosta, who had also directed the stage version, isn't comfortable with the camera, and the material seems too literal, too practical, too set. But the star, Robert Preston, has a few minutes of fast patter—conmanship set to music—that constitute one of the high points in the history of American musicals. This is one of those triumphs that only a veteran performer can have; Preston's years of experience and his love of performing come together joyously. With Shirley Jones as the librarian who reforms the roué hero, and Paul Ford, Hermione Gingold, Buddy Hackett, Pert Kelton, and Ronny Howard. Screenplay by Marion Hargrove. Warners. color

The Music Room *Jalsaghar* (1958)—Satyajit Ray's extraordinary study of pride carried to extremity. A great, flawed, maddening film—hard to take but probably impossible to forget. It's often crude and it's poorly constructed, but it's a great experience. Worrying over its faults is like worrying over whether *King Lear* is well constructed; it doesn't really matter. Ray made this film between the second and third parts of the Apu Trilogy, for respite. With Chhabi Biswas as the aristocrat who has nothing left but his love of music—he holds a musicale in his decaying mansion. Ray's script is based on a story by T. S. Bannerjee. In Bengali. b & w

Mutiny on the Bounty (1935)—A stirring 18th-century sea adventure in the big M-G-M manner, freely adapted from the Charles Nordhoff and James Norman Hall books. The story of H.M.S. Bounty, its brutal Captain Bligh, and the mutineers who fled to Pitcairn Island, has narrative push and a popular theme—the revolt against a tyrant. The movie doesn't fall into the usual trap of setting strong heroes against weak, cowardly villains. As Charles Laughton plays him, the corrupt, sadistic Bligh is the strongest person on the screen; it is not merely that Bligh is a great sailor, capable of remarkable feats of navigation, and a man who is defiant even when defiance takes courage—it's that Laughton has a genuinely horrible mad power. He's a great villain—twisted and self-righteous—and you can't laugh him off. He transcends campiness. Clark Gable (looking a little tubby in white pants) is well cast as Fletcher Christian, leader of the mutineers; Gable's Americanness works to his advantage—makes him seem more of a plain,

rough-hewn man. Franchot Tone plays the pivotal character—the highborn officer who is taken back to England to stand trial; Tone is perhaps a shade too engaging and decent, and when he delivers his courtroom speech, he seems carried away by his own eloquence. The director, Frank Lloyd, goes after "human interest" details in a broad, conventional manner, and some of the bits of business of the minor characters are tediously simpleminded. But for the kind of big budget, studio controlled romantic adventure that this is, it's very well done; it took the Academy Award as Best Picture of the year. With Herbert Mundin and Eddie Quillan (there could be less of both), and Douglas Walton, Donald Crisp, Dudley Digges, Ian Wolfe, Movita, Mamo, Henry Stephenson, Spring Byington, and Francis Lister. Script by Talbot Jennings, Jules Furthman, and Carey Wilson; cinematography by Arthur Edeson; music by Herbert Stothart. Produced by Irving Thalberg, assisted by Albert Lewin. (Remade in 1962, with Trevor Howard as Bligh and Marlon Brando as Fletcher Christian). b & w

My American Cousin (1985)—Set in the summer of 1959 on a ranch in British Columbia, this first feature by the writer-director Sandy Wilson is a fictionalized account of her experiences at 12, when she developed a crush on her flashy, mixed-up boy cousin, who was 17. In the movie, he arrives from L.A. in a red Cadillac convertible, and he's a dreamboat—a tanned, golden-haired ringer for James Dean. The lively, restless Sandy, who wishes she were 16, is very well played by Margaret Langrick—there's nothing actressy about her. The picture has humor and it's perceptive; it's even fair to the helplessly stuffy adults (though it crudely caricatures the boy's rich-American parents). There's nothing much wrong with it, except that it's levelheaded in a terribly conventional way. It's too mild, it's too pokey, and it's a little dull. The fine cinematographer Richard Leiterman gives the paradisiacal terrain its due. With John Wildman as the tormented young Adonis, and Richard Donat and Jane Mortifee as the girl's parents. color

My Apprenticeship *V Lyudyakh* Also known as *Out in the World*. (1939)—This is part two of the Mark Donskoi Trilogy based on the memoirs of Maxim Gorky. In this section, the teen-age Alexei (who is to become Gorky) works as a cook's helper on a Volga ship (he washes dishes), and, at the end, he leaves the grandparents who raised him— the hated grandfather and the deeply loved grandmother. This second film retains the major characters (and the actors) of the first, and Alexei Lyarsky still plays the boy; it is as fine as the first (*The Childhood of Maxim Gorky*). But the third film (*My Universities*) is disappointing. In Russian. b & w

My Beautiful Laundrette (1985)—A startlingly fresh movie about life in South London among the surly white street gangs who live on the dole and feel that they're in a dead-end society and the Pakistani immigrants who know that this society is the best they can hope for, and try to move upward by wriggling through the cracks. In the foreground is a love affair between a dark-eyed, softly handsome, almost flowerlike Pakistani teen-ager, Omar (Gordon Warnecke), who grew up in this neighborhood, and a young blond street lout, Johnny (Daniel Day-Lewis). They become partners when Omar persuades his slumlord uncle (Saeed Jaffrey) to let him have a ratty-looking failed launderette, and the two boys, using stolen money, turn it into the launderette of their flashy dreams. Directed by Stephen Frears, from a witty script by the young playwright Hanif Kureishi, who was born in South London to a Pakistani father and a white English mother, the film catches you up in the racketeering and decay

of modern big-city life; you feel that your blinders have been taken off. Frears has a sensual, highly developed visual style, and he's responsive to the uncouthness and energy in English life—he's responsive to what went into the punk-music scene and to what goes into teen-age gang life. It's an enormous pleasure to see a movie that's really about something, and that doesn't lay on any syrupy coating to make the subject go down easily. (It's down before you notice it.) Written for British television, on a budget of under $850,000, the film was shot in 16-mm; the blowup to 35-mm is near-miraculous. The cast includes Shirley Anne Field, Roshan Seth, Rita Wolf, and Souad Faress. The cinematography is by Oliver Stapleton. color (See *Hooked*.)

My Brilliant Career (1979)—This Australian film—the pictorial re-creation of a late-Victorian novel—shows considerable charm and craft, though it's essentially taxidermy. The impoverished, 16-year-old heroine, Sybylla (Judy Davis), spends most of the movie pursuing a wealthy, aristocratic bachelor (Sam Neill)—a tall, thin "man of the world." He seems to be the only thing on her mind; she publicly displays her jealousy, and she is a thoroughgoing sexual tease. But when she has him half crazy and he proposes, she hits him with a whip. It seems she intends to have her own career as an artist. The appeal of this material to the modern women filmmakers (the 27-year-old director Gillian Armstrong, the screenwriter Eleanor Witcombe, the producer Margaret Fink) must be in Sybylla's desire for independence, but they don't clarify what's going on in their heroine. From the evidence of the film, the book, which was written by a 16-year-old girl under the name Miles Franklin, is a gothic feminist fantasy: feisty Cinderella wins Prince Charming but turns him down and goes off to fulfill herself. Though the movie doesn't go any deeper into the material than this sort of feminine self-infatuation, Sybylla is treated as if she were a precursor of the new woman: a model of the woman who resists conventional blandishments. The 23 year-old Judy Davis (in her first major screen role) is memorable: she suggests a blooming, broad-faced version of Katharine Hepburn's tomboy Jo in *Little Women*. Sam Neill manages to give some grit to the role of a romantic ideal, and the fine cast includes Wendy Hughes. The cinematography is by Don McAlpine; the production design is by Luciana Arrighi; the editing is by Nick Beauman. color

My Brother Talks to Horses (1946)—Americana, with humor and an easygoing style, set in an indefinite past. Fred Zinnemann was still relatively unknown when he directed this low-budget charmer for M-G-M. It never developed much of a reputation—maybe because it's so fluky. Jackie (Butch) Jenkins, who has a quiet, loner quality, is the freckled little kid who's happiest when he's talking to horses. His older brother is played by the English-accented Peter Lawford—a peculiar matchup, yet the movie is so pleasantly odd that it doesn't seem to matter. Spring Byington is the two boys' widowed mother, and the cast includes Charles Ruggles, Beverly Taylor, and Edward Arnold. The screenplay, by Morton Thompson, was based on part of his book *Joe the Wounded Tennis Player*. b & w

My Dinner with André (1981)—It's like a mad tea party or a mad, modern Platonic dialogue about the meaning of life. Self-effacingly directed, by Louis Malle, it flows smoothly, creating the illusion that we are simply listening in on the dinnertime conversation of the playwright Wallace Shawn and the former avant-garde theatre director André Gregory. The premise of the movie is that they haven't seen each other since 1975, when André dropped out—took off on a spiritual quest for "reality," which led him around the world. (Actually, they taped their conversations two or three times a week for three months, and then Shawn worked for a year shaping the material into a script, in which they play comic distillations of aspects of themselves.) Wally persuades André to tell him what he has been up to, and the suave, hawklike André, who's like the sum of all the crackpot glittery-eyed charmers in the world, pours out the record of his transcendental experiences. He keeps going, in wave after impassioned wave, describing astonishing, preposterous adventures in the Polish forests, in Scotland, in India and Tibet and in the Sahara, and even in Montauk, where he was buried alive in a death-and-rebirth ceremony. What he acts out for us is the questing that has torn so much of the modern theatre apart, when the men and women of the theatre became dissatisfied with the limits of stage performance and began to delve into para-theatrical cults. Wally, the pragmatist and sensualist, throws in an occasional sceptical dart, and then, when he begins to talk, he plays warthog to André's soaring flights of mysticism and offers the grubbiest of small comforts as proof of the fullness of his life. The two are perfect foils. This is a bizarre and surprisingly entertaining satirical comedy—the story of the search beyond theatre turned into theatre, or, at least, into a movie. color (See *Taking It All In*.)

My Fair Lady (1964)—The Lerner and Loewe musical staggers along in this large production, directed by George Cukor and designed by Cecil Beaton. The film seems to go on for about 45 minutes after the story is finished. Audrey Hepburn is an affecting Eliza, though she is totally unconvincing as a guttersnipe, and is made to sing with that dreadfully impersonal Marni Nixon voice that has issued from so many other screen stars. Rex Harrison had already played Higgins more than a bit too often. With Stanley Holloway, as buoyant as ever, Wilfrid Hyde-White, and Gladys Cooper. Warners. color

My Favorite Wife (1940)—Tennyson wrote *Enoch Arden* in 1864, and the movies have been making versions of it ever since D.W. Griffith did it in 1908 (and again in 1911). This one is the most famous and the funniest. On the day Cary Grant (as Nick Arden) marries Gail Patrick, his wife, Irene Dunne, shipwrecked seven years before, comes home. She follows the newlyweds on their honeymoon, prevents the consummation of the marriage, and, like a smart kitty, purrs herself to an ultimate victory. Garson Kanin was 27 (and at his liveliest) when he directed this screwball-classic hit. Randolph Scott plays the vegetarian scientist who was Dunne's companion on the island. Written by Bella and Samuel Spewack, with Leo McCarey, who was also the producer. R K O. b & w

My Favorite Year (1982)—The year is 1954, when Sid Caesar was the king of live TV comedy, and this movie is a fictional treatment of life backstage during the days when many soon-to-be-famous writers worked on his shows, brainstorming together. As the brawny, truculent King Kaiser, Joe Bologna suggests an introverted ox, and Peter O'Toole is King's guest star from Hollywood—the notorious womanizing boozer Alan Swann, who is part John Barrymore and part Errol Flynn. Bologna has an authentic boss-comic aura, and O'Toole is simply astounding. Ravaged and liquefied as Swann is, he still has his feelers out—he's always aware of the impression he's making; even when Swann is drunk, he's acting a great actor drunk. This show-business farce is the first film directed by Richard Benjamin, and it's a creaky job of moviemaking, but it has a bubbling spirit; Benjamin is crazy about actors—not a bad

start for a director. Bill Macy, Lainie Kazan, Cameron Mitchell, and Anne DeSalvo all have a crack at fresh material. In the tricky role of the youngest of the gag writers, Mark Linn-Baker is button-eyed and skinny—a snookums; it's an inventive performance yet borderline ghastly. And Jessica Harper's scenes don't pan out. But overall, it's a very funny picture. Also with Selma Diamond, Adolph Green, Lou Jacobi, Tony Di Benedetto, Gloria Stuart, and Basil Hoffman. From a terrific script by Norman Steinberg (who appears in a bit as Sandy) and Dennis Palumbo. M-G-M/United Artists. color (See *Taking It All In.*)

My Friend Flicka (1943)—As a piece of moviemaking it's ordinary—and that's putting it kindly. But when Roddy McDowall is on the screen, that doesn't seem to matter; he has a magical seriousness. This is the story of a dreamy boy and his strange colt Flicka, and the West Point–type father (Preston Foster) who understands neither boy or horse. It's one of the rare children's films—old or new—that doesn't make you choke up with rage. With Rita Johnson and Jeff Corey. Mary O'Hara wrote the script, from her novel; Harold Schuster directed. (A sequel, in 1945, was called *Thunderhead—Son of Flicka.*) 20th Century-Fox. color

My Gal Sal (1942)—A composer named Paul Dresser (he had a distinguished brother, Theodore, who spelled the family name "Dreiser") wrote some songs, including "On the Banks of the Wabash" and the title one. In this big, drawn-out, lachrymose musical bio, set in the 1890s, he is impersonated by Victor Mature, and his beloved is Rita Hayworth. Dresser's songs are supplemented by some nondescript numbers by Leo Robin and Ralph Rainger. The cast includes Phil Silvers, James Gleason, and Carole Landis. Directed by Irving Cummings. 20th Century-Fox. color

My Left Foot (1989)—The greatness of Daniel Day-Lewis's performance as the Dubliner Christy Brown, a victim of cerebral palsy who became a painter and a writer, is that he pulls you inside Christy's frustration and rage (and his bottomless thirst). There's nothing soft or maudlin about this movie's view of Christy: he's anguished and locked in yet excitingly insolent. The movie may tear you apart, but it's the story of a triumphantly tough guy who lived it up, and Day-Lewis's interpretation has some of the sexual seductiveness that was so startling in Olivier's *Richard III.* This is the first film of the Irish playwright-director Jim Sheridan, who wrote the superb screenplay with another Irish playwright, Shane Connaughton. With Brenda Fricker, Ray McAnally, Fiona Shaw, Cyril Cusack, Ruth McCabe, and Hugh O'Conor playing Christy as a child. Academy Awards: Best Actor (Day-Lewis), Supporting Actress (Fricker). Released by Miramax. color (See *Movie Love.*)

My Little Chickadee (1940)—A classic among bad movies; despite the presence of Mae West and W. C. Fields (it's the only time they acted together), this satire of Westerns never really gets off the ground. But the ground is such an honest mixture of dirt, manure, and corn that at times it is fairly aromatic. Mae West is hampered by the censors breathing down her décolletage; but even though she is less bawdy, and rather more grotesque, than at her best, she is still overwhelming. Fields is in better form: whether cheating at cards, or kissing Mae West's hand ("What symmetrical digits!"), or spending his wedding night with a goat, he remains the scowling, snarling misanthrope. Fields and West, who wrote most of their own vehicles, collaborated on the script. Directed by Edward Cline; with Joseph Calleia, Margaret Hamilton, and Dick Foran. Universal. b & w

My Man Godfrey (1936)—In this entertaining (and hugely successful) screwball comedy about the Depression, Carole Lombard is a rich, gorgeous nit who goes to the city dump to find a "forgotten man." The man she finds—a suave, bitter victim of the economic collapse—is played by William Powell. When she tells him she needs to take him back to a party in order to win a scavenger hunt, he asks what that is, and, sighing, she says, "A scavenger hunt is just like a treasure hunt, except in a treasure hunt you find something you want and in a scavenger hunt you find things you don't want and the one who wins gets a prize, only there really isn't any prize, it's just the honor of winning, because all the money goes to charity if there's any money left over, but then there never is." Lombard has a delirious, breathless plaintiveness at a moment like this—recognition dawning in her. The movie starts out with a promising satiric idea and winds up in box-office romance, but it's likable and well-paced even at its silliest. Lombard shrieks happily and Powell modulates impeccably. With Mischa Auer doing a simian imitation to amuse his patron, Alice Brady. Also with Franklin Pangborn, Grady Sutton, Jean Dixon, Gail Patrick, Alan Mowbray, Eugene Pallette, and, in a bit part, Jane Wyman. Directed by Gregory La Cava, from a screenplay by Eric Hatch and Morrie Ryskind. Like several of the Astaire-Rogers musicals, this film has a sleek and silvery Art Deco look; the black-and-white cinematography is by Ted Tetzlaff. Universal.

My Sister Eileen (1942)—Ruth McKenney's *New Yorker* stories about her and her younger sister's experiences in Greenwich Village were turned into a Broadway hit, and then into this less than dazzling romantic comedy (and later into a Broadway musical, which was also filmed, in 1955). As Ruth, leggy Rosalind Russell is too boisterously aware that she's the life of the party, and as Eileen, Janet Blair is very pretty but not much else. (The actual Eileen McKenney married Nathanael West and died with him in an automobile crash in 1940.) Alexander Hall directed. With Brian Aherne, Allyn Joslyn, George Tobias, June Havoc, Elizabeth Patterson, and Richard Quine (who directed the 1955 version, with Bob Fosse as choreographer). Columbia. b & w

My Sister, My Love *Syskonbädd 1782* (1966)—The writer-director Vilgot Sjöman, who later became famous for *I Am Curious*, directed this Jacobean story of incest (derived from John Ford's 1633 play *'Tis Pity She's a Whore*) in a tense, sensuous style that is morbidly effective. Movie incest usually seems just trivial sport, but in this film the love of the brother and sister (Per Oscarsson and Bibi Andersson) is terrifying and fills one with anxiety and dread. It's a strong movie: Sjöman gets you on a hook and won't let you off. He updates the material to the 18th century. With Jarl Kulle and Gunnar Björnstrand. In Swedish. b & w

My Uncle Antoine *Mon Oncle Antoine* (1971)—When it opened in Washington, D.C., Russell Baker wrote a column saying that it was "the most extraordinary movie," and adding, "It is almost impossible to explain why." He came close, though, when he said, "It is like walking into one of Wren's small London churches just when you have come to believe that the entire world looks like the Pentagon." Seen through the eyes of a boy (Jacques Gagnon), who lives with his ribald storekeeper-undertaker uncle (Jean Duceppe), it's a reminiscence of Christmastime in an asbestos-mining town in Quebec, in the 40s. In one sequence, the mineowner rides through town in his carriage tossing trinkets at the children of the mineworkers, and the parents are torn, not wanting to deprive their children of the toys yet humiliated to see them pick up this miserly beneficence. We watch the hesitant, eager children and the parents divided against themselves, and we, too, are divided—between the beauty of perception that brings us such moments and the anguish of having, from this time on, to live with this perception. Claude Jutra, who made this plangent, simple masterpiece, plays the role of Fernand, the store clerk, who dallies with the uncle's wife (Olivette Thibault) and loves the townspeople, without illusions, for what they are. (Jutra is present in the film the way Jean Renoir is present in *The Rules of the Game*; Fernand is the soul of the movie.) The screenplay, by Clément Perron and Jutra, is based on incidents in Perron's early life. The cinematography is by Michel Brault; the music is by Jean Cousineau. Made on a budget of $250,000. In French. color

My Universities *Moi Universiteti* (1940)— In this third film of the Mark Donskoi Trilogy, based on the memoirs of Maxim Gorky, the young hero, Alexei (now played, less successfully, by Y. Valberg), goes to work in a bakery, where the men go out on strike; he mingles with revolutionaries and intellectuals, and becomes, at last, the writer we know as Maxim Gorky. This lyric, epic group of films is the only work in movie history that is roughly comparable to Satyajit Ray's Apu Trilogy; however, Donskoi falls into pompousness in the third film and the joyous revolutionary spirit seems programmed, while Ray soars. With Stepan Kaynkov as the bakery boss Semyonov. In Russian. b & w

Le Mystère Koumiko, see *The Koumiko Mystery*

Le Mystère Picasso *The Mystery of Picasso* (1956)—Picasso and Henri-Georges Clouzot (*The Wages of Fear, Diabolique*) collaborate. The result is one of the most joyful of all records of an artist at work. (It was a disastrous failure, though, when it opened in a few American theatres.) Picasso has a volatile, explosive presence. He seems to take art back to an earlier function, before the centuries of museums and masterpieces; he is the artist as clown, as conjurer, as master funmaker. For most of the film the screen is his paper or canvas, and in 75 minutes he draws or paints 15 pictures. When he complains to Clouzot that the canvas is too small, the screen expands to CinemaScope size. Some sequences use time-lapse photography to compress the working time on a canvas to a few minutes: the changes and developments (when, for example, a goat's head becomes a skull and then a head again) suggest what animation might be but isn't. In one sequence he does a really bum picture and you watch to see what he can possibly do to salvage it; he reworks it, making it more and more complicated, and it gets worse and worse. Finally he gives up in disgust and scribbles over it, and you feel relieved that he didn't like it any better than you did. Cinematography by Claude Renoir; score by Georges Auric. (Don't be put off by the fatuous narrator who tells us that we will see what is in the mind of a genius at work, and exclaims, "We would give much to know what was in Joyce's mind while he was writing *Ulysses!*") color

The Mysterious Island (1929)—Imaginative undersea fantasy based on an 1874 Jules Verne novel and starring sinister monsters, weird fish, Lionel Barrymore as a 19th-century inventor, and Montagu Love as a wicked nobleman. This ill-fated production was begun in 1927 by the greatly gifted Maurice Tourneur, who was fired by M-G-M and replaced by Benjamin Christiansen, and it was finally credited to Lucien Hubbard—by which time sound had come in, so the film is part silent, part sound. The plot twists are silly, but the film presents the invention, launching, and kidnapping of the first submarine, and then the real capper: a mammoth octopus with tentacles long enough to embrace that submarine in its entirety. And surely no one who saw the film as a child has completely forgotten a horror scene on the ocean floor: the wreck of a Roman galley with the skeletons of slaves still chained to the oars. With Lloyd Hughes, Harry Gribbon, Gibson Gowland, and Snitz Edwards. Art direction by Cedric Gibbons. (There were several subsequent versions of the novel: a Russian film in 1941, a serial made by Columbia in 1951, a British film in 1961 starring Michael Craig, and in 1974, a version called *The Mysterious Island of Captain Nemo*, starring Omar Sharif.) color, with b & w sequences

The Mystery of Kaspar Hauser *Jeder für Sich und Gott Gegen Alle* Also known as *Every Man for Himself and God Against All*. (1975)—The story of Kaspar Hauser, who appeared in a German town in the 1820s, is a factually based variant of the lost-or-abandoned-child, Mowgli-Tarzan myth; Kaspar wasn't raised among wolves, bears, or apes but, rather, in isolation. In this nightmare version, written and directed by Werner Herzog, Kaspar (Bruno S.) is a grunting lump of a man, chained in a dungeonlike cellar from infancy. Covered with sores and welts, unable to stand, he is fed by a black-caped man who beats him with a truncheon. One day, the man carries him to a town square and leaves him there. The townspeople train him in human habits and try to educate him, but as he begins to learn, he balks at what he is taught, and becomes obstinate, trying to retain his new, mesmerized pleasure in nature. Before the issues are resolved, he is struck down by the caped figure, who returns, first to maim him, then to murder him. The film is a double fable, intermingling the stultifying effects of bourgeois society and the cruelty of a demonic universe. Herzog achieves a visionary, overcast style; his images look off-balance, crooked, as if the cameraman were wincing. Herzog is a film poet, all right, but he's a didactic film poet, given to heavy, folk-art ironies; he says that society puts you through pain in order to deform you, and he makes it impossible for you to identify with anyone but Kaspar, who hasn't lost his innocent responses. The other people are alone, immobilized, unanimated; life is dormant in them. Though one could not fault this in a painter's vision, in a filmmaker's it is numbing. In Herzog's conception Kaspar is the only one who has still got his soul. This conception has a flower-child fashionableness, but Bruno S. (who was once believed to be a mental defective himself) is amazing. His Kaspar has sly, piggy eyes, yet he's so totally absorbed in experiencing nature, his head thrust out ecstatically, straining to grasp everything he was denied in his cave existence, that he becomes Promethean; the light dawning in that face makes him look like a peasant Beethoven. In German. color (See *When the Lights Go Down*.)

The Mystery of Picasso, see *Le Mystère Picasso*

The Mystery of the Wax Museum (1933)— Marvellously grisly chiller, directed by Michael Curtiz and shot in an early Technicolor process, with the color contributing to the general creepiness. Lionel Atwill is the murderous curator who pours hot wax over his manacled, still-living victims and then exhibits them as sculpture. With Glenda Farrell, Fay Wray, Gavin Gordon, Frank McHugh, Edwin Maxwell, and Arthur Edmund Carewe. From a play by Charles S. Belden. (Remade in 1953 in 3-D as *House of Wax*, and probably the source of the 1959 *A Bucket of Blood*.) Warners.

Nachts, Wenn der Teufel Kam, see *The Devil Strikes at Night*

Naciala, see *The Début*

Nadine (1987)—The picture features such faded thrills as a shack full of dynamite, a box packed with rattlesnakes, and an ancient, rickety ladder stretched horizontally between two rooftops. You have to keep reminding yourself that you're not just watching the trailer. Kim Basinger is Nadine, a manicurist in a beauty parlor in Austin, Texas, in 1954, who stalls on giving her small-time dreamer husband (Jeff Bridges) a divorce, because she still loves him. When she has been at the scene of a murder and, by mistake, got hold of copies of state plans for a superhighway—inside information that real-estate speculators could parlay into big money—she turns to him for help, and they're both trapped by the local crook (Rip Torn) who arranged for the copies in the first place. Written and directed by Robert Benton, the picture is like a genteel variant of a redneck hillbilly burlesque about how it pays to be lucky and dumb. Basinger is peculiarly muted as an actress and Bridges no longer has the manic,

boyish spontaneity his role calls for. As a scuzzball photographer, Jerry Stiller, who has only one scene before he turns into the murder victim, conveys a lifetime of self-disgust; that's more felt life than anyone else shows. With Glenne Headly, Mickey Jones, and Gwen Verdon. Tri-Star. color (See *Hooked*.)

The Naked and the Dead (1958)—Norman Mailer's Second World War novel, turned into a third-rate action movie. Under Raoul Walsh's direction, the action itself—the assault-craft landings on tropical beaches, the thick, steamy jungle where American patrols reconnoitre behind Japanese lines—is impressive; it's the characterizations (plus the lacklustre casting) that prevent this movie from being in any way memorable. The Denis and Terry Sanders script spells out the men's motivations: there's the maniacal sergeant (Aldo Ray), who steals gold from the teeth of dead Japanese; the starched, too-noble lieutenant (Cliff Robertson); the dedicatedly militaristic brigadier general (Raymond Massey); and assorted types played by Richard Jaeckel, William Campbell, James Best, Joey Bishop, Jerry Paris, L. Q. Jones, and, in flashbacks, Lili St-Cyr and Barbara Nichols. Music by Bernard Herrmann; produced by Paul Gregory, for R K O. color

The Naked City (1948)—After the success of their *Brute Force*, the producer, Mark Hellinger, and the director, Jules Dassin, returned with this fast-jabbing, empty, Manhattan-set melodrama about the Homicide Squad. The drab script is by Albert Maltz and Malvin Wald; the film is visually impressive only. (William Daniels is the cinematographer.) With Barry Fitzgerald, Howard Duff, Don Taylor, Ted de Corsia, Frank Conroy, and Tom Pedi. (Not to be confused with an infinitely superior film Dassin made in London in 1950 called *Night and the City*.) Universal. b & w

The Naked Edge (1961)—A stilted, witless English thriller that you watch stupefied, trying to figure out how and why it got made, and how Gary Cooper (looking aged and ill—he has huge bags under his eyes) and Deborah Kerr got suckered into doing it. The picture has fancy lighting and tricky camera positions, but they're no fun: you get very tired of the closeups of Kerr's distraught, finely modelled face and her upswept, ladylike hairdo as she agonizes nobly. She suspects that her husband (Cooper) has committed a murder. After a while a viewer may be more perplexed by mysteries such as why is each room made to look huge? Michael Anderson directed; the script (by Joseph Stefano, from Max Ehrlich's novel *First Train to Babylon*) seems to have picked up the least entertaining aspects of Hitchcock's *Suspicion*. With Michael Wilding, Eric Portman, Peter Cushing, Diane Cilento, Hermione Gingold, Wilfrid Lawson, and Ronald Howard. b & w

The Naked Night *Gycklarnas Afton* In England, *Sawdust and Tinsel*; in France, *La Nuit des forains*. (1953)—Written and directed by Ingmar Bergman, the film is set in the circus world at the turn of the century. It opens with a flashback shot on different film stock: a clown's wife—a dumpy, middle-aged woman—bathes exhibitionistically in view of a whole regiment of soldiers; the clown comes and takes her away. From there the story moves to the circus owner, Åke Groenberg, and his voluptuous mistress, Harriet Andersson; this swinish Circe betrays him, and is in turn betrayed, and they go on together. The atmosphere suggests E. A. Dupont's 1925 film, *Variety*, with Emil Jannings, but has upsetting qualities all its own. There is an erotic scene between Miss Andersson and Hasse Ekman, as a seducer-actor, that leaves audiences slightly out of breath. *The Naked Night* is one of the bleakest of Bergman's films: no one is saved from total damnation; life is a circus, and the people are gross clowns; it is a round of frustration, humiliation, and defeat. Yet this heavy, mawkish Expressionism, of a kind widespread in Germany in the 20s, was extraordinarily popular with young Americans in the late 60s. With Anders Ek, Gunnar Björnstrand, and Åke Fridell. In Swedish. b & w

The Naked Runner (1967)—Why didn't Frank Sinatra take the professional pride in his movies that he took in his recordings? This implausible, unconvincing spy story doesn't have a single witty idea, and he's cast in the role of an anxious lifeless mouse. The director, Sidney J. Furie, provides enormous vistas for small bits of dialogue, closeups of cups of creamy brown coffee, fancy simulations of Magritte. What on earth for? Done straightforwardly this movie would still be nothing, but it would be half the length. It's stretched out by having the characters address each other as Mr. So-and-So, and it's full of footsteps: that should be the audience leaving. The screenplay, by Stanley Mann, is based on Francis Clifford's novel. A British production, released by Warners. color

The Naked Truth, see *Your Past Is Showing*

The Nanny (1965)—A small-scale English thriller, directed by Seth Holt—deft enough to be tantalizingly suggestive of what it might have been. Though Jimmy Sangster's script, from Evelyn Piper's novel, is just a routine horror job, there's real promise in the conception of the nanny as a mush-mouthed tyrant, with fraudulent sentiments substituting for feeling. The characters are amusingly "modern": the children are "cool," the father insufferable, the mother weak, the aunt self-centered. So far, so good. The exception is Bette Davis, trying to give a restrained performance as the dowdy, repressed nanny, whose 10-year-old charge suspects her of having killed his little sister. Restraint is what Davis has not got much of. Antennae flailing wildly, she signals us that she's being self-effacing, that she's holding back. Everything she does is out of key with the other performers; her thick eyebrows look false, and she treats her hair like a wig, patting it. You have to hand it to Davis, though: she *is* a star. When she can't dominate by a good performance, she dominates by a bad one. With Jill Bennett, Wendy Craig, James Villiers, Pamela Franklin, Maurice Denham, Jack Watling, and William Dix. b & w

Nanook of the North (1921)—Robert Flaherty, who began as an explorer and anthropologist, once remarked that in the usual travelog, the filmmaker looks down on and never up to his subject. By looking up, Flaherty created a new genre. He began to record the life of a people with a camera, and then, in editing, to distill the meaning. What Flaherty—a great storyteller—distilled was the heroic beauty in simple everyday experience. Instead of going to a culture with a

story, he developed his stories out of what he observed; his films have no human villains, yet they have great drama and a surprising amount of comedy. (Like all great documentarians, he imparts his own spirit to his films.) His feature-length study of the Eskimo Nanook, who lives where nothing grows and who depends on what he can kill, was made in 1920 and 1921. Two years later, while people all over the world were applauding this smiling man in his cold and hostile environment, Flaherty's hero died of starvation. He lives on in this movie in a different way from screen actors of the past: Flaherty closes the distance between Nanook and the audience. Financed by Revillon Frères. Silent. b & w

Napoléon (1927)—Presented in a reconstructed version in 1981. Abel Gance originally made it as a 6-hour silent film, in color (the prints were tinted and toned by a dye process), and with sections designed to be run on a triple-width screen, by a process called Polyvision. His conception was far more complex than what directors later did with Cinerama, since Gance frequently used the images at the left and right of the central image for contrapuntal effects—history became an avalanche of armies, battles, and crowds. The film is both avant-garde and old-fashioned. In Gance's view Napoleon (Albert Dieudonné) is a Man of Destiny. Before that, when he's still a boy (Vladimir Roudenko), he's a Boy of Destiny. As a thinker Gance is essentially a fantasist, a mythmaker enslaved by his own schoolboy gush. And when Napoleon is treated as the embodiment of the French Revolution, you know you're in the grip of a crazy. Gance isn't rounded (as, say, Renoir was). His films are superb in glimpses or in sequences, but they're not unified by simple emotion, as Griffith's epics were. They're held together by obsession, by fervor. (When Gance tries for simple, ordinary feelings, he's usually at his worst.) But he's a great moviemaker. In the opening section, a fortresslike military school is in the distance, while in the foreground the courageous 12-year-old Napoleon commands his outnumbered troops in a snowball fight. The camera seems to encompass miles of landscape, yet there's so much activity within the shots, and the movement of the boys is so quick and darting and funny, that the effect is of your eyes clearing—of everything becoming bright. Gance cuts from the long shots to closeups, and adds superimpositions, and then the cutting becomes fast and rhythmic, with Napoleon's face flashing by in one frame of every four, and you realize that the principal purpose of this jazzy blinking is to give you a feeling for speed and movement—and for the possibilities of the medium. Gance doesn't dawdle; he starts off with pinwheels, sparks, madness. The film was chopped down into so many different versions (some of them re-edited by Gance himself) that it took the English filmmaker and film historian Kevin Brownlow years to assemble this new, relatively complete version. Francis Ford Coppola served as impresario for its release in the United States, and a score was prepared by Carmine Coppola. With Gina Manès as Josephine, Pierre Batcheff as her lover General Hoche, Nicolas Koline as Fleuri, Annabella as his daughter Violine, Antonin Artaud as Marat, and Gance himself as Saint-Just. (See *Taking It All In*.)

Napoli Milionaria, see *Millionaires of Naples*

Nära Livet, see *Brink of Life*

The Narrow Margin (1952)—Richard Fleischer directed this ingenious little sleeper set on a train. It's about a gangster's widow (Marie Windsor—she was the destructive floozy in *The Killing*) on her reluctant way from Chicago to Los Angeles to testify before a grand jury. The gimmick is that she's being stalked by two mobsters, but they don't know what she looks like. This isn't a first-rate thriller; it's rather drab. Yet the train ride and that gimmick help to provide suspense, and a lot of people remember the movie fondly. (It was made for $188,000.) With Charles McGraw and Queenie Leonard. The screenplay is by Earl Felton. (Remade in 1990 by Peter Hyams.) R K O. b & w

Nashville (1975)—The funniest epic vision of America ever to reach the screen. Robert Altman's movie is at once a *Grand Hotel*–style narrative, with 24 linked characters; a country-and-Western musical; a documentary essay on Nashville and American life; a meditation on the love affair between performers and audiences; and an Altman party. In the opening sequences, when Altman's people—the performers we associate with him because he has used them in ways no one else would think of, and they've been filtered through his sensibility—start arriving, and pile up in a traffic jam on the way from the airport to the city, the movie suggests the circus procession at the non-ending of *8½*. But Altman's clowns are far more autonomous; they move and intermingle freely, and the whole movie is their procession. The basic script is by Joan Tewkesbury, but the actors have been encouraged to work up material for their roles, and not only do they do their own singing but most of them wrote their own songs—and wrote them in character. The songs distill the singers' lives, as the pantomimes and theatrical performances did for the actors in *Children of Paradise*. With Ronee Blakley as a true folk artist and the one tragic character, and David Arkin, Barbara Baxley, Ned Beatty, Karen Black, Timothy Brown, Keith Carradine, Geraldine Chaplin, Robert Doqui, Shelley Duvall, Allen Garfield, Henry Gibson, Scott Glenn, Jeff Goldblum, Barbara Harris, David Hayward, Michael

Murphy, Allan Nicholls, Dave Peel, Cristina Raines, Bert Remsen, Lily Tomlin, Gwen Welles, and Keenan Wynn. Also with Richard Baskin (who arranged and supervised the music) and Elliott Gould and Julie Christie who do bits as themselves. Cinematography by Paul Lohmann. (161 minutes.) Paramount. color (See *Reeling*.)

Nastasia Filipovna, see *The Idiot* (1958)

Nasty Habits (1977)—At its best—high wit and inspired silliness—it's a dream of a satire, reminiscent of Bea Lillie's brand of madness. Adapted from *The Abbess of Crewe*, Muriel Spark's 1974 Watergate travesty set in a convent, the film features a coiffed little wolf pack—Glenda Jackson, flashing her claws, as Nixon, Geraldine Page and Anne Jackson as Haldeman and Ehrlichman, and, in an inspired bit of casting, Sandy Dennis as their flunky, John Dean. In her first real crack at screen farce, Dennis turns tactlessness and blurting into woozy slapstick; it's a blissful performance—she's such a drip she's creepy. As Kissinger, Melina Mercouri doesn't help much, but the scenarist, Robert Enders, has added a Gerald Ford figure— Anne Meara, who is such a brassy, good-humored top banana that everything she does is funny. The script tapers off toward topicality and obviousness, but Michael Lindsay-Hogg's directing has a balmy gracefulness to it. With Edith Evans, Susan Penhaligon, Eli Wallach, Jerry Stiller, and Rip Torn. Cinematography by Douglas Slocombe. color (See *When the Lights Go Down*.)

National Velvet (1944)—One of the most likable movies of all time. Under the direction of Clarence Brown, the 12-year-old Elizabeth Taylor rings true on every line she speaks; she gives what is possibly her most dedicated performance as Velvet Brown, a little English girl who wins a horse in a village

lottery and is obsessively determined to enter him in the Grand National. The film is a high-spirited, childish dream; like *The Wizard of Oz*, it makes people smile when they recall it. As the jockey who coaches Velvet, Mickey Rooney is very fine in some scenes; in others, he's a shade too professional, too ready with his lines. As Velvet's mother, who was the first woman to swim the English Channel, Anne Revere is convincingly strong and daring, even though she is made all-wise, in the M-G-M parental tradition. Donald Crisp is Velvet's father, Angela Lansbury is Velvet's dreamy, out-of-it older sister, and Jackie "Butch" Jenkins is the little brother of everyone's dreams. With Arthur Treacher, Reginald Owen, Norma Varden, Terry Kilburn, and Arthur Shields. The 1935 novel, by Enid Bagnold, was adapted by Theodore Reeves and Helen Deutsch. Produced by Pandro S. Berman. (A 1978 sequel, *International Velvet*, starred Tatum O'Neal as Velvet's niece.) color

Nattlek, see *Night Games*

The Natural (1984)—Robert Redford as Roy Hobbs, who feels he has it in him to be the greatest baseball player there ever was. With the forces of evil (Kim Basinger) and good (Glenn Close) contending for his soul, this inspirational fantasy asks: Will Redford hold on to his dream, will he be strong enough to triumph? There isn't a whisper of surprise in Redford's performance, and he's photographed looking like a wary, modest god, with enough backlighting and soft focus to make him incandescent even when he isn't doing a thing. Each time Roy is about to pitch or hit with supernatural help, he's glorified in slow motion, and the rhythm of the shots is unvarying. And we're supposed to sit there oohing and ahing over Robert Redford lifting his leg. Directed by Barry Levinson, in a picturesque, prose-poetry style, the movie turns its source material—Bernard Malamud's lively, magical first novel—into primordial hokum. A few performers—Barbara Hershey, Joe Don Baker, and John Finnegan—stand apart from the sludge of moral uplift; the cast also includes Robert Duvall, Wilford Brimley, Richard Farnsworth, Robert Prosky, Darren McGavin, Michael Madsen, and George Wilkosz as the bat boy. The overly showy, overly dark cinematography is by Caleb Deschanel; the tender, drippy, hymnlike music is by Randy Newman; the script is by Roger Towne, with a credit also to Phil Dusenberry, who wrote an earlier version. Tri-Star. color (See *State of the Art*.)

Naughty Marietta (1935)—It's an atrocity, of course, and one of the most spoofed of all the Jeanette MacDonald–Nelson Eddy operettas, and yet it has vitality and a mad sort of appeal. When those two profiles come together as they sing "Ah, Sweet Mystery of Life," it's beyond kitsch, it's in a realm of its own. She's a princess who has fled France and come to the New World and he's a valiant Indian scout. With Elsa Lanchester, Douglass Dumbrille, Frank Morgan, Joseph Cawthorn, and Cecilia Parker. W. S. Van Dyke directed, from a script by John Lee Mahin, Frances Goodrich, and Albert Hackett based on Rida Johnson Young's operetta. The music is by Victor Herbert. Hunt Stromberg produced, for M-G-M. b & w

The Navigator (1924)—Arguably, Buster Keaton's finest—but amongst the Keaton riches can one be sure? What isn't subject to debate is that this movie about a useless young millionaire (Keaton), who can't even shave himself, and his rich dizzy girlfriend (Kathryn McGuire) adrift on an enormous, deserted ocean liner without lights or steam is one of the greatest comedies ever made. It was also his biggest box-office success. Keaton (and Donald Crisp) directed. According to Keaton, Crisp was to take care of the dra-

matic scenes but lost interest in them and "turned into a gagman. Well, that we didn't want, but we did manage to pull the picture through." Keaton pulled it through all right, while playing with the abstract possibilities of the film image the way a violin virtuoso uses his fiddle. Noble Johnson is the cannibal chief; Crisp's face appears in a scene. Metro-Goldwyn. Silent. b & w

Nazarin (1958)—The hero is a gentle Mexican priest—a Candide who is robbed and cheated—in this simple, masterly, ambiguous film by Luis Buñuel which is (perhaps in spite of his intention) his most tender. A woman offers Nazarin a pineapple and her blessing. Nazarin is so stubbornly proud that it's a struggle for him to accept, and Buñuel himself is so proud that he will hardly allow the scene to have any weight. Humility is very difficult for him; he just tosses in the pineapple. He's determined not to give in to the folly of tenderness, but it's there. With Francisco Rabal. In Spanish. b & w

Near Dark (1987)—The vampires here are a gang of outlaws travelling by van, drifting around the country, hibernating in motels during the sunlight hours. Most of the time they pick off a chance victim, but when they're really bloodthirsty they take over a roadside bar and slaughter everybody in it. This thriller, directed by Kathryn Bigelow, has a nocturnal, erotic atmosphere, shards of wit, and some better performances than are customary in the genre. And it becomes more intense as it goes along. Vampirism is reversible here, so the characters' fates aren't sealed, and this allows for curiosity about what will happen to the melancholy heroine, appealingly played by Jenny Wright. (She bites reluctantly and almost mournfully, yet hungrily.) Bill Paxton, as the most rambunctious of the gang, has a biker's gusto that energizes his scenes. Jenette Goldstein makes an impact, too—she's the mom figure of the pack. The cast includes Lance Henriksen as the dad figure, Joshua Miller as the little brother, Adrian Pasdar as the new inductee, Tim Thomerson, and Marcie Leeds. A painter turned filmmaker, Bigelow (who was a graduate student in film at Columbia) shows a talent for the uncanny; the cinematography, by Adam Greenberg, contributes to the exploitation-movie lyricism that draws you into the horror. The script is by Eric Red and Bigelow; music by Tangerine Dream; editing by Howard Smith. Released by De Laurentiis. color

Neko to Shozo to Futari no Onna, see *A Cat and Two Women*

Network (1976)—Television, Paddy Chayefsky says, is turning us into morons and humanoids; people have lost the ability to love. Who has—him? Oh, no, the blacks, the revolutionaries, and a power-hungry executive at the fictional UBS network named Diana Christensen (Faye Dunaway). The cast of this messianic farce includes William Holden, Peter Finch, Robert Duvall, Beatrice Straight, and Ned Beatty, and they all take turns yelling at us soulless masses. Sidney Lumet directed. Academy Awards: Best Actor (Finch), Actress (Dunaway), Supporting Actress (Straight), Screenplay (Chayefsky). United Artists. color (See *When the Lights Go Down*.)

Nevada Smith (1966)—A Western, derived from material in the Harold Robbins novel *The Carpetbaggers* that wasn't used in the 1964 film. Steve McQueen plays a half-breed boy who devotes his adolescence and early manhood to tracking down the men who killed his parents. (The boy's Indian mother is mutilated in a shockingly violent scene; it isn't staged to give you a kick but rather to make you understand the boy's helpless rage and

his long search for revenge.) McQueen gives an earnest performance, though he is too often openmouthed and slack-jawed; that seems to be his way of acting youthful. The other characters are too conventional—they're bad guys and good, sweet women. The script (by John Michael Hayes) isn't rich enough for the loving care that the veteran director, Henry Hathaway, and the veteran cinematographer, Lucien Ballard, lavish on it. They provide the look of authenticity and the proficiency and beauty of a well-made movie. Ballard's images are like his extraordinary work in *The Magnificent Matador* (1955)—a discovery and celebration of blue. With Brian Keith, Suzanne Pleshette, Karl Malden, Raf Vallone, Arthur Kennedy, Martin Landau, Janet Margolin, Howard Da Silva, Pat Hingle, John Litel, Gene Evans, Josephine Hutchinson, Lyle Bettger, Bert Freed, Val Avery, and Ted de Corsia. (Not to be confused with the 1975 made-for-TV movie, also called *Nevada Smith*.) A Joseph E. Levine Production/Avco. color

Never Cry Wolf (1983)—Adapted from Farley Mowat's autobiographical book, this Carroll Ballard film is about a young biologist (Charles Martin Smith) working for the Canadian government who is sent to spend a year in the sub-Arctic North. His mission is to find a way to get rid of the wolves that have supposedly been devastating the caribou herds, but he learns that men, rather than wolves, are the predators. Visually (and aurally, too), the film is magnificent. It needs a more stirring script and a central actor with more range (and some depth). But there's a lot of free-floating transcendence, and though it doesn't serve the prosaic story, it certainly holds you. Everything that Ballard (working with Hiro Narita as the cinematographer) shoots seems new, and it has a distinctive, shimmering purity. With Brian Dennehy as Rosie, Zachary Ittimangnaq as

Ootek, and Samson Jorah as Mike. Disney. color (See *State of the Art*.)

Never Give a Sucker an Even Break (1941)—W. C. Fields in his prime. Like *The Bank Dick* of the year before, this one deals with making a movie. The movie Fields wants to make is set in a Ruritania in the clouds that is native American surrealism—comic-strip foolishness and then some. Up there, he encounters the great-bosomed comic divinity, Margaret Dumont. The film has also its horror: an erstwhile ingenue named Gloria Jean. You can't just shut your eyes because she *sings*. With Leon Errol; directed by Edward Cline. Universal. b & w

Never on Sunday (1960)—Melina Mercouri, as the happy whore who goes to bed only with men she likes, in Jules Dassin's clumsy fable about the joys of amorality and the stupidity of virtue. Pinheaded Shavian ironies and an exhaustingly robust heroine, but a great success. Made in Greece, with bouzouki music by Manos Hadjidakis. In English and Greek. b & w

The New Land *Nybyggarna* (1972)—At the end of *The Emigrants*, the viewer wanted to go on to find out if the survivors of the mid-19th-century emigration from Sweden found what they had hoped for. In this second half, the master director Jan Troell shows what happened to them in Minnesota. Together, the two halves offer the pleasures of a rich, overflowing epic novel. Max von Sydow has never given a better performance. (In his case, that's saying something.) And Liv Ullmann, pale and fragile, intense and determined, has a delicacy that isn't evident in her performances for Ingmar Bergman. Both films were directed, photographed, and edited by Troell, who also wrote the scripts with the producer, Bengt Forslund, based on novels by Vilhelm Moberg. With Eddie Axberg

and Monica Zetterlund. In Swedish. color (See *Reeling*.)

A New Leaf (1971)—Elaine May adapted and directed this harmlessly doddering comedy about an aristocratic American playboy (*Walter Matthau?*) who must marry a fortune in six weeks and finds a rich botanist (May). It's an unusually ugly-looking movie, and one can't be sure that much of anything in it was intended, but there is a sweetness about its absence of style and about its shapeless, limp comic scenes. William Redfield and George Rose help. Paramount. color (See *Deeper into Movies*.)

New York, New York (1977)—An honest failure. This United Artists big-budget musical film, directed by Martin Scorsese, suffers from too many conflicting intentions. Scorsese works within the artifices of 40s movie-musical romances and stylizes the sets in order to emphasize the shot-on-a-soundstage look. Evoking the movie past, he's trying to get at the dark side that was left out of the old cliché plots. But the improvisational, Cassavetes-like psychodrama that develops between the stars (Robert De Niro and Liza Minnelli) seems hollow and makes us uneasy, and sequences go on covering the same uncertain ground; the director seems to be feeling his way through a forest of possibilities (he shot a much longer film and then cut it down to 2 hours, 33 minutes). The effect is of desperately talented people giving off bad vibes. De Niro plays a restless hipster, a tenor-sax player who's frustrated in the big-band era—he's already into the progressive bop that's not yet accepted. Minnelli is a big-band singer who becomes popular with a wide audience through records and in musical movies. The story is about their meeting at a VJ Day celebration, their marriage, its dissolution, and their diverging musical paths. Though his role lacks depth and likability, De Niro, sleek and handsome and jumpy, brings it a locked-in, hotheaded intensity that almost holds the picture together—for the first half, anyway. But the story loses momentum once the girl gets pregnant. Trying to be subdued, Minnelli seems somewhat dazed—openmouthed and vacuous, and unpleasantly overripe. She pushes her scenes; in her hyper way, she's as false as Julie Andrews. Her two big numbers ("But the World Turns Round" and the title song) are, however, in their own wildly hysterical show-biz terms, smashing (and she's in superb voice). With Diahnne Abbott as the Harlem Club singer, Lionel Stander, Barry Primus, Mary Kay Place, Lenny Gaines, George Memmoli, and George Auld, who gives a good, sour performance as the jaundiced band leader and also dubs De Niro's sax. In addition to some mellow big-band standards, there are new songs by John Kander and Fred Ebb. The screenplay started with Earl Mac Rauch; then Mardik Martin, the cast, and others worked on it. The cinematography is by Laszlo Kovacs. Irving Lerner and Marcia Lucas were the editors; the film is dedicated to Lerner, who died during the final editing stages. (In 1981, a longer version—2 hours, 43 minutes—was released, with Minnelli's number "Happy Endings" restored.) color

New York Stories (1989)—A three-part anthology film, with sections by Martin Scorsese, Francis Coppola, and Woody Allen. Scorsese's intensely enjoyable *Life Lessons* features a masterly performance by Nick Nolte as an Action painter who needs tumult in his life. (Richard Price wrote the script.) Coppola's *Life Without Zoe* is a forgettable attempt to use New York as a city out of the Arabian Nights. Woody Allen's *Oedipus Wrecks* is a Freudian vaudeville about a Jewish lawyer (played by Allen) who feels that if he marries a Gentile (Mia Farrow) he'll escape his mother (Mae Questel). (He doesn't stand a chance.) This short-story comedy is a bit too long and schematic, but it has some genuine laughs, and a lovely performance by Julie Kavner as a hopeless involuntary comic. All told, the movie is a two-base hit. Touchstone (Disney). color (See *Movie Love*.)

The Next Man (1976)—Glamour and gore, featuring an international-playgirl assassin (Cornelia Sharpe, who speaks tonelessly and slits her eyes to express emotion). The ludicrous story is about a war between oil cartels and a visionary Saudi Arabian diplomat (Sean Connery) who's trying to bring about world peace (by making gaseous speeches). Anti-terrorist sentiments are tossed in between the cheesecake and the bombs, bullets, and knives. The picture teeters on the edge of parody without giving itself the relief of falling over. The producer, Martin Bregman, originated this project; Richard C. Sarafian directed. With Marco St. John, Albert Paulsen, Adolfo Celi, Ted Beniades, Charles Cioffi, and Bregman; cinematography by Michael Chapman. Released by Allied Artists. color (See *When the Lights Go Down*.)

Next Stop, Greenwich Village (1976)—Paul Mazursky's wonderful autobiographical lyric satire about a young comedian's life in the Village in the early 50s. With a tip-top cast headed by Lenny Baker, Ellen Greene, Christopher Walken, and Antonio Fargas, and with Shelley Winters giving perhaps her best performance—as the comedian's mother, whose unused brains and talent have turned her into a morose, irrepressible, howling freak. Also with Jeff Goldblum, Dori Brenner, Lois Smith, Mike Kellin, Michael Egan, John Ford Noonan, Lou Jacobi, Rochelle Oliver, and John C. Becher. 20th Century-Fox. color (See *When the Lights Go Down*.)

Next Time We Live, see *Next Time We Love*

Next Time We Love Also known as *Next Time We Live*. (1936)—Margaret Sullavan and James Stewart are magnetic together in this story of two careers that don't mesh. She's an actress and he's a war correspondent, and despite their love for each other their marriage doesn't work. The movie is unusually delicate and touching. This first pairing of Sullavan and Stewart is memorably romantic. In some scenes she seems miraculous, and though his line readings aren't up to hers, he's remarkably good—he's even sensual here. The film has grace notes, such as Sullavan's being superbly outfitted most of the time. It also has its embarrassments, such as a scene with the pair's too-adorable son learning French; a ludicrously clipped conversation toward the end, when Stewart's ill; and the very last scene, on a train. With Ray Milland, Grant Mitchell, and Robert McWade. Directed by Edward H. Griffith, from a script, by Melville Baker and (uncredited) Preston Sturges, based on stories by Ursula Parrott. Universal. b & w

Niagara (1953)—This isn't a good movie but it's compellingly tawdry and nasty—the only movie that explored the mean, unsavory potential of Marilyn Monroe's cuddly, infantile perversity. There's no affection for her here. This picture was made just before she won Hollywood over with *Gentlemen Prefer Blondes*, and her amoral, destructive tramp—carnal as hell—may represent Hollywood's lowest estimate of her. Monroe's wet-lipped lasciviousness is enough to keep the first half of this murder melodrama going, but by the second half there's nothing but plot twists, centering on Niagara Falls. Joseph Cotten plays the husband whom she plans to kill; Richard Allan is her lover. With Jean Peters and Denis O'Dea. Directed by Henry Hathaway, from a script by Charles Brackett, Walter Reisch, and Richard Breen. Brackett produced, for 20th Century-Fox. color

Nibelungen Saga (1923, 1924)—Utterly extraordinary: gigantic heroes, acres of studio-built sets, trailing processions, and a romantic mystique. Fritz Lang's bizarre, monumental German silent film, conceived as a tribute to the nation, is in two full-length parts—*Siegfried* and *Kriemhild's Revenge*—and the second, made a year after the first, is the madder of the two. The first tends to be static and ornamental; the second is packed with contrapuntal visual rhythms. It makes a picture like *Caligari* seem as routine as a TV sit-com. At the ending of *Siegfried*, Brünnhilde has had Siegfried killed, and his widow, Kriemhild, swears revenge. In the second picture, Kriemhild marries Attila the Hun and begins the devastation—massacres, flames, chaos. The influence of the painter Arnold Böcklin is evident; this film, in turn, was a strong influence on Eisenstein and Leni Riefenstahl. There's a fine analysis of it in Lotte Eisner's book *The Haunted Screen*. b & w

Nicholas and Alexandra (1971)—As obsequiously respectful as if it had been made about living monarchs who might reward the producer with a command performance. Viewers are put in the position of celebrity-lovers eager to partake of the home life of the dullest of the Czars. Nicholas and Alexandra (Michael Jayston and Janet Suzman) appear to be two dunces sitting on a volcano, and the solemnly square movie is more interested in the dunces than in the volcano. When one is asked to watch them for over 3 hours with no object but to feel sorry for them one's sympathies dry up. The faith healer and "holy man" Rasputin was a very funky monk, but you'd never know it from this movie, which skips the triumph of that crude peasant libertine over the court. It *avoids* drama, and the death of Rasputin (Tom Baker) is so badly staged that it doesn't seem as if he's hard to kill because he has so much rotten life in him—it just seems as if his murderers are incompetent. Directed by Franklin J. Schaffner, without the sweeping mastery of large-scale visual imagery he has shown in the past. With Laurence Olivier, Michael Redgrave, Jack Hawkins, Harry Andrews, and Alexander Knox. Adapted from Robert K. Massie's book, by James Goldman; cinematography by Freddie Young. Columbia. color (see *Deeper into Movies*.)

Nicholas Nickleby (1947)—Alberto Cavalcanti, the Brazilian who was active in the French film avant-garde of the 20s, is best known in this country for his direction of the ventriloquist episode in *Dead of Night*. His fast-moving, English-made version of the early Dickens novel has been undeservedly neglected. It's darker, more grotesque and melodramatic than the other Dickens films, with more attention paid to the visual design and the lighting than to any affectionate qualities in the characters, but the style has its own excitement, and the cast is almost everything it should be. Dickens' heroes never seem to come to much on the screen, and Derek Bond's Nicholas is no exception, but his villainous uncle (Cedric Hardwicke) is a beauty, and there are Stanley Holloway as a travelling actor, Sybil Thorndike as bawdy old Mrs. Squeers, Alfred Drayton as the properly horrible Wackford Squeers, Bernard Miles as Noggs, Aubrey Woods as Smike, and Jill Balcon and Sally Ann Howes. The action moves from Dotheboys Hall, where the odious Squeerses board unwanted children, to the King's Bench Prison, where debtors not yet utterly destitute are held. John Dighton did the adaptation. b & w

Nickelodeon (1976)—Peter Bogdanovich's slapstick homage to early fly-by-night moviemaking begins in 1910 and ends in 1915, when the director hero (Ryan O'Neal) attends the L.A. première of *The Birth of a Nation* and realizes the inadequacy of the pictures he's been churning out. It sounds promising, but Bogdanovich attempts an exercise in style, and the result is sustained clutter. It's like *Once in a Lifetime* played at the wrong speed, and it makes you feel terrible, because you realize how deeply involved the director must have been to go so blindly wrong. With Tatum O'Neal, Burt Reynolds, Jane Hitchcock, Stella Stevens, and Brian Keith. Everyone seems to be on his own. The cinematography is by Laszlo Kovacs. Columbia. color (See *When the Lights Go Down*.)

Night and Day (1946)—William Bowers, one of the three scenarists, said later that he was so ashamed of this picture that about a year after it came out he called Cole Porter, whose biography it purported to be, and told him how sorry he was, and Porter said, "Love it. Just loved it. Oh, I thought it was marvellous." Bowers says that he told Oscar Hammerstein how puzzled he was by this, and Hammerstein said, "How many of his songs did you have in it?" Bowers answered "Twenty-seven," and Hammerstein said, "Well of course he loved it. They only turned out to be twenty-seven of the greatest songs of all time. You don't think he heard that stuff that went on between his songs, do you?" This utterly wretched movie is possibly endurable to others who can blank out on that stuff in between, which involves Cary Grant, as the composer, starting as an excruciatingly unconvincing bouncy Yale undergraduate. Later on, Grant embraces Alexis Smith from time to time, but nervously, unwillingly—as if she were a carrier of Rocky Mountain spotted fever. No doubt the movie was trying to tell us something. Grant looks constrained and distracted—as if he would give anything to get out of this mess; he relaxes briefly when he sings "You're the Top" with Ginny Simms. With Monty Woolley and many other unfortunates—Mary Martin, Jane Wyman, Victor Francen, Dorothy Malone, Selena

Royle, Eve Arden, Donald Woods, Alan Hale, Paul Cavanagh, Henry Stephenson, Clarence Muse, Sig Rumann, and Herman Bing. Arthur Schwartz produced, for Warners, and Michael Curtiz directed. color

Night and the City (1950)—Several years before he made *Rififi*, Jules Dassin directed this less flamboyant thriller, which is much less well known, but, in some ways, better. Dassin's shocking specialty—a kind of stifled violence that one fears will explode—finds the right milieu in the Gerald Kersh novel, a complex view of the underside of London entertainment. An Anglo-American cast is headed by Richard Widmark, who has possibly his best role as Harry Fabian, "the artist without an art," a tout with a creative passion for fantastic, shady schemes. The victims of his double-crossing artistry include Googie Withers, Francis L. Sullivan, Gene Tierney, Herbert Lom, and—as the old-time wrestler pitted against Mike Mazurki—Stanislaus Zbyszko. With Hugh Marlowe. Script by Jo Eisinger; cinematography by Max Greene. b & w

A Night at the Opera (1935)—The Marx Brothers sometimes said that this was their best film; it isn't, but it was their greatest hit. Two beautifully stuffed American targets—grand opera and high society—are left dismantled, flapping like scarecrows. (If you ever could listen to *Il Trovatore* with a straight face, you can never do so again.) Many writers have tried to analyze Marx Brothers wit, coming up with little monographs on "dissociated thinking," "disguised social protest," or "commedia dell'arte." Think about it too much and sanity, like a lettuce leaf, begins to wilt and curl at the edges. The Marx Brothers keep turning corners you didn't know were there, and while you're trying to break down the content of lines like Groucho's "You big bully, why are you hit-

ting that little bully?", you miss the series of non sequiturs that are piling up on top of it. George S. Kaufman and Morrie Ryskind did the script, from a story by James Kevin McGuinness, and with additional material by Al Boasberg; Sam Wood directed. The cast includes Groucho's perennial grand-dame inamorata, Margaret Dumont, the most stately of stooges (her smirking dowager is rather like a comic derivative of Edna Purviance in Chaplin's movies). There are also the vocalizing lovers, Kitty Carlisle and Allan Jones, whom Irving Thalberg, the producer and a master diagnostician of popular taste, put in for people (*what* people?) to "identify with," and the cruel villain, Walter Woolf King. (Incredible as it may seem, the banal romantic melodrama which intermittently wrecks the movie proved sound at the box office.) This comedy has its classic sequence: the stateroom scene, which is widely regarded as the funniest five minutes in screen history. It will sustain you through the dreadful duets. With Sig Rumann. M-G-M. b & w

A Night in Casablanca (1946)—Standing on the sidewalk, Harpo pushes against a wall. A policeman accosts him: "What do you think you're doing—holding up the building?" Harpo nods, and the angry policeman pushes him away. The building collapses. In this comedy the Marx Brothers dismantle the international-intrigue thriller; the Warner Brothers, producers of the movie *Casablanca*, were indignant and tried to stop the production. Though not as famous as the Marx Brothers' films of the 30s, this picture is funnier than all but a handful of their earlier ones. Groucho manages the hotel in Casablanca where all the spies hang out, and Chico runs a fleet of camel taxis. With Sig Rumann, Dan Seymour, Charles Drake, Lisette Verea, and Lois Collier. Directed by Archie Mayo, from a script by Joseph Fields, Roland Kibbee, and Frank Tashlin. Produced by David L. Loew; released by United Artists. b & w

Night Games *Nattlek* (1966)—It's set in a castle in Sweden and it features the kind of depraved upper-class partying at which the question "Don't you wish you were dead?" is answered by "I'm dead already." A jazz ensemble plays as Ingrid Thulin gives birth (to a dead child, of course), and at a wedding-night party the groom (Keve Hjelm), who can't make it, gets up from bed, lets the birds out of their fancy cage and puts the cage on himself. And he vomits great gushing torrents—i.e., his whole past life. At a final party, he dynamites the castle which, because it is where his childhood took place, is presumably the block to his potency. He literally blasts through. It all seems like a huge joke but Mai Zetterling directs in a stark, grand manner, and, despite the posturing (out of Fellini and Bergman), she's gifted. The movie is ludicrous, but it isn't dead. There's a startling sequence of the groom as a child caught masturbating. The mother and the wife are look-alikes, but the wicked bitch mother is excitingly played by Thulin as a fierce despot, the wife (Lena Brundin) is a Reformation madonna with sad eyes and heavy breasts. And while the wanly virtuous young couple are having their anguished wedding-night roll, the "degenerates" run a porny home movie they've made, and it's quite lively. With Naima Wifstrand. The screenplay, by Zetterling and David Hughes, is based on her novel. (The picture caused scandals at a couple of film festivals.) In Swedish. b & w

Night Must Fall (1937)—Robert Montgomery, the foremost romantic light comedian of the early talkies, startled movie audiences when he took this role of a baby-faced killer— a Cockney psychopath carrying a sinister hatbox. Adapted (just barely) by John van Dru-ten from the Emlyn Williams play, this shocker, set in an isolated cottage, is stagebound but very scary. Intelligent, repressed Rosalind Russell is drawn to the smiling, thick-lipped Montgomery but becomes frightened when she sees him wheedling his way into the affections of a silly, spoiled old lady (Dame May Whitty). The direction, by Richard Thorpe, is somewhat ponderous (in the we-want-to-be-sure-you-are-catching-every-single-detail M-G-M manner), but the penny-dreadful theatrics are gruesomely effective. This is one of the rare movies in which the viewer loathes the potential victim (Whitty) and still doesn't want to see her get it. With Alan Marshal, Merle Tottenham, Kathleen Harrison, and E. E. Clive. (A 1964 English version, directed by Karel Reisz and starring Albert Finney, was insistently cinematic, and a mess.) b & w

Night Nurse (1931)—There's a memorable moment in this hardboiled early talkie melodrama when a drunken rich woman has passed out on the floor of her home, and Barbara Stanwyck, the nurse who is tending the woman's sick children, stands over her and says disgustedly, "You mother!" William Wellman directed this picture in his fast, unvarnished style; it has a grungy likability. Clark Gable is the sexy villain, a thieving gigolo-chauffeur in a black uniform; his specialty is socking women. Stanwyck gets it right on the jaw. But Wellman knew how to use Stanwyck for her unsentimental strength, and she does some no-nonsense slugging of her own that startled audiences at the time—and helped make her a public favorite. With Joan Blondell, who is funny and vivacious as the heroine's pal, and Ben Lyon, Charles Winninger, Ralf Harolde, Edward Nugent, and Marcia Mae Jones. From a novel by Dora Macy; adapted by Oliver H. P. Garrett, with additional dialogue by Charles Kenyon. Warners. b & w

The Night of the Following Day (1969)—
Fancy kidnapping-for-ransom movie, with
the production designed in gold and brown
and blue and black, and the characters sil-
houetted against white walls and talking in
pseudo-casual gangster jargon. Playing card-
board-cutout thugs, Marlon Brando (gold-
haired to match the visual scheme) and
Richard Boone have an edge of irony that
makes the bad movie seem a joke we're all
partly in on. Rita Moreno (also gold-haired),
who plays a ticky little drug addict, gives an
expert, stylized performance. With Pamela
Franklin and Jess Hahn. Directed by Hubert
Cornfield, who wrote the script with Robert
Phippeny, based on Lionel White's novel *The
Snatchers*. Cinematography by Willy Kurant.
Universal. color (See *Going Steady*.)

The Night of the Hunter (1955)—Despite its
peculiar overtones of humor, this is one of
the most frightening movies ever made (and
truly frightening movies become classics of a
kind). Robert Mitchum is the murderous, sex-
obsessed, hymn-singing soul-saver with
hypnotic powers, and his terrified new wife
(Shelley Winters), who has a boy and a little girl from an earlier marriage, becomes his
fervent disciple. He is something of a Pied
Piper in reverse: adults trust him, children
try to escape. The two kids' flight from the
madman is a mysterious, dreamlike episode—a deliberately "artistic" suspense fantasy, broken by the appearance of a Christian
variety of fairy godmother (Lillian Gish). The
adaptation of Davis Grubb's novel was James
Agee's last film work, and this shadowy horror fable was the first and only movie directed
by Charles Laughton; it was a total financial
disaster, and he never got a chance to direct
again. With Evelyn Varden, James Gleason,
Don Beddoe, and Peter Graves. Cinematography by Stanley Cortez; produced by Paul
Gregory. United Artists. b & w

The Night of the Iguana (1964)—Richard
Burton is the defrocked clergyman working
as a tour guide; Ava Gardner is the strumpety
widow who operates the rundown Mexican
hotel where the action centers; Deborah Kerr
is the saintly, middle-aged spinster from
Nantucket, travelling with her 97-year-old
poet-grandfather (Cyril Delevanti); Sue Lyon
is the teen-ager out to seduce the minister;
and Grayson Hall is the head of the schoolteachers' tour group. The director, John Huston, brings some coarse melodramatic vitality
to the Tennessee Williams play, but whatever
poetry it had seems to have leaked out. And
without that the movie is terribly obvious,
sentimental, and plain dumb. It's also indifferently made. M-G-M. b & w

Night of the Living Dead (1968)—It would
be fun to be able to dismiss this as undoubtedly the best movie ever made in Pittsburgh,
but it also happens to be one of the most
gruesomely terrifying movies ever made—
and when you leave the theatre you may
wish you could forget the whole horrible experience. It's about a night when the dead
rise and eat the living; seven people (the most
resourceful one is played by Duane Jones)
take refuge in a farm house, and we watch
as the relentlessly marching, hungry corpses
come in and tear at them—and we see, in
closeup, the devouring of hearts, lungs, entrails. Made by George A. Romero, who photographed and directed on a budget of
$114,000. The film's grainy, banal seriousness
works for it—gives it a crude realism; even
the flatness of the amateurish acting and the
unfunny attempts at campy comedy add,
somehow, to the horror—there's no art to
transmute the ghoulishness. (The dead also
rise and come toward us at the climax of Abel
Gance's pacifist film *J'Accuse*, but the effect
there goes far beyond the grisly-scary; the
horror has grandeur.) At first this film received almost no attention, but in two or

three years it became a hit at midnight showings after the regularly scheduled feature—and not just in the U.S. but in Tokyo, Paris, and other centers. b & w

The Night of the Shooting Stars *La Notte di San Lorenzo* (1982)—In its feeling and completeness, this film by Paolo and Vittorio Taviani may rank close to Jean Renoir's bafflingly beautiful *Grand Illusion*, and maybe because it's about the Second World War and Renoir's film was about the First, at times it's like a more deracinated *Grand Illusion*. The story is a woman's memories of her adventures as a 6-year-old in a Tuscan village and its environs during the summer of 1944, when the American troops were rumored only days away, and the Germans who had held the area under occupation were preparing to clear out—preparations that included mining the houses so they could blow them up. Yet this setting is magical, like a Shakespearean forest, and the woman's account has the quality of folklore and legend, and even its most tragic moments can be dizzyingly comic. The full fresco treatment that the directors give to the events of that summer is based on their own wartime experiences as adolescents, and on the accounts of others; it's this teeming, fecund mixture, fermenting in their heads for almost 40 years, that produces the film's giddy, hallucinated realism. With Omero Antonutti (who was the father in *Padre Padrone*) as the leader of the group of two or three dozen villagers who sneak away in the night to find the Americans. The script is by the Tavianis and the producer, Giuliani G. De Negri, with the collaboration of Tonino Guerra; the score is by Nicola Piovani; the cinematography is by Franco di Giacomo. In Italian. color (See *Taking It All In*.)

Night People (1954)—It's set in Berlin: a U.S. soldier is kidnapped; he is rescued by a U.S. Intelligence Officer (Gregory Peck) who knows how to deal with the Russians. They are "a methodical bunch of lice" and "head-hunting cannibals." That's the level of the film's anti-Communism; it's simply a reworking of the anti-Nazism of the previous era. Nunnally Johnson, who wrote the screenplay and produced and directed this melodrama, referred to it as "Dick Tracy in Berlin." Efficiently put together, on a large scale, the film is basically part of America's public relations romance with itself. With Broderick Crawford, Anita Björk, Buddy Ebsen, Rita Gam, Walter Abel, Jill Esmond, and Peter Van Eyck. 20th Century-Fox. CinemaScope, color (See *I Lost it at the Movies*.)

The Night Porter (1974)—A porno gothic, set in Vienna in 1957 and veneered with redeeming social values. As Max, a former Storm Trooper, Dirk Bogarde presides over an s & m Grand Hotel; Charlotte Rampling, who got her sexual education from him when she was a 14-year-old in a concentration camp, arrives and wants more of Max's brand of love. The film's claim that it's saying something important is offensive, but the picture is too crudely trumped up to be a serious insult. Directed by a woman, Liliana Cavani—which proves no more than that women can make junk just as well as men. With Philippe Leroy and Gabriele Ferzetti; produced by Robert Gordon Edwards. color (See *Reeling*.)

Night Shift (1982)—This isn't much of a movie but it manages to be funny a good part of the time anyway. The comedian Michael Keaton is a human whirligig with saucer eyes and quizzical eyebrows—the face of a puzzled adolescent satyr. As attendants at the morgue, he and Henry Winkler play off each other very gently. Keaton is part hipster, part innocent lost soul; he's the idea man, and he seems to have all the screwed-up big-city energy in his jive talk and his jiggling move-

N

ments, but when he has to carry through on any of his schemes he falls apart. That's where the shy, steady nerd Winkler comes in. Though this comedy is based on a newspaper item about two young men who were caught operating a prostitution ring, using a city morgue as their headquarters, it seems wildly improbable and about two-thirds of the way through, the situations begin to have the TV blahs. Still, Keaton, in his movie début, is an original, the director, Ron Howard, is one of the few young directors who know how to set up a scene so that gags can blossom, and there are a lot of attractive performers, especially the talented Shelley Long as a satiric version of the girl next door. Also with Gina Hecht, Bobby Di Cicco, and Richard Belzer. From a script by Lowell Ganz and Babaloo Mandel. Produced by Brian Grazer; a Ladd Company Release through Warners. color (See *Taking It All In*.)

The Night They Raided Minsky's (1968)— An affectionate parody tribute to burlesque, with a minimum of plot and a maximum of evocative stage routines. It's lightweight and disorganized; it's a shambles, yet a lot of it is charming, and it has a wonderful seedy chorus line—a row of pudgy girls with faces like slipped discs. Jason Robards and Norman Wisdom play a comedy team, Joseph Wiseman (memorably, elegantly funny) is the senior Minsky, Elliott Gould is the junior Minsky, and as the country girl who does interpretive dancing, Britt Ekland has her warm, big smile that is a happy substitute for acting. Directed by William Friedkin; choreographed by Danny Daniels; score by Charles Strouse and Lee Adams; cinematography by Andrew Laszlo. The script by Arnold Shulman, Sidney Michaels, and Norman Lear is based on an entertaining book (of the same title) by Rowland Barber. Also with Denholm Elliott, Harry Andrews, Forrest Tucker, Jack Burns, and Bert Lahr, whose role was re-

duced to little more than a glimpse because he died during the shooting. Produced by Lear; United Artists. color (See *Going Steady*.)

A Night to Remember (1958)—Tear-stained melodrama has an undeniable power; the 1953 American film *Titanic*, which centers on the marital miseries of Clifton Webb and Barbara Stanwyck, attracted large audiences and still attracts TV watchers. This version of the disaster, made by the English, has been generally ignored here. It's a straightforward account of how, in 1912, the scientifically constructed, "unsinkable" liner set out for New York on its first voyage with 2207 people on board, struck an iceberg, and sank in 2 hours and 40 minutes (just 37 minutes longer than it takes to see the movie). Eric Ambler's screenplay, derived from the book by Walter Lord, is well-written in a solid, unsurprising way. You come out with a clear perception of what, according to fairly reliable evidence, actually happened. This, it turns out, is far more exciting than the usual screenwriter's contrivances. Roy Baker directed this shrewd, slick job of historical reconstruction, using 200 actors with Kenneth More as the linking figure among them. There are no big-star roles, but the movie is full of small dramas. The cast includes the skinny-faced young David McCallum, Honor Blackman, Anthony Bushell, Frank Lawton, George Rose, Ralph Michael, Laurence Naismith, and Alec McCowen. The cinematography is by Geoffrey Unsworth. b & w

The Nightcomers (1971)—Ingenious but literal-minded prelude to Henry James's *The Turn of the Screw*, showing how Peter Quint (Marlon Brando) and Miss Jessel (Stephanie Beacham) corrupted the children. Quite well done—Brando is shockingly sadistic as the working-class lout and Beacham is very fine—yet pointless, since it is effective neither as a horror story nor as a psychological study. It leaves the viewer cold—perhaps even repelled. How could anyone think this movie would be entertaining? Michael Winner directed the English production, from a script by Michael Hastings. With Thora Hird and Harry Andrews. color

Nightmare Alley (1947)—A tough-minded treatment of telepathy. It opens in the carnival world, where the ultimate in how low a man can sink is represented by the Geek, who bites the heads off live chickens; shuddering dipsomaniacs take the job, for a bottle a day. We know that this is what is in store for the smart, smiling young climber Stan (Tyrone Power); this shrewd, absorbing movie is about how he gets to that point. Stan eagerly and ruthlessly learns everything he can from the plump mind reader Zeena (Joan Blondell, in a rich, intensely likable performance), after getting rid of her burnt-out partner (Ian Keith, who brings unexpected depth to his small role). Using Zeena's tricks, Stan becomes a headliner in a Chicago nightclub and begins to sample the possibilities of spiritualist rackets. The film loses its imaginative energy once it moves out of the ripe, sleazy carny milieu, and from the start the technique of the director, Edmund Goulding, is conventional, even a little stodgy. Still, the material, adapted from William Gresham's novel by Jules Furthman, is unusual and the cast first-rate. Power, who persuaded 20th Century-Fox to let him play the double-crossing heel-charlatan, puts his black-Irish good looks to ambivalent effect. With Coleen Gray giving one of her freshly thought-out performances as Stan's girl; Helen Walker as Lilith, the blackmailing psychologist who outsmarts him; Taylor Holmes as the aged industrialist who is conned into believing that Stan can help him communicate with his dead sweet-

heart; and Mike Mazurki as the carny strong man. Cinematography by Lee Garmes. b & w

Nights of Cabiria *Le Notti di Cabiria* (1957)—Possibly Federico Fellini's finest film, and a work in which Giulietta Masina earns the praise she received for *La Strada*. The structure is a series of episodes in the life of Cabiria (Masina), a shabby, aging, dreamy little Roman streetwalker—a girl whose hard, knowing air is no protection against her fundamental gullibility, which, we finally see, is her humanity and her saving grace. A famous actor (Amedeo Nazzari) picks her up and takes her to his luxurious villa; she goes to a cheap vaudeville show, and when the magician hypnotizes her, the innocent dreams of her adolescence pour out; a young man in the audience (François Périer) meets her and proposes to her, etc. Though the film seems free and almost unplanned, each apparent irrelevance falls into place. (It was the basis for the Broadway musical—and the movie musical—*Sweet Charity*.) In Italian. b & w

Nine Days a Queen Also known as *Tudor Rose*. (1936)—When Henry VIII died, his small son, Edward VI, succeeded him; when the boy died, the Warwicks and Seymours placed Lady Jane Grey on the throne, and for nine of the bloodiest, most chaotic days in England's history, she was queen. The English film version of these events is a restrained, unimaginative dramatization of the conspiratorial trap, with the young, hapless Jane (played by the gifted Nova Pilbeam) at its center. Robert Stevenson directed, and Miles Malleson wrote the dialogue. Desmond Tester is little Edward, and you'll find the familiar, welcome faces—almost like a royal family by now—Cedric Hardwicke, Sybil Thorndike, and inevitably, Felix Aylmer, and John Mills, as well. b & w

N

Nine to Five (1980)—A feminist revenge fantasy in which three office workers—Lily Tomlin, Dolly Parton (in her film début), and Jane Fonda—each with a complaint against the lecherous, petty-tyrant boss (Dabney Coleman), kidnap him, get the business humming, and institute reforms, such as equal pay for equal work, flexible hours, hiring the handicapped, and providing day-care services. Tomlin confirms herself as a star whenever she gets the material, and Dolly Parton's dolliness is very winning, but it's easy to forget that Jane Fonda is around—she seems to get lost in the woodwork. The director, Colin Higgins, is a young fossil who sets up flaccid, hand-me-down gags as if they were hilarious, and damned if the audience doesn't laugh. Written by Patricia Resnick and then reworked by Higgins. A production of IPC (the company formed by Fonda and Bruce Gilbert); released by 20th Century-Fox. color (See *Taking It All In*.)

1900 *Novecento* (1977)—Bernardo Bertolucci's utopian folly is about two boys born in the North Italian region of Emilia-Romagna on the same day in 1901. Alfredo (Robert De Niro) is the heir to the vast landholdings of his grandfather (Burt Lancaster), and Olmo (Gérard Depardieu) is the bastard grandson of the patriarch (Sterling Hayden) of the peasant clan that lives on those holdings and labors for a share of the crop. Bertolucci is trying to transcend the audience appeal of his lyrical, psychological films. He is trying to make a people's film by drawing on the mythology of movies, as if it were a collective memory. *1900* is a romantic moviegoer's vision of the class struggle—a love poem for the movies as well as for the life of those who live communally on the land. (The belief that permeates the movie is that Communism will preserve the folk culture of the peasants.) In form, it's an opera-novel, and its homage is to Verdi, the great Emilian who died on the day of the two boys' birth; it has all of Bertolucci's themes and motifs, and one could call it the Portable Bertolucci, though it isn't portable. It's like a course to be enrolled in, with a guaranteed horror every hour; there are also sequences as great as any ever filmed. The cast includes Dominique Sanda, Alida Valli, Donald Sutherland, Stefania Sandrelli, and Laura Betti. Cinematography by Vittorio Storaro; music by Ennio Morricone. The European version (it opened in 1976) ran over 5 hours; the version that Bertolucci (under duress) prepared for the U.S. runs 4 hours and 5 minutes, plus intermission. color (See *When the Lights Go Down*.)

1941 (1979)—Steven Spielberg tried out new things in this intricate slapstick farce, from a script by Robert Zemeckis and Bob Gale. The movie has a choppy beginning: it seems to start with the story (about civil defense and a long Japanese submarine off the West Coast) already under way. And Spielberg overdoes some of the broad, cartoon aspects—several of the performers seem to be carrying placards telling you what's wacko about them. But the movie gets better and better: the U.S.O. jitterbug number is a great piece of film choreography and the film overall is an amazing, orgiastic comedy, with the pop culture of an era compacted into a day and a night. There are such surprising slapstick payoffs that the film's commercial failure in this country didn't make much sense. It was accused of gigantism, and it did seem huge, though part of what was so disarmingly fresh about it was the miniature re-creation of Hollywood Boulevard at night in 1941, with little floodlights illuminating the toy cars tootling around the corners and toy planes flying so low they were buzzing through the streets. The movie gives you the feeling of a madly happy playroom. The cast includes John Belushi, Dan Aykroyd, Nancy Allen (as the girl who has a thing for planes), Robert Stack (as

General Stilwell he anchors the action), Bobby Di Cicco (the terrific dancer), Patti LuPone, Wendie Jo Sperber, Frank McRae, Ned Beatty, Tim Matheson, Lorraine Gary, Dianne Kay, John Candy, Penny Marshall, Toshiro Mifune, Christopher Lee, Eddie Deezen, Elisha Cook (Jr.), Warren Oates, Murray Hamilton, Slim Pickens, Lionel Stander, Lucille Benson, Dub Taylor, Treat Williams, and Joe Flaherty. The cinematography is by William A. Fraker; the editing is by Michael Kahn; the witty score is by John Williams. (The story was devised by the scriptwriters and John Milius.) Universal. color

Ninotchka (1939)—"Garbo Laughs," said the original ads, but there is by now a widespread story that when the time came for her laughing scene she pantomimed laughter beautifully, but no sound emerged; it was later provided by someone anonymous. The rest of her performance is her own—and she brings her incredible sensual abandon to the role of a glum, scientifically trained Bolshevik envoy who succumbs to Parisian freedom—i.e., champagne. The film includes a historic encounter, when the great instinctual artist of the screen meets the great stylist and technician of the stage—Ina Claire, as a Russian grand duchess. The fur flies exquisitely. Directed by Ernst Lubitsch, this light, satirical comedy has the nonchalance and the sophistication that were his trademark—but it also reveals that this time the trade marked him too high. There's an obviousness here; we can feel that we're being played down to. And there's a jeering cynicism built into the script: the Russians don't defect for freedom but for consumer goods. With Melvyn Douglas, Sig Rumann, Felix Bressart, Bela Lugosi, Alexander Granach, George Tobias, and Edwin Maxwell. Screenplay by Charles Brackett, Billy Wilder, and Walter Reisch, from a screen story by Melchior Lengyel. (The material is no more than a musical-

comedy turn, which it became in the stage musical *Silk Stockings*, filmed in 1957.) M-G-M. b & w

No Minor Vices (1948)—A glossy little oddball—part sophisticated farce, part nothing in particular. Louis Jourdan, bouncing around as a volatile young artist, has considerable charm. Dana Andrews plays a fatuous, psychologically oriented physician who disapproves of the artist's "decadent" painting and "immoral" way of life. The artist gets back at him by appealing to the sympathy of his wife (Lilli Palmer); the doctor is quickly twisted into knots. There's a wonderful sequence, involving an attempt to cook lobsters—a precursor of the episode in *Annie Hall*. Directed by Lewis Milestone, from a script by Arnold Manoff that doesn't have enough going on. (Milestone has nothing to cut away to.) With Jane Wyatt and Norman Lloyd. Cinematography by George Barnes. Released by M-G-M. b & w

No Time for Comedy (1940)—S. N. Behrman's romantic comedy about life in the theatre, adapted by Julius J. and Philip G. Epstein. The film is halfway between play and movie and it doesn't quite work as either; it lacks a spark, but it has amusing repartee and good New York "types," and it starts out well. A boyish Minnesota hick (James Stewart) writes a sophisticated drawing-room comedy about titled lords and ladies; it becomes a hit and he marries his star (Rosalind Russell) and writes a succession of hits. But he meets a rich, blond muse (Genevieve Tobin) who flutters her eyelids while telling him that he has deeper possibilities—that he's a "latent artist"—and his head gets puffed up. At this point the picture stalls and becomes more forced. The supporting players are very assured in the way they hit their laugh lines, especially Allyn Joslyn as a wiseguy Broadway director, Clarence Kolb as a producer, Charlie Ruggles as the muse's husband, and Louise Beavers as an actress who, between jobs, works as a maid. But Rosalind Russell's line readings are too rhythmic and mannered, and her no-nonsense, sceptical modern-woman role is tiresomely true-blue, and although James Stewart dominates the film with ease, there's not much excitement in what he does. The film recalls that period when people could stroll in Central Park at night while waiting for their reviews, and then flip to the theatre page in one newspaper after another. Lamely directed by William Keighley, for Warners. With J. M. Kerrigan, Lawrence Grossmith, and Frank Faylen as a cab-driver. b & w

No Way Out (1987)—This is a *film noir* without malevolence or mystery. It's a Yuppie thriller: it has no psychological layers. Mostly it involves chasing around the glass offices and corridors of the Pentagon (actually Stage 27 at the old M-G-M studios in Culver City). But many people respond to it with hot, jumpy enthusiasm—especially to the high-level friskiness and the display of thigh in a stretch limo. A reworking of the plot of the Kenneth Fearing novel *The Big Clock* (filmed in 1948, with Charles Laughton as a Henry Luce figure) the Robert Garland script features Gene Hackman as an arrogant Secretary of Defense who discovers that his mistress (Sean Young) has a lover—though not who it is—and, in a rage, accidentally kills her. His wormy yes-man aide (Will Patton) dreams up the idea that the lover is an as yet undiscovered—perhaps only hypothetical—Russian agent named Yuri, who can be blamed for the murder. Needing a front man for this coverup, they arrange to have a naval hero (Kevin Costner) put in charge of the search to find the lover and "neutralize" him. This naval hero is, of course, the lover, and the movie, told from his point of view, is about his peril. There's a surprise at the end—a twist that has a logic, if you take the whole movie as a wacko joke on Oliver North as the Manchurian Candidate. But it's a surprise you don't want—a fizzle. The director, Roger Donaldson, whips the action along, with camera angles changing so fast you hardly have time to ask what the chases are for or why the story points don't follow through. He can't do much about Young's archness though, or her peals of phony laughter; she may look like Kay Kendall, but she acts like a nutbird Ali McGraw. With Howard Duff, George Dzundza, Iman, and Fred Dalton Thompson. Cinematography by John Alcott; editing by Neil Travis. Orion. color (See *Hooked*.)

Nobi, see *Fires on the Plain*

None but the Lonely Heart (1944)—This was made at Cary Grant's instigation. He acquired the rights to the Richard Llewellyn novel, set in the East End of London, and he played Ernie Mott, a young Cockney drifter who grew up in oppressive poverty and lacked the will to leave the ghetto for good. Grant's friend Clifford Odets wrote the script and directed (for the first time). It was an extraordinary début film: Odets brought off some hard-earned effects with an élan that recalled Orson Welles' first movies. He also gave the material the rich melancholy of his best plays. Too much of it, however: the dirge-like, mournful, fogged up atmosphere seemed fake and stagey, and the film failed at box offices. It made a pervasive, long-lasting impression, though. And as Ernie's mother, who runs a secondhand furniture shop, Ethel Barrymore had perhaps her greatest screen role. In a few scenes, she and Grant touched off emotions in each other which neither of them ever showed on screen again. But he's not as vivid in the memory as she is. This precursor of the 50s rebel-hero was the only character Grant ever played that he is known to have consciously identified with, yet he seems somewhat miscast. With June Duprez, of the plaintive, puzzlingly perverse face and voice, as Ernie's girl; Barry Fitzgerald; George Coulouris; Roman Bohnen; Dan Duryea; Rosalind Ivan; Konstantin Shayne; and Jane Wyatt. The cinematography is by George Barnes; the musical score is by Hanns Eisler. R K O. b & w (See *When the Lights Go Down*.)

El Norte (1983)—An independently made epic about the flight of two oppressed, terrorized young Guatemalans—Rosa (Zaide Silvia Gutierrez) and her brother Enrique (David Villalpando)—who travel from their Mayan village in the highlands, which probably hasn't changed much since pre-Columbian times, to modern Los Angeles, where they pass themselves off as Mexicans and become part of the Hispanic cheap-labor force. Within a matter of days, Rosa goes from carrying a large jug of water on her head to trying to operate an electronic washing machine in a Beverly Hills mansion. Written by the director, Gregory Nava, and his wife, Anna Thomas, who was the producer, the film tries to cover all the bases—the typical difficult, wrenching experiences of Central American refugees. It's uninspired, but the subject has so much resonance that the picture doesn't leave you feeling quite as empty as an ordinary mediocre movie does. With Stella Quan as Josefita, Trinidad Silva as the L.A. job broker, and Lupe Ontiveros as Nacha. In Spanish. color (See *State of the Art*.)

North by Northwest (1959)—The title (from Hamlet's "I am but mad north-northwest: when the wind is southerly, I know a hawk from a handsaw") is the clue to the mad geography and improbable plot. The compass seems to be spinning as the action hops all over the U.S., people rush about in the wrong direction, and, for no particular reason, the hero—played by Cary Grant—heads north (by Northwest Airlines). Though not as cleverly original as *Strangers on a Train*, or as cleverly sexy as *Notorious*, this is one of Hitchcock's most entertaining American thrillers. It goes on too long, and the script seems shaped to accommodate various set pieces (such as the chase on Mount Rushmore) that he wants to put in. But it has a classic sequence, in which a crop-dusting plane tries to dust Grant, and it has a genial, sophisticated, comic tone. Just about everybody in it is a spy or a government agent (except Grant, who is mistaken for one). His performance is very smooth and appealing, and he looks so fit that he gets by with having Jessie Royce Landis, who was born the same year he was, playing his mother. The heroine is Eva Marie Saint, who doesn't seem quite herself here; her flat voice and affectless style suggest a Midwestern Grace Kelly, and a perverse makeup artist has turned her face into an albino African mask. With James Mason, Leo G. Carroll, Martin Landau as the blue-eyed menace Leonard, and, in smaller roles, Josephine Hutchinson, Philip Ober, Carleton Young, Adam Williams, and Ned Glass. The music is by Bernard Herrmann; the script, by Ernest Lehman, has a family resemblance to Hitchcock's *The 39 Steps* (and bits of it turn up again, slightly transposed, in Lehman's script for Mark Robson's *The Prize*). M-G-M. color

The North Star Also known as *Armored Attack*. (1943)—Samuel Goldwyn produced this Second World War monstrosity in his typical shiny prestige format. Anne Baxter, Farley Granger, Walter Huston, Dana Andrews, Ann Harding, Walter Brennan, and Jane Withers are Russians living in a village that fights back against its German invaders. Lillian Hellman wrote the script, Aaron Copland composed the music, James Wong Howe did the careful, studio-style cinematography, and Lewis Milestone, who had made his reputation with *All Quiet on the Western Front*—which was about the humanity of the young German soldiers who proudly went off to die in the First World War—disgraced himself by directing this slick piece of propaganda, which dehumanizes the Germans and, in the process, romanticizes the Russians so fondly that they're turned into Andy Hardy's neighbors. Among the stock characters are Erich von Stroheim, Dean Jagger, Martin Kosleck, Tonio Selwart, Esther Dale, Paul Guilfoyle, and Carl Benton Reid. The film was doctored to change its political slant and reissued in 1957 under the title *Armored Attack*. Released by R K O. b & w

Northwest Passage (1940)—Plodding adventure story with a rather queasy point of view. Even those Boy Scouts who revel in the hardships of the stalwart martinet Major Rogers (Spencer Tracy) and his Rangers in this pre-Revolutionary story may become uncomfortable when these heroes attack and burn a village of sleeping Indians. Directed by King Vidor, from the novel by Kenneth Roberts. With Walter Brennan, Robert Young, Ruth Hussey, Nat Pendleton, and an endless Technicolor landscape of the Lake Champlain district. M-G-M.

Nosferatu (1922)—Directed by F. W. Murnau, the original, superbly loathsome German version of Bram Stoker's novel *Dracula* is a concentrated essay in horror fantasy, full of weird, macabre camera effects. Though ludicrous at times (every horror film seems to become absurd after the passage of years, and many before—yet the horror remains), this first important film of the vampire genre has more spectral atmosphere, more ingenuity, and more imaginative ghoulish ghastliness than any of its successors. The movie often seems more closely related to demonic painting than to the later, rather rigid vam-

pire-movie genre. Because Murnau concentrated on scenes of suggestive and horrible beauty and didn't make the narrative line very clear, those who have had little contact with bloodsuckers may be helped by a bit of outline. Henrik Galeen's adaptation of the novel changes the setting from Victorian England to Bremen in 1838. A real-estate agent in Bremen sends his young, recently married clerk to the Carpathian woods to settle some property matters at the castle of Nosferatu (the Vampire). An emaciated skeleton of a man with a rodent face, Nosferatu spends his days in his coffin, his nights sucking blood. The clerk, though weakened by the nightly loss of blood, escapes and returns to his wife. But Nosferatu follows: he boards a sailing ship for Bremen and, incarnating and carrying pestilence, he infects the whole crew. The phantom ship reaches Bremen, and Nosferatu meets the wife, who, knowing that vampires cannot survive the dawn, surrenders herself to him. As the morning sun breaks into her bedroom, Nosferatu dissolves. The influence of this film can be seen in movies as disparate as Bergman's *The Magician* (the opening sequences of the coach) and Godard's *Alphaville* (the use of negative film). With Max Schreck as Nosferatu. (In 1978, Werner Herzog made *Nosferatu the Vampyre*, in homage to Murnau's film.) Silent. b & w

Nothing but the Best (1964)—Though enormously talented, the English writer Frederic Raphael (*Darling*, *Two for the Road*, TV's *The Glittering Prizes*) falls back on facile, brittle irony. Pictures made from his scripts have a distinctive tone—a bitchy cleverness that tends to go sour—and there's a self-satisfied air about them. In this satirical comedy about the class system, Jimmy (Alan Bates), a young clerk in a real-estate company—a working-class climber—is eager to learn how to pass for a member of the upper class. Denholm Elliott plays an aristocratic scrounger, a cynically cheerful rotter who moves in with the go-getter and tutors him in bad manners and casual arrogance. As the agent—a quick study—rises in the world, the movie suggests a satiric *Room at the Top*, but then it turns melodramatic (Jimmy's amorality includes murder) and it deflates, losing whatever impudent charm it had. All along, the material is shallow: everybody is class-conditioned, in the most obvious ways, and they're no more than their conditioning—it's poison-pen writing. Directed by Clive Donner, who seems to have an oral fixation—Jimmy's dream rich-girl (creamy-skinned, red-headed Millicent Martin) has a sexy toothy smirk, and his lecherous landlady (Pauline Delaney) has a big lewd mouth, which we see so often that it's like a seal of doom on the movie. Bates is skillful, though, and Elliott (who has the best role) is close to inspired. With Harry Andrews, James Villiers, Lucinda Curtis, and a glimpse of Bernard Levin. From a short story by Stanley Ellin; cinematography by Nicolas Roeg; the title song is sung by Millicent Martin. color

Nothing in Common (1986)—As the boyish advertising man who says, "It's economically unsound to grow up," Tom Hanks is like an updated version of the cocky reporter heroes of 30s movies, but the script puts him in a mawkish situation. After 36 unhappy years, his unworldly housewife mother (Eva Marie Saint) leaves his garment-salesman father (Jackie Gleason), and the son is thrust into the grown-up role of being a mainstay to each of them. He discovers that he has a bond with his sour, self-centered father, once a wizard at selling, who loses his job and is losing his sight, too. The movie is *Death of a Salesman* as a sit-com, with the father's misery used as a lesson to the swinging Yuppie son. Through helping his father—even when it means risking some of his standing in the advertising world—he grows up and devel-

ops a sense of values. Directed by Garry Marshall, from a script by Rick Podell and Michael Preminger, this Chicago-set comedy-weepie (in the manner of *Terms of Endearment*) is best in its hard-edged parodies of advertising. Its moralizing is insufferable, and so is the way everything is flagged for you. This isn't a movie; it's television on a big screen. With Hector Elizondo, Barry Corbin, Bess Armstrong, Sela Ward, and Conrad Janis and the Unlisted Jazz Band. The cinematography, by John Alonzo, is an awful mixture of glossy and drab. Tri-Star. color (See *Hooked*.)

Nothing Sacred (1937)—A screwball satire that was a huge success. What are generally sentimentalized as "the little people" are the targets of this famous 30s comedy. Ben Hecht, who wrote the script, has them dripping crocodile tears over a girl they think is dying of radium poisoning, and enjoying every minute of it. The audience may begin to wonder what makes the reporter-hero, Fredric March, and the girl, Carole Lombard—who was by that time "the Duse of daffy comedy"—any different. The answer can only be that they, like the author, hate phoniness. William Wellman's direction is more leisurely than usual; he has such good material here that he takes his time. There are classic sequences: March, the New York City sophisticate, arrives in a small town and learns how the natives feel about strangers when a small boy runs up and bites his leg; the swozzled Lombard passes out while showgirls impersonating the heroines of history parade in her honor. And a great slugging match between March and Lombard. With Walter Connolly as the dyspeptic big-city editor, Charles Winninger as the alcoholic small-town doctor, Slapsie Maxie Rosenbloom in his acting début, and Frank Fay, Margaret Hamilton, Monty Woolley, Hattie McDaniel, John Qualen, Hedda Hopper, and Sig Rumann. (The film spawned a Broadway

N

musical, *Hazel Flagg*, as well as a movie with Jerry Lewis in the Lombard role.) A David O. Selznick Production. Color

Notorious (1946)—Alfred Hitchcock's amatory thriller stars Ingrid Bergman as the daughter of a Nazi, a shady lady who trades secrets and all sorts of things with American agent Cary Grant. The suspense is terrific: Will suspicious, passive Grant succeed in making Bergman seduce him, or will he take over? The honor of the American male is saved by a hairbreadth, but Bergman is literally ravishing in what is probably her sexiest performance. Great trash, great fun. With Claude Rains, Louis Calhern, Madame Konstantin, and Reinhold Schunzel. Script by Ben Hecht; cinematography by Ted Tetzlaff; music by Roy Webb. A David O. Selznick Production, for R K O. b & w

La Notte (1962)—In Antonioni's earlier *L'Avventura*, which was also about the moral and spiritual poverty of the rich, his architectural sense was integral to the theme and characters; here, the abstract elements take over, and the drama becomes glacial. And his conception is distasteful: his characters seem to find glamour in their own desolation and emptiness. They are cardboard intellectuals—a sort of international café society—and their lassitude seems an empty pose. Marcello Mastroianni plays a blank-faced famous novelist; as his wife, Jeanne Moreau walks endlessly, with the camera fixated on her rear; and Monica Vitti is a brunette with money up to her ears and nothing to do. In Italian. b & w (See *I Lost it at the Movies*.)

Le Notti di Cabiria, see *Nights of Cabiria*

La Notte di San Lorenzo, see *The Night of the Shooting Stars*

Novecento, see *1900*

Now Voyager (1942)—A campy tearjerker variation on the Cinderella story: a psychiatrist (Claude Rains) enables the sexually repressed, neurotically dowdy Bostonian Charlotte Vale (Bette Davis) to become an attractive, confident woman. The scenarist, Casey Robinson, adapted the novel by Olive Higgins Prouty, the genius of kitsch who also wrote *Stella Dallas*; both novels are about the glories of female self-sacrifice. A couple of the most quoted bits in film history come from this movie: Paul Henreid lighting two cigarettes and tenderly handing one to Davis, and her parting line to him: "Don't ask for the moon—we have the stars." The best scene may actually be Charlotte's brisk dismissal of her priggish suitor, played by John Loder—"Let's not linger over it." The score, by Max Steiner, aims right for the jugular; the director, Irving Rapper, is just barely competent, and the action plods along, yet this picture is all of a piece, and if it were better it might not work at all. This way, it's a schlock classic. (Mary Gordon's novel *Final Payments* has the markings of an 80s equivalent.) With Gladys Cooper, Bonita Granville, Lee Patrick, Ilka Chase, Charles Drake, Franklin Pangborn, James Rennie, Frank Puglia, and Janis Wilson as Tina. Warners. b & w

La Nuit américaine, see *Day for Night*

La Nuit de Varennes (1981)—Descended from a long line of "Gallic romps," this is a creakingly cultured historical pageant set in the time of Louis XVI. For diverse reasons, assorted historical and fictional personages are travelling by stagecoach to Varennes; the King, who has fled with the Queen, is also on the road, in a coach ahead of them. And what do the ladies and gentlemen who are trailing behind the King do? For two and a half hours, they look knowingly at each other and talk literately. As the decaying Casanova, Marcello Mastroianni (who is made to look toweringly tall) has a couple of superb moments—one with Laura Betti as a jolly touring opera singer, and one with Andrea Ferreol as a wealthy woman who declares her passion for him. Jean-Louis Barrault looks great as the scandalously popular, often pornographic writer Restif de la Bretonne, but the role has been written to make Restif a darling old reprobate, and Barrault just keeps smiling. Also with Hanna Schygulla as a royalist countess; Jean-Claude Brialy, who is almost a comic archetype as her devoted hairdresser; Harvey Keitel as Thomas Paine; and Daniel Gélin and Jean-Louis Trintignant. Written by the director, Ettore Scola, and Sergio Amidei. A French-Italian co-production. In French. color (See *Taking It All In*.)

Nutcracker, The Motion Picture (1986)—There's a sensuousness about seeing ballet on a big screen, and Carroll Ballard, who directed, uses it so that we identify with the young heroine's dreams of romantic fulfillment, and identify, too, with the way she fights off the kinds of recognition that growing up involves. The movie is poised at that moment in childhood when this child longs to go to adults' parties and be treated as a lovely young lady but also wants to escape and run upstairs to play with her toys. It's a fairy-tale Christmas-party movie that avoids confectionary innocuousness—partly because the designs, by Maurice Sendak, have his low-down, bad-boy klunkiness. The movie has an enchantment that's distinct from that of the stage versions—even, no doubt, from that of the production it's based on, the one choreographed for the Pacific Northwest Ballet by its artistic director, Kent Stowell, and designed by Sendak, that had its première in Seattle late in 1983. Ballard's is an ideal sensibility for a movie that tells its story primarily in non-verbal terms. The landscape of this film is childhood before the hormones begin to rage. Yet your responses to things are already being affected. You have strange thoughts about dirty old men who compete with princes, and you accuse the old men of putting rodents in your dreams. But the accusation itself is part of a dream. The dancers of the Pacific Northwest Ballet are a fresh, well-trained group. From the E.T.A. Hoffmann story "The Nutcracker and the Mouse King." Music by Tchaikovsky. color (See *Hooked*.)

The Nutty Professor (1963)—Jerry Lewis in a Jekyll-and-Hyde story that provides him with one of the best gimmicks of his career: as Julius Kelp, he's a shy, clumsy chemistry professor, a simp with specs and rabbity teeth, but when he drinks his formula he turns into a brash, domineering hipster singer named Buddy Love—i.e., a cartoon of Dean Martin. Lewis has reconstituted his former team but now plays both halves, and working within this format he has some scenes that can hold their own with the classic silent comedies. The picture is very erratic, and it's too long and repetitive; Lewis, who also directed and wrote the script (with Bill Richmond), has always had trouble knowing when to drop something. But he had the good taste to cast Stella Stevens as the heroine; with her just faintly infantile sexiness, she's a remarkably curvy and pert straight woman. Lewis plays the hapless Julius for childlike pathos, and Buddy for hollow-man Las Vegas loathsomeness; yet in his TV appearances in the years that followed he moved even closer to Buddy Love—even down to singing loudly and off-key, and being aggressively maudlin as he milked the audience for approval. With Kathleen Freeman, Howard Morris, Henry Gibson, and Les Brown and his band. Paramount. color

Nybyggarna, see *The New Land*

Obchod na Korze, see *The Shop on Main Street*

Occupe-toi d'Amélie, see *Oh, Amelia!*

October *Oktyabr'* Also known as *Ten Days That Shook the World.* (1927)—Eisenstein followed *Potemkin*, made in 1925, with this epic celebrating the 10 days in 1917 during which the Bolsheviks overthrew the Kerensky government. It continues his striking experimental methods—the violent juxtapositions, the use of visual symbols to communicate abstract ideas, and the concept of the masses as hero. The movie also has a niche in the history of political falsification: the Soviet government commissioned the film for the 10th anniversary of the Revolution, but it was not shown. Trotsky was one of the main characters in Eisenstein's original version, and Trotsky at the time was organizing demonstrations against the Communist Party; Eisenstein had to spend five months re-editing the work to dislodge Trotsky from his place in the making of the Revolution. Even this edited version was later banned, as "formalist." Maybe because of the pressures Eisenstein experienced, the film lacks excitement, and it may leave you cold. (It's almost impossible to feel cold about *Potemkin*.) Eisenstein's 1924 film, his brutal, bloody *Strike*, has a charge and a sense of a new direction. The satire in *October* is heavy-handed, and its visual puns are too simpleminded; it seems already the end of his youthful, revolutionary period. Silent. b & w

Octopussy (1983)—This is probably the most casual of the James Bond series, and in some ways it's more like the Bob Hope and Bing Crosby *Road* comedies than it is like the Bonds. It features a chase sequence in a crowded marketplace, with a great camera angle on a camel looking up and doing a double-take as an automobile flies over its head. And among the disguises that Bond—Roger Moore—uses are a gorilla suit and an alligator outfit that doubles as a boat. Moore gets most of his effects here by the spark in his worried, squinched-up eyes; he may not be heroic, but he's game. This 14th in the Bond series (or 13th, if you don't include *Casino Royale*) is set against a tourist-paradise India. It's not the latest-model Cadillac; it's a beat-out old Cadillac, kept running with junkyard parts. But it rattles along agreeably, even though the director, John Glen, seems to lose track of the story, and neither he nor the writers (George

MacDonald Fraser, with Richard Maibaum and Michael G. Wilson) appear to have thought out the women's roles. The picture doesn't deliver on the chic perversities suggested by the inelegant title (and some of the decor). As Octopussy, the beautiful amazon Maud Adams is disappointingly warm and maternal—she's rather mooshy. (At one moment, she's a leader, and the next moment she's a dupe who doesn't know what's going on around her.) With Kristina Wayborn as the tall greasy-lipped blonde, and Louis Jourdan, Kabir Bedi, Steven Berkoff, Vijay Amritraj, and David and Tony Meyer as the knife-throwing twins. Produced by Albert R. Broccoli. M-G-M/United Artists. color (See *State of the Art*.)

Odd Man Out (1946)—Wounded at noon, the Irish rebel Johnny MacQueen (James Mason) stumbles through the streets of Belfast until midnight—the object of an intense, widespread manhunt. The tormented, delirious man, bleeding to death, seeks (but does not find) refuge on his way to the grave. Despite the reservations we may feel about his final denunciation of a world without charity, it's a memorable scene. Though the director, Carol Reed, doesn't quite succeed in creating a masterpiece (the inflated ideas in the script don't allow him to), there are bravura visual passages, the sound is often startlingly effective, and the film provides an experience that can't be shrugged off. Mason isn't only a resourceful actor; he's also a superb camera subject, and Reed and the cinematographer, Robert Krasker, draw us so close to his Johnny MacQueen that we want to save him to save ourselves. With Kathleen Ryan, W. G. Fay, Maureen Delany, Denis O'Dea, F. J. McCormick, William Hartnell, Dan O'Herlihy, Fay Compton, Cyril Cusack, and, regrettably, Robert Newton, in a badly misconceived performance in a badly misconceived role—the drunken mad painter

Lukey. From F. L. Green's novel, adapted by Green and R. C. Sherriff. Score by William Alwyn. (A 1969 American version, *The Lost Man*, starred Sidney Poitier.) b & w

Odd Obsession, see *Kagi*

Oedipus Rex (1957)—With co-directing help from Irving Lerner, Tyrone Guthrie transcribed his famous production, as it was performed at Stratford (Canada) in 1954 and 1955. Guthrie uses the Yeats translation of Sophocles' tragedy, and the cast performs in masks. This is certainly authentic, and no doubt onstage it helped to suggest that the actors represented figures larger than life. The hypnotic effect of the masked, endlessly moving robed figures does begin to suggest a ritual experience, and the readings are very fine, but the camera destroys even ordinary stage distance and brings us smack up against painted, sculpted papier-mâché. One may feel benumbed, looking at the mouth openings for a sign of life underneath. With Douglas Campbell in the lead. color

Oeil pour oeil, see *An Eye for an Eye*

Of Human Bondage (1934)—Bette Davis had a great slouch in the role of Mildred, the scheming, deceitful Cockney waitress who sinks her hooks into the sensitive hero, Leslie Howard. (Howard was the man-born-to-be-betrayed until Dirk Bogarde came along.) Davis makes her role work through sheer will; she doesn't let it happen, she makes it happen—and, boy, you'd better watch! Her peroxide-blond Mildred may be too showily *mean* to be convincing, but Davis's energy was, for the first time, fully released on the screen, and the role made her a star. John Cromwell directed this careful, rather stilted version of the Somerset Maugham novel. The other women in the hero's life are played by the lovely young Frances Dee and the unusual, wry Kay Johnson. With Reginald Denny, Reginald Owen, and Alan Hale. (Remade by Edmund Goulding in 1946, with Paul Henreid and Eleanor Parker, and by Ken Hughes—with additional scenes by Henry Hathaway—in 1964, with Laurence Harvey and Kim Novak.) R K O. b & w

Of Mice and Men (1940)—When Lewis Milestone prefaced the credits of his version of the John Steinbeck play and novel with George (Burgess Meredith) and Lennie (Lon Chaney, Jr.) fleeing a posse, he was, no doubt, aiming for economy and tension. He couldn't have guessed that he was starting a new vogue, and that it would become almost standard practice for a film's action to precede the credit information even when the action made no particular sense as a prologue. The story, about the friendship between two lonely, vagrant ranch hands—the small, bedraggled, intelligent George and the simpleminded giant Lennie—is gimmicky and highly susceptible to parody, but it is emotionally effective just the same. The film was beautifully put together, and has a fine Aaron Copland score. Betty Field's silly, vain, hapless Mae is a small acting classic, and the cowboy star Bob Steele is amazingly good as her sadistic husband, Curley. With Leigh Whipper, memorable as the lean, bitter Crooks (an unjolly black man), and Charles Bickford. A Hal Roach Production, released by United Artists. b & w

An Officer and a Gentleman (1982)—This formula romantic melodrama, which involved the regenerative moral powers of military discipline, seems to come out of a time warp, but the director, Taylor Hackford, has done a smashing job of making the retrograde love story whiz by. He has a headlong style; he gives the picture so much propulsion that it gains a momentum of its own. It's crap, but crap on a motorcycle. Richard Gere

is the tightly wound-up loner who is determined to become a flyer; the movie centers on his 13-week basic-training ordeal at the Naval Aviation Officer Candidate School in the Northwest, near Puget Sound. Gere has a striking moment when the character cracks, after the tough drill sergeant (Louis Gossett, Jr.) has caught him in some petty chiselling and has punished him. But after he has broken down—when you expect him to be emotionally transfigured—he's still Richard Gere, lost in his own placid beauty. As the millworker heroine, Debra Winger brings the film sultriness; you pull for this heroine because her tough-chick little-girl insolence plays off the avid look in her eyes that tells you she longs to make human contact. Winger convinces you that this girl really believes her life would be empty if she didn't share it with the hero. Gossett plays the sergeant bone hard; it's a beautifully hammy austere performance. There are also impressive characterizations by David Keith as the hero's friend and Robert Loggia as the hero's father, and there are entertaining flashes of Tony Plana as an officer candidate with a Mohawk haircut and Lisa Eilbacher as a woman candidate. They all work under a handicap: the script, by Douglas Day Stewart, is schematic in the manner of TV drama, circa 1955. Paramount. color (See *Taking It All In*.)

Oh, Amelia! *Occupe-toi d'Amélie* Also known as *Look After Amelia*. (1950)—A Parisian cocotte (Danielle Darrieux) agrees to a mock marriage ceremony, is deceived by a genuine ceremony but manages to outwit the fate worse than death—respectability. Georges Feydeau, "the father of French farce," wrote about 40 of these beautifully constructed follies; this is one of his most famous. Claude Autant-Lara's direction is all speed and artifice, a surprising change of pace from his other work (*Devil in the Flesh, The Game of Love*). He emphasizes the stylization by setting the action behind the footlights and moving in and out of the theatre. With Jean Desailly, Carette, and Grégoire Aslan, in what's probably his best screen role, as Le Prince de Palestrie. In French. b & w

Oh, God! (1977)—Basically a single-joke movie. George Burns is God in a baseball cap; He appears to John Denver, a mild supermarket manager with a Dutch-boy hairdo that makes him look as if he has no ears, and tells him to spread His Word. The movie isn't exactly painful to watch—Burns has his superb quirky timing, and he gets everything imaginable out of his lines—but listening to God's bland messages (which sound like est philosophy) is like sinking in a mountain of white flour. The picture is so cautious about not offending anyone that it doesn't rise to the level of satire, or even spoof. It's very thin and quiet—a soft-sell religious lecture—and there's a vaudeville piety about it, a greeting-card shallowness. (Give brotherly love a chance.) It seems to congratulate the audience for laughing at its harmless little jokes. With Teri Garr, who has a funny moment or two when she squinches her eyes in suffering (she's like a pretty, blond Olive Oyl), and Donald Pleasence, Ralph Bellamy, William Daniels, Barnard Hughes, Barry Sullivan, Jeff Corey, George Furth, Paul Sorvino (in a caricature of a religious faker), and Dinah Shore and Carl Reiner as themselves. From Larry Gelbart's adaptation of Avery Corman's novel. As the director, Reiner is no more than a caretaker (he kept his toupee on), and the cinematographer, Victor Kemper, has thrown the same bright light over everything, as if he thought the picture would play only in drive-ins. Actually, it played widely and was a huge success. The sequel was called *Oh God! Book II*. Warners. color

Oh! What a Lovely War (1969)—A big, heavy anti-war musical in the pukka-sahib tradition of English moviemaking, with John Mills, Laurence Olivier, Ralph Richardson, John Gielgud, Michael and Corin and Vanessa Redgrave, Maggie Smith, Dirk Bogarde, John Clements, Susannah York, Jack Hawkins, Edward Fox, Cecil Parker, Ian Holm, et al.; if a bomb had fallen on the set, the English theatre would have been wiped out. The conception is a music-hall revue in which the songs of the First World War are counterpointed with the battle statistics to evoke the myths and facts of war. There's a suggestion of how things should go in a number with naïve young chorus girls luring the boys to do their duty. And when Maggie Smith delivers a raucous patriotic song, she's startling and vivifying and you can see that the movie, which is based on the stage production by Joan Littlewood's company, is meant to stir your sentiments, evoke nostalgia, and make you react to the obscenity of battles and bloodshed. Apparently it does do all that for some people. But as in Richard Lester's *How I Won the War* and Tony Richardson's *The Charge of the Light Brigade*, the specific target is the follies of the upper classes, and the explanation of war is the British equivalent of the adolescent *Mad*-magazine approach: wars are made by the officers, who are homicidal imbeciles interested only in personal ambition and indifferent to the death of their men. At times, when these movies positively exult in imbecility (Gielgud's scenes in *Light Brigade* and Olivier harrumphing around in this one) the satire is effective, because the actors can give these monster-ninnies such a glow that their stupidity has a real, Marx Brothers madness to it. But most of the time, particularly in *How I Won the War* and here, the moviemakers just keep demonstrating the same proposition as outrageously as possible. The ritual exhumations of historical figures become as elaborate as their funerals once were; the English pick at their old dead leaders, pounding and jabbing—toreros trying to draw blood from stuffed toy bulls. Directing a movie for the first time, Richard Attenborough has a stately, measured approach—just what the 50 musical numbers don't need. color (See *Deeper into Movies*.)

Oil for the Lamps of China (1935)—The muckraking novel by Alice Tisdale Hobart had been a best-seller, and her account—sentimental but basically sound—of how the American oil companies recruited idealistic young men, used them, and then dumped them, seemed a natural for the movies. But with a bathetic script (by Laird Doyle), the apathetic direction of Mervyn LeRoy, and a lacklustre cast (Pat O'Brien, Josephine Hutchinson, Lyle Talbot, Jean Muir, Donald Crisp, John Eldredge, Arthur Byron, Henry O'Neill), the picture fell into the deadly "worthwhile" category. Also with Willie Fung, Keye Luke, Christian Rub, and Willard Robertson. Warners. b & w

Les Oiseaux vont mourir au Pérou, see *Birds in Peru*

Oktyabr', see *October*

Old Acquaintance (1943)—Trashy fun, on an unusually literate level. One of the rare dry-eyed "women's pictures," it features bitchery and keeps its passages of self-sacrifice fairly tart. Bette Davis is an admirably tough-minded, no-nonsense serious writer, and Miriam Hopkins is her flouncy, butterfly-brained friend, who, out of envy, becomes the author of slovenly big best-sellers. Adapted from John van Druten's play, it spans 18 years of their love-hate friendship, including a glorious scene in which Davis shakes the catty, hysterical Hopkins. John Loder is Hopkins' husband, who wants to leave her for Davis; Dolores Moran is Hopkins' rebellious daughter; Phillip Reed is a playboy seducer; and Gig Young is the young

man who falls in love with the middle-aged Davis. With Esther Dale, Anne Revere, and Roscoe Karns. Directed by Vincent Sherman. (Remade in 1981, as *Rich and Famous*.) Warners. b & w

The Old Dark House (1932)—This wonderful deadpan takeoff of horror plays was directed by the eccentric James Whale in the witty, perverse, and creepy manner he also brought to *The Bride of Frankenstein*. Five travellers (Charles Laughton, Melvyn Douglas, Raymond Massey, Gloria Stuart, and Lilian Bond) are caught in a storm in Wales. They seek shelter in a gloomy mansion, which is inhabited by a prize collection of monsters and decadent aristocrats; a mute, scarred brute of a butler (Boris Karloff) attends a prissy madman (Ernest Thesiger), his religious-fanatic hag of a sister (Eva Moore), his pyromaniac-dwarf younger brother (Brember Wells), and their father—a 102-year-old baronet. (The performer is listed as "John Dudgeon," but the part is actually played by a woman, Elspeth Dudgeon.) Based on J. B. Priestley's novel *Benighted*, this camp comedy-fantasy was adapted by Benn W. Levy, with additional dialogue by R. C. Sherriff. Universal. b & w

The Old Maid (1939)—Bette Davis doesn't have much talent for masochism. When she attempts the sacrificial-mother roles that were meat and potatoes to many a trouper, she builds the character so painstakingly that she loses her flair and turns mealy. In this costume picture, taken from Zoë Akins' Pulitzer Prize play version of the Edith Wharton novel, she's an unwed mother, forced to turn over her 5-year-old daughter to—of all people—Miriam Hopkins, as her married cousin, and then she must stand by and watch as the daughter grows up treating her contemptuously as a spinster aunt. Full of tight-lipped renunciation, Davis gives what might be called a creditable performance; the picture isn't bad, but it trudges along and never becomes exciting. Edmund Goulding directed smoothly, from Casey Robinson's screenplay. With Jane Bryan as the daughter, and George Brent, James Stephenson, Louise Fazenda, Jerome Cowan, William Lundigan, and Donald Crisp. Warners. b & w

Oliver! (1968)—On the stage *Oliver!* was an undistinguished musical that people took their children to, dutifully; it was an English variant of Broadway Americana. The movie transforms the material; it's not only a musical entertainment but an imaginative version of the novel as a lyrical, macabre fable. The tone is set in the opening sequence, in the children's workhouse, when Oliver's "Please, sir, I want some more" leads into a choreographed children's riot. The stylization seems to put quotation marks around everything Dickensian, in a way that makes you more aware of the qualities of Dickens' art. It's as if the movie set out to be a tribute to Dickens and a comment on his melodramatic art as well as to tell the story of Oliver Twist. The songs (by Lionel Bart) provide the distancing that enables us to appreciate Dickens' pathos intellectually, and the director, Carol Reed, gives a superb demonstration of intelligent craftsmanship; he doesn't urge us to tears—he leaves us our pride. Typically, the best moment is a quiet one. Oliver (Mark Lester), who has been listening to "Who Will Buy?," the lovely early-morning song of the tradespeople in Bloomsbury, walks along singing a few bars to himself, and it is probably the most delicately beautiful reprise in movie-musical history. The score isn't great, but it's certainly well sung. With Ron Moody as Fagin; Harry Secombe as Mr. Bumble; Shani Wallis as Nancy; Oliver Reed, who finds the right outlet for his peculiar talents as Bill Sikes; and Jack Wild as the Artful Dodger. The musical sequences were choreographed by Onna White; the cinematography

is by Oswald Morris; the set designs are by John Box; the screenplay is by Vernon Harris. Produced by John Woolf. color (See *Going Steady.*)

Oliver Twist (1948)—In the person of Alec Guinness, Fagin the Viper, the corrupter of youth, has a sly, depraved charm. David Lean directed this phantasmagoric version of the Dickens novel right after he did *Great Expectations* (that was Guinness's first film; this is his second), but it ran into some troubles over here: Fagin, the master pickpocket, is Jewish, and pressure groups objected to such a low Jewish character; with seven minutes of offending closeups and profiles plucked, a somewhat assimilated Fagin was allowed to enter the country in 1951. In a later period, the film would probably have been protested by gay activists as well, because Fagin comes across as a malignant old homosexual. The book is, of course, an attack on cruelty, and the movie in its fidelity is sometimes cruel to the audience, especially in the terrifying scene when Bill Sikes (Robert Newton) murders Nancy (Kay Walsh) because she tried to help Oliver, while his dog scratches at the door, and in the sequence when Sikes has Oliver in his clutches. With John Howard Davies as Oliver, Francis L. Sullivan as Bumble, Anthony Newley as the Artful Dodger, and Diana Dors, Kathleen Harrison, Henry Stephenson, Mary Clare, Ivor Barnard, and Peter Bull. Produced by Ronald Neame, for J. Arthur Rank; screenplay by Lean and Stanley Haynes; production design by John Bryan; music by Arnold Bax; cinematography by Guy Green; camera operator, Oswald Morris. b & w

Olivia, see *Pit of Loneliness*

Los Olvidados Originally released in the U.S. as *The Young and the Damned.* (1950)—Set in Mexico, Luis Buñuel's ruthless—almost surgical—examination of how the poor prey on one another is the most horrifying of all films about juvenile crime. The one masterwork on this subject, it stands apart from the genre by its pitilessness, its controlled passion. Buñuel doesn't treat his characters as ideas but as morally responsible human beings; there is little of the familiar American-movie cant that makes everyone responsible for juvenile crimes except the juveniles. There's no pathos in this film; it's a squalid tragedy that causes the viewer to feel a moral terror. Buñuel, whose early work fascinated Freud, creates scenes that shock one psychologically. Among them here is the mother-meat dream—perhaps the greatest of all movie dream sequences; it is disturbing long after the lacerations of the more realistic material have healed. Buñuel had intended much more in this surreal vein but he did not have a completely free hand. For example, in the scene in which one of the boys goes to beat up and kill another boy, the camera reveals in the distance a huge 11-story building under construction; Buñuel had wanted to put an orchestra of a hundred musicians in the building. The cast includes Estela Inda and Roberto Cobo; cinematography by Gabriel Figueroa. In Spanish. b & w

Olympia, see *Olympiad*

Olympiad Also known as *Olympia*. (1938)— (Sometimes Part I and Part II are shown separately.) During the 30s the international press ridiculed Hitler's supposed infatuation with the red-haired dancer-skier-actress turned movie director, Leni Riefenstahl, to whom he had entrusted the production of movies on his political conventions and on the 1936 Olympic Games. The results were the two greatest films ever directed by a woman. Out of the Nuremberg Rally of 1934, Riefenstahl made the most outrageous political epic of all time, the infamous, hypnotic *Triumph of the Will*; out of the Berlin Olympics she made a great lyric spectacle. *Olympiad* is only incidentally a record of the actual games: she selected shots for their beauty rather than for a documentary record. After 18 months of editing she emerged with over 3 hours of dazzling quality—a film that affects one kinesthetically in response to movement, and psychologically in response to the anguish and strain of men and women competing for a place in history. Despite Hitler's Aryan myth, she knew beauty when she saw it: in the throbbing veins of Jesse Owens' forehead (in her book on *Olympiad*, Riefenstahl has a simple caption for his picture—"Jesse Owens, *der schnellste Mann der Welt*"); in the lean Japanese swimmers; in the divers soaring in flight so continuous that they have no nationality. Viewed now, *Olympiad* is an elegy on the youth of 1936: here they are in their flower, dedicated to the highest ideals of sportsmanship—these young men who were so soon to kill each other. b & w

On Approval (1943)—A dadaist English comedy. Clive Brook, Beatrice Lillie, Roland Culver, and Googie Withers hold to the drawing-room style of an antique play by Frederick Lonsdale so relentlessly that the old, arch clichés of "daring" dialogue are reactivated. You can't help responding to these old quips when they are delivered by actors who appreciate their absurdity. Groomed by Cecil Beaton, the quartet of players is surrealistically elegant. As the stiff-backed shrew, Bea Lillie delivers what has been acclaimed as the perfect Lillie line: "You will find the dinghy by the jetty." As the heroine, an American heiress, Googie Withers demonstrates that an actress can be utterly charming even while parodying romantic charm. Everyone who has seen the movie seems to remember the great proposal scene and the great refusal, and Googie Withers asking, "What color are my eyes?" The real star of the piece is the fantastically adroit Clive Brook; his timing is perfection, both in the role of the exhausted, effete Duke, and in the direction. He also did the adaptation (with Terence Young). b & w

On Golden Pond (1981)—The kind of uplifting twaddle that traffics heavily in rather basic symbols: the gold light on the pond stands for the sunset of life, and so on and on. Directed by Mark Rydell, from Ernest Thompson's adaptation of his own 1978 play, the movie is a doddering valentine in which popsy Norman (Henry Fonda), who's having his 80th birthday, and mopsy Ethel (Katharine Hepburn), who's nearing her 70th, crack jokes, weather domestic crises, and show us the strength of solid Yankee values. Or is it "good American stock," or Hepburn's pedigreed cheekbones? The movie is shaped so that it seems to be getting at the problems of old age (Norman's eyes and ears are failing, his memory is spotty, and his body is becoming more and more unreliable), but then his crankiness is made to appear sly—a form of one-upmanship. He's meant to be a lovable curmudgeon. With Jane Fonda, who gives a tense performance in the terrible role of the neurotic daughter of the lovey-dovey old pair; and Dabney Coleman, Doug McKeon, and William Lanteau. Produced by Bruce Gilbert; released by Universal. color (See *Taking It All In*.)

On Her Majesty's Secret Service (1969)— This Bond thriller—the sixth, and set mainly in Switzerland—introduces a new Bond, George Lazenby, who's quite a dull fellow, and the script, by Richard Maibaum, isn't much, either, but the movie is exciting, anyway. In some ways, it's the most dazzling of the series up to this time. The director, Peter Hunt, looks to be a wizard at action sequences, particularly in an ethereal ski chase and a mean, fast bobsled chase. Diana Rigg

is a tall, amusing Mrs. Bond, and Gabriele Ferzetti (from *L'Avventura*) is an amiable gangster-tycoon; he and Ilse Steppat, the indefatigable villainess, help give the picture some tone. With Telly Savalas as Blofeld. The second unit work is by John Glen; there's additional dialogue by Simon Raven. Produced by Harry Saltzman and Albert R. Broccoli. United Artists. color

On the Avenue (1937)—One of the best of the 20th Century-Fox musicals of the 30s, despite its unevenness and lack of sophistication. If it had nothing else, it might still be worth seeing for Alice Faye singing the memorable "This Year's Kisses," and it has a lot more: Dick Powell in ebullient voice, the Ritz Brothers doing a parody number, and a first-rate Irving Berlin score that includes "I've Got My Love to Keep Me Warm," "Slumming on Park Avenue," and "You're Laughing at Me." The love interest involves ever-beautiful, ever-coy Madeleine Carroll, who gurgles when she means to talk, but the director, Roy Del Ruth, doesn't linger on her. He does, blessedly, linger on Harry Ritz, and when this great manic vaudevillian puts on drag and does an imitation of Alice Faye, or when he exercises his eyeballs, you can just barely gasp "dada." With John Davis, George Barbier, Cora Witherspoon, Walter Catlett, E. E. Clive, Alan Mowbray, and Billy Gilbert. Written by Gene Markey (who was also the producer) and William Conselman; choreography by Seymour Felix. b & w

On the Beach (1959)—Linus Pauling was quoted as saying, "It may be that some years from now we can look back and say that *On the Beach* is the movie that saved the world." The greatest ability of the director, Stanley Kramer, may have been for eliciting fatuous endorsements from eminent people. This cautionary tale brings together a group of stars and puts them on the littoral of Australia, to await the lethal hydrogen-bomb cloud that has wiped out the rest of the world's population. Gregory Peck plays the commander of an American submarine with his customary relentless dignity, even when he's cuddling up with Ava Gardner, a lovable wildflower "who has lived too hard and drunk too much." Anthony Perkins, one of the submarine officers, gangles, and wrestles, wet-eyed, with the problem of whether to give suicide pills to his wife (Donna Anderson) and child; Fred Astaire is a civilian scientist who explains the disaster by saying that somebody has pulled a boner. Somebody has; his initials are S. K. Adapted from the Nevil Shute novel by John Paxton; cinematography by Giuseppe Rotunno and Daniel Fapp; music by Ernest Gold. United Artists. b & w

On the Bowery (1956)—The derelicts of New York's enormous skid row were persuaded to act out a story that is essentially their own. This is the technique Flaherty used in *Man of Aran* and *Nanook of the North*—but how different the results were! The basic truth of this story may be gauged by the fact that the man who plays the derelict hero later refused a Hollywood contract with the words "I just want to be left alone. . . . There's nothing else in life but the booze." Yet, as it's played, the script seems all wrong, and the work is awkward, hesitant, without the revelations the material cries out for. However, some reviewers evoked the names of Dostoevski and Christ. Produced by Lionel Rogosin. b & w

On the Town (1949)—This musical about three sailors with 24 hours leave in New York has an undeserved high reputation. Yes, Gene Kelly, Frank Sinatra, Betty Garrett, Ann Miller, Jules Munshin, Vera-Ellen (as Miss Subways), and Florence Bates, Tom Dugan, and Alice Pearce are all in it, and it's the Com-

den and Green musical with the remnants of the Bernstein score. But its exuberant love of New York seems forced, and most of the numbers are hearty and uninspired. Kelly and Stanley Donen choreographed and directed. Produced by Arthur Freed, for M-G-M. color

On the Waterfront (1954)—The director, Elia Kazan, and the writer, Budd Schulberg, start out to expose racketeering in the waterfront unions, and wind up trying to make the melodrama transcend itself. They fail, but the production took eight Academy Awards anyway, and most of them were deserved. It is one of the most powerful American movies of the 50s, and few movies caused so much talk, excitement, and dissension—largely because of Marlon Brando's performance as the inarticulate, instinctively alienated bum, Terry Malloy. Some of Brando's scenes, such as his having a beer with Eva Marie Saint in a bar and his conversation with Rod Steiger in a car, have real vibration. (The latter one has been imitated to the point of notoriety.) The attempt at dynamic Christian symbolism and Karl Malden's big scenes as a conscientious priest are far below the imaginative level of the simpler, more realistic scenes, and Kazan hypes up the hollowest parts of the melodrama, achieving some effects of shrieking emptiness. (In order to have a triumphant, audience-pleasing finish what actually happened in the dock situation that the film was based on has been falsified; the model for Terry Malloy did not succeed in toppling the crooked bosses.) It's a near-great film, though. Score by Leonard Bernstein; cinematography by Boris Kaufman; based on articles by Malcolm Johnson. With Lee J. Cobb as an avaricious union boss, and Leif Erickson, Martin Balsam, Tony Galento, Fred Gwynne, Pat Hingle, Nehemiah Persoff, Clifton James, and Michael V. Gazzo. Columbia. b & w (See *I Lost it at the Movies.*)

On with the Show (1929)—For anyone who wants to know what the Broadway musical comedy of the 20s was like, this film is indispensable. Made by Warners, it was the first all-color (rather than just sequences-in-color) talking picture. It provides a backstage story about a producer (Sam Hardy) trying to put on a musical while fighting off his creditors; the star is Betty Compson, and her understudy is Sally O'Neil. The same basic story turns up later in *42nd Street*. This extravagant version, however, also provides the onstage musical with its own plot; the backstage story is smoothly intercut with this onstage material, which is lighthearted and parodistic, and which features tall showgirls. Perky (very short) Sally O'Neil is hard to take, but the compensations include Ethel Waters, slender and torchy, singing "Am I Blue?" and "Birmingham Bertha"; Joe E. Brown dancing; and the superb black dancers, the Four Covans. Also with Louise Fazenda, Arthur Lake, William Bakewell, Purnell Pratt, Angelus Babe, and the Harmony Four Quartette. Directed by Alan Crosland; dances staged by Larry Ceballos; adapted from Humphrey Pearson's play, by Robert Lord. The songs are by Harry Akst and Grant Clarke, including a ditty called "Lift the Juleps to Your Two Lips."

Once in a Lifetime (1932)—The young, unknown Moss Hart wrote a satire of Hollywood in the transition from silents to talkies. The Broadway producer Sam Harris accepted it and signed George S. Kaufman, the reigning young playwright, to collaborate. After nine nerve-racking months of revisions, Kaufman and Hart had the "smash" of 1930, and the team lasted for 10 historic and incredibly profitable years (what Broadway joined together, psychoanalysis put asunder). They created bustling, congested wisecrack-piled-on-wisecrack comedies; their calculated silliness adds more than enough to each situation and in going beyond your expectations, it can double you up and put you helplessly at the mercy of the next excess. This particular play was considered too rough for Hollywood, but in 1932 Universal brought the enemy within the gates, and, of course, pulled some of its satirical teeth. With moon-faced Jack Oakie as the goodhearted imbecilic vaudevillian who in Hollywood is taken for a genius; Gregory Ratoff as the producer, Herman Glogauer; Aline MacMahon as the sceptical, witty voice coach; Onslow Stevens as the playwright; ZaSu Pitts as the studio receptionist; Louise Fazenda as the critic; and Sidney Fox, Russell Hopton, and Mona Maris. Russell Mack directed, from Seton I. Miller's adaptation. The picture isn't particularly well-made, but it's a true period piece—a reminder of the beginnings of a type of Broadway lampoon-comedy, and it has a lovely corny triviality and innocence. (Twenty years later, another famous team, Betty Comden and Adolph Green, took the same period for their *Singin' in the Rain*.) b & w

Once in Paris (1978)— A tepid, moderately engaging brief-encounter movie about a married American screenwriter (Wayne Rogers) who arrives alone in Paris to doctor the script of a film that is going into production and falls in love with an Englishwoman (Gayle Hunnicutt) who's staying at his hotel. He also makes a friend of his French chauffeur (Jack Lenoir), who has a shady past, and they're all three terribly kind and considerate of one another. The writer-director, Frank D. Gilroy, thinks small and in 50s terms, but Rogers has a gift for pantomime (each time he sees a sexy woman he looks surprised and hurt—almost stricken) and Lenoir has a slight sullenness and complication under his charm, and this saves him when he's given French wisdom to spout. The picture might have more substance if Hunnicutt weren't such an expensive-looking, high-toned sex object; her suffering looks like something she bought in a swank shop, to match her bracelet. Independently financed and released. color (See *When the Lights Go Down*.)

Once Is Not Enough (1975)—This adaptation of Jacqueline Susann's infatuated exposé of the scandalous goings-on among celebrities wants so badly to be shocking and is actually so naïve that you begin to feel some affection for its silly sleaziness. The picture lacks the nerve to be crudely flamboyant, and so it isn't the smashing trash it should have been, but it has its moments, such as George Hamilton, as a celebrated stud, luring a virgin named January Wayne (Deborah Raffin) into his lecher's pad, which is equipped with red couches, blazing fires, and a Sinatra record at the ready. Brenda Vaccaro is entertainingly spunky as a Helen Gurley Brownish editor, and David Janssen gives a surprisingly energetic performance as a Norman Mailer–like brawling writer. The others include Kirk Douglas, and Alexis Smith and Melina Mercouri, who have an excruiating lesbian scene. Guy Green directed, unevenly, from a too-sober script by Julius J. Epstein. Howard Koch produced, for Paramount. color

Once Upon a Honeymoon (1942)—This clammily contrived anti-Nazi comedy-melodrama, set in Europe, attempts to show the public the evils of Nazism while sugar-coating the message. Ginger Rogers is an American burlesque queen married to an Austrian baron (Walter Slezak) who is a Nazi agent. Cary Grant is the American radio correspondent who tries to show her the miseries that her husband and his associates are causing. Grant twinkles with condescending affection when the (supposedly adorable) nitwit stripper develops a political consciousness and helps a Jewish hotel maid escape from danger. With Albert Dekker, Albert Basserman, and Hans Conried. Directed by Leo McCarey,

who also wrote the script, with Sheridan Gibney. They must have been very eager to be done with this abomination, because they finally dispatch the Nazi baron by means of a casual sick joke so they can have Rogers and Grant together. R K O. b & w

Once Upon a Time in America (1984)—Just about all the incidents in this 3-hour-and-47-minute film echo scenes in Hollywood gangster movies, but the director, Sergio Leone, inflates them, slows them down, and gives them a dreamy obsessiveness. He transmutes the lower East Side settings of those gangster movies to give the genre a richer, more luxuriant visual texture. His widescreen view of a group of Jewish kids who start with petty crime and move into big-time racketeering is set in 1921, 1933, and 1968, but not in that order. His theme is the betrayal of the immigrants' dream of America, and the story begins and ends in an opium den where Noodles (Robert De Niro) puffs on a pipe while episodes of his life of killings and rapes and massacres drift by and a telephone rings somewhere in the past. This epic is a compendium of kitsch, but it's kitsch aestheticized by someone who loves it and sees it as the poetry of the masses. It isn't just the echoing moments that keep you absorbed—it's the reverberant dreamland settings and Leone's majestic, billowing sense of film movement. With Jennifer Connelly, who's marvellously vivid as the young Deborah; Darlanne Fluegel as the beautiful streamlined blond Eve; and Tuesday Weld, who brings a gleam of perversity to the role of a nympho moll. Also with Elizabeth McGovern, who's badly miscast as the adult Deborah, and James Woods, Larry Rapp, James Hayden, William Forsythe, Treat Williams, Burt Young, and Joe Pesci. Many writers worked on the screenplay, which is loosely based on the novel *The Hoods*, by Harry Grey; the final credits go to Leone and five Italians, plus

Stuart Kaminsky (for additional dialogue). The cinematography is by Tonino Delli Colli; the score by Ennio Morricone uses "Amapola" as the theme song. (A studio-shortened version that runs 2 hours and 15 minutes is disastrously incoherent.) A Ladd Company Release, through Warners. color (See *State of the Art*.)

One-Eyed Jacks (1961)—Marlon Brando, the Great Unpredictable, is both star and director of this Western about a bandit whose only purpose in life is to kill his former partner. As the prospective victim, Karl Malden makes a tough antagonist. Katy Jurado and Pina Pellicer, a lovely young Mexican actress, give aid and comfort to the two enemies. Also with Slim Pickens, Timothy Carey, Ben Johnson, and Elisha Cook, Jr. The picture is of variable quality: it has some visual grandeur; it also has some bizarrely brutal scenes. It isn't clear why Brando made this peculiarly masochistic revenge fantasy, or whether he hoped for something quite different from what he finished with. From a script by Guy Trosper and Calder Willingham, based on Charles Neider's novel *The Authentic Death of Hendry Jones*. Cinematography by Charles Lang; music by Hugo Friedhofer. Paramount. color

One Flew Over the Cuckoo's Nest (1975)— Smashingly effective version of Ken Kesey's novel about a rebel outcast, McMurphy (Jack Nicholson), who is locked in a hospital for the insane. The book was a lyric jag, and it became a nonconformists' bible. Published in 1962, it contained the prophetic essence of the whole Vietnam period of revolutionary politics going psychedelic. Miloš Forman, who directed the movie version, must have understood how crude the poetic-paranoid vision of the book would look on the screen after the 60s paranoia had lost its nightmarish buoyancy, and he and the scenarists—Law-

rence Hauben, and then Bo Goldman—did an intelligent job of loosening Kesey's schematism. Set in 1963, the movie retains most of Kesey's ideas but doesn't diagram them the way the book does. Louise Fletcher gives a masterly performance as Nurse Ratched— she's the company woman incarnate. And Will Sampson, a towering full-blooded Creek, is very impressive as Chief Broom, the resurrected catatonic. Forman's tentative, literal-minded direction lacks the excitement of movie art and there's a callousness running through his work; he gets laughs by pretending that mental disturbance is the same as ineptitude. But the story and the acting make the film emotionally powerful. And Nicholson, looking punchy, tired, and baffled—and not on top of his character (as he often is)—lets you see into him, rather than controlling what he lets you see. With William Redfield, Brad Dourif, Scatman Crothers, Danny DeVito, Vincent Schiavelli, Sydney Lassick, Louisa Moritz, Marya Small, and Christopher Lloyd; cinematography by Haskell Wexler. Produced by Saul Zaentz and Michael Douglas. Academy Awards: Best Picture, Director, Actor (Nicholson), Actress (Fletcher), Screenplay (Hauben and Goldman). Released by United Artists. color (See *When the Lights Go Down*.)

One from the Heart (1982)—Francis Ford Coppola's jewelled version of a film student's experimental pastiche—the kind set in a magical junkyard. You get the feeling that the movie grew by accretion—that he piled so many visual ideas and comedy bits on top of the small story he started with that it disappeared from sight and the movie turned into something like a poet's salute to the banal silver screen. It's set in a metaphorical Las Vegas (constructed at Zoetrope Studios) on Independence Day, when Frannie (Teri Garr), who works at the Paradise Travel Agency, walks out on the man she has been living with—Hank (Frederic Forrest), who runs Reality Wrecking. The holiday is treated like Mardi Gras, with crowds dancing through the street. All we're asked to care about is whether Hank, who's in love with Frannie, will win her back. Or, rather, this story being negligible, what we're asked to respond to is Coppola's confectionery artistry. The movie is very pretty and sometimes eerily charming, but the effects don't have any emotional meaning in terms of the characters, and the video editing techniques that Coppola uses seem to destroy the dramatic definition of the scenes; a day later the film is as blurry in the mind as the memory of a psychedelic light show. With Nastassia Kinski, Raul Julia, Harry Dean Stanton, and Lainie Kazan. From a script by Armyan Bernstein and Coppola; there's a song track, with Tom Waits and Crystal Gayle telling us the meaning of what we're seeing and wailing words of wisdom. Dean Tavoularis designed the production. Zoetrope. color (See *Taking It All In*.)

One Sings, the Other Doesn't *L'Une chante l'autre pas* (1977)—Agnès Varda brings a Disney touch to this account of women finding their independence. The lives of Pomme (Valérie Mairesse) and Suzanne (Thérèse Liotard) between 1962 and 1976 are supposed to indicate the evolution of modern women's consciousness, but these two don't seem to have any consciousness—the way Varda skims over their lives, they could be butterflies or duckies. The singer, Pomme, and her combo tour provincial towns, performing educational songs, with lyrics (by Varda) such as "I'm neither a tough cookie nor a busy beaver nor a Utopian dreamer—I'm a woman, I am me." Decked out in harlequin colors that suggest a French child's dream of what Haight-Ashbury was like, they chant "My Body Is Mine." They sing about the joys of pregnancy when it's "your choice and your

pleasure"; they sing about their "ovules." The sunshiny simplicity of the feminist movement celebrated here is so laughable that you can't hate the picture. You just feel that some of your brain cells have been knocked out. In French. color (See *When the Lights Go Down*.)

One Touch of Venus (1948)—Robert Walker kisses a statue in Macy's and it comes alive—or, to describe more accurately the performance by the ravishing young Ava Gardner, half alive. Her songs are dubbed (by Eileen Wilson), which adds to the sloe-eyed sleepwalker effect. The film creaks; it's a bowdlerized version of the Broadway show by S. J. Perelman, Ogden Nash, and Kurt Weill. With Olga San Juan, Eve Arden, Tom Conway, and Dick Haymes. Directed by William A. Seiter, from a script by Harry Kurnitz and Frank Tashlin. Universal. b & w

One, Two, Three (1961)—Machine-gun paced topical satire of East-West relations, in which the characters shout variations of stale jokes at each other—people are described as sitting around on their assets, and we're invited to laugh at the Russians for rejecting a shipment of Swiss cheese because it is full of holes. The director, Billy Wilder, shot this example of an assembly-line approach to gags in Berlin and Munich (where a full-scale replica of the Brandenburg Gate was constructed). James Cagney expertly mugs his way through the role of an American Coca-Cola executive in Europe; he complains that the East Germans are hijacking his shipments, "and they don't even return the empties." When his wife (Arlene Francis) says that their marriage has gone flat, like a stale glass of beer, Cagney replies, "Why do you have to bring in a competing beverage?" The gags are almost all on this level, and the little sops to sentiment are even worse; the film was a huge success. With Horst Buchholz, Pamela Tiffin, Lilo Pulver, and Red Buttons.

Wilder and I.A.L. Diamond wrote the script, based on a Ferenc Molnár one-act play. A Mirisch Production, for United Artists. b & w (See *I Lost it at the Movies*.)

Open City *Roma, Città Aperta* (1945)—Roberto Rossellini burst open the world with this film, made just after the Allies took Rome. The fame of his brutal, melodramatic account of the underground resistance to the Nazi occupation rests on its extraordinary immediacy and its rough, documentary look; at its most startling, it seems "caught" rather than staged. Many Americans, used to slick war films, reacted to it as if it actually were caught, documentary footage, and mistook the great Anna Magnani and Aldo Fabrizi, Maria Michi, and the other actors for non-professionals—this despite such stock elements as a rapacious lesbian Gestapo agent and a Hollywood-and-Vine-type Gestapo chief. The plot devices are often opportunistic, but there's a unifying fervor: shot on odds and ends of film stock, with fluctuating electricity, and showing people who a few weeks before had been part of the events, the movie gave us a cross-section of a city under terrible stress. When the initial $25,000 that Rossellini had raised was used up, he and Magnani sold their clothes; Maria Michi, who had hidden men like Togliatti—and the scriptwriter, Sergio Amidei—in her flat, now provided the flat for some of the sequences. Federico Fellini assisted Amidei on the script. In Italian. b & w

Operation Mad Ball (1957)—The perennial war of enlisted men and officers is joined again, luckily under the direction of Richard Quine. The setting is Normandy, where the American troops are stationed; the soldiers aren't allowed to fraternize with the nurses, but Jack Lemmon, the buck-private hero, is determined to stage a mad ball where the men and the nurses can get together. Ernie

Kovacs is the maddeningly unctuous, obnoxious officer determined to thwart him—a barracks Malvolio. Dick York is the liaison man between the two factions, Mickey Rooney the sergeant who pulls together a jazz group for the ball. The four of them are good—occasionally so good they seem inspired. If Arthur O'Connell as the commanding officer, Kathryn Grant as the nurse Lemmon adores, and a French maman-concierge could have been eliminated, this might have been a classic American comedy. As it is, it's an often uninhibited farce, and one of the funniest pictures of its period. Rooney, with his hot band, gives the picture some of the wild charge it needs more of. (He and Quine had worked together as performers when they were adolescents.) Written by Arthur Carter, Jed Harris, and Blake Edwards, based on a play by Carter. Produced by Harris, for Columbia. b & w

Orchestra Wives (1942)—Livelier than the title (which sounds like a satirical classification) suggests. It's the swing era, the band is Glenn Miller's (with Tex Beneke and The Modernaires), and the screenwriters, Karl Tunberg and Darrell Ware, use the shopworn love triangle of an innocent small-town girl (Ann Rutherford) who marries a musician (George Montgomery) and then comes up against his old flame, the band vocalist (Lynn Bari), as a framework for all the snappy repartee they can pile on. Archie Mayo directed this musical for 20th Century-Fox, and the picture has a seedy, unassuming pungency. Best of all, the moviemakers were prepared to jettison the story line for the sake of entertainment: suddenly, at the end of the picture, the Nicholas Brothers, that great team of dancers, come out of nowhere and do one of their most dizzying acrobatic tap routines, to "I've Got a Gal in Kalamazoo." The number is such a feat of sustained high flying that you hold your breath in tense admiration.

The cast includes Glenn Miller, Jackie Gleason, Carole Landis, Cesar Romero, Virginia Gilmore, and Mary Beth Hughes; the tunes include "Serenade in Blue," "At Last," "Chattanooga Choo Choo," and "Bugle Call Rag"; among the musicians are Bobby Hackett and Ernie Caceres, and when Jackie Gleason plays the bass you're actually hearing Doc Goldberg. Cinematography by Lucien Ballard. b & w

Orchids and Ermine (1927)—Lively, gifted Colleen Moore, the best comedienne of the silent flapper period, wore her dark hair short and straight with bangs—it was an almost abstract frame for the games she played with her eyes and mouth. No mere personality girl but a light, unaffected, inventive actress, in style she was a little like Buster Keaton. In this romantic comedy she's a telephone operator who has just about given up her hopes of landing a rich husband. She works in a swank New York hotel, which is called the Ritz, but which is actually the Plaza, and there's nostalgic charm in the sequences shot in and around the hotel and on top of an old double-decker Fifth Avenue bus. Jack Mulhall plays a young millionaire, and Gwen Lee and Sam Hardy are a gold-digger and a valet. There is a sequence at the hotel switchboard when a midget addresses Miss Moore—the "midget" is one of the first screen appearances of Mickey Rooney. Alfred Santell directed; the script is by Carey Wilson and Mervyn LeRoy; the wisecracking titles have a fine patina—they're by Ralph Spence. With Hedda Hopper as a modiste, and Yola D'Avril as another telephone operator. First National. Silent. b & w

Orders to Kill (1958)—Anthony Asquith attempts to use the thriller structure for an ironic drama of conscience; the hero (Paul Massie) is an American bomber pilot sent to German-occupied Paris to assassinate a trai-

tor to the Allies. But this pilot, though capable of murder from the air, is torn by nerves and scruples when he actually confronts a potential victim, and the victim, it turns out, was not a traitor. This pacifist study of individual responsibility involves also a different sort of irony—craft, not correspondence to historical facts, gives a film the look of truth, and this picture, which is based on actual incidents, always seems far-fetched. The cast includes Eddie Albert, Lillian Gish, Irene Worth, James Robertson Justice, Lionel Jeffries, Jacques Brunius, and Leslie French. Written by Paul Dehn. b & w

Ordet (1955)—Carl Dreyer made two emotionally overpowering great films—*The Passion of Joan of Arc* and *Day of Wrath*. He also made the visually and conceptually daring *Vampyr*. But *Ordet*, which the world press greeted as his masterpiece, may be considerably less than that. Kaj Munk, author of the play, was a Danish pastor, famed for such statements as "It is better that Denmark's relations with Germany should suffer than that her relations with Jesus Christ should suffer." In 1944, the Nazis shot him through the head and tossed him in a ditch. His play, written on the text "O ye of little faith," deals with a modern Resurrection, and Dreyer treats it with extreme literalness. Some of us may find it difficult to accept the holy-madman protagonist (driven insane by too close study of Kierkegaard!), and even more difficult to accept Dreyer's use of the protagonist's home as a stage set for numerous entrances and exits, and altogether impossible to get involved in the factional strife between bright, happy Christianity and dark, gloomy Christianity—represented as they are by people sitting around drinking vast quantities of coffee. In Danish. b & w

Ordinary People (1980)—Autumn leaves and wintry emotions. This is an academic exercise in catharsis; it's earnest, it means to improve people, and it lasts a lifetime. The story is about the Jarretts—Donald Sutherland, Mary Tyler Moore, and their son, Timothy Hutton—a Protestant family living in an imposing brick house in a wealthy suburb of Chicago. There is so little communication in this uptight family that the three Jarretts sit in virtual silence at the perfectly set dinner table in the perfectly boring big dining room. From time to time, the father, with a nervous tic of a smile, tries to make contact with his son and urges him to see a psychiatrist recommended by the hospital where he was treated after a recent suicide attempt. The movie is about the harm that repression can do, but the movie is just as repressive and sanitized as the way of life it means to expose, and it backs away from anything messier than standard TV-style psychiatric explanations. Making his début as a film director, Robert Redford shows talent with the actors, the younger ones especially; Alvin Sargent's adaptation of the popular Judith Guest novel is heavy on psychobabble. The joker about this movie is that part of the audience weeps for the unloving Wasp-witch mother, who cares only for appearances and who can't change because of the pride and the privacy she was trained in; she seems the gallant last standard-bearer for the Wasp family ethic, and the picture somehow turns into a nosegay for Wasp repression. With Judd Hirsch as the idealized warm, friendly Jewish psychiatrist, Elizabeth McGovern as the son's girlfriend, and Meg Mundy as the grandmother. Paramount. color (See *Taking It All In*.)

Les Orgueilleux   Also known as *The Proud and the Beautiful*. (1953)—The China Coast of Sartre's *L'Amour redempteur* has become Veracruz in Yves Allégret's film, but the milieu is still the depths: heat, squalor, disease, and desperation, exotic but unbearable. A bored French woman (Michèle Morgan) searches for a doctor to take care of her dying husband (André Toffel); she finds a drunken derelict (Gérard Philipe) who refuses to treat him. Through founding a plague hospital, the woman and the doctor redeem themselves and, incidentally, find love. Allégret uses this story atmospherically in an effort to approximate the ironies, inconsequences, accidents, and stupidities of life, and the atmosphere *almost* redeems the movie. (Audiences gasp at one shot: the camera is still, intoxicated, as a hypodermic is slowly inserted.) In French. b & w

The Original Sin, see *Der Apfel Ist Ab*

L'Oro di Napoli, see *The Gold of Naples*

Orphans of the Storm (1921)—It's almost unbelievable, but this D. W. Griffith spectacle set during the French Revolution was not a financial success. It's a marvellous, expensively produced mixture of melodrama and sentimentality, with duels, kidnappings, the storming of the Bastille, and Lillian Gish being saved from the guillotine. It's not one of Griffith's greatest; in a way, it seems dated, even for a 1921 movie. (Not in its technique—in its thinking.) But those who saw it as children never forgot the sequence in which Lillian hears the voice of her long-lost blind sister, played by Dorothy Gish. Griffith sequences like this go beyond heart-wringing into some arena of theatrical sublimity. The huge cast includes the handsome young Joseph Schildkraut, Monte Blue as Danton, Louis Wolheim as the executioner. Cinematography by Hendrik Sartov, Billy Bitzer, and Paul Allen. (It's a big picture—14 reels when it opened, cut to 12 reels a few months later.) Based on a 19th-century melodrama, *The Two Orphans*. United Artists. Silent. b & w

Orphée, see *Orpheus*

Orpheus *Orphée* (1949)—A masterpiece of magical filmmaking. Though it is a narrative treatment of the legend of Orpheus in a modern Parisian setting, this film, written and directed by Jean Cocteau, is as inventive and as enigmatic as a dream. Orpheus (Jean Marais), the successful poet who is envied and despised by younger poets, needs to renew himself; he tries to push beyond the limits of human experience, to reach the unknowable—the mystery beyond morality. Dark, troubled, passionate Maria Casarès is his Death: attended by her roaring motorcyclists, the hooded messengers of death, she is mystery incarnate. The jazzy modern milieu has urgency, and Cocteau uses emblems and images of the then recent Nazi period and merges them with more primitive images of fear—as, indeed, they are merged in the modern consciousness. This gives the violence and mystery of the Orpheus story a contemporaneity that, in other hands, might seem merely chic; Cocteau's special gift was to raise chic to art. The death figure and much of the film's imagery derive from the American movie *Death Takes a Holiday* (1934), starring Fredric March; the only modern film image of death that, visually and psychologically, stands comparison with Maria Casarès is in Ingmar Bergman's *The Seventh Seal* (1956). The glazier in the "zone" (a variant of the angel in Cocteau's *Blood of a Poet*) must be a tribute to (or a memory of?) Chaplin as the angelic glazier of *The Kid*. With Marie Déa as the sickly-sweet Eurydice, François Périer as Heurtebise (part chauffeur, part guardian angel, he suggests the ferryman Charon), and Edouard Dermithe and Juliette Greco. Music by Georges Auric; the sumptuous cinematography with its velvety dark and light contrasts is by Nicholas Hayer. In French. b & w

The Oscar (1966)—Joseph E. Levine's style of tawdriness, as in *The Carpetbaggers, Harlow*, and this picture, rivals the triumphs at M-G-M in the 40s. The Levine beds and draperies were already deluxe. Here he has added Harlan Ellison's incomparable bedroom conversations and it's such a perfect commingling that the words might have sprouted from the coverlets. Meant to be hard-hitting, the picture is florid-fancy, and so energetically overacted that it was instantly hailed as a classic of unintentional comedy. It's no accident that all three of these Levine productions are set in Hollywood: this gives their decor and dialogue a certain authenticity—after all, it's derived from the movies. The characters here are also taken from the movies. The heel-hero (Stephen Boyd, intense every minute) is the movie gangster relocated as a Hollywood actor; instead of pushing a grapefruit in his moll's face, he dumps a salad on a star's lap. This picture is a wonder; it's of a lurid badness that has to be experienced. With Tony Bennett as the rotter Boyd's kind, grovelling pal, and Milton Berle, Eleanor Parker, Joseph Cotten, Ernest Borgnine, Jill St. John, Edie Adams, Merle Oberon, Walter Brennan, Broderick Crawford, James Dunn, Peter Lawford, Ed Begley, Bob Hope, Frank Sinatra, Edith Head, and Hedda Hopper. It leaves one sweet memory: Elke Sommer, or rather the way she enunciates—squeezing the words out between lips always puckered for a kiss. Russel Rouse directed and also worked on the script with Ellison and Clarence Greene; it's from a novel by Richard Sale. Released by Paramount. color

Ostre Sledovane Vlaky, see *Closely Watched Trains*

Otchi Tchornyia, see *Dark Eyes*

Othello (1965)—A filmed record of the National Theatre of Great Britain production starring Laurence Olivier; the techniques employed are pitifully inadequate. But there he is: the most physical Othello imaginable—deep voice, with a trace of foreign music in it; happy, thick, self-satisfied laugh; rolling buttocks. He's grand and barbaric and, yes, a little lewd. As a lord, this Othello is a bit vulgar—too ingratiating, a boaster, an arrogant man. Who can afford to miss this performance? With Frank Finlay as the pale, parched little Iago—a man consumed with sexual jealousy—and Maggie Smith as the quietly strong, willful Desdemona. Also with Joyce Redman, Derek Jacobi, and Robert Lang. Stuart Burge, who directed this filming, doesn't always protect the actors: they speak as if they were on a stage and they're sometimes seen very close (in stage makeup) when the camera should be at a discreet distance. The cinematography is by Geoffrey Unsworth. color (See *Kiss Kiss Bang Bang*.)

Our Blushing Brides (1930)—The title is deceptive: it's a popular film of the period, about whether working girls ought to Take the Easiest Way or Wait for Mr. Right. Joan Crawford, Anita Page, and Dorothy Sebastian are the roommates who work in the same department store (the vivacious Crawford as a model, the other two as clerks). Their dreams of luxury get them in trouble with, respectively, Robert Montgomery, Raymond Hackett, and John Miljan. It's high-mindedly moral but not seriously so, with an arrest for theft, a suicide, a fashion show on a Long Island estate, and an Albertina Rasch ballet all tossed in together. Harry Beaumont directed; the writers were Bess Meredyth and a pre-Marxist John Howard Lawson. With Hedda Hopper, Martha Sleeper, Albert Conti, Edward Brophy, and, among the mannequins, Claire Dodd. M-G-M. b & w

Our Daily Bread (1934)—About how a young couple (Karen Morley and Tom Keene) make a go of life on a bankrupt farm by turn-

ing it into a co-op. King Vidor—restless, never satisfied by his commercial successes—borrowed up to his ears to make this movie, and it's innovatively well directed. He experiments with Russian ideas of montage, and manages to make a grand finale out of the co-operative farmers digging a ditch to irrigate a cornfield—cheating only a little by heightening the scene with an orchestral score. The rhythmic visual conceptions are beautifully realized, but the acting and writing are awful; sophisticated in film terms, it's a primitive picture in dramatic terms. The earnest title indicates where Vidor went wrong; the film suffers from awkwardly simple thinking and from the excessive virtue ascribed to the common-man characters. With John Qualen and Barbara Pepper. Written by Elizabeth Hill, Joseph L. Mankiewicz, and Vidor; cinematography by Robert Planck; released by United Artists. b & w

Our Man Flint (1966)—When he plays comedy, James Coburn is often a grinning, stylized original, but in this starring role he's so spoofy he becomes infantile. As a super-spy imitation of James Bond, Coburn is really Little Boy Flint: a good little boy stretched tall, like a young Uncle Sam. And the movie is a little boy's fantasies, with his little physical fitness exercise and all his little toys. With Lee J. Cobb. Directed by Daniel Mann, from a script by Hal Fimberg and Ben Starr. It was a hit (and was followed by *In Like Flint*, in 1967). 20th Century-Fox. CinemaScope, color

Our Man in Havana (1960)—Though Alec Guinness's name is Wormold and he is the Havana representative of a vacuum cleaner company, he is the hero. This hero, recruited into the British secret service (by dry, hunched Noël Coward—the mandarin as secret agent), has no idea what is wanted of him. He must send in reports, however; so he fills them with inventions and fantasies.

This satirical comedy turns into a nightmarish thriller when his phony reports precipitate actual reprisals and murders. Adapted by Graham Greene, from his novel, the picture is almost too clever and maybe that's why it was a box-office failure, but its naughtiness is terribly funny. It appears to be a travesty of the international spy story, like *Beat the Devil*, except that it has a pinprick of purpose; the deep thought that innocence can lead to evil is not likely to keep you up nights. The director, Carol Reed, employs the Cuban locations (with cinematography by Oswald Morris) as wittily as he does the actors— Ralph Richardson, Burl Ives, Ernie Kovacs, Maureen O'Hara, Grégoire Aslan (he takes Wormold's washroom spying overtures for an indecent proposition), Jo Morrow, Paul Rogers, and Duncan Macrae. The farce is perhaps too straight-faced, low-keyed, and tenuous—it needs more exuberance. One reason it isn't as good as *Beat the Devil* is that everything is so beautifully held in check. It might be better if it were sloppier, but it does have some first-rate sequences and it's very entertaining. (Kovacs wasn't allowed to wear a beard, because of fear that it might offend Castro.) The music is by the Hernanos Deniz Cuban Rhythm Band. Produced by Reed; Columbia. CinemaScope, b & w

Our Modern Maidens (1929)—The big-eyed, energetic young Joan Crawford in the jazz age. She and her friends give expensive parties where now and then someone jumps on a piano, sings a song, makes a speech, or does an imitation. With Douglas Fairbanks, Jr., as Crawford's young husband, Rod La Rocque as the older man of the world who complicates her life, Anita Page as the girl who complicates Fairbanks' life, and Edward Nugent and Josephine Dunn. One of the "shocking-youth" pictures that audiences flocked to; the surprise in this one is that Crawford leaves her husband and winds up

with La Rocque. Directed by Jack Conway. A silent, though some prints had a musical score and sound effects. M-G-M. b & w

Our Town (1940)—Despite all one's conscious objections—the sentiment, the stagey techniques that don't really work on film— the movie version of the Thornton Wilder play stays with one. Partly that's because of the beauty of many of the lines, and partly, too, because of the acting. In conception, the play is similar to Dylan Thomas's later *Under Milk Wood*, but in Wilder's New England setting the dialogue is laconic, the wit dryly humane. The young William Holden is warm and skillful as the adolescent hero. Martha Scott, who plays opposite him, repeats her stage performance; she didn't take the camera well, and her readings are a little too arch and finished, but she gets her laughs. Frank Craven, also from the original cast, is the omniscient spokesman of the piece; if Wilder had to be omniscient, nobody could come as close to getting away with it as Craven. With Fay Bainter, Beulah Bondi, Thomas Mitchell, and Guy Kibbee. Sam Wood, who did another view of small-town life in *Kings Row*, directed; he can't be blamed for the Hollywoodization of the ending. Produced by Sol Lesser for Principal Artists Productions, released by United Artists. b & w

Out Cold (1989)—Teri Garr is Sunny, who murders her husband. John Lithgow is the husband's business partner, a big, shy dope with a slow-motion brain who thinks he accidentally did the killing. And Randy Quaid is a lunkhead private detective. This trim, smart, evenly paced murder comedy is set mostly in and around San Pedro, California, but the calm with which the young English director, Malcolm Mowbray (who made the 1984 *A Private Function*), keeps everything in check doesn't seem American, exactly. Mowbray's deliberateness has a lunar dimension.

The smoothness keeps you giggling. With Bruce McGill and Fran Ryan. The screenplay is by Leonard Glasser and George Malko. A Hemdale Production, released by Tri-Star. color (See *Movie Love*.)

Out in the World, see *My Apprenticeship*

Out of Africa (1985)—Adult, cryptic, self-conscious, and unsatisfying, it attempts to romanticize the lives of the high-strung Danish woman (played by Meryl Streep), who ran a coffee plantation in Kenya, saw herself as a patrician, and wrote under the name Isak Dinesen, and the handsome English big-game hunter Denys Finch Hatton (Robert Redford). Directed by Sydney Pollack, from a script by Kurt Luedtke, the picture squirms around trying to make these people morally acceptable to a modern audience. Streep is animated in the early scenes, but Redford doesn't give out with anything for her to play against, and the energy goes out of her performance. These two are meant to be lovers, but when they address each other they talk into a void, as if the other weren't there, and when she demands that he marry her, it's as if a couple of pages from a bad novel about a possessive woman had been pasted into the middle of a *National Geographic* photo essay. This is "classical" big-star narrative movie-making, but without the logic, the easy-to-read surface, and the sureness that contribute to the pleasure of that kind of picture. It seems to be about something nebulous. The film hums a little when Klaus Maria Brandauer (as Baron Blixen-Finecke) or Michael Kitchen (as Berkeley Cole) or Suzanna Hamilton (as Felicity) is on the screen; they're recognizably human. And several of the black performers are great subjects for the David Watkin's camera—Malick Bowens (as the majordomo Farah), in particular. Academy Awards: Best Picture, Direction, Adapted Screenplay, Art Direction, Cinematography, Score, Sound. Universal. color (See *Hooked*.)

Out of the Past (1947)—A thin but well-shot suspense melodrama, kept from collapsing by the suggestiveness and intensity that the director, Jacques Tourneur, pours on. It's empty trash, but you do keep watching it. Kirk Douglas, a gangster, hires Robert Mitchum to find Jane Greer, who has run away from him. Predictably, she gets Mitchum (at his most somnolent-sexy droopy-eyed) in her clutches, and there are several killings before matters are resolved. The screenplay is by Geoffrey Homes (a pseudonym of Daniel Mainwaring), from his novel *Build My Gallows High*. Cinematography by Nicholas Musuraca; with Rhonda Fleming and Dickie Moore. R K O. b & w

Outback (1970)—A good subject: comradeship among white men in the Australian desert, their boredom, and their erratic, senseless destructiveness. They keep acting out adolescent rituals of virility. They guzzle all day and all night; they garland themselves with the pull tabs from the beer cans. They smash things for excitement or brawl, or shoot anything that moves, or run it down with their cars. Their blood sport is boxing with wounded kangaroos and then slitting their throats. The film, directed by Ted Kotcheff, spends too much time on the melodramatic—and Conradian—ordeals of a sensitive yet arrogant male schoolteacher (Gary Bond) who hates the coarse life he's trapped in. His inadequacies are the focal point, but the butch boomtown atmosphere (without a trace of culture) is more vivid and authentic and original. You remember the red eyes of the kangaroos in the glare of car headlights, not the schoolteacher's disintegration and self-discovery. Even though the movie retreats into its narrow story line, you come out with a sense of epic horror and the perception that this white master race is retarded. With Donald Pleasence and Chips Rafferty. The script, by Evan Jones, is based on Kenneth Cook's novel *Wake in Fright*. color (See *Deeper into Movies*.)

An Outcast of the Islands (1951)—A marvellous film (drawn from Joseph Conrad's work) that relatively few people have seen. It's probably the only movie that has ever attempted to deal in a complex way with the subject of the civilized man's ambivalence about the savage. It also contains some of the most remarkable sequences ever filmed by the English director Carol Reed; it's an uneven movie, but with splendid moments throughout. Trevor Howard is superb as Willems, who makes himself an outcast first through contemptible irresponsibility and through betrayal of those who trust him, and finally and hopelessly when, against his will, he is attracted to the silent, primitive girl, the terrifying Aissa (played by Kerima). Willems is wrong in almost everything he does, but he represents a gesture toward life; his enemy, Almayer (Robert Morley), is so horribly, pathetically stuffy that his family unit (with Wendy Hiller as his wife and Annabel Morley as his child) is absurdly, painfully funny. With Ralph Richardson, whose role is possibly ill-conceived, and George Coulouris, Wilfrid Hyde-White, and Frederick Valk. The screenplay is by William Fairchild; cinematography by John Wilcox. b & w

Outland (1981)—Science fiction set in a morally grimy future that is conceived as a continuation of capitalist exploitation in space. Sean Connery is the new federal district marshal on Io (a volcanic moon of Jupiter), who learns that Peter Boyle, the boss of the mines on Io, is selling the workers amphetamines that keep them speeding for 10 or 12 months, until they go berserk and kill themselves or attack others. When Connery destroys a shipment of the drug, Boyle sends for hired killers, and, just as in *High Noon*, the one lone good man finds he has to fight by himself. The sets are great—the industrial-nightmare city on Io is like the offspring of a gigantic pipe organ and an oil rig. And Peter Hyams, who directed, knows how to stage chases and fights. But he also wrote the script, which deadens everything and doesn't even make sense. (It's insane that the miners refuse to help Connery—that they don't mind being exploited, going crazy, and destroying themselves.) It's a noisy, somber film, with an element of the repugnant (the high spots are the horrible deaths), but with good performances by Connery, Frances Sternhagen as a sour, snappish doctor, and James B. Sikking as Connery's sergeant. Also with Kika Markham. The production designer was Philip Harrison; the art director was Malcolm Middleton; the cinematographer was Stephen Goldblatt. A Ladd Company Production; released by Warners. color (See *Taking It All In*.)

The Outlaw (1941)—As producer-director and bra designer, Howard Hughes managed to create the definitive burlesque of cowtown dramas, and without even trying. Jane Russell swings her bosom around and shows her love for frail, seedy Billy the Kid (Jack Buetel) by hitting him over the head with a coffeepot and putting sand in his water flasks when he is setting out across the desert. To reciprocate, he ties her up with wet thongs and leaves her out in the sun. Walter Huston and Thomas Mitchell provide a little relief from the amorous games. Written by Jules Furthman; cinematography by Gregg Toland; smarmy music by Victor Young. Though completed in 1941, the film was tied up in heavily publicized censorship battles and wasn't shown until 1947. Released by United Artists. b & w

Outrageous Fortune (1987—Two young New York actresses of contrasting types— Shelley Long is a lofty ditz and Bette Midler is a vulgarian-sexpot Kewpie doll—discover they've been sharing a lover (Peter Coyote). When he disappears, they chase him across the country to the cliffs and mesas of New Mexico, becoming friends along the way. Near the start, there are a few snappers for Midler, and she gets to shoot some wonderful derisive looks at Long. Though the gags aren't fresh, the screenwriter, Leslie Dixon, knows how to construct them. With a director who had an appetite for elemental belly-laugh farce, maybe even the claptrap plot about spies and terrorists would have something like the self-mocking giddiness of the plot in *Romancing the Stone*. But with Arthur Hiller in charge, much of the dialogue turns into squawking, and the movie is flattened out and rackety, with Midler doing her damnedest to pump sass and energy into it. (Pregnant when the picture was shot, she sticks out her chest and charges into her scenes.) Peter Coyote gives a polished and wily performance in the first section, before he gets lost in the noise; also with Robert Prosky, George Carlin, Florence Stanley, John Schuck, Ji-Tu Cumbuka, and Jerry Zaks. Cinematography by David M. Walsh. Touchstone (Disney). color (See *Hooked*.)

Over 21 (1945)—Ruth Gordon wrote the play on which it is based, and she opened on Broadway as the heroine, America's most spectacular woman wit, a Dorothy Parker–ish refugee from the Algonquin and the fleshpots of Hollywood, who accompanies her middle-aged husband, the editor of a liberal paper, to officers' training camp. Unfortunately, this heroine (played here by Irene Dunne) is extremely articulate but not nearly as funny as she's meant to be; many of the jokes turn on the mad, charming inconsequence of the feminine mind, and the whole comedy is too obviously set up, and rather self-congratulatory. With Alexander Knox, effective as the husband until he reads us an editorial sermon on the brotherhood of man, and Charles Coburn, Cora Witherspoon, Jeff Donnell, and Lee Patrick. Directed by Charles Vidor, from Sidney Buchman's adaptation. Produced by Buchman; Columbia. b & w

The Owl and the Pussycat (1970)—George Segal and Barbra Streisand give this romantic comedy about a self-deceiving would-be writer who works in a bookstore and a hooker a good, fast, raucous spirit. There's an air of festivity about their teamwork. Her works come out impetuously fast and hit such surprising notes that she creates her own suspense—she's a living, talking cliff-hanger. And he supplies a steadying grace. The picture is just a doodle, but it's one of the most enjoyable comedies of its era. Streisand and Segal charge right through the "lonely little people" stuff, and they bull their way through the bad spots (though no one could redeem one sour sequence in Central Park, in which Segal is called upon to humiliate her). Their energy and the director Herbert Ross's sense of pace just about overcome the principal dramatic weakness of the material (Bill Manhoff's two-character play, adapted by Buck Henry)—that it starts high. This takes a while to get used to; then you don't want it to let down. Ross does a fine job of helping you adjust to the subsequent changes in tone and tempo. (What's funny about the scene in which the two of them are bombed out of their heads in a bathtub together is how *romantic* it is.) With Robert Klein and Allen Garfield. Produced by Ray Stark; Columbia. color (See *Deeper into Movies*.)

The Ox-Bow Incident (1943)—A Western set in Nevada in 1885 that is also an attempt at a poetic tragedy about mob violence. Two cowboys (Henry Fonda and Harry Morgan)

ride into a small, lonely cattle town and become involved in the hysteria of a lynch mob. Three innocent men (Dana Andrews, Anthony Quinn, and Francis Ford) are hanged, while we see not only their fear and despair, but the varied motives of the members of the posse who take justice into their own hands. It's easy to be put off by the studio sets and lighting and by the 40s approach to a "serious" subject, but the director, William Wellman, has made the characters so vivid that after many years people may still recall Frank Conroy as the sadistic Southern major, and the rapid changes of expression of William Eythe, as his son. With Harry Davenport as Mr. Davies, Leigh Whipper as Sparks, and Jane Darwell as the cackling, lewd old woman who enjoys the excitement—a much better performance than her Ma Joad in *The Grapes of Wrath*. From the very fine novel by Walter Van Tilburg Clark—it has ambiguities that Lamar Trotti's script couldn't encompass; reading the book expands the movie. 20th Century-Fox. b & w

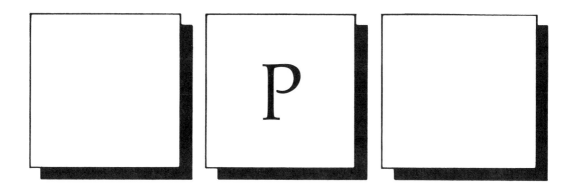

P

Pacific Heights (1990)—It's supposed to be a thriller, but it's more like an executive decision to make a thriller. The director, John Schlesinger, has his professionalism—it shows in the clean, efficient staging. But the fun is missing: he scares you only by making you nervous. Melanie Griffith and Matthew Modine are the San Francisco lovers who fix up a Victorian house (on Potrero Hill); Michael Keaton is the sicko scam artist who takes over one of their two rental units and calls the police when they try to evict him. It's a drag that we're expected to identify with the dull young couple; the tenant with the perverted legalistic mind and the fiendish cupid's-bow smile provides the only gleams of interest. A promising cast—it includes the uncredited Beverly D'Angelo, and Laurie Metcalf, Dorian Harewood, Carl Lumbly, Mako, Tracey Walter, Dan Hedaya, Luca Bercovici, Guy Boyd, and Tippi Hedren as rich Florence—is all but thrown away. The screenplay is by Daniel Pyne; the cinematography is by Amir Mokri. A Morgan Creek Production, released by 20th Century-Fox. color (See *Movie Love*.)

Padre Padrone (1977)—The Taviani brothers, who wrote and directed this film version of Gavino Ledda's 1974 autobiography, have learned to fuse political commitment and artistic commitment into stylized passion. Ledda's story is about how he was enslaved as a child, imprisoned in a sheepfold, and forced to tend the family flock, and of how he fought his way out of the isolation and silence—how he struggled for words. The spirit of the film isn't naturalistic—it's animistic. And the Tavianis' technique is deliberately barbaric; their vision is on the nightmare side of primitivism, where the elements themselves are the boy's enemies. The grotesquely natural cruelty is mythological—almost rhapsodic. Though made in 16 mm, for Italian television, this extraordinary work—pungent and carnal, and in faintly psychedelic Romanesque color—took the two top prizes at Cannes (the Golden Palm and the International Critics' Prize). With Saverio Marconi, Omero Antonutti, Margella Michelangeli, and Ledda, as himself, at the beginning and the end. In Italian. (See *When the Lights Go Down*.)

Paisan (1946)—Roberto Rossellini made this episodic film after his breakthrough with *Open City* the year before. Each of the six parts has a story and deals with an aspect of the war that had just ended. The present-tense semi-documentary visual style is innovative, the content less so. Some of the stories have a tidy O. Henry finish, and there's a lot of sentimentality, though the film gives the impression of being loose and open. The script by Federico Fellini and Rossellini was based on stories they and others had written. (The Florence episode is by Vasco Pratolini, who isn't credited.) With Maria Michi and Gar Moore in the Roman episode, and Dots M. Johnson as the black soldier in Naples. Cinematography by Otello Martelli. In English, French, Italian, and German. b & w

Pal Joey (1957)—Blighted Hollywoodization of the musical by John O'Hara, Richard Rodgers, and Lorenz Hart, with the score purified along with Joey's character. The heel-hero—a hoofer in the Broadway version—is now a crooner, in line with the talents of Frank Sinatra. His singing helps things along, and he also does the only acting, though Kim Novak's vacuity is rather touching and isn't as laborious as Rita Hayworth's performance. (It is said that the studio was out to break Hayworth; she certainly doesn't seem to be getting a fair shake here.) This sad botch was directed by George Sidney; choreography by Hermes Pan. The songs include "I Didn't Know What Time It Was," "Bewitched," "The Lady Is a Tramp," and "There's a Small Hotel." With Elizabeth Patterson and Barbara Nichols. Script by Dorothy Kingsley, based on O'Hara's stage version of his stories in *The New Yorker*, written as a series of letters, signed "Your Pal Joey." The singing voice of Novak was dubbed by Trudy Erwin; Hayworth's singing was dubbed by Jo Ann Greer. Columbia. color

Pale Rider (1985)—Clint Eastwood's art Western, shot in art color—shades of dirt, with gray, brown, and black trimmings, and interiors so dark you can barely see who's onscreen in the middle of the day. Eastwood himself, a ghost who materializes as the answer to a 14-year-old girl's prayer for a miracle, seems to be playing some spectral combination of Death, Jesus, Billy Jack, and the Terminator. Set in the California Sierras during the gold-rush era before the Civil War, the movie is full of recycled mythmaking (*Shane*, *High Noon*, and Sergio Leone's spaghetti Westerns), but Eastwood goes through his motions like someone exhumed, and in his directing he numbs out what he borrows. There isn't a gleam of good sense anywhere in this picture. With Michael Moriarty, Carrie Snodgress, Richard Dysart, Christopher Penn, Sydney Penny, Richard Kiel, John Russell, and Doug McGrath. From a script that Eastwood commissioned from Michael Butler and Dennis Shryack, based on his own story idea; filmed in Idaho. Cinematography by Bruce Surtees. A Malpaso Production, for Warners. (See *Hooked*.)

Palm Beach Story (1942)—One of the giddiest and most chaotic of Preston Sturges's satiric orgies. The romantic problems of the leads (Joel McCrea and Claudette Colbert) get shoved aside by the secondary characters. Colbert, travelling by train, becomes involved with a bunch of drunken millionaires—members of the "Ale and Quail Club," on board with their hounds and guns—who stage an informal skeet shoot in the club car and demolish the glassware. Sturges's comic invention soars, but the picture is too wild to be sustained; still, it's a joy, despite the lulls of waggish humor. With Mary Astor, Rudy Vallee, and the Sturges stock company, including William Demarest, Franklin Pangborn, and Jimmy Conlin. Paramount. b & w

Panama Hattie (1942)—A sad disappointment, though Lena Horne is ravishing, and when she sings you can forget the rest of the picture. The 1940 Broadway musical (which had starred Ethel Merman) underwent the usual Hollywood bowdlerization; the movie still has some energy, but only a couple of the Cole Porter songs remain. Ann Sothern is in the Merman role, supported by Ben Blue, Red Skelton, and Rags Ragland as sailors, as well as by the Berry Brothers, Jackie Horner, Marsha Hunt, Virginia O'Brien, Dan Dailey, Alan Mowbray, and Carl Esmond. The songs (from various sources) include ''Did I Get Stinking at the Club Savoy!'' by E. Y. Harburg and Walter Donaldson. Directed by Norman Z. McLeod; produced by Arthur Freed, for M-G-M. b & w

Pandora and the Flying Dutchman (1951)—Certifiably one of a kind. Albert Lewin, who produced, directed, and wrote the story and screenplay, shows more visual feeling than common sense. James Mason, in his gloomily romantic period, is, literally, the doomed sailor, and Ava Gardner (looking unspeakably luscious) is an American playgirl in evening clothes who wanders through exotic, poetic landscapes before sacrificing herself to save him. Lewin's direction is static, yet his staging is so luxuriantly mad that it's easy to get fixated on what, if anything, he could have had in mind. Sally Bowles might have called it divinely incoherent—it's as nutty-fruity as another Ava Gardner film, *The Barefoot Contessa*, but without as much talk. The English production, shot in Spain, has a mostly British cast—Nigel Patrick, Pamela Kellino (Mason), Marius Goring, and John Laurie. Cinematography by Jack Cardiff. An Anglo-American co-production; released by M-G-M. color

Pandora's Box *Die Büchse der Pandora* (1928)—Louise Brooks, a great—almost impersonal—beauty who set styles in the flapper period, and whose straight hair and bangs were imitated all over the world (and were used as the model for the Dixie Dugan comic strip), left Hollywood in 1928 at the height of her career and went to Germany for the role of a lifetime. G. W. Pabst had selected her to play Lulu in this film, adapted from the Wedekind plays *Erdgeist* and *Die Büchse der Pandora* (the same source material that Alban Berg used for his opera *Lulu*). Pabst, one of the giants of the screen, is perhaps most famous for his treatment of sex, violence, and abnormal psychology, and Wedekind's sex tragedy provided startling material. Lulu is the sexually insatiable female, the archetype of voracious, destructive woman. She has no moral sense and no interests beyond sensuality; when a man is exhausted, she leaves him. The film is episodic; it's in an Expressionist style, with rapid cutting and surprising kinds of almost violent visual tension, particularly in the first half. For sheer erotic dynamism, the backstage scenes on the opening night of a show Lulu is in have never been equalled; the later scenes, in Marseilles, are comparatively drab. Moving through the chiaroscuro, Louise Brooks, with her straight back and strong shoulders, seems to have her own form of sexuality—preconscious yet intuitively all-knowing. She's like a cool, beautiful, innocently deadly cat that people can't keep their hands off. With Fritz Kortner as Dr. Schön, Francis Lederer as his son, Alice Roberts as the lesbian Countess Geschwitz, and Gustav Diessl as Jack the Ripper. Adaptation by Ladislaus Vajda. The German censors made extensive cuts in the film (Brooks indicated that they cut about 15 minutes); a reconstituted version was assembled a half-century later. (The Wedekind material was first filmed in 1919 with Asta Nielsen; the most recent version was probably the 1962 *Lulu* with Nadja Tiller.) Silent. b & w

The Panic in Needle Park (1971)—Boy (Al Pacino) meets girl (Kitty Winn), but he is a heroin addict and she becomes one. The New

York–set movie doesn't tell you much you don't know. Worthy, but a drag—despite the many incidents, it feels undramatic. It shows a lot of care, though. It has an authentic look and a thoughtfully selected cast that includes Richard Bright, Alan Vint, Kiel Martin, Michael McClanathan, Raul Julia, Warren Finnerty, Paul Sorvino, Sully Boyar, and Joe Santos. Directed by Jerry Schatzberg, from the script by Joan Didion and John Gregory Dunne, based on a novel by James Mills. Cinematography by Adam Holender; produced by Dominick Dunne. 20th Century-Fox. color

Panic in the Streets (1950)—Elia Kazan took a fairly conventional thriller script and made a tense, high-powered movie of it. Seeing this film, one wouldn't know that he had ever worked in the theatre: everything is kept moving, in a feverish, seething way, yet the performances are never sacrificed to the action. The setting is the New Orleans waterfront; a murder victim is discovered to be carrying plague, and a Public Health doctor (Richard Widmark) and a city detective (Paul Douglas) hunt for everybody who came into contact with him. Mean Jack Palance (then billed as Walter Jack Palance) and frightened, sweaty Zero Mostel are the thugs they're after. With Barbara Bel Geddes, who is exceedingly likable as Widmark's wife, Tommy Rettig as their son, and Alexis Minotis. The writers involved were Richard Murphy, Edward and Edna Anhalt, and Daniel Fuchs; Joe MacDonald shot the picture in and on actual bars and wharfs. 20th Century-Fox. b & w

Panique (1946)—Julien Duvivier's psychological thriller is a devastatingly effective job of visual storytelling. Michel Simon is the stranger in a Paris suburb who is framed for murder; Viviane Romance and her lover, Paul Bernard, are the ones who frame him. The sordid, intriguingly nasty movie—taken, inevitably, from a Simenon novel—has some pretensions toward being a parable of sadistic injustice; on that level, it can't be taken very seriously. But in terms of how the sequences are planned, and how they build, it's an unusual, near-perfect piece of film craftsmanship. In French. b & w

The Paper Chase (1973)—Blurry Timothy Bottoms, who looks like a romantic anarchist who has lost his bombs, as a first-year law student at Harvard, and John Houseman as the professor he idolizes. Bottoms meets the professor's daughter (Lindsay Wagner), who's derisive about everything, and he becomes confused about why he's studying. The picture, written and directed by James Bridges, tries to be thoughtful and provocative, but it has nothing to say. Houseman shines because he's the only one who suggests that he was formed by experience. He brings it his air of eminence, and the film led to a TV series featuring him. Cinematography by Gordon Willis; music by John Williams; based on a novel by John Jay Osborn, Jr. 20th Century-Fox. color (See *Reeling*.)

Paperback Hero (1975)—There is an idea behind this Canadian film, set in Saskatchewan: it's an attempt to show how a small-town hockey hero and womanizing brawler (Keir Dullea) is destroyed by his fantasy that he's a mythic hero figure as big as the hero of "Gunsmoke." And the Western Canadian prairie country is an unusual locale. But the film is feebly written, and the director, Peter Pearson, can't do anything with the scenes involving a college girl (Dayle Haddon) who speaks what are clearly meant to be bitter truths. The film was very successful in Canada, where its view of prairie life and of living on American fantasies probably strikes nerves. Here, the film's intentions look wobbly: for example, Pearson's periodic reliance on cut-in reaction shots of the townspeople is an amateurish embarrassment. The film also makes passes at the soft-core porno market in scenes between Dullea and Elizabeth Ashley (his long-suffering, still hopeful girlfriend), but though these scenes are fairly explicit they are so unerotic that it's difficult to know why they're there at all. color.

Papillon (1973)—A methodical, pointlessly gruelling movie in which Steve McQueen keeps trying to escape from Devil's Island and fellow-convict Dustin Hoffman keeps financing his attempts. There isn't a laugh in its 2½ hours. The moviemakers have approached the subject of Papillon (a French safecracker who was sentenced to prison for life for killing a pimp and who, 30-odd years after he broke out, trumped up his adventures into a best-seller) as if they were making an important historical biography—about a pope, at the very least. The material has been treated not as if it were an escape story but as if it were *the* escape story. This is a movie Mount Rushmore, though it features only two heads. If ever there was a wrong actor for a man of great spirit, it's McQueen; as Robert Mitchum once remarked, "Steve doesn't bring too much to the party." He seems to inspire Hoffman to underplay, too. Theirs is the only emotional bond in the movie, and there's hardly any emotion in it. Directed by the immaculately literal-minded Franklin Schaffner; the script, by Dalton Trumbo and Lorenzo Semple, Jr., is based on the book by Henri Charrière. With Anthony Zerbe and George Coulouris. Cinematography by Fred Koenekamp; music by Jerry Goldsmith. Allied Artists. color (See *Reeling*.)

The Paradine Case (1947)—There are few thrills in this big misconceived courtroom thriller, directed by Hitchcock and ornately produced by David O. Selznick. Talky and stiff, the film never finds the passionate tone that it needs. The story (taken from a Robert Hichens novel) is about a barrister (Gregory Peck) who louses up a murder case because he falls in love with the defendant, his mysterious client, Mrs. Paradine (Alida Valli). The judge is played by Charles Laughton, and Ethel Barrymore (looking very elegant) is his sensitive, mistreated wife. Also with Ann Todd, Louis Jourdan, Charles Coburn, Isobel Elsom, and Leo G. Carroll, who are mostly miserably miscast. The characters and their problems don't make much imprint on a viewer; if you can't remember whether you've seen the picture or not, chances are that you did and forgot it. The script was pinned on Alma Reville, but probably her husband (Hitchcock) and James Bridie and Selznick himself also struggled with it. Cinematography by Lee Garmes; music by Franz Waxman. Selznick International. b & w

Paradise Lagoon   Also known as *The Admirable Crichton*. (1957)—James M. Barrie's comedy about class distinctions was turned into the epic *Male and Female* by Cecil B. De Mille in 1919 (the shipwrecked Gloria Swanson looked wonderful in wet satin). The best qualities of this English version derive from Barrie's original—solid construction, a sense of fun, and well-turned phrases at the expense of the English aristocracy (who seem to be more useful to the theatre than to the country). However, the director, Lewis Gilbert, works somewhat heavily and for rather boisterous effects, as if Barrie's gentle, expert style could be updated by noise. Kenneth More is "the perfect butler"—stuffy, tyrannical Crichton, and Cecil Parker is the democratic, liberal Lord Loam. Cast on a desert island where there are no classes, where skill and aptitude count, the servant becomes master, the master servant. This will hold few surprises for audiences; still there's something rather satisfying in the demonstration. *Paradise Lagoon* is an interesting example of the way movies scavenge on themselves and their theatrical ancestors, and an indication of why: there's a solid nugget of entertainment in many of the old repertory items. The cast includes Martita Hunt, Sally Ann Howes, and Diane Cilento. color

Paramount on Parade (1930)—A lavish "all-star" musical revue, directed by Dorothy Arzner, Ernst Lubitsch, Rowland V. Lee, Edward Sutherland, and others, and supervised by Elsie Janis. The numbers include Ruth Chatterton singing "My Marine" to a quartet that includes Fredric March; Clara Bow, with Jack Oakie and Skeets Gallagher, in "I'm True to the Navy Now"; Helen Kane as a schoolteacher singing "What Did Cleopatra Say?" to the children, who reply "Boop Boopa Doop"; Maurice Chevalier, with his practiced street-urchin charm (he was past 40, but he got by with it), doing a song number while surrounded by a troupe of girls also dressed urchin-style; William Powell as Philo Vance and Clive Brook as Sherlock Holmes in "Murder Will Out." Among the other stars are Nancy Carroll, Nino Martini, Jean Arthur, Gary Cooper, Fay Wray, Lillian Roth, Dennis King, Kay Francis, and Buddy Rogers. Shows like this, in which the studios showed off their contract players, were a form of institutional advertising that paid for itself. And these revues did actually reveal the distinctive tone and style of the studios—Paramount was the giddiest, the least self-serious. b & w and color

Parents (1989)—This first feature directed by the actor Bob Balaban is a stunning début, even though the story, which starts as a satiric comedy about the conformism of the Eisenhower 50s, lapses into gory horror-movie banality. The terrifyingly outsize Nick (Randy Quaid), a defoliation expert, and his adoring, obedient Lily (Mary Beth Hurt) are a lovely-dovey pair of married sweethearts. All's right with the world—a man's world—except for their miserable, finicky, little 10-year-old son (Bryan Madorsky), who won't eat his meat to grow up as big and strong as Daddy. He's a budding version of the counterculture hippies. The boy's scenes with Sandy Dennis, as the blowsy school psychologist, go into comedy heaven, and his moments with Juno Mills-Cockell, as his new school friend, are inexplicably flaky. The script is by Christopher Hawthorne; the art direction is by Andris Hausmanis. Vestron. color (See *Movie Love*.)

Les Parents terribles Also known as *The Storm Within*. (1949)—One of Jean Cocteau's two or three greatest films, and one of the finest examples of group acting ever photographed. He took his play about the disorderly, unpredictable parents (Marcel André and Yvonne de Bray) who cannot accept the fact that their son (Jean Marais) is growing up and re-created it for the screen with such skill that a true claustrophobic family atmosphere is achieved. In structure, this is a coincidence-ridden boulevard comedy, but Cocteau lifts it to the realm of tragicomic Oedipal fable. The mother screams for the police when she learns that her son has a girl; Yvonne de Bray's performance is so magically convincing that Marais's actual mother is said to have developed a jealous hatred of her. Gabrielle Dorziat plays the boy's aunt, and Josette Day his girl. Designed by Christian Bérard; cinematography by Michel Kelber; music by Georges Auric. In French. b & w

Paris Does Strange Things, see *Eléna et les hommes*

Une Partie de campagne, see *A Day in the Country*

Partner *Il Sosia* (1968)—Two years before *The Conformist*, Bernardo Bertolucci made this inventive but bewildering political vaudeville—a modernization of Dostoevski's *The Double*, in which a young drama teacher (Pierre Clémenti) has fantasies of extending the theatre of cruelty into political revolution. Clémenti doesn't convey enough intellectuality for an audience to understand the character, who seems to be a comic-strip Artaud. Visually extraordinary, but the meaning appears to get lost in the vivid pop color, the daring tricks of style, and the profusion of great images—in one scene books are piled up in heaps on the floor of a room, like the Roman ruins outside. (It's the most Godardian of Bertolucci's films.) With Stefania Sandrelli, Tina Aumont, and Sergio Tofano. The script is by Bertolucci and Gianni Amico; cinematography by Ugo Piccone. There are versions in French and in Italian. CinemaScope, color

The Party (1968)—Peter Sellers plays a bungling actor from New Delhi who accidentally blows up an expensive Hollywood set. Intending to blacklist him, the studio head writes his name down on a slip of paper; a secretary assumes that the name is to be added to a party guest list, and so the actor arrives at the home of the studio head who wants to kill him. It's a promising beginning—too promising for what follows. Most of this Blake Edwards slapstick farce records the way the Indian innocently destroys the party, and it's too long for its one-note jokes, and often too obvious to be really funny. But it's agreeable in tone, though as it goes on, the gags don't have any particular connection with the touching, maddening Indian character that Sellers plays so wickedly well. With Claudine Longet, Marge Champion, Steve Franken, Gavin MacLeod, Buddy Lester, and Denny Miller; written by Edwards and Tom and Frank Waldman. United Artists. color

Pas si méchant que ça, see *The Wonderful Crook*

Pasqualino Settebellezze, see *Seven Beauties*

Pass the Ammo (1988)—Set in an Ozark community, this lampoon of television evangelists is a piece of rollicky backwoods Americana. It was shot in Eureka Springs, Arkansas, where the civic auditorium was converted into the studios of the Tower of Bethlehem, a ministry that lays claim to an audience of 20 million people and is systematically bilking them. A young woman (Linda Kozlowski) from the hill country is trying to recover $50,000 that her family was stung for. Her fiancé (Bill Paxton) organizes what's meant to be a small, quiet robbery of the Tower's counting room but finds himself holding the congregation of a couple of thousand people hostage, and on satellite TV. The movie straggles a bit, but it has a klunky freshness, and it has a whole slew of terrifically talented actors: Tim Curry as the bratty con artist, the charismatic Reverend Ray Porter who dallies with the ladies of the choir; Annie Potts as his exhibitionist wife, Darla, who wiggles like the best cootch dancer in Heaven while delivering a sales pitch for expensive Bibles; Anthony Geary; Glenn Withrow; Dennis Burkley; Leland Crooke; and others. Directed by David Beaird, from a script by Neil Cohen and Joel Cohen (no relation). Cinematography by Mark Irwin. color (See *Hooked*.)

A Passage to India (1984)—This admirable version of E. M. Forster's 1924 novel about the tragicomedy of British colonial rule was adapted, directed, and edited by David Lean, who knows how to do pomp and the moral hideousness of empire better than practically anybody else around. He enlarges the scale of Forster's irony, and the characters live in more sumptuous settings than we might have expected. But they do live. Peggy Ashcroft comes through with a transcendent piece of acting as Mrs. Moore, and Judy Davis is close to perfection as the repressed Miss Quested, who longs for adventure; they are the two women whose attempt to get to know the Indians socially results in a charge of attempted rape against Dr. Aziz, played by Victor Banerjee, a fine, fluid actor who's like a piece of erotic sculpture. If Lean's technique is to simplify and to spell everything out in block letters, this kind of clarity has its own formal strength. It may not be the highest praise to say that a movie is orderly and dignified or that it's like a well-cared-for, beautifully oiled machine, but of its kind this *Passage to India* is awfully good, until the last half hour or so. Having built up to the courtroom drama, Lean isn't able to regain a narrative flow when it's over; the emotional focus is gone, and the concluding scenes wobble all over the place. With the exception of Alec Guinness (whose caricature of an inscrutable Brahmin is simply in the wrong movie), the cast is just about irreproachable. It includes James Fox as the dogged liberal Fielding and Nigel Havers as Ronny, and also Art Malik, Michael Culver, Saeed Jaffrey, Roshan Seth, and Sandra Hotz as Stella. Cinematography by Ernest Day; music by Maurice Jarre; production design by John Box. (2 hours and 43 minutes.) Columbia. color (See *State of the Art*.)

Passages from Finnegans Wake (1965)—Not great, certainly, but a pleasant and inoffensive attempt to convey the fun of the jokes and enigmas and metamorphoses of the Joyce dream book. Martin J. Kelley is Finnegan, Peter Haskell is Shem, and Jane Reilly is Anna Livia Plurabelle. Directed by Mary Ellen Bute; based on the play version by Mary Manning. b & w

La Passion de Jeanne d'Arc, see *The Passion of Joan of Arc*

The Passion of Joan of Arc *La Passion de Jeanne d'Arc* (1928)—One of the greatest of all movies. The director, Carl Dreyer, based the script on the trial records, and the testimony appears to be given for the first time. (Cocteau wrote that this film "seems like an historical document from an era in which the cinema didn't exist.") As the five gruelling cross-examinations follow each other, Dreyer turns the camera on the faces of Joan and the judges, and in giant closeups he reveals his interpretation of their emotions. In this enlargement Joan and her persecutors are shockingly fleshly—isolated with their sweat, warts, spittle, and tears, and (as no one used makeup) with startlingly individual contours, features, and skin. No other film has so subtly linked eroticism with religious persecution. Falconetti's Joan may be the finest performance ever recorded on film. With Silvain as Cauchon, Michel Simon, André Berley, Maurice Schutz, and the young Antonin Artaud—as Massieu he's the image of passionate idealism. The staging, and the cinematography by Rudolph Maté, are in a style that suggests the Stations of the Cross. The film is silent but as you often see the (French) words forming you may have the illusion that you've heard them. b & w

Passport to Pimlico (1949)—British comedy with a fine flavor and wonderful details, though the whimsey is rather self-congratulatory. An ancient royal charter ceding Pimlico to the Dukes of Burgundy is unearthed in a London shell hole, and the people of Pimlico are "just British enough to fight for our rights to be Burgundians." Margaret Rutherford is the historian who gives scholarly sanction to an independent Pimlico; Basil Radford and Naunton Wayne are the protocol-ridden bureaucrats trying to handle the crisis; Stanley Holloway and Hermione Baddeley are shopkeepers. The ingenious author, T.E.B. Clarke, got the idea from a wartime newspaper item: the Canadian government transferred title to the room in which the exiled Princess Juliana was about to bear a child to the Netherlands; in this way the child would technically be born on Dutch soil and thus be a legal heir to the throne. Henry Cornelius directed; music by Georges Auric. With Raymond Huntley, John Slater, Jane Hylton, and Sydney Tafler. b & w

Pat and Mike (1952)—Katharine Hepburn and Spencer Tracy play together so expertly that their previous films seem like warmups. The script, by Ruth Gordon and Garson Kanin, isn't up to the best of *Adam's Rib*, but the stars have achieved such teamwork that their sparring is more beautiful than punch lines. Hepburn plays a phenomenal all-around athlete, and in the course of the picture she takes on Gussie Moran, Babe Didrikson Zaharias, and other professionals, touching off the comic possibilities in various sports with grace and ease. Tracy, who plays a sports promoter (with a streets-of-the-big-city accent—"cherce" for "choice") has a lighter, funnier tone than in the other Tracy-Hepburn pictures. With Aldo Ray as a sulky boxer, William Ching, Jim Backus, Phyllis Povah, Sammy White, Chuck Connors, Charles Bronson, and Don Budge. George Cukor directed—beautifully. It's as close to perfect as you'd want it to be. Produced by Lawrence Weingarten, for M-G-M. b & w

Pat Garrett and Billy the Kid (1973)—Ambitious, erotic, peculiarly unrealized account of how Garrett (James Coburn) hunts down his best friend Billy (Kris Kristofferson), with Bob Dylan (who sings the score, written by him) appearing as a buddy of Billy's. Sam Peckinpah directed, from a screenplay by Rudolph Wurlitzer. With an amazing cast that includes Jason Robards, Katy Jurado, Rita Coolidge, Emilio Fernandez, Slim Pickens, Chill Wills, John Beck, Richard Jaeckel, Matt

Clark, Richard Bright, Jack Elam, Harry Dean Stanton, John Davis Chandler, L. Q. Jones, Peckinpah, Wurlitzer, and Elisha Cook (Jr.). Probably nobody involved was very happy about the results; Dylan doesn't come off at all. M-G-M. color

Pather Panchali (1955)—(Variously translated as "Song of the Road," "The Lament of the Path," etc.) This first film by the masterly Satyajit Ray—possibly the most unembarrassed and natural of directors—is a quiet reverie about the life of an impoverished Brahman family in a Bengali village. Beautiful, sometimes funny, and full of love, it brought a new vision of India to the screen. Though the central characters are the boy Apu (who is born near the beginning) and his mother and father and sister, the character who makes the strongest impression on you may be the ancient, parasitic, storytelling relative, played by the 80-year-old Chunibala, a performer who apparently enjoyed coming back into the limelight after 30 years of obscurity—her wages paid for the narcotics she used daily. As "auntie," she is so remarkably likable that you may find the relationship between her and the mother, who is trying to feed her children and worries about how much the old lady eats, very painful. Ray continued the story of Apu in *Aparajito* and *Apur Sansar* (*The World of Apu*), and the three films, all based on a novel by B. B. Bandapaddhay, became known as The Apu Trilogy. (Robin Wood's study, *The Apu Trilogy*, does the films justice.) Cinematography by Subrata Mitra; music by Ravi Shankar. In Bengali. b & w

Paths of Glory (1957)—Just after he made his racetrack robbery picture *The Killing*, Stanley Kubrick directed this version of Humphrey Cobb's novel, photographed in Germany. It is not so much an anti-war film as an attack on the military mind. Some of the press went all out for it ("searing in its intensity," and that sort of thing), but it wasn't popular. The movie has a fascinating jittery quality, especially when Timothy Carey, who's like a precursor of the hipster druggies of the 60s, is on the screen, and the strong, liberal-intellectual pitch makes it genuinely controversial, though it was certainly easier to be anti-militaristic in a film (made in peacetime) set during the First World War than it would have been in a film set during the Second World War. The story is about the class structure within the French army—the aristocratic generals in their spacious, sunlit châteaux and the proletarian soldiers in the dark trenches; trapped between them is Colonel Dax (Kirk Douglas), who commiserates with the men but is powerless—he carries out the orders of the high command. When the soldiers refuse to fight in a battle that is almost certain death, three of them are selected to be tried for cowardice; Dax has the task of defending them. The film's rhythm is startling—you can feel the director's temperament. And there's an element of relentlessness in the way he sets out to demonstrate the hopeless cruelty of the "system." (The film was banned in France for some years.) It's an angry film that seems meant to apply to all armies. Watching it is very frustrating: Kubrick, who wrote the script with Calder Willingham and Jim Thompson, doesn't leave you with anything. He must have felt this, because he tacks on a scene at a cabaret, with a German girl (Susanne Christian) singing and the soldiers singing along, as they weep. (It just makes you uncomfortable.) With Adolphe Menjou—a cartoon of a wily general, George Macready as another general, and Ralph Meeker, Wayne Morris, Richard Anderson, Joseph Turkel, Bert Freed, Emile Meyer, Peter Capell, and John Stein. Produced by James B. Harris of Harris-Kubrick Productions, for United Artists. b & w

Patton (1970)—The film is enormous in scale and runs almost three hours; it was directed by Franklin J. Schaffner in a style that might be described as imperial—incredibly long, wide shots that take in vast areas, with the human figures dwarfed by the terrain. There's so much land and air—and it's so clear—that we seem to be looking at the action from God's point of view. The landscapes are full of men, but they're all essentially extras—even men like Omar Bradley (Karl Malden), who *should* be important. There's really nobody in this movie except George C. Scott's Patton. He is what people who believe in military values can see as the true military hero—the red-blooded American who loves to fight and whose crude talk is straight talk. He is also what people who despise militarism can see as the worst kind of red-blooded American mystical maniac; for them, Patton can be the symbolic proof of the madness of the whole military complex. The picture, from a script by Francis Ford Coppola and Edmund H. North, plays him both ways—crazy and great—and more ways than that, because he's a comic-strip general, and even those who are anti-war may love comic strips. Patton is treated as if he were the spirit of war, yet the movie begs the fundamental question: Is this the kind of man a country needs when it's at war? This movie is both a satirical epic and a square celebration, yet the satire backfires. Scott's Patton is so much stronger than anyone else that he has glamour and appeal. The film's style itself validates Patton the war lover as a hero. With Karl Michael Vogler as Rommel. Produced by Frank McCarthy, for 20th Century-Fox; adapted from L. Farago's *Patton: Ordeal & Triumph* and Bradley's *A Soldier's Story*; cinematography by Fred Koenekamp. color (See *Deeper into Movies*.)

Patty Hearst (1988)—It's unlikely that this stylized movie of ideas will appeal to a large audience, but on its own terms it's a lean, impressive piece of work. Directed by Paul Schrader, from a bilge-free script by Nicholas Kazan, it's a distanced presentation of the kidnapping of the 19-year-old heiress, in 1974, by an eight-member terrorist group that called itself the Symbionese Liberation Army, and of her subsequent participation in the group's holdups, and of her trial. The whole series of events is like a nightmare that's all of a piece—a kid's nightmare that no one is on your side. And it answers the question that people asked before, during, and after the trial: Did Patty Hearst become part of the S.L.A. willingly, out of conviction, or was she simply trying to save her life? The movie shows you that, in the state she was in, there was no difference. Natasha Richardson, who plays Patty, has been handed a big unwritten role; she feels her way into it, and she fills it. We feel how alone and paralyzed Patty is— she retreats to being a hidden observer. Patty is a girl who is raped in mind and body, and no longer knows when it started. The picture seems flat for a long time, but when Patty's capture by the S.L.A. is followed by her capture by the police, everything starts to add up, and suddenly the film is overwhelming. With William Forsythe, Dana Delany, Jodi Long, and Ving Rhames. The score is by Scott Johnson. color (See *Movie Love*.)

Pauline at the Beach   *Pauline à la plage* (1982)—The writer-director Eric Rohmer serves up this innocuous sex roundelay with exquisite control. It's all low-key conversation, and there's a thin veneer of chic over everybody. Rohmer contrasts the belle of the beach, the voluptuous blond divorcée Marion (Arielle Dombasle), with her dark-eyed 15-year-old cousin Pauline (Amanda Langlet). The self-centered, self-deluding Marion flirts and babbles, and Rohmer lets us know what he thinks of her by showing her walking away from the camera in a tight, wet bathing

suit that's squeezing her. Pauline is quiet and intelligent and her bathing suit has nary a wrinkle or a crease. Rohmer has an amazing gift for finding (or creating) actors who embody the tiny, precise psychological observations that he wants to make, and, with the help of the cinematographer Nestor Almendros, he establishes a loose, summery atmosphere that the characters fit right into. But he offers a tedious message ("A wagging tongue bites itself"), and he can't resist setting up the little girl as our moral instructor. (She and her adolescent lover, played by Simon de la Brosse, are so "natural" they go to bed together without a stab of fear or self-consciousness; does anybody believe this?) The six characters involved in the bedroom-farce misunderstandings include a suave, 40ish stud (Féodor Atkine); a handsome young windsurfer (Pascal Greggory), who's a ninny; and a girl (Rosette) who sells candy on the beach. In French. color (See *State of the Art*.)

The Pawnbroker (1965)—Rod Steiger plays a benumbed Jewish survivor of the concentration camps who lives on in Harlem running a pawnshop—fat, sagging, past pain, past caring. Adapted from the Edward Lewis Wallant novel and directed by Sidney Lumet, the film is trite, and you can see the big pushes for powerful effects, yet it isn't negligible. It wrenches audiences, making them fear that they, too, could become like this man. And when events strip off his armor, he doesn't discover a new, warm humanity, he discovers sharper suffering—just what his armor had protected him from. Most of the intensity comes from Steiger's performance and from the performance of the great old Juano Hernández, as a man who comes into the shop to talk. With Geraldine Fitzgerald, Brock Peters, and Jaime Sanchez; cinematography by Boris Kaufman; score by Quincy Jones. Released by Allied Artists. b & w

Payday (1973)—Shot entirely on location in Alabama, it's an acrid, hardboiled melodrama with a feeling for authentic characters and details. An exceptionally functional script, by the novelist Don Carpenter, makes it possible for the director, Daryl Duke, to cover the grimy country music scene of a small-time recording star—a goaty, rancidly unromantic third-rate Johnny Cash. Rip Torn, with his smirking satyr grin, will probably never have a role that suits him better than the barnstorming Maury Dann. In the back of his Cadillac between two girls, Maury Dann is a sweating rajah, drinking Coke and beer and bourbon, smoking pot and popping pills. Made by an independent company, with Ralph J. Gleason, the veteran writer on jazz, as executive producer, and financed by Fantasy Records (Saul Zaentz and Gleason), the film didn't get the distribution it deserved. Its only real flaw is the flaw that's also present in hardboiled fiction: when a world is this clearly defined, our imagination is frustrated. With Michael C. Gwynne as Maury's manager, Cliff Emmich as his fat, loyal driver and cook who takes a prison rap for him, Elayne Heilveil as a teen-age groupie who works in a dime store, and Ahna Capri as Maury's blond mistress who goads him at the wrong moment and is deposited in the middle of the highway. color (See *Reeling*.)

Payment on Demand (1951)—This Bette Davis picture—the story of a hideously bad marriage—was made just before *All About Eve*, though it wasn't released until afterward. Davis plays a wrong-headed, treacherous, racist wife who drives her husband (Barry Sullivan) to success and into the arms of another woman (Frances Dee). Davis has so many outbursts that Sullivan, who has to listen to them, looks benumbed. By the time the celebrated stage actress Jane Cowl turns up, as a broken-down divorcée who is reduced to sharing her life with a grubby poet—a spectacle that shatters Davis's wicked complacency and causes her to reform—the special damp rot of dull "women's pictures" has set in. With Kent Taylor, John Sutton, Otto Kruger, Natalie Schaefer, Richard Anderson, and, in the flashback sequence, Davis's own daughter, playing her child. Directed by Curtis Bernhardt; screenplay by Bruce Manning and Bernhardt. R K O. b & w

The Pearls of the Crown *Les Perles de la couronne* (1937)—The writer-director-actor Sacha Guitry made one-of-a-kind movies, and he made them one after another—quickly, tossing them off. They're glittering trifles; they reek of boulevard insouciance, of chic. And they're among the wittiest and most innovative movies ever made. This one is a comic pageant, a casual succession of jokes and incidents, shifting from ironic high style to low-down put-ons. The picture follows the career of a group of matching pearls over several centuries and several continents; it involves such personages as Mary of Scotland, Empress Eugenie, Napoleon, Henry VIII, Madame DuBarry, and the Queen of Abyssinia—seeing it is rather like flipping the pages of a history book while drinking champagne. Guitry himself plays four roles and is assisted by Arletty, Jean-Louis Barrault, Marguerite Moreno, Cecile Sorel, Jacqueline Delubac, and Jean Coquelin (many of them also play more than one role). *Pearls* isn't as simply made as, say, Guitry's 1936 *The Story of a Cheat* or even his very last film, the 1956 *Lovers and Thieves*; it's a 2-hour spectacle (Christian-Jaque served as co-director) and it's slower and plushier. But it has some of his farthest-out campy jokes. (As the Queen of Abyssinia, Arletty wears black-face and black-body, too; she also screeches in "Abyssinian.") A trilingual production in French, Italian, and English. b & w

Peccato che Sia una Canaglia, see *Too Bad She's Bad*

The Pedestrian *Der Fussgänger* (1974)—Maximilian Schell takes the year's Stanley Kramer Prize for a Movie on the Theme of War Guilt Which Confuses More Issues Than It Raises. The protagonist (Gustav Rudolf Sellner) is a powerful industrialist who is exposed as the man responsible for the massacre of an entire Greek village during the Second World War. In writer-director Schell's hazy reasoning, however, the industrialist shouldn't really feel bad; nobody in particular is guilty, because everybody is guilty. The film has been praised in the U.S. as if it were a deep probe into serious issues; no doubt, it can be praised in Germany as a very comforting view. Schell loves fanciness and abstractions and imprecision; this film is about so many things that it's finally not about anything. Sellner has a strong presence and holds the camera; Schell turns up in a minor role, and so does the English director Peter Hall. In one clumsy, gratuitous sequence, Peggy Ashcroft, Elisabeth Bergner, and Françoise Rosay appear, along with several other famous actresses, and are shamefully wasted. In German. color

Pee-wee's Big Adventure (1985)—This slapstick novelty starring the grown-up yet prepubescent Pee-wee Herman—a Peter Pan of the shopping-mall era—is somewhere between a parody of kitsch and a celebration of it, and it has the bouncing-along inventiveness of a good cartoon. It's set in a candy-colored period of its own—a 50s-80s Twilight Zone, where you might not be surprised to bump into Harry (the baby) Langdon or Steve Martin as the Jerk. When Pee-wee's bike—the love of his life—is stolen, his search to recover it takes him from L.A. to Texas, to the Alamo, and back. Hitching rides, he encounters a series of American-movie arche-types (an escaped convict, a waitress out of *The Petrified Forest* who dreams of going to Paris, truckers, hoboes, rodeo riders, a mean, wild motorcycle gang) and the 26-year-old director Tim Burton shows his flair for the silly-surreal. The movie is full of slobby, hairy giants—they make you think of Paul Bunyan or Bluto—and you see them from Pee-wee's point of view. He looks at the dirty, uncouth, threatening men and would rather remain a 10-year-old. With Jan Hooks, who has a juicy comedy routine as the tour guide at the Alamo; Mark Holton as Pee-wee's rival Francis; Judd Omen as the convict; Elizabeth Daily as Dottie; Alice Nunn as Large Marge; Diane Salinger as the waitress; Tony Bell; and, as movie stars, James Brolin and Morgan Fairchild. Pee-wee Herman shares the writing credit (with Phil Hartman and Michael Varhol) under his own name, Paul Reubens. Warners. color (See *Hooked*.)

Peggy Sue Got Married (1986)—Distressed by her marital troubles, Peggy Sue (Kathleen Turner), the mother of two grown-up children, collapses at the 25th reunion of her high-school class, and when she wakes up she discovers that she has gone back in time to the spring of 1960. Directed by Francis Coppola, this is a dream movie that asks whether Peggy Sue, knowing what she does at 43, should marry the same boy—passionate Charlie (Nicolas Cage), the only man she ever dated, and the one who got her pregnant on her 18th birthday—knowing that he won't go on to have the singing career he talks about, that he'll go into his father's business and turn into the man who introduces himself on television as Crazy Charlie, the Appliance King. (It's perfectly clear what Peggy Sue will do because, of course, if she doesn't marry Charlie her children will never be born.) The underlying question is: Should Peggy Sue reconcile with her husband or go ahead and get a divorce? And the picture answers it the way Hollywood movies used to, by showing us that as teen-agers Peggy Sue and Charlie were physically attracted to each other—as if that meant that they were destined to live together forever, in the best of all possible worlds. The script, by Jerry Leichtling and Arlene Sarner, lacks the mechanical ingenuity of a *Back to the Future*, yet the characters are almost as superficial, and Coppola's efforts to bring depth to this material that has no depth make the picture seem groggy. It's as if he were trying to reach through a veil of fog, trying to direct the actors to bring something out of themselves when neither he nor anyone else knows what's wanted. (Cage does bring something touching and desperate to Charlie the small-town hotshot.) With Barbara Harris, Barry Miller, Kevin J. O'Connor, Catherine Hicks, Joan Allen, Don Murray, Maureen O'Sullivan, Sofia Coppola, Leon Ames, and John Carradine. Cinematography by Jordan Cronenweth. A Rastar Production, released by Tri-Star. color (See *Hooked*.)

Penn & Teller Get Killed (1989)—There's a terrific opening sequence with the pair of prankster magicians on a live late-night talk show; the screen is full of hoopla and graphics, and it's as if some new kind of bludgeoning, hip comedy were being invented— as if the Three Stooges had taken over "Saturday Night Live." But when the TV show is over, the snap goes out of the movie. It's meant to take off from Penn's remark that it would be fun if a killer were stalking him, but basically it's about the two magicians playing murderous practical jokes on each other, and it's extremely laborious. Caitlin Clarke does appealing backup work as the team's manager, and Christopher Durang turns up as a sneaky nut with a gun concealed in a hollowed-out Bible. Directed by Arthur Penn (no relation), from a script by Penn and Teller. Shot mostly in Atlantic City, by the

Danish cinematographer Jan Weincke, who's great on black backgrounds. Warners. color (See *Movie Love*.)

Pennies from Heaven (1936)—The cheerful tone of this Bing Crosby film grates on one like canned laughter. Sample dialogue: "Are you married?" "No, I'm sane." The story has something to do with an orphanage, and Madge Evans plays a welfare worker. There are some pleasant, mostly inconsequential songs, though, and Louis Armstrong turns up, with his orchestra, and Lionel Hampton is around. Directed by Norman Z. McLeod; with Edith Fellows. Columbia. b & w

Pennies from Heaven (1981)—A startling, stylized big M-G-M musical, set in the mythology of the Depression. When the characters can't say how they feel, they open their mouths, and the voices on hit records of the 30s come out of them. And as they lip-sync the lyrics their obsessed eyes are burning bright. Their souls are in those voices, and they see themselves dancing just like the stars in movie musicals. The dance numbers are funny, amazing, and beautiful all at once; several of them are just about perfection. And though some of the dialogue scenes are awkwardly paced and almost static, they still have a rapt, gripping quality. There's something new going on—something thrilling— when the characters in a musical are archetypes yet are intensely alive. Steve Martin, Bernadette Peters, Christopher Walken, Vernel Bagneris, Jessica Harper, Tommy Rall, Robert Fitch, and Jay Garner all seem to be working at their highest capacities. This is also true of Danny Daniels, who did the choreography; Ken Adam, who designed the production; Bob Mackie, who did the costumes; Gordon Willis, who was the cinematographer; and Dennis Potter, who wrote the script, which is adapted from his six-segment BBC series. The film was directed by Herbert

Ross, who took a plunge but didn't go far enough. The material is conceived in terms of extremes—melodrama and pathos on one side and the dream world on the other. Normal life is excluded. Yet Ross keeps trying to sneak normal life back in: he treats the piled-on sentimental gloom tenderly, as if it were meant to be real. As a result, the picture doesn't come together (as *Cabaret* did). But it's extraordinary. (There are breathtaking re-creations of paintings by Edward Hopper and Reginald Marsh and of famous photographs of the 30s.) color (See *Taking It All In*.)

Penny Serenade (1941)—Irene Dunne and Cary Grant, who had made audiences laugh in *The Awful Truth* and *My Favorite Wife*, jerked tears this time. They play a childless couple who adopt an infant, learn to love it and then lose it. The director, George Stevens, dragged his feet (the picture is over 2 hours long) and he wasn't very subtle; it's "sincere" in an inert and horribly pristine way. Yet he made the sentimental story convincing to a wide audience; many people talk about this picture as if it had really been deeply moving. It may be that the unrealistic casting does the trick: the appeal to the audience is that two glamorous stars play an ordinary couple and suffer the calamities that do in fact happen to ordinary people. When tragedy strikes Irene Dunne and Cary Grant, it hurts the audience in a special way. (And Grant could hardly have been better. Using his dark eyes and his sensuous, clouded handsomeness as a romantic mask, he gave his role a defensive, not quite forthright quality, and he brought out everything that it was possible to bring out of his warmed-over lines, weighing them perfectly, so that they almost seemed felt.) With Edgar Buchanan, Beulah Bondi, and Ann Doran; the screenplay is by Morrie Ryskind. Columbia. b & w (See *When the Lights Go Down*.)

Pépé le Moko (1937)—Superb entertainment. A classic romantic melodrama of the 30s, and one of the most compelling of all the fatalistic French screen romances, yet seen by few Americans because it was remade in Hollywood two years later as *Algiers*, starring Charles Boyer and "introducing" Hedy Lamarr. *Algiers* was so closely copied from *Pépé le Moko* that look-alikes were cast in many of the roles, and some sequences were followed shot by shot. But *Algiers* is glamorous pop that doesn't compare to the original, directed by Julien Duvivier and starring Jean Gabin as the gangster who finds love but can't find his freedom. No one who saw *Pépé* is likely to forget the scene in which the homesick-for-Paris Gabin looks at a Métro ticket and recites the names of the stations. Ironically, Duvivier had hoped to make an American-style gangster film and had drawn some of this characters from *Scarface*. With Mireille Balin, Marcel Dalio, Gaston Modot, Gabriel Gabrio, Line Noro, Saturnin Fabre, and Charpin. The script by Henri Jeanson is based on a novel by Ashelbé (Henri La Barthe), at one time commissioner of the Paris police. (The American version was remade as the musical *Casbah* in 1948.) In French. b & w

Perfect Friday (1970)—A modish trifle from England—a suspense film about how an amoral trio (Ursula Andress, and David Warner, her husband, and Stanley Baker, her lover) rob a bank. It's rather humdrum. The only thing it has going for it is that the Swiss Ursula Andress, who was always sensational looking and also indicated a certain amount of humor, improved her English and she comes across as a witty deadpan comedienne. With her face and figure, the addition of technique makes her dazzling—she's seductive and funny, like the larcenous Dietrich of *Desire*, but the director, Peter Hall, doesn't know how to set her off. The script is by

P

Anthony Greville-Bell and J. Scott Forbes; the music is by Johnny Dankworth. color

Les Perles de la couronne, see *The Pearls of the Crown*

Persona (1967)—In this film, as in his very early *Prison*, the writer-director Ingmar Bergman involves us in the making of a movie. He gives us a movie within a movie, but he seems hardly to have made the enclosing movie, and then he throws away the inner one. (You can *feel* it go—at the repeated passage, when the director seems to be trying an alternate way of shooting a sequence.) It's a pity, because the inner movie had begun to involve us in marvellous possibilities: an actress (Liv Ullmann) who has abandoned the power of speech is put in the care of a nurse (Bibi Andersson), and the nurse, like an analysand who becomes furious at the silence of the analyst, begins to vent her own emotional disturbances. The two women look very much alike, and Bergman plays with this resemblance photographically by suggestive combinations and superimpositions. Most movies give so little that it seems almost barbarous to object to Bergman's not giving us more in *Persona*, but it is just because of the expressiveness and fascination of what we *are* given that the movie is so frustrating. There is, however, great intensity in many of the images, and there's one great passage: the nurse talks about a day and night of sex on a beach, and as she goes on talking, with memories of summer and nakedness and pleasure in her voice and the emptiness of her present life in her face, viewers may begin to hold their breath in fear that the director won't be able to sustain this almost intolerably difficult sequence. But he does, and it builds and builds and is completed. It's one of the rare truly erotic sequences in movie history. With Gunnar Björnstrand, and Jörgen Lindström as the

boy. Cinematography by Sven Nykvist. In Swedish. b & w (See *Kiss Kiss Bang Bang*.)

Personal Best (1982)—There has probably never been a growing-up story presented on the screen so freely and uninhibitedly. Set in the world of women athletes, this film, written, produced, and directed by Robert Towne, tells most of the story non-verbally and character is revealed in movement. When Towne shows the two heroines—Mariel Hemingway and Patrice Donnelly—armwrestling, he concentrates on their throbbing veins and their sinews and how the muscles play off one another. He breaks down athletic events into specific details; you watch the athletes' calves or some other part of them, and you get an exact sense of how their bodies work—it's sensual and sexual, and it's informative, too. There's an undercurrent of flabbergasted awe in this celebration of women's bodies, and everything in the movie is physically charged. The women athletes are all great looking and all funny, because they have advanced so much faster than men's thinking about them has. They razz men flirtatiously, flaunting their own strength. This is a very smart and super-subtle movie, in which the authenticity of the details draws us in. It should be one of the best dating movies of all time, because it pares away all traces of self-consciousness. With Scott Glenn and Kenny Moore; cinematography by Michael Chapman, with a few scenes by Caleb Deschanel. Warners. color (See *Taking It All In*.)

Personal Services (1987)—An astonishingly cheerful high and low comedy, starring Julie Walters as a London brothelkeeper. Walters is a human carnival; at times, she's as spirited as Mel Brooks on a good day. When this madam, called Christine Painter, thinks about the undignified actions that her dignified old gentlemen like to engage in, she giggles, and she carries you along with her. Her giddy hysteria seems the only appropriate response to the sexual habits of the English—it seems a higher normality. Christine Painter, grounded on Cynthia Payne, London's famous Mme. Cyn (who acted as consultant to the film), is a great subject for the director, Terry Jones, of the Monty Python group, and the writer, David Leland (who co-wrote the 1986 *Mona Lisa*). With Julie Walters at the center of things, the soft spots don't matter much. She seems to energize the whole film—to give it a rare kind of screwball fizziness—though she actually gets a lot of help from Alec McCowen, Shirley Stelfox, and Danny Schiller (as Dolly, the elderly maid at the brothel). Cinematography by Roger Deakins. (The film *Wish You Were Here* is loosely based on Cynthia Payne's earlier life.) Released by Vestron. color (See *Hooked*.)

Pete 'n' Tillie (1972)—Carol Burnett and Walter Matthau in a low-key modern equivalent of old semi-forgettable, semi-memorable pictures like *Penny Serenade*, about decent people trying to live their lives somewhat rationally. Pete and Tillie speak in an epigrammatic style derived from the Peter De Vries short novel *Witch's Milk*, on which the movie is based, but their good life together is so aseptically the middle-class ideal that it looks like death. Martin Ritt directed, from Julius J. Epstein's screenplay. With Geraldine Page, René Auberjonois, and Barry Nelson. Universal. color (See *Reeling*.)

Peter Ibbetson (1935)—A romantic fantasy in which the hero (Gary Cooper) is visited by his dead beloved (Ann Harding, as Mary, Duchess of Towers), who comes drifting down from Heaven. The five screenwriters failed to lick the datedness of the material (a George Du Maurier story, filmed as a silent, in 1921). This is an essentially sickly gothic, and yet the director, Henry Hathaway, brings off some of the ethereal moments, and the film tends to stay in the memory. With Ida Lupino, John Halliday, Douglass Dumbrille, Donald Meek, and Leonid Kinskey. Paramount. b & w

Le Petit Soldat (1960)—Jean-Luc Godard's first foray into politics, with romance and political extremism and torture and talk of cinema all suspended in an existential mixture. Technically an innovative work, but humanly a baffling one. With Anna Karina and Michel Subor; cinematography by Raoul Coutard. In French. b & w

The Petrified Forest (1936)—Leslie Howard is all forehead as a world-weary, desiccated intellectual who arrives on foot at a gas station and Bar-B-Q in the Arizona desert; Bette Davis is an ardent, fresh American girl, eager for experience, who lives there with her grandfather (Charley Grapewin). For a guy who's supposed to be burnt out, Howard sure has a lot of talk in him, and it's fancy and poetic as all getout. ("All this evening I've had the feeling of destiny closing in," and so on.) There's no way to say this stuff without sounding affected, and every now and then Howard hits really embarrassing false notes—but who else could embody this Robert E. Sherwood literary conceit and do it as well? Davis, surprisingly, plays her part very simply and doesn't overdo it. In a jumper with a white blouse, wearing bobby-sox and a ribbon in her hair, she's very appealing, and she says her lines as if for the first time—she's almost the only one in the cast (except for Grapewin) who does. The movie is famous for Humphrey Bogart's "dangerous" performance as Duke Mantee, the gangster who is using the Bar-B-Q to rendezvous with his moll and the members of his mob, and who, out of mercy, gives the exhausted, idealistic intellectual the peace of death that he seeks. Bogart does look great, but you feel that his performance was worked out for the stage (he had played the part on Broadway). His moves are almost stylized from repetition, and he gives some of his lines overstated, overscaled readings—particularly his laugh lines, when this public enemy expresses conventional moral sentiments by reprimanding the intellectual for talking to an old man without sufficient respect. As moviemaking, this is a pedestrian piece of work; the director, Archie Mayo, gives you the feeling that he has even retained the stage blocking. Every move seems rehearsed, and the Sherwood play loses its stage vitality without losing its talkiness. But the actors in minor roles are a considerable asset, and there's a tense exchange between a black mobster and a black chauffeur. The cast includes Genevieve Tobin, Joe Sawyer, Porter Hall, Dick Foran, Slim Thompson, Eddie Acuff, Paul Harvey, John Alexander, Adrian Morris, and Nina Campana. Adapted by Charles Kenyon and Delmer Daves. This melodrama spawned a whole genre of imitations (such as *When You Comin' Back, Red Ryder,* from the play by Mark Medoff) and was also remade in 1945 as *Escape in the Desert.* Warners. b & w

Phaedra (1962)—Jules Dassin's glossy, novelettish version, set in modern Greece, of the classic story that was dramatized by Euripides, Seneca, Racine, and many others. Here, it's undermined by a lunatic piece of miscasting: when Melina Mercouri leaves her rich, powerful bull of a husband, Raf Vallone, to run away with his skinny young son, Anthony Perkins, the audience can't imagine why. She scoops him up in her arms, like a toy. With its snazzy cars and fabulous jewels that can be casually thrown into the sea, this is like a Joan Crawford picture, only more so. Dassin appears as Christo. b & w

The Phantom Baron *Le Baron fantôme* (1943)—Somehow or other, Cocteau got involved in writing the script for this silly romantic adventure, which was directed by Serge de Poligny and has little connection to Cocteau's own screen work. Set in the early 19th century, it's about a hidden treasure. Cocteau played the title role; possibly he inveigled Gabrielle Dorziat into appearing in it also; in any case, she looks as if she's not sure what she's doing here. With Alain Cuny and Jany Holt. In French. b & w

Phantom Lady (1944)—The mood and pacing lift this low-budget thriller out of its class, but the ideas, the dialogue, and the ending that the studio insisted on prevent it from being a first-rate B-picture. Ella Raines is the girl in danger, Franchot Tone is the psychopathic killer, Alan Curtis is the man wrongly convicted of murder, Thomas Gomez is the police inspector, and Elisha Cook, Jr., is the drummer in the jam session that is the film's high point of excitement. Robert Siodmak directed, and the producer was Joan Harrison, who had worked as an assistant to Hitchcock. From a William Irish novel, adapted by Bernard C. Schoenfeld; with Fay Helm, Regis Toomey, Virginia Brissac, and Doris Lloyd. (The drumming was actually done by Dave Coleman.) Universal. b & w

The Phantom of the Opera (1925)—If you're in a temple of the arts and see someone looking up furtively at the chandelier with a faint shudder, you can be fairly sure he has seen this tacky yet unforgettable piece of Guignol claptrap—or, at least, one of the remakes of it. The story is from a French penny dreadful (by Gaston Leroux); the first half is a botch and dreary, but then the mixture of the morbid, the gaudy, the ornate, and the rotted becomes scary and, in a way that may be peculiar to movies, thrilling. Lon Chaney is the diabolical genius, Erik, who lives in the dripping cellars of the Paris opera house; hypnotically, he lures the young singer (Mary Philbin) he loves into his bedroom in the sewers and shows her his coffin bed. Norman Kerry is the blundering, deadhead hero, Arthur Edmund Carewe is the Persian, and Snitz Edwards, John Miljan, and Gibson Gowland are in the cast. The director was Rupert Julian, but things were not going well, and Edward Sedgwick was brought in to finish the film; Chaney himself directed some of his own sequences. (He must have cut quite a figure on the set, giving orders to the crew while in his grisly, cadaverous makeup.) Universal. Silent. b & w, with color sequences

The Phantom of the Opera (1943)—Someone at Universal had the brainstorm of redoing the 1925 silent Lon Chaney horror picture and taking advantage of the fact that it was set in an opera house to make it not only a sound picture but a high-toned musical. The result is this flaccid, sedate version, directed by Arthur Lubin, with Claude Rains as the faceless horror and Nelson Eddy and Susanna Foster as the singing pretty people. Even masked, Rains is more expressive than they are; they seem too polite, too nice to show a trace of personality. But there's something in the morbid kitschy material that really hooks people, and there was a surprisingly scared, enthusiastic response to this bummer. With Edgar Barrier, Leo Carrillo, J. Edward Bromberg, and Hume Cronyn. The Gaston Leroux novel was served up this time by Erich Taylor and Samuel Hoffenstein. (An English remake, by Hammer in 1962, starred Herbert Lom.) color

Phantom of the Paradise (1974)—This satire of horror movies is also a rock musical comedy. The writer-director, Brian De Palma, has an original comic temperament; he's drawn to rabid visual exaggeration and to sophisticated slapstick comedy. William Finley is the idealistic young composer who is robbed of his music, busted for drugs, and sent to Sing Sing, all at the instigation of Swan (creepy Paul Williams), the entrepreneur of Death Records, who has made a pact with the Devil for eternal youth. The composer escapes from prison, is maimed by a record-pressing machine, and becomes the Phantom, who haunts Swan's new rock place, the Paradise, where the girl he loves (Jessica Harper) becomes a star. This mixture of *The Phantom of the Opera* and *Faust* isn't enough for De Palma. He heaps on layers of acid-rock satire and parodies of *The Cabinet of Dr. Caligari, The Hunchback of Notre Dame, Psycho,* and *The Picture of Dorian Gray*—and the impacted plots actually function for him. The film is a one-of-a-kind entertainment, with a kinetic, breakneck wit. The cinematographer, Larry Pizer, keeps the images full to overflowing, and the set designer, Jack Fisk, supplies striking takeoffs of the frenzied decor of German silent films. The singer, Beef, is played by Gerrit Graham, who gives the single funniest performance; Harold Oblong, Jeffrey Comanor, and Archie Hahn turn up as three different groups—the Juicy Fruits, the Beach Bums, and, with black-and-white expressionist faces, the Undeads. 20th Century-Fox. color (See *Reeling.*)

The Phantom President (1932)—This musical political satire was George M. Cohan's first talking picture; for anyone who cares about American theatrical history it's an indispensable record of Cohan's style—which is almost nothing like the styles of James Cagney and Joel Grey when they played Cohan (on the screen and the stage, respectively). Cohan is dapper and bland; he seems to wear a mask of ordinariness, and only the droopy-lidded eyes, and sometimes the awareness in the smile, clue us in to the theatrical instinct at work. One doesn't know quite what to make of him or his smooth technique. There's a good satirical idea here: Cohan plays a double role—a quiet Presidential candidate and the extroverted look-alike who campaigns for him. With Claudette Colbert, Jimmy Durante, Alan Mowbray, George Barbier, Sidney Toler, and Jameson Thomas. Norman Taurog directed, for Paramount. The songs are by Cohan, except for Rodgers and Hart's "Give Her a Kiss." Walter De Leon and Harlan Thompson did the screenplay, based on a novel by George F. Worts. b & w

Phèdre (1968)—Marie Bell has been acclaimed as the greatest Phèdre since Bernhardt. Most Americans must take this judgment on faith, but at least it's possible to see her legendary performance and to glean an idea of the sound and look of the classic French style of acting from this somewhat shortened version of the Racine tragedy in Alexandrine verse, directed by Pierre Jourdan. In French. color

The Philadelphia Story (1940)—Philip Barry wrote this romantic comedy for Katharine Hepburn, shaping it for her tense patrician beauty and her eccentricities, and she had her greatest popular triumph in it on Broadway (in 1939) and on the screen. There's conventional Broadway shoddiness at its center: the material plays off Hepburn's public personality, pulling her down from her pedestal. As Tracy Lord, a snow maiden and a phony— which is how the movie public regarded Hepburn, according to the exhibitors who in 1938 had declared her "box-office poison"—she gets her comeuppance. The priggish, snooty Tracy is contemptuous of everyone who doesn't live up to her high standards (and that includes her father, played by John Halliday, and her ex-husband, played by Cary

Grant); in the course of the action, she slips from those standards herself, learns to be tolerant of other people's lapses, and discovers her own "humanity." Shiny and unfelt and smart-aleck-commercial as the movie is, it's almost irresistibly entertaining—one of the high spots of M-G-M professionalism. There isn't much real wit in the lines, and there's no feeling of spontaneity, yet the engineering is so astute that the laughs keep coming. This is a paste diamond with more flash and sparkle than a true one. The director, George Cukor, has never been more heartlessly sure of himself. With James Stewart, who took the Academy Award for Best Actor for his performance as the journalist who has a sudden romantic fling with Tracy, and Ruth Hussey, John Howard, Roland Young, Mary Nash, Henry Daniell, and Virginia Weidler. The additions by the adaptor, Donald Ogden Stewart, are brief and witty; Hepburn's gowns are by Adrian. Produced by Joseph L. Mankiewicz. b & w

The Pick-up Artist (1987)—An airy romantic comedy with Robert Downey, Jr., as a buoyant young New Yorker who races through his days, chasing women compulsively, as if he were under a spell and could never relax. Then he propositions a long-legged, nimble-witted redhead (Molly Ringwald), who's only 19 but is a few leaps ahead of him. Downey, whose soul is floppy-eared, gives the movie a fairy-tale sunniness, and Ringwald, who has acquired lusher, deeper colors, is essentially a girl in distress. They match up like Pierrot and Pierrette. The film doesn't build the rush of excitement that's needed when the action moves to Atlantic City, but it's bright and blithe, like the sound of the 60s girl groups on the track; the flimsy plot hardly matters, because new, undreamed-of characters turn up, and they keep things bubbling. The cast includes Victoria Jackson, Bob Gunton, Christine Baranski, Mildred Dunnock, Robert Towne, Dennis Hopper, Harvey Keitel, Danny Aiello, Lorraine Bracco, and Tom Signorelli (as a used-car salesman). Among the women the hero tries to pick up are Anne Marie Bobby, who tells him she's studying for the priesthood, and Vanessa Williams, whose dog gives him the brushoff. Written and directed by James Toback; the cinematography is by Gordon Willis. 20th Century-Fox. color (See *Hooked*.)

Pickup on South Street (1953)—Richard Widmark as a scroungy petty gangster who sneaks a look into a woman's handbag, turns up some microfilm, and finds himself dealing with Communist agents. Samuel Fuller wrote the script (adapted from Dwight Taylor's story written for the screen) and directed, in his fast, flashy, essentially empty-minded style. The film isn't boring—there's always something going on—but you come away with nothing. (It isn't that Fuller's insensitive, exactly; it's that he's totally unconcerned with sensitivity—it would get in his way.) With Jean Peters, Thelma Ritter, Richard Kiley, Murvyn Vye, Milburn Stone, and George E. Stone. 20th Century-Fox. b & w

The Pickwick Papers (1953)—Dickens' episodic book almost defies a simple continuity, but the adaptor-director, Noel Langley, has been surprisingly successful at cutting through the labyrinth and keeping the enormous collection of characters rattling along. The best is Nigel Patrick's Jingle—swaggering, staccato, outrageously amoral, and finally, because of Patrick's creative characterization, the most sympathetic of the company. As the duelling Winkle, James Donald has moments so ethereally absurd that he seems to have emerged from *A Midsummer Night's Dream*. James Hayter's Pickwick is more of a reasonable facsimile than a person, but the only really bad casting is the lamentably immodest Harry Fowler as Sam Weller.

With Donald Wolfit, Hermione Gingold, and Joyce Grenfell. This is one of the most enjoyable of the films derived from Dickens. b & w

Picnic on the Grass *Le Déjeuner sur l'herbe* (1959)—Jean Renoir, but at neither his best nor even his second best. His themes are reduced to crotchets in this story about a scientist (Paul Meurisse) who preaches artificial insemination until he catches sight of Catherine Rouvel bathing nude. Some sequences were filmed at Les Collettes, the home where Auguste Renoir spent his last years. Cinematography by Georges Leclerc; music by Joseph Kosma. In French. color

The Picture of Dorian Gray (1945)—It has its ludicrous side. Hurd Hatfield's Dorian (who sells his soul to keep his youth) doesn't look fresh; he looks glacéed. And the other characters don't seem to age with the years either, so there's no contrast with him. But the Oscar Wilde story has its compelling gimmick and its cheap thrills, and despite the failings of Albert Lewin as writer and director, he has an appetite for decadence and plushy decor. Neither Hatfield, who tries scrupulously hard, nor George Sanders, who plays the epigrammatic Wilde figure, Lord Henry Wotton, rises above Lewin's chic gothic conception, but as Dorian's victim, gullible Sibyl Vane, the young Angela Lansbury gives her scenes true depth of feeling. This may be her most intuitive and original screen performance. When she sings "Little Yellow Bird" in a pure, sweet voice, the viewer grasps that the man who would destroy this girl really is evil. With Donna Reed, Lowell Gilmore, and Peter Lawford. The cinematography is by Harry Stradling; the Albright brothers—Ivan and Zsissly—painted the series of portraits. (A 1970 version, starring Helmut Berger and released by A.I.P. under the name *Dorian Gray*, is more like

Fanny Hill.) M-G-M. b & w, with color for the portrait.

Picture Snatcher (1933)—A B-picture starring James Cagney; he plays a cocky ex-con turned reporter. The story is lifted from the exploit of the newspaper photographer of the 20s who sneaked a picture of Ruth Snyder's electrocution. In the movie, the reporter goes back to the prison where he served time and does a comparable dirty deed. Lloyd Bacon directed, from a script by Allen Rivkin and P. J. Wolfson; it's all fairly snappy until the reporter has to expiate his crime. Chesty Patricia Ellis is the heroine; also with Ralph Bellamy, Alice White, and Ralf Harolde. Warners. b & w

Pierrot le fou (1965)—Jean-Luc Godard's unresolved, disturbing film: it gets to you. The narrative encompasses a satire of advertising, an existential stalemate, political violence, and romance, all shot—in color—in a hard-edge style. With Jean-Paul Belmondo as Ferdinand, who leaves his rich wife in Paris and goes off to the South of France with the restless Marianne (Anna Karina); he comes to an unforgettably explosive end. Also with Jimmy Karoubi as the dwarf, and Samuel Fuller as himself, and a glimpse of Jean-Pierre Léaud. The cinematography is by Raoul Coutard; the script (by Godard) has its origins in the novel *Obsession*, by Lionel White. In French. Released by Pathe Contemporary.

Pig Across Paris, see *Four Bags Full*

Pigeons (1971)—It has been said that this movie about an alienated youth turned New York cab-driver improves as it goes along, but who wants to stick around long enough to find out? Static direction by John Dexter. The cast includes Jordan Christopher, Jill O'Hara, Kate Reid, and William Redfield. Produced by Richard Lewis. color

Pigskin Parade (1936)—It's beyond belief—atrocious and yet funny and enjoyable. A 20th Century-Fox musical—and that's not exactly a recommendation, as anyone who went to musicals knows. But there was often a lot going on in them, and this one centers on a rowdy (if somewhat extended) football game and features the young, pudgy, budding talent, Judy Garland (three years before *The Wizard of Oz*), as a farm girl. (This was her feature film début.) Also, Patsy Kelly, Betty Grable, Stuart Erwin, Dixie Dunbar, Johnny Downs, Jack Haley, and the Yacht Club Boys. David Butler directed; the songs include "Balboa." b & w

The Pink Panther Strikes Again (1976)—Inspector Clouseau's clenched-jaws politesse is a joke that had already run its course. Playing Clouseau for the fourth time, Peter Sellers is required to imitate himself, and his fish-eyed deadpan is joyless. In this one Herbert Lom as Dreyfus (Clouseau's former boss, the Chief Inspector of the Sûreté, who was driven to nervous collapse in both *A Shot in the Dark* and *The Return of the Pink Panther*) turns into a criminal mastermind and threatens to destroy the world if the major powers don't hand Clouseau over to him. The director, Blake Edwards, sets up promising slapstick situations, and then the payoffs are out of step (and, worse, repeated); after the first half hour or so, the film loses momentum. Edwards seems to be flipping through the pages of the script (which he himself wrote, with Frank Waldman). The picture was a hit, though. The cast includes Burt Kwouk as Cato, Lesley-Anne Down, Colin Blakely, Michael Robbins, Leonard Rossiter, Marne Maitland, Richard Vernon, and Dick Crockett (as Gerald Ford) and Byron Kane (as Kissinger). Omar Sharif, who turns up for a gag, shows more spirit than he does in his starring roles. United Artists. color (See *When the Lights Go Down*.)

Pinky (1949)—Pinky is so light-skinned she passed for white while studying nursing in Boston; when she returns to her washerwoman grandmother's Southern shack, she is terrified and enraged by a fresh awakening to what she has almost forgotten—what it's like to be treated as a Negro, not only by contemptuous whites but by self-hating Negroes. Elia Kazan directs this material with a fine eye for the vicious undercurrents of Southern decay. The film garnered a little too much praise for its courage; it isn't overwhelmingly courageous—Pinky isn't played by a Negro actress, she's played by petite, delicate-faced Jeanne Crain, and at the end Pinky renounces her white fiancé, William Lundigan, thereby sparing 20th Century-Fox no end of awkwardnesses. But the film hasn't been given its due for the tense dramatic sequences and the pressures we're made to feel. *Pinky* is slick and Hollywoodized, but it's also pretty good. Under Kazan's direction, Jeanne Crain is vibrant; she lacks conflict, but she shows qualities that don't turn up in her romantic comedy performances. And though Ethel Barrymore plays her image of herself as a wise liberal (not her best role), Ethel Waters, Nina Mae McKinney, and Frederick O'Neal have compelling moments. Also with Evelyn Varden, Kenny Washington, and Basil Ruysdael. The screenplay, by Philip Dunne and Dudley Nichols, is based on the novel *Quality*, by Cid Ricketts Summer; the cinematography is by Joe MacDonald; produced by Darryl F. Zanuck. b & w

The Pirate (1948)—Judy Garland is a 19th-century maiden on a Caribbean island, dreaming of a famous pirate, and Gene Kelly, bouncing with élan in the manner of Fairbanks, is a travelling actor who pretends to be that pirate. This Vincente Minnelli musical, based on an S. N. Behrman play that the Lunts performed, is flamboyant in an innocent and lively way. Though it doesn't quite work, and it's all a bit broad, it doesn't sour in the memory. The Nicholas Brothers join Garland and Kelly in the celebrated "Be a Clown" number. The score is by Cole Porter. With Walter Slezak, Reginald Owen, Gladys Cooper, and George Zucco. M-G-M. color

Pit of Loneliness *Olivia* (1951)—The American title for this study of lesbianism was an obvious attempt to connect it to the then still scandalous novel by Radclyffe Hall, *The Well of Loneliness*. The period is fin-de-siècle. Edwige Feuillère and Simone Simon play two unmarried women who run a finishing school; the students adore the more elegant and seductive Feuillère, and she takes a "special" interest in the lovely young English girl, Olivia (Marie-Claire Olivia). The film doesn't compare with that earlier study of lesbianism at school, *Mädchen in Uniform*. Born in 1908, the director, Jacqueline Audry, worked her way up from script girl and made a number of popular films, including two based on material by Colette (*Mitsou* and the French non-musical version of *Gigi*), and Colette wrote this script, adapted from the English novel *Olivia*. But Audry was more adept at light comedy than at this sort of subtle sensuousness. Feuillère has superb presence but the movie is so determinedly "delicate" that it seems to move at a snail's pace. With Yvonne de Bray. In French. b & w

Pixote (1980)—A shockingly lyrical Brazilian film about the life of abandoned children who learn to pick pockets and grab purses and hustle—it's their only way of surviving. Thrown into a reformatory, the 10-year-old Pixote watches as several of the larger boys gang-rape a kid not much older than he is, and his truculent baby face is indifferent, but he's a little camera taking it all in. A group of boys, including Pixote, break out, and he and three others snatch enough purses and wallets to make their way to Rio de Janeiro and begin dealing cocaine. Outsmarted by the adult criminals, the kids buy an aging, drunken prostitute from a pimp and go into business with her: she brings men home, and they rob them at gunpoint. As the director, Hector Babenco (who appears in a prologue), sees it, Pixote is a snub-nosed infant asserting his wants, and when they're denied he changes into a baby gangster—a runt Scarface, who kills innocently, in the sense that he doesn't understand the enormity of the crime. The thesis is too pat, but two of the characters—Lilica (Jorge Julião), a flamingly nelly 17-year-old transvestite homosexual, and the whore Sueli, the whoriest whore imaginable (Marília Pera)—transcend it. Dusky and aquiline-faced, Marília Pera has an Anna Magnani–like presence—horrifying and great. Her display of passion wipes the little non-actor kids off the screen. She's the whore spawned out of men's darkest imaginings, and in her scenes the movie achieves a raw garish splendor. The script by Babenco and Jorge Duran is based on the novel *Infância dos Mortos* by Jose Louzeiro; cinematography by Rodolfo Sanchez. In Portuguese. color (See *Taking It All In*.)

The Pizza Triangle *Dramma della Gelosia* Also known as *A Drama of Jealousy*. (1970)— A genial mutt of a movie—an extroverted romantic satire with sight gags, jokes about the pollution in Rome and modern sex mores. As Oreste, a moon-faced, bushy-haired Communist bricklayer who doesn't always smell good, Marcello Mastroianni holds it all together. Married to a battle-axe, a fat hag with a topknot, Oreste falls in love with a young flower seller, whom Monica Vitti plays with a soulful silliness that is a parody of generations of comic waifs and neo-realist heroines. When she betrays him with his best friend, a Tuscan pizza cook (Giancarlo Giannini), he becomes obsessed with the idea that there's a class basis for the betrayal, and the

movie turns into a slapstick tragedy. Oreste, the great *stupido*, whose face reflects a mind that has been emptied of everything but fluky ideas, commits a crime of passion and becomes a comic-strip parody of an operatic figure—the crazed lover. (This is one of Mastroianni's least-known great performances.) The color is warm and bright, the music is light and nostalgic, and the cutting has a quick rhythm. There's an original comic temperament here. The director, Ettore Scola, doesn't seem to be anxious; the picture is spotty but nothing is forced, so one can relax even when the ideas misfire. From a script by Age and Scarpelli, and Scola. In Italian. (See *Deeper into Movies*.)

A Place in the Sun (1951)—This George Stevens version of Dreiser's *An American Tragedy*, updated to the 50s, features Elizabeth Taylor—in one of her most sensitive (yet steamy) performances—as the rich girl whom a poor, rather weak young man (Montgomery Clift) is drawn to. Perhaps because Stevens' methods here are studied, slow, and accumulative, the work was acclaimed as "realistic," though it's full of murky psychological overtones, darkening landscapes, the eerie sounds of a loon, and overlapping dissolves designed to affect you emotionally without your conscious awareness. Stevens and his scriptwriters (Michael Wilson and Harry Brown) pre-interpret everything, turning the basically simple story into something portentous and "deep." The film is mannered enough for a gothic murder mystery, while its sleek capitalists and oppressed workers seem to come out of a Depression cartoon; the industrial town is an arrangement of symbols of wealth, glamour, and power versus symbols of poor, drab helplessness. The hero's jilted working-class girlfriend (Shelley Winters) is not allowed even to be attractive; part of the horror of the 1931 von Sternberg version, in which Sylvia

Sidney was the victim, was that despite her beauty, her poverty made her, finally, undesirable. If Elizabeth Taylor had played the working girl in this production, then the poor could at least be shown to have some natural assets. But Shelley Winters makes the victim so horrifyingly, naggingly pathetic that when Clift thinks of killing her he hardly seems to be contemplating a crime: it's more like euthanasia. (And Clift himself is perhaps a shade too soft and shrinking—an over-directed pawn.) The conclusion of the film in which the hero (and presumably the audience) is supposed to be convinced that a man should pay with his life for a murder he didn't commit—but wanted to commit—is bizarre. "Who doesn't desire his father's death?" asked Ivan Karamazov. Stevens and company would send us all up for it. But whatever one's reservations about this famous film, it *is* impressive, and in the love scene between Taylor and Clift, physical desire seems palpable. With Raymond Burr, Fred Clark, Keefe Brasselle, Shepperd Strudwick, and Ted de Corsia. Academy Awards for Best Director, Screenplay, Cinematography (William C. Mellor), Editing (William Hornbeck), Score (Franz Waxman), Costume Design (Edith Head). Paramount. b & w

Places in the Heart (1984)—The title refers to the places where our roots are, and this inspirational film, written and directed by Robert Benton, is set in his home town, Waxahachie, Texas, in 1935. Sally Field plays a good Christian woman, secure in her faith. A homebody with two children, she is suddenly widowed and left without enough money to meet the next mortgage payment; she holds her family together and hangs on to her house and 40 acres by, of course, grit and total determination. (The story actually centers on a cotton-pickin' contest.) The film isn't just about the widow—it's about family, community, America, and Christian love. It's

about decency, which this mean town is very short of. But Benton's gentle, nostalgic presentation muffles this. His craftsmanship is like an armor built up around his refusal to outrage or offend anyone; it's an encrusted gentility. Danny Glover gives a humorous eccentric force to the all-too-endearing role of Moze, an itinerant, black laborer whose efforts on the widow's behalf get him in trouble with the local branch of the Ku Klux Klan, and John Malkovich gives a hushed performance as Mr. Will, a blind First World War veteran who becomes the widow's boarder. Benton has conceived Mr. Will as if blindness purified him and drove out ordinary faults; blackness does the same for Moze. The cast includes Amy Madigan (she brings a passionate delicacy to the role of a married schoolteacher who's having a guilt-ridden affair), Lindsay Crouse, Ed Harris, Lane Smith, and Bert Remsen as a country singer—he lip-syncs "Cotton-Eyed Joe" to a Doc Watson record. Cinematography by Nestor Almendros. Academy Awards: Best Actress (Field), Original Screenplay. Tri-Star. color (See *State of the Art*.)

Le Plaisir (1952)—This Max Ophuls omnibus film, based on three de Maupassant stories, sounds better than it is; the stories allow Ophuls to display his virtuoso technique, but two of the three turn out too thin and hokey. The first, "The Mask," famous for the Palais de la Danse sequence, is about a man trying to retain the illusion of youth; Gaby Morlay and Claude Dauphin are in it. "The Model" is about an artist (Daniel Gélin) who quarrels with his mistress-model (Simone Simon). The most satisfying, "The House of Madame Tellier," is about the temporary closing of a brothel when the madam (Madeleine Renaud) and her girls go to the country to attend the first Communion of the madam's niece. The cast includes Jean Gabin, Danielle Dar-

P

rieux, Pierre Brasseur, Ginette Leclerc, Mila Parély, and Louis Seigner. In French. b & w

Planet of the Apes (1968)—This is a slick commercial picture, with its elements carefully engineered—pretty girl (who unfortunately doesn't seem to have had acting training), comic relief, thrills, chases—but when expensive Hollywood engineering works, the results can be impressive. This is one of the most entertaining science-fiction fantasies ever to come out of Hollywood. The writing, by Michael Wilson and Rod Serling, who adapted Pierre Boulle's novel *Monkey Planet*, is often fancy-ironic in the old school of poetic disillusion, but the construction is first-rate. An American astronaut finds himself in the future, on a planet run by apes; the audience is rushed along with this hero, who keeps going as fast as possible to avoid being castrated or lobotomized. All this wouldn't be so forceful or so funny if it weren't for the use of Charlton Heston in the role. With his perfect, lean-hipped, powerful body, Heston is a godlike hero; built for strength, he's an archetype of what makes Americans win. He doesn't play a nice guy; he's harsh and hostile, self-centered and hot-tempered. Yet we don't hate him because he's so magnetically strong; he represents American power—and he has the profile of an eagle. The director, Franklin Schaffner, has thought out the action in terms of the wide screen, and he uses space and distance dramatically. The makeup (there is said to be a million dollars' worth) and the costuming of the actors playing the apes are rather witty, and the apes have a wonderful nervous, hopping walk. The best little hopper is Kim Hunter, as an ape lady doctor; she somehow manages to give a distinctive, charming performance in this makeup. With Roddy McDowall, Maurice Evans, James Whitmore, James Daly, and Linda Harrison. The movie

spawned four sequels and a TV series. 20th Century-Fox. color (See *Going Steady*.)

Platinum Blonde (1931)—Frank Capra's early talkie about a glib newspaper reporter (Robert Williams) who marries an aristocratic heiress (Jean Harlow, ludicrously miscast but fun to watch anyway). Almost a catalogue of the movie conventions of the period, complete to an effete valet (Claude Allister) and a comic butler (Halliwell Hobbes). The film's considerable attractions include Robert Riskin's uninhibited dialogue and ravishing Loretta Young, who, as a tough-minded girl reporter (prototype of the later Jean Arthur roles), is a natural aristocrat. With Louise Closser Hale, Reginald Owen, and Walter Catlett. From a story by Harry E. Chandlee and Douglas W. Churchill, which had been adapted by Jo Swerling, with continuity by Dorothy Howell; Riskin, a former playwright, livened it all up, and went on to do a series of hits with Capra. (The central performer, Robert Williams, whose style suggests that of Lee Tracy, was on the verge of stardom, but this was his last film; he died of a ruptured appendix.) Columbia. b & w

Platoon (1986)—Vietnam, as seen by the writer-director Oliver Stone, who dropped out of Yale and, feeling, he says, that he needed to be an anonymous common soldier, enlisted and saw action with the 25th Infantry along the Cambodian border. The film has been widely acclaimed, but some may feel that Stone takes too many melodramatic shortcuts, and that there's too much filtered light, too much poetic license, and too damn much romanticized insanity. Charlie Sheen plays Chris, the autobiographical figure (who, regrettably, narrates the movie by reading aloud the letters he writes home to his grandmother). Chris finds two authority figures in two sergeants who represent good and evil. Willem Dafoe's Sergeant Elias is a supersensitive hippie pothead, who cares about the men—he's a veteran fighter who's kept his soul. Tom Berenger's Sergeant Barnes is a kickass boozer—a psycho, whose scarred, dead-eyed face suggests the spirit of war. There are fine, scary scenes, but there are others where you think, It's a bit much. The movie crowds you; it doesn't give you room to have an honest emotion. And when Chris calmly, deliberately shoots a fellow soldier, and the murder is presented as an unambiguous justified execution you may wonder at the mixture of war elegy and pulp revenge fantasy. With Keith David, Forest Whitaker, and Kevin Dillon. The score, by Georges Delerue, includes a soupy orchestration of Samuel Barber's "Adagio for Strings." Cinematography by Robert Richardson; editing by Claire Simpson. Academy Awards: Best Picture, Director, Film Editing, Sound. Orion-Hemdale. color (See *Hooked*.)

Play It As It Lays (1972)—About empty lives, acute anguish, Hollywood and Hell. As Joan Didion's hurting waif-heroine who has discovered the nothingness of life, Tuesday Weld wanders around numbly, looking like a great pumpkin-headed doll. The movie is a touchstone, like the book: people have different levels of tolerance for stories celebrating soulless high life, and catatonic alienation has never been more poshly narcissistic than in this one. Frank Perry directed; it's visually handsome but a peculiarly passive viewing experience. With Tony Perkins, Tammy Grimes, Adam Roarke, and Ruth Ford. Universal. color (See *Reeling*.)

The Pleasure Garden (1925)—The first film that Alfred Hitchcock (previously a movie designer and writer) directed. It's about two chorus girls from the Pleasure Garden Theatre; the parts are played by two American actresses—Virginia Valli is the virtuous one, Carmelita Geraghty the villainous one. The picture has ingenious sequences, and it's good to look at, though the story is vintage melodramatic hokum; actually, some of that hokum is hilariously campy now, such as the sequence about a depraved white man in the tropics. With another American, Nita Naldi, and Miles Mander. Silent. b & w

Plein Soleil, see *Purple Noon*

Plenty (1985)—David Hare's sick-soul-of-England play, which he adapted for the screen and Fred Schepisi directed, turns his own preachiness into the intellectual clarity of an abrasive woman. After serving courageously as a British courier for the French Resistance, Susan Traherne (Meryl Streep) has her youthful idealism destroyed by the hypocrisy and materialism of postwar life. She keeps exercising her gift for cultured, sardonic invective, and her outspokenness turns her into a scourge, and eventually into a basket case. Schepisi works with his usual team—the cinematographer Ian Baker and the composer Bruce Smeaton—and also with the celebrated production designer Richard MacDonald; together they give the movie a lustrous, sensuous texture. Their craftsmanship is superb. But Hare's means in this movie are every bit as constricted as what he's attacking. Angry Young Manhood has become mannerism. And as Streep plays Susan there's no imploded energy in her rudeness and no force in the film. She just isn't there. With John Gielgud, Tracey Ullman, Charles Dance, Ian McKellen, Sam Neill, Burt Kwouk, and Sting. color (See *Hooked*.)

Poil de carotte (1932)—(It could be translated as "Carrot Top.") Julien Duvivier established his mastery of the sound film with this remake of his 1925 silent about the desperate estrangement of a young red-headed boy. Harry Baur plays the father and skinny little Robert Lynen is the boy who tries to hang himself; their performances are delicate and psychologically complex, but the film achieves its lyric intensity largely through the rhythmic use of imagery. (There's none of the didactic dialogue that might have marred an American film of the period, with a doctor or analyst explaining that the mother felt unloved and so she rejected the child, and so on.) Here, Duvivier isn't the masterly entertainer that he became a few years later; this film is more exploratory, more searching. From a novel by Jules Renard, adapted by the director. In French. b & w

Point Blank (1967)—Showoffy, brutal, somewhat inexplicable account of a crook (Lee Marvin) who seeks justice on his own murderous terms. But it's director John Boorman's virtuosity that is the star. Intermittently dazzling, the film has more energy and invention than Boorman seems to know what to do with. He appears to take the title literally; one comes out exhilarated but bewildered. With Angie Dickinson (she has her best scene slapping Marvin repeatedly—to no effect), Carroll O'Connor, Keenan Wynn, Michael Strong, and John Vernon. The West Coast settings include the actual (though no longer in use) prison on Alcatraz. Cinematography by Philip Lathrop. M-G-M. color

Poltergeist (1982)—Steven Spielberg's suburban gothic about a family besieged by nasty, prankish ghosts is no more than an entertaining hash designed to spook you. It's *The Exorcist* without morbidity, or, more exactly, it's *The Amityville Horror* done with insouciance and high-toned special effects. Because Spielberg is a dedicated craftsman and a wit, he can make a much better low-grade, adolescent entertainment than most directors. But he isn't really thinking in this film—he's just throwing ideas and effects at

us, and there's no rationale for the forms that the poltergeists (there seem to be multitudes of them) take on or for what they do. If the picture succeeds to a degree, it's because of the warmth of the family itself in its tract home, full of toys, in a fast-expanding new subdivision. The cool, jazzy mother (JoBeth Williams) and the blandly handsome father (Craig T. Nelson) are terrific, groovy people—they're kids at heart. When the ghostly manifestations start in the kitchen, what happens seems so benign that the mother reacts as if her household objects were staging a vaudeville show for her—she's turned on by it. The 4-foot-3-inch actress Zelda Rubinstein, as the psychic Tangina who comes to "cleanse" the house, gives the movie new life and makes a large chunk of it work. With Beatrice Straight, who, as a doctor of parapsychology, bores the audience blind and brings the film to a momentary halt, and, as the two younger kids, Oliver Robins and Heather O'Rourke. The credits indicate that Tobe Hooper is the director, but Steven Spielberg wrote the initial story, rewrote the other writers' work on the script, storyboarded the shots, produced the picture, and supervised the final edit. It appears that he also took over, in considerable part, on the set. M-G-M. color (See *Taking It All In*.)

Poor Cow (1967)—An English film with Carol White as Joy, a young London barmaid who learns about life as she drifts from one thief to another. But she doesn't learn enough to keep one's attention from drifting in this ambitious but flat version of Nell Dunn's novel, directed by Kenneth Loach in a semi-documentary style. He uses the poor cow Joy as an example of modern urban anomie. Joy is having a baby pulled out of her and is crying in pain as the movie opens, and Donovan is singing Christopher Logue's words: "Be not too hard/For life is short/And nothing is given to man . . . Be not too hard/For soon he'll die/Often no wiser than he began.'' So you can't say Loach hasn't warned you. Adapted by Dunn and Loach. With John Bindon as the cloddish burglar who impregnates her, and Terence Stamp as the thief she takes up. color (See *Going Steady*.)

Popcorn (1969)—It's a trap: hardly enough footage of the Rolling Stones and a few other groups to make a short has been stretched to feature length with surfing, shots of Twiggy, a disc jockey mugging for the camera, a sickeningly cheery singer named Johnny Farnham, a Western gundown, fictional shorts, travelogs, and documentary footage of a cremation in India. The rock footage is intercut with animals being butchered and views of Vietnam and the atomic bomb—you'd have to be a real ninny to accept the film's claims to significance. color (See *Deeper into Movies*.)

The Pope of Greenwich Village (1984)—An entertaining but shallow movie that gives itself heavyweight airs. Based on Vincent Patrick's adaptation of his own 1979 novel about the ties among small-time Italian and Irish hoods, it's a candied *Mean Streets*, evenly and impersonally directed by Stuart Rosenberg. It has no temperament—it doesn't even have any get-up-and-go. But Patrick supplies colorful "ethnic" dialogue, and the actors run with it. As the two young pals who get into trouble together, Mickey Rourke is fatherly and protective (and a little repetitive), while Eric Roberts tries for something outré—he brings off some wild, androgynous effects, and gives the film whatever drive and point it has. As a crooked cop's tough old mother, Geraldine Page gives an enthrallingly hammy performance—smoking, boozing, and picking horses. As her son, Jack Kehoe has just the right kind of cagey, sallow anonymity. Kenneth McMillan is sly and astute as an ex-con safecracker. Playing a detestable Mafia

boss, Burt Young has mad little porcine eyes. And Tony Musante, M. Emmet Walsh, Philip Bosco, and several other actors have big moments. Daryl Hannah plays Rourke's girlfriend—the one Wasp in the picture. The cinematography (which has a shine) is by John Bailey. M-G-M/United Artists. color (See *State of the Art*.)

Popeye (1980)—Sometimes the components of a picture seem miraculously right and you go to it expecting a magical interaction. That's the case with *Popeye*, with Robin Williams as the squinting sailor, and Shelley Duvall as the persnickety Olive Oyl, and Robert Altman directing, from a screenplay by Jules Feiffer. The picture doesn't come together, though, and much of it is cluttered, squawky, and eerily unfunny. But there are lovely moments—especially when Olive is loping along or singing, and when she and Popeye are gazing adoringly at the foundling Swee'Pea (Wesley Ivan Hurt). The songs—an uneven collection—are by Harry Nilsson. With Paul Dooley as Wimpy, Paul L. Smith as Bluto, and, as Pappy, Ray Walston, whose rambunctious Broadway pizzazz cheapens everything. A Paramount and Walt Disney Presentation; released by Paramount. color (See *Taking It All In*.)

Poppy (1936)—W. C. Fields did not write this script on the back of an envelope. It was a play first, and Fields himself had had a hit with it on Broadway in 1923—how could he miss in the role of the con man Eustace McGargle? He had even appeared in a silent movie version in 1925, directed by D. W. Griffith, with *Poppy*, the title of the original play by Dorothy Donnelly, changed to *Sally of the Sawdust*. (It was Fields' first success with the movie public.) But the talkie version doesn't allow for the way Fields had developed: the public now enjoyed him because he snarled at sentimentality. He was given sticky-sweet, cow-eyed Rochelle Hudson for his ward, and she was given sticky-sweet, cow-eyed Richard Cromwell for a sweetheart, and really they're not the sort of people Fields should be mucking around with. Or maybe he should—if he could just show us how he really feels about them. With Fields, you want any indication of virtue in his character to be a fraud or a momentary aberration; damned if this picture doesn't make him just a scowling angel. The adaptors, Waldemar Young and Virginia Van Upp, and the director, Eddie Sutherland, give the old heart-of-gold stuff a workout, and Fields never gets a chance to cut loose and be mean and dirty-minded. With Lynne Overman, Maude Eburne, and Catherine Doucet. Paramount. b & w

Port of Shadows *Quai des brumes* (1938)—This film was the first of the three major collaborations of director Marcel Carné and writer Jacques Prévert—followed by the infinitely superior *Daybreak* in 1939 and by *Children of Paradise* in 1944—the movies which helped to create the French film style of poetic fatalism. In *Port of Shadows*, which is a drearily predictable film, the central figure of the French movies of the period was, nevertheless, created—the hopelessly rebellious hero, the decent man trapped by society; it was the beginning of the Jean Gabin era. A man (Gabin) is running away from the police; he arrives at a dock-side backstreet looking for a ship in which to escape. He meets a girl, the exquisite, raincoated Michèle Morgan, and tries to free her from her disreputable guardian (Michel Simon) and his crony (Pierre Brasseur). He doesn't escape. *Port of Shadows*, rather like Robert E. Sherwood's *The Petrified Forest*, is gloomy and shallow, but at the time the defeatism of the film was like a breath of fresh air to American filmgoers saturated with empty optimism. In French. b & w

Porte des lilas *Gates of Paris* (1957)—An easygoing idler (Pierre Brasseur) lives off his mother and whiles away his time with drink; suddenly, he is a reformed man, busy and self-important—he has found a purpose in life. The purpose is hiding a gangster-killer (Henri Vidal) from the police. René Clair's small, ironic film is set in an ancient quarter of Paris; it's almost a reverie on loneliness, and it's rather languorous, but the change in Brasseur is entertaining, and there's one marvellous scene, in which the children in the street outside the hideout re-enact a crime at the same time that it's of central importance inside. With the popular French singer Georges Brassens, Dany Carrel, and Raymond Bussières. Written by Clair and Jean Aurel, from René Fallet's novel *La Grande Ceinture*. In French. b & w

Portrait of Jason (1967)—A monologue film, in which a black homosexual hustler and sometime entertainer (Jason Holliday) talks directly to Shirley Clarke's camera crew. The idea is that, faced with the camera, his defenses will be stripped away and the "inner" man revealed—an idea both sadistic and naïve. b & w

Portrait of Jennie (1949)—At the start, a glorious con of a preface, designed to soften the audience for the fantasy to come, states, "Since the beginning, Man has looked into the awesome reaches of infinity. . . . Out of the shadows of knowledge, and out of a painting that hung on a museum wall comes our story, the truth of which lies not on our screen but in your heart." What follows is a story about a painter (Joseph Cotten) who spends his life in love with the spirit of a dead girl (Jennifer Jones). David O. Selznick's deluxe exercise in mystical romanticism was taken from a Robert Nathan novel. William Dieterle directed, but Selznick poured on the gloppy grandeur—a Dmitri Tiomkin score based on themes from Debussy, an impressively large-scale skating scene, a hyperdramatic hurricane sequence—and though the story may not make much sense, the pyrotechnics, joined to the dumbfounding silliness, keep one watching. Cinematography by Joseph August; with Ethel Barrymore, Lillian Gish, Cecil Kellaway, David Wayne, Florence Bates, Henry Hull, and Felix Bressart. b & w, with sepia and color

The Poseidon Adventure (1972)—Expensive pop disaster epic, manufactured for the market that made *Airport* a hit. An ocean liner turns turtle, and the logistics of getting out of an upside-down ship are fairly entertaining; the script is the true cataclysm in this waterlogged *Grand Hotel*. The writers (Stirling Silliphant and Wendell Mayes) achieve real camp only once: just before the ship capsizes, a crewman says to the captain (Leslie Nielsen), "I never saw anything like it—an enormous wall of water coming toward us." With Gene Hackman, Ernest Borgnine, Stella Stevens, Red Buttons, Carol Lynley, and Arthur O'Connell. There's also a lot of Shelley Winters, who yearns to see her grandson in Israel and makes endless jokes about her bloated appearance. (She's so enormously fat she goes way beyond the intention to create a warm, sympathetic Jewish character. It's like having a whale tell you you should love her because she's Jewish.) Ronald Neame directed, with dull efficiency. Based on a novel by Paul Gallico; the score is by John Williams. 20th Century-Fox. color (See *Reeling*.)

Possessed (1947)—" 'I love you' is such an inadequate way of saying I love you," the impassioned Joan Crawford murmurs to her sweetheart (Van Heflin). When Heflin, who is an engineer as well as a cold-hearted lady-killer, points out, in a passage of technological ecstasy, that he finds a girder he has devised more beautiful than Miss Crawford, she whimpers, "Why don't you love me like that? I'm a lot nicer than a girder." Heflin can't see it her way, and presently, in despair, she marries Raymond Massey, a big oil man with a lively daughter (Geraldine Brooks). Watching Heflin fall in love with her stepdaughter proves too much for Crawford, who comes down with a case of schizophrenia that really rattles the walls of the Massey homestead. Then psychiatrists take her in tow. In terms of suspense, this picture, directed by Curtis Bernhardt, is often very striking, and, clearly, he and the cast are doing their damnedest. Insanity is used, in the usual 40s Hollywood manner, to provide an excuse for high-on-the-hog melodrama; there isn't a trace of believability—that's part of what makes it enjoyable. With Stanley Ridges, Moroni Olsen, John Ridgely, and Monte Blue. Cinematography by Joseph Valentine; music by Franz Waxman; art direction by Anton Grot; editing by Rudi Fehr. The script by Sylvia Richards and Ranald MacDougall is based on Rita Weiman's *One Man's Secret*. Jerry Wald produced, for Warners. b & w

Postcards from the Edge (1990)—This tale of a sorrowful, wisecracking starlet (Meryl Streep) whose brassy, boozing former-star mother (Shirley MacLaine) started her on sleeping pills when she was 9 is camp without the zest of camp. It's camp played borderline straight—a druggy-Cinderella movie about an unformed girl who has to go past despair to find herself. The director, Mike Nichols, is a parodist who feigns sincerity, and his tone keeps slipping around. What's clear is that we're meant to be enthralled by the daughter's radiant face, her refinement, her honesty. Nichols keeps the camera on Streep as if to prove that he can make her a popular big star—a new Crawford or Bette Davis. (She remains distant, emotionally atonal.) The tacky, bright-colored film—a near-plotless version of a woman's picture—

is weightless, yet it's watchable. Its jadedness appeals to the narcissism of show-biz insiders and to the would-be insider in the rest of us. (Nichols is acclaimed for being hip to the Zeitgeist.) There are a lot of people to look at: Gene Hackman, Dennis Quaid, Richard Dreyfuss, Annette Bening, Robin Bartlett, C. C. H. Pounder, Oliver Platt, Gary Morton, Mary Wickes, Rob Reiner, Simon Callow, Michael Ontkean, Pepe Serna, and Dana Ivey. The screenplay, by Carrie Fisher (with Nichols' uncredited collaboration), is based on her novel; cinematography by Michael Ballhaus. Columbia. color (See *Movie Love*.)

The Postman Always Rings Twice (1946)—Entertaining, though overlong. The director, Tay Garnett, knew almost enough tricks to sustain this glossily bowdlerized version of the James M. Cain novel, and he used Lana Turner maybe better than any other director did. Cain's women are, typically, calculating, hot little animals, and his men doom-ridden victims. Here, Lana Turner's Cora—infantile in a bored, helpless, pre-moral way—is dressed in impeccable white, as if to conceal her sweaty passions and murderous impulses; John Garfield plays the drifter who becomes her lover. Cora's harmless husband (Cecil Kellaway) seems a nuisance to have around, so they decide to finish him off while he's relaxing in the bathtub. The shoddy, ironic twist signified in the title is that the killers get away with their crime but retribution comes anyway. As opposing lawyers, Hume Cronyn and Leon Ames have a show-offy courtroom clash. With Audrey Totter. The script is by Harry Ruskin and Niven Busch. (A French version, *Le Dernier Tournant*, was directed by Pierre Chenal in 1939 with Fernand Gravet, Corinne Luchaire, and Michel Simon; Visconti made an Italian version, *Ossessione*, in 1942.) M-G-M. b & w

The Postman Always Rings Twice (1981)—Taste and craftsmanship have gone into this Bob Rafelson version of James M. Cain's hot tabloid novel, but Rafelson's detached, meditative tone is about as far from Cain's American tough-guy vernacular as you can get. The impulsiveness and raw flamboyance that make the book exciting are missing, and the cool, elegant visuals (Sven Nykvist is the cinematographer) outclass the characters right from the start. As Frank, the drifter whose passion for Cora leads him to kill her husband, Jack Nicholson does a run-through of his overdeliberate, sly, malevolent expressions from *The Shining* while still lobotomized from *Cuckoo's Nest*. (His performance could have been given by a Nicholson impersonator.) As Cora, who does the cooking at her husband's roadside café, Jessica Lange is the best reason to see the movie. She looks good-sized—muscular but rounded—and with her short, curly blond hair, a Japanese silk wrapper pulled tight, and a lewd, speculative smile, she's both seraphic and steamy. The film needs to be propelled by a growing intensity in the sex scenes, but the first sex, on the table in the café kitchen, is the hottest. So things go downhill. With John Colicos as greasy Nick, the husband; Michael Lerner as Katz, the lawyer; and a highly expendable episode that features Anjelica Huston as a lion tamer. The sparse yet maundering script is by David Mamet. An international co-production; released by Paramount. color (See *Taking It All In*.)

Pot-Bouille Also known as *Lovers of Paris* and *The House of Lovers*. (1957)—Julien Duvivier's lavish satire on the triumph of business values over bourgeois morals was only a moderate success in the United States. Perhaps art-house audiences, still recovering from the anguish of *Gervaise*, were reluctant to face more Zola. But, Mendelian that he was, Zola allowed the Rougon-Macquart series one sport: an unscrupulous young fortune hunter from the provinces who climbs to respectability over the beds of satisfied bourgeois ladies. Duvivier's re-creation of Paris in the overstuffed 1880s is one of the most unusual historical evocations in movies: ugly, ludicrous, conspicuous expenditure dominates the enormous apartment house, the shops, the streets. In the best sequence, a group of merchants gather to discuss a matter of honor and load themselves with food and drink. Duvivier keeps his balance on the tightrope over the dangerous material— human mediocrity, bad taste, the middle-class man as animal—but sometimes you may get the feeling that the tightrope is suspended much too low. Gérard Philipe is the dimply, curly-haired seducer, the man who accepts venality so simply and instinctively that he has no need of hypocrisy. With Danielle Darrieux, Dany Carrel, Anouk Aimée, Claude Nollier, Henri Vilbert, and Jane Marken. In French. b & w

Potemkin *Bronenosets Potyomkin* Also known as *The Battleship Potemkin*. (1925)— Voted the greatest film of all time by an international panel of critics in Brussels in 1958, as it had been in 1950, *Potemkin* (Russians and purists pronounce it Po-*tyom*-kin) has achieved such an unholy eminence that few people any longer dispute its merits. Great as it undoubtedly is, it's not really a likable film; it's amazing, though—it keeps its freshness and its excitement, even if you resist its cartoon message. Perhaps no other movie has ever had such graphic strength in its images, and the young director Sergei Eisenstein opened up a new technique of psychological stimulation by means of rhythmic editing— "montage." The Odessa Steps sequence, the most celebrated single sequence in film history, has been imitated in one way or another

in countless television news programs and movies with crowd scenes; it has also been parodied endlessly. And yet the power of the original is undiminished. Montage is used in this film for revolutionary political purposes: the subject is the 1905 mutiny of the sailors of the battleship Potemkin, and the massacre of the people who sympathized with them. But policies in the U.S.S.R. changed: mutiny could no longer be sanctioned, nor could experimental film techniques, and under Stalin, Eisenstein was purged, partially reinstated, and then fell from grace over and over. *Potemkin* looks astonishingly like a newsreel, and the politically naïve have often taken it as a "documentary." The more knowing have a graceful euphemism: Eisenstein, they say, "sacrificed historical facts for dramatic effect." Silent, with added musical soundtrack. b & w

The Power (1968)—Sci-fi about a couple of men with superhuman mental powers; they can think somebody to death. Naturally, one of them is the villain and the other the hero, but the film is so lacklustre you don't care which one wins. Byron Haskin directed this George Pal production, based on a novel by Frank M. Robinson. The cast includes George Hamilton, Nehemiah Persoff, Yvonne De Carlo, Aldo Ray, Gary Merrill, Earl Holliman, and Arthur O'Connell. M-G-M. Cinema-Scope, color

The Power and the Glory (1933)—Preston Sturges wrote the script (which is sentimental and heavy-handed but is nevertheless almost a warmup for *Citizen Kane*), and the producer, Jesse L. Lasky, who considered it "the most perfect script" he'd ever seen, insisted that the director, William K. Howard, shoot it word for word. Spencer Tracy is the railroad tycoon who has killed himself, and the story is told from his funeral by Ralph Morgan.

P

With Colleen Moore and slinky Helen Vinson. Cinematography by James Wong Howe. Fox. b & w

Practically Yours (1945)—Fred MacMurray, a presumably doomed aviator in the Pacific, broadcasts a last message to the other members of his combat group. "I wish I could walk with Peggy through Central Park again and kiss the tip of her nose," he says. His friends naturally assume that he is talking about a girl, although the Peggy he has in mind is a little dog (with a passionate disposition). Norman Krasna wrote this comedy of confusion in his usual pushy madcap style; when MacMurray gets back, he finds he is engaged to Claudette Colbert, who's a complete stranger to him. There's one funny sequence with a self-inflating boat inflating in the subway. Mitchell Leisen directed; with Robert Benchley, Cecil Kellaway, Gil Lamb, Rosemary DeCamp, and Tom Powers. Paramount. b & w

Prenom: Carmen, see *First Name: Carmen*

Préparez vos mouchoirs, see *Get Out Your Handkerchiefs*

The President's Analyst (1967)—James Coburn, as the psychoanalyst to the President of the United States, is pursued by a Russian spy (Severn Darden), an American agent (Godfrey Cambridge), and everybody else. This erratic political spoof, written and directed by Theodore Flicker, has sly, ingenious sequences (one involves a super-automated phone company) and sour sequences (William Daniels as the head of an upper-middle-class liberal family obsessed with the threat of right-wing neighbors). Very lively when Flicker is just making sophomoric jokes, but he doesn't seem to know what he's good at, or how to stick to it. Paramount. color

Pretty in Pink (1986)—Molly Ringwald is enshrined as the teen-age ideal in this romantic movie for kids—it's slight and vapid, with the consistency of watery Jell-O. The spoiled-rotten richies are mean to Ringwald's Andie, a poor-girl high-school senior who lives in a dinky, rattletrap house on the wrong side of the tracks. But she's the opposite of trashy: blessed with quiet good taste, she's proudly conventional. And so she wins both a college scholarship and the rich boy of her dreams. John Hughes, who wrote the script and supervised the work of the first-time director, Howard Deutch, never goes beyond a kid's point of view; this picture isn't actually about teen-agers—it's closer to being a pre-teen's idea of what it will be like to be a teen-ager. In its sociological details, it might have been made by little guys from Mars. With the winsome comedienne Annie Potts as Andie's closest friend, Andrew McCarthy as her rather passive young prince, Jon Cryer as the smartmouth nerd who follows her around, Harry Dean Stanton as her daddy, and James Spader as a snobby hunk. Cinematography by Tak Fujimoto. A John Hughes Production, for Paramount. color (See *Hooked.*)

Pretty Poison (1968)—An unobtrusive little psychological thriller, subtle and very smart. Anthony Perkins gives what may be his most sensitively conceived performance; he's a character who develops from a quirky, sneaky, funny boy into a decent, sympathetic man. He toys with fantasies but knows they're fantasies. Tuesday Weld plays a small-town girl, crazy for excitement, who accepts his fantasies in a matter-of-fact way and proceeds to act on them. Lorenzo Semple, Jr., wrote a beauty of a script (based on Stephen Geller's novel *She Let Him Continue*); the horror in the movie isn't just in the revelation of what the pretty young girl is capable of—it's in your awareness that the man's future is being destroyed. Directed by

Noel Black. With John Randolph and Beverly Garland. Shot on location in Western Massachusetts; the river that is carrying poisonous red dye is the once "mighty" Housatonic. 20th Century-Fox. color (See *Going Steady*.)

Prick Up Your Ears (1987)—Joe Orton wrote some of the most highly regarded farces of the English-speaking theatre in this century, but you could come out of this movie about him without any sense of their vengeful, bawdy originality. Directed by Stephen Frears from a screenplay by Alan Bennett, based on the literary biography of the same name by John Lahr, the film is honest and watchable. But, unlike Orton, it takes no real delight in misbehaving. And though the moviemakers don't try to conceal the facts of the 16 years that Orton (Gary Oldman) spent with Kenneth Halliwell (Alfred Molina), who bludgeoned him to death and then killed himself, the relationship between the two hasn't been made convincing. What you come out with is some modern-style psychosexual moralizing about how Orton's pansexuality liberated his talent whereas the inhibited Halliwell was driven to murder. You don't feel Orton's pulse, but Vanessa Redgrave, who plays his smart, ribald agent, has never been sexier or more spontaneous. With Wallace Shawn as Lahr, Lindsay Duncan as Anthea Lahr, Margaret Tyzack as the elocution teacher, Janet Dale as Mrs. Sugden, and Julie Walters as Orton's mother. Cinematography by Oliver Stapleton. Released by the Samuel Goldwyn Company. color (See *Hooked*.)

Pride and Prejudice (1940)—This literate movie is a reasonably faithful transcription of Jane Austen's sparkling comedy of manners, adapted from Helen Jerome's play by Aldous Huxley and Jane Murfin. But when Jane Austen's characters are brought to life at M-G-M, everything is changed—broadened. Ani-

mated and bouncing, the movie is more Dickens than Austen; once one adjusts to this, it's a happy and carefree viewing experience. The movie belongs to Laurence Olivier, who plays Darcy, and to that great old dragon Edna May Oliver, as Lady Catherine. In the role of Elizabeth Bennet, Greer Garson is not as intolerably noble as she became later. She's effective and has nice diction, though she's arch and incapable of subtlety, and a viewer can get weary watching that eyebrow that goes up like the gold curtain at the old Met. The cast includes Mary Boland, Edmund Gwenn, Melville Cooper, E. E. Clive, Bruce Lester, and a batch of girls in overstarched dresses (Marsha Hunt, Maureen O'Sullivan, Karen Morley, Ann Rutherford, Heather Angel), and a villain (Edward Ashley) and a villainess (Frieda Inescort, of the slurpy voice). Directed by Robert Z. Leonard. (Those dresses, which are plastered with ribbons and bows, look as if they were designed for an operetta.) b & w

Prima della Rivoluzione, see *Before the Revolution*

The Prime of Miss Jean Brodie (1969)—Maggie Smith as Muriel Spark's witty caricature of a romantic crackpot teacher in an Edinburgh school in the 30s. She wants to inspire the girls rather than teach them—she's the kind of teacher little girls get crushes on. The movie has been too conventionally directed by Ronald Neame, but Maggie Smith, with her gift for mimicry and her talent for mannered comedy, makes Jean Brodie very funny—snobbish, full of affectations, and with a jumble shop of a mind. Miss Brodie is so entertaining that you can't accept it when the plot becomes melodramatic and you're asked to take her seriously as a dangerous influence. Celia Johnson has a genuine triumph as her implacable adversary, Miss Mackay, and Robert Stephens does a lot with the role of her lover, the art instructor. The script is by Jay Presson Allen, who also wrote the stage version. With Pamela Franklin (her big confrontation scene is a clinker, but the fault isn't hers—it goes back to the novel) and Gordon Jackson. Made in London and Edinburgh. 20th Century-Fox. color (See *Going Steady*.)

The Prince and the Showgirl (1957)—This Ruritanian romance, directed by Laurence Olivier, is slanted to show off the talents of Marilyn Monroe as an innocent abroad. Olivier, perhaps with excess gallantry, makes his prince something of a cold cod, but even in this uningratiating role he has a high gloss—an irony that shines. Monroe's breathy little-girl voice and polymorphous-perverse non-acting have a special mock-innocent charm that none of her imitators seem able to capture. With Sybil Thorndike, Richard Wattis, and Daphne Anderson. The drawback of the film is that Terence Rattigan's script, though it improves on his play *The Sleeping Prince*, still lacks invention and wit. Warners. color

Prince of the City (1981)—Treat Williams has a very closed face—the kind of opaque face that is like a brick wall in front of the camera. And that may be why Williams, as a New York City police officer who agrees to be wired and to obtain evidence about corruption in his unit, plays each scene as an acting exercise—going through so much teary, spiritual agony that you want to throw something at him. He acts all over the place yet the movie—2 hours and 47 minutes of pseudo-documentary seriousness—is so poorly structured that you keep wondering what's going on and why he has agreed to inform on his friends. Things don't begin to come together until you're heading into the third hour, when the cross suspended from Williams' neck lights up, like a balloon above his head, announcing "Penance! Absolution!" There's one remarkable performance (it's mostly in the last section): Jerry Orbach, as the tough-minded cop, Gus Levy, acts with such sureness and economy that while Williams is flailing about Orbach magnetizes the camera. Directed by Sidney Lumet, the film has a super-realistic overall gloom, and the people are so "ethnic" and yell so much that you begin to long for the sight of a cool blond in bright sunshine. Lumet and Jay Presson Allen wrote the screenplay, based on the book by Robert Daley about the New York City police officer Bob Leuci. With Lindsay Crouse, who's stuck with one of those speeches about how we're all guilty, Bob Balaban, and Ron Maccone as Nick. The cinematography is by Andrzej Bartkowiak; the music, by Paul Chihara, suggests an existentialist fugue by Schubert. Orion; released by Warners. color

The Princess and the Pirate (1944)—This elaborate Technicolor romp that Bob Hope did with Virginia Mayo isn't the best setting for his casual wit; the situations are too strained, the fooling around is too buffoonish. Kids probably enjoy this Hope movie more than adults do. It's set in the early 19th century. Hope is Sylvester the Great, a quick-change artist, Mayo is a princess travelling incognito, and they get kidnapped by pirates. Victor McLaglen and Walter Slezak are the sinister villains; also with Maude Eburne, Hugo Haas, Walter Brennan, and Marc Lawrence. A whole slew of writers were involved; David Butler directed. A Samuel Goldwyn Production, for R K O.

The Princess Bride (1987)—The director Rob Reiner doesn't have the craft to bring off the kinetic daredeviltry he tries for, and the movie is ungainly—you can almost see the chalk marks it's not hitting. But it has a loose, likable slobbiness. Set in the late Middle Ages in the mythical kingdom of Florin, the picture, from a script written in 1973 by William Goldman, and based on the 1973 novel that he wrote for his children, is an affectionate composite parody of the high points in adventure movies: the duels, the feats of strength, the rope climbing, the black-masked heroes, the swamps, the dungeons with medieval Rube Goldberg torture machines. Cary Elwes, who has a gift for giddy slapstick, is Westley, the blond farm boy who goes to seek his fortune so that he can claim his true love, blond Buttercup (Robin Wright). Westley is captured by pirates, and Buttercup, selected by Crown Prince Humperdinck (Chris Sarandon) to be his bride, is abducted by a trio of ruffians: Wallace Shawn, Mandy Patinkin, and all 7 feet 5 and 525 pounds of the French-born wrestler André the Giant. The cast includes Christopher Guest as a smarmy six-fingered sadist, Mel Smith as the Albino, Margery Mason as the ancient woman who boos the royal family, and, in scenes that are show-biz bliss, Billy Crystal and Carol Kane, wearing makeup that adds centuries to them, as the retired Miracle Max and his nagging crone, Valerie. These two give the movie a lift that puts it all into perspective. It's shtick softened by childlike infatuation. Peter Falk appears in the framing device. Photographed partly on locations in England and Ireland; Florin Castle is actually Haddon Hall, parts of which date back to the 12th century. 20th Century-Fox. color (See *Hooked*.)

The Prisoner (1955)—As the proud cardinal induced to make a false confession of treason (in an unnamed Communist country), Alec Guinness gives a powerful, almost agonized performance. (It was probably the most intense acting he had done in movies up to that time.) Though Bridget Boland's script (from her play) and Peter Glenville's direction leave a great deal to be desired, Guinness achieves

what they inadequately reach for. This English film is really nothing but his performance—which is perhaps enough. With Jack Hawkins as the interrogator, Wilfrid Lawson as the warden, and Kenneth Griffith and Raymond Huntley. b & w

The Prisoner of Second Avenue (1975)—Jack Lemmon, as a New York advertising executive, gets fired, feels worthless, and has a nervous breakdown; Anne Bancroft is his devoted wife. Vaguely about urban despair, full of bad jokes. From Neil Simon's adaptation of his own play. Melvin Frank directed in his usual sagging, 50s style, but probably there isn't a filmmaker in the world who could substantially improve this picture except by throwing out the play altogether. With Gene Saks and Elizabeth Wilson. Warners. color (See *Reeling*.)

The Prisoner of Zenda (1937)—Amiable, though familiar, romantic swashbuckler, set in a mythical country, with Ronald Colman in the double role of the King and the smiling, gentlemanly look-alike who takes his place for a while, and plushy Madeleine Carroll as the sweetly dutiful Princess Flavia, who puts crown before love. Lewis Stone and Alice Terry played the roles in 1922, and Stewart Granger and Deborah Kerr did them in 1952, but this 1937 version has the advantage of dashing, grinning Douglas Fairbanks, Jr., as the naughty Rupert of Hentzau. Fairbanks steals the show from the restrained Colman. It's a well-paced production, directed by John Cromwell and W. S. Van Dyke, and shot by James Wong Howe, with banter supplied by Donald Ogden Stewart, among others. With Raymond Massey, David Niven, Mary Astor, and C. Aubrey Smith. (Peter Sellers did a feeble parody version in 1979, playing the King as a twit and giving the look-alike a Cockney accent that made him sound exactly like Michael Caine.) Produced by David O. Selznick; released by United Artists. b & w

The Private Affairs of Bel Ami (1947)—Albert Lewin, a writer who became head of Irving Thalberg's story department and then functioned as a producer for Thalberg, seemed to stand for the same values as his boss: carefully mounted, prestigious entertainment. But when he turned director, in 1942 (writing his own scripts as well), he showed a predilection for ultra-literary material, and his style—a mixture of sophistication, romanticism, and stiff, awkward staging—finally led him to the visual poetry and high camp of *Pandora and the Flying Dutchman* and the peerless, posh silliness of *Saadia*. The Newark-born director suffered from an almost obsequious lust for everything European and an excess of taste that resulted in tastelessness. *Bel Ami*, taken from a de Maupassant story that had been filmed in Germany in 1938, is a flaccid, overdressed production about a 19th-century cad who makes his way in the world by taking advantage of women. Lewin got an interesting ambivalence out of George Sanders in *The Moon and Sixpence*, and then typecast him amusingly as Lord Henry Wotton in *The Picture of Dorian Gray*, but here Sanders seems heavy and monotonous. With Angela Lansbury, Ann Dvorak, Frances Dee, Marie Wilson, Katherine Emery, Albert Basserman, Hugo Haas, and John Carradine. The score is by Darius Milhaud; cinematography by Russell Metty. United Artists. b & w

Private Benjamin (1980)—A women's-liberation service comedy, in which Goldie Hawn plays a spoiled honey bunch—a rich blond Jewish girl from Philadelphia—who becomes a real woman in the Army. The script goes from one formula to the next, and it reworks the pranks of generations of male service comedies, but the director, Howard Zieff, refurbishes the stale material with smart small touches, and Goldie Hawn has such infectious frothy charm that she manages to get laughs out of ancient routines about a tenderfoot going through the rigors of basic training. Her likableness makes the picture moderately amusing until the last third, when she gets involved with a dream prince (Armand Assante) who turns out to be a thickheaded chauvinist, and she has to be liberated all over again; the picture seems to be stuck in a revolving door. This is the sort of feminist movie in which almost every man is an insensitive boor or a fool, yet the heroine gets what she wants by manipulation and the shrewd use of sexual blackmail—which we're meant to find adorable. Basically, it's just Daffy Duck–TV sit-com. With Albert Brooks, Eileen Brennan, Harry Dean Stanton, Hal Williams, Toni Kalem, Damita Jo Freeman, Mary Kay Place, P. J. Soles, Robert Webber, and Sam Wanamaker and Barbara Barrie as the heroine's parents. Written by Nancy Meyers, Charles Shyer, and Harvey Miller. Released by Warners. color (See *Taking It All In*.)

A Private Function (1984)—This joint début film by the celebrated British television playwright Alan Bennett and the young director Malcolm Mowbray keeps adding greedy eccentrics and scatological jokes until everything is interconnected and the action seems on the verge of exploding into lewd farce. It never quite makes the final leap, but it's pretty funny anyway. The action is set in a small Yorkshire town in 1947, during the worst of the postwar austerity, and the plot involves the efforts of the local pillars of society (Denholm Elliott, John Normington, Richard Griffiths) to fatten a hidden, "unlicensed" pig for a banquet celebrating the nuptials of Princess Elizabeth and Prince Philip. The run into trouble when the pig is stolen by a mild-mannered chiropodist (Michael Palin), who is encouraged by his Lady Macbeth of a wife (Maggie Smith). The movie is trivial, but alive and unruly; the characters cheat and conspire on such a low level that it suggests *Volpone* set in a cabbage patch. Maggie Smith can bring you up short with a devastating inflection, and as her aged mother, Liz Smith (no relation) is like a bleary, befuddled mirror image of the daughter's pretensions. Also with Bill Paterson as the inspector for the Ministry of Food and Rachel Davies as his seductive landlady. A HandMade Film. color (See *State of the Art*.)

The Private Life of Don Juan (1934)—A relatively motionless Douglas Fairbanks, Sr., in a rueful, satirical movie analogy to his then domestic problems. His Don Juan, past his heyday, is in his 40s and has to watch his diet and sneak in a masseur. The story is about how he frees himself from the demands of philandering. It's one of those films that lumbers along and never really takes off, though the gimmick—he is believed dead and comes back in disguise—appears promising. With Merle Oberon, Benita Hume, Binnie Barnes, Melville Cooper, Joan Gardner, and Athene Seyler. Directed by Alexander Korda, from a script by Lajos Biro and Frederick Lonsdale, based on a play by Henri Bataille. The picture features sumptuous Spanish costumes; some look cribbed from Goya. b & w

The Private Life of Henry VIII (1933)—Charles Laughton as the robust, gluttonous monarch; among the ladies he marries are Merle Oberon, Binnie Barnes, Wendy Barrie, and Elsa Lanchester. Alexander Korda directed this war-horse of the movie repertory, which is still alive and in good spirits. With Robert Donat and John Loder. b & w

The Private Life of Sherlock Holmes (1970)—Billy Wilder's detective picture is meant to be a put-on of the Sherlock Holmes mythology, concentrating on a case that Holmes (Robert Stephens) fouls up, because he's distracted by the treachery of a smart charmer (Geneviève Page). But for this idea to have bounce and suspense we need to see the clues and draw our own inferences, so that we can spot where Holmes is going wrong and enjoy his mistakes. And for it to be somewhat romantic, as it's intended to be, we need to see much more of how the woman deceives him. Instead, one must content oneself with the occasional archly amusing lines, the handsome Victorian decor, and Christopher Challis's lovely (if somewhat dark) tinted-looking cinematography. It's a graceful picture, but it dawdles, and Stephens doesn't seem to have the star presence that Holmes requires. Made in England. With Colin Blakely, Christopher Lee, Clive Revill, Stanley Holloway, and Catherine Lacey. Written by Wilder and I.A.L. Diamond; art direction by Alexander Trauner; music by Miklós Rózsa. United Artists. color

Private Lives (1931)—Early talkie attempt at glittering theatrical sophistication, and, somehow, in its own terms, it works. This M-G-M version of the Noël Coward play was made soon after the play came out, and perhaps the play's style and excitement carries the cast along. Norma Shearer isn't so bad, and Robert Montgomery is very, very good. It was a dazzling success. A performance of the play was filmed so that the stars, the director, Sidney Franklin, and a raft of adaptors would get the idea; that may explain Franklin's showing a little zip, for a change, and Shearer's acting halfway human. With Reginald Denny, Una Merkel, and, in a role added in the film, Jean Hersholt. b & w

The Private Lives of Elizabeth and Essex (1939)—Bette Davis, well painted and dressed for the role of the shrewd old Queen, looks the part and gives a magnetic, tough performance, but an impossible task was set for her, since as Essex, Errol Flynn couldn't come halfway to meet her. His talents were in other directions; the role was totally outside his range, and the poor man seemed to know it. Davis's performance is bound to suffer from comparison with Glenda Jackson's multifaceted Elizabeth on television, but Davis's Elizabeth is a precursor of Jackson's— it might almost be a sketch for the Jackson portrait. Michael Curtiz directed this adaptation of the Maxwell Anderson play. With Olivia de Havilland, Henry Daniell, Leo G. Carroll, James Stephenson, Vincent Price, Donald Crisp, and Ralph Forbes. Music by Erich Wolfgang Korngold. Warners. color

The Prize (1964)—It opens badly but then becomes a lively, blatant entertainment— cheerful in a shameless sort of way. (It's the sort of movie you may not want to own up to enjoying.) Paul Newman plays an American writer (with oddly slurry diction) who wins the Nobel Prize, goes to Stockholm for the ceremonies, and gets caught up in a spy plot. Ernest Lehman wrote the script, based on the Irving Wallace novel; the movie may remind you of Hitchcock's *North by Northwest*, which Lehman also wrote. Pieces of that earlier script turn up here, transposed only slightly. Mark Robson directed, and the cast includes Edward G. Robinson (in a dual role), Elke Sommer puckering up, and Leo G. Carroll, Kevin McCarthy, Diane Baker, Micheline Presle, Gerard Oury, John Qualen, and the sinister Sacha Pitoëff. Produced by Pandro S. Berman, for M-G-M. color

Prizzi's Honor (1985)—Adapted from Richard Condon's prankish satire of American corruption, this John Huston picture has a ripe and daring comic tone. It revels voluptuously in the murderous finagling of the members of a Brooklyn Mafia family, and re-

joices in their scams. It's like *The Godfather* acted out by The Munsters. Jack Nicholson's average-guyness as Charley, the clan's enforcer, is the film's touchstone: this is a baroque comedy about people who behave in ordinary ways in grotesque circumstances, and it has the juice of everyday family craziness in it. Everything in this picture works with everything else—which is to say that John Huston has it all in the palm of his big, bony hand. With William Hickey as the shrunken old Don Corrado, ghouly and wormy, with tiny, shocking bright eyes; Anjelica Huston as the don's scheming granddaughter, a high-fashion Vampira who moves like a swooping bird and talks in a honking Brooklynese that comes out of the corner of her twisted mouth; Kathleen Turner as Charley's ravishingly pretty bride; John Randolph as Pop, the Prizzis' *consigliere* and Charley's beaming, proud father; and Lee Richardson and Robert Loggia as the don's two sons, and Lawrence Tierney as a corrupt cop, Tomasina Baratta as an opera singer, and Alexandra Ivanoff as the soprano in the wedding scene. The script is by Condon and Janet Roach; the cinematography is by Andrzej Bartkowiak. Alex North's score, with its lush, parodistic use of Puccini, and some Rossini, a little Verdi, and a dash of Donizetti, too, actively contributes to the whirling texture of the scenes. An ABC Production, released through 20th Century-Fox. color (See *State of the Art*.)

Procès de Jeanne d'Arc, see *Trial of Joan of Arc*

The Producers (1968)—Zero Mostel as a producer who sells 25,000 per cent of a play, intending to produce a flop so that he won't have to pay the backers anything. Naturally, he produces a hit. Some of the material is funny in an original way, but Mel Brooks, who wrote and directed (both for the first time), doesn't get the timing right and good gags fall apart or become gross or just don't develop. The sequence consisting of tryouts for the role of Hitler in the play, which is called "Springtime for Hitler," is potentially so great that what he does with it lets you down. Still, terrible as this picture is, a lot of it is very enjoyable. For satire of the theatre as inspired as Brooks' gags at their best, it's not hard to put up with the ineptitude and the amateurish camera angles. It's even possible to put up with Zero Mostel in closeup. (He was not one to tone his effects down for the camera.) With Dick Shawn, Estelle Winwood, Renée Taylor, Kenneth Mars, and Gene Wilder, whose whining, strangled-voice bit is almost a shtick of genius. Produced by Sidney Glazier; released by Embassy Pictures. color (See *Going Steady*.)

The Professionals (1966)—The title is accurate. This action-Western, written and directed by Richard Brooks, with Burt Lancaster, Lee Marvin, Robert Ryan, Woody Strode, Jack Palance, and Claudia Cardinale, has the expertise of a cold old whore with practiced hands and no thoughts of love. There's something to be said for this kind of professionalism: the moviemakers know how to provide excitement and they work us over. We're not always in the mood for love or for art, and this film makes no demands, raises no questions, doesn't confuse the emotions. It's as modern a product as a new car; it may be no accident that Ryan, the man in this Western who loves horses, is treated as some sort of weakling. Cinematography by Conrad Hall; music by Maurice Jarre; based on Frank O'Rourke's novel *A Mule for the Marquesa*. Columbia. color

Promise at Dawn (1971)—Jules Dassin has tried to turn Romain Gary's nostalgic celebration of his loving mother into a vehicle for Melina Mercouri. But she seems, as usual, to be playing a normal hearty, hot nympho-maniac. The different parts of the past run together in a blur in this generally unsatisfying film, but there are a few good satirical sequences with Dassin acting the role of a silent-movie idol. With Assaf Dayan; cinematography by Jean Badal; music by Georges Delerue. Avco. color

The Promoter Also known as *The Card*. (1952)—Denry the audacious, the opportunist who rises from washerwoman's son to town mayor through devious and ingenious scheming, is one of Alec Guinness's most winning roles—he even gets the girl (Petula Clark, looking very pretty at this stage in her career, though she doesn't sing). His performance is neatly matched against Glynis Johns's portrait of a female opportunist—a babyfaced, husky-voiced dancing teacher who latches on to wealth and a title. Eric Ambler adapted Arnold Bennett's 1911 satire on business methods and class barriers; it makes a blithe, wonderfully satisfying comedy. Directed by Ronald Neame; cinematography by Oswald Morris. With Valerie Hobson as the Countess of Chell. b & w

The Proud and the Beautiful, see *Les Orgueilleux*

Providence (1977)—Alain Resnais, working in English, directed this intricately planned Freudian-puzzle movie, mostly set inside the mind of a dying writer (John Gielgud). Alone at night, in pain, the elderly writer drunkenly plots a novel about the members of his family (Dirk Bogarde, Ellen Burstyn, David Warner, Elaine Stritch). The effect of the pearl-gray tones and the swift, smooth cutting is peculiarly fastidious and static; you feel as if the movie, with all its technique and culture, were going to dry up and blow away. With a longer death scene than Camille's, Gielgud is the only one who looks alive. He's lean and wiry, turkey-faced, a tough old bird; he bounces through his bitchy role, savoring every mean syllable. David Mercer wrote the script, which is impossibly elocutionary. Gielgud delivers himself of flourishes like "How darkness creeps into the blood—darkness, the chill obsidian fingers." No doubt Mercer intended this writer's thoughts to have an edge of florid fatuity. But when Bogarde—a barrister—is asked (by his mistress) how he and his wife live, he answers, "In a state of unacknowledged mutual exhaustion, behind which we scream silently." Is this, too, only part of the old man's second-rate novel? Some people have a surprising tolerance for this sort of thing; the movie is widely regarded as a masterpiece, and it was chosen as the greatest film of the 70s by an international jury of critics. Music by Miklós Rózsa. color (See *When the Lights Go Down*.)

The Public Enemy (1931)—William Wellman's gangster classic, with James Cagney, Jean Harlow, Joan Blondell, and Mae Clarke as the girl who gets the grapefruit shoved in her kisser. A good picture, even if the theme music *is* "I'm Forever Blowing Bubbles." Warners. b & w

The Public Eye (1972)—Traipsing around London followed by a private detective, Mia Farrow is the most graceful, romantic comedienne one could hope for. She has a sure light touch, and so does the director, Carol Reed, who comes up with visual gags that fill out Peter Shaffer's script, based on his one-act play. As the accountant husband who hires the detective, because he can't believe his American wife simply enjoys poking about in the city, Michael Jayston is too tight-faced and stagey (he's a priss). The conception would probably have worked better if he'd played a charming man gone dry; instead, he seems a dry man trying to act charming. But as the Greek detective, Topol

gets to play his own age (35), and he's likably bearish—he's warm. Looking for the wife's concealed lover, this private eye watches the wife—a young woman with expressive wandering hands, a woman with poetry in her and a tender, slightly forlorn humor—and soon he's in love. This triangle comedy is totally artificial, yet it has a lovely, small, carefree quality. The cinematography, by Christopher Challis, is a happy love letter to London. A (British) Hal B. Wallis Production, released by Universal. color

I Pugni in Tasca, see *Fists in the Pocket*

Pumping Iron (1977)—Competently made documentary about the grotesque, comic subculture of bodybuilding. It holds the viewer's interest, but it does so by setting up the bodybuilding champions for you to react to in a certain way, and then congratulating you for seeing them in that psychologically facile way. The directors, George Butler and Robert Fiore, treat Arnold Schwarzenegger, Mike Katz, Franco Columbu, and Louis Ferrigno and his parents as if they were fictional characters, and there are elements of presumption, cruelty, and condescension in this. The film never transcends its own slickness. color

The Pumpkin Eater (1964)—Jack Clayton's underrated version of the Penelope Mortimer novel, with a script by Harold Pinter and a fine cast headed by Anne Bancroft. Her performance as the (compulsive childbearing) Englishwoman whose nerves are giving out has an unusual tentative, exploratory quality. (It ranks with her more straightforward acting in *The Miracle Worker*.) With Peter Finch as the screenwriter husband who plays around, and James Mason, Maggie Smith, Cedric Hardwicke, Alan Webb, Richard Johnson, and Yootha Joyce. It's a stunning, high-style film—fragmented yet flowing. The murky sexual tensions have a fascination, and there are memorable moments: Bancroft's crackup in Harrods; glimpses of Mason being prurient and vindictive, and Maggie Smith being a troublemaking "other woman." The cinematography is by Oswald Morris; the music is by Georges Delerue. Released in the U.S. by Columbia. b & w

Punchline (1988)—Pop-psych moral uplift, about standup comics. The writer-director, David Seltzer, wants us to see Steven Gold, the compulsive young spritzer, played by Tom Hanks, as "troubled"; Seltzer points up Steven's hostility, his inability to relate to other people, his not understanding what love is. And everything that Seltzer points up is soggy and only partway believable. Sally Field plays Lilah, a New Jersey housewife and mother of three who hopes to become a comic: Lilah looks at the restless, driven Steven and sees the soft, suffering child within. The movie gives Lilah an insipid radiance while it pulls back from Steven's aggressive twisted smile and his stabbing vocal rhythms. (These two are Lenny Bruce and Erma Bombeck.) We're supposed to dislike Steven's brashness and desperation, and approve of Lilah because she has a wholesome, normal outlook. We're also supposed to be charmed by the naughty vibrator jokes that pop out of her little head and "embarrass" her. Seltzer's sit-com style of humor is just like Lilah's. The bedraggled plotting forces Hanks into maudlin situations, but he manages to get under some of his material and darken it. He's what keeps you watching. Good performances by John Goodman, Mark Rydell, and Kim Greist. Columbia. color (See *Movie Love.*)

Le Puritain, see *The Puritan*

The Puritan *Le Puritain* (1939)—Jean-Louis Barrault was not yet an internationally known actor, and those of us who saw this unheralded young man in *The Puritan* experienced a sense of discovery. His bony, thin young face was perfect for Liam O'Flaherty's psychological study of the murderer Ferriter, a righteous reformer and sexually obsessed religious fanatic. Barrault's acting was so unusually objective that one respected this poor devil even at his most hopelessly self-deceived. The film, condemned by New York's State Board of Censors in toto as "indecent, immoral, sacrilegious, tending to incite to crime and corrupt morals," is in perfectly good taste, but the censors had a reason for their stand: Ferriter is not only conceived as a censor type, he's actually engaged in this work in the film. The production, which also features Pierre Fresnay and Viviane Romance, was made in Paris by the director, Jeff Musso, for a total cost of $27,000. In French. b & w

Purple Noon *Plein Soleil* (1960)—Maurice Ronet and Alain Delon as decadent Americans loafing in Italy—Ronet rich and vicious, Delon poor, amoral, and murderous. When Delon tries on Ronet's clothes, it's clear that they look better on him. The director, René Clément, keeps this thriller in the sun-drenched-holiday style of travel posters, with homosexual hatred and envy festering. All it has going for it is this sensuous, kicky atmosphere; you feel as if you're breathing something beautiful and rotten. With Marie Laforêt as the shared girlfriend. Adapted from Patricia Highsmith's *The Talented Mr. Ripley*. Cinematography by Henri Decaë; music by Nino Rota. In French. color

Purple Rain (1984)—In this fictional bio, Prince, the 26-year-old pansexual rock star, appears as the Kid, a vulnerable loner and struggling musician. The son of a self-pitying black man who beats his white wife, because he blames her for his failure to achieve success as a composer, the moody Kid is a tortured soul. When he falls in love with Apollonia (the overpoweringly sultry Patty Apollonia Kotero), he begins to repeat the pattern, but, of course, the love that is the source of his torment is also the source of his redemption. It's not difficult to see the attraction that the picture has for adolescents: Prince's songs are a cry for the free expression of sexual energy, and his suffering is a supercharged version of what made James Dean the idol of young moviegoers—this Kid is "hurting." And this picture knows no restraint. It was directed by Albert Magnoli (who also wrote the final script and was the co-editor), but Prince is in charge, and he knows how he wants to appear—like Dionysus crossed with a convent girl on her first bender. And his instinct is right: if he had performed the role more realistically, the picture would be really sodden. This way, his impudent pranks make the audience laugh and his musical numbers keep giving the picture a lift. It's pretty terrible (there are no real scenes—just flashy, fractured rock-video moments), but those willing to accept Prince as a sexual messiah aren't likely to mind. The film introduces a full-fledged young comedian, Morris Day, the lead singer of The Time, who suggests a Richard Pryor without the genius and the complications. When the giggling Day and his handsome sidekick, Jerome Benton, dance to The Time's funk rock they have a loose, floppy grace. There's also a good straight performance by Clarence Williams III as the Kid's father. Cinematography by Donald Thorin; shot in Minneapolis. Released by Warners. color (See *State of the Art*.)

The Purple Rose of Cairo (1985)—The 13th movie that Woody Allen directed, this comedy has a small, rapt quality; he wrote it for Mia Farrow, and it seems scaled to her cheekbones. The time is 1935; and she is Cecilia, who lives in a small town in New Jersey and can't hold a job for long because her thoughts wander away to the glamorous worlds she sees on the screen at the Jewel Theater. This is the first Woody Allen movie in which a whole batch of actors really interact and spark each other. Jeff Daniels plays a dashing young screen character who bounds down from the black-and-white image and into color, and takes Cecilia out of the theatre with him; he's also the ambitious actor who arrives in the town to try to persuade the character to go back up on the screen where he belongs. Also with Danny Aiello, Stephanie Farrow, Zoe Caldwell, John Wood, Edward Herrmann, Van Johnson, Deborah Rush, Annie Joe Edwards, Karen Akers, Irving Metzman, Milo O'Shea, Alexander H. Cohen, and, in a spectacular cameo, Dianne Wiest. Cinematography by Gordon Willis; the original music is by Dick Hyman. Orion. color (See *State of the Art*.)

Puzzle of a Downfall Child (1971)—The title is enough to warn you that this is going to be literary in the worst sense, and it turns out to be about the anguished life of a high-fashion model (Faye Dunaway)—a lapsed Catholic, striving for grace and sleeping with strangers. The script by Carol Eastman (under the pseudonym Adrian Joyce) is reminiscent of her script for *Five Easy Pieces*; it's another tribute to alienation. Jerry Schatzberg has directed it in a fractured, prismatic style. Put them together and you've got the high-flown chic of soullessness. After you've looked at the heroine's teeny marble features for almost two hours, you're offered the conceit that perhaps she's an empty wreck because every time someone takes a picture of her she loses a piece of her soul. (At 24 frames a second, this movie must have devastated Dunaway.) With Barry Primus, Emerick Bronson, Roy Scheider, and Viveca Lindfors.

Cinematography by Adam Holender; music by Michael Small. Universal. color (See *Deeper into Movies*.)

Pygmalion (1938)—First-rate romantic comedy, and certainly the best G.B.S. picture ever done. It doesn't seem weighted down with talk, like most of the others, and though a trifle slow in spots, it has a very satisfying tempo. Wendy Hiller is triumphant in the role of Eliza, the Covent Garden flower girl, and Leslie Howard is marvellously high-spirited and combative as the smug Professor Higgins, who trains Eliza to speak like a lady. Gabriel Pascal produced, Anthony Asquith and Leslie Howard directed, David Lean edited, Arthur Honegger did the score, and Harry Stradling shot it. The costumes are by Czettell, Worth, and Schiaparelli. The cast includes Wilfrid Lawson as Doolittle, Marie Lohr as Mrs. Higgins, Scott Sunderland as Colonel Pickering, Jean Cadell as Mrs. Pearce, David Tree as Freddy, Esmé Percy as Count Karpathy, and Leueen MacGrath, Everley Gregg, Violet Vanbrugh, Iris Hoey, Stephen Murray, Irene Brown, Cathleen Nesbitt, and Ivor Barnard. Though several writers worked on the adaptation (and received an Academy Award for it), the award for the screenplay was given to Shaw (who wrote some new scenes for the movie). (The play was later turned into the musical-comedy *My Fair Lady*, which was filmed in 1964.) b & w

Q & A (1990)—Sidney Lumet has made some exciting, dramatic New York movies (*Serpico*, *Dog Day Afternoon*). He also made the hard-to-sit through *Prince of the City*, a murky indictment of big-city graft, which he co-scripted. This is in the same mode: it's about the city's ethnic humor and anger, and about police corruption. Lumet wrote the script alone, and he's so busy laying on the rancorous, bantering atmosphere that he waits too long to get to the plot; the movie becomes torpid. (You have to concentrate to figure out what's supposed to be going on—that's the only suspense.) Nick Nolte, in dark hair that makes him look like a vampire, is a big, bulky Irish cop with a vicious streak; a repressed homosexual, he especially enjoys intimidating and murdering transvestites. The co-star is Timothy Hutton as an assistant D.A., also Irish, who's expected to cover up one of the cop's killings. But the standout performance is given by Luis Guzman as a Hispanic police detective who's pressured to be "dirty." Also with Patrick O'Neal, Armand Assante, Lee Richardson, Charles S. Dutton, Jenny Lumet, Fyvush Finkel, Paul Calderon, and International Chrysis. Cinematography by Andrzej Bartkowiak; music by Rubén Blades. Based on the book by Edwin Torres. Tri-Star. color

Q Planes   Also known as *Clouds Over Europe*. (1939)—A likable, nonsensical British spy thriller about secret rays, mysterious enemies, and dastardly plots against Britain's aircraft. It's charmingly light in tone. Laurence Olivier and Ralph Richardson play in just the right spirit. Olivier has an engaging romantic-comedian manner and Valerie Hobson shows her gift for looking beautiful in a distinguished way. (She's definitely not a broad or a chick.) Tim Whelan directed this Alexander Korda production, written by Ian Dalrymple, Brook Williams, Jack Whittingham, and Arthur Wimperis. b & w

Quai des brumes, see *Port of Shadows*

Quai des Orfèvres   Also known as *Jenny Lamour*. (1947)—A stunningly well-made entertainment, this detective film by Henri-Georges Clouzot features the master actor Louis Jouvet in the role of a police inspector. His world is contrasted with that of the music hall, represented by the full-blown, hypersexual Suzy Delair. When this voluptuous slut sings "Avec Son Tra-la-la," she may make you wonder if the higher things in life are worth the trouble. With Bernard Blier as Delair's worshipful-masochist husband, Charles Dullin in the role of a lecherous hunchback, and, as a lesbian photographer, Simone Renant, at the time said to be the most beautiful actress in Paris. From a novel by S. A. Steeman, adapted by Clouzot and Jean Ferry. The film took the top prize at Venice, but in this country it never got the audience it deserved.

Quality Street (1937)—It isn't really so long ago—though it seems like another age—that the heroine of a Hollywood movie could say, "I could bear all the rest, but I've been unladylike." It should be recorded that even in the 30s, the audience rejected this quaintness. Set in an English village during the Napoleonic wars, the film is from the James M. Barrie play about a street where gentlemen are an event, and where a dashing, gallant officer (Franchot Tone) devastates the maiden ladies. As in so much of Barrie, the sensitive, all-knowing woman (Katharine Hepburn) gets the vain, infantile male. Underneath all the twittering proprieties, there's a dismaying and rather grim view of human relations. The director, George Stevens, seems to lumber through some of the scenes—they turn stiff and silly; the picture was one of several costume romances that turned Hepburn into box-office poison, and one can see why—it's impossibly arch. Yet she brings surprising feeling to the stylized material—she does wonders with it, and she looks lovely in the Regency gowns. With Cora Witherspoon as the belligerent servant, Fay Bainter, Eric Blore, Joan Fontaine, Florence Lake, Helena Grant, Bonita Granville, and—in a lace cap and tall hat—Estelle Winwood. Adapted by Allan Scott and Mortimer Offner; costumes by Walter Plunkett; produced by Pandro S. Berman, for R K O. b & w

Il Quartetto Basileus, see *Basileus Quartet*

Quatre Nuits d'un rêveur, see *Four Nights of a Dreamer*

Que He Hecho Yo Para Merecer Esto, see *What Have I Done to Deserve This!*

Que la bête meure, see *This Man Must Die*

Que Viva Mexico, see *Time in the Sun*

The Queen (1968)—A documentary centering on the transvestites entered in a "Miss All-American" beauty contest for female impersonators held at Town Hall in 1967. Directed by Frank Simon, the film (which runs just over an hour) has considerable humor and drama, as well as that mixture of perversity and sadness distinctive to the drag scene. Released by Grove Press. color

Queimada!, see *Burn!*

Quest for Fire (1982)—Set 80,000 years ago, this science fantasy is a full-length version of the ape-man prologue to *2001*; it's a heavy dose of Desmond (*Naked Ape*) Morris, with blaring Dawn of Consciousness music. Naoh, Amoukar, and Gaw (Everett McGill, Ron Perlman, and Nameer El-Kadi), three warriors of the spear-carrying Ulam tribe, go out on the sacred mission of finding fire. As they fight off predatory animals and hideous, apier men you begin to wish you could detect famous actors under all the makeup, the way you could in the Biblical spectaculars. If it weren't for the grisly closeups of torn flesh and the composer, Philippe Sarde, letting himself go in the Stravinsky and Wagner department, the picture might be taken for a put-on. (If it were double-billed with the comedian Carl Gottlieb's *Caveman*, its overblown solemnity might backfire.) The director, Jean-Jacques Annaud, has his own primitivism: he doesn't seem to have discovered crosscutting yet. What's fun in the movie is the makeup, and the way that the faces of the three warriors are simian and yet attractive; the 60s have made the ape look seem hip—these fellows might be rock stars. The hero Naoh falls in love with the smooth-skinned, bluish-looking Ika (Rae Dawn Chong) of the mud-people, the Ivaka, who have pottery and the beginnings of a culture and know how to *make* fire. Ika also teaches Naoh a few other things—such as a basic, mutually satisfying sex position. It's almost impossible to guess what the tone of much of this Stone Age love story is meant to be. At times Amoukar and Gaw are baggy-pants comics without the pants. Anthony Burgess "created" the "special languages" and Desmond Morris "created" the "body languages and gestures." Script by Gérard Brach, based on a 1911 French novel by J. H. Rosny, Sr. A Canada-France co-production. color (See *Taking It All In*.)

The Quiet American (1958)—It was a commercial failure, and it's also an artistic failure, but the theme and the principal characters are of such immediacy and interest that it's far more absorbing than many successful movies with a more conventional subject matter. Graham Greene's 1956 novel was based on his experiences as a correspondent in Indo-China, and Joseph L. Mankiewicz, who adapted the book and directed the movie, shot most of it in Saigon. It is a study of the American (Audie Murphy) as do-gooder, and of the harm that innocent and crusading idealism can do, and it is a study of the Englishman (Michael Redgrave) as cynical, convictionless neutralist. There are so many fine things in the film (especially Red-

grave's portrait of a man whose cold exterior is just a thin skin over his passionate desperation) that perhaps one can put to the side the offending compromises by which Mankiewicz turned Greene's novel upside down and made the American heroic. With Claude Dauphin, Georgia Moll, Kerima, Richard Loo, and Bruce Cabot. The cinematography is by Robert Krasker (who also shot *The Third Man*) and the film has a great deal more visual richness and style than most Mankiewicz films. This one moves with an almost documentary freedom. United Artists. b & w

The Quiet Man (1952)—One of John Ford's most popular films—but fearfully Irish and green and hearty. John Wayne plays an American prizefighter who returns to Ireland and courts a ripe, fiery beauty, Maureen O'Hara. In the best scene, on the morning after the wedding, the fighter's driver (Barry Fitzgerald) comes in through the smashed bedroom door and looks at the broken-down bed, and says something indecipherable that sounds like "Impetuous! Homeric!" There's a big brawl between Wayne and Victor McLaglen, who plays the bride's brother; with Ward Bond, Mildred Natwick, Francis Ford, Arthur Shields, Jack MacGowran, Sean McClory, May Craig, Mae Marsh, Ken Curtis as the ballad singer, and four of Wayne's children. From Maurice Walsh's short story "Green Rushes," adapted by Frank S. Nugent. Produced by Ford and Merian C. Cooper. Filmed in Ireland and at Republic Pictures. color

Quintet (1979)—When Robert Altman enters his allegorical, poetic phase, he goes into his own fugal version of dreamtime, which means, in practice, that he puts the audience in such a depressed state that people are fighting to stay awake even before the titles come on. Electronic sounds and a lot of white on the screen can do it—especially when the camera travels with one person trudging along in the snow, offering views of nothingness for our admiration. You get a sense of eternity fast. The picture is like a Monty Python show played at the wrong speed. It's set in a post-apocalypse ice age in which the scattered survivors of a highly technological society live without hope in decaying, vandalized structures that suggest public housing designed by a drunken spider. (The interiors were shot in the remnants of Expo 67 in Montreal, with the "Man and His World" photo-murals still visible; they enrich the visual texture in an accusatory way— we're made to feel vaguely guilty.) To alleviate the boredom of survival, the last men and women play a death game called Quin-

tet, which appears to be an elaborate form of Arctic roulette. The corpses of the losers are tossed outside into the frozen waste, to be devoured by packs of Rottweilers. Paul Newman plays Essex the seal hunter, who seems to be the last potent man left; Brigitte Fossey is lovely in a too brief appearance as his fresh-faced, pregnant companion. Also with Bibi Andersson, Vittorio Gassman, Fernando Rey (who seems crippled by his struggle to speak in English), Nina Van Pallandt, Monique Mercure, and Craig R. Nelson. Cinematography by Jean Boffety; the ominous, dissonant score is by Tom Pierson. Screenplay by Frank Barhydt, Patricia Resnick, and Altman. A Lion's Gate Film, released by 20th Century-Fox. color

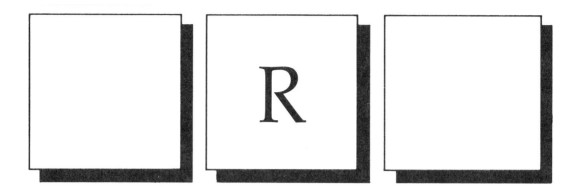

R

Racing with the Moon (1984)—It's Christmas, 1942, and Sean Penn and Nicolas Cage are two Northern California small-town boys who are due to report to the Marines in six weeks; Penn falls in love with a new girl in town (Elizabeth McGovern), and Cage gets a girl pregnant. That's the whole movie. Penn brings his role emotional crosscurrents and creates a lived-in character; you see the full person, with nothing closed off. And Richard Benjamin directs all three lovingly, so that the nuances they bring to their roles sustain our interest. But the picture isn't enough of anything; there isn't a thing in it that you can get excited about or quarrel with. The script, written by Steven Kloves (when he was 22), might be an exercise in conventional fine writing; it's a reminiscence based on earlier reminiscences. And the movie doesn't feel firsthand. It's too smooth, and it's square. With the lively Shawn Schepps as a girl that McGovern double-dates with, Carol Kane as an agreeable flooze, Arnold Johnson as a tattoo artist, and also Max Showalter as the piano teacher, John Karlen as Penn's father, Rutanya Alda as his mother, and Suzanne Adkinson as the pregnant Sally. Cinematography by John Bailey. Paramount. color (See *State of the Art*.)

Radio Days (1987)—Woody Allen looks back fondly, in a warm, amber-toned reminiscence of what radio meant to him and his family at the start of the Second World War. The actors who make up the 11-year-old hero's lower-middle-class Jewish family in Rockaway Beach are a wonderful group of comedians—Michael Tucker, Julie Kavner, Josh Mostel, Renee Lippin, Joy Newman, Dianne Wiest—yet they're never up close, at the center of our attention. Allen has reduced everyone to harmlessness. It's pure nostalgia—the past sweetened and trivialized. The mood is soft regret: he treats the old songs (the film incorporates a generous assortment of hits) as a value that we've lost. As he spells it out, the public's memories of the stars of radio become dimmer each year. The question the film asks—its theme—is "Will our fame last?" Implicitly, he's saying that we movie stars (and TV stars) must learn humility. With Mia Farrow as the one character whom we follow over a period of years, as she rises from cigarette girl to jewel-decked radio star, and Seth Green as the boy, Gina DeAngelis, Danny Aiello, Denise Dummont, Tito Puente, Jeff Daniels, Tony Roberts, Wallace Shawn, and Diane Keaton. The cinematography is by Carlo Di Palma. Orion. color (See *Hooked*.)

Rafferty and Gold Dust Twins (1975)—A charmingly inconsequential film with a side-wise vision that sneaks up on you. Two girls (Sally Kellerman as an aspiring singer, and softer and more flexible than in her earlier performances, and Mackenzie Phillips, as a hard-shelled, foul-mouthed teen-ager) kid-nap a man (Alan Arkin) and force him, at gunpoint, to drive them from Los Angeles to Arizona; the film is about how they begin to care for each other. The script, by John Kaye, is slight but it sustains a half-fantasy, balloon-going-up mood and the director, Dick Rich-ards, shows a feeling for momentary en-counters; what might be throwaways for another director are his most acutely realized moments. He's a very companionable sort of director here, with humor based on affection for rejects and outsiders. Well acted by the three principals (Alan Arkin loosens up, for a change), and also by Alex Rocco as a scrounger who attaches himself to the scruffy trio, and by Harry Dean Stanton, with his hollowed face (as if he'd worn away whatever life was in him). Warners. color (See *Reeling*).

The Rage of Paris (1938)—Hollywood's at-tempt to make an American star of the rap-turously beautiful young Danielle Darrieux—it's easy to see why it failed. In this innocuous bedroom farce, the arch frilliness of Univer-sal's conception of a *jeune fille* robs her of any depth. She is cast as a poor French girl work-ing as a model in New York; financed by Helen Broderick and Mischa Auer, she sets out to capture a millionaire. Under the direc-tion of Henry Koster (who, after leaving Ger-many, had made his reputation here on the Deanna Durbin musicals), Darrieux pouts re-lentlessly, and after many misadventures wins Douglas Fairbanks, Jr. b & w

Raggedy Man (1981)—Sissy Spacek gives a delicate performance—one of her softest and least eccentric—as the telephone operator who runs the phone company out of her two-room house, in a little town in Texas, during the Second World War. Deserted by her hus-band, she's raising her two small boys alone and she's cooped up—tied to the switch-board—and feeling desperate. (She dances with a broom, to the Andrews Sisters' "Rum & Coca Cola.") A young sailor on leave (Eric Roberts) drops by to make a long-distance call, and a warm friendship begins to build. Spacek and Roberts and the two child actors have surprising, evocative, believable dia-logue, and their vocal inflections and rhythms are lovely. But then Roberts is sent away, and the story takes a literary, gothic turn that violates the film's best qualities. And some of the scenes have been so lyrically fresh and involving that when the tone goes off, a viewer can feel really affronted. The first-time director, Jack Fisk, who early on worked with David Lynch and then made his name as an art director (*Badlands, Phantom of the Paradise, Carrie, Days of Heaven*), gives us flowing, expressive images that linger in the memory. (There are dissolves with an orange-pink light.) What also lingers in the memory are some of the performances Fisk gets: Spacek in particular, who seems grown up (she's married to Fisk, and he brings out another side of her), and Roberts, who is un-expectedly simple and open. (He has a won-derful listening-on-the-phone scene that's like a Dear John letter.) And the kids (Henry Thomas, who went on to play Elliott in *E.T.*, and Carey Hollis, Jr.) are unaffected. The cast includes R. G. Armstrong as Spacek's boss (he seems too loud), and, in hopelessly melo-dramatic roles, Sam Shepard, Tracey Wal-ter, and William Sanderson. The screenplay is by the talented William D. Wittliff; he wrote a farewell scene for Roberts and the kids that's too pixilated to be sentimental—it's a beauty. The cinematography is by Ralf Bode; the music is by Jerry Goldsmith. Universal. color

Raging Bull (1980)—Martin Scorsese's film based on the life of the former middleweight champ Jake La Motta (played by Robert De Niro) is a biography of the prizefight genre; it's also about movies and about violence, it's about gritty visual rhythm, it's about Brando, it's about the two *Godfather* pictures—it's about Scorsese and De Niro's trying to top what they've done and what everybody else has done. Scorsese puts his unmediated obsessions on the screen, trying to turn raw, pulp power into art by removing it from the particulars of observation and narrative. He loses the lowlife entertainment values of prizefight films; he aestheticizes pulp and kills it. De Niro put on more than 50 pounds to play the older, drunken La Motta; he seems a swollen puppet. With Cathy Moriarty, whose Vickie La Motta is a beautiful icon—a big, lacquered virgin-doll of the 40s—and Joe Pesci as Joey La Motta. (De Niro won the Academy Award for Best Actor.) An Irwin Winkler–Robert Chartoff Production; released by United Artists. b & w (See *Taking It All In*.)

Ragtime (1981)—The movie doesn't have an impudent slapstick vision, isn't a pop epic, or even a satiric fling. It's limp—it always seems to be aiming about halfway toward the effects that E. L. Doctorow achieved in his literary extravaganza. Is it possible that the director, Miloš Forman, thought that if he didn't go for razzle-dazzle what was left would be "truth"? If so, he started from the wrong book. He has made a seriously intended eccentric movie about a black piano player (Howard E. Rollins, Jr.) who demands redress for an insult. (Dog excrement has been put on the seat of his shiny new Model T Ford.) When the piano player can't find a

legal remedy, he becomes a bomb-planting terrorist. But the picture isn't even socially conscious: this character is so totally, aberrantly unbelievable that there's no social milieu that could account for him, and we don't know on what conceivable basis he could have recruited his band of urban guerrillas. Forman is not—to put it courteously—strongly visual. His extras are generally posed frozen faced in a row in the background—they look exactly like extras. The narrative shifts are jerky; the film seems chewed up rather than edited. With James Cagney as the New York Police Commissioner; returning to the screen after a 20-year retirement, Cagney has the faint, satisfied smile of an old tiger. Also with Pat O'Brien, Donald O'Connor, Norman Mailer, Elizabeth McGovern, Mary Steenburgen, Mandy Patinkin, Kenneth McMillan, Moses Gunn, Brad Dourif, Robert Joy, and James Olson. Script by Michael Weller. Produced by Dino De Laurentiis; Paramount. color (See *Taking It All In*.)

Raiders of the Lost Ark (1981)—Steven Spielberg directed this high-powered cliffhanger about the exploits of Indiana Jones (Harrison Ford), an adventurer-archeologist. The time is 1936, and Indy, working for the United States government, is trying to find the Ark of the Covenant (a chest holding the broken stone tablets of the Ten Commandments) ahead of his arch-enemy, the suave, amoral Belloq (Paul Freeman), who is in cahoots with the Nazis. Hitler means to use the Ark's invincible powers to lay waste opposing armies and proclaim himself the Messiah. Conceived by George Lucas, the picture is an amalgam of Lucas's follies—plot for its own sake, dissociated from character or drama; the affectless heroine, Marion (Karen Allen), who's a tougher version of spunky Princess Leia in *Star Wars*—and effects that Spielberg the youthful magician has already dazzled us with. Kinesthetically, the film gets to you, but there's no exhilaration, and no surge of feeling at the end. It seems to be edited for the maximum number of showings per day. With John Rhys-Davies as Sallah, Ronald Lacey as Toht, and Denholm Elliott. Cinematography by Douglas Slocombe; score by John Williams. Written by Lawrence Kasdan, from a story idea worked up by Lucas and Phil Kaufman. *Raiders of the Lost Ark* was the first film of a trilogy; it was followed by *Indiana Jones and the Temple of Doom* (1984) and *Indiana Jones and the Last Crusade* (1989). A Lucasfilm, released by Paramount. color (See *Taking It All In*.)

Rain (1932)—Joan Crawford is the innocent-at-heart tramp Sadie Thompson in this version of the Somerset Maugham wheezer, adapted by Maxwell Anderson and directed by Lewis Milestone. Crawford is the most unnuanced actress imaginable, and her interpretation of Sadie has absolutely no delicacy. Yet this time her desperate earnestness is fixating. With all the emotion she pours on, and her flashing eyes and twisted-scar mouth and strained voice, she's so totally affected that the affection begins to seem natural. Her vitality is undeniable. As the sanctimonious Reverend Davidson (Hollywood's archetypal lustful hypocrite), Walter Huston has some startlingly shrewd moments, but the production is stilted and claustrophobic—obviously, the dated stage version of the Maugham story dominated the moviemakers' thinking. With William Gargan, Beulah Bondi, Guy Kibbee, and Matt Moore. United Artists. b & w

Rain Man (1988)—Dustin Hoffman is Raymond, an autistic savant who lives in an institution in Cincinnati, and Tom Cruise is his huckster brother Charlie, an L.A. car dealer, who kidnaps him, hoping to get hold of some of the $3 million that their father has left in trust for Raymond's care. Hoffman keeps his actor's engine chugging and upstages the movie; Cruise's performance consists of not smiling too much—so as not to distract his fans from watching Hoffman. The director, Barry Levinson—it's his temperament—stretches out the scenes until they yawn. But the picture has its effectiveness: people cry at it. Of course, they cry at it—it's a piece of wet kitsch. With Valeria Golino; Ronald Bass was the principal screenwriter. Academy Awards: Best Picture, Director, Actor (Hoffman), Original Screenplay. United Artists. color (See *Movie Love*.)

The Rain People (1969)—There's a prodigious amount of talent in Francis Ford Coppola's unusual, little-seen film, but it's a ponderously self-conscious effort; the writer-director applies his film craftsmanship with undue solemnity to material that suggests a gifted college student's imitation of early Tennessee Williams. The result is academic, and never believable. Shirley Knight is atrociously mannered as a pregnant woman who leaves home and picks up a brain-damaged hitchhiker (James Caan). With Robert Duvall as a motorcycle cop. Warners. color

The Rainbow (1989)—The pastoral locations are grassy vistas that seem to melt before your eyes, and the images suggest that the material—the second half of the D. H. Lawrence novel about marriage—is being approached with humility and seriousness. This isn't one of the director Ken Russell's lurid, campy pictures. But his underlying attitudes haven't really changed; the campiness is simply more restrained, and the movie is amorphous and unsatisfying. As Ursula Brangwen, who (in the novel) yearns for sexual and spiritual union, Sammi Davis seems merely petulant. One of the pioneering feminist heroines—a woman who represents an advance on previous generations, a woman on a quest—has been turned into a snippy, closed-off brat. Glenda Jackson and Christopher Gable are surprisingly relaxed (and effective) as Ursula's parents, and David Hemmings is very smooth as her smiling, corrupt uncle. Also with Paul McGann as Ursula's conventional-minded fiancé, who hates her whenever she expresses her feelings, and Amanda Donohoe and Dudley Sutton. The adaptation is by Russell and his wife, Vivian. Cinematography by Billy Williams. (Russell filmed *Women in Love*, the successor to *The Rainbow*, in 1969.) Vestron. color (See *Movie Love*.)

The Rainmaker (1956)—The cowtown spinster suffering from drought is Katharine Hepburn, and the man who delivers the rain is Burt Lancaster. The casting is just about perfect. Lancaster has an athletic role, in which he can also be very touching. His con man isn't a simple trickster; he's a poet and dreamer who needs to convince people of his magical powers. Hepburn is stringy and tomboyish, believably plain yet magnetically beautiful. This is a fairy tale (the ugly duckling) dressed up as a bucolic comedy and padded out with metaphysical falsies, but it is also genuinely appealing, in a crude, good-spirited way, though N. Richard Nash, who wrote both the play and the adaptation, aims too solidly at lower-middle-class tastes. Once transformed, the heroine rejects the poet for the deputy sheriff (Wendell Corey); if there were a sequel, she might be suffering from the drought of his imagination. With Lloyd Bridges, Earl Holliman, Cameron Prud'homme, and Wallace Ford. The director is Joseph Anthony, who also staged it on Broadway; the movie barely exists as a movie, but if you accept it as an "opened-out" play it's highly enjoyable. Music by Alex North. Produced by Hal B. Wallis, for Paramount. color

Raintree County (1957)—A full-scale mess set during the Civil War. Based on the 1948 novel by Ross Lockridge, the script is so literary and chaotic it seems demented. At the start, the movie is all chatter and there's no hook to get us into the story; later, the sequences don't flow together. As a rich, orphaned Southern belle (whose part-black ancestry is concealed), Elizabeth Taylor is soft-faced, with a ripe, full-lipped smile, and in the early scenes she's amusingly flirty and squealy. But as a handsome abolitionist Yankee, Montgomery Clift is in real trouble. It was in 1956, in the middle of making this picture, that he was disfigured in a car accident; he looks awful, he seems in agony, and his acting is mannered and odd. (Taylor, who's relatively unaffected, gives a better performance, even though all the fun goes out of her role.) The director, Edward Dmytryk, let by two major booby-prize performances: Walter Abel (actory-phony) and Agnes Moorehead (fake-jolly) as Clift's parents. But then this is the kind of movie in which a heavenly choir is heard while Taylor and Clift talk about the legendary magical rain tree. The cast includes Eva Marie Saint (who looks incredibly pretty), Rod Taylor, Lee Marvin, Nigel Patrick, Tom Drake, DeForest Kelley, and Gardner McKay. The screenplay is by Millard Kaufman; Johnny Green's music seems to be trying to create moods, but you get the feeling he's unsure what they should be. M-G-M. color

Raising Arizona (1987)—This broad farce is no big deal, but it has a cornpone-surreal quality and a rambunctious charm. It's about baby love—about people who feel they can't live without an infant to cuddle. When Edwina, or Ed—played by Holly Hunter—discovers she can't have a child, she's a wreck until she hears about male quintuplets that have been born to a woman who took fertility drugs; then she torments her husband, Hi (Nicolas Cage), until he goes to steal one of them. As soon as Hi plunks a quint into her arms, she yowls, "I love him so much!" Hi and Ed live in a yellow mobile home in a Tempe, Arizona, trailer park at the edge of a Pop-art version of the desert. Everything in the film is warped and flipped out; the light seems fluorescent, as if the world were a 24-hour supermarket. Joel and Ethan Coen, who did the writing together—Joel directed and Ethan produced (with Mark Silverman)—have a knack for hick-suburban dialogue (it's backed up by banjos and, sometimes, a yo-deller). And the film is storyboarded like a comic strip; it has a galumphing tempo. With John Goodman and William Forsythe as the escaped-convict brothers who become gaga over the babe, Trey Wilson as the quints' hardheaded father, Randall (Tex) Cobb as the biker, and Frances McDormand and Sam McMurray. Cinematography by Barry Sonnenfeld. Released by 20th Century-Fox. color (See *Hooked*.)

Rambo: First Blood Part II (1985)—Jump-cutting from one would-be high point to another, *Rambo* is to the action film what *Flashdance* was to the musical, with one to-be-cherished difference: audiences are laughing at it. (They hoot at it and get a little charged up at the same time.) The proceedings are directed by George P. Cosmatos and he gives the near-psychotic material—a mixture of Catholic iconography and *Soldier of Fortune* pulp—a veneer of professionalism, but the looniness is always there. The film's star and progenitor is Sylvester Stallone, and the way he's photographed he's huge—our national palooka. This humanoid Christ figure with brown leather skin and symmetrical scars goes into Vietnam and brings out a bunch of our missing-in-action men. The film specializes in scenes such as Rambo spread-eagled on an electrified rack, Rambo branded on the face with a red-hot knife, Rambo immersed in pig glop while hanging crucifixion-style. With Julia Nickson, Richard Crenna, Charles Napier, Steven Berkoff, George Kee Cheung, and Martin Kove. Cinematography by Jack Cardiff; screenplay by Stallone and James Cameron, from a story by Kevin Jarre, based on the characters from David Morrell's novel *First Blood*. Tri-Star. color (See *State of the Art*.)

Ran (1985)—Set in the 16th century, Akira Kurosawa's epic spectacle, a variation on the theme of *King Lear*, is static, but it deepens, and it has its own ornery splendor. It's a totally conceptualized work—perhaps the biggest piece of conceptual art ever made. For the first 40 minutes or so, the picture is all preparation, and it seems dead, but then the preparation begins to pay off, and by the end the fastidiousness and the monumental scale of what Kurosawa has undertaken can flood you with admiration. With Mieko Harada as Lady Kaede, the vengeful demon who brings down the House of Ichimonji; Tatsuya Nakadai as the warlord head of the clan; the Japanese transvestite pop star known as Peter as the Fool; and Hisashi Ikawa as Kurogane, who defies Lady Kaede. The fine, harsh, percussive score is by Toru Takemitsu. (2 hours and 41 minutes.) In Japanese. A French-Japanese co-production, released in the U.S. by Orion. color (See *Hooked*.)

Rancho Deluxe (1975)—Tom McGuane wrote the script for this flip, absurdist modern Western. Jeff Bridges plays a dropout from the upper middle class, and Sam Waterston plays a wryly bemused Indian. These two pranksters rustle cattle because the facetious machismo of it appeals to them; they do it "to keep from falling asleep." Their sly asides are too kicky, too pleased; the self-conscious cleverness isn't as charming as it's meant to be. McGuane sets up some funny situations, but the film's deadpan distancing makes everything seem anticlimactic. Things brighten up whenever Harry Dean Stanton or Richard Bright or Slim Pickens is on the screen. Frank Perry directed; with Elizabeth Ashley, Charlene Dallas, and Clifton James. United Artists. color (See *When the Lights Go Down*.)

Rancho Notorious (1952)—Not one of the films that Fritz Lang will be remembered for. Lang said that this Western was conceived for Marlene Dietrich (she plays an aging femme fatale, a retired dance-hall hostess who operates a hideout for outlaw gangs) but that by the time it was finished he and Dietrich had stopped speaking to each other. Financed by Howard Hughes, though on a small scale, it was shot mostly in the studio; the picture was to be called "Chuck-a-Luck" and Lang used the ballad "The Legend of Chuck-a-Luck" as an integral theme song, but afterward Hughes changed the title. (The picture was also recut.) Possibly even under the best of circumstances the mixture of Lang's conspiratorial motifs with the Western characters and locale might not have worked out. Arthur Kennedy is a cowpuncher obsessed with getting revenge for the rape and murder of his fiancée, and Mel Ferrer is Frenchy, a Western variant of Lang's master criminals. With Gloria Henry, William Frawley, Jack Elam, Dan Seymour, George Reeves, Lloyd Gough, and Fuzzy Knight. R K O. color

Random Harvest (1942)—Ronald Colman is the amnesiac who falls in love with Greer Garson, having forgotten that he'd been in love with her before; he must be the only person lucky enough to forget that sticky, arch great lady of the screen. The only reason to see this hunk of twaddle is the better to savor the memory of the Carol Burnett–

Harvey Korman parody, which also was shorter. Mervyn LeRoy, who directed many a big clinker, also gets the blame for this one; it's taken from a James Hilton novel, and M-G-M gave it the full false-English treatment. The cast includes Philip Dorn, Susan Peters, Reginald Owen, Margaret Wycherly, Peter Lawford, Henry Daniell, Una O'Connor, Jill Esmond, Ian Wolfe, and Bramwell Fletcher. b & w

Rashomon (1951)—In 9th-century Kyoto, a nobleman's bride is raped by a bandit; the nobleman is murdered, or possibly he is a suicide. This double crime is acted out four times, in the versions of the three participants, each giving an account that increases the prestige of his conduct, and in the version of a woodcutter who witnessed the episode. Continuously reconstructing the crime, *Rashomon* asks, How can we ever know the truth? This great enigmatic film was directed by Akira Kurosawa, from stories by Ryunosuke Akutagawa (who died from an overdose of veronal). The introductory and closing sequences are tedious; the woman's whimpering is almost enough to drive one to the nearest exit. Yet the film transcends these discomforts: it has its own perfection. With Machiko Kyo, Toshiro Mifune as the bandit, Masayuki Mori as the samurai, Takashi Shimura as the woodcutter. First Prize, Venice; Academy Award, Best Foreign Film. (There was a Broadway version with Rod Steiger, and a 1964 movie, with Paul Newman, appropriately called *The Outrage*.) In Japanese. b & w

Rasputin and the Empress (1932)—The only film with all three Barrymores—John, Ethel, and Lionel—and they all seem to be stuffed. John had played the mesmerist Svengali the year before, so Lionel was decked out in a beard to play Rasputin. (The brothers seemed to have swapped chin hair.) The hammiest actor in the family, Lionel, who doddered even in his youth, is so unhypnotic that Ethel, as the Empress, appears less mesmerized than bored stiff. But when Rasputin, after being poisoned and shot and beaten, still refuses to die, there really seems to be something vile and supernatural about him. John finally gets to choke his brother, to everyone's immense satisfaction. With Ralph Morgan, as Nicholas, and Diana Wynyard. Directed, pompously, by Richard Boleslawski; the script is attributed to Charles MacArthur. M-G-M. b & w

The Raven, see *Le Corbeau*

Raw Deal (1986)—It's reprehensible and enjoyable, the kind of movie that makes you feel brain dead in two minutes—after which point you're ready to laugh at its mixture of trashiness, violence, and startlingly silly crude humor. As a lawman who infiltrates the biggest mob in Chicago, Arnold Schwarzenegger is a puzzling, cartoon phenomenon, like a walking brick wall, and the director, John Irvin, sets the other characters to bouncing off that wall. The cast includes Kathryn Harrold, who shows the physical abandon of a good slapstick comedienne, Sam Wanamaker, who has some juicy, egocentric moments as the gangland boss, and Paul Shenar, Steven Hill, Darren McGavin, Ed Lauter, Robert Davi, Joe Regalbuto, and Blanche Baker. The script, cooked up by a couple of Italians (Luciano Vincenzoni and Sergio Donati), written by the erratic Norman Wexler, and then rewritten by Gary M. DeVore, still retains some of Wexler's rowdy spirit. The cinematography is by Alex Thomson. De Laurentiis. color (See *Hooked*.)

The Razor's Edge (1946)—Almost as irresistibly funny and terrible as *The Fountainhead*. Tyrone Power plays the Somerset Maugham hero who journeys all the way to India and figures that he has hit upon a mystical bonanza when he hears a bewhiskered yogi murmur, "There is in every one of us a spark of the infinite goodness." Nobody in the film seems to be very agile mentally, from the Chicago débutante (beautiful Gene Tierney) whom the hero leaves behind when he sets out in pursuit of an inscrutable gleam to the girl he almost marries—poor, sad Sophie (Anne Baxter), who has tried to forget the death of her husband and child by surrendering herself to half the male population of the Parisian underworld. There are quantities of Chicago mansions and country clubs, French bistros and Indian lamaseries, and thousands of extras to keep the sets from looking bare. The performers move about in a vague, somnambulistic manner befitting a literary masterpiece, especially Herbert Marshall, who plays Maugham himself. Clifton Webb does a memorable high-camp number as an expatriate snob. Edmund Goulding directed. 20th Century-Fox. (Remade in 1984 by John Byrum.) b & w

Razumov (1937)—Three of France's greatest actors appear in this little-known film adaptation of Conrad's *Under Western Eyes*. Jean-Louis Barrault is the revolutionary assassin; Pierre Fresnay, subtle and tense, is Razumov, the student who is forced to inform on his friends; Jacques Copeau is the head of the secret police. Marc Allégret directed; he doesn't try to soften the malevolent, tragic material. In French. b & w

Razzia sur la chnouf (1957)—America's movie gangsters of the 30s and 40s, adored by the French and imitated by them, come back to us with strange accents, more refined sadistic and erotic habits, and a whole new vocabulary of exotic gangster argot. This cultural crossfertilization produces an amusingly plodding pseudo-documentary like *Razzia*. The French are very serious about vice, and the dedicated authenticity with which the director Henri Decoin follows Jean Gabin and his hoods and pushers through dingy waterfront cafés, beat bistros where glistening African bodies writhe in the hashish smoke, gay bars presided over by bass-voiced lesbians, lonely subway stops, and opium dens where ambiguous-looking men recline among Orientalia, would probably shock the American directors who, in their innocence, created the genre. As the ring's enforcer, snarling, shiv-eyed Gabin is the familiar, inexorable tough of the French tradition. One may wonder whether the teeth he sinks into Magali Noel's magnificent neck are his own; in the film's final moment, when morality triumphs and the audience is cheated, one knows the answer. With Lila Kedrova. In French. b & w

Re-Animator (1985)—Adapted from a series of six stories that H. P. Lovecraft published in 1922, this horror film about a medical student with a fluorescent greenish-yellow serum that restores the dead to hideous, unpredictable activity is close to being a silly ghoulie classic—the bloodier it gets, the funnier it is. It's like pop Buñuel; the jokes hit you in a subterranean comic zone that the surrealists' pranks sometimes reached, but without the surrealists' self-consciousness (and art-consciousness). This is indigenous American junkiness, like the Mel Brooks–Gene Wilder *Young Frankenstein*, but looser and more low-down. (*Re-Animator* wasn't submitted to the Ratings Board.) This is the first movie directed by Stuart Gordon (one of the founders of the Organic Theatre, in Chicago); the actors he picked perform with a straight-faced, hip aplomb. Herbert West, the re-animator, is played by Jeffrey Combs with pursed lips and a clammy-prissy set of the jaw. David Gale is the hypocritical lecher who loses his head, Robert Sampson is the Dean, Barbara Crampton is the Dean's creamy-pink

daughter (who's at her loveliest when she's being defiled), and Bruce Abbott is her adoring fiancé. The screenplay is by Dennis Paoli, William J. Norris, and the director. Music by Richard Ban; cinematography by Mac Ahlberg, with additional work by R. F. Ebinger. Produced by Brian Yuzna; released by Empire Pictures. color (See *Hooked*.)

Rebecca (1940)—Magnificent romantic-gothic corn, full of Alfred Hitchcock's humor and inventiveness. It features one of Laurence Olivier's rare poor performances; he seems pinched and too calculated—but even when he's uncomfortable in his role he's more fascinating than most actors. Joan Fontaine gives one of her rare really fine performances—she makes her character's shyness deeply charming. And with Judith Anderson, George Sanders, and Florence Bates—all three showing their flair for playing rotten people. Also with Gladys Cooper, Nigel Bruce, Leo G. Carroll, Reginald Denny, C. Aubrey Smith, and Melville Cooper. From Daphne du Maurier's novel, adapted by Robert E. Sherwood and Joan Harrison; the cinematography is by George Barnes; music by Franz Waxman. A David O. Selznick Production. b & w

Rebel Without a Cause (1955)—As Jim, a high-school boy, James Dean was the archetypal misunderstood teen-ager in this generation-gap soap opera of the 50s, which had more emotional resonance for the teen-agers of the time than many much better movies. With Natalie Wood as Judy, Sal Mineo as Plato, Corey Allen as Buzz, Nick Adams as Moose, Dennis Hopper as Goon, Jim Backus and Ann Doran as Jim's parents, Virginia Brissac as his Grandma, William Hopper and Rochelle Hudson as Judy's parents, and Ian Wolfe, House Peters, and Gus Schilling. Directed by Nicholas Ray; written by Stewart Stern and Irving Shulman, based on Ray's story; music by Leonard Rosenman; cinematography by Ernest Haller. Warners. CinemaScope, color

The Red and the Black *Le Rouge et le noir* (1954)—The director, Claude Autant-Lara, tried to encompass the full span of the Stendhal novel, and when the movie opened in Paris it was 2 hours and 50 minutes long. When the "international version" was prepared, the film lost 30 minutes. Almost four years elapsed before American distribution was arranged; it opened there in 1958 to superb reviews (*Time* called it "a shot of straight perfume"), but it drew such meager audiences that it disappeared before the people who might have wanted to see it even knew it was around. In addition, it's a film with a special problem: Stendhal's ironic romanticism is interpreted in so many different ways by readers that any visualization is bound to be distressing to some of them. The movie has been lauded as a perfect achievement, but you may feel that Stendhal's spirit doesn't come through—that Autant-Lara's fidelity and taste cancel out the dash of the novel and that the pretty pastel colors are too delicate. Gérard Philipe plays the proud opportunist, Julien Sorel, analytic and calculating in his priestly cassock, but at heart a redcoated romantic. No doubt Philipe was the obvious choice for the role, because he had been playing spin-offs of Julien Sorel for 20 years; he no longer had Julien's young, rapturous foolishness, though, and he wasn't fired up. The casting of Danielle Darrieux as Madame de Rênal and Antonella Lualdi as Mathilde de la Mole doesn't set off any sparks either. The picture is intelligent but pallid. It should have been called "The Pink and the Gray." With Jean Mercure, Jean Martinelli, and Balpêtré as Abbé Pirard. In French. color

The Red Badge of Courage (1951)—Despite the mutilation (recorded in Lillian Ross's *Pic-*

ture), some 70 minutes remain of John Huston's film version of Stephen Crane's Civil War classic, and much of it is breathtaking. Audie Murphy plays the hero and Bill Mauldin is his sidekick; with Royal Dano, John Dierkes, Andy Devine, Douglas Dick, and Arthur Hunnicutt. Cinematography by Harold Rosson; music by Bronislau Kaper; the script is by Huston. Produced by Gottfried Reinhardt, for M-G-M. b & w

The Red Balloon *Le Ballon rouge* (1956)—Albert Lamorisse's celebrated 34-minute film without dialogue, about a small boy (his son, Pascal) who wanders all over Paris trailed by a balloon. It's an allegory of innocence and evil, set in a child's dream world. Elegantly photographed and with a durable appeal to children, though it lacks the passionate beauty of the director's other film on the same theme, *White Mane*. Lamorisse wrote and directed. Also with Sabine Lamorisse. color

Red Desert *Il Deserto Rosso* (1964)—Boredom in Ravenna, and it seeps into the viewer's bones. Antonioni's hazy illustration of emotional chaos may or may not have something to do with industrialism; he makes the hazy, polluted atmosphere so ethereal that one can't decide. With Monica Vitti and Richard Harris. In Italian. color

Red Dust (1932)—A sexy jungle melodrama from M-G-M, with Jean Harlow as a bawdy, tough girl who has been around, and an unshaven Clark Gable who thinks he prefers cool, ladylike Mary Astor. Harlow is intensely likable, delivering her zingy wisecracks with a wonderful dirty good humor, and Gable is at that early peak in his career when he is so sizzlingly sexual that it seems both funny and natural for the two women to be fighting over him. M-G-M remade the film in 1953 as *Mogambo*, with Ava Gardner in the Harlow role and Grace Kelly as the lady, but by then Gable, still manfully holding down his old role, didn't bring much heat to it. The original was directed by Victor Fleming in a racy, action-packed style, from a script by John Lee Mahin, based on Wilson Collison's story. With Gene Raymond, Tully Marshall, and Donald Crisp. (*Red Dust* was also recycled in 1940 as *Congo Maisie*.) b & w

Red-Headed Woman (1932)—Jean Harlow (with tinted hair) as a girl who exploits her charms and makes the climb from the wrong side of the tracks to a rich marriage and then up higher and higher. She's a smart cookie, and the picture, written by Anita Loos (based on a novel by Katherine Brush), is tough and funny. It caused a scandal in the movie industry, because she didn't suffer for her sins. Directed by Jack Conway. With Chester Morris, Leila Hyams, Una Merkel, Lewis Stone, Henry Stephenson, May Robson, and briefly, Charles Boyer. M-G-M. b & w

The Red Inn   *L'auberge rouge* (1951)—A popular macabre comedy, rather like a more refined French equivalent of *Arsenic and Old Lace* and *The Old Dark House*. Set in 1833 in the Ardèche Mountains, the story is about a group of travellers in a public carriage who take refuge in a remote inn. Fernandel plays a licentious monk who hears confession from the innkeeper's wife (Françoise Rosay); she nonchalantly reveals that all guests who come to the inn are robbed and murdered, and he sets about the task of getting the guests to leave, without violating the confessional. This Claude Autant-Lara film, from a script by Jean Aurenche and Pierre Bost, is generally considered to be a highly sophisticated satire, but it isn't really as funny as one might wish. With Julien Carette as the innkeeper, Grégoire Aslan, and Marie-Claire Olivia. In French. b & w

Red River (1948)—A magnificent horse opera—one of the more elaborate celebrations of those trail-blazing episodes that Hollywood used to glorify as "historical events"—this time it's the mid-19th-century first cattle drive up the Chisholm Trail. (The cattle in this production are not to be passed over lightly: they are impressive and they were very expensive. 6,000 head were rented at $10 a day each—and then it rained and rained while the cattle waited and the film's cost rose from $1,750,000 to $3,200,000. Figures like that help make a movie an epic.) The director, Howard Hawks, structures the drive as an exciting series of stampedes, Indian battles, and gunfights, with a ferocious climax in the fight between the two principals—John Wayne, as the father, and Montgomery Clift, as the adopted son. A lot of it is just terrible, but Clift—in his most aggressively sexual screen performance—is angular and tense and audacious, and the other actors brawl amusingly in the strong-silent-man tradition. Russell Harlan's photography makes the rolling plains the true hero; the setting has epic grandeur. The screenplay is by Borden Chase and Charles Schnee, from Chase's story "The Chisholm Trail," but as Chase admitted, it's actually *Mutiny on the Bounty* turned into a Western, with Wayne as Captain Bligh and Clift as Fletcher Christian. The cast includes Walter Brennan, Harry Carey, Coleen Gray, John Ireland, and frantic Joanne Dru, who acts as if the Old West were Greenwich Village. Music by Dmitri Tiomkin. United Artists. b & w

The Red Shoes (1948)—The most "imaginative" and elaborate backstage musical ever filmed, and many have called it great. The film contains a 14-minute ballet, also called "The Red Shoes," based on a Hans Christian Andersen story about a wicked shoemaker who sells an enchanted pair of slippers to a young girl. Delighted at first with the slippers in which she dances joyously, she discovers that the slippers will not let her stop dancing—and the bewitched, exhausted girl dies. The film's story is, of course, the same story, spelled out in more complicated terms, with the shoemaker of the ballet (Léonide Massine) replaced by the megalomaniac ballet impresario (Anton Walbrook). The exquisite young Moira Shearer is the ballerina; the cast includes Marius Goring as the young composer, Robert Helpmann, Albert Basserman, Ludmilla Tcherina, and Esmond Knight. Blubbery and self-conscious, but it affects some people *passionately*, and it's undeniably some kind of classic. Written, produced, and directed by Michael Powell and Emeric Pressburger—master purveyors of high kitsch. Choreography by Helpmann; music by Brian Easdale; conducted by Sir Thomas Beecham. color

Reds (1981)—Warren Beatty, who was the producer, the director, and the co-writer (with Trevor Griffiths), also plays the hero, the American journalist John Reed, who took part in the Bolshevik Revolution and wrote *Ten Days That Shook the World*. Diane Keaton plays Reed's wife, the independent-minded Louise Bryant. The film, which runs 3 hours and 27 minutes, is conceived as a love story set against a background of bohemian living and revolutionary fervor. But the writers didn't work out a scrutable character for Louise. In the first half, she's presented as a tiresome, pettishly hostile, dissatisfied woman, and the film moves on the messy currents of sexual politics. In the second half, she is made to set off on a (fictitious) dangerous journey to go to Reed, who has been imprisoned in Finland; she makes her way across the icy tundra in scenes that seem to belong to a different picture (something Zhivagooey), and then the film embraces her, because she's doing what a woman is supposed to do—go through any hardship to be

with her man. This second half moves more swiftly but with conventional epic situations and very familiar visual rhetoric. Beatty is often touching, and he does some of the best acting he has ever done, but he doesn't let his energy come through; he plays so much on what the audience responds to in him—the all-American combination of innocence and earnestness—that he's in danger of turning into Li'l Abner. The subject—the romantic life of an American Communist—may be daring, but the moviemaking is extremely traditional, with Beatty playing a man who dies for an ideal. It's rather a sad movie, because it isn't really very good. With Jack Nicholson as Eugene O'Neill, and Gene Hackman, Paul Sorvino, the novelist Jerzy Kosinski as Zinoviev, Edward Herrmann, and Max Wright. Best of all: Maureen Stapleton as Emma Goldman, and a group of contemporaries of the Reeds (e.g., Rebecca West, Henry Miller, Dora Russell), who appear in documentary interviews as "witnesses." Academy Awards: Best Director, Supporting Actress (Stapleton), Cinematography (Vittorio Storaro). Paramount. color (See *Taking It All In*.)

Reflections in a Golden Eye (1967)—John Huston directed this sensuous and intense version of Carson McCullers' Georgia-set short novel of 1941; the visual style, which suggests paintings made from photographs, has a measured lyricism. The movie doesn't find a way to give us the emotional texture of the interrelationships and dependencies in the book (one can probably enjoy the film much more if one knows the book) but the principal actors (Marlon Brando, Brian Keith, Elizabeth Taylor, Julie Harris) were able to do some startling things with their roles. The stifled homosexuality of Brando's duty-bound Major Penderton is grotesque and painful. This is one of Brando's most daring performances: the fat, ugly Major putting cold cream on his face, or preening at the mirror, or patting his hair nervously when he thinks he has a gentleman caller is so pitiful yet so ghastly that some members of the audience invariably cut themselves off from him by laughter. Taylor is charming as the Major's silly, ardent, Southern-"lady" wife, who makes love to Keith in a berry patch. Keith, underplaying, has one of his rare opportunities to show depth; at moments he seems the most *believable* of actors—these are great moments. The movie is most garishly novelistic just when it departs most from McCullers—when it attempts to clarify the original and bring it up to date, which means bringing in the sexual platitudes that in 60s movies were considered Freudian modernism. The story has been furbished with *additional* fetishes, as if McCullers' material weren't Southern and gothic enough. The Major's wife gives him a horsewhipping and then explains that the whipping cleared the air; we are cued to crank out the Freudian explanation "Oh, yes, he wanted to be beaten." With Robert Forster and Zorro David. The script is by Chapman Mortimer and Gladys Hill; the offensive score is by Toshiro Mayuzumi; the cinematography is by Aldo Tonti. The first release prints were in a "desaturated" color process—they were golden hued, with delicate sepia and pink tones; when the movie didn't do well at box offices, this stylized color was blamed, full-color prints were substituted, and the film lost its dreamy, mythic ambiance. The picture's bad luck was capped when it was condemned by the National Catholic Office for Motion Pictures. A Ray Stark Production for Warner–Seven Arts.

Regain, see *Harvest*

La Règle du jeu, see *The Rules of the Game*

The Reivers (1969)—Nostalgic, affectionate Southern Americana out of Faulkner; the style is a little too "beguiling" but it's an awfully pleasant comedy anyway. When Ned McCaslin (Rupert Crosse), Negro kin to a white family, who hasn't learned to drive, takes the family's gleaming new 1905 Winton Flyer on a wild course through town (Jefferson, Mississippi), you may be afraid that you'll be embarrassed by what happens. But when the car comes to a halt, the family's white handyman and official chauffeur, Boon (Steve McQueen), is so beside himself with rage at Ned for endangering the car that he wants to kill him—he starts punching away at Ned without the slightest condescension. In the central story, Ned and Boon and another McCaslin, 12-year-old Lucius (Mitch Vogel), steal that same yellow Winton Flyer—a dream of a car—for a trip to Memphis, the nearest sin city. Rupert Crosse's Ned, who has a snaggle-toothed grin, is supremely likable; he seems to skip through life without a care—he's like a living, walking sense of humor. McQueen is ingratiating and Sharon Farrell plays his harlot bride-to-be with a nice pungency. Ruth White is the madam of a Memphis whorehouse and the great Juano Hernández turns up as Uncle Possum. When the director, Mark Rydell, isn't sure how to do things, he overdoes them; at times the picture seems to be rogue Disney. It's certainly rollicking enough without the score's constantly reminding us to appreciate how darling everything is. But the script, by Irving Ravetch and Harriet Frank, Jr., has great charm, though the narration, by Burgess Meredith, in a jocular-avuncular style, is dismaying—and the fiction that his voice belongs to Lucius as a grown man is just silly. (We all recognize Meredith's lyrical scratchiness.) With Will Geer, Clifton James, Vinette Carroll, Michael Constantine, John McLiam, Dub Taylor, Diane Ladd, and Allyn

Ann McLerie. Released by National General. color (See *Deeper into Movies*.)

Rembrandt (1936)—Perhaps because Charles Laughton's performance lacked the crowd-pleasing exuberance of his other major roles, the picture was not a commercial success, though it's a fine example of its genre and was obviously made (by Alexander Korda) with love and dedication. At times, the visual style seems more Vermeer than Rembrandt, but that's closer than most movies about painters get. Gertrude Lawrence plays the artist's shrewd housekeeper, and lovely young Elsa Lanchester is the kitchenmaid who becomes his mistress. Also with Roger Livesey, Marius Goring, John Clements, Gertrude Musgrove, and Raymond Huntley. Korda produced and directed; his brother Vincent was the art director; the script involved Karl Zuckmayer, Lajos Biro, and others; the cinematography was by Georges Périnal and Richard Angst, with Robert Krasker as camera operator. b & w

Remember the Day (1941)—Claudette Colbert, wearing glasses and walking with a stoop, is the elderly schoolteacher who attends a banquet honoring a former pupil, now a candidate for the Presidency (John Shepperd, otherwise known as Shepperd Strudwick). Then we swing back to the days when the candidate was a child in her schoolroom and she was a young beauty, in love with the gym director (John Payne), who went off to war and was killed. No doubt Tess Slesinger and her husband, Frank Davis, who worked on the script along with Allan Scott, hoped for a sensitive treatment of a working woman's life, but the film came out swathed in a reverential sentiment. It's fairly awful—your basic fantasy about an unmarried schoolteacher's romantic youth. Henry King directed; with Anne Revere, Frieda Inescort,

Chick Chandler, George Chandler, and the child actress Ann Todd. 20th Century-Fox. b & w

Renaldo & Clara (1978)—Bob Dylan made this 3-hour-and-52-minute film, which was mostly shot during a Bicentennial (1975–76) tour. (The show was called the "Rolling Thunder Revue.") The performance footage is handsomely photographed, but it doesn't build up the excitement that one can sometimes feel at a performance film, because the movie keeps cutting away from the stage to *cinéma-vérité* fantasies of Dylan's life, which occupy more than two-thirds of the running time. Dylan has given himself more tight closeups than any actor can have had in the whole history of movies. color (See *When the Lights Go Down*.)

Repo Man (1984)—The L.A. of freeways and off ramps and squarish pastel-colored buildings that could be anything and could turn into something else overnight is the perfect setting for a movie about men who take out their frustrations by repossessing other people's cars. This low-budget fantasy gives you the feeling that you've gone past alienation into the land of detachment—a punkers' wasteland where you never know where you are, and nobody cares to make things work, and everybody you see is part of the lunatic fringe. The film takes off from Godard's *Weekend*, with (probably) some help from Aldrich's *Kiss Me Deadly* and Zemeckis and Gale's *Used Cars*, but its catatonic, shoofly humor is all its own. The young English writer-director Alex Cox keeps his dazed sociopaths speeding around—always on the periphery. There's nothing at the center. He has underhand ways of being funny, and the jokes don't often jump out at you—sometimes they barely peek out at all, because of the film's ramshackle ineptness. But the whole comic atmosphere of druggy burnout gets to you, and Cox never once slips—he never lets things get sentimentalized or organized. With Harry Dean Stanton, Emilio Estevez, Tracey Walter as the acidhead philosopher, Vonetta McGee as Marlene, and Fox Harris as a lobotomized scientist (who drives a 1964 Chevy Malibu, with a metallic gold paint job). Robby Müller's cinematography sustains the flat grunginess of the conception; so does a song by the L.A. group The Circle Jerks. Produced by Michael Nesmith; released by Universal. color (See *State of the Art*.)

Report to the Commissioner (1975)—Another entry in the *French Connection* sweepstakes, smartened up with the newer *Serpico* theme, but to no avail. It's a slovenly production, and the suspense never gets going. Michael Moriarty plays the hippie undercover detective destroyed by his blundering, callous superiors in the New York City Police Department. Moriarty is required to fall apart at the end, but he can't wait for the climactic collapse, and he begins disintegrating before you've settled in your seat. With Yaphet Kotto, giving a respectable performance, against all odds, and a twittering blond ingenue, Susan Blakely, who is supposed to be a hotshot narc. Adapted from James Mills' novel; directed by Milton Katselas; score by Elmer Bernstein. With Hector Elizondo, Bob Balaban, and Tony King; cinematography by Mario Tosi. United Artists. color (See *Reeling*.)

Repulsion (1965)—Roman Polanski's British-made, London-set horror film records the deterioration of a murderous, terrified Belgian girl, played by Catherine Deneuve. The script, by Polanski and Gérard Brach, seems completely shaped for the camera; the approach is so objective, so external, that the film doesn't raise questions about this foreign girl's estrangement and loneliness, doesn't offer explanations of her madness. It just stays on her—on her hallucinations and her fantasies of being in danger, and on the actual reprisals she takes against anyone who comes her way. It's clinical Grand Guignol, and the camera fondles the horrors: the high spot is a man being slashed in the face with a straight razor—until he's cut to death. (If you're too scared to look you still hear the slashing sounds.) Undeniably skillful and effective, all right—excruciatingly tense and frightening. But is it entertaining? You have to be a hardcore horror-movie lover to enjoy this one. With Yvonne Furneaux, John Fraser, Ian Hendry, Patrick Wymark, Renée Houston, James Villiers, and Polanski in a bit. Music by Chico Hamilton; cinematography by Gilbert Taylor. b & w

Resurrection (1931)—Serious, stupefying version of Tolstoy's novel, featuring the stolid musical-comedy singer John Boles and the Mexican spitfire comedienne Lupe Velez. Boles' speaking voice never changes its mellow tone throughout, but Siberia seems to agree with Velez; she does a little acting and looks radiant. Directed by Edwin Carewe. Universal. b & w

Resurrection (1980)—Ellen Burstyn dies, has an ''out of body'' experience, then returns with the gift of healing through the power of love. The picture is even and smoothly tasteful—a vat of non-denominational caramel custard. Lewis John Carlino was commissioned to write the script for Burstyn, and he shaped it to her; she bestrides the movie, glowing with love and wholesome humor. (Her simulation of beatific ordinariness is a little frightening.) The director, Daniel Petrie, does some very polished, fluid work, but you're always aware of the planning and calculation. Mysticism doesn't come easy to him. Carlino's script, which attempts to combine holistic healing and feminism, is an amazing fusion of old corn and modern cant. With Sam Shepard, who brings the film some sexy tension as a hell-raising kid whom Burstyn heals after he has been stabbed in a drunken fight, and Richard Farnsworth, Roberts Blossom, Lois Smith, Madeleine Thornton-Sherwood, and Pamela Payton-Wright. And as Burstyn's grandmother, Eva Le Gallienne wrinkles her nose and lifts her head so she can look out of her half-blind eyes, and she spouts homilies as if she'd lived her whole life onstage. Cinematography by Mario Tosi; music by Maurice Jarre. Universal. color (See *Taking It All In*.)

Le Retour de Don Camillo, see *The Little World of Don Camillo*

The Return of a Man Called Horse (1976)— The stirring early Westerns had a narrative push forward, a belief in the future of a people. That epic spirit—understandably missing from most 70s Westerns—came back in a new form in this surprising film; here, the surge of elation comes from the spiritual rebirth of an Indian tribe. The hero is John Morgan, an English lord, played by Richard Harris. In *A Man Called Horse* (1970), directed by Elliot Silverstein, Morgan was captured by the Yellow Hand, a tribe of the Sioux nation; he was accepted as a brother, and free, chose to return to his own country. This sequel, directed by Irvin Kershner, shows that Morgan, once having known that brotherhood and accepted its magical religion, is lost as a white man; when he's in his English mansion he's split off from the life around him—his soul has become Indian. The early part of the film, which cuts from an attack on the Yellow Hand to a foxhunt in England, has an emotional power that is almost comparable to that of the early scenes of *The Godfather Part II*. Later, there's a memorable sequence with the dark shapes of buffalo running over blinding

pale-green meadows. Despite a pulpy script (by Jack DeWitt) and a lot of awkward, unconvincing acting, this Western, with its Old Testament mysticism, which appears to be authentically Indian as well, is a startling affirmative vision. (When Morgan and some of the Indian children take on themselves the burden of suffering, the mutilation scene is very powerful but it's not disgusting, because you can see how the rituals work in the lives of the people. This sequence has been cut from some prints, though it's vital to the story.) Harris comes through with a strong— and often subtle—performance, especially in his early scenes. With Gale Sondergaard (overacting), Geoffrey Lewis, Claudio Brook, and Enrique Lucero as Raven. Music by Laurence Rosenthal; cinematography by Owen Roizman. United Artists. color

Return of the Jedi (1983)—Some of the trick effects in this concluding film of the *Star Wars* trilogy might seem miraculous if the imagery had any luster, but this is an impersonal and rather junky piece of moviemaking. It's packed with torture scenes, and it bangs away at you. And every time there's a possibility of a dramatic climax—a chance to engage the audience emotionally with something awesome—the director Richard Marquand trashes it. In *The Empire Strikes Back*, the three central figures seemed capable of real exhilaration and real suffering. Here, they're back to being what they were in the first film—comic-strip characters wandering through a jokey pastiche of the Arthurian legends. But children who have lived their imaginative lives with the Star Wars characters may be so eager to get the payoffs to the story that they'll hardly notice. And they'll probably be charmed by some of the new characters, especially the tribe of potbellied woodland creatures, the furry, cuddly Ewoks, who suggest a cross between koala bears and puli dogs—they're like living

Teddy bears. With Mark Hamill, Carrie Fisher, Harrison Ford, Billy Dee Williams, Anthony Daniels as C-3PO, and Peter Mayhew as Chewbacca. A Lucasfilm, from a screenplay by Lawrence Kasdan and Lucas, based on Lucas's story; music by John Williams. Released by 20th Century-Fox. color (See *Taking It All In*.)

The Return of the Soldier (1982)—Adapted by Hugh Whitemore, and directed by Alan Bridges, this film version of Rebecca West's first novel, published in 1918, when she was 25, isn't great or exciting, but it's very enjoyable. With its re-creation of an era when Freudianism was new, it's like a piece of intellectual history, and it gives you the feeling that you sometimes get when you read an "advanced" novel of the 20s and are touched and charmed by its streamlined Victorianism. Julie Christie, Glenda Jackson, and Ann-Margret play the three women who love the shell-shocked amnesiac Captain Chris Baldry (Alan Bates), who has forgotten the last 20 years of his life, and regressed to the time of his greatest joy. The conflict is: Should he be allowed to remain in his boyish state of happiness, or should he be forced to confront the truth? Julie Christie is a ravishing camera subject who knows how to use her beauty against herself—as Chris's wife, she's so outrageously vain that she's funny. Glenda Jackson takes Rebecca West's literary conception of an instinctual, loving woman and plays it with an ease and leanness that's fairly astounding. Ann-Margret has a thankless role, but her bone structure has an aristocratic quality, and she acquits herself with likable dignity. And in a role that could seem ludicrous Alan Bates has a weight and an aura of middle-aged bewilderment that you don't laugh off. The dated modernity of the novel is faithfully reproduced, and it's a fascinating reminder that it has only been a few decades since Freud and Victoria walked arm in arm:

in this material, Chris's return to reality doesn't mean learning what his repressed feelings are and freeing himself from a dead marriage—it means going back to being a proper husband and a good soldier. The cast includes Ian Holm, Frank Finlay, and Jeremy Kemp. Cinematography by Stephen Goldblatt; music by Richard Rodney Bennett; production design by Luciana Arrighi; costume design by Shirley Russell. color (See *State of the Art*.)

The Revolt of Mamie Stover (1956)—William Bradford Huie's novel *The Revolt of Mamie Stover* had to do with a woman who, after being tossed out of San Francisco, went on to Honolulu and put sex on an assembly-line basis. But the studio executives, who in the 50s were still trying to comply with the provisions of the Production Code, sometimes produced outlandish stories. The film Mamie (Jane Russell) is a poor, misguided kid who wants to make a lot of money to impress the folks back home in Mississippi. When she gets to the islands, she decides that she will join a pal in a dime-a-dance joint. The place is a little raucous, but nothing untoward ever happens to the danseuses. Even so, they are looked down upon by everybody. Mamie, though, manages to cultivate a well-bred writer (Richard Egan), who has a fine home on a hill in Oahu, and she also manages to save a huge packet of cash from her commissions on dancing. When Pearl Harbor is attacked, the writer is taken off to war, and Mamie promises she won't dance anymore but will wait for him stolidly. The lure of money is too much for her, however, and shortly after his departure she's dancing all over the place again. When he returns, he renounces her, and she comes to the realization that money isn't everything and as she can never take up residence with him on his tony hilltop she wends her lonely way back to Mississippi. This synopsis is provided in

R

the event you don't make it to the end—you might be called away to perform delicate heart surgery. Egan gives a performance that would be memorably bad if only one could remember it; with Joan Leslie, Agnes Moorehead, and Michael Pate. The director, Raoul Walsh, seems baffled and eager to get home for dinner; the script is by Sidney Boehm. Produced by Buddy Adler, for 20th Century-Fox. color

Revolution (1985)—Everything in this picture, which goes from the beginning of the American War of Independence in 1776 to the end of combat in 1783, seems dissociated. The director, Hugh Hudson, plunges us into gritty, muddy restagings of famous campaigns, but we don't find out what's going on in these campaigns, or what their importance is in the course of the war. As Tom Dobb, a Glasgow-born fur trader from the Adirondack wilderness who turns guerrilla fighter, Al Pacino wears 18th-century homespun and talks with a Scots accent but in the rhythms of the Bronx. Nastassja Kinski (Daisy McConnahay is her name here, and Joan Plowright is her mother) assists at field amputations and runs supply wagons through redcoat lines, but she seems hectic and feverish and keeps oozing tears. Hudson and the scriptwriter, Robert Dillon, present the war as a primal Oedipal revolt of the Colonies against the parent country, and the relationships of the characters are designed in Oedipal pairs; Hudson also stages torture orgies to indicate how sadistic the redcoats are, and scenes are devised to set up echoes of the *Rocky* series and *Rambo*. This is a certifiably loony picture; it's so bad it puts you in a state of shock. With Donald Sutherland, sporting a big, black, hairy mole on his jowl, as a redcoat sergeant major who's a sexual psychopath; and Annie Lennox, Sid Owen as Tom's young son Ned, and Dexter Fletcher as Ned grown up. Filmed in England. An

Irwin Winkler Production; released in the U.S. by Warners. color (See *Hooked*.)

Rich and Famous (1981)—Twenty years in the lives of two women writers, pals from their college days. Bland Jacqueline Bisset is the "modern" artist—perpetually dissatisfied, self-conscious, hard-drinking. Candice Bergen is the gusher—as a housewife and mother, she writes a roman à clef about her Malibu Colony neighbors, and then she just keeps pouring out her fantasies and getting richer and richer. Bisset is unvaringly intense; she reads her puffed-up lines straight, and all with the same intonation. If she doesn't know that the picture is a comedy, this may be because Gerald Ayres, who wrote the script, seems to mean everything she says. (Her character is intended to be fearfully intelligent.) Bergen is much the livelier, but her caricature of a shallow bitch is too busy; she's a good sport rather than an actress, though she probably does as much for the role as anybody could. This remake of the 1943 film *Old Acquaintance* (which was based on John van Druten's 1940 play) isn't camp, exactly; it's more like a homosexual fantasy. Bisset's affairs with young men are creepy, because they don't seem like what a woman would get into. And Bergen is used almost as if she were a big, goosey female impersonator. Directed by George Cukor, this movie has an unflagging pace, but it's full of scenes that don't play, and often you can't even tell what tone was hoped for. It's a tawdry self-parody. With David Selby, Hart Bochner, Steven Hill, Matt Lattanzi, Fay Kanin, and Michael Brandon, who makes an uncredited appearance as the man who has sex with Bisset in an airplane washroom. Among the guests in the party scenes are Christopher Isherwood, Don Bachardy, Roger Vadim, Paul Morrissey, Ray Bradbury, Nina Foch, and Gavin Lambert. M-G-M. color (See *Taking It All In*.)

Richard Pryor Live in Concert (1979)—Probably the greatest of all recorded-performance films. Pryor has characters and voices bursting out of him. He personifies objects, animals, people, the warring parts of his own body, even thoughts in the heads of men and women—black, white, Oriental; when he tells us about his heart attack, he is, in almost the same instant, the helpless body being double-crossed by its heart, the heart itself, a telephone operator, and Pryor the aloof, dissociated observer. Watching this mysteriously original physical comedian you can't account for his gift and everything he does seems to be for the first time. The film retains the impetus of a live performance. Directed by Jeff Margolis. color

Richard Pryor Live on the Sunset Strip (1982)—The master of physical comedy and lyrical obscenity in a one-man show. To those of us who thought his 1979 film, *Richard Pryor Live in Concert*, was one of the greatest performances we'd ever seen or ever will see, it may be disappointing yet emotionally stirring. That earlier movie made him a legend, and the vast public outpouring of affection for him after his near-fatal accident in June, 1980, when (as he acknowledges here) the dope he was freebasing exploded and set him on fire, has changed him and his relation with the audience. He knows that all he has to do is stand on the stage and be adored. And he knows there's something the matter with this new situation, but he doesn't know how to deal with it. This film isn't in the class of the first, but it has superb bits. Produced by Ray Stark; directed by Joe Layton; cinematography by Haskell Wexler. Columbia. color (See *Taking It All In*.)

Richard III (1956)—Laurence Olivier makes Shakespeare's "son of hell" such a magnetic, chilling, amusing monster that the villainy arouses an almost immoral delight. As director and star, Olivier succeeds with the soliloquies as neither he nor anyone else ever did on film before; they're intimate, yet brazen. If the film were all malevolent crookback Richard, it would be a marvel; unfortunately, he was plagued with quantities of associates and relations, and even when impersonated by Ralph Richardson, John Gielgud, Cedric Hardwicke, etc., they're a dull lot. The William Walton score is unimaginative, and the Book-of-Hours camera setups decompose into common calendar art. But none of this matters very much when you can watch Olivier's lewd courtship of Claire Bloom and hear the inflections he gives lines like "I am not in the giving vein today." With Stanley Baker, Norman Wooland, Pamela Brown, Alec Clunes, Nicholas Hannen, Laurence Naismith, John Laurie, Helen Haye, Michael Gough, and Esmond Knight. Produced by Alexander Korda and Olivier; the adaptation is by Olivier and Alan Dent; the design and costumes are by Carmen Dillon and Roger Furse; the cinematography is by Otto Heller. color

The Richest Girl in the World (1934)—Miriam Hopkins is the rich girl who is wary of fortune hunters; so she persuades her secretary, Fay Wray, to swap places with her whenever they're in public. Joel McCrea is the young man who falls crazily in love with Miriam, but thinks he'd better be practical and go after Fay. This surprisingly sexy romantic comedy has been almost forgotten. It's not exactly a classic but it's pretty nifty. Hopkins was still in her most seductive phase; this was made just a couple of years after *Trouble in Paradise*, and she has her distinctive flash and wit. With Reginald Denny, Henry Stephenson, George Meeker, and Beryl Mercer as the maid. Directed by William A. Seiter, from a story and script by Norman Krasna. The cinematography is by Nick Musuraca; the music is by Max Steiner. Produced by Pandro S. Berman, for R K O. b & w

Ride in the Whirlwind (1965)—Monte Hellman directed this film and *The Shooting* in Utah during a seven-week period on a budget of $160,000 (from Roger Corman) for both. Jack Nicholson, who acts in both, was also Hellman's co-producer, and wrote the script for this one. The cast includes Millie Perkins and Cameron Mitchell, and the story has something to do with three cowboys on the run—a metaphysical run. The picture was a critical success in Paris, but Hellman (he later made *Two-Lane Blacktop*) bakes the Western in the sun too long for most Americans. Maybe the person who wrote the subtitles in the French version added something to the austerity and the bleak riddles. color

Ride the High Country (1962)—Perhaps the most simple and traditional and graceful of all modern Westerns. Sam Peckinpah's small (and humane) classic is unassuming, and its elegiac poetry is plainer than that of Altman's *McCabe & Mrs. Miller*, although the emotional complexity is comparable. That unpublicized fine actor Joel McCrea plays a former marshal who gets a job transporting gold; he signs up another former lawman, Randolph Scott, who has been working as a carnival sharpshooter, to help him. In the film's most astonishing and original sequence, the marriage of an innocent young girl (Mariette Hartley) takes place in a brothel in a mining camp, and the terrified bride realizes that the groom's brothers expect to share her; McCrea and Scott help her escape. In the film's most memorable single image, the old Westerner (McCrea) sinks to the bottom of the frame to die. The cinematography is by Lucien Ballard at his peerless best. M-G-M. CinemaScope, color

Ride the Pink Horse (1947)—One of a kind; no one in his right mind would imitate it. Starting from a novel by Dorothy B. Hughes, Ben Hecht and Charles Lederer concocted this baroque folly about gangsters in the Southwest. Some of the characters speak standard-Hollywood broken English in order to convey the information that they're Mexican; the hero, Robert Montgomery (who also directed), speaks in a tough-guy lingo that isn't just broken—it's smashed. He says of a woman he doesn't like, "She has a dead fish where her heart ought to be." This doesn't quite satisfy him, and he expands the idea. "A dead fish," he goes on, "with a bit of perfume on it." That may be cruel to the woman, but it's a fair summary of the picture. Wanda Hendrix, in dark makeup, gets a ride on a merry-go-round, thus giving the film its inappropriate title. But nothing else would have been appropriate either. With Thomas Gomez, Fred Clark, and Andrea King. Produced by Joan Harrison, for Universal. b & w

Riffraff (1935)—Jean Harlow and Spencer Tracy as cocky working-class people in love, and Joseph Calleia as the wily Greek who runs the tuna fleet and the cannery. Anita Loos was on the script, and the wisecracks fly, but the direction (by J. Walter Ruben) is weak. M-G-M produced, and the corporate hand is clearly visible: the labor troubles are the result of an outside agitator who comes in with bombs. The film might be used as an index to Hollywood-movie social attitudes of the period. b & w

Rififi *Du Rififi chez les hommes* (1955)—A quartet of thieves breaks into a jewelry store, and for a tense half-hour we watch as they work, silently. It is like a highly skilled documentary on how to disconnect a burglar alarm and open a safe, and it is thoroughly engrossing, because we see the criminals as craftsmen, and we celebrate their teamwork, their finesse, their triumph. Ironically, we find ourselves sympathizing with their honest exhaustion after their dishonest labor. From then on, this movie, made in France, by the American director Jules Dassin, follows the tradition of *Scarface, Public Enemy*, and *The Asphalt Jungle* (and of *Macbeth* before them), bringing the tragic, trapped figures (now symbols of our own antisocial impulses) to a cadaverous finish. Along the way, Dassin keeps things actively vicious, with glimpses of underworld prostitutes and hopheads and a murder, a kidnapping, and the thrashing of a faithless mistress, who is stripped. *Rififi* is the granddaddy of a batch of suspense films featuring how to knock over safes or break into banks and museums, but its own chief distinction is its nasty tone. With Jean Servais, Robert Manuel, Carl Mohner, and Dassin as the four; and Robert Hossein, Marie Sabouret, Magali Noel. In French. b & w

The Right Stuff (1983)—Based on Tom Wolfe's 1979 book, this often satirical epic—a re-enactment of the early years of the space program (1947–63)—gives off a pleasurable hum. The writer-director Philip Kaufman is working on a broad canvas and it excites him—it tickles him. The movie has the happy, enthusiastic spirit of a fanfare, and it's astonishingly entertaining considering how divided it is in spirit. It contrasts Chuck Yeager (Sam Shepard) and the other early test pilots who risk their lives in secrecy with the seven publicly acclaimed astronauts who replace the chimps that were sent up in the first American space capsules. The movie is more than a little skewed: it's Kaufman's—and Tom Wolfe's—dreamy vision of the nonchalant Yeager and a past that never was set against a comic view of the modern hype-bound world. Then, it turns out, the astronauts are not quite the square-jawed mannikins they pretend to be; they're phony

only on the outside. But whatever one's reservations, the film is great fun to watch. The action zigzags from old-movie romance to cock-eyed buffoonery to the courage (and exaltation) of men alone in tiny capsules orbiting the earth at 18,000 miles an hour. And Kaufman doesn't take the bloom off space by knocking us silly with the grandeur of it all. With Dennis Quaid, who has a devilish kid's smile, with his upper lip a straight line across his face, as Gordon Cooper; the pale-eyed Ed Harris as John Glenn; Fred Ward as Gus Grissom; and Scott Glenn, Pamela Reed, Veronica Cartwright, Mary Jo Deschanel (as Annie Glenn), Jeff Goldblum, Barbara Hershey, Levon Helm, Scott Wilson, Kim Stanley, Jane Dornacker, and many others, including Brigadier General Chuck Yeager as a bartender, Donald Moffat as Lyndon Johnson, and Robert Beer, who's an uncanny look-alike, as Eisenhower. (There are some pretty awful scenes featuring Royal Dano as a black-clad minister.) Cinematography by Caleb Deschanel; special visual effects by Jordan Belson. A Chartoff-Winkler Production, for the Ladd Company; released by Warners. color (See *State of the Art*.)

Rio Bravo (1959)—Howard Hawks directed this semi-satiric Western pastiche (mainly of old Hawks movies), with John Wayne as John T. Chance, Dean Martin as a drunk called Dude, Ricky Nelson as Colorado, Walter Brennan as Stumpy, and Angie Dickinson as Feathers. Jules Furthman and Leigh Brackett provided the script, Dmitri Tiomkin the score. Silly, but with zest; there are some fine action sequences, and the performers seem to be enjoying their roles. Warners. color

Rio Grande (1950)—In this John Ford Western, John Wayne is a lieutenant colonel in the cavalry and Maureen O'Hara is his estranged wife, whom he hasn't seen for 16 years; she arrives at the post he commands because their son (Claude Jarman, Jr.) is among the new recruits there. The action involves an Apache uprising, but the conflict is the emotional one between the colonel's sense of duty and his love of his wife; Wayne and O'Hara are very effective together, so that the viewer deeply wants the final reconciliation. The script is by James Kevin McGuinness, based on James Warner Bellah's *Mission with No Record*. With Ben Johnson, Harry Carey, Jr., Victor McLaglen, Chill Wills, J. Carrol Naish, Grant Withers, and the Sons of the Pioneers as the regimental singers. Republic. b & w

Rio Lobo (1970)—There's a lot of chatter and not much conviction or feeling for the period (the Civil War and after) in this undistinguished Western, made late in the careers of Howard Hawks and John Wayne. The plot requires Wayne to rout a bunch of bad guys who have taken over Rio Lobo, down in Texas. Hawks could sometimes redeem routine material by fresh performances, but he doesn't seem to get with it this time. The picture is lackadaisical, with tiresome (and demeaning) jokes about Wayne's age and girth, a spoofy tone, and sudden bursts of violence. The women are Shasta, played by Jennifer O'Neill, who gets to act like a tomboy daredevil, and Amelita, played by Sherry Lansing, who gets to shampoo her hair and weep a lot and have her face cut by a sadistic villain. It's hard to remember anything the men do; the cast includes Jack Elam, Jorge Rivero, David Huddleston, Chris Mitchum, Victor French, Mike Henry, Bob Steele, and George Plimpton. The script, which suggests a weary rehash of *Rio Bravo* and *El Dorado*, was written by Burton Wohl and Leigh Brackett. A Malabar Production, for National General. color

Rio Rita (1942)—For masochists. They get the works in this one: Kathryn Grayson shrill-ing her songs from that quivering heart-shaped mouth, John Carroll acting virile, and Abbott and Costello acting funny. S. Sylvan Simon directed this pitiful version of a good old musical show. M-G-M. b & w

Riot (1969)—Though made by whites, this is one of the first of the films shaped to exploit the anger of the black audience. Based on Frank Elli's book and partly shot in the State Penitentiary in Florence, Arizona, with the warden and the inmates in many of the roles, it stars Jim Brown (his character is virtue incarnate), who is in almost every scene, outwitting the weak and/or sadistic whites. The plotting of the action is poor, but Brown's easy manner has its humorous charm. With Gene Hackman, and Ben Carruthers as a psychotic Indian. Buzz Kulik directed. Paramount. color

Risky Business (1983)—At 17, the high-school-boy hero (Tom Cruise) is equally worried about what college he'll get into and when and how he'll make out with a girl. When his parents go off on a week's vacation and he's left alone in their expensive ersatz-Colonial house on the North Shore of Chicago, he phones for the services of a call girl named Lana (Rebecca De Mornay). Up until her arrival, he is desperate, horny, and ingratiating; imagining himself a rock star dancing, he's a charmingly clunky dynamo. But once Lana glides in, the pictures shifts into an enamelled dreamtime; it gets a vacuous soft-core porno look, and everything is dark and slightly unreal. The movie aims to be hypnotically sexy while satirizing the materialistic values of the affluent. The boy grows up sexually, and financially, too, when the purringly seductive Lana turns him into a pimp and his home into a bordello. There's a stale cuteness in the idea; it's like a George Bernard Shaw play rewritten for a cast of ducks and geese. Directing his first feature, the screenwriter Paul Brickman is overdeliberate, and his control is so tight that there are no incidental pleasures—there's nothing but the one thin situation. De Mornay's Lana is the only person left with any trace of individuality; she's mysterious, supple—a golden blonde with an inward-directed smile, like Veronica Lake, but taller and with a greater range of expressiveness. With Joe Pantoliano, Nicholas Pryor, and Richard Masur. The jangling electronic mood music is by Tangerine Dream. Warners. color (See *State of the Art*.)

The River (1951)—Jean Renoir's first color film, made in India, in English, was adapted from Rumer Godden's novel about a British family in India and shot along the banks of the Ganges by Renoir's great cinematographer nephew, Claude Renoir. It's a poetic study of the contact of two civilizations. Renoir does not usurp the position of an insider; he sees India with western eyes—eyes so sensitive and highly trained that his vision of India is a mythic poem set in the midst of the Indian river of life. This river encompasses death (the Goddess Kali episode, the holy cobra that kills the child) in a way that American audiences tend to find disturbing. Rumer Godden's themes and story line are part of the texture, interwoven with the ritual feasts, the festivals, the rhythms of native music, and some people, accustomed to films edited for dramatic crescendo, dislike the serene flow—so much is going on that they feel nothing happens. There are static patches of dialogue, and some of the casting is questionable, but the theme (outsiders in a culture) meshes perfectly with the director's own position as a moviemaker in India, and visually the film is serenely yet passionately beautiful. With the dancer Radha, Nora Swinburne, Esmond Knight, Adrienne Corri, Patricia Walter, Arthur Shields, and Thomas Breen. Adapted by Renoir and Rumer Godden.

River's Edge (1987)—Teen-age anomie and the indifference of selfish, corrupt adults. The subject might suggest a movie made for TV if it weren't for the explicitly sexual pulp elements and the woozy poetry. The script, by Neal Jiminez, which takes off from an incident in Milpitas, California, in 1981, appears to have been conceived as an exploitation melodrama, but the director, Tim Hunter, has a fuzzy, naturalistic approach, and the movie is a slack mixture of "important" and mediocre—a blur that viewers can project onto. Big-bellied John (Daniel Roebuck), a high-school pothead, strangles his girlfriend, Jamie, and leaves her lying nude on the riverbank. Soon all the members of his pack of six or seven stoned kids have viewed their dead friend, but nobody speaks of notifying the authorities, because Layne (Crispin Glover), the high-strung leader of the group, pressures them to believe that it would be a violation of their code to let any adults know what happened. The movie doesn't deal with the facts of the Milpitas case. It tells us next to nothing about why John killed Jamie and shows us very little of how the other kids react to her death. Then this vacancy at the heart of the film is used as proof of the kids' heartlessness. Glover gives a weird, grimacing, hand-waving performance; other garish elements include Dennis Hopper as a one-legged ex-biker dope dealer who waltzes with an inflatable sex doll and Joshua Miller as a malicious 12-year-old who drowns his baby sister's dolly. Also with Keanu Reeves, Ione Skye, and Jim Metzler as the teacher. Cinematography by Frederick Elmes. color (See *Hooked*.)

Road to Morocco (1942)—Maybe you have to have seen the Bob Hope–Bing Crosby road movies (comedies with songs and a lot of patter) when they came out to understand the affection people felt for them, and to appreciate how casually sophisticated the style seemed at the time. The pictures haven't weathered as well as 30s comedies, because they were satirizing melodramas that are already forgotten. The series spoofed the fancy backgrounds of adventure movies; Hope and Crosby ambled through exotic, nonsensical lighthearted situations with no pretense to believability. They took the thud out of the dumb gags and topical jokes by their amiable comic intimacy. And the rare good jokes shone in the unpretentious atmosphere. Hope and Crosby's rapport has great charm, and every once in a while Hope does something—a gesture or a dance movement—that is prodigiously funny. Dorothy Lamour is their joint inamorata and the foil of the series; inimitably out of it, she was taken over from the pictures being satirized, and she played in the same coy, eager-to-please manner. The best song here is "Moonlight Becomes You." David Butler directed; Frank Butler and Don Hartman did the script. Paramount. b & w

Road to Singapore (1940)—Bob Hope and Bing Crosby sauntering along, singing and playing innocent practical jokes, while Dorothy Lamour keeps house for them on a South Sea island. She wears an expression of intense domesticity, a trim sarong, and a hibiscus; a frown of chaste speculation darkens her brow when she must decide which of these two nice boys she will specifically love, honor, and obey. In spite of this problem of sentiment, it's a happy, unpretentious farce with Jerry Colonna—grinning, wild-eyed, and manic—and Charles Coburn. Directed by Victor Schertzinger; the oddball songs include "Sweet Potato Piper." Paramount. b & w

Road to Utopia (1946)—Perhaps the farthest out of the Bob Hope–Bing Crosby road pic-

tures. Some of the patter is pure, relaxed craziness, but the topical jokes (about Paramount Pictures, about Crosby's rivalry with Frank Sinatra, about Hope's radio sponsor, a toothpaste company) and the awful quips ("Don't be facetious." "Keep politics out of this.") keep pulling it down. In this one, the boys whoop around Alaska in search of a gold mine owned by Dorothy Lamour. Robert Benchley turns up but, unfortunately, he didn't write his own material. The songs include "Would You?" Hal Walker directed; Norman Panama and Melvin Frank did the script. Paramount. b & w

The Road Warrior (1982)—Set in a postapocalyptic Wasteland, this Australian film, a sequel to the 1979 *Mad Max* and known as *Mad Max 2* in other countries, is a mutant, sprung from virtually all action genres. George Miller, who directed, may have been content to make an openly sophomoric bash in *Mad Max*—it was a revenge fantasy turned into a futuristic cartoon—but this time he's in the mythmaking business. The film is one continuous spurt of energy, and the jangly, fast editing suggests wit; so does the broad blacktop highway that cuts across the desert nothingness. And the rampaging vandals—punkish post-nuclear-war bikers, led by a masked bodybuilder called the Humungus—are s-m comic-strip terrors; they menace the decent folk, in more barbarous and gaudier versions of the way the wild motorcyclists in Roger Corman pictures did. But the picture is abstract in an adolescent way. Miller's attempt to tap into the universal concept of the hero (as enunciated by Jung and explicated by Joseph Campbell in *The Hero with a Thousand Faces*) makes the film joyless. He consciously uses his hero, Max (Mel Gibson), as an icon; that's enough to squeeze the juice out of any actor, and Max seems bland and apathetic. There are perhaps 10 minutes of spectacular imagery, and if you think of

George Miller as one of the kinetic movie-makers, such as John Carpenter and George A. Romero, he's a giant, but he's pushing for more and he apparently doesn't see the limitations of the kind of material he's working with. For all its huffing and puffing, this is a sappy sentimental movie. With Bruce Spence as the stork-legged aviator and Vernon Wells as Wez; the script is by Terry Hayes and Miller, with Brian Hannant. (The third in the trilogy, *Mad Max Beyond Thunderdome*, was released in 1985.) color (See *Taking It All In*.)

The Roaring Twenties (1939)—The title and the names of the stars—James Cagney and Humphrey Bogart—make it sound like a lot more fun than it is. They play underprivileged kids who grow up together, come back from the First World War, and get into the rackets. The movie has a very mechanical and moralistic view of character; nobody ever says or does anything that surprises you. If you fed the earlier gangster movies into a machine and made a prototype, you'd come up with this picture. With Gladys George, Priscilla Lane, Paul Kelly, Jeffrey Lynn, Frank McHugh, and Elisabeth Risdon. Directed by Raoul Walsh, from a script by Jerry Wald, Richard Macaulay, and Robert Rossen, based on a Mark Hellinger story; produced by Hal B. Wallis. Warners. b & w

Robin and Marian (1976)—Sean Connery and Audrey Hepburn are wittily matched, and their dark-brown eyes of full of life, but the picture's revisionist approach to legends results in a series of trivializing attitudes and whimsical poses. As the Sheriff of Nottingham, Robert Shaw makes speeches about Robin Hood's death fixation, and Marian poisons herself and Robin because he's a fool who lives to fight. The line between tragic horror and joking make-believe has got smudged; the film is so sententious that it's difficult to gauge when to laugh and when

to be appalled. Richard Lester directed, from James Goldman's script; cinematography by David Watkin. With Nicol Williamson and Richard Harris. Columbia. color (See *When the Lights Go Down*.)

Robin Hood (1922)—The big, handsome Douglas Fairbanks, Sr., version, directed by Allan Dwan, and featuring extraordinarily expensive sets and Fairbanks' beautiful athletic prowess. With Wallace Beery as Richard the Lion-Hearted, Enid Bennett as Marian, and Alan Hale as Little John (the same role he played 16 years later in the Errol Flynn version). Silent. b & w

RoboCop (1987)—In this punk sci-fi revenge fantasy, the near future is played for depravity, for kicks. Set in a Detroit of cloud-topped skyscrapers and a decaying older part of the city where rapists and vandals run wild and every day is open season on cops, the movie is shot in a deliberate sick-sleazo comic-book style. (Body parts are treated as if they were auto-body parts.) When Murphy (Peter Weller), a young cop employed by the all-powerful conglomerate OCP, is blown apart by a gang of scummy sadists, OCP's scientists use his remains as part of a cyborg—an experimental model for an organic, automated cop that requires food but is virtually indestructible and is programmed to keep order. Part man, part tank, this virtuous knight in heavy metal clumps through the city. The picture keeps telling you that its leering brutishness is a terrific turn-on, and maybe it is if you're hooked on Wagnerian sci-fi comic books. The Dutch director, Paul Verhoeven, was nastily witty in *The 4th Man*, but here, working in English, he doesn't have the timing or the spirit for that. This isn't gallows humor—it's just gallows pulp. As Murphy's woman-cop partner, Nancy Allen has the right soft tones to give the movie a little differentiation; it makes sense that she would get through to RoboCop's human memory. (When he removes his steel hood, his tense, pained face has the imaginative beauty that stirs audiences at classic horror films.) With Kurtwood Smith, Miguel Ferrer, Daniel O'Herlihy, Ronny Cox, and Robert Doqui. Written by Edward Neumeier and Michael Miner. Shot in Dallas (with added matte paintings of skyscrapers) and in a rusted abandoned steel mill outside Pittsburgh. Orion. (A sequel, *RoboCop II*, directed by Irvin Kershner, was released in 1990.) color (See *Hooked*.)

Rocco and His Brothers *Rocco e i Suoi Fratelli* (1961)—Luchino Visconti's strange sprawling epic—a flamboyant melodrama about how a poor Sicilian family (a mother and her five sons) is corrupted and eventually destroyed by life in Milan. Visconti's methods are still partly neo-realist, but the scale of the film is huge and operatic, and it loses the intimacy of the best neo-realist films, and their breath of life. This is more like a hollow, spectacular version of a Warners movie of the 30s (three of the sons take turns in the prize-fight ring) but the characters aren't as vivid and individualized as the Warners actors made them. The movie is memorable largely because of Annie Girardot's stunning performance as a prostitute; her role suggests that of Dostoevski's great heroine in *The Idiot*, while her final scene suggests *Woyzeck*. The weirdest aspect of the film is the casting of Alain Delon (who at times seems to be lighted as if he were Hedy Lamarr) as a saintly, simple Prince Myshkin. Renato Salvatori plays the most forceful of the brothers—it's actually his sexual passion rather than the horrors of urban existence that destroys the family. Also with Katina Paxinou as the mother, and Roger Hanin, Paolo Stoppa, Suzy Delair, and Claudia Cardinale. The script is adapted from the novel *The Bridge of Ghisolfa*, by Giovanni Testori; there are also

suggestions of the Biblical story of Joseph and his brethren. Cinematography by Giuseppe Rotunno; music by Nino Rota. In Italian. b & w

Rockabye (1932)—As in rockabye baby. Constance Bennett, it may be recalled, was the 30s' leading interpreter of sinners with babies. This isn't much of a movie, but at least she doesn't drudge and suffer this time; she's a stage star with a glamorous existence, and in the best scene, a suitor fills her boudoir with balloons. George Cukor directed from a negligible script; he doesn't appear to have been able to keep several of the performers from competitive bouts of overacting—a key offender is Jobyna Howland as the heroine's alcoholic mother. With Joel McCrea, Paul Lukas, Walter Pidgeon, Walter Catlett, and Sterling Holloway. R K O. b & w

The Rocking Horse Winner (1949)—An intelligent, little-known version of the D. H. Lawrence story. A child (the marvellous John Howard Davies, who also played Oliver Twist in the David Lean film) uses his second sight to rescue his parents; the painful part is that he lacks first sight—the judgment that would enable him to see that they are already destroyed. The enduringly beautiful but not notoriously gifted Valerie Hobson gives her best (maybe her only) performance as his mother. (She is phenomenal in the pawnshop episode.) With John Mills and Ronald Squire. Directed by Anthony Pelissier. b & w

Rocky (1976)—A low-budget winner—a romantic fable about a Philadelphia palooka who gains his manhood, written by and starring muscle-bound Sylvester Stallone, who is repulsive one moment, noble the next. He's amazing to watch: there's a bull-necked energy in him, smoldering, and in his deep caveman's voice he gives the most surprising, sharp, fresh shadings to his lines. The picture is poorly made, yet its naïve, emotional shamelessness is funny and engaging. Directed by John G. Avildsen. With Talia Shire, Carl Weathers, Burt Young, and Burgess Meredith. Cinematography by James Crabe; music by Bill Conti; produced by Irwin Winkler and Robert Chartoff. Academy Awards: Picture, Director. (A 1979 sequel, *Rocky II*, written and also directed by Stallone, featured the same cast.) United Artists. color (See *When the Lights Go Down*.)

Rocky III (1982)—Whatever oddball charm and silliness the first *Rocky* had is long gone. *Rocky III* starts with the hyped climax of *II* and then just keeps going on that level; it's packaged hysteria. The movie really works you over. You're pummelled by the noise and the rock music and the images of bodies being whammed. The pace is accelerated by a crude, hustling shorthand—montages of Rocky in the ring defending his title against a series of contenders, Rocky doing commercials, Rocky with his family, Rocky's training intercut with his opponent Clubber's training, and so on. The first *Rocky* was primitive in a relatively innocent way. This picture is primitive, but it's also shrewd and empty and inept. Written and directed by its star, Sylvester Stallone; with Carl Weathers, whose physique makes Rocky look like a lump, and who gives a likable, unaffected performance; and an actor called Mr. T as Clubber Lang; and Burgess Meredith, Talia Shire, and Burt Young. Produced by Robert Chartoff and Irwin Winkler, for M-G-M/ United Artists. color (See *Taking It All In*.)

Roger & Me (1989)—Michael Moore's widely praised muckraking documentary is about his 2½-year pursuit of Roger Smith, the chairman of General Motors, who, according to the film, is directly responsible for closing 11 plants and bringing about the destruction of Flint, Michigan—GM's birthplace and Moore's home town. The film purports to show what was happening in Flint from February, 1987, to August, 1989, but what happens is that Moore, a big shambling joker who's the director, producer, writer, and star, deadpans his way through interviews with an assortment of unlikely people, who are used as stooges. He chases gags and improvises his version of history: in his account of the plant closings, the worker layoffs, and the construction of tourist attractions, he compresses the events of many years and fiddles with the time sequence. He comes on in a give-'em-hell style, but he breaks faith with the audience. And he does something that is humanly very offensive: *Roger & Me* uses its leftism as a superior attitude. Members of the audience can laugh at ordinary working people and still feel that they're taking a politically correct position. Released by Warners. color (See *Movie Love*.)

Roma, Città Aperta, see *Open City*

Roman Holiday (1953)—Charming. This is the picture that made Audrey Hepburn a movie star. Probably no one could have brought out her skinny, long-necked gamine magic as winningly as the director William Wyler did; his calm, elegant style prepares the scenes and builds the character until she has the audience in thrall, and when she smiles we're all goners. She plays a Central European princess on an official tour of Rome. The princess flies the royal coop and has her first experiences of freedom with an American reporter (Gregory Peck, who is at his most animated and likable) and his photographer-sidekick (Eddie Albert). The plot is banal, and the movie is no more than a Cinderella-style romantic comedy, but it's enough. (Children adore this fairy tale about a modern princess.) With Harcourt Williams, Hartley Power, Margaret Rawlings, and Tullio Carminati. Much of the film was shot on

Roman locations. The cinematography was by Franz Planer until he fell ill and Henri Alekan took over; the music is by Georges Auric; the editing is by Robert Swink. The story is credited to Ian McLellan Hunter and the script to him and John Dighton, though Ben Hecht also worked on it, at one stage, and Ennio Flaiano and Suso Cecchi d'Amico are said to have rewritten it for Wyler when he was in Rome. (And Hollywood folklore has it that Hunter, who picked up an Academy Award for his contribution, may have been serving as a front for the blacklisted Dalton Trumbo.) Paramount. b & w

Roman Scandals (1933)—Posh and popular musical comedy, starring Eddie Cantor, with the luscious, ripe Ruth Etting, and Gloria Stuart, David Manners, Verree Teasdale, Alan Mowbray, Edward Arnold, and the Goldwyn Girls. They're a toothsome bunch of sirens in this one—parading in revealing dresses or just in long, blond, calendar-art wigs, and with their dances choreographed by Busby Berkeley. (It's easy to spot Lucille Ball and Paulette Goddard among them.) The picture has a wonderful, silvery bright light; the cinematographer, Gregg Toland, keeps everything sparkling—everything visual, that is. It's the star, Eddie Cantor, who's stale. The material is credited to half a dozen writers (including George S. Kaufman and Robert E. Sherwood, who wrote the stage version), but Cantor's material is one thudder after another. As the American who dreams himself back in ancient Rome, he's a limp presence, telegraphing how darling and naughty he is, especially when he sings and rolls his eyes. He can't seem to do anything but play the sissy who's always in panic. Frank Tuttle directed; the score by Al Dubin and Harry Warren includes "No More Love," which Ruth Etting sings, and "When We Build a Little Home." A Samuel Goldwyn Production. b & w

The Roman Spring of Mrs. Stone (1961)— The Tennessee Williams novella is in the tradition of D. H. Lawrence's *Lovely Lady* stories; it's about an aging widow, a proud, cold-hearted bitch without cares or responsibilities, who learns that sex is all that holds her to life—that it's the only sensation that temporarily saves her from the meaningless drift of her existence. And so she picks up young men and pays them. José Quintero, who directed, and Gavin Lambert, who wrote the adaptation, seem to think this idea so daring and unusual that they fumble around with it almost as much as the doctor in the movie of *Suddenly, Last Summer*, who couldn't seem to cope with the simple facts of Sebastian's homosexuality and kept saying, "You *don't* mean *that?*" . . . "No, it *can't* be *that.*" *The Roman Spring* is so insistent about the "shocking" mechanics of buying love that this is what the film seems to be about, and by trying so diligently to make Mrs. Stone (Vivien Leigh) sympathetic and understandable the moviemakers kill all interest in her. Though the role seems ideal for Vivien Leigh, the director was a novice in films, and she comes across as parched and monotonous. (She was infinitely superior in a similar role in *The Deep Blue Sea*.) The picture is a disappointment, but it's a try at a sexual study, and there are good moments—especially when Warren Beatty is on the screen. As the young man Mrs. Stone becomes addicted to, the boyish young Beatty shows his gift for slyness. The cast includes Lotte Lenya, Ernest Thesiger, Coral Browne, Jill St. John, and Jeremy Spenser. Warner–Seven Arts. color

Romancing the Stone (1984)—This slapstick adventure comedy is in the commercial genre of *Raiders of the Lost Ark*, but it's a simpler, more likable entertainment than *Raiders*; it doesn't leave you feeling exhausted. The picture's greatest asset is its taking-off place: a woman's wanting a more exciting life. Kathleen Turner plays the timid, pleasantly slobby author of best-seller romances who is thrust into the kind of perils she has dreamed up for her books. The picture has a bravura opening and a jolly kind of movement, but it becomes too slam-bang; the score is cheesy and loud, and there are a few too many unrealized gags. Still, the director, Robert Zemeckis, sustains the carefree tone; and the widescreen imagery, which is stunning at the start, is always good to look at. (Dean Cundey was the cinematographer.) Turner knows how to use her dimples amusingly and how to dance like a woman who didn't know she could; her star performance is exhilarating. As Zolo the knifer, Manuel Ojeda is a terrific swinish villain, and Alfonso Arau has an affable spaciness as a Colombian drug-trade chieftain who's hooked on the heroine's novels. It's too bad that when the heroine's fictional hero materializes he's Michael Douglas, the producer of the film, who isn't a comedian and tries too hard. His face exaggerates everything and registers nothing, and no matter how fast he moves he seems to slow down whatever is going on around him. Written by Diane Thomas; the handsome production design is by Lawrence G. Paull. With Danny DeVito (who's used for his cuteness and as if our hearing him deliver commonplace expletives would knock us silly), Zack Norman, Holland Taylor as Gloria, the heroine's publisher, and Mary Ellen Trainor who doesn't exactly light up the screen as the heroine's sister. (The Colombian scenes were shot in Mexico.) 20th Century-Fox. color (See *State of the Art*.)

The Romantic Englishwoman (1975)—Michael Caine is the pulp-writer husband, and Glenda Jackson is the discontented wife, and this is another flaccid essay on infidelity, with prissy-mouthed Helmut Berger as the gigolo-intruder. The director, Joseph Losey, persuaded Tom Stoppard to do the rewrite on Thomas Wiseman's adaptation of his own novel, and Stoppard has given the dialogue a few Noël Cowardish bitch-nifties, but not enough to keep the viewer's blood coursing. It's a mystification melodrama with leftish overtones; the title is ironic—the film's oblique message is that the bourgeois wife consumes everything, even her lover. Cinematography by Gerry Fisher. color. (See *When the Lights Go Down*.)

Romeo and Juliet (1936)—Expensively devotional, in the literal-minded and heavily overproduced Irving Thalberg manner, but the readings are often clear and sensible, and there is an audacious, controversial, florid performance by John Barrymore as Mercutio. Leslie Howard is an anemic, overage Romeo, while Norma Shearer, never much of an actress, makes a valiant effort at Juliet, but never rises above conventional adequacy. With Basil Rathbone (Tybalt), Edna May Oliver (the Nurse), C. Aubrey Smith (Capulet), Ralph Forbes (Paris), Violet Kemble-Cooper (Lady Capulet), Reginald Denny (Benvolio), Katherine De Mille (Rosaline). Directed by George Cukor; the play was simplified by Talbot Jennings. Totally made in a studio Italy, it remains a chief example of the pasteboard M-G-M style in full decadence. b & w

Romeo and Juliet (1954)—The dramatic rhythm of the play is lost, but this Anglo-Italian production, directed by Renato Castellani, is extraordinarily rich and voluptuous, photographed in the golden remnants of the High Renaissance in Verona, Venice, and Siena, and with costumes by Leonor Fini that are derived from Piero della Francesca, Pisanello, Carpaccio, and Fiorenzo di Lorenzo. The Capulets' ball, where Romeo and Juliet meet and quiveringly touch, amid masked dancers in heavy, ornate costumes, has such sensuality that it conveys a better idea of what the play is *about* than conventional stage presentations do; when the boy sopranos begin to sing, the atmosphere is magical. There are other, sudden miracles in this production—like the way Mervyn Johns transforms tiresome old Friar Laurence into a radiantly silly little man. And there are miracles of sight and sound—the clanging of the great church doors, the sudden recognition that the servants carrying food are right out of Botticelli, or that, dressed by Fini, a big lug like Bill Travers is a Benvolio that Italian painters might have fought over. Laurence Harvey (at 26) is Romeo and his readings are often exciting; the 20-year-old Susan Shentall, a nonprofessional, is lovely as Juliet but lacks voice and presence. With Flora Robson as the Nurse, and Sebastian Cabot as Capulet; John Gielgud is the chorus. Music by Roman Vlad. color

Romeo and Juliet (1968)—Franco Zeffirelli goes in for strenuous knockabout stuff—for brawling, cavorting young men and for revels and roistering that have an awful way of suggesting the supers at the opera trying to keep the stage "active." In this bowdlerization, Zeffirelli loads on what academic bowdlerizers used to take out; the lusty, rambunctious film even provides a fashion show in codpieces—two-toned, with fringe and bows and laces. The one element Zeffirelli removes that the other bowdlerizers also removed is Shakespeare's language. Only about half the play is left, and what's there doesn't build up the rhythm of a poetic drama. Heard in isolated fragments, the lines just seem a funny way of talking that is hard to understand. The movie was sold on its "youth appeal" and on teen-agers playing teen-agers. But you can always make a movie with kids playing kids; the feat would be if the kids could read Shakespeare. Here, the lines are unintelligible because the actors' faces and bodies aren't in tune with the words. Olivia Hussey (Juliet), her childish eyes wide open and her mouth open, too, and Leonard Whiting (Romeo), his hair cut like a suburban hippie's, are not really bad; they're rather sweet. But they're as banal in their youth and innocence as the high-school students in the TV series "Peyton Place." In Shakespeare's version, Romeo and Juliet played together at poetry and at love; they made love through poetry, matching each other's conceits. Here the actors seem dear little children playing at the director's notion of teen-age sex hunger. Then, suddenly, Nino Rota's music is poured on in emotional torrents and the movie is filled with weeping and lamentation and carrying-on. Romeo flings himself to the floor while Juliet, hair streaming, bangs herself against the wall. All this violence and hysteria appear to come out of nowhere, because these little child lovers, with their baby talk, hardly seem to have the grand passion to go mad this way. The movie gets so bizarre and excessive in a 19th-century melodramatic fashion that it begins to be rather fascinating; it supplies an operatic love-death for a romantic teen-age audience. With John McEnery as a freaked-out Mercutio, Michael York as Tybalt, Pat Heywood as the Nurse, and Milo O'Shea, Natasha Parry, and for the prologue, Laurence Olivier's voice. color (See *Going Steady*.)

Room at the Top (1958)—It's the good, familiar story of the bright, ambitious boy from the provinces who wants to make good in the big city. Stendhal set it in the post-Napoleonic period in *The Red and the Black*; Theodore Dreiser set it in the beginnings of industrialization in *An American Tragedy*. Here, the boy comes from the modern industrial slums of Yorkshire; he has acquired a cynical education in a Second World War German prison camp; and he has become a civil servant. Like Julien Sorel and Clyde Griffiths, Joe Lampton is on the make; unlike them, he doesn't get killed for his sexual transgressions, though he does get beaten up in a manner which suggests a ritual punishment. Like its predecessors, the novel is about class, money, and power—and about how sex, which is used to get them, traps the user. Joe (Laurence Harvey) is an aggressive young parvenu, a slum-bred man who wants to break through the class structure and get into the Establishment. The movie helped bring American adults back into the theatres—partly, no doubt, because of the unusually intelligent treatment of Joe's drives and the unusually blunt dialogue, but mostly because of the superb love scenes between Harvey and Simone Signoret. She's magnificent as the older woman whom he loves yet sacrifices to his ambition. Her sensuality is contrasted with the virginal shallowness of Heather Sears, as the rich girl he marries. With Donald Wolfit, Hermione Baddeley, Raymond Huntley, Donald Houston, and Ambrosine Philpotts. Directed capably, and with great emotional tact, by Jack Clayton, from Neil Paterson's adaptation of the John Braine novel; cinematography by Freddie Francis. Signoret won the Academy Award for Best Actress. (A sequel, *Life at the Top*, also with Harvey, was made in 1965; it was directed by Ted Kotcheff, from a script by Mordecai Richler.) b & w

Room Service (1938)—The Marx Brothers in the Broadway farce about bankrupt theatrical producers holed up in a hotel room with their stranded players, fighting off famine and creditors. Unfortunately, the play (by John Murray and Allen Boretz, adapted by Morrie Ryskind) fits them like a strait jacket. With Lucille Ball, Ann Miller, Frank Albertson, and Donald MacBride grinning his great bulldog grin. Directed (lamely) by William Seiter. R K O. b & w

A Room with a View (1986)—Adapted from the early novel by E. M. Forster, this is a whimsical social comedy about a muddled young English girl (Helena Bonham Carter) who desires yet fears sexual love; she runs away from the man (Julian Sands) who stirs her emotions, and becomes engaged to a rich twit (Daniel Day-Lewis). Bonham Carter lacks the carriage and presence of a trained actress, and Sands, though likable, is playing Forster's flimsy—almost abstract—dream of a natural, uninhibited lover, and is rather vague. But the movie is well paced, and it never loses its hold on a viewer's affections, because it's so thoroughly inhabited. The actors who circulate around the heroine create a whirring atmosphere—a comic hum. They include Denholm Elliott (playing the novel's resident saint), Maggie Smith, Judi Dench, Simon Callow, and Rosemary Leach; the young Italian lovers are played by Isabella Celani and Lucca Rossi. Full of allusions to art and literature, the movie is more than a little precious, but it's a piece of charming foolishness. It was produced by Ismail Merchant and directed by James Ivory, from a script by Ruth Prawer Jhabvala that pares down the text skillfully and takes much of its lively, dizzy dialogue directly from Forster. Shot in England and Florence, by Tony Pierce-Roberts. Released by Cinecom International. color (See *Hooked*.)

Rooster Cogburn (1975)—Pretty bad. A Western shoot-'em-up, with John Wayne wallowing in the role of the one-eyed U.S. marshal carried over from *True Grit*. Katharine Hepburn—her role lifted bodily from *The African Queen*—plays the schoolteacher-daughter of a missionary to the Indians. When Wayne and Hepburn spar, it's mortifyingly blunt vaudeville, and their inevitable mutual admiration comes all too coyly soon. Stuart Millar directed, from a script written by the producer Hal B. Wallis, his wife, Martha Hyer, and others; they all hid—as well they should have—under the pseudonym Martin Julien. Universal. color (See *When the Lights Go Down.*)

Rosalie (1938)—Eleanor Powell, in her big smiles and big puffed sleeves, and Ray Bolger dance together—sort of. She also has a sort of romance with Nelson Eddy, who looks even more uncomfortable about the whole thing than she does—and romance was never her forte. W. S. Van Dyke directed this berserk M-G-M extravaganza, which was vaguely derived from a 1928 Ziegfeld show, and produced and adapted to the screen by William Anthony McGuire, a former Ziegfeld aide, who swamped the cameras with a cast of over 2,000 people. Sometimes there are so many showgirls surrounding Powell that you have to strain to see her tapping away, like a wholesome automaton. Bolger redeems a few moments, and the Cole Porter songs (which replaced the original Romberg and Gershwin numbers) are a choice group, including "In the Still of the Night," "I Know It's Not Meant for Me," and "It's All Over But the Shouting"—which are, however, staged execrably. Porter is said to have hated the title song, which Louis B. Mayer loved; Mayer's ear matched his eye—the sets are to make a person of taste weep. The cast includes Frank Morgan (as a Ruritanian king), Ilona Massey (making her film début), and Edna May Oliver, Jerry Colonna, Janet Beecher, Virginia Grey, Reginald Owen, Billy Gilbert, and George Zucco. The choreography is by Albertina Rasch. b & w

The Rose (1979)—Bette Midler makes her starring début as an orgiastic rock 'n' roll singer in the last stages of burning herself out. This musical is set in the smoky, psychedelic night world of a young star who has leapt into the big money. Her story is told in hot Day-Glo pinks and reds and lavenders, with orange for her frizzy halo. (The cinematography is by Vilmos Zsigmond.) She sings frenziedly, trying to reach her emotional limits; she lives in planes, and when she lands she totters on high heels and blinks, bleary-eyed, at the sunshine. Directed by Mark Rydell and written by Bill Kerby and Bo Goldman, the picture is shaped to tear you up, and as one of the Dionysian stars (such as Janis Joplin) who ascended to fame in the 60s and OD'd, all within a few years, Midler gives a paroxysm of a performance—it's scabrous yet delicate, and altogether amazing. The movie is hyper and lurid, yet it's also a very strong emotional experience, with an exciting visual and musical flow, and there are sharply written, beautifully played dialogue scenes. Its largest weakness is in the conception of the bullying manager (Alan Bates); he simply isn't convincing—he seems to be in the movie for melodramatic purposes. But there's a scarily effective scene with Harry Dean Stanton as a stern, self-righteous country-music man, and Frederic Forrest is original and likable as the singer's army-deserter lover. Also with Barry Primus, David Keith, and four female impersonators—Claude Sacha, Michael St. Laurent, Sylvester, and Pearl Heart—who do a wonderfully loose, ribald number with Midler. She has eight others that she does virtually alone—"Midnight in Memphis," "Whose Side Are You On?," "When a Man Loves a Woman," "Love Me with a Feeling," "Stay with Me," "Sold My Soul to Rock and Roll," "The Rose," and "Let Me Call You Sweetheart," which she never finishes. She's a great performer. 20th Century-Fox.

Rose Marie (1936)—Singing "The Indian Love Call," Jeanette MacDonald and Nelson Eddy are in a class of their own; the wholesome, hearty fakery of it is matchless. This is one of the liveliest and most popular of their kitschfests. It's set in the Pacific Northwest; she's an opera star and he's a Mountie who has arrested her brother (skinny young James Stewart). With Allan Jones and Reginald Owen. Directed by W. S. Van Dyke. M-G-M. b & w

Rose of Washington Square (1939)—This movie, starring Alice Faye, is quite clearly cribbed from the life of Fanny Brice; the contrast would be entertaining if it were double-billed with *Funny Girl*. When Alice sings the title song (an old Brice number), the lyrics are changed and "Roman nose" becomes "turned-up nose"; when Alice sings "My Man," her voice is lovely and velvety, but the song isn't very intense. The young bail-jumping sharper (based on Nicky Arnstein) who gives her her heartaches is played by Tyrone Power, who's more entertaining and plausible in the role than Omar Sharif was in the Streisand version. The period of the Ziegfeld Follies and speakeasy raids is re-created in the somewhat tacky 20th Century-Fox manner; the cinematographer, Karl Freund, gives the material some style, even though the director, Gregory Ratoff, doesn't seem to have a grip on the story. Fortunately, Al Jolson turns up and gives the film an authentic connection to its Broadway sources. Nunnally Johnson wrote the script (from a story by John Larkin and Jerry Horwin) and produced (under Zanuck). The cast includes Hobart Cavanaugh, Joyce Compton, Moroni Olsen, William Frawley, and Louis Prima and his band; among the many songs are "April Showers," "I'm Just Wild About Harry," and "Rockabye Your Baby with a Dixie Melody." The choreographer was Seymour Felix. b & w

The Rose Tattoo (1955)—Tennessee Williams' Serafina (Anna Magnani) is a Sicilian-American widow still in love with the fantasy of her dead husband's perfection, a woman cut off from the life around her because nothing is as good as that dream (and, from the way it looks, the squalid Gulf Coast town around her isn't up to anybody's dream). Magnani's virtuoso display of vitality makes it almost frighteningly clear that her husband's perfection was his sexual potency. The weakness of the material is that the reduction of all human needs to sex is handled only semi-comically. Burt Lancaster is rather embarrassing as Serafina's not-too-smart suitor, though he has a funny scene when he chases a goat. Magnani won an Academy Award for her performance; Tennessee Williams reputedly wrote the role for her, though Maureen Stapleton played it on Broadway. Directed by Daniel Mann, the picture comes across as a rather foolish, good-hearted romp; with Jo Van Fleet, Marisa Pavan, Ben Cooper, and Virginia Grey. The cinematographer, James Wong Howe, also won an Academy Award. Paramount. b & w

Roseland (1977)—Three stories set inside the famous, still functioning dance hall on 52nd Street off Broadway, now a haven for nostalgic, aging people. In its hushed concern for their dignity, the movie denies them any spirit. According to the press, when this film was shown at the New York Film Festival it received a seven-minute standing ovation. Did those people stand up and cheer to get their circulation going again? The picture makes you feel that it was produced in 1936 but didn't reach the screen for decades because nobody had the vitality to thread the projector. Christopher Walken and Don De Natale, an actual m.c. at Roseland, are the only performers who manage to transcend the film's faded genteel sensitivity. With Teresa Wright, Lou Jacobi, Geraldine Chaplin, Helen Gallagher, Lilia Skala, and David Thomas. Directed by James Ivory, from Ruth Prawer Jhabvala's script; produced by Ismail

Merchant. color (See *When the Lights Go Down*.)

Rosemary *Das Mädchen Rosemarie* (1958)—The American reviews suggested that it was a witty, stylized musical satire; it was widely compared to early René Clair—probably by people who hadn't seen much early René Clair. The film makes some attempts at musical satire and rhythmic editing, but it's fairly simpleminded stuff. Nine capitalists in their black Homburg hats step out of nine black Mercedes-Benz limousines and snap the doors shut in time to the music—that's about as close to the style of René Clair as the Rockettes at Easter. And as for the reviewers' enthusiastic idea that *Rosemary* was some *Threepenny Opera* of the 50s, well it's easy enough to see how they got the idea—the score is just a reprise of Kurt Weill's music, and the subject matter is social corruption. But who wants to eat a sausage when he can see what's being ground up into it? Rolf Thiele, the director, and his scenarist, Erich Kuby, are so busy stuffing in irony, horror, songs, and farce that we sit coldly examining the ingredients. The actual Rosemary Nitribitt was a high-class call girl who became a favorite of Frankfurt's postwar industrialists; it was thought that she dabbled in blackmail and sold information about the industrial manipulations of her clients, and she was found dead in 1957. Nadja Tiller, who plays the role, is a former Miss Austria; she—or perhaps her publicity agent—felt it necessary to explain that she had accepted the role because the film was not intended simply to show "the tragic fate of a prostitute but rather to produce a critique of our modern times. That takes courage. And since courage seems to be at a premium in our film industry, I felt morally bound to cooperate." The irony is that the best element of the film is precisely Nadja Tiller as a prostitute: she's one of the best whores who ever walked the screen. The critique of our modern times is labored and silly. With the suave Peter Van Eyck, and Gert Fröbe, Mario Adorf, Werner Peters, and Carl Raddatz. In German. b & w

Rosemary's Baby (1968)—Pregnant women sometimes look at their men as if to say, "What did you do to me?" Rosemary (Mia Farrow), the Omaha-born girl who's now living in Manhattan, has reason to wonder, and this satirical gothic thriller, written and directed by Roman Polanski, from Ira Levin's novel, is told from her point of view. Rosemary's actor-husband (John Cassavetes) conspires with a coven, drugs her, and mates her with Satan, in exchange for a Broadway hit. It's genuinely funny, yet it's also scary, especially for young women: it plays on their paranoid vulnerabilities. The queasy and the grisly are mixed with its entertaining hipness. (It's probably more fun for women who are past their childbearing years.) Mia Farrow is enchanting in her fragility: she's just about perfect for her role. And the darkly handsome Cassavetes is ideal as the narcissist who makes the deal for a cloven-hoofed infant. Also with Ruth Gordon, Sidney Blackmer, Maurice Evans, Ralph Bellamy, Patsy Kelly, Charles Grodin, and Elisha Cook (Jr.). The cinematography is by William Fraker; the production design is by Richard Sylbert; the editing is by Sam O'Steen. Paramount. color

Le Rosier de Madama Husson (1932)—First released here as *He* and later as *The Virgin Man*. These titles are a disguise for Bernard Deschamps' classic French comedy, based on the Guy de Maupassant story, and starring Fernandel and Françoise Rosay. The setting is a small provincial town: the committee formed to select the virgin to be crowned Rose Queen cannot locate a single female virgin; but they locate a male—the village fool,

Isidore (Fernandel)—and he is crowned Rose King. The festivities prove too much for the virtuous young man, and he winds up in Paris—a city that imperils even a fool's virtue. This isn't the tired, mugging Fernandel of the 50s; his wit and spontaneity are the real thing. In French. b & w

Le Rouge et le noir, see *The Red and the Black*

'Round Midnight (1986)—Most of Bertrand Tavernier's mournful, blue-toned movie, which, an opening title tells us, was "inspired by incidents in the lives of Francis Paudras and Bud Powell," is set in Paris in 1959. The French jazz enthusiast Paudras is now called Francis Borier and is played by François Cluzet, and Powell, the great bebop pianist, who suffered frequent nervous breakdowns and then made a new life abroad, is now the dazed, alcoholic tenor-sax man Dale Turner, and is played by the near-legendary Dexter Gordon. The enthusiast is a saintly groupie. You know what kind of movie it's going to be when you see this guy out in a drenching rain, crouched against the building where the American is playing, because he doesn't have the money to go in. Cluzet is soaking wet, but his eyes shine and he listens to Dexter Gordon's music worshipfully. Soon he has become a friend of the black American giant. (Gordon is 6 feet 5 or 6.) Cluzet follows him around, takes care of him, and rescues him when he goes on a bender and is hospitalized; Cluzet becomes Gordon's keeper, treating the expatriate with the respect he didn't get in his own country. He treats him as the artist he is, and Gordon flowers into a courtly, gentle fellow, and begins to compose agian. But his self-destructiveness runs very deep, and so the picture is one crisis after another, with the saintly groupie running through the streets, searching for the imperilled saintly bopper.

The way the picture is conceived, the musician is always on the verge of collapse or death. (Afterward, in the lobby, a woman said to her friend, "I'm worn out from worrying about him.") The French are pretty hard to take when they celebrate how much they love American art. The film is "respectfully dedicated to Bud Powell and Lester Young." Tavernier clearly identifies with the fan, and he probably cast Cluzet in the role because of his resemblance to Truffaut. (We're being told that Tavernier loves American movies as well as American jazz; he even shows us Cluzet making home movies of his idol.) Tavernier seems to be enshrining his own idolatry. The music itself has none of the mysterious teeming vitality of great bebop—it's lifeless. With Sandra Reaves Phillips, who shakes things up when she sings a good low-down version of Bessie Smith's "Put It Right Here," and Lonette McKee, John Berry, Martin Scorsese, Philippe Noiret, and many well-known musicians, including Herbie Hancock, who arranged and conducted the music. The script, which attempts to achieve a musical flow (and allows for improvised dialogue), is by David Rayfiel and Tavernier. A Franco-American film, produced by Irwin Winkler, released by Warners. color

Roxanne (1987)—Steve Martin is improbably light on his feet in this airy, modern love comedy based on Rostand's *Cyrano de Bergerac*. He seems to crossbreed the skills of W. C. Fields and Buster Keaton, with some Fred Astaire mingled in. And as the stargazer Roxanne, Daryl Hannah gives off a womanly radiance—a combination of carnality and moonglow. Directed by Fred Schepisi, from Martin's script, this film is unabashedly romantic. It's set in the ski-resort town of Nelson, Washington (nestled against the mountains, it seems a dream-built locale, but it's actually Nelson, British Columbia). You want to go to the town; you want to go back to the movie. It has a mellow, dotty charm. With Shelley Duvall, Rick Rossovich, Shandra Beri, and a squad of volunteer firefighters who are like Keystone Cops. Cinematography by Ian Baker; music by Bruce Smeaton. Columbia. color (See *Hooked.*)

Roxie Hart (1942)—Roxie (Ginger Rogers) is the 1926 sensation of Chicago—a flapper on trial for her life who has the time of her life while on trial. She is coached and defended by Adolphe Menjou—"Roxie's simple, barefoot mouthpiece"—in sequences that may be the funniest courtroom buffoonery ever filmed. The scriptwriter, Nunnally Johnson, provides a loving, satiric look at the speakeasies, floozies, and tabloids, with a glance at the forsaken rural boredom. (Roxie's farmer father, summoned to the long-distance phone and informed that she has been arrested on a murder charge, returns to the rocker on his porch, rocks for a while, and then says to his wife, "They're going to hang Roxie." The mother murmurs approvingly, "What did I tell you?") William Wellman directed, in a fast, broad, spirited style (though the end is the kind of studio-factory finish that no director can do anything with). The cast is first-rate: Iris Adrian is Two-Gun Gertie ("Got a butt, buddy?"); the reporters and photographers include Lynne Overman (whose vocal inflections could do as much for dialogue as Lee Tracy's), Phil Silvers, George Montgomery, William Frawley, and Spring Byington as a sob sister. Sara Allgood is the prison matron, Nigel Bruce is a theatrical agent, and George Chandler is Roxie's husband. Even Jeff Corey turns up in a bit. Adapted from the Maurine Watkins play *Chicago*, which was also filmed in 1927, with Phyllis Haver in the lead, and which also provided the basis for the 1975 Bob Fosse stage musical *Chicago*. 20th Century-Fox. b & w

The Royal Family of Broadway (1930)—Fredric March in one of his best comedy roles—a flamboyant burlesque of great-lover actor John Barrymore. The gossipy, thinly disguised satire of the Barrymore-Drew clan was a Broadway hit in 1927; Herman J. Mankiewicz and Gertrude Purcell adapted (and improved) the Kaufman-Ferber play, and the young George Cukor (co-directing with Cyril Gardner) had the right theatrical instincts for the material. The film presents actors as childishly vain and narcissistic; as Cukor has said, "It represented what people at that time liked to believe about the theatre." The picture is stagebound and awkward, but good fun anyway. As Ethel Barrymore, the expert, sophisticated stage comedienne Ina Claire doesn't come through fully on screen (she did only once—in *The Greeks Had a Word for Them*), but some of her legendary technique is in evidence. With Henrietta Crossman as the family matriarch, Frank Conroy, Mary Brian, and the stodgy juvenile Charles Starrett. Paramount. b & w

Royal Flash (1975)—Richard Lester directs George MacDonald Fraser's adaptation of one of his novels celebrating the inglorious career of Captain Harry Flashman, of the 11th Hussars (Malcolm McDowell), a rotten, snivelling Victorian coward. It's a parody of movie heroics, especially of *The Prisoner of Zenda*, but Lester is on his own antic wavelength, and he doesn't try to tune us in. The characters don't care about each other, and we don't care about any of them. Lester has done all this carousing and pratfalling before; his inventiveness is beginning to seem desperate, compulsive—as if he kept piling on the jokes because he was bored. With Oliver Reed, Alan Bates, Britt Ekland, Florinda Bolkan, Alastair Sim, and Lionel Jeffries; cinematography by Geoffrey Unsworth. 20th

R

Century-Fox. color (See *When the Lights Go Down*.)

The Royal Hunt of the Sun (1969)—As the Inca king, Christopher Plummer arrives carried on a litter and dressed in feathers, and he hisses and prances like a mad queen; Robert Shaw, trying to play Pizarro straight, is howlingly upstaged. (Shaw keeps staring at Plummer and his pale-blue eyes get more and more bewildered.) No doubt Plummer should be chastised, but he's so outlandishly entertaining, and the movie is a mess, anyway. Peter Shaffer's play is an exercise in the heroic style of historical confrontation: he trumped up reasons for the Inca king and Pizarro to be trapped together. This theatrical convention stops the film cold—people stand on rocks and make speeches. With Leonard Whiting as the boy-put-there-to-be-disillusioned. Directed by Irving Lerner, from Philip Yordan's script. Though Lerner was himself a highly respected editor (his last work was on *Close Encounters of the Third Kind*, which is dedicated to him), the editing here is the kind that gives you the shot an instant before anything happens in it. Cinema Center. color (See *Deeper into Movies*.)

A Royal Scandal (1945)—Tallulah Bankhead gave this sex farce about Catherine the Great a sort of low glitter, but it's not much of a vehicle. (Unhappily, poor as it is it's one of the few halfway decent screen roles she ever got.) She does wonders with a few line readings, and the fine young actor William Eythe (he died at 38) has some splendid comic moments with her. The cast includes Charles Coburn, Anne Baxter, Vincent Price, Sig Rumann, and Mischa Auer. The script, which is marred by horseplay and dumb wisecracks, is by Edwin Justus Mayer; directed by Otto Preminger. 20th Century-Fox. b & w

Royal Wedding (1951)—The director, Stanley Donen, tries to make this musical buoyant, and Fred Astaire, Jane Powell, Sarah Churchill (yes, the daughter), Peter Lawford, and Keenan Wynn all work at it, but the magic isn't there. It's jaunty at times but not more than that. The script by Alan Jay Lerner is weak and the songs by Lerner and Burton Lane are not all they are sometimes said to be. Produced by Arthur Freed, M-G-M. color

Ruby Gentry (1952)—A feverishly—almost campily—operatic story of passion turning to fury. The setting is North Carolina. Blue-blooded Charlton Heston loves Ruby (Jennifer Jones), but she's a poor swamp girl, so he marries a woman from a proper background. Ruby lands the richest man in town, is widowed, and proceeds to avenge herself on everyone who has ever done her dirt. Heston is her prime target; he has been involved in a large-scale endeavor to reclaim marshland. She terminates the project with the order "Stop the pumps." That may sound like a put-on, but the movie doesn't mean to be funny. King Vidor directed, in the seething, extravagant style he employed in parts of *Duel in the Sun* and in such outré items as *Beyond the Forest* and *The Fountainhead*. With Karl Malden, Josephine Hutchinson, and Tom Tully. Russell Harlan did the cinematography; Sylvia Richards wrote the screenplay, from a story by Arthur Fitz-Richard. 20th Century-Fox. b & w

Ruggles of Red Gap (1935)—Charles Laughton starred in this justly honored version of the venerable comedy by Harry Leon Wilson. (There were two earlier versions—one in 1918, and one in 1923 with Edward Everett Horton—and a later version in 1950, called *Fancy Pants*, with Bob Hope.) The Laughton film, directed in a calm, restrained style by Leo McCarey, is just about irresistible, even with its big scene—Laughton, an English valet in the Old West, reciting the Gettysburg Address in a saloon, as the camera pans across the awed faces of the cowhands. It's a bit much, but it works like magic. The cast could hardly be better: Roland Young is the Englishman who loses the valet in a poker game, Mary Boland and Charlie Ruggles are the rich American couple who win him, and ZaSu Pitts is the widow the valet courts. With Maude Eburne, Lucien Littlefield, Willie Fung, Libby Taylor, and Leila Hyams. Paramount. b & w

The Rules of the Game *La Règle du jeu* (1939)—Perhaps the most influential of all French films, and one of the most richly entertaining. Jean Renoir's legendary butchered and then restored masterpiece is a farce about a large houseparty, gathered for a hunt, where the servants and masters begin to chase and shoot each other. The party at the country château is a tragicomic world in motion; ironically, once the whole mechanism is spinning the man who begins at the center of it—the romantic aviator (Roland Toutain)—is flicked off. With Marcel Dalio as the Marquis, Julien Carette as the poacher, Gaston Modot as the gamekeeper, Nora Gregor as Christine, Mila Parély as Genevieve, Paulette Dubost as Lisette, and Renoir as Octave. The script, by Renoir, assisted by Carl Koch, was derived from Alfred de Musset's *Les Caprices de Marianne*. Cinematography by Jean Bachelet and J. P. Alphen; costumes by Chanel; Cartier-Bresson served as an assistant director. Released in Paris in 1939 after being cut by the distributors; cut again after violent audience reactions; banned as demoralizing by the Vichy government and then banned by the Nazis. The original negative was destroyed when the Allies bombed the studios at Boulogne; the picture was reassembled (from 200 cans of film and bits of soundtrack) and restored in the late 50s. Selected by the 1962 international poll of critics as the third

greatest film ever made. In French. b & w (See *Kiss Kiss Bang Bang*.)

Rumba (1935)—Paramount, having succeeded at the box office with the pseudo-primitive sexuality of *Bolero*, pushed its luck the next year in this attempt at a follow-up. George Raft and Carole Lombard carry on some wriggling activity that is meant to be dancing. The film is beyond disaster. With Lynne Overman, Margo, Iris Adrian, Gail Patrick, Monroe Owsley, and Samuel S. Hinds. Directed, in a spirit of hopelessness, by Marion Gering. b & w

The Russians Are Coming, the Russians Are Coming (1966)—Alan Arkin as a Russian sailor, and Carl Reiner as a vacationing New York writer, in a comedy about a Russian submarine going aground on an island just off Cape Cod. Norman Jewison directed this too warmly rambunctious entertainment, which was actually shot in Northern California. With Doro Merande hanging on a wall (the best gag in the movie), Brian Keith, Jonathan Winters, Eva Marie Saint, Ben Blue, John Phillip Law, Paul Ford, Theodore Bikel, and Tessie O'Shea. The script, by William Rose, is based on Nathaniel Benchley's novel *The Off-Islanders*. United Artists. color

Ruthless People (1986)—A lot of normally bright people seem to like getting dumbed-out when they go to movies in the summer, and that may explain the whooping-it-up hot-weather audience for this cheesy low farce, with Danny DeVito as a thieving millionaire who wants to kill his heiress wife (Bette Midler) and is overjoyed when she's kidnapped. With Judge Reinhold and Helen Slater (who has good eyes for rolling) as the warmhearted kidnappers; Anita Morris as the husband's mistress (she looks as if she could do considerably better); Bill Pullman as the mistress's ninny of a lover; and William G. Schilling as the police commissioner. Directed by the *Airplane!* threesome—Jim Abrahams, David Zucker, and Jerry Zucker—from a script, by Dale Launer, that provides a semblance of clever construction, though you see each complication being set in place. (The plot is a reworking of an O. Henry story that has served many other screenwriters, as in the 1958 *Too Many Crooks* and the 1967 *The Happening*.) Touchstone (Disney). color

Ryan's Daughter (1970)—Gush made respectable by millions of dollars tastefully wasted. Sarah Miles marries Robert Mitchum but experiences rapture with Christopher Jones. Directed by David Lean, on a cosmic scale, from Robert Bolt's script. With John Mills, Trevor Howard, and Leo McKern. Cinematography by Freddie Young; music by Maurice Jarre. M-G-M. color (See *Deeper into Movies*.)

S

Sabotage Also known as *The Woman Alone*. (1936)—Hitchcock thought that he erred in this one, and that that explained why the picture wasn't a hit. But he was wrong: this adaptation of Conrad's *The Secret Agent* may be just about the best of his English thrillers, and if the public didn't respond it wasn't his fault. Sylvia Sidney and Oscar Homolka are a married pair, the Verlocs, who manage a small movie house; Desmond Tester plays Mrs. Verloc's younger brother, who, unknowingly, carries a bomb in the package her husband has given him to deliver. There's a breathtaking sequence when Mrs. Verloc, who has just learned of her brother's death, watches the cartoon *Who Killed Cock Robin?* With John Loder as a police detective, Sara Allgood, Martita Hunt, Peter Bull, and Torin Thatcher. b & w

Saboteur (1942)—A mixed-up and overloaded American spy thriller by Alfred Hitchcock, with the unengaging Robert Cummings in the lead and an unappealing cast, featuring Priscilla Lane and Otto Kruger. Nothing holds together, but there are still enough scary sequences to make the picture entertaining. Universal. b & w

Sabrina (1954)—Audrey Hepburn is forced to overdo her gamine charm in this horrible concoction about a Cinderella among the Long Island rich. She's the chauffeur's daughter who's in love with the playboy son (William Holden) of her father's employer (Walter Hampden). There's also an older son—an earnest magnate—and Humphrey Bogart got trapped in the role. Billy Wilder directed, and he had a hand in adapting the Samuel Taylor play (*Sabrina Fair*), though Bogart is said to have accused Wilder's 3-year-old offspring of having written the script. With John Williams, Martha Hyer, Marcel Dalio, Nella Walker, and Francis X. Bushman. Paramount. b & w

The Saga of Gösta Berling (1924)—Garbo, when she was an entrancingly soft-faced, full-bodied young girl, and the dashing Byronic Lars Hanson in Mauritz Stiller's stirring, romantic film version of the Selma Lagerlöf novel. Stiller was a master at unifying visual beauty and emotional effect; the complicated narrative is blurry, but there are sequences as lovely and expressive as any on film. Silent. b & w

Sahara (1943)—Bogart and an all-male supporting cast that includes J. Carrol Naish and Rex Ingram, in a lost-patrol-type story set during the Second World War. Bogart is a sergeant in command of an American tank that's been cut off from the rest of the Army during the British retreat to El Alamein. The tank keeps rolling, picking up strays along the way until it has a full Hollywood ethnic complement—a Texan, a Brooklynite, a white Southerner, a black Sudanese, and so on. Excitingly staged and stunningly photographed, the film might have been a classic wartime melodrama if it weren't so offensively didactic. John Howard Lawson and the director, Zoltán Korda, wrote the screenplay, based on an incident in a Soviet screenplay, and the picture has the self-righteous, uplifting formula of many Soviet films—Bogart and his buddies capture a complete Nazi battalion. Cinematography by Rudolph Maté. Columbia. b & w

St. Louis Blues (1929)—Bessie Smith appeared in only this one movie; it has an all-black cast and runs 16 minutes. Whatever one might say about the limitations of the story line, derived from the W. C. Handy song by the director, Dudley Murphy, and Handy himself (who served as musical director), seems irrelevant. Even in this folklorish film, made when sound recording was still primitive, she comes through. Here she is, the greatest of all our jazz singers, all 5 feet 9 inches and 200 pounds of her, crowned with a little 20s hat, and when she lets out her harsh, thick voice, full of gin and sensuality and humor, she's one of the most beautiful images that ever filled the screen. With James P. Johnson's Orchestra (most of them were members of the Fletcher Henderson Band); the pianist on the screen is Johnson. Made in Astoria, Long Island. R K O. b & w

Le Salaire de la peur, see *The Wages of Fear*

Salome (1922)—One of the true curiosities of film history. Rudolph Valentino's wife, the designer Natacha Rambova (she designed her own name, also), loved Aubrey Beardsley's drawings. She arranged to make this film with Alla Nazimova in the lead and Charles Bryant directing, and she did the decor and costumes, based on Beardsley's drawings. The bizarre results are undramatic and boring, and yet often so decorator-dream-born they're fascinating. Nazimova, one of the greatest actresses of her time, shows almost nothing of her talents here. She has a surprisingly boyish figure in the outré garments, and throughout much of the film her hair seems to be covered with ball fringe. The movie looks better in stills than when one actually sees it, but a folly like this should probably be experienced. Silent. b & w

Salt of the Earth (1954)—The raw material for this social realist movie, made in a semi-documentary style, is a 1951–52 strike of Mexican-American zinc miners in New Mexico. The picture was sponsored by the International Union of Mine, Mill and Smelter Workers (expelled from the C I O in 1950 as Communist dominated), made by blacklisted filmmakers, and financed by money "borrowed from liberal Americans." The miners are supposedly striking for equality with the "Anglos," but the strike is not a bargaining weapon for definite limited objectives. It's inflated with lessons, suggestions, and implications. "Strike" here is used in its revolutionary meaning as a training ground in solidarity, a preparation for the big strike to come; it's a microcosm of the coming revolution. And a pedagogical tone, reminiscent of the 30s, is maintained throughout much of the movie: these strikers are always teaching each other little constructive lessons, and their dialogue is blown up to the rank of folk wisdom. Rosaura Revueltos, the Mexican actress who has the leading role, is nobility incarnate—the Madonna on the picket line. Directed by Herbert J. Biberman; written by Michael Wilson. b & w (See *I Lost it at the Movies*.)

Salto nel Vuoto, see *Leap Into the Void*

Salut l'artiste (1976)—The creeping mediocrity of the poetic approach to "ordinary" people makes the film a fairly numbing experience. Marcello Mastroianni plays a wilted, second-rate actor who's also a second-rate person; his mistress sums him up when she says that he doesn't have a presence, he has absence. This is meant to be not a joke but a tragic perception. *Salut l'artiste* is a hollow pop film, with a little gas from undigested Antonioni. There isn't much Mastroianni can do but look depressed. Françoise Fabian, as the mistress, and Carla Gravina, as his wife, are very low-key. The only spark in the film comes from Jean Rochefort, as an actor who gets fed up, takes a business job, and then, being thought a nonprofessional, is offered a job in a movie. Yves Robert directed. In French. color

Salvador (1986)—The director, Oliver Stone, is probably aiming for a Buñuelian effect—a vision so intensely scummy that it clears the air. If the result, with its grime and guilt, comes closer to suggesting a hyperkinetic, gonzo version of Graham Greene, that's still nothing to be ashamed of. Written by Stone and the free-lance foreign correspondent Richard Boyle, the movie presents the civil war in El Salvador during the years 1980 and 1981 as some kind of ultimate bad trip. James Woods, perhaps the most hostile of all American actors, plays Boyle as a scroungy hustler who knows how to function in chaos: the squalid confusion wires him up, and he feels on top of things. The title doesn't refer just to the country: "Salvador" means "savior," and Woods' Boyle is the one who needs to

be saved. What Stone has here is a right-wing macho fantasy joined to a left-leaning polemic. He writes and directs as if someone had put a gun to the back of his neck and yelled "Go!" and didn't take it away until he'd finished. With Elpidia Carrillo as the peasant madonna, Jim Belushi as Doctor Rock, John Savage as the dedicated photojournalist, and Michael Murphy, Tony Plana, and Cynthia Gibb. Cinematography by Robert Richardson; music by Georges Delerue. Released via Hemdale; the film was shot in Mexico except for a few scenes set in the U.S. color (See *Hooked*.)

Salvatore Giuliano (1961)—Francesco Rosi is one of the great modern directors, but he has a tendency to be both political and abstract, and often when seeing a Rosi movie one is awed by the compositions and the vividness of the incidents while being flummoxed by the conception. As writer-director of this account of the life and death of the famous Sicilian outlaw, Rosi develops the semi-documentary style that Rossellini had used in *Paisan*. The images are never less than arresting, but the ambitious, Marxist point of view is bewildering; somehow Rosi fails to invite us into the story. It may be that his brilliance does not include a gift for simple dramatization. Cinematography by Gianni Di Venanzo. In Italian. b & w

Same Time, Next Year (1978)—A tepid sweet meal. Genteel lifelong adultery by two ciphers, played by Ellen Burstyn and Alan Alda. The time span is from 1951 to 1977. The gimmick is the way that social changes and fashions in dress and ideas are reflected in these two, and the single joke is that adultery can be regulated and celebrated, just like marriage. Of course it can be, if you remove every ounce of passion and sexual tension from it, which is what the writer, Bernard Slade, and the director, Robert Mulligan, have done. If someone you make the mistake of caring about insists on your going to this movie, take a small flashlight and a book. From Slade's two-character, one-set Broadway hit. Universal. color (See *When the Lights Go Down*.)

Sammy and Rosie Get Laid (1987)—This second film by the director Stephen Frears and the writer Hanif Kureishi, who made *My Beautiful Laundrette*, has so much going on that it keeps losing track of what it's about. Sammy (Ayub Khan Din) and Rosie (Frances Barber) and their friends are Third World bohemians who live in a decaying, racially mixed part of London. Sammy's father, Rafi (Shashi Kapoor), who was a minister in the repressive government of Pakistan and is fleeing threats on his life, thinks he can return to the courteous, law-abiding England he remembers from 30 years before. He comes from the airport straight into a race riot—the movie is his nightmare experience of the new London. Houses and cars have been set on fire and we are supposed to see the flames as a destructive-creative element. (Sammy explains the rioting in the streets to Rafi: "Rosie says these revolts are an affirmation of the human spirit. A kind of justice is being done.") What we see is an apocalyptic carnival that's like street theatre. At times, it's as if Swinging London had come back as a race riot. Made in a documentary manner as stylized as a Hollywood musical, the movie is hyperconscious of art, of politics, of itself, and at times it's exasperatingly affectless. At its best, it's playfully Godardian, as in the sequence with the screen split horizontally and three multiracial couples stretched out on top of each other, and the Ghetto Lites singing a reggae version of "My Girl." There are two marvellous performances: by Kapoor, and by Claire Bloom, as a woman he deserted long ago. Wendy Gazelle is likable as an American photographer; Roland Gift (of

Fine Young Cannibals) is dimply. Released by Cinecom. color (See *Hooked*.)

Samson and Delilah (1949)—De Mille, with God as his co-maker. In general, the plot follows the Bible story, though Victor Mature's Samson, costumed in terry-cloth leotards and a monstrous wig, looks bilious and flaccid, as if he couldn't pull down even the papiermâché temple. He does it, though, and he also wrestles a moth-eaten lion and crowns several extras with the jawbone of an ass. Hedy Lamarr's Delilah would be more at home in a Yorkville bar than in a high-toned Philistine residence. All in all, this film does not enhance the glory of De Mille or his Associate; its splendors are purely in the camp division. Among them are George Sanders as the head man of the Philistines, Henry Wilcoxon looking as nobly baffled as ever, and Angela Lansbury as the woman for whom Mature yearns, to the inexplicable despair of Lamarr. The sets are wondrous chintzy. Paramount. color

San Pietro, see *The Battle of San Pietro*

Sanders of the River (1935)—One of those all-for-the-glory-of-the-British-Empire specials. Paul Robeson plays Bosambo, a trustworthy Congo chieftain, so loyal to the British that he helps the colonial officials crush a native revolt. Robeson, who had apparently expected this English film—an Alexander Korda production, directed by Zoltán Korda—to have a very different point of view, fought its release. However, despite the junkiness of the Edgar Wallace story on which it is based, and despite the flagrant racism of the noble-savage conception, Robeson himself has a nobility that transcends the picture's terms. He's magnificently stirring in his African bangles, especially when his chants roll out over the waters. Bosambo and Robeson's similar role in *King Solomon's Mines* were among his most popular performances. With the elegant Nina Mae McKinney, and Leslie Banks. b & w

The Sandpiper (1965)—At the time it was released, Richard Burton and Elizabeth Taylor, who had been the world's most highly publicized scandalous lovers during the making of *Cleopatra* only a couple of years before, had finally got married, and as the massive-headed Burton, looking more foreshortened than ever, eyed the portly Taylor in her Irene Sharaff poncho, and they delivered such lines as "I never knew what love was before" and "I've lost all my sense of sin," the people in the theatres could not contain themselves. The movie will probably never be quite as hilarious again, but it's a classic, no matter when you see it. Burton, an Episcopal clergyman, makes high-toned literary remarks to beatnik-atheist-artist Taylor, such as "I can't dispel you from my thoughts," and then, when he hates himself in the morning, she reassures him with "Don't you realize that what happened between us is *good*?" At the last, the clergyman, redeemed by contact with the atheist's spiritual values, casts off the temptations of wealth and worldly success and finds his simple faith again. If that isn't enough, there's Charles Bronson playing a sculptor (posing for him, Taylor demurely cups her breasts with her hands—though they seem inadequate to the task). Vincente Minnelli directed from a script by Dalton Trumbo and Michael Wilson. With Eva Marie Saint as the clergyman's wife; she says bright things like "Thinking is a kind of prayer, isn't it?" M-G-M. color

Le Sang d'un poète, see *The Blood of a Poet*

Sans mobile apparent, see *Without Apparent Motive*

Sans toit ni loi, see *Vagabond*

Santa Fe Trail (1940)—One of Hollywood's careless, shameless distortions of American history. The team of Errol Flynn and Olivia de Havilland had thrived under the direction of Michael Curtiz in such films as *Captain Blood*, *The Adventures of Robin Hood*, and *Dodge City*, and so this bloated Western was confected. Flynn plays a monolithically brave Jeb Stuart, and Ronald Reagan is young George Armstrong Custer; they're both after dainty Olivia. The offensive plot pits the two handsome young blades, fresh from West Point, against a rabid, fanatic John Brown (Raymond Massey, at his most burning-eyed hypertense, and photographed to inspire fear and revulsion in the audience). The black men whom Brown seeks to liberate appear to be childish dupes. It's a romantic, action-filled, screwed-up epic; you get the feeling that maybe nobody intended it to be as reactionary as it turned out, with Olivia looking especially fetching in front of the gallows where Brown is hanged. At the end, some good liberal appears to have had a fit of remorse: when the heroine goes on her wedding trip with Stuart, the sound of "John Brown's Body" rises above the rhythm of the moving train. The large cast includes Van Heflin (a dirty villain), Douglas Fowley, Gene Reynolds, Alan Hale, Alan Baxter, Susan Peters, and Ward Bond. The screenplay is by Robert Buckner; music by Max Steiner. Warners. b & w

Saratoga Trunk (Made in 1943, but not released until 1946.)—A brunette Ingrid Bergman plays the fabulous adventuress Clio Dulaine in this exhilarating travesty of Edna Ferber's costume romance about the railroad robber barons. Flanked by Flora Robson in incredible blackface as the mulatto maid Angelique and Jerry Austin as the dwarf manservant Cupidon, Bergman is a demimondaine raised in Paris, who returns to plague her father's respectable Creole family in New Orleans and then invades fashionable Saratoga Springs and conquers all, including Gary Cooper, as the gambling Texan Clint Maroon. This is a lavish piece of frivolous, ebullient moviemaking—replete with details dear to the readers of tempestuous fiction (i.e., the heroine enjoys champagne with peaches in the afternoon), and those who abandon themselves to it for two hours can have a marvellous time. Clio the trollop is Bergman's flirtiest, funniest role; the dark hair seems to liberate her from her usual wholesome blandness. There's a lovely moment when a pompous little lawyer (Curt Bois) looks at her, his eyes misting with admiration, and says, "Madame, you're very beautiful. I mean . . . *beautiful*." She smiles, "Yes, isn't it lucky?" Directed by Sam Wood, from Casey Robinson's screenplay. With Florence Bates, John Warburton, John Abbott, and Ethel Griffies. A bad, coy three minutes at the very end. Hal B. Wallis produced, for Warners. b & w

Sasame Yuki, see *The Makioka Sisters*

Satchmo the Great (1956)—In one scene, 100,000 Gold Coasters celebrate the "return" of the hero—Louis Armstrong. In another scene, a smile hovers on Prime Minister Nkrumah's face as Louis sings, "What did I do to be so black and so blue?" This record of the contact of civilizations was originally prepared for television by Edward Murrow and Fred Friendly; it covers Armstrong's trip to Europe, Africa, and his coming home. At the end there is a sad demonstration of what Dwight Macdonald calls the homogenization of culture: Armstrong performs with the lagging, dragging New York Philharmonic under the direction of Leonard Bernstein, and he looks very proud. But whatever he's doing—blowing the horn or singing "Mack the Knife" in England—the man with the voice that somebody said was "as smooth as a tired piece of sandpaper calling to its mate" is a spellbinder. (63 minutes.) b & w

Saturday Night and Sunday Morning (1961)—It's set entirely in working-class locations, the hero is a Nottingham factory worker, and the film is all told from his point of view. That may help to explain why English critics called it everything from "the finest picture of the year" to "the greatest English picture of all time." It's superbly photographed (by Freddie Francis) and Albert Finney is remarkable as the hero whose vitality has turned to belligerence. But this study of working-class energies and frustrations has been overdirected (by Karel Reisz). Everything is held in check; every punch is called and then pulled. When the hero and his cousin are fishing, the caught fish signals the end of the scene; a dog barks for a fade out. The central fairground sequence is like an exercise in cinematography, and the hero's beating is just another mechanical plot necessity. The fine cast includes Rachel Roberts, Norman Rossington, and Shirley Anne Field. Alan Sillitoe adapted his own novel; music by Johnny Dankworth. b & w (See *I Lost it at the Movies*.)

Saturday Night Fever (1977)—How the financially pinched 70s generation that grew up on TV attempts to find its own forms of beauty and release. John Travolta plays Tony, a 19-year-old Italian Catholic who works selling paint in a hardware store in Brooklyn's Bay Ridge; on Saturday nights, he's off to the local disco dream palace, where he's the champion dancer. It's Tony's pent-up physicality—his needing to dance, his becoming himself only when he dances—that draws us into the pop rapture of this film. The mood, the beat, and the trance rhythm are so purely entertaining, and Travolta is such an original presence, that a viewer spins past the crudeness in the script (by Norman Wexler, based on Nik Cohn's June 7, 1976, *New York* cover story, "Tribal Rites of the New Saturday Night"). Karen Lynn Gorney plays opposite Travolta as Stephanie, who is trying to climb out of Brooklyn and onto Manhattan, which is seen as the magic isle of opportunity—not ironically but with the old Gershwin spirit. Young moviegoers saw themselves expressed in this film, as earlier generations had seen themselves in *The Wild One, Rebel Without a Cause, The Graduate, Easy Rider*; Travolta became a national cult hero, almost overnight. John Badham directed. With Donna Pescow, Fran Drescher, Barry Miller, Joseph Cali, Paul Pape, Bruce Ornstein, Martin Shakar, Julie Bovasso, Val Bisoglio, and Monti Rock III. The music is by Barry, Robin, and Maurice Gibb, with additional music by David Shire. Choreography by Lester Wilson; cinematography by Ralf D. Bode. A Robert Stigwood Production, for Paramount. color (See *When the Lights Go Down*.)

Sauve qui peut/La Vie, see *Every man for Himself*

The Savage Is Loose (1974)—George C. Scott, Trish Van Devere, and John David Carson, as their son, are shipwrecked on a jungle island, and so is the audience. Agonizing. Produced and directed by Scott. color (See *Reeling*.)

Savage Messiah (1972)—Another of Ken Russell's unstable satires on romantic artists: it's Henri Gaudier-Brzeska's turn this time. Russell makes prankish, venomous jokes about the Vorticists, the suffragettes, and sensual art lovers. As the hero, Scott Antony is like a young, even less talented Rock Hudson or Stewart Granger, but as his platonic lover, Sophie Gaudier-Brzeska, Dorothy Tutin is a brilliant shrew—comic, high-powered, and erotically nasty. M-G-M. color (See *Reeling*.)

Save the Tiger (1973)—The picture asks us to weep for Harry the garment manufacturer (Jack Lemmon), who pimps for his customers so they'll give him their orders, and who plans to set fire to his warehouse so the insurance money will finance filling these orders. The picture is a moral hustle that says this high-living showoff is a victim of American materialism. Harry suffers and jabbers; the writer and producer, Steve Shagan, appears to think he has created a modern tragic hero, and he's determined to puff the movie up with wit and wisdom. Directed by John G. Avildsen. With Jack Gilford, Laurie Heineman, Norman Burton, and William Hansen. Paramount. color (See *Reeling*.)

Sawdust and Tinsel, see *The Naked Night*.

Say Amen, Somebody (1982)—A sensitive and absorbing documentary about the lives of the pioneers of gospel music. It features Thomas A. Dorsey, an 83-year-old hepcat who is still bouncing to the jazz rhythms that he brought into black people's churches in the late 20s and the early 30s—the Depression years—when he fused their profane and their sacred music and called the result gospel. The music keeps its singer-evangelists young, radiant, hearty. That's the film's unspoken message. At 78, Willie Mae Ford Smith, the matriarch of gospel, has astonishingly firm and strong contralto tones. And the three middle-aged Barrett Sisters—dramatic, physically striking women with ample figures in shiny, clinging blue gowns—sing so exhilaratingly that they create a problem for the young filmmaker, George T. Nierenberg. They bring the film to an emotional pitch, and we in the audience want to go on soaring; we feel let down when we get more reminiscences and only snatches of song. Talented as he is, Nierenberg may be too genteel for his subject. The movie doesn't acknowledge that for a lot of people the rhythmic excitement and spiritual uplift of gospel make it an overpoweringly pleasurable combination that leads to the convulsive writhing and muttering of religious possession. With the twin O'Neal brothers, and a sensationally attractive St. Louis singer, Zella Jackson Price (she looks better than she sounds). color (See *Taking It All In*.)

Say Anything (1989)—Lloyd Dobler (John Cusack) is a high-school senior who doesn't know what he wants to do yet. And he's so in awe of Diane (Ione Skye), the class valedictorian and prize student, that when he phones to ask her to the graduation party he can't keep up a sequential conversation—he babbles, and talks in spurts. Yet when they're out together he makes Diane feel happier than she has ever been. As for Lloyd, he's found bliss. He wants to hang on to Diane—for life. This first picture directed by Cameron Crowe (who wrote *Fast Times at Ridgemont High*) is unabashedly romantic about Lloyd Dobler's capacity to make a commitment. Crowe is great here on oddity and fringe moments; the comedy helps to dry out the romanticism—to give it lightness and a trace of enchantment. And Cusack is a wonder: Lloyd's (nearly) blank look tells you that a lot of things are going on inside him—he has a buzz in his blank face. Crowe's script has some central flaws, and there's no special moviemaking excitement in the picture, but it's a lovely piece of work. Clearly, Crowe loves actors. There's a compelling performance by John Mahoney as Diane's father; there are a couple of astonishingly fluid scenes between Cusack and his real-life sister Joan, playing Lloyd's sister. And the cast includes Lili Taylor as the girl who has written 65 songs about her ex-boyfriend's perfidiousness, Kim Walker, Loren Dean, Jason Gould, Eric Stoltz, Amy Brooks, Chynna Phillips, Lois Chiles, Philip Baker Hall, and a terrific 3-year-old, Glenn Walker Harris, Jr. Cine-

matography by Laszlo Kovacs. Released by 20th Century-Fox. color (See *Movie Love*.)

The Scalphunters (1968)—A rousing comedy-Western with an amiable tone. Ossie Davis is a runaway slave who is captured by Indians and Burt Lancaster is a stubborn-minded fur trapper. Lancaster gives one of those performances of his that really work and yet are so odd that it's hard to know why they work. Ossie Davis and he play quarrelling buddies, and they're peculiarly funny together, maybe because they're both such physical performers. (At the end they fight in mud and emerge the same color.) Shelley Winters chomps on a stogie and bones up on astrology in the covered wagon she shares with her temporary sweetie, Telly Savalas. Under Sydney Pollack's direction they all perform with wit and—for these four—restraint. The movie becomes a shade idiotic near the end, but it's too enjoyable for that to matter much. With Nick Cravat, Dabney Coleman, and Armando Silvestre. Script by William Norton; music by Elmer Bernstein; cinematography by Duke Callahan and Richard Moore. Produced by Levy-Gardner-Laven, and Roland Kibbee (who also had a hand in *The Crimson Pirate*). United Artists. color

Scandal (1989)—Tepid. The director, Michael Caton-Jones, and the writer, Michael Thomas, who dig up the Profumo affair, might have used it as the basis for a satirical slice of history; instead, they've made a sentimental docudrama—one more English film about the cruelty of the class system. What sustains a viewer is the narrative, with its evocative details of life in London from 1959 to 1963—how teen-age showgirl Christine Keeler (Joanne Whalley-Kilmer), bored with the middle-aged dignitaries that the society osteopath Stephen Ward (John Hurt) introduced her to, took on a West Indian lover and then another West Indian, and how, as a result of a violent quarrel between the two, a newspaperman got on her trail. She then offered up the story of her earlier gentlemen callers, the Tory Secretary of State for War, John Profumo (Ian McKellen), and the assistant naval attaché of the Soviet Embassy (Jeroen Krabbé). And bang! The tabloids whipped up indignation over the decadence of the Establishment—over sadomasochism and spies and naked bathing in Lord Astor's pool. Along the way there's Ward introducing Christine to hash and her becoming spacey, and the music changing, and the kinky Victorian repressiveness giving way to London's Swinging 60s. But Whalley-Kilmer's Christine is opaque, unreadable. She comes to life a bit in her scenes with her showgirl pal, Mandy Rice-Davies, played by Bridget Fonda, who brings a gamine crispness to the role. She's the movie's only wild card. With Daniel Massey, Roland Gift, Britt Ekland, Leslie Phillips, and Trevor Eve. Miramax. color (See *Movie Love*.)

Le Scandale, see *The Champagne Murders*

Scarface (1932)—The gangster classic, with Paul Muni as the dangerous hood with the scar on his cheek, and dark, huge-eyed Ann Dvorak as his sister. The writer, Ben Hecht, and the director, Howard Hawks, said that they wrote the story by treating the Capone family "as if they were the Borgias set down in Chicago." Overall, it's a terrific movie, even though the pacing doesn't always seem quite right. The opening sequence is a beauty: the camera moves from a street lamp with stylized skyscrapers in the background and follows a milkman into a speakeasy, where we see the remnants of a gangland New Year's Eve party and finally pick up the shadow of Scarface, who kills the gangland leader. The film's violence has the crazy, helter-skelter feeling of actual gun battles, and Paul Muni, with a machine gun in his

arms, is brutal and grotesque, in a primal, childlike, fixating way. Truffaut suggests that Hawks "deliberately directed Paul Muni to make him look like a monkey, his arms hanging loosely and slightly curved, his face caught in a perpetual grimace." The cast includes George Raft, Osgood Perkins, Karen Morley, Boris Karloff, Vince Barnett, Edwin Maxwell, C. Henry Gordon, Tully Marshall, Henry Armetta, and Purnell Pratt. Here's Truffaut again: "The most striking scene in the movie is unquestionably Boris Karloff's death. He squats down to throw a ball in a game of ninepins and doesn't get up; a rifle shot prostrates him. The camera follows the ball he's thrown as it knocks down all the pins except one that keeps spinning until it finally falls over, the exact symbol of Karloff himself, the last survivor of a rival gang that's been wiped out by Muni. This isn't literature. It may be dance or poetry. It is certainly cinema." The story, based on a novel by Armitage Trail, is credited to Hecht, and the continuity and dialogue to Seton I. Miller, John Lee Mahin, and W. R. Burnett. The cinematography is by Lee Garmes and L. W. O'Connell. The film was ready for release in 1930, but was held up for two years by censorship problems; the scene in the publisher's office wasn't directed by Hawks—it was inserted to appease pressure groups. The title *Scarface* bore the subtitle *Shame of the Nation*. Presented by Howard Hughes; United Artists. b & w

Scarface (1983)—Directed by Brian De Palma from a script by Oliver Stone, this 2-hour-and-49-minute remake of the 1932 *Scarface* has the length of an epic but not the texture of an epic, and its dramatic arc is faulty. Al Pacino's Tony Montana, a Cuban who scrambles to the top of the Miami drug world, is just starting to learn the ropes and then, sated with wealth and dope, he's moldy. The middle of the movie is missing; we get the aftermaths but not the capers. For the first three-quarters of an hour, the film feels like the beginning of a new-style, post-*Godfather* gangster epic—hot and raw, like a spaghetti Western. But when Tony gets everything he wants, he's a pig rooting around in money and cocaine, and, as things go wrong, he snorts more and more. Probably all this excess is intended to be satirical—snorting coke turns into a running gag. But the scenes are so shapeless that we don't know at what point we're meant to laugh. The picture is peddling macho primitivism and at the same time making it absurd. It's a druggy spectacle—manic yet exhausted, with De Palma entering into the derangement and trying to bring something larger than life out of Tony's debauchery. The whole feeling of the movie is limp. This may be the only action picture that turns into an allegory of impotence. With F. Murray Abraham as Omar, Steven Bauer as Manolo, Robert Loggia as Frank Lopez, Michelle Pfeiffer as Elvira, Mary Elizabeth Mastrantonio as Gina, Paul Shenar as Sosa, Harris Yulin as Bernstein, Arnaldo Santana as Ernie, Richard Belzer as the nightclub m.c., and some highly expendable scenes with Miriam Colon as Tony's poor-but-proud mother. Cinematography by John A. Alonzo; the designer Ferdinando Scarfiotti served as visual consultant; the score is by Giorgio Moroder—it's reminiscent of his music for *Cat People*. Produced by Martin Bregman, for Universal. color (See *State of the Art*.)

The Scarlet Empress (1934)—Josef von Sternberg turned the story of Catherine the Great into what he himself called a "relentless excursion into style"; the decor and the visual motifs became the stars, and Marlene Dietrich was used as a camera subject instead of as a person. She's photographed behind veils and fishnets, while dwarfs slither about and bells ring and everybody tries to look degenerate. Von Sternberg had a peculiar no-

tion that this showy pomposity proved that film was an art medium. The picture is egocentric and empty of drama, yet it has the fascination (and the tediousness) that bizarre, obsessional movies often have. Sam Jaffe, in a fright wig and smiling like a death's-head, plays mad, crippled Peter; Dietrich's daughter, Maria Sieber, appears in the opening scenes as the young Catherine; in the role of Count Alexei, John Lodge wears dashing long hair and a mustache and swaggers about in furs. With Louise Dresser, strangely folksy as the old Empress, and Jane Darwell, Gavin Gordon, C. Aubrey Smith, Olive Tell, and Edward Van Sloan. The script by Manuel Komroff was presumably based on a diary of Catherine's; the music is definitely based on Tchaikovsky and Mendelssohn. Paramount. b & w

The Scarlet Letter (1926)—"I wanted to make a film of *The Scarlet Letter* . . . I was asked which director I would like, and I chose Victor Sjöström, who had arrived at M-G-M some years earlier from Sweden. I felt that the Swedes were closer to the feelings of New England Puritans than modern Americans." With historic simplicity, Lillian Gish described the background to this film. She leaves it for us to explain her extraordinary taste and judgment—and her acting genius. Her Hester Prynne is one of the most beautifully sustained performances in screen history—mercurial, delicate, passionate. There isn't an actress on the screen today, and perhaps there never was another, who can move like Lillian Gish: it's as if no bones, no physical barriers, stood between her intuitive understanding of the role and her expression of it. Sjöström chose the Swedish actor Lars Hanson for Arthur Dimmesdale; Henry B. Walthall plays Prynne. Karl Dane is also in the cast. The cinematography is by Hendrik Sartov, who had earlier worked with Griffith; the adaptation—or diminution—of Hawthorne is by Frances Marion. Sjöström presents a heroine struggling against moralistic conventions; his conception is so strong that the coy elements in the scenario and the cloying titles almost disappear from consciousness. He stages Lars Hanson's final revelation scene with a power and conviction that justifies Lillian Gish's hunch: these two Swedes understand Hawthorne's guilt and suffering. (There have been numerous versions of the novel—the first in 1908.) Silent. b & w

The Scarlet Pimpernel (1935)—One of the most romantic and durable of all swashbucklers—maybe because Leslie Howard was such a wonderfully unlikely hero for this sort of derring-do about spies and aristocrats and the French Revolution. With Merle Oberon looking almost inhumanly beautiful, and Raymond Massey as the snarling villain, and Nigel Bruce, Bramwell Fletcher, Joan Gardner, Gertrude Musgrove, and Anthony Bushell. Script by S. N. Behrman, Robert Sherwood, and others, based on the novel by Baroness Orczy. Directed by Harold Young; an Alexander Korda Production. b & w

Scarlet Street (1946)—Fritz Lang directed this American version of Renoir's *La Chienne*; in the American setting it's a sordid, lowlife melodrama about illicit love, and it never takes root—it's not one of Lang's best American movies. (It was originally banned in New York State—that is, denied a license—as "immoral, indecent, corrupt, and tending to incite crime," a judgment that seemed off the wall even then.) Edward G. Robinson is a frustrated, gray-haired cashier married to a nag (Rosalind Ivan); his only pleasure is in painting on Sundays. He falls for a tart (Joan Bennett) and sets her up in a Greenwich Village apartment, on stolen money. But the tart is in love with a lout (Dan Duryea), who beats her. The script, by Dudley Nichols, is heavy-

handed, and Lang's emphatic style pounds home the ironies and the murder-plot devices. (Robinson kills the girl, and Duryea is electrocuted for the crime.) Robinson's paintings are actually by John Decker. Universal. b & w

Lo Sceicco Bianco, see *The White Sheik*

Scenes from the Class Struggle in Beverly Hills (1989)—The script, by Bruce Wagner, from a satirical sex-farce plot he devised with the director, Paul Bartel, calls for something like the goosey stylized acting that Charles Ludlam perfected at the Ridiculous Theatrical Company, but Bartel has directed with his usual home-movies sluggishness. Two houseboys, a cynic (Ray Sharkey) and a romantic (Robert Beltran), who work in adjacent mansions, bet on which one will be first to make out with the other's employer—one a divorcée (Mary Woronov), the other a widow (Jacqueline Bisset). The households include various siblings, offspring, and hangers-on (Arnetia Walker, Ed Begley, Jr., Wallace Shawn, Paul Mazursky, Rebecca Schaeffer, Edith Diaz, and others)—all of them libidinous or gaga. Scenes that should have some fizz and revelations that should be delirious are bland and flat, like filmed theatre. Arnetia Walker manages to bring in some zesty horseplay, and Bisset's amused calm is occasionally pleasant, but mostly this is just mistimed, failed camp, and some of the lines that are meant to be screamingly dirty-funny come out screamingly sour. (The sound recording is poor.) A Cinecom release. color

Sciuscià, see *Shoeshine*

Scrooge (1970)—Innocuous musical version of *A Christmas Carol,* starring Albert Finney looking glum. The Leslie Bricusse music is so forgettable that your mind flushes it away while you're hearing it. Ronald Neame directed. color (See *Deeper into Movies*.)

Scrooged (1988)—Bill Murray, in a striking, outsize entertainment based on Dickens' *A Christmas Carol*. Murray's Frank Cross, who's the youngest network president in history, is the meanest man in television. (That's the same as the meanest man in the world.) The performance is a triumphant parody of Yuppie callousness. And it's much more: Murray's freewheeling, screwy generosity is what makes the huge contraption of a movie work. With production design by J. Michael Riva and cinematography by Michael Chapman, this satirical extravaganza is set in a stylized, made-up universe with deep blues and black backgrounds—suave and velvety. The heartlessness of the film's beauty is exciting: you're looking at life in an executive's dark mirror. And the picture keeps popping surprises: David Johansen (also known as the lounge singer Buster Poindexter) is the grinning cabbie whose identification card reads "Ghost of Christmas Past." John Glover, who sports a collegiate "Tennis, anyone?" haircut, is the new executive who's bucking to replace Frank. Carol Kane, as the Ghost of Christmas Present, is a weirdly dainty Sugar Plum witch. Also with Robert Mitchum, John Forsythe, Alfre Woodard, Michael J. Pollard, Karen Allen, and many other famous performers. Directed by Richard Donner; the script is credited to Mitch Glazer and Michael O'Donoghue. (Elaine May and others also worked on it.) Paramount. (See *Movie Love*.)

The Sea Gull (1968)—This carelessly made version of the Chekhov play gives one an almost Chekhovian sense of missed opportunities; people come and go more rigidly than on a stage—they're practically swept away when they have spoken their lines. But Vanessa Redgrave is an extraordinarily grave and girlish Nina. She's almost too brilliant; she does so many marvellous things that at times they cancel each other out. James Mason is very fine as Trigorin, and because he is a quiet, somewhat passive actor, he seems more at home in Chekhov country than the rest of the cast does. Still, there are suggestions of what the other roles should be in the performances of David Warner, Denholm Elliott, Kathleen Widdoes, Eileen Herlie, Harry Andrews, and the miscast Simone Signoret. Directed by Sidney Lumet; cinematography by Gerry Fisher. Warners. color (See *Going Steady*.)

The Sea Hawk (1940)—Errol Flynn, playing a hero based on Sir Francis Drake, in a rousing swashbuckler directed by Michael Curtiz. The Spaniards talk peculiar slang, considering that the year is 1585, but Flora Robson's Queen Elizabeth is a vigorous shrewdie. The cast includes Brenda Marshall, Claude Rains, Gilbert Roland, Henry Daniell, Alan Hale, Una O'Connor, Donald Crisp and many other well-known performers. Seton I. Miller and Howard Koch were the writers; the music is by Erich Wolfgang Korngold. Warners. b & w

The Sea of Grass (1947)—A big clinker that Elia Kazan would probably just as soon forget. Spencer Tracy plays a grim Southwestern cow-country baron who tries unsuccessfully to keep homesteaders off the land he considers his own. His wife (Katharine Hepburn) finds his antipathy for the homesteaders almost as trying as his mooning over his "sea of grass"; she has a brief fling with the homesteaders' dour lawyer (Melvyn Douglas) and presents her husband with a chubby boy. Tracy throws her out but keeps the child, who grows up to be Robert Walker. It takes a wild burst of melodramatics to bring Tracy and Hepburn together again, and they wind up preparing to spend the twilight of their lives peering at the grass. The scriptwriters (Marguerite Roberts and Vincent Lawrence) should have been run out of Hollywood, or maybe the guilty party is whoever bought the novel (by Conrad Richter). With Edgar Buchanan, Robert Armstrong, and Harry Carey. Produced by Pandro S. Berman, for M-G-M. b & w

The Sea Wall *Barrage contre le Pacifique* Also known as *This Angry Age.* (1958)—Marguerite Duras's novel is a study of decaying colonialism, set on the Pacific Coast of Indo-China. A Frenchwoman struggles to keep her rice fields safe, but the Pacific is too strong for the flimsy sea wall she has put up; her son and daughter are too busy with their sexual fantasies to care about the land or the wall. There are a great many crosscurrents in the book, and in trying to convey them all, the film turns into a fiasco, but it is in many ways a dazzling fiasco. It has photographic sequences (shot in Thailand) that suggest Renoir's *The River*, and some brother-sister scenes between Tony Perkins and Silvana Mangano that suggest Cocteau. The too-ambitious, too-international project was directed by René Clément, with Jo Van Fleet as the mother, and Alida Valli, Nehemiah Persoff, and Richard Conte. Screenplay by Irwin Shaw and Clément; cinematography by Otello Martelli; music by Nino Rota. A Dino De Laurentiis Production. color

The Search (1948)—Both Marlon Brando and Montgomery Clift made their screen débuts with the director Fred Zinnemann—Brando in *The Men* (1950) and Clift in this film, which was made in a quasi-documentary style (using actors as if they were documentary subjects and mixing them in with non-professionals) in a Zurich studio and in the U.N.R.R.A. camps in the U.S. Occupied Zone of Germany. It's about the terrors of the refugee children of the Second World War. A group of them panic when they're being put in a Red Cross ambulance, because they think they're being tricked into a motorized gas chamber, and a terrified, inarticulate little boy (played by 9-year-old Ivan Jandl, from Prague) runs away. As the American soldier who finds the boy, takes him in, gradually wins his trust, and restores him to speech, Clift gives the movie (which has that postwar U.N.–Marshall Plan piety running through it) a shot of excitement. His gestures and vocal rhythms and his emotional rapport with the child are different from the acting that moviegoers had been familiar with; he's sensitive and engaging in a new stylized, yet realistic, way. The movie crosscuts between what is happening to the boy and scenes of his desperate, persistent Czech mother (played by the singer Jarmila Novotna), who is trudging from camp to camp in search of him. The emotion got to many viewers, even though the manipulated suspense and the sentimental softening prevent the film from doing anything like justice to its subject. With Aline MacMahon radiating motherly warmth as a U.N.R.R.A. worker, and Wendell Corey. Zinnemann had been working in Hollywood since 1930, but many people who saw this film thought him a brilliant new European director, and his reputation was made. Produced by Lazar Wechsler, for M-G-M. b & w

The Searchers (1956)—John Wayne is the taciturn loner, Ethan Edwards, a Confederate veteran who arrives at his married brother's ranch in Texas in 1868. Learning that there are Comanches in the area, Ethan and Martin (Jeffrey Hunter), a part Cherokee young man who lives with the brother's family, go off to look for them. While they're away the Comanches attack the ranch; they return to a scene of horror—the house has been burned down and the family slaughtered, all except Ethan's two nieces, who have been abducted. The ravaged body of the older girl is found and buried; the search for the little one (played by Lana Wood) goes on. It's a peculiarly formal and stilted movie, with Ethan framed in a doorway at the opening and the close. You can read a lot into it, but it isn't very enjoyable. The lines are often awkward and the line readings worse, and the film is often static, despite economic, quick editing. What made this John Ford Western fascinating to the young directors who hailed it in the 70s as a great work and as a key influence on them is the compulsiveness of Ethan's search for his niece (whose mother he loved) and his bitter, vengeful racism. He's surly and foul-tempered toward Martin, who accompanies him during the five years of looking for the girl (who by then has turned into Natalie Wood, in glossy makeup, as if she were going to a 50s prom), and he hates Indians so much that he intends to kill her when he finds her, because she will have become the "squaw" to what he calls a "buck." The film doesn't develop Ethan's macho savagery; it's just there—he kills buffalo, so the Comanches won't have meat, and he shoots out the eyes of a dead Comanche. The sexual undertones of Ethan's character almost seem to belong to a different movie; they don't go with the many crude and corny touches in this one. Ford's attempts at comic relief are a fizzle—especially the male knockabout humor, an episode involving a fat Indian woman called Look (Beulah Archuletta), and the scenes with Hank Worden overacting the role of a crazy man. Throughout, the performances are highly variable. With Vera Miles, Dorothy Jordan, Ward Bond who wears a fine top hat, Henry Brandon as Chief Scar, Ken Curtis as Charlie the singing guitarist, Peter Mamakos as Futterman, Olive Carey, John Qualen, Antonio Moreno, Harry Carey, Jr., Walter Coy, Pippa Scott, Pat Wayne, Nacho Galindo, and in a small part, Mae Marsh. From a novel by Alan LeMay, adapted by Frank S. Nugent; music by Max Steiner; filmed in Colorado and in Monument Valley. (There are allusions to this film in *Star Wars,* *Mean Streets, Hardcore,* and many others.) Warners. color

Sebastian (1968)—Dirk Bogarde as a master decoder, in a London-set romantic thriller about espionage that's tolerably amusing whenever John Gielgud is on the screen demonstrating his flair for self-parody. The suspense never gets going, and the characters are literate according to a peculiarly illiterate theatrical convention: they make references to mythology and the classics. A few small jokes come off, or maybe we laugh just because they're so very small. When the picture tries to be Mod and posh and sexy it's extremely bad; *Modesty Blaise* already did what the director, David Greene, and the scriptwriter, Gerald Vaughan-Hughes, seem to be just barely considering. With Susannah York being kinky and smirky, and Lilli Palmer, Nigel Davenport, and Ronald Fraser. Cinematography by Gerry Fisher. color

Second Chorus (1940)—A misbegotten Fred Astaire musical. At the time, it was generally considered his worst picture, and Astaire himself later concurred in the judgment. He plays an overage undergraduate—a swing bandleader who keeps flunking his exams so that he can stay in college. The band is actually Artie Shaw's, considerably augmented. Astaire's romantic and tap partner is Paulette Goddard, who manages the band, and his rival for her affections is Burgess Meredith. The funnymen, Charles Butterworth and Jimmy Conlin, don't compensate for the scarcity of good numbers. The most memorable song is the one known by the line "I ain't hep to that step but I'll dig it." H. C. Potter directed; Bobby Hackett dubbed Astaire's trumpet, and Billy Butterfield dubbed Meredith's trumpet. Paramount. b & w

Second Fiddle (1939)—Mary Healy steals the picture clean away when she sings "I'm

Sorry for Myself." Then we're left with Sonja Henie skating and pouting and making pretty little faces to show that she's thinking. It's a padded little nothing about Hollywood life and publicity trickery, but the cast (Tyrone Power, Edna May Oliver, and Rudy Vallee) and the Irving Berlin songs keep it from being as lethally offensive as the Sonja Henie–John Payne movies. Sidney Lanfield directed, in his routine, straightforward manner; the script is by Harry Tugend. 20th Century-Fox. b & w

Seconds (1966)—John Frankenheimer's macabre sci-fi thriller about a diabolical conspiratorial organization that arranges for people to be "reborn" via plastic surgery. There are some good ideas tucked away inside the scrambled unpleasantness; the best of them concerns a banker (John Randolph) who is vaguely dissatisfied with his life and arranges a Faustian bargain for a second chance (he comes back as Rock Hudson) but doesn't have any conception of a new life. Unfortunately, Hudson seems dull to us as well as to himself. Frankenheimer shows off (he even stages a bacchanal), and James Wong Howe displays his camera pyrotechnics as if they were going on sale in the nation's supermarkets; Lewis John Carlino did the screenplay, from David Ely's novel. With Salome Jens, Jeff Corey, Murray Hamilton, Wesley Addy, and Will Geer. Paramount. b & w

Secret Agent (1936)—Not altogether successful Hitchcock version of Somerset Maugham's spy thriller, *Ashenden*, but it has a bright, quick, fresh touch, and it's fixating, partly because the two male leads, John Gielgud and Peter Lorre, are so ill-used. Gielgud looks like a tailor's dummy for Leslie Howard, and Lorre plays a cheerful little killer who speaks with a Mexican accent and wears a single earring. With Madeleine Carroll, Robert Young, and Lilli Palmer. b & w

Secret Honor (1984)—As Richard Milhous Nixon, Philip Baker Hall delivers a wild rumination on his life—a mixture of confession and self-exoneration. Directed by Robert Altman, the movie has a heightened quality, as if all the tumult of Nixon's last year in the White House, his resignation, and his pardon—all the news that we devoured from magazines and the papers and TV, and the constant stream of revelations—were compacted into this frazzled monologue. It's a seizure, a crackup, and the near-pornographic excess of the display is transfixing. There's a virtuoso naughtiness about the sureness of Altman's touch here; he has a small, weird triumph with this gonzo psychodocudrama. From the play by Donald Freed and Arnold M. Stone; cinematography by Pierre Mignot. color (See *Hooked*.)

The Secret Life of Walter Mitty (1947)—Worse than there's any excuse for, considering that the James Thurber story seems like simple, foolproof movie material. But this was to be a big Sam Goldwyn production, and somebody decided that it wasn't enough simply to show the extravagant daydreams of a timid, harried man (Danny Kaye), so a plot was invented that plunges him into a string of adventures that are as unbelievable as any of his dreams. Kaye is often very funny—fantasizing himself as a grim-faced captain battling a typhoon or as an eminent surgeon saving a patient's life—but when the picture gets derailed and he starts chasing crooks, it's tedious. The scriptwriters, Ken Englund and Everett Freeman, don't do too well by the domestic episodes, either. The cast includes Boris Karloff, Florence Bates, Virginia Mayo (she's not much help), Ann Rutherford, Reginald Denny, and Fritz Feld. Norman Z. McLeod directed; Sylvia Fine provided two patter numbers, which seem rather inappropriate. R K O. color

The Secret of My Success (1987)—The story of how the farm-bred Brantley (Michael J. Fox) comes to Manhattan, is given a lowly mailroom job by his distant uncle (Richard Jordan), and takes over his uncle's wife (Margaret Whitton), mistress (Helen Slater), and conglomerate. The picture is stupid and often perfunctory; at the same time it's moderately enjoyable. It has a let's-try-it cheerfulness, a knockout performance by Whitton, who's like a Lubitsch vamp, and nonchalant bits of artifice that are like Lubitsch touches. The director, Herbert Ross, seems to take the derivative, jumbled material as a challenge, and he gives the adventures of Fox's polite Yuppie hustler a spinning, light-headed quality. With standout "character" performances by Elizabeth Franz as Brantley's mother, John Pankow as his mailroom pal, Christopher Murney as the boss of the mailroom, Susan Kellerman and Carol Ann Susi as secretaries, and Mercedes Ruehl as a waitress. The script is credited to Jim Cash & Jack Epps, Jr., and A. J. Carothers, though the dialogue was reworked by others—principally by Peter Stone, and by Christopher Durang, who appears as the most petulant member of the corporate board. The cinematography is by Carlo Di Palma; the editing is by Paul Hirsch. The movie is painless, except for the music (by David Foster). Universal. color (See *Hooked*.)

The Secret of Santa Vittoria (1969)—Anthony Quinn and Anna Magnani are Italo Bombolini and his wife, Rosa; he's the town drunkard and buffoon, and she's a virago, rolling pin in hand. If you want to know more, you deserve everything you get—even the cast of thousands of hairy, warty, wine-loving peasants, waving their funny Italian arms, in the way they do only in American movies. When the director is Stanley Kramer they make their funny Italian sounds extra loud. United Artists. color (See *Deeper into Movies*.)

Secret People (1951)—The use of violence for idealistic purposes is the theme of this English suspense film. Valentina Cortese plays a refugee from totalitarianism who becomes involved in an underground movement in London; her revulsion and guilt when she employs brutal methods are contrasted with the attitude of her lover (Serge Reggiani), a hardened revolutionary. With the very young Audrey Hepburn in a sizable role (it's rather like seeing Cinderella before the transformation), and Irene Worth, Athene Seyler, Charles Goldner, and Megs Jenkins. The expressive camera movements and the editing techniques of the director, Thorold Dickinson, were much discussed at the time, yet the film isn't very gripping. Written by Dickinson and Wolfgang Wilhelm. b & w

The Secret Sharer (1952)—Joseph Conrad's story of the new master of a ship (James Mason) who must decide what to do with a murderer (Michael Pate) makes an intense, eerie mood piece. This short-story film was directed by John Brahm; it was originally presented, along with *The Bride Comes to Yellow Sky*, under the title *Face to Face*. Produced by Huntington Hartford; released by R K O. b & w

Secrets of Women *Kvinnors Väntan* (1952)—Eva Dahlbeck, Anita Björk, and Maj-Britt Nilsson tell the stories of their marriages, in this cloyingly middle-class comedy-melodrama, written and directed by Ingmar Bergman. With Gunnar Björnstrand, Jarl Kulle, and Birger Malmsten. In Swedish. b & w

S

Section spéciale, see *Special Section*

Semi-Tough (1977)—Starting from Dan Jenkins' popular 1972 novel, an anecdotal burlesque about professional football players, the director, Michael Ritchie, and the screenwriter, Walter Bernstein, made a movie that's a loose series of riffs on the human-potential, consciousness-raising movement, with the two football stars (Burt Reynolds and Kris Kristofferson) involved in a romantic comedy triangle with the team owner's daughter (Jill Clayburgh). The film ambles along in a sunshiny, woozy, hit-or-miss way. Ritchie has an offhand visual slapstick sense, and he supplies about 20 minutes of funny bits that you catch out of the corner of your eye; with that and Reynolds' polished good-ol'-boy Cary Grant performance, the movie is like a low-grade fever—you slip in and out of it painlessly. With Bert Convy and Robert Preston; cinematography by Charles Rosher, Jr. Produced by David Merrick; released by United Artists. color (See *When the Lights Go Down.*)

The Senator Was Indiscreet (1947)—This satirical farce about political corruption is the only movie that the famous comedy writer George S. Kaufman ever directed. He doesn't show much talent for the medium; he gets his laughs by broad spoofing and overemphatic wisecracks that seem pitched to the last row in the balcony. The film is disappointingly short on wit, especially if one considers that Nunnally Johnson was the producer and Charles MacArthur wrote the script (from a story by Edwin Lanham), but it's still tolerable in a dumb, burlesque sort of way. William Powell flails about, trying to be funny in the tired slapstick role of a windbag senator running for President; with Ella Raines, Peter Lind Hayes, Hans Conried, Allen Jenkins, Arleen Whelan, Ray Collins,

Norma Varden, and an unbilled appearance by Myrna Loy. Universal. b & w

A Sense of Loss (1972)—Marcel Ophuls gets into what the struggle in Northern Ireland is about in a far deeper sense than a mere account of the factions or the recent political moves would: he observes the living roots of the hatred in family folklore, in the schools, and on the streets, and shows how it is passed from generation to generation, and how it feeds upon violence and repression. The structure of this documentary film is defective, but for the gifts of feeling that Ophuls offers, a little discomfort is a small price. This is perhaps the first film to demonstrate how the original crimes against a people go on festering. color (See *Reeling.*)

A Separate Peace (1972)—Not shameful, exactly; not much of anything. John Knowles' prep-school novel hasn't been dramatized; the director, Larry Peerce, seems to think that conversations in lyrical places are all that's needed to make a movie. It's all chatter. The nonprofessional cast acts "natural" enough, but there's no depth of character to this kind of acting, and no excitement. John Heyl, who plays Fearless Finny, bears on amusing resemblance to Burt Lancaster. Paramount. color

September (1987)—Woody Allen wrote and directed (but does not appear in) this roundelay of unrequited love. The general anguish spans 24 hours at the end of summer, just before September, and the setting is the tasteful yellow-beige interior of the Vermont house that belongs to Lane (Mia Farrow). She's a crushed, suicidal mouse, presumably because at 14 she shot her playgirl mother's brutal lover. The film's limp refinement suggests a generic Chekhov play drained of humor and mixed with Ingmar Bergman's

Autumn Sonata; the only thing that locates Woody Allen in the real world is that he wrote a screenplay about being haunted by the Johnny Stompanato–Lana Turner scandal. With Elaine Stritch as the belting, domineering life-force mother, and Dianne Wiest, Sam Waterston, Jack Warden, Denholm Elliott, and Rosemary Murphy. Orion. color (See *Hooked.*)

The Serpent's Egg (1977)—Set in Berlin in 1923, this Ingmar Bergman film, made in English in Munich, is about a Jewish-American trapeze artist (David Carradine) and his sister-in-law (Liv Ullmann), who are entrapped by a mad doctor (Heinz Bennent)—a prophet who dreams of what the Nazis will accomplish in the 30s. The movie, which fills the screen with images of fear and blood, of head-splitting pain and death, and then throws in gothic political theories, is a crackpot tragedy. Everything is strained, insufficient, underfelt. Cinematography by Sven Nykvist. color (See *When the Lights Go Down.*)

Serpico (1973)—Al Pacino as Frank Serpico, the New York City policeman whose incorruptibility alienated him from his fellow-officers and turned him into a messianic hippie freak. The theme is richly comic, and the film is great fun, even though it sacrifices Serpico's story—one of the rare hopeful stories of the time—for a cynical, downbeat finish. Norman Wexler (who wrote *Joe*) is responsible for most of the hip humor; he writes virulent lowlife dialogue with a demented lift. The screenplay is by Waldo Salt and Wexler, based on the book by Peter Maas. Directed, sloppily but effectively, by Sidney Lumet—he sends the comic lines across. The picture has a cartoon stridency, and the laughter isn't deep or lasting, but it's good and rude, and there's lots of it. Paramount. color (See *Reeling.*)

The Set-Up (1949)—This intelligently modest, low-budget film about a shabby, aging prizefighter (Robert Ryan) is generally considered a classic. It's not a great movie, or even a very good one (it's rather mechanical), but it touches one's experience in a way that makes it hard to forget. (Maybe that's why so many movies have imitated it, even though it wasn't a commercial success.) Based on a narrative poem by Joseph Moncure March and written by Art Cohn, it was directed by Robert Wise and shot (by Milton Krasner) in actual locations. Ryan—his face never more craggily heroic than in defeat—raised the picture above its poetry-of-realism aspirations. With Audrey Totter as the fighter's perceptive, harried wife, George Tobias, Wallace Ford, and Alan Baxter. R K O. b & w

Seven Beauties *Pasqualino Settebellezze* (1975)—The writer-director Lina Wertmüller's slapstick-tragedy investigation of an Italian common man's soul, set during the Second World War, with flashbacks to the 30s. Pasqualino, or as he's called, Pasqualino Seven Beauties (Giancarlo Giannini), deserts the Italian Army in Germany, is captured by the Germans, and is sent to a concentration camp. In flashbacks, we see his prewar life as a two-bit mafioso, with fat sisters—the "seven beauties." Pasqualino is everybody's dupe—a man who has swallowed all the lies that society hands out. He believes what the Mafia tells him, what Mussolini tells him, what anybody in authority tells him. As Giannini plays him, he's a Chaplinesque Fascist—the Italian Everyman as a pathetic worm. He's the man who never fights back—the one who wheedles and whimpers and crawls through. Wertmüller reactivates the entire comic-opera view of Italians as cowards who will grovel to survive. The picture is full of flashy ideas, cruelty, moist wistfulness, and pious moralizing, and Wertmüller presents it all in a goofy, ebullient mood. The box-office success of this film represents a triumph of insensitivity. With Elena Fiore, Fernando Rey, Enzo Vitale, Mario Conti, and Shirley Stoler as the gross commandant of the concentration camp (though no woman in Nazi Germany could rise to such a post—Ilse Koch's power at Buchenwald derived from her being the commandant's wife). Cinematography by Tonino Delli Colli; art direction by Enrico Job; music by Enzo Iannacci. In Italian. color (See *When the Lights Go Down*.)

Seven Brides for Seven Brothers (1954)— Stanley Donen directed this big, highly praised musical, set in Oregon in 1850, and adapted from Stephen Vincent Benét's story "The Sobbin' Women" (based on Plutarch's *The Rape of the Sabine Women*). It's marred by a holiday family-picture heartiness—the M-G-M back-lot Americana gets rather thick. Howard Keel is the lead, with Jane Powell opposite him. The picture is ambitious in its use of dance, and was unusual in that it features male dancers (Jacques d'Amboise, Tommy Rall, Marc Platt, Matt Mattox, Jeff Richards, and Russ Tamblyn), who are most memorable in the "Lonesome Polecat" ballet in the snow. The most prominent among the women is Julie Newmar (then Newmeyer). The choreography is by Michael Kidd; the script is by Frances Goodrich and Albert Hackett; the score is by Gene dePaul and Johnny Mercer. CinemaScope, color

Seven Chances (1925)—The plot gimmick— the hero must be married in a few hours in order to collect an inheritance—is an antique, and the play flopped on Broadway, but what Buster Keaton and his gag writers managed to do with the material will be everlastingly fresh. When the news of the shy hero's need

to wed is published in the papers, prospective brides arrive, singly at first and then in droves, and the distraught man, fleeing them, dislodges a boulder, which dislodges others, and soon he is pursued by hundreds of huge boulders. It's a lovely comedy, imaginatively—possibly faultlessly—directed by Keaton. With Snitz Edwards and Ruth Dwyer. Silent. b & w

The Seven-Per-Cent Solution (1976)—The plot starts from two pieces of common knowledge—that Sherlock Holmes used cocaine, and that Sigmund Freud took the drug for a period. The fictional Holmes "lived" at the same time as the historical Freud; they're both myths by now, and by crossing these mythologies the film, adapted by Nicholas Meyer from his 1974 best-seller, gives us a luxuriant straight-faced parody, in which the two great detectives—Nicol Williamson's Sherlock Holmes and Alan Arkin's Sigmund Freud—pool their deductive skills to solve the mysterious kidnapping of one of Freud's patients (Vanessa Redgrave). The film is somewhere between the genial "little" English comedies of the 50s, with their nifty plots and overqualified performers, and the splashy, stylized James Bond pictures. Chief among the overqualified performers, who seem to be having an actor's holiday, is Laurence Olivier, in high form as the criminal mastermind Professor Moriarty—a prissy, complaining old pedagogue. Olivier plays the role with the covert wit that is his specialty. The others include Robert Duvall as Dr. Watson, Joel Grey, Anna Quayle, Samantha Eggar, Jill Townsend, Regine, Gertan Klauber, Georgia Brown, Jeremy Kemp, and Charles Gray. Directed by Herbert Ross, this is a highly civilized light entertainment. The production was designed by Ken Adam; the cinematography is by Oswald Morris; "The Madame's Song" is by Stephen Sondheim.

Universal. color (See *When the Lights Go Down*.)

The Seven Samurai *Shichi-Nin No Samurai* (1954)—Seven hired knights defend a village against 40 mounted bandits—their pay a few handfuls of rice. This 3½-hour epic on violence and action—Akira Kurosawa's masterpiece—has been widely imitated, but no one has come near it. With Toshiro Mifune and Takashi Shimura. (For a period in the 50s it circulated, in a much shorter version, under the title *The Magnificent Seven*, but in 1960 that title was appropriated by an American version of the story, with the samurai changed to gunmen.) In Japanese. b & w (See *I Lost it at the Movies*.)

Seven Sinners (1940)—Marlene Dietrich's name is Bijou in this one, and her theme song is "I Can't Give You Anything but Love, Baby." The picture is a rowdy mediocrity. Bijou, who entertains in a South Seas café, the Seven Sinners, is so attractive to the U.S. Navy that the commander of the fleet finds her a problem. "The Navy has enough destroyers," he says. Tay Garnett's direction keeps the melodrama tolerable, but there's not much glamour in the material. John Wayne is the male lead, and the picture's big moment is a barroom brawl. With Albert Dekker, Broderick Crawford, Anna Lee, and Mischa Auer. Universal. b & w

The Seven Year Itch (1955)—All that most people remember of this labored farce is the sequence with Marilyn Monroe standing on a New York subway grating when a train whooshes by; the air sends her skirt swirling up to her shoulders. The director, Billy Wilder, and George Axelrod reshaped Axelrod's Broadway hit about the summertime flirtation of a shy married man (Tom Ewell) in order to build up Monroe's role. Wilder flails away at such gags as a plumber (Victor Moore) dropping a wrench in a bathtub occupied by Monroe, who has caught her toe in the faucet. With Evelyn Keyes, Sonny Tufts, Robert Strauss, Oscar Homolka, Carolyn Jones, and Doro Merande. 20th Century-Fox. CinemaScope, color

1776 (1972)—A Broadway operetta featuring those lovable old codgers, the Founding Fathers, gathered at the Second Continental Congress. It's shameless: first it exploits them as clodhopping fools, and then it turns pious and reverential, asking us to see that their compromise on the issue of slavery may look like a sellout but was the only way to win the unity needed to break away from England—that what they did we would have done, too. Yocks and uplift—that's the formula. We get toilet jokes, frisky anachronisms, double-entendres, and the signing of the Declaration of Independence; the insulting dumb, crusty jocularity may have you shrinking in your seat. Peter Stone wrote the original show and adapted it for the screen, and Sherman Edwards conceived it and did the music and lyrics. The actors are like kids dressed up: John Adams (the prim William Daniels) is the sarcastic schoolboy, and his snoozing sidekick is Ben Franklin (that blue-ribbon coy attention-getter and overactor Howard Da Silva). The cast includes the lovely Blythe Danner as Martha Jefferson, Ken Howard as Jefferson, and John Cullum, Virginia Vestoff, Ron Holgate, Donald Madden, Ray Middleton, and Roy Poole. The director Peter H. Hunt's idea of camera movement is to follow them all as they scamper about. His camera is as busy as a nervous puppy chasing its master. Produced by Jack L. Warner, for Columbia. color (See *Reeling*.)

The Seventh Seal *Det Sjunde Inseglet* (1956)—Ingmar Bergman's medieval morality play about man in search of the meaning of life is set in 14th-century Sweden. But it's a magically powerful film—the story seems to be playing itself out in a medieval present. A knight (Max von Sydow), tormented and doubting, returns from 10 wasted years in the Crusades, and Death (Bengt Ekerot) comes to claim him. Hoping to gain some revelation or obtain some knowledge before he dies, the knight challenges Death to a game of chess. As they play, the knight observes scenes of cruelty, rot, and suffering that suggest the tortures and iniquity Ivan Karamazov described to Alyosha. In the end, the knight tricks Death in order to save a family of strolling players—a visionary, innocent, natural man, Joseph (Nils Poppe), his wife (Bibi Andersson), and their infant son. The knight, a sane modern man, asking to believe despite all the evidence of his senses, is childlike compared with his carnal atheist squire (Gunnar Björnstrand). The images and the omens are medieval, but the modern erotic and psychological insights add tension, and in some cases, as in the burning of the child-witch (Maud Hansson), excruciation. The actors' faces, the aura of magic, the ambiguities, and the riddle at the heart of the film all contribute to its stature. In Swedish. b & w

The Seventh Veil (1945)—In the mid-40s, when the New York critics said a film was for "adult minds" they were referring to something like *The Seventh Veil*—a rich, portentous mixture of Beethoven, Chopin, kitsch, and Freud. Ann Todd is the shy young pianist obsessed with the idea that she can never hit those keys again, and Heathcliff-Svengali James Mason is the smoldering cause of it all (his fires always seem to be banked). Herbert Lom performs that marvellous 40s-movie type of psychoanalytic cure: he discovers which of her suitors the heroine really loves. All this nonsense is highly entertaining: maybe, with a few veils stripped away, most of us have a fantasist inside who gobbles up this sadomasochistic sundae, with its culture sauce. Directed by Compton Bennett; screenplay by Muriel and Sydney Box. b & w

Shadow of a Doubt (1942)—The setting is quiet, clean, sleepy Santa Rosa, California; it is invaded by a psychopathic killer (Joseph Cotten), who comes to visit his unsuspecting and adoring relatives. Until Alfred Hitchcock made *Strangers on a Train,* he considered this fine thriller (from a script principally by Thornton Wilder) to be his best American film. It's very well worked out in terms of character and it has a sustained grip, but it certainly isn't as much fun as several of his other films. With Patricia Collinge, Teresa Wright, Hume Cronyn, and Henry Travers. Cinematography by Joe Valentine; music by Dmitri Tiomkin. Universal. b & w

Shadow of the Thin Man (1941)—Hardly even a shadow; Myrna Loy, William Powell, and Asta go through their paces for the fourth time, but the jauntiness is gone. This one is about a murder involving racetrack crooks, and the only thing that gives it any distinction is the cast. The most amazing people keep turning up: Stella Adler as a gambler's blond floozy, Barry Nelson as a muckraking reporter, Joseph Anthony, Donna Reed, Sam Levene, Louise Beavers, Alan Baxter, and many others. Too bad Harry Kurnitz, who wrote the story, didn't give them more to do; W. S. Van Dyke directed. M-G-M. b & w

The Shadow Warrior, see *Kagemusha*

Shalako (1968)—As the hero of this Western, Sean Connery is tough, like the Clark Gable heroes but smarter and smoother—somewhat less fatuous. Like Charlton Heston, Connery plays conventional heroes the way most actors play villains—scowling and sullen and insolent, not so much the good guy as the rugged superman casually contemptuous of the amenities observed by mere good guys. He has more presence and style (even in his indifference) than this picture deserves. It's one of those movies in which the hero has to be a man of few words because if he ever explained anything to the other characters they wouldn't get into the trouble they get into that he has to get them out of, and there wouldn't be a movie. There isn't much of one anyway. Taken from a Louis L'Amour novel, it's about a group of European aristocrats on safari in New Mexico Territory in the 1880s (with Connery as their guide); it's tidily rigged so that the bad people and the expendable servants get killed off by the Indians and each other, the half-bad people reform, and the good ride away into the bright future. Through the insanities of casting for the international market, that appealing slutty gamine Brigitte Bardot is a countess, delicately wringing her hands while Connery fights an Apache (Woody Strode!). The director, Edward Dmytryk, doesn't even try to bring out Bardot's comic sparkle. The woman who set the style for modern girls to look like amoral teen-age whores is supposed to act highborn; she's left stranded on the screen with her smudged, pouty mouth open and the dark roots showing in her yellow hair. With Honor Blackman, Jack Hawkins, Stephen Boyd, Peter Van Eyck, Eric Sykes, Alexander Knox, and Victor French. Made in Spain. color

Shame *Skammen* (1968)—Ingmar Bergman's simple, masterly vision of normal war and what it does to survivors. Set a tiny step into the future, the film has the inevitability of a common dream. Liv Ullmann is superb in the demanding central role—one that calls for emotional involvements with her husband (Max von Sydow) and her lover (Gunnar Björnstrand). One of Bergman's greatest films, this is one of the least known. Cine-matography by Sven Nykvist. In Swedish. b & w (See *Going Steady*.)

The Shameless Old Lady *La Vieille Dame indigne* (1964)—An agreeable though thin comedy about how an old lady discovers the pleasures of the modern world after her husband's death. A little too lulling and gratifying; it encourages the audience to chuckle in condescension at miserliness and meanness. With that great old screen-stealer Sylvie occupying center stage for a change. Written and directed by René Allio; based on a story by Brecht. With Malka Ribovska, Victor Lanoux, and Jean Bouise; cinematography by Denys Clerval. In French. b & w

Shampoo (1975)—This sex roundelay is set in a period as clearly defined as the jazz age—the time of the Beatles and miniskirts and strobe lights. When George (Warren Beatty), the hairdresser hero, asks his former girlfriend, Jackie (Julie Christie), ''Want me to do your hair?'', it's his love lyric. When George gets his hands in a woman's hair, it's practically sex, and sensuous, tender sex—not what his Beverly Hills customers are used to. The film opens on Election Eve, November 4, 1968, and ends the day after Nixon and Agnew's victory; it deals with George's frantic bed-hopping during those 40-odd hours, in which he tries to borrow the money to open his own shop, so he can settle down with his current girlfriend, Jill (Goldie Hawn). The script by Robert Towne, with the collaboration of Beatty (who also produced), isn't about the bondage of romantic pursuit—it's about the bondage of the universal itch among a group primed to scratch. The characters (the others are played by Jack Warden, Lee Grant, Tony Bill, and Carrie Fisher) have more than one sex object in mind, and they're constantly regrouping in their heads. When they look depressed you're never sure who exactly is the object of their misery. The director, Hal Ashby, has the deftness to keep us conscious of the whirring pleasures of the carnal-farce structure and yet to give it free play. This was the most virtuoso example of sophisticated, kaleidoscopic farce that American moviemakers had yet come up with; frivolous and funny, it carries a sense of heedless activity, of a craze of dissatisfaction. With Jay Robinson, George Furth, Brad Dexter, William Castle, and, in a bit, Susan Blakely. Cinematography by Laszlo Kovacs. Columbia. color (See *Reeling*.)

Shane (1953)—The Western stranger in town consciously turned into Galahad on the range. Superficially, this is a Western, but from Shane's knightly costume, from the way his horse canters, from the Agincourt music, it's all too recognizable as an attempt to create a myth. With chivalric purity as his motivation, the enigmatic Shane (Alan Ladd) defeats enemies twice his size—the largest is the Prince of Darkness himself, Jack Palance. The earth-loving Wyoming homesteaders befriended by Shane include Van Heflin, Jean Arthur as his wife, and Brandon deWilde as their child. This George Stevens film is overplanned and uninspired: Westerns are better when they're not so self-importantly self-conscious. However, audiences wept over the scene in which a dog mourns at his master's coffin, and Jean Arthur's farewell handshake to Shane—whom she loves—brought forth sniffles. Brandon deWilde's final cry, "Shane," was heard for years wherever kids played. With Edgar Buchanan, Elisha Cook, Jr., Ben Johnson, and Emile Meyer. The screenplay is by A. B. Guthrie, Jr., from Jack Schaefer's novel. The cinematography by Loyal Griggs won the Academy Award; this must have struck him as a black joke, because Paramount, in order to take advantage of the new fashion for the wide screen, had mutilated the compositions by cutting off the top and bottom. color

Shanghai Express (1932)—Irresistibly enjoyable. Marlene Dietrich gets to deliver what is perhaps her most memorable line: "It took more than one man to change my name to Shanghai Lily." In this glossy mixture of sex and intrigue, Shanghai Lily and her exquisitely stoic beloved (Clive Brook) fall into the hands of sinister Chinese revolutionaries led by Warner Oland. (He gets to deliver a camp classic—"The white woman stays with me.") When this Oriental chieftain questions Lily about why she's going to Shanghai, she answers "To buy a new hat." The scriptwriter, Jules Furthman, must have had a special affection for that line, because he gave it to Lauren Bacall, in her début film, *To Have and Have Not*, in 1944. Directed by Josef von Sternberg, this movie has style—a triumphant fusion of sin, glamour, shamelessness, art, and, perhaps, a furtive sense of humor. With Anna May Wong, Gustav von Seyffertitz, Eugene Pallette, Louise Closser Hale, Lawrence Grant, and Emile Chautard. Cinematography by Lee Garmes; art direction by Hans Dreier; based on a story by Harry Hervey. Paramount. b & w

The Shanghai Gesture (1941)—Hilariously, awesomely terrible. Pressure groups were so strong at the time that the moviemakers had to clean up John Colton's old melodrama about night-life depravities in Shanghai; Mother Goddam became Mother Gin Sling (Ona Munson), and her establishment became nothing more disreputable than a gambling den. Josef von Sternberg proceeded to pack the orgiastic, smoky atmosphere with crowds of coolies, diplomats, roulette players, and "bird-cage" girls, and in the foreground he put one of the most ridiculous casts ever assembled. Victor Mature, in a burnous, as the languid Dr. Omar—his eyes welling with mysterious passions—is worth the price of admission, and when you throw in Gene Tierney, as Poppy, a rich girl going to the dogs (Tierney acts as if she's having a tantrum in Schrafft's over the fudge sauce), you've got a gorgeous travesty. Some of this effect is probably intentional, but the total effect couldn't have been. Walter Huston stalks through as Mother Gin Sling's former lover, and the cast includes Maria Ouspenskaya, Phyllis Brooks, Ivan Lebedeff, Mike Mazurki, Albert Basserman, Eric Blore, Marcel Dalio, Mikhail Rasumny, and John Abbott. Cinematography by Paul Ivano; art direction by Boris Leven. Produced by Arnold Pressburger; released by United Artists. b & w

She (1935)—Hilarious, terrible, essential. Over the land of Kor rules She (Helen Gahagan Douglas, before her political career), kept young throughout five centuries by her Flame of Eternal Youth. The stagey decor of Kor is in the Art Deco style of Radio City Music Hall, and you keep expecting the Rockettes to turn up. The dialogue, however, belongs to an earlier age: the great She addresses her subjects with such lines as "You haunters of darkness, how you try my patience!" A pair of lovebirds (Helen Mack and Randolph Scott) intrude upon the realm, and She, who takes a fancy to Scott and plans to make a human sacrifice of her rival, tries one too many dips in the Flame. No one but H. Rider Haggard could have dreamed up the story; Irving Pichel and Lansing C. Holden directed. With Nigel Bruce. Camp like this is a rarity. Adapted by Ruth Rose, with some assistance from Dudley Nichols; produced by Merian C. Cooper, for R K O. (There were versions in 1908, 1911, 1916, and 1917, and a later one, with Ursula Andress, in 1965.) b & w

She Done Him Wrong (1933)—Mae West, the great shady lady of the screen, wiggles and sings "Easy Rider" and seduces virtuous young Cary Grant. A classic comedy and a classic seduction. Written by the star, from her play *Diamond Lil*, with some help on the script by Harvey Thew and John Bright; directed by Lowell Sherman. With Rafaela Ottiano as the woman who gets herself killed, and Gilbert Roland, Owen Moore, Rochelle Hudson, Dewey Robinson, Noah Beery, and David Landau. Paramount. b & w

She Married Her Boss (1935)—The flat title tells the whole story of this uninspired office romance. Claudette Colbert, a chic, hyper-efficient secretary, is in love with her rich, miserable department-store-owner boss (Melvyn Douglas). He has a spoiled brat (Edith Fellows) by a previous marriage and a rotten sister who keeps house for him. When he finally marries Claudette, she takes on his domestic mess and discovers that he expects her to be Miss Efficiency forever. This is one of those movies in which all problems are finally solved by the hero and heroine getting drunk and throwing bricks through plate-glass windows. Gregory La Cava directed. Columbia. b & w

She Wore a Yellow Ribbon (1949)—John Ford's film begins with Custer and the disgrace of Little Big Horn, and it has the handsome, faintly melancholy look of Frederic Remington's work. The subject is the burden of command, and the cavalry-captain hero (John Wayne), an officer on his last mission before retirement, is a man who, unlike Custer, is worthy of his office. Like Ford's other large-scale, elegiac Westerns of this period, it's not a plain action movie but a pictorial film with slow spots and great set pieces. There's some tedious Irish comedy (Victor McLaglen is around too much) and an irksome pair of lovers—John Agar and Joanne Dru. The cast includes Ben Johnson, Mildred Natwick, Noble Johnson, George O'Brien, Francis Ford, and Arthur Shields. Based on James Warner Bellah's *War Party*; screenplay by Frank Nugent and Laurence Stallings. Filmed in Monument Valley. R K O. color

Sheena (1984)—Some of the best animal actors ever to grace a movie—a stately elephant, a rhino, chimps, an amiable lion with a gigantic head—form a peaceable kingdom around Sheena (Tanya Roberts), a female Tarzan who rides a zebra-striped horse. This lighthearted, slightly loony adventure film is a takeoff of the late-30s comic-strip heroine who was featured in a mid-50s syndicated television series. Raised in "Zambuli territory" by a hyper-cultured black woman shaman, played by the majestically beautiful Elizabeth of Toro, the Cambridge-educated lawyer princess from Uganda who went into exile in Kenya (where this movie was shot), Sheena can communicate telepathically with animals and creatures of the sea and sky. Tanya Roberts is too tense and earnest for her blond-goddess, queen-of-the-jungle role, but she has the face of a ballerina, and a prodigious slim, muscular form, and she gazes into space with exquisitely blank pale-blue eyes. She's pretty funny when she presses her fingers on the center of her forehead and summons legions of waterbucks or swarms of tall birds. The script, by David Newman and Lorenzo Semple, Jr., has a central reversal-of-sex-roles joke—Sheena has the skills to survive in the environment, while the city-boy hero (Ted Wass), a TV sports producer, is lovestruck and helpless. The plot involves the efforts of a Westernized and corrupted African prince (Trevor Thomas) to seize the valuable lands of the Zambulis. The film is stilted and on some level it isn't quite awake—moments that could be effective are muffled (despite the use of fiery effects). But there are some good silly gags, and the animals look relaxed even in their dizziest slapstick scenes. And the picture certainly never starves the eye; the cinematography is by the celebrated Pasqualino

De Santis. Directed by John Guillermin; the cast includes Donovan Scott (regrettable as a comical TV cameraman) and Frances Zobda as Countess Zanda. Columbia. color (See *State of the Art*.)

Sheila Levine Is Dead and Living in New York (1975)—Gail Parent's novel is in the form of a fat girl's jokey suicide note, full of one-liners. Parent and her TV writing partner, Kenny Solms, rewrote it for the movies. Now it's the Romance of Liberation. No longer fat but clumsy and easily flustered, Sheila (Jeannie Berlin) comes to New York and meets a handsome doctor (Roy Scheider); it isn't until she becomes a successful career woman that he extricates himself from an involvement with her roommate (Rebecca Dianna Smith) and proposes. The film says that Sheila's finding herself entitles her to a first-class fella—the libbers get the princes. Jeannie Berlin, understandably, has nothing to express but bewilderment, and frequently she looks openmouthed comatose. Sidney J. Furie directed. Paramount. color (See *Reeling*.)

Sherlock Jr. (1924)—The title of this Buster Keaton comedy doesn't do justice to what the movie is about: Keaton plays a projectionist who, while running a movie—"Hearts and Pearls"—enters the screen and becomes involved with the characters. Directed by Keaton, it's a wonderfully imaginative film, full of extraordinary tricks so immaculately executed that they look simple. It's a piece of native American surrealism. With Kathryn McGuire as the heroine, and Keaton's father, Joe Keaton, as the heroine's father. Silent. b & w

She's Gotta Have It (1986)—The voluptuous, easygoing Nola (Tracy Camila Johns), a graphic designer who lives in the black bohemian world in Brooklyn, is happily juggling three lovers when she's faced by a mock crisis: each of the three men has turned possessive and wants to be her one and only. That's the premise of this quick-witted sex comedy written, directed, and edited by the 29-year-old Spike Lee, who shot it in 16-mm in twelve days, on an almost nonexistent budget. Nola, her three lovers, and her family and friends explain themselves directly to the camera, and the film's basic set is Nola's bed; you can't shoot a movie much cheaper or faster than that. Lee's economies become part of what's enjoyable about the film, and he keeps it all sparking and bouncing along. He gave the script the structure (and title) of an exploitation picture for the soft-core market, but his own exuberance and the soft lighting that the cinematographer Ernest Dickerson uses for the sex scenes transcend that structure and give the movie a lyrical, lilting feeling. Lee doesn't appear to know how to develop the story, and he fumbles toward the end. But by then the picture has built up so much good will that you don't feel too let down. With Tommy Redmond Hicks as the conventional narrow-minded middle-class romantic Jamie, John Canada Terrell as the vain and pretentious Greer, and Spike Lee himself as the jive artist Mars. The jazz score is by his musician father, Bill Lee. (The picture was completed on a final budget of $175,000, of which all except about $60,000 was deferred.) color (See *Hooked*.)

Shichi-Nin No Samurai, see *The Seven Samurai*

The Shining (1980)—Stanley Kubrick's gothic about the primal fear of a 5-year-old boy (Danny Lloyd) that his father (Jack Nicholson) will hurt his mother (Shelley Duvall) and him. The father, who wants to write, brings his wife and child to spend the winter in an isolated, snowbound, haunted hotel in Colorado, where he is to be the caretaker—and where he goes mad and acts out his son's fears. Though taken from a pulp best-seller, by Stephen King, the movie isn't the scary fun one might hope for from a virtuoso technician like Kubrick. It has a promising opening sequence, and there is some spectacular use of the Steadicam, but Kubrick isn't interested in the people on the screen as individuals. They are his archetypes, and he's using them to make a metaphysical statement about the timelessness of evil. He's telling us that man is a murderer through eternity. Kubrick's involvement in technology distances us from his meaning, though, and while we're watching the film it just doesn't seem to make sense. Nicholson gives the first hour its buzz, but then his performance begins to seem cramped, slightly robotized; Duvall's performance, however, becomes stronger as the film goes on, and she looks more like a Modigliani than ever. With Scatman Crothers, Joe Turkel, Barry Nelson, and Anne Jackson; script by Kubrick and Diane Johnson. Released by Warners. color (See *Taking It All In*.)

The Shining Hour (1939)—Elaborately staged, sanctimonious melodrama about a nightclub dancer (Joan Crawford) who marries into a feudal landowning family in Wisconsin and by disrupting the members' lives causes their spiritual regeneration. Melvyn Douglas is her husband, but his brother (Robert Young) is also in love with her, and this naturally creates difficulties for the brother's wife, Margaret Sullavan. Fearfully noble, she attempts to immolate herself, so that her husband will be free. The Keith Winter play had been set among quiet English farm people; the adaptors, Jane Murfin and Ogden Nash, gave the material the grand scale more appropriate to an M-G-M production, as well as the then practically mandatory happy ending. It's an unconvincing, overly classy film, with the selfish characters being ennobled by love in a way that nobody gets ennobled in movies anymore. Margaret Sullavan is a considerable asset, even in her do-gooding role. The cast also includes Fay Bainter as a smart, neurotic spinster, Hattie McDaniel, Allyn Joslyn, Frank Albertson, and Harry Barris. Directed by Frank Borzage. b & w

Ship Ahoy (1942)—Bert Lahr and Red Skelton turn up in this M-G-M musical starring Eleanor Powell; she taps all the way through, and at the end she taps out a message in Morse code. There are some relatively lively numbers, although Virginia O'Brien isn't as funny as she's meant to be. With John Emery, and Tommy Dorsey and his band, and its unbilled vocalist, Frank Sinatra. Some of the orchestrations are by Sy Oliver, and the number "I'll Take Tallulah" features Buddy Rich, along with Eleanor Powell. Directed by Eddie Buzzell, from Harry Clark's just barely functional script. b & w

Ship of Fools (1965)—A German ship travelling from Veracruz to Bremerhaven—an ocean-liner *Grand Hotel*. Katherine Anne Porter's novel was set in 1931, and though she explained the title as referring to the "simple almost universal image of the ship of this world on its voyage to eternity" (adding, "I am a passenger on that ship"), her vessel was also a microcosm of the pre-Nazi world, and the director, Stanley Kramer, and the scenarist, Abby Mann, move the date to 1933 and turn her conception into a pompous cartoon. The fools are those who do not see what is coming, and we're supposed to observe how the passengers' character flaws will lead to the Holocaust; Kramer and Mann give us dinner-party snubs as foreshadowings of the gas chambers. The movie is staccato, loud, and crude, and the relationships in the book are deformed. The novel's central sexual entanglement is that of two young artists—

Jenny, who is trying to be free, and puritanical David, who wants to own her. In the movie, George Segal's David (modelled, Abby Mann acknowledged, on himself) is a proletarian artist of great animal vitality who is being kept by neurotic, rich-bitch Jenny (Elizabeth Ashley). She is jealous of his genius, and he sums her up with "You're so full of competition. You're so full of God knows what kind of sickness." One can enjoy the movie by giggling over its florid swoony trash, such as the doomed lovers—the ship's doctor (Oskar Werner) smiling mistily, and compassionately giving injections and adoring love to La Condesa (Simone Signoret), who has met him too late. (Doctor: "You're so strange—sometimes you're so bitter, then you're like a child, soft and warm." La Condesa: "I'm just a woman.") The international star cast includes Vivien Leigh as an aging divorcée (this may be her most embarrassing screen performance—she's like a jerky Pinocchio), and Lee Marvin as a comical baseball player, José Ferrer as a Jew-baiting German businessman, Michael Dunn, Jose Greco, Charles Korvin, Lilia Skala, Heinz Ruhmann, Werner Klemperer, Alf Kjellin, and Kaaren Verne. Greeted with widespread enthusiasm by the press, as "powerful." Columbia. b & w (See *Kiss Kiss Bang Bang*.)

Shoah (1985)—Claude Lanzmann's 9-hour-and-23-minute documentary epic is made up of interviews with people who have knowledge of the Nazi extermination centers—whether as slave laborers, railroad workers, technicians, bureaucrats, or just onlookers. The film has fine, painful moments, and it's widely regarded as a masterpiece. But some may feel that it lacks the moral complexity of a great work, and may also find it logy and diffuse, and exhausting right from the start. Divided into Part I (4 hours and 33 minutes) and Part II (4 hours and 50 minutes). In Polish, French, German, English, Hebrew, and

Yiddish, with English subtitles where necessary. color (See *Hooked*.)

Shoeshine *Sciuscià* (1946)—Vittorio De Sica's lyric study of how two boys betrayed by society betray each other and themselves. It has a sweetness and a simplicity that suggest greatness of feeling, and this is so rare in films that to cite a comparison one searches beyond the medium. If Mozart had written an opera set in poverty, it might have had this kind of painful beauty. The two young shoeshine boys sustain their friendship and their dreams amid the apathy of postwar Rome, but they are destroyed by their own weaknesses and desires when they're sent to prison for black-marketeering. Cesare Zavattini wrote this study of the corruption of innocence; it is a social-protest film that rises above its purpose. In Italian. b & w (See *I Lost it at the Movies*.)

Shoot the Moon (1982)—As Faith and George Dunlap, whose marriage has become poisoned because she knows all his weaknesses and failures, and her knowledge eats away at his confidence, Diane Keaton and Albert Finney give the kind of performances that in the theatre become legendary. And, in its smaller dimensions, Dana Hill's performance as their 13-year-old daughter is perhaps equally fine. This unapologetically grown-up movie about separating is perhaps the most revealing American movie of its era. Though the director, Alan Parker, doesn't do anything innovative in technique, it's a modern movie in terms of its consciousness. The characters in the script written by Bo Goldman aren't taken from the movies, or from books, either. Their emotions are raw, and rawness is what makes this film get to you. It goes way past coolness. Diane Keaton has no vanity; Faith's angry misery is almost like a debauch—it makes her appear sodden. And both as a character and as an actor, Fin-

ney seems startled and appalled by what has been let loose in him. He's an actor possessed by a great role—pulled into it kicking and screaming, by his own guts. With Peter Weller, Karen Allen, George Murdock, and three child actresses—Viveka Davis, Tracey Gold, and Tina Yothers. Filmed on locations in Northern California; cinematography by Michael Seresin; production design by Geoffrey Kirkland; editing by Gerry Hambling. M-G-M. color (See *Taking It All In*.)

Shoot the Piano Player *Tirez sur le pianiste* (1960)—This François Truffaut film is based on David Goodis's *Down There*, a trim, well-written American crime novel. The movie busts out all over—and that's what's wonderful about it. Comedy, pathos, and tragedy are all scrambled up. Charlie, the sad-faced little piano player (Charles Aznavour), is the thinnest-skinned of modern heroes: each time he has cared about someone he has suffered, and now he just wants to be "out of it." This is a comedy about melancholia—perhaps the only comedy about melancholia. Truffaut is freely inventive here—a young director willing to try almost anything—and Charlie's encounters with the world are filled with good and bad jokes, bits from old Sacha Guitry films, clowns and thugs, tough kids, songs and fantasy and snow scenes, and homage to the American Grade-B gangster pictures of the 40s and 50s. The film is nihilistic in attitude yet by its wit and good spirits it's totally involved in life and fun. Nothing is clear-cut; the ironies crisscross and bounce. With Nicole Berger, Marie Dubois, Albert Rémy, Michèle Mercier, and Daniel Boulanger. Written by Truffaut and Marcel Moussy; cinematography by Raoul Coutard. In French. b & w (See *I Lost it at the Movies*.)

The Shooting (1965)—The low-budget Monte Hellman film shot in Utah at the same time as *Ride in the Whirlwind*. Carol Eastman, who sometimes uses the name Adrien Joyce and who later wrote *Five Easy Pieces*, did the enigmatic script. Millie Perkins, on horseback, is searching for something unspecified in the desert; she has a gunman riding behind her, on a leash. The cast includes Jack Nicholson, Warren Oates, and Will Hutchins. They use a dialect that may be authentic to something but is largely indecipherable. To lift from Henry James, Monte Hellman asks a lot for the little he gives. color

The Shooting Party (1984)—Working with Julian Bond's adaptation of Isabel Colegate's novel and a dream of a cast—James Mason (in his final movie), John Gielgud, Dorothy Tutin, Edward Fox, Gordon Jackson, Cheryl Campbell, Judi Bowker, Rupert Frazer, Aharon Ipalé—the director Alan Bridges carries the Masterpiece Theatre approach to the level of art. In the English countryside in the autumn of 1913, a large number of landed gentry, aristocrats, servants, gamekeepers, beaters, and loaders gather for a three-day shoot. Once again we get a vision of an aristocracy reduced to playing games of death, and once again a shooting party foreshadows the greater violence to come. But Colegate's tone is lightly self-mocking, and the film is full of the English affection for gentle lunacy. This is one of the rare movies that can be said to be for an educated audience without that being a putdown. As the host, an aging baronet who's conscious that he's losing his grip, Mason gives the film its immediacy. His face and, especially, that plangent voice are so deeply familiar that when we see him in a role that does him justice there's something like an outpouring of love from the audience to the man on the screen. His performance validates our feelings. Produced by Geoffrey Reeve; cinematography by Fred Tammes. With Robert Hardy, Rebecca Saire, and Sarah Badel. color (See *State of the Art*.)

The Shootist (1976)—In this movie that sets out to be a classic, the setting is a Nevada town in 1901, and John Wayne is a legendary Western gunslinger suffering from cancer. Wayne wears a noble hat and acts with dignity, but the script, by Miles Hood Swarthout and Scott Hale, is a mechanical demonstration of how greedy and unfeeling the townspeople are, and Don Siegel's directing lacks rhythm—each scene dies a separate death. Lauren Bacall is unnecessarily tight-faced as a widow; as her adolescent son, Ron Howard overdoes the anguish of learning to become a man, and as the town doctor who treats Wayne, James Stewart talks too loudly, as if he thought we'd all gone deaf. With Richard Boone, Sheree North, Scatman Crothers, Hugh O'Brian, Richard Lenz, and Harry Morgan. Paramount. color (See *When the Lights Go Down*.)

The Shop Around the Corner (1940)—Close to perfection—one of the most beautifully acted and paced romantic comedies ever made in this country. It is set in the enclosed world of the people who work together in a small department store; Margaret Sullavan and James Stewart are the employees who bicker with each other, and in no other movie has this kind of love-hate been made so convincing. Their performances are full of grace notes; when you watch later James Stewart films, you may wonder what became of this other deft, sensitive, pre-drawling Stewart. As for Sullavan, this is a peerless performance: she makes the shopgirl's pretenses believable, lyrical, and funny. The script by Samson Raphaelson is a free adaptation of a play by Nikolaus Laszlo, and though it's all set in a Hollywood Budapest, the director, Ernst Lubitsch, sustains a faintly European tone. With Frank Morgan, Joseph Schildkraut, William Tracy, Sara Haden, Edwin Maxwell, and Inez Courtney. (A 1949 musical remake starring Judy Garland and Van Johnson was called *In the Good Old Summertime*.) M-G-M. b & w

The Shop on Main Street *Obchod na Korze* (1965)—An apocalyptic folk tale set in a German-occupied Slovakian village in 1942. A simple, poor carpenter (Josef Kroner) with a nagging wife is appointed by his brother-in-law to be the "Aryan controller" of a button shop run by an aged Jewish woman (Ida Kaminska), and he expects to make his fortune. But the old woman is penniless, has nothing to sell, and is so deaf she doesn't understand that he has come to take over. She assumes he has been sent to be her assistant; he slips into that role, and the two innocents become friends. The story deals with his confusion and spiritual crisis when the Jews are deported. This film has been much honored, though it pulls at the viewer's emotions and its folkishness is laboriously whimsical. Ján Kadár and Elmar Klos, who co-directed, allow us to be too aware of the acting; Kroner's impersonation of a "little man" looks like hard work—in the Paul Muni tradition. Based on a story by Ladislav Grossman. In Czech. b & w

The Shopworn Angel (1938)—The material is shopworn, too; it's another version of Dana Burnet's play (based on his 1918 *SatEvePost* story, "Private Pettigrew's Girl"), which had been filmed in 1919 with Ethel Clayton and in 1929 with Nancy Carroll (who was lovely in it) and Gary Cooper. Margaret Sullavan manages to be poetically believable in the outdated role of the cynical, chainsmoking Broadway actress who is so touched by the adoration of an innocent soldier (James Stewart) that she marries him before he goes off to war. There are too many shots of Stewart, in doughboy uniform, looking yearningly at her, and her character reformation pulls the movie down, but Sullavan and Stewart always had a special rapport—a tenderness

that seemed to allow for her hard edges and conflicts. (She always played the more complex role in their pictures together.) Produced by Joseph L. Mankiewicz for M-G-M, and directed by H. C. Potter, who creates the right sort of romantic atmosphere. The young Waldo Salt did the subtle screenplay—tart yet plaintive. With Walter Pidgeon as the rich man who has been "keeping" the actress, and Hattie McDaniel, Sam Levene, Alan Curtis, and Nat Pendleton. Margaret Sullavan's songs were dubbed by Mary Martin. b & w

Short Circuit (1986)—Ally Sheedy had a comic spark in *WarGames* (1983), and as the skittish wacko she pepped up *The Breakfast Club* (1985), but she's painfully adorable here, and so is the whole movie. She's a girl who takes in stray animals, and she plays opposite Steve Guttenberg, perhaps the least likely of all the young actors who have been cast as scientific prodigies. One of the robots that this genius has invented for army use as "the ultimate soldiers"—Number Five—is hit by lightning and comes alive, and his wide-spaced big round eyes (they're like coy headlights) tell you that the moviemakers had him designed to be a lovable robot version of E.T. Robot Number Five escapes from the military compound. Sheedy takes him in, Guttenberg comes after him, and they try to save Number Five (who is charmed by butterflies) from being slaughtered by the government meanies. The picture is smoothly directed; it required a lot of craftsmanship to make it, but it has so little individuality that it seems merely an example of a simpering new genre: sci-fi for the teen market. In one sequence, Number Five watches TV, sees John Travolta dance in John Badham's *Saturday Night Fever* (1977), and imitates his moves; since Badham also directed *Short Circuit*, the scene may make you uncomfortable. It reminds you that the characters in his films (he did *WarGames*, too, and also *Blue Thunder* and *American*

Flyers) have become more and more mechanized. As a scientist from India who has assisted Guttenberg in the creation of the robots, Fisher Stevens is the film's resident comic; he keeps misusing American expressions. It's such an obvious and repetitive gag that when you laugh you feel contempt for yourself. Also with Austin Pendleton, Brian McNamara, and Tim Blaney's voice (for Number Five). The sucking-up-to-youth script is by S. S. Wilson and Brent Maddock. Tri-Star. color

Short Eyes (1977)—Robert M. Young directed Miguel Piñero's adaptation of his own play—an insider's view of life in a men's house of detention, centering on the revulsion that prisoners feel toward child-molesters ("short eyes"). The play shows through the documentary surface, and the film's potency is in its words, yet parts of this disorganized, somewhat pedestrian movie seem as good as they could possibly be, and the neo-Cagney cocky humor and the moments of pain, danger, and cruelty suggest that this may be the most emotionally accurate—and so most frightening—movie about American prisons ever made. Shot entirely in the Tombs; with Piñero as Go Go, Bruce Davison as the child-molester, Joe Carberry as Longshoe Murphy, and José Perez, Nathan George, Tito Goya, Don Blakely, Shawn Elliot, and Kenny Steward. Produced by Lewis Harris; released by the Film League. color (See *When the Lights Go Down.*)

Show Boat (1936)—This classic musical-melodrama with the Jerome Kern songs and the novelistic Edna Ferber plot, full of heartbreaks and miscegenation and coincidences, is hard to resist in any of its versions. This one from Universal has a believability that was lost in the 1951 M-G-M version. It features Irene Dunne and Allan Jones, but its greatest attractions are Paul Robeson as Joe,

and singing "Ol' Man River," and the marvellous Julie of Helen Morgan, who sings "Bill" and "Can't Help Lovin' Dat Man." James Whale directed, and the cast includes Charles Winninger, Helen Westley, Hattie McDaniel, Donald Cook, Eddie "Rochester" Anderson, Clarence Muse, Queenie Smith, E. E. Clive, and Harry Barris. The screenplay is by Oscar Hammerstein II, from the 1927 Ziegfeld musical that Kern and he wrote, based on the Ferber novel. The lyrics for "Bill" were written by P. G. Wodehouse—the song was a reject from one of the 10 musicals on which Kern and Wodehouse had collaborated; Kern is said to have taken the inspiration for "Ol' Man River" from Mark Twain's *Life on the Mississippi*. (A 1929 version, also from Universal, starred Laura La Plante, Alma Rubens, Joseph Schildkraut, and Stepin Fetchit as Joe.) b & w

Show Boat (1951)—Manufactured (by M-G-M) and embarrassingly lacking in innocence. The most lavish and least convincing of the three movie versions of Edna Ferber's novel, with the singing valentine Kathryn Grayson mangling the Jerome Kern songs. Marge and Gower Champion come through with some lively dancing, but almost everyone else sinks. Howard Keel is too good for what he's given to do, Ava Gardner (at her most beautiful as Julie) looks as if she's dying to parody her lines, and Joe E. Brown is allowed only one brief dance. With William Warfield, Robert Sterling, and a shameful performance by the miscast Agnes Moorehead. George Sidney directed, from John Lee Mahin's adaptation; the cinematography is by Charles Rosher; produced by Arthur Freed. (Ava Gardner's singing was dubbed by Annette Warren.) color

Show People (1928)—William Randolph Hearst insisted that Marion Davies appear in costume pictures; he liked her to be a romantic maiden, and—what was irreconcilable with her talent—dignified. But in the late 20s she broke out and made some funny pictures: *The Red Mill, The Fair Coed,* the wonderfully good-humored *The Patsy,* and this slapstick parody of Gloria Swanson's career—how fame went to her head. Hearst wouldn't let Davies do a custard pie sequence, despite her pleas and those of the director, King Vidor, and of Laurence Stallings, who was one of the writers. (Many years later Vidor described the conference that Louis B. Mayer called so that Vidor could make his case to Hearst for the plot necessity of the pie.) The film is light and deft and charming. William Haines plays opposite Davies, and the cast includes Dell Henderson, Polly Moran, and Harry Gribbon. There are also glimpses of Hollywood's fashionable celebrities as themselves: John Gilbert, Mae Murray, Charles Chaplin, Douglas Fairbanks, Elinor Glyn, and Davies the cutup looking very chic. M-G-M. Silent, but with sound effects and a musical score. b & w (See *The Citizen Kane Book.*)

Side Street Story, see *Millionaires of Naples*

Siegfried, see *Nibelungen Saga*

The Sign of the Cross (1932)—Looking at the plump young actor in an English film, Cecil B. De Mille must have clutched his chest ecstatically and cried out "My Nero!" Charles Laughton fulfilled De Mille's juiciest dreams. Sitting in the imperial box at the arena, and using an emerald as a lorgnon, this Nero peers at the Christians and lions at their games. He's a voluptuous connoisseur of agonies, and childishly appreciative of any novelty, such as the frolicsome spiking of a Pygmy on a fork by a wild woman from the North. As the wicked Empress Poppaea, Claudette Colbert looks wryly amused to find herself bathing in asses' milk, but her svelte

figure in Roman scanties explains the casting; she must have had the best shape on the Paramount lot. Elissa Landi is mushmouthed and tiresome as the virtuous Christian heroine, and Fredric March (Marcus Superbus!) was always better in pants than in short skirts hovering above his knees, but there are enough howling lines of nonsensical dialogue to compensate for the goody characters. De Mille's bang-them-on-the-head-with-wild-orgies-and-imperiled-virginity style is at its ripest; the film is just about irresistible. With Ian Keith, Vivian Tobin, Arthur Hohl, Ferdinand Gottschalk, and Nat Pendleton. Adapted from Wilson Barrett's play by Waldemar Young and Sidney Buchman. b & w

Signal 7 (1983)—Directed by Rob Nilsson and shot in three-quarter-inch videotape (using two cameras during six nights), which was then blown up to 35 mm, this semi-improvisational movie is about a group of San Francisco taxi drivers from the start of the night shift until dawn, 6 P.M. to 6 A.M. Between calls, the men sit around playing cards and swapping stories at the De Soto Cab Company garage on Geary Street; the rest of the film was shot on location, too—on the streets and inside the cabs as they move through the city. The title refers to an alert that a driver isn't responding to the dispatcher and may be in distress; metaphorically, it refers to the distresses that beset us all. The movie is about the anguish of men who know they're failures—in particular, the genial sad-sack Marty (Dan Leegant) and the ravaged hammy-handsome Speed (Bill Ackridge). Long-time friends, they have both done some acting, and in the course of the night they audition for roles in a local theatre production of Odets' *Waiting for Lefty* (which is about a cab-drivers' strike). These auditions are straight-faced satire, and they're the movie's high spot, with the theatre director (Bob

Elross) a solemn high-muck-a-muck and the producers and others involved huddled in chairs around him and leaning in to confer in whispers. The actors auditioning are like miscreants at the bar of justice. Conceived in the manner of Cassavetes (to whom the film is dedicated), *Signal 7* often gives us parts of lined faces filling the screen. They're heavily lined, because videotape doesn't have the sensitivity to light that film has, and when Nilsson shoots outdoors at night, using available light, the images simply don't have the depth of field that we're used to. The faces look flattened out and they're grainy and greenish. Used this way, video itself adds to the anguish. But the film has its fascination. The small talk at the garage has a comedy rhythm that a director isn't likely to get in a scripted movie, and the drawn-out sequence in which the probably impotent Speed tries to put the make on a young Israeli passenger (Hagit Farber) is compelling in its awkwardness and embarrassment. This video-to-film method cuts down costs in a major way, though as with early Cassavetes, the time gained in shooting is lost in editing; Nilsson had 33 hours of tapes, and it took eight months to edit them down to 92 minutes. Coppola lent the film his name; the credits read "Francis Ford Coppola Presents." color

The Silencers (1966)—Crude but good-natured super-spy nonsense with Dean Martin (as Matt Helm) and Stella Stevens. Their best sequence together has been lifted from the 1948 *Julia Misbehaves*. With Cyd Charisse, Daliah Lavi, and Victor Buono. Directed by Phil Karlson. Columbia. color

Silk Stockings (1957)—A paralyzed version of the Cole Porter Broadway musical based on the Greta Garbo film *Ninotchka*. The director, Rouben Mamoulian, manages to do practically nothing with a cast that includes Fred Astaire, Cyd Charisse (as Ninotchka),

Barrie Chase, Janis Paige, Peter Lorre, Jules Munshin, Joseph Buloff, George Tobias, and Ivan Triesault. M-G-M. CinemaScope, color

Silkwood (1983)—An absorbing but cloudy and unfocussed account of Karen Silkwood's union activism, her contamination by plutonium, and her death in a single-car crash. Directed by Mike Nichols, this passive advocacy film raises suspicions of many kinds of nuclear-age foul play; it's permeated with paranoia and hopelessness. As the heroine, Meryl Streep tousles her shag-cut brown hair, chews gum, and talks with a twang; she eyes a man, her head at an angle. She has the external details of "Okie bad girl" down pat, but something is not quite right. She has no natural vitality; she's like a replicant—all shtick. Her performance is muted, and Nichols, whose work here is erratic, soft-pedals everything around her. Kurt Russell, who plays Karen's lover, is used mostly for his bare chest and his dimples. Cher (as Karen's friend and roommate) has a lovely, dark-lady presence, but she's used as a lesbian Mona Lisa, all faraway smiles and shrugs. It's a wan, weak role. As a cosmetician in a mortuary, Diana Scarwid rouses the audience from its motion-picture-appreciation blues. She gets laughs out of her tight walk and her line readings; when she prolongs syllables and twists meanings, she sounds like Jean Harlow as a Valley Girl. Some scenes appear to relate to passages that have been cut, and the end is chopped short. The script is by Nora Ephron and Alice Arlen; the cinematography is by Miroslav Ondříček. The cast includes Craig T. Nelson, Ron Silver, E. Katherine Kerr, Sudie Bond, Josef Sommer, and Fred Ward. An ABC Motion Picture. color (See *State of the Art*.)

Silver Streak (1976)—Some studio executive must have looked at the Colin Higgins script, noticed that most of the action took place on board the train from Los Angeles to Chicago, and said, "Who the hell travels by train?" The movie starts with a mess of exposition, explaining why each of the principal characters didn't take a plane. Jill Clayburgh, Gene Wilder, and Richard Pryor are 1970s performers trapped in this fake 30s mystery-comedy, which is so inept you can't even get angry: it's like the imitations of sophisticated entertainment that high-school kids put on. For about 15 minutes Pryor gives the picture some of his craziness. His comedy isn't based on suspiciousness about whites, or on anger, either; he's gone way past that. Whites are *unbelievable* to him. He's stupefied at the ignorance of the hero (Wilder), and he can't believe the way this white man moves. His attempt to teach Wilder how to move like a black man is genuinely funny, but then the picture relapses and when Pryor is required to show pure-hearted affection for Wilder you have never seen such a bad actor. The villains, headed by Patrick McGoohan, are art forgers. (Has there ever been a good movie about art forgery? The idea is even more hopeless than having an amnesiac hero.) Arthur Hiller directed, lamely; the film features pathetic double-entendres—horticultural and barnyard—and there's a callously unfunny gag—a plane buzzing a flock of sheep just for the fun of it. The picture was a considerable success at the box office. With Ned Beatty, Clifton James, Richard Kiel, Scatman Crothers, Valerie Curtin, Ray Walston, Lucille Benson, Len Birman, and Stefan Gierasch. 20th Century-Fox. color (See *When the Lights Go Down*.)

Silverado (1985)—Probably, to enjoy this roguish, mechanically plotted Western, you'd have to accept the fights and shootouts as decorative, as part of the scenery. The director, Lawrence Kasdan (who wrote the script with his brother Mark), uses accomplished actors: the four heroes journeying west to Silverado in the 1880s are played by Kevin Kline, Scott Glenn, Kevin Costner, and Danny Glover, and they're variously involved with Linda Hunt, Rosanna Arquette, Brian Dennehy, John Cleese, and Jeff Goldblum. But the atmosphere is arch and uninvolving, and these actors don't seem sure what their characters are meant to be. The film is so opulent it has a nouveau riche aura about it; it's a counterfeit Western, without the feel of the memorable ones. The pounding orchestral score is a bad mistake; it tries to inflate the emotions that the movie intended to arouse. The cinematography is by John Bailey. Columbia. color (See *Hooked*.)

Simon of the Desert *Simon del Desierto* (1965)—Luis Buñuel made this short satirical feature (45 minutes) in Mexico, just before he did *Belle de Jour*. It's a jovial comedy about the temptations of St. Simeon Stylites, the 5th-century desert anchorite who spent 37 years preaching to pilgrims from his perch on top of a column; in both a literal and figurative sense, it's a shaggy-saint story. Simon (Claudio Brook) performs his miracles, and the crowds evaluate them like a bunch of New York cab-drivers discussing a parade: whatever it was, it wasn't much. He restores hands to a thief whose hands have been chopped off; the crowds rate the miracle "not bad," and the thief's first act with his new hands is to slap his own child. The Devil, in the female form of Silvia Pinal (much more amusing as the Devil than she was in her guises in other Buñuel films), tempts Simon, and at one point frames him in front of the local priests, who are more than willing to believe the worst of him. He falls, of course, because of the animal instincts he has tried to deny. Buñuel couldn't raise the money to finish the film, and he resorted to a bummer of a jokey ending in which the foolish saint is transported to the modern world and left, a lost soul, in a Greenwich Village disco-

S

thèque full of dancing teen-agers. Up to then, this little film ranks with Buñuel's finest; his technique here is so simple and direct that the movie is an aesthetic assault on bourgeois taste. In Spanish. b & w (See *Going Steady*.)

Since You Went Away (1944)—David O. Selznick must have had a reverent desire to do for the American home front what Hollywood had already done for the British home front in *Mrs. Miniver*—that is, to package a "typical" genteel home (in this case, in the Middle West) in a wishful, postcard version. He wrote the script himself, intending his story to be moving and simple, along epic lines; the result is pedestrian in a peculiarly grandiose manner. Claudette Colbert is the mother of the family, Neil Hamilton is her husband, Jennifer Jones and Shirley Temple are her daughters, Joseph Cotten is her old suitor who still hovers about, and Hattie McDaniel is her cook; others involved in this self-righteous salute to idealized American middle-class values include Nazimova, Robert Walker, Agnes Moorehead, Guy Madison, Monty Woolley, and Lionel Barrymore. The 2-hour-and-51-minute film, directed by John Cromwell, is perhaps more memorable for the James Agee review it occasioned (not the one in *Time* but the one in the *Nation*—see his book *Agee on Film*) than it is for itself: if one reads Agee first, the film may actually become entertaining. Released by United Artists. b & w

Singin' in the Rain (1952)—This exuberant satire of Hollywood in the late 20s, at the time of the transition from silents to talkies, is probably the most enjoyable of all American movie musicals. The teamwork of the stars, Gene Kelly, Donald O'Connor, and Debbie Reynolds, is joyful and the material is first-rate—ranging from parodies of the Busby Berkeley style of choreography to the Charleston and Black Bottom performed

straight. The film falters during a too-long love song on a deserted studio stage (later cut from some of the prints) and during a lavish oversize Broadway ballet, but these sequences don't seriously affect one's enjoyment. With Jean Hagen as an imbecile movie-queen, Millard Mitchell as a producer, Cyd Charisse as a dancer, Rita Moreno as a flapper actress, Madge Blake as a syrupy columnist, Douglas Fowley as a distraught director. Directed by Kelly and Stanley Donen from the witty, affectionate script by Betty Comden and Adolph Green. The songs by Nacio Herb Brown with lyrics by Arthur Freed include "All I Do Is Dream of You," "Make 'Em Laugh," "I've Got a Feeling You're Fooling," "Wedding of the Painted Doll," "Fit as a Fiddle," "Should I?," "You Were Meant for Me," "Good Mornin'," "You Are My Lucky Star," and, of course, "Singin' in the Rain." The song "Moses" is by Comden and Green and Roger Edens. Cinematography by Harold Rosson. Produced by Freed, for M-G-M. color

The Sisters (1938)—A costume melodrama beginning, in Montana, on the evening of Theodore Roosevelt's election and ending on the evening of Taft's election. During those years, a benign Bette Davis elopes with a transient newspaperman (Errol Flynn) who drinks. He deserts her For Her Own Good, and she undergoes strenuous hardships, including the San Francisco earthquake, which drives her to take brief refuge in an Oakland brothel, where a goodhearted whore (Lee Patrick) and a kindly madame (Laura Hope Crews, in a frilly negligée) nurse her back to health. The marital fortunes of the heroine's sisters (Anita Louise and Jane Bryan) are interwoven. It's an inoffensive but rather pointless story, with a good deal of attention to realistic detail. Hal B. Wallis produced, for Warners, and Anatole Litvak directed; from a novel by Myron Brinig, adapted by Milton Krims. With Beulah Bondi, Donald Crisp, Ian

Hunter, Alan Hale, Patric Knowles, Dick Foran, Henry Travers, Harry Davenport, and Mayo Methot. b & w

Sisters (1973)—Brian De Palma's low-budget horror movie about a psychotic ex-Siamese twin has its share of flaked-out humor (as in the TV game-show parody at the beginning) and De Palma does some virtuoso stunts though not in the dream-slapstick style of his later thrillers, *Carrie* (1976) and *The Fury* (1978). This is a much more primitive scare picture. He lurches his way through; he can't seem to get two people talking to make a simple expository point without its sounding like the drabbest Republic picture of 1938. The facetious dialogue is a wet blanket, and De Palma isn't quite up to his apparent intention—to provide cheap thrills that are also a parody of old corn. He manages the thrills, though (there are some demented knife-slashings), and audiences seemed to be happily freaked by Bernard Herrmann's score, with its old radio-play throb and zing. With Margot Kidder, who knows how to turn on sexiness with a witch's precision, and Jennifer Salt, who gives a feeble performance as a nitwit girl reporter. Also with Charles Durning, Lisle Wilson, Mary Davenport, Bill Finley, and Barnard Hughes. Shakily written by De Palma and Louisa Rose. A Pressman-Williams Production, released by A.I.P. color (See *Reeling*.)

Sitting Pretty (1948)—Clifton Webb became a big box-office hit in this dumb yet lively and, on some levels, satisfying comedy. He plays a supercilious gentleman who moves in on an average disorderly family as a baby-sitter and brings discipline to the household. Actually, he becomes a domestic tyrant, cowing his charges with his haughtiness and reducing their parents (Robert Young and Maureen O'Hara) to the status of peasants. Audiences guffawed happily when he glared

at the family's youngest, who was making a mess with his porridge, and placed the bowl over the baby's head. Webb is abetted by Richard Haydn as the adenoidal neighborhood gossip. Walter Lang directed, from F. Hugh Herbert's screenplay. 20th Century-Fox. b & w

Sixteen Candles (1984)—Samantha (Molly Ringwald), a high-school sophomore, is having the worst day of her life. It's her 16th birthday, and, in the midst of preparations for her older sister's wedding, the whole family has forgotten about it. And in the evening, when she goes to a school dance and longs to be noticed by the handsome senior (Michael Schoeffling) who's the man of her dreams, she's subjected to the humiliating attentions of a scrawny freshman (Anthony Michael Hall), who's known as Geek—a pesty, leering smartmouth with braces on his teeth. Less raucous than the usual 80s pictures about teen-agers, this comedy by the young writer-director John Hughes is closer in tone to the gentle English comedies of the 40s and 50s. Hughes devised too much of a farcical superstructure, and a lot of the characters function at a sit-com level, but he brings off some fresh scenes, and he has a feeling for teen-agers' wacko slang. (Geek confesses that he has never "bagged a babe.") Molly Ringwald has a lovely, offbeat candor, and Hall's Geek, with his pitchman's hard sell, is a truly weird creation. With Paul Dooley, Carlin Glynn, Blanche Baker, Justin Henry, Gedde Watanabe, Haviland Morris, Liane Curtis, and, in bits, Brian Doyle-Murray and Zelda Rubinstein. Universal. color (See *State of the Art*.)

Det Sjunde Inseglet, see *The Seventh Seal*

Skammen, see *Shame*

The Ski Bum (1971)—Some U.C.L.A. film students took over the Romain Gary novel, soaked it in Fellini and Buñuel, and stuffed it with pot. Weird is a mild word for the result, but a few sequences are also weirdly effective. With Zalman King and Charlotte Rampling. Directed by Bruce Clark; cinematography by Vilmos Zsigmond. Avco Embassy. color

The Skin Game (1971)—Lighthearted and charming story of a black and white team of con artists in the Old South. Very enjoyable. With Lou Gossett, Jr., James Garner, and Susan Clark. Directed by Paul Bogart, from a script by Peter Stone and Richard Alan Simmons. Warners. color

The Sky Above, The Mud Below *Le Ciel et la boue* (1959)—You learn a lot about the expedition—about the courage and loyalty of the porters, the height of the mountains to be crossed, the bridges that must be built over the swift rivers, the incredible cold and the prostrating heat, the dysentery and malaria and leeches, the jungle that no white men before had ever charted, and the incredible heroism of the intrepid men who made the movie. You learn surprisingly little about the Stone Age men, the headhunters of New Guinea who are, presumably, the film's subject. One explorer looks very much like another explorer, and their photography of themselves is rarely adventurous. It's a mediocre film with a few informative sequences; it also includes some obviously staged footage. The "poetic" narration is very fancy and may have influenced those who gave this French documentary an Academy Award. Written and directed by Pierre-Dominique Gaisseau. color

The Sky's the Limit (1943)—Dreary R K O musical, with Fred Astaire as a Flying Tiger war hero. He's cast, unfortunately, opposite the wholesome Joan Leslie, with her girl-next-door big smiles. But Astaire does some beautiful solo work, including the memorable "One for My Baby (and One More for the Road)." With Robert Benchley, Robert Ryan, Eric Blore, Elizabeth Patterson, Marjorie Gateson, Paul Hurst, Clarence Kolb, and Freddie Slack's orchestra. Directed by Edward H. Griffith; written by Frank Fenton and Lynn Root; songs by Johnny Mercer and Harold Arlen. b & w

The Slap *La Gifle* (1974)—Isabelle Adjani playing a charmingly thoughtless, petulant, fibbing teen-ager in a heartwarming French comedy of the sort that generally isn't imported because it's assumed that Americans who go to foreign films won't be attracted by the French equivalent of the Debbie Reynolds and Sandre Dee movies of the late 50s. (Adjani was a big hit in France in this role.) Claude Pinoteau directs competently, but the movie is contrived out of spun sugar and endless misunderstandings. Lino Ventura and Annie Girardot are the heroine's estranged parents. With François Perrin, Nicole Courcel, Jacques Spiesser, and Georges Wilson. Written by Jean-Loup Dabadie and Pinoteau; music by Georges Delerue. In French. color

Slap Shot (1977)—Fast, noisy, profane comedy set in the world of minor-league ice hockey. The theme is that the public no longer cares about the sport—it wants goonish vaudeville and mayhem. The director, George Roy Hill, has heated up his technique, and the picture is also geared to giving the public "what it wants"—it has a forced, antagonistic feeling. Hill is making a farcical hymn to violence. Dede Allen's hot-foot editing moves the action along from zinger to zinger, and the Maxine Nightingale record "Right Back Where We Started From" punches up the pacing. The beat gives the film a relentlessness, and expletives are sprinkled around like manure to give it funky seasoning. (Perhaps as a result, the public rejected the film.) Hill lacks the conviction or the temperament for all this brutal buffoonishness, and he can't hold the picture together; what does is the warmth supplied by Paul Newman, as Reggie, a player-coach. Reggie is scarred and bruised, and there are gold rims on his chipped teeth; you don't see much of his eyes. He has never grown up—he's a raucous American innocent, an overage jock, thin-skinned but a little thickheaded. Newman's likableness in the role is infectious. With Michael Ontkean, Lindsay Crouse, Jennifer Warren, Allan Nicholls, Yvon Barrette, M. Emmet Walsh, Paul Dooley, and Jeff and Steve Carlson and David Hanson as the three Hanson brothers, and Kathryn Walker, Swoosie Kurtz, Jerry Houser, Strother Martin, and Melinda Dillon—there's a luscious infantile carnality about her scene in bed with Newman, who's nuzzling her. Screenplay by Nancy Dowd; cinematography by Victor Kemper. Produced by Robert J. Wunsch and Stephen Friedman; distributed by Universal. color (See *When the Lights Go Down.*)

Sleeper (1973)—A modern slapstick-comedy classic, directed by and starring Woody Allen. Set 200 years in the future, it's the most stable and sustained of his comedies, with a clean visual style and an elegant design. It's a very even work, with no thudding bad lines and no low stretches, but it doesn't have the loose, manic highs of some of his other films. You laugh all the way through and come out smiling and happy, but you're not driven crazy—not really turned on the way his messier movies can turn you on. With Diane Keaton and John Beck. Written by Allen, and Marshall Brickman; cinematography by David M. Walsh; editing by Ralph Rosenblum; costume design by Joel Schumacher. The music is by Woody Allen with the Preservation Hall Jazz Band and the New Orleans Funeral and Ragtime Band. United Artists. color (See *Reeling.*)

Sleuth (1972)—At first, the elation of seeing Laurence Olivier in a big role is sufficient to give this Joseph L. Mankiewicz transcription of the Anthony Shaffer play (about an eccentric author of detective novels and his prey—Michael Caine) a high spirit, and Olivier seems to be having a ripsnorting old time. But the cleverness of Shaffer's excessive literacy wears down, and the stupid tricks that the two characters play on each other keep grinding on. It's Olivier in the kind of material he outgrew more than 30 years ago—it's Olivier in a George Sanders role. Cinematography by Oswald Morris. color (See *Reeling.*)

A Slight Case of Murder (1938)—A black farce in the manner of *Arsenic and Old Lace*. It's a burlesque of gangster films, with Edward G. Robinson as a bootlegger who turns legitimate and faces one mortifying mess after another. He drives his family out for a weekend in a country house, and finds the corpses of four gangsters sitting around a table in the spare bedroom. Eventually, at a party back in town, the four are brought in and strung up on hooks in a closet. The director, Lloyd Bacon, succeeds in getting giggles out of some of these scenes, but his style is too broad, and the tone of the film is archly childish. With Allen Jenkins as a beer salesman, Jane Bryan, Bobby Jordan, Ruth Donnelly, Harold Huber, Edward Brophy, John Litel, and Willard Parker. From a play by Damon Runyon and Howard Lindsay, adapted by Earl Baldwin and Joseph Schrank. Warners. b & w

Slither (1973)—The first feature directed by the advertising ace Howard Zieff is a suspense comedy with a prickly, flea-hopping humor—a sort of fractured hipsterism. As the thick-witted hero looking for the fortune promised him by an embezzler, James Caan demonstrates some of the best double-takes in modern movies. The plot is tired, and the picture never delivers on its promise, but the gags are sneaky and offbeat, and the cast is full of crazies. With Peter Boyle, Louise Lasser, Allen Garfield, Richard B. Shull, and Sally Kellerman, as a speed freak. From an original script by W. D. Richter. M-G-M. color (See *Reeling*.)

Slow Dancing in the Big City (1978)—A boxing-movie-type ballet movie—Rocky as a young ballerina (Anne Ditchburn), who has to learn that she's a champion inside. The man who teaches her is a Jimmy Breslin–like columnist (Paul Sorvino), who works for the *News*. This is a feminine fantasy (written by Barra Grant), yet it's inspired by the tough-guy-with-a-soft-heart school of journalism, and the film aims for our hearts with brass knuckles, in the Breslin manner. It never once lands on target, and almost all the actors seem to be impaled by the camera. The earnestness and shamelessness of the director, John G. Avildsen (whose previous picture *was Rocky*), are so awesome, though, that if the picture fails as romance it succeeds as camp. The ballerina, who has a prissy little-girl voice, talks to her parakeet, whose name is Orville Wright, and when she's loosening her muscles she thrashes around passionately to Carole King's "I Feel the Earth Move Under My Feet"—she's the Patti Smith of ballet, pouring sweat and suffering ecstatically for her art. You don't get scenes like this in every movie. With Nicolas Coster, Anita Dangler, Hector Jaime Mercado, and the Manhattan Dance Company. Cinematography by Ralf D. Bode; music by Bill Conti. United Artists. color (See *When the Lights Go Down*.)

Small Change   *L'Argent de poche* (1976)— François Truffaut's series of sketches on the general theme of the resilience of children turns out to be that rarity—a poetic comedy that's really funny. Truffaut's deadpan, disjointed style is quicker and surer than ever before; the kids seem to be photographed in the act of inventing slapstick. There's a serious side (the story of a mistreated boy) that's a failure, and Truffaut's view of childhood innocence has elements of middle-class preciousness, but the jokes make the film worth seeing. In French. color (See *When the Lights Go Down*.)

Smash Palace (1981)—A remarkable film from New Zealand on the theme of separating. The husband and wife, played by Bruno Lawrence and Anna Jemison, embody a basic male-female conflict. He's flesh-and-blood and growing bald; she's French-born and fine-boned and fastidious. He runs the business he inherited from his father—the Smash Palace, a vast wrecking yard in an isolated area in New Zealand—and, except for the pleasure he takes in watching their 7-year-old daughter Georgie scooting around in miniature cars, he lives like a single man, puttering with motors, burning up the country roads in the Grand-Prix Formula One racer he's restoring, and drinking beer with his pals. He ignores his wife's complaints, but when she leaves him and, enjoying the upper hand, gets a legal order to prevent him from seeing Georgie, he goes a little crazy. This affable, intelligent man isn't driven mad in the funny, cuckoo sense but in a special, modern, obsessed way. The rage of fathers deprived of their children—something that few men experienced in the past—is no doubt a key madness of our age. The director, Roger Donaldson, has the kind of neo-neorealist technique that a viewer is unconscious of; the director disappears into the story. Even the easy, dry wit seems to belong to the material, along with the summery light. This film can pull you in deep, but some people don't like its almost documentary surface and the fact that the characters are believably real and not unusual—they feel it's too much like life, and that they see it going on all the time. Donaldson's handling of the little girl (Greer Robson) who plays Georgie is beyond praise. He wrote the script with Peter Hansard and Bruno Lawrence; the cinematography is by Graeme Cowley. color (See *Taking It All In*.)

Smash-Up (1947)—Alcoholism became a hot, gaudy movie subject after the success of *The Lost Weekend* (1945), and Susan Hayward had her turn at no-holds-barred drunkenness and suffering in this dismal, overwrought melodrama, directed by Stuart Heisler. At the end, half stewed but valiant, she rescues her little daughter from a burning house and promptly hops on the wagon. It may be hard to believe, but the writers who worked on this included Dorothy Parker and John Howard Lawson, and it was presented with some solemnity as a prestige picture. (It was originally called *Smash-Up—The Story of a Woman*.) With Lee Bowman, Marsha Hunt, Eddie Albert, Carleton Young, and Carl Esmond. Universal. b & w

Smile (1975)—A fresh, mussed-up comedy about the California finals of a national "Young American Miss" contest. A cousin to *Lord Love a Duck*, the film is an affectionate satirical salute to the square; though we laugh at the gaffes of the rawboned teen-age girls, the laughter isn't cruel. Bruce Dern plays the chief judge, a booster who talks in homilies that express exactly how he feels; he's a donkey, but he doesn't have a mean bone in his body. With Barbara Feldon as the girls' den mother, Michael Kidd as the choreographer brought in to stage the beauty pageant, and several talented new actresses—Annette O'Toole, Joan Prather, and Maria O'Brien. Michael Ritchie's direction is highly variable in quality, but he's a whiz at catching details of frazzled behavior. The script is by Jerry

Belson; the cinematography is by Conrad Hall. The cast includes Nicholas Pryor, Geoffrey Lewis, Melanie Griffith, Colleen Camp, and Paul Benedict. United Artists. color (See *When the Lights Go Down*.)

Smiles of a Summer Night *Sommarnattens Leende* (1955)—Ingmar Bergman achieves one of the few classics of carnal comedy: a tragicomic chase and roundelay that raises boudoir farce to elegance and lyric poetry. This film is the culmination of Bergman's "rose" style; as writer and director, he ties up his persistent, early battle-of-the-sexes themes in an intricate plot structure. And in this fin-de-siècle houseparty setting, with its soft light, its delicate, perfumed atmosphere, and its golden pavilion, the women are all beautiful and epigrams shine. The film becomes an elegy to transient love; a gust of wind, and the whole vision may drift away. As the hostess, the stage actress trying to win back the lawyer she loves, there is the great Eva Dahlbeck (in one inspired, suspended moment she sings "Freut Euch des Lebens"). Ulla Jacobsson is the lawyer's virgin wife; Harriet Andersson, a blonde here but as opulent and sensuous as in her earlier roles, is the impudent, love-loving maid; Margit Carlquist is the proud, unhappy countess. Gunnar Björnstrand is the lawyer, Björn Bjelvenstam is his son, Jarl Kulle is the strutting count, and Naima Wifstrand is the actress's aged mother, who is carried about for her game of croquet. With Åke Fridell as the groom, and, in a bit part, Bibi Andersson. Cinematography by Gunnar Fischer. (Used as the basis for the American stage and screen musical *A Little Night Music*.) In Swedish. b & w (See *I Lost It at the Movies*.)

Smooth Talk (1985)—It has lovely touches in its first half, when the director, Joyce Chopra, shows us the restless and narcissistic 15-year-old Connie (Laura Dern), who acts seductive and teases boys her own age or a year or two older, because she doesn't know what else to do about the way she feels. Connie and her friends (Sarah Inglis and Margaret Welch) parade happily around the shopping plaza for hours and hours—testing their skills at attracting boys and bantering with them. Tom Cole, who wrote the script, expanding the brief Joyce Carol Oates story "Where Are You Going, Where Have You Been?," has a fine ear for teen-age talk. But the movie's texture is thin from the start—especially in the scenes at Connie's home, where she and her mother (Mary Kay Place) bicker. And the second half isn't just stretched out—it's a little screwy. The Oates story is a young girl's sex-and-horror fantasy: a sordid creep (an older man) arrives at Connie's house when she's alone; he's like the materialization of her ugliest fears, and he terrorizes her and lures her into his car. End of story and, the reader assumes, probably the end of poor Connie. Unaccountably, Chopra and Cole try to turn this material into a coming-of-age movie with a happy resolution. Their ending suggests that Connie has grown up—matured—via what amounts to terrorization and (possibly) rape; the experience seems to have made her a better person. As the creep, Treat Williams gives a neo-Method performance that's all affectation. With Levon Helm as Connie's pleasant-goofball father, and Elizabeth Berridge as Connie's older sister, though, confusingly, she looks more like a kid sister. color (See *Hooked.*)

Smultronstallet, see *Wild Strawberries*

So Ends Our Night (1941)—There are some lovely qualities in this film about anti-Nazi refugees, and Frances Dee, who plays the wife of a disaffected fugitive German officer (Fredric March), is so remarkably beautiful in a key passage that her image stays with one,

like that of Garbo at the end of *Queen Christina.* March gives the romanticizing picture suggestions of realism and some needed weight. With Margaret Sullavan (the part doesn't do her justice, and she falls back on things she's done before) and, opposite her, the soft-eyed, lanky young Glenn Ford (in his first important role), as a sensitive Jewish boy. Also Anna Sten, Erich von Stroheim, Alexander Granach, Sig Rumann, Leonid Kinskey, and Roman Bohnen. From Erich Maria Remarque's novel *Flotsam,* well adapted by Talbot Jennings. The action, which starts in Vienna before the Anschluss, moves from Prague to Zurich and Paris and Berlin through the skill of the set designer, William Cameron Menzies. Though the film was not a commercial success, the director, John Cromwell, rightly regards it as one of his best pieces of work. Produced by David L. Loew and Albert Lewin, for United Artists. b & w

So Fine (1981)—This is the first film directed by the comedy writer Andrew Bergman, and it's a visual insult: crudely lighted and framed, and jumping out at you. Jack Warden is Jack Fine, a Seventh Avenue dress manufacturer in debt to the mob; his most frequent line is "Holy shit," which he delivers whenever Bergman thinks the movie needs a really big laugh. The central gimmick is that Jack's college-teacher son (Ryan O'Neal) splits a pair of jeans and stuffs see-through plastic into the cheeks, and that this turns into a fashion craze. There are potentially funny scenes, but Bergman doesn't know how to give timing and polish to his own jokes. Stuck with frantic gags, O'Neal just revamps his tight-mouthed professorial priss from *What's Up, Doc?* The film's only freshness comes from the lovely, tiny Italian blonde Mariangela Melato, making her American début as a mobster's wife. In her deep voice she garbles her English charmingly; she's an erotic imp—she looks a bit like Harpo Marx, and she's always flying, like Carole Lombard in a hurricane. With Richard Kiel, Fred Gwynne, and Irving Metzman, who gives likable readings to his role as an accountant, Bruce Millholland as Sir Alec, the world's greatest poet, and Mike Kellin as the smiling, ever-hopeful salesman. The assaultive cinematography is by James A. Contner. Produced by Mike Lobell, for Warners. color (See *Taking It All In.*)

So This Is New York (1948)—Henry Morgan plays the Indiana cigar-salesman hero in this adaptation of Ring Lardner's *The Big Town*. The movie is a satire of New York in the 20s—a deadpan farce that's uneven, but frequently very funny. Morgan and his wife (Virginia Grey) take her sister (Dona Drake) to the big city to find a husband: the prospects include Rudy Vallee as a millionaire, Hugh Herbert as an explorer, Leo Gorcey as a jockey, and Bill Goodwin as an egomaniac actor. Directed by Richard Fleischer, from a screenplay by Carl Foreman. A Stanley Kramer Production; released by United Artists. b & w

S.O.B. (1981)—A sour mixture of slapstick, cynicism, and sentimentality. Robert Preston covers his thick head of graying hair with glory in the role of a hearty, imperturbable Dr. Feelgood, who gives all-purpose injections; Larry Storch has a bright scene as a guru; and Richard Mulligan is involved in a few funny sight gags. He plays a producer who cracks up after his hugely expensive film starring his wife (Julie Andrews) opens and closes practically simultaneously; wandering about his Malibu home in a suicidal stupor, he sinks through a hole in the second-story bedroom floor that has been covered with a large rug and lands gracefully in the middle of an orgy. But Blake Edwards, who wrote and directed this broadside against Holly-

wood, uses a tired plot about turning the disastrous picture into a hit by having Julie Andrews bare her breasts. Edwards is snide in a square, unfunny way—he thinks he's showing us how corrupt the movie business is by casting Shelley Winters as a treacherous woman agent who wears tent-size caftans and shares her bed with a cutie-pie black woman. The picture is acknowledged to be based on Edwards' own experiences when his picture *Darling Lili* was a colossal flop. But *Darling Lili* wasn't a flop for the reason suggested—that it was innocent and charming at a time when the dirty-minded public wanted nudity and sex. (As a matter of bleak record, Julie Andrews did a striptease in *Darling Lili* that wasn't so very different from the breast-baring here.) With William Holden, Marisa Berenson, Larry Hagman, Stuart Margolin, Robert Loggia, Loretta Swit, Benson Fong, Robert Vaughn, Robert Webber, John Pleshette, and the director's daughter, Jennifer Edwards, as Lila. Released by Paramount. color

Soil, see *Earth*

A Soldier's Story (1984)—This tense, wholehearted combination of melodrama and psychodrama is set in and around an Army base in Louisiana in 1944. A black drillmaster, Sergeant Waters (played, in flashbacks, by Adolph Caesar), has been murdered, and a black lawyer, Captain Davenport (Howard E. Rollins, Jr.)—the first black commissioned officer ever to be seen in this part of the country—has been sent down from Washington, D.C., to investigate. Charles Fuller (who did the adaptation of his *A Soldier's Play*) uses the structure of a whodunit for an inquiry into the psychological dynamics of racism, and there's some daring in his perception that in a racist society the temptation toward self-hatred is part of being black. The material is overexplicit; it's like the trumped-up, creaky yet powerful socially conscious plays-into-movies of the past. But the director, Norman Jewison, has given it an atmosphere that recalls his crack 1967 comedy-mystery *In the Heat of the Night*, and he has also given it a beautiful sense of pace, and brought out all the humor he can find. Since Captain Davenport is one-on-one with the people he questions, a number of actors get to dominate the screen for a scene or two. The standouts are Denzel Washington (as the best educated of the black soldiers), Art Evans, Larry Riley, David Harris, and, among the white officers, Dennis Lipscomb. The cinematographer, Russell Boyd, knows how to photograph black men: their skins seem iridescent, and Rollins has a heroic, sculptural presence. Columbia. color (See *State of the Art*.)

The Solid Gold Cadillac (1956)—Richard Quine directed Abe Burrows' adaptation of the George S. Kaufman–Howard Teichmann Broadway play about the little-old-lady stockholder in a giant corporation; though her holdings are minuscule, her questions about corporate salaries cause an uproar at the annual meeting, and pretty soon she has enough proxies to take over the business. In the movie, this eccentric stockholder becomes a woman of marriageable age, and Judy Holliday brings the role her familiar cartoon mixture of wide-eyed primordial simplicity and complacent urban abrasiveness. She's a funny woman, yet lacking in variety; her truculent voice and glassy eyes and shrewd innocence are wonderful in a sketch but a little monotonous in a starring role like this one. However, the fault here isn't primarily hers: it's in the formula Broadway comedy, with its predictable situations and sledgehammer laugh lines. With Paul Douglas, Fred Clark, Hiram Sherman, John Wil-

liams, and Arthur O'Connell. Columbia. b & w

I Soliti Ignoti, see *The Big Deal on Madonna Street*

Some Call It Loving (1973)—Illusion-and-reality games, or thumb-twiddling. James B. Harris wrote and directed this drowsy whimsey (based on a John Collier story) about a jazz-musician prince (Zalman King) who buys a sleeping beauty (Tisa Farrow) at a carnival and takes her to his castle, which is presided over by wicked Scarlett (Carol White). Everyone in this picture about romantic enchantment seems to be sleepwalking, and the director, too. Richard Pryor turns up briefly, acting amiably stoned. color

Some Like It Hot (1959)—A comedy set in the Prohibition era, with transvestism, impotence, role confusion, and borderline inversion—and all hilariously innocent, though always on the brink of really disastrous double-entendre. Tony Curtis and Jack Lemmon are the musicians who witness the St. Valentine's Day Massacre and then hide out from the mobsters by disguising themselves as women and joining an all-girl band. Marilyn Monroe and Joe E. Brown are their somewhat confused love partners. Curtis demonstrates a parodistic gift with an imitation of Cary Grant (which he went on doing for years afterward), and Lemmon is demoniacally funny—he really gives in to women's clothes, and begins to think of himself as a sexy girl. Monroe gives perhaps her most characteristic performance, which means that she's both charming and embarrassing; Brown is inspired, the way he was years before in Max Reinhardt's movie of *A Midsummer Night's Dream*, when he made some of us weep from laughter. With George Raft, Pat O'Brien, Nehemiah Persoff, Mike Mazurki,

Tom Kennedy, George E. Stone, and, on the soundtrack, Matty Malneck's orchestra, with Art Pepper, Shelly Manne, Barney Kessel, and Leroy Vinegar. Directed (unevenly) by Billy Wilder, who also collaborated on the screenplay with I.A.L. Diamond. For collectors of useless movie memorabilia: in one of the earlier versions of this material, a German musical film, the orchestra girls were called The Alpine Violets. United Artists. b & w

Somebody Killed Her Husband (1978)—A romantic suspense comedy that resembles the pictures that Ginger Rogers did in the late 30s—the ones about ordinary, pleasant people falling in love and getting into farfetched scrapes. But when this dishy blonde (Farrah Fawcett-Majors, in her first movie as a star) walks through the toy department of Macy's with her toddler son in a stroller and spills a bag of pretzels, and a clerk (Jeff Bridges) rushes to her assistance and looks into her teeth and it's love at first sight, everything seems a little custardy and congealed. Did the screenwriter, Reginald Rose, pull the script out of a filing cabinet where it had rested for decades? Bridges probably does better by the dated romantic badinage than anybody else could have, and he makes the movie semi-watchable. John Glover's pinched-faced, amused craziness is also entertaining, and John Wood and Tammy Grimes try for a stylish arch ghoulishness, though they don't have the witty lines that are needed to support that style. With Mary McCarty, Laurence Guittard, Patricia Elliott, and Beeson Carroll. Directed by Lamont Johnson, on location in New York City. Produced by Martin Poll for Melvin Simon; released by Columbia. color (See *When the Lights Go Down*.)

Someone to Watch Over Me (1987)—A Manhattan socialite (Mimi Rogers), who writes about art and looks expensively asymmetrical, witnesses a murder; a police detective (Tom Berenger), a warmhearted, decent, uncultivated fellow who lives in Queens with his wife and child, is assigned to protect her. He falls for her, and she for him, and the murderer tries to get at her. That's essentially all there is, except for the high-class hauntedness supplied by Ridley Scott, who directed. He draws you into a dull, sensual daydreaminess, but after watching Tom Berenger and Mimi Rogers for a while, you look around for the stars. With so much buildup—so much terror-tinged atmosphere—you expect actors with some verve, and you wonder why the script (credited to Howard Franklin) doesn't sneak in a few jokes. (Has a good thriller ever been this solemn? Or this simple?) Daniel Hugh Kelly brings some kick to the small role of a cop who has split up with his wife; the only performer who really stands out, though, is Lorraine Bracco, as the detective's wife—her line readings have a hardheaded urban earthiness, and her comedy timing sparks the movie. With Jerry Orbach, Andreas Katsulas, and John Rubinstein. Cinematography by Steven Poster; the title song (by the Gershwins) is performed at the start by Sting, then by Roberta Flack, then by Gene Ammons. Columbia. color (See *Hooked*.)

Something to Shout About (1943)—Clumsy, chaotic little musical taken from a Cole Porter Broadway show. Janet Blair has too much to do; Jack Oakie doesn't have enough. With William Gaxton, Hazel Scott, Cyd Charisse, and Don Ameche. One good Cole Porter song: "You'd Be So Nice to Come Home To." Directed by Gregory Ratoff. Columbia. b & w

Something to Sing About (1937)—The title represents unjustified optimism. James Cagney plays a bandleader who goes to Hollywood to make a musical. Cagney gets a chance to do some of that hoofing of his that's not like anybody else's, but the story is a leaden satire of Hollywood, with a feeble suggestion of *A Star Is Born*. Mona Barrie, in a blond wig, does a refreshing parody of Garbo; the heroine is overpowering Evelyn Daw, of whom not much more was heard. With William Frawley and Gene Lockhart. Direction, music, and story by Victor Schertzinger. First National. b & w

Something Wild (1986)—Jonathan Demme's romantic screwball comedy isn't just about a carefree kook (Melanie Griffith) and a pompous man from Wall Street (Jeff Daniels). The script—a first by E. Max Frye—is like the working out of a young man's fantasy of the pleasures and punishments of shucking off middle-class behavior patterns. The movie is about getting high on anarchic, larcenous behavior and then being confronted with ruthless, sadistic criminality. This rough-edged comedy turns into a scary slapstick thriller. Demme weaves the stylization of rock videos into the fabric of the movie. Starting with David Byrne and Celia Cruz singing Byrne's ''Loco De Amor'' during the opening credits, and ending with a reprise of Chip Taylor's ''Wild Thing'' by the reggae singer Sister Carol East, who appears on half of the screen while the final credits roll on the other half, there are almost 50 songs (or parts of songs), several of them performed onscreen by The Feelies. The score—it was put together by John Cale and Laurie Anderson—has a life of its own that gives the movie a buzzing vitality. This is a party movie with both a dark and a light side. With Ray Liotta as the dangerous, menacing Ray; Dana Preu as the kook's gloriously bland mother; and Margaret Colin as bitchy Irene. Also with Jack Gilpin, Su Tissue, and Demme's co-producer Kenneth Utt, and, tucked among the many performers, John Waters and John Sayles.

Cinematography by Tak Fujimoto. Orion. color (See *Hooked*.)

Sommarlek, see *Summer Interlude*

Sommarnattens Leende, see *Smiles of a Summer Night*

Son of Frankenstein (1939)—The third and last in the Boris Karloff series, directed by Rowland V. Lee, rather than James Whale, who did *Frankenstein* and the more whimsical *Bride of Frankenstein*. The conception here doesn't have the resonance of the first two films; this one slips out of the memory, except for a few individual scenes and Bela Lugosi's affecting Ygor, the shepherd and grave robber who becomes the Monster's only friend. Karloff has a few inventive moments—the Monster's revulsion when he sees himself in a mirror, his agonized scream when he discovers that Ygor is dead. (Lugosi returned as Ygor in *The Ghost of Frankenstein*, but without Karloff.) The set designs contribute to the dreamy, unworldly mood, and actors such as Basil Rathbone as the Baron, Lionel Atwill as the Police Inspector (whose artificial arm gets torn out), Edgar Norton, and Gustav von Seyffertitz give the production a certain amount of class. Emma Dunn and timid, terrified Josephine Hutchinson don't. Universal. b & w

Song of Norway (1970)—Self-parody is built into operettas and is part of their innocent, campy charm. But this one isn't authentic kitsch of the Wiener-schnitzel variety, it isn't a dated crowd-pleaser squeezed for the remaining box-office juice; it's second-generation kitsch—an imitation operetta, on the joys and tribulations of Edvard Grieg's life, that combines the worst of *The Sound of Music* with the worst of *A Song to Remember* and *Song Without End*. Even if you're prepared for dirndls and roguish smiles you're not likely to be ready for the distorted sound, the pasty, pudgy faces, and the bewildering use of dance as if it were mood music. (When the picture isn't showing you waterfalls, flaxen-haired dancers go leaping by—a few frames at a time—to maintain a frolicsome Norwegian mood.) The movie is of an unbelievable badness; it brings back clichés you didn't know you knew—they're practically from the unconscious of moviegoers. You can't get angry at something this stupefying; it seems to have been made by trolls. With T. Maurstad as Grieg, Florence Henderson as Nina Grieg, and Harry Secombe, Robert Morley, Edward G. Robinson, Oscar Homolka, and James Hayter. Directed by Andrew L. Stone, who also wrote the script, suggested by the stage show *Song of Norway* by Milton Lazarus, based on a play by Homer Curran. Music and lyrics by Robert Wright and George Forrest, based on Grieg's work. An Andrew and Virginia Stone Production, for ABC and Cinerama. color

Song of Songs (1933)—At the start, Marlene Dietrich is a pure young peasant, with angelic big blond braids around her head; after falling in love with a sculptor (Brian Aherne) and being carelessly discarded by him, she marries a nastily decadent old baron (Lionel Atwill), who takes her to his big *Schloss*, which is presided over by a villainous housekeeper (Helen Freeman). After much anguish, she becomes a flamboyant woman of the world, wearing great splashy hats, and is finally reunited with the guilt-ridden sculptor. All this is given the full spiritual-suffering treatment, with lyric, pictorial symbolism and quotes from the Song of Solomon. It was unbelievably dated when it came out; if the director, Rouben Mamoulian, hadn't been so ponderously artistic, it might have been delirious camp. Dietrich looks blankly beautiful—she seems to be wondering what the devil she's doing here. With Alison Skipworth and Hardie Albright. Vaguely derived from Hermann Sudermann's novel (which had also served as the basis for a silent film with Pola Negri, and, even earlier, for one with Elsie Ferguson); it comes via a play version by Edward Sheldon, adapted to the screen by Leo Birinski and Samuel Hoffenstein. Paramount. b & w

Song Without End (1960)—A gigantic calamity. The standard movie life of an artistic genius deals with the simple conflict between normal family life, respectability, and success on the one hand and the creative drive, poverty, and misunderstanding on the other. This life of Franz Liszt (played by Dirk Bogarde) has three conflicting elements: his career as Europe's greatest performing pianist, his desire to compose (when inspired by a beautiful Russian princess), and his pledge (to mama) to become a priest. Prepared by the director Charles Vidor, the film was completed after his death by George Cukor who, out of respect for Vidor's reputation, or for his own, declined screen credit. Among the historical impersonations are Capucine as Princess Carolyne, Patricia Morison as George Sand, Martita Hunt as the Grand Duchess, Geneviève Page as Countess Marie, Marcel Dalio as Chelard, Ivan Desny as Prince Nicholas, Walter Rilla as the Archbishop, and Robert Warwick as the Emissary. Featuring the music of Liszt, Wagner (Lyndon Brook), Chopin (Alex Davion), and Bach, Paganini, Handel, Beethoven, Mendelssohn, Verdi, and Schumann. Photographed (principally in Europe) by James Wong Howe. Columbia. CinemaScope, color.

Songwriter (1984)—Unpublicized by the company that made it, this is a terrifically enjoyable movie—a freewheeling, sophisticated comedy about how artists are driven to become con artists in order to survive. As the wily Doc Jenkins who turns to "mogulling,"

Willie Nelson is a country-music version of Alec Guinness's scalawag painter Gulley Jimson in *The Horse's Mouth*. Working with a witty script by Bud Shrake, the director Alan Rudolph is able to bring out the scrounginess and the ribaldry of the down-home music scene; the picture offers a wide range of rowdy slapstick, and some that's fairly highbrow and still rowdy. The performers are up for everything that's handed to them. The cast includes Nelson's co-star, the silver-bearded Kris Kristofferson, as a vain, happy sensualist; Lesley Ann Warren in a stunning performance as a sweet, insecure, boozing hysteric; Rip Torn, who makes everything he says sound mean and dirty; Melinda Dillon, who has a way of blending right in with the gags; Richard C. Sarafian (the director of *Vanishing Point*) as a Nashville gangster entrepreneur; and a blond newcomer, Rhonda Dotson, a romantic comedienne with awesome poise. The cinematography is by Matthew Leonetti; the production design is by Joel Schiller; the song score is by Nelson and Kristofferson. Tri-Star. color (See *Hooked*.)

Sons and Lovers (1960)—A sensitive and intelligent (though not altogether satisfying) version of D. H. Lawrence's autobiographical novel, adapted by Gavin Lambert and T.E.B. Clarke, and directed by Jack Cardiff. Visually, it's extraordinarily fine, though the visual beauties aren't informed by Lawrence's passionate sense of life. The artist's fire simply isn't here—the movie is temperate, earnest, episodic. But Dean Stockwell does well in the role of Lawrence, and Wendy Hiller as the mother and Trevor Howard as the drunken-miner father are superb; it's possible that Howard has never done anything to match his work here. There are scenes—such as the one of the father getting his weekly bath—that are so remarkable they almost do Lawrence justice; other scenes are merely conscientious. The most embarrassing sequences are two post-coital discussions. In the book they're the culminations of relationships that have been developed over hundreds of pages; in the film it's as if as soon as two people hit the sack, they know exactly what's wrong with the relationship and why it has got to end. With Mary Ure as Clara the suffragette, Heather Sears as Miriam, Rosalie Crutchley as Miriam's mother, and Ernest Thesiger and Donald Pleasence. Cinematography by Freddie Francis; the assistant director was Peter Yates. CinemaScope, b & w (See *I Lost it at the Movies*.)

Sophie's Choice (1982)—This unusually faithful adaptation of William Styron's Holocaust gothic comes to us stuffed with literary references and encrusted with the weighty culture of big themes: evil, tortured souls, guilt. The director, Alan J. Pakula, did the screenplay himself. He didn't write it, he penned it, and the film tells us that (1) survivors of the death camps carry deathly guilt within them and (2) William Styron is right up there on Parnassus with Thomas Wolfe, Walt Whitman, Emily Dickinson, and Hart Crane. Meryl Streep plays Sophie the Catholic; Kevin Kline is Nathan the mad-genius Jew, who is her lover and tormentor; and Peter MacNicol is Stingo the Protestant, the young heir to Southern chivalry (and stand-in for Styron)—he moves into the Brooklyn house they live in and becomes involved in their sadomasochistic trials. Styron got these three central characters so gummed up with his idea of history that it's hard for us to find them even imaginable, and Pakula can't get all the crazed romanticism in motion. The movie is a novel being talked to us, and it has the kind of plotting that points relentlessly at a character's secret and then has to have the character lying constantly, so that the lies can be stripped away. As Sophie, Meryl Streep is colorful in the first, late-40s scenes when, red-lipped and with bright-golden curls, she dimples flirtatiously and rattles on in Polish-accented broken English; she does amusing, nervous bits of business, like fidgeting with a furry boa—her fingers twiddling with our heartstrings. But when the flashbacks to Sophie's past start up and the delayed revelations are sprung on us, it's apparent that the whole plot is based on a connection that isn't there—the connection between Sophie and Nathan's relationship and what the Nazis did to the Jews. The narrator is Josef Sommer; the cinematography is by Nestor Almendros. Academy Award for Best Actress (Streep). Produced by Keith Barish and Pakula; released by Universal. color (See *Taking It All In*.)

Sorok Pervyi, see *The Forty-First*

The Sorrow and the Pity (1970)—Magnificent documentary epic on the German Occupation of France. Directed by Marcel Ophuls, this study in the psychology of history makes us ask what we and our friends and families would actually have done if our country had been invaded, like France. It's both oral history and essay: people who lived through the German Occupation tell us what they did during that catastrophic period, and we see and hear evidence that corroborates or corrects or sometimes flatly contradicts them. What makes the film innovative is the immediate annotation of what has just been said. As the perspectives ramify, we begin to get a fuller sense of what it was like to participate in the moral drama of an occupied nation than we have ever had. (4½ hours.) b & w (See *Deeper into Movies*.)

Sorry, Wrong Number (1948)—Lucille Fletcher wrote this overextended treatment of her radio play about a bedridden hypochondriac who calls her husband at his office, overhears a couple of men arranging a murder, and slowly comes to realize that she is to be the victim. Barbara Stanwyck is the terrified and, finally, whimpering woman; Burt Lancaster is her morose husband. The director, Anatole Litvak, seems to be defeated by the extravagantly jumbled, shallow script. With Ann Richards. Paramount. b & w

S.O.S. Iceberg *S.O.S. Eisberg* (1933)—An international production (Danish, German, American), this adventure melodrama about a shipwrecked group of explorers hanging on to a glacier that's breaking up was an international hit. Made in Greenland in 1932 and 1933 by the director, Dr. Arnold Fanck, it starred Leni Riefenstahl and a German cast; the American version, with Tay Garnett given the director's credit, retains much of Fanck's footage, and Riefenstahl is still the star, but the other German leads are replaced by Rod La Rocque and Gibson Gowland. From the start, the production doesn't appear to have been taken too seriously by those involved (not, at least, in the way they took *The White Hell of Pitz Palu* seriously), and it's far from a great epic, but it has an entertainingly perilous situation, and there are marvellously photographed sequences. Ernst Udet, who had appeared in *Pitz Palu* and other Fanck films, does some exhibition-style stunt flying here, as he comes to the rescue. By the time she appeared in this film, Riefenstahl, discovered by Fanck when he saw her dancing the lead role in a ballet when she was 17, had already made her own début as a director, with *The Blue Light*, in 1932. b & w

Il Sosia, see *Partner*

La Souffle au coeur, see *Murmur of the Heart*

Souls at Sea (1937)—Swashbuckling action film, based on a trial for a crime on a sailing ship in the early 19th century. The director, Henry Hathaway, can't get the confused script elements to mesh, and the sentimental manipulation is cloying; this is the unlamented type of movie in which a mortally wounded tough guy steals back to die with his sweetheart and slips a wedding ring on her finger. However, Hathaway gets all the panic and fury he can out of the slave trade, a mutiny, a fire at sea, and a crowded lifeboat. The three principals are Gary Cooper, George Raft, and Frances Dee, and the huge cast includes Henry Wilcoxon, Olympe Bradna, Robert Cummings, Joseph Schildkraut, Harry Carey, Porter Hall, and George Zucco. Paramount. b & w

The Sound Barrier, see *Breaking the Sound Barrier*

The Sound of Music (1965)—Set in Austria in 1938, this is a tribute to freshness that is so mechanically engineered and so shrewdly calculated that the background music rises, the already soft focus blurs and melts, and, upon the instant, you can hear all those noses blowing in the theatre. Whom could this operetta offend? Only those of us who, despite the fact that we may respond, loathe being manipulated in this way and are aware of how cheap and ready-made are the responses we are made to feel. We may become even more aware of the way we have been turned into emotional and aesthetic imbeciles when we hear ourselves humming the sickly, goody-goody songs. The dauntless, scrubbed-face heroine (Julie Andrews), in training to become a nun, is sent from the convent to serve as governess to the motherless Von Trapp children, and turns them into a happy little troupe of singers before marrying their father (Christopher Plummer). She says goodbye to the nuns and leaves them outside at the fence, as she enters the cathedral to be married. Squeezed again, and the moisture comes out of thousands—millions—of eyes and noses. Wasn't there

perhaps one little Von Trapp who didn't want to sing his head off, or who screamed that he wouldn't act out little glockenspiel routines for Papa's party guests, or who got nervous and threw up if he had to get on a stage? The only thing the director, Robert Wise, couldn't smooth out was the sinister, archly decadent performance by Christopher Plummer—he of the thin, twisted smile; he seems to be in a different movie altogether. With Eleanor Parker, Richard Haydn, Peggy Wood, Anna Lee, and Marni Nixon. The music is by Richard Rodgers and Oscar Hammerstein II; the script by Ernest Lehman is based on the stage version by Howard Lindsay and Russel Crouse. Academy Awards: Best Picture, Director, Editing (William Reynolds), Musical Scoring (Irwin Kostal), Sound (the 20th Century-Fox Sound Department). color (See *Kiss Kiss Bang Bang*.)

Sounder (1972)—Extraordinarily simple, since it starts from an inspirational story much like *The Corn Is Green*, yet deeply, emotionally rich. Perhaps the first movie about black experiences in America that can stir people of all colors. With Cicely Tyson (playing the first great black heroine on the screen), Paul Winfield, Kevin Hooks, and Janet MacLachlan. Directed by Martin Ritt, from a script by Lonne Elder III, based on a novel by William H. Armstrong. The score is by Taj Mahal, who also plays the comedy role of Ike. Cinematography by John Alonzo. 20th Century-Fox. color (See *Reeling*.)

Sous les toits de Paris *Under the Roofs of Paris* (1930)—René Clair's first sound film was one of the first imaginative approaches to the musical as a film form. Clair keeps dialogue to a minimum and uses music and sound effects to create a carefree, poetic style. More lyric, less comic, than his other films of this period, *Sous les toits* isn't the fun that his 1931 *Le Million* is; it may be a little too pure, too "cinematic." It tells the story of two inseparable friends and the girl they both love. With Albert Préjean as the street singer. In French. b & w

Southern Comfort (1981)—The members of a National Guard squad lost in the maze of the green-gray Louisiana marshlands are hunted down and ambushed by vengeful Cajuns. Walter Hill has a dazzling competence as an action director; he uses the locale for its paranoia-inducing strangeness (it suggests Vietnam), and he uses the men to demonstrate what he thinks it takes to survive. The movie is built like an infernal machine; it closes in on the characters, who are designed to be trapped. (Each of the men seems to shed his anonymity and be given an identity just before he's picked off.) The film is very intense, and there's an unusual sequence, edited to Cajun dance music, in which the two principal characters (Keith Carradine and Powers Boothe) take refuge in a village that is having a celebration. Its limitation is that there's nothing underneath the characters' macho masks, and—partly because there were so many fine, shallow action films made in the studio-factory era—we want more from movies now. The action format colors everything with its own brand of action politics: you get the feeling that the world is threatening your manhood every minute of the day. With a good cast: T. K. Carter as the live-wire dope dealer, Carlos Brown as the high-school teacher, and Peter Coyote, Lewis Smith, Fred Ward, Franklyn Seales, and Les Lannom. (Even the Cajuns—usually a joke in movies—are fairly convincing.) Cinematography by Andrew Laszlo; music composed and arranged by Ry Cooder. Written by Michael Kane, Hill, and the producer, David Giler. 20th Century-Fox. color (See *Taking It All In*.)

The Southerner (1945)—Jean Renoir's poetic tribute to some of the patterns of American life. It's an account of the year of a poor white Texas family—a chronicle of seasons and conflicts, adapted from the book *Hold Autumn in Your Hand*, by George Sessions Perry. Zachary Scott, who usually played lounge lizards, is almost unrecognizable as a young tenant farmer; it was the performance of his career. Betty Field plays his wife, and his relatives and neighbors include Percy Kilbride, Blanche Yurka, J. Carrol Naish, Norman Lloyd, and, regrettably, Beulah Bondi, who is more than a bit much as Granny. The picture has beautiful, evocative moments, mysteriously solemn. Having agreed to release this uneven but affecting picture, United Artists tried to sell it by a campaign of astonishing irrelevance—"She was his woman . . . and he was her man! That's all they had to fight with—against the world, the flesh, and the devil!" Though William Faulkner worked on the screenplay, Renoir is the only one listed, with Hugo Butler credited for the preliminary adaptation. Werner Janssen did the music. Produced by David Loew and Robert Hakim. b & w

Souvenirs d'en France, see *French Provincial*

Sparkle (1976)—As Sister, the hell-bent lead singer of a trio (made up of the three daughters of a domestic servant), the young singer-actress Lonette McKee has the sexual brazenness that stars such as Susan Hayward and Ava Gardner had in their youth. Sister puts the dirty fun of sex into her songs, with the raw charge of a rebellious, nose-thumbing girl making her way. She's terrific, but she has barely had a taste of singing in public when she falls for a sadistic pusher who degrades her. She goes downhill unbelievably fast, and the picture loses its zing when the action shifts to the rise of her docile and dewy-eyed little sister, Sparkle (Irene Cara), who is guided by a hardworking, dimply manager (Philip Michael Thomas). His almost canine devotion defeats the attempts of gangsters to muscle in on her career. The director, Sam O'Steen, may have got a little carried away by the smoky theatrical milieu, but he keeps the movie full of atmospheric detail, and the tawdry black-vaudeville scenes have the teeming, bodies-spilling-out-the-edges quality of Toulouse-Lautrec. The crowded look of the film helps to compensate for the skeletonic Joel Schumacher script, which seems heavily indebted to the story of the Supremes. As a teen-age boy who nonchalantly steals a car to take Sister out, Dorian Harewood has the vitality to match McKee's. The songs are by Curtis Mayfield. A Robert Stigwood Production; released by Warners. color (See *When the Lights Go Down.*)

Spartacus (1960)—This may be the best-paced and most slyly entertaining of all the decadent-ancient-Rome spectacular films. It's a great big cartoon drama, directed by Stanley Kubrick, with Kirk Douglas at his most muscular as the slave gladiator Spartacus who leads a rebellion of his fellow-slaves against the might of Rome. Spartacus makes some conscientious speeches—out of Howard Fast (who wrote the novel) by way of Dalton Trumbo (who did the screenplay)—but there's so much else going on that it's easy to brush off the moralizing. Laurence Olivier is Spartacus's antagonist, Crassus, a devious patrician who wants to rule Rome in the name of order—he is designed as a super-subtle fascist. Crassus is a wonderfully gaudy character: he takes Tony Curtis, a young "singer of songs," as his sexual favorite, but he also has a fancy for the slave girl whom Spartacus loves—Jean Simmons. She has never been more beautiful, and the emotions that appear on her humor-filled face are blessedly sane. Peter Ustinov is superb as a slave dealer, who along with his grovelling sycophancy and his merchant's greed has his resentments; and Charles Laughton, amusingly wide in his toga, is a wily old Roman senator. (The two of them have a chat about the beneficial effects of corpulence.) As a gladiator who is Spartacus's friend and who is forced to fight him, Woody Strode has the quietest, most elegant physical presence in the movie. The large cast seems to be having a high good time; it includes Nina Foch, Herbert Lom, John Ireland, John Dall, John Hoyt, and John Gavin as the young Julius Caesar, and Charles McGraw, who has a strongman-of-the-comics jaw, like Kirk Douglas's, as the sadistic master of the gladiators. After the rebellion, Spartacus's group of men, women, children, and animals march to the sea, and it's like a giant kibbutz on the move; they're all hearty and earthy and good to each other—a bunch of picnicking folk singers. Is Kubrick dozing at the controls? He wakes up sharply. Crassus, who has taken command of the armies of Rome, is out to kill the spirit of revolutionary fervor; suddenly, Spartacus's people are confronted with a demonstration of Roman might—acres and acres of soldiers in perfect military formation. Cinematography by Russell Metty; music by Alex North. Hearst's San Simeon was used for some of the locations. (196 minutes.) Universal. color

Spawn of the North (1938)—Entertaining action melodrama, dealing with Russian predators becoming involved in the Alaskan salmon-fishing industry. The script shows the happy hand of the wizardly Jules Furthman, especially in the friendship and rivalry of the two heroes (Henry Fonda and George Raft) and their dealings with the heroine (Dorothy Lamour). Directed by Henry Hathaway, this film has many of the elements usually associated with the lusty, romantic movies of Howard Hawks, which Furthman also worked on. Handsomely produced, it includes a surprising sequence: a documentary montage, very well done, showing how the salmon industry works. The other elements are all commercially calibrated in a frank, likable way, with John Barrymore, Akim Tamiroff, Lynne Overman, and Vladimir Sokoloff strutting their stuff in a cast that also includes Louise Platt, Fuzzy Knight, Duncan Renaldo, and a good-natured trained seal. Co-written by Talbot Jennings; cinematography by Charles Lang; music by Dmitri Tiomkin. Produced by Albert Lewin, for Paramount. (Remade in 1954 as *Alaska Seas*.)

A Special Day   *Una Giornata Particolare* (1977)—A schematic romance that takes place in Rome on May 8, 1938, during Hitler's visit with Mussolini. Sophia Loren, without visible cosmetics, wears a drab housedress. But with your husband as the producer and Pasqualino De Santis as the lighting cameraman, who needs makeup and fancy clothes? She has never looked more richly beautiful or given such a completely controlled great-lady performance. This movie is perfectly calibrated for its teeny bit of courage: the big stars playing uncharacteristic roles. She's an oppressed working-class housewife, the mother of six children, and Marcello Mastroianni is a suspected homosexual who has just been dismissed as a radio announcer and is about to be interned in Sardinia. Their humiliation draws them together for a few hours, and we see that society has wronged them, cruelly. It's neo-realism in a gold frame. This strenuous exercise in sensitivity was directed by Ettore Scola in a style that might be called genteel shamelessness—the brief encounter turf so well tended by Noël Coward when he was being "real." There's one miscalculation, though: when Mastroianni is in bed with Loren, he lies there

politely, as she puts his hand on her magnificent melon breast. And how can you have any feeling for a man who doesn't enjoy being in bed with Sophia Loren? You lose any interest in the radio announcer; he just fades away. In Italian. color (See *When the Lights Go Down*.)

Special Section   *Section spéciale* (1975)—Costa-Gavras's melodrama, set in Vichy France, raises the question of why highly placed Cabinet ministers, judges, and prosecutors, who were in no immediate danger themselves, carried out measures that flagrantly violated the system of justice they had been trained to uphold. But the casting and the writing are so prejudicial that this purpose is undercut: the collaborators are cartoon figures—vain, ambitious weaklings, easily soft-soaped. Their victims, however, shine with humanity. The film lacks temperament; it seems lifelessly worthy. With Louis Seigner, Michel Lonsdale, Henri Serre, Pierre Dux, Julien Bertheau, Jean Bouise, Julien Guiomar, Heinz Bennent, Michel Galabru, Yves Robert, Eric Rouleau, Bruno Cremer, Jacques Perrin, and many other well-known performers. In French. color (See *When the Lights Go Down*.)

Specter of the Rose (1946)—Ben Hecht wrote, directed, and produced this amusingly florid melodrama about a great mad dancer (Ivan Kirov) who is suspected of having murdered his dancing-partner wife. He marries his new partner (Viola Essen), and it isn't long before George Antheil's music is suggesting horrors to come. Lionel Stander plays a moody poet with a broken heart, and he rasps out the gaudiest *mots* ever heard in an American movie, while Judith Anderson, as a ballet teacher, and Michael Chekhov, as a shoestring impresario, engage in dialogues about the deep-down-under meaning of art and life. Such ironic asides as "My heart is dancing a minuet in the ashcan" may leave you unsure whether all this high thought is meant to be funny. Kirov, a California high jumper, was a shudderingly bad dancer to have been cast in this Nijinsky ripoff, but Viola Essen is lovely. Cinematography and co-direction by Lee Garmes. Republic. b & w

Spellbound (1945)—The idea is intriguing: a murder mystery set among a group of psychoanalysts, with a solution to be arrived at by clues found in a dream. It was carried out by one of the most highly publicized collaborations of all time: Alfred Hitchcock and Salvador Dali, with Ben Hecht writing the script. Ingrid Bergman is the analyst, Gregory Peck her amnesiac patient—the murder suspect. Yet, with all the obvious ingredients for success, *Spellbound* is a disaster. It was fitting that the actress who was once described as a "fine, strong, cow-country maiden" should be cast as a good, solid analyst, dispensing cures with the wholesome simplicity of a mother adding wheat germ to the family diet, but Bergman's apple-cheeked sincerity has rarely been as out of place as in this confection whipped up by jaded chefs. With Michael Chekhov, John Emery, Leo G. Carroll. Academy Award for Best Original Score (!), to Miklós Rózsa. Produced by David O. Selznick, released by United Artists. b & w

The Spider's Stratagem *Strategia del Ragno* (1970)—Before he made *The Conformist*, Bernardo Bertolucci made this adaptation of Jorge Luis Borges' enigmatic "Theme of the Traitor and Hero" for Italian television. Shot in Sabbioneta, a miniature city between Mantua and Parma, with colonnades that suggest de Chirico, the film is mysteriously beautiful; it has heightened colors and evocative imagery. But Giulio Brogi, playing both the son and the hero-father whose death the son is investigating, is given no character as either, and he lacks energy. The film itself is ener-

vated, and the themes are frustratingly elusive; it's all atmosphere and no strength. With Alida Valli, still splendidly handsome, and with that same secret look she had in *The Third Man*. Cinematography by Vittorio Storaro. In Italian.

The Spiral Staircase (1946)—Set in New England in 1906, it's about the activities of a finical strangler engaged in eliminating young women who don't measure up to his ideas of physical perfection. His preoccupation sets him in murderous pursuit of Dorothy McGuire, a harmless, attractive mute who serves as companion to gruff Ethel Barrymore, the bedridden mistress of a spooky mansion decorated with the hides of various wild animals and full of creaking doors, gates, and shutters. Robert Siodmak directed this little horror classic; it has all the trappings of the genre—a stormy night and a collection of psychopaths. But the psychopaths are quite presentable people, and this, plus the skillful, swift direction, makes the terror convincing. With George Brent, Kent Smith, Sara Allgood, Elsa Lanchester, and Rhonda Fleming. Produced by Dore Schary. R K O. b & w

Splash (1984)—This romantic comedy-fantasy about a mermaid (Daryl Hannah) who falls in love with a New Yorker (Tom Hanks) has a friendly, tantalizing magic. Hannah has long blond tresses, wide blue eyes, smiling curvy lips, and the look of a beatifically sexy Nordic goddess, yet her flashing tail and fins are like a butterfly's wings—they're her most ravishing feature; she moves like the glistening vision of mermaids that we all carry from childhood. The director, Ron Howard, has a knack for bringing the sweetness out of his performers without lingering on it. He's also the first film director who has let John Candy loose. As the hero's debonair playboy brother, Candy

S

is a mountainous lollipop of a man, and preposterously lovable. There is a whole cartoonish side of the film, involving a nuthead scientist and a lot of dumb chasing around that has the familiarity of TV humor, but Eugene Levy, who plays the nut case, is inspired; he exults in the comic-book eccentricity of his role, and everything he does is insanely deliberate. The picture is frequently on the verge of being more wonderful than it is—more lyrical, a little wilder. That verge isn't a bad place to be, though. The day after you've seen this movie, you may find yourself running the images over in your mind, and grinning. Written by the team of Lowell Ganz and Babaloo Mandel, along with Bruce Jay Friedman. With Bobby Di Cicco, Shecky Greene, Dody Goodman, Howard Morris, Richard B. Shull, and Tony Di Benedetto. Produced by Brian Grazer, for Disney. color (See *State of the Art.*)

Splendor in the Grass (1961)—William Inge wrote the baroque primer-Freud screenplay about the frustrations of adolescent sexuality, set in a small town in Kansas in the 20s, and Elia Kazan whipped it up. The picture is hysterically on the side of young love, and this hysteria seems integral to the film's moments of emotional power, its humor, and its beauty. Natalie Wood and Warren Beatty are high-school sweethearts whose parents think they are too young to marry. And so, deprived of love together, the boy turns to a floozy and the girl, maddened by loss of him, goes to a mental institution. The parents are the mean, hypocritical monsters you expect in this sort of youth-slanted picture that pretends to deal with real adolescent problems but actually begs the issue by having the two kids tenderly in love; the movie doesn't suggest that adolescents have a right to sexual experimentation—it just attacks the corrupted grown-ups for their failure to value love above all else. It's the old corn, fermented in a new way, with lots of screaming and a gang-bang sequence and girls getting pawed on their twitching little schoolgirl behinds; Natalie Wood probably has the most active derrière since Clara Bow. The extraordinary cast includes Sandy Dennis, Barbara Loden, Zohra Lampert, Pat Hingle, Martine Bartlett, Audrey Christie, Fred Stewart, Gary Lockwood, and Phyllis Diller as Texas Guinan, and Inge himself as the reverend. Cinematography by Boris Kaufman; production design by Richard Sylbert; music by David Amram. Warners. color

The Spoilers (1942)—The fourth version (a fifth came out in 1955) of the Rex Beach story about the brawling Nome of 1898, with its gold miners, crooked lawyers, and fancy women in feather boas. The climax of each version is always a bone-breaking furniture-smashing fight between the two strong men who are battling for the love of the same woman, and in this one John Wayne and Randolph Scott go at each other like mastodons fighting to the death. You know that the fight will turn out the right way for the lady (Marlene Dietrich, decked out in Gay Nineties plumage, like a more willowy Mae West), but the way the whole story builds to it makes it exciting, anyway. However, the man's-man material has been somewhat softened to turn the story into a vehicle for Dietrich, and with Ray Enright directing, the film doesn't have the brutish, raw vitality of the earlier versions. It's tired, a little ordinary; too many Westerns had already lifted the story's most colorful touches. With a brief appearance by the poet of the Yukon, Robert W. Service, and Richard Barthelmess, Harry Carey, Margaret Lindsay, Samuel S. Hinds, and William Farnum, the star of the first version. Adapted by Lawrence Hazard and Tom Reed; produced by Frank Lloyd, for Universal. b & w

The Sporting Club (1971)—Thomas Mc-Guane's surreal woodland comedy, in which the "aristocracy" of Michigan revert to base animality, fell into the hands of Larry Peerce, who has directed the entire picture in the style of the Jewish wedding party of his *Goodbye, Columbus.* An atrocity. With Robert Fields, Maggie Blye, Nicolas Coster, Jack Warden, and Richard Dysart. A Lorimar Production, for Avco Embassy. color (See *Deeper into Movies.*)

The Spy Who Loved Me (1977)—A glitter sci-fi adventure fantasy that balances the indestructible James Bond with an indestructible cartoon adversary, Jaws (Richard Kiel), who is a great evil windup toy. This is the best of the Bonds starring the self-effacing Roger Moore—there's a robust perversity in the way the film gets you rooting for the bionic monster Jaws when he tears a truck apart in a childish temper. He's 7 feet 2 and has razor-sharp steel teeth; Moore gets the chance to look scared—an emotion that suits him and makes him more likable. The film is a little long, but as the heroine—the Russian-spy counterpart of Bond—Barbara Bach is both luscious and self-parodying; there are magnificent views of Egypt; and the arch-villain Stromberg (Curt Jurgens) has a vast underwater domain and a supertanker that swallows submarines—the sets recall Fritz Lang's *Metropolis.* The designer, Ken Adam, the director, Lewis Gilbert, and the cinematographer, Claude Renoir, have taken a tawdry, depleted form and made something flawed but funny and elegant out of it; they use their sets and locations choreographically, turning mayhem into a comic dance. The last 45 minutes is a spectacular piece of sustained craftsmanship: you see the faces of imperilled men and you feel the suspense, but you're also drinking in the design of the machinery, the patterned movements, and the lavender tones, the blues and the browns.

The lavishness isn't wasted—it's entertaining. For Adam, Gilbert, and Renoir the film must have been a celebration of delight in mechanical gadgetry and in moviemaking itself; the sumptuous visual style functions satirically. The script is by Christopher Wood and Richard Maibaum; Carly Simon sings the theme song by Marvin Hamlisch and Carole Bayer Sager. Produced by Albert R. Broccoli; United Artists. color

Stage Door (1937)—One of the flashiest, most entertaining comedies of the 30s, even with its tremolos and touches of heartbreak. As roommates in a New York boarding house for girls aspiring to a stage career, Katharine Hepburn and Ginger Rogers are terrific wise-cracking partners. (Rogers, at her liveliest, holds her own with apparent ease.) The other girls waiting for their lucky breaks include Eve Arden (who wears a cat around her neck like a tippet), Lucille Ball, Ann Miller, Andrea Leeds, and Gail Patrick. The cast includes the supremely regal (and supremely funny) Constance Collier as an aged actress who does coaching, Adolphe Menjou as a producer with a roving eye, Franklin Pangborn as his valet, and Samuel S. Hinds, Jack Carson, William Corson, Grady Sutton, Phyllis Kennedy, Katharine Alexander, Ralph Forbes, Mary Forbes, Huntley Gordon, and Theodore Von Eltz. Directed by Gregory La Cava; from the Broadway hit by George S. Kaufman and Edna Ferber, adapted by Morrie Ryskind and Anthony Veiller. Produced by Pandro S. Berman, for R K O. b & w

Stage Door Canteen (1943)—Patriotism, entertainment, and romance mix badly in this celebration of the 44th Street canteen run for servicemen by stage folk during the Second World War; many famous performers make fools of themselves, and six bands provide the music—those of Count Basie, Benny Goodman, Xavier Cugat, Kay Kyser, Freddy

Martin, and Guy Lombardo. When this movie first came out, James Agee said that it was a gold mine for those who were willing to go to it in the wrong spirit. It's depressing, though. Frank Borzage directed; the horribly elaborate narrative by Delmer Daves is about a group of soldiers (Lon McCallister is among them) about to be sent overseas. They go to the canteen on their last night of leave in New York and fall in love with hostesses there. When the embarkation is postponed, they go back for another night, and then a third; by the time their farewells are final, the audience's tears could float them to the war zone. Katharine Cornell, Katharine Hepburn, and Paul Muni fare a shade worse than most of the other 50-odd famous performers; Ray Bolger and Ed Wynn come off rather better. Some other breaks: Ethel Waters sings "Quicksand" with the Basie orchestra, and Peggy Lee sings "Why Don't You Do Right?" with the Goodman band. With Cheryl Walker and William Terry as the young lovers. United Artists. b & w

Stagecoach (1939)—Perhaps the most likable of all Westerns, and a *Grand Hotel*-on-wheels movie that has just about everything—adventure, romance, chivalry—and all of it very simple and traditional. John Ford directed, from a script by Dudley Nichols (with, it's said, uncredited work by Ben Hecht), based on a story by Ernest Haycox—"Stage to Lordsburg." The cast includes John Wayne, at his most appealing as the Ringo Kid, and Claire Trevor as the goodhearted whore, Dallas, and skinny-faced John Carradine as the gambler, Hatfield, and Louise Platt, George Bancroft, Thomas Mitchell as Doc, Andy Devine, Donald Meek, Berton Churchill, Tom Tyler, Chris-Pin Martin, Tim Holt, Francis Ford, Florence Lake, and the second-unit director, Yakima Canutt, as the white scout, and Chief White Horse as the Indian chief.

Cinematography by Bert Glennon; filmed in California, Arizona, and Monument Valley, Utah. (There was a pitiful remake, by Gordon Douglas, in 1966; a big, brawling action picture, it featured Ann-Margret as the whore.) A Walter Wanger Production, for United Artists. b & w

Stakeout (1987)—Wanting to be loved isn't necessarily the worst thing in an actor: Richard Dreyfuss makes his adorableness amusing here, and gives his most confident star performance to date. He and Emilio Estevez play two Seattle police detectives who are assigned to the night shift on a stakeout, watching the former girlfriend (Madeleine Stowe) of an escaped convict (Aidan Quinn). The Dreyfuss character finds himself falling in love with the woman he's spying on, and when he breaks the rules and spends time with her he's aware that his partner, Estevez, is watching him. Hypnotized by the soft-lipped Irish-Mexican beauty played by Stowe, he's also mugging for the benefit of the young worrywart Estevez. All this is a jolly setup for amorous farce, and Dreyfuss has a Chaplinesque glee in some of the scenes; he's fun to watch. The director, John Badham, does his most entertaining work in years, but you feel the pressure of engineering underneath. You know that the movie is scheduled to deliver action, and Badham keeps everything dark and grungy, with frequent cuts to the cop-hating escaped convict, who is committing a few murders as he makes his way to Seattle. For all the nippiness in the dialogue (the script is by Jim Kouf) and the comic interplay of the actors, the picture doesn't leave you with anything. Aidan Quinn, who first appears heavily bearded, has a dashing, bulging-blue-eyed scariness. With Forest Whitaker, Dan Lauria, and Ian Tracey. (Shot in and around Vancouver.) Touchstone (Disney). color (See *Hooked*.)

Stalag 17 (1953)—In this rowdy comedy about Americans in a German prisoner-of-war camp during the Second World War, William Holden's hair-trigger performance as the crafty, cynical heel who turns into a hero won him a new popularity, as well as the Academy Award for Best Actor. He had been a sensitive but milder actor before, and even the despairing range he demonstrated in *Sunset Boulevard* hadn't prepared audiences for the abrasive edge and distinctively American male energy he showed in this role, which is rather like the parts that catapulted Bogart to a new level of stardom in the early 40s. The melodramatics of the plot are low-grade, and the material, taken from a play by Donald Bevan and Edmund Trzcinski—two ex-G.I.s who were interned in the actual Stalag 17—is still structured and performed like a play, but the gallows humor is entertaining, despite some rather broad roughhouse effects. Billy Wilder directed and had a hand in the adaptation, and it's a safe bet that he'd taken a long look at *La Grande Illusion*—Otto Preminger does an Erich von Stroheim–*Kommandant* number. With Don Taylor, Robert Strauss, Harvey Lembeck, Neville Brand, Peter Graves, and Sig Rumann. Paramount. b & w

Stand by Me (1986)—On a summer weekend in 1959, four 12- and 13-year-old boys from the fictional Castle Rock, Oregon (pop. 1,281), go on an overnight hike in the woods outside town to look for the body of a boy their age who has been missing for several days. The four, misfits who feel rejected, keep intuiting one another's emotions, and they're plucky—when they get in tight spots, they stand by each other. They're like a pastoral support group, quick to perceive signs of trouble and to lay gentle, firm hands on needy shoulders. Rob Reiner's film, taken from Stephen King's autobiographical no-

vella *The Body*, overdoses on sincerity and nostalgia. Seeing it is like watching an extended Christmas special of "The Waltons" and "Little House on the Prairie"—it makes you feel virtuous. All that stays with you is the tall tale that Gordie, the central character, tells his friends around the campfire; it's a stupendous gross-out about a fat boy known as Lardass (Andy Lindberg) who enters a blueberry-pie-eating contest. With Wil Wheaton as the little Gordie and Richard Dreyfuss as the adult Gordie who narrates the story, and River Phoenix, Jerry O'Connell, Corey Feldman, Kiefer Sutherland, and, in a flashback, John Cusack. The screenplay is by Raynold Gideon and Bruce A. Evans. Columbia. color (See *Hooked*.)

Stand-In (1937)—An erratic script about a high-strung Hollywood director (Humphrey Bogart, howlingly miscast); a classy efficiency expert (Leslie Howard) trying to make sense of the motion-picture business; and a sensible girl (Joan Blondell) who was once a child star. At one point, she does a wicked imitation of Shirley Temple. The movie was moldy even when it came out, but it's harmless and rather likable. With Alan Mowbray, Jack Carson, and Marla Shelton. Directed by Tay Garnett; script by Gene Towne and Graham Baker, based on a Clarence Budington Kelland story; produced by Walter Wanger. United Artists. b & w

The Star (1953)—Very bad. Bette Davis as a star who once won an Academy Award but is now down on her luck; she lands in jail for drunken driving, and is saved by Sterling Hayden, a boat-builder who once acted with her. Others who wander about in this lachrymose, exploitative treatment of the lives of aging stars (it was originally written for Joan Crawford) are Natalie Wood, Minor Watson, Barbara Lawrence, and Warner Anderson.

Directed—feebly—by Stuart Heisler. Davis throws her weight around but comes through in only a few scenes. Script by Katherine Albert and Dale Eunson. 20th Century-Fox. b & w

Star! (1968)—Cast as Gertrude Lawrence in this biographical musical, Julie Andrews lacks the insolent confidence and the elusive, magical sophistication that can make mannerisms into style; she's pert and cheerful in some professional way that is finally cheerless. Trying for glamour, she merely coarsens her shining, nice-girl image, becoming a nasty Girl Guide. The director, Robert Wise, and the writer, William Fairchild, appear to be aiming for a dispassionate portrait of an archetypal empty ratfink kind of star—a female Citizen Kane of the theatre and high society. But the ambivalence doesn't come across successfully, partly because Andrews is never convincing as a magnetic, tough-sentimental performer. Some of the best songs of Cole Porter and Noël Coward and Kurt Weill and the Gershwins are mangled, while audiences inside the movie go mad with enthusiasm. As Coward, Daniel Massey (who is Raymond Massey's son and Coward's godson) has the best lines and gives an amiable parody-impersonation. With Richard Crenna, Michael Craig, Beryl Reid, Jenny Agutter, Robert Reed, and Roy Scheider in a bit. Choreographed by Michael Kidd; the ugly, unflattering swell clothes ($347,000 worth) that Andrews wears are by Donald Brooks. At a cost of $14 million, *Star!* was a catastrophic box-office failure. 20th Century-Fox. color (See *Going Steady*.)

Star 80 (1983)—Written and directed by Bob Fosse, this movie is based on Teresa Carpenter's "Death of a Playmate," in the *Village Voice*, and other accounts of the murder of the *Playboy* playmate Dorothy Stratten by her estranged bodybuilder husband, Paul Snider, a pimp and a two-bit promoter, who, after killing her, sodomized the corpse and then shot himself. Fosse uses the case as evidence that murder is inherent in pornography and that the whole world is scummy. As Paul Snider, Eric Roberts uses a wet, mushy voice here, and he makes you feel the man's squirminess and rage. He gets the film's central idea across: that Paul Snider represents a mutation of the *Playboy* "philosophy," and that it's his frustration at not becoming a success like his idol, Hugh Hefner, that's driving him crazy. But Fosse keeps Roberts shouting and sweating and twisting his face for what seems an eternity. Mariel Hemingway tries hard as Dorothy, but she's all wrong for the part—she's simply not a bunny type. Fosse must believe that he can make art out of anything—that he doesn't need a writer to create characters, that he can just take the idea of a pimp murdering a pinup and give it such razzle-dazzle that it will shake people to the marrow. He uses his whole pack of tricks—flashbacks, interviews, shock cuts, the works—to keep the audience in a state of dread. He piles up such an accumulation of sordid scenes that the movie is nauseated by itself. With Carroll Baker, who, as Dorothy's mother, manages to suggest that the woman has some substance; Josh Mostel as a private detective; and Cliff Robertson and Roger Rees. Cinematography by Sven Nykvist. A Ladd Company Release through Warners. color (See *State of the Art*.)

A Star Is Born (1937)—The first version, starring Janet Gaynor and Fredric March. The director, William Wellman, had a hand in the story, and Dorothy Parker, Alan Campbell, and Robert Carson devised the script, which purports to tell the true inside story of Hollywood and the perils of fame—how the fresh young actress, Vicki Lester, becomes a great star, while her spoiled, big-headed husband, Norman Maine, falls from stardom and sinks via alcoholism and despair. The film is peculiarly masochistic and self-congratulatory. The cast includes Adolphe Menjou, Lionel Stander, May Robson, Edgar Kennedy, Andy Devine, and Owen Moore. Produced by David O. Selznick; released by United Artists. Selznick acknowledged that the 1932 film *What Price Hollywood* was the source material. color

A Star Is Born (1954)—Grandiose, emotionally charged musical version of the 1937 tearjerker. Judy Garland and James Mason are the leads (although she looks tired and worn, and he gives such a remarkable performance as the washed-up, decaying star that he brings a bloom to the movie). This updated version is a terrible, fascinating orgy of self-pity and cynicism and mythmaking. Garland's jagged, tremulous performance is nakedly intense; her musical numbers include the capering "Born in a Trunk" and the dark, heavy torch song "The Man That Got Away." With Charles Bickford, Jack Carson, and Tommy Noonan. George Cukor directed, from Moss Hart's acerbic rewrite of the 1937 film. George Hoyningen-Huené served as color consultant, and the strikingly sumptuous color design gives the film deep, neurotic, emotional tones. Warners. CinemaScope

A Star Is Born (1976)—The Barbra Streisand–Kris Kristofferson musical version, with the milieu switched to the rock world, is sentimental, without being convincing for an instant. Those in the mood for an emotional extravaganza can swoon and weep, and giggle, too. Directed by Frank Pierson; adapted by John Gregory Dunne and Joan Didion, and Pierson. With Paul Mazursky and Gary Busey. Songs by Paul Williams, Streisand, and others. Warners. color (See *When the Lights Go Down.*)

Star Spangled Girl (1971)—Sandy Duncan's comic talent shines through—she has a troll-like spark of genius in her timing—and Tony Roberts' and Todd Susman's talents almost shine through, too, but the material is atrocious Neil Simon. The situations are so contrived that the wisecracks aren't funny even when they're funny. But when they're sour they're certainly sour. Directed at breakneck speed by Jerry Paris, but the picture can't go by fast enough. Paramount. color

Star Trek II: The Wrath of Khan (1982)—Wonderful dumb fun. The director, Nicholas Meyer, hits just the right amused, slightly self-mocking note in the opening scenes, and the same actors who looked flabby and embarrassed in the 1979 *Star Trek—The Motion Picture* turn into a troupe of confident, witty professionals. The theme of this endlessly inventive movie is death and rebirth, with the prim, smug Admiral Kirk (William Shatner), who has become stiff from sitting at his administrative post, taking a three-week cruise on his old starship, the Enterprise, encountering his old enemy, the maniacal Khan (Ricardo Montalban), and waking up. Montalban plays his fiery villainy to the hilt, smiling grimly as he does the dirty; his bravado is grandly comic. The regulars are all present: Mr. Spock, "Bones" McCoy, Sulu, Uhura, Scotty, and the fuddled Chekov. And the crew has acquired a voluptuous half-Vulcan—Saavik, played by Kirstie Alley. Such guest performers as Paul Winfield, Bibi Besch, and Judson Scott shine in their roles, and DeForest Kelley makes the prickly Bones more crisply funny than he used to be; his performance helps to compensate for the disappointment of Leonard Nimoy's ashen, dried-out Spock. The pieces of the story fit together so beautifully that eventually the director has you wrapped up in the foolishness. By the end, all the large, sappy, satisfying emotions get to you. The story is credited to

Jack B. Sowards and Harve Bennett, and the script to Sowards, yet it isn't hard to detect Meyer's hand (especially when he leaves his signature—at a crucial point he has the hero echo the words of the hero in *Time After Time*). Paramount. color (See *Taking It All In*.)

Star Trek III: The Search for Spock (1984)—With Leonard Nimoy at the helm, this is the first movie directed by a Vulcan; maybe we shouldn't be surprised that it's achingly prosaic. This one is really only for Trekkies; others are likely to find it tolerable but yawny. Its predecessor, *Star Trek II: The Wrath of Khan*, ended with Spock's casket's being sent to a newly created planet, the paradisiacal Genesis, where, the audience could assume, Spock would be reborn. But this new film seems to take a churlish attitude toward its lighthearted, delicately self-mocking predecessor; almost vindictively, the new film requires that Genesis disintegrate. Admiral Kirk (William Shatner) and his venerable crew must steal the now mothballed Enterprise to rescue Spock—whatever form he's in—and take him home to Vulcan. The principal diversion comes from the Klingons, a bunch of ogres whose brains appear to be on the outside of their foreheads, and their Lord (Christopher Lloyd), who manages to be droll despite the absolute nonexistence of comedy scenes. There's also a ceremony conducted by a Vulcan priestess, played by Judith Anderson (in her 87th year); her voice is so commandingly intense it's scary, and she brings a spot of high style to this movie—her huge, pointy ears only add to her grandeur. The rest of the time there's not much to look at besides the collection of hairpieces on the crew of the Enterprise. From a script by the producer, Harve Bennett. Paramount. color (See *State of the Art*.)

Star Trek IV: The Voyage Home (1986)—Things are fairly comatose in space, and you may start feeling passive and depressed, but then the seven crewmates travel from the 23rd century back to 20th-century San Francisco to save a pair of humpback whales, and the encounters there between the seven and the more primitive San Franciscans allow for a few modest jokes. Here's a typical scene: Chekov (Walter Koenig) has been badly injured and is unconscious in a hospital, where he is about to undergo an emergency operation. In order to save him from the barbarities of 20th-century surgery, Bones (DeForest Kelley) hurriedly—and furtively—cures him by placing a small disk on his forehead. The scene is meant to be comic, but, with Leonard Nimoy directing, Chekov doesn't wake immediately—he wakes gradually; and when he's asked his name and rank he takes so long answering that any possible humor leaks out of the scene (which has no other reason for existence). Some of the kidding around is fairly genial, and William Shatner's Kirk is less stoic here than in *III*—he's pleasantly daffy. The others in the crew also have an easy, parodistic tone. But the picture doesn't have much beyond the interplay among them and the jokey scenes in San Francisco. The crewmates are supposed to be technical wizards of the 23rd century, but they deliver their lines as if they were ancient tortoises who had to get their heads out and up before they could say anything. It's a relief to hear two San Francisco garbagemen talk, because there's some energy in their voices, and when Madge Sinclair turns up for a minute, as the captain of the S. S. Saratoga, her crisp, urgent tone is like a handclap. Screenplay by Steve Meerson, Peter Krikes, Harve Bennett, and Nicholas Meyer; story by Nimoy and Bennett. Catherine Hicks is the teary-eyed marine biologist; Jane Wyatt and John Schuck also turn up. Paramount. color

Star Wars (1977)—One of the biggest box-office successes in movie history—probably because for young audiences it's like getting a box of Cracker Jack that is all prizes. Written and directed by George Lucas, the film is enjoyable in its own terms, but it's exhausting, too: like taking a pack of kids to the circus. There's no breather in the picture, no lyricism; the only attempt at beauty is in the image of a double sunset. The loudness, the smash-and-grab editing, and the relentless pacing drive every idea from your head, and even if you've been entertained, you may feel cheated of some dimension—a sense of wonder, perhaps. It's an epic without a dream. Maybe the only real inspiration involved was to set its sci-fi galaxy in the pop-culture past, and to turn old-movie ineptness into conscious Pop Art. And maybe there's a touch of genius in keeping the film so consistently what it is, even if this is the genius of the plodding. Lucas has got the tone of bad movies down pat: you never catch the actors deliberately acting badly; they just seem to be bad actors, on contract to Monogram or Republic, their klunky enthusiasm polished at the Ricky Nelson school of acting. In a gesture toward equality of the sexes, the high-school-cheerleader princess-in-distress (played by Carrie Fisher) talks tomboy-tough—Terry Moore with spunk. (Is it because the picture is synthesized from the mythology of serials and old comic books that it didn't occur to anybody that *she* could get the Force?) With Mark Hamill as Luke Skywalker, Harrison Ford as Han Solo, Peter Mayhew as Chewbacca, Anthony Daniels as C-3PO, Kenny Baker as R2-D2, and Alec Guinness as Ben Obi-Wan Kenobi. A Lucasfilm, released by 20th Century-Fox. (*Star Wars* was the first film of a trilogy; it was followed by *The Empire Strikes Back* [1980] and *Return of the Jedi* [1983].) color

Stardust (1975)—A hyperbolic English melodrama about the rise of a working-class rock group which never invites the viewer into the story. At first, the central character, played by David Essex, seems to be a fairly ordinary grubby kid, pushed to the top by shrewd mercenaries, but by the time he has acquired riches and stardom, the film's nastiness turns against the crowds who pursue him and he is presented as a doomed hero. The director, Michael Apted, shows his usual flashes of talent, but he overreaches. The editing is irritatingly mannered, and the exposé aspects are fuzzy-minded. The hipness and bitterness aren't entertaining, and they don't serve any serious purpose, either. When the hero OD's on a big international live TV show, the neo-Nazi grandiloquence of the spectacle is too sodden to be satirical. Written by Ray Connolly, the film continues the story of the 1973 *That'll Be the Day*, which dealt with the hero's earlier days. With Adam Faith as the manager, Keith Moon, Marty Wilde, Edd Byrnes, Ines Des Longchamps, and Larry Hagman. Cinematography by Tony Richmond; produced by David Puttnam and Sanford Lieberson, for EMI. color

Stardust Memories (1980)—Woody Allen wrote, directed, and stars in this obsessional pastiche, modelled on Fellini's *8½* and shot in black-and-white that suggests a dupe of a dupe of *8½*. Allen plays Sandy Bates, a comedian-writer-director who goes to the Hotel Stardust, a resort on the New Jersey seashore, to be the celebrity-in-residence for a weekend film seminar and is besieged by his fans, who want him to make more comedies, though he doesn't feel like it, because all he sees is human suffering. The pushy fans are photographed as Diane Arbus grotesques—big-nosed, fat-lipped, with outsized thick goggles—and Sandy Bates is presented as their victim. To say this picture isn't funny is putting it mildly; it isn't good, either. Everything in it turns uncomfortable, morose, icky. With Charlotte Rampling, Marie-Christine Barrault, Jessica Harper, and, as Sandy's sister, Anne DeSalvo. United Artists. (See *Taking It All In*.)

Starman (1984)—This sci-fi romance, directed by John Carpenter, has something of the sentimental paranoia of *Easy Rider* transposed to the 80s. With Karen Allen as a young widow with sad, glazed eyes and Jeff Bridges as a gentle extraterrestrial whose spacecraft has been shot down near her cabin in Wisconsin, and who takes the form of the husband she mourns, the picture has a melancholy gooeyness. He will die if he doesn't make it to a designated spot in Arizona in three days, to be picked up by his mother ship, so the two of them set out in her souped-up 1977 Mustang. En route, her fear of him changes to love, and he experiences some of the pleasures and pangs of being human, male, and American. And we experience some of Carpenter's idea of tenderness: when the two are in a roadside restaurant, he asks her to define "love," and she tries helplessly, wet-eyed, thinking of her dead husband, while a synthesized heavenly choir in the distance makes wistful, whimpering sounds. In this victimization fantasy, it's all sweet innocence between the starman and the widow because everything else has been displaced onto some violent hunters and the government, which pursues the two flower children with a dozen or so helicopters—embodiments of evil. Bridges is mildly amusing at the start, but the picture is muted and draggy; it lacks vitality. With Charles Martin Smith, who is likably sane, Lu Leonard as a friendly waitress, and Richard Jaeckel. From a script by Bruce A. Evans and Raynold Gideon (rewritten by the uncredited Dean Riesner). Columbia. color (See *State of the Art*.)

The Stars Look Down (1939)—Carol Reed was only 33 when he made this film and he had not yet acquired the technical virtuosity of his later style; it contains nothing as imaginative as the first sequences of his *Odd Man Out* when the Irish conspirators stage their robbery, and lose their leader in the getaway. But this straightforward film is, in some ways, his finest. It's a remarkably beautiful work, and until the 60s it was one of only a few English movies with a strong contemporary subject. It sustains an emotional tone like that of a Thomas Hardy novel, and the hero (Michael Redgrave, in his first really distinguished screen performance) is a frustrated idealist, not unlike Hardy's Jude. Growing up in a Welsh mining town, this hero dreams of improving the life around him, but marries naïvely, and disastrously. Margaret Lockwood plays the stupid, vulgar, unhappy girl who snares him, and Emlyn Williams is the little sharpie she's instinctively drawn to. One sequence is almost pure Hardy: a group of men are trapped in a mine; the conscience-stricken, criminally irresponsible mine owner, on his way to the rescue squad with the plans that will save the men, has a fatal stroke; the plans fall from his hand, and the trapped men die. With Edward Rigby as the hero's father, Nancy Price as his mother, Desmond Tester as his younger brother, and Ivor Barnard and Cecil Parker. From a novel by A. J. Cronin. The film met with a hostile reaction from organized labor, partly because the miners are seen to be contemptuous of their own union, and few people in the U.S. saw it when it finally arrived here in 1941. b & w

Start the Revolution Without Me (1970)—A parody of swashbucklers that begins bouncingly with the birth of Donald Sutherland and Gene Wilder as two sets of identical twins, mismatched by a harried obstetrician—one pair to be raised as peasants, the other pair as aristocrats. But the script doesn't hold up, the directing (by Bud Yorkin) is flaccid, and Sutherland smirks and mugs through his dual role. The picture turns silly, yet, at least, it doesn't turn sour, and Wilder has a fantastic shtick. He builds up a hysterical rage about nothing at all, upon an imaginary provocation, and it's terribly funny. It's the sort of thing you wouldn't expect to work more than once, but it works each time and you begin to wait for it and hope for it—his self-generated neurasthenic rage is a parody of all the obscene bad temper in the world. With a lovely poignant performance by Hugh Griffith as a befuddled Louis XVI, and Billie Whitelaw, Jack MacGowran, and Victor Spinetti. Written by Fred Freeman and Lawrence J. Cohen. Warners. color

State Fair (1933)—Will Rogers in a homey, good-natured comedy-romance that was a huge popular success. He is the farmer who takes his big black-and-white hog, Blue Boy, to compete at the fair. (When the hog feels poorly, Rogers accuses him of shamming.) At the fair, the farmer's daughter, Janet Gaynor, meets a newspaperman, Lew Ayres, and the farmer's son, Norman Foster, encounters a trapeze performer, Sally Eilers; meanwhile, the farmer's wife, Louise Dresser, wins prizes for her pickles, jams, and mincemeat. Frank Craven has a leading role, playing a storekeeper, and Victor Jory appears as a barker. The romance of Foster and Eilers is dismal, but the rest is highly satisfying. Henry King directed; the script by Paul Green and Sonya Levien is based on Phil Stong's novel. Has been remade a couple of times, but this version is the best by far. It's folksy stuff, all right, but Will Rogers and Frank Craven know how to satirize the characters they embody, and Janet Gaynor, sticky-sweet as she is, knows how to sneak into the audience's heart. Fox. b & w

State Fair (1945)—Rodgers & Hammerstein take over. Cheerful is probably the word for it—if you're in the mood for cheerful. The story has lost the folk humor it had in its 1933 version, and the Americana has been poured on. Everything is too clean and bright and smiley; it all reeks of manufacture, especially Charles Winninger. The principal actors trying to fake their way through are Fay Bainter, Jeanne Crain, Dana Andrews, Dick Haymes, and Vivian Blaine. Walter Lang directed. The score includes "It Might As Well Be Spring" and "It's a Grand Night for Singing." It would have been a better musical if the lyricist (Hammerstein, who also wrote the script) hadn't been fond of words like "grand." 20th Century-Fox. color

State of the Union (1948)—Katharine Hepburn and Spencer Tracy in a large, expensive political melodrama with satirical and romantic overtones, based on the play by Howard Lindsay and Russel Crouse, and directed by Frank Capra. Tracy is the Republican candidate for the Presidency, and Hepburn is his estranged wife, who agrees to come home for appearance' sake to help him win the election. It's a shallow but generally entertaining show, with lots of devious characters (such as Angela Lansbury and Adolphe Menjou) doing dirty deeds. Hepburn is wasted in her pillar-of-rectitude role, but she's still a dervish of a performer, and more fun to watch than just about anybody else who might have played it. Van Johnson, Lewis Stone, Raymond Walburn, and Charles Dingle are in the cast, along with such troupers as Marion Martin and Tom Pedi. The ending has the Capra sentimentality familiar from the 30s: the little people always know the truth—they can spot a phony or a sellout, and they know when a man is on the level. If you care to see what Arthur O'Connell looked like when he was younger, watch for the reporter who turns up. Adapted by Anthony Veiller and Myles Connolly. M-G-M. b & w

Stavisky (1974)—Alain Resnais's death song for 30s elegance, featuring a silver Hispano-Suiza, an Art Deco diamond necklace, baskets of white hothouse flowers, a white plane with a red-circle nose, a white-on-white animal in the snow. Even the buildings and the skies are silvery white, and the slightly acrid neo-Gershwin score, by Stephen Sondheim, enhances the design. The film seems to be a reverie on facades and contrasts, in which the international king of crooks, the swindler-charmer Stavisky (Jean-Paul Belmondo), who hides his origins and his past, who lives as if he had no memories, is paired with his friend Baron Raoul (Charles Boyer), who lives secure in the protection that class provides. Stavisky's adventurism, which weakened France and helped to destroy her in the Second World War, is also balanced against the revolutionary hopes of Leon Trotsky, exiled by Stalin, who was living near Fontainebleau. But Resnais directs as if vitality would be a sin against art, and the characters are no more than emblems. Each shot, each camera movement, is thought out in design terms; Resnais has a beautiful technique, but it's not an expressive technique. This is an icy, high-minded, white-telephone movie. The script is by Jorge Semprun, the cinematography by Sacha Vierny. With Anny Duperey, François Périer, Michel Lonsdale, Claude Rich, and Gérard Depardieu as a young inventor. In French. color (See *Reeling*.)

Staying Alive (1983)—Ludicrous. As producer-writer-director, Sylvester Stallone turns everything into a fight, and this sequel to John Badham's *Saturday Night Fever*, with John Travolta once again playing the dancer Tony Manero from Brooklyn's Bay Ridge, is a weirdly stripped-down-for-action musical. The whole movie seems designed to pound the audience into submission. Stallone doesn't bother much with characters, scenes, or dialogue. He just puts the newly muscle-plated Travolta in front of the cameras, covers him with what looks like oil slick, and goes for the whambams. Travolta still has his star presence; he holds the screen more strongly than ever—but too flagrantly. The film gives the audience such a pounding that if it weren't for the final two minutes of Travolta on the street, moving to the theme music from *Saturday Night Fever*, people might not have the strength to crawl out of the theatre. With Cynthia Rhodes, Finola Hughes, and Julie Bovasso, who has a couple of remarkable scenes as Tony's mother. Paramount. color (See *State of the Art*.)

Steamboat Bill, Jr. (1927)—One of the least known of the Buster Keaton features, yet it possibly ranks right at the top. It is certainly the most bizarrely Freudian of his adventures, dealing with a tiny son's attempt to prove himself to his huge, burly, rejecting father. Ernest Torrence is the father—a tough Mississippi-steamboat captain, who does not conceal his disgust when Junior (Keaton) arrives to join him, nattily dressed in bell-bottoms, a polka-dot tie, and a beret. When the father is in jail, Keaton tries to hand him a gigantic loaf of bread containing tools for breaking out, but the father doesn't understand what's in it and refuses the bread; Keaton mutters, "My father is ashamed of my baking." The film features a memorable comic cyclone, and a peerless (and much imitated) sequence in which Keaton tries on hats and changes personality with each, becoming a series of movie stars of the period. Directed by Charles Riesner. Silent. b & w

Steamboat Round the Bend (1935)—There's a romantic story in this pleasant John Ford comedy, but the picture is carried by Will Rogers (just before his death), as a patent-medicine peddler along the Mississippi; Irvin S. Cobb, as a steamboat captain; Eugene Pallette, as a sheriff; and Berton Churchill, as a stray evangelist. These four character actors get an assist now and then from Stepin Fetchit. With Anne Shirley as the girl in love with John McGuire, who has to be saved from hanging; Will Rogers—his uncle—goes up and down the river, searching for the witness who can clear him. Ford felt that Darryl F. Zanuck, who had just taken over as studio chief and who high-handedly recut this picture, picking up the pace, had ruined it. (It was popular, though.) Also with Raymond Hatton, Roger Imhof, Francis Ford, and Hobart Bosworth. The script, by Dudley Nichols and Lamar Trotti, is adapted from a novel by Ben Lucien Burman; music by Samuel Kaylin; cinematography by George Schneiderman. 20th Century-Fox. b & w

Steelyard Blues (1973)—Blithe exuberance turned into cant. Donald Sutherland, Jane Fonda, and Peter Boyle are among the band of friendly outlaws who are persecuted by the stupid, vindictive straights, and who fly away to a better world. With Alan Myerson's amateurish direction, the film never gets a rhythm going, and its adolescent anarchism just seems smug. Warners. color (See *Reeling*.)

Stella (1956)—Young men dance in a row in the sunlight and a solemn, solitary man dances in front of a high-pitched, almost metallic bouzoukia orchestra. The streets and bistros of Athens are much more memorable than the story of this crude, vigorous Greek film, written and directed by Michael Cacoyannis. The story is rather like *Camille* crossed with *Carmen*—an overcharged melodrama about a fiery young woman (the leonine Melina Mercouri) and her uncompromising determination to be emotionally independent of her lovers. She refuses to marry the weak,

insomniac aristocrat (Aleko Alexandrakis), outrages his condescending relatives, and drives him to his death; she falls in love with a young peasant athlete (Georges Foundas), but she stands him up at the altar, and he kills her. This movie doesn't have the grace of Cacoyannis's later, more subdued *A Girl in Black*, but it's a triumph of temperament. Cinematography by Costa Theodorides. In Greek. b & w

Stella Dallas (1937)—A celebrated tearjerker of the stage and screen, particularly effective in this version, starring Barbara Stanwyck and directed by King Vidor. Stanwyck plays the uncouth, down-to-earth young woman who can't live up to the socially prominent fellow (John Boles) she marries; they separate. Stella is loud and overdressed, but she's also sensitive, and when she realizes that she's an embarrassment to the daughter she loves (Anne Shirley), she gives her up to the husband. Tim Holt, Marjorie Main, Alan Hale, and Barbara O'Neil are also in the cast, but the picture is all Stanwyck's, and worth seeing for her brassy, touching, all-out performance (possibly her greatest), even if pictures about maternal love and self-sacrifice give you the heebie-jeebies. Also with Nella Walker, Ann Shoemaker, and in a bit at a soda fountain, Laraine Day. Adapted from the novel by Olive Higgins Prouty and also from a theatre version; screenplay by Sarah Y. Mason and Victor Heerman. Cinematography by Rudolph Maté. Produced by Samuel Goldwyn, who had also produced the 1925 silent version, with Belle Bennett. United Artists. (A remake, *Stella*, starring Bette Midler, was released in 1990.) b & w

Step Lively (1944)—An R K O musical version of the John Murray and Allen Boretz stage farce *Room Service*, which had already been filmed (to generally dismal results) with the Marx Brothers in 1938. This time, instead of the gang of characters running back and forth in one hotel room, they run clockwise and counterclockwise, through many hotel rooms. The star is Frank Sinatra, so calmly self-possessed that whenever the pack closes in he lies down on a bed or a dance floor and the thundering feet pass over him. Between times, he sings some Sammy Cahn and Jule Styne songs, including "As Long As There's Music." His cool head saves him in a movie that would be enough to eclipse the career of an ordinary singing star. With Gloria De Haven, Adolphe Menjou, Anne Jeffreys, Walter Slezak, Eugene Pallette, and George Murphy, who, directed to be idiotically rambunctious, sinks in this morass. Tim Whelan directed. b & w

The Stepfather (1987)—A first-rate, cunning, shapely thriller, directed by Joseph Ruben (*Dreamscape*), from a nifty screenplay by the crime novelist Donald E. Westlake. The blandly handsome perfectionist (Terry O'Quinn) wants to be the head of an ideal family; he's attracted to widows with children, in picture-postcard houses. Everything's going smoothly for him in his new marriage, except that his 16-year-old stepdaughter (Jill Schoelen) recoils from his touch. She knows right down to her toes that he's got some kind of fix on her and that he doesn't love her bamboozled mother (Shelley Hack). This movie has a deceptively placid surface: the horror is there waiting all the time. It's in what's missing from the man we see, and the skill of the picture is that it keeps us creepily conscious of what's missing. With the Vancouver area doubling for Seattle in the opening section, and then for the fictitious towns nearby, Ruben uses everyday settings, and the film's scariness is almost cruelly plausible; luckily, he and Westlake are entertainers. With Charles Lanyer, Stephen Shellen, and Jeff Schultz; cinematography by John W. Lindley. Story by Carolyn Lefcourt

and Brian Garfield and Westlake, suggested by the John List case. An ITC Production. color (See *Hooked.*)

The Stepford Wives (1975)—The first women's-lib gothic—hardly the landmark the world had been waiting for. Besides, it's so tastefully tame that there's no suspense. Taken from an Ira Levin novel that might have been written by a computer, it's about the encroaching horror of suburban blandness; in this account, the responsibility for suburban women's becoming overgroomed deadheads, obsessed with waxed, antiseptic households, is placed totally on the men. Katharine Ross plays the young New Yorker who moves to Stepford and discovers that the wives have been robotized by their husbands. Written by William Goldman and directed by Bryan Forbes, the picture is literal in a way that seems a wasting disease. With Paula Prentiss, Nanette Newman, Peter Masterson, and Patrick O'Neal. A Palomar Production, released by Columbia. color (See *Reeling.*)

The Sterile Cuckoo (1969)—Liza Minnelli's sad, quizzical persona—the gangling body and the features that look too big for the face—are ideal equipment for the role of a desperate, funny, imaginative college girl in this surprisingly gentle, surprisingly good film, directed by Alan J. Pakula. The screenplay is by Alvin Sargent; adapted from John Nichols' novel. With Wendell Burton. Paramount. color (See *Deeper into Movies.*)

Stick (1985)—Adapted from an Elmore Leonard novel, this picture about an ethical tough guy who returns to Miami after seven years in the slammer is a mess. It doesn't make sense and it shows its director and star, Burt Reynolds, at a low ebb. It has a wild stunt, though. Dar Robinson plays an albino killer who falls off the balcony of a high building; while plunging to his death he keeps firing his revolver all the long way down. And George Segal gives a rip-roaringly manic performance as a cigar-chomping millionaire who likes to pal around with hoods. Some of Segal's old joy in acting comes out, and each time he appears he gives the movie a shot of energy. The cast includes Richard Lawson, who, as the millionaire's houseman, has a good relaxed comedy touch, and Candice Bergen, Charles Durning, Tricia Leigh Fisher, Castulo Guerra, Alex Rocco, José Perez, and Sachi Parker. Shot in 1984, the film was put through some alterations and reshooting during postproduction. Universal. color (See *State of the Art*.)

Still of the Night (1982)—The writer-director Robert Benton is unquestionably intelligent, but he seems to have misplaced his sense of humor, and this murder mystery set in Manhattan shows almost no evidence of the nasty streak that's part of the pleasure of a good thriller, or of the manipulative skills that might give us a few tremors. Meryl Streep plays the icy hot woman suspected of murder, and her performance is all about her hair. It's platinum-white, it hangs bone straight like a curtain, and part of her face is hidden behind it; from time to time she peers up and shakes it back a little. This femme fatale is meant to be guileful and slinky—a woman with neurotic wiles. But Streep's high-strung emotionality isn't fun in the way that Faye Dunaway's has often been. She seems pale and gaunt, and more zombified than anything else. And as the psychologist who is attracted to her yet is afraid that she's a killer, Roy Scheider is competent but colorless; he brings nothing to his role but his physical frame—some sinews, a profile. In the early part, we do get some prickly sensations from Josef Sommer as Scheider's patient and Streep's lover, who works in an art-and-antiques auction house that resembles

Sotheby Parke Bernet. Sommer here is like a snide and slightly dirty Trevor Howard; he and Sara Botsford—she's one of the women who work at the auction place—are lovely (in a creepy-crawly way). Shot by Nestor Almendros, the film looks sterile and feels static. With Jessica Tandy, Joe Grifasi, and Irving Metzman; the story line was worked out by David Newman and Benton. Produced by Arlene Donovan. M-G-M/United Artists. color (See *Taking It All In*.)

The Sting (1973)—After their hit film *Butch Cassidy and the Sundance Kid*, Paul Newman and Robert Redford swapped mustaches and got together again with the director George Roy Hill. They were darling desperadoes in their previous match; now they're hearty hoods. The cardsharps-and-swindlers-of-the-30s mood isn't as coyly lyrical as before, but it's coy, all right; the script by David S. Ward is a collection of Damon Runyon hand-me-downs with the flavor gone. This is a visually claustrophobic, mechanically plotted movie that's meant to be a roguishly charming entertainment, and many people probably consider it just that. It was hugely successful, and the music—Scott Joplin's piano rags, as adapted by Marvin Hamlisch—was heard throughout the land, and heard and heard. Robert Shaw plays the sullen, stiff-necked menace with a brogue and some bullying force, but the whole movie is full of crooks as sweeties. With Eileen Brennan, Charles Durning, Dimitra Arliss, Ray Walston, John Heffernan, Harold Gould, Dana Elcar, Jack Kehoe, Robertearl Jones, Avon Long, and Sally Kirkland. Produced by Tony Bill and Michael and Julia Phillips. A Zanuck-Brown film, for Universal. color (See *Reeling*.)

Stolen Kisses *Baisers volés* (1968)—This first romantic comedy by François Truffaut is charming and likable, but maybe too easily likable. (The tenderness is a little flabby.) It's a series of improvisations on the young man-hood and love life of Antoine Doinel (Jean-Pierre Léaud), who was first presented at 12, suffering from the callousness of the adult world, in *The 400 Blows,* and later appeared as an adolescent in Truffaut's episode of *Love at Twenty.* Here, Truffaut seems to start with the assumption that we already love his little Antoine and will find his ineptness and in-competence adorable. The feat of a master of improvisation would be to achieve the loose-ness and texture of "life" and the "magic" of movie art simultaneously—to tell a story as if it had been found. This story seems to have been planted; we're conscious of the players trotting around the streets of Paris playacting for the camera. It's a pleasantly negligible movie, with free, idiosyncratic touches: a lit-tle documentary interpolation on the speedy mail service, a lovely moment when the her-oine (Claude Jade) teaches Antoine a method of buttering toast, and, best of all, a marvel-lous character invention—Michel Lonsdale as the man who hires detectives to find out why nobody likes him. (He thinks there must be a conspiracy.) With Delphine Seyrig and Marie-France Pisier. The script is by Truffaut, Claude de Givray, and Bernard Revon; the music is by Antoine Duhamel. In French. Re-leased by United Artists. color (See *Going Steady.*)

Stop Making Sense (1984)—Directed by Jon-athan Demme, this concert film by the New York New Wave rock band Talking Heads is a continuous rock experience that keeps building, becoming ever more intense and euphoric. In its own terms, the movie is close to perfection. The lead singer, David Byrne, is a stupefying performer who gives the group its modernism—the undertone of re-pressed hysteria, which he somehow blends with freshness and adventurousness and a driving beat. He designed the stage lighting and the elegantly plain performance-art en-vironment (three screens used for backlit slide projections); there's no glitter, no sleaze. The sound seems better than live sound: it *is* better—it has been filtered and mixed and fussed over, so that it achieves ideal clarity. The movie was shot during three performances at the Hollywood Pantages Theatre, in December, 1983; the cinematog-raphy is by Jordan Cronenweth. Released by Cinecom. color (See *State of the Art.*)

Det Stora Äventyret, see *The Great Adven-ture*

The Storm Within, see *Les Parents terribles*

Stormy Weather (1943)—Vague, wandering show-biz story—a fictionalized bio of Bill Robinson—but marvellous musical numbers. With Robinson, Fats Waller (doing "Ain't Misbehavin' "), Lena Horne, Cab Calloway, Dooley Wilson, Katherine Dunham and her dancers, the great Nicholas Brothers, Zutty Singleton, Ada Brown, Eddie "Rochester" Anderson, Benny Carter, and many other black performers and musicians. There are so many famous people in this movie that some-times there are three or four "greats" packed together in the drably staged scenes. Andrew Stone directed, and Clarence Robinson and Nick Castle staged the dances. The script by Frederick Jackson and Ted Koehler is about as bad as a script can be. 20th Century-Fox. b & w, originally released in sepia (In *Hi, Mom!,* De Palma parodies the use of sepia for black subjects.)

The Story of Adèle H. *L'Histoire d'Adèle H.* (1975)—A François Truffaut film to rank with *Shoot the Piano Player, Jules and Jim,* and *The Wild Child*—and perhaps his most pas-sionate work. The picture is damnably intel-ligent—almost frighteningly so, like some passages in Russian novels which strip the characters bare. And it's deeply, disharmoniously funny—which Truffaut has never been before. The story, about romantic love fulfilled by self-destruction, is based on the journals of Adèle, the daughter of Victor Hugo; she's played by the prodigious young actress Isabelle Adjani. The visual consistency attained by the cinematographer, Nestor Almendros, enables Truffaut to achieve a new concentration on character. In French. color (See *When the Lights Go Down.*)

The Story of Robin Hood (1952)—Not as stirring a piece of mythology as the Errol Flynn version (*The Adventures of Robin Hood*), but a robust, handsome production; made in England, it's a Disney film that doesn't look or sound like one. (That is a compliment.) Richard Todd is a likable Robin, and his Maid Marian (Joan Rice) is surprisingly spirited. The first-rate cast includes Peter Finch, Michael Hordern, Martita Hunt, James Hayter, and James Robertson Justice. Directed by Ken Annakin; cinematography by Guy Green and Geoffrey Unsworth. color

The Story of Vernon and Irene Castle (1939)—This was the last (and ninth) of the Fred Astaire and Ginger Rogers R K O pictures. The re-creations of the Castles' dances are painstakingly authentic, and most of them are fun to watch, but the movie is cursed with the dullness of big bios—especially those produced when some of the key figures are alive. And there's another problem—Astaire and Rogers lose their giddy personalities and their romantic breeziness when they're playing husband and wife, and in a period picture (the First World War) at that. With Edna May Oliver, Walter Brennan, Lew Fields, Victor Varconi, Etienne Girardot, Janet Beecher, Donald MacBride, Douglas Walton, Leonid Kinskey, Frances Mercer, and Marge Champion (in those days she was called Marjorie Bell). This may be the only musical in which Astaire ever looked unin-

tentionally funny: when he does a brief Spanish dance he's a howl, because he hasn't the macho fire and anger that it requires. H. C. Potter directed, from a script by Richard Sherman, Oscar Hammerstein II, and Dorothy Yost, based on Irene Castle's memoirs. b & w

La Strada (1954)—The theme of Federico Fellini's spiritual fable is that everyone has a purpose in the universe. It is acted out by three symbolic characters. Giulietta Masina is the waif Gelsomina (soul, innocence, spirit, dreams); Anthony Quinn is the strong man Zampanò (brute physical strength, man as animal); Richard Basehart is an artist-fool (mind). Though the background of the film is neo-realist poverty, it is transformed by the romanticism of the conception. Giulietta Masina's performance has been compared variously to Chaplin, Harry Langdon, Stan Laurel, Barrault, and Marceau, and the comparisons are just—maybe too just. Basehart's performance as the fool, which is not like the work of other performers, is possibly more exciting. Even if one rejects the concepts of this movie, its mood and the details of scenes stay with one; a year or two later, a gesture or a situation suddenly brings it all back. Winner of at least 50 prizes, including the Academy Award for Best Foreign Film. In Italian. b & w

Straight, Place, and Show (1938)—The Ritz Brothers. Not at their manic, surreal best (that was *Kentucky Moonshine*, the year before), and there's too much distraction from them in the horse-racing story that involves Phyllis Brooks, Richard Arlen, and Ethel Merman, but still it's the Ritz Brothers. Merman has a twinkle in her hard eyes as she belts out "Why Not String Along with Me" and "With You on My Mind"; her belting wasn't nearly as brassy in those days. She's a knockout. She also gets to proposition Richard

Arlen in a passage of double-entendre dialogue that became more famous when it was lifted for Bacall and Bogart in *The Big Sleep*—remember when they suddenly started talking about horses? Directed by David Butler. 20th Century-Fox. b & w

Straight Time (1978)—Dustin Hoffman gives what is possibly his finest (and most demanding) performance up to this time as Max Dembo, a paroled robber. Based on the novel *No Beast So Fierce* by Edward Bunker, a former convict (who plays the part of Mickey), the film provides a ruthlessly objective view of Max—a man with closer psycho-sexual relations to people from the prison world, such as his viciously zealous parole officer (M. Emmet Walsh), than he could ever have with outsiders, such as the scrubbed-faced girl (Theresa Russell) who takes up with him. The script (a synthesis of the efforts of Alvin Sargent, Bunker, and Jeffrey Boam) has first-rate, hardheaded, precise, sometimes funny dialogue, but it errs in bringing this girl too much to the center. Dramatically, the film lacks snap; there isn't enough tension in the way Max destroys his freedom, and so the story drags—it seems to have nowhere to go but down. The director, Ulu Grosbard, falters in most aspects of film technique and he doesn't shape the material; he doesn't enable us to feel what we recognize intellectually—that the movie is really about life *inside* prison. But he excels in handling actors: scenes between Hoffman and Harry Dean Stanton (as an ex-convict) and between Hoffman and Gary Busey (as a junkie ex-convict) are performed superlatively. And Hoffman's acting suggests that he could have gone much further in *Lenny*—could have given it the dangerous, almost homicidal streak it needed—if he'd been encouraged to; as the mean and unyielding Max, he even uses his voice well—softening it for a held-in, distrustful-of-talk effect. With Sandy Baron, Kathy Bates, Rita Taggart, Corey Rand, and Jacob Busey. Produced by First Artists and Warners. color

Strange Cargo (1940)—Strange is putting it mildly. Joan Crawford and Clark Gable are the amorous stars of this hilariously steamy melodrama set in a French penal colony. Peter Lorre and Paul Lukas are the cutthroat villains. There's also a Mysterious Stranger. You might as well know the worst: right in the middle of a convict's escape, with his girlfriend bustling along, up turns the Messiah. The Presence, in human guise (Ian Hunter), leads to the most untoward spiritual spasms; even the most hardened mystics may blush. Frank Borzage directed Lawrence Hazard's adaptation of the Richard Sale novel *Not Too Narrow, Not Too Deep*. Well, not too deep, anyway. With Albert Dekker, J. Edward Bromberg, Eduardo Ciannelli, Victor Varconi, and John Arledge. Produced by Joseph L. Mankiewicz, for M-G-M. b & w

Strange Deception, see *Il Cristo Proibito*

The Strange Love of Martha Ivers (1946)—Enjoyable glossy melodrama that reaches a boil. At the outset, the moody, adolescent Martha prevents her rich, sadistic aunt from killing her pet cat with a cane by using it to kill Auntie. Regrettably for Martha, a couple of her playmates, both boys, are around the house when the old lady is done in. Boy One (whom Martha loves) leaves town and becomes Van Heflin, a gambler. Boy Two, a sheepish sort in glasses, stays on, marries Martha (Barbara Stanwyck) and becomes Kirk Douglas, the district attorney. Robert Rossen, who wrote the script from a story by John Patrick, knew how to grab the audience, and the director, Lewis Milestone, knew how to hold it. With Lizabeth Scott, Judith Anderson, Darryl Hickman, and Roman Bohnen. A Hal B. Wallis Production, for Paramount. b & w

The Strange One Also known as *End as a Man*. (1957)—Jack Garfein's version of Calder Willingham's novel *End as a Man* serves up Ben Gazzara as the most polymorphous-perverse young sadist of the year. (The competition was keen.) This psychopathology of morale in a Southern military academy is a grisly—often effective—fusion of Freud and Actors' Studio. With George Peppard, Pat Hingle, Arthur Storch, Larry Gates, Mark Richman, James Olson, Geoffrey Horne, Clifton James, and Julie Wilson. Adapted by Willingham; cinematography by Burnett Guffey; music by Kenyon Hopkins. Produced by Sam Spiegel, for Columbia. b & w

The Strange Ones, see *Les Enfants terribles*

The Stranger (1946)—The only conventionally made narrative film that Orson Welles ever directed. He undertook it, apparently, in order to prove that he could stay on a schedule and make the same sort of movies that other directors did; he has said that there is nothing of himself in it, and that it's his "worst" picture. What he meant was, probably, that it's impersonal—that it has little of the specific Wellesian moviemaking excitement. It's a smooth, proficient, somewhat languorous thriller, handsomely shot (by Russell Metty), with some showy long takes. It's quite watchable, but the script (by Anthony Veiller and, though uncredited, John Huston, from a story by Victor Trivas and Decla Dunning) is clever in a shallow way: the people need more dimensions. Edward G. Robinson plays an F.B.I. war-crimes investigator on the trail of a Nazi arch-criminal (Welles) who has taken a false identity and is living in a small town in Connecticut, teaching in a prep school; his wife (Loretta Young) knows nothing of his past. The small-town details are entertaining, especially the scenes involving Billy House as the canny, fat drugstore proprietor, and Welles introduces some baroque touches and a garish finale, in which he's impaled on a sword at the top of a clock tower. His performance is so flagrantly, boyishly unconvincing—the Nazi seems preoccupied by his evil superman thoughts—that it's rather amusing. With Konstantin Shayne, Philip Merivale, Richard Long, and Brian Keith. Produced by S. P. Eagle (Sam Spiegel), for R K O. b & w

The Stranger *Lo Straniero* (1967)—Marcello Mastroianni plays Meursault, the Camus hero, very simply, with scrupulous intelligence and concentration. Directed by Luchino Visconti, the movie has great passages and is highly effective in suggesting the atmosphere of the novel—the Algerian heat, the sudden, unpremeditated violence. What's missing is the psychological originality that made the book important. The novel was a definitive new vision—a more honest view of human behavior. But by the time the movie was made, that vision had already entered into the modern sensibility, and the concept of alienation had become cut-rate and conventional in movies. And so, although the film is set in the correct period—the 30s—this doesn't help to relate it to what Camus's vision meant in the post–Second World War years, and the movie seems merely a factual account of Meursault's crime and trial. With Anna Karina, Bruno Cremer, and Bernard Blier; cinematography by Giuseppe Rotunno. Produced by Dino De Laurentiis. In French. color

Strangers in the House *Les Inconnus dans la maison* (1941)—Raimu has a good tragicomic role as a dipsomaniac lawyer in this Henri Decoin film, from a script by Henri-Georges Clouzot, based on a Simenon murder mystery. The crime becomes the peg on which to hang bourgeois hypocrisy and various social evils. As this attack on French corruption was made during the Occupation, Clouzot was censured as an appeaser of the Nazis. Not released in the U.S. until 1949, the film has had surprisingly few showings. With Pierre Fresnay as the narrator, Jean Tissier, Mouloudji, Juliette Faber, and Noel Roquevert. In French. b & w

Strangers on a Train (1951)—Hitchcock's bizarre, malicious comedy, in which the late Robert Walker brought sportive originality to the role of the chilling wit, dear degenerate Bruno; it's intensely enjoyable—in some ways the best of Hitchcock's American films. The murder plot is so universally practical that any man may adapt it to his needs: Bruno perceives that though he cannot murder his father with impunity, someone else could; when he meets the unhappily married tennis player Guy (Farley Granger), he murders Guy's wife for him and expects Guy to return the favor. Technically, the climax of the film is the celebrated runaway merry-go-round, but the high point of excitement and amusement is Bruno trying to recover his cigarette lighter while Guy plays a fantastically nerve-racking tennis match. Even this high point isn't what we remember best—which is Robert Walker. It isn't often that people think about a performance in a Hitchcock movie; usually what we recall are bits of "business"—the stump finger in *The 39 Steps*, the windmill turning the wrong way in *Foreign Correspondent*, etc. But Walker's performance is what gives this movie much of its character and its peculiar charm. It is typical of Hollywood's brand of perversity that Raymond Chandler was never hired to adapt any of his own novels for the screen; he was, however, employed on *Double Indemnity* and *Strangers on a Train* (which is based on a novel by Patricia Highsmith). Chandler (or someone—

perhaps Czenzi Ormonde, who's also credited) provided Hitchcock with some of the best dialogue that ever graced a thriller. With Marion Lorne as Bruno's doting, dotty mother, and Leo G. Carroll, Ruth Roman, Patricia Hitchcock, Laura Elliott, and Howard St. John. Warners. b & w

Stranger Than Paradise (1984)—The young writer-director Jim Jarmusch (who raised the $120,000 to make the movie) uses a minimalist aesthetic for low-key comic effects. This punk picaresque is in black-and-white, and each scene is a single take followed by a blackout; the three anomic principal characters—deadpan deadbeats—live in dead space. Jarmusch keeps the picture formal and cool, and it has an odd, nonchalant charm; it's fun. But it's softhearted fun—shaggy-dog minimalism—and it doesn't have enough ideas (or laughs) for its 90-minute length. It's so hemmed in that it has the feel of a mousy Eastern European comedy. With John Lurie as Willie, Eszter Balint as Eva, and Richard Edson as Eddie. Cinematography by Tom DiCillo. (See *State of the Art*.)

Lo Straniero, see *The Stranger* (1967)

Strategia del Ragno, see *The Spider's Stratagem*

A Stravinsky Portrait (1966)—Richard Leacock's too-little-known documentary portrait shows Stravinsky at work and in conversation with Christopher Isherwood, Pierre Boulez, Nicolas Nabokov, Balanchine, and Suzanne Farrell. The film was shot in Los Angeles, Hamburg, and London, with Stravinsky speaking English, French, and German salted with Russian; more than a simple record of his activities, it is an attempt to illuminate his creativity. b & w

Straw Dogs (1971)—Dustin Hoffman plays a weakling mathematician who finds his manhood when he learns to kill to protect his home, and Susan George is his snarling, pouty wife—a little beast who wants to be made submissive. Machismo, sold under the (then) fashionable guise of the territorial imperative, and directed by Sam Peckinpah in a way that apparently affects many men at a very deep, fantasy level. Probably one of the key films of the 70s. Its vision is narrow and puny; Peckinpah sacrifices the flow and spontaneity and the euphoria of spaciousness that have made him a legend—but not the savagery. The only beauty he allows himself is in eroticism and violence, which he links by an extraordinary aestheticizing technique. When the wife is raped, the rape has heat to it and what goes into that heat is the old male barroom attitude: she's asking for it. With David Warner. Screenplay by David Zelag Goodman and Peckinpah, adapted from the novel *The Siege of Trencher's Farm* by Gordon M. Williams. Cinematography by John Coquillon; editing by Paul Davies, Roger Spottiswoode, and Tony Lawson. Filmed in England. Produced by Daniel Melnick; released by Cinerama. color (See *Deeper into Movies*.)

The Strawberry Statement (1970)—How a student (Bruce Davison) gets radicalized by falling in love (with Kim Darby), directed by Stuart Hagmann, in TV-commercial style, so it looks like a super-duper beach-party revolution. The big confrontation scene seems to have been done after a quick look at the work of Busby Berkeley and Eisenstein; pretty patterns shot from overhead plus a lot of gas and screaming and blood. Screenplay by Israel Horovitz, based on the novel by James Kunen; they both also play roles. Also with James Coco, Bob Balaban, Jeannie Berlin, and Edra Gale. M-G-M. color

Street of Chance (1930)—William Powell, very cool and very sure as a gentleman rack-

eteer, in a well-written, deftly plotted melodrama about gambling. In order to cure his younger brother, Babe (Regis Toomey), of gambling fever, he sets up a game with the slickest cardplayers in New York. When Babe cleans them out and makes off with all the cash in the pot, the gamblers think big brother has put one over on them, and they go after him. Jean Arthur and Kay Francis are the women; directed by John Cromwell, who also plays Imbrie. Paramount. b & w

The Street of Sorrow, see *The Joyless Street*

Street Smart (1987)—Morgan Freeman may be the greatest American actor in movies. He gives the role of a Times Square pimp, Fast Black, a scary, sordid magnetism that gives the picture some bite. Magically, he sustains Fast Black's authenticity; it's like sustaining King Lear inside *Gidget Goes Hawaiian*. The ostensible star is Christopher Reeve; he appears as a Harvard-educated free-lance writer who fabricates a story about "24 hours in the life of a pimp," and then becomes enmeshed in Fast Black's efforts to get clear of a murder charge. The director, Jerry Schatzberg, can make viewers feel the beauty and excitement of everyday grit, and he makes the script (by David Freeman) look and play better than it deserves to, but he can't give it conviction, rootedness—he can't conceal the author's thin, brassy attitudes. Reeve is willing to play a suck-up who's trying to make his name, yet as an actor he's physically too inexpressive to play inexpressiveness; it isn't the character who's a lug—it's Reeve. And when we're told that this journalist has gained the cunning to out-street-smart Fast Black, it's a white boy's dream of glory. The screenwriter did, in fact, fabricate "The Lifestyle of a Pimp," in *New York*, May 5, 1969; there were no dire results. In the movie, he piles on fantasies of all the things that could or should have happened. Most of the performers do their damnedest. Kathy Baker brings a sexy intelligence to the role of the prostitute Punchy, and André Gregory is terrific as Reeve's smug, dryly self-amused editor. (He's his own yes-man.) Schatzberg and his cinematographer, Adam Holender, bring off the trick of using Montreal for most of the Manhattan locations. The funky jazz score (by Robert Irving III) features Miles Davis, and Kathy Baker seduces Reeve to Aretha Franklin singing "Natural Woman." Released by Cannon Films. color (See *Hooked*.)

A Streetcar Named Desire (1951)—Vivien Leigh gives one of those rare performances that can truly be said to evoke pity and terror. As Blanche DuBois, she looks and acts like a destroyed Dresden shepherdess. No one since the early Lillian Gish and the almost unknown, plaintive Nadia Sibirskaya of *Menilmontant* (1926) has had this quality of hopeless, feminine frailty; Shakespeare must have had a woman like this in mind when he conceived Ophelia. Blanche's plea "I don't want realism . . . I want magic!" is central to *Streetcar*. When Marlon Brando, as the realist Stanley Kowalski, cuts through her pretensions and responds to her flirting with a direct sexual assault, the system of illusions that holds her together breaks down, and he is revealed as a man without compassion—both infant and brute. Elia Kazan's direction is often stagey, the sets and the arrangement of actors are frequently too transparently "worked out," but who cares when you're looking at two of the greatest performances ever put on film and listening to some of the finest dialogue ever written by an American? When Vivien Leigh says "The Tarantula Arms!" or "It's Della Robbia blue," you know how good Tennessee Williams can be. He adapted his play himself, with additional adaptation work by Oscar Saul; the music is by Alex North; the cinematography is by Harry Stradling. Academy Awards: Best Actress (Leigh), Supporting Actress (Kim Hunter), Supporting Actor (Karl Malden), Art Direction and Set Direction (Richard Day, G. J. Hopkins). But initially theatre managers complained that more customers left than came in. (It took a while for this movie to reach its audience.) Made by Charles K. Feldman Group Productions; released through Warners. b & w

Strike Up the Band (1940)—Judy Garland and Mickey Rooney, that hard-to-forget teenage vamp June Preisser, and Paul Whiteman and his orchestra, in an M-G-M musical directed by Busby Berkeley that is so klunky and poorly paced, and so loaded with sanctimonious moral lessons, that even the George and Ira Gershwin score doesn't save it. (The Andy Hardy pictures were never this square.) The script, by John Monks, Jr., and Fred Finklehoffe, is like a noose around everybody's neck. Rooney is the drummer in the high-school band that turns itself into a swing orchestra, with Garland as the vocalist; the group is trying to raise money to compete in a national contest. Rooney's flamboyant energy makes some sequences fairly bright, but in a number of scenes he's photographed so that he's foreshortened, and he's given hopelessly awkward moments; his mother (big-bosomed Ann Shoemaker) urges him to become a doctor, and he says to Garland, "Now, do I look like a doctor?" Garland is rather dreary in a role which requires her to have romantic longings for Rooney though he thinks of her only as a pal; even her songs lack bounce—the arrangements are too sweet and too slow. The siren Preisser (who also does acrobatics) is much livelier than Garland; she's like a baby Mae West and her eyes rove with mischief. With the ebullient William Tracy, who is often funny; Larry Nunn in the sad-sack role of the boy who is hurt; and Virginia Brissac. In the "Drummer Boy" number, Rooney hits the drums with manic exhibitionistic joy, and he takes a crack at a xylophone, too. But in the other musical numbers (including a real Berkeley ghastly oddity—a marionette orchestra made out of pieces of fruit) Berkeley doesn't know when to end things; he keeps them going until he runs out of ideas. The score includes "Our Love Affair" by Arthur Freed and Roger Edens. Produced by Arthur Freed. (Lee Young dubbed Rooney's percussion work.) b & w

Stripes (1981)—Bill Murray as a wreck of a hipster who has screwed up his life and is in terrible physical condition. Having nothing better to do, he enlists in the Army to get back in shape, and he cons his buddy, played by Harold Ramis, into joining up, too. The picture is just a flimsy, thrown-together service comedy about smart misfits trying to do things their own way in the Army. But it has a lot of snappy lines (the script is by Len Blum, Dan Goldberg, and Ramis), the director, Ivan Reitman, keeps things hopping (it's untidy but it doesn't lag), and the performers are a wily bunch of professional flakes. The story comes to a natural end with the recruits' commencement exercises; afterward, when the platoon is whipping around Europe, the action is standard farce. Yet even when the plot goes all over the place some funny lines turn up. With John Candy (the big-blob charmer from the Second City), Warren Oates as the drill sergeant, Sean Young, P. J. Soles, and Second City people—such as Joseph P. Flaherty, as a border guard spouting Slavic gibberish. Columbia. color (See *Taking It All In*.)

The Stripper (1963)—This film adaptation of William Inge's *A Loss of Roses* has the dreary, liberal Freudian Sunday School neatness of second-rate serious drama: it's necessary for the characters to be shallow so that the audience can see them learning their little life's lessons and *changing*. Still, Joanne Woodward is at the center of this picture, and everything she does here is worth watching. Skinny and platinum blond, with an infantile, vulnerable manner and a bouncy walk, she's a small-town beauty queen who went off to Hollywood, failed, and is now passing through her home town with some seedy carnival entertainers—except that she gets stranded and stays on for the summer at the house where she once worked as a babysitter. The baby is now an 18-year-old (Richard Beymer), and she has an affair with him. It's the film's thesis that this affair causes her to grow up and learn to stand on her own two feet. Woodward doesn't do anything conventional; she gives the Marilyn Monroe–ish role a nervousness that cuts through its pathos. Even when the movie was first released, audiences were so familiar with the mechanics of homiletic writing that there was hooting each time the boy's mother (Claire Trevor) demonstrated her possessiveness. With Robert Webber, Gypsy Rose Lee, Louis Nye, Carol Lynley, and Michael J. Pollard. Directed by Franklin Schaffner (fresh from TV); the screenplay is by Meade Roberts; the handsome cinematography is by Ellsworth Fredericks. 20th Century-Fox. CinemaScope, b & w

The Strong Man (1926)—At the time this picture (his best) came out, Harry Langdon—innocent, moronic, infantile, saintly, cunning—was widely held to be in the class of Chaplin, Keaton, and Lloyd. It was his second long comedy and his last box-office success; perhaps not coincidentally, it was almost his last association with Frank Capra, who had been instrumental in shaping Langdon's comic character. Langdon plays a Belgian soldier in the First World War who has become a pen pal of an American girl and comes to find her after the war; he eventually has to clean out the corrupt town she lives in. At one point he falls into the grip of a

S

tough broad who is trying to steal some money from the lining of his coat; he misinterprets her action and gives a glorious rendition of outraged virtue. Written and directed by Capra. Silent. b & w

Studs Lonigan (1960)—Irving Lerner directed this small-scale version of the James T. Farrell material, set among the Chicago Irish in the 20s; clearly, Lerner didn't have the resources to do Farrell's characters and milieu justice, but it's an honorable low-budget try by a group of people trying to break the Hollywood molds, and there are a few passages of daring editing that indicate what the film was aiming for. It's an under-financed American attempt at an *I Vitelloni*. Christopher Knight was miscast as Studs, and even at the time the picture came out audience interest centered on his teen-age pals—Frank Gorshin as Kenny, and the very young Jack Nicholson as Weary Reilly, who is arrested for rape. With Madame Spivy as Mother Josephine, Jack Kruschen as Charlie the Greek, and Jay C. Flippen as Father Gilhooey. Also with Helen Westcott, Dick Foran, Robert Casper, Snub Pollard, Carolyn Craig, and Venetia Stevenson as Lucy, the girl Studs dreams about. Among the people who worked on the production were Haskell Wexler and, in the editing, Verna Fields and Melvin Shapiro. The music was by Gerrald Goldsmith; the adaptation (not inspired) was by Philip Yordan, who also produced. b & w

The Stunt Man (1980)—A virtuoso piece of kinetic moviemaking. Working with material that could, with a few false steps, have turned into a tony reality-and-illusion puzzle, the director, Richard Rush, has kept it all rowdy and funny—it's slapstick metaphysics. Lawrence B. Marcus's script, based on Rush's free adaptation of the Paul Brodeur novel, is about paranoia and the making of movies; Steve Railsback is the fugitive who becomes a stunt man, and Peter O'Toole is the flamboyant, fire-eater director who the stunt man thinks is out to kill him. Playing a protean figure—visionary, fierce-tempered, and ornery, yet ethereal and fey, O'Toole gives a peerless comic performance. With Allen Goorwitz, as the dumpling scriptwriter who plays Sancho Panza to O'Toole's Don Quixote, Barbara Hershey, Sharon Farrell, Adam Roarke, Alex Rocco, and Chuck Bail. Cinematography by Mario Tosi; music by Dominic Frontiere. Released by 20th Century-Fox. color (See *Taking It All In*.)

Such Good Friends (1971)—About the self-abasement of a modern woman (Dyan Cannon). The director, Otto Preminger, shows us the heroine's subservience to her demanding son-of-a-bitch husband (Laurence Luckinbill); we see that he exploits her and that he's sexually indifferent to her, but we never find out what she wants done about it. Why she allows herself to be used is the missing center of the story. When she makes snide remarks while an impotent man works away on her, and when she services a fat doctor (James Coco), is she getting even with her husband or proving her independence or just intensifying her masochism? "Sensitive" is not a word that is often applied to Preminger; still, one is unprepared for the rancid, fake-smart Manhattan atmosphere, and the ugliness of the malicious jokes. With Burgess Meredith, Jennifer O'Neill, Louise Lasser, Ken Howard, Sam Levene, Nina Foch, Rita Gam, Nancy Guild, and William Redfield. From Lois Gould's novel, adapted by Elaine May, under a pseudonym. Paramount. color (See *Deeper into Movies*.)

Sudden Impact (1983)—Clint Eastwood as Dirty Harry Callahan of the San Francisco Police Department for the fourth time. The pic-

S

ture is a slightly psychopathic version of an old Saturday-afternoon serial, with Harry sneering at the scum and cursing them before he shoots them with his king-size custom-made "44 Auto mag." The murderer he's on the trail of is played by Sondra Locke, who, it turns out, is a saintly executioner, much like him; she's taking care of her quota of scum, and might just as well be called Dirty Harriet. The script, by Joseph C. Stinson, features lines such as the main sadistic, rotten villain's laying claim to Harriet with "The bitch is mine." The whole thing is so obvious that people in the audience applaud and hoot; it might be mistaken for parody if the sledgehammer-slow pacing didn't tell you that the director (Eastwood) wasn't in on the joke. With Pat Hingle, Audrie J. Neenan, Bradford Dillman, Albert Popwell, Paul Drake, Jack Thibeau, Mara Corday, and Michael V. Gazzo. Released by Warners. color (See *State of the Art*.)

Suddenly, Last Summer (1959)—One of Tennessee Williams' feverous fantasies, padded out by Joseph L. Mankiewicz, the director, and by Williams and Gore Vidal, who did the screenplay. They should never have allowed the audience so much time to think about what's going on: the short play turns into a ludicrous, lumbering horror movie. Katharine Hepburn is rather amusing as the Southern-belle dragon lady whose homosexual poet-son, Sebastian, was killed and partly eaten by the North African boys he'd preyed upon. Elizabeth Taylor is her distraught niece, whom she's trying to get lobotomized so that the girl won't be able to tell the story. Taylor works hard at her big monologue, trying to give us the shudders, but Mankiewicz has delayed her revelations too long. Montgomery Clift, in possibly his worst performance, is the dimwitted neurosurgeon

who can't seem to get anything into his eminent head. Columbia. b & w

The Sugarland Express (1974)—This is one of the most phenomenal début films in the history of movies; the 26-year-old director, Steven Spielberg, is a wizard at action sequences, and this picture has so much eagerness and flash and talent that it just about transforms its scrubby ingredients. Lou Jean (Goldie Hawn) and her husband (William Atherton) are petty thieves who lost custody of their infant son while they were in jail; their attempt to get him back involves taking a highway patrol officer (Michael Sacks) hostage. The child is with his adoptive parents in the town of Sugarland, and as Lou Jean and her husband drive there in the patrol car they've commandeered, other cars follow. It's implicit in the movie's whole scheme that vast numbers of police cars pursue them, and that townspeople join the procession and encourage the young parents to retrieve their child, because that gives them all an opportunity to get in their cars and whiz across Texas. Spielberg patterns the cars; he makes them dance and crash and bounce back. The cars have tiffs, wrangle, get confused. And so do the people. These huffy characters, riled up and yelling at each other, are in the combustible comedy style of Preston Sturges; the movie sees the characters' fitful, moody nuttiness as the American's inalienable right to make a fool of himself. We wind up feeling affectionate toward some highly unlikely people—particularly toward Lou Jean, who started it all. She's the American go-getter gone haywire. Surprisingly, the film was not a box-office success. With Ben Johnson, Louise Latham, and Harrison Zanuck as the child. From a script by Hal Barwood and Matthew Robbins. The cinematography—full of shimmering, eerie effects—is by Vilmos Zsigmond; score by John Williams. Produced by

Richard D. Zanuck and David Brown, for Universal. color (See *Reeling*.)

Sullivan's Travels (1941)—Writer-director Preston Sturges's comedy about a popular—slightly fatuous—Hollywood director (Joel McCrea), who feels that his hits, such as "Ants in Your Plants of 1939," aren't worthy of a war-devastated world. To research his next project, a relevant film to be called "O Brother, Where Art Thou?", he gets dressed as a tramp and goes out to investigate the lower depths. Sturges is more at home in slapstick irony (as in *The Lady Eve*, earlier in '41) than in the mixed tones of this comedy-melodrama, but it's a memorable film nevertheless. With Veronica Lake, underacting with perfect composure, and Margaret Hayes, and many of the actors Sturges delighted in and used repeatedly—William Demarest, Franklin Pangborn, Robert Warwick, Porter Hall, Eric Blore, Esther Howard, Jimmy Conlin, Willard Robertson, J. Farrell MacDonald, Roscoe Ates, Dewey Robinson, Chester Conklin, Arthur Hoyt, Robert Greig, Frank Moran, Harry Rosenthal, Monte Blue, and others. Sturges himself can be glimpsed behind Veronica Lake on a set inside the movie studio. Paramount. b & w

Sult, see *Hunger*

Summer and Smoke (1961)—There's supposed to be something on fire inside Alma, Tennessee Williams' lonely, inhibited preacher's daughter, but from Geraldine Page's performance and Peter Glenville's direction 'tain't smoke that rises—just wispy little old tired ideas goin' to rejoin the Holy Ghost. Page is all delicate shadings and no surprises, her performance is so meticulously worked out it's dead. Laurence Harvey is the virile doctor's son who represents flesh to her spirit. With Una Merkel, Thomas Gomez sweating and shouting, Rita Moreno being

tigerish, and Pamela Tiffin dimpling, and also John McIntire, Earl Holliman, Lee Patrick, and Malcolm Atterbury. The play, written in 1948, was adapted by James Poe and Meade Roberts; music by Elmer Bernstein. (Williams' rewritten version, *The Eccentricities of a Nightingale*, was given a far superior production on TV in 1976, with Blythe Danner as Alma.) Produced by Hal B. Wallis, for Paramount. color

Summer Holiday (1948)—Rouben Mamoulian directed this essentially ghastly musical version of *Ah Wilderness!*, Eugene O'Neill's nostalgic comedy about adolescence, set in a small town at the turn of the century. The play unfortunately lends itself to the wholesome-Americana-good-clean-dances approach. Mamoulian has a heavy touch, and perhaps because of that Mickey Rooney, in the lead, mugs offensively. The cast includes Walter Huston, Gloria De Haven, Agnes Moorehead, Marilyn Maxwell, Frank Morgan, Selena Royle, Anne Francis, Virginia Brissac, and Butch Jenkins, in the role Rooney had played in the 1935 *Ah Wilderness!* The disastrous script was adapted from the 1935 script by Irving Brecher and Jean Holloway; the undistinguished music is by Harry Warren. Shot in 1946, this film spent a couple of years in the editing room and on the shelf. M-G-M. color

Summer Interlude *Sommarlek*, literally "Summerplay." Also known as *Illicit Interlude*. (1951)—This early Ingmar Bergman film is about the loss of love: a tired ballerina of 28 (Maj-Britt Nilsson), who has ceased to feel or care, is suddenly caught up by the memory of the summer when her life ended. We see her then as a fresh, eager 15-year-old, in love with a frightened, uncertain student (beautifully played by Birger Malmsten), and we watch the delicate shades of their "summerplay," interrupted by glances at adult relatives, as Bergman contrasts decadence and youth, corruption and beauty. In the early part, an old woman appears for just a moment in a road, walking—and this image, like the croquet game in the later *Smiles of a Summer Night*, seems to be suspended in time. Bergman found his style in this film, and it is regarded by cinema historians not only as his breakthrough but also as the beginning of "a new, great epoch in Swedish films." Many of the themes (whatever one thinks of them) that Bergman later expanded are here: the artists who have lost their identities, the faces that have become masks, the mirrors that reflect death at work. But this movie, with its rapturous yet ruined love affair, also has a lighter side: an elegiac grace and sweetness. With Alf Kjellin as the ballerina's suitor, Stig Olin as the ballet master, George Funkquist as the lecherous uncle. Cinematography by Gunnar Fischer. In Swedish. b & w

Summer Stock (1950)—The emotional rapport of Judy Garland and Gene Kelly transforms the corny, simpleminded story material—a reworking of the Judy Garland–Mickey Rooney pictures about adolescents staging a show in a barn. Though Garland is overweight and obviously uncomfortable in much of the picture, she and Kelly bring conviction to their love scenes and make them naïvely fresh. As a team, they balance each other's talents: she joins her odd and undervalued cakewalker's prance to his large-spirited hoofing, and he joins his odd, light, high voice to her sweet deep one. Their duet on "You Wonderful You" has a plaintive richness that stays with one. The most famous sequence is Garland's rakish "Get Happy," shot almost three months after the rest of the picture; exultantly thin, in a black hat and short jacket, she flaunts her spectacular long legs. It is one of the great cheerful numbers of her career. For all the messiness, this

is a likable picture, with lots of good songs and dances; they were staged by different hands—Kelly, Nick Castle, and the director, Charles Walters (he choreographed "Get Happy"). With Phil Silvers, Gloria De Haven, Eddie Bracken, Marjorie Main, Hans Conried, and Carleton Carpenter; the dancers include Carol Haney and Jeannie Coyne. Most of the songs are by Harry Warren and Mack Gordon. From a screenplay by George Wells and Sy Gomberg. M-G-M. b & w

Summer Wishes, Winter Dreams (1973)—Dun-colored earnestness about a middle-aged Manhattan housewife's coldness, unfulfillment, and regrets; Joanne Woodward is less lively than in her other suffering-women roles. The screenwriter, Stewart Stern, following the structure of *Wild Strawberries*, tries to equate the American woman's supposed incapacity for love with the whole American screwup of recent years but never shows the connection. Gilbert Cates directed; with Martin Balsam and Sylvia Sidney. Columbia. color (See *Reeling*.)

Summertime (1955)—Katharine Hepburn, prim and gaunt as an aging American virgin vacationing in corrupt, sensual Venice, and Rossano Brazzi as a soft, thickening Venetian art dealer who makes love to her. There is an element of embarrassment in this pining-spinster role, but Hepburn is so proficient at it that she almost—though not quite—kills the embarrassment. It's hard to believe that the coming together of a withered Puritan and a middle-aged roué would light up the sky with the fireworks that the director, David Lean, provides, but this is one of those overwrought, understated, romantic movies (like Lean's *Brief Encounter*) that many people remember with considerable emotion. From Arthur Laurents's play *The Time of the Cuckoo*; with Isa Miranda and Darren McGavin; the cinematography is by Jack Hildyard. color

The Sun Shines Bright (1953)—John Ford returns to the Irvin S. Cobb stories that he filmed in *Judge Priest*, starring Will Rogers, in 1934. At one point, Ford said that this remake was his favorite picture, but it doesn't feel right to a viewer—not the way the earlier version did. As the fair-minded, humorous Kentucky judge who defends a black man accused of rape, circa 1905, Charles Winninger can't get the character across the way Will Rogers did, and the actors never seem to blend with the period setting. Everything's a little stiff and creaky. With a large cast, including Stepin Fetchit, Arleen Whelan, Clarence Muse, Russell Simpson, Milburn Stone, Slim Pickens, Mae Marsh, James Kirkwood, Dorothy Jordan, Jane Darwell, Grant Withers, and Patrick Wayne. Screenplay by Laurence Stallings; music by Victor Young; cinematography by Archie Stout. Republic. b & w

Sun Valley Serenade (1941)—Sonja Henie skates and skis to such colossal triumphs that Lynn Bari, her jealous rival for John Payne's affection, can do nothing more than call her a "Scandinavian hillbilly" and take off in a huff. Sonja Henie probably has to be seen once, just as the infant Shirley Temple has to be seen once. There's no way of explaining what made either of them a top star, but when you see them you understand it perfectly; they may be beyond satire but they're undeniably stars. This picture is as strong a dose of adorable Sonja Henie as anyone could wish; it even includes the number "The Kiss Polka." With Milton Berle, Joan Davis, the Nicholas Brothers, Dorothy Dandridge, Ray Eberle, Tex Beneke and the Modernaires, and Glenn Miller and his orchestra, who come through with "Chattanooga Choo-Choo." Directed by H. Bruce Humberstone. (Lynn Bari's vocals were dubbed by Lorraine Elliott.) 20th Century-Fox. b & w

Sunday Bloody Sunday (1971)—John Schlesinger directed this complex, remarkably modulated English movie about three Londoners and the breakup of two love affairs, from a delicate, pungent screenplay by Penelope Gilliatt, and it may be his finest work. It's an unusual film—perhaps a classic. A homosexual doctor in his 40s, played by Peter Finch, and an employment counsellor in her 30s, played by Glenda Jackson, are both in love with a boyish, successful kinetic sculptor, played by Murray Head, who casually divides his time and affections between them. He has no special sexual preferences and doesn't understand what upsets the two older people about sharing him, since he loves them both. The film is a curious sort of plea on behalf of human frailty—it asks for sympathy for the non-heroes of life who make the best deal they can. People can receive solace from it—it's the most sophisticated weeper ever made. There is perhaps a little too *much* sensibility; compassion is featured. "People can manage on very little," the doctor says to relatives of an incapacitated patient. "Too late to start again," a sad, heavy-lidded woman who looks like Virginia Woolf says of her miserable marriage. Schlesinger has a gift for pacing and the energy to bring all the elements of a movie together, but he uses his technique so that it's just about impossible for you to have any reaction that he hasn't decreed you should. The film is full of planted insights; you can practically count the watts in the illuminations. With Peggy Ashcroft, Vivian Pickles, Tony Britton, and Maurice Denham. Cinematography by Billy Williams. color (See *Deeper into Movies*.)

Sunday Woman *La Donna della Domenica* (1976)—This semi-satirical whodunit set in Turin among the bored, decadent rich is equipped with three star names (Jean-Louis Trintignant, Marcello Mastroianni, Jacqueline Bisset), but the social observations are too small and too archly obvious to have any bite, and it doesn't have suspense—just complication. On Bisset's face even an amused deadpan looks good; it adds to her high-fashion glaze. But everybody else walks through this blankly, too. It's a poshly made bummer. Directed by Luigi Comencini; written by Age and Scarpelli; music by Ennio Morricone. With Claudio Gora, who is done in by a big ceramic phallus, Aldo Reggiani as a young homosexual, and Pino Caruso. An Italian-French co-production. In Italian. color

Sundays and Cybèle *Les Dimanches de Ville d'Avray* (1962)—A moist, romantic pastiche about a brain-damaged young man (Hardy Krüger) and a girl of 12 (Patricia Gozzi, who has the eyes of a Keane painting). With Nicole Courcel. Directed by Serge Bourguignon; cinematography by Henri Decaë. In French. b & w

The Sundowners (1960)—This major film by a major director (Fred Zinnemann) was neglected when it came out—possibly because Warners didn't believe that people would go to see a movie set in Australia—and it has never achieved the reputation it deserves. It's a large, episodic movie, with a strong emotional texture—an epic about the space and emptiness of the country, and about Robert Mitchum as a man who doesn't want to stay in one place, and Deborah Kerr as the wife who keeps moving with him, raising a son (Michael Anderson, Jr.) who has never known a settled existence. There are marvellous sequences: one involving a race horse who's like a pipe dream of a horse; another, a great sheep-shearing contest, with Mitchum pitted against a wizardly little old geezer (Wylie Watson). And though the story builds slowly (and the first half may seem a little pokey), the characters are more redblooded and vigorous and eccentric than in most other Zinnemann films. Deborah Kerr

isn't at all aristocratic or mannered here; this may be her richest performance. Peter Ustinov and Glynis Johns play a secondary, contrasting pair of lovers, and the cast includes Dina Merrill, Chips Rafferty, Ronald Fraser, John Meillon, and Mervyn Johns. The script, by Isobel Lennart, is based on a novel by Jon Cleary; the cinematography is by Jack Hildyard. color

Sunrise (1927)—A near masterpiece, made in Hollywood by the great German director F. W. Murnau, who was given contractual assurance that there would be no interference by the studio (Fox). The script, freely adapted from Hermann Sudermann's *A Trip to Tilsit*, was prepared in Berlin by Carl Mayer, and Murnau planned the whole film there, on the basis that the story was universal. The opening title reads, "This story of a Man and his Wife is of nowhere and everywhere, you might hear it anywhere and at any time." The man (George O'Brien) and his wife (Janet Gaynor) are rural Americans; their happiness is disrupted by a city temptress (Margaret Livingston) who seduces the man and persuades him to drown his wife. The story is told in a flowing, lyrical German manner that is extraordinarily sensual, yet is perhaps too self-conscious, too fable-like for American audiences. (Huge stylized sets were built.) The film failed commercially, and on his next two Fox projects Murnau didn't have the same freedom. There are some masterly sequences: the seduction under a full moon, the wife's flight (she boards a trolley). Cinematography by Karl Strüss and Charles Rosher; art direction by Rochus Gliese, with Edgar Ulmer as one of his assistants. Silent. b & w

Sunset Boulevard (1950)—A young scriptwriter (William Holden), speeding away from the finance-company men who have come to repossess his car (it is Los Angeles, where a man can get along without his honor, but not without his car), turns into a driveway on Sunset Boulevard and finds himself at the decaying mansion of the once great silent star Norma Desmond (Gloria Swanson). Attended by her butler (Erich von Stroheim), who was once her husband and her director, she lives among the mementos of her past, and plots her comeback in her own adaptation of *Salome*. The rapacious old vamp persuades the young man to stay and work with her on the script; he becomes her kept man, her lover, her victim. The details are baroque: the rats in the empty swimming pool, the wind moaning in the organ pipes, the midnight burial of a pet chimpanzee. Glint-eyed Swanson clutches at her comeback role almost as if it were Salome, yet the acting honors belong to Holden. When he makes love to the crazy, demanding old woman, his face shows a mixture of pity and guilt and nausea. This brittle satiric tribute to Hollywood's leopard-skin past—it's narrated by a corpse—is almost too clever, yet it's at its best in this cleverness, and is slightly banal in the sequences dealing with a normal girl (Nancy Olson) and modern Hollywood. Billy Wilder directed; Charles Brackett produced; the script is by Brackett, Wilder, and D. M. Marshman, Jr. With Buster Keaton, H. B. Warner, Anna Q. Nilsson, Hedda Hopper, Cecil B. De Mille, Jack Webb, Fred Clark, and Lloyd Gough. Paramount. b & w

The Sunshine Boys (1975)—Neil Simon's extended sketch about two quarrelsome vaudevillians (Walter Matthau and George Burns) who, 11 years back, broke up after 43 years together and haven't spoken to each other since; they're brought together to appear on a TV special. It's all one-liners; Matthau keeps blasting us with his bullhorn voice; Burns has the repose of a tortoise, his eyes gleaming and alert, and he has a rhythmed formality in his conversation, as an old trouper might. (He was rewarded with the Academy Award for Best Supporting Actor.) The director, Herbert Ross, doesn't bring enough invention to the material, and it's just shouting, when it needs to be beautifully timed routines. (It was a big hit, though.) With Richard Benjamin. Produced by Ray Stark, for M-G-M; released by United Artists. color (see *When the Lights Go Down*.)

Super Fly (1972)—Gaudy black-exploitation film with explicit racism and some that's implicit (the hero deals in cocaine, which is supposed to be O.K., since most of the users are white). Partly slick, partly amateurish. With Ron O'Neal and Carl Lee; directed by Gordon Parks, Jr. Warners. color

Superman (1978)—Christopher Reeve, the young actor chosen to play the lead, is the best reason to see the picture: he's immediately likable, with an open-faced, deadpan style that's just right for a windup hero. The film is likable but disappointing—it gives the impression of having been made in panic, in fear that style or "too much" imagination might endanger its appeal to the literal-minded. Though one of the two or three most expensive movies made up to that date, it's cheesy-looking, and the plotting is so hit-or-miss that the story never seems to get started; the special effects are far from wizardly, and the editing often seems hurried and jerky just at the crucial points. Directed by Richard Donner, though there's so little consistency that each sequence might have had a different director and been color-processed in a different lab. (Richard Lester was said to have worked on parts of it.) With an enormous cast that includes Marlon Brando, Gene Hackman, Margot Kidder, Valerie Perrine, Ned Beatty, Glenn Ford, Phyllis Thaxter, Terence Stamp, Susannah York, Jeff East, Marc McClure, Trevor Howard, Harry Andrews, Maria Schell, Jackie Cooper, and Aaron Smolinski, who plays Superman as a child. The writers involved in adapting the comic strip created by Jerry Siegel and Joe Schuster include Mario Puzo, David Newman, Leslie Newman, Robert Benton, Tom Mankiewicz, and Norman Enfield. Cinematography by Geoffrey Unsworth; music by John Williams. An Alexander & Ilya Salkind Production. color (See *When the Lights Go Down*.)

Superman II (1981)—It has charm and a lot of entertaining kinkiness, too. Richard Lester, who directed this sequel to *Superman*, brings it one light touch after another, and pretty soon the movie has a real spirit—what you wished the first had had. Christopher Reeve, who brings emotional depth to Superman, pulls a switch on the material: Kryptonian that he is, Superman is the only human being in the movie. By the end, he's no longer a square; he has suffered humiliation and grown up—you come out of the picture thinking about Superman's feelings. And Reeve has become a smoothie: his transitions from Clark Kent to Superman and back are now polished comedy routines. Gene Hackman gives a juicy performance as the bald, shyster clown Lex Luthor, who tries to make a deal with the three arch-fiend Kryptonians in their black high-punk jumpsuits—Terence Stamp as General Zod, Jack O'Halloran as Non, and Sarah Douglas as the sadistic tease Ursa. This Ursa has the kind of face cameras worship, and she does her dirty deeds with blasé nonchalance and the merest flick of a malicious smile. The picture grows faster and quirkier as it moves along. With Margot Kidder as Lois Lane. Written by Mario Puzo, David Newman, Leslie Newman, and Tom Mankiewicz. (The special effects are highly variable in quality, and the whole film—blown up from 35 mm to 70 mm for the big-theatre showings—is grainy and bleached and often poorly framed. You're much better off if you see it in 35 mm.)

Released by Warners. color (See *Taking It All In*.)

Superman III (1983)—The star is Richard Pryor, who acts as if he were trying not to be noticed. He plays Gus Gorman, a computer wizard who is ordered by his boss (Robert Vaughn), the slimy-suave head of a conglomerate, to work out the elements of kryptonite, the only substance that can destroy Superman (Christopher Reeve). Gus fakes one element, and his near-kryptonite doesn't kill Superman; it demoralizes him and he begins to perform dirty deeds. Richard Lester, who directed (he also did *Superman II*), provides agreeable visual humor, and the film begins promisingly, but Lester wants us to see Superman as a virtuous clod, and this drains the mythic life out of the movie. What Superman and the other characters do doesn't seem to have any weight. Too many scenes are treated as if they were just obligatory, and because of this air of indifference, verging on disdain, the movie's sight gags and special effects—even the biggest ones—aren't particularly exciting. The scattered impulses behind the picture cancel each other out—everything feels marginal. As Lana Lang, the girl from Smallville who has had a crush on Clark Kent since high school, Annette O'Toole is the only member of the cast who appears to believe in his or her role yet stays in a comic-book frame. Also with Gavan O'Herlihy as Lana's jock suitor, Pamela Stephenson as the floozy-intellectual Lorelei Ambrosia, Annie Ross as the witchlike Vera (a real mistake), and—fleetingly—Margot Kidder as Lois Lane, Jackie Cooper, and Marc McClure. The script is by David and Leslie Newman. Produced by the Salkinds; released by Warners. color. (See *State of the Art*.)

The Survivors (1983)—Robin Williams may be that rarity, a fearless actor; his cock-a-doodle-doo eagerness transcends the flaws in this slapstick social satire. He plays a junior executive in New York who gets fired on the same day that Walter Matthau, the owner of a service station, loses his business. They meet at a lunch counter, where each man is trying to drown his sorrow in a cup of coffee, and when a bullying thug (Jerry Reed) tries to rob the place, they disarm him and, briefly, become media heroes. Being fired seems to have thrown a switch in the young executive's skull, and after the attempted robbery he goes gun-crazy, buys an arsenal, and goes off for a course of training in survival tactics at a parafascist camp in New England; he wants to learn how to be violent, so he can live in the wild and protect himself when the social order collapses. The best thing about this framework is that it permits Robin Williams to be himself and yet to be in character. He sputters out his short-circuited thoughts; he seems to be free-associating 24 hours a day, and this spritzing never seems false or prepared. (It's Matthau's function to soothe him.) There's a lot of unconventional humor in the script by Michael Leeson, though he doesn't appear to be experienced in building a plot to a climax, and the director, Michael Ritchie, tends to be at his sharpest in divertissements on a theme rather than on the theme itself. Jerry Reed (better known as a country musician) has a fine handsome, maniacal presence—he has scary, deep-set eyes; and Kristen Vigard is fresh and entertaining as Matthau's spacey redhead daughter. The unusually gifted supporting cast includes Anne Pitoniak and Joseph Carberry (who has the presence of a young Bogart), as well as Marian Halley, Annie McEnroe, and James Wainwright. Columbia. color (see *State of the Art*.)

Susan and God (1940)—Susan, the upper-crust religious quack of Rachel Crothers' comedy of manners, is not really in Joan Crawford's range. Crawford can't provide the charm that Gertrude Lawrence reportedly gave the role on Broadway—when Crawford is being intellectually frivolous, it's merely tiresome. The director, George Cukor, and the scenarist, Anita Loos, must certainly have been aware of the problem, because Loos supplied some new characters, and Cukor lavished affection on the actresses—Marjorie Main and Constance Collier—who played them. As the caretaker, Marjorie Main practically walks off with the picture. Fredric March does all he can in the role of Susan's husband, who has sensibly taken refuge in drink; with Rita Hayworth, Ruth Hussey, Rose Hobart, John Carroll, Gloria De Haven, and Nigel Bruce. It's not a good comedy, but it has a certain fascination, because the theme is such an odd one for Hollywood to have attempted at all. M-G-M. b & w

Susan Lenox, Her Fall and Rise (1931)—This was Garbo's only film with Clark Gable. They were both at M-G-M, but Gable's rough, right-out-there physical appeal didn't quite fit Garbo's pictures—it didn't allow for the spirituality that was a key element in the passion that she awakened in her other screen lovers. With Gable she wasn't a goddess; she was sex-hungry, just like Crawford in the early Gable-Crawford movies. Garbo plays a young Swedish-American farm girl who runs away from the brute (Alan Hale) she is being forced to marry and takes refuge in the cabin of a construction engineer (Gable); they fall in love, sleep together, and plan to marry. But when unlucky circumstances separate them, and she has an affair with a carnival owner (John Miljan), her engineer won't forgive her. Over the years, she does very well as the mistress of rich men, but she keeps locating her true love and begging forgiveness until, at last . . . Still, one can sit through all this without too much pain, because of Garbo's beauty and the raw heat that she and Gable generate. Their love scenes in the cabin redeem a lot of bad writing and bad acting. Directed by Robert Z. Leonard. The novel by David Graham Phillips was adapted by Wanda Tuchock, with dialogue provided by Zelda Sears and Leon Gordon. With Ian Keith, Jean Hersholt, Hale Hamilton, Cecil Cunningham, Theodore Von Eltz, and Russell Simpson. b & w

The Suspect (1944)—Robert Siodmak's craftsmanship keeps this period suspense film satisfyingly tense. It's realistic, yet bone-chilling. And Siodmak directed a fine cast. Charles Laughton is restrained and moving as a patient man goaded to murder by his harpy wife (Rosalind Ivan). Henry Daniell has his best (evil) role since he shared the piano bench with Garbo in *Camille*, and Ella Raines brings some individuality to the part of the sympathetic woman. The screenplay, by Bertram Millhauser, is based on James Ronald's novel. Universal. b & w

Suspect (1987)—Is there a piece of casting more ineffably Hollywood than Cher as a busy, weary public defender? She's all wrong for this role: her hooded, introspective face doesn't give you enough—she needs a role that lets her use her body. With the camera on her steadily here, you might be watching a still picture. This laboriously set-up thriller has her defending a deaf-mute (Liam Neeson) accused of murder, in a Washington, D.C., courtroom, before a rigid, cold-eyed judge (John Mahoney). It's impossible to know how we're meant to interpret the lame-brained job this lawyer does at the trial. She'd be lost if one of the jurors—a young lobbyist (Dennis Quaid)—didn't do the detective work that helps her out. Probably the director, Peter Yates, and the scriptwriter, Eric Roth, were just so proud of not having made the woman a bimbo that they didn't notice they'd made her a lummox. The way Washington is shot it looks like a shopping mall.

With Joe Mantegna, Philip Bosco, and E. Katherine Kerr. Tri-Star. color (See *Hooked*.)

Suzy (1936)—Jean Harlow in a pasted-together story about an American showgirl barging about London and Paris during the First World War. She marries Irish inventor Franchot Tone in London, then, thinking him dead, goes to Paris and marries famous French aviator Cary Grant. Naturally, Tone comes to Paris to work for Grant. . . . It's negligible, all right, but it isn't too awful, because Dorothy Parker and the other writers tossed in some dexterous badinage, and Grant brings an elfin bounce to his role, especially in the sequence in which Harlow is trying to sing and he demonstrates that he knows how. His song seems to tickle her—she smiles in a fresh, open way. (The clip appears in *That's Entertainment!*) Benita Hume is the delectable villainess; with Lewis Stone, Inez Courtney, and Una O'Connor. Directed by George Fitzmaurice; based on a novel by Herbert Gorman. M-G-M. b & w

Svengali (1931)—John Barrymore's love of bizarre roles and outré makeup (no man had less reason to cover his face) led him to take on George Du Maurier's wonderful hokum about the sly, sinister musician who hypnotizes beautiful, blue-eyed little Trilby (Marian Marsh) into becoming a great singer. In one startling sequence, Svengali, his eyes a blank white, stands at a window and casts his spell over the rooftops to the room where Trilby lives, and there are affecting moments, too, like the failure of Trilby's voice when Svengali's influence wanes. Barrymore, long and lank here, with greasy locks, never needed occult powers to be magnetic; one's interest flags when he's offscreen, however. Physically perfect for Trilby, Marian Marsh is a classic example of type-casting. But it would have taken more of a hypnotist than Archie Mayo, who directed, to get a performance out of her. In some sequences the imaginative scene designs (which re-create Paris in the 1890s) and Mayo's staging suggest the German Expressionist films of the preceding decade. With Bramwell Fletcher, Donald Crisp, Lumsden Hare, Luis Alberni, Paul Porcasi, and Carmel Myers. Adapted from Du Maurier's *Trilby* by J. Grubb Alexander. (There are at least five film versions—the first in 1914.) Warners. b & w

Swann in Love *Un Amour de Swann* (1984)—Of all the imaginable material for the screen, Proust's writing requires the most subtle feeling for rhythms—the meaning is in his rhythm—and neither the director (Volker Schlöndorff) nor the scriptwriters (Peter Brook, Jean-Claude Carrière, Marie-Hélène Estienne) seem to do anything to draw us in. The movie doesn't even have the force of real desecration; it's easy to forget you've seen these stiff arrangements of people in ornate, cheerlessly lighted rooms that every instinct tells you they never lived in. Ornella Muti is a wily, plausible Odette, and Alain Delon is, at least, amusing as the Baron de Charlus. But as Swann, Jeremy Irons doesn't suggest intelligence or feeling; he's a stick, a dried-out Wasp, with dead eyes. Also with Fanny Ardant, Marie-Christine Barrault, Jacques Boudet, Roland Topor, and Jean Aurenche. Cinematography by Sven Nykvist; music by Hans-Werner Henze. Released in the U.S. by Orion Classics. In French. color (See *State of the Art*.)

Sweet Bird of Youth (1962)—Paul Newman as the gigolo Chance Wayne and Geraldine Page as the battered, fading star Alexandra Del Lago, in Richard Brooks' slicked-up version of Tennessee Williams' flamboyant pop fantasy. When Newman's bare chest isn't being fumbled at and crooned over by Page, it's being pawed and picked at by Shirley Knight, who plays his fresh-faced girlfriend,

Heavenly Finley. This hysterical twaddle features a sadistic attack on Newman, engineered by Heavenly's father (Ed Begley), a crooked political boss, and a climactic telephone soliloquy by Page (we hear her part of a long-distance conversation with Walter Winchell, who convinces her that, far from being a flop in her last picture, she has scored her greatest hit). Rip Torn and Mildred Dunnock are also involved in the madness. M-G-M. CinemaScope, color

Sweet Charity (1969)—Based on what is possibly Fellini's finest film, *Nights of Cabiria*, about a gullible, softhearted prostitute, this big musical, starring Shirley MacLaine, may have been too ambitious a project for Bob Fosse's début as a movie director. The tricky camera effects that Fosse later brought off in *Cabaret* and in the TV special "Liza with a Z" are jangling here, and although Shirley MacLaine tries hard, it's obvious that her dancing isn't up to the demands of the role. It's a disaster, but zoom-happy Fosse's choreographic conceptions are intensely dramatic, and the movie has some of the best dancing in American musicals of the period. With Sammy Davis, Jr., Paula Kelly, Chita Rivera, Ricardo Montalban, Barbara Bouchet, Stubby Kaye, and John McMartin. Peter Stone did the screenplay, based on the version Neil Simon did for Broadway; with songs by Cy Coleman and David Fields. Universal. color

Sweet Dreams (1985)—As the pop-and-country singer Patsy Cline, Jessica Lange has a raw physicality that's challenging and heroic; she wants pleasure out of life, and she's happiest and rowdiest and most fully alive when she's singing, and when she's rolling in the hay. The singing voice that comes out of her is from the vocal tracks of recordings that Patsy Cline made between 1960 and 1963, and Lange's body lives up to the sound.

The weakness of this kind of bio-pic is that once it's on the rails you can see where it's heading, and the basic story seems banal. The film doesn't transcend this limitation, yet scene by scene, the script by Robert Getchell has a funny, edgy spontaneity, a tang. And the director, Karel Reisz, doesn't step back from Patsy; she's taken on her own terms. As Patsy's husband, Ed Harris comes on at first bristling with sexual confidence, and he and Lange are great at mean low-down banter that nips at you and makes you laugh. The essence of Harris's acting style is the intensity he brings to quietness, and he gives the role a tragic, pitiable sweetness. The soft-faced Ann Wedgeworth, a marvellous comedienne, plays Patsy's mother, who's disturbed and titillated—in about equal parts—by Patsy's swinging hips and uncouth language. The cinematography is very ordinary, and most of the staging is uninspired, but Lange has real authority, and the performance holds you emotionally. People cry at this movie though it isn't sentimental—it's an honest tearjerker. With David Clennon and P. J. Soles. Tri-Star. color (See *Hooked*.)

Sweet Hours *Dulces Horas* (1981)—Another graceful, measured Freudian-fantasy game by the Spanish writer-director Carlos Saura. The hero (Iñaki Aierra) is a playwright so obsessed with memories of his childhood that he has written a new play that contains the key scenes of his early life. The play (*Sweet Hours*) is in rehearsal, and he attends the sessions watchfully, rapt. He's searching for something. (Can it be the clue to what's always missing from Saura's films—the final burst of energy that would make everything count?) Eventually, the searching playwright dredges up the repressed material, and his Oedipus complex is resolved. Saura has given his hero a bonus—a perfect wish fulfillment—by having him fall in love with Berta (Assumpta Serna), the stunning young

actress who is rehearsing the role of his mother. This might seem like an exploding Buñuelian joke, but the entire movie is cultured and dignified; it's on gliders—it's smooth and languorous, and with intricately choreographed shifts from the present to the theatrically performed past and to the remembered past. What saves it from pedantry is that from time to time the images have an erotic tingle. Something sexual hovers in the atmosphere, especially when the tall, wide-eyed Assumpta Serna is on the screen. Her smile has a teasing elusiveness a bit like that of Vanessa Redgrave. In Spanish. color (See *Taking It All In*.)

Sweet Liberty (1986)—Alan Alda is the writer, the director, and the star of this satirical comedy about moviemaking. He plays a history professor whose Pulitzer Prize–winning book on the American Revolution is to be filmed during the summer in the area where the events he wrote about took place—in and around the fictional college town of Sayeville, North Carolina, where he teaches. Alda's conception of this professor—as smug and insecure but basically a representative of solid, enduring values—casts a pall over the proceedings; still, if you don't expect too much and just ride along with the movie's conventionality there are enough enjoyable scenes to put you in a good mood. The fun comes from the Hollywood contingent of show folk who invade the community: Michael Caine as the skirt-chasing star, Michelle Pfeiffer as the leading lady who believes in staying "in character" as fully as possible, Bob Hoskins as the vulgarian screenwriter, and Saul Rubinek as the wily director. And it comes from Lois Chiles as the college president's wife—the star's first local conquest. Also with Lise Hilboldt and Lillian Gish. Cinematography by Frank Tidy; the film was shot on Long Island, around Sag Harbor and Southhampton. Universal. color (See *Hooked*.)

Sweet Rosie O'Grady (1943)—By the time Betty Grable became a full-fledged musical star at 20th Century-Fox, the studio was grinding out routinized nostalgic celebrations of the rowdy old music-hall days. This one is no better than most of the others; in fact, it's one of the worst. With Robert Young, Adolphe Menjou, Phil Regan, Virginia Grey, and Reginald Gardiner. The songs by Mack Gordon and Harry Warren are not of their best; Irving Cummings directed. color

Sweet Smell of Success (1957)—For several years, Tony Curtis had been a virtual guarantor of box-office success, and the New York locations for this film were invaded by thousands of teen-agers, who broke through police barricades to get to their idol. But these throngs ignored the completed picture, in which Curtis grew up into an actor and gave what will probably be remembered as the best performance of his career. Even the presence of that other box-office guarantor, Burt Lancaster, did not lift the picture from the red ink. This is understandable, because the movie is a slice of perversity—a study of dollar and power worship, with Lancaster as a Broadway gossip columnist and Curtis as an ingratiating, blackmailing press agent. Clifford Odets never came through more pungently as a screenwriter; his distinctively idiomatic dialogue generally seems like bad poetry when it's spoken from the screen, but here it's harshly expressive and taut. The director, Alexander Mackendrick, has a crisp *film-noir* style: the production is shaped by a zest for the corrupt milieu, the pulsating big-city life (what used to be called "the symphony of a city")—the streets, the nightclubs, the cynical types, the noise and desperation. His temperament enables us to respond to the vitality in this decadence. The weakest part is in the contrasting sweetness and light of the young lovers, Martin Milner and Susan Harrison. The melodrama is somewhat synthetic and is pitched very high, but the film has body and flavor; even Tony Curtis's name (Sidney Falco) stays with one—that, and the inflection he gives to "avidly." With Barbara Nichols, Sam Levene, and Emile Meyer; script by Odets and Ernest Lehman, from a short story by Lehman. Score by Elmer Berstein, with considerable assistance from the Chico Hamilton Quintet; cinematography by James Wong Howe. United Artists. b & w

Sweethearts (1938)—One of the liveliest of the Jeanette MacDonald and Nelson Eddy musicals. The title is ironic; they are husband-and-wife operetta stars, trading lovey-dovey lines that were given an edge by the writers, Dorothy Parker and Alan Campbell. The Parker-Campbell script has nothing to do with the original story of Victor Herbert's 1913 operetta; the songs are retained as part of the long-running show, *Sweethearts*, that the couple is appearing in. This was M-G-M's first three-color-process Technicolor feature, and it has startling color costuming by Adrian. Directed by W. S. Van Dyke; choreographed by Albertina Rasch. With Ray Bolger, Reginald Gardiner, Mischa Auer, Frank Morgan, Allyn Joslyn, Herman Bing, Florence Rice, Berton Churchill, Terry Kilburn, Lucile Watson, George Barbier, Gene and Kathleen Lockhart, Barbara Pepper, Raymond Walburn, and Jimmy Conlin.

Swept Away by an Unusual Destiny in the Blue Sea of August *Travolti da un Insolito Destino nell'Azzuro Mare d'Agosto* (1974)—A Sicilian Communist deckhand (Giancarlo Giannini) working on a yacht and the rich blond shrew (Mariangela Melato) who chartered the ship for a pleasure cruise are marooned on an island. She gave him a bad time when she had the upper hand, so when he takes charge on the island and starts whacking her around maybe one can say that he isn't hitting a woman, he's hitting the capitalist class. However, when she kisses his feet and gathers flowers to garland his phallus she isn't the capitalist class, she's a woman who finds fulfillment in recognizing a man as her master. She not only experiences new sexual bliss, she wins the prize that has often been said to be woman's highest goal: because of her submissiveness, the man loves her and worships her as his goddess. Uncorrupted by social forces the couple live the "true" relations of the sexes and find paradise. But they go back, she can't resist returning to her life of privilege, and he is left heartbroken. Under the guise of a Socialist parable about the economic determinism of personal behavior (class interests determine sexual choice, etc.) the writer-director, Lina Wertmüller, has actually introduced a new version of the story of Eve, the spoiler. Despite the clamor of politics in Wertmüller's movies, her basic pitch is to popular prejudice. This erotic fantasy is like a modern version of Valentino's *The Sheik*—blissful rape for the trendy, dissatisfied liberated woman. And solid reassurance for the men in the audience that women only want to be mastered, yet are sly little beasts, never to be trusted. The picture stays on the same high energy level throughout. The characters never stop yelling and shrieking, and since the post-synchronization is so careless that their voices are several beats off from their lip movements, the effect is as irritating as if the movie were dubbed, even though it's subtitled. In Italian. color

Swimming to Cambodia (1987)—Jonathan Demme directed this concert film of Spalding Gray's stage performance; it was shot before live audiences during three consecutive evenings (and one day) in November 1986, at the Performing Garage, in lower Manhattan. Working on a minimalist basis, with nothing but Gray and his props, Demme uses the lighting and shifts in camera angles and a musical score by Laurie Anderson to virtuoso rhythmic effect. The result is an apotheosis of Gray, who calls himself a "poetic reporter." (He gives you old news as if it were the subject of an investigative report; it's new to him.) Cagey in his use of his naïveté, Gray presents a droll, vaguely stream-of-consciousness report of his life as an actor, and of how he happened to be cast in the small role of an American diplomat in *The Killing Fields*. Some of his material (his firsthand observations, his voice mimicry) is legitimately effective. But the high point of his monologue comes when he hears about our secret bombing of Cambodia, and what the Khmer Rouge did to the Cambodian people in 1975, driving them out of the cities and to their deaths. He's incredulous and horrified as he describes the exodus; he's an actor who has discovered strong material, and he builds the tension—his words come faster, his voice gets louder. He thinks like an actor; he doesn't know that heating up his piddling stage act by an account of the Cambodian misery is about the most squalid thing anyone could do. color (See *Hooked*.)

The Swindlers, see *Il Bidone*

Swing Shift (1984)—This film about the home front during the Second World War was a tragedy for its director, Jonathan Demme. A bootleg cassette of his original cut reveals a delicate masterpiece. But what was released was a re-edited, rescored, and reshot botch. The studio version has a glazed lyricism; the performers look stuffed and posed, as if they were consciously trying to re-create themselves in the images of the shiny-faced teen-age servicemen and girls-next-door in old movies and the 40's issues of *Life*. The film's nostalgic fixation on the ambiance of the war years seems to exclude any real interest in the lives of the women workers; this feminist fairy tale sees the characters as precursors of the women's movement of the 60s and 70s rather than as people. As the cuddlebug housewife who becomes a riveter in a Santa Monica aircraft factory and learns to be a competent person, Goldie Hawn dampens the picture; she's trying to make herself simple and passive and ordinary—she thinks that she will become typical by flattening herself out. The insubstantiality of the film may make you feel as if you were dozing. The scenes rarely last more than 20 seconds. They don't quite come to anything; they abort—with a sometimes audible pop—and you sit there wondering what nothing is going to happen next. As the heroine's pal, Christine Lahti delivers a few wisecracks and gives the picture whatever spark and intensity it has. With Kurt Russell, Ed Harris, Fred Ward, Holly Hunter, and also Lisa Pelikan, Sudie Bond, Charles Napier, Belinda Carlisle, and Roger Corman as the head of the factory and Beth Henley in a bit part. The writing credit went to the pseudonymous Rob Morton; the writers who were listed before and during production were initially Nancy Dowd, then Bo Goldman, then Ron Nyswaner, and there was also last-minute patch-up work by Robert Towne. Cinematography by Tak Fujimoto. Warners. color (See *State of the Art*.)

Switching Channels (1988)—It's adapted from *His Girl Friday*, the 1940 film version of the 1928 play *The Front Page*, but it has lost most of the inspired engineering that gave the material its snap, and the attempt to update the plot to the era of television seems halfhearted. Still, this disreputable, burlesque version has its own rambunctious, sloppy humor, and the director, Ted Kotcheff—short as he may be on visual invention—

has a sense of tempo. Things don't stall. Burt Reynolds reins himself in and shows some sly grace as Sully, the news director of a Chicago-based cable outfit called Satellite Network News; as Sully's ex-wife and star reporter, Kathleen Turner is lusty and likable even when she doesn't hit the right tones; and Christopher Reeve is enjoyably silly as the manufacturer of athletic equipment—a hulking, vain twerp—that the star reporter means to marry. (He crinkles his face in the grin of a goofus.) Ned Beatty is marvellously piggish as the corrupt D.A., and when Henry Gibson, who plays a convicted cop-killer, turns his stare on us, we feel a frazzled, poetic rapport with him. Also with George Newbern as Sully's assistant, Laura Robinson as the Twinkie, Al Waxman, Fiona Reid, Joe Silver, and several fresh performers from Toronto (where most of the movie was shot). The script (erratic, but with some good gags) is by Jonathan Reynolds; the Michel Legrand score is just litter on the soundtrack. Tri-Star. color (See *Hooked*.)

Sylvia Scarlett (1936)—This Katharine Hepburn film, directed by George Cukor, was not a success—and, fascinating as it is, you'll know why. Taken from a Compton Mackenzie novel, and set in Cornwall but actually shot on the California coast, it features an oddly erotic transvestite performance—Hepburn is dressed as a boy throughout most of the film—and a peculiarly upsetting love affair between Edmund Gwenn, as her conman father, and an uncouth young tease (Dennie Moore). The movie seems to go wrong in a million directions, but it has unusually affecting qualities. Cary Grant plays a brashly likable product of the British slums—this was the picture in which his boisterous energy first broke through. He and a fearfully smirky Brian Aherne are the male leads, and the beautiful Natalie Paley is the bitch-villainess. The extraordinarily free cinematography is by Joseph August; no other Cukor film of the 30s ever looked like this one. But this is a one-of-a-kind movie in any case: when the con artists weary of a life of petty crime, they become strolling players, and at one lovely point, Hepburn, Grant, Gwenn, and Dennie Moore sing a music-hall number about the sea. Script by Gladys Unger, John Collier, and Mortimer Offner. Hepburn tells the story that after the disastrous preview at Cukor's house, she and Cukor offered to do another picture for the producer, Pandro S. Berman, for nothing, and he said, "I don't want either of you ever to work for me again." (They did, though.) R K O. b & w

Sylvie and the Phantom *Sylvie et le fantôme* (1945)—In Claude Autant-Lara's graceful but extremely slight fantasy, Odette Joyeux plays a 16-year-old girl who falls in love with a ghost. The film is such a delicate pastry that you can hardly remember eating it. With François Périer. In French. b & w

La Symphonie pastorale (1946)—André Gide supervised this too little known version of his early, subtly disquieting novel. The director Jean Delannoy is, as usual, careful and literal, and this time his sensitivity enables Pierre Blanchar and Michèle Morgan to give perhaps their most memorable performances; the film itself is emotionally overwhelming. Blanchar plays a Swiss pastor who finds an ignorant, neglected blind girl (Morgan) and teaches her to live without sight. The pastor's passion for the blind girl destroys his wife and family, and when the girl gains her sight she realizes the damage she has caused and becomes tormented and withdrawn. The film is about the spiritual and psychological blindness that people cannot overcome. Filmed in the Swiss Alps. With Jean Desailly and Line Noro; score by Georges Auric. Truffaut did homage to this film in Marie Dubois's death scene in the snow in *Shoot the Piano Player*, and also in *The Wild Child*, and he used Desailly in the central role of *The Soft Skin*. In French. b & w

Syskonbadd 1782, see *My Sister, My Love*

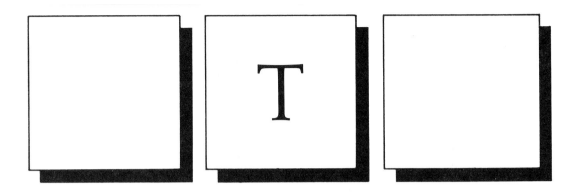

Tabu (1931)—Working together, two great directors—Robert Flaherty and the German Expressionist F. W. Murnau—began this South Seas picture; they disagreed and Flaherty split. Murnau was killed in an auto accident before the opening of this marvellous, deeply flawed classic. It has some of the worst scenes that have ever been part of a work of screen art—cavorting natives and a creaking plot and a heroine with plucked eyebrows—and its musical score combines plaintive, moaning choirs, bits of Schubert, and "The Moldau," but the dancing is superlative and there are extraordinary pictorial effects. Murnau's mysticism may be alien to the islands, but it does wonders for the movie: the old chieftain of the village becomes as chilly a figure of doom as the emaciated vampire of Murnau's *Nosferatu*, and at the end, the ghostly little boat does not seem to be sailing like an ordinary boat. . . . It is headed for nothing so commonplace as land. Floyd Crosby won the Academy Award for Cinematography. Silent. b & w

Take Me Out to the Ball Game (1949)—This big M-G-M musical, set in the early part of the century, began with a not too inspired script idea from Gene Kelly and Stanley Donen, and after it went through a series of cast changes and then got assigned to Busby Berkeley to direct, it was a full-scale mess. Kelly and Frank Sinatra are vaudevillians who are also baseball players; Esther Williams, the manager of the baseball team, is in love with Kelly, but Sinatra is in love with her. And there are gangsters trying to get the boys to double-cross her and lose a game. This asinine story just about smothers the good-natured hoofing. Comden and Green and Roger Edens did the songs, but the musical numbers have that flag-waving Irish-American cheeriness which also blighted many Fox musicals made in the same period. With Betty Garrett and Jules Munshin, who work well with Kelly and Sinatra. They all got together—*sans* Esther Williams—the following year in *On the Town*. The finale here isn't by Berkeley; it was co-directed by Kelly and Donen, and served to persuade the studio to let them co-direct *On the Town*. Script by Harry Tugend and George Wells; with Edward Arnold and Tom Dugan. color

The Taking of Pelham One Two Three (1974)—The director, Joseph Sargent, doesn't just make points—he drops weights. The picture is full of noise and squalling and "dirty"

words used for giggly shock effects; the one element that keeps it going is the plot, taken from John Godey's thriller about how a New York subway train is hijacked and the passengers held for ransom. As the Transit Authority Police detective, Walter Matthau, who just coasts through, seems an oasis of sanity. With Robert Shaw and Martin Balsam; screenplay by Peter Stone. United Artists. color (See *Reeling*.)

A Tale of Two Cities (1935)—In this most popular version of the least typical of Dickens' novels, Ronald Colman is Sydney Carton, who gives up his life so that another man may live. As Madame Defarge, Blanche Yurka dominates the film; a menace in the grand manner, she knits like a house afire and takes the Bastille practically single-handed. The story has been simplified so that it can be told very clearly. It's a creditable though unadventurous film, handsomely staged in the M-G-M backlot style for classics. It's not likely that adults will be eager to see it, but if they sit down to watch it for a few minutes with their children, they'll probably find themselves sitting until the sacrificial end—which isn't as gooey as they may fear. Jack Conway directed, with Val Lewton and Jacques Tourneur working on the Revolution sequences; W. P. Lipscomb and S. N. Behrman wrote the script. The immense cast includes Edna May Oliver as Miss Pross, Elizabeth Allan, Basil Rathbone, Billy Bevan, Reginald Owen, Isabel Jewell, Fritz Leiber, Donald Woods, H. B. Warner, Tully Marshall, Lucille LaVerne, Claude Gillingwater, and Henry B. Walthall. Reputedly there were 17,000 extras used in the mob scenes. Produced by David O. Selznick. b & w

Tales of Hoffmann (1951)—This choreographic spectacle, based on the Jacques Offenbach light opera, stars Moira Shearer, Léonide Massine, Robert Helpmann, and Ludmilla Tcherina in the dancing roles, with singers Robert Rounseville and Ann Ayars. Pamela Brown contributes her silent, disconcerting presence; Sir Thomas Beecham conducts (rather phlegmatically); the Sadler's Wells Chorus fills out the larger dance sequences. After the success of *The Red Shoes*, the producers, Michael Powell and Emeric Pressburger, found themselves in a position to employ first-rank people in all the technical departments and to fulfill their most lavish appetites, and they really laid on a spread. It's apparent that the decor and color were intended to create moods, but the whole thing seems to be the product of an aberrant, second-rate imagination that confuses decor with art. Moira Shearer is lovely; it's a long film, though, and it seems structured almost as a series of divertissements. Powell directed.

Tales of Manhattan (1942)—This five-episode film was planned by its producers, Boris Morros and S. P. Eagle (Sam Spiegel), as a flamboyant, star-filled, gimmicky package. Ten top screenwriters, including Ben Hecht, Donald Ogden Stewart, and Ferenc Molnár, concocted the script (which resembles a series of O. Henry rejects), and the performers who were hired include Charles Boyer, Henry Fonda, Paul Robeson, Rita Hayworth, Edward G. Robinson, Ginger Rogers, Charles Laughton, Ethel Waters, Roland Young, Thomas Mitchell, James Gleason, Cesar Romero, Gail Patrick, Elsa Lanchester, Victor Francen, Eddie Anderson, Eugene Pallette, George Sanders, Harry Davenport, Christian Rub, and the Hall Johnson Choir. The story is about the jacket of a full-dress suit; as this tailcoat, cursed by its cutter, passes from one owner to the next, it changes the luck of those who handle it. One director, Julien Duvivier, wrestled with the hyperactive, overextended vignettes, bringing the film a gaudy unity, but not a single episode is convincing on any level. The Edward G. Robinson portion has, at least, a little suspense and irony; in competition for the most embarrassing section are the ones with Laughton as a symphony conductor and a heaven-sent miracle featuring Robeson and Waters. 20th Century-Fox. b & w

Tales of Ordinary Madness (1981)—Not for people who are disturbed by four-letter words or sexual acts performed with lewd gusto. Made in English by the Italian director Marco Ferreri, it's about many of the same themes as an Ingmar Bergman picture but it isn't stark—it has the matter-of-fact, one-thing-after-another plainness of an Abbott and Costello movie. The script is based on the stories and the spirit of the American poet and novelist Charles Bukowski, a master of rut who writes about the gutbucket pain and elation of being human. The artist-bum hero, who is based in L.A., is played by Ben Gazzara, who gets to cut loose and do things that probably nobody has done onscreen before. Ferreri gets right down inside Bukowski's self-mocking lust and self-dramatizing temperament. As the convent-bred prostitute, Cass, "the most beautiful woman in town," Ornella Muti is as lithe as a cat, and has the soft radiance of the young Hedy Lamarr in the coital scenes of *Ecstasy*. The early sequences don't have much impetus and the dialogue is often flatulent, but there's genuine audacity and risk-taking in this movie. It may not have the energy of great art, but its nakedness has an aesthetic force. With Susan Tyrrell as the gamiest and funniest of the women the hero has bouts with, and Judith Drake. The script, by Ferreri, Sergio Amidei, and Anthony Foutz, is based on Bukowski's stories in the City Lights book *Erections, Ejaculations, Exhibitions and General Tales of Ordinary Madness*. color (See *Taking It All In*.)

The Talk of the Town (1942)—The combined writing talents of Irwin Shaw and Sidney Buchman resulted in a script about one Leopold Dilg (Cary Grant), a vaguely radical factory worker falsely accused of arson and manslaughter by the management. He breaks jail and is hidden in the home of a vacationing judge (Ronald Colman) by the judge's soft-hearted, fuzzy-headed landlady (Jean Arthur), who is convinced of Dilg's innocence. The judge takes a more dogmatic legalistic view, but is persuaded to relax his scruples. Did the authors think they were writing a Shavian comedy of ideas? The ideas are garbled and silly, but the people are so pleasant that the picture manages to be quite amiable and high-spirited anyway. George Stevens directed. With Glenda Farrell, Edgar Buchanan, Rex Ingram, Emma Dunn, and Charles Dingle. Columbia. b & w

The Tall Guy (1989)—Jeff Goldblum as an American actor in London who has spent six years playing stooge to a detestably smug English comic (Rowan Atkinson) and has lost his confidence and most of his sex drive. Then this gangling wreck is cast as the lead in an Andrew Lloyd Webber–style version of *The Elephant Man—Elephant!* the musical. Directed by Mel Smith, from a script by Richard Curtis, this satire of the life of the theatre has a loose, inventive dottiness. Goldblum's wild-eyed sloppy good nature sets off Atkinson's lethal genius at playing an articulate swine, and the whole cast appears to be acting in clover. That includes Emma Thompson, who seems stripped down to pure flakiness, and Geraldine James as a nympho landlady, Hugh Thomas as a diphead doctor, Anna Massey as a gleaming smart agent, Kim Thomson as a curly-haired singer, and the insidious Peter Kelly as the smarmy mountebank who stages *Elephant!* Mel Smith turns up in several bits; he's the blobby-faced fellow who looks like a pixie Alfred Hitchcock. A Working Title Production, released by Miramax. color (See *Movie Love*.)

Tampopo (1986)—Written and directed by Juzo Itami, this understated farce has its own brand of dippy enchantment. It's about noodles, pleasure, and the movies. The title, which is Japanese for "dandelion," is the name of a 40ish widow (Nobuko Miyamoto) who is trying to make a go of a run-down noodle shop on the outskirts of Tokyo. A courtly truck driver (Tsutomu Yamazaki), who wears a dark-brown cowboy hat straight across his brow, like the righteous hero of a solemn Western, makes it his mission to help her become a real noodle cook. The film crosscuts between the story of Tampopo and her cowboy samurai and the culinary-erotic adventures of a pair of lovers: a gangster (Koji Yakusho) in a white suit and his ready-for-everything cutie (Fukumi Kuroda). These two demonstrate that eating and sex can be the same thing. The movie is constructed like a comic essay, with random frivolous touches, and much of it is shot in hot, bright color that suggests a neon fusion of urban night life and movie madness. The subtexts connect with viewers' funnybones at different times, and part of the fun of the movie is listening to the sudden eruptions of giggles—it's as if some kids were running around in the theatre tickling people. In Japanese. (See *Hooked*.)

Target (1985)—Gene Hackman plays a quiet fellow who runs a lumberyard in Dallas; his son (Matt Dillon), who doesn't get along with the old man, thinks he's a fud—that he never had the nerve to go anywhere or do anything. It's not until the boy's mother (Gayle Hunnicutt) is kidnapped while she's on a Paris vacation and the father and son are in Europe looking for her that the boy discovers his fa-

ther is a whirlwind—a tough former C.I.A. agent who had to be relocated in order to protect the family. By that time the picture, which started out as if it were going to be about a father-son relationship, is all spies, shootings, corpses, and stupidly spectacular car chases. (It takes a lot of killing to make the son respect his dad.) The whole idea is pretty bad, and Arthur Penn, who directed, keeps going off key. Many of the scenes, especially Dillon's and Hunnicutt's, are so maladroitly staged that you find yourself staring at them blankly. (The son comes across as a callow loudmouth.) With Victoria Fyodorova, Josef Sommer, Ilona Grubel, Herbert Berghof, and Guy Boyd (who's amusing as a crude C.I.A. man). The screenplay, by Howard Berk and Don Petersen, is based on a story by Leonard Stern. Cinematography by Jean Tournier; score by Michael Small. A Zanuck/Brown Production, for CBS; released by Warners. color (See *Hooked*.)

Targets (1968)—Peter Bogdanovich wrote, directed, and appears in this lame melodrama about a clean-cut all-American boy (Tim O'Kelly) who turns sniper. The picture is rather naïvely made, and one begins to wait for the sniper to hit his targets, because there's nothing else of interest going on. Boris Karloff, in one of his last screen appearances, plays a veteran horror-film actor. Produced by Roger Corman. Paramount. color

The Tarnished Angels (1958)—Rock Hudson said that this movie was not like his others—that he disapproved of it, and that such nasty stories shouldn't be presented to the American public. The nasty material is William Faulkner's *Pylon*, adapted by George Zuckerman. Set in New Orleans in 1931, the movie attempts to re-create Faulkner's hectic, feverish atmosphere and heroes—the ex-war pilots who will do anything to sustain the thrill of flying. The daredevils are played by Robert Stack, Dorothy Malone as his promiscuous parachutist wife, and Jack Carson as a mechanic; Hudson, pooped as ever, is the heavy-drinking reporter who wants to do a story on the trio. This movie would have been better—in its odd, neo-30s sort of way—if the last quarter hour had been left out. It's the kind of bad movie that you know is bad—and yet you're held by the mixture of polished style and quasi-melodramatics achieved by the director, Douglas Sirk. Universal. CinemaScope, b & w

Tarnished Lady (1931)—Limp. George Cukor's first directorial solo, Tallulah Bankhead's first talkie, and a flop for both. Donald Ogden Stewart shaped the script for Bankhead (from his story "New York Lady"), and it was conceived on the elegant model of her stage successes; she's a socialite who marries Clive Brook for money and is torn when she falls in love with a Greenwich Village writer (Alexander Kirkland). But the Bankhead of tubercular hollows and *soigné* sagging posture who had become a stage idol was never to become popular in movies; only the later boisterous, bellowing Bankhead succeeded with the public. And you can see why. As Cukor has said, "She had beautiful bones, but her eyes were not eyes for movies. They looked somehow hooded and dead. . . . Her smile didn't illuminate." With Osgood Perkins and Elizabeth Patterson; about half of the picture was shot in New York City locations. Paramount. b & w

Tarzan and His Mate (1934)—Johnny Weissmuller and Maureen O'Sullivan in the carefully prepared follow-up to the 1932 hit *Tarzan, the Ape Man*. It's cheerful and outrageously preposterous. You are right in the heart of the craziest Africa ever contrived for your entertainment; no wild beast ever

misses a cue. Tarzan's mate has adapted herself to her husband's mode of living with true Victorian propriety; snug in her tree houses, she has a devoted gorilla for her personal maid. Everything is idyllic, though some old Mayfair friends of hers turn up and make trouble for a while. With Neil Hamilton, Paul Cavanagh, and Forester Harvey. Produced by Bernard Hyman; directed by Cedric Gibbons and Jack Conway, using location footage blended with a studio jungle; written by James K. McGuinness, Howard Emmett Rogers, and Leon Gordon. M-G-M. b & w

Tarzan, the Ape Man (1932)—Johnny Weissmuller of the body beautiful—making his movie bow in a loincloth—and pretty, likably coy Maureen O'Sullivan. There is something irresistibly funny about the predicament of a ladylike young lady abducted by a man who has lived like an ape, and who pokes and pummels her with the gestures of an ape. The picture, which is (and always was) great, parodistic fun, doesn't attempt to be realistic about jungle life; it's an entertaining romantic adventure—lighthearted and agreeable. W. S. Van Dyke directed this M-G-M film, based on Edgar Rice Burroughs' durable kitsch. Weissmuller was by no means the first movie Tarzan, but he was the first Tarzan of the talkies; he played the character in almost a dozen films, and others also got into the act: Buster Crabbe, Herman Brix (later known as Bruce Bennett), Lex Barker, Glenn Morris, Gordon Scott, Jock Mahoney, and Mike Henry. In 1959, M-G-M did a color remake of the first Weissmuller film, starring Denny Miller, and in 1981 another remake—this time with the emphasis on Bo Derek as Jane. b & w

Taxi Driver (1976)—Robert De Niro is in almost every frame of Martin Scorsese's feverish, horrifyingly funny movie about a lonely New York cab-driver. De Niro's inflamed, brimming eyes are the focal point of the compositions. He's Travis Bickle, an outsider who can't find any point of entry into human society. He drives nights because he can't sleep anyway; surrounded by the night world of the uprooted—whores, pimps, transients— he hates New York with a Biblical fury, and its filth and smut obsess him. This ferociously powerful film is like a raw, tabloid version of *Notes from Underground*. Scorsese achieves the quality of trance in some scenes, and the whole movie has a sense of vertigo. The cinematographer, Michael Chapman, gives the street life a seamy, rich pulpiness. From Paul Schrader's script; with Harvey Keitel, Cybill Shepherd, Jodie Foster, Peter Boyle, Albert Brooks, Leonard Harris, Harry Northup, Joe Spinell, Diahnne Abbott, and Scorsese himself. Columbia. color (See *When the Lights Go Down*.)

The Teahouse of the August Moon (1956)— John Patrick's Pulitzer Prize–winning play, adapted from Vern J. Sneider's novel, is a whimsical comedy fantasy about the foolishness of the American military bureaucracy's attempts to impose American ideas on occupied countries—in this case Okinawa. Many people thought the play magical, but this M-G-M version, miserably directed by Daniel Mann, is an almost total mistake. Everybody in it, whether American or Okinawan, seems childish and stupid; the squeals and giggles of the native women are enough to drive one out of the theatre. Marlon Brando starved himself to play the pixie interpreter Sakini, and he looks as if he's enjoying the stunt—talking with a mad accent, grinning boyishly, bending forward, and doing tricky movements with his legs. He's harmlessly genial (and he is certainly missed when he's offscreen), though the fey, roguish role doesn't allow him to do what he's great at and it's possible that he's less effective in it than a lesser actor might have been. But

this whole production is so talky and rhythmless that it's hard to see how even a specialist in the fey arts could have got the role airborne. As the American captain who tries to turn an Okinawan village into a well-scrubbed Yankee community and then is converted by the natives, Glenn Ford grimaces, twitches galvanically, and stutters foolishly. It's the kind of role and the kind of performance that make you hate an actor. With Machiko Kyo, Paul Ford, Eddie Albert, and Henry Morgan. The adaptation is by the playwright himself. color

Teen Kanya, see *Two Daughters*

Teenage Mutant Ninja Turtles (1990)—A tacky, lighthearted parody of crime-wave movies—camp for kiddies. As babies, the four turtles were let loose in radioactive muck; they mutated into hip, English-speaking, people-size turtles who live in the dark sewers of New York City and send out for pizza. Their mentor, the wise old rat Splinter, has trained them in the martial arts; they fight the criminal legions led by the Japanese, Darth Vader–like Shredder. Their human friends are the TV newswoman April O'Neil (Judith Hoag) and the daredevil Casey Jones (Elias Koteas). Everything in the movie has a playful, pop familiarity, and the jokey allusions to other movies are easy for young kids to grasp. The four turtles (stunt men in getups devised by Jim Henson's Creature Shop) are not as individualized as one might hope, but Splinter has an Alice-in-Wonderland creepiness. The director, Steve Barron, is casual with Hoag and Koteas, who blend in gracefully; he can't do much for the preachy subplot involving a father and son who misunderstand each other. (The flashbacks are the most fun.) The story is based on the comic-book characters devised in 1983 by Peter Laird and Kevin Eastman. Golden Harvest, released by New Line. color

Tell Them Willie Boy Is Here (1969)—Ideology on horseback. The writer-director Abraham Polonsky has taken a Western story about an Indian, Willie (Robert Blake), who, in 1909, kills another Indian, the father of his girl (Katharine Ross), and grafted onto it enough schematic Marxism and Freudianism and New Left guerrilla Existentialism and late-60s American self-hatred so that every damned line of dialogue becomes "meaningful." There isn't a character who doesn't make points and represent various political forces, and the sheriff (Robert Redford) is named Coop so that his actions will symbolize the ultimate cowardice and failure of the Gary Cooper hero figures. The woman doctor (Susan Clark) who is superintendent of the reservation is a patronizing-to-Indians liberal—the ultimate villainess. Ashamed of her sexuality (like all liberals), she is given such lines as—to Redford—"I use you the way you use me." (Most women in the audience will probably think, Lucky you.) The picture is solemnly measured, and its color is desaturated for barren, dusty landscapes. It says that since a black man (the Indian pretense isn't kept up for long) can't trust any white man and there can be no reconciliation of the races, he should try to bring everything down. That is the only way he can make the whites know he was here. A strange notion, because there wouldn't be anybody around to remember him. This picture isn't likely to be very satisfying except to black kamikazes and white masochists. With Barry Sullivan, John Vernon, and Charles McGraw. Cinematography by Conrad Hall; based on the novel *Willie Boy*, by Harry Lawton. Universal. (See *Deeper into Movies*.)

Tempest (1982)—Taking off from Shakespeare and the idea of a world-famous American architect of Greek ancestry who is having a mid-life crisis, Paul Mazursky tries for a free, airborne mix of comedy, musical, psychodrama, and dream play. The film has a flickering wit and there are charming bits by Susan Sarandon and the talented young actress Molly Ringwald, but Mazursky doesn't find an original tone that the audience can respond to, and he has put John Cassavetes—one of the most dour and alienating of actors—at the film's center. And worse, the picture has delusions of pain-in-the-soul glamour; set mostly in Manhattan and on a Greek island, it's overblown and luxuriantly elegant. You feel you should ooh and ah the vistas (courtesy of the cinematographer, Don McAlpine). It has the polished pictorial extravagance of stupe classics, such as Albert Lewin's 1951 *Pandora and the Flying Dutchman*. (It even has the swank blue skies that *Pandora* had.) And it's a sophisticated fantasy in the same mode: the images might be used to advertise a new *parfum*. This is an absurd movie, but what an artifact! It takes a high degree of civilization to produce something so hollow. With Raul Julia, Gena Rowlands, Vittorio Gassman, Lucianne Buchanan, Sam Robards, Paul Stewart, Jackie Gayle, Tony Holland, Jerry Hardin, and Paul and Betsy Mazursky. From a script by Mazursky and Leon Capetanos; with a modern score by Stomu Yamashta. Columbia. color (See *Taking It All In*.)

Ten Cents a Dance (1931)—The hardboiled sentimentality of many early talkie melodramas could be crackling, and even daring, when a good craftsman was in charge, but here the director, Lionel Barrymore, fails to shape the scenes, and the film drags heavily. In the role of a no-nonsense taxi-dancer, Barbara Stanwyck fends off sailors and rough guys and raps out her lines believably; she's a miraculously natural actress, but without a director she doesn't show anything like the gifts she demonstrated in this same period in *Ladies of Leisure* and *The Miracle Woman*. Here she marries a thieving weakling (Monroe

Owsley), and then saves him from prison by borrowing money from a rich (and worthy) gentleman (Ricardo Cortez). When her ungrateful husband turns nasty, she quite sensibly leaves him and goes off to marry the gent. With Sally Blane and Martha Sleeper. Script by Jo Swerling. Columbia. b & w

The Ten Commandments (1956)—Charlton Heston is the highly athletic Moses; Anne Baxter is the kittenish princess who loves him; Judith Anderson is the sinister slave who knows the secret of his Jewish birth; Cedric Hardwicke is the likable old Pharaoh; Yul Brynner is the prince who beats Moses to the Egyptian throne; Edward G. Robinson is the traitor to the Jews; Debra Paget is the young slave old Robinson has got his eyes on. Stir them all together, throw in stone tablets, a whopping big Golden Calf, part the Red Sea, and you've got Cecil B. De Mille's epic—3 hours and 38 minutes of it. As old-fashioned hokum, it's palatable and rather tasty. Also with Yvonne de Carlo, John Derek, John Carradine, Nina Foch, Douglass Dumbrille, Martha Scott, Vincent Price, Henry Wilcoxon, and H. B. Warner. Paramount. color

Ten Days That Shook the World, see *October*

Ten from Your Show of Shows (1973)—A sampling of the 160 90-minute weekly shows produced and directed by Max Liebman from 1950 to 1954, starring Sid Caesar and Imogene Coca, with Carl Reiner and Howard Morris. A few of the skits are classic, and if you saw Caesar when you were young enough, maybe he'll always be the greatest clown for you. b & w (See *Reeling*.)

Tender Mercies (1983)—This bare-bones "art" movie is about the healing of Mac Sledge (Robert Duvall), a legendary country-

and-Western singer who has become an alcoholic wreck. The film is said to be honest and about real people, and it affects some viewers very powerfully; audiences are unusually still—almost reverent—as the born-again Mac is baptized at the church of the Vietnam widow (Tess Harper) whose frontier-woman steadfastness has made his redemption possible. The Australian director, Bruce Beresford, making his American début with this inspirational film, has shot it in bright sunshine out in the middle of nowhere; the widow's motel–gas station is as isolated as the mansion in *Giant*. (It's a mystery how she could ever make a living from it.) Mostly the picture consists of silences; long shots of the bleak, flat land, showing the horizon line (it gives the film integrity); and Duvall's determination to make you see that he's keeping his emotions to himself; and Tess Harper staring out of her cornflower-blue headlights. (These two have matching deep-sunk eyes.) The theme song—which Duvall sings in a dry, unmusical voice—is called "It Hurts to Face Reality." Written by Horton Foote, master of arid realism, the script recalls the alleged Golden Age of Television. With the fine young actress Ellen Barkin, whose few scenes as Mac's daughter by an earlier marriage are the film's high points, and Betty Buckley, who stirs things up a bit as the brassy, country-star earlier wife, and also Wilford Brimley. Produced by Foote and Duvall; Foote won the Academy Award for Best Original Screenplay and Duvall won for Best Actor. Universal. color (See *Taking It All In*.)

The 10th Victim *La Decima Vittima* (1965)—Marcello Mastroianni and Ursula Andress are the stars of this sometimes witty science-fiction extravaganza about licensed killing in the 21st century. Inventive at the start, but it gets out of hand. Directed by Elio Petri. In Italian. color

Tenue de soirée, see *Ménage*

Teorema (1969)—Some people profess to find spiritual sustenance in this movie; others break up on lines such as "You came to destroy me" and "I was living in a void," and they find Pasolini's platitudes and riddles and the is-this-man-Christ-or-a-devil game intolerably silly. With Terence Stamp and Silvana Mangano. In Italian. color

Tequila Sunrise (1988)—You have to be able to enjoy trashy shamelessness to enjoy old Hollywood and to enjoy this picture. Robert Towne, who wrote and directed, is soaked in the perfume of 30s and 40s Hollywood romanticism. This is a lusciously silly movie; it has an amorous shine. The three talented stars are smashing: Mel Gibson is a former drug dealer who longs for a decent, respectable life and is trying to succeed in the irrigation business. Kurt Russell is his friend who's the head of the narcotics squad in L.A. County. And Michelle Pfeiffer is the woman they both love. The crime plot often seems to be stalled, and by rational standards the stars' triangular shuffle is flimsy and stupid, but by romantic standards the whole thing is delectable. With Raul Julia, who has a big, likable, rumbling presence as a scoundrel, J. T. Walsh as a quintessential flatfoot, Ann Magnuson, Arliss Howard, Ayre Gross, and, in a bit as a judge, Budd Boetticher. The golden cinematography is by Conrad Hall; the aggressively offensive score is by Dave Grusin. Warners. color (See *Movie Love*.)

The Terminal Man (1974)—One of those errors-of-science thrillers; it's an even worse error of moviemaking. Pitifully miscast, George Segal is a man implanted with a computer that's supposed to regulate his violent temper; it goes haywire and he runs around stabbing people uncontrollably. Mike Hodges, who directed, also is guilty of the adaptation of the Michael Crichton novel. Of all the bad sci-fi movies of the 70s, this one probably has the least charm. With Joan Hackett as a soulful-eyed doctor, Richard Dysart, Jill Clayburgh, Michael C. Gwynne, and Ian Wolfe as a priest. If you close your eyes you can just listen to Glenn Gould playing Bach. Warners. color

Terms of Endearment (1983)—Retro-40s virtue piled on the cartoon underpinnings of TV comedy shows. The movie—which spans 30 years—is a Freudian story of role reversals between mother (Shirley MacLaine) and daughter (Debra Winger), told in a slap-happy style. The mother comes across as a parody of an anti-life monster and the daughter as a natural woman—a life force. The two actresses might be playing in two different movies. Adapted (from Larry McMurtry's novel) and directed by James L. Brooks, this is the kind of bogus picture that gets people to say, "I saw myself in those characters." Of course they see themselves there; Brooks guides the actors with both his eyes on the audience. The mother is a pixie horror—a rich skinflint with a blond dye job and pastel frills. She's a TV-museum piece, like the characters in "Mary Hartman, Mary Hartman" or "Soap"; she's warped. And so is the pie-eyed lecher who's her next-door neighbor—a former astronaut, played by Jack Nicholson. But the emotion she feels for him transforms her, and when a tragic illness strikes her family she shows her mettle, and his fundamental decency rises to the surface. This real-life tragedy movie uses cancer like a seal of approval. Cancer gives the movie its message: "Don't take people for granted; you never know when you're going to lose them." At the end, the picture says, "You can go home now—you've laughed, you've cried." What's infuriating about it is its calculated humanity. What makes it tolerable are the performers. Debra Winger is incredibly vivid;

Nicholson is alert and polished. And the cast includes John Lithgow, Jeff Daniels, and Troy Bishop and Huckleberry Fox as Tommy and Teddy. Academy Awards: Best Picture; Best Director; Best Screenplay, Adaptation; Best Actress (MacLaine); Best Supporting Actor (Nicholson). Paramount. color

La Terra Trema (1947)—Luchino Visconti's neo-realist tragedy, set among the exploited Sicilian fishermen, is long and full of political clichés, and yet in its solemnity and beauty it achieves a true epic vision. The film is lyrical yet austere, and it's beautifully proportioned. It may be the best boring movie ever made: although you might have to get up and stretch a few times, you're not likely to want to leave. Filmed on location in Aci-Trezza, Sicily. Director of photography, G. R. Aldo; camera operator, Gianni Di Venanzo. The assistant directors were Francesco Rosi and Franco Zeffirelli. The script is by Visconti. (160 minutes.) In Sicilian dialect. b & w

Tess (1979)—Roman Polanski's version of Thomas Hardy's *Tess of the D'Urbervilles* is textured and smooth and even, with lateral compositions subtly flowing into each other; the sequences are beautifully structured, and the craftsmanship is hypnotic. But the picture is tame. There's a visual turmoil in Hardy when he describes the Wessex countryside; Polanski's tastefully cropped compositions and unvaried pacing make nature proper. For a reader, the shock of the 1891 book is that Tess isn't simply a woman at the mercy of men, society, and nature; she's also at the mercy of her own passions. Polanski's Tess (the lovely young Nastassia Kinski, 17 when she played the role) is strictly a victim of men and social conventions. The film takes a sympathetic, feminist position toward her—in a narrow and demeaning sense. She isn't a protagonist; she is merely a hapless, frail creature, buffeted by circumstances. And Kinski—a

soft, European gamine—isn't rooted in the earth of England or any other country; she's a hothouse flower, who manages the West Country sounds in a small, uninflected schoolgirl voice. She's affecting and sensitive, but she's in the wrong movie. With fine performances by Leigh Lawson as Alec and by Peter Firth as Angel Clare, and amazingly sharp, clear performances by John Collin as the drunken Durbeyfield, Tony Church as Parson Tringham, and by just about everyone else in the supporting cast. Made in English; shot in France, with cinematography by Geoffrey Unsworth and Ghislain Cloquet. color (See *Taking It All In*.)

Des Teufels General, see *The Devil's General*

Tex (1982)—An oddly quiet, tepid, soft film about adolescent travail in Oklahoma. Making his début as a director, Tim Hunter uses setups that are drably simple, and the locations are hazy—the cinematographer (Ric Waite) might be in some personal watery-pastel fog. The movie has no strong images; everything is flattened out. Yet this adaptation of one of the S. E. Hinton novels that became favorites of high-school kids in the 70s has an amiable, unforced good humor that takes the curse off the film's look and even off its everything-but-the-bloodhounds plot. As the prankish 15-year-old Tex, Matt Dillon radiates a mysteriously effortless charm; Dillon has a gift for expressing submerged shifts of feeling—we may feel that we're actually seeing Tex's growth process. The earnest naïveté of this movie has its own kind of emotional fairy-tale magic. Too bad that there's nothing in the very likable *Tex* to make it linger in the mind—it's visually so fuzzy that it drifts away like a TV show. As Tex's older brother, the promising Jim Metzler has been kept too monotonous, and as the heavy, Ben Johnson gives an unrelieved performance. But there's some lively, smart acting by Meg Tilly as Johnson's daughter, and some good shading in the acting of Pamela Ludwig as a high-school-age mother and Bill McKinney as the boys' rodeo-bum father. The author, Susan Hinton, appears in a bit as the typing teacher; the script is by Charlie Haas and the director. Disney. color (See *Taking It All In*.)

Thank Your Lucky Stars (1943)—Wartime patriotic musical, featuring the Warners stable—somewhat livelier than most of the other revues of this ilk. The high point is Bette Davis complaining of the lack of civilian males in the song "They're Either Too Young or Too Old." With Humphrey Bogart, John Garfield, Dinah Shore, Ida Lupino, Ann Sheridan, Errol Flynn, Hattie McDaniel, Dennis Morgan, Spike Jones and His City Slickers, Eddie Cantor, and many others. David Butler directed, from a not-too-constricting script by Norman Panama, Melvin Frank, and James V. Kern. b & w

That Certain Feeling (1955)—Bob Hope's relaxed skill buoys up this adaptation of the Broadway play *King of Hearts*, by Jean Kerr and Eleanor Brooke. The lines are light and amusing, though the slim contrivance of a plot is overlabored by the heavy hands of the directing team, Norman Panama and Melvin Frank. It's Hope's show: he has some good material and he stays in character as an anxiety-ridden comic-strip artist. Except for one good drunk scene, Eva Marie Saint is a dismayingly flat, uninspired heroine; George Sanders' role as an obnoxious success is too close to low comedy for his suave, jaded style; Pearl Bailey is a rather dubious deus ex machina. Also with Al Capp. Adapted by the directors and I.A.L. Diamond. Paramount. color

That Cold Day in the Park (1969)—It is certainly well directed (by Robert Altman), it's well written (by Gillian Freeman), and it is beautifully shot (by Laszlo Kovacs). But does anybody want to see a movie about a desperately lonely spinster (Sandy Dennis) who traps a young man (Michael Burns) and walls him up in her home? There may be something in the film medium itself that works against these stories of obsessional incarceration (*The Collector* also failed): we in the audience are trapped along with the prisoner, and we long to get away. One can admire this film for its craftsmanship; it has a cold brilliance. But that's all. With Luana Anders, John Garfield, Jr., Suzanne Benton, and Michael Murphy. From a novel by Richard Miles; music by Johnny Mandel; art direction by Leon Ericksen. A Canadian production, filmed in Vancouver. color

That Man from Rio *L'Homme de Rio* (1963)—Philippe de Broca's immensely successful parody-fantasy on thrillers and adventure films. With Jean-Paul Belmondo, Françoise Dorléac, and Jean Servais. High spirits and bravura and extravagance, but maybe too much of each. In French. color

That Night in Rio (1941)—Alice Faye could dance and she had a lush contralto voice (no lover of movie musicals will forget her "This Year's Kisses" in *On the Avenue*), but this low-camp musical is one of her co-starring jobs with Don Ameche, the cipher that sings, in a double role. That's twice nothing. As the wife of a Brazilian baron (Ameche) she is weighed down by huge glassy necklaces and by the other characters' references to her great beauty; she keeps staring, in misery and embarrassment. The mistaken-identity plot, with the neglected wife falling in love with the nightclub entertainer (also Ameche) hired to impersonate her husband, is just a farce variation on *The Prisoner of Zenda*. The film, directed by Irving Cummings, for 20th Century-Fox, features the studio's Brazilian Bombshell, Carmen Miranda—it would be a euphemism to describe her as volatile. She plays the entertainer's girlfriend, wears fruit on her head, and sings "I Yi Yi Yi Yi (I Like You Very Much)." The movie was remade 10 years later as the Danny Kaye vehicle *On the Riviera*; those with really long memories may recall that it was done for the first time back in 1935 as a Maurice Chevalier–Merle Oberon musical called *Folies-Bergère*. Of the three versions *That Night in Rio* takes the booby prize. With Maria Montez as Inez, and S. Z. Sakall, J. Carrol Naish, Curt Bois, Leonid Kinskey, Fortunio Bonanova, and Frank Puglia. From a play by Rudolph Lothar and Hans Adler; at least five writers worked on the script. (garish) color

That Obscure Object of Desire *Cet Obscur Objet du désir* (1977)—Luis Buñuel's style here is peerlessly urbane, but the film is a little monotonous. Fernando Rey plays a rich, worldly French widower of perhaps 50, who loves a young Spanish girl; she alternates between promises and postponement—she teases him, fleeces him, enrages him. She claims to love him but says, "If I gave in, you wouldn't love me anymore." In this fifth movie version of *La Femme et le pantin*, Pierre Louÿs' short novel about a femme fatale, the role is played by two actresses—Carole Bouquet, a tall French girl, poker-faced except for a squint of amusement and a foxy, crooked smear of a smile, and Angela Molina, a shorter, more rounded Spanish girl, who's physically impulsive, and sensual in a traditional heavy-eyed way. This doubling-up stunt doesn't add any meaning: perhaps there's less than if there were a single actress who could capture our imaginations. Buñuel sets up the Louÿs story, then treats it glancingly as a joke to hang other jokes on—and his jokes now don't have the violence un-

derneath to make connections for us. His style is too serene for his subject. In French. color (See *When the Lights Go Down*.)

Themroc (1973)—This anarchistic, deliberately bestial black comedy-fantasy grew out of the post-1968 period in France, when it was fashionable to attack all "structures." It's about sex and the family and revolution, and it stars Michel Piccoli as Themroc (pronounced Temroc), a middle-aged factory worker who revolts, goes back to his flat, throws his material goods into the courtyard, and walls himself up in it, along with his pretty young sister (Béatrice Romand), whom he has been lusting after. He lives like an animal (what animal we'll never know) feasting on pigs—i.e., policemen—roasted on a spit. Soon, others in the block of flats follow suit and join in the orgy. The characters don't speak in any known language; they grunt and squeal and make "animal" sounds. In its assault on taboos, this work somewhat resembles Makavejev's *WR—Mysteries of the Organism*; unlike Godard's *Weekend*, it revels in barbarism, cannibalism, and bestiality. The director, Claude Faraldo, is ingenious and talented, though the pacing is often too slow and the thinking suggests a dirtier, French *Steelyard Blues*. The usually suave Piccoli is surprisingly effective in his caveman, King Kongish role; the result is much funnier than if a normally crude actor had played the part. The cast includes members of the Théâtre de la Gare; among them are Miou-Miou and Patrick Dewaere. color

Theodora Goes Wild (1936)—Irene Dunne was better in comedy than in her smug, sacrificial roles, and in this movie and *The Awful Truth* she was at her best. She's too bright—she's almost shrill in her brightness—and she does something clever with her teeth that makes one want to slap her, but she has energy, and this comedy about a small-town girl who writes a best-seller and charms a city sophisticate (Melvyn Douglas) has a corny vitality that almost passes for wit. It was a hugely successful popular entertainment. Richard Boleslawski directed, from Sidney Buchman's screenplay. With Thomas Mitchell and Spring Byington. Columbia. b & w

There Was a Crooked Man . . . (1970)— This example of commercialized black-comedy nihilism seems to have been written by an evil 2-year-old, and it has been directed in the Grand Rapids style of filmmaking. The story plays murderous double-crossing games until any characters with a decent impulse are dead fools or have become crooked. There's nobody to root for but Kirk Douglas, a red-haired jokester-killer who is sent to a territorial prison in the Arizona desert in the 1880s; he makes a fool of Henry Fonda, the warden, who is changing the prison from a brutalizing place into a decent one, and he makes corpses of his buddies. Written by David Newman and Robert Benton; directed by Joseph L. Mankiewicz. With Hume Cronyn, Warren Oates, Burgess Meredith, Lee Grant, Alan Hale, Arthur O'Connell, John Randolph, Martin Gabel, Bert Freed, and Gene Evans. Cinematography by Harry Stradling, Jr. Warners. color (See *Deeper into Movies*.)

There's a Girl in My Soup (1970)—A would-be scintillating comedy about a girl who can't decide between a dapper older man and a young hippie—the sort of thing that requires the audience to be enchanted by an elfin kook. Goldie Hawn bats her goldfish eyes, but she seems to have a hook in her mouth; Peter Sellers struggles manfully, trying to find her irresistible. Mechanically directed by Roy Boulting; written by Terence Frisby, from his play. Columbia. color

There's No Business Like Show Business (1954)—Square and garish. Conceived as entertainment for the whole family, this musical is about a family of Irish vaudevillians—the Five Donahues; Ethel Merman and Dan Dailey are the parents, and Donald O'Connor, Mitzi Gaynor, and Johnnie Ray are their progeny. The plot is almost insultingly sentimental; it involves a misunderstanding between O'Connor and the girl he loves— Marilyn Monroe, as a seductive but good-hearted Broadway star. You have to put up with Johnnie Ray, who sings like a rutting cat and then—as if to win our indulgence— announces he is going to be a priest. But there's good, fast hoofing by Dailey and O'Connor and Mitzi Gaynor, who has a gleeful bounciness; she and O'Connor are wonderful together. And the Irving Berlin songs can carry you through a lot of tedious silliness. The costumes are so grotesquely tasteless, they become enjoyable—Ethel Merman sings the title song in a monstrous white gown that looks as if it's going to attack her. With Hugh O'Brian. The choreography is by Robert Alton and Jack Cole; the script is by Henry and Phoebe Ephron, from a story by Lamar Trotti. Directed by Walter Lang. 20th Century-Fox. color

Thérèse (1986)—Shot in a diorama in a richly austere visual style—the actors appear against a mottled, opaque backdrop—this Alain Cavalier film is undoubtedly a feat of some sort. (But perhaps it's no more than an art curiosity.) It concentrates our attention on the bare, masterly images (lighted by Philippe Rousselot) that come out of the darkness, and on tiny sounds and whispered bits of conversation. The script, by Cavalier and his daughter, Camille de Casabianca, is a minimalist version of the story of the young girl who at 15 got permission to enter the Carmelite order; she died of tuberculosis in 1897, at 24, and was canonized and became popular as St. Theresa of Lisieux, the Little Flower of Jesus, and the model of the pure woman. (This is at least the fourth French movie she has inspired.) What Cavalier's version gives us is the beaming eagerness of a girl (Catherine Mouchet) who seems born to be a nun. She takes completely literally her marriage to Christ, and burns with love for her bridegroom. For Thérèse, carnal passion and spiritual passion seem fused. But Cavalier's formal, noncommittal style is too measured for you to get any sense that you're observing life in a convent. He walls off Thérèse's inner struggle, and since nothing happens to her outwardly, she becomes only an aesthetic or possibly erotic object. And after a while the film's austerity may begin to seem as repressive as the cloistered life. In French. color (See *Hooked*.)

Thérèse Desqueyroux (1962)—Emmanuèle Riva (of *Hiroshima, mon amour*) as François Mauriac's Thérèse, the provincial bourgeois lady who attempts to murder her gross, prosperous husband (Philippe Noiret) for the best and worst of reasons: he is dull. Directed by Georges Franju, and filmed in the cold Bordeaux of marshes and moors; it was shot on Mauriac's own estate. It's an oblique yet almost painfully lucid account of the stifled emotions that lead to attempted murder. You see bourgeois comfort and hypocrisy through the eyes of the sensitive intelligent person who registers exactly what it all is—you see through Thérèse the poisoner's eyes. The film is measured and relentless, and very beautiful in an ascetic way—but when it's over you're not likely to say, "Let's sit through it again." Riva is an ideal screen actress in the way that Jeanne Moreau and Annie Girardot are ideal: beyond their skills, they're fascinating just to look at. Riva is perfectly balanced against Noiret (whose performance here was prized and celebrated). Mauriac wrote the dialogue; he, his son

Claude, and Franju did the adaptation. Cinematography by Christian Matras; with Edith Scob and Sami Frey. In French. b & w

These Three (1936)—A beautifully made early version of the Lillian Hellman play *The Children's Hour*, which effectively transposes the lesbian accusation to a heterosexual accusation. (Hellman did the adaptation.) Merle Oberon (in one of her better performances), Joel McCrea, and Miriam Hopkins are the three leads; Bonita Granville is the ghastly, tale-bearing child who claims to have seen sexual carryings-on; and Catherine Doucet is Hopkins' aunt. William Wyler, who directed, also made the 1962 version (with Shirley MacLaine and Audrey Hepburn, and Hopkins in the aunt role), which restored the original charge, but *These Three* is the better movie. Wyler seems more confident and relaxed in this version; he doesn't hover over things as much. With Alma Kruger, Marcia Mae Jones, Margaret Hamilton, and Walter Brennan. Cinematography by Gregg Toland. A Samuel Goldwyn Production. b & w

They All Kissed the Bride (1942)—"You're a machine—not a woman," Melvyn Douglas, the bohemian journalist, tells Joan Crawford, the boss-lady with the wrong slant on life. It was the refrain of Hollywood comedies after the Second World War: the heroine has to learn that running things isn't feminine. Joan, the head of a trucking company, proves she's fit to be a bride by doing a jitterbug number and getting drunk. It's grimly unfunny: Crawford, glowering, strides through the role that Carole Lombard's death saved her from. With Roland Young, Billie Burke, Helen Parrish, and Allen Jenkins; directed by Alexander Hall, from P. J. Wolfson's script. Columbia. b & w

They Drive by Night (1940)—The director, Raoul Walsh, probably had little to do with the film's schizoid nature. The first half, involving George Raft, Humphrey Bogart, and Alan Hale, is an action-filled, realistic good story about free-lance truck drivers who run fruit and vegetables to the big-city markets. In the second half, Raft, neat, shaved, and respectably at work in an office, is pursued by Ida Lupino, his employer's wife, but manages to hold out, because he is engaged to Ann Sheridan. Nobody cares anymore whether the oranges and lettuce get to market on time; they're busy watching Lupino go off her scheming nut in a big courtroom scene (much like the one Bette Davis had played in 1935 in *Bordertown*). This part is standard movie melodrama and not particularly well done. With Roscoe Karns, George Tobias, Gale Page, and Joyce Compton; from a novel by A. I. Bezzerides. Warners. b & w

They Knew What They Wanted (1940)—The Sidney Howard play was highly regarded in 1924, and Hollywood was drawn to this adulterous drama of the San Francisco waitress who agrees to marry Tony Patucci, an Italian grape grower in the Napa Valley, and then, in spite of herself, is seduced by the bridegroom's hired man. It was filmed in 1928 with Pola Negri and in 1930 with Vilma Banky. In this version, Carole Lombard sucks in her gorgeous cheeks and tries to look as if she's desperate to escape a life of poverty and drudgery; while Charles Laughton, as the goodhearted Tony, wears overalls and a droopy mustache, waves his arms ebulliently, and laughs with so much Latin gusto that even Anthony Quinn might be stunned. Lombard and Laughton work at their roles seriously, but who wants to see her in dowdy clothes thinking thoughts, and who wants to see him being earthy and simple and wise? (He has some ingenious moments but his "ethnic" acting isn't remotely Italian-American—at times he might be playing Charlie Chan.) Directed by Garson Kanin, from Rob-

ert Ardrey's adaptation; edited by John Sturges. With William Gargan as the hired hand, Harry Carey as the virtuous Doc, and Frank Fay, in one of the least convincing performances of all time, as a purehearted padre. Everybody involved seems to be working against the grain. The picture, which is permeated with spiritual sentiments of the tackiest variety, is like a fake antique. R K O. b & w

They Live by Night (1948)—Nicholas Ray made his début as a director with this near-hallucinatory, hardboiled, expressionist version of Edward Anderson's too little known 1937 novel *Thieves Like Us*. The film—designed as a social tragedy—was ready for release in 1948 (under the title "The Twisted Road"), but R K O apparently thought it lacking in entertainment values and shelved it; released in England, it became a critical and box-office success, and so the studio relented and opened it here, in 1949. A variation of such earlier Bonnie-and-Clyde, on-the-road movies as *You Only Live Once*, it presents the girl, Keechie (Cathy O'Donnell), and her young escaped-convict lover, Bowie (Farley Granger), as doomed innocents, trying to escape the forces pursuing them, looking for a refuge where their baby can be born. Ray's tense choreographic staging and tightly framed compositions give the film a sensuous, nervous feeling of imminent betrayal. Yet this *film-noir* stylization, elegant in design terms and emotionally powerful, is also very simplistic; the movie suffers from metaphysical liberalism—social injustice treated as cosmic fatalism. With Jay C. Flippen and Howard Da Silva, as Bowie's bank-robber friends, Helen Craig, Ian Wolfe, and Marie Bryant. Script by Charles Schnee; produced by John Houseman, under the aegis of Dore Schary. (Robert Altman made another version of *Thieves Like Us*, in 1974.) b & w

They Made Me a Criminal (1939)—The screenwriter must have gone berserk on this one, or maybe it was some higher-up's idea to cast John Garfield as a New York prize-fighter on the lam from a murder charge, who gets a job on a date ranch in Arizona, which is run by a kindly old lady (May Robson) as a work farm for delinquent boys—the Dead End Kids. When the do-gooding old broad is about to be evicted, the redeemed Garfield enters a local prizefight, and is spotted by a New York detective (Claude Rains). To add to the unlikeliness, Busby Berkeley was the director. The melodrama is mawkishly familiar, but there are watchable bits along the way, and it's tolerable. Barbara Pepper and Ann Sheridan figure in the big-city dirty glitter at the beginning, and on the ranch there's twisty-mouth Gloria Dickson as the good-woman blonde—she's an odd one, even by Warners' 30s standards. James Wong Howe was the cinematographer. The script, credited to Sig Herzig, is a reworking of the 1933 Warners movie *The Life of Jimmy Dolan.* b & w

They Shoot Horses, Don't They? (1969)— Horace McCoy's hardboiled 1930s novel about the Hollywood extras who enter a marathon dance contest is turned into a macabre allegory, with the paranoid, apocalyptic vision of American rottenness that was typical of movies in the Vietnam era. Though the picture staggers under its heavy load of symbolism and is marred by flash-forwards, and even flashbacks triggered by flash-forwards, it's still striking, with vestiges of the hard sarcasm of 30s lower-depths humor—those acrid sick jokes that make one wince and laugh simultaneously. As the defiantly self-destructive, sharp-tongued Gloria, the girl who is so afraid of being gullible that she can't live, Jane Fonda gives a startling, strong performance. She shows the true star's gift of drawing one to her emotionally even when the character she plays is repellent; her Glo-

ria, like Bogart's Fred C. Dobbs, is one of those creations who live on as part of our shared moviegoing experience. The screen-writers, James Poe and Robert E. Thompson, wrote a good role for Gig Young as the promoter-m.c.; he's a crude barker who, in his pitches on the microphone, cheapens every human emotion, but he's also sensitive and empathic. He knows how to handle people in crises—partly, one gathers, because he has been among people in ugly messes all his seamy life. The director, Sydney Pollack, isn't particularly inventive, but he has tight control of the actors. They work well for him, and he keeps the grisly central situation going with energy and drive. The cast includes Michael Sarrazin (his role—that of a man who commits a murder from which he is totally estranged—is the adaptors' worst failure, and he just looks weak, calf-eyed, and vaguely benumbed), Susannah York, Bonnie Bedelia, Bruce Dern, Red Buttons, Allyn Ann McLerie, and Severn Darden. Cinerama Releasing Corporation. color (See *Deeper into Movies.*)

Thief (1981)—Grandiloquent masochism of the kind an adolescent boy might fantasize. With rain outside and smoke inside, this Chicago-set movie is almost a parody of *film noir*: it's the underworld movies of the 40s and 50s made volcanic and abstract and existential. This is the first theatrical feature by the writer-director Michael Mann, and he has designed it like a choo-choo train to the box office. James Caan is the big-time safecracker who wants to take his bundle and retire, marry, have a nice house, and raise a family. But the corrupt System won't let him. The film is hyper-animated by this conception of existential tragedy: the thief—a loner in pain, the embodiment of a macho mystique—must learn that he's free only when he doesn't care about life and has nothing to lose. The film sets up an improbable character in a series of rigged situations and then leaps to universal despairing conclusions. Mann belongs to the pressure-cooker school of filmmaking: Tangerine Dream's synthesized electronic music pulsates like mad, and the cinematography (by Donald Thorin) is so snazzy it overwhelms the action. (Maybe because of all this high-powered look-at-me filmmaking the picture was a box-office failure.) With Tuesday Weld as the dazed, burnt-out woman whom Caan marries; Willie Nelson, oozing sincerity as Caan's only friend, who dies; and Robert Prosky and James Belushi. United Artists. color (See *Taking It All In*).

The Thief of Bagdad (1924)—Douglas Fairbanks, Sr., in a lavish Arabian Nights spectacle, designed by William Cameron Menzies and directed by Raoul Walsh. It's slow, dreamy, magically pretty, and enduringly enjoyable. With Anna May Wong, Julanne Johnston, Noble Johnson, Snitz Edwards, Sadakichi Hartmann, and Brandon Hurst. Silent. b & w

The Thief of Bagdad (1940)—Magical Arabian Nights adventures, on enormous, spacious sets and in brilliantly clear Maxfield Parrish colors; the screen seems to be made of velvet. Sabu is the boy thief who befriends Ahmed (John Justin), the prince who has been blinded and has had his kingdom usurped by the evil magician, the Grand Vizier Jaffar (Conrad Veidt). Though Justin is a wan embodiment of virtue, Veidt sparkles with villainy; in his dashing black ensembles, he makes superb entrances in the calendar-art vistas that the designer, Vincent Korda, supplied for this essentially cheery Alexander Korda production. Sabu seems most appealing when the wicked Jaffar has turned him into a dog; the dog seems to represent the essence of Sabu, and it even looks like him. Best of all is the deep-rumbling-voiced Rex Ingram as the Djinni of the bottle; this Djinni

is not only giant-sized but giant voiced, with a big roaring, threatening laugh and a grin that suggests trouble. (He also has a Southern accent.) Bare except for a loincloth, he has talon fingernails and great quizzical eyebrows, and is bald-headed except for a ponytail. As the heroine, June Duprez—with her soft-lipped pout and sensual, edgy diction—is an unusual enough choice to catch one's interest. And Miles Malleson does a quirky turn as the Sultan, her toy-loving senile father; Malleson is like a toy himself, and when he becomes enchanted by a mechanical flying horse, he and the machine seem a perfect pair. But as a writer, Malleson, who, along with Lajos Biro, did the script, lacks enchantment; the flashback device at the beginning is unnecessarily complicated, and the dialogue throughout is distressingly flat. This adds to the film's other problems—the uneven rhythms and the occasional dead spots, the stagey use of the spectacular sets. Yet considering how many directors took turns on this picture (Ludwig Berger, Michael Powell, and Tim Whelan are all credited, and Zoltán Korda and William Cameron Menzies, who are credited only as associate producers, also directed, as did Alexander Korda), it's surprising how well it holds together. The Miklós Rózsa score is intrusive and mood-shattering, but the cinematography by Georges Périnal (with Osmond Borradaile on the outdoor footage, and Robert Krasker as camera operator) and the costumes by Oliver Messel, John Armstrong, and Marcel Vertès have a fairy-tale richness. (This version takes off from the 1924 silent film that starred Douglas Fairbanks, Sr., as the thief, but it's very different.) Vincent Korda, Périnal, and the special-effects team all won Academy Awards.

The Thief of Paris *Le Voleur* (1967)—Jean-Paul Belmondo in Louis Malle's slow-paced, romanticized view of the state of mind of a nihilist thief in late-19th-century France. This thief hates the bourgeoisie, yet is so successful he becomes part of it. Malle shows none of the seaminess of thievery; this is a study of compulsion, and though it's well shot by Henri Decaë, it lacks substance and is tedious. Screenplay by Malle and Jean-Claude Carrière, with dialogue by Daniel Boulanger; based on a novel by Georges Darien. With Geneviève Bujold, Marie Dubois, Charles Denner, Françoise Fabian, Julien Guiomar, Paul Le Person, Marlène Jobert, and Bernadette Lafont. In French. color

The Thief Who Came to Dinner (1973)—A more cynical version of old Hollywood escapist fantasies about nonchalant gentleman thieves. Now the whole society is seen as crooked ("everybody cheats" on expense accounts, we're told), and we're supposed to root for the young, attractive crook who outsmarts all those cheaters. As a swinger jewel thief, Ryan O'Neal turns on the charm; he's got it, all right, but it's processed—he's so assured that he looks spoiled. As his sexy socialite girlfriend, Jacqueline Bisset is so velvety a projection of masculine fantasies that she doesn't have enough rough edges to be alive. The movie is faintly diverting, but the vacuity becomes oppressive. With Warren Oates as a tenacious insurance investigator; Charles Cioffi; Jill Clayburgh, who supplies some bits of humor as O'Neal's ex-wife; and Austin Pendleton as a tormented sissy who writes a chess column. Directed by Bud Yorkin, from a script by Walter Hill, who also wrote *The Getaway* on the same formula. Set in Houston; score by Henry Mancini; adapted from a novel by Terrence Lore Smith. Warners. color (See *Reeling*.)

Thieves (1977)—New York ghetto schoolteacher Marlo Thomas lectures her sellout husband, Charles Grodin, who has lost his wild, free spirit, about the glories of a carefree existence—with full dedication to the underprivileged. The author, Herb Gardner (he also took over the direction from John Berry), specializes in the urban poetry of craziness; the characters don't talk—they make speeches, every one of them profound. The husband and wife are followed around by mute ghosts of the city—an emblematic ragpicker (Mercedes McCambridge) and a token skid-row bum (Gary Merrill). With Irwin Corey as the wife's cab-driver father—a 78-year-old leprechaun who chases "tootsies" because tootsies are "hopefulness itself." There's not a believable minute. Paramount. color (See *When the Lights Go Down.*)

Thieves Like Us (1974)—Robert Altman finds a sure, soft tone in this movie and never loses it. His account of Coca-Cola-swigging young lovers in the 30s is the most quietly poetic of his films; it's sensuous right from the first pearly-green long shot, and it seems to achieve beauty without artifice. Keith Carradine is Bowie, the boy who escapes from prison with two bank robbers, Chicamaw and T-Dub (John Schuck and Bert Remsen), and Shelley Duvall is Keechie, the girl whose drunken father runs the gas station the convicts hide in. The film is adapted from a neglected 1937 novel by Edward Anderson, which also served as the basis of the Nicholas Ray 1948 picture *They Live by Night.* Although Calder Willingham gets a screen credit for the script, his script didn't have the approach Altman wanted, and Altman's former script girl, Joan Tewkesbury, devised another script, in collaboration with the director, which stays on Edward Anderson's narrative line and retains much of his dialogue. Made in the vegetating old towns of Mississippi, the movie has the ambiance of a novel, yet it was also the most freely intuitive film Altman had made up to that time. Carradine and Duvall have the easy affinity that they showed in their much smaller roles in *McCabe*

& *Mrs. Miller*; when Keechie and Bowie fall in love it's two-sided, equal, and perfect. As the heavy-drinking, half-mad Chicamaw, Schuck—who has a suggestion of bulldog in his face—gives a performance that in some scenes rivals Bogart's Fred C. Dobbs in *The Treasure of the Sierra Madre*; he has a comic, terrifying scene when he's in a home and insists on playacting a robbery with a couple of small children and then explodes in a murderous rage when the kids lose interest. Louise Fletcher is impressively strong as the kids' mother—the no-nonsense Mattie. Cinematography by Jean Boffety. United Artists. color (See *Reeling*.)

The Thin Man (1934)—Directed by the whirlwind W. S. Van Dyke, the Dashiell Hammett detective novel took only 16 days to film, and the result was one of the most popular pictures of its era. New audiences aren't likely to find it as sparkling as the public did then, because new audiences aren't fed up, as that public was, with what the picture broke away from. It started a new cycle in screen entertainment (as well as a *Thin Man* series, and later, a TV series and countless TV imitations) by demonstrating that a murder mystery could also be a sophisticated screwball comedy. And it turned several decades of movies upside down by showing a suave man of the world (William Powell) who made love to his own rich, funny, and good-humored wife (Myrna Loy); as Nick and Nora Charles, Powell and Loy startled and delighted the country by their heavy drinking (without remorse) and unconventional diversions. In one scene Nick takes the air-gun his complaisant wife has just given him for Christmas and shoots the baubles off the Christmas tree. (In the 70s Lillian Hellman, who by then had written about her long relationship with Hammett, reported that Nora was based on her.) A married couple, Albert Hackett and Frances Goodrich, wrote the script; James Wong Howe was the cinematographer. The cast includes the lovely Maureen O'Sullivan (not wildly talented here), the thoroughly depressing Minna Gombell (her nagging voice always hangs in the air), and Cesar Romero, Harold Huber, Edward Brophy, Nat Pendleton, Edward Ellis (in the title role), and a famous wirehaired terrier, called Asta here. Warning: There's a lot of plot exposition and by modern standards the storytelling is very leisurely. Produced by Hunt Stromberg, for M-G-M. b & w

The Thin Man Goes Home (1945)—This came late in the series but it's still fairly cheerful. It features William Powell, Myrna Loy, Asta, and Anne Revere, who, carrying a rifle and wearing a felt hat that looks as if it might have been discarded by a janitor, makes a fascinating lunatic. Directed by Richard Thorpe; written by Robert Riskin and Dwight Taylor; cinematography by Karl Freund. With Helen Vinson, Gloria De Haven, Lucile Watson, and Harry Davenport. M-G-M. b & w

The Thing Also known as *The Thing from Another World*. (1951)—Scarily effective sci-fi. It's a kind of flying-saucer ghost story, set in the cold—in a remote station at the North Pole. The Thing (played by James Arness) is like a more abstract Frankenstein monster. The events surrounding its appearance are wonderfully well staged; they're so banal and economic and naturalistic they have a kick. Howard Hawks was listed as "presenting" the film, with Christian Nyby listed as director, but chances are that Hawks also had a sizable share in the directing. The amusing, ingenious script, by Charles Lederer (with a possible assist by Ben Hecht), is loosely based on a 1938 story, "Who Goes There?," by John W. Campbell, Jr. (under the name Don A.

Stuart). With Kenneth Tobey, Margaret Sheridan, Dewey Martin, Eduard Franz, Douglas Spencer, William Self, John Dierkes, and Robert Cornthwaite as Professor Carrington. The bluish looking b & w cinematography is by Russell Harlan; the music is by Dmitri Tiomkin. R K O.

The Thing (1982)—This remake of the 1951 version, by the director, John Carpenter, and the special makeup effects wizard, Rob Bottin, was a folie à deux. They went back to the chameleon idea of the original story, so they seem to be trying to outdo the monster from Ridley Scott's *Alien* (1979)—the one who could take any form and, at one horrifying point, erupted from John Hurt's chest. In its own putting-the-squeeze-on-the-audience terms, *Alien* was effective. This picture isn't (except for an early episode with a husky trying to escape the hunters shooting at it from a plane). It appears to be a film of limited imagination with unlimited horror effects. A new landmark in gore, it features oozing, jellied messes of blood and entrails and assorted parts of the people and serpents and animals that the mutating Thing devours. And it's grimly serious. Carpenter seems indifferent to whether we can tell the characters apart; he apparently just wants us to watch the apocalyptic devastation. With Kurt Russell, Wilford Brimley, David Clennon, Keith David, Tom Waites, Richard Dysart, Richard Masur, and Donald Moffat. The script—the station is now at the South Pole—is by Bill Lancaster; the music is by Ennio Morricone. Universal. color

The Thing from Another World, see *The Thing* (1951)

Things Change (1988)—A modernist version of a sentimental fable: David Mamet, who directed and was the co-writer (with Shel Silverstein), gives you the blueprint but not the feeling. The story is essentially a heart-warmer: Sicilian-born Gino (Don Ameche), a dignified old Chicago shoeshine man who gets mixed up with mobsters and is mistaken for a Mafia don, emerges unscathed because of his simple goodness—his humanity. Gino becomes the buddy of a blundering mafioso, Jerry (Joe Mantegna); there's nothing to look at except Gino and Jerry's mummified skits, which are directed at a deliberate and unvarying pace. Mamet piles on improbabilities in a matter-of-fact style; flatness of performance seems to be part of the point. This minimalist approach— it suggests a knowingness—takes the fun out of hokum. The result is like a Frank Capra– Damon Runyon comic fairy tale of the 30s in slow motion. With Robert Prosky, Mike Nussbaum, W. H. Macy, and Jonathan Katz. Columbia. color (See *Movie Love*.)

Things to Come (1936)—The most elaborate science-fiction movie ever made in England until *2001*. H. G. Wells wrote the tendentious screenplay (based on his book *The Shape of Things to Come*); the celebrated designer William Cameron Menzies directed, Vincent Korda (with László Moholy-Nagy) worked on the sets, Georges Périnal was the cinematographer, and Arthur Bliss wrote the score. Wells peers ahead through a century of devastation to the cold, abstract architecture of 2055. The whole "scientific" phantasmagoria is posh and modernistic—an amusingly dated view of the future. (It suggests the 20s.) The movie is more handsome than dramatic, with spacious sets and great costumes (they're like what actors in Greek tragedies wore in avant-garde productions of the 20s), and some wonderful howlers in Raymond Massey's and Ralph Richardson's dialogue and acting. With Cedric Hardwicke, John Clements, Ann Todd, Margaretta Scott, and

Derrick de Marney. Produced by Alexander Korda. b & w

The Third Man (1950)—The most famous collaboration of the director Carol Reed and the screenwriter Graham Greene has the structure of a good suspense thriller and an atmosphere of baroque, macabre decadence. The simple American, Joseph Cotten, arrives in postwar Vienna to meet an old friend, only to be told that the friend has been killed in an accident. In trying to discover the facts, Cotten learns so much about his friend that when he finally finds him alive, he wants him dead. Orson Welles' portrait of the friend, Harry Lime, is a study of corruption—evil, witty, unreachable. It's balanced against Trevor Howard's quietly elegant underplaying of the Army officer who teaches the simple American some of the uglier facts of life. There is an ambiguity about our relation to the Cotten character: he is alone against the forces of the city and, in a final devastating stroke, he is even robbed of the illusion that the girl (Alida Valli) is interested in him, yet his illusions are so commonplace that his disillusion does not strike us deeply. Greene has made him a shallow, ineffectual, well-meaning American. Robert Krasker's cinematography won the Academy Award. The zither music is by Anton Karas. b & w

13 Rue Madeleine (1946)—The producer Louis de Rochemont, known for his work on the "March of Time" series, had a popular success in 1945 with *The House on 92nd Street*, an anti-Nazi spy picture, based on an actual case and shot in New York locations, in a semi-documentary style. Working with the same director (Henry Hathaway) and the same cinematographer (Norbert Brodine), de Rochemont attempted *another* anti-Nazi spy picture in the same pseudo-realistic format, but this time the script (by John Monks, Jr.,

and Sy Bartlett) was listless and hokey, and the film had no tension. Even its star, James Cagney, whips through his scenes, as if he knew that all he could hope for was to pick up the pace. Cast as the noble American, he has just one flashy moment: there's a shot of him laughing triumphantly at his Nazi torturers as the Allies blow them all to bits. With Walter Abel (it's true his lines are righteous and earnest but still his readings are inexcusably bland), Annabella, Richard Conte, Frank Latimore, Sam Jaffe, Melville Cooper, Blanche Yurka, Alexander Kirkland, Karl Malden, and a "March of Time" narrator. The title refers to the Gestapo headquarters in Le Havre. 20th Century-Fox. b & w

Thirty-Day Princess (1934)—A pleasant, trifling romantic comedy. Sylvia Sidney plays Caterina of Taronia, visiting the United States to get some economic help for her country. Sylvia Sidney also plays Nancy Lane, an American actress hired to impersonate the princess (who has come down with mumps), and to captivate New York's leading newspaper publisher (Cary Grant), who has taken a strong position against aid to Taronia. Grant, still a leading man in this picture (he didn't become a full comedy star until about three years later), is handsome and very engaging, and Sidney—in one of her rare lighthearted performances—is such a skillful technician that you can't distinguish between her technique and her personal charm. (She operates in that area where acting and witchcraft come together.) Marion Gering directed; Preston Sturges, Frank Partos, Sam Hellman, and Edwin Justus Mayer all worked on the inventive, witty script, which was adapted from a Clarence Budington Kelland story. The cast includes Edward Arnold, Vince Barnett, Henry Stephenson, Robert McWade, and Lucien Littlefield. Cinematography by Leon Shamroy. A B. P. Schulberg Production, for Paramount. b & w

30 Is a Dangerous Age, Cynthia (1968)—Not only does Dudley Moore star in this movie—and he really eats up the camera, which holds him in closeup for unconscionably long periods—but he wrote the score and he collaborated on the script with John Wells and the director, Joseph McGrath. Everything in the picture is shaped to show off Moore's "multiple talents." He plays a pianist-composer who sells a musical—a puckish little fellow who goes through skit after skit, cavorting like crazy, with lots of wig changes and jokey dreams. Some of the gags aren't bad, but they don't further the plot, and McGrath's direction leaves almost every performer exposed in the desperate attempt to be hilarious. Shot in London and Dublin; with Eddie Foy, Jr., Suzy Kendall, John Bird, Patricia Routledge, Duncan Macrae, and John Wells. Columbia. color

The 39 Steps (1935)—At the time, Alfred Hitchcock explained the point of view behind the picture: "I am out to give the public good, healthy, mental shake-ups. Civilization has become so screening and sheltering that we cannot experience sufficient thrills at first hand. Therefore, to prevent our becoming sluggish and jellified, we have to experience them artificially." What fun to make a movie in an era when people still needed a bit of a jolt! Even now, Hitchcock's little jolts are more surprising than most of the shocks engineered to stun modern audiences. This suave, amusing spy melodrama is directed with so sure a touch that the suspense is charged with wit; it's one of the three or four best things Hitchcock ever did. The lead, Robert Donat, was that rarity among English actors: a performer with both personal warmth and professional skill. The heroine is Madeleine Carroll. Hitchcock paired them off by the mischievous use of a gimmick: a man and a woman who detest each other are handcuffed together; as day wears into night,

they fall in love. The movie thus contains an extra—implicit, as it were—element of bathroom-humor suspense. Among Hitchcock's other pleasing perversities was the casting of Godfrey Tearle, who looked astonishingly like Franklin Delano Roosevelt, as the chief enemy agent. The film also has one of his rare emotionally felt sequences: the brief, chilling scenes between Peggy Ashcroft and John Laurie as a mismated couple joined together by real chains. John Buchan's novel was adapted by Charles Bennett, Ian Hay, and Alma Reville. b & w

This Angry Age, see *The Sea Wall*

This Gun for Hire (1942)—Glossily amusing Paramount version of the Graham Greene spy-intrigue thriller, *A Gun for Sale*; the film's sentimentality has a satisfying underlayer of perversity. Alan Ladd is the nervous, gentle, and sensitive gunman without a trace of human kindliness; what heart he has he gives to the care of sad cats, mongrels, and such. Laird Cregar is the sinister stout villain with fussy habits; the proprietor of a nightclub, he hires Veronica Lake to entertain the patrons. This was Veronica Lake's first big starring role, and she is the most stylized character of all. Her face is so impeccably blank that when she smiles, as she does perhaps twice in the film, hearts can be heard to break—smack—in the theatre. With Robert Preston, Tully Marshall, Marc Lawrence, and Mikhail Rasumny. Directed by Frank Tuttle; adapted by Albert Maltz and W. R. Burnett. b & w

This Is Elvis (1981)—A mixture of footage of Presley himself (seen in films, concert clips, TV kinescopes, newsreels, and home movies) and material that Malcolm Leo and Andrew Solt have written and directed, with four actors impersonating Presley at periods of his life that weren't recorded on film, and with the voice of a fifth actor to impersonate him as a narrator. What the actors dish up is a batch of inanities, generalities, and—arguably—fabrications. It doesn't add to the powerful images of Presley—it takes away. Almost everything that Leo and Solt have done to the raw footage makes you cringe. But Presley is the star in his life that he never was in his Hollywood movies; he commands the screen. It's overwhelming to see a life spread out on film—especially the life of someone who peaked a couple of years after finishing high school, when he still had the look of a white-trash schoolboy sheik. Presley showed the strength to peak again when he quit Hollywood, and then just slid. The film is hair-raising because of what Elvis turns into. A David L. Wolper Production, released by Warners. color and b & w (See *Taking It All In*.)

This Is the Army (1943)—The celebrated patriotic stage revue, with music by Irving Berlin, originally performed by enlisted men, was given a story line for the movie, and the cast was padded out with civilian screen actors and other notables. The plot spans two wars and features the curious, near-beer prophetic father-son pairing of George Murphy, as Jerry Jones, a First World War soldier who writes an Army show called "Yip, Yip, Yaphank," and Ronald Reagan, as Johnny Jones, who writes the Second World War show "This Is the Army." Having presented these fictitious authors, when it comes time for Irving Berlin to appear (as Irving Berlin) and sing "Oh, How I Hate to Get Up in the Morning," the film has the devil's own time explaining who *he* is. It's a huge 2-hour musical that reeks of uplift, but there are a few funny lines, an impressive soldier chorus, and many tolerable, if wholesome, numbers. This is not the Army of *From Here to Eternity*. Michael Curtiz directed; with Joe Louis, Kate Smith, George Tobias, Joan Leslie, Charles Butterworth, Gertrude Niesen, Frances Lang-

ford, Ruth Donnelly, Dolores Costello, Una Merkel, and from the original cast, the tap-dancer Private James Cross and the singer Sergeant Robert Shanley. Warners. color

This Man Must Die *Que la bête meure* (1969)—Claude Chabrol directed this suspense movie about a father who sets out to avenge the hit-and-run murder of his son, but his technique sags, and the movie is so attenuated and so unhurried that it dies on the screen. When you hear that the father's quest for the child's murderer is like looking for a needle in a haystack, you want to giggle, because practically the only other man in the movie is the hit-and-run driver. With Michel Duchaussoy as the father, and Jean Yanne, who gives the picture a breath of life, as the uncouth villain. From Nicholas Blake's novel *The Beast Must Die*. In French. color (See *Deeper into Movies*.)

This Sporting Life (1963)—Lindsay Anderson's movie about an inarticulate professional rugby player (Richard Harris) and a "bruised" woman (Rachel Roberts) was hailed as the best feature ever made in England—maybe because it suggests all sorts of passion and protest, like a group of demonstrators singing "We Shall Overcome" and leaving it to you to fill in your own set of injustices. Like Anderson's later work, it draws its considerable power from what one can only assume is unconscious and semi-conscious material. The film is heavy with multiple meanings that the director doesn't sort out, and even the best sequences are often baffling. The rugby games were said to be a "microcosm of a corrupt society," and you can certainly tell that the movie is meant to be bold and tragic. (It has something of the disturbing brute force of Scorsese's *Raging Bull*.) It's a mixture of the powerful, the inexplicable, and the dislikable, with the hurt in Rachel Roberts' face lingering in the memory. The cast includes Colin Blakely, Alan Badel, William Hartnell, and Arthur Lowe. The script is by David Storey, based on his novel. The cinematography is by Denys Coop. b & w (See *I Lost it at the Movies*.)

This Strange Passion, see *El*

This Thing Called Love (1940)—One of those 40s comedies in which the independent-minded heroine has no common sense. Rosalind Russell is the insurance-company executive who insists on a companionate "trial" marriage and a kissless honeymoon, and Melvyn Douglas is her unlucky groom. The picture—it opened at Radio City Music Hall—aimed at nothing more than light hilarity (which it achieves only fitfully), but it was banned by the Catholic Legion of Decency, probably because of Douglas's energetic scrambling efforts to seduce his wife. This is the sort of bedroom farce in which by the time she's ready to say yes he's got poison oak. With Binnie Barnes, Allyn Joslyn, Lee J. Cobb, Gloria Dickson, Don Beddoe, and Gloria Holden. Alexander Hall directed; based on a 1928 play by Edwin Burke, adapted by George Seaton, Ken Englund, and P. J. Wolfson. Columbia. b & w

The Thomas Crown Affair (1968)—Seeing it is like lying in the sun flicking through fashion magazines and (as used to be said) feeling rich and beautiful beyond your wildest dreams. As the man who has everything but craves danger and turns to crime out of boredom, Steve McQueen is artful and glamorous; there's a self-awareness in his performance that makes his elegance funny. When he robs a Boston bank and outwits a mercenary woman insurance investigator (Faye Dunaway, in gaudy clothes), he's a hero for the little romantic, adolescent fascist lurking in most of us. Dunaway is so over-coiffed and overdressed, she's like a teenybopper playing at being a great lady, but she and McQueen are amusing together. What gives this trash a life, what makes it entertaining is clearly that the director, Norman Jewison, and some of those involved, knowing of course that they were working on a silly, shallow script—it's by Alan R. Trustman—used the chance to have a good time with it. The cinematographer, Haskell Wexler, lets go with a whole bag of tricks, flooding the screen with his delight in beauty, shooting all over the place and sending up the material. The multiple-screen effects at the beginning are by Pablo Ferro; the dazzling editing is by Hal Ashby; the less dazzling music is by Michel Legrand. With Yaphet Kotto, Jack Weston, and Paul Burke. A Mirisch Production, released by United Artists. color (See *Going Steady*.)

Thoroughly Modern Millie (1967)—Produced by Ross Hunter, this lavish, oversized musical spoof, set in the 20s, was directed in a desperately with-it style by George Roy Hill, and the players work so hard that one begins to suffer for them and, finally, to feel numb. The picture sank Mary Tyler Moore's screen career for a decade, and it certainly didn't help Julie Andrews (though she looks her best in the 20s clothes), James Fox, John Gavin, or a rather weary Beatrice Lillie. As for Carol Channing, who gets shot out of a cannon and, as usual, grins like an albino Louis Armstrong, she projects too big for even this elephantine movie. Screenplay by Richard Morris; cinematography by Russell Metty. Universal. color

Those Lips, Those Eyes (1980)—This stage-struck-boy's-coming-of-age movie has no nerve center. Frank Langella plays a song-and-dance man who is the leading performer of a summer-stock theatre that's doing a season in Cleveland in 1951 and Thomas Hulce is a local pre-med student who signs on with the theatre as prop boy and loses his innocence. He is also fired with the ambition to become a playwright and, like the screenwriter David Shaber, to grow up to write this maudlin, autobiographical movie. Directed by Michael Pressman, this production is every bit as tacky and enervated as the stage productions of war-horse operettas that it parodies. There are only a few performances that can be watched without squirming: Glynnis O'Connor as a dancer with the company; Joseph Maher as an aging, alcoholic actor; and Kevin McCarthy as a lecherous New York agent who shows up at the theatre. Released by United Artists. color (See *Taking It All In.*)

Thousands Cheer (1943)—An army camp puts on a big show, culminating in "United Nations on the March"—a work by Shostakovich that was specially commissioned by M-G-M. Gene Kelly tries hard in this all-star extravaganza, Lena Horne sings "Honeysuckle Rose," and Judy Garland tackles "The Joint Is Really Jumpin'," but nothing could save it. Maybe José Iturbi put the seal of doom on the venture when he sat down to play boogie-woogie; he hits the notes all right, but his boogie-woogie is (arguably) the most mechanical ever recorded. The dull, dull plot involves Mary Astor, John Boles, and Kathryn Grayson. With Mickey Rooney, June Allyson, Gloria De Haven, Ben Blue, Eleanor Powell, Lucille Ball, Red Skelton, and many others, plus the bands of Kay Kyser, Benny Carter, and Bob Crosby. Written by Paul Jarrico and Richard Collins; produced by Joe Pasternak. George Sidney directed. color

Three Broadway Girls, see *The Greeks Had a Word for Them*

Three Brothers *Tre Fratelli* (1981)—Three Italian brothers who have emigrated to the cities go back south to their father's farm in the Apulia region for their mother's funeral. The modern-folktale structure is somewhat schematic, but it's a wonderful film that moves on waves of feeling. Directed by Francesco Rosi, from a script he wrote with Tonino Guerra, it might be said to be an inquiry into the terrorist chaos of the country. That's the underlayer: it's about the violence in the cities, the split between the North and the South, the break between the generations. Yet it's set in the old father's world, where the cycle of nature is what matters. It's about ideas, yet it's saturated with emotion. The old man (Charles Vanel, at 89) has lived his life without ever needing to worry about terrorism, crime, chaos; the sons' thoughts and fantasies all come out of their anxieties. The father has his place in the larger ritual; when the sons come back, they realize they've lost their place. Working with his longtime cinematographer, Pasqualino De Santis, Rosi, who has one of the greatest compositional senses in the history of movies, keeps you in a state of emotional exaltation. A simple image—such as that of the old man just walking—has the kind of resonance that most directors never achieve. Though the actors who play the brothers—Philippe Noiret, Vittorio Mezzogiorno, and Michele Placido—are less than exciting, while you're watching this film it envelops you. Grateful for its intelligence, you sink into it. You're led by the camera—something more is always going to be revealed. In Italian. color (See *Taking It All In.*)

Three Comrades (1938)—Scott Fitzgerald worked on many films, but this is one of the rare ones that actually retain his spirit. (*Winter Carnival* is another.) Bits of the dialogue are elegantly romantic, and the atmosphere has his distinctive chivalrous quality. Margaret Sullavan, slender and special, and with her ravishing huskiness, is an ideal Fitzgerald heroine—a perfect Daisy—and she brings her elusive, gallant sexiness to this First

World War romance, taken from a Remarque novel. It's conventional and heavy and false in the M-G-M manner, but with this delicate Fitzgerald feeling rising out of it at times. The movie is still awful; it has a particularly offensive tearjerking score by Franz Waxman. Produced by Joseph L. Mankiewicz. (Fitzgerald's letter imploring him not to change the dialogue has been published.) The script is credited to Fitzgerald and Edward A. Paramore. Directed by Frank Borzage. With Robert Taylor, Franchot Tone (who is tight-faced here—he's probably conscious of how terrible he is), Robert Young, Monty Woolley, Lionel Atwill, Guy Kibbee, Charley Grapewin, and Henry Hull. b & w

Three Daring Daughters (1948)—Joe Pasternak had a monstrous gift for producing relentlessly perky films for the whole family; sometimes, the damned things got to you— all those toothy smiles made you smile back. This one, though, can make you feel your jaw is wired shut. It's a musical that features the full horror of Jeanette MacDonald and José Iturbi; Jane Powell and Edward Arnold also traipse around. Fred M. Wilcox directed; a sizable troupe of screenwriters concocted the script about three girls who are upset by the news that their mother is planning to remarry, and decide to take action. Howard Dietz and Sammy Fain came up with "The Dickey Bird Song." With Larry Adler, Harry Davenport, and a redeemer—Moyna MacGill. M-G-M. color

Three Days of the Condor (1975)—The director, Sydney Pollack, doesn't have a knack for action pulp; he gets some tension going in this expensive spy thriller (and it was a box-office success), but there's no real fun in it. It may leave you feeling depressed or angry. Robert Redford plays a New York–based researcher for the C.I.A. who accidentally turns up a clue to the existence of a ren-egade conspiratorial network within the C.I.A. organization and becomes everybody's target. With a miscast, subdued Faye Dunaway as a photographer who shoots bare, wintry scenes and is meant to be half in love with death. Not a girl to jazz things up. In the film's high point of flossy artistry, Redford and Dunaway go to bed together, and their coitus is visualized for us in a series of her lonely, ghostly pictures. Also with Max von Sydow, Cliff Robertson, and John Houseman. Cinematography by Owen Roizman; the script by Lorenzo Semple, Jr., and David Rayfiel was adapted from James Grady's *Six Days of the Condor*. A Dino De Laurentiis Production, for Paramount. color (See *When the Lights Go Down*.)

The Three Faces of Eve (1957)—Joanne Woodward's big one—her Academy Award–winning role as the drab Southern housewife and mother with a splintered personality. The heroine calls herself Eve White when she's good and Eve Black when she's bad and sexy, and has yet another personality—that of the upstanding, intelligent woman whom the writer-producer-director, Nunnally Johnson, approves of. Shallow, but the gimmick is appealing, and Woodward's showmanship is very likable. With Lee J. Cobb and David Wayne, and an introduction by Alistair Cooke. Adapted from a book by two doctors: C. H. Thigpen and H. M. Cleckley. 20th Century-Fox. CinemaScope, b & w

Three for the Show (1955)—Betty Grable started singing and dancing in Hollywood musicals in 1930 (when she was 13), and she was thrown into so many dumb, garish pictures, especially during the Second World War when she was known as the number one pin-up girl, that her film career ended before she was 40. This picture was made in her last year in films, and she shows the comedy style of a buoyant veteran. It's a surprisingly bright musical version of the 1940 Jean Arthur comedy *Too Many Husbands*, which was derived from Somerset Maugham's play *Home and Beauty*. (He wrote it in the winter of 1917–18, while he was recovering from tuberculosis; he did it, he said, to amuse himself and war-weary audiences.) Grable plays a widowed, remarried Broadway star who discovers that her first husband is still alive. With Jack Lemmon, Marge and Gower Champion, Myron McCormick, and Paul Harvey. Directed by H. C. Potter, from the script by Edward Hope and Leonard Stern. Some of the dances (choreographed by Jack Cole) have a charge to them, and the songs include "How Come You Do Me Like You Do" and "Someone to Watch Over Me." Columbia. CinemaScope, color

Three Fugitives (1989)—A crumbum farce by the French writer-director Francis Veber, working in the U.S. (It's a remake of his *Les Fugitifs*.) Nick Nolte plays a veteran armed robber who goes to a bank to open an account and is taken hostage by Martin Short, a terrified twerp of an amateur holdup man. He needs money to keep his 6-year-old daughter (Sarah Rowland Doroff) in a special school—she has been mute since her mother died, two years earlier. That's the setup: the three are variously chased, and chase each other. Nolte keeps whamming Short on the head, and the tot ignores her devoted father. He's too small for her. She's smitten by big, blond, blue-eyed Nolte; queasy pedophiliac overtones hover in the air. Everything in the picture seems designed to humiliate the father, and you can't tell what's going on when Short—ostensibly for purposes of disguise—is dressed as a woman and the three form a nuclear family. This salute to macho has cinematography by Haskell Wexler; he lighted something that shouldn't have seen the light of day. With Kenneth McMillan, James Earl

Jones, and Bruce McGill. Touchstone (Disney). color (See *Movie Love*.)

Three in the Attic (1969)—Christopher Jones as Paxton Quigley, the unredeemed, self-centered, carnal frat boy who can't abandon promiscuity even after he has discovered love (with Yvette Mimieux). The college humor in this youth-oriented sex-exploitation film is unabashedly coarse and frequently funny. There's too much soft-focus lyricism and leaping about, and the last third is poor, and some of the trying-to-be-bright lines are real thudders, but it has a pleasantly open attitude. Directed by Richard Wilson; the script, by Stephen Yafa, is based on his novel *Paxton Quigley's Had the Course*. Filmed on location at the University of North Carolina at Chapel Hill, and in Durham. A.I.P. color (See *Going Steady*.)

Three Little Words (1950)—A big M-G-M musical bio of the songwriting team of Bert Kalmar (Fred Astaire) and Harry Ruby (Red Skelton). It's a rags-to-riches-and-contentment story, with few opportunities for Astaire to dance and with no more drama than the screenwriter (George Wells) can squeeze out of Kalmar's infatuation with magic and Ruby's obsessive enthusiasm for baseball. The two men have a childish quarrel and the team breaks up, but their devoted wives (Vera-Ellen and Arlene Dahl) soon put that to rights. The movie is witless and totally uninspired but good-natured, especially during the 14 Kalmar-Ruby songs, which include "Nevertheless," "I Love You So Much," "Who's Sorry Now," and "Hooray for Captain Spaulding." With Debbie Reynolds, who plays the boop-a-doop cutie, Helen Kane, and is dubbed by her; Gloria De Haven, who impersonates her mother, Mrs. Carter De Haven; a luscious, red-headed band vocalist, Gale Robbins, as the gold-digger who almost snares Ruby; and Keenan Wynn, Carleton Carpenter, Phil Regan, Paul Harvey, and Harry Shannon. Produced by Jack Cummings, directed by Richard Thorpe, and with dances staged by Hermes Pan. Vera-Ellen's songs are dubbed by Anita Ellis. color

The Three Musketeers (1948)—In grinning, leaping homage to Douglas Fairbanks, Gene Kelly plunges his sword into dozens of extras, vaults onto more horses than there are in a rodeo, swings from assorted drapes and chandeliers, and hops about 17th-century rooftops. His D'Artagnan veers between romance and burlesque, but is always enjoyable. However, the lavish M-G-M production is a heavy, roughhousing mess. As Lady de Winter, Lana Turner sounds like a drive-in waitress exchanging quips with hot-rodders, and, as Richelieu, Vincent Price might be an especially crooked used-car dealer. (The studio didn't want to offend anyone, so this Richelieu doesn't wear clerical trappings, and is never addressed by his ecclesiastical title.) Angela Lansbury wears the crown of France as if she'd won it in a milking contest at a county fair, and, as Lady Constance, June Allyson looks like a little girl done up in Mama's clothes. Kelly's amorous grapplings don't seem as strenuous as they actually were: he threw Lana Turner on her bed so hard that she fell off it and broke her elbow. He should have thrown the director, George Sidney, and the costume designer, Walter Plunkett, who swaddled the performers. Among them are Van Heflin, Gig Young, Frank Morgan, Keenan Wynn, John Sutton, Ian Keith, Patricia Medina, Robert Coote, and Reginald Owen. Produced by Pandro S. Berman, from Robert Ardrey's script. color

The Three Musketeers (The Queen's Diamonds) (1973)—This Richard Lester version was produced in the counterculture period—a time when some of the most talked about films made corruption seem inevitable and hence something you learn to live with; Lester saw corruption as slapstick comedy, and he turned out an absurdist debauch on swashbuckler themes. He keeps his actors—Michael York, Oliver Reed, Richard Chamberlain, Frank Finlay, Faye Dunaway, Raquel Welch, Geraldine Chaplin, Charlton Heston, Spike Milligan, Roy Kinnear, Christopher Lee, Simon Ward, Jean-Pierre Cassel, Michael Gothard, and Victor Spinetti—at a distance and scales the characters down to subnormal size. They're letching, carousing buffoons. Their derring-do isn't subverted; it's just cancelled out. Lester's decorative clutter is the best thing about the film: he loves scurrilous excess. But the whole thing feels hectic and forced. You want some gallantry and charm; you don't want joke, joke, joke. The second half was shot together with the first but released separately, as *The Four Musketeers* (*The Revenge of Milady*). The screenplay, based on Dumas, is by George MacDonald Fraser; the cinematography, by David Watkin, is ravishing (though Lester devalues the images by throwing them together so fast); the production design is by Brian Eatwell; the costumes are by Yvonne Blake de Carretero; the music is by Michel Legrand. Toledo, in Spain, is used for 17th-century Paris. Released by 20th Century-Fox. color

Three on a Match (1933)—Bette Davis, Joan Blondell, and Ann Dvorak (who goes through some steamy emotions) are the girls who grew up together and, after several years, meet again in the big city. At lunch one day, they light three cigarettes on one match, and, according to the superstition (which is said to have been invented and publicized by Ivar Kreuger, the Swedish match king), there's bad luck ahead. A modest, entertaining little melodrama from Warners, directed by Mervyn LeRoy. With Warren William, Glenda Farrell, Lyle Talbot, Humphrey Bogart, Patricia Ellis, Edward Arnold,

Jack La Rue, Grant Mitchell, Clara Blandick, and Allen Jenkins. Written by Lucien Hubbard, Kubec Glasmon, and John Bright. (Remade in 1938, as *Broadway Musketeers*, with Marie Wilson in the Davis role.) b & w

Three Smart Girls (1937)—Deanna Durbin's début picture, in which the happy, toothsome 14-year-old soprano conquered audiences and rescued Universal Pictures. And you can see why. This is the definitive "family picture": three shiny-eyed sisters (Deanna and Barbara Read and Nan Grey) swing into action when they see the tears of their divorced mother (Nella Walker), who has learned that their father (Charles Winninger) is about to marry a gold-digging blonde. There are solid pros in the surrounding cast—Binnie Barnes as the blonde, Alice Brady as her scheming mother, Ray Milland, Mischa Auer, Ernest Cossart, Lucile Watson, and Hobart Cavanaugh—and they do a lot of grinning. The picture is idiotically turned on to wholesome happiness, but it isn't boring. That master of sentimental engineering, Joe Pasternak, produced; Henry Koster directed. The script is by Adele Comandini, with some assistance from Austin Parker. b & w

Three's a Crowd (1927)—James Agee wrote that Harry Langdon looked "as if he wore diapers under his pants." This was fine as long as Langdon was doing slapstick, but when he sought pathos the results were horrible—sickly whimsical. He directed himself in this Chaplin imitation. He plays the Odd Fellow, who lives by himself and longs for romance and a happy home. On a stormy winter's night, The Girl he has loved, who has married another, comes to his shack and has her baby there. On Christmas Eve, just as happiness begins shedding its tender rays, The Girl's husband arrives and takes her and the child away. Having prepared for the role of Santa Claus, The Odd Fellow is left with torn heartstrings—and a box-office calamity. Silent. First National. b & w

Threshold (1981)—This hospital drama about the implanting of an experimental artificial heart in a desperately ill young woman (Mare Winningham) is perhaps too antiseptic and quietly intelligent; it's underdramatized—the dramatic excitement doesn't start until about an hour and a quarter in, and the end doesn't seem to take you anywhere. Yet it's very well written, by James Salter, and though it has a tedious self-conscious side, it develops its own kind of intensity. The cool imagery (the cinematographer is Michel Brault) has a beautiful formality, and the director, Richard Pearce, works well with the cast. Donald Sutherland is somewhat sacramental as the risk-taking surgeon (based on Dr. Denton Cooley, who was the subject of a *Life* cover story that Salter wrote); Jeff Goldblum provides some comedy in the role of a publicity-hound biologist (and heart inventor) who talks too much, especially on TV. Also with Sharon Acker, Robert Joy, Michael Lerner, John Marley, Allan Nicholls, and a glimpse of Dr. Cooley, who served as technical adviser. (His presence may account for the restraint—and the excess of spirituality—in Sutherland's performance.) A Canadian production, the film was shot mostly in Toronto but is set in Los Angeles. The score is by Mickey Erbe and Maribeth Solomon. Released by 20 Century-Fox. color

The Throne of Blood *Kumonosu-jo* (1957)—Kurosawa's version of *Macbeth* is a virtuoso exercise, as stylized and formalist in its way as Eisenstein's *Ivan the Terrible* movies, though not as ponderous or as inexplicably strange. This is like a demonstration of the uses of violence, decor, pageantry, and costuming, and it's almost a textbook in the techniques for making a movie move. Besides that, it has the great Isuzu Yamada washing her bloody hands, and West or East, there may never be a more chilling Lady Macbeth. Kurosawa is at his playful best when Birnam Wood advances on the castle, and that's just it—he loves this sort of effect so much it's all play. The ending, with Toshiro Mifune's Macbeth stuck full of arrows, like a porcupine-quill cushion, suggests the wildest Kabuki tradition. (Eisenstein was also fascinated by Kabuki.) The action for its own sake can seem like an orgy of masculine delight in warfare. Its greatness is in Kurosawa's glorious bad taste; he flings mad, absurd images on the screen. He has the courage to go over the top. Just one effect seems a mistake: when he uses a mechanical device (slowing down the sound) to simulate a witch's voice. (It's too obvious a trick.) With Takashi Shimura. In Japanese. b & w

Thunder Rock (1944)—Michael Redgrave, perhaps the finest exponent of neurotic tensions in movies of the period, as a young war correspondent who becomes disillusioned and retires to an ivory tower—a lighthouse. He is haunted by immigrants whose ship was lost there a century before, and they talk to him and restore his ideals. Adapted by Jeffrey Dell and Bernard Miles from Robert Ardrey's play, this ambitious movie is spectacularly handsome (especially the scenes outside the lighthouse); yet the situation is very theatrical—those dead people seem an awfully elaborate contrivance just to re-invigorate the hero. There are some fine, photogenic performers among them, though: Lilli Palmer (who's very touching), Barbara Mullen, Frederick Valk, and Finlay Currie. And James Mason, who plays a live visitor to the lighthouse, provides a strong, clashing presence; when he and Redgrave speak together, their voices ring out. At one point, Redgrave loses control and smacks him, and Mason says something on the order of "That's the trouble with Irish whiskey—you don't know you've been drinking until you're delirious," and there's surprising power in the scene. It's too bad that there isn't more of Mason and less of those worthy immigrants. Produced and directed by, respectively, John and Roy Boulting; cinematography by Mutz Greenbaum. b & w

Thunderball (1965)—Sean Connery as James Bond. The setting is Caribbean; the enemy is Adolfo Celi, the mastermind of SPECTRE, who stoops to using sharks. Terence Young directed. Not bad, but not quite top-grade Bond. A little too much underwater war-ballet. With Claudine Auger and Luciana Paluzzi, and, of course, Bernard Lee and Lois Maxwell. The script was written by Richard Maibaum and John Hopkins. United Artists. color

Thunderbolt (1929)—This Josef von Sternberg underworld melodrama (which he did just before he went to Germany and made *The Blue Angel*) was filmed as a silent and released in that form in some places, but sound was added after the film was completed, and it was more generally released as a talkie. George Bancroft is the gang leader known as Thunderbolt; Fay Wray is his gun moll, Ritzy; Richard Arlen is the bank clerk who knew her before she took up with Thunderbolt, and wants to marry her. Bancroft was such a genial, large-spirited actor that he makes Thunderbolt likable even while he's framing the bank clerk for murder. The two men wind up facing each other in opposite cells on death row. Tully Marshall is very funny as the agitated, sly, vaguely philanthropic warden. The picture is an imitation of von Sternberg's 1927 hit, *Underworld*, also starring Bancroft, and it isn't in the same class, but the first half isn't bad. After that, the contrivances are threadbare. With Eugénie Besserer as Arlen's mother, and Fred

Kohler as Bad Al. Written by Jules Furthman and Herman J. Mankiewicz. Paramount. b & w

The Thundering Sword, see *Cartouche*

Thursday's Children (1954)—This short film was made by Lindsay Anderson and Guy Brenton at the Royal School for Deaf and Dumb Children in England. It's a documentary that seems to transcend the documentary form: it becomes a fresh, almost lyric series of visual impressions of intent, observant faces and small bodies in movement. Cinematography by Walter Lassally. b & w

THX 1138 (1971)—George Lucas's first feature—a psychedelic view of the horrors of the 25th century, which turns out to be an abstract version of *1984.* The compulsorily drugged characters are shaven-headed, wear white, and are photographed against white; the effect is both gloomy and blinding. Maggie McOmie and anxious-eyed Robert Duvall are the lovers; Donald Pleasence is the nasty, as usual. Some talent but too much "art." Movie lovers may enjoy ticking off the homages or steals—Cocteau's *Orpheus*, Dreyer's *The Passion of Joan of Arc*, and so on. With Ian Wolfe, Marshall Efron, and Irene Forrest. Screenplay by Lucas and Walter Murch, from Lucas's story; titles and animation by Hal Barwood; editing by Lucas, with sound montages by Murch; cinematography by Dave Myers and Albert Kihn; music by Lalo Schifrin. An American Zoetrope Production (the executive producer was Francis Ford Coppola) for Warners. color

Thy Kingdom Come, Thy Will Be Done (1987)—This powerful and thoughtful documentary has a great subject: the union of Christian fundamentalism and the political right, which was engineered in the 80s by the use of computers, direct mail, and organized phone campaigns. The English producer-writer-director Antony Thomas comes on too strong at first, but he settles down quickly. He knows how to ask piercing questions without being hostile, and how to keep the footage tense and dramatic. And he shows deep-felt empathy with the people drawn into the born-again movement. In the second half, in which he examines the First Baptist Church of Dallas—the "richest and most powerful stronghold" of the religious right— he gets into the subject of how rich Christians keep themselves comfortable in their faith while abandoning the core of Christ's teachings. The film's central character is Dr. W. A. Criswell, the dignified white-haired pastor of First Baptist, who preaches the Gospel of Success. The crew was American, headed by the cinematographer Curtis Clark. Co-financed by Britain's Central Television and by WGBH (the PBS station in Boston). color (See *Hooked*.)

Ticket to Heaven (1981)—A Canadian film on a hot, dramatic subject. On a trip to San Francisco, the hero (Nick Mancuso), a handsome young Toronto schoolteacher, is sucked into a religious cult that worships its Oriental founder. Deprived of sleep, of food, and of any solitude for reflection, he gradually shrinks into a smiling child-zombie panhandler, part of a team selling flowers on the streets. It's a plausible metamorphosis: his independent spirit is visibly drained away until his greatest excitement is joining with the others in the chant "Bring in the money! Stay awake! Smash out Satan!" As the hero's friend, a would-be standup comic who organizes a kidnapping plot to rescue him, Saul Rubinek rescues the movie, too, by providing it with some personality. Rubinek has a wry, affectionate manner and bright, brimming eyes that register double-takes. After the kidnapping, when the bullying de-programmer (R. H. Thomson) stalks in and takes over, the dramatic logic collapses, because the director, Ralph L. Thomas, and his co-writer, Anne Cameron, haven't clarified the steps in the de-programming process (if it is a process, rather than just hit or miss). The picture could have used a better script and more taut direction, but the subject in itself makes it fairly compelling. Based on Josh Freed's 1978 newspaper series and on his 1980 book *Moonwebs*. With Meg Foster, Guy Boyd, and Robert Joy. color (See *Taking It All In*.)

A Ticket To Tomahawk (1950)—Written by Mary Loos and directed by Richard Sale, this is a pleasantly offbeat railroad comedy. The train in it may be the only one you'll ever see that takes its track with it. With Dan Dailey, Anne Baxter, Rory Calhoun, Walter Brennan, Sen Yung, Connie Gilchrist, and, though you might miss her if you're distracted for a minute, Marilyn Monroe. 20th Century-Fox. color

Tiger Shark (1932)—The material of this brisk (80-minute) Howard Hawks melodrama is naïve and far from virgin-new, but the movie is freshly and powerfully directed, and the tired plot is filled out by surprisingly exciting footage of tuna fishing in the Pacific. Edward G. Robinson gives a shrewd, energetic performance as the Portuguese captain of a tuna boat; the beautiful, sullen, dark-eyed Zita Johann is his wife, and his best friend (Richard Arlen) is, inevitably, in love with her. Wells Root did the script, from *Tuna*, by Houston Branch. With Vince Barnett and J. Carrol Naish. Warners. b & w

Tight Little Island Also known as *Whisky Galore*. (1949)—The only amusing famine in movie history is the whiskey famine on the mythical Scottish island of Todday; the wartime ration of whiskey has run out, and the island is devastated by drought. Then a ship bound for the United States with 50,000 cases of Scotch is wrecked on the shore, and the parched islanders take on the sweet task of salvage. Alexander Mackendrick directed this convivial little classic, based on Compton Mackenzie's novel *Whisky Galore*, adapted by Mackenzie and Angus MacPhail. With Joan Greenwood, Gordon Jackson, Basil Radford, Catherine Lacey, James Robertson Justice, A. E. Matthews, Jean Cadell, John Gregson, Mackenzie himself, and a contingent of gloomy Scots. Photographed on Barra, the Hebrides. b & w

Tightrope (1984)—Clint Eastwood is Homicide Inspector Wes Block, of the New Orleans Police Department, who is investigating a series of murders: young prostitutes are being tortured, raped, and strangled. The gimmick is that Wes is struggling with dark, sexist impulses, and that the killer is his doppelgänger and carries out his sadistic fantasies. The writer-director Richard Tuggle keeps whomping us on the skull with good-evil symbolism, but the movie has no more depth than the usual exploitation film in which pretty girls are knocked off. (Their naked corpses are photographed more tenderly than their live bodies.) And the movie has a queasy (unexplored) aspect: Eastwood's own 12-year-old daughter, Alison, who looks like him and acts like him, plays Wes's daughter Amanda, whom the doppelgänger means to rape. There's no progression in the plot—it's just one body after another—and the picture just grinds along. Eastwood seems to want to be fiery, but he doesn't have it in him—there's no vigor or puritan grandeur in Wes Block's character. And there's nothing in the psycho doppelgänger (played by Marco St. John)—he's just a bogeyman. The movie is like a sombre, pedestrian *Halloween*. With Geneviève Bujold, Janet MacLachlan, and Jamie Rose; cinematography by Bruce Surtees. A Malpaso Production, for Warners. color (See *State of the Art*.)

Till the Clouds Roll By (1946)—This monster thing, spawned at M-G-M, was meant to be the life of Jerome Kern. Robert Walker was the actor given the role (unlucky Walker was also miscast as Brahms), and he was surrounded by an all-star troupe that included Judy Garland, Lena Horne, Van Johnson, Dinah Shore, Tony Martin, June Allyson, and Frank Sinatra, who, in perhaps the most ill-conceived sequence in this staggeringly ill-conceived venture, sings "Ol' Man River" in white tie and white tails. There are 22 songs by Kern, most of them reasonably well performed, but not one performed memorably. Richard Whorf directed; Vincente Minnelli staged some of the sequences. color

Time After Time (1979)—Nicholas Meyer, the author of several popular novels (among them *The Seven-Per-Cent Solution*, which he also adapted for the screen), turned director with this tall tale about H. G. Wells (Malcolm McDowell) and Jack the Ripper (David Warner). The movie doesn't fully succeed: McDowell's shy, flustered Wells doesn't fit the Wells of our recollections, and the Ripper, with his big, bony hands, is too frighteningly sociopathic to fit into the film's romantic framework. (His murders are gruesome.) But most of the plotting is ingenious, and soft-faced Mary Steenburgen, as the woman from 20th-century San Francisco who is charmed by the Victorian Wells, makes it all semi-engaging. She's very sweet in an out-of-it way—a stoned cupcake—and she and McDowell seem to belong together in an enchanted playroom. With Patti D'Arbanville, who's terrific as a hooker, and Charles Cioffi, Joseph Maher, and Corey Feldman. From a story by Karl Alexander and Steve Hayes; the cinematography is by Paul Lohmann; the production design is by Edward C. Carfagno; the music is by Miklós Rózsa. An Orion Release through Warners. color

Time Bandits (1981)—Written by two members of the "Monty Python" group, Michael Palin and the American expatriate Terry Gilliam, who also directed, this surreal adventure fantasy has been conceived as a movie for children and adults. It's about a little English boy who is hurtled from one era to another by a pack of six dwarfs who have stolen The Supreme Being's map of the holes in the space-time continuum, and it's as picaresque as you can get, with Ian Holm as Napoleon, John Cleese as Robin Hood, Sean Connery as Agamemnon, Ralph Richardson as The Supreme Being, who's too busy to get his three-piece-suit pressed, and David Warner, who's a great-looking Evil Genius—he wears talons and a Nixon nose out of a David Levine drawing. (The light shining up from hell makes his nostrils red.) All this seems to do something for the 8- to 12-year-old boys in the audience—the ones known to be very high on d & d (Dungeons and Dragons)—that it may not do for adults, who will probably see and hear a lot of jokes without feeling much impulse to laugh. The whimsical rhythms of the vaudeville-skit humor often seem to be the result of mistiming; the interludes with Palin and Shelley Duvall as wonky sweethearts are especially musty—the two of them seem more amused than the audience. Gilliam has a cacophonous imagination; even the magical incongruities are often cancelled out by the incessant buzz of cleverness. It's far from a bad movie, but it doesn't quite click together, either. The director doesn't shape the material satisfyingly; this may be one of those rare pictures that suffers from a surfeit of good ideas. With David Rappaport, Kenny Baker, Jack Purvis, Mike Edmonds, Malcolm Dixon, and Tiny Ross as the bandits; the boy is Craig Warnock, and Peter Vaughan and Katherine Helmond are The Ogre and his wife. Songs by George Harrison. color

Time in the Sun *Que Viva Mexico* (1946)—The only film that Eisenstein directed outside the Soviet Union was never completed. But out of the fabulous footage that he and his cinematographer, Eduard Tisse, shot in Mexico in 1930 and 1931 the film *Time in the Sun* was edited by his disciples, who attempted to approximate his original plan—from Aztec cults through Conquistadores and peonage to Christian feasts. The footage imposes its vision of the Indian faces and the Mexican landscape; these faces are perhaps too noble and eternal, but they are marvellous to look at. b & w

The Time Machine (1960)—Entertaining George Pal sci-fi, loosely derived from the H. G. Wells novel and set at about the time the book was written—1895. The plush Victorian furnishings in the home of the time-travelling scientist (Rod Taylor) are contrasted with the catacombs of the cannibalistic future, where Yvette Mimieux is a dainty morsel on the menu. The machine itself is a beauty, with a red velvet seat and gadgets made of ivory and rock crystal, and the time-travel effects help to make this film one of the best of its kind. However, it deteriorates into comic-strip grotesqueries when the fat, ogreish future race of Morlocks torments the effete, platinum-blond, vacant-eyed race of Eloi. With Alan Young, Sebastian Cabot, and Whit Bissell. M-G-M. color

Times Gone By *Altri Tempi* (1951)—This is a lavish episodic film, based on stories, plays, and sketches by well-known Italian writers of the 19th and early 20th centuries. Peasants argue about "a matter of property"; would-be lovers go to great pains to achieve a clandestine meeting and then fritter away their time quarrelling; two children who are separated feel the first stirrings of love. There's a Pirandello one-act play, *The Vise*, and there's a witty finale, *The Trial of Phryne*, in which Vittorio De Sica as an arm-waving lawyer defends Gina Lollobrigida, the amiably loose woman of the town who is charged with murder. It's florid, with great verve—it's the only real reason to see the (tolerable but uneven) movie. Alessandro Blasetti directed. In Italian. b & w

Tin Men (1987)—Written and directed by Barry Levinson, this movie about aluminum-siding salesmen in Baltimore in 1963 (the year that the state cracked down on their bunco games) is a middle-aged echo of his 1982 film *Diner*. He's making essentially the same point—that guys relate better to guys than they do to girls. His basic theme here is the stunted imaginative life of the businessman who hangs out at the racetrack because he can feel good about himself when he's joking with his business pals. (The men's get-togethers are a form of consciousness-lowering.) The picture centers on a feud between two strutting tin men—Richard Dreyfuss and Danny DeVito—who work for different outfits, and on Dreyfuss's trying to score off DeVito by seducing his wife (Barbara Hershey). The salesmen's scams are entertaining, but their spritzing is too tame, and the action is prolonged with limp, wavering scenes. Levinson wants to be on the humane side of every issue. The best work is done by the supporting players. Dreyfuss's sales team includes John Mahoney as his partner, and Seymour Cassel, Matt Craven, Richard Portnow, Alan Blumenfeld, and Michael Tucker as the boss. DeVito's team includes Jackie Gayle as his partner, and Stanley Brock, Bruno Kirby, and J. T. Walsh as the boss. Touchstone (Disney). color (See *Hooked*.)

Tin Pan Alley (1940)—Big, splashy, pinheaded musical in the tasteless 20th Century-Fox style, with Alice Faye (the Fox queen of the 30s, on her way down), Betty Grable (scheduled to become the Fox queen of the 40s), the Nicholas Brothers, Jack Oakie, Billy Gilbert, and that Fox inevitable John Payne. The numerous songs include "Honeysuckle Rose," "You Say the Sweetest Things," "The Sheik of Araby," "On Moonlight Bay," and "K-K-K-Katy." Walter Lang directed. b & w

Tirez sur le pianiste, see *Shoot the Piano Player*

Titanic (1953)—In 1912, the Titanic, the largest ship in the world, struck an iceberg while on its maiden voyage from Southampton to New York and sank. Of the 2,207 people board, only 690 survived. The disaster was one of the most terrifying and fascinating in maritime history, but one wouldn't guess it from this movie. The scriptwriters (Charles Brackett, Walter Reisch, and Richard Breen) describe the emotional ups and downs of an unbelievable American fop (Clifton Webb); his estranged wife (Barbara Stanwyck), whom he is trying to win back; and their dreary kids. While the Titanic goes racing along, Webb and Stanwyck argue the respective merits of the Continent and the Middle West as a place to bring up children, until Stanwyck gets so heated about the advantages of the prairie that she informs him that she's cuckolded him and his son isn't even his. Unstrung by this information, Webb dashes to the ship's bar and plays bridge furiously for many hours. It should be funny, but it isn't even that. In standard variations of *Grand Hotel* style, the cast includes an unfrocked priest (Richard Basehart), an obtrusive bore (Allyn Joslyn), a rich and salty Western lady (Thelma Ritter), and the doomed master of the ship (Brian Aherne). Jean Negulesco directed; the actual sinking looks like a nautical tragedy on the pond in Central Park. Also with Robert Wagner and Audrey Dalton. Brackett produced, for 20th Century-Fox. b & w

Titicut Follies (1967)—Fred Wiseman's first documentary, photographed in the state hospital for the criminally insane at Bridgewater, Massachusetts. Crude in technique, but a revealing (and shocking) piece of visual muckraking. It has some unforgettable scenes. b & w

To Be or Not to Be (1942)—Some people have great affection for this anti-Nazi comedy-melodrama, with its knockabout seriousness. The stars are Carole Lombard and Jack Benny, bizarrely cast as a famous Polish actress and her actor-husband; the plot involves actors disguising themselves as Nazis in order to foil the Nazis. Ernst Lubitsch, who directed, starts off on the wrong foot and never gets his balance; the performers yowl their lines, and the burlesque of the Nazis, who cower before their superior officers, is more crudely gleeful than funny. With Robert Stack, Lionel Atwill, Stanley Ridges, Felix Bressart, Tom Dugan (as Hitler), Sig Rumann, Maude Eburne, Halliwell Hobbes, and Miles Mander. Produced by Lubitsch and Alexander Korda, for United Artists. Edwin Justus Mayer wrote the script, from a story conceived by Lubitsch and Melchior Lengyel. Cinematography by Rudolph Maté. It was Lombard's last film; two weeks after completing it, she was killed in a plane crash while on a tour to sell defense bonds. b & w

To Be or Not to Be (1983)—This remake of Ernst Lubitsch's 1942 picture about a Polish theatre troupe that outwits Nazi officialdom is a mild farce—benign but not really very funny. The roles once played by Jack Benny and Carole Lombard—the husband and wife who run the theatre and are its stars—are now filled by Mel Brooks and Anne Bancroft. With her thick, dark curly hair cut short, pencil-line 30s eyebrows, a broad, lascivious smile, and her body jiggling in silver lamé, Bancroft is friendly and sexy, and she seems more at ease in the general silliness than Brooks does. He rushes around in one disguise after another, pretending to be a whole series of Nazis; he never cuts loose. The tall, dazed Christopher Lloyd has a good moment or two, and Charles Durning (as a Nazi colonel) keeps his energy up high enough to give the picture a boost. Others in the cast include José Ferrer, Jack Riley, Tim Matheson, George Gaynes, and, in a new subplot, James Haake as a fey homosexual. Directed by Alan Johnson, who doesn't seize his opportunities to work up a head of steam; the film's high spot is its opening number—"Sweet Georgia Brown," sung in Polish. The semi-new script is by Thomas Meehan and Ronny Graham. Produced by Mel Brooks, for 20th Century-Fox. color (See *State of the Art.*)

To Catch a Thief (1955)—The later, jaded Hitchcock leans to malice and manner. He gets by with it here, largely because of Cary Grant's elegance as a retired cat burglar, and the luscious, sunny Riviera scenery, and Grace Kelly—she actually looks alive, and she's sexier than she is in anything else. The suspense plot (reprised in the 1974 *The Return of the Pink Panther*) isn't much; there are few thrills in this romantic comedy-thriller—it's no more than a pleasant minor diversion, but it does have a zingy air of sophistication. With Jessie Royce Landis, Charles Vanel, John Williams, and Brigitte Auber. The screenplay by John Michael Hayes is based on a novel by David Dodge. Paramount. color

To Die in Madrid *Mourir à Madrid* (1965)— A French-made documentary about the Spanish Civil War, compiled by Frédéric Rossif. Fancy, highly emotional, and not as informative as it might be, but some of the footage is very fine. With an English narration. b & w

To Die of Love *Mourir d'aimer* (1970)—This thinly fictionalized version of the Gabrielle Russier case has an unconvincing air of high-minded rectitude. It turns what appeared to be a gleaming social tragicomedy (in Mavis Gallant's reporting, especially) into one more bathetic, sacrificial love story, set in the French equivalent of our counterculture. As the schoolteacher in love with her teen-age student, Annie Girardot acts like a cross between Greer Garson as a mother superior and Greer Garson as the Maid of Orleans in love. Bruno Pradal brings youthful sensuality to the boy and gives the only halfway decent performance—though he seems to be used as a stand-in for Gérard Philipe. The boy's parents (who bring charges against the teacher) specialize in cold, malignant looks, while the rest of the adult cast is stereotyped for life-denying callousness or cynicism or impotence. The students are so life-enhancing they look stuffed; love is coming out their ears. Directed by André Cayatte, from a script he and Russier's lawyer concocted. In French. color (See *Deeper into Movies.*)

To Each His Own (1946)—Illegitimacy tearjerker. This time it's Olivia de Havilland who gives up her bouncing baby so he'll have a name. John Lund bats his eyelashes as her dashing aviator lover, and also as the son when, in the inevitable progression of events, she becomes a successful businesswoman (she operates a cosmetics outfit, like Elizabeth Arden's) and meets up with him (wearing wings like his father before him). As an example of the "woman's picture" this doesn't have any of the grubbiness or conviction of the Barbara Stanwyck *Stella Dallas*, but de Havilland works hard confecting cold cream, and her exertions won her the Academy Award. The atmosphere of lugubrious sensitivity is probably just about what the director, Mitchell Leisen, wanted. (He had a better side that came out in comedy.) With

Roland Culver, Phillip Terry, Mary Anderson, and Bill Goodwin. Charles Brackett, who produced this glossy package, also wrote the script, with Jacques Théry. Paramount. b & w

To Have and Have Not (1944)—In this picture, Humphrey Bogart, the greatest cynical hero of them all, found himself in Martinique, where a beautiful big cat of a girl named Lauren Bacall slouched across the screen for the first time and managed to make the question "Anybody got a match?" sound like the most insolent and insinuating of demands. Howard Hawks directed this slickly professional, thoroughly enjoyable Second World War melodrama, which was taken from what Warner Brothers advertised as Ernest Hemingway's novel, with William Faulkner listed as co-writer (with Jules Furthman) of the screenplay—making this the only movie on record with two Nobel Prize–winning authors. Don't be misled: it's the Warners mixture as before—sex and politics—but better this time. Asked to explain the genesis of this film, Hawks explained that once when he and Ernest Hemingway were hunting together, he had claimed that he could take Hemingway's worst story and make a movie of it. Hemingway asked which was his worst, and Hawks said *To Have and Have Not*. According to Hawks, Hemingway then explained that he had written it in one sitting when he needed money. Hawks made good on his boast, but he and the screenwriters cheated a bit: the movie deals with what may have occurred in the lives of the characters before the novel begins. (Footnote for somebody's Ph.D. thesis on "Novel into Film": the novel's ending was used to polish off John Huston's film version of Maxwell Anderson's dreary play *Key Largo*; the novel's plot was used for another movie, *The Breaking Point*, directed by Michael Curtiz, in 1950; and the short story "One Trip Across," which Hem-

ingway had expanded into *To Have and Have Not*, was used for an Audie Murphy movie, *The Gun Runners*, directed by Don Siegel, in 1958. And no doubt the Hawks version altered the Hemingway original in order to combine elements that had made big box office of Curtiz's *Casablanca*.) This film belongs to the movie era in which characters were clearly defined, and if a man was perverse, you knew he was a Nazi. The refreshingly, daringly sexy Bacall burst through the conventions of the era. A writer said of her that her "husky, underslung voice, which is ideal for the double-entendre, makes even her simplest remarks sound like jungle mating cries." Hoagy Carmichael provides the music and accompaniment for Bacall's facial exercises; the singing voice is that of Andy Williams, and it never sounded sexier than when coming out of her. Lauren Bacall's début had, in a sense, been pre-tested: Jules Furthman had worked out that good-bad girl act for Betty Compson in *Docks of New York* (1928) and perfected it on Marlene Dietrich in *Morocco* (1930). With Walter Brennan, Dolores Moran, Sheldon Leonard, Marcel Dalio, and Dan Seymour (literally, the heavy). b & w

To Kill a Mockingbird (1962)—When Gregory Peck got the Academy Award for Best Actor for his performance as an upstanding widowed lawyer practicing in a small Alabama town in the early 30s, there was a fair amount of derision throughout the country: Peck was better than usual, but in that same virtuously dull way. (There was the suspicion that Peck was being rewarded because the Lincolnesque lawyer shot a rabid dog and defended an innocent black man accused of raping a white woman.) Robert Mulligan directed, from Horton Foote's adaptation of Harper Lee's Pulitzer Prize novel, and it's all terribly conscientious—the clapboard houses, the slatted porch swings on rusty chains, the Chevy phaetons on dusty streets, the high moral sentiments, the specs on Peck's nose. Mulligan slows the pace down when he wants to suggest the mysteries of childhood or to arouse warm emotions; this works only intermittently. The movie is part eerie Southern gothic and part Hollywood self-congratulation for its enlightened racial attitudes. Brock Peters, who flares his nostrils mightily, is the black man on trial, and Robert Duvall is the brain-damaged Boo Radley, of whom the lawyer's children (Mary Badham and Philip Alford) are terrified. With John Megna, Ruth White, Rosemary Murphy, James Anderson, Collin Wilcox, William Windom, Alice Ghostley, Crahan Denton, Frank Overton, and Richard Hale. Cinematography by Russell Harlan; music by Elmer Bernstein; art direction by Alexander Golitzen and Henry Bumstead. Universal. b & w

To Sir with Love (1967)—James Clavell wrote and directed this feebly well-intentioned English movie. It's *Blackboard Jungle* reshaped to bring mist to your eyes. This time Sidney Poitier is the teacher—a West Indian—and he inspires and reforms the whole bunch of tough East End teen-agers (and their teachers, too). The film's awkwardness and naïveté seemed to be what made it a box-office favorite. In movies like this one, Poitier's self-inflicted stereotype of goodness cancels out his acting. Adapted from a novel by E. R. Braithwaite; with Judy Geeson, Suzy Kendall, and Christian Roberts. Columbia. color

The Toast of New Orleans (1950)—Sheer excruciation. Mario Lanza, as a boy from Bayou country, singing the execrable "Be My Love," and such minor horrors as "The Bayou Lullaby" and "Boom Biddy Boom Boom." Whoever it was who thought of teaming Lanza with Kathryn Grayson had a streak of malignant humor: when those voices collide

and his big chest meets her big bosom, pop culture is at climax. With David Niven, James Mitchell, Rita Moreno, J. Carrol Naish, and J. Clinton Sundberg. Directed by Norman Taurog, from a script by Sy Gomberg and George Wells; with choreography (of sorts) by Eugene Loring. Produced—inevitably—by Joe Pasternak; that man has a lot to answer for. M-G-M. color

Tobacco Road (1941)—Erskine Caldwell's novel turned into a folksy comic strip. The director, John Ford, and the scenarist, Nunnally Johnson, were up against censorship problems; still, that doesn't account for the broad pointlessness of the rustic humor or the glossy studio lighting of the poor whites cavorting in front of their Georgia shacks. The whole thing seems deranged. Charley Grapewin plays Jeeter Lester as a familiar corn-liquored old scamp, Gene Tierney is a glamourized Ellie May, Marjorie Rambeau is Sister Bessie, and Elizabeth Patterson is Ada. With William Tracy, Dana Andrews, Ward Bond, Zeffie Tilbury, Russell Simpson, Grant Mitchell, and Slim Summerville. Based on Jack Kirkland's theatre version of the novel; the play—considered hot and sensational—was a huge success. 20th Century-Fox. b & w

Today We Live (1933)—William Faulkner wrote a story called "Turn About," which had to do with the First World War rivalry between the aviators and the men in the torpedo boats; it had no heroine. Adapted to the screen, it became a vehicle for Joan Crawford, and the subject became how she can be freed from her old love so that she can give herself (in marriage) to Gary Cooper. There are some (uninspired) flying scenes, and some tolerable sequences on the high seas; the personal relationships are heavy-handed and rather baffling—maybe because although Crawford is the star, she really doesn't seem to have a place in the picture. The director, Howard Hawks, must have been confused, too; he gets minimal results from the cast. Cooper and Roscoe Karns aren't bad, but Robert Young and Franchot Tone use most of their energy trying for clipped British accents. Also with Louise Closser Hale. M-G-M. b & w

Together Again (1944)—The title refers to the earlier pairing of Irene Dunne and Charles Boyer in *Love Affair* and *When Tomorrow Comes*. This time, she's a widow, a small-town mayor who doesn't know that she needs love, and he's a sculptor from the big city, commissioned to do a commemorative statue of her late husband. During their various misunderstandings, each becomes engaged to a high-school student, and a million laughs ensue, all of them from the people in the picture. With Charles Coburn, Mona Freeman, and Elizabeth Patterson. Directed by Charles Vidor; among the many writers employed were Virginia Van Upp and Herbert Biberman. Columbia. b & w

Tom, Dick, and Harry (1941)—Ginger Rogers, a telephone operator, has three suitors: Alan Marshal is the millionaire of her dreams, George Murphy is a car salesman sure to get on in the world, and Burgess Meredith is a happy-go-lucky mechanic somewhat loose in the head. The movie is a series of sketches, as the heroine, trying to choose among them, dreams of her future life with each. (Her final choice leaves the viewer sceptical.) A nice detail: when she imagines marrying the millionaire, she sees newspaper headlines announcing her marriage; just under the large type there is a small heading, in quite insignificant type, reading, "Adolf Hitler Assassinated." Garson Kanin directed this Cinderella comedy from a script by Paul Jarrico. It's a little too jaunty and much too comfy in its sterotypical assumptions, but a lot of people enjoyed it. Phil Silvers turns up in a bit.

(Remade in 1958 as *The Girl Most Likely*.) R K O. b & w

Tom Jones (1963)—Tony Richardson whizzes through the Henry Fielding novel, but he pauses long enough for a great lewd eating scene. With Albert Finney as the foundling hero, Hugh Griffith, Joyce Redman, Edith Evans, Joan Greenwood, Susannah York, Diane Cilento, David Warner, Wilfrid Lawson, Rachel Kempson, and George Devine. The script is by John Osborne. Academy Awards: Best Picture, Director, Adapted Screenplay, Score. United Artists. color

Tomorrow Is Forever (1946)—One of the most preposterous of the many variants on the *Enoch Arden* theme. A cherub-faced chemist named MacDonald (Orson Welles) gets so badly shot up in the First World War that he prefers to let his wife (Claudette Colbert) think he's dead; he returns, transformed bewilderingly into a shattered European, to find that she has married the industrialist for whom he's going to work. Wearing a wig and false whiskers, dragging a gimpy leg, and rolling gutturals around on his tongue, Welles is so transparently Welles that it's pretty funny that Colbert doesn't recognize him. That's the only humor in this pallbearer-paced weeper. With Natalie Wood as the child the poor goof can't reveal himself to, and George Brent, Lucile Watson, and Richard Long. Directed by Irving Pichel, from Lenore Coffee's script, based on Gwen Bristow's novel. R K O. b & w

Tonight at 8:30 (1953)—Three of Noël Coward's light, corrosive social comedies are performed by excellent casts in this production, directed by Anthony Pelissier. The bill includes: *The Red Peppers*—two vaudeville hams bicker their way through a Saturday night, with Kay Walsh, Ted Ray, Martita

Hunt; *Ways and Means*—at a Côte d'Azur houseparty, a bankrupt couple persuade a burglar to rob the rich American down the hall and split with them, with Valerie Hobson, Nigel Patrick, Jack Warner, Jessie Royce Landis; *Fumed Oak*—a hag-ridden suburbanite tells off his in-laws, with Stanley Holloway. Too patently "clever" and "ribald" to be taken very seriously, these playlets are nevertheless models of skillful entertainment. color

Too Bad She's Bad *Peccato che Sia una Canaglia* (1955)—Alberto Moravia's divertissement on the cops and robbers theme features a prodigious family of thieves—father Vittorio De Sica is a dignified and accomplished pickpocket, his big pussycat daughter Sophia Loren is a happy delinquent who can't understand people who work for a living, and his two little sons can strip an automobile in 30 seconds flat. As several critics pointed out, this comedy has only one drawback: when the magnificent Sophia sails across the screen, one forgets to read the subtitles. With Marcello Mastroianni. Directed by Alessandro Blasetti. In Italian. b & w

Too Hot to Handle (1938)—A busy, forgettable Clark Gable–Myrna Loy screwball melodrama. He's a daredevil newsreel cameraman who fakes war stories and will do anything for a scoop and she's a celebrated "aviatrix." One of his dirty tricks wrecks her reputation, and they carry on a love-hate affair that jumps around from China to the Amazon jungle. The director, Jack Conway, flails about trying for laughs and he settles for facetiousness. The movie looks as if it were made up of odds and ends of scrap footage, and it's crudely racist, in a casual, dumb-jokey way; in the jungle Gable projects a reel of disaster footage in order to frighten the natives, and he jeers at their response—he refers to them as "jitterbugs" and calls the

medicine men "monkeys." This hero's cockiness and unscrupulousness seem intended to be likable, but Gable can't bring it off, though Myrna Loy, who is simply dressed and fairly quiet, manages to be very charming, despite the idiotic things she has to do. With Walter Pidgeon, Leo Carrillo, Walter Connolly (in perhaps his worst performance—as Gable's expostulating, dyspeptic boss), Marjorie Main (who has a nice, dry way with her few lines), Virginia Weidler, Willie Fung, Johnny Hines, Al Shean, Henry Kolker, Frank Faylen, and a couple of accomplished black actors whose names are not easy to come by. Laurence Stallings and John Lee Mahin wrote the script; Lawrence Weingarten produced, for M-G-M. b & w

Too Many Crooks (1958)—Michael Pertwee, who wrote such English comedies as *Laughter in Paradise* and *Your Past Is Showing* for the director Mario Zampi, had a good idea here, too. (It bears some relationship to an O. Henry story.) A gang of crooks (George Cole, Sidney James, and company) kidnap the wife (Brenda de Banzie) of a tycoon (Terry-Thomas) and discover they are holding a cold potato. The tycoon, who is having an affair with his secretary, is delighted to be rid of his wife and has no intention of ransoming her. Furious, the wife becomes the mastermind of the gang. Zampi didn't do the gimmick justice; he directed clumsily, confusing shouted dialogue with wit. Elliot Silverstein handled the same idea (and did worse by it) in the 1967 *The Happening*; the plot turned up again in the 1986 *Ruthless People*, with Bette Midler in the Brenda de Banzie role. b & w

Too Many Husbands (1940)—In *My Favorite Wife* and its many variations, the husband with two wives is generally frantic. Here, Jean Arthur, caught between Fred MacMurray and Melvyn Douglas, loves the dilemma. A well-written, light-spirited comedy, adapted by Claude Binyon from Somerset Maugham's play *Home and Beauty*. The cast includes Harry Davenport, Melville Cooper, Edgar Buchanan, and Dorothy Peterson. Directed by Wesley Ruggles. (A musical version in 1955 starred Betty Grable and was called *Three for the Show*; it was one of Grable's last and best pictures.) Columbia. b & w

Tootsie (1982)—Marvellous fun. Dustin Hoffman is both the hero and the target of this satirical farce about actors. He plays Michael Dorsey, a brilliant, "uncompromising" New York actor whom no one wants to hire because he makes things hell for everybody. When Michael's girlfriend (Teri Garr) goes up for an audition for a role in a soap and is rejected, he makes himself up as a woman, presents himself as "Dorothy Michaels," and lands the job. And Michael finds himself when he's Dorothy—not because he has any secret desire to be a woman but because when he's Dorothy he's acting. He's such a dedicated, fanatical actor that he comes fully alive only when he's playing a role—you can see it in his intense, glittering eyes. Michael is in the guise of Dorothy when he meets his dream girl—Jessica Lange, who's like a shock absorber to him; she says her lines in such a mild, natural way that it makes perfect sense for him to stop in his tracks and stare at her in wonder. With Bill Murray, Charles Durning, George Gaynes, Geena Davis, Doris Belack, Dabney Coleman, and, as Michael's agent, Sydney Pollack, who also directed. Pollack does some of his best work yet in the opening sequences—a crackling, rapid-fire presentation of the hopes versus the realities of out-of-work actors' lives. The script is credited to Larry Gelbart and Murray Schisgal, but Don McGuire wrote the first draft, and Elaine May and many others worked on it. Columbia. color (See *Taking It All In*.)

Top Gun (1986)—It features MTV motivation: I pose, therefore I am. The strapping Kelly McGillis is an astrophysicist employed to teach the elite fighter pilots in training at San Diego's Miramar Naval Air Station; she sidles into rooms and slouches, so she won't overpower her co-star, the relatively diminutive Tom Cruise, who is supposed to be the most daring of her students. When McGillis is offscreen, the movie is a shiny homoerotic commercial: the pilots strut around the locker room, towels hanging precariously from their waists. It's as if masculinity had been redefined as how a young man looks with his clothes half off, and as if narcissism is what being a warrior is all about. In between the bare-chested maneuvers, there's footage of ugly snub-nosed jets taking off, whooshing around in the sky, and landing while the soundtrack calls up Armageddon and the Second Coming—though what we're seeing is training exercises. What is the movie selling? It's just selling, because that's what the producers, Don Simpson and Jerry Bruckheimer, and the director, Tony (Make It Glow) Scott, know how to do. Selling is what they think moviemaking is about. The result is a new "art" form: the self-referential commercial. With Val Kilmer, Anthony Edwards, Tom Skerritt, Meg Ryan, Rick Rossovich, and Tim Robbins. The script is credited to Jim Cash and Jack Epps, Jr., though the producers acknowledge that other writers were involved. Paramount. color (See *Hooked*.)

Topaz (1969)—Hitchcock's 51st feature is a larger, slower, duller version of the spy thrillers he made in the 30s. Apparently he expects us to identify with the waxwork Cuban rightists who are spying for the U.S.; he expects us to accept the creaking late-late-show romances, and the Arrow-collar-shaving-cream-ad hero (Frederick Stafford), and all the people who look like cutouts and behave like drab, enervated versions of spies in his earlier films. Per-Axel Arosenius, Michel Piccoli, and Philippe Noiret have a few moments, and Roscoe Lee Browne perks things up briefly, but most of the other performers waste away in their roles. With John Vernon, John Forsythe, Dany Robin, Karin Dor, Claude Jade, and Michel Subor. From a Leon Uris novel, adapted by Samuel Taylor. Universal. color (See *Deeper into Movies*.)

Topaze (1933)—John Barrymore is completely charming as the shabby, unworldly science teacher who is bounced from his academic environment and lands in the business world of delightful depravity; handed his first martini, he gulps the olive with the liquid. The film was made in the period when teachers were considered virtuous recluses and the academic world was called the ivory tower. At the time—which really wasn't so long ago—the attitudes in this gentle comedy were thought very modern and sly and cynical. Produced by David O. Selznick, it's an elegantly designed picture; it was directed by Harry d'Abbadie d'Arrast in his too leisurely, "continental" style—everything is a little too slow. With Myrna Loy as the sophisticated woman who is attracted by the teacher's innocence. Adapted from Marcel Pagnol's play by Benn W. Levy and (though uncredited) Ben Hecht. There have been several other screen versions; Louis Jouvet, Fernandel, and Peter Sellers have all played the teacher. Music by Max Steiner. R K O. b & w

Topkapi (1964)—Comic grand larceny in Eric Ambler terrain—Istanbul. The gang in this Jules Dassin thriller includes Peter Ustinov, Melina Mercouri, Maximilian Schell, Robert Morley, and Akim Tamiroff, and they all work too hard at being merry, lovable scoundrels. Music by Manos Hadjidakis. United Artists. color

El Topo (1971)—A spaghetti Western in the style of Luis Buñuel, and tinsel all the way. The writer-director-star, Alexandro Jodorowsky, plays with symbols and ideas and enigmas so promiscuously that the confusion may be mistaken for depth. He has some feeling for pace and for sadistic comedy, but the principal appeal of the movie is as a violent fantasy—head comics. Cinematography by Rafael Corkidi; produced by Roberto Viskin. In Spanish. color (See *Deeper into Movies*.)

Topper (1937)—Much fun; a sophisticated fantasy, with Cary Grant and Constance Bennett as a high-stepping married couple, George and Marion Kirby. Killed in an automobile accident, they return as elegant, ectoplasmic pranksters and drive banker Cosmo Topper (Roland Young) to happy distraction. Norman Z. McLeod directed this adaptation of a Thorne Smith novel; the picture was such a hit that it led to a series of movies and then to a TV series, but don't judge this one by what followed. This is the one to see, and for those who don't know why Constance Bennett was a big movie star, her provocative, teasing Marion Kirby should provide the answer. With Billie Burke, Alan Mowbray, Hedda Hopper, Arthur Lake as a bellboy, and Eugene Pallette as a house detective. A Hal Roach Production; released by M-G-M. b & w

Topper Returns (1941)—The third in the vaporish series doesn't have the style or wit of the first two; it's a standard mystery with spooky trimmings, mostly set in an old mansion, with hands in the dark, sliding panels, and trap doors. Constance Bennett is gone, and the heroine is Joan Blondell; she's a blessing, as always, but she doesn't have much help from the plot. Stabbed to death, she reappears as a facetious phantom who expects Topper (Roland Young again, looking tired) to find her killer. Roy Del Ruth directed. The cast includes Billie Burke (still Mrs. Topper), Carole Landis, Eddie Anderson (as an all-too-easily-scared chauffeur), and bulldog-jawed Donald MacBride, as a choleric policeman. Produced by Hal Roach; released by United Artists. b & w

Topper Takes a Trip (1939)—A sequel to *Topper*, but this time Cary Grant has vanished altogether (except in the introductory footage lifted from the first film). Constance Bennett, as Marion Kirby, and Roland Young, as Topper, are still around, however, and the film, though talky and overextended, is generally bright. Topper goes to Paris for a divorce, and Marion follows him; the action takes place mostly in a Riviera hotel. As before, Norman Z. McLeod is the director, and Billie Burke and Alan Mowbray are on hand. Also with Verree Teasdale, Franklin Pangborn, Alex D'Arcy, and the dog known as Asta in the *Thin Man* pictures, who turns up here as Mr. Atlas. A Hal Roach Production; released by United Artists. b & w

Torch Song (1953)—The viewer is asked to admire Joan Crawford's legs and her acting, which consists of pushing her mouth into positions meant to suggest suffering. The first is easy; the second impossible. In this misbegotten melodrama with some musical numbers, she finally settles for a blind musician (Michael Wilding). Which, all things considered, is a remarkably sensible decision. With Gig Young, Marjorie Rambeau, and Eugene Loring. Directed by Charles Walters. M-G-M. color

Torment *Hets* (1944)—Alf Sjöberg directed this famous study of adolescent despair and mean-spirited, authoritarian education. It was written by the 25-year-old Ingmar Bergman, who worked on it as Sjöberg's assistant. Stig Järrel plays the sadist schoolmaster; the student and the shopgirl whom he victimizes

are played by Alf Kjellin and Mai Zetterling (who also became directors). Gunnar Björnstrand and others of Bergman's troupe may be glimpsed in small roles, looking very young. In Swedish. b & w

Torn Curtain (1966)—Sloppy, clumsy Hitchcock thriller with Paul Newman as an American nuclear scientist who says he's defecting, and Julie Andrews as the girl who tags along—pure heart, piping voice, and all. With Lila Kedrova, Tamara Toumanova, and Ludwig Donath. Brian Moore is credited with the original screenplay, but probably his friends don't mention it. Universal. color

Torrid Zone (1940)—Steamy hot and very funny. This tropical comedy-adventure, set in a Warners mockup of a plantation in Honduras, has James Cagney, Ann Sheridan, and Pat O'Brien shouting double-entendres at breakneck speed. Sheridan is sultry and rowdy as a vagrant nightclub entertainer wandering through the jungle nightclub circuit and taking the natives' minds off banana picking. O'Brien plays the tough plantation manager, and Cagney, with a mustache, is the breezy, belligerent foreman who deals with a crisis a minute, including George Tobias as a revolutionary, Andy Devine as a hopelessly incompetent No. 1 Boy, and cucumber-cool Helen Vinson, always a troublemaker. The picture borders on satirical farce; the target is the typical Hollywood treatment of South American bandits and tropical passions. William Keighley directed, from a script by Richard Macaulay and Jerry Wald; cinematography by James Wong Howe. b & w

Tortilla Flat (1942)—A good-natured and engaging minor novel by Steinbeck, turned into a good-natured and engaging (though corny and quaint and picturesque) film at M-G-M. Spencer Tracy, John Garfield, John

Qualen, Sheldon Leonard, Akim Tamiroff, and Allen Jenkins are among the wine-drinking *paisanos* of a studio version of a shantytown section of Monterey, California. Jenkins doesn't even try to pass, but the others make a stab at acting ignorant and talking in a folk rhythm—they sound like Broadway wiseguys out of Damon Runyon. Tracy is meant to be a scrounger loafer who leads the others astray. An unusually animated Hedy Lamarr plays a hot-tempered Portuguese girl (in pigtails) who works in a cannery and keeps a goat. The only performer who really gets into his role is Frank Morgan, bearded, as a saintly old beggar who talks to the stray dogs he takes into his chicken-coop home. Morgan is very effective, but the moviemakers know it and they milk it; he is rewarded by a vision of St. Francis of Assisi. By the time that Tracy pleads for a miracle to save the injured Garfield's life and is overheard by a silver-haired padre (Henry O'Neill), the picture's charm has become cloying. Victor Fleming directed. With Donald Meek and Connie Gilchrist. The script is by John Lee Mahin and Benjamin Glazer; Sam Zimbalist produced. It says something about M-G-M's attitude toward *paisanos* that it was made in sepia.

Touch and Go (1986)—It has a terribly virtuous idea: it's about the chance meeting of a tough 11-year-old "ethnic" boy (Ajay Naidu), who's economically handicapped, and the career-centered all-star forward (Michael Keaton) of a Chicago hockey team, and how they change each other's lives. But the director, Robert Mandel, who finished the film in 1984 (after his first, *Independence Day*, and before his third, *F/X*), takes the drivelling story and informs it with honesty and sensibility. Keaton gives a grown-up-male performance of a kind you don't often see. As Bobby Barbato, a local boy from the South Side, he's in fighting trim, and he's quick and impudent in conversation. High up in his ex-

pensive lakefront apartment, he watches the VCR, studying replays of his moves. He's a real pro, and Keaton, who got in shape for the role, is on top of it. Blessedly, the movie isn't preachy about Bobby's single life. But when he meets the kid's mother in the person of the volatile Maria Conchita Alonso, Keaton shows us the deepening of Bobby's feelings. And Alonso has the uninhibited sexiness of the young Sophia Loren. She brings a happy sizzle to the role of the openhearted single mother who's so eager for experience that she walks tilted forward, almost at a run. The picture is stuck with crude plot turns, but Keaton and Alonso have a lovely, spinning rapport. With Max Wright, Maria Tucci, and Lara Jill Miller; the handsome cinematography is by Richard H. Kline. Screenplay by Alan Ormsby and Bob Sand and Harry Colomby. Tri-Star. color (See *Hooked*.)

Touch of Evil (1958)—As the madam of a Mexican bordello, Marlene Dietrich (done up in her Gypsy makeup from *Golden Earrings* of 1947), greets the grotesquely oversized, padded, false-nosed Orson Welles with a glorious understatement—"You're a mess, honey. You've been eating too much candy." When the final bullet punctures him and he is floating in the water like a dead whale, she eulogizes—"What can you say about anybody? He was some kind of a man. . . ." That may be one of the worst lines ever written or a parody of bad writing—the funeral scene in *Death of a Salesman*. Welles' first American production in a decade, this marvellously garish thriller has something, but not very much, to do with drugs and police corruption in a border town. What it really has to do with is love of the film medium, and if Welles can't resist the candy of shadows and angles and baroque decor, he turns it into stronger fare than most directors' solemn meat and potatoes. It's a terrific entertainment. The cast, assembled as perversely as in a nightmare, includes Charlton Heston, Joseph Cal-leia, Akim Tamiroff, Joseph Cotten, Zsa Zsa Gabor, Mercedes McCambridge, Janet Leigh, Dennis Weaver, Valentin De Vargas, Joanna Moore, Harry Shannon, and Ray Collins. Cinematography by Russell Metty; filmed at Universal Studios and partly on location at Venice, California. The script, credited to Welles, is supposed to be a free adaptation of Whit Masterson's novel *Badge of Evil*. When the picture opened in 1958 it was 93 minutes long and some scenes were said to have been added that were directed by Harry Keller; in 1976 a version was released that runs 108 minutes and is said to represent Welles' original intentions. Universal. b & w

A Touch of Larceny (1960)—Few people appear to have seen or even heard of this pleasantly adult Anglo-American comedy; it's a little too thin to be memorable, but it's surprisingly light and debonair. James Mason gives one of his best comic performances as the naval commander, weary of his desk job at the British Admiralty, who makes it appear that he has gone over to the Russians, in order to sue the papers for libel. The best scene is one of the quietest: Mason, who has carefully shipwrecked himself on an uninhabited island, sees a passing vessel; he sips champagne while murmuring, "Help, help!" With George Sanders, Robert Flemyng, Harry Andrews, Duncan Lamont, and Vera Miles, who acts in an aloof, low-keyed manner which is apparently meant to be highly suggestive—she's not totally objectionable. Guy Hamilton directed; the script by Roger MacDougall, Peter Winterton, Hamilton, and the producer, Ivan Foxwell, is based on Andrew Garve's novel *The Megstone Plot*. b & w

Tough Guys Don't Dance (1987)—Norman Mailer directed and did the adaptation of his murder-mystery novel. The setting is Prov-

incetown in November, and we're meant to feel the wintry corruption that has seeped into the town—it involves five or six killings. The writer hero (Ryan O'Neal) is ravaged from hard living with a rich wife and three years in the pen for dealing drugs, but he can tell his tough old father (Lawrence Tierney) that in those three years no man used him for a punk. His having remained anally inviolate is the proof of his manhood. Women victimize him, though—at least, the dirty-sex, Pia Zadora blondes (like Debra Sandlund) do. He has a love-hate bond to them. He needs to escape to a true-love earth-mother brunette (Isabella Rossellini). This is paltry stuff; it has an eerie, dated quality, like a copy of *Playboy* left out in the sun for 15 years. The women are subhuman, and most of the actors look stranded—lost and undirected. Yet the tawdriness of Mailer's self-exposure and self-glorification has a low-level fascination. After a while, the movie turns into a burlesque of itself. It's thin—thinner than pulp, lacking the shock and suggestiveness of pulp. Mailer isn't enough of a moviemaker to draw us in on a primitive level: we're not caught up in the hero's fear that he may be a murderer, and so we're outside the movie from first to last. What Mailer provides is an intellectual's idea of a pulp thriller. You stare at it knowing it's hopeless yet not really wanting to leave. With Wings Hauser and John Bedford Lloyd (who gives the best performance). Cinematography by John Bailey. Cannon Films. color (See *Hooked*.)

Tout va bien (1972)—Not as deadly in its pedagogical tone as other Jean-Luc Godard–Jean-Pierre Gorin films of the period. There's some relaxation and humor in this story of a workers' takeover of a sausage factory, but the way Jane Fonda, as an American journalist, and Yves Montand, as her French filmmaker-husband, are radicalized by the situation seems mechanical and naïve. In French. color

Tovarich (1937)—The 30s stage play about a penniless Russian prince and his grand-duchess wife who are happy to get jobs as servants in a Paris household. It's the sort of vehicle that comes to life in the theatre, because of the opportunities it affords dazzling technicians, but in the movie version, although Charles Boyer has a devilish cuckoo quality and Claudette Colbert is very charming, the whole thing seems rather attenuated. It's pleasant, but there's no energy in it, and the director, Anatole Litvak, who had demonstrated a highly developed visual style when he worked with Boyer only the year before (in *Mayerling*), seems paralyzed by the stagey material. With Basil Rathbone, Isabel Jeans, Anita Louise, Morris Carnovsky, Melville Cooper, Montagu Love, and Fritz Feld. From the play by Jacques Deval, adapted for the American stage by Robert E. Sherwood; the screenplay is by Casey Robinson. (Another version was made in France, in 1935.) Warners. b & w

The Towering Inferno (1974)—Disaster blockbuster, with each scene of someone horribly in flames presented as a feat for the audience's delectation. The picture practically stops for us to say, "Yummy, that's a good one!" These incendiary deaths and the falls from high up in the 138-floor tallest skyscraper in the world are the film's only feats. Paul Newman and Steve McQueen mutter heroic sentiments, and Faye Dunaway manages to look goddessy-beautiful through it all, wandering through the chaos in puce see-through chiffon. John Guillermin directed and Irwin Allen produced. Stirling Silliphant wrote the series of bloopers that make up the script, which is based on two books—Richard Martin Stern's *The Tower* and Thomas M. Scortia's *The Glass Inferno*—that were sold to Hollywood studios. The plots were so similar that the two studios—20th Century-Fox and Warners—got together and jointly financed this one expensive (and highly profitable) movie. The picture asks us to believe that the tallest building in the world—a golden glass tower that's a miracle of flimsiness, as it turns out—would have been set down in San Francisco, of all places. With William Holden, Susan Blakely, Robert Vaughn, Jennifer Jones, Fred Astaire, Robert Wagner, O. J. Simpson (he gets to rescue a pussycat), and Richard Chamberlain as a rat-fink electrical contractor—can you imagine him negotiating with the electricians' local? Cinematography by Fred Koenekamp. (160 minutes.) color (See *Reeling*.)

Toys in the Attic (1963)—This Freudian Southern gothic is well done for what it is—one of those hyped-up unflinching movies in which a family that is "living a lie" suddenly finds its glass house crashing down. ("You never really loved me. . . . It was Jed, your own father, you really wanted. . . . Go on, say it.") The main characters in James Poe's adaptation of Lillian Hellman's play are an incestuous trio of two sisters (Geraldine Page and Wendy Hiller) and a dependent, weakling brother (Dean Martin, pitiably miscast). Page shows considerable brio, as she makes her transitions from fluttering Dixie charm to granitic cruelty; Hiller has the trembling-lip role. There's no shortage of dramaturgy, such as a crucial overheard conversation. And Martin has to perceive the psychological truth of Page's attachment to him, and walk out a man. Whatever made anyone think there'd be an audience for this? George Roy Hill directed. With Yvette Mimieux and Gene Tierney. United Artists. b & w

T. R. Baskin (1971)—Baroque in its stupidity. Candice Bergen, looking like a million dollars, as an alienated, friendless typist in

Chicago. The movie feminizes alienation by turning it into whimsy. Herbert Ross directed, from a script by Peter Hyams, who also produced. With Peter Boyle, James Caan, and Marcia Rodd. Paramount. color (See *Deeper into Movies*.)

Trade Winds (1939)—Hedy Lamarr was the rage in Hollywood the year this was made, and she had also just married Joan Bennett's ex-husband. So Bennett, in a witchy, prankish mood, turned from blonde into sultry brunette, *à la* Lamarr—and had no trouble at all outacting her. This picture is made from glamour and jokes and scraps of old melodrama, and the trashy mixture is pretty lively, with Bennett on a ship, trying to escape a charge of murder, Fredric March as the detective whose job it is to take her back, and Ann Sothern on hand as a cynical, wisecracking blonde. The script was written by Dorothy Parker, Alan Campbell, and Frank R. Adams, and they supplied Sothern with some real zingers. Audiences liked her so much that there was a spin-off—she went on to star in the *Maisie* series. With Ralph Bellamy, Thomas Mitchell, and Sidney Blackmer. Directed by Tay Garnett, who seems to give it spurts of energy—he dozes in between; the cinematography is by Rudolph Maté. Produced by Walter Wanger; United Artists. b & w

Trading Places (1983)—Dan Aykroyd plays a snooty young blueblood who runs a Philadelphia brokerage house and Eddie Murphy plays a con man–beggar who disguises himself as a blind, legless Vietnam veteran. The two don't exactly trade places; they're traded, by a pair of heartless, rich old brothers (Ralph Bellamy and Don Ameche) who have made a heredity-versus-environment bet—something we've been spared in movies of the past few decades. John Landis directed this comedy in a mock-30s formal style; it's eerily arch

and static. But the picture has its big, chugging structure working for it; the whole apparatus picks up speed toward the end and comes to a rousing, slapstick finish, with the younger guys rich and the old skinflints punished. And the audience appears to enjoy the premeditated obviousness. With Denholm Elliott, who deserves better than his role as a butler; Jamie Lee Curtis, who deserves better than her role as a prostitute named Ophelia; and Paul Gleason and Kristin Holby. From a script by Timothy Harris and Herschel Weingrod. Paramount. color (See *State of the Art*.)

Traffic (1971)—This time Jacques Tati's M. Hulot is a car designer on his maundering way to an international automobile exposition in Amsterdam. As a comic figure, Tati had a nice spare bouyancy in *Jour de fête* and was poignantly quick and eccentric in *Mr. Hulot's Holiday*, but here his whimsical bumbling seems precious and fatuous. And as the director, he keeps the actors at a distance—an oddly depersonalizing technique for a movie that is commenting on modern depersonalization. Still, the color and design are pretty, and Tati's style is in his purest form—evocative and bittersweet—in the sequence where two garage mechanics simulate walking on the moon. Released by Columbia; in English. (See *Reeling*.)

La Tragedia di un Uomo Ridicolo, see *Tragedy of a Ridiculous Man*

Tragedy of a Ridiculous Man *La Tragedia di un Uomo Ridicolo* (1981)—Bernardo Bertolucci's movie about a left-wing terrorist kidnapping in Parma centers on the father (Ugo Tognazzi) who is required to give up everything he has worked for—a big cheese factory, a villa, and a yacht—to recover a son, who he suspects may be in on the plot. Tognazzi does his robust-life-force and peasant-cunning number. He does have more energy than anything else in the movie, but it's the hollow kind of actor's energy you want to get away from. The movie is logy—complex yet undramatic; there's no urgency, no tension, and you sense that you're not going to find out what's going on, that it's all metaphorical. Bertolucci's vision is grayed-out here; there's no feeling of discovery in the acting, no zest in the editing—it's like an old man's movie. Screenplay by Bertolucci. With Anouk Aimée, Laura Morante, Victor Cavallo, and Riki Tognazzi; cinematography by Carlo Di Palma. In Italian. color (See *Taking It All In*.)

The Trail of the Lonesome Pine (1935)— Made in pale picture-postcard colors (blue hills and green trees), this folk Western about the feud of the Tollivers and the Falins is awfully pokey and loaded with fake myth-making, yet it has lovely, affecting qualities— some attributable to Henry Hathaway's direction; more to Sylvia Sidney's and Henry Fonda's youth and talent; and some to Fuzzy Knight's singing of "Twilight on the Trail." Fred MacMurray plays the young mining engineer who comes into the Kentucky backwoods community and falls in love with Sylvia Sidney (so does the entire audience). The producer, Walter Wanger, provided a big cast, including Fred Stone, Beulah Bondi, Nigel Bruce, Alan Baxter, Robert Barrat, Spanky McFarland, and Richard Carle, for this first three-color-process outdoor movie. The screenplay by Grover Jones, Horace McCoy, and Harvey Thew was based on a novel by John Fox, Jr. Paramount.

Tramp, Tramp, Tramp (1926)—Harry Langdon's first full-length comedy. Not quite the picture that his second, *The Strong Man*, is, but the restrained slapstick is charming. In this one, he enters a footrace across the continent and gets caught in a chain gang and a cyclone before winning. Harry Edwards directed, with Frank Capra on the script. With Joan Crawford. Silent. b & w

Transatlantic Tunnel (1935)—Though actually a remake of a much better German sci-fi adventure film, this melodramatic English production, directed by Maurice Elvey, has some memorable and gripping sequences once it gets under way—which takes a while. The title tells the story: it's about trying to drive a tunnel under the Atlantic, with all the floods and eruptions imaginable. Iron-jawed Richard Dix, one of the most appealing early screen stars, is the lead, with Madge Evans opposite him. b & w

Trapeze (1956)—Trapeze work is so graceful, so scary, and so marvellously photogenic that it has always been a source of regret that circus movies generally slight the high flyers and dwell on the seamy side (the sad-faced-clown-loves-the-beautiful-bareback-rider-who-loves-the-strong-man sort of thing). The script of *Trapeze* doesn't have much distinction; the characters aren't likely to be called deep, and their fates seem to be determined by theatrical convenience, but one is, nevertheless, caught up in the excitement. There's vitality in Carol Reed's direction, and an exuberant sweep in Robert Krasker's camera work. Burt Lancaster and Gina Lollobrigida function as stars—they're magnetic. And Tony Curtis shows the beginnings of acting skill (the later *Sweet Smell of Success* showed how much he could learn). While the film is going on, you're too absorbed to consider how banal the story is; after it's over, you've had too good a time to care. Filmed in large part at the Cirque d'Hiver in Paris. United Artists. CinemaScope, color

Trash (1970)—Absurdist porno-comedy about an impotent junkie (Joe Dallesandro) who drags himself around while various women try to arouse him. His sort-of-wife is played by a goofy female impersonator, Holly Woodlawn, whose intensity amidst the general dejection is crazily—and entertainingly—incongruous. The wife's highest aspiration is to get on welfare, and to accomplish this she pretends to be pregnant, but the welfare investigator (Michael Sklar) wants the fabulous-40s shoes that the wife found in a garbage can, and she refuses to give them up. The picture is steeped in a sense of grotesque parody, though most of the time it's as enervated and limp as its hero. The knocked-out couple do their put-on of marriage, and we are invited to laugh at their outcast status and their meaningless lives and to feel sorry for them. This Andy Warhol production was directed by Paul Morrissey, who lingers over needles going into flesh and puts a nimbus around the messiest head of hair. With Jane Forth, as the indolent housewife in the modern apartment that the hero tries to burglarize. color (See *Deeper into Movies*.)

Travels with My Aunt (1972)—Maggie Smith gives a desperate, flustered performance as the disreputable Augusta, a woman in her 70s who induces her stuffy nephew (Alec McCowen) to accompany her on her travels. Whatever private joke Graham Greene was working out in the novel, the message here is "Live, live, live!" But the movie itself has no real zing; it seems to run down before it gets started, and just about everyone in it looks miscast. With Lou Gossett, Jr., Cindy Williams, Robert Stephens, and Robert Flemyng. Directed by George Cukor; written by Jay Presson Allen and Hugh Wheeler; cinematography by Douglas Slocombe. M-G-M. color (See *Reeling*.)

La Traversée de Paris, see *Four Bags Full*

Travolti da un Insolito Destino nell'Azzuro Mare d'Agosto, see *Swept Away by an Unusual Destiny in the Blue Sea of August*

Tre Fratelli, see *Three Brothers*

The Treasure of the Sierra Madre (1948)—One of the strongest of all American movies. Three Americans stranded in Mexico dig for gold and strike it rich—and the writer-director, John Huston, "looks on," as he says, and "lets them stew in their own juice." Bogart is the paranoid tough guy, Fred C. Dobbs; Walter Huston is the toothless, shrewd old prospector; Tim Holt is a blunt, honest young man. With Alfonso Bedoya as a primitive bandit who makes one appreciate civilization, Robert Blake as a Mexican boy, and Bruce Bennett, and the director himself as the victim of Bogart's cadging. From the B. Traven novel; Ted McCord was the cinematographer; Max Steiner wrote the terrible score. The first section (about 20 minutes), set in Tampico, with Bogart getting a haircut and fighting Barton MacLane in a bar, is so sure and lucid it's as good as anything John Huston ever did—maybe even better than *The Maltese Falcon*. But there he sustained the hard, economic style; here, he doesn't. And an episode involving the reading of a letter written by Bruce Bennett's wife is so false and virtuous that it's hard to believe that it's in the same movie as those scenes in Tampico. The picture is emotionally memorable, though—it has a powerful cumulative effect; when it's over you know you've seen something. (It was a box-office failure in 1948; apparently audiences resented Bogart's departure from the immensely popular *Casablanca* stereotype.) Warners. b & w

The Trial (1962)—Orson Welles' theatricality and bravado would seem to be especially unsuited to the matter-of-fact comic horror of the Kafka novel, but he manages some striking effects that aren't at all jarring. This little-seen film has effective passages; it's more than an honorable try, though the hollow sound (that is, of the English-language version) is sometimes off-putting. With Anthony Perkins, Jeanne Moreau, Romy Schneider, Akim Tamiroff, Fernand Ledoux, Elsa Martinelli, Jess Hahn, Suzanne Flon, Madeleine Robinson, Michel Lonsdale, and Welles. Cinematography by Edmond Richard; the pin-screen animation of the prologue is by Alexandre Alexeieff and Claire Parker. Made in Europe. A French-Italian production. b & w

The Trial of Billy Jack (1974)—A maudlin sequel to the 1971 *Billy Jack* which for 2 hours and 50 minutes expands on the most melodramatic elements of the earlier film. Once again, Delores Taylor, who made both pictures with her husband, Tom Laughlin (he plays Billy Jack), is the founder of the Southwestern interracial Freedom School, built on Indian land, which is being harassed by crooked and bigoted townspeople. This time, the Laughlins give the director's credit to their 19-year-old-son Frank, and from the look of this film he may actually have done it, though more likely he assisted his father. An orgy of victimization, the movie tosses together My Lai, Wounded Knee, Kent State, and battered children. The half-breed Billy Jack is also involved in Carlos Castaneda spin-offs; he turns red and blue, walks among serpents, is attacked by bats, and listens to doggerel wisdom supplied by Indian maiden guides. This big Pentecostal tub-thumping show brings together the worst of mass culture and the worst of the counter-culture. Released by Warners. color (See *Reeling.*)

Trial of Joan of Arc *Procès de Jeanne d'Arc* (1962)—Terse, spare, and oddly perfunctory. Robert Bresson's hour-long précis of the trial is based on the historical records but it's directed as unemotionally as if Joan were a philosophy student taking an oral examination for which she's overprepared. (She rattles off her answers.) The actors are not merely non-professionals, they're also non-actors—this is by Bresson's choice. Unexplained: why Bresson sticks to the trial testimony but then introduces melodramatic behind-the-scenes material. (Also unexplained: What's the dog for?) With Florence Carrez; cinematography by L.-H. Burel. In French. b & w

Trick Baby (1973)—Mel Stewart as a black con artist who enjoys shearing the sheep, and Kiel Martin as his partner, the Trick Baby—the child of a black whore and her white trick. He can pass for white but *chooses* to be black. (Both blacks and whites should be able to enjoy the joke when a rich white woman, taking him for white, is astounded by his sexual prowess.) But, for the racial-switch-hitter premise of the picture to be effective, he needs to have some recognizable "soul," which we in the audience can perceive, even if the whites in the movie are blind to it, and Kiel Martin, with his dimply, spoiled-baby face, doesn't have it. Shot in Philadelphia, the film strikes some fresh sparks; Mel Stewart gives his role the black equivalent of old-world grace, and the first half is entertaining. Then, disappointingly, he's killed, and the picture shifts from comedy to melodrama. The director, Larry Yust, has a good feel for street life, but he's weak in his handling of the actresses, both black and white, who are unnecessarily degraded. From the novel by Iceberg Slim—Robert Beck, the black pimp turned writer. Universal. color (See *Reeling.*)

The Trip (1967)—Exploitation, late 6os style. Roger Corman takes his hero, Peter Fonda (playing a TV-commercials director who lives in Los Angeles), on an extended LSD trip, during which he is reborn. (He may not look any different to you.) Fonda's hallucinations provide Corman with the chance to imitate several styles of filmmaking, and to introduce what appear to be brief clips from his own horror movies. With Dennis Hopper, Susan Strasberg, and Bruce Dern. Written by Jack Nicholson. A.I.P. color

The Trip to Bountiful (1985)—Geraldine Page gives a controlled, all-out performance as Carrie Watts, an old-age pensioner who wears seat-sprung housedresses and lives in a tiny apartment in Houston with her sad, defeated son and his shrill wife, who keeps picking on her. The movie—a weeper—is about Carrie's longing to escape and return to Bountiful, the Gulf Coast town where she grew up; she runs away, gets on a bus headed in the right direction, and lives out her dream. Directed by Peter Masterson, from Horton Foote's adaptation of his 1953 teleplay (Lillian Gish starred in it on TV and Broadway), it's a "spiritual" picture—a tribute to the decency of the common people who endure by doing the best they can, and it has the glow that movies get when they're about the need to have compassion. The camera is meant to be the mirror of Carrie's soul, but we look in that mirror for so long that finally all we see is Geraldine Page acting. Foote can't make poetry out of material as laundered and denatured as what he comes up with here. The movie is intended to be a hymn, but all he and Masterson can do is give some of the characters a limp, anesthetized grace. With John Heard as the son, Carlin Glynn as the daughter-in-law, Rebecca De Mornay as a soldier's young wife, and Richard Bradford as a Texas sheriff. Cinematography by Fred Murphy. Academy Award for Best Actress (Page). Released by Island Pictures. color (See *Hooked*.)

Triple Echo (1972)—Grim (but absurd) pastoral tragedy—isolated Wiltshire farm in the 40s, ailing dog, lonely woman (Glenda Jackson), and an AWOL soldier (Brian Deacon). He becomes her lover and she protects him by dressing him as a woman and passing him off as her sister. The gimmick is he begins to dig it. Unfortunately the movie is not played for comedy; it's lugubriously stark, except for Oliver Reed (gross, yet funny) as a no-neck bullying brute of a sergeant, who takes a fancy to sister. The soldier idiotically agrees to be Reed's date for the Christmas ball at the barracks, and when Reed tries to deflower him, the tragedy winds up fast. Sister-soldier has used a shotgun to put the old dog out of its misery, so when he has been exposed and is being horribly beaten, the woman uses the shotgun on him. Everyone is put out of his misery but the audience. It's a very weird picture; spiky-thin Glenda Jackson, who speaks as if she were biting on a bullet, is so masculine here that she gives it an extra dimension of sexual ambiguity. (When you see the shy soldier in frilly clothes and padded breasts, you wonder whom he's imitating.) Michael Apted directed; from an H. E. Bates novel, adapted by Robin Chapman. Cinematography by John Coquillon. color (See *Reeling*.)

Trog (1970)—Joan Crawford plays Stella Dallas with an ape instead of a baby girl. Some actors will do anything to be in movies: she probably would have played the ape. An English horror film, directed by Freddie Francis, from a script by Aben Kandel. With Michael Gough and Bernard Kay. Released by Warners. color

The Trojan Women (1971)—The Euripides play is the greatest lament for the loss of freedom ever written; it is not just the first but the one great anti-war play, and, despite the makeshift style of the film, the material catches you by the throat, and by the most legitimate of all means—its simplicity and its intensity. Katharine Hepburn, always forthright, starts as a fine, tough Hecuba, plainspoken and direct; she's splendid when she's angry. (Later, she comes to seem pitiful and mummified.) A false nose gives Geneviève Bujold's mad seeress Cassandra a classical look, and the actress plays with a bursting conviction; though the performance doesn't fully come off, she makes a stunning try. As Andromache—as anything—Vanessa Redgrave never does the expected. Her Andromache is being freshly thought out as you watch—a dazed, pale-golden matron, unflirtatious, free from guile. A tiny half-sob gurgles from her throat. Redgrave gives the finest performance in the film, and the director, Michael Cacoyannis, demonstrates his love of the material and his right to film it, in casting her as Andromache, and not in the obvious role for her—Helen. Because it is Irene Papas as a demonic Helen of Troy who lifts the movie out of the women's-college virtuous cultural ambiance that plagues stage productions. Helen is introduced prowling behind the slats of the stockade that protects her, and all you see are her brownblack eyes, as fiercely alive as a wolf's. While the other women mourn their dead, Helen uses all her animal cunning to survive. This is a cast that one could never hope to see on the stage. Released by Cinerama. color (See *Deeper into Movies*.)

Trollflöjten, see *The Magic Flute*

Tropic of Cancer (1970)—A trivial but entertaining sex comedy derived from the Henry Miller novel about expatriates in Paris. This series of vignettes and fantasies, with bits of Miller's language rolling out, may be closer to Russ Meyer's *The Immoral Mr. Teas* than to its source, but at least it isn't fusty. It makes you laugh. With Rip Torn, and Ellen Burstyn, James Callahan, David Bauer, Magali Noel, and Ginette Leclerc. There's a glimpse of Henry Miller standing in front of a church. Directed by Joseph Strick; written by Strick and Betty Botley. (The story is up-

dated.) Released by Paramount. color (See *Deeper into Movies*.)

Trouble in Mind (1985)—Written and directed by the gifted high-flyer Alan Rudolph at his most art-conscious, this is a reworking of what he did much better in *Choose Me*. The mixed-up lovers have been replaced by mixed-up gangsters, and what was comic and lyrical is now fatalistic. He's got the *film-noir* bug, and the picture is a pile of poetic mush set in some doom-laden, vaguely universal city of the past and/or the future. (It was shot mostly in Seattle.) As Hawk, Kris Kristofferson is supposed to be the gallant Bogart hero living in an evil semi-fascist era. Joe Morton is a bitter, ironic crook called Solo who recites verses; Keith Carradine is a greedy young hood named Coop, who appears in a series of ever more gross and gooey pompadours— punk-fop styles, with matching cosmetic jobs and earrings; and the actor known as Divine plays Hilly Blue, an epicene gangster who's made up to look like a plump plucked chicken. Geneviève Bujold is Hawk's old flame Wanda, who runs the café where the gangsters plan their heists, and Lori Singer is Georgia, the country girl whom Coop brings into this moody stew. Rudolph probably aimed to create a glamorous, funky trance-world, but his control fails him; the scenes often start with a shimmer that makes you feel hopeful, but they become stagnant, and you have no way of knowing how to interpret the flossy hipster-philosopher babble that the characters speak. With John Considine (who's rather funny), Antonia Dauphin, George Kirby, and, in a bit, Allan Nicholls. The lushly beautiful cinematography is by Toyomichi Kurita; the score is by Mark Isham, with songs performed by Marianne Faithfull. color (See *Hooked*.)

Trouble in Paradise (1932)—Perhaps the most shimmering of the romantic comedy collaborations of the director Ernst Lubitsch and the writer Samson Raphaelson, this film is a make-believe world of the 30s preserved intact. Herbert Marshall is so adept at the silky tricks written into his lines that he creates a hushed atmosphere. He plays a career jewel thief and, as his partner, Miriam Hopkins, quick and darting, always has her feelers out, along with her kittenish claws. These two are accomplished seducers, and in this movie witty seduction is indistinguishable from love itself. Kay Francis is the wealthy widow whose face takes on a yearning expression once she sees Marshall; desire makes her warm and languid. The movie is full of suave maneuvers and magical switcheroos; in its light-as-a-feather way, it's perfection. With Charles Ruggles, Edward Everett Horton, C. Aubrey Smith, Robert Greig, Leonid Kinskey, Luis Alberni, Nella Walker, and Tyler Brooke as the singing Venetian garbageman. Remotely based on a Hungarian play by Aladar Laszlo. Paramount. b & w

The Truck *Le Camion* (1977)—Marguerite Duras's control of film technique here suggests that she has become a master. But there's a joker in her mastery: though her moods and cadences and her rhythmic phrasing, with its emotional undertow, might seem ideally suited to the medium, they don't fulfill moviegoers' expectations. There are only two people in this film: Duras herself and Gérard Depardieu, and they sit at a round table in a room in her home, and never leave it. Serene, half-smiling, she reads aloud the script of a film in which Depardieu would act the role of a truck driver who picks up a woman hitchhiker. The film alternates between sequences in the room and sequences of a rolling truck, seen always at a distance. Each time Duras cuts from the room to the truck, we're drawn into the hypnotic flow of the road imagery—we half-dream our way

into a "real" movie—and each time she pulls us back into the room we feel an emotional wrench, a rude awakening. Duras makes us aware of our mechanisms of response, and it's tonic and funny to feel the tensions she provokes. Her picture has been thought out with such supple discrimination between the values of sound and image that you could almost say it's *perfectly* made—an ornery, glimmering achievement. Cinematography by Bruno Nuytten. In French. color (See *When the Lights Go Down*.)

True Believer (1989)—A nifty thriller—fast and tense—about a Manhattan lawyer (James Woods) who was a hero of the counterculture but is now defending drug dealers and getting paid in cash. When he's goaded by his new law associate (Robert Downey, Jr.) into taking on a murder case, his eyes widen at the bare possibility that the man he's defending might be innocent. The movie makes us share the lawyer's energy and charge as he investigates the crime. He doesn't want to sleep: he lives off the excitement of having a cause. It's a pick-me-up of a movie. Nothing great, nothing terribly distinctive, but the aliveness of the texture can quicken your senses and keep you fascinated. Directed by Joseph Ruben (*Dreamspace*, *The Stepfather*), from a script by Wesley Strick. With Yuji Okumoto, Margaret Colin, Kurtwood Smith, Tom Bower, Luis Guzman, and Miguel Fernandes. The cinematography, by John W. Lindley, has a tabloid harshness, and the editing, by George Bowers, doesn't let you feel you're ahead of the story. (The interiors were shot in San Francisco and Oakland.) Columbia. color (See *Movie Love*.)

True Confession (1937)—It rarely turns up, though it's one of the most affable of Carole Lombard's screwball comedies. She plays an extravagant, compulsive liar—a young wife whose confession to a murder fools even her prim lawyer-husband (Fred MacMurray). John Barrymore, who had brought out Lombard's slapstick talent in *Twentieth Century*, plays an eccentric, tippling criminologist and swipes the picture; "She'll fry," he chuckles to himself during her trial. The characters of the husband and wife are too simplified and their comic turns too forced, but the general giddiness and Barrymore keep the picture going. The director, Wesley Ruggles, was one of the original Keystone Cops; Claude Binyon adapted the play by Louis Verneuil and Georges Berr; cinematography by Ted Tetzlaff. With Una Merkel, Edgar Kennedy, Lynne Overman, Porter Hall, and Fritz Feld. Paramount. b & w

True Confessions (1981)—The idea is to take the lovable Irish brothers of 30s movies—the cop and the priest—and turn them inside out. Robert Duvall plays an L.A. police detective who finds evidence linking his brother (Robert De Niro), a monsignor who is chancellor of the Los Angeles archdiocese, to corrupt business deals and, indirectly, to the murder of a hooker. Repelled by the hypocrisy, the detective brings his brother down. But the movie is in a stupor; everything is internalized. Duvall is locked in, and De Niro is in his chameleon trance—he seems flaccid, preoccupied. The director, Ulu Grosbard, dulls out the material, and the writers—John Gregory Dunne, who wrote the 1977 novel that the film is based on, and his wife, Joan Didion, who collaborated with him on the script—carry their hardboiled detective fiction to a virtually abstract level. You have to put up a struggle to get anything out of this picture. What we need to know—what the movie is supposed to be about—is what the brothers are mulling over on their silent, troubled walks alone and together (and still alone). With Kenneth McMillan, who gives the only performance with any juice in it, and Charles Durning, Ed Flanders, Burgess Mer-

edith, Cyril Cusack, Rose Gregorio, Jeanette Nolan, and Louisa Moritz. Produced by Robert Chartoff and Irwin Winkler, for United Artists. color (See *Taking It All In*.)

True Heart Susie (1919)—A lovely, simple pastoral romance—one of the most charming of all D. W. Griffith films. Close to perfection, on a small scale. Lillian Gish is Susie, Robert Harron is William, and Clarine Seymour is Bettina, William's pleasure-loving bride, who sneaks out to a party and can't get back into her house. Scott Fitzgerald must have seen this film before he wrote "Babylon Revisited." Silent. b & w

True Stories (1986)—This first feature directed by David Byrne, of Talking Heads, is laid out like a musical-comedy documentary about a town, except that the town—Virgil, Texas—is imaginary. Byrne, the narrator and observer, introduces us to the townspeople, who are about to take part in the pageantry of the Texas Sesquicentennial with their own "Celebration of Specialness." Byrne is looking for a true mythic image of America; Virgil is Our Town, it's Anytown, U.S.A., and the movie is about banality and eccentricity and consumerism—it's about the manners and mores of the shopping mall, where fashion shows are staged and miming contests are held to see who is best at lip-synching to records. In his polite, formal, and slightly ghostly matter-of-fact way, Byrne is trying for something large scale: a postmodern *Nashville*. Byrne sets up the material for satirical sequences, yet he doesn't give it a subversive spin. His unacknowledged satire is like a soufflé that was never meant to rise. But, working with the crack cinematographer Ed Lachman, Byrne shows a respect for pared-down plainness, and after a rather shaky opening the characters themselves begin to engage us—especially John Goodman as the big, friendly bachelor with a "Wife Wanted" sign on his lawn, who gets to sing the film's anthem, "People Like Us." Jo Harvey Allen is terrific as a crackpot liar, and Tito Larriva's high-speed dancing has a comic dazzle. Singing "Papa Legba," Roebuck (Pops) Staples has a juicy richness about him; when he's onscreen a viewer can be completely happy. Also with Swoosie Kurtz, Spalding Gray, Annie McEnroe, and Alix Elias. The nine songs by Byrne are conceived as rock or country, Tex-Mex or gospel, depending on which character sings them. The Heads provide the instrumental work, and can be heard now and then on the words; it's their voices that the lip-synchers weave and sway to. The script is by Byrne, Beth Henley, and Stephen Tobolowsky. An Edward R. Pressman Production, released by Warners. color (See *Hooked*.)

The Truth About Women (1957)—This English comedy was directed by Muriel Box, who also wrote it, with Sydney Box; it wobbles in both departments. You may long to sit back and look at many of your favorite actors and actresses, sumptuously costumed by Cecil Beaton, as they act out a series of anecdotes about ladies and love, but the picture is deadly. With Julie Harris, Diane Cilento, Mai Zetterling, Eva Gabor, Catherine Boyl, Jackie Lane, Elina Labourdette, and Ambrosine Philpotts (as the mother in *Room at the Top* she delivered a remark that she is peculiarly fitted to deliver: "Where do some of these people get their names?"), and Laurence Harvey, Christopher Lee, Roland Culver, Marius Goring, Wilfrid Hyde-White, Michael Denison, Derek Farr, Griffith Jones, and the irreplaceable Ernest Thesiger. It's amazing that with all those talented people nothing happens on the screen. Cinematography by Otto Heller. color

Tudor Rose, see *Nine Days a Queen*

Tunes of Glory (1960)—An English film starring Alec Guinness and John Mills as two colonels in a peacetime Scottish regiment who are out to destroy each other. There are times when the two virtuoso performances are completely overpowered by the clumsy staging, but the acting and the unusual theme help to compensate for the muddy exposition and mediocre film techniques. It's an ugly-looking movie, though. Ronald Neame directed, from James Kennaway's script, based on his own novel. With Susannah York, Kay Walsh, Dennis Price, Gordon Jackson, Duncan Macrae, and John Fraser. color

The Turning Point (1977)—This is a 40s women's picture (like *Old Acquaintance*, in which a noble Bette Davis and a catty Miriam Hopkins played scrapping lifelong friends) transferred to a backstage-ballet milieu, with Anne Bancroft as a gallant, aging ballerina and Shirley MacLaine as her friend and rival, who quit to raise a family. The script is by Arthur Laurents, who writes sodden expository dialogue in which these two are forever revealing truths to each other. We get a glimpse of something great in the movie— Mikhail Baryshnikov dancing—and these two harpies out of the soaps block the view. In his screen acting début, Baryshnikov plays a Russian dancer with whom MacLaine's young aspiring-ballerina daughter (Leslie Browne) falls in love; this swoony romance helped to make the film a box-office hit. Herbert Ross directed, unexcitingly; there's no visual sweep, no lift. The effort here is to domesticate ballet—to remove the taint of European decadence; most of the characters are so heartland ordinary that they disinfect one's imagination. With Tom Skerritt, Alexandra Danilova, Anthony Zerbe, Martha Scott, Lisa Lucas, Phillip Saunders, James Mitchell, Marshall Thompson, Daniel Levans, Starr Danias, and Suzanne Farrell,

Peter Martins, Antoinette Sibley, Marcia Haydée, Richard Cragun, Lucette Aldous, Martine Van Hamel, and other dancers. Nora Kaye was the executive producer; Robert Surtees was the cinematographer. 20th Century-Fox. color (See *When the Lights Go Down.*)

Turtle Diary (1986)—Glenda Jackson and Ben Kingsley play the two Londoners who separately develop the fantasy of liberating the three giant turtles from the Aquarium at the London Zoo and taking them back to the sea. John Irvin directed this low-key, fastidious version of the 1975 Russell Hoban novel (a counterculture fable), from a script by Harold Pinter. It's like a *Brief Encounter* between turtles; the two strangers come out of their shells a bit, but not with each other. Jackson and Kingsley give their lines an especially tight-lipped, staccato reading; these two are so private and tense and minimalist that it's amusing to see how they vary their performances enough to keep going. They manage to give the middle of the movie—the weekend drive to the coast with the turtles—a balmy comic spirit of adventure. But the picture verges on the deliberately quaint, and the story has been given the same maudlin orchestration as in the novel; it's full of sad and lonely people reaching out. The awful artfulness of this stuff! With Michael Gambon, Jeroen Krabbé, Harriet Walter, Richard Johnson, Rosemary Leach, Eleanor Bron, and Pinter, in a bit in a bookstore. Cinematography by Peter Hannan. Released by the Samuel Goldwyn Company. color (See *Hooked.*)

Tutto a Posto e Niente in Ordine, see *All Screwed Up*

Twelfth Night (1956)—The Russians sometimes bring an epic sweep to Shakespeare's tragedies, but the comedies don't fare too well. This attempt, in color, to capture the charm and delight of Shakespeare's Illyria gets heavily frolicsome, and the whole crew of dukes, clowns, and countesses who are entangled in his folly of mistaken sex and identity look a little overweight. The picture isn't terrible, just very literal-minded. Klara Luchko plays Viola-Cesario; Yakov Fried directed. In Russian.

Twelve Angry Men (1957)—This ingenious melodrama set in a jury room generates more suspense than most thrillers; the battle begins with the jury 11 to 1, and the spectator is keyed to watch for those points in the heat and frustration of argument when each juror will begin to seek the truth. Both Reginald Rose's script (a reworking of his teleplay) and Sidney Lumet's direction are so sure-fire that the movie has the crackle of a hit; it was, however, a commercial failure. The social psychology of the film is attuned to the educated audience. The hero, Henry Fonda, the 1 against the 11, is its hero—a liberal, fairminded architect. And the victim is its dream victim: he is a slum product who never had a chance; he's a member of some unspecified minority; and to clinch the case, his father didn't love him. The 11 are a cunningly selected cross-section of humanity. With Lee J. Cobb, Jack Warden, E. G. Marshall, Ed Begley, Martin Balsam, Jack Klugman, Robert Webber, George Voskovec, Edward Binns, John Fiedler, and Joseph Sweeney. Cinematography by Boris Kaufman. United Artists. b & w

The Twelve Chairs (1970)—Mel Brooks, who wrote and directed this comedy-fable, has given himself only a small role at the beginning, and the picture never quite recovers from the loss of him. The plot, which is about three men hunting for a fortune stuffed into one of 12 chairs, is set in prerevolutionary Russia. This gives Brooks an opportunity to show his affection for the innocent nuttiness of earlier periods—such as burlesque and the mad Russian accents of early radio—but, gifted as he is, he still doesn't go beyond gag comedy. The exteriors, which were shot in Yugoslavia, have a sprightly, picturesque Grandma Moses atmosphere; the whole enterprise is a little forlorn, though. Not bad, really—just so-so. The three leads are Ron Moody, who has a great moment toward the end clutching a piece of chair; Dom DeLuise; and Frank Langella, who comes across as supercilious in the witlessly written role of the handsome juvenile. Based on the same Ilf and Petrov novel as the 1945 Fred Allen picture *It's in the Bag*. Produced by Michael Hertzberg. color (See *Deeper into Movies*.)

Twentieth Century (1934)—A first-rate hardboiled farce about theatrical personalities. John Barrymore was a great farceur, and his performance as the egomaniac producer Oscar Jaffe is a roaring caricature of theatrical drive and temperament. It was Carole Lombard's performance as Jaffe's protegée, Lily Garland (née Mildred Plotka), who has become a movie star, that established her as a comedienne. Lombard's talents here are not of the highest, but her spirits are, and in her skin-tight satins she incarnates the giddy glamour of 30s comedy. Most of the action takes place on the crack train of the title—the Twentieth Century, going from Chicago to New York—which represented the latest thing in speed and luxury. The script, by Hecht and MacArthur from their play (which was a reworking of Bruce Millholland's play *Napoleon on Broadway*), is freely, carelessly irreverent, with affectionate, corny ethnic humor and wisecracks about religion. Howard Hawks directed in a fast, entertaining style—punching up the lines; it's the style he later perfected in *His Girl Friday* (from Hecht and MacArthur's *The Front Page*). With Ralph Forbes, and a batch of character actors whose faces were once as familiar to audiences as the faces with great names: Walter Connolly, Roscoe Karns, Charles Levison, Etienne Girardot, Edgar Kennedy, Edward Gargan, and Herman Bing. (The material was recycled in the 1978 Broadway musical *On the Twentieth Century*.) Columbia. b & w

20,000 Years in Sing Sing (1933)—Spencer Tracy as a wise-guy hood, and Bette Davis as his vulnerable, sweet-tough moll. This Warners mixture of social reform, comedy, and sentimentality was very loosely based on a book by Warden Lewis E. Lawes; the plot creaks, but the director, Michael Curtiz, keeps things moving. The cast includes Lyle Talbot, Louis Calhern, Arthur Byron, and Warren Hymer as Hype. b & w

Twice in a Lifetime (1985)—This miracle of psychobanality presents the basic story of a long-married middle-aged man (Gene Hackman, as a Seattle steelworker) who experiences a renewal of vitality when he has an affair with a younger woman (Ann-Margret), but the story is now so dressed up in the language of self-help books that the man is a life-affirming force—and not only for himself but also for his wife of 30 years (Ellen Burstyn), whom he leaves. The movie could be every errant husband's self-justifying fantasy. (And the way Burstyn overacts, a man would have to be a saint to have stayed with her so long.) Directed by Bud Yorkin, from a script by Colin Welland, the picture is like a sermon on the therapeutic value of adultery, divorce, and remarriage, given by a minister who learned all he knows from watching TV. As Hackman's intensely angry daughter, Amy Madigan brings a spark of fierceness to her performance, and a comic flair. Also with Brian Dennehy, Ally Sheedy, Stephen Lang, and Darrell Larson. Bud Yorkin Productions. color (See *Hooked*.)

Twilight Zone—The Movie (1983)—Four young directors—John Landis, Steven Spielberg, Joe Dante, and the Australian George Miller (who made *The Road Warrior*)—pay homage to the Rod Serling TV series "Twilight Zone." It's disappointing that they didn't attempt to engineer more modern and artful macabre games than the ones on the old shows; what they've given us is an overproduced remake, but with some redeeming elements. The prologue, written and directed by John Landis, and featuring Dan Aykroyd as a hitchhiker and Albert Brooks as a driver, is a beauty, but the happy rush of fright we get from it has to sustain us for a long stretch, because the first two episodes are embarrassments. The first (by Landis) is a painfully blunt sermon on the evils of racism and prejudice, starring Vic Morrow, who, along with two Vietnamese-American children, was killed in a helicopter accident during the filming; it's like an unconscious parody of the old shows, and its straightness is a deadweight on the viewer's head. The second, a lump of ironclad whimsey directed by Spielberg, is about how a group of people in a home for the aged have their minds magically refreshed; it's coy and twinkling, with gloppy rich music—it's horribly slick. The third, directed by Joe Dante, is a risky attempt at using a style derived from animated cartoons for an insidious, expressionist effect; it has an insane atmosphere—it's eccentric and unsettling, with startling good things in it. (Among them is the alert, graceful Kathleen Quinlan as a strong-willed schoolteacher.) The subject—how horrible life might be if a 10-year-old boy (Jeremy Licht) could run everything just as he liked, on the basis of what he has learned from TV—may be too fertile for the half-hour form. There are also too many different kinds of spookiness and parody buzzing around in the material. For those people in the audience whose childhood included a TV set that was always going, this half hour may reawaken all sorts of childhood feelings. But even for them it's probably better when they think it over than when they're watching it. The fourth episode, directed by Miller, from a script by Richard Matheson, is the best reason to see the movie; it's a classic shocker of the short form. Almost all the action takes place in the confines of an airliner during a storm, where a passenger, played by John Lithgow, is seated, squirming and thrashing about, sick with fear. The whole episode is about this one passenger's freaking out. Miller builds the kind of immediacy and intensity that the high points of *Jaws* had. The images rush at you; they're fast and energizing. And Lithgow does something that's tough for an actor to do: he shows fear without parodying it and yet makes it horrifyingly funny. With his white face all scrunched up, and anxiety burning out his brain, he takes us with him every step of the way, from simple fear to dementia to stupor. This episode is a comic orgy of terror. Warners. color (See *State of the Art*.)

Twilight's Last Gleaming (1977)—A suspense melodrama, set in 1981, about a U.S. Air Force general (Burt Lancaster) who, because of his anti–Vietnam war attitudes, is framed on a murder charge and sent to prison. He breaks out, takes control of a nuclear-missile site, and threatens to send out nine missiles and start a nuclear war if the President (Charles Durning) and the Joint Chiefs don't make public disclosure of the secret goals of the war. The action built up in the first hour has some urgency, but when the director, Robert Aldrich, gets to the serious message part—when the President and his advisers discuss the general's demands—it falls apart, and drags on and on. The screenplay by Ronald M. Cohen and Edward Huebsch is a mixture of tacky cynicism and political naïveté—it suggests an overextended episode of a TV series, and the attempts at wit are pathetically gross. With Paul Winfield, Richard Widmark, Burt Young, Melvyn Douglas, Roscoe Lee Browne, Joseph Cotten, William Marshall, and Richard Jaeckel. Released by Allied Artists. color

Two Cents Worth of Hope *Due Soldi di Speranza* (1952)—Love laughs in the face of disaster in Renato Castellani's neo-realist account of the abysmally poor on the slopes of Vesuvius. The hero comes back from army service to a series of frustrations—his sisters are hungry, his mother is a thieving busybody, he can't hold a job, and his overenthusiastic tigress of a girl causes no end of trouble. He works as a chauffeur and as a sexton, he sells lemonade, he sells his blood. When he marries his girl they have literally nothing but 2¢ worth of hope, yet it seems more than enough to live on . Castellani, who wrote the script with Titina de Filippo, is said to have been told the story by Vincenzo Musolino, who plays the hero, and most of the roles are played by nonprofessionals from the lice-ridden area that the movie was shot in. Surprisingly it has a picaresque charm—the lives here have gone past tragedy into black comedy. Some of the episodes, including one set in a shabby Naples movie theatre, have a believable everyday craziness about them. With Maria Fiore as the tigress. In Italian. b & w

Two Daughters *Teen Kanya* (1961)—Originally the film had three stories and was called *Three Daughters*. Satyajit Ray at his most splendid in two short-story films based on works by Rabindranath Tagore. The first, "The Postmaster"—a story of betrayal—is a pure and simple small masterpiece; the second, "The Conclusion," has some memorable scenes, beauty, and wit but also has some

defects of rhythm, so it is merely wonderful—and a little wearying. In Bengali. b & w

Two English Girls *Les Deux Anglaises et le continent* (1972)—François Truffaut tries for gaiety and gentleness and charm in this adaptation of the only other novel by Henri-Pierre Roché, the author of *Jules and Jim*, but everything is muffled, almost repressed. The story is about the messed-up lives of two English sisters who love the same man—a Frenchman (Jean-Pierre Léaud, badly miscast). The picture is uncomfortable and, when it's over, unresolved yet emotionally affecting. A bewilderingly sad movie. With Kika Markham as Anne, the emerging independent bohemian, and Stacey Tendeter as Muriel, the rigidly—exhaustingly—high-principled virgin, and Philippe Léotard and Sylvia Marriott. Script by Truffaut and Jean Gruault; cinematography by Nestor Almendros; music by Georges Delerue (who appears as the Frenchman's business agent). In French. color (See *Reeling*.)

Two for the Road (1967)—Other films by the director, Stanley Donen, are not so edgy. It's the self-consciously witty English scriptwriter, Frederic Raphael, who set his brittle stamp on this story of a husband and wife—Albert Finney and Audrey Hepburn—seen on European trips at different periods of their lives, not consecutively but shifting back and forth. The intention is to show a modern marriage in which ideal people, in love, and successful, are still not happy. Yet there's always a swimming pool for the characters to take their pratfalls in. Raphael is too much in love with old-movie comedy romances: he puts in tedious running jokes, such as the wife's forever turning up with the passport the husband loses. And at the same time the film is trying for a bitter comment on modern marital ennui, of the *La Notte* variety. The facile, comic bits set off audience expectations that are then betrayed, and the clever, bitter stuff just seems sour. Still, at times Hepburn is surpassingly beautiful—particularly at the end, when she's meant to be roughly the age she actually is, and her hard, lacquered mini-face is set off by a shining-disk gown. As the husband, Finney seems surly and beefy and rather infantile—which makes Hepburn look all the more gallant and poignant when the wife tries to make the best of things. The caricatures of Americans, played by William Daniels and Eleanor Bron, which would be embarrassingly overdone at 50 yards, are in closeup. With Jacqueline Bisset, Claude Dauphin, and Nadia Gray. Cinematography by Christopher Challis. 20th Century-Fox. color

The Two Jakes (1990)—Directed by and starring Jack Nicholson, this sequel to *Chinatown* (1974) begins absorbingly, with hard-edged dialogue and muffled echoes of the earlier film. Nicholson's Jake Gittes, the private detective specializing in divorce, takes on a client, Jake Berman (Harvey Keitel), a budding real-estate developer, and finds himself caught up in a murder case that somehow involves Katherine Mulwray, the daughter of Evelyn Mulwray, the Faye Dunaway character he loved in *Chinatown*. But when we've got the setup clear in our heads and expect the movie to rouse itself, to develop a present tense and get going, it remains airless and murky. It proceeds phlegmatically, bringing in more and more characters and complications, and losing us. We don't get the *film-noir* thrill of mystery and resolution. By the time the plot comes together (more or less), we're benumbed. As the director, Nicholson doesn't give the characters any snap and he doesn't build the scenes; it's as if he were scratching his head each time the camera got turned on. As Gittes he wears a bitter half-smile and gives a groggy performance. It's a spiritless movie, dark and mannered. There

are good people in the cast—Meg Tilly, Madeleine Stowe, Rubén Blades, Frederic Forrest, Eli Wallach, David Keith, Joe Mantell, Richard Farnsworth—but they're emotionally distanced from us, and they don't seem to matter. The script (though not the narration) is mostly by Robert Towne; the cinematography is by Vilmos Zsigmond. Paramount. color

Two Men and a Wardrobe *Dwaj Ludzie z Szafa* (1958)—Roman Polanski's 15-minute fable about nonconformity, made when he was still a student at the Lodz film school. At the start two men emerge from the sea with a wardrobe. It's a huge wardrobe; it won't fit in anywhere, and the men won't relinquish it. They try to do the ordinary things that men do in a city—eat, travel about, find lodgings—and they are mistreated, kicked, and beaten. They carry their wardrobe back into the sea. This is the sort of screen comedy Kafka might have written. The feeling is both fantastic and logical, and the film is rounded—it's complete, in a classic way. b & w

Two People (1973)—Peter Fonda and Lindsay Wagner are lovers who meet in Marrakesh and take the train to Casablanca. He's an American who deserted in Vietnam and has finally decided to go home and serve his prison sentence; she's a successful model. The picture is meant to be a sensitive modern romance and the director, Robert Wise, tries to simulate spontaneity and improvisation and a documentary surface. But it's all dead smooth—impersonal, inexpressive, and without interest, except for the handsome travelogue footage of Morocco shot by Henri Decaë. Though Fonda's acting is well-controlled here, he doesn't have a core of tension; something in him is still asleep and perhaps always will be—he's the Richard Carlson or David Manners of the 70s. With

Estelle Parsons, Frances Sternhagen, Geoffrey Horne, and Alan Fudge. From a painstaking, lethally bland script by Richard De Roy. Universal. color (See *Reeling*.)

Two Rode Together (1961)—A disorienting cynical, tragicomic Western by John Ford, in which the hero, played by James Stewart, is a mercenary sheriff. This sheriff and an Army officer (Richard Widmark) go off to rescue some white captives of the Comanches; the captives, it turns out, might be better off left where they are. From a script by Frank Nugent, based on Will Cook's novel *Comanche Captives*, this reworking of some of the themes of *The Searchers* doesn't engage the audience. With Shirley Jones, Linda Cristal, Anna Lee, Andy Devine, Jeanette Nolan, Woody Strode, and Ted Knight. Columbia. color

2001: A Space Odyssey (1968)—Stanley Kubrick's slow, precise yet dreamy sci-fi epic. The ponderous, blurry appeal of the picture may be in its mystical vision of a graceful world of space, controlled by superior, godlike minds, where the hero (Keir Dullea) is reborn as an angelic baby. It says that man is just a tiny nothing on the stairway to paradise; something better (i.e., non-human) is coming, and it's all out of your hands anyway. Kubrick's story line—which accounts for evolution by an extraterrestrial intelligence—is probably the most gloriously redundant plot of all time. The sulky, peevish voice of Hal, the computer—the only amusing character, he suggests a rejected homosexual lover—was supplied by Douglas Rain; the soft-spoken cast includes Gary Lockwood, Margaret Tyzack, and Leonard Rossiter. The script is by Kubrick and Arthur C. Clarke; the chief cinematographer was Geoffrey Unsworth, with additional work by John Alcott. M-G-M. color

Two Weeks in Another Town (1962)—The producer, John Houseman; the director, Vincente Minnelli; the screenwriter, Charles Schnee; the composer, David Raksin; and the star, Kirk Douglas, had all worked together 10 years before on *The Bad and the Beautiful*, a flashy hit movie about Hollywood moviemaking. This time they give us an oversophisticated, overheated view of Hollywood has-beens gathered in Rome, trying to make a comeback. Gnashing his teeth and twitching, Kirk Douglas plays a self-destructive former star who cracked up and was institutionalized for three years; Cyd Charisse (spangled by Pierre Balmain) is his nymphomaniac ex-wife; Edward G. Robinson is the cynical famous director he used to work with—now the director is down on *his* luck, too. All the characters are seen at a time of extreme strain and extravagant disorder. They drive maniacally and do mean things to each other; they also take part in orgies designed to outdo *La Dolce Vita*. And at one point they run excerpts from *The Bad and the Beautiful*, which is discussed as a model of creative moviemaking; the scenes show Lana Turner having hysterics and her performance is described—with awe—as an example of great screen acting. Hysteria is predominant in *Two Weeks*, and it takes a peculiarly pictorial form—the stylized compositions, the sumptuous gorgeousness, the decorator delights run away with the movie. The dialogue has its own foolish swank: on a beach where, presumably, people speak the truth, the young "fresh" heroine (Daliah Lavi) asks Douglas what he was like when he was a star. "Lonely," he answers. "So famous and alone?" she queries. He replies, "Everybody's alone. Actors more so." And she asks, "Why would anyone want to be an actor?" Douglas responds with a straight face, "That's a good question. To hide from the world. What's the audience doing there but hiding . . . trading their problems for mine on the screen." And how do we know that this girl is really as sweet and sympathetic as she looks? When Douglas kisses her, she touches the scar on his face, thus demonstrating that it is the hurt man rather than the famous man that she cares about. In the circumstances, Douglas and Robinson do surprisingly good work. With George Hamilton as a sulky new star, and Claire Trevor, James Gregory, Rosanna Schiaffino, Erich von Stroheim, Jr., George Macready, and Leslie Uggams as a chanteuse. The picture was an almost total box-office failure. Adapted from the novel by Irwin Shaw. Cinematography by Milton Krasner. M-G-M. CinemaScope, color

Two Women *La Ciociara* (1960)—There isn't much conviction in this movie. It's a commercial, warmed-over Vittorio De Sica–Cesare Zavattini collaboration, but probably more people went to see it than ever went to see their finest films—*Shoeshine, Miracle in Milan*, or *Umberto D.*—or even their most famous one, *The Bicycle Thief*. The chief attraction here is Sophia Loren, deglamourized, playing an Anna Magnani role—a woman in wartime who can't save herself or her daughter from rape. There's nothing to mark the picture as a work by De Sica, except perhaps that this man so gifted at calling up great performances from nonprofessionals has worked his magic and *almost* made Loren appear to be a great professional. The film scholar Mira Liehm has suggested that "the film became what *Bicycle Thief* might have become if Cary Grant had played the role of the unemployed Roman worker." The Nazis, the Russians, and the Moors all seem to be planted for the sake of the plot; Loren's lusty affair with Raf Vallone is coy; the intellectual played by Jean-Paul Belmondo is a tired conception; and the daughter (Eleanora Brown) is written to be pale and standard. Based on a novel by Alberto Moravia. Academy Award for Best Actress (Loren). In Italian. b & w

Ugetsu (1954)—This subtle, violent yet magical film is one of the most amazing of the Japanese movies that played American art houses after the international success of *Rashomon* in 1951. The director, Kenji Mizoguchi, handles the narrative in two styles: barbaric sequences dealing with greed and civil war that seem realistic except that the characters are deliberately animalistic and are symbolically acting out the bestial side of man; and highly stylized sequences dealing with the aesthetic, luxurious, and romantic modes of life. When the hero (Masayuki Mori), a grunting peasant potter, develops self-awareness and becomes an artist, the meanings multiply. The film is upsetting and unspeakably cruel at times, and then so suggestive and haunting that it's confounding. When, in the midst of serene elegance, the phantom Lady Wakasa (Machiko Kyo) offers the potter-artist rarefied sensual delights, you know how he feels as he cries, "I never imagined such pleasures existed!" Heavy going in spots, but with marvellous passages that are worth a bit of patience. With Kinuyo Tanaka as the potter's wife. In Japanese. b & w

The Ugly American (1963)—This attempt to deal with some of the peculiarities of American foreign policy in Asia is only marginally successful, and the director, George Englund, has zero style, but the film is entertaining anyway. The plot is about the mythical Asian country of Sarkhan, divided by factional disputes and torn between American aid and Communist influence. Its star, Marlon Brando, clearly enjoys the joke of his playing a proper career statesman in a pinstriped suit, who sports a neat little mustache. He's the new U.S. Ambassador to Sarkhan (concocted out of Thailand and Universal's back lot), whose premier is played by the extraordinarily handsome Kukrit Pramoj, who was later to become the Thai premier in fact. He was hired as the film's technical consultant, but Brando and Englund persuaded him to turn actor, and he saves the later part of the action, when Brando's role is dim. With Eiji Okada, Pat Hingle, Sandra Church, Jocelyn Brando, George Shibata, Reiko Sato, Stefan Schnabel, Philip Ober, and Arthur Hill. The screenplay, by Stewart Stern, has fairly remote connections to its credited source, the novel by William J. Lederer and Eugene Burdick. Cinematography by Clifford Stine. color

Ultimo Tango a Parigi, see *Last Tango in Paris*

Ulysses (1967)—No doubt the director, Joseph Strick, hoped for a great deal more, but the film he made is merely an act of homage to Joyce's novel in the form of readings from the book plus illustrated slides. A surface map of the comings and goings in town and "Nighttown," and some plausible facsimiles of Joyce's characters (Buck Mulligan, particularly), it seems both static and jerky. On the soundtrack are the lines we want to hear and it's good to be reminded of them, but they don't have the sensuality or the weight that they had in the novel; they're merely quotations from a classic, well-selected, intelligently read. Joyce gives us the drama within Stephen's consciousness; the film stays on the outside, and so Leopold Bloom, who is easier to represent, takes over. With Maurice Roeves as Stephen, Milo O'Shea as Bloom, Barbara Jefford as Molly, and T. P. McKenna, Anna Manahan, and Maureen Potter. Adapted by Strick and Fred Haines. Shot in Dublin. b & w (See *Kiss Kiss Bang Bang*.)

Umberto D. (1952)—Vittorio De Sica's Umberto D. is a stubborn old gentleman with bourgeois standards and no means, isolated in an impersonal modern city, unable to communicate with anyone, except his dog (Flick in the subtitles but pronounced Flike). Umberto's alienation has pride and spirit in it, even though his skinny frame is stiffening. Someone has said that this picture goes a long way toward making us aware of what it is to be a man—and also, for that matter, of what it is to be a dog. There are graceful, beautiful episodes—such as a sequence of a young servant girl rising—that would be unthinkable in a conventional movie, or even in a documentary of the time, since the sequence doesn't illustrate any social thesis but is there for itself, for what Cesare Zavattini, who wrote the script with De Sica, called "the love of reality." This work stands apart from De Sica's other films, with the possible excep-

tions of *The Children Are Watching Us* and *Shoeshine*—its moral passion has a special purity. Zavattini wrote that "No other medium of expression has the cinema's original and innate capacity for showing things . . . in what we might call their 'dailiness.' " Perhaps what makes this film singular is that its "dailiness" is infused with so much awareness that the screen seems luminous. There isn't a minute of banality in this simple, direct film, and there's none of the usual Italian post-synching—even the background sound is live and was recorded at the time. Cinematography by G. R. Aldo. With Carlo Battisti, a retired professor, as Umberto, Maria Pia Casilio as the servant, and Lina Gennari as the landlady. In Italian. b & w

The Unbearable Lightness of Being (1988)— Glorious. Directed by Philip Kaufman, this adaptation of Milan Kundera's novel is touching in sophisticated ways that you don't expect from an American director. A prankish sex comedy, it treats modern political events with a delicate—yet almost sly—sense of tragedy. It's the way the variations of jealousy and erotic attraction are played out by the three principal actors—an Englishman (Daniel Day-Lewis), a Swedish woman (Lena Olin), and a Frenchwoman (Juliette Binoche), all playing Czechs—that gives the movie its wonderfully unresolved texture. The story begins in Prague in 1968, during the period of freedom of expression and artistic flowering known as "socialism with a human face." Day-Lewis's Tomas is a hedonist, a womanizer, and an eminent young brain surgeon; Olin's Sabina, a painter who is his longtime sex partner, and Binoche's Tereza, whom he marries, represent the two poles of his life—lightness and weight. Kaufman has an exuberant temperament, and the spirit of the film is younger and looser than that of the book; a short 173 minutes, the picture has a whirling beauty. With Derek de Lint as the professor who's too virtuous for Sabina, Pavel Landovsky as the man with the tiny pet pig, Erland Josephson as the barroom janitor who was formerly the Czech ambassador in Vienna, Donald Moffat as the chief surgeon, Stellan Skarsgard as the engineer, and Daniel Olbrychski as the interior ministry official. Script by Jean-Claude Carrière and Kaufman; editing by Walter Murch; cinematography by Sven Nykvist. (The Prague scenes were shot in Lyon and Paris.) A Saul Zaentz Production, released by Orion. color (See *Hooked.*)

Uncommon Valor (1983)—This realistic action fantasy, in which a group of seven former Marines get together for an expedition into Southeast Asia to bring out the missing-in-action men from their Vietnam unit who have been slave laborers for ten years, is right-wing and racist, but the director, Ted Kotcheff, keeps the grandiosity in check and the movie is understated and surprisingly enjoyable. It moves on a strong emotional current. In the film's terms, the ex-Marines' defiance of the United States government—they keep going even after the C.I.A. fingers them to officials in Bangkok and their weapons are confiscated—is enough to make their mission honorable and make them heroes. As their leader, Gene Hackman treats soldiering in a businesslike way, and he offers a range of held-in, adult emotion that you don't expect to see in an action movie. The cinematography by Stephen H. Burum and Ric Waite and the smooth authority of the editing also help to undercut the cheap jingoism. With the heavyweight prizefighter Randall (Tex) Cobb, who gives an endearing, uninhibited performance as a slobby, self-destructive biker called Sailor (because he used to "take a lot of red wine and uppers and sail away"), and Fred Ward, Harold Sylvester, Reb Brown, Tim Thomerson, Patrick Swayze, and also Robert Stack, Alice Lau, Debi Par-

ker, Kwan Hi Lim, and Gail Strickland. The script is by Joe Gayton. Paramount. color (See *State of the Art.*)

The Unconquered (Helen Keller in Her Story) (1954)—Snapshots, old newsreels, and specially prepared sequences reconstruct the activities of more than 70 years. We see Helen Keller with Mark Twain, G. B. Shaw, Jascha Heifetz, Caruso, and many others; we see her in her Hollywood acting fling in 1919, in Martha Graham's studio, and, finally, in her home life. Through it all there is the mobile, glowing face that in the closing scenes acquires the luster of a legend. Narrated by Katharine Cornell. b & w

Under Capricorn (1949)—A Hitchcock stinker, set in Australia in the early 19th century (though shot in England). High-born English Ingrid Bergman (!) is Lady Henrietta, who elopes with a stable-man, Joseph Cotten (!), becomes alcoholic, and falls in love with her visiting cousin, Michael Wilding. The casting in this movie defies all reason, and includes Margaret Leighton as a servant, and Cecil Parker, Denis O'Dea, and Jack Watling. Script by James Bridie, based on Helen Simpson's novel. Released in the U.S. by Warners. color

Under Fire (1983)—A beautiful piece of new-style classical moviemaking. Everything is thought out and prepared, but it isn't explicit, it isn't labored, and it certainly isn't over-composed. Set in Nicaragua in 1979, during the last days of Somoza's dictatorship, the film is a little like Peter Weir's *The Year of Living Dangerously*, but visually and in its romantic revolutionary spirit it's more like Pontecorvo's *The Battle of Algiers* and *Burn!* With his subdued impassioned manner, the director, Roger Spottiswoode, brings the Nicaragua of countless news stories right to the center of our consciousness, by showing us how three grown-up Americans react to the Sandinist revolution. The stars are the unostentatiously fine actor Nick Nolte as the photojournalist hero—part artist, part automaton; Joanna Cassidy, strong and stunning as a radio reporter; and Gene Hackman in one of his wonderfully expansive performances as a jaunty, professionally likable war correspondent. The characters around them include Jean-Louis Trintignant as a suave, sleazo Frenchman who works for the C.I.A., Ed Harris as a mercenary with the grin of a happy psychopath, René Enriquez as a Teddy-bear Somoza, and Richard Masur as his American publicity expert. The often edgy and maliciously smart script, by Ron Shelton (working from a first draft by Clayton Frohman), gives the actors some very knowing material. The cinematography is by John Alcott; the Jerry Goldsmith score, which features a bamboo flute from the Andes with a barely perceptible electronic shadow effect, is a beauty. Shot in Mexico. Orion. color (See *State of the Art*.)

Under Milk Wood (1973)—An affectionate and beautiful reading of Dylan Thomas's radio play—a celebration of the originality and eccentricity in "ordinary" life. Andrew Sinclair, who adapted and directed, provides a fairly modest visual accompaniment. Richard Burton is the principal speaker and performer; Peter O'Toole is the blind Captain Cat; Elizabeth Taylor is the Captain's lost love, Rosie Probert. Also with Victor Spinetti, Glynis Johns, Sian Phillips, Ann Beach, Vivien Merchant, in the cast of about 70. Seeing the people seems to clarify and set the play in one's mind, though one may lose the unkempt luxuriance of Thomas's vision, and perhaps also lose the freedom not to think of the voices in terms of characters—the freedom not to visualize the material. The play was already complete in its original form, as a radio play—a play for voices. For some of

us, it took place nowhere but in the poet's unruly head, and the disembodiment played a part in its glorious windiness. Who could handle the sensations this language produces and take in rich visual imagery, too? The only strong visual images in the movie—some superb dark shots of seals—may, on one level, extend the poetry, but they also add something foreign, because they, too, have a life of their own. The adaptation includes a bit lifted from Thomas's short story "Just like Little Dogs." color (See *Reeling*.)

Under the Roofs of Paris, see *Sous les toits de Paris*

Under the Volcano (1984)—Malcolm Lowry, who wrote the novel, had a mystique about booze: he somehow got himself to believe that alcoholic self-destruction would give him access to the states of mind necessary to set words on fire. And his hero, Geoffrey Firmin, the former British Consul in Cuernavaca, is meant to be a genius with the courage to destroy himself so that he can transcend the limits of ordinary men and see things more intensely. For the movie to mean anything resembling the novel, we would have to see something of what Firmin—with his psyched-up consciousness—perceives. But all that it does is take a literal approach to the novel, as if it were no more than an account of the final binge of a drunk who becomes suicidally careless and gets himself killed. Since there's almost no attempt to find equivalents of Firmin's visions or of the excitement of Lowry's incendiary prose, the film puts a terribly heavy burden on Albert Finney, who plays Firmin. The drama has to come from his performance, in a big yet virtually unwritten role, and Finney can't help making us aware that he's giving the role more than his best shot—that he's pushing too hard (frequently in closeup), and overusing his facial muscles. Directed by John Huston, from a script by Guy Gallo, the movie has a deep-toned flossy and "artistic" clarity and a peculiarly literary tone—the dialogue doesn't sound like living people talking. With Jacqueline Bisset, Anthony Andrews (who gives an arch, acting-by-the-manual performance), James Villiers, Emilio Fernandez, Katy Jurado, and Ignacio Lopez Tarso. The cinematography is by Gabriel Figueroa; the score, by Alex North, ages the material, gives it a pompous emotionalism. Filmed in Mexico. color (See *State of the Art*.)

L'Une chante l'autre pas, see *One Sings, the Other Doesn't*

Unfaithfully Yours (1948)—One of the most sophisticated slapstick comedies ever made, this classic, written and directed by Preston Sturges, got terrible reviews and failed at the box office. The hero, a symphony conductor (a parody of Sir Thomas Beecham), is played by Rex Harrison, who is at one of his comic peaks. During a concert the conductor, convinced that his wife (Linda Darnell) has been unfaithful to him, fantasizes how he will handle the situation in three different ways, according to the style of the music on the program—Rossini's Overture to *Semiramide*, the "Pilgrim's Chorus" from Wagner's *Tannhäuser*, and Tchaikovsky's "Francesca da Rimini." After the concert, he tries to carry them out, scrambling them hopelessly. There are so many great lines and situations in this movie that writers and directors have been stealing from it for years, just as they've been stealing from Sturges's other work, but no one has ever come close to the wild-man deviltry of the best Preston Sturges comedies. With Edgar Kennedy, Rudy Vallee, Kurt Kreuger, Barbara Lawrence, and Lionel Stander. 20th Century-Fox. b & w

Unfaithfully Yours (1984)—Sloshed, Dudley Moore is a star (as he proved in *Arthur*,

which kept him happily stewed throughout); this film takes too long getting him there. It's an uninspired remake of Preston Sturges's 1948 film, which was a great musical joke. Directed by Howard Zieff, from an ingenious script by Valerie Curtin, Barry Levinson, and Robert Klane, this version isn't a total dud, but it's a coarser piece of slapstick, and not at all memorable. Moore is the symphony conductor who thinks his young wife (Nastassja Kinski) is betraying him; he fantasizes how he will handle the situation while he conducts the Tchaikovsky Violin Concerto, with his supposed betrayer (Armand Assante) as the soloist. Assante's bedroom voice and sleek, well-pleased-with-himself manner are a serviceable contrast to Moore's apoplectic (and ineffectual) rage, and Albert Brooks, who plays the conductor's manager, is really brilliant; he gives the film a crazed, hip subtext. (He came up with some of his own dialogue.) Toward the end, Moore shows his slapstick virtuosity, but he hasn't been as well protected by the director (or by the script) as he might have been; he's rather too pitiable and elfin—and at the very end, he's needlessly infantilized. With Richard B. Shull, Richard Libertini, Cassie Yates, and Magda Gyenes as the giddy, tempestuous Hungarian singer. (The Russian Tea Room footage was shot on a Los Angeles sound stage; so were the interiors of Carnegie Hall and the Plaza Hotel.) 20th Century-Fox. color (See *State of the Art*.)

Unfinished Business (1941)—It starts as a frothy comedy, with Robert Montgomery and Irene Dunne being madcap and frivolous, and there's an entertainingly preposterous inside view of nightclub life, but the froth curdles. Once sentiment gets the upper hand, look for an exit. Before then, Walter Catlett has a few choice moments as the proprietor of a luxurious resort. With Eugene Pallette, as a playboy's butler. Gregory La

Cava directed, from Eugene Thackery's screenplay. Universal. b & w

The Unholy Three (1930)—Lon Chaney, in a talkie remake of one of his grotesque, horrifying silent hits. He plays Echo, a crooked ventriloquist, who works in a dime museum along with a malevolent midget (Harry Earles, later the star of *Freaks*) and a strong man (Ivan Linow). They sell parrots who, with Echo's aid, appear to be great talkers; when dissatisfied customers complain, the three visit the customers' homes, which they subsequently burglarize. (Surely the most outlandish burglary scheme on film.) This sound version, directed by Jack Conway, isn't as nightmarishly well done as the Tod Browning silent, but Chaney ("the man of a thousand faces") demonstrates that he also has a variety of voices (he uses four), and the sound is particularly effective in the courtroom climax when, masquerading as an old woman, he suddenly gives himself away by speaking like a man. With Lila Lee, John Miljan, and Elliott Nugent. M-G-M. b & w

The Uninvited (1944)—Ray Milland and Ruth Hussey are the brother and sister who buy a house on the Cornish coast only to find it inhabited by a spooky evil presence. Sexy-eyed Gail Russell never could act worth a damn, but she had an eerie luster, and she's lovely as the mysterious young girl who helps in the exorcism. The picture was popular, though it doesn't come anywhere near fulfilling one's initial hopes that it will be a first-rate ghost movie. Charles Brackett produced; Lewis Allen directed; from Dorothy Macardle's novel *Uneasy Freehold*, adapted by Dodie Smith and Frank Partos; musical score by Victor Young. With Cornelia Otis Skinner (playing the usual Gale Sondergaard role), and Donald Crisp, Alan Napier, Dorothy Stickney, and Barbara Everest. Paramount. b & w

An Unmarried Woman (1978)—Paul Mazursky wrote and directed this buoyant, enormously friendly comedy about Erica (Jill Clayburgh) and her attempt to get back into "the stream of life" after her marriage of 16 years breaks up. It's a tenderhearted feminist picture. What may be disappointing to those who love Mazursky's earlier work is that in trying to identify with Erica and tell the story from a woman's point of view, he shies away from having her look foolish; in crucial parts, he suppresses his sense of satire, and the picture becomes virtuous. With Michael Murphy, Lisa Lucas, Pat Quinn, Kelly Bishop, Linda Miller, Cliff Gorman, Mazursky himself, as Hal, and Alan Bates, whose fine comic, expansive performance as Saul Kaplan, a famous painter, overpowers the movie. Saul is such a rich, loamy Father Earth figure that when Erica resists him in order to satisfy her yearnings for independence she seems puny and a bit of an idiot. 20th Century-Fox. color (See *When the Lights Go Down.*)

The Untouchables (1987)—Set in Chicago circa 1930—Al Capone's capital of crime—this Brian De Palma movie, from a script by David Mamet, is like an attempt to visualize the public's collective dream of Chicago gangsters. Our movie-fed imagination of the past is enlarged and given a new vividness. De Palma is a showman here. Everything is neatly done in broad strokes, and the slight unbelievability of it all makes it more enjoyable. Robert De Niro's Capone is a plump peacock with receding hair and a fat cigar in his mouth. The four men who fight to restore the honor of a corrupted society—the four who can't be bribed, the Untouchables—are the fresh-faced young Special Agent Eliot Ness, played by Kevin Costner; a smart, ornery veteran cop, played (magnificently) by Sean Connery; a rookie-cop sharpshooter (Andy Garcia); and a small, middle-aged accountant (Charles Martin Smith). It's not a great movie; it's too banal, too morally comfortable—the script is too obvious. But it's a great audience movie—a wonderful pot-boiler. It's a rouser. The architectural remnants of the era (including solid traces of Louis Sullivan and Frank Lloyd Wright) have been refurbished to provide a swaggering showcase for the legend. Cinematography by Stephen H. Burum; music by Ennio Morricone. (Every now and then you may wonder what Morricone's throbbing disco-synthesizer beat is doing in this period.) With Jack Kehoe, Billy Drago, and Richard Bradford. Paramount. color (See *Hooked*.)

Up in Central Park (1948)—A misery from Universal. The subject of how the Tweed ring was busted isn't exactly ideal musical-comedy material, and with smiley, suave Vincent Price as Boss Tweed, and that most juvenile of all singing juveniles, Dick Haymes, as the reporter who blows the lid off, there's no redemption. Deanna Durbin plays a colleen (yes, really) who is smitten with love for Haymes, and she sings some of the undistinguished songs by Dorothy Fields and Sigmund Romberg. Directed by William Seiter, from Karl Tunberg's script. With Tom Powers. b & w

Up in Smoke (1978)—You don't have to be an insider to see the humor in dopers' single-minded, never-ending quest for great grass. This piece of stoned-hippie foolishness, starring the comedy team Cheech and Chong, who wrote the script, is fairly consistently funny. It's an exploitation slapstick comedy, rather than a family picture, such as *Blazing Saddles* or *High Anxiety*—which means that it's dirtier, wilder, and sillier. (It's also better paced.) With Zane Buzby as the speed-freak, June Fairchild as the woman who snorts Ajax, and Otto Felix, Tom Skerritt, Stacy Keach, Louisa Moritz, Strother Martin, and Edie Adams. Produced and directed by Lou

Adler. Paramount. color (See *When the Lights Go Down.*)

Up the Down Staircase (1967)—Sandy Dennis, blinking as if she'd taken pills and been awakened in the middle of the night. As the teacher in Bel Kaufman's account of education in a tough New York school, she reacts confusedly before the situations even develop, but the audience is ahead of her, anyway: this is *Blackboard Jungle* with a woman sweating it out. Even in her dopey state, Dennis stumbles with what must be embarrassment on the obligatory speech: "I came here to teach. . . ." There are touching but too heavily pointed vignettes, peculiarly affectless readings from some of the young actors, and a coy score; still, it holds a viewer's attention. An Alan J. Pakula–Robert Mulligan Production, directed by Mulligan, from Tad Mosel's script. With Ruth White, Eileen Heckart, Jean Stapleton, Roy Poole, Patrick Bedford, Frances Sternhagen, Ellen O'Mara, and Sorrell Booke. Warners. color

Up the River (1930)—The setting is Sing Sing, and damned if the inmates don't file into their cells at night and break into melodious lullabies, their trained voices ringing in the stone corridors. In this co-educational prison, gracious women prisoners engage in badinage—and occasional dalliance—with the men. The picture—a true curiosity—started out to be something quite different. A highly publicized uprising in Auburn Prison in New York led to a spate of plays and movies about prison life. On Broadway, Spencer Tracy had a great success in *The Last Mile*; M-G-M rushed to prepare *The Big House*, a melodrama, and Fox commissioned Maurine Watkins to write *Up the River*, which was also to be a melodrama. But *The Big House* came out first and Fox was going to cancel *Up the River* when John Ford, who was scheduled to direct it and had already hired Tracy, came up with the idea of turning it into a spoofy comedy featuring prison baseball instead of a riot. In the finale, Tracy and Warren Hymer, who have broken out in order to help their buddy, Humphrey Bogart, who had got caught in a jam after he'd been released, go back in, so they can play in a big baseball game. Bogart here is not much more than a shiny-faced, gum-chewing, smiling juvenile with a long, skinny jaw, but Tracy, making his film début, is assured and lively as a cocky, tough mug—he keeps his scenes going by a lot of by-play with the other actors. Still, the big galoot Warren Hymer, playing a blissful sort of innocent stupe, gets most of the laughs. The picture—which is slow and bizarrely corny, especially when Bogart is at home with his proper Mom, or goes on a hayride with his convict pals—was very popular. With Claire Luce, William Collier, Sr., Ward Bond, Sharon Lynne, Noel Francis, Wilbur Mack, Morgan Wallace, Robert E. O'Connor, and two actors known as Slim and Clem playing Black and Blue. (Remade in 1938, with Preston Foster.) b & w

Up the Sandbox (1972)—Barbra Streisand has never seemed so radiant as in this joyful mess, taken from the Anne Richardson Roiphe novel and directed by Irvin Kershner. The picture is full of knockabout urban humor, though it doesn't seem to have settled on what it's meant to be about. The heroine is the wife of a Columbia instructor, and the movie is a hip, free-association treatment of her daydreams and conflicting desires, and of a variety of women's-lib problems. With David Selby, Paul Benedict, Paul Dooley, Carl Gottlieb, Moosie Drier, and Jacobo Morales as Fidel Castro. Script by Paul Zindel; cinematography by Gordon Willis. Warners. color (See *Reeling*.)

Up Tight (1968)—An updated version of *The Informer*, set in the black community of Cleve-

land, in the days following the death of Martin Luther King. Everybody tries hard, but the material doesn't transfer successfully, and the movie lacks spirit. With Raymond St. Jacques, Julian Mayfield, Ruby Dee, Roscoe Lee Browne, Juanita Moore, and Frank Silvera. Directed by Jules Dassin in a 40s melodrama style; Dassin also wrote the script, with Ruby Dee and Mayfield. Cinematography by Boris Kaufman. Paramount. color

Urban Cowboy (1980)—Aaron Latham's 1978 *Esquire* article, "The Urban Cowboy," was subtitled "Saturday Night Fever, Country & Western Style," and it was quite clearly a set of variations on *Saturday Night Fever* (1977). According to Latham, the headquarters of the young hardhats who worked in the petrochemical plants around Houston was a vast honky-tonk, Gilley's, which featured a mechanical bull, and these anomic young Southwesterners had no way to prove their manhood except by dressing up in boots and jeans and cowboy hats and trying to live out the myths of the West by riding this contraption. The film, directed by James Bridges, from a script he wrote with Latham, views its young hero, Bud (John Travolta), as rootless and ignorant. But on the assumption (probably false) that the audience believes in those antiquated macho values and wants to see them on the screen, the movie also tries to reactivate the cowboy mythology. It dredges up an ex-convict villain (Scott Glenn) out of an ancient Western, so Bud can defeat him on the bucking machine and beat him up in a fistfight as well. The picture is scrappily edited, and the director seems willing to do almost anything for an immediate effect. It's only in the best scenes that satire and sultriness work together. With Debra Winger, who gives a steamy and very appealing performance as the girl Bud marries, and Madolyn Smith as a slumming rich bitch, and Brooke Alderson and Barry Corbin as Bud's aunt and uncle. The country music doesn't supply much excitement. Paramount. color (See *Taking It All In*.)

Used Cars (1980)—A classic screwball fantasy—a neglected modern comedy that's like a more restless and visually high-spirited version of the W. C. Fields pictures. (The Fields title *Never Give a Sucker an Even Break* sums up the theme.) The director, Robert Zemeckis, and his co-writer and producer, Bob Gale, have developed a homegrown surrealism out of earlier American slapstick routines. Set in the world of competing used-car dealers in the booming Southwest, this picture has a wonderful, energetic heartlessness; it's an American tall-tale movie in a Pop Art form. The premise is that honesty doesn't exist; if you develop a liking for some of the characters, it's not because they're free of avarice but because of their style of avarice. Kurt Russell is the hero—a fast-talking supersalesman who's so rambunctiously, ingeniously crooked that he's a standout—a star in the world of the mendacious. With Jack Warden as twin brothers who run rival lots across the street from each other, and Gerrit Graham, Frank McRae, Deborah Harmon, Al Lewis, Alfonso Arau, Harry Northup, and David L. Lander and Michael McKean as the electronic wizards who devise a way to cut into a Presidential address with used-car commercials. Cinematography by Donald M. Morgan; editing by Michael Kahn. Columbia. color (See *Taking It All In*).

Utu (1983)—Fresh and surprising. The New Zealander Geoff Murphy treats the conventions of the colonial-epic form with offhand audacity. Set in 1870, this movie about the relations between the Maori, the dark-skinned Polynesians who settled in New Zealand about a thousand years ago, and the British, who began to migrate there in the 19th century and became their rulers, centers on Te Wheke (Anzac Wallace), an English-speaking Maori scout with the British colonial forces. When his people are slaughtered, he feels the need to exact *utu*—the Maori word that means honor and includes ritualized revenge. Te Wheke becomes a guerrilla leader and runs his army as a parody of the white man's army; he and his guerrillas turn themselves into the Europeans' image of them as butchers and buffoons. Mimicry goes on at so many levels in this horror comedy of colonialism that the viewer may be laughing, exhilarated by constant discovery, yet be a little discombobulated and scared. Murphy throws you at the start and keeps you in a state of suspension. He has an instinct for popular entertainment and a deracinated kind of hip lyricism. The film has sweep, yet it's singularly unpretentious—irony is turned into slapstick. Murphy and his co-writer Keith Aberdein keep skewering your expectations, bringing to the foreground one and then another of the leading characters, played by Bruno Lawrence, Kelly Johnson, Wi Kuki Kaa, Tania Bristowe, and Ilona Rodgers. The score, written by John Charles, was recorded by a traditional Maori flautist and the New Zealand Symphony Orchestra; much of the film was shot in high country in wet weather, and the cinematographer, Graeme Cowley, shows you an Arcadian beauty that makes your head swim. color (See *State of the Art*.)

Utvandrarna, see *The Emigrants*

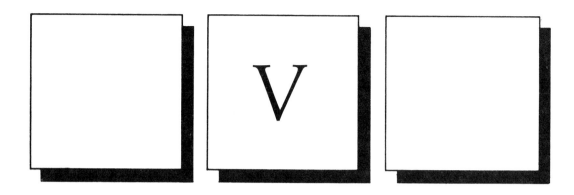

V Lyudyakh, see *My Apprenticeship*

Les Vacances de Monsieur Hulot, see *Mr. Hulot's Holiday*

Vagabond *Sans toit ni loi* (1985)—Agnès Varda wrote and directed this scrupulously hardheaded film about an 18-year-old girl on the road, a deliberately homeless drifter who lives on handouts, thefts, a little prostitution, and the occasional odd job. At the opening, her frozen body is discovered in a ditch in the countryside near the city of Nîmes. Varda presents the movie as a documentary investigating how this happened; the characters are the sullen, suspicious, vacant-eyed young girl (played immaculately by Sandrine Bonnaire) and the witnesses to her last weeks. The purity and boldness of Varda's approach may call Robert Bresson to mind, and it's perfectly evident why this film won the Golden Lion at the 1985 Venice Film Festival; it's the work of a visual artist. But we see the closed-off girl strictly from the outside, and this factual, objective view isn't enough. Varda's flat-out approach excludes the uses of the imagination—both hers and ours. With Macha Méril. Cinematography by Patrick Blossier. In French. color (See *Hooked*.)

Valentino (1977)—By attaching the names of actual people to his sadomasochistic fantasies, the director, Ken Russell, gives the picture a nasty inside-joke appeal. The only redeeming element is Rudolf Nureyev in the title role; he doesn't evoke Valentino, but from time to time he has a captivating, very funny temperament of his own. Despite his inexperience in speaking lines, he is not a novice performer—and he knows how to laugh at himself. His eagerness to please is at war with Russell's spitefulness—Russell turns the great Alla Nazimova (Leslie Caron) into nothing more than a cheap, vengeful, blackmailing bitch, and he shows no feeling for Valentino's wife, Natacha Rambova (Michelle Phillips), who was a superb Art Nouveau designer. In this movie everybody is out to defame Valentino's manhood and he is punched to a pulp while trying to defend himself against the charge of effeminacy. (He hemorrhages.) With Anthony Dowell as Nijinsky, and Carol Kane, Seymour Cassel, Felicity Kendal, and Huntz Hall. Shot in England and Spain, with little attempt (or small success) at matching the sleekness of the remembered Valentino—the beautifully dressed, almond-eyed Latin in his California Spanish, streamlined decor. Writ-

V

ten by Russell and Mardik Martin. United Artists. color (See *When the Lights Go Down*.)

Valmont (1989)—A version of the Choderlos de Laclos novel *Les Liaisons dangereuses*, directed by Miloš Forman, from the script he prepared with the writer Jean-Claude Carrière. In the novel, the Marquise de Merteuil and the Vicomte de Valmont, French aristocrats in the late 1770s, plan their sexual conquests with the cold calculation that might be given to war games—they turn innocent people into pawns. Here, their manipulations are so lightweight and offhand there's no sting to them. There has always been the danger that period movies will become intoxicated with jesters and fire-eaters and village fairs. *Valmont* has its share, but it's really into candlelit interiors and pale-rose bodices and rose-and-gold furniture. The story disappears among the cushions. As Valmont, the blandly handsome Colin Firth doesn't have the energy to be a lecher or even to make contact with the audience. With Annette Bening as the Marquise, Meg Tilly as Mme. de Tourvel, Fairuza Balk as Cécile, Fabia Drake as Valmont's aunt, and Jeffrey Jones, Henry Thomas, Aleta Mitchell, and Sian Phillips. The costumes were designed by Theodor Pištek. Orion. (see *Movie Love*.)

Les Valseuses, see *Going Places*

Vampire's Kiss (1989)—Nicolas Cage is airily amazing here. As a Manhattan literary agent—a poseur with a high-flown accent and a pouty, snobbish stare—he does some of the way-out stuff that you love actors in silent movies for doing. Something between a horror picture and a black comedy, this may be the first vampire movie in which the modern office building replaces the castle as the site of torture and degradation. The young British director Robert Bierman works well with the performers, and despite some narrative confusion (that may be the result of the cutting done by Hemdale, the producing company) the movie has an effective scary wackiness. With Maria Conchita Alonso, Jennifer Beals, Kasi Lemmons, and Elizabeth Ashley. The script is by Joseph Minion; Colin Towns provides an eerie score; Stefan Czapsky's cinematography suggests a madman's city. color (See *Movie Love*.)

Vampyr (1932)—Most vampire movies are so silly that this film by Carl Dreyer—a great vampire film—hardly belongs to the genre. Dreyer preys upon our subconscious fears. Dread and obsession are the film's substance, and its mood is evocative, dreamy, spectral. Death hovers over everyone. The cast is headed by Julian West (the movie name of Nicolas de Gunzburg), with Henriette Gérard as the vampire, and Rena Mandel and Sybille Schmitz as her potential victims. The incomparable photographic effects are the work of Rudolph Maté. Movie-lovers may cherish what appears to be Dreyer's homage to Cocteau—the use of the little heart from *The Blood of a Poet*. (Roger Vadim's 1960 exercise in supernatural chic, *Blood and Roses*, is based on the same story by Sheridan Le Fanu that Dreyer used.) In German. b & w

Il Vangelo Secondo Matteo, see *The Gospel According to St. Matthew*

Variété, see *Variety*

Variety *Variété* Also known as *Vaudeville*. (1925)—A German classic of sadomasochism in a circus setting, with the master masochist actor Emil Jannings as an acrobat who leaves his wife for a foreign girl (plumply erotic, saucer-eyed Lya de Putti); he forms a trapeze act with the girl and a younger acrobat (Warwick Ward)—who inevitably seduces her. The enduring power of the movie, directed by E. A. Dupont and photographed by Karl

Freund, is not in its far from original story but in the restless, subjective camera and the fast editing which make it an almost voluptuous experience. Von Sternberg's *The Blue Angel* and Ingmar Bergman's *The Naked Night* are both indebted to it. (A remake in 1935, with Hans Albers and Annabella, was negligible.) Silent. b & w

Variety Lights *Luci del Varietà* (1949)—This first film directed by Federico Fellini (working with Alberto Lattuada as co-director) has a backstage story with a theme that he returned to later in the big, trashy phantasmagoria *Juliet of the Spirits*. Giulietta Masina plays the aging mistress of the head of a touring company; he goes off with a younger woman, then returns to her. It's a very simple and, in some ways, tawdry film, but Fellini shows his extraordinary talent for the dejected setting, the shabby performer, the fat old chorine, the singer who will never hit the high note. Though he deals with "artists," he doesn't deal with talent or artistry; his specialty is revealing the shoddiness of theatrical life and the forlorn hopes of the performers. For Fellini, the magic of show business is in self-delusion. He achieves some of his most memorable images in the sequence with a troupe on a backcountry road at night and in the stage show representing the glorification of a sex goddess. With Peppino de Filippo, Carla del Poggio, Folco Lulli, and John Kitzmiller. In Italian. b & w

Vaudeville, see *Variety*

The Verdict (1982)—The camera sits like Death on the dark, angled images of this anguished movie about a Boston Irish lawyer, played by Paul Newman, who was hurt by those closest to him and became a booze-soaked failure. Lest anybody miss the point, the director, Sidney Lumet, puts dirges on the soundtrack. When the lawyer goes into court to fight the powerful Archdiocese of Boston, his faith in the judgment of the ordinary people who sit on the jury enables him to redeem himself. It's a Frank Capra setup given art-film treatment. (There's plenty of drizzle and brown gloom.) Newman plays his role for all it has got, making himself look soft and heavier, and even a little jowly, but it's a tired old show-business view of "a good man." In its own sombre, inflated terms, the picture is effective, but it's dragged out so self-importantly that you have time to recognize what a hopelessly naïve, incompetent, and untrustworthy lawyer the hero is. With Charlotte Rampling, James Mason, Jack Warden, Lindsay Crouse, Milo O'Shea, Edward Binns, Julie Bovasso, Lewis Stadlen, and Wesley Addy. The script, by David Mamet, is based on a novel by Barry Reed; the cinematography is by Andrzej Bartkowiak. Produced by Richard D. Zanuck and David Brown. 20th Century-Fox. color (See *Taking It All In*.)

A Very Private Affair *Vie privée* (1961)—Brigitte Bardot as a spoiled, bratty sex kitten who floats from modelling into movies, becomes a great star, takes innumerable lovers, finds fame and a multiplicity of beds equally unrewarding, and becomes suicidal. The director, Louis Malle, provides prankish, lively moments, though the story, with its many parallels to Bardot's own life, produces a sense of discomfort. It's one of the least interesting of Malle's films: he seems to be trying to show what's under a star's myth, but we don't experience the myth—only the shallowness underneath. With Marcello Mastroianni. Screenplay by Malle and Paul Rappeneau; cinematography by Henri Decaë. In French. color

Viaggio in Italia, see *A Voyage to Italy*

V

Victim (1961)—This pioneering attempt to create public sympathy for homosexuals and to publicize the English laws that put them in jeopardy is ingenious, moralistic, and moderately amusing. Structurally, it's a slick thriller about a blackmail ring that preys on homosexuals. There's a terribly self-conscious attempt to distinguish between the "love" that the barrister hero (Dirk Bogarde) feels for his wife (Sylvia Syms) and the physical desire—presumably a lower order of emotion—that he once felt for a young man (Peter McEnery), who appears to be more interesting in every way than the wife. The plot requires the barrister to sacrifice his career—to confess his own homosexuality—in order to trap the blackmailers. Basil Dearden directed, from a screenplay by Janet Green and John McCormick. With Dennis Price and Hilton Edwards. The film marked a turning point in Bogarde's career; having been an actor for over 20 years, he was tired of playing boyishly charming, happy, bouncy roles ("I was the Loretta Young of England," he said), and this time he acted his age in what was, in those years, a daring role. b & w (See *I Lost it at the Movies*.)

Victor/Victoria (1982)—The writer-director Blake Edwards' rough-and-tumble boudoir farce centers on Julie Andrews as Victoria, an English singer stranded in Paris in 1934, who pretends to be a man so that she can get work as a female impersonator. The picture is at its yeastiest in the slapstick embellishments of the preparatory sequences; when the infuriatingly sane and distant Julie Andrews finally gets into men's clothes, there's nothing remotely funny about it. And you don't believe that she could successfully impersonate a woman on the stage. Edwards pulls laughs, though. He does it with the crudest setups and the moldiest, most cynical dumb jokes. As an aging homosexual entertainer who trains Victoria to pass as Victor, Robert

Preston brings an unholy glee to his work. He plays a sentimental stereotype so heartily and likably that he redeems the musty material. (This is yet another movie in which a girl's best friend is a homosexual.) James Garner, in a mustache and acting like a funny, scowly Clark Gable, is a nightclub owner from Chicago, and, as the girlfriend he discards when he falls for Victoria, Lesley Ann Warren, gone blond, does dippy, exaggerated versions of Jean Harlow's nasal petulance. She's a comic-strip eccentric, and you feel her sweetness, but Edwards ties tin cans to her tail—he makes her into a nasty, screeching floozy. This picture features speeches about sexual politics that are the latest in show-biz enlightenment; it also features a chorus line, headed by Lesley Ann Warren, that may be the most contemptuous display of women's bodies ever seen in a major-studio movie. With Alex Karras as Garner's bodyguard. The songs by Henry Mancini and Leslie Bricusse are bland and forgettable. Based on the 1933 German film comedy *Viktor und Viktoria*; this is at least the fifth version. M-G-M. color (See *Taking It All In*.)

Victory (1940)—An ambitious attempt to bring the Conrad novel to the screen, which failed both artistically and commercially. The movie tries to stick with the action-adventure aspects of the Dutch East Indies story, yet a queasiness—a sinister unpleasantness—comes through, and the viewer, not given the explication one gets from Conrad, doesn't know quite what to make of it. Fredric March is the morose, handsome hero, and Betty Field is a distressed young girl in a travelling orchestra. The film is dominated by Cedric Hardwicke as the eerie, diseased epicure, Mr. Jones, who plausibly makes a hell's corner of Java and the world around it. This is an unsatisfying film at almost every level, yet it's unusual and disturbing, too. Margaret Wycherly plays the hotelkeeper's weird wife. John Cromwell directed, from John L. Balderston's screenplay. (Maurice Tourneur did a version in 1919 with Jack Holt; William Wellman did another, called *Dangerous Paradise* and starring Richard Arlen, in 1930; there were also French and German versions that year.) Produced by Anthony Veiller, for Paramount. b & w

Vie privée, see *A Very Private Affair*

La Vieille Dame indigne, see *The Shameless Old Lady*

De Vierde Man, see *The 4th Man*

A View from the Bridge (1962)—A complicatedly wrong-headed attempt to make a neo-realist Greek tragedy about a longshoreman in Brooklyn who neglects his wife, because he's in love—although he doesn't know it—with his wife's 18-year-old niece. Sidney Lumet directed, from Arthur Miller's play; acted by Raf Vallone, Maureen Stapleton, Raymond Pellegrin, Carol Lawrence, and Jean Sorel. Shot in France in two versions—French and English. b & w (See *I Lost it at the Movies*.)

A View to a Kill (1985)—The James Bond series has had its bummers, but nothing before in the class of this one. The way the daredevil feats are set up, they don't give you the irresponsible, giddy tingle they should, and the dumb police-car crashes seem to have got in by mistake—they belong to a back-roads chase comedy. The villain, Christopher Walken, is the ultra-blond psychopathic product of a Nazi doctor's experiments, and his major endeavor is to flood Silicon Valley. All that keeps the picture going is that it needs to reach a certain heft to fit into the series. With Roger Moore in his seventh go-round as Bond, Grace Jones, Tanya Roberts, Patrick Macnee, Patrick Bauchau, and a stunning young model named Alison Doody. The action is set mostly in Chantilly, Paris, and San Francisco. Directed (dispiritedly) by John Glen; written (with an air of hopelessness) by Richard Maibaum and Michael G. Wilson. Cinematography by Alan Hume; title song by Duran Duran. M-G-M/ United Artists. color

Vigil in the Night (1940)—This adaptation of an A. J. Cronin novel was a mistake from the word go, but the director, George Stevens, plodded ahead valiantly, dressing up the hopeless. Given the most resplendent makeup and lights, Carole Lombard glows with foolish nobility in the role of a trained nurse who takes the blame for a frivolous—and fatal—mistake by her student-nurse kid sister (Anne Shirley), also lighted phosphorescently; you expect the two girls to rise to Heaven by their cheekbones. After a solemn while, a busload of people are maimed, and eventually the beautiful nurses and Brian Aherne, as the doctor Lombard loves, become involved in an epidemic of cerebrospinal fever. With Robert Coote, Peter Cushing, Brenda Forbes, Doris Lloyd, and Ethel Griffies. R K O. b & w

Village of the Damned (1960)—A rarely shown thriller about wicked kids. It's clever and has some really chilling moments. George Sanders is the lead, and Martin Stephens is the scariest of the cold-eyed children from outer space. From John Wyndham's novel *The Midwich Cuckoos*; made in England and directed by Wolf Rilla (a terrific name for the director of this particular film). M-G-M. b & w

Vincent, François, Paul, and the Others *Vincent, François, Paul, et les autres* (1974)—A fabulous all-star cast that includes Yves Montand, Michel Piccoli, Serge Reggiani, Gérard

Depardieu, Stéphane Audran, Marie Dubois, and Antonella Lualdi, in an undeservedly neglected movie about a group of people who take refuge in friendship. All hell breaks loose in their lives, but the friendship pads their falls. The director, Claude Sautet, is a wizard at juggling and balancing the complex *Dinner at Eight* situation, and he's got the control and refinement of a master—the film may be too impersonally crafted, but it moves rhythmically, as if it were a melancholy, romantic tune. Cinematography by Jean Boffety. In French. color (See *When the Lights Go Down.*)

Violets Are Blue (1986)—A slim, undeveloped movie in which Sissy Spacek, as a globe-trotting photojournalist, is a vaporous figure standing in for all the women who got into what they once thought were the glamorous occupations and find themselves shading 35 or 40 and alone. The movie raises the question: Can this modern woman who has given up the simpler, more basic satisfactions go back to her home town (Ocean City, Maryland) and retrieve the man she left behind? That is, can she have everything—the excitement of her work and the solidity represented by Kevin Kline as the editor of the local paper? And does this man who has been a useful, contented stick-in-the-mud for so long really want to ditch his responsibilities—which include a wife (Bonnie Bedelia) and a son (Jim Standiford)—and become a risk-taker? The director, Jack Fisk, modulates the dialogue so it has a gentle tone, and he uses the oceanside-resort-town locale, with its sailboats and its amusement park, to get the love scenes between the two retro-adolescents moving, but all he can accomplish is to keep the movie lightweight and pretty. Spacek plugs away at her non-role, although, with tendrils of her long red-gold angel hair forever spilling over her face, you wonder how the hell she takes pictures. Kline is

doughy and unmagnetic; he gives you the feeling he's an actor with nothing inside. But Bedelia, who has the advantage of playing anger, comes through with a lovely performance. The picture doesn't really get started—to the degree that it ever gets started—until she's around. Based on an idea by Marykay Powell, who was the producer; the script is credited to Naomi Foner (it probably started out as hers). With John Kellogg. Cinematography by Ralf Bode. A Rastar Production, for Columbia. color (See *Hooked.*)

Les Violons du bal (1974)—A romantic memoir by the French writer-director Michel Drach about his childhood during the Occupation, and about the efforts of his gracious and beautiful mother to save the family—which is Jewish—from the Nazis. Drach re-creates the Nazi period in terms of what his vision was when he was a little boy, and his memory seems to burnish everything: everyone in the family is tender, cultivated, and exquisitely groomed. The film gets off to a fast start as the bearded, intense-looking Drach tries to arrange financing to make this autobiography; this first sequence is done in a playful, jump-cutting shorthand, but afterward everything is lyrical and glassy smooth. The incidents have a warmed-over old-Hollywood look, and the smartly tailored hat that the mother wears for the escape across the border and the fine gloves with which she parts the strands of barbed wire are the height of refugee chic. (If this is what the child experienced, he must have had the soul of a couturier.) Drach has cast his wife, the lovely Marie-José Nat, as his mother, and his own son as the blithe little treasure he imagines he was. With Jean-Louis Trintignant and Nathalie Roussel. In French. color (See *Reeling.*)

The Virgin Man, see *Le Rosier de Madame Husson*

The Virginian (1929)—Gary Cooper's first all-talking picture, and the one in which, with the help of the director, Victor Fleming, he found the laconic, straight-arrow character that he was to represent through much of his later career. He plays a Wyoming rancher-lawman in the 1870s who hangs his charmingly weak best friend (Richard Arlen, in a very engaging performance) for cattle rustling. Walter Huston glories in his opportunities as the film's mustachioed bad guy. He and Cooper have a celebrated encounter in a saloon: Huston mutters something not quite audible but beginning "son of a," and the super-calm Cooper, fondling his gun, says, "If you want to call me that, smile." With Chester Conklin and Eugene Pallette. Mary Brian is the pretty schoolteacher from Vermont who wins Cooper, but it's the relationship of Cooper and Arlen which, like the later friendship of Newman and Redford, gives the film its emotional resonance. The movie has an enduring charm; it was the third version of the Owen Wister novel, which also became a TV series in the 60s. Adaptation by Howard Estabrook; dialogue by Edward E. Paramore, Jr. Paramount Famous Lasky. b & w

Les Visiteurs du soir *The Devil's Envoys* (1942)—A fantasy romance set in the 15th century and based on a French legend: "And so in the beautiful month of May, 1485, the Devil sent on earth two of his creatures in order to drive the human beings to despair." The director, Marcel Carné, and the writers, Jacques Prévert and Pierre Laroche, intended a magical and seductive film poem, and they certainly had the cast for it—Arletty with her great, lustrous eyes, Jules Berry as the Devil, Marie Déa, Alain Cuny (unfortunately, he's young and looks like a wooden Indian), Fernand Ledoux, Gabriel Gabrio, and Marcel Herrand. There are wonderful images (such as a medieval ball, with the dancers suddenly frozen) but the movie is heavy on the allegorical and becomes rather slow and over-stylized. Perhaps the sentiments (the Devil himself, i.e., Hitler, is unable to corrupt true lovers) are a little too fragrant. Art direction by Alexandre Trauner and Georges Wakhévitch; cinematography by Roger Hubert; music by Joseph Kosma and Maurice Thiriet. In French. b & w

Viskningar och Rop, see *Cries and Whispers*

I Vitelloni Originally released in the U.S. as *The Young and the Passionate*; an idiomatic translation of the title would be something like "Adolescent Slobs." (1953)—Frustrated small-town boys with big ideas, the central characters are sons of indulgent, middle-class families, who cadge off their parents, loaf, and dream of women, riches, and glory. Their energies are wasted in idiotic pursuits; whatever dreams or ideals they have are pathetically childish or rotten. The director, Federico Fellini, observes the farce of their lives without condescension; his tone is satirical, yet warm and accepting—the distinctive Fellini tone, in his first fully confident piece of direction. The group suggests an American wolf pack. There is Fausto the flirt (Franco Fabrizi), who will become another unhappy, middle-class family man; plump, ludicrous Alberto the buffoon (Alberto Sordi, Fellini's "White Sheik" of the previous year, and before that a music-hall actor who first achieved recognition as the dubbed voice of Oliver Hardy); Leopoldo the poet (Leopoldo Trieste), whose naïve artistic illusions wilt when he is propositioned by an ancient homosexual actor; and Moraldo (Franco Interlenghi, who a few years earlier had been one of De Sica's two great child stars in *Shoeshine*). Fellini's autobiographical hero, he is the only one who finds the guts to say goodbye to this futile provincial life. There was, as yet, no indication that the road Moraldo took would lead to the corruption of *La Dolce Vita*. Screenplay by Fellini and Ennio Flaiano; score by Nino Rota. In Italian. b & w

Viva Maria! (1965)—After Louis Malle made the masterly but anguished and claustrophobic *The Fire Within* (1963), he did a flipover to the outdoors and the New World. He made this frivolous picaresque, a spoof of revolutionary politics set in the Latin America of La Belle Epoque and starring Brigitte Bardot and Jeanne Moreau. At the opening, the child who will become Bardot helps her imperialist-hating father dynamite a British fortress in Ireland, and the contrast between the father's act and the child's blooming, innocent happiness as she plays in the fields planting explosives is rapturously comic. The picture is lavish and visually beautiful (it was shot superbly, by Henri Decaë), and it has a spirit of abandon, but the subsequent bombings and shootings aren't as pointed. And the central conceit involved in the pairing of Bardot and Moreau as carnival striptease artists, both named Maria, doesn't work out. So the slapstick facetiousness is just left there, with nothing under it. But Bardot has never been more radiant than in parts of this film. When she's a tomboy looking for fun, wearing boys' clothes, with a cap (and a smudge on her cheek), she takes the picture clean away from the great Moreau. With George Hamilton, Paulette Dubost, and Claudio Brook. The screenplay is by Malle and Jean-Claude Carrière; the music is by Georges Delerue. In French. Released by United Artists. color

Viva Zapata! (1952)—Before the rifles of that infamous concealed regiment get poor Zapata (Marlon Brando), John Steinbeck's script has thoroughly done him in. Land and liberty, the simple slogans of the Mexican civil wars of 1911–19, are transformed into the American liberal clichés of 1952 and phrased in that slurpy imitation of simplicity and grandeur which some high-school English teachers and TV producers call "poetry." The virtues of the production are in Elia Kazan's slam-bang direction: some of the scenes have startling immediacy; the fighting is first-rate; even the phony folklore holds one's interest. And the actors are fun to watch: there's the magnetic young Brando (age 27) impersonating a great revolutionary leader—an illiterate young titan, a peasant and a thinker (and, in the time-worn actor-peasant tradition, he screws up his face when he has to think). And there are Anthony Quinn (his performance took the Academy Award for Best Supporting Actor) as Zapata's older brother; Jean Peters as Josefa; Joseph Wiseman, acting like some sinister mixture of Judas Iscariot and a junkie, as Fernando the journalist; Alan Reed as Pancho Villa; Lou Gilbert as Pablo; Margo as Soldadera; Harold Gordon as Madero; Frank Silvera as Huerta; and Mildred Dunnock, Abner Biberman, Philip Van Zandt, Henry Silva, and Arnold Moss. The film includes Steinbeck's folly: the famous, supposedly terribly touching wedding-night scene in which Zapata asks Josefa to teach him to read. (To deflower his virgin mind?) Cinematography by Joe MacDonald. A Darryl F. Zanuck Production. 20th Century-Fox. b & w

Vivacious Lady (1938)—A good-natured, unpretentiously entertaining comedy, with Ginger Rogers (supremely likable here) as a nightclub singer who marries an assistant professor of biology (James Stewart). The movie is about the collision of cultures. When the newlyweds arrive at his college town—Old Sharon—they discuss the problem of breaking the news to his parents (Beulah Bondi and Charles Coburn), and Ginger finds the perfect solution. "You go tell them how wonderful I am," she says, "and I'll come over later." George Stevens directed in a relaxed style that derives from his early work with Laurel and Hardy, and he coached Ginger Rogers to do some of Stan Laurel's routines. The cast (which includes James Ellison, Grady Sutton, Franklin Pangborn, Jack Carson, Willie Best, and Maude Eburne) all seem to be having a good time. P. J. Wolfson and Ernest Pagano did the script, based on I.A.R. Wylie's story. R K O. b & w

La Voie lactée, see *The Milky Way*

Le Voleur, see *The Thief of Paris*

Volpone (1939)—Louis Jouvet is the shameless, swindling Mosca to the crafty, raucous old Volpone of the great Harry Baur, but they both seem tired. Maurice Tourneur directed this fairly straightforward version of the Ben Jonson satire, which is, however, weighed down by the lavish production, and maybe also by the threat of Hitler. Neither Baur nor Jouvet seems to be in a comic spirit. (It was Baur's last film—he was sent to prison in 1940 and died soon after being freed. Jouvet left France in 1940, with part of his acting company, and went to South America; his flight served as part of the basis for Truffaut's *The Last Metro*.) The play was adapted and modernized by Stefan Zweig and Jules Romains, though the setting remains Renaissance Venice. With Jacqueline Delubac and Charles Dullin. In French. b & w

Voyage of the Damned (1976)—This movie is based on the actual 1939 voyage of the S.S. St. Louis with 937 German-Jewish refugees aboard, yet there is not a single moment in the star-packed epic that carries any conviction. As the lines drone on—paced with a sledgehammer—you may feel you could die for a little overlapping dialogue. But with this material you can't even have the frivolous pleasure of derision. Cast as a woman who doesn't excite her husband, Faye Dunaway must have decided that she'd better give the public *something*, and she comes on looking absolutely smashing, and at one point appears dressed to outdo the Nazis—she wears jackboots and a monocle. As the ship's captain, Max von Sydow acts with some distinction; most of the others—Oskar Werner, Malcolm McDowell, Katharine Ross, Janet Suzman, Maria Schell, Victor Spinetti, Julie Harris, Wendy Hiller, Orson Welles, James Mason, Helmut Griem, Nehemiah Persoff, Sam Wanamaker, Donald Houston, Jonathan Pryce, Leonard Rossiter, Denholm Elliott, José Ferrer, Lee Grant, Ben Gazzara, Luther Adler, Lynn Frederick, Fernando Rey, et al.—are crippled by the dreary script, written by Steve Shagan and David Butler, and the ponderous directing by Stuart Rosenberg. You sit there wondering how there can be so many bad actors in one picture; if you hadn't seen these performers in other roles, you'd assume they were the dregs of the profession. Based on the book by Gordon Thomas and Max Morgan Witts; cinematography by Billy Williams. A Sir Lew Grade Production; released by Avco/Embassy. color

Voyage Surprise (1946)—The Prévert brothers—director Pierre and scenarist Jacques—got together on this offhand comedy, and there's nothing comparable to its poetic eccentricity in other French movies of the period; the humor suggests early Marx Brothers, but the improvisatory style is that of Mack Sennett 2-reelers, or a looser, more amateurish version of René Clair's *The Italian Straw Hat*. It can be tedious, but it has a loony, antique grace. In competition with a tourist bureau, a mad old man (Sinoël) collects a busload of uninhibited people, and they go on a "mystery" tour—the route and destination unknown. The surprises follow: they become fugitives from the law; they spend a night in a sumptuous brothel; they are mistaken for a theatrical troupe. Kosma did the music. With Martine Carol, and the dwarf Pierre

Piéral, who's like a miniature Bette Davis. In French. b & w

A Voyage to Italy *Viaggio in Italia* (1953)—Roberto Rossellini made this study of a marriage in trouble, starring Ingrid Bergman and George Sanders; in the film's finest scene, the couple visit Pompeii and see two petrified embracing bodies that have just been uncovered. An influential film (there are echoes of it in both Godard's *Contempt* and Bergman's *The Touch*), which is marred by banality and clumsiness. Screenplay by Rossellini and Vitaliano Brancati; cinematography by Enzo Serafin. In Italian. b & w

Vredens Dag, see *Day of Wrath*

Vynalez Zkazy, see *The Deadly Invention*

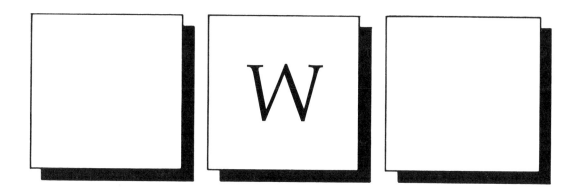

Wachsfigurenkabinett, see *Waxworks*

The Wages of Fear   *Le Salaire de la peur* (1953)—An existential thriller—the most original and shocking French melodrama of the 50s. The opening sequence shows us a verminous South American village and the Europeans trapped in it; they will risk everything for the money to get out. An oil well 300 miles away has caught fire, and the oil company offers four of them $2,000 each to drive two trucks loaded with nitroglycerine (to explode out the fire) over primitive roads. The four are a Corsican (Yves Montand), a Frenchman (Charles Vanel), an Italian (Folco Lulli), and a German (Peter Van Eyck), and the film is about their responses to the gruelling test of driving the trucks. When you can be blown up at any moment only a fool believes that character determines fate. In this situation, courage and caution are almost irrelevant, and ordinary human responses are futile and archaic—yet nothing else is left. If this isn't a parable of man's position in the modern world, it's at least an illustration of it. Henri-Georges Clouzot directed his own adaptation of Georges Arnaud's novel. His most controversial film, it is also his most powerful; the violence is not used simply for excitement—it's used as in Eisenstein's and Buñuel's films: to force a vision of human experience. With Vera Clouzot and William Tubbs. The music is by Georges Auric; the cinematography is by Armand Thirard. Awarded the Golden Palm at Cannes. Originally released in the U.S. in a cut version, partly because of the film's length (156 minutes), and partly because of nervousness about how Americans would react to the sequences touching on the exploitative practices of American oil companies; the footage trimmed was later restored. (You can see the influence of this picture in Peckinpah's *The Wild Bunch*.) In French. b & w

A Walk in the Sun (1945)—This account of an American infantry platoon in Italy has a great big inexplicable reputation. Maybe people were impressed by its serious and poetic intentions, evidenced by the film's having no one higher in rank than the sergeants who take over when their lieutenant is killed, and by the stylized recurrence of such lines as "There's no sense in it—no sense at all" and "That's the way it is—sure as little apples, that's it." The director, Lewis Milestone, brought the film a visual style, and Robert Rossen's script (from the Harry Brown novel) emphasizes that these civilians turned soldiers are just stumbling about, wondering what's going on. But this is the kind of literate movie that is more impressive than enjoyable. With Dana Andrews, Richard Conte, Lloyd Bridges, John Ireland, Huntz Hall, Herbert Rudley as the psycho, and blond, cracked-voice Sterling Holloway, who gets a death scene. The ballad on the soundtrack, which adds to the air of fanciness, is by Millard Lampell and Earl Robinson. 20th Century-Fox. b & w

A Walk with Love and Death (1969)—An unusual and relatively little known fable of love in a time of destruction, directed by John Huston. A student (Assaf Dayan) and a young girl of noble birth (Anjelica Huston) try to find an escape hatch from the Hundred Years' War. This romantic idyll is unusually tough-minded, and effective because it is. The movie lacks urgency, but it's compelling, nevertheless. It has at least one superb image—a great, clumping white horse, a dream horse—and when this fairy-tale beast is slaughtered war becomes truly obscene. With Michael Gough, John Hallam, and Robert Lang. The rather literary screenplay is by Dale Wasserman, from a novel by Hans Koningsberger; music by Georges Delerue; costumes by Leonor Fini. color (See *Deeper into Movies*.)

Walking Tall (1974)—The implied system of values in the early, heroic Westerns and action-adventure films began to be treated satirically in the "counterculture" movies of the Vietnam and Watergate years. But there were also some hugely popular 70s films, such as this one and *Dirty Harry*, in which the old values returned in a corrupt, vigilante form under the banner of "law and order." This rabble-rousing movie appeals to a deep-seated belief in simple, swift, Biblical justice; the visceral impact of the film makes one know how crowds must feel when they're being swayed by demagogues. It was sold as the true story of crusading Tennessee sheriff Buford Pusser, who cleaned out the moonshining, gambling, and prostitution in his county. But it's a tall tale: a fiction derived from early Westerns. The director, Phil Karlson, is brutally effective; he makes the battle of virtuous force against organized evil seem primordial. Karlson pulls out all the stops of classical cheapie melodrama, right down to the murder of the Pusser family dog and the weeping face of a bereaved child. The picture's crudeness and its crummy cinematography give it the illusion of honesty. With Joe Don Baker, who gives a powerful performance as Pusser, the gifted Elizabeth Hartman as Mrs. Pusser, and Rosemary Murphy, Gene Evans, Brenda Benet, Felton Perry, Kenneth Tobey, Lurene Tuttle, Ed Call, and Noah Beery, who acts Hollywood-cornpone-Southern. Shot in Tennessee; written by Mort Briskin. It spawned sequels and imitations. Released by Cinerama. color (See *Reeling*.)

The Walls of Malapaga *Au-delà des grilles Le Mure di Malapurga* (1949)—Jean Gabin and Isa Miranda are the restless, lonely lovers in this Franco-Italian production, directed by René Clément. Gabin plays a Frenchman, wanted for homicide, who has fled to Genoa; there he spends a few days with the troubled Miranda and her impressionable daughter (Vera Talchi) before the police close in on him. Though the film won international recognition (the Best Director and Best Actress Awards at Cannes, and the Academy Award for Best Foreign Film), it's a rather uneasy mixture of the romantic, melodramatic prewar French style and the harsh, poetic postwar Italian style (especially in the semi-documentary use of the Genoa-waterfront locations and in the attempt at a fresh approach to character). There was gossip that the French team of Jean Aurenche and Pierre

Bost, who had worked on some of Gabin's fatalistic, atmospheric prewar successes, rewrote Cesare Zavattini's and Suso Cecchi d'Amico's neo-realist script. Whatever the reasons, Clément seems to be pulled in different directions; his "sensitivity" is like a glue holding the picture together. Music by Roman Vlad. In French and Italian. b & w

Wanda (1971)—Barbara Loden wrote, directed, and stars in this story of the minimal love affair of a passive, bedraggled girl from a mining town and a nervous wreck of a small-time crook (Michael Higgins). The director never falls back on coy tricks or clichés and the performances are admirable, but the movie is such an extremely drab and limited piece of realism that it makes Zola seem like musical comedy. Shot in 16 mm, in color. (See *Deeper into Movies*.)

WarGames (1983)—The people who made it had half an idea. The film begins as a comedy about a teen-age boy in Seattle who is caught up in the fascination of computers and video games; he has all this miracle-working technology and not a thought in the world about what to do with it. Matthew Broderick plays the role with great charm; the boy is like an American Antoine Doinel, and he's the life of the movie. But when this boy accidentally plugs into the Defense Department's wargames system and gets into what he thinks is just another video game—Global Thermonuclear War—the machines take over, especially a huge box of flashing light that sounds like an 18-wheel truck rumbling down the highway. There's also the noise of speechmakers—the director, John Badham, loses his easy touch, and the picture goes flooey. It's at its worst when John Wood is onscreen as a saintly computer scientist who's so brainy and bitter that he rolls his eyes from side to side and wears his hair in bangs. With Ally Sheedy, who has some nifty

lines in the first part, and Dabney Coleman, Barry Corbin, and Eddie Deezen as Mr. Potato Head. From a script by Lawrence Lasker and Walter F. Parkes. M-G-M/United Artists. color (See *Taking It All In*.)

The Warriors (1979)—Walter Hill's spectacle takes its story from Xenophon's *Anabasis* and its style from the taste of the modern urban dispossessed—in neon signs, graffiti, and the thrill of gaudiness. The film enters into the spirit of urban-male tribalism and the feelings of kids who believe that they own the streets because they keep other kids out of them. In this vision, cops and kids are all there is, and the worst crime is to be chicken. It has—in visual terms—the kind of impact that "Rock Around the Clock" had when it was played behind the titles of *Blackboard Jungle*. It's like visual rock, and it's bursting with energy. The action runs from night until dawn, and most of it is in crisp, bright Day-Glo colors against the terrifying New York blackness; the figures stand out like a jukebox in a dark bar. There's a night-blooming, psychedelic shine to the whole baroque movie. Adapted from the Sol Yurick novel. With Michael Beck, Deborah Van Valkenburgh, David Patrick Kelly, David Harris, Dorsey Wright, James Remar, Thomas Waites, Roger Hill, and Marcelino Sanchez. Cinematography by Andrew Laszlo; art direction by Don Swanagan and Bob Wightman. Paramount. (See *When the Lights Go Down*.)

Warui Yatsu Hodo Yoku Nemuru, see *The Bad Sleep Well*

Watch on the Rhine (1943)—Lillian Hellman's 1941 Broadway play—a cautionary polemical melodrama about the danger of Fascism in the U.S.—is housebound and fearfully lofty. She performs staggering melodramatic tricks in order to get a big confrontation scene; Dashiell Hammett is credited with the screenplay, but from the theatrical look and sound of things he can't have changed much. Paul Lukas is the European Underground leader who brings his American wife (Bette Davis) and three children home to the Washington mansion of her mother (Lucile Watson). The film has some inadvertent humor: the children of this liberal couple are the most highly disciplined little prigs imaginable. Lukas, repeating his stage role, won an Academy Award; Davis is subdued and unexciting. With George Coulouris as a suave, vile Fascist, Geraldine Fitzgerald, Donald Woods, Henry Daniell, and Beulah Bondi. Directed by Herman Shumlin. Warners. b & w

Waterloo Bridge (1940)—A great many people are inexplicably hooked on this weeper about the unlucky wartime love affair of a duke's nephew (Robert Taylor, trying to act aristocratic) and a dancer (Vivien Leigh). She becomes the saddest-eyed fallen woman ever. The director, Mervyn LeRoy, uses candlelight and rain more effectively than he does the actors, although Vivien Leigh does manage to give a beautiful performance. With Lucile Watson, Maria Ouspenskaya, C. Aubrey Smith, Steffi Duna, and Virginia Field. Adapted from a Robert E. Sherwood play, by S. N. Behrman, Hans Rameau, and George Froeschel. (There was a Universal version in 1931, with Mae Clarke and Kent Douglass—also known as Douglass Montgomery—and an M-G-M version in 1956, called *Gaby* and starring Leslie Caron and John Kerr. By far the best version is the parody done by Carol Burnett and Harvey Korman on TV.) Produced by Sidney Franklin, for M-G-M. b & w

Waxworks *Wachsfigurenkabinett* (1924)— The three episodes of this engaging, too-little-known German horror-fantasy incorporate extravagantly villainous performances—

Conrad Veidt as Ivan the Terrible, Emil Jannings (in one of his rare comic portraits) as Haroun-al-Raschid, and Werner (*Caligari*) Krauss as Jack the Ripper. In the Veidt-Ivan sequence, which was obviously a major influence on Eisenstein's *Ivan the Terrible*, Ivan is a jokester-poisoner who enjoys presenting his victims with hourglasses timed to run out at the precise moment of their deaths; one day he discovers an hourglass labelled "Ivan." The director, Paul Leni, a former Max Reinhardt collaborator, was an extraordinarily gifted scenic artist; the macabre Expressionistic decor for the Jack the Ripper sequence is made entirely from sheets of painted paper. William Dieterle is also in the cast. Silent. b & w

Way Down East (1920)—The plot is Victorian, but the treatment is inspired. D. W. Griffith took a creaking, dated stage melodrama and turned it into a melodramatic epic. Lillian Gish is the girl betrayed by Lowell Sherman and eventually rescued from an icy river by Richard Barthelmess. Audiences giggle at bits here and there, but not at the sequence in which she refuses to part from her dead baby. Griffith stole from Thomas Hardy, but he stole beautifully. One of Griffith's greatest box-office successes, and a film that influenced several Russian epics. (The play by Lottie Blair Parker and Joseph R. Grismer was so popular that Griffith paid $175,000 for the right to adapt it.) Silent. b & w

Way Out West (1937)—This satire of Westerns is probably Laurel and Hardy's most comically sustained feature, and it shows off their vaudeville skills in a couple of musical interludes. They do a classic soft-shoe shuffle outside a saloon; Hardy's lolling elephantine grace has never been more ingratiating. And they sing "In the Blue Ridge Mountains of Virginia." As Mickey Finn, the villain in love with his own villainy, James Finlayson is practically a co-star, and Sharon Lynne is the voluptuous blond saloon girl. The film is leisurely in the best sense; you adjust to a different rhythm and come out feeling relaxed, as if you'd gone on vacation. James Horne directed. A Hal Roach Production, for M-G-M. b & w

The Way We Were (1973)—Robert Redford is a straw-haired jock from Virginia who wants to have a good time, and Barbra Streisand is a frizzy-haired Communist who's always sure she's right. The picture has some atrocious sequences set in Hollywood during the blacklisting troubles, but the romantic star chemistry of Redford and Streisand turns a half-terrible movie into hit entertainment— maybe even memorable entertainment. Sydney Pollack directed; from Arthur Laurents's novel. With Patrick O'Neal, Viveca Lindfors, Bradford Dillman, and Lois Chiles. Produced by Ray Stark, for Columbia. color (See *Reeling*.)

We Still Kill the Old Way *A Ciascuno il Suo* (1966)—Based on Leonardo Sciascia's novel, *A Man's Blessing*, this tense, unusual thriller directed by Elio Petri has a nightmare realism that suggests Kafka. The professor-hero (Gian Maria Volonte)—a man who has always been an outsider—finds himself involved in a crime in his own Mafia-ridden Sicilian home town, and this familiar region becomes as terrifying and incomprehensible as the desert in a Paul Bowles story. His life begins to resemble paranoid fantasy—which, the movie suggests, is what life is for people who live in a corrupt society. It's easy to present fantasy on the screen, but to show a man's life in completely realistic terms as this film does and make us experience it as fantasy is difficult. Petri keeps us tense and uneasy, wary, expecting the worst at each moment. The island looks hot and barbaric,

ominous and teeming with life. Volonte is a powerful actor who draws you inside his character, and the film is marvellously well-sustained. Gabriele Ferzetti (the weak hero of *L'Avventura*) is the politician who knows how to get along, and Irene Papas is scarily effective as a survivor—at the end, in her white wedding dress, her black eyes shining, she seems as strong as corruption. Also with Leopoldo Trieste. In Italian. color

We Were Dancing (1942)—A misbegotten attempt by M-G-M to embroider on Noël Coward's *Tonight at 8:30* playlets and put them together. (A much better British version came out in the early 50s under the original title.) With Norma Shearer, Melvyn Douglas, Gail Patrick, Marjorie Main, Florence Bates, Lee Bowman, Reginald Owen, Alan Mowbray, Sig Rumann, and Ava Gardner (in her début). None of them have the brittle sentimentality necessary for Coward's brand of light social comedy. Besides, Americans don't move their mouths right for that British chat. Directed by Robert Z. Leonard. b & w

Web of Passion, see *Léda*

Wednesday's Child Also known as *Family Life*. (1971)—Valuable as an attack on the use of shock therapy and drugs in the care of disturbed people, but simplistic in its brief for R. D. Laing's methods of treatment. Ken Loach directed this *cinéma-vérité*-style English movie, which centers on a passive, weak-willed 19-year-old girl (Sandy Ratcliff) crushed by her rigid family and falling apart because of her regimented existence. Sent to a hospital, she is at first treated in a relaxed, informal experimental ward run by a Laingian, and it appears that she merely needs to learn to stand up to her family. But the Laingian is dismissed and she is given shock treatment and is left, at the end, a vegetable. David Mercer wrote the script, from his play

In Two Minds. There are a few striking performances in the simulations of documentary footage. If you're not convinced by the Laing thesis, though, you may get very impatient. color

Wee Geordie   Also known as *Geordie*. (1955)—A runty little bit of a boy, the son of a Scottish gamekeeper, sees an ad for a body-building course: "Are you undersized? Let me make a man of you!" When we next see the boy, 10 years of sweat and exercise have turned him into a strapping 6 feet 6 inches of solid muscle—muscle even between his ears. He's a dour giant obsessed with his giantism. Bill Travers (after a course of muscle development and a steak diet) was assigned the role of Geordie, who takes up hammer-throwing and meets his match at the Olympics: a 6-foot woman shotputter. Alastair Sim turns up as the Laird, and the Scottish Highlands provide the background for this gentle satire of man's mania for bodybuilding. Too gentle. In its period this was one of the most popular English imports, though it really isn't very lively. The idea is so promising that you keep expecting more pleasure than you get. With Miles Malleson, Norah Gorsen, and Raymond Huntley. Sidney Gilliat and Frank Launder wrote the script; Launder, who seems as muscle-bound as the hero, directed—he's slow and heavy. Based on a novel by David Walker. color

Weeds (1987)—Nick Nolte plays a holdup man serving "life without possibility"—that is, without possibility of parole. After flunking a couple of suicide attempts, he begins to write plays about imprisonment and then to stage them, and his activities win him his release. He organizes an acting troupe made up of former cons he worked with—a shoplifter (William Forsythe), a murderer (Ernie Hudson), an embezzler (Lane Smith), a pimp (John Toles-Bey), a flasher (Mark Rolston)—

and they go on tour in a camper, with no money. The movie is about the men's impulses to revert to their former crime patterns, and about their efforts to become professional men of the theatre. It encompasses way too much, and it never goes very far into the issues it raises, but the messy collision of energies keeps a viewer feeling alive. The picture grew out of the director John Hancock's contacts with the convict Rick Cluchey and his San Quentin Drama Group (whose late-60s show *The Cage* toured the U.S. and Europe); Hancock and his wife, Dorothy Tristan, who collaborated with him on the script, also did research into other prison theatre groups, and the movie gives the impression that they piled together the stories and anecdotes they liked best, and left the job of unifying them to Nolte. (He does it.) With Joe Mantegna, Rita Taggart, J. J. Johnson, and Anne Ramsey. A Kingsgate Film, released by De Laurentiis. color (See *Hooked*.)

Weekend (1967)—Only the title of this extraordinary poetic satire is casual and innocent. The writer-director Jean-Luc Godard has a gift for making the contemporary satiric and fantastic. He begins with just a slight stylization of civilized living now—the people are more adulterous, more nakedly mercenary, touchier. They have weapons, and use them at the slightest provocation, and it seems perfectly logical that they should get into their cars and bang into one another and start piling up on the roads. The traffic jam is a prelude to highways littered with burning cars and corpses. As long as Godard stays with cars as the symbol of bourgeois materialism, the barbarity of these bourgeois—their greed and the self-love they project onto their possessions—is exact and funny. The picture goes much further—sometimes majestically, sometimes with surreal details that suggest an affinity between Godard and Buñuel, sometimes with methods and ideas that miss, badly. There are extraordinary passages, such as a bourgeois wife's erotic confession and a long virtuoso sequence of tracking shots of cars stalled on the highway, with the motorists pressing down with all their might on their car horns, which sound triumphant, like trumpets in Purcell. Though deeply flawed, this film has more depth than any of Godard's earlier work. It's his vision of Hell and it ranks with the greatest. As a mystical movie *Weekend* is comparable to Bergman's *The Seventh Seal* and *Shame* and Ichikawa's *Fires on the Plain* and passages of Kurosawa, yet we're hardly aware of the magnitude of the writer-director's conception until after we are caught up in the comedy of horror, which keeps going further and further and becoming more nearly inescapable, like *Journey to the End of the Night*. With Mireille Darc and Jean Yanne. Score by Antoine Duhamel. In French. color (See *Going Steady*.)

Weekend in Havana (1941)—Probably the cheerfullest weekend in Havana's history, what with Carmen Miranda, Alice Faye, John Payne, Cesar Romero, Leonid Kinskey, George Barbier, and everybody else on the 20th Century-Fox lot beaming with fatuous good will. Carmen Miranda wears a headgear of grapefruit, grapes, apples, oranges, bananas, lemons, pineapples, and an occasional small plum. Walter Lang directed; Hermes Pan did the choreography. The songs (mostly by Harry Warren and Mack Gordon) are not top drawer. color

Die Weisse Hölle vom Piz Palü, see *The White Hell of Pitz Palu*

Welcome to L.A. (1977)—The writer-director, Alan Rudolph, is literary in a subliterate way; he overvalues mournful poetic thoughts. And Richard Baskin, whose suite of rock songs "City of the One Night Stands"

was the starting point for this sick-soul-of-Los Angeles movie, growls his guru-wisdom lyrics on the soundtrack. Their whimsical, laid-back alienation is stagnant and irritating; the picture seems drugged. Keith Carradine, Geraldine Chaplin, Lauren Hutton, Harvey Keitel, John Considine, Sissy Spacek, Sally Kellerman, and others perform attentively, but they're undirected, and you can sense their unease as they trudge from one cheerless affair to the next. Cinematography by Dave Myers. Produced by Robert Altman. color (See *When the Lights Go Down*.)

The Well-Digger's Daughter *La Fille du puisatier* (1940)—The most famous French comedy about illegitimacy stars Raimu as the well-digger, Fernandel as his assistant, and the lovely Josette Day (the beauty of *Beauty and the Beast*) as the erring daughter. Undeservedly popular, this pastoral romp, written and directed by Marcel Pagnol, did much to convince a generation of art-house patrons that the French who lived close to the soil were warm, witty, and wise. Actually, Raimu and Fernandel, both products of the Marseilles music halls, were about as representative of indigenous peasant humor as an American burlesque graduate like Bert Lahr was of rural humor. But Pagnol knew not only how to use his actors, but how to use traditional, stylized comedy plots in a natural setting and make them look as if they grew there. He also knew how to rework a hit; this movie is a spin-off of *The Baker's Wife*. (It took Clouzot to shatter the image of French character that Pagnol had given to the world.) In French. b & w

We're No Angels (1955)—Humphrey Bogart, Peter Ustinov, and Aldo Ray trying very hard to be funny as a trio of convicts who escape from Devil's Island late in the 19th century. They take refuge in the home of a none too bright merchant (Leo G. Carroll)

and his opaque wife (Joan Bennett), and coyly busy themselves protecting the kindly dumb merchant from his mean, rich cousin and boss (Basil Rathbone). Michael Curtiz directed this oppressive, misbegotten venture, adapted from the French play *La Cuisine des anges*, from which the Broadway play *My 3 Angels* was also taken. Paramount. color

We're Not Dressing (1934)—Light, easy-going Paramount musical comedy about the wreck of a yacht on a desert island, taken (very loosely) from J. M. Barrie's *The Admirable Crichton*, one of the most serviceable of screen sources. Bing Crosby is the sailor; the spoiled heiress is Carole Lombard; he doesn't bat her around the way the hero of Lina Wertmüller's shrill *Swept Away* does. The other passengers are lecherous Ethel Merman (who sings "It's Just an Old Spanish Custom"), and Ray Milland and Leon Errol as rich prigs. The island, fortunately, isn't deserted; Gracie Allen and George Burns turn up, as naturalists living there. Norman Taurog directed; the Harry Revel and Mack Gordon songs include "Love Thy Neighbor" and "She Reminds Me of You." b & w

West Side Story (1961)—The film begins with a blast of stereophonic music, and everything about it is supposed to stun you with its newness, its size. The impressive, widely admired opening shots of New York from the air overload the story with values and importance—technological and sociological. And the dance movements are so sudden and huge, so portentously "alive" they're always near the explosion point. Consider the feat: first you take Shakespeare's *Romeo and Juliet* and remove all that cumbersome poetry; then you make the Montagues and Capulets modern by turning them into rival street gangs of native-born and Puerto Ricans. (You get rid of the parents, of course;

America is a *young* country—and who wants to be bothered by the squabbles of older people?) There is the choreographer Jerome Robbins (who conceived the stage musical) to convert the street rumbles into modern ballet—though he turns out to be too painstaking for high-powered moviemaking and the co-director Robert Wise takes over. The writers include Ernest Lehman, who did the script, Arthur Laurents, who wrote the Broadway show, and, for the lyrics, Stephen Sondheim. The music is by Leonard Bernstein. The irony of this hyped-up, slam-bang production is that those involved apparently don't really believe that beauty and romance *can* be expressed in modern rhythms, because whenever their Romeo and Juliet enter the scene, the dialogue becomes painfully old-fashioned and mawkish, the dancing turns to simpering, sickly romantic ballet, and sugary old stars hover in the sky. When true love enters the film, Bernstein abandons Gershwin and begins to echo Richard Rodgers, Rudolf Friml, and Victor Herbert. There's even a heavenly choir. When Romeo-Tony meets his Juliet-Maria, everything becomes gauzy and dreamy and he murmurs, "Have we met before?" When Tony, floating on the clouds of romance, is asked, "What have you been taking tonight?" he answers, "A trip to the moon." Match *that* for lyric eloquence! (You'd have to go back to Odets.) With Natalie Wood as Maria, Richard Beymer as Tony, and Rita Moreno, George Chakiris, Russ Tamblyn, Eliot Feld, Gus Trikonis, Ned Glass, John Astin, Bill Bramley, and Simon Oakland. Natalie Wood's songs were dubbed by Marni Nixon, Richard Beymer's by Jim Bryant, and Rita Moreno's by Betty Wand. Academy Awards: Best Picture, Director (Wise, Robbins), Supporting Actor (Chakiris), Supporting Actress (Moreno), Cinematography (Daniel L. Fapp), Art Direction and Set Direction (Boris Leven and Victor Gangelin),

Sound, Scoring, Costume Design (Irene Sharaff.) United Artists. color (See *I Lost it at the Movies*).

The Westerner (1940)—There are agreeable overtones of Mark Twain tall tales in this good-humored, though uneven, version of the paradoxical life of Judge Roy Bean, with Walter Brennan in the part. The hero, Gary Cooper, a travelling saddle bum, delays being hanged by the Judge (on a false charge of horse thieving) by spinning a yarn about his close friendship with Lily Langtry (the Judge's obsession). The handsome production was directed by William Wyler. With Fred Stone, Doris Davenport, Dana Andrews, Lilian Bond (as Langtry), Chill Wills, Forrest Tucker, Paul Hurst, and Tom Tyler. Script by Jo Swerling and Niven Busch, from a story by Stuart N. Lake. Cinematography by Gregg Toland; music by Dmitri Tiomkin. Produced by Samuel Goldwyn; released by United Artists. b & w

Westworld (1973)—Michael Crichton wrote and directed this sci-fi movie; it's set in Delos, a Disneyland for adults, where vacationers can play out their movie-fed fantasies by living in total environments that simulate past ages—ancient Rome, the medieval world, or the West of the 1880s. Computer-programmed humanoids satisfy the guests' vanity and lust and aggression. The idea is ingenious, and the film might have been marvellous: it isn't, quite (it has the skimped TV-movie look of a too-tight budget), but it's reasonably entertaining, and the leads (Richard Benjamin and Yul Brynner) are far superior to the actors in the usual sci-fi films. With James Brolin. M-G-M. color (See *Reeling*.)

Wetherby (1985)—It's about a younger generation whose souls are bombed out, and a middle-aged middle class that's spiritually desiccated. David Hare, who wrote and directed this English film, is out to show a society where nobody connects with anybody. He devised a who-is-to-blame mystery structure, with interlocking flashbacks. A sallow, dead-eyed graduate student (Tim McInnerny) comes to the Yorkshire village of Wetherby, crashes a dinner party given by an emotionally repressed secondary-school English teacher (Vanessa Redgrave), and the next day returns to her cottage to blow out his brains right in front of her, in her kitchen. The only real mystery is the radiant starshine that Redgrave gives off; she saves the movie from being a totally arid puzzle. With Suzanna Hamilton, Ian Holm, Judi Dench, Stuart Wilson, and Redgrave's daughter Joely Richardson, who plays the teacher as a young woman in love. color (See *Hooked*.)

What a Woman! (1943)—Another of the 40s movies about a career girl who isn't interested in men. Of its sort, it's better than some, largely because Rosalind Russell has a clown's all-out silliness and wildness in the way she gets some of her effects. This time, she plays the country's No. 1 hotshot literary agent. Brian Aherne is a writer assigned to do a magazine profile of her, and Willard Parker is a college professor–author whom she wants to star in the movie of his best-seller. Aherne acts in his usual asexual, bemused manner, and Parker (a huge man, on the order of Randolph Scott) is frenzied yet stolid. With Alan Dinehart and Ann Savage. Directed by Irving Cummings; the script by Therese Lewis and Barry Trivers is based on a story by Erik Charell. Columbia. b & w

What Every Woman Knows (1934)—Helen Hayes making nice. The mousiest First Lady of the theatre in a classic mouse role. Gregory La Cava directed this version of the James M. Barrie play, a prestigious little number from

M-G-M with a cast that includes Brian Aherne as the opaque husband of the little darling. With Dudley Digges, Donald Crisp, and David Torrence. b & w

What Have I Done to Deserve This! *Que He Hecho Yo Para Merecer Esto* (1984)—This Spanish film by the bad-boy writer-director Pedro Almodóvar has an Off Off Broadway informality. It's a generally likable dadaist farce about working-class family life in Madrid's housing projects—huge block buildings of dinky, cramped apartments. The heroine, Gloria (Carmen Maura), drags herself through 18-hour days with the help of No Doz and an occasional sniff of glue or detergent. She goes out to work as a cleaning woman and also cooks and scrubs for her taxi-driver husband (who's a gifted forger and is involved in a scheme to fake Hitler's memoirs) and her two sons—a 14-year-old drug dealer and a 12-year-old hustler who seduces his schoolmates' fathers. You'll probably never see a woozier treatment of the breakdown of the family and the decay of the society. The picture is like a flip, slaphappy version of *The Threepenny Opera*. With Chus Lampreave as the mother, and Verónica Forqué as the prostitute. In Spanish. color (See *State of the Art*.)

What Price Hollywood (1932)—The story line of this film, directed by George Cukor for the producer David O. Selznick, is basically the same as that of Selznick's later *A Star is Born* (1937), which he admitted was a reworking of this material. (Cukor also got back to the material when he directed the 1954 version of *A Star is Born*.) Constance Bennett is a waitress at the Brown Derby who meets a brilliant alcoholic director (Lowell Sherman); she rises to fame as his career collapses. Sherman probably patterned his interpretation on the self-destructive drinking of his brother-in-law John Barrymore.

Many of the scenes are like sketches for scenes in the later versions, but this film has its own interest, especially because of its glimpses into the studio world at the time. Screenplay by Jane Murfin, Ben Markson, Gene Fowler, and Rowland Brown; from a story by Adela Rogers St. John. With Neil Hamilton, Louise Beavers, Eddie Anderson, and Gregory Ratoff. R K O. b & w

What's New Pussycat? (1965)—The script for this lavish production, set in Paris, is by Woody Allen, and his oblique humor is occasionally weird and alienating in this expensive context. It's a frenetic but generally funny psychiatric farce. Peter O'Toole plays a fashion-magazine editor who consults a psychiatrist (Peter Sellers) about how to cure his susceptibility to the girls who pursue him; inevitably, Sellers goes berserk trying to discover the secrets of O'Toole's success. Sellers is in the Woody Allen role, but Woody turns up, too, and there is a trio of beautiful, zingy comediennes—Paula Prentiss (who gets to read a poem called "Ode to a Pacifist Junkie"), Romy Schneider, and Capucine. Directed by Clive Donner. United Artists. color

What's Up, Doc? (1972)—Rehashed humor. Peter Bogdanovich tries to resuscitate screwball comedy; his chief source is the 1938 *Bringing Up Baby*, with Cary Grant and Katharine Hepburn—an extended absent-minded-professor joke that's a lovely piece of lunacy. That film's underlying assumption is that if you repress your instincts you can get so disjointed you can forget your own name. Grant, a square pedant engaged to a bossy girl pedant, was a paleontologist, putting together the bones of a dinosaur. Hepburn was a live-animal lover, an uninhibited girl with a fluffy wild mane. She undermined the orderly absent-mindedness of Grant's life, and everything in the movie flowed from that. Bogdanovich takes the plot and the externals of the characters but loses the logic. His picture goes every which way; he restages gags from Buster Keaton and Laurel & Hardy and W. C. Fields, plus a lot of cornball devices. Ryan O'Neal and Barbra Streisand are asked to play Grant and Hepburn. They're given no other characters, and O'Neal is embarrassing as he diligently goes through the Grant motions and mannerisms; Streisand comes off better because she sticks to her own rapid, tricky New Yorkese line readings. As the fiancée, Madeline Kahn does a traditional bossy-female caricature that is strident but sometimes funny, and Liam Dunn has a pleasant bit as a judge—another facsimile. There are a couple of wonderful fresh moments (seconds, really) when Sorrell Booke trips Mabel Albertson and when they wrestle together in a hotel corridor. Though the picture works only fitfully and at a rather infantile, imitative level, that was enough to make it a box-office hit. Also with Austin Pendleton, Kenneth Mars, Michael Murphy, John Hillerman, Randy Quaid, and M. Emmet Walsh. Script by Buck Henry and David Newman & Robert Benton, from Bogdanovich's story line; cinematography by Laszlo Kovacs. Warners. color (See *Deeper into Movies*.)

What's Up, Tiger Lily? (1966)—(The discreet comma was not always in the title.) Woody Allen provides dubbed dialogue for a chopped-up Japanese sexy-spy thriller; the jokes get rather desperate, but there are enough wildly sophomoric ones to keep this pop stunt fairly amusing until about midway. It would have made a terrific short. A.I.P. color

When Comedy Was King (1960)—The high spots are great: Wallace Beery chains Gloria Swanson to the railway track, and Bobby Vernon dances, in sequences from *Teddy at the Throttle*; Laurel and Hardy go through routines taken from *Big Business* (directed by Leo McCarey, photographed by George Stevens). And there are nostalgic (often remarkable) glimpses of Chaplin and Keaton and Langdon, and Ben Turpin, Charlie Chase, Fatty Arbuckle, Mabel Normand, Mack Swain, Edgar Kennedy, and the Keystone Cops. Robert Youngson compiled these clips, after the success of his *The Golden Age of Comedy*. Though both these anthologies of silent comedy have an irritating sentimental commentary, they contain pieces of film that you can't easily see elsewhere. b & w

Where's Charley? (1952)—Ray Bolger's earlier film roles never gave him a full-scale star opportunity, but this time he was able to transfer one of his most famous Broadway performances to the screen. The movie preserves the airy grace of (very likely) the greatest comic dancer this country ever produced. The vehicle is a deftly made musical, taken from the sturdy old farce *Charley's Aunt*, with Bolger as Oxford's favorite female impersonator. He has a charming partner in Allyn Ann McLerie as Amy, as well as a suitor in Horace Cooper as Mr. Spettigue. There are a pair of lovers—Robert Shackleton and Mary Germaine—but you can find some excuse to step outside during their duet. Frank Loesser wrote the lighthearted score (which includes "Make a Miracle" and "Once in Love with Amy"). This is one of the most pleasing of Hollywood musicals—maybe because it's so unostentatious and unambitious; it seems just right. David Butler directed; John Monks, Jr., did the adaptation of George Abbott's musical version of the Brandon Thomas play. With Margaretta Scott. Warners. color

Where's Poppa? (1970)—Two New York brothers (George Segal and Ron Leibman) who have promised their dying father they won't put their mother (Ruth Gordon) in a home for the aged are stuck with a demanding senile psychopath. Segal, the unmarried son who lives with her, is in an agony of sexual frustration and walks in a stooped position under his Oedipal load. This Freudian farce was adapted by Robert Klane from his own novel and directed by Carl Reiner. It's full of hip energy and talent, and it's intermittently very funny, though it goes any which way for a gag. The skits tend to fall apart for want of aim, and the unlimited, omni-destructive satirical humor doesn't leave us anything to hold on to—there's nothing for our laughs to bounce off. The high point is perhaps the quietest moment: when Segal, in a near trance of romantic longing, sings "Louise" to the charmingly comic ingenue, Trish Van Devere. With Vincent Gardenia, Paul Sorvino, Rae Allen, Garrett Morris, Rob Reiner, and Barnard Hughes. United Artist. color (See *Deeper into Movies*.)

Whirlpool (1950)—A real stinker, with Richard Conte as a psychoanalyst whose wife (Gene Tierney) is an insomniac kleptomaniac with a father fixation. The obtuse Conte doesn't spot any of this, but a thieving, bug-eyed hypnotist (José Ferrer) reads her mind fast, and starts throwing her into trances. He decides to throttle an old flame of his and put the blame on the sticky-fingered Tierney. The plot goes from confusion to chaos when he arranges an ironclad alibi for himself: he has his gall bladder removed just a few hours before the murder. The scriptwriters, Ben Hecht (hiding in shame under the pseudonym Lester Barstow) and Andrew Solt, must have really had it in for the director, Otto Preminger. Others swimming in this stew, taken from a Guy Endore novel, are Charles Bickford, Constance Collier, Barbara O'Neil, Eduard Franz, and Fortunio Bonanova. 20th Century-Fox. b & w

Whisky Galore, see *Tight Little Island*

The Whisperers (1967)—Essentially a character portrait of a lonely old pensioner (Edith Evans) in a grimy English industrial town who chats to herself and has moved into a fantasy world, this film gives one the feeling that it should be loose, discovered material. But though the director, Bryan Forbes, is talented, everything—the furniture, the streets, the people's expressions—looks planned for the camera, and we are led to see things in such a limited way that even what is intelligent and well acted seems false. Not Edith Evans, however. Her performance is so varied—so commanding and noble even when she's rummaging around in old newspapers or talking paranoid nonsense—that she transcends the melodramatic incidents involving a criminal son (Ronald Fraser), a seedy husband (Eric Portman) who deserted her, and a sympathetic social worker (Leonard Rossiter, so conscious of playing kindness you want to smack him). Evans' full-scale performance—the creation of a senile woman's inner life—confers greatness on this otherwise mediocre British film. Forbes wrote the screenplay, from Robert Nicolson's novel. With Nanette Newman, Avis Bunnage, Margaret Tyzack, and Kenneth Griffith. b & w

Whistle Down the Wind (1961)—Although the story about a group of children who discover a murderer hiding in their barn and take him for Jesus Christ is a modern parallel of Christ's progress to the cross, this English film isn't nearly as embarrassing and sickly as that sounds. The directing, writing, and acting are all better than the basic idea. In some peculiar double-edged way the movie is both satirical and straight; Keith Waterhouse and Willis Hall, who adapted Mary Hayley Bell's novel, kidded the idea in a way that almost make the idea work. *Saturday Night and Sunday Morning* began with the working-class hero in a machine shop counting "900 and 90-bloody-9"; in this picture, a

6-year-old boy, every bit as cynical as that hero, attacks his morning boiled egg with a muttered "178." Though the central figure is Hayley Mills, who gives her standard lip-licking performance, she isn't offensive and you can forget about her. The pleasures of the film relate to the egg-eater—the ancient-looking Alan Barnes—and to Diane Holgate, who has unbelievably old, all-seeing, beautiful eyes, and to the dozens of amazing unchildish children who keep filling the screen. They're already wearing the faces they'll be wearing for the rest of their lives, and the startlingly sensible lines they speak are as good as just about anything in English movies of the period. The director, Bryan Forbes, makes them perhaps the least sentimental collection of children you've ever seen in a film, and when the disillusioned egg-eater says, "He's not Jesus. He's just a feller" he's amazingly like that working-class hero with his "What I'm out for is a good time. All the rest is propaganda." With Alan Bates and Bernard Lee. b & w

White Cargo (1942)—After starting Hedy Lamarr off big in this country (in *Algiers*), Hollywood could never quite figure out what to do with her. So here she is in her eleventh American picture, in dark suntan makeup and bangles, as a sexy savage who drives white men wild. She wiggles tropically and announces "I am Tondelayo"—a line which served a generation of female impersonators. The setting of this meant-to-be-steamy melodrama is Africa, but you wouldn't know it except for the portentous drums that accompany the credits; nobody ever seems to go outside the headquarters of the rubber plantation. The actors sweat profusely and deliver a succession of howlers—each remark seems to have a long theatrical pedigree. Sample: "The natives have been looking at me lately in a queer sort of way." Walter Pidgeon is cast in what was usually the Clark Gable role

(the tough cynic); the others are Frank Morgan as the genial drunken doctor, Richard Carlson as the new arrival, Leigh Whipper as the black servant, and Bramwell Fletcher, Henry O'Neill, Richard Ainley, and Reginald Owen. Directed by Richard Thorpe—so routinely that even the lighting looks stagey. Leon Gordon did the adaptation of his popular play, which was based on the novel *Hell's Playground* by Ida Vera Simonton. (There was a British film version in 1929.) M-G-M. b & w

The White Cliffs of Dover (1944)—Sentimental patriotism, in the *Mrs. Miniver* mold, and a truly monstrous cultural artifact. Irene Dunne (looking rather mature) plays a young, small-town girl from Tulsa who is courted by Sir John (Alan Marshal), an English aristocrat; they are married on the eve of the First World War, amid much speechifying about the ties that bind the English (represented by Gladys Cooper as Sir John's indomitable, upper-crust mother and Dame May Whitty as his devoted old nanny) and the Americans (represented by the bride's wise, jolly father, Frank Morgan). Sir John goes directly from his honeymoon to the war; Irene and the English women sit around waiting for the soldiers to come home, and when Gladys Cooper receives word that her other son—Reggie—has been killed in action, she crosses her drawing room, walking straighter than ever. Irene's husband has a few days' leave in Paris, so she takes her baby boy and the silliest hat you've ever seen (it has a floral doodad that sticks up a full six inches), and meets him there, and the three of them watch proudly as the Americans, who have entered the war, march into the city. (That's the movie's emotional peak.) Irene resumes her waiting; Sir John is killed in action, and she goes into a decline, with hysterical seizures. But she regains her self-control and the baby grows into serious-faced little Roddy Mc-

Dowall, who becomes attached to beautiful little Elizabeth Taylor, whose family lives on the land he will inherit. The picture becomes really grotesque when two horrid, blond German boys show up; they're junior-Nazi types and they seem privy to Hitler's war plans. Watching their ugly behavior, old Frank Morgan, who has been visiting, *knows* the truth; he tells Irene there's another war coming. Desperate to save Roddy from his father's fate, she packs him up and they head for Tulsa. He's a virtuous tyke, though, and on the train he convinces her that they mustn't run away—they must go back and do what's right. Years pass; he turns into Peter Lawford, Elizabeth Taylor turns into June Lockhart, he goes off to the Second World War, and old Irene, now a Red Cross nurse, finds him among the wounded brought in to her hospital. Probably the movie only appears to go on for several more generations. With Van Johnson, C. Aubrey Smith, John Warburton, Jill Esmond, Brenda Forbes, Norma Varden, and is that Tom Drake as a dead American soldier? Based on a narrative poem by Alice Duer Miller; the screenplay is by Claudine West, George Froeschel, and Jan Lustig. Directed by Clarence Brown (he sinks to the level of the material—this must be his worst-paced movie); produced by Sidney Franklin. M-G-M. b & w

White Heat (1949)—This Freudian gangster picture, directed by Raoul Walsh, is very obvious, and it's so primitive and outrageous in its flamboyance that it seems to have been made much earlier than it was. But this flamboyance is also what makes some of its scenes stay with you. James Cagney plays the tough guy who sits on the lap of his mother (Margaret Wycherly), and goes berserk in the prison mess hall when he learns of her death—a horrible sobbing whine comes out of him, and it just keeps coming, as he punches out anyone who gets near him. This

is perhaps the most daring sequence Cagney ever performed; he does his most operatic acting in this film, and he has his wildest death scene: he literally explodes. With Virginia Mayo, Edmond O'Brien, Steve Cochran, Paul Guilfoyle, and Fred Clark. The script by Ivan Goff and Ben Roberts was based on a story written for the screen by Virginia Kellogg. Warners. b & w

The White Hell of Pitz Palu *Die Weisse Hölle vom Piz Palü* (1929)—The German geologist-filmmaker Dr. Arnold Fanck made a series of six "mountain films"—all popular successes—starring the young dancer Leni Riefenstahl. This one is the most famous, perhaps because although Fanck directed the outdoor sequences (a celebration of heights, vastness, ordeal, purity), the overall story was in the hands of G. W. Pabst, who obtained marvellously sensual performances from Riefenstahl and Gustav Diessl. It's a passionate, romantic outdoor epic full of that Promethean Alpine idealism about the conquest of the peaks which was soon after to become identified with Nazi mysticism. The celebrated German daredevil ace of the First World War, Ernst Udet (whose later experiences, during the Nazi period, were used as the basis for the 1955 film *The Devil's General*), appears as himself; when the principal characters are trapped on a mountain peak, Udet arrives in a tiny rescue plane. An example of a genre that died, this film of precipices, avalanches, and suffering produces very mixed emotions, but however one feels about it, it is visually stunning. When it opened in the U.S., it had a tremendous success, though its fame was diminished by a bastardized sound version, with sequences shot in a studio replacing the authentic originals. b & w

White Mane *Crin blanc* (1953)—One of the most beautiful films ever made. Shot in the Camargue, France's wildest, loneliest region, it's a fable—a tragic fairy tale—about a boy's love for the horse he alone is able to tame. Hunted down by a band of men who want the animal, the boy and his horse head out to sea rather than face capture. The film-maker was Albert Lamorisse; his intentions were clearly to achieve a piece of visual po-etry—unlike most filmmakers who head that way he succeeded. James Agee wrote the En-glish narration. (40 minutes.) b & w

White Nights (1985)—The magnificent Mi-khail Baryshnikov, who might have been cre-ated for the movie camera, shames the movie he's in. He plays a Russian ballet star who defected from the Soviet Union to the U.S. in the 70s and is on his way to dance in Tokyo when his plane crash-lands in Siberia. The movie's central gimmick is that the ballet dancer is put in the care of a black American tap dancer (Gregory Hines, acting morose and embittered) who defected from the U.S. Army during the Vietnam war. Except for the happiness he has found with his Russian wife (Isabella Rossellini), the tap dancer is miser-able, and now a K.G.B. colonel tells him that if he can't persuade the ballet star to renounce the U.S. and perform in just a few days at a Kirov gala, he'll be taken out of the Siberian playhouse where he has been performing and sent to work in the mines. This cheap melodramatic plot is like a straitjacket that the director, Taylor Hackford, got into vol-untarily and can't wriggle out of. The film is meant to be about two dancers who, each in his own way, have fled their countries in quest of freedom of movement, but it turned into a movie about dancers in a funk. It's often ludicrously bad, but Rossellini, a great beauty hidden in a mousy role, evokes her mother (Ingrid Bergman), around the time of *Casablanca*, and there's enough footage of Ba-ryshnikov to carry you past the embarrass-ments of the tacky script. The opening sequence—a performance of the Roland Petit

ballet *Le Jeune Homme et la mort*—is superb; Twyla Tharp choreographed the Baryshni-kov-Hines duet to David Pack's "Prove Me Wrong." With Jerzy Skolimowski as the colo-nel, and Geraldine Page, Helen Mirren, and John Glover. Cinematography by David Wat-kin. The script is credited to James Goldman and Eric Hughes. Columbia. color (See *Hooked*.)

White Savage (1943)—Jon Hall, Maria Mon-tez, and Sabu, with their marvellous mix of accents, having implausible adventures in the South Sea Islands; they all sound just as they did in *Arabian Nights*. The writer, Rich-ard Brooks, subversively put a character named Tamara in the story; the way it works out, other, serious-minded characters say things like "Well, how are you feeling today, Tamara?" Arthur Lubin directed this hunk of low camp. It may be that these semi-bur-lesques were more fun to make than to watch. With Turhan Bey, who somehow puts his seal on them, and Sidney Toler, Thomas Gomez, and Paul Guilfoyle. Produced by George Waggner, for Universal. color

The White Sheik *Lo Sceicco Bianco* (1951)—This affectionate satire on glamour and delusion is probably the most gentle and naturalistic of Federico Fellini's films, but it was not a success, maybe because it is a little flat in places. (Fellini is still clumsy, and the storytelling is rather drawn out.) The hero-ine, Brunella Bovo (also the heroine of De Sica's *Miracle in Milan*), has come to Rome for her honeymoon, but the devotion of the groom (Leopoldo Trieste) is much less im-portant to her than her infatuation with the White Sheik—the hero of a photographic comic strip. She rushes off to find her ideal, and the cheap, crude actor (Alberto Sordi, in a marvellous performance) tries to rise above himself, to the level of her fantasies. The White Sheik, it turns out, is far more a creature of self-delusion than the star-struck bride. The groom, deserted, sad, and anxious, wandering at night in the piazza, finds solace in conversation with a lively, friendly little prostitute (Giulietta Masina; Fellini later developed this episode into *Nights of Cabiria*). Among those who worked on the story and script were Fellini, Ennio Flaiano, Tullio Pinelli, and Michelangelo Antonioni. Music by Nino Rota. (It was the source idea of Gene Wilder's *The World's Greatest Lover*.) In Italian. b & w

Who Is Killing the Great Chefs of Europe? (1978)—Robert Morley's legs, his arms, and even his head are appendages of his stomach. In this macabre farce, he plays Max, the editor of a gourmet magazine, and he enters his scenes by pointing his gut and then following it—the legs are a distance behind, holding it up. Max is an imperious child, ruling the world of haute cuisine. At 70, the incomparable Morley is clearly overjoyed at having this chance to play an enfant terrible. It's a completely controlled debauch: he knows the precise effects of his pendulous scowl, his sagging lower lip and trembling jellyfish chins; he knows that his eyes are so close together that when he knits his bushy brows the wiry hairs commingle and he's a cartoon. The tone of the film is meant to be debonair slapstick ghoulishness, but the director, Ted Kotcheff, doesn't have the reserve intended by the scriptwriter, Peter Stone; Kotcheff's work is pushed and bumpy. But messy as the film is, it's spirited, it's fun. With Jacqueline Bisset, Jean-Pierre Cassel, Stefano Satta Flores, Philippe Noiret, Jean Rochefort, Madge Ryan, and, as the romantic lead, George Segal, who looks as if he hasn't slept for four years—his smile is like a wince. There are good bits by John Le Mesurier, Kenneth Fortescue, Daniel Emilfork, and many others. From the book *Someone Is Killing the Great Chefs of Europe* by Nan and Ivan Lyons; cin-

ematography by John Alcott. Warners. color (See *When the Lights Go Down*.)

The Whole Town's Talking (1935)—John Ford directed this likable comedy about a gentle clerk, his gangster double (Edward G. Robinson in a dual role), and the hardboiled girl, Bill, whom the clerk adores. Bill is Jean Arthur, the comedienne with the wistful-husky voice; that voice was one of the best sounds in the romantic comedies of the 30s and 40s. (Talkies made her a star, but in the silent period she was already a popular leading lady; Ford had directed her in 1923 in a John Gilbert vehicle, *Cameo Kirby*.) Adapted from a W. R. Burnett story, by Jo Swerling and Robert Riskin. With Wallace Ford, Etienne Girardot, Donald Meek, Arthur Byron, and Edward Brophy. Columbia. b & w

Wife Versus Secretary (1936)—Clark Gable, Jean Harlow, James Stewart, and Myrna Loy in the kind of hit picture M-G-M was famous for. It's taken from one of the love-triangle magazine stories that Faith Baldwin ground out, and though Norman Krasna, John Lee Mahin, and Alice Duer Miller all worked on it, it's just glossy, contrived, and moralistic. There's no wisecracking here; it's a melodrama, a cautionary tale about temptation. What makes it so fundamentally dull is that Jean Harlow, who's the central character, is cast as a nice hardworking girl. Harlow talks nasal baby talk, her voice rises to a high rasp when she means to show stress, and she walks with a sexual swagger, but she's supposed to be the hyper-efficient executive secretary to Gable, a millionaire publisher. He's in love with his adoring wife, Myrna Loy, who is misled into thinking that he's having an affair with the secretary. Gable overacts rather fatuously and makes the publisher seem very stupid; Loy's role gives her no chance to do anything but fret graciously; and

James Stewart, who plays the secretary's poor-boy fiancé, is a high-minded type, who wants her to quit her glamorous job when they get married. Whatever interest the movie has is in the secretary's role, because although innocent of any adulterous wrongdoing, she is half in love with her boss, and she's not happy about her prospects with the virtuous Stewart. Harlow has some moments, but likably brassy as she is, Jean Harlow is nobody's secretary, and when she tries to seem natural and sincere, she is a truly terrible actress. The hairdresser who did her up in rigid little platinum curls didn't help. Clarence Brown directed. With May Robson, Gilbert Emery, George Barbier, Hobart Cavanaugh, John Qualen, Marjorie Gateson, Tom Dugan, and, in a bit, Jack Mulhall. b & w

The Wilby Conspiracy (1975)—Wearing a mustache and speaking with a rhythmic Bantu accent, Sidney Poitier is a black revolutionary leader on the lam (from Cape Town to Johannesburg) in this little-known tense, intelligent melodrama. Michael Caine is the British mining engineer who helps him; Nicol Williamson is the Afrikaaner tailing them, and he's scary because he's smart and hideously prejudiced. This Anglo-American production doesn't go in for romance or comedy; it sticks to suspense, and it's really good at what it does (except for a rather tacky escape by air). Directed by Ralph Nelson; the script, based on a novel by Peter Driscoll, is by Rod Amateau and Harold Nebenzal. (Amateau also directed the action sequences.) With Saeed Jaffrey, Persis Khambatta, Prunella Gee, and Helmut Dantine, who was one of the producers. Released in the U.S. by United Artists. color

The Wild Angels (1966)—A crude A.I.P. wheeler that was aimed at the drive-in and male-loner audience but wound up reaching so large an international audience that the major studios began to imitate it. It's loaded with pot-smoking, orgies, rumbles, and whatever else the producer-director, Roger Corman, and his scenarist, Charles B. Griffith, could work in. Their big number is set in a chapel at a funeral service for a member of a motorcycle gang—Loser (played by Bruce Dern), who was hooked on Nazi insignia. Loser's buddies tie up the minister, rape the young widow, and take the body from its coffin in order to wrap it in a Nazi flag. Corman and Griffith seem to know only one way to entertain an audience: by sensationalism. And it's a very square idea of sensationalism—you're supposed to be thrilled by each demonstration of how gross and violent the gang members are. (There's a good moment, though, when Loser, dying, asks, "Anybody got a straight cigarette?") With Peter Fonda as Heavenly Blues, Nancy Sinatra as Mike, Michael J. Pollard as Pigmy, and Diane Ladd and Gayle Hunnicutt. Edited by Monte Hellman. color

Wild Boys of the Road (1933)—The freight-hopping excerpt, which has become a standard of anthology films, gives the impression of a very powerful Depression melodrama, but there's a load of sentimentality, too. William Wellman directed, from an uninspired script by Earl Baldwin. With Frankie Darro, Rochelle Hudson, Arthur Hohl, Sterling Holloway, Robert Barrat, Minna Gombell, Ward Bond, and Willard Robertson. Warners. b & w

The Wild Bunch (1969)—It's a traumatic poem of violence, with imagery as ambivalent as Goya's. By a supreme burst of filmmaking energy Sam Peckinpah is able to convert chaotic romanticism into exaltation; the film is perched right on the edge of incoherence, yet it's comparable in scale and sheer poetic force to Kurosawa's *The Seven*

Samurai. There are images of great subtlety and emotional sophistication: a blown-up bridge, with horses and riders falling to the water in an instant extended (by slow motion) to eternity; a vulture sits on a dead man's chest and turns his squalid, naked head to stare at the camera. The movie is set in the Texas and Mexico of 1913, and, in Peckinpah's words, "I was trying to tell a simple story about bad men in changing times. *The Wild Bunch* is simply what happens when killers go to Mexico. The strange thing is that you feel a great sense of loss when these killers reach the end of the line." That's accurate, as far as it goes. But Peckinpah has very intricate, contradictory feelings, and he got so wound up in the aesthetics of violence that what had begun as a realistic treatment—a deglamourization of warfare that would show how horribly gruesome killing really is—became instead an almost abstract fantasy about violence. The bloody deaths are voluptuous, frightening, beautiful. Pouring new wine into the bottle of the Western, Peckinpah explodes the bottle; his story is too simple for this imagist epic. And it's no accident that you feel a sense of loss for each killer of the Bunch: Peckinpah has made them seem heroically, mythically alive on the screen. With William Holden, Ernest Borgnine, Robert Ryan, Ben Johnson, Edmond O'Brien, Warren Oates, Bo Hopkins, L. Q. Jones, Strother Martin, Jaime Sanchez, Emilio Fernandez, Albert Dekker, and Dub Taylor. With cinematography by Lucien Ballard, editing by Lou Lombardo, and music by Jerry Fielding. The script is by Walon Green and Peckinpah, based on story material by Green and Roy N. Sickner; the film was possibly influenced by Clouzot's 1953 *The Wages of Fear*. (Peckinpah's cut runs 2 hours and 23 minutes; the studio's cut runs 2 hours and 15 minutes. Both versions are in circulation.) A Phil Feldman Production for Warners–Seven Arts. CinemaScope, color

Wild in the Streets (1968)—This blatant, insensitive, crummy-looking American International Pictures movie is entertaining in a lot of ways that more tasteful movies aren't; it has wit without any grace at all, and is enjoyable at a pop, comic-strip level. The story (by Robert Thom) is a satiric fantasy about the freaked-out young as a new breed of fascist; it's treated with lunatic relish and enough mockery to make it funny. Barry Shear's direction isn't up to the playful paranoia of the script, but the cast is good—Christopher Jones, Shelley Winters, Millie Perkins, Diane Varsi rattling a tambourine, Hal Holbrook as a congressman who has a faint twitch when he smells trouble, and a very young Richard Pryor in his first screen appearance. color

The Wild One (1954)—Based on the 1947 events in Hollister, California, when a convention of 4,000 motorcyclists took over the town, this film offers a nightmare image: the "Black Rebels," an outlaw motorcycle gang—a leather-jacketed pack who resemble storm troopers—terrorize a town. Their emblem is a death's head and crossed pistons and rods, and Marlon Brando, in his magnetic, soft-eyed youth, is their moody leader. The picture seemed to be frightened of its subject—the young nihilists who said "no" to American blandness and conformity—and reduced it as quickly as possible to the trivial meaninglessness of misunderstood boy meets understanding girl (Mary Murphy), but the audience savored the potentialities, and this clumsy, naïve film was banned and argued about in so many countries that it developed a near-legendary status. In this country, young men were saying "It's the story of my life" for several years afterward. Some of the scenes, such as the one in which the cyclists circle around the frightened heroine, have considerable power. And the film has that memorable moment when a woman asks

Brando, "What are you rebelling against?" and he answers, "What have you got?" With Lee Marvin as Brando's rival for control of the pack, Robert Keith, Jay C. Flippen, and Ray Teal. Directed by Laslo Benedek, from a sceenplay by John Paxton, based on the story "The Cyclists' Raid" by Frank Rooney. Cinematography by Hal Mohr; produced by Stanley Kramer for Columbia. b & w (See *I Lost it at the Movies*.)

The Wild Party (1929)—The manic, wide-eyed flapper Clara Bow, in her first talkie, set in a women's college; she's a student and Fredric March is a young professor. It's silly stuff, yet charming. Clara Bow, whose vitality was awesome and was combined with a childlike vulnerability, was for her period something like what Marilyn Monroe was for hers. (And when she was past her peak she, too, was celebrated by intellectuals.) Bow's infantile sexuality is high-voltage; she's both repulsive and irresistible. Dorothy Arzner directed; with Joyce Compton, Jack Oakie, Shirley O'Hara, and Marceline Day. (A 1956 film and a 1974 film use the same title, but are not remakes.) Paramount Famous Lasky. b & w

Wild Strawberries *Smultronstallet* (1957)—Ingmar Bergman's first big popular success in the United States. It's a very uneven film: an eminent physician (Victor Sjöström) looks back over his life, which is tricked up with gothic effects and contrasts (there are resemblances to passages in *Dead of Night* and Dreyer's *Vampyr*) and with peculiarly unconvincing flashbacks and overexplicit dialogue. It's a very lumpy odyssey, yet who can forget Sjöström's face, or the vicious, bickering couple who rasp at each other in the back seat of a car, or the large-scale mask of the beautiful Ingrid Thulin as the physician's unhappy daughter-in-law? Few movies give us such memorable, emotion-charged images. One can try to forget the irritations: the in-

credibly callow representatives of youth, the "cold" rigid son (Gunnar Björnstrand), the disappointingly vacuous parts assigned Bibi Andersson as the two Saras, the expendable role of Naima Wifstrand as the ancient mother. With Max von Sydow, Gunnel Lindblom, Folke Sundquist, Maud Hansson, Gertrude Fridh, Björn Bjelvenstam, Åke Fridell. Cinematography by Gunnar Fischer. In Swedish. b & w

Will Penny (1968)—A "realistic" Western, in the sense that the cowhand hero (Charlton Heston) is dirty, ignorant, not overly courageous, and 50 years old. This film, written and directed by Tom Gries, is trying to be a classic—you can tell because all that the hero really hopes to do is survive, and though he meets a woman (Joan Hackett, who gives the film its only freshness), he goes back to his dull, solitary existence. It's static and overextended, to put it generously, and Donald Pleasence does one of his more obnoxious performances; as the religious-maniac villain, he stares fixedly—and persistently. The cast includes Bruce Dern as Pleasence's gigglykiller son, Ben Johnson, Slim Pickens, Anthony Zerbe, Lee Majors, Clifton James, G. D. Spradlin, Luke Askew, and Jon Francis as the young boy. Gries stages the action so that it all seems to start 10 feet from the camera and then rush toward it dead center; after a while the mountains and blue skies begin to seem like a painted backdrop. Heston does a solid job, however. Paramount. color

Willie & Phil (1980)—Writer-director Paul Mazursky's homage to *Jules and Jim* is also an overview of the psycho-social fashions of the 70s, but there's no texture to the lives of the characters. We have no idea why Willie, a high-school teacher (Michael Ontkean), and Phil, a go-getting fashion photographer (Ray Sharkey), who meet at a revival showing of *Jules and Jim* in Greenwich Village, become inseparable friends, or why they both fall in love with Jeannette (Margot Kidder), rather than with any other stray pretty girl in Washington Square. Jeannette doesn't live up to what Willie and Phil say about her, and they don't live up to what the narrator (Mazursky) says about them. In Mazursky's best films, everyone is satirized, and the characters' foolishness makes them more likable; Mazursky brings people to life only when he makes fun of them. But he presents everything that Jeannette does at face value, and, having held back his feelings about her (or not having sorted them out), he muffles his satiric feelings about the men and the triangular situation. The whole movie becomes neutral. Apparently looking for an escape from his principal characters, Mazursky drags in ethnic humor and never lets up on it—Willie's Jewish parents, Phil's Italian-Catholic parents, and Jeannette's Protestant mother in Kentucky. The liveliest, funniest performance—it's just a small one—is by Kaki Hunter as Jeannette's cutie younger sister. With Helen Hanft as a used-car saleswoman, Julie Bovasso as Phil's mother, Jan Miner as Willie's mother, Kathleen Maguire as Jeannette's mother, Laurence Fishburne III as the student who recites "To be or not to be," and Kristine DeBell as Rena. Cinematography by Sven Nykvist. 20th Century-Fox. color (See *Taking It All In*.)

Willow (1988)—The evil sorceress Queen Bavmorda (Jean Marsh) is killing all the newborn babies in the Daikini domain, because of a prophecy that an infant born with a special mark will bring about her downfall. Placed on a raft of rushes, the savior baby girl drifts downriver into the land of a peaceful, elflike people, the Nelwyns. A young Nelwyn farmer, Willow (Warwick Davis), tries to protect her, and eventually, with the help of an outlaw Daikini swordsman, Madmartigan (Val Kilmer), and a rebel Daikini,

Airk (Gavan O'Herlihy), Willow storms the evil queen's black castle. This tale involves trolls, vicious black boars, 9-inch-tall men called Brownies, platinum-wigged Tinker Bells, a two-headed dragon, and some 400 special-effects shots. Before it's over, you feel as if you'd fallen into a pile of mixed metaphors. Produced by George Lucas, who also wrote the story, the movie seems to be one stale idea after another. The director, Ron Howard, shows his gentle talent only in his handling of the 3-foot-4-inch Willow, whose sweet-faced humility could make parts of the movie appealing to kids. (Adults may observe that Lucas, who underwent a costly divorce, has made a sword-and-sorcery epic in which all the power is in the hands of women.) With Billy Barty—triumphant as usual—as the High Aldwin of the Nelwyns, and Joanne Whalley, Julie Peters, and Patricia Hayes. Made in England, Wales, and New Zealand. M-G-M. color (See *Hooked*.)

Willy Wonka and the Chocolate Factory (1971)—A fantasy with music for children that never finds an appropriate style; it's stilted and frenetic, like Prussians at play. With Gene Wilder, Jack Albertson, and Roy Kinnear; directed by Mel Stuart; adapted by Roald Dahl, from his own story; songs by Leslie Bricusse and Anthony Newley. Produced by David Wolper; released by Paramount. color

The Wind and the Lion (1975)—The flamboyance of the writer-director, John Milius, is initially startling; this film opens with such a flourish and bang that the viewer may really expect a beautiful, old-fashioned swords-in-the-desert epic. However, when the actors begin to talk (which they do incessantly), the flat-footed dialogue and the amateurish acting (especially by the secondary characters) take one back to the low-budget buffoonery of Maria Montez and Turhan Bey. Milius doesn't seem to be a very gifted storyteller: he lets the actors toss away the information that the audience needs to make sense of the action, and people are killed so arbitrarily that the whole epic seems dissociated. There isn't enough conviction behind this movie to hold it together. The plot involves Brian Keith as Theodore Roosevelt (ordering a fictitious invasion), Sean Connery as the last of the Barbary pirates, and Candice Bergen as a kidnapped American. Connery seems to be having a good time playing Yul Brynner in *The King and I*, and Vladek Sheybal, as something called the Bashaw, is clearly doing a parody. With John Huston as John Hay. Cinematography by Billy Williams. M-G-M; released by United Artists. color

Wings of Desire   *Der Himmel über Berlin* (1987)—The director, Wim Wenders, who wrote the script with the collaboration of Peter Handke, had a theme: in an approximation of Rilke's words, "Joy has gone astray." We're told that "when the child was a child," stories held together. Now all we have is fragmentation, entropy. Two angels—Damiel (Bruno Ganz) and Cassiel (Otto Sander)—hover over the bleak, divided city and move among the forlorn Berliners, listening to what's in their minds: listening to the questions about existence that these people ask themselves. Our overhearing what the angels hear—the thoughts chanted on the track, all in even, quiet tones, as grayed out as the sunless skies—works on us like a tranquillizer. The dim whimsey, the recitations of prose poetry that recall the Beats—it all produces a blissed-out stupor that feels vaguely avant-garde. Eventually, Damiel falls in love with a beautiful French aerialist (Solveig Dommartin), and gives up his wings. With Peter Falk, who brings some funky warmth to the role of an American movie star, and Curt Bois as a sad-faced old man called Homer. The cinematography (tinted black-and-white, and color) is by Henri Alekan. This Franco-German production is in English, French, and German. (See *Hooked*.)

Winterset (1936)—Maxwell Anderson's most famous verse drama—a blend of *Romeo and Juliet* and the Sacco-Vanzetti case—was widely held to be the supremely eloquent last word on the unconquerable soul of man. Burgess Meredith, who mastered the cadences for Broadway, made his first screen appearance as Mio, giving fine voice and excellent interpretation to the soaring banalities that one might—in a romantic mood—mistake for poetry. Even with Anderson's poetics slightly trimmed by the adaptor, Anthony Veiller, the play is still in a grand manner that just won't do on the screen. But there are fine moments in the performances, and there's something childishly touching in the florid dramatic effects. With Edward Ellis as Judge Gaunt, Margo as Miriamne, Eduardo Ciannelli as Trock Estrella, Stanley Ridges as Shadow, Maurice Moscovitch as Esdras, Paul Guilfoyle as Garth Esdras. It's a clue to Anderson's popularity at the time that these actors have been forever identified with the characters they play here. Also with Mischa Auer, Myron McCormick, and John Carradine. Directed by Alfred Santell. R K O. b & w

Wise Guys (1986)—Danny DeVito, as the bumptious Italian Harry, and Joe Piscopo, as the Jewish simpleton Moe, are the two clownish underdogs who come out on top in this Mafia burlesque—a broad, slapstick farce, set in Newark and spattered with boyish grossout humor. The directing, by Brian De Palma, is canny and smooth, but this musty genre calls for fresh jokes and sharp, colorful personalities, and that's not what he's working with. The frankness of the picture's grubby anti-glamour is its only claim to charm. Maybe you'd have to be part of what is delicately referred to as the undemanding audience—say, somebody who watches every rerun of the Abbott and Costello pictures—to succumb and find the antics and the mugging as uproarious as they're meant to be. The script is credited to George Gallo. With Dan Hedaya, Captain Lou Albano, and, in brief appearances, Harvey Keitel, Ray Sharkey, Patti LuPone, Julie Bovasso, Mimi Cecchini, Antonia Rey, and Anthony Holland. Cinematography by Fred Schuler. M-G-M/United Artists. color (See *Hooked*.)

Wish You Were Here (1987)—Set in a seaside town on the south coast of England and shot in warm, sunny flesh tones, this English comedy has a satirical yet dreamlike texture. It's about an uncontrollably ribald girl who flaunts her sexuality the same way she flaunts taboo words. It's 1951; she lifts up her skirts to show off her Betty Grable legs and gives men a good look at her knickers. The 16-year-old Emily Lloyd, who plays the part, has the kind of freshness and youthfulness that can't be faked on camera; she embodies everything that the writer-director David Leland is trying to say about the spontaneity, the honesty, and the happy, rude extroversion that kids have pressured out of them. The film is based on the early years of Cynthia Payne, who was the inspiration for the madam in *Personal Services* (which Leland wrote). The first-rate cast includes Tom Bell as the girl's bookie lover, Geoffrey Hutchings as her father, Jesse Birdsall as her bus-conductor boyfriend, Pat Heywood as her aunt, and Heathcote Williams as the psychiatrist she's taken to. The film has its banal side, but it's never visually banal; the cinematography is by Ian Wilson. Channel Four and its theatrical arm, Film Four International. color (See *Hooked*.)

The Witches (1990)—The ads say "From the imagination of Jim Henson and director Nicolas Roeg." It would be more accurate to say "From the imagination of the writer Roald Dahl." This quirky fairy-tale movie is about the diabolical, gleeful evil that's hidden behind normality. (It's about women who secretly hate children.) What Henson and Roeg supply is their craftsmanship and their affection for the novel's adult, calmly macabre tone. (The movie promises to be an enduring, slightly scandalous joy.) As the Grand High Witch of the World, the black-clad Anjelica Huston lifts her arm up high in a towering salute and, addressing the witches of England at their annual meeting, held at a seacoast hotel, she outlines her plan: all the children in the land are to be turned into mice. The 9-year-old Luke (Jasen Fisher), who overhears her speech, is hunted down and transformed, but, blessed with a practical-minded Norwegian granny (Mai Zetterling) who's an expert on witches, he sets out to foil the plan. The movie doesn't have Dahl's narrative confidence and it goes in for a little sweetening, but it has major compensations. Pale, bespectacled Luke is rather mousy to start with, and when he becomes a light-brown critter who can be cradled in his granny's hand it seems almost a fulfillment. His greedy pal Bruno (Charles Potter) seems fulfilled, too—as a blobby gray rodent. The two mice are triumphs for Henson's workshop. Zetterling is the hypnotic storytelling granny of our dreams; Huston is a gutsy, camp witch, with an accent that slips like her features; her terrified underlings—bald, drag-queen witches—are like a child's drawings of the devil. With Bill Paterson and Brenda Blethyn as Bruno's parents, Rowan Atkinson as the hotel manager, and Jane Horrocks as Miss Irvine. The script is by Allan Scott; the exteriors were filmed in Bergen, Norway, and at the Headland Hotel, Newquay, Cornwall. Warners. color

The Witches of Eastwick (1987)—It wavers between satirizing a hyper-sexed male's misogyny and revelling in it. Directed by George Miller (of the *Mad Max* movies), from a rickety script credited to Michael Cristofer, the movie resembles its source, John Updike's 1984 novel, only in its high gloss, the general outlines of the leading characters, some purloined lines of dialogue, and Jack Nicholson's entertainingly uncouth turns of phrase. As "your average horny little devil" he is so repulsive he's funny, and he has invented some furiously demented slapstick; he's an inspired buffoon. The three beauties whose combined longing for a man is potent enough to lure this devil from New York City to the (fictional) New England town of Eastwick are Cher as a sculptor, Susan Sarandon as a cellist and music teacher, and Michelle Pfeiffer as a reporter on the *Word*. (A brunette, a redhead, and a blonde, they have lost their husbands by death, divorce, and desertion.) About half the scenes don't make much sense, and the final ones might as well have a sign posted: "We're desperate for a finish." But even at its trashiest the movie keeps bumping along. And those women are a supple trio—not a brittle bone among them. Nicholson has waited all his acting life for a harem like this. With Veronica Cartwright as an unlucky puritan. Cinematography by Vilmos Zsigmond. Warners. color (See *Hooked*.)

Without Apparent Motive *Sans mobile apparent* (1971)—An affectionate imitation of *The Big Sleep*, set in the sunny baroque of Nice and directed with finesse by Philippe Labro. Jean-Louis Trintignant is the Bogart-style detective with a snarl-grin, and Dominique Sanda is the tawny-blond big pussycat. The cast includes Sacha Distel, Stéphane Audran, Laura Antonelli, Jean-Pierre Marielle, Erich Segal, and the stunning, sad-eyed Carla Gravina. Understated and too refined to be hugely entertaining, but pleasant enough.

The plot is some gimcrackery derived form Ed McBain's *Ten Plus One*, but at least it creates suspense and it doesn't fizzle out. Segal, who plays an astrologer, has a wonderful moment (it doesn't require acting): seated on a luxurious patio, he looks out and spots a sniper just an instant before the bullet reaches his heart. Cinematography by Jean Penzer. In French. color (See *Deeper into Movies*.)

Without Love (1945)—One of the dreariest films in the Katharine Hepburn–Spencer Tracy series; it has a metallic flavor. Philip Barry had shaped the play for Hepburn, but it had never worked and she just barely squeaked by with it on Broadway in 1942; for the movie, the material was extensively rewritten by Donald Ogden Stewart and it still didn't work, though the picture was a box-office success anyway. Tracy is a homespun scientist working on a helmet for high-altitude flying, and Hepburn is a widow with a big house in Washington. The wartime housing shortage is the plot excuse for his moving in with her, on the understanding that they'll have a platonic marriage. And guess what happens. Hepburn comes off as a weird cross between an old maid and a tomboy; she's at her most cultured and affected, yet she keeps exclaiming "By gum!" The dialogue tries to be sophisticated; it doesn't match the desperate plot maneuvers, such as the one requiring Tracy to be a sleepwalker. Sleepwalking in movies is almost as tacky as amnesia, and with the sturdy Tracy there's not enough difference between awake and asleep. Keenan Wynn and Lucille Ball, who play a second pair of lovers, are much more likable than the stars. With Patricia Morison, Carl Esmond, Felix Bressart, and Gloria Grahame in a bit as a flower girl. The pedestrian direction is by Harold S. Bucquet; cinematography by Karl Freund; produced by Lawrence Weingarten, for M-G-M. b & w

Witness (1985)—An 8-year-old Amish boy (Lukas Haas), on his first trip to a city, sees a murder taking place in the men's room of Philadelphia's 30th Street train station. In order to protect the boy and his widowed mother (Kelly McGillis) from the killers, the police captain (Harrison Ford) who's in charge of the investigation tries to hide their identities, and, with a bullet wound in his side, drives them back to their farm in Lancaster County before he collapses. Ford's stay at the Amish farm is like a vacation from the real world. Directed by the Australian Peter Weir (filming in the U.S. for the first time), the movie seems to take its view of the Amish from a quaint dreamland, a Brigadoon of tall golden wheat, and to take its squalid, hyped-up view of life in Philadelphia from prolonged exposure to TV cop shows. (Murder is treated as if it were a modern, sin-city invention.) And, of course, Ford comes to love McGillis and her bonnet too much to want to expose her to the ugliness outside. The picture is like something dug up from the earliest days of movies; it has a bland, seductive lyricism, and one familiar, "mythic" scene after another. Lukas Haas is a good little actor (even though the boy is so idealized it's as if the moviemakers had never been driven nuts by the antics of a real, live child), and Ford gives a fine, workmanlike performance. McGillis shifts uneasily between the heroic naturalness of Liv Ullmann and the dimpled simpering of the young Esther Williams. With Alexander Godunov as the widow's galumphing Amish suitor, Patti LuPone, Josef Sommer, Danny Glover, and Jan Rubes. The script is by Earl W. Wallace and William Kelley, from a story they wrote with Pamela Wallace; the cinematography is by John Seale. Paramount. color (See *State of the Art*.)

Witness for the Prosecution (1958)—Billy Wilder's inane yet moderately entertaining version of an Agatha Christie courtroom thriller, with Charles Laughton wiggling his wattles, and Marlene Dietrich, Tyrone Power, Elsa Lanchester, Una O'Connor, Henry Daniell, Norma Varden, and Ian Wolfe. Script by Wilder and Harry Kurnitz. United Artists. b & w

The Wiz (1978)—With Diana Ross in the lead, Dorothy is now a shy schoolteacher in Harlem, and Diana Ross's shy is like Sergeant Bilko's modest. Fervently wet-eyed, she sings songs of preachy uplift in relentlessly slow arrangements. Nipsey Russell (as the Tinman) is able to ride right over the film's muddy carelessness, and a sweetness comes through the Pagliacci makeup that Michael Jackson wears as the Scarecrow, and Mabel King, who plays the Wicked Witch, has a hot growly song. But this film brings out all the weaknesses of its director, Sidney Lumet, and none of his strengths. The whole production has a stagnant atmosphere, and the big dance numbers are free-form traffic jams. Charlie Smalls' score for the Broadway show has been padded out with some new music, and adapted by Quincy Jones; the maladroit script is by Joel Schumacher. With Lena Horne, Richard Pryor, and Ted Ross. Universal. color (See *When the Lights Go Down*.)

The Woman Alone, see *Sabotage*

Woman in a Dressing Gown (1957)—Yvonne Mitchell is extraordinary as the desperately disorganized wife of a neat, rising office worker (Anthony Quayle); she achieves an unusual balance of sensitivity and insensitivity, the painful and the absurd. This English movie, well written in the semi-angry mode, was adapted by Ted Willis from his TV play, and proficiently directed by J. Lee Thompson, though it carries unpretentiousness to a fault. With Sylvia Syms and Andrew Ray. b & w

The Woman in the Painting, see *Amici per la Pelle*

The Woman in the Window (1944)—One of the best of Fritz Lang's American movies—a thriller with the logic and plausibility of a nightmare. Lang's technique is so sure and so seductive that the viewer completely identifies with the safe, serene protagonist (Edward G. Robinson), an associate professor of psychology at a New York City college, and shares his shock and fear when he's caught in a trap. The professor is interested in the relation of motive to homicide—an interest that's purely a matter of intellectual curiosity. Then, when his wife and child are out of town, he visits a woman's apartment; her lover comes in and unexpectedly attacks him, and he kills the intruder with a pair of scissors. Joan Bennett is the woman in the case, Dan Duryea is a blackmailer, and Raymond Massey is an assistant district attorney. Nunnally Johnson produced, and adapted J. H. Wallis's novel *Once Off Guard*. With Dorothy Peterson and Bobby (later Robert) Blake. Cinematography by Milton Krasner. R K O. b & w

A Woman of Affairs (1928)—Greta Garbo was never more rapturous than in this adaptation of Michael Arlen's 1924 novel *The Green Hat*. She and Douglas Fairbanks, Jr., are cast as sister and brother, and with their matching profiles they're probably the most glamorous sister and brother look-alikes in film history. Garbo plays a daring, sleekly groomed woman of the 20s who isn't considered good enough to marry the handsome aristocratic stiff (John Gilbert) whom she loves. It turns out that she has the finer code of honor. But Garbo transcends this moral framework: as a woman in love, she has a sensuality that's dreamlike—it knows no bounds. (Watch her in the hospital scene.) The cast includes John Mack Brown, Lewis Stone, Hobart Bosworth, and Dorothy Sebastian. Directed by Clarence Brown, from a script by Bess Meredyth. It's an elegantly sumptuous M-G-M production, with cinematography by William Daniels, art direction by Cedric Gibbons, and gowns by Adrian. Silent, but it was also made available in a version with added sound effects and music. b & w

Woman of Dolwyn Also known as *The Last Days of Dolwyn*. (1949)—Edith Evans gives one of her most remarkable performances as the woman who inundates a village in Wales in order to conceal a murder committed by her son—Richard Burton, in his first screen appearance. (His face is thinner and far more open than in his later, Hollywood films; he seems beautiful rather than just handsome.) Emlyn Williams wrote, directed, and also appears in this unusual film, which is very loosely based on an actual 19th-century incident; it's melodramatic in an affecting, emotional way, and it's really Welsh—the landscapes, the voices, the whole feeling. (Some years earlier, Williams had coached Edith Evans for a play in which she had to sound Welsh—her accent here certainly fools Americans.) With Hugh Griffith. Cinematography by Otto Heller. An Alexander Korda film, produced by Anatole de Grunwald. b & w

Woman of the Year (1942)—The first of the films co-starring Katharine Hepburn and Spencer Tracy. The chemistry is great, but the plot and the tone are wobbly. He's a sportswriter, and she's a celebrated political journalist (probably modelled on Dorothy Thompson) who doesn't know how to be a woman. The comedy goes sour whenever the movie scores points against her, and the slapstick resolution has an air of desperation. George Stevens directed, from a script by Ring Lardner, Jr., and Michael Kanin. With

Fay Bainter, Reginald Owen, and William Bendix. M-G-M. b & w

The Woman on the Beach (1947)—This Hollywood film by Jean Renoir was cut, re-edited, and partly reshot after a disastrous sneak preview in Santa Barbara. Renoir has said that he was trying to do "a love story in which there was no love," in which the attractions "were purely physical," but that after he remade it, it was "neither flesh nor fish," having "lost its raison d'être." What's left suggests that Renoir was attempting an American film with the sensual atmosphere of his French work, such as *La Bête humaine*; it's a 71-minute melodrama, but it's slow-rhythmed and full of dreamlike ambiguities, tensions, suspicions. Joan Bennett is the petulant femme fatale, married to a great painter (Charles Bickford) who has gone blind. Robert Ryan is the Coast Guard lieutenant who finds her so irresistible that she has him trying to do in her husband. The film, hampered further by a fiercely obtrusive Hanns Eisler score, was a box-office calamity, and finished Renoir in Hollywood; he didn't make another movie until the 50s, when he went to India for *The River*. Some critics (most notably Jacques Rivette) consider this mutilated film a masterpiece and that's an appealing idea, but one may have to strain to see it as more than an over-aestheticized, interesting failure. The script by Frank Davis and Renoir was adapted from Mitchell Wilson's novel *None So Blind*. R K O. b & w

A Woman Rebels (1936)—Arguably Katharine Hepburn's worst picture (most serious rival: *Mary of Scotland*), and the central issue—the freedom of women—is made to seem tired, dated, and convictionless. This time Hepburn is Pamela Thistlewaite, daughter of an autocratic judge (Donald Crisp). After an affair (with Van Heflin), she has an illegitimate child; though she's the crusading editor of a women's magazine and a campaigner for women's rights, she fibs about the baby. After much suffering, she realizes she's in love with her longtime faithful suitor (Herbert Marshall). Despite what Hepburn goes through in this movie, she looks great and she *has* something; she does a lot for her more amusing speeches. Mark Sandrich directed; from Netta Syrett's *Portrait of a Rebel*, adapted by Anthony Veiller and Ernest Vajda. With Lucile Watson, Doris Dudley, Elizabeth Allan, and David Manners. Pandro S. Berman produced, for R K O. b & w

A Woman Under the Influence (1974)—The writer-director, John Cassavetes, presents his morose yet romantic view of mental disorder, with Gena Rowlands as the helpless victim of a bullying blue-collar husband (Peter Falk) and a repressive society. She's a frantic, wilted Los Angeles housewife who is endowed with a clarity of vision that the warped society can't tolerate, and so she's persecuted. The scenes are often unshaped, and so rudderless that the meanings don't emerge. Rowlands externalizes schizophrenic dissolution; she fragments before our eyes. But her prodigious performance is enough for half a dozen tours de force—it's exhausting. With Katherine Cassavetes. (2 hours and 35 minutes.) color (See *Reeling*.)

A Woman's Face (1941)—Joan Crawford as a woman whose soul is blighted by the horrible disfigurement of one side of her face, in a remake of a Swedish film (based on a French play) that the very young Ingrid Bergman had been a hit in. The Swedish setting has been retained—rather inexplicably, since the story is about Crawford's ruthless blackmailing activities, and then her spiritual transformation, once a surgeon (Melvyn Douglas) has healed her face. As her mad, treacherous lover, who wants to involve her in the murder of a child, Conrad Veidt is the gaudiest character. Too bad that the director, George Cukor, doesn't have a little more feeling for the loony baroque; the story is treated much too soberly. However, Cukor toned down Crawford's notorious emotionalism—no small feat. Funniest sequence: a Swedish folk dance, with Crawford in a peasant get-up. With Marjorie Main, Osa Massen, Albert Basserman, Reginald Owen, Connie Gilchrist, and Donald Meek. The screenplay is by Donald Ogden Stewart; cinematography by Robert Planck; music by Bronislau Kaper. Produced by Victor Saville, for M-G-M. b & w

The Women (1939)—Clare Boothe Luce's ode to wisecracking cattiness, given the full, expensive M-G-M treatment in its first movie version. It confirms rich men's worst suspicions and fantasies of what women want (money) and what they're like when they're together (clawing beasties). With Rosalind Russell, Joan Crawford, Paulette Goddard, Joan Fontaine, Mary Boland, Marjorie Main, Hedda Hopper, Margaret Dumont, Virginia Grey, Virginia Weidler, Ruth Hussey, Phyllis Povah, Lucile Watson, and noble Norma Shearer, weeping, weeping. George Cukor directed—surprisingly coarsely; it's a kicking, screaming low comedy, with a quiet character such as Joan Fontaine coming across as a female wimp. Goddard is a standout—she's fun. And audiences at the time loved Russell's all-out burlesque of women as jealous bitches. Adapted by Anita Loos and Jane Murfin. b & w

Women in Love (1970)—Ken Russell's movie could perhaps be described as a gothic sex fantasy on themes from D. H. Lawrence's novel. Visually and emotionally, it's extravagant and, from time to time, impressive. Because Lawrence was one of the most purple of all great writers (perhaps the most, though rivalled by Conrad), Russell's style might de-

ceive one into imagining that he is providing an equivalent to Lawrence's prose. But though Lawrence's passionate imprecision is what's bad in his writing, one can pass right through it in his *Women in Love*, because he was reaching for clarity; he might make a fool of himself groping around his characters' psycho-sexual insides like a messianic explorer, but he was opening up new terrain. Russell, on the other hand, heads right for the purple, and his overheated virtuoso tableaux are piled on for our admiration, not for our understanding. The movie is a highly colored swirl of emotional impressions, bursting with intensity that isn't really grounded in anything. Probably to see this particular movie before reading the book is desecration; the novel is a staggering accomplishment—the sort of book that leaves one dumbfounded at how far its author got—and since there are few English novels of this stature, it's mad to jeopardize one's vision of it by reading it in terms of the actors and images of the film. (The movie is rather like Lawrence's accounts of bad sex.) With the bold, tense Glenda Jackson as Gudrun; Jennie Linden as her unimaginative sister, Ursula; Alan Bates as Birkin; Oliver Reed, glum and bilious, as Gerald; and also Vladek Sheybal, Eleanor Bron, Alan Webb, Catherine Willmer, Richard Heffer, Christopher Gable, and Michael Gough. The adaptation is by Larry Kramer, who also produced. The cinematography is by Billy Williams; the score is by Georges Delerue; the set designer is Luciana Arrighi; the costume designer is Shirley Russell. color (See *Deeper into Movies*.)

Women in Revolt (1972)—Three transvestites (Candy Darling, Holly Woodlawn, Jackie Curtis) in a porno burlesque of women's liberation. It sounds like fun, but it isn't. The subject is really the fantasies of Andy Warhol's "superstars"; the dialogue is flat and the camera seems glued to the blemishes on the performers' rumps and thighs. The credits list Andy Warhol as director and Paul Morrissey as executive producer. With Jane Forth. color

Women on the Verge of a Nervous Breakdown *Mujeres al Borde de un Ataque de Nervios* (1988)—The most original pop writer-director of the 80s, Pedro Almodóvar is Godard with a human face—a happy face. The artificial is what sends him sky-high, and the Madrid of this film is (as the closing song has it) "Puro Teatro." This comedy looks as if it had been made by a mad scientist playing with chemical rainbow colors—John Lithgow in his lab in *Buckaroo Banzai*. It's all coincidences, and each new one adds to the crazy brio. What seem to be incidental jokes turn out to be essential parts of one big joke. This is a movie where after a while you can't tell sexy from funny. Pepa (Carmen Maura), an actress who works in TV and commercials, turns on her answering machine and learns that she has been jilted. Infuriated, she dashes around, on spike heels, in a short, tight skirt, trying to confront her longtime live-in lover, the elegant, vain Iván (Fernando Guillén). The women of the title include Iván's early lover (Julieta Serrano), his new lover (Kiti Manver), and two (Rossy De Palma and María Barranco) who are involved with his son (Antonio Banderas). Sleek-legged and chic, they run the theatrical gamut. Cinematography by José Luis Alcaine. In Spanish. color (See *Movie Love*.)

The Wonderful Crook *Pas si méchant que ça* (1975)—Gérard Depardieu as a petit-bourgeois Robin Hood, a man who commits robberies in order to meet the payroll of his family business, a small furniture factory. The Swiss writer-director, Claude Goretta, develops the small stresses and breaks of feeling; we know we're seeing a film made by artists. But Goretta's wheels grind so fine that we become impatient; the hero's arrest is our reprieve. With Philippe Léotard, Marlène Jobert, Dominique Labourier, and Jacques Debary. Cinematography by Renato Berta. In French. color (See *When the Lights Go Down*.)

Words and Music (1948)—Double bio of Richard Rodgers and Lorenz Hart, with Tom Drake and Mickey Rooney insanely miscast in the roles. The story part is painfully embarrassing to watch, but some of the musical numbers are just fine. The huge cast includes Judy Garland, Cyd Charisse, Perry Como, Janet Leigh, Gower Champion, Gene Kelly (who choreographed the "Slaughter on Tenth Avenue" ballet that he dances with Vera-Ellen), and June Allyson, whose "Thou Swell" with the Blackburn Twins is a bright spot in her career. Also with Lena Horne singing "The Lady Is a Tramp," and Ann Sothern, Mel Tormé, Betty Garrett, Allyn Ann McLerie, and Marshall Thompson. Norman Taurog directed, from a script by Fred Finklehoffe, based on a story by Guy Bolton and Jean Holloway. Robert Alton and Kelly staged the dances. The roughly two dozen Rodgers and Hart songs include "Where or When," "There's a Small Hotel," and "This Can't Be Love." M-G-M. color

Working Girl (1988)—Mike Nichols made this Yuppie Cinderella romance, with Melanie Griffith as Tess McGill, a poor but enterprising girl from Staten Island who fights off the sleazoid bosses and struggles to break through the educational-background barriers and climb from Wall Street secretary to executive. We're supposed to be cheered by watching Tess become part of the establishment: she makes it into the world of mergers and acquisitions, and Carly Simon's choral music soars exultantly. Nichols may have been planning to let in a little bit of funk and tackiness, and then backed off; that might explain the double-entendre of the title and

W

some of the plot details. Griffith is very appealing, and she carries what there is of the picture, but this is the kind of star performance in which the heroine's misty eyes and soft-focus smiles (which suggest bleariness) are supposed to turn our brains to jelly. After a bouncy, promising opening, the staging becomes so broad you can't tell whether satire is intended or just dumb jokes. The lines have a lot of surprise, but the situations (and digressions) are moldy. With Sigourney Weaver, Harrison Ford, Joan Cusack, Kevin Spacey, Nora Dunn, Alec Baldwin, Philip Bosco, and Olympia Dukakis. The script is by Kevin Wade; the cinematography is by Michael Ballhaus. 20th Century-Fox. color (See *Movie Love*.)

The World According to Garp (1982)—The movie version of John Irving's novel, directed by George Roy Hill, from a script by Steve Tesich, has no center; it's a simple series of vignettes, spanning Garp's life from his beginning to his end. This isn't necessarily bad—Hill's pastel, detached, and generally meaningless comedy may, in some ways, be preferable to the baroque apparatus that Irving constructed—but in recounting the book's key incidents Hill and Tesich lay bare the pattern of mutilations in the plot. Tongues, ears, penises, eyes, lives—everybody on the screen is losing something. If you listen to what Garp (Robin Williams) says, the movie is about love of family; if you look at what happens, though, it's a castration fantasy. The masochistic gifted-victim game has been played in recent American writing on just about every conceivable level, but Irving's novel is still something special: he created a whole hideous and deformed women's political group (the Ellen Jamesians) in order to have his author-hero, his alter ego, destroyed by it, and the film is faithful to Irving's "vision." With John Lithgow, who gives an appealing performance as the big-

bruiser transsexual Roberta Muldoon, Glenn Close as Garp's mother, Mary Beth Hurt as his wife, and, in a bit, Amanda Plummer as Ellen James. Cinematography by Miroslav Ondříček. Warners. color (See *Taking It All In*.)

A World Apart (1988)—Set in 1963, it's about a 13-year-old girl (Jodhi May), who lives a well-ordered, ruling-class life in a fine home in suburban Johannesburg until her father (Jeroen Krabbé), who's a Communist, flees the country in the middle of the night to escape arrest, and her mother (Barbara Hershey), the editor of a small anti-apartheid newspaper, is "detained" for 90 days, and then another 90 days. Based on a semi-autobiographical script by Shawn Slovo, the daughter of the journalist Ruth First and Joe Slovo, the leader of the then-banned South African Communist Party, the movie deals with the girl's feeling confused and resentful, because her parents have never explained anything to her—they've treated her like a baby. Forced to grow up, she perceives the ugliness of apartheid, and wants to join in the fight against it, yet that fight is also her competitor. In prison or out, her mother is not all there for her. When the girl needs her mom, she bashes her head against a principled person. The theme of the movie is the conflict between fighting injustice and what we owe to our families—or, more poignantly, a young girl's pain at the loss of her mother and father, though she knows the reason for it. Shot in Zimbabwe, this remarkable first feature directed by the noted cinematographer Chris Menges (pronounced men-ghees) has a visual snap to it. It's luminous yet very informal. And though, toward the end, it falls into chanting slogans, it has a radiant intelligence. The cast includes Linda Mvusi, who shared the best-actress award at Cannes with May and Hershey, and Tim Roth, Yvonne Bryceland, Albee Lesotho, David

Suchet, and Nadine Chalmers. color (See *Hooked*.)

The World of Apu   *Apur Sansar* (1959)—Satyajit Ray's protagonist, Apu, whose consciousness developed from the village life of *Pather Panchali* and the university in *Aparajito*, marries the exquisite Sharmila Tagore and grows beyond self-consciousness. Rich and contemplative, and a great, convincing affirmation. The full-grown Apu is played by the remarkable Soumitra Chatterji, who starred in several other Ray films. Adapted from a novel by B. B. Bandapaddhay, by Ray; music by Ravi Shankar. In Bengali. b & w

The World of Henry Orient (1964)—Odd and erratic but often touching tragicomedy about two young New York girls who go celebrity hunting. With Peter Sellers, Angela Lansbury, Paula Prentiss, and Tippy Walker and Merrie Spaeth. Directed by George Roy Hill, from a script by Nora and Nunnally Johnson, based on Nora Johnson's novel. United Artists. color

World Première (1941)—John Barrymore, in his self-parodying period, doing an entertaining lampoon of a movie producer in an insignificant contraption of a movie, directed by Ted Tetzlaff. With Frances Farmer, Sig Rumann, Ricardo Cortez, and Eugene Pallette. Paramount. b & w

The World's Greatest Lover (1977)—Gene Wilder's slapstick farce may not be long, but ''long'' is a relative term, and a half hour of this is eternity enough. It's set in the 20s and has to do with a Milwaukee baker (Wilder) who goes to Hollywood for a screen test, hoping to become a rival to Rudolph Valentino. Infantile humor, for young, slow kids, who want everything pounded at them. With Carol Kane, Dom DeLuise, and Fritz Feld. Script by Wilder, with a ''thank you'' credit

to Fellini (for the use of part of the plot of *The White Sheik*). 20th Century-Fox. color

The Would-Be Gentleman, see *Le Bourgeois Gentilhomme*

WR—Mysteries of the Organism   *WR—Misterije Organizma* (1971)—Controversial, comic collage-movie by Dusan Makavejev that mixes and parodies left-wing politics and Wilhelm Reichian psychology; the point of view is so unstable that it seems to be more sophomoric than anything else. With the gifted actress Milena Dravić, as well as Jackie Curtis and Tuli Kupferberg. A Yugoslavian film, filmed in Europe and the U.S. English subtitles and dialogue. color

Written on the Wind (1957)—A Texas oil millionaire (Robert Stack) sweeps a secretary (Lauren Bacall) off her feet, marries her, and then gets to wondering whether the baby that she's going to have is really his or if it's the child of his best friend, a geologist (Rock Hudson). The Texan's nympho sister (Dorothy Malone) encourages his suspicions while trying to trap the geologist, who is, indeed, in love with the wife. The director, Douglas Sirk, shows his talent for whipping up sour, stylized soap operas in posh settings. With Robert Keith. The script by George Zuckerman is based on Robert Wilder's novel. Universal. color

The Wrong Man (1956)—An unusually drab Hitchcock film, based on a true story about an innocent man (Henry Fonda) sent to prison. The picture has an almost Kafkaesque nightmare realism to it, but the story line wanders diffusely instead of tightening, and the developments become tedious (though the final discovery of the right man is chillingly well done). With Vera Miles, Anthony Quayle, Esther Minciotti, and Harold J. Stone. Written by Maxwell Anderson and

Angus MacPhail; music by Bernard Herrmann. Warners. b & w

WUSA (1970)—A garish example of liberal exhibitionism. Stuart Rosenberg overdirected this over-written story of a right-wing political plot in New Orleans. Joanne Woodward has a scar on her face, Paul Newman drinks because he can't face himself, Tony Perkins is quietly going mad, and Cloris Leachman is a crippled newsy. Also with Laurence Harvey, Moses Gunn, Wayne Rogers, Pat Hingle, and Bruce Cabot. The score is by Lalo Schifrin; Robert Stone's script is based on his novel *Hall of Mirrors*. (After Newman's girl has hanged herself, he visits her grave—in a potter's field, no less—and savagely addresses the departed lady: "I'm a survivor and I'm leaving these flats for the mile-high city. When I get up there, baby—when I look down—I'll have a few regrets." The rhetoric suggests a mixture of *Winterset* and *The Oscar*.) Paramount. color (See *Deeper into Movies*.)

Wuthering Heights (1939)—Laurence Olivier has said that in this film the director, William Wyler, taught him how to act on the screen, and there's no doubt that, as Heathcliff, he shows new passion and power. Unfortunately, Merle Oberon's Cathy—though exquisite—lacks the complementary passion; she's a bit chill and dainty for the character hewn in Emily Brontë's "wild workshop" (to use sister Charlotte's phrase). But it's a beautifully made gothic-romantic classic, with many memorable scenes. Hecht and MacArthur did the script; Gregg Toland was the cinematographer; Alfred Newman did the music. The cast includes Flora Robson, David Niven, Geraldine Fitzgerald, Donald Crisp, Hugh Williams, Leo G. Carroll, Miles Mander, Cecil Kellaway, and Alice Ehlers at the harpsichord. The Ventura area (about 40 miles north of Los Angeles) was used for the Yorkshire moors. (The novel was first filmed, in England, in 1920; the many movie versions include one that Buñuel made in Mexico in 1953, an Egyptian production, and another English version, directed by Robert Fuest in 1970 and starring Timothy Dalton and Anna Calder-Marshall. And there have been at least seven TV versions—the Heathcliffs have included Richard Burton, Keith Michell, Charlton Heston, Richard Boone, and Tom Tryon, and the Cathys have included Rosemary Harris and Claire Bloom.) A Samuel Goldwyn Production. b & w

W. W. and the Dixie Dancekings (1975)—Burt Reynolds is once more being chased by a sheriff and once more using his beefy, child-like grin, but he gives perhaps his most ingratiating comic performance. He's a con man in this redneck fairy tale set in and around Nashville, in the late 50s. There's a genial, romantic script by Thomas Rickman, and Reynolds seems more human than usual. At times, you can see him working to keep the picture alive—trying to give it some juice and sweetness and humor. He has to work extra hard because the director, John G. Avildsen, seems erratic and outright sloppy. With Art Carney, Conny Van Dyke, Jerry Reed, and Ned Beatty. 20th Century-Fox. color

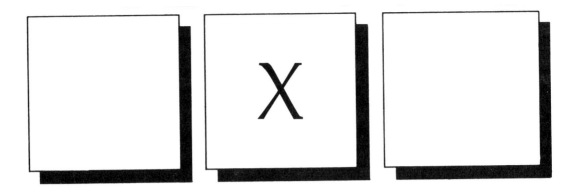

X—The Man with the X-Ray Eyes (1963)—Not as cut-and-dried as most low-budget science-fiction thrillers; some novel ideas help to sustain interest in this one, though eventually it goes the tired old moralizing route, and scientific "transgression" results in doom. A solemnly serious Ray Milland is Dr. Xavier, the scientist whose experiments result in the X-ray vision that torments him; Don Rickles helps to redeem the stereotyped role of the greedy carny man who exploits poor Xavier. With John Hoyt, Diana Van Der Vlis, Harold J. Stone, and John Dierkes. Cinematography by Floyd Crosby; written by Robert Dillon and Ray Russell. Produced and directed by Roger Corman, for A.I.P. color

X Y & Zee The English title is *Zee and Co.* (1971)—Elizabeth Taylor in an all-out, let-it-bleed performance that shows her talent for comic toughness. She appears to be having a roaring good time on camera and she's so energetic that Michael Caine and Susannah York (it's a triangle movie) have to work hard to hold their own. The subject is the shocking messiness of love, and the director, Brian G. Hutton, aims each shot at the jugular; nothing is implied, nothing is suggested—everything belts you. Set in London, it's an entertaining plush circus of a "women's picture," with cinematography in Billy Williams' ripest palette. Edna O'Brien wrote the script and her dialogue has a sardonic tickle to it. With Margaret Leighton. A Kastner-Ladd-Kanter Production; released by Columbia. color (See *Deeper into Movies*.)

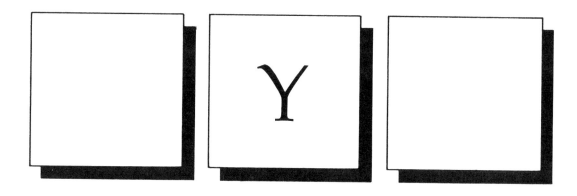

The Yakuza (1975)—An attempt to sell a romantic view of gangsterism in an exotic setting. The yakuza are Japanese mobsters, and one of the items in their "code" is that you can show penitence for an offense against the mob chieftain by slicing off your little finger and presenting it to him. Robert Mitchum plays an American private eye who goes to Japan to rescue an American girl kidnapped by yakuza; he enlists the aid of a "retired" yakuza, a master-teacher of swordsmanship (Takakura Ken, or, if you prefer, Ken Takakura), and they fight side by side, the gun and the sword. At the end, Mitchum realizes that he has offended the swordsman and commits his act of penance. This is a swaggeringly meretricious fairy tale, overloaded with exposition, and solemn when it means to be Orientally inscrutable. Richard Jordan, as Mitchum's bodyguard, gives the film its only fresh, unexpected moments; the director, Sydney Pollack, doesn't seem to understand how action-film mechanisms operate. The script by Paul Schrader, from Leonard Schrader's story, was given a rewrite by Robert Towne. With Brian Keith and Eiji Okada. Warners. color (See *Reeling*.)

Yankee Doodle Dandy (1942)—The astonishingly versatile James Cagney as the prodigious actor-playwright-songwriter George M. Cohan, in a big, enjoyable musical biography, well directed by Michael Curtiz. Made during the Second World War, it's packed with jingoistic Americanism, but this ties in with Cohan's own attitudes and with the unself-conscious Irish-American sentimentality of his songs, and Cagney's stiff-backed hoofing is so spirited that the moldy plot turns hardly bother one. He gets to dance more in this movie than in any of his previous films, and though he was born in 1899 and is somewhat portly here, he is so cocky and sure a dancer that you feel yourself grinning with pleasure at his movements. It's quite possible that he has more electricity than Cohan himself had. (He took the Academy Award for Best Actor.) With Walter Huston, Joan Leslie, Rosemary DeCamp, Frances Langford, Richard Whorf, George Tobias, Jeanne Cagney, Eddie Foy, Jr., Walter Catlett, Irene Manning, S. Z. Sakall, and George Barbier. The script is by Robert Buckner and Edmund Joseph; the cinematography is by James Wong Howe. Warners. b & w

The Year of Living Dangerously (1983)—Peter Weir's romantic adventure film is set in Indonesia in 1965, during the political upheavals that shook President Sukarno's unstable government, and centers on the Caucasian community of journalists and diplomats in Djakarta. Linda Hunt has the pivotal male role of the goblinlike Billy Kwan, a half-Chinese, half-Australian cameraman who plays matchmaker and brings together Mel Gibson, as a newly arrived Australian foreign correspondent, and Sigourney Weaver, as the assistant military attaché at the British Embassy. To a degree, Weir is the victim of his own skill at creating the illusion of authentic Third World misery, rioting, and chaos; the emaciation of the natives overwhelms the made-up problems of the Caucasians. But movie squalor has its own glamour, and scene by scene this film is fascinating; despite a certain amount of mystical-East blather, it's alive on the screen. A new-style old-time "dangerous" steaminess builds up as Gibson and Weaver eye each other. And though Billy Kwan is the movie's walking conscience and higher moral purpose, Linda Hunt's lyric intensity and concentration help to purify the lines she speaks. Filmed in the Philippines and Australia. With Bill Kerr, Michael Murphy, Bembol Roco, and Noel Ferrier. The score is entertaining, with records that range from Richard Strauss to Little Richard, and background music by Maurice Jarre, in which gamelan gong sounds are never far away; the script by David Williamson, Weir, and C. J. Koch is based on Koch's highly readable 1978 novel. M-G-M. color (See *Taking It All In.*)

Year of the Dragon (1985)—Stan White (Mickey Rourke), a New York police captain, is assigned to put a damper on the murderous youth gangs who are disrupting life in Chinatown. But Stan—a synthesis of Rambo and Dirty Harry—can't live with compromise; he

starts to create chaos in the community so that (in some unexplained way) he can tear out the roots of crime. The movie is a form of hysterical, rabble-rousing pulp, yet it isn't involving; it doesn't have the propulsion of good pulp storytelling. It's sunk in torpor, and Stan, who seems to be continuing the Vietnam war in Chinatown, has no core; he's all blowhard pose. Loosely derived from the novel by Robert Daley, the tawdry script—it gives the characters a flat, stunted vocabulary of about 25 words, most of them the basic four-letter expletives—was written by Oliver Stone, along with Michael Cimino, who directed. The only performance that has any intensity is the quiet one given by John Lone as the sneaky, new young Chinese Godfather—he's Cimino's Heart of Darkness and Yellow Peril, too. Lone is so fine-drawn and elegant he just about turns the movie upside down; this gangster comes across as the only character with any brains or emotional life. The grating-voiced Ariane, a model of Dutch and Japanese parentage, is the TV-newscaster heroine; she's officious and nostrilly, like an Oriental Ali MacGraw. With Raymond J. Barry, Caroline Kava, Dennis Dun, and Leonard Termo. Cinematography by Alex Thomson; music by David Mansfield; production designed by Wolf Kroeger. Parts of Chinatown's Mott Street were re-created in Dino De Laurentiis' studios in Wilmington, North Carolina. A De Laurentiis Production, released by M-G-M. color (See *Hooked.*)

The Yearling (1946)—The yearling is a boy's pet deer, and it represents the freedom of the boy's childhood. But when the deer becomes destructive, the boy's mother shoots him. Claude Jarman, Jr., plays the boy Jody, Gregory Peck is his farmer father, and Jane Wyman is surprisingly effective as the hard-bitten, unimaginative mother. An actor named Donn Gift plays the boy's friend—a strange little creature called Fodderwing.

What the director, Clarence Brown, does with the material is surprising even if you're familiar with other fine Brown films, such as *National Velvet* and *Intruder in the Dust*. When Jody and Fodderwing are together, something quirky and magical seems to be happening on the screen; when Jody and his deer are together the boy's emotion has a fairy-tale glitter; and when Jody's mother reveals a streak of humor she's so pleased at her dumb joke that you find yourself staring in disbelief—and laughing. Even Peck seems to blend into the atmosphere. From Marjorie Kinnan Rawlings' book, adapted by Paul Osborn. With Chill Wills, Forrest Tucker, Henry Travers, June Lockhart, Clem Bevans, and Margaret Wycherly. Shot on location; cinematography by Charles Rosher and Leonard Smith. Produced by Sidney Franklin, for M-G-M. color

Yellow Submarine (1968)—A Pop Art animated feature with hippie heroes (cartoon versions of the Beatles) going to the rescue of the people of Pepperland and saving them from the Blue Meanies by using the weapons of love and music. Good-natured, full of verbal-visual jokes, and surprisingly entertaining, though the love is less impressive than the music (10 songs by the Beatles). The brightly colored animation is so blatantly derivative that it's an amusing catalogue of 20th-century graphic design. One sequence—the dancing couple for "Lucy in the Sky with Diamonds"—is a stunning use of stylized human figures, an apotheosis of Rogers and Astaire. Directed by George Dunning; the chief designer was Heinz Edelmann. United Artists. (See *Going Steady*.)

Yentl (1983)—Barbra Streisand directed, produced, co-wrote, and stars in this musical version of the Isaac Bashevis Singer story "Yentl the Yeshiva Boy," and it has a distinctive and surprising spirit. It's funny, delicate, and intense—all at the same time. Set in the thriving Polish-Jewish communities of an imaginary, glowing past, it tells of a young woman with a passion for religious study who grows up in a tradition-bound society where women are excluded from scholarship; when her widower father (who has secretly taught her) dies, she dresses as a boy and goes off to enroll in a yeshiva in a distant town. There's a running theme in Singer: human beings keep trying to flirt with God, hoping that someday a line of communication can be established, but sex always gets in the way. Dressed as a boy, Yentl is no longer resentful of male privileges, and for the first time she feels attracted to a man—the virile, bearded Avigdor, played by Mandy Patinkin, who can hardly wait for his wedding to Hadass, played by Amy Irving. When these three repressed characters become entangled, the movie (like Singer's story) brushes up against darkness on the one hand and sex farce on the other. The director keeps her balance; her vision is sustained until the end (which is a misstep), and as the yeshiva boy she's a wonderful, giddy little shrimp. The music by Michel Legrand isn't varied enough and the lyrics by Alan and Marilyn Bergman are tainted with feminist psychobabble and Broadway uplift, but Streisand sings with passionate conviction, and as the director she does graceful tricks with the songs. She also brings out the other performers' most appealing qualities; the cast includes Nehemiah Persoff as Yentl's papa, and Steven Hill as Hadass's father. The diffuse, poetic lighting is by the cinematographer David Watkin; the film was shot on Czech locations and in English studios. Streisand's co-writer was the English playwright and television writer Jack Rosenthal. United Artists. color (See *State of the Art*.)

Les Yeux sans visage, see *Eyes Without a Face*

Y

Yojimbo (1961)—Akira Kurosawa's boisterous, exuberant comedy-satire about violence, with Toshiro Mifune as an unemployed samurai, a sword for hire. When our Westerner came into town, although his own past was often shady, he picked the *right* side—the farmers against the gamblers and the cattle thieves. This samurai walks into a town divided by two rival merchants quarrelling over a gambling concession, each supporting a gang of killers. He has his special skills and the remnants of a code of behavior, but to whom can he give his allegiance? He hires out to each and systematically eliminates both. We might expect violence carried to extremity to be sickening; Kurosawa, in a triumph of bravura technique, makes it explosively comic and exhilarating. There is so much displacement of the usual movie conventions that we don't have the time or inclination to ask why we are enjoying the action; we respond kinesthetically. One of the rare Japanese films that is both great and funny to American audiences. (Sergio Leone made his own version of it, *A Fistful of Dollars*.) In Japanese. b & w (See *I Lost it at the Movies*.)

Yolanda and the Thief (1945)—Fred Astaire was paired with Lucille Bremer in this stupefyingly baroque M-G-M musical set in a mythical South American country and encumbered with what its director, Vincente Minnelli, once called "an insane plot." Astaire is cast howlingly against type as a crooked gambler; when he learns that the beautiful heiress Yolanda believes she has a guardian angel, he pretends to be the angel in order to swindle her. The picture is the most extreme of the big-musical mistakes of the 40s; it's full of surreal dreams and fiestas, and because it goes beyond parody, it perhaps needs to be seen by anyone who wants to know what killed the M-G-M musicals. Yolanda's bathroom has cascading fountains, and the ballets, staged by Eugene Loring and costumed by Irene Sharaff at her maddest, include such decorator delights as laundresses washing linen in a pool of gold coins. The cast includes Frank Morgan, Mildred Natwick, Mary Nash, and Leon Ames. The script by Irving Brecher is based on a story by Ludwig Bemelmans and Jacques Théry. The songs, by Harry Warren and Arthur Freed, are best forgotten. Produced by Freed. color

You and Me (1938)—It starts with attractive Art Deco titles, and the sets and stylized cinematography would suggest high comedy, but as soon as the action starts (in a department store where parolees are hired), you can smell disaster. Sylvia Sidney is the overly sweet and demure ex-convict employee who marries another ex-convict employee (George Raft), even though it violates her parole. This clompingly coy movie was the result of studio interference with a great director (Fritz Lang), who had got himself into what was probably a hopeless project, even if it hadn't been interfered with. Bertolt Brecht had great influence on Lang at the time, and in several episodes, Lang, with the help of the composer Kurt Weill, tried to escape from the pedestrian script (by Virginia Van Upp, from Norman Krasna's story) with musical numbers in the pedagogic Brecht vein. Lang later explained that he didn't get to work out his ideas with Weill, and that with Boris Morros on the scoring, he couldn't get what he'd hoped for. The movie turns out to be a gangster-comedy fairy tale, botched in every department. Lang seems to be trying to be Lubitsch, but without the requisite lightness of touch. With Robert Cummings, Roscoe Karns, Harry Carey, Barton MacLane, George E. Stone, Bernadene Hayes, Willard Robertson, Joyce Compton, Warren Hymer, Guinn Williams, Jack Mulhall, Cecil Cunningham, Arthur Hoyt, and

Carol Paige as the torch singer. Paramount. b & w

You Light Up My Life (1977)—If the producer-director-composer-writer, Joseph Brooks, had written a script with a few more strands woven into it, he wouldn't have had to overwork the gamine vulnerability of his star, Didi Conn. The single plot thread has her trying to break away from a career as a comic, which her borscht-belt comedian father (Joe Silver) shoved her into in childhood, and find her own way as a composer-singer-actress. The movie is both amateurish and slick—it oozes heart. The scenes go on too long, and there isn't enough in them—they're stretched out with closeups of the heroine grinning or singing (she's dubbed by Kasey Cisyk)—yet it's all so unabashedly on her side that many in the audience (young girls, especially) seem to respond happily. The whole thing is like a commercial for the insistent title song. With Stephan Nathan, who is amusingly relaxed as the fiancé born to be jilted, and Melanie Mayron and Michael Zaslow. Independently made, released by Columbia. color

You Only Live Once (1937)—This early version of the Bonnie and Clyde story, starring Sylvia Sidney and Henry Fonda (neither has ever been better), is perhaps the finest of Fritz Lang's American movies, and certainly one of the finest American melodramas of the 30s. In this version, the young outcasts are seen as innocent victims of the indifference and cruelty of society—a view the audiences of the period readily shared. Even though the social slant may seem like Lang pushing his view of doom, and even though the end seems maudlin, the details and many of the individual sequences are so clearly directed that the social melodrama is transcended. With Jean Dixon, Barton MacLane, Margaret Hamilton, Warren Hymer, Guinn Williams,

Charles (Chic) Sale, and regrettably, William Gargan as Father Dolan. The script is by Gene Towne and Graham Baker. United Artists. b & w (See *Kiss Kiss Bang Bang*.)

You Only Live Twice (1967)—The fifth of the Bonds, it can easily be differentiated from the others because it's the Japanese one. It's a product, but probably the most consistently entertaining of the Bond packages up to the time—not as startling as parts of *Goldfinger* but much superior to *Thunderball*. Ken Adam's sci-fi production designs (including a hollow volcano) seem almost perfectly calculated for the genre. Lewis Gilbert is a rather more humanistic director than his predecessors and he's a reasonably efficient traffic manager; he doesn't let the actors loiter on the sets too long. And Sean Connery's James Bond isn't the sleek, greasy-lipped dummy of the earlier films; playing the super-hero as a paunchy, rather bemused spectator, Connery gives him more character than he's ever had before. This casual, human Bond is rather tender in his sex relationships—one might almost call them love relationships this time. The Roald Dahl screenplay (out of Jules Verne and old movies) is clever enough, and Donald Pleasence, as Blofeld, pets his white cat ominously. With Alexander Knox as the American president. The cinematography is by Freddie Young. United Artists. color

You'll Never Get Rich (1941)—Fred Astaire and Rita Hayworth, and it doesn't work out too well, partly because she's too physical—too radiantly, youthfully overpowering for him (she works better with Gene Kelly in *Cover Girl*)—and partly because the mixture of the backstage-musical plot and the Second World War enlistment-in-the-Army theme weighs down the songs and dances. Cole Porter did the lyrics and music (which don't stick in the mind); Robert Alton was dance director; Michael Fessier and Ernest Pagano wrote the script; Sidney Lanfield directed. The cast includes Robert Benchley, John Hubbard, Osa Massen, Donald MacBride, Frieda Inescort, Guinn Williams, the singer Martha Tilton, and, among the guardhouse inmates, the Delta Rhythm Boys and a jazz group that contains Chico Hamilton. Rita Hayworth's songs were dubbed by Nan Wynn. Columbia. b & w

Young and Innocent Also known as *The Girl Was Young.* (1937)—Hitchcock reworks *The 39 Steps*, this time using a very young hero and heroine. Once again, the hero (now Derrick de Marney) is accused of a murder he didn't commit; he tries to track down the real killer while the police track him. The bewildered teen-age girl (Nova Pilbeam) who tries to help him is too earnest a conception to be very amusing; the film is pretty fair Hitchcock, though not as sexy or as witty as *The 39 Steps*. The bravura sequences include the hero's crashing of a children's party and a nifty sinister joke at the climax: the heroine knows only one thing about the villain—that his eyes twitch. She goes to a dance at a big hotel, and we see the blackface band; the drummer's eyes fill the screen—and twitch. Hitchcock takes the joke even further: as the drummer sees the police enter, he gets nervous, and his rhythm goes so crazily off that the people have to stop dancing. With Basil Radford, Percy Marmont, and Mary Clare. Hitchcock turns up, looking very young, as a press photographer, holding a tiny camera in front of him, like a talisman. b & w

The Young and the Damned, see *Los Olvidados*

The Young and the Passionate, see *I Vitelloni*

Young at Heart (1954)—A remake of the 1938 *Four Daughters*, with Frank Sinatra taking over the John Garfield role, the daughters reduced to three, and songs added. It isn't the monstrosity that it might have been, but in the 30s when Garfield, a rootless product of the big city and the Depression, encounters the cozy life of a small-town middle-class family it enrages him by making him feel how deprived he has been; in the 50s when Sinatra, an orphan who has never found a place for himself, expresses the same kind of chip-on-the-shoulder bitterness he seems just a sorehead and a loser. Still, the first half is watchable; Sinatra handles his cynical lines well and there's a lot of activity around the family as you get to know the daughters— Doris Day, Dorothy Malone, and Elizabeth Fraser—and their suitors. But after Sinatra and Day go off to the city together, there's nothing much to look at but their suffering in drab rooming houses. Doris Day is too competent looking to play a passive wifey who just wrings her hands while her husband keeps failing in his singing jobs; from the look of the back of her stiff head and her ducktail bob, you expect her to take over or, at least, do something. And because the period isn't right the story (it comes from Fannie Hurst's novel *Sister Act*) seems dated. Gig Young gives an appealingly flamboyant performance as the hotshot composer who brings Sinatra to the town to work with him; whenever Gig Young is onscreen, the movie's energy level goes up. With Ethel Barrymore, Robert Keith, and Alan Hale, Jr. Directed by Gordon Douglas; the script is by Julius J. Epstein and Lenore Coffee. The songs include "Someone to Watch Over Me," "Just One of Those Things," and "Hold Me in Your Arms." Warners. color

Young Cassidy (1965)—John Ford was to have directed this film, which is based on portions of Sean O'Casey's autobiography and was shot in and around Dublin, but he fell ill, and Jack Cardiff (who directed *Sons*

and Lovers) took over. The movie is far from fully realized, and it's much too genteel and discreet, but it has stirring scenes of strikes and political uprisings and some of the same sort of intelligent reticence as parts of *Sons and Lovers*. Rod Taylor gives a surprisingly good performance as the brawling dreamer-hero—a husky revolutionary who digs ditches to support his stoic mother (Flora Robson) and desperately exhausted sister (the remarkable Sian Phillips). The hero has an affair with a chorus-girl trollop (Julie Christie) and becomes involved with a timid librarian (well played by Maggie Smith); in the Dublin literary world he meets Lady Gregory (Edith Evans) and Yeats (Michael Redgrave). One may want to snicker at the hero's quick rise to literary eminence, but compared to other movies about a famous writer's youth, this one is highly intelligent. The script is by John Whiting. M-G-M. color

Young Frankenstein (1974)—A farce-parody of Hollywood's mad-scientist movies. You have to let this Mel Brooks comedy do everything for you, because that's the only way it works. If you accept the silly, zizzy obviousness, it can make you laugh helplessly. Gene Wilder is the old Baron's scientist-grandson, Peter Boyle is the new Monster, and Madeline Kahn is the scientist's fiancée, who becomes the Monster's bride. The picture is in black-and-white, which holds it visually close to the films it takes off from. It's Brooks' most sustained piece of moviemaking—the laughs never let up. The script is by Wilder and Brooks. With Cloris Leachman, Marty Feldman, Teri Garr, Liam Dunn, Richard Haydn, Kenneth Mars, and Gene Hackman, bearded, in a masterly bit as a blind man. 20th Century-Fox. (See *Reeling*.)

The Young in Heart (1938)—The title is slightly sickening, and the movie does have a mushy messagey side, but the story about a family of con artists (Roland Young and Billie Burke are the parents; Douglas Fairbanks, Jr., and Janet Gaynor are the children) has some good bright moments. There's a posh automobile, the "Flying Wombat," and a memorable sequence in which Fairbanks and Young set out to look for work and pause to watch the honest labor of hod carriers as if they were observing a strange kind of insect activity. Gaynor's peculiarly saccharine charms may be trying but she's held in check; Paulette Goddard is in it too, and she's shiny and attractive. With Minnie Dupree, and Richard Carlson, in his screen début. Directed by Richard Wallace; adapted from I.A.R. Wylie's novella *The Gay Banditti*, by Charles Bennett and Paul Osborn. The Art Deco sets (and the Wombat) were designed by Lyle Wheeler. Selznick International, released by United Artists. b & w

The Young Lions (1958)—This piece of heavyweight kitsch is fairly entertaining, what with Marlon Brando as a fearfully handsome German ski instructor turned Nazi (he's also the blondest blond ever seen), Montgomery Clift as a forlorn, romantic American Jew, and Dean Martin as a Broadway playboy. The three meet before the Second World War and then again during it. Directed by Edward Dmytryk and adapted by Edward Anhalt from an Irwin Shaw novel, the film is episodic and overproduced, like a wartime *Grand Hotel*. Maximilian Schell plays a mean Nazi, in contrast to Brando's misguided, agonized idealist, and Hope Lange, Mai Britt, and Barbara Rush are among the women. Also with Lee Van Cleef. Cinematography by Joe MacDonald; music by Hugo Friedhofer. (167 minutes.) 20th Century-Fox. Cinema-Scope, b & w

Young Mr. Lincoln (1939)—One of John Ford's most memorable films, and not at all the tedious bummer that the title might suggest. The film is an embroidery (by the scenarist Lamar Trotti) on an actual murder trial in which Lincoln was the defense lawyer. Henry Fonda, in one of his best early performances, is funny and poignant as the drawling, awkward young hero, and Alice Brady plays the mother of the two defendants, Richard Cromwell and Eddie Quillan. With Pauline Moore as Ann Rutledge, Marjorie Weaver as Mary Todd, and Arleen Whelan, Ward Bond, Donald Meek, Robert Lowery, and assorted members of the Ford stock company. 20th Century-Fox. b & w

The Young Savages (1961)—John Frankenheimer made this melodrama about juvenile gangs in Spanish Harlem, recruiting some of the boys on location. You're awfully conscious that the picture means to be hard-hitting; it sometimes succeeds, but a lot of it is just worthy. Burt Lancaster is the assistant D.A. who came out of the slums and has now got himself married to Dina Merrill, no less. Others involved include Shelley Winters, Telly Savalas, and John David Chandler. Script by Edward Anhalt and J. P. Miller, based on Evan Hunter's novel *A Matter of Conviction*; cinematography by Lionel Lindon. United Artists. b & w

Young Scarface, see *Brighton Rock*

Young Sherlock Holmes (1985)—There's a coziness about the familiar murk and gloom of Victorian London around 1870. The schoolboy Holmes—Nicholas Rowe, a 6-foot-4 adolescent, with a slender, ascetic face—has a gentle, sweet precociousness. As his stocky, loyal chum Watson—a junior version of an old duffer—little Alan Cox has to keep stumbling and sprawling, and he takes his falls like a pro. And with a fiendish killer who is armed with an Egyptian blowgun (which is basically a peashooter), this promises to be a funnier, zestier picture than it turns out to be. Directed by Barry Levinson, from a script by Chris Columbus, it's mildly, blandly amusing as long as it stays within the conceits of the Holmesian legends. It falls apart when it starts turning Holmes into an action-adventure hero, and it lets you down with a thump when it rips off *Indiana Jones and the Temple of Doom*. Levinson's temple of doom (where a fanatic religious sect offers up human sacrifices) has a choir chanting solemnly; the pomposity of this music is lethal—it's like a High Mass for a dead mouse. With Nigel Stock as the smiling, dotty Professor Waxflatter; Earl Rhodes as the slimy, blond young rotter Dudley; Anthony Higgins as a fencing master and all-around smoothie; and Sophie Ward as the too sugary ingenue Elizabeth. Handsomely lighted by Stephen Goldblatt. Amblin Entertainment, for Paramount. color (See *Hooked*.)

Young Winston (1972)—A few parts pop psychiatry, a few parts adventure, a few parts politics, and a dash of family scandal: that's a basic pop mixture, and at least the movie isn't sluggish. Simon Ward is fine-boned, with a face that holds the camera, and his intelligent impersonation of Churchill from ages 17 to 26 is fun to watch; Anne Bancroft's eye-popping, haughty Jennie Jerome is the stuff of parody. Richard Attenborough directed, from Carl Foreman's adaptation of Churchill's *My Early Life*. Foreman, who was also the producer, has not merely a popularizing mind but a popularized one, coarsened by conventional plotting, yet bouncingly full of high spirits and remembered twists. You can grow fond of the fertility of the bad ideas. With Robert Shaw as the high-strung father going mad from syphilis, Anthony Hopkins, Ian Holm, Jack Hawkins, John Mills, Pat Heywood, Maurice Roeves, and Patrick Magee. The whole picture seems to be in faded pinks, with lulling mauve-grays and pale pinkish browns; the cinematography is by Gerry Turpin. Released by Columbia. (See *Reeling*.)

Your Past Is Showing   Also known as *The Naked Truth*. (1957)—Michael Pertwee's English-comedy scripts are sometimes based on such nifty ideas that the films are moderately entertaining despite indifferent directing. In this one Dennis Price has one of his best roles since *Kind Hearts and Coronets*. He's the blackmailing publisher of a *Confidential*-type magazine. His victims, who get together to kill him, include: Peter Sellers as a peculiarly nasty television celebrity—Sellers captures the horror and hypocrisy of the role with great finesse (particularly in a sequence with an old man from the Gorbals); Terry-Thomas as a racketeering peer; Shirley Eaton as a model; and the formidable Peggy Mount (a female Charles Laughton crossed with a young Margaret Rutherford) as a novelist. No one could describe the director Mario Zampi's style as subtle, but it's loose enough to allow for good bits by Miles Malleson and Joan Sims, who plays the novelist's daughter. b & w

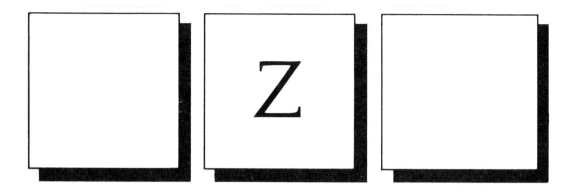

Z (1969)—How a political murder is made to look like an accident. Costa-Gavras's extraordinary thriller—one of the fastest, most exciting melodramas ever made—was based on contemporary events in Greece. The picture never loses emotional contact with the audience; it derives from the traditions of the American gangster movies and prison pictures and anti-Fascist melodramas of the 40s. The young Greek expatriate director uses a searching, active camera style that's a little too self-consciously dynamic, and his staccato editing style and the use of loud music to build up suspense for the violent sequences put a lot of pressure on you. He gets you in his grip and squeezes you to react the way he wants you to. The story is based on the Lambrakis affair, as it was presented in fictional form in the novel Z, by the Greek exile Vassili Vassilikos. In 1965, Lambrakis, a professor of medicine, was struck down by a delivery truck as he left a peace meeting; the investigation of his death uncovered such a scandalous network of corruption and illegality in the police and in the government that the leader of the opposition party, George Papandreou, became Premier. But in 1967 a military coup d'état overturned the legal government. The movie re-enacts the murder and the investigation in an attempt to show how the mechanics of fascist corruption may be hidden under the mask of law and order. It was shot in Algeria, in French, as a French-Algerian co-production, with a score by Mikis Theodorakis (who was under house arrest in Greece at the time), and a script by Jorge Semprun, an exile from Spain. When the picture is over and you've caught your breath you know perfectly well that its techniques of excitation could as easily be used by a smart fascist filmmaker, if there were one. Luckily there isn't. With Yves Montand, Jean-Louis Trintignant, Irene Papas, François Périer, Renato Salvatori, Charles Denner, Pierre Dux, Marcel Bozzufi, Magali Noel, and Georges Geret. The cinematography is by Raoul Coutard. In French. color (See *Deeper into Movies*.)

Zabriskie Point (1970)—Antonioni's American-made movie is about a semi-political boy (Mark Frechette) and an uncommitted girl (Daria Halprin) and how everything they encounter of American life is cruel and rotten. (They meet in Death Valley.) When the boy is (implausibly) killed by a "pig," the girl sees what must come: the destruction of America (which turns out to be a ravishingly pretty apocalypse). It's a very odd sensation to watch a message movie by a famous European artist telling us what is wrong with America while showing us something both naïve and decrepit; if it weren't for this peculiar sense of dislocation and the embarrassment you feel for Antonioni, this would be just one more "irreverent" pandering-to-youth movie, and (except visually) worse than most. He can't animate the young performers—he can't, it seems, truly connect with them. He falls back on the youth mythology so popular in the mass media (the young are good guys and the older white Americans are bad guys), and this rigid, schematic point of view doesn't fit his deliberately open-ended, sprawling style. The movie seems unconsciously snobbish—as if Antonioni thought America should be destroyed because of its vulgarity. With Rod Taylor. Cinematography by Alfio Contini; script by Antonioni, Fred Gardner, Sam Shepard, Tonino Guerra, and Clare Peploe. Produced by Carlo Ponti; released by M-G-M. color

Zachariah (1971)—A rock Western, and, as if that weren't mixture enough, it also tries to be both spoof and morality play. Nothing quite works, yet it's a relaxed and generally inoffensive movie; the hero (John Rubinstein) has an open, smiling manner, and the menace (Elvin Jones) does a smashing drum solo—the high point of the film. Directed by George Englund, from a script by Joe Massot, and an improvisational troupe of four called The Firesign Theatre—they didn't like the way the script had been edited, and referred to the movie as "Zacharooka." With Pat Quinn (the Alice of Arthur Penn's *Alice's Restaurant*). A Cinerama release. color

Zandy's Bride (1974)—The Swedish director Jan Troell proved his enormous talent in the two-part epic *The Emigrants* and *The New Land*, but he had terrible luck when he worked on Hollywood projects. His first, the Western *Zandy's Bride* (which was drastically shortened), was a commercial failure and his second, the 1979 *Hurricane*, was an all-around fiasco. Set in California's Big Sur region in the 1870s, *Zandy's Bride*, with Gene Hackman as the cattle rancher Zandy and Liv Ullmann as his mail-order bride, is a respectable piece of work. But it feels too worthy: the story material simply isn't original enough for the unrelieved serious tone. Troell's background isn't theatrical, and he doesn't provide the pleasures that people expect from a Western—the comic and romantic sweetening, the fun. Zandy is a hard man and close-mouthed; his bride suffers from loneliness and from his brutal indifference to her feelings. It's almost impossible to warm up to the glum Zandy; Hackman seems defeated by the way the character is written, and Ullmann is left to carry the picture. And either because of the script (by Marc Norman, based on the 1942 novel *The Stranger*, by Lillian Bos Ross) or the re-editing, the melodramatic action that develops has very little to do with the core of the movie—which is the wife's gradual civilizing influence on Zandy. With Eileen Heckart, Susan Tyrrell, Sam Bottoms, Harry Dean Stanton, and Joe Santos. Cinematography by Jordan Cronenweth; produced by Harvey Matofsky, for Warners. color

Zardoz (1974)—Sean Connery in a loincloth as the only virile man in an elitist commune of the future, dominated by hyperintellectual immortal women. John Boorman, who wrote, produced, and directed this lushly photographed piece of twaddle, appears to be worried about mankind's losing its fighting strength. With ideas skimmed off the top of various systems of thought, *Zardoz* is a glittering cultural trash pile, and probably the most gloriously fatuous movie since *The Oscar*—though the passages between laughs droop. With Charlotte Rampling, whose gim-

Z

let eyes and sensual hauteur inspire Connery to found a new race, and Sara Kestelman as May. Cinematography by Geoffrey Unsworth. 20th Century-Fox. color (See *Reeling*.)

Zaza (1939)—Overdressed, stultifying "period" picture, heavy on recriminations and renunciations. Claudette Colbert is miscast as a rowdy wench, the darling of the French music halls, who becomes involved with a married gentleman—Herbert Marshall, so respectable and courteous and boringly nice that his adulterous duplicity is scarcely believable. Colbert wears big feathered hats and works herself up to the appropriate tantrums and spasms of nobility, but it's all mild and lifeless. (The script, which had to be laundered to get through the Hays office, fades away.) Bert Lahr blooms (briefly) as Zaza's manager, and Helen Westley, liquored up and besequinned, plays her greedy stage mother; Constance Collier and Genevieve Tobin are also in the cast. George Cukor directed; the musical numbers have a little more flair than the rest of the movie. Screenplay by Zoë Akins, from the play by Pierre Berton and Charles Simon. Produced by Albert Lewin; Paramount. b & w

Zazie dans le Métro (1960)—Movies are said to be an international language, but sometimes a film that is popular in one country finds only a small audience in another. This anarchistic, impudent comedy (from Raymond Queneau's novel), a great success in France in 1960, was hardly heard of in the United States. The film, which is like a Mack Sennett 2-reeler running wild, seemed to be peculiarly disturbing for American critics and audiences alike. To Americans, *Zazie* seemed to go too far—to be almost demonic in its inventiveness, like a joke that gets so complicated you can't time your laughs comfortably. The editing, which is very fast, may be too clever; some critics have suggested that

for Americans this comedy sets off some kind of freakish, fantastic anxiety. Putting it as squarely as possible, Bosley Crowther wrote in the *New York Times*: "There is something not quite innocent or healthy about this film." Yet it's like *Alice in Wonderland*: Zazie (Catherine Demongeot) is a foul-mouthed little cynic, age 11, who comes to Paris for a weekend with her uncle (Philippe Noiret), a female impersonator, and nobody and nothing are quite what they seem. Louis Malle, who directed, includes satirical allusions to *La Dolce Vita* and other films, and a parody of his own *The Lovers*. Many of the modern styles in film editing, which were generally thought to derive from Alain Resnais or Richard Lester, have an earlier source in *Zazie*. In French. color

Zee and Co., see *X Y & Zee*

Zelig (1983)—Woody Allen's intricately layered parody—a mock documentary about a celebrity of the 20s, Zelig the Human Chameleon (Allen), who takes on the characteristics of whatever strong personalities he comes in contact with. The film seems small, and there's a reason: there aren't any characters in it, not even Zelig. Allen shafts the almost universally accepted idea that everyone is someone. This is a fantasy about being famous for being nobody. The whole movie is an ingenious stunt: it has been thought out in terms of the film image, turning the American history we know from newsreels into slapstick by inserting the little lost sheep Zelig in a corner of the frame. Zelig's story couldn't have been told any other way—the pathos would have been crushing. The documentary fakery dries it out and keeps it light. Zelig is always just glimpsed and the movie darts on. It's made up of artful little touches. With Mia Farrow as Zelig's analyst, and Stephanie Farrow and Ellen Garrison. Narrated by Patrick Horgan; cinematography by Gordon Willis; edited by Susan E. Morse. Orion; released byWarners. b & w (See *State of the Art*.)

Zemlya, see *Earth*

Zero for Conduct *Zéro de conduite* (1933)— School as seen through the eyes of children. Jean Vigo's 44-minute comedy-fantasy about a schoolchildren's revolt is one of the most poetic films ever made and one of the most influential, both in theme (as in Truffaut's *The 400 Blows* and Lindsay Anderson's *If . . .*) and in its leaping continuity (as in Godard's *Breathless*). Vigo, himself, was clearly influenced by Abel Gance's pillow-fight sequence in *Napoléon*. In French. b & w

Ziegfeld Follies (1944)—Vincente Minnelli directs an extraordinary cast in this plotless, often tedious M-G-M musical revue. It features a peculiar Hollywood-40s style of decor (chorus boys with jewelled antler-shaped branches, chorus girls clad in vermillion, and so on). Some high spots: Fred Astaire dances "Limehouse Blues" in a set left over from *The Picture of Dorian Gray*; he and Gene Kelly do a routine together ("The Babbitt and the Bromide," by George and Ira Gershwin); and Judy Garland appears at her most light-hearted in the dance-and-patter number—"A Great Lady Has an Interview." The other performers include Lena Horne, Fanny Brice, Victor Moore, Red Skelton, Esther Williams, Keenan Wynn, Jimmy Durante, Lucille Ball, Lucille Bremer, James Melton, Hume Cronyn, Edward Arnold, and William Powell as Ziegfeld up in heaven dreaming this big bash. The fastidious are advised to head for the lobby while Kathryn Grayson sings "There's Beauty Everywhere" against magenta foam skies. Produced by Arthur Freed. color

Ziegfeld Girl (1941)—An odd, rather fascinating M-G-M musical that mixes melodrama with big production numbers. The story involves Judy Garland, James Stewart, Hedy Lamarr, and Dan Dailey, as a sadistic prize-fighter who gives Lana Turner a bad time. (Dailey is scarily good.) The cast includes the great dancers Antonio and Rosario, who were known at the time as The Kids from Seville, and Tony Martin, Al Shean, Charles Winninger, Ian Hunter, Jackie Cooper, Eve Arden, and Edward Everett Horton. Produced by Pandro S. Berman; directed by Robert Z. Leonard; the dance numbers were staged by Busby Berkeley; the costumes are by Adrian; the script is by Sonya Levien and Marguerite Roberts, from a story by W. A. McGuire; the songs, from various sources, include "You Stepped Out of a Dream," "I'm Always Chasing Rainbows," and "You." b & w

Zoo in Budapest (1933)—A lovely, romantic fantasy, with the radiant Loretta Young as a girl who runs away from an orphanage, spends the night in a zoo, and meets a handsome, nonconformist zoo attendant (Gene Raymond). The entire beautifully produced movie takes place during that night in the zoo. Rowland V. Lee directed, and Lee Garmes did the memorable cinematography—tranquil visions of swans and herons on a moolit lake, and, at the end, when the police arrive and the whole zoo has gone mad, a glimpse of the porcupines in a panic. With O. P. Heggie; written by Dan Totheroh, Louise Long, and the director. Fox. b & w

Zorba the Greek (1964)—A violent old Greek (Anthony Quinn) tries to teach a tame young Englishman (Alan Bates) how to live. The central Life Force conception is banal and pushy, yet there *is* life force in Quinn's performance. The setting is the harshly beautiful island of Crete. Irene Papas is the magnificent widow the young man is drawn to, and Lila Kedrova plays the coquettish old ruin who thinks she can cheat death if she's still attractive enough to get a man. The director, Michael Cacoyannis, lingers too long over this great old tart, wanting a little too much of a good thing; his more serious weakness is for choreographed set pieces—theatrical "classic" sequences. He presses down too hard; the film has its moments, though. From the novel by Nikos Kazantzakis; cinematography by Walter Lassally; music by Mikis Theodorakis. b & w

Zorro, the Gay Blade (1981)—A wonderful giddy farce. If you could combine the screen images of Douglas Fairbanks, Sr., and Peter Sellers, the result might be pretty close to the slinky, self-mocking George Hamilton as Zorro. This gleaming-eyed Zorro, with his idiotic leering grin and his idiosyncratic Spanish accent, and Paco (Donovan Scott), his plump, teddy-bear servant, set out to help the people of old Los Angeles, who are being taxed to death by the villainous Esteban (that actory actor Ron Leibman, sporting a thick head of hair and a full beard, and giving a rambunctious, likable performance). Directed by Peter Medak, from Hal Dresner's script, this is the kind of silly movie at which you laugh so hard that when something misfires it's just a little rest. With Brenda Vaccaro (doing a Madeline Kahn), Lauren Hutton, James Booth, and Clive Revill. A Melvin Simon Production; released by 20th Century-Fox. color (See *Taking It All In*.)

INDEX

Domínguín, 109
Dommartin, Solveig, 841
Donaggio, Pino, 90, 203
Donahue, Troy, 290
Donald, James, 102, 123, 443, 581
Donaldson, Roger, 96, 465, 532, 687
Donaldson, Walter, 563
Donat, Peter, 334
Donat, Richard, 506
Donat, Robert, 138, 157, 284, 296, 599, 761
Donath, Ludwig, 782
Donati, Danilo, 240, 241, 250
Donati, Sergio, 617
Donen, Stanley, 25, 59, 80, 130, 159, 271, 287, 362, 374, 427, 443, 500, 546, 646, 667, 683, 740, 798
Donizetti, Gaetano, 600
Donlan, Yolande, 229
Donlevy, Brian, 51, 57, 75, 185, 287, 302, 360, 399, 483
Donnell, Jeff, 359, 559
Donnelly, Donal, 177, 401, 482
Donnelly, Dorothy, 580
Donnelly, Patrice, 576
Donnelly, Ruth, 81, 255, 316, 487, 489, 686, 762
Donner, Clive, 535, 830
Donner, Richard, 297, 406, 660, 730
D'Onofrio, Vincent, 271
Donoghue, Mary Agnes, 56
Donohoe, Amanda, 614
Donovan, 588
Donovan, Arlene, 715
Donovan, King, 220
Donskoi, Mark, 132–33, 506, 510
Doody, Alison, 361, 815
Dooley, Paul, 589, 684, 686, 809
Doqui, Robert, 516, 635
Dor, Karin, 781
Doran, Ann, 11, 35, 318, 473, 575, 618
Doran, Mary, 105
Doré, Edna, 331
Dorfman, Robert, 151
Dorfman, Ron, 309
Dorléac, Françoise, 72, 750
Dorn, Philip, 224, 351, 616
Dornacker, Jane, 630
Doroff, Sarah Rowland, 766
Dörrie, Doris, 475
Dors, Diana, 393, 543
Dorsey, Jimmy, 336, 349, 404
Dorsey, Thomas A., 655
Dorsey, Tommy, 106, 286, 675

Dorville, 197
Dorziat, Gabrielle, 425, 489, 495, 566, 578
Dos Passos, John, 187
Dostoevski, Feodor, 225, 264, 354, 567
Dotrice, Roy, 110
Dotson, Rhonda, 695
Doty, Douglas, 413
Doucet, Catherine, 590, 753
Douglas, Gordon, 185, 319, 359, 704, 858
Douglas, Helen Gahagan, 672
Douglas, John, 480
Douglas, Kirk, 4, 35, 46, 123, 186, 187–88, 273, 419, 423, 443, 500, 548, 557, 570, 599, 718, 752, 800
Douglas, Lawrence, 393
Douglas, Lloyd C., 306, 451
Douglas, Melvyn, 26, 30, 72, 118, 156, 298, 341, 344, 351, 531, 542, 660, 672, 674, 752, 753, 763, 779, 798, 825, 846
Douglas, Michael, 147, 239, 549, 638
Douglas, Paul, 140, 330, 419, 564, 691
Douglas, Robert, 7, 262, 376
Douglas, Sarah, 731
Douglass, Kent, see Montgomery, Douglass
Douglass, Robyn, 431
Dourif, Brad, 87, 207, 230, 486, 549, 612
Dove, Billie, 77
Dovzhenko, Alexander, 35, 209
Dowd, Nancy, 150, 686, 738
Dowell, Anthony, 811
Dowling, Allan, 346
Dowling, Doris, 86, 437
Down, Lesley-Anne, 66, 303–4, 427, 582
Downey, Robert, Jr., 45, 580, 792
Downs, Johnny, 14, 582
Doyle, Arthur Conan, 341
Doyle, Laird, 171, 542
Doyle-Murray, Brian, 143, 684
D'Oyly Carte players, 480
Drach, Michel, 816
Drago, Billy, 808
Dragoti, Stan, 437
Drake, Charles, 11, 19, 35, 287, 524, 536
Drake, Dona, 30, 67, 690

Drake, Fabia, 812
Drake, Frances, 259, 445, 484
Drake, Judith, 742
Drake, Paul, 725
Drake, Tom, 614, 834, 848
Drake, William A., 300
Draper, Peter, 110
Dratler, Jay, 413
Dravić, Milena, 850
Drayton, Alfred, 523
Dreier, Hans, 107, 187, 198, 671
Dreiser, Theodore, 23, 121, 584
Drescher, Fran, 22, 655
Dresdel, Sonia, 234
Dresner, Hal, 34, 866
Dresser, Louise, 658, 711
Dresser, Paul, 508
Dressler, Marie, 28, 190, 337
Drew, Ellen, 136, 298, 355, 372
Drew, Lowell, 307
Dreyer, Carl, 176, 552, 568, 812
Dreyfuss, Richard, 21, 33, 70, 142, 150, 199, 296, 365, 378, 592, 704, 705, 773
Drier, Moosie, 23, 809
Drimmer, John, 353
Driscoll, Bobby, 318
Driscoll, Peter, 837
Dru, Joanne, 19, 620, 672
Druon, Maurice, 470
Drury, Allen, 8
Drury, David, 183
Drury, Norma, 366
Dryden, Wheeler, 494
Dubin, Al, 255, 262, 288, 291, 292, 637
Dubois, Marie, 364, 385, 676, 739, 757, 816
Du Bois, Marta, 95
Dubost, Paulette, 647, 818
Duceppe, Jean, 510
Duchaussoy, Michel, 241, 762
Dudgeon, Elspeth (John), 542
Dudley, Doris, 846
Dufaux, Guy, 182
Duff, Howard, 17, 108, 412, 514, 532
Duff, Warren, 27
Duffell, Peter, 221
Duffy, Jack, 202
Dugan, Dennis, 343
Dugan, Tom, 195, 296, 546, 740, 774, 837
Duggan, Andrew, 91, 129, 359

Stanwyck, Barbara, 30, 48, 75, 140, 198, 243, 251, 257, 292, 336, 403, 404, 405, 445, 473, 478, 483, 525, 528, 696, 713, 718, 746, 774, 775
Staples, Roebuck (Pops), 794
Staples, the, 411
Stapleton, Jean, 808
Stapleton, Maureen, 12, 111, 144, 325, 366, 448, 621, 815
Stapleton, Oliver, 3, 506, 595
Stark, Graham, 14
Stark, Ray, 29, 76, 115, 238, 272, 296, 559, 622, 628, 730, 825
Starling, Lynn, 322
Starr, Ben, 555
Starr, Blaze, 80
Starr, Ringo, 117, 127, 411, 450; see also Beatles
Starrett, Charles, 469, 645
Starrett, Jack, 141
Steadman, Alison, 7
Steel, Anthony, 413
Steele, Barbara, 78, 213
Steele, Bob (Robert), 220, 540, 631
Steele, Freddie, 258, 313
Steele, Karen, 467
Steele, Marjorie, 101
Steele, Tommy, 244
Steeman, S. A., 607
Steenburgen, Mary, 164, 290, 474, 479, 485, 612, 772
Stefanelli, Simonetta, 289
Stefano, Joseph, 514
Steibel, Warren, 339
Steiger, Rod, 4, 70, 126, 195, 317, 360, 440, 467, 546, 571, 616
Stein, John, 570
Stein, Joseph, 242
Stein, Margaret Sophie, 219
Stein, Paul L., 482
Steinbeck, John, 209, 301, 421, 540, 782, 818
Steinberg, Norman, 81, 508
Steiner, Max, 36, 67, 74, 99, 130, 137, 155, 250, 278, 306, 363, 380, 392, 419, 428, 536, 628, 653, 662, 781, 788
Steinhilber, Budd, 273
Stelfox, Shirley, 577
Stellman, Martin, 183
Stemmle, R. A., 184
Sten, Anna, 689
Stendhal, 61, 619
Stephan, Aram, 268

Stéphane, Nicole, 220
Stephens, Harvey, 225–26
Stephens, Martin, 365, 815
Stephens, Robert, 206, 329, 332, 497, 595, 599, 788
Stephenson, Henry, 72, 118, 130, 153, 428, 505, 524, 543, 620, 628, 760
Stephenson, James, 419, 543, 600
Stephenson, Pamela, 731
Steppat, Ilse, 545
Sterling, Jan, 4, 382
Sterling, Robert, 382, 679
Sterling, Thomas, 339
Stern, Bert, 379
Stern, Daniel, 87, 190, 316
Stern, Isaac, 242, 345
Stern, Leonard, 743, 766
Stern, Miroslava, see Miroslava
Stern, Richard Martin, 785
Stern, Stewart, 409, 618, 727, 802
Sternhagen, Frances, 103, 361, 558, 800, 808
Stevenin, Jean-François, 197
Stevens, Andrew, 97, 273
Stevens, Cat, 320
Stevens, Craig, 345
Stevens, Fisher, 679
Stevens, George, 14, 30, 284, 292, 310, 351, 391, 497, 575, 584, 607, 671, 742, 815, 818, 831, 845
Stevens, Gösta, 366
Stevens, Inger, 310
Stevens, K. T., 89
Stevens, Leslie, 416
Stevens, Onslow, 156, 547
Stevens, Stella, 48, 523, 537, 591, 681
Stevens, Warren, 51
Stevenson, Parker, 422
Stevenson, Robert (actor), 352
Stevenson, Robert (director), 60, 529
Stevenson, Robert Louis, 393
Stevenson, Venetia, 724
Steward, Kenny, 679
Stewart, Alexandra, 77, 266
Stewart, Charlotte, 224
Stewart, Donald, 486
Stewart, Donald Ogden, 52, 190, 336, 391, 400, 413, 421, 580, 597, 741, 744, 843, 847
Stewart, Douglas Day, 86, 540
Stewart, Elaine, 46, 103

Stewart, Fred, 702
Stewart, James, 9, 93, 107, 185, 287, 305, 343, 353, 373, 374, 448, 460, 461, 488, 522, 531, 580, 642, 677, 678, 800, 818, 836, 865
Stewart, Mel, 407, 418, 789
Stewart, Michael, 111
Stewart, Nick, 120
Stewart, Paul, 46, 138, 144, 382, 488, 746
Stewart, Sophie, 36
Stickney, Dorothy, 126, 351, 496, 502, 807
Stiers, David Ogden, 3, 31
Stigwood, Robert, 655, 699
Stiller, Jerry, 313, 513, 517
Stiller, Mauritz, 649
Stine, Clifford, 802
Stine, Harold E., 469
Sting (Gordon Sumner), 7, 207, 587, 692
Stinson, Joseph C., 725
Stock, Nigel, 423, 860
Stockwell, Dean, 25, 87, 151, 200, 207, 279, 409, 432, 695
Stockwell, Guy, 58
Stoker, Bram, 201, 534
Stokowski, Leopold, 236
Stoler, Shirley, 183, 185, 339, 667
Stoltz, Eric, 656
Stone, Andrew L., 304, 694, 716
Stone, Arnold M., 663
Stone, Christopher, 343
Stone, David C., 314, 480
Stone, Dee Wallace, see Wallace, Dee
Stone, Fred, 15, 787, 829
Stone, George E., 137, 262, 425, 462, 581, 692, 856
Stone, Grace Zaring, 75
Stone, Harold J., 129, 850, 852
Stone, Irving, 11, 443
Stone, James, 52
Stone, Lewis, 134, 299, 353, 438, 469, 597, 620, 711, 733, 845
Stone, Milburn, 581, 728
Stone, Oliver, 93, 213, 479, 586, 651, 657, 854
Stone, Peter, 130, 239, 664, 668, 685, 734, 741, 836
Stone, Robert, 851
Stone, Virginia, 694
Stong, Phil, 711
Stoppa, Paolo, 9, 59, 417, 483, 635